W9-AZY-308

Museum of Broadcast Communications

Encyclopedia of Television

Second Edition

Museum of Broadcast Communications

Encyclopedia of TELEVISION

SECOND EDITION

Volume 1

A–C

Horace Newcomb

EDITOR

FITZROY DEARBORN
New York • London

Published in 2004 by
Fitzroy Dearborn
An imprint of the Taylor & Francis Group
270 Madison Avenue
New York, New York 10016

First published by
Fitzroy Dearborn Publishers
70 East Walton Street
Chicago, Illinois 60611
U.S.A.

Library of Congress Cataloging-in-Publication Data:

Encyclopedia of television / Museum of Broadcast Communications ; Horace
Newcomb, editor.—2nd ed.
p. cm.
Includes bibliographical references and index.
ISBN 1-57958-394-6 (set : alk. paper) -- ISBN 1-57958-411-X (v. 1 :
alk. paper) -- ISBN 1-57958-412-8 (v. 2 : alk. paper) -- ISBN
1-57958-413-6 (v. 3 : alk. paper) -- ISBN 1-57958-456-X (v. 4 : alk.
paper)
1. Television broadcasting--Encyclopedias. I. Title: Encyclopedia of
television. II. Newcomb, Horace. III. Museum of Broadcast
Communications.
PN1992.18.E53 2005
384.55'03--dc22

2004003947

Contents

Advisory Board

Preface

The Museum of Broadcast Communications is proud to continue its commitment to educating about, and providing a better understanding of, electronic media in our world with this second edition of the *Museum of Broadcast Communications Encyclopedia of Television.* We also continue our collaboration with Dr. Horace Newcomb as Editor of the *Encyclopedia.* Dr. Newcomb is the Lambdin Kay Distinguished Professor for the Peabodys and Director of the George Foster Peabody Awards Program in the Grady College of Journalism and Mass Communication at the University of Georgia.

The first edition the *Encyclopedia of Television* was recognized throughout the world of reference book reviewers, librarians, scholars, teachers, and students as a powerful addition to their resources for understanding this most important medium. As an accompaniment to the Arthur C. Nielsen, Jr. Research Center at the Museum, it makes a major contribution to our ongoing educational mission. Television, as Dr. Newcomb writes in his Introduction, is constantly changing. Our efforts, both at the Museum and in this important reference work, mark those changes and look to the future of the medium.

The MBC is dedicated to preserving the history of television, analyzing its present state, and assisting in shaping its future. This edition of the *Encyclopedia of Television,* completely updated and containing almost 200 new entries, is central to those tasks. We believe it makes a truly significant contribution and are pleased to collaborate with our new publisher, Routledge, in making it available to the public.

This second edition of the *MBC Encyclopedia of Television* will also usher in a new era for the Museum. In 2006 the MBC will move into its new 50,000 square foot home on State Street at Kinzie in downtown Chicago. At this new location, visitors will be able to explore radio and television history in comfort. They will also be able to interact with our digitized collection in the MBC Media Cafe. The digitization of the MBC collection began in early 2004. It will allow us to offer greater access to our archives, our public programs and our seminars, both onsite and online at www.museum.tv. With extensive streaming content, standardized lesson plans for teachers, online exhibitions and our *Flashback* series of historic events, the MBC website is on the "favorite list" of many television scholars around the world.

Happy reading, happy browsing and please plan to visit us at our new home in Chicago in 2006.

Bruce DuMont
Founder/President/CEO
Museum of Broadcast Communications

Acknowledgments

Once again this project would not have been possible without the confidence and support of Bruce DuMont, Founder and President of the Museum of Broadcast Communications in Chicago. His continued efforts on behalf of those committed to understanding the history of electronic media are deeply appreciated by anyone involved in the educational enterprises that continue to grow in this area.

My thanks also go to Elizabeth Nishiura, who served as house editor for the project when it was initiated at Fitzroy Dearborn Publishers. She started this revision in the best possible manner. The project would not have been completed, however, without the amazing efficiency of Kristen Holt and Josh Pasternak at Routledge. They have made my work as editor both better and easier.

I am very grateful to the staff of the George Foster Peabody Awards Program in the Grady College of Journalism and Mass Communication at the University of Georgia. Tom Hoover, Program Coordinator for the Peabodys, Danna Williams, Senior Administrative Assistant, and Eric Holder, Public Relations Coordinator, have been aware of my efforts to complete this project and have made space and time available in the midst of a very demanding schedule. I also appreciate the support received from my many colleagues in the Telecommunication Department and throughout the Grady College. Moving to a new institutional setting in the midst of a project such as this one could have caused major problems. Fortunately, all mine have been minor and of my own doing.

Thanks also go to all the colleagues who assisted this project by suggesting new entry topics, writing new entries, revising existing ones, and offering general advice.

As always, special thanks to Sara Newcomb, whose ongoing support makes work such as this possible.

Horace Newcomb
Athens, Georgia

Introduction to the Second Edition

This second edition of the *Museum of Broadcast Communications Encyclopedia of Television* contains almost 200 new entries. Additionally, approximately 500 entries from the first edition have been revised and updated to account for developments since 1997, including changes in cast or other personnel, industrial developments, changes in executive ranks, series endings, or, in some cases, with the addition of new readings or other ancillary materials.

As it was for the first edition, the selection of additional entries has been a difficult process. Some new entries are included because they should or could have been placed in the first edition. That is, their absence from that edition was an oversight. In most cases, however, they are here because they add depth and breadth to the overall attempt to represent television in the fullest possible manner. Others, however, do reflect new developments in the television industries, such as new programs, new companies, merged conglomerates, and individuals who have risen to prominence.

Satellites, videocassette recorders, cable systems, and computers continue to alter the profiles and processes related to the medium of television. By the end of the century these technologies had all but obviated any necessity for the locally familiar transmitting tower, the antenna, and even conventional forms of tuners and receivers. Regularized program schedules had given way in most cases to an array of choices, even in regions where official agencies still attempted to control access to televised content. Moreover, the shifts in technology, with consequent alterations in economic underpinnings, and the power alignments accompanying them, showed up new failures—shortcomings, really—in policies and legal arrangements designed to monitor and rationalize the systems of broadcasting commonly thought of as "television."

Still, some aspects retain familiar outlines. The GE/NBC purchase of Vivendi Universal in late 2003 was a clear example of old strategies of increased vertical and horizontal integration in the media industries. Whatever new technologies are applied in production or used in transmission and reception, it was in the interest of the network to own a major production facility, especially one that produced one of its "bread and butter" program franchises, the *Law and Order* "brand" of television fictions. Moreover, that brand may be popular precisely because it maintains "older" styles of narrative, marked by contained episodes in which familiar characters deal with issues of the day within a crime and punishment format.

In the case of both the more heavily revised and the many new entries, then, the variable, mutable, strategically positioned definitions of "television" mentioned in the Introduction to the first edition, including the most traditional as well as the more innovative, experimental, or postmodern, come into play. One fundamental question can be framed in terms of degrees of change: has "television" truly changed in less than a decade, or has it merely shifted shape? And in either case, has the type and degree of control by corporate and state interest or the type and degree of use by "viewers" and "audiences" been significantly altered? I have no intention of attempting a firm answer to those questions. Rather, I call attention to a few examples that could be fruitfully examined in such an attempt.

In the Introduction to the first edition, I noted the increasing use of personal video recorders, digitally based devices for recording television programs from broadcast or cable transmission. This topic is examined much more fully in a specific entry in this edition ("Digital Video Recorder"), where William Boddy outlines the development of the devices and explores some of the implications of their diffusion and uses. Interestingly, however, the same devices are mentioned in numerous other entries on topics such as "Advertising," "Time Shifting," "Programming," and "Zapping," among others. From discussions of dire predictions to comments about ease of use, the significance of the device is demonstrated in large and small shifts in our understanding of "television." Is "television" in the U.S. the same thing if commercials, so long a topic of anger, delight, scorn, and profit, are easily avoided? Will the entire financial structure of the industries falter? Will producers be influenced more directly by advertising agencies desirous of placing their products inside fictional narratives? Such questions indicate that the personal video recorder is perhaps more significant than its predecessor, the video cassette recorder, which seems now so basic, so useful primarily for recording programs and skipping a few commercials (if only it could be more easily programmed by someone in the house).

In other developments, programming decisions have altered the material that might be available for such recordings. Despite the claims of HBO, for example, that "it's not TV," original programming for cable television has adopted and adapted narrative strategies long familiar to viewers. In terms of content, however, cable television offerings have also pushed boundaries set by cultural restrictions and social expectations, opening television to subject matters and treatments long restricted in the era dominated by network broadcasting. Moreover, in response to the attraction of these newer programs, more conventional television venues have relaxed these restrictions in their own programming.

In part, these variations in content are made possible by the continuing segmentation of audiences. As more distribution outlets are developed with the capacity afforded by digitalization, as technologies make it easier to record for private viewing, and as creative communities take advantage of new freedom to experiment and challenge, the notion of the "mass audience" recedes in the design and dissemination of televisual material. While it is the case that the largest number of viewers can still be reached within the conventional network structure familiar since the days of radio, television programs remain available on schedules with far smaller numbers of regular viewers. As a result of some of these factors, corporate strategies also shift. New entries in this edition note the presence of new television networks such as The WB. The expanded holdings of conglomerates such as Viacom and Disney are discussed here as is the trend capped, for the time being, by the aforementioned GE/NBC purchase of Vivendi Universal studios, cable channels, and ancillary services.

These alterations are best understood, I believe, as evidence of incremental change, rather than completely new developments, and many were in some degree of progress at the time of publication of the first edition of the *Encyclopedia of Television.* They indicate the complexity of social attitudes and cultural patterns, and even more significantly the strength and flexibility of the powerful forces that exercise some forms of control over the multiple contexts in which "television" is made and experienced. Radical shifts, whether in the realm of policy, economics, creativity, or technology, are hard to come by.

In some ways, then, the new entries and revisions published here represent a best effort at "keeping up" with the topics that are very likely already in a process of transformation. More than that, however, they also represent an ongoing attempt to *understand* these processes. The selection of entries, then, continues to represent a useful map of the surface of television rather than a complete analysis of the entire phenomenon. The *Encyclopedia of Television* does not pretend to provide final answers for these questions. It offers no definition of its own for "television." Instead, it offers a multitude of beginning points from which to trace the intersections, conflicts, struggles, and convergences that can be applied, and used as partial explanations for particular events, policies, developments—even for the existence of particular television "shows."

In the second edition of the *Encyclopedia of Television* as in the first, connections are pervasive. Multiple explanations are essential. Comparisons are to be expected. Contradictions are inevitable. With a thorough analytical **Index,** and a network of **Cross-References** in the form of **See alsos** following most entries, an apparatus enabling the user to explore these connections is built into the structure of the work. The presence of **750 Photographs** accompanying entries (486 of which are entirely new to the second edition) further enhances usage of the encyclopedia. In every case the connections, cross-references, explanations, comparisons, and contradictions should be sought out and used to understand any particular item presented here. These items are starting points on that surface map of television. Radiating from any single entry, crossing many others, are lines of inquiry. But they are also lines of influence. Providing those connections is the aim of this work. Pursuing them should be the delight of the user.

Horace Newcomb
Athens, Georgia
January, 2004

Contributors

Gina Abbott
Daniel Abram
Bram Abramson
Charles Acland
Henry B. Aldridge
Alison Alexander
Erika Tyner Allen
Robert C. Allen
Robert S. Alley
Martin Allor
Manuel Alvarado
Mark Alvey
Hussein Y. Amin
Christopher Anderson
Danielle Aron
Sanjay Asthana
Paul Attallah
Patricia Aufderheide
Albert Auster
Philip J. Auter
Robert K. Avery

Robert Babe
Vidula V. Bal
Tino Balio
Miranda Banks
Warren Bareiss
Eduardo Barrera
Richard Bartone
John Bates
Vanessa B. Beasley
Giovanni Bechelloni
Christine Becker
Robert V. Bellamy Jr.
Louise Benjamin
Harry M. Benshoff
Arthur Asa Berger
Daniel Bernardi
Alina Bernstein
Daniel Biltereyst
J. B. Bird
William L. Bird Jr.
Thomas A. Birk
Gilberto M. Blasini
Joan Bleicher
Jay G. Blumler
William Boddy
Aniko Bodroghkozy
Stuart Borthwick
J. Dennis Bounds
Stephen Bourne
Marian Bredin
Myles P. Breen
Dwight Brooks
Carolyn N. Brooks-Harris
Sue Brower
James A. Brown
Charlotte Brunsdon
Steve Bryant
Gary Burns
Mary Margaret Butcher
Jeremy G. Butler
Richard Butsch
Rodney A. Buxton

John Thornton Caldwell
Steven Carr
James Castonguay
Christine R. Catron
Frank J. Chorba
Miyase Christensen
Kathryn Cirksena
Kevin A. Clark
Lynn Schofield Clark
Kathleen Collins
John Cook
Lez Cooke
John Cooper
John Corner
Michael Couzens

Robert Craig
Sean Cubitt
Jan Čulik
Paul Cullum
Stuart O. Cunningham
Ann Curthoys
Michael Curtin

Kathryn C. D'Alessandro
Daniel Dayan
Roger de la Garde
Pamala S. Deane
Michael DeAngelis
Mary Desjardins
George Dessart
Robert Dickinson
John Docker
Thomas Doherty
David F. Donnelly
Bonnie Dow
Kevin Dowler
John D.H. Downing
Phillip Drummond
Mark Duguid
J.A. Dunn

Ross A. Eaman
Gary R. Edgerton
Greg Elmer
Susan Emmanuel
Michael Epstein
Anna Everett
Robert Everett

Jaqui Chmielewski Falkenheim
Irving Fang
Norman Felsenthal
Robert Ferguson
John P. Ferré
Dick Fiddy
Robert G. Finney
Frederick J. Fletcher
James E. Fletcher
Terry Flew
Nicola Foster
Eric Freedman
Katherine Fry

Ursula Ganz-Blaetller
Ronald Garay
Paula Gardner
Frances K. Gateward
Susan R. Gibberman
Mark Gibson

Joan Giglione
William O. Gilsdorf
Ivy Glennon
Kevin Glynn
Peter Goddard
Donald G. Godfrey
Douglas Gomery
Hannah Gourgey
Nitin Govil
August Grant
Sean Griffin
Alison Griffiths
Lynne Schafer Gross
David Gunzerath
Karen Gustafson

Bambi Haggins
Jerry Hagins
Daniel C. Hallin
Geoffrey Hammill
Susan Hamovitch
Keith C. Hampson
Denis Harp
Cheryl Harris
Roderick P. Hart
John Hartley
Amir Hassanpour
Tim Havens
Mark Hawkins-Dady
James Hay
Richard Haynes
Michele Hilmes
Hal Himmelstein
Olaf Hoerschelmann
Todd Holden
Jennifer Holt
Junhao Hong
Stewart M. Hoover
W.A. Kelly Huff
Ed Hugetz
Olof Hultén
David Humphreys
Darnell M. Hunt

Elizabeth Jacka
Matt Jackson
Jason J. Jacobs
Randy Jacobs
Sharon Jarvis
Henry Jenkins
Ros Jennings
Victoria E. Johnson
Jeffrey P. Jones
Judith Jones

Lisa Joniak
Garth Jowett
Guy Jowett

Michael Kackman
Lynda Lee Kaid
David Kamerer
Nixon K. Kariithi
Michael B. Kassel
Janice Kaye
Mary C. Kearney
†C.A. Kellner
Douglas Kellner
Brendan Kenny
Vance Kepley Jr.
Kelly Kessler
Lahn S. Kim
Won-Yong Kim
Howard M. Kleiman
Derek Kompare
Beth Kracklauer
Robert Kubey

Antonio C. La Pastina
Manon Lamontagne
Christina Lane
Jim Leach
Stephen Lee
Nina C. Leibman
Debra A. Lemieux
Robert Lemieux
Lisa Anne Lewis
Tamar Liebes
Lucy A. Liggett
Val E. Limburg
Sonia Livingstone
Guy E. Lometti
Amy W. Loomis
Amanda Lotz
Lynn T. Lovdal
Chris Lucas
Moya Luckett
Kathleen Luckey
Catharine Lumby

Ted Magder
Sarita Malik
Brent Malin
Chris Mann
David Marc
P. David Marshall
William Martin
Tom Mascaro
Michael Mashon
Kimberly B. Massey
Richard Maxwell
Sharon R. Mazzarella
Matthew P. McAllister
Anna McCarthy
Tom McCourt
Mark R. McDermott
Alan McKee
Lori Melton McKinnon
Susan McLeland
Peter McLuskie
John McMurria
Philippe Meers
Bishetta D. Merritt
Fritz J. Messere
Walter Metz
Cynthia Meyers
Andrew Miller
Mary Jane Miller
Toby Miller
Bob Millington
Jason Mittell
Margaret Montgomerie
Nickianne Moody
Albert Moran
James Moran
Albert Moretti
Anne Morey
Michael Morgan
David Morley
Margaret Morse
Megan Mullen
Seung-Hwan Mun
Graham Murdock
Matthew Murray
Susan Murray

Diane M. Negra
Horace Newcomb
Darrell Mottley Newton
Jonathan Nichols-Pethick
Joan Nicks
Poul Erik Nielsen
Dawn Michelle Nill
Kaarle Nordenstreng

Cary O'Dell
Peter B. Orlick
David Oswell

Lindsy E. Pack
Lisa Parks
Chris Paterson
Tony Pearson

Alisa Perren
Lance Pettitt
Jennie Phillips
David Pickering
Joanna Ploeger
Gayle M. Pohl
Robbie Polston
Rodolfo B. Popelnik
Vincent Porter
Julie Prince

Andrew Quicke

Marc Raboy
Michael Real
Jimmie L. Reeves
Jef Richards
William Richter
Jeremy Ridgman
Karen E. Riggs
Trudy Ring
Madelyn Ritrosky-Winslow
America Rodriguez
Stacy Rosenberg
Karen Ross
Robert Ross
Sharon Ross
Pamela Rostron
Lorna Roth
Eric Rothenbuhler
David Rowe
Steve Runyon
Paul Rutherford

Michael Saenz
Avi Santo
Eric Schaefer
Thomas Schatz
Sherra Schick
Christine Scodari
Jeffrey Sconce
Elizabeth Seaton
Peter B. Seel
Krishna Sen
Jan Servaes
Scott Shamp
Mitchell E. Shapiro
Marla L. Shelton
Shawn Shimpach
Jeff Shires
Mayra Cue Sierra
Jane Sillars
Ismo Silvo
Ron Simon
Nikhil Sinha
Jeannette Sloniowski
B.R. Smith
Christopher Smith
Paul A. Soukup
Nigel Spicer
Lynn Spigel
Michael Sragow
Janet Staiger
Laura Stein
Christopher H. Sterling
Joel Sternberg
Nicola Strange
Joseph Straubhaar
Daniel G. Streible
Sharon Strover
John Sullivan
Trine Syvertsen

Zoe Tan
Lora Taub-Pervizpour
Julia Taylor
Gisèle Tchoungui
John C. Tedesco
David J. Tetzlaff
Robert J. Thompson
David Thorburn
Bernard M. Timberg
Paul J. Torre
Raul D. Tovares
Liza Treviño
John Tulloch
Marian Tulloch
J.C. Turner
Rob Turnock
Joseph Turow

Peter Urquhart

Tise Vahimagi
Hanna Bjork Valsdottir
Leah R. Vande Berg

Clayland H. Waite
Cynthia W. Walker
James R. Walker
Kay Walsh
Charles Warner
Jody Waters
Mary Ann Watson
James Wehmeyer
Tinky "Dakota" Weisblat

Gary Whannel
Mimi White
Phil Wickham
D. Joel Wiggins
Karin Gwinn Wilkins
Carol Traynor Williams
Kevin D. Williams
Mark Williams
Suzanne Williams-Rautiolla
Pamela Wilson
Brian Winston
Richard Worringham

Thimios Zaharopoulos
Rita Zajacz
Sharon Zechowski
Nabeel Zuberi

Alphabetical List of Entries

Volume 1

Volume 2

Volume 3

Volume 4

Abbensetts, Michael (1938–)

British Writer

Michael Abbensetts is considered by many to be the best black playwright to emerge from his generation. He has been presented with many awards for his lifetime achievements in television drama writing and, in 1979, received an award for an "Outstanding Contribution to Literature" by a black writer resident in England. His work emerged alongside, and as part of, the larger development of black British television drama.

Abbensetts was born in Guyana in 1938. He began his writing career with short stories but decided to turn to playwriting after seeing a performance of John Osborne's *Look Back in Anger.* He was further inspired when he went to England and visited the Royal Court Theatre, Britain's premier theater of new writing, where he became resident dramatist in 1974. *Sweet Talk,* Abbensetts's first play, was performed there in 1973.

In the same year, *The Museum Attendant,* his first television play, was broadcast on BBC 2. Directed by Stephen Frears, the drama was, Abbensetts says, based on his own early experiences as a security guard at the Tower of London. After these two early successes, Abbensetts, unlike most black writers in Britain at the time, was being offered more and more work. He wrote *A Black Christmas,* which was broadcast on the BBC in 1977 and featured Carmen Munroe and Norman Beaton. Like *The Museum Attendant, A Black Christmas* was based on actual experience and was shot on location for television.

During the 1970s and 1980s, a number of Abbensetts's plays were produced for the London theater. *Alterations* appeared in 1978, followed by *Samba* (1980), *In the Mood* (1981), *Outlaw* (1983), and *El Dorado* (1983). *Inner City Blues, Crime and Passion, Roadrunner,* and *Fallen Angel* were produced for television.

Abbensetts's success led to participation in British television's first black soap opera, *Empire Road* (1978–79), for which he wrote two series. Horace Ove was brought in to direct the second series, establishing a production unit with a black director, black writer, and black actors. The television series was unique not only because it was the first soap opera to be conceived and written by a black writer for a black cast but also because it was specifically about the British-Caribbean experience. Set in Handsworth, Birmingham (United Kingdom), it featured Norman Beaton as Everton Bennett and Corinne Skinner-Carter as his long-suffering screen wife. Although *Empire Road* was a landmark program on British television, it managed to survive only two series before it was axed. Beaton said of the program, "It is perhaps the best TV series I have been in."

Beaton continued to star in many of Abbensetts's television productions, including *Easy Money* (1981) *Big George Is Dead* (1987), and *Little Napoleons* (Channel 4, 1994). *Little Napoleons* is a four-part comic-drama depicting the rivalry between two solicitors, played by Saeed Jaffrey and Beaton, who become Labour councillors. The work focuses on a number of themes, including the price of power, the

Michael Abbensetts.
Photo courtesy of Michael Abbensetts

relationship between West Indian and Asian communities in Britain, and the internal workings of political institutions.

Much of Abbensetts's drama has focused on issues of race and power, but he has always been reluctant to be seen as restricted to issue-based drama. His dialogue is concerned with the development and growth of character, and he is fundamentally aware of the methods and contexts for his actors. Abbensetts has always actively involved himself in the production process, and his dramatic works have provided outstanding roles for established black actors in Britain (Carmen Munroe, Rudolph Walker, and Beaton), giving them the chance to play interesting and realistic roles as well as creating stories about the everyday experiences of black people. Abbensetts's work thrived at a time when there was very little drama on television that represented the lives of black British people, and his television plays have created new perspectives for all his viewers.

SARITA MALIK

Michael Abbensetts. Born in British Guiana (now Guyana), June 8, 1938; became British citizen, 1974. Educated at Queen's College, Guyana, 1952–56; Stanstead College, Quebec; Sir George Williams University, Montreal, 1960–66. Security attendant, Tower of London, 1963–67; staff member, Sir John Soane Museum, London, 1968–71; resident playwright, Royal Court Theatre, London, 1974; visiting professor of drama, Carnegie Mellon University, Pittsburgh, Pennsylvania, 1981; Royal Literary Fellow, University of North London, 2000–01 and 2001–02. Recipient: George Devine Award, 1973; Arts Council bursary, 1977; Afro-Caribbean Award, 1979.

Television Series

1978–79 *Empire Road*
1994 *Little Napoleons*

Television Plays

1973 *The Museum Attendant*
1975 *Inner City Blues*
1976 *Crime and Passion*
1977 *A Black Christmas*
1977 *Roadrunner*
1981 *Easy Money*
1987 *Big George Is Dead*

Radio

Home Again, 1975; The Sunny Side of the Street, 1977; Brothers of the Sword, 1978; The Fast Lane, 1980; The Dark Horse, 1981; Summer Passions, 1985.

Stage

Sweet Talk, 1973; Alterations, 1978; Samba, 1980; In the Mood, 1981; The Dark Horse, 1981; Outlaw, 1983; El Dorado, 1984; Living Together, 1988; The Lion, 1993.

Publications

Sweet Talk (play), 1976
Samba (play), 1980
Empire Road (novel), 1979
Living Together (play), 1988
Four Plays (including *Sweet Talk, Alterations, El Dorado,* and *In the Mood*), 2001

Further Reading

Leavy, Suzan, "Abbensetts an Example," *Television Today* (May 19, 1994)
Walters, Margaret, "Taking Race for Granted," *New Society* (November 16, 1978)

Abbott, Paul (1960–)

British Writer

Paul Abbott is one of a new generation of British television writers whose work owes much to the strong tradition of social realism in British television drama. His upbringing in the northwest of England, as the ninth of ten children in a poor working-class family, has clearly had a formative influence, yet the zest and vitality of series like *Clocking Off* and *Linda Green* belie the deprivations of his childhood.

Writing stories was a means of escape for the teenage Abbott and after having a story published in the local *Weekly News* he began to think he could make a living from it. In 1980 Abbott enrolled at Manchester University to study psychology but he didn't give up hopes of a writing career, and when, in 1982, he had a radio play accepted by the BBC he decided to leave the university and concentrate on writing.

Abbott got a job at Granada Television as a story editor on *Coronation Street* and it was there, like many writers before him, that he served his apprenticeship, graduating to writing episodes for the serial in 1989. Given his background, the nuances of working-class life in *Coronation Street* were something Abbott could easily relate to. His upbringing in a large family also drew him to writing for and about children and his first televised script was for Granada's children's series *Dramarama,* an episode called "Blackbird Singing in the Dead of Night," written with Kay Mellor, who was also working on *Coronation* Street. Following this Abbott and Mellor developed *Children's Ward* for Granada TV. The series, which Abbott had originally wanted to set in a children's home, enabled him to draw on his experience of growing up in a large family and sharing a bedroom with seven brothers.

After working on *Coronation Street* for more than ten years Abbott decided to move on in 1994, producing the second series of Jimmy McGovern's *Cracker* before writing two stories for the third series in 1995, one of which involved a psychology student stalking Fitz, the criminal psychologist played by Robbie Coltrane. The *Cracker* scripts marked Abbott's growing maturity as a writer and saw him following in the footsteps of McGovern, branching out from soap opera to series drama.

Following *Cracker* Abbott spent the next year working on three serials, all screened in 1997, an unusually prolific spell for a writer in contemporary television. The first of these was the six-part romantic drama *Reckless,* starring Francesca Annis and Robson Green, which was nominated for Royal Television Society (RTS) and Writers Guild awards, followed by the four-part *Springhill,* a soap opera about a large Liverpool family, and the six-part crime drama *Touching Evil,* also nominated for RTS and Writers Guild awards. This period saw Abbott establish himself on ITV as a successful writer of popular generic drama—a talent much sought after by television companies increasingly concerned with maximizing audiences. After the limitations of the half-hour soap episode these serials enabled Abbott to extend himself with longer, original stories. A sign of his emerging reputation was that high-profile actors were attracted to his scripts; Peter Postlethwaite starred in the 1999 two-part police drama *Butterfly Collectors.*

In 1998 Abbott signed a two-year contract with the BBC and his first commission was the series that really established him as a leading writer of contemporary television drama, *Clocking Off.* Based on the lives of a group of workers at a textile factory in Manchester, with each episode focusing on a different character, *Clocking Off* was in the BBC *Play for Today* mold, serious single dramas about working-class life in the north of England. While its factory setting, working-class characters, and urban locations suggested social realism, Abbott's stylish treatment gave *Clocking Off* an altogether different flavor. The series was highly acclaimed, winning British Academy of Film and Television Arts (BAFTA) and RTS awards for Best Drama Series, with Abbott receiving the RTS Best Writer award for the series.

The first series of *Clocking Off* in early 2000 was followed by *The Secret World of Michael Fry,* an off-beat two-part drama starring Ewen Bremner, Abbott's second drama for Channel 4 following the pilot episode for the 1999 series *Love in the 21st Century.* The move from ITV to the BBC and Channel 4 liberated Abbott, enabling him to broaden his repertoire and experiment with different styles, but the three-part BBC 1 serial, *Best of Both Worlds* (2001), about an air hostess with marriages in two different countries, was disappointing, suggesting that Abbott was less comfortable with material that did not arise from his own working-class experience. *Linda Green* (2001), by contrast, was an inspired return to form. Featuring Liza Tarbuck as the brash, uninhibited car salesperson, out for a good time, it marked a return to more familiar territory.

As if to prove his ability to deal with "serious" drama material Abbott spent the next two years working on a major drama for the BBC. *State of Play* (2003) was a six-part political thriller, a genre with an illustrious history but little seen on British television since the 1980s. With a rapturous critical reception *State of Play* cemented Abbott's reputation as a serious dramatist and, while the "human interest" story may have eclipsed the politics in an overly complex plot, it was enough of a success for a second series, this time concentrating on the investigative journalists, to be commissioned by the BBC.

Also in 2003, ITV screened *Alibi,* a two-part drama that confirmed Abbott's standing as a highly accomplished television dramatist. Essentially a crime thriller leavened with comedy, the three-hour drama worked well thanks to excellent performances from Michael Kitchen and Sophie Okonedo, two of British television's best actors.

With *Shameless,* a seven-part autobiographical drama, also screening in 2004, Paul Abbott has established himself as one Britain's most prolific and original screenwriters. His success may suggest that the days of the writer as an important figure in British television are not yet numbered.

LEZ COOKE

Paul Abbott. Born in Burnley, England, 1960. Worked as story editor and scriptwriter on *Coronation Street,* writer and producer on *Cracker,* then creator and writer of several acclaimed series and serials, including *Touching Evil, Clocking Off,* and *State of Play.* Recipient: Royal Television Society Award for Best Writer, for *Clocking Off,* 2001.

Television

1988	*Dramarama,* "Blackbird Singing in the Dead of Night" (with Kay Mellor)
1989–94	*Coronation Street*
1989–95	*Children's Ward*
1995	*Sharman: Hearts of Stone*
	Cracker
1997	*Reckless*
	Springhill
	Touching Evil
1999	*Butterfly Collectors*
2000–02	*Clocking Off*
2000	*The Secret World of Michael Fry*
	Love in the 21st Century, "Reproduction"
2001	*Best of Both Worlds*
	Linda Green
2003	*State of Play*
	Alibi
2004	*Shameless*

Theater

1989	*Binnin' It*
1993	*Possession*

Further Reading

Abbott, Paul, "Making a Drama Out of a Crisis," *Observer* (December 21, 2003)

Abbott, Paul, "Spinners and Losers," *Guardian* (May 12, 2003)

Brown, Maggie, "The Best Stuff Comes from Real Life," *Daily Telegraph* (April 25, 1997)

Dessau, Bruce, "Watching the Clock," *Time Out* (January 19–26, 2000)

Keighron, Peter, "Master of the Scene," *Broadcast* (February 16, 2001)

O'Carroll, Lisa, "Abbott Turns His 'Sub-Working Class' Life into Drama," *Guardian Unlimited* (May 16, 2003)

ABC. *See* **American Broadcasting Company**

ABC Family Channel

When the Walt Disney Company bought the Family Channel from FOX in October 2001, the acquisition came with an unusual condition: two or three times a day, the cable channel now known as ABC Family Channel must provide time for the Christian evangelist Pat Robertson to air his religious talk show, *The 700 Club*. To understand the origin of this decree, one must look back to 1960, when a then-unknown Robertson bought a run-down UHF TV station in Portsmouth, Virginia, for $37,000 and called his operation the Christian Broadcasting Network (CBN). Robertson was a pioneer in satellite-delivered cable programming, since he saw that it was really the only way he could reach 60 million homes with his evangelical programming. CBN built its own satellite Earth station in 1977, bought $13 million worth of satellite time when it was sold cheaply, and began providing round-the-clock religious programming to a growing network of cable stations. By 1980 the Continental Broadcasting Network, an alternative name for CBN Cable, reached more than 5 million homes, and cable operators were paid eight cents a month per subscriber to provide the religious cable channel in their area.

Robertson financed the early days of his channel by allowing other religious broadcasters to buy his airtime, but the number of viewers was low. He then decided to boost his audience size by providing a broad channel of wholesome entertainment based on reruns of successful old shows from the 1960s and to get rid of all religious shows other than his own *700 Club*, which received a boost in viewership when CBN made the format change. On August 1, 1968, CBN Cable changed its name to the Family Channel.

Two years later, the U.S. Internal Revenue Service forced CBN to sell its profitable subsidiary. Pat Robertson and his son Tim arranged a leveraged buyout, with a new group, International Family Entertainment (IFE), purchasing the Family Channel from CBN for $250 million in cash and $43 million in program commitments. IFE was controlled and partially owned by Pat and Tim Robertson, and, under the terms of the sale, IFE and its successors were required to provide airtime for *The 700 Club* in perpetuity. It was good deal for everyone; CBN claimed that the transaction provided the company with $600 million in benefits (which included everything from cash to airtime), and IFE, brilliantly managed by Tim Robertson, Larry Dantzler, and John de Moose from Chrysler, soon became a profitable entity. Launched on the New York Stock Exchange in 1992, IFE became a publicly held $150 million company.

IFE flourished, buying a chain of theaters in the southern United States and starting the Games Channel, with a format of original game shows and reruns of such series as *Crosswits, Let's Make a Deal,* and *Truth or Consequences.* IFE also began a cable Health Club Channel, with limited success. Tim Robertson's most inspired move was to negotiate the 1993 acquisition of the United Kingdom operation Television South (TVS) for a modest $85 million. TVS had lost its license to broadcast in the ITV awards of 1992 but still had impressive holdings, including MTM Productions (which TVS had bought for approximately $285 million four years earlier) and Maidstone Studios, which IFE later sold for a profit. Ownership of MTM gave IFE not only the production company's library of programs but also its production facilities in Los Angeles; in addition the TVS acquisition presented an opportunity to establish a British version of the Family Channel.

IFE grew into a variety of entertainment divisions, which included production, live-entertainment, and syndication groups. The MTM catalog provided the channel with such notable programs as *The Bob Newhart Show, Lou Grant,* and *Evening Shade.* IFE revenues rose from $242 million in 1994 to $273 million in 1995 to $315 million in 1996. Cable analyst Breck Wheeler suggested that IFE was "poised to ride a wave of worldwide cable system growth that will push demand for both original and syndicated programming." Big groups like Disney and FOX looked toward the Family Channel as an attractive acquisition, while at the same time the Robertsons doubted whether they had the long-term capital resources to compete for new programming with the giants who surrounded them. For Pat Robertson, the real incentive to own the Family Channel remained its ability to carry *The 700 Club* to a nationwide audience; if the terms of any sale included the provision that the new owners must carry this show, he reasoned, why not sell? The issue then became who would pay the highest price, Disney or FOX?

In 1996 it was an Israeli entrepreneur with a huge library of cartoons for kids, Haim Saban of Saban Entertainment, who started serious negotiations to acquire IFE, with the enthusiastic backing of the FOX Children's Network. The new company was called FOX Kids Worldwide, jointly owned by FOX Broadcasting and Saban Entertainment. FOX saw the merger as a necessary ingredient for future success in their worldwide expansion plans. Margaret Loesch, chief executive officer of FOX Kids Networks Worldwide, was quoted as saying that, "Together, we are greater than the sum of our parts.... By bringing [Saban] on board, it gives us an insurance policy and the tools we need to build a very strong international television company. I think it makes the difference between success and failure." In hindsight, the Saban presence did make a difference, but not the one for which Loesch had hoped: Saban's total lack of cable programming experience doomed FOX Kids Worldwide to relative failure.

Still, back in June 1997 Rupert Murdoch, chairman and CEO of FOX's parent company, News Corporation, was congratulated on his wisdom in buying IFE for the price of $1.9 billion. At that point, the Family Channel reached 59 million homes in the United States. Now known as FOX Family Worldwide, the channel thus provided the Saban/Murdoch team with a cable base of roughly equal standing to that of the two other main children's cable enterprises in the United States: Viacom's Nickelodeon channel (reaching 66.8 million homes at that time) and Time Warner's Cartoon Network (cablecast in 28.3 million households). However, the good times promised did not materialize, for the audience accustomed to the Family Channel format did not like drastic changes in programming instituted by the new owners. Sinking ratings and restless affiliates led to an immediate crisis; within a month Saban removed FOX Kids founder and creative head Loesch from all operations.

IFE staff members left in droves, while Saban struggled desperately to stop the disintegration of his audience by hiring Rich Cronin, a 13-year Nickelodeon veteran, as FOX Family president, but Nickelodeon's owners, MTV Networks, went to court and prevented Cronin from taking the position until his old contract terminated in July 1998. Tim Robertson stepped down from his duties as adviser to the network, and Saban was left without the guidance he needed. He decided to change everything he inherited from IFE and spent $100 million on promotion, promising another $125 million for 26 original movies.

Cronin only survived two years under Saban. By May 2000 ratings for FOX Family remained static at 0.3; viewing by children was up 6 percent, but the adult audience 18 to 49 years, a demographic so important to advertisers, declined 0.6 percent. The company lost $86 million and was forced to borrow $125 million from another News Corporation unit at a high interest rate of 20 percent. Saban and News Corporation denied they were looking to sell, but rumors abounded. Salvation for the ailing network came in July 2001, when Disney paid an amazing $5.3 billion ($3 billion in cash and $2.3 billion in assumed debt), an amount 32 times the annual cash flow generated from FOX Family's 81 million basic-cable subscribers. Disney executives openly acknowledged that one way they expected to justify the high price was through license-fee hikes to operators.

Disney's purpose in buying FOX Family Worldwide and renaming it ABC Family was to provide an outlet for "repurposed content." In plainer language, Disney intends to repeat its programming from the ABC network and other Disney subsidiaries on the ABC Family Channel, a strategy some media analysts think can succeed. One thing remains from the old Family Channel days, however; whether Disney likes the program or not, *The 700 Club* is now carried by the ABC Family Channel.

ANDREW QUICKE

Aboriginal People's Television Network

Aboriginal People's Television Network's (APTN) inaugural broadcast on September 1, 1999, from Winnipeg, Canada, marked a watershed in North American and international television. APTN is the first national network controlled and operated by indigenous peoples carrying primarily aboriginal content. The Canadian Radio-television and Telecommunications Commission's (CRTC) February 1999 license decision established APTN as a mandatory service distributed to nearly 8 million households on basic cable, satellite, and wireless cable.

In regions and nations with significant "Fourth

Courtesy of APTN

World" populations like Canada, the United States, Australia, New Zealand, Scandinavia, and several Central and South American countries, indigenous minority groups have recently included access to media among their other struggles, such as political rights, land entitlement, and cultural autonomy. APTN can be situated within this global emergence of indigenous media and demonstrates First Peoples' desire to use television and other media as tools to sustain aboriginal languages and cultures.

Aboriginal television in Canada has its roots in community radio projects in the 1970s, interactive satellite experiments in the 1980s, and the consolidation of regional native broadcasting organizations across the north in the 1990s. Throughout this period, aboriginal groups (including Indian, Inuit, and Metis) actively lobbied various government jurisdictions for more direct control over television production and distribution as a means of counteracting the flow of nonnative media and its cultural influences upon native communities.

Beginning in 1985, television produced by federally funded native communications societies was distributed to northern native audiences on the basis of ad hoc and often unstable agreements with existing networks such as the Canadian Broadcasting Corporation (CBC) or TV Ontario. In 1992 the CRTC licensed a consortium of native broadcasters and northern educational institutions to operate a dedicated northern native satellite channel called Television Northern Canada (TVNC). TVNC was APTN's immediate predecessor, but the service was not widely available in southern and urban Canada, and it was limited by declining government support for the native broadcasters supplying programs.

In 1997 TVNC implemented a strategy to re-create the network as a national television channel with a secure financial base and renewed mandate to represent aboriginal people across Canada. In its license application to the CRTC, APTN emphasized the need to see Canada through aboriginal eyes in order to strengthen national unity and contribute to the country's cultural development. The network fulfills key requirements for participation of aboriginal peoples laid out by the 1991 Broadcasting Act. APTN is also a response to recommendations of the1990–96 Royal Commission on Aboriginal Peoples, which called for a new relationship between aboriginal and nonaboriginal Canadians.

APTN is a unique hybrid of several elements in Canada's mixed broadcast economy. Constituted as a nonprofit, native-controlled entity, it fulfills public service and cultural policy objectives, while its mandatory carriage and reliance on subscription fees adapts the financial model of specialty cable channels. In the tradition of earlier native broadcasting, APTN remains connected to aboriginal communities through its 21-member volunteer Aboriginal Board of Directors, drawn from all regions of Canada.

Although the eight northern native broadcasters who contribute regional programming to APTN receive some operating funds from the federal government, the network itself depends primarily on the $.15 per month, per residential subscriber, collected from cable and satellite distributors in combination with a small percentage of advertising income.

The majority of APTN programming is uplinked from its Winnipeg headquarters; a smaller portion originates in Yellowknife. APTN broadcasts in English (60 percent), French (15 percent) and a variety of aboriginal languages (25 percent). The network has less proprietary interest in its programs than conventional networks and functions as a distributor for locally and regionally produced aboriginal programming. By acquiring much of its new programming from independent aboriginal production companies, APTN is generating the growth of a distinctive aboriginal television sector. In 2001 APTN successfully applied to increase its non-Canadian content from 10 percent to 30 percent, allowing the network to reflect the diverse perspectives and cultures of the world's indigenous peoples through a greater proportion of international programming.

While its first season consisted primarily of "shelf product" and contributions from former TVNC members, by October 2000 APTN was able to launch 20 new programs. The network mounted its own in-house news and current affairs programs in April 2000. *APTN National News* now contains segments from all regions, with bureaus in major Canadian centers. A live national call-in program, *Contact,* covers a wide range of topical issues relevant to First Peoples, from aboriginal content on the Internet to a public "town hall" debate in Ottawa on proposed revisions to Canada's Indian Act. Northern native broadcasters contribute news and current affairs programming in aboriginal languages including Inuktitut, Inuvialuktun, Dene, Oji-Cree, and Cree.

Programming for children and young people includes: *Takuginai,* an Inuktitut puppet show that teaches young children values of respect and sharing; *Longhouse Tales,* a combined puppet and live action program for older children; and *Seventh Generation,* profiles of aboriginal youth who excel in their fields. APTN also schedules several arts and entertainment programs. *Buffalo Tracks* is a talk show featuring aboriginal guests in a wide range of fields. *The Rising Sun Café* presents interviews with aboriginal talent in sports, theater, and music from Edmonton. In *Cooking with the Wolfman,* chef David Wolfman demonstrates aboriginal fusion cuisine.

Part of APTN's mandate is cross-cultural communication with a nonaboriginal audience. Reception immediately after its launch was mixed, with some nonnative critics welcoming the unique perspectives offered by aboriginal television, others dismissing the new network as another instance of government handouts. While APTN is included in the basic-cable package, it competes for attention with the second and third cable tiers as well as with a new slate of digital specialty channels launched in September 2002. APTN has been given channel assignments in the 50s and 60s in many areas, making it that much harder to locate by the casual channel surfer. The network risks being marginalized within rapidly expanding television choices in Canada. Still in its infancy, APTN offers Canadian audiences a tantalizing model of how television can communicate cultural differences. Presenting the nation through aboriginal eyes subtly relocates the center, so that viewers can begin to imagine more inclusive local, national, and global cultural spaces.

MARIAN BREDIN

See also **First People's Television Broadcasting in Canada; Television Northern Canada**

Further Reading

David, Jennifer, "Seeing Ourselves, Being Ourselves: Broadcasting Aboriginal Television in Canada," *Cultural Survival Quarterly,* Vol. 22 (1998)

Haggarty, Dolores, "APTN's Long Road to the Air," *Globe and Mail* (September 1, 1999)

Regan, Tom, "Aboriginal Network Tests Idea of Niche TV," *Christian Science Monitor* (January 21, 2000)

Rice, Harmony, "Don't Touch That Dial!" *Aboriginal Voices,* Vol. 6 (1999)

Roth, Lorna, "Bypassing of Borders and Building of Bridges: Steps in the Construction of the Aboriginal Peoples Television Network in Canada," *Gazette: International Journal for Communication Studies,* Vol. 62 (2000)

Roth, Lorna, "First Peoples' Television in Canada's North: A Case Study of the Aboriginal Peoples Television Network," in *Mediascapes: New Patterns in Canadian Communications,* edited by Paul Attallah and Leslie Regan Shade, Scarborough, Ontario: Nelson, Thomson Canada Ltd., 2002

Absolutely Fabulous

British Situation Comedy

A half-hour BBC sitcom with a large cult following, *Absolutely Fabulous* debuted in 1992 with six episodes. Six additional episodes appeared in 1994, six more in 1995, and still another half-dozen in 2001. The U.S. cable channel Comedy Central began running the series in 1994.

Ab Fab, as fans call it, is about idle-rich Edina Monsoon (Jennifer Saunders), a 40-ish spoiled brat who owns her own PR business but works at it only rarely (and incompetently). Stuck in the self-indulgences of the 1960s but showing no sign of that decade's political awareness, Edina refuses to grow up. Her principal

Absolutely Fabulous, Joanna Lumley, Jennifer Saunders, 1992–2001, episode "The Last Shout" aired November 6–7, 1996.
Courtesy of the Everett Collection

talent is making a spectacle of herself. This she achieves by dressing gaudily, speaking loudly and rudely, and lurching frantically from one exaggerated crisis to the next. All the while, she overindulges—in smoking, drinking, drugs, shopping, and fads (Buddhism, colonic irrigation, various unsuccessful attempts at slimming down). She lives extravagantly off the alimony provided by two ex-husbands.

Edina's best friend, Patsy Stone (Joanna Lumley), is equally a caricature. Employed as "fashion director" of a trendy magazine, she almost never works (she has the job because she slept with the publisher). She is even more of a substance abuser than Edina and trashier in appearance with an absurdly tall, blond hairdo and far too much lipstick. Most disturbingly, Patsy is overly dependent upon Edina for money, transportation, and especially companionship.

Patsy often behaves like an unruly daughter, thereby displacing Edina's real daughter, Saffron (Julia Sawalha), of whom Patsy is extremely jealous. Edina humors Patsy's excesses and seems parental only by virtue of her money and domineering personality. The real "mother" of the house is Saffron, a young adult who, in being almost irritatingly virtuous, is both a moral counterweight to Patsy and a comic foil for the two childlike adults.

Thus, Saffron represents conscience and serves a function similar to that of Meathead in *All in the Family,* except that in *Ab Fab* the generational conflict is not one of conservative versus liberal so much as bad versus good liberalism. Neither Saffron nor Edina is conservative. Although Saffron is somewhat nerdy in the manner of Alex Keaton of *Family Ties,* she lacks his predatory materialism and serves as a reassuring model of youth. While Patsy and Edina illustrate a pathological mutation of 1960s youth culture, Saffron provides hope that liberalism (or at least youth) is redeemable.

Ab Fab's focus on generational issues also plays out in Edina's disrespect for her mother (June Whitfield). The relationships among the four female main characters are all the more interesting because of the absence of men. Edina's father puts in only two appearances in the series (most noticeably as a corpse), and only Saffron cares that he has died. Similarly, Edina's son is never seen in the first 12 episodes and is only mentioned a few times. It is not that men are bad; rather, they are irrelevant.

This allows *Ab Fab* to have a feminist flavor even as it portrays women in mostly unflattering terms. Edina and Patsy are certainly not intended as role models, and in presenting them as buffoonish and often despicable, series creator-writer Saunders ridicules not only bourgeois notions of motherhood and family life but also media images of women's liberation. For example, Edina and Patsy, although "working women," actually depend upon the largesse of men to maintain their station in life. This cynical vision of professionalism may seem regressive, but at the same time, it is a refreshing critique of advertising and fashion, two industries invariably depicted by TV as "absolutely fabulous."

Ab Fab developed from a sketch on the *French and Saunders* show and is a fine example of the flowering of Alternative Comedy, the post-*Monty Python* movement that also produced *The Young Ones.* Rejecting what Roger Wilmut and Peter Rosengard have called the "erudite middle-class approach" of the *Python* generation, the new British comics of the 1980s approached their material with a rude, working-class, rock-and-roll sensibility (see Wilmut and Rosengard). *Ab Fab,* while focusing on the concerns of middle age, nonetheless has a youthful energy and eschews sentimentality. Flashbacks and dream sequences contribute to this energy and give the show a mildly anarchic structure.

A smash hit in Britain, *Ab Fab* won two International Emmy Awards and gave the somewhat obscure

Comedy Central channel a significant publicity boost. Camp elements of the series were especially appreciated by gay viewers, among whom the Edina and Patsy characters achieved icon status. Comedian Roseanne began developing an American adaptation of *Ab Fab* in 1995 but was unable to find a network willing to air it. Meanwhile, Saunders kept the franchise alive by producing a half-hour mock documentary, *How to Be Absolutely Fabulous* (1995), and a reunion movie, *Absolutely Fabulous: The Last Shout* (1996). Six new episodes of the sitcom aired on the BBC in 2001 and debuted on Comedy Central in November of that year.

The success of *Ab Fab* and other mid-1990s series such as *Politically Incorrect* has encouraged Comedy Central to venture even further in the direction of topicality and taboo breaking. For the cable channel, this programming strategy has resulted in additional success *(South Park)* as well as the occasional failure *(That's My Bush!).*

GARY BURNS

See also **Comedy Central; Lumley, Joanna; Saunders, Jennifer**

Cast

Edina Monsoon	Jennifer Saunders
Patsy Stone	Joanna Lumley
Saffron Monsoon	Julia Sawalha
June Monsoon (Mother)	June Whitfield
Bubble	Jane Horrocks

Producer

Jon Plowman

Programming History

BBC

November 1992–December 1992	Six episodes
January 1994–March 1994	Six episodes
March 1995–May 1995	Six episodes
August 2001–October 2001	Six episodes

Further Reading

"An Absolutely Fabulous Finale," *New Yorker* (March 20, 1995)

Kroll, Gerry, "The Women," *Advocate* (April 16, 1996)

Lyall, Sarah, "Absolutely Catching, Bad Habits and All," *New York Times* (July 13, 1995)

O'Connor, John, "Absolutely Fabulous," *New York Times* (June 12, 1995)

Putterman, Barry, *On Television and Comedy: Essays on Style, Theme, Performer, and Writer,* Jefferson, North Carolina: McFarland, 1995

Saunders, Jennifer, *Absolutely Fabulous,* London: BBC Books, 1993

Saunders, Jennifer, *Absolutely Fabulous 2,* London: BBC Books, 1994

Wilmut, Roger, and Peter Rosengard, *Didn't You Kill My Mother-in Law? The Story of Alternative Comedy in Britain from the Comedy Store to Saturday Live,* London: Methuen, 1989

A.C. Nielsen Company

Media Market Research Firm

Under the banner of Nielsen Media Research, AC-Nielsen measures and compiles statistics on television audiences. It sells this data in various formats to advertisers, advertising agencies, program syndicators, television networks, local stations, and cable program and system operators. Marketing research comprises the primary activity of ACNielsen, which provides a variety of standard market analysis reports and engages in other market research on many different consumer products and services for clients worldwide. By some reports, only 10 percent of ACNielsen's total business relates to the television audience, although it is well known to the general public for that work. This is due, of course, to the ubiquitous reporting and discussion of program and network ratings produced by ACNielsen.

The A.C. Nielsen Company was started in 1923 by A.C. Nielsen, an engineer, and bought by Dun and Bradstreet in 1984 for $1.3 billion. On February 16, 2001, the company was acquired by VNU N.V., an international media and information corporation based in the Netherlands. Thus, ACNielsen is no longer an independent entity but a subsidiary of the larger conglomerate.

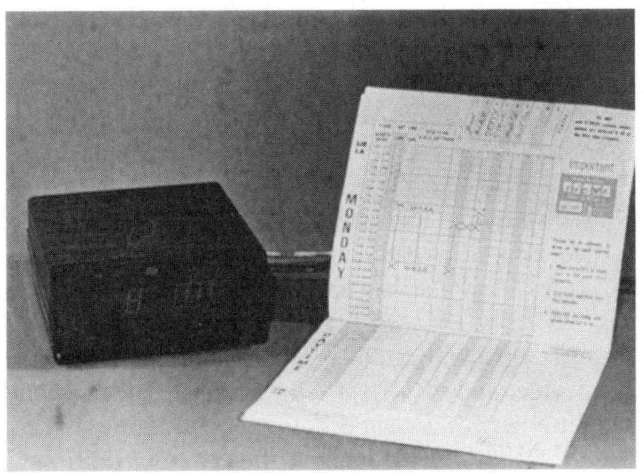

A Nielsen viewing diary.
Courtesy of Nielsen Media Research

A Nielsen "Peoplemeter."
Courtesy of Nielsen Media Research

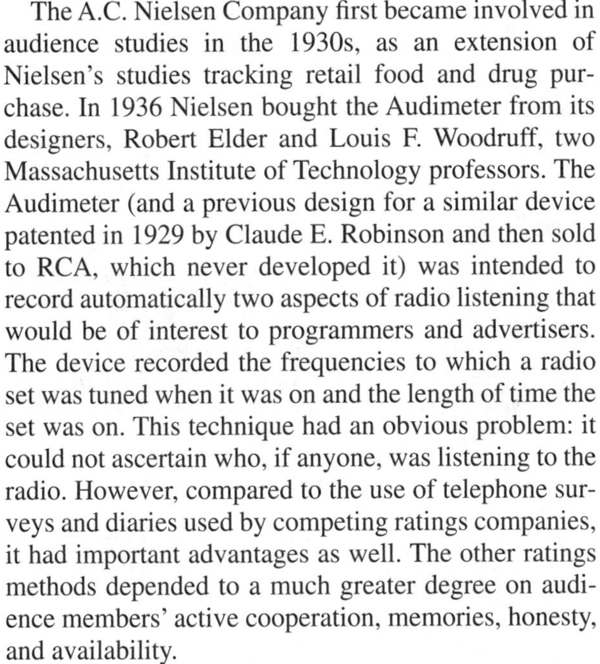

The A.C. Nielsen Company first became involved in audience studies in the 1930s, as an extension of Nielsen's studies tracking retail food and drug purchase. In 1936 Nielsen bought the Audimeter from its designers, Robert Elder and Louis F. Woodruff, two Massachusetts Institute of Technology professors. The Audimeter (and a previous design for a similar device patented in 1929 by Claude E. Robinson and then sold to RCA, which never developed it) was intended to record automatically two aspects of radio listening that would be of interest to programmers and advertisers. The device recorded the frequencies to which a radio set was tuned when it was on and the length of time the set was on. This technique had an obvious problem: it could not ascertain who, if anyone, was listening to the radio. However, compared to the use of telephone surveys and diaries used by competing ratings companies, it had important advantages as well. The other ratings methods depended to a much greater degree on audience members' active cooperation, memories, honesty, and availability.

After a period of redesign and a four-year pilot study, the Nielsen Audimeter was introduced commercially in 1942 with an 800-home sample in the eastern United States. The number of Audimeters and the sample size and coverage were expanded after World War II, eventually, by 1949, representing 97 percent of U.S. radio homes. The Cooperative Analysis of Broadcasting had ceased providing ratings in 1946; in 1950 the A.C. Nielsen Company bought Hooper's national radio and television ratings services and thus became the single national radio-rating service. This allowed the company to increase rates, and the new capital was used to increase sample size. As the television industry grew, the Nielsen Company's attention to television grew with it, and the company left the radio field in 1964.

In 1973 the Nielsen Company began using the Storage Instantaneous Audimeter, a new and more sophisticated design for the same purposes as the original (although surely not the only modification to the Audimeter made over the years, this one was much publicized). Set in a closet, designed with battery backup for power outages, and hooked to a dedicated telephone line for daily data reports to a central office, the device kept track of turn on, turnoff, and channel setting for every television in a household, including battery-operated and portable units (through radio transmitter).

Although the Audimeter, widely known as the "Nielsen black box," was the company's most famous device, it was used only for household television ratings. For ratings by people and demographic descriptions of the audience, the Nielsen Company required supplementary studies of audience composition based on a separate sample using the diary technique. This separate sample was smaller, and there was concern in the industry that the people who cooperated with the diaries were not representative of the population in general.

In the 1970s the Nielsen Company experimented with Peoplemeters, a system for measuring the viewing of individuals without diaries, but brought no new services to market. In 1983 AGB Research of Great Britain proposed a commercial Peoplemeter service in the United States similar to the system that organization was using in other countries. This proposal attracted funding from a group of networks, advertising agencies, and others for an evaluation study in Boston. In 1985, in response to this competitive threat, the

Nielsen Company initiated its own Peoplemeter sample, as a supplement to its existing samples. Reports became available beginning in January 1986. The system depends on a box sitting atop the television set that keeps track, in the usual way, of what channel is tuned in. However, the meter is also programmed with demographic descriptions of individual viewers in the household and their visitors. Viewers are asked to push a button indicating when they begin or end viewing the television, even if the set is left on when they leave. The data then indicate which (if any) viewers are present as well as set tuning. (There have also been experiments with passive meters that use infrared sensing rather than requiring viewers to cooperate by pressing buttons, but so far these devices have not been sufficiently reliable.)

Because the Peoplemeters produced different numbers than diaries, they generated controversy in the industry. Ratings points are the reference for negotiations in the purchase of advertising time, in deciding which programs are syndicated, and other issues vital to the television industry. Thus, when different measurement techniques produce different ratings, normal business negotiations become complicated and less predictable. For this reason, many participants in the television business actually prefer one company to have a monopoly on the ratings business, even if it does allow that company to charge higher rates for its services. Even if this service provides inaccurate numbers, those numbers become agreed-upon currency for purposes of negotiation. Eventually, the most recent controversies were settled, and AC-Nielsen's Peoplemeter system now dominates the production of national television ratings.

The Audimeter was originally conceived as a means to the testing of advertising effectiveness. To at least some extent, A.C. Nielsen's own interest in broadcast audiences was originally motivated by his marketing and advertising clients. However, the ratings have grown to be an end in themselves, a product sold to parties interested in the composition of audiences for broadcasting.

Among the ratings reports provided by the Nielsen Company were, until 1964, the Nielsen Radio Index (NRI) for network radio audiences. Currently, AC-Nielsen provides the Nielsen Television Index (NTI) for network television audiences, the Station Index (NSI) for local stations and for designated market areas (DMAs), the Syndication Service (NSS) for the audiences of syndicated television shows, and the Homevideo Index (NHI) for the audiences of cable and satellite networks, superstations, and home video. More recent systems include the Nielsen/NetRatings Internet audience measurement service (in partnership with NetRatings).

ACNielsen periodically produces reports on special topics as well, such as videocassette recorder (VCR) usage, viewership of sports programming, or television viewing in presidential election years. In 1992 ACNielsen launched the first national Hispanic television ratings service (Nielsen Hispanic Television Index) in the United States.

ERIC ROTHENBUHLER

Further Reading

Beville, Hugh Malcolm, *Audience Ratings: Radio, Television, and Cable,* Hillsdale, New Jersey: Erlbaum, 1985; revised edition, 1988

Buzzard, Karen, *Electronic Media Ratings,* Boston: Focal, 1992

Clift, Charles III, and Archie Greer, editors, *Broadcast Programming: The Current Perspective,* Washington, D.C.: University Press of America, 1981

Dominick, Joseph R., and James E. Fletcher, *Broadcasting Research Methods,* Boston: Allyn and Bacon, 1985

Webster, James G., and Lawrence W. Lichty, *Ratings Analysis: Theory and Practice,* Hillsdale, New Jersey: Erlbaum, 1991

What TV Ratings Really Mean, How They Are Obtained, Why They Are Needed, New York: Nielsen Media Research, 1993

Academy of Television Arts and Sciences

The Academy of Television Arts and Sciences (ATAS) is known primarily for bestowing Emmys, the top awards for television. These are peer awards, selected by vote of members of the academy, individuals who work in the television industry. In addition to presenting this most public face of the television industry in an annual award ceremony, the academy also engages in a number of other educational and public functions.

The academy was founded in 1946 in Los Angeles by Syd Cassyd, a trade journal writer who recognized the need for a television organization similar to the Academy of Motion Picture Arts and Sciences. Cassyd

The Emmy Award.
Courtesy of the Everett Collection

and a group of associates held several exploratory meetings and then decided they needed a major television industry figure to support the project. They succeeded in interesting ventriloquist Edgar Bergen, who became the academy's first president in 1947.

One of the earliest activities of the new academy was to establish a creative identity (and a degree of publicity and prestige) for the developing television industry by presenting awards, the Emmys, in recognition for outstanding work in the medium. Originally, the awards were to be called "Ikes," an abbreviation for the television iconoscope tube. Because "Ike" was so closely associated with Dwight D. Eisenhower, however, the group decided on "Emmy," a feminine form of "Immy," nickname for the television camera image orthicon tube. A contest was held for the design of the statuette and the winner was Louis McManus, an engineer, who used his wife as the model for the winged woman holding up the symbol of the electron.

In the first year of the award, Emmys were presented in only five categories. And because television did not yet have a coast-to-coast hookup, they were given only to Los Angeles programs and personalities. Shirley Dinsdale (and her puppet Judy Splinters) was the Most Outstanding Television Personality and *Pantomime Quiz* the Most Popular Television Program. By the second year, any show seen in Los Angeles could receive an award and New York-based personalities such as Milton Berle and Ed Wynn were winners.

At this point, there was more intrigue backstage in the academy than onstage. In 1950 Ed Sullivan, host of *Toast of the Town,* produced in New York, initiated a rival TV awards program, but these lasted only until 1953. No awards were presented in 1954 (the only year there have been no Emmys), because the Los Angeles group had decided the show had become too expensive. By 1955, however, the television networks were interested and the Emmys were broadcast nationally for the first time. Sullivan, realizing the Hollywood-based Emmys were a success, became upset and called together New York's television leaders. They demanded, and were granted, a New York chapter of the academy. They then asked for another academy, with equal "founding chapters" in both New York and Hollywood. Thus, in 1957 a newly formed and newly named National Academy of Television Arts and Sciences (NATAS) was created with Sullivan as the first president.

The animosity between the East and West Coasts continued. In the early years, New York had the upper hand because the networks were based there and much early live dramatic programming, as well as news and documentaries, emanated from New York. From 1955 to 1971, the Emmys were simulcast with cameras cutting between New York and Los Angeles, often creating technical blunders that left screens blank for several minutes.

By 1971, however, Hollywood was firmly established as the predominant site for television program production. New York was no longer producing live dramas, and, although it was still the seat of news and documentaries, audiences tuned in to the Emmys to see Hollywood stars. In addition, the Emmys were growing in number and the telecast in length, so in 1973 and 1974 the news and documentary categories were removed from the regular show (now produced totally in Hollywood) and given their own telecast. Ratings were low, however, and the show was dropped.

During this period, other cities such as Atlanta, Chicago, and Cincinnati organized academy chapters. Hollywood producers resented the fact that academy members, scattered throughout the country, all had equal votes in determining the Emmy Awards. From their beginning, the Emmys were conceived as peer awards, and the powerful Hollywood community hardly considered a cameraperson in Cincinnati to be a peer. New York, however, sided with the smaller chapters.

In 1976 the Hollywood chapter of NATAS decided to split from that organization. A year of lawsuits followed, but the end result was two academies: the National Academy of Television Arts and Sciences comprised of New York and outlying cities, and the Hollywood-based Academy of Television Arts and Sciences. NATAS would bestow daytime, sports, news, and documentary Emmys, and ATAS would oversee prime-time awards, using its Hollywood member base as voters.

The two academies remain separate, although from time to time they hold meetings regarding reunification, and ATAS has assisted NATAS in the production of the Daytime Emmy Awards. When those prizes first aired nationally in 1991, they achieved higher ratings than the prime-time awards. During this period, ATAS was having its own problems with the prime-time show. For many years, the telecast rotated sequentially among ABC, CBS, and NBC. When the upstart FOX network went on the air, it offered the academy more money for the telecasts than the other networks had been paying, and from 1987 to 1992 the Emmys were shown exclusively on the new network. Ratings plummeted, largely because FOX programming did not appear on local stations throughout the entire country. Eventually the academy returned to the rotation concept, with FOX as one of the participants.

ATAS's membership is based on peer groups: writers, art directors, performers, sound editors, production executives, and so forth. Each peer group establishes its own requirement for membership, usually defined in terms of the number of shows or number of hours of television the person has to his or her credit. The board of governors is composed of two members from each peer group.

Voting for prime-time Emmys is also conducted on a peer group basis, so that only members of the music peer group vote for awards involving music, directors vote for directing awards, and so on. Some "Best Program" awards can be voted on by much of the membership. Individuals may nominate themselves for awards, and producers may nominate individuals or programs. All nominated material is then judged by the appropriate peers, who come to a central location to view the tapes or are mailed tapes to view at home. Their votes are tabulated and the winners are announced, either during the on-air telecast or at a luncheon ceremony. In general, the awards that the public is most likely to find interesting (performers, outstanding shows, directors) are presented during the prime-time telecast.

While the Emmy Awards are the most visible of its projects, the academy undertakes many other activities including sponsoring a paid student internship program, through which outstanding students from around the country spend eight weeks working with Hollywood professionals; conducting a contest for student TV productions with the winners receiving cash sums; inducting outstanding industry professionals into a hall of fame; holding an annual faculty seminar, where college teachers come to Hollywood and are introduced to people and ideas related to TV programming; hosting luncheons and meetings at which people from within and without the industry share ideas and information; participating, with the University of California Los Angeles, in overseeing a television archives; and publishing *Emmy,* a magazine devoted to articles about the TV industry.

In 1991 ATAS moved into new headquarters containing office space as well as a state-of-the-art theater in which to screen television materials and hold large meetings.

LYNNE GROSS

See also **National Academy of Television Arts and Sciences**

Further Reading

Michael, Paul, and James Robert Parish, *The Emmy Awards: A Pictorial History,* New York: Crown, 1970

O'Neil, Thomas, *The Emmys: Star Wars, Showdowns, and the Supreme Test of TV's Best,* New York: Penguin, 1992

Acquisitions. *See* **Mergers and Acquisitions**

Action/Adventure Programs

"Action/Adventure" is a loose generic categorization that encompasses a range of programming types, all of which celebrate bodies and objects in action across the television screen. Action/adventure is not a formal or technical term, but this melding of two Hollywood film genres can been seen as a staple within American television production. It is often considered a quality or stylistic mode within other, more popular genres: detective series, westerns, science fiction, fantasy, police shows, war dramas, spy thrillers, and crime stories.

Whether a particular program can be deemed an action/adventure show is somewhat arbitrary; what qualifies as action- or adventure-oriented enough to fit within the genre has changed over the course of television history. While there are many series that have not followed these larger programming patterns, there have been certain types of action/adventure shows that have been particularly popular during specific eras. In the 1950s, westerns and detective programs ruled the genre and the screen, while in the 1960s, during the height of the cold war, American television viewers saw a larger trend toward international spy stories. Tough, urban undercover cops became popular in the early 1970s, while in the later half of the decade, the trend was toward fantasy and mild titillation. The 1980s action/adventure show centered around the group or the crime-fighting couple, while in the 1990s the action heroine emerged as a popular new lead. In the new millennium, the emphasis seems to be on reality action/adventure programming, with a return to the international action/adventure thriller also discernible.

Because of its emphasis on violence, the genre has often served as an easy target for public criticism. As a genre, action/adventure shows celebrate spectacle, often based on violence, from elaborate fight sequences, to the representation of people in physical jeopardy, to car chases, to explosions, to the dramatization of crimes. In 1961, United States Federal Communications Commission chief Newton Minow decried television as "a vast wasteland," singling out as the arbiters of mediocrity

> a procession of game shows, violence, audience participation shows, formula comedies about unbelievable families, blood and thunder, mayhem, violence, sadism, murder, western badmen, western good men, private eyes, gangsters, more violence, and cartoons.

Besides his disdain for game shows, cartoons, and domestic comedies, most of his comments seemed directed toward a genre that was dominating prime-time network programming during this era, the action/adventure show. Nevertheless, the genre has remained popular because of its ability to thrill, shock, and ultimately entertain television viewers.

Advancements in the technology of television production have often had their greatest showcase in the action/adventure show. Technical innovations in film stock, cameras, and sound equipment have lead to greater flexibility for television producers in designing the look of their programs. The syndicated adventure series *Sea Hunt* (1957–61) made use of underwater camera equipment to follow the show's hero, Mike Nelson (Lloyd Bridges), on his deep-sea adventures. Programs such as the buddy espionage series *I Spy* (NBC, 1965–68) began using location shooting to create more exciting visuals and dramatic chase sequences. The early 1980s saw great changes as handheld cameras brought a more gritty, realistic feel to programs such as *Hill Street Blues* (NBC, 1981–87). With the knowledge that the average viewer's television screen size is increasing, television programs are becoming more visually complex. A program like Michael Mann's *Miami Vice* (NBC, 1984–89), which was shot much like an MTV video, or the hybrid science fiction police drama *The X-Files* would film sequences outdoors in low light, knowing that color technology on television sets could still register the image clearly on modern television screens. In order to keep track of multiple, simultaneous actions, the television program *24* uses split screens to follow as many as five different characters' movements at the same time. Since its inception, the action/adventure show has virtually been defined by its fast-paced style: a detective show becomes action/adventure simply by an increase in motion of the bodies represented—both by actors and the editor.

While there were a few programs that could be considered action/adventure in the early years of television, it was not until the mid-1950s that the genre became defined for television. By the middle of the decade, action/adventure programming was extremely popular, manifesting itself in the form of westerns, crime shows, and children's programming. The late

Sea Hunt, Lloyd Bridges, 1957–61, water.
Courtesy of the Everett Collection

1950s saw an exponential rise in the number of action-oriented westerns on television, including *Cheyenne, Gunsmoke, Maverick, Have Gun—Will Travel,* and *The Rifleman.* These westerns featured the exploits of a strong man of the West, and episodes often involved dramatic, violent confrontations. The second most popular dramatic prime-time program of the era was the detective show. While some programs featured more thrills than others, the detective program always offered a few sequences filled with action and danger. Focusing more on the individual, the detective show, from *Peter Gunn,* to *77 Sunset Strip,* to *Route 66,* offered access to a world of drama, intrigue, and adventure. The police procedural *Dragnet* (NBC, 1952–59, 1967–70), proved to be one of the most successful action/adventure series, lasting over eight years and making the program's laconic actor-director Jack Webb into a household name. For four years, Desilu Productions offered perhaps the most violent program of the era, *The Untouchables* (ABC, 1959–63), which celebrated the crime-fighting work of Eliot Ness and his gang and emphasized audience-pleasing action over historical accuracy. Children's programming of the era also offered a number of action/adventure series, a number of which were mined from popular children's books or comic book series, including *The Adventures of Rin Tin Tin, Zorro, The Lone Ranger, The Adventures of Superman,* and *Sheena, Queen of the Jungle.*

The popularity of action/adventure programming increased in the 1960s, with an emphasis on international espionage and detection. From *I Spy,* to *The Man from U.N.C.L.E.,* to *Mission: Impossible,* spy stories that seemed to echo real-life cold war experiences were extremely popular. Two programs from the United Kingdom both stood out as significant contributions to the genre—*The Avengers* and *The Prisoner.* Produced from 1961 to 1969, the British television import *The Avengers* promised a world of fashion, pop culture, and witty repartee, along with the typical espionage plots. (*The Avengers* reemerged in the 1970s again with a new female lead, but with less success.) *The Prisoner* (1968–69) was a personal tour de force for Patrick McGoohan, who created, produced, wrote, and starred in the series as its protagonist, the ex-spy, known only as Number Six, who is stuck in a merry-go-round world unable to escape. Another significant player in the genre emerged in the 1960s, television producer Aaron Spelling. First with his series featuring a young martial arts-trained female private detective, *Honey West* (ABC, 1965–66), and then a few years later with *The Mod Squad* (ABC, 1968–73), which followed street kids turned undercover cops, Spelling gave audiences hip, stylish, youthful heroes along with action-packed theatrics. The decade also offered a range of action/adventure programming that included war dramas, in particular *Combat* (ABC, 1962–67), as well as the cult hit *Star Trek* (NBC, 1966–69), a franchise that has been known for its dedicated fan following throughout all of its television, as well as cinematic, variations.

The genre began moving off the soundstage and onto the streets starting in the late 1960s. One program that capitalized on its location was *Hawaii Five-O* (CBS, 1968–80), the longest continually running police show, which featured tough, often brutal, violence along Hawaii's most beautiful beaches. After the program ended, CBS's production studio based in Hawaii was taken over by another action/adventure series, *Magnum, P.I.* (1980–88). Along with exciting locales came more youthful protagonists—a continuing trend that virtually guarantees the coveted 18–35 audience for the genre. *Starsky and Hutch* (ABC, 1975–79) featured two plainclothes cops, celebrating their swinging bachelorhood, catching criminals after long chase sequences in their bright red hot rod. As part of a similar tactic to bring

Macgyver, Richard Dean Anderson, 1985–92.
©Paramount/ Courtesy of the Everett Collection

Tarzan, Ron Ely, 1966–69.
Courtesy of the Everett Collection

in more youthful audiences, the 1970s saw a great surge in the number of high-concept, fantasy-oriented action/adventure shows. *The Six Million Dollar Man* (ABC, 1974–78) was the first in a line of heroes and heroines imbued with special powers who began saving the day on a weekly basis. From *The Bionic Woman,* to *Wonder Woman,* to *The Incredible Hulk,* superheroes promised great thrills and fearless characters, if often somewhat simplistic plotlines. The heroines could also be included in what Julie D'Acci has referred to as the "jiggle era" of the late 1970s, epitomized in the series *Charlie's Angels* (ABC, 1976–81), which featured young, sexy, fashionable women fighting crime. While the action/adventure heroine in the 1970s was negotiating a position of power, she was often quite conventional in comparison to the type of characters being developed in other television genres of the era, in particular, the sitcom. A few years later, *Cagney and Lacey* (CBS, 1982–88) countered the one-dimensional characters in 1970s jiggle programs by presenting female cops as both professionally and emotionally strong, well-rounded characters—but, like many of the female heroines of action/adventure programming, they were also less physically active.

The 1980s saw a rise in the number of crime-fighting buddies or teams. In 1983 Stephen Cannell, a veteran of the action/adventure genre, who had been involved in *Adam 12, Baretta,* and *The Rockford File,* as well as the superhero spoof *The Greatest American Hero,* began producing a show about four unjustly persecuted Vietnam veterans in the program *The A Team* (NBC, 1983–87). Each episode featured massive explosions, grand displays of firepower, but very little blood or death. Urban crime dramas such as *Miami Vice, Hill Street Blues,* and *Hunter* highlighted the intensity of city life and featured gritty, typically male cops who often had to break the rules in order to catch the most heinous criminals. The end of the 1980s saw an increase in reality programming, and for the action/adventure genre, in particular, an increased interest in police documentary programs, such as *COPS* (FOX, 1989–). *COPS* offered a view of real police tracking down and arresting ordinary criminals and seemed to celebrate the sordid, unsavory nature of the United States's underworld of crime.

Unlike these more violent action/adventure shows, a number of buddy programs featuring male-female private investigation firms began appearing on television

Wonder Woman, Lynda Carter, 1976–79.
Courtesy of the Everett Collection

screens. Starting with *Hart to Hart* (ABC, 1979–84), which featured wealthy, married supersleuth millionaires, buddy programs proved popular with male and female audiences. The success of *Remington Steele* (NBC, 1982–87) and the more comical than action-oriented duo in *Moonlighting* (ABC, 1985–89) soon lead to more crime-fighting couples, all of whom promised light action/adventure along with the prospect of romance. Even children's programming of the era played into the trend of team-oriented heroes, as evidenced by the great ratings and merchandising success of programs like *The Mighty Morphin Power Rangers* and *Teenage Mutant Ninja Turtles,* which were targeted primarily to young boys.

While there was a variety of action/adventure shows in the 1990s, many questioned the authority of what had often been, within the genre, a guaranteed acceptance of the government and the law as moral and just. Particularly popular with Generation X viewers (loosely defined as those born between 1965 and 1980), *The X-Files* (FOX, 1993–2002) was another buddy series but within a story arc that found the pair uncovering hidden government conspiracies about alien abductions.

Another trend that was decidedly broken in the mid-1990s was the focus on the male action hero. Up until the mid-1990s, the overwhelming number of action/adventure shows had starred male leads. Over the years there have been notable exceptions, but the 1990s saw a great rise in the number of action/adventure heroines on television, in particular *Xena: Warrior Princess* (syndicated, 1995–2001) and *Buffy the Vampire Slayer* (WB, 1997–2001, UPN, 2001–3). *Xena: Warrior Princess,* a syndicated, campy action/adventure show created as a spin-off to *Hercules: The Legendary Journeys* (syndicated, 1995–99), became a cult classic, with a strong female fan base. Two years later, the WB premiered *Buffy the Vampire Slayer* in an attempt to bring in the teen audience. These female action/adventure heroines gained strong audience followings, and soon more female heroines began to emerge on the small screen, from the animated series *The Powerpuff Girls,* to James Cameron's postapocalyptic *Dark Angel.*

The action/adventure show continues to be one of the most popular genres on American television. The early 2000s saw the development of the international crime show as well as the genre's blending with reality programming. Television shows like *24* (FOX, 2001–), which follows a government agent's attempt to thwart a presidential candidate's assassination; *Alias* (ABC, 2001–), whose heroine is both a graduate student and an international double agent, and *The Agency* (CBS, 2001–3), the first program created with the support of the CIA, all use federal agents as their heroes. While all of these programs went into production before the terrorist attacks of September 11, 2001, this progovernment trend in programming has only helped to increase their audience share. On an entirely different programming spectrum, the qualities of the action/adventure show can be seen within a reality series such as *Survivor* (CBS, 2000–), where contestants must brave physical challenges as well as the cutthroat competition among their peers.

At the turn of the century, the action/adventure show continued to morph to fit producers' whims and audiences' tastes. The genre has maintained its status as a television staple due to its flexibility in adapting various styles and genres. But always, at is core, is the pleasure of excess, from fights, to explosions, to awesome displays of power and bravura. The low-brow nature of the genre has led to much condemnation by politicians and cultural critics, and programs have often been cited for their emphasis on action and violence over narrative or character development. Yet for television scholars, the action/adventure shows' bold visual style, narrative conventions, and emphasis on a clear symbolic iconography have offered compelling points of entry for the study of American popular culture.

MIRANDA J. BANKS

See also **Avengers, The; Buffy the Vampire Slayer; Cagney and Lacey; Charlie's Angels; Cheyenne; COPS; Detective Programs; Dragnet; Gunsmoke; Have Gun—Will Travel; Hawaii 5–0; Hill Street Blues; I Spy; Man from U.N.C.L.E., The; Magnum, P.I.; Maverick; Miami Vice; Mission: Impossible; Moonlighting; Police Programs; Prisoner, The; Reality Programming; Star Trek; Starsky and Hutch; Survivor; Untouchables, The; Western; X-Files, The; Xena: Warrior Princess**

Further Reading

Buxton, David, *From the Avengers to Miami Vice: Form and Ideology in Television Series,* Manchester: Manchester University Press, 1990
Creeber, G., *The Television Genre Book,* London: British Film Institute, 2001
D'Acci, Julie, "Nobody's Woman?: *Honey West* and the New Sexuality," in *The Revolution Wasn't Televised: Sixties Television and Social Conflict,* edited by Lynn Spigel and L.M. Curtin, London: Routledge, 1997
Giles, Dennis, "A Structural Analysis of the Police Story," in *American Television Genres,* edited by Stuart M. Kaminsky, with Jeffrey H. Mahan, Chicago: Nelson-Hall, 1985
Higashi, Sumiko, "Hold It! Women in Television Adventure Series," *Journal of Popular Film and Television* (Fall 1980)
Inness, S.A., *Tough Girls: Women Warriors and Wonder Women in Popular Culture,* Philadelphia: University of Pennsylvania Press, 1999
Miller, T., *The Avengers,* London: British Film Institute, 1997
Osgerby, B., and A. Gough-Yates, *Action TV: Tough Guys, Smooth Operators and Foxy Chicks,* London: Routledge, 2001
Vahimagi, T., *The Untouchables,* London: British Film Institute, 1998

Action for Children's Television

U.S. Citizens' Activist Group

A "grassroots" activist group, Action for Children's Television (ACT) was founded by Peggy Charren and a group of "housewives and mothers" in her home in Newton, Massachusetts, in 1968. The members of ACT were initially concerned with the lack of quality television programming offered to children. In 1970 ACT petitioned the Federal Communications Commission (FCC), asking that television stations be required to provide more programming for the child viewer. In that year the organization also received its first funding from the John and Mary R. Markle Foundation. ACT later received funding from the Ford and Carnegie Foundations as well, grants that allowed the group to expand from volunteers to between 12 and 15 staff members at the height of its activity.

ACT was not generally viewed as a radical or right-wing group advocating censorship. According to Charren, "too many people who worry about children's media want to do it in. ACT was violently opposed to censorship." Partially due to this attitude, the group was able to gain support from members of the public and from many politicians.

ACT also became concerned with issues of advertising within children's programming. Of particular concern was their finding that one-third of all commercials aimed at children were for vitamins. Partially due to their efforts, the FCC enacted rules pertaining to program-length commercials, host selling, and the placement of separation devices between commercials and children's programming.

ACT was responsible for many cases brought before the courts involving the FCC and its policies concerning children's television. These cases include a major case in media law, *Action for Children's Television, et al. v. Federal Communications Commission and the United States of America* (821. F. 2d 741. D.C. Cir. 1987).

One of the major successes of ACT was the passage of the Children's Television Act of 1990. Shortly after the passage of this act, Charren announced the closing

Peggy Charren.
Photo courtesy of Peggy Charren

of Action for Children's Television, suggesting that it was now up to individual citizens' groups to police the airwaves. In recent years Charren, a strong supporter of the First Amendment, has fought against FCC regulations limiting "safe harbor" hours; she has also lobbied for government regulation of digital broadcasting to ensure that digital TV serves and protects the interests of children.

WILLIAM RICHTER

See also **Activist Television; Children and Television**

Further Reading

Alperowicz, Cynthia, and R. Krock, *Rocking the Boat: Celebrating 15 Years of Action for Children's Television,* Newtonville, Massachusetts: Action for Children's Television, 1983

Cole, Barry G., and Mal Oettinger, *Reluctant Regulators: The FCC and the Broadcast Audience,* Reading, Massachusetts: Addison-Wesley, 1978

Duncan, Roger Dean, "Rhetoric of the Kidvid Movement: Ideology, Strategies, and Tactics," *Central States Speech Journal* (Summer 1976)

Activist Television

Although it has antecedents in earlier print, radio, and film activism, activist television first arose in the late 1960s. A confluence of technological and social factors inspired activists of that era to use television as a tool for political, social, and cultural change. The advent of consumer video cameras, cable television, and video recorders/players opened up new possibilities in television production and distribution. Ordinary people could use inexpensive, portable production equipment to make their own messages in the video medium. Public access cable channels and consumer VCRs provided the means of viewing these messages. The growth of contemporaneous social movements and the founding of a new documentary tradition also spurred the rise of activist television. The New Left, the women's movement, and the civil rights movement all recognized the value of using television to communicate to their members and the society at large. In addition, a broad movement for participatory democracy advocated citizen involvement in public policy formation and access to the media. Participatory democrats thought that popular media, including television, should play a role in mobilizing people, disseminating information, and improving political and social life. At the same time, a new documentary tradition, known as "community media," began using film and video as a tool for political organizing within communities and for conveying community concerns to government authorities.

Over the years, various media-centered groups have attempted to use television for activism. Media scholars have called the resulting media by various names, including grassroots or community television, guerilla television, radical alternative television, and advocacy video. Differing mainly in their relative emphasis on a range of strategies and goals for media activism, these groups share an overarching interest in TV as a catalyst

Paper Tiger Television.
Courtesy of Paper Tiger TV Collective

Paper Tiger Television.
Courtesy of Paper Tiger TV Collective

for change, a medium for community expression, and a forum for democratic communication and representation.

The Canadian "Challenge for Change" project of the late 1960s and early 1970s was an early impetus for activist television. Grounded in the Canadian social democratic tradition and funded by the Canadian government and National Film Board, the project established and refined the concept of community media. Hoping to increase citizen involvement in social and cultural development, "Challenge for Change" sent video makers into impoverished or socially troubled locales to train already active citizens groups to communicate their needs. These groups used video to help establish community leaders, prioritize social agendas, tell their stories, catalyze local action, and demand better government programs and services. In its later years, the project promoted the creation of community video centers. A former executive producer on the project, George Stoney, cofounded the Alternative Media Center in New York in the early 1970s and began advocating for the establishment of community television in the United States and for public access cable television as a means of distributing community programming. Today, community television often stresses local outreach, organization, and participation; direct expression unmediated by industry professionals; and small scale, locally based initiatives and projects. This model of television activism has analogs in many other parts of the world, including Aboriginal community television in Australia, TV Maxambomba from the marginalized and impoverished neighborhoods of Rio de Janeiro, Brazil, and Video SEWA, produced by working women in Ahmedabad, India, to name a few.

Guerilla television groups in the United States were another impetus for activist television. Video collectives, such as Global Village, Videofreex, People's Video Theater, and Raindance, sought to use new technologies to create a more democratic and Utopian society. In the book *Guerilla Television,* Michael Shamberg of the Raindance collective laid out his ideas for the philosophy and practice of activist media. The book, which became known in the United States as the "Bible" of guerilla media, covered a range of issues, including the dynamics of the information economy, the nature of media bias, and practical tips on video production. Shamberg criticized the undemocratic, centralized, and monotonous character of the mainstream media and proposed a re-democratization of the media through political and cultural guerilla warfare waged with video, cable TV, and computers.

Activist television today also finds expression in radical alternative television and advocacy video projects. Radical alternative television includes noncommercial and noncorporate media that have a content, aesthetics, and organization that is fundamentally different from the mainstream media. These media address topics and represent viewpoints often excluded from mainstream television, sport a visual look that purposefully defies televisual norms and conventions, and adhere to a more democratic though less efficient and professionalized production process. In addition, these videos place their audience in a different relationship to the product they're viewing, often aiming at smaller and more specific audiences than their mainstream counterparts. Radical alternative television projects are activist in that they pose challenges to

Paper Tiger Television.
Courtesy of Paper Tiger TV Collective

dominant power structures, give voice to diverse communities and classes, enable like-minded groups to speak to one another, and aim to move and motivate their viewers. U.S. projects in this vein include: Paper Tiger Television, a video collective that produces a series of media critiques that deconstruct both the content and aesthetic of conventional media; *Labor Beat,* a news and public affairs show that covers labor issues for working people; and *Dyke TV,* a show made by and for lesbians.

Advocacy video refers to the production of works closely connected to specific political campaigns. These videos aim to motivate people to take direct action on issues such as environmental protection, human rights, animal rights, and corporate responsibility. Often in the form of short documentaries, advocacy videos focus on a particular problem intending to evoke a response, initiate debate, build constituencies, and shape legislation. There are many successful examples of advocacy video. The United Farm Workers video, *No Grapes* (1992), was part of an effective campaign to boycott California table grapes and ultimately to restrict the use of harmful pesticides. *Not in Our Town* (1995), a film produced in response to a series of hate crimes in Billings, Montana, was part of a national initiative to fight hate crimes. *Deadly Deception* (1991), an Academy Award–winning documentary designed to hold the General Electric (GE) corporation responsible for the health effects of its nuclear production facilities, helped win a drive to push GE out of the nuclear weapons business.

The ability to produce activist television has increased with developments in technology. In the 1980s, relatively cheap and lightweight video cameras became available. In the 1990s, digital formats and computer-based editing substantially reduced the time and cost of postproduction. These developments are beginning to erode the gap in production values between mainstream media and activist television. Although the means of production has become widely available, the same cannot be said for distribution. Activist television is largely excluded from mainstream broadcast and cable television channels. Since the late 1960s and early 1970s in the United States, public access cable television has been a primary source of distribution for activist television, but these channels are hard-won concessions obtained from cable operators by cities during cable franchise negotiations. The diffusion of home videocassette recorders/players in the 1970s and 1980s offered another avenue for viewing this mode of television. Both public access cable and VCRs require that producers distribute individual tapes to potential audiences and programmers. Since the 1980s, there have been some notable efforts to distribute activist television more efficiently and broadly by satellite. Deep Dish TV Network began using satellite in the mid-1980s to deliver activist programming to public access stations and home dish owners around the United States. In 2000 Free Speech TV began its own channel for activist-oriented programming on the direct broadcast satellite system the Dish Network.

The Internet is the newest frontier for activist television distribution. Numerous activist groups have put the Internet to innovative uses. Free Speech TV uses the World Wide Web to stream program segments, provide additional information on program topics, coordinate discussion forums, and connect viewers with activist organizations. The Witness program works with partner groups in 50 countries to produce and distribute short advocacy videos on human rights abuses. Internet users can view Witness program videos on the Internet that deal with such topics as state-supported executions in Jamaica, police abuse and torture in Tamil Nadu, India, and the women's right movement in Afghanistan. Independent Media Centers (IMCs) may constitute the most ambitious use of the Internet for both local and global activism. Since the establishment of the first IMC in Seattle in 1999, over 100 others have sprung up throughout the world, including Africa; Canada; Europe; Latin America; the Pacific; and South, East, and West Asia. IMCs provide activists interested in initiating debate, spreading information and analysis, and organizing political action with open forums for the distribution of video and other media online. IMC activists frequently couple online with established offline methods of video distribution to achieve maximum circulation of their work.

LAURA STEIN

Further Reading

Dagron, Alfonso Gumucia, *Making Waves: Stories of Participatory Communication for Social Change,* New York: Rockefeller Foundation, 2001

Downing, John, editor, *Radical Media: Rebellious Communication and Social Movements,* Thousand Oaks, California: Sage, 2001

Engelman, Ralph, "The Origins of Public Access Cable Television, 1966–1972," *Journalism Monographs* No. 123 (October 1990)

Jankowski, Nicholas, and Ole Prehn, editors, *Community Media in the Information Age: Perspectives and Prospects,* Cresskill, New Jersey: Hampton Press, 2002

Kidd, Dorothy, "Indymedia.org: A New Communications Commons," in *Cyberactivism: Online Activism in Theory and Practice,* edited by M. McCaughey and M. Ayers, New York: Routledge, 2003

Marcus, Daniel, editor, *ROAR! The Paper Tiger Television Guide to Media Activism,* New York: Paper Tiger Television Collective, 1991

Stein, L., "Access Television and Grassroots Political Communication in the United States," in *Radical Media: Rebellious Communication and Social Movements,* edited by John Downing, Thousand Oaks, California: Sage, 2001

Adaptations

Since programming began in the 1940s, adaptations have become a mainstay of commercial television. All manner of preexisting written properties have been turned into adapted teleplays. Short stories, novels, plays, poems, even comic books have been altered for presentation on television. To name just one example, in 2001 the WB began producing a hip version of the comics' Superboy story with *Smallville,* updating Clark Kent's teenage travails to the present and adding an *X-Files* flavored reliance on weird, Kryptonite-induced phenomena. Adaptations appear in formats ranging from half-hour shows, as in some episodes of *The Twilight Zone,* to 30-hour epic miniseries, as in 1988's *War and Remembrance.*

Adaptations are attractive to producers for a variety of reasons. In many cases, audiences for such fare are "presold," having purchased or read the original text or having heard of the work through word of mouth. Sources for adapted works may come from public domain materials drawn from classical literary sources, or, more frequently, from hotly pursued novels by best-selling writers. Authors such as Judith Krantz, John Jakes, Alex Haley, and Stephen King have solid book sales and loyal audiences; adaptations of their works typically generate good ratings and audience share. Synergy between book publishers and networks may also be a factor in the purchasing or optioning of works for adaptation; a successful miniseries can prolong the life of a book currently in print and may resurrect older books that are out of print or no longer readily available in the mass market. When Herman Wouk's *War and Remembrance* was adapted in 1988, not only were that book's sales improved but an unexpected million copies of the first book in the series, *The Winds of War,* were also ordered.

Another reason for television's reliance on adaptations, especially in the form of miniseries, is the lack of good scripts, along with television's voracious need for sponsor-attractive, time slot-filling product. Few miniseries are produced from wholly original concepts; experts estimate that 75 to 90 percent of all miniseries use novels for source material. Novels have overcome basic, yet essential dilemmas in constructing narratives: they have well-defined characters; interwoven subplots filled with ideas and events that can be rearranged, highlighted, or deleted by scriptwriters; and enough story for at least two hours of product. A producer holding something complete and tangible, in the form of an already written story, can feel more confident when searching for financing; in turn, sponsors and networks are more likely to commit money and resources to a finished property, even one that is not yet a best-seller. Consequently, producers option many books that are never produced for television or film, in the belief that some of these unknown and untried works may become popular.

What producers see as a "sure thing," however, professional screenwriters often view as a challenge. Adaptation is far more than slavishly reproducing a previously constructed story in a different format. The requirements of the two forms are significantly different. From the perspective of screenwriters, novels take characters and subplots and let them careen willy-nilly into unstructured chaos. Screenwriters rearrange and augment material to stress the visual and storytelling requirements of the television medium. They purge the script of unnecessary characters or combine the traits and experiences of several characters into one. They try to structure the script so it moves from crisis to cri-

Little Lord Fauntleroy.
Photo courtesy of Rosemont Productions

sis, keeping in mind the constraints imposed by the presence of commercial breaks. They find opportunities to make the internal world of thoughts and feelings more external, through dialogue and action. The process of adaptation requires a level of creativity that may be equal to that expended in the writing of the source material, as writers hone, pare, expand, and modify concepts from one medium to the other.

Possibly the most frequently adapted works are those of William Shakespeare; the BBC produced adaptations of MacBeth as early as 1949 and as late as 1983. These adaptations take many forms; PBS's 2001 adaptations of *The Merchant of Venice* and *Othello* were updated with contemporary settings and costumes. HBO has created a series of short animations for middle school-age viewers based on the Bard, and popular shows as diverse as *Star Trek, The Simpsons,* and *Clueless* have derived individual episodes from Shakespearean plays.

Because novels frequently include dozens of characters interacting over extended periods of time, screenwriters often find the miniseries format essential in marshaling the scope and flavor of the original text. PBS, considered the "godfather" of the miniseries, introduced the United States to the concept of long-form sagas with its imports of British productions, presented in such series as *Masterpiece Theatre, Mystery,* and *Great Performances.* The audience for upscale adaptations of *The Forsyte Saga, Brideshead Revisited,* and *The First Churchills* was small, but the form was successful enough to encourage the adaptation of more popular, less highbrow novels such as Irwin Shaw's *Rich Man, Poor Man* (ABC, 1976–77). It was the phenomenal success of Alex Haley's *Roots,* a 12-hour adaptation broadcast over eight consecutive evenings in 1977, however, which cemented this form of adaptation and established it as a staple of television production.

Most genres of television have had their adaptations: children's programming (Showtime's 1982–87 *Faerie Tale Theater;* NBC's 1996 *Gulliver's Travels*); the western (CBS's 1989 *Lonesome Dove*); historical romance (NBC's 1980 *Shogun;* ABC's 1985–86 *North and South*); science fiction (episodes of CBS's 1959–64 *The Twilight Zone*) are a few of the genres featured in outstanding adaptations produced for television. The adaptation continues to be popular, lucrative, and entertaining; as long as the genre holds an audience, this narrative form will remain an essential element in broadcasting.

KATHRYN C. D'ALESSANDRO

See also **Brideshead Revisited; Forsyte Saga, The; I, Claudius; Jewel in the Crown; Miss Marple; Poldark; Rich Man, Poor Man; Road to Avonlea; Roots; Rumpole of the Bailey; Sherlock Holmes; Thorn Birds, The; Tinker, Tailor, Soldier, Spy; Women of Brewster Place**

Further Reading

Brady, Ben, *Principles of Adaptation for Film and Television,* Austin: University of Texas Press, 1994

Bulman, J.C., and H.R. Coursen, editors, *Shakespeare on Television: An Anthology of Essays and Reviews,* Hanover, New Hampshire: University Press of New England, 1988

Davies, Anthony, and Stanley Wells, editors, *Shakespeare and the Moving Image: The Plays on Film and Television,* Cambridge: Cambridge University Press, 1994

Edgar, David, *Ah! Mischief: The Writer and Television,* London: Faber and Faber, 1982

Giddings, Robert, Keith Selby, and Chris Wensley, *Screening the Novel: The Theory and Practice of Literary Dramatization,* New York: St. Martin's Press, 1990

Leonard, William T., *Theatre: Stage to Screen to Television,* Metuchen, New Jersey: Scarecrow, 1981

Marill, Alvin H., *More Theatre: Stage to Screen to Television,* Metuchen, New Jersey: Scarecrow, 1993

Willis, Susan, *The BBC Shakespeare Plays: Making the Televised Canon,* Chapel Hill: University of North Carolina Press, 1991

Adolescents. *See* **Teenagers and Television**

Advanced Television Systems Committee

The Advanced Television Systems Committee (ATSC) was formed in 1982 by representatives of the Joint Committee on Inter-Society Coordination (JCIC). The purpose of the ATSC is to facilitate and develop voluntary technical standards for an advanced television system to replace the aging American NTSC television standard. Originally, the ATSC also made recommendations to the U.S. Department of State regarding standards at the International Radio Consultative Committee (CCIR). ATSC membership consists of 146 organizations, including representatives from the National Association of Broadcasters, the National Cable and Telecommunications Association (NCTA), the Institute of Electrical and Electronics Engineers, broadcasting organizations, manufacturers, and the Society of Motion Picture and Television Engineers (SMPTE).

In 1981 Japan's NHK broadcasting organization demonstrated a working high-definition television (HDTV) system called MUSE, which produced startling clear, rich color images of exceptional resolution. The MUSE system utilized analog technology that was incompatible with the American NTSC color television standard. The MUSE system also required substantially larger spectrum allocations than current NTSC signals. The ATSC accepted the recommendations of the SMPTE by calling for U.S. and worldwide acceptance of Japan's 1,125/60 standard for HDTV production. In 1986 the CCIR refused to accept the standard, claiming that adoption would be detrimental to the interest of many of its members and participants. Renewed recommendations by the ATSC in 1988 for adoption of the 1,125/60 Japanese standard met with opposition from U.S. network broadcasters because the system requirements were not easily convertible for NTSC usage.

In 1987 the Federal Communications Commission (FCC) invited proponents of HDTV to propose a system that would provide terrestrial HDTV to the United States. By 1990 several U.S. entrants proposed all-digital transmission systems that proved preferable to the analog MUSE system. Perhaps the biggest advantage of these digital systems was the potential for scaling HDTV signals into a 6-megahertz bandwidth allowing transmission by terrestrial broadcasters. The ATSC advisory committee developed test procedures to evaluate the different proposed systems. Later, various proponents of digital systems merged their proposals into a compromise hybrid digital system. In 1996 the FCC adopted the ATSC standard and authorized digital television (DTV) broadcasting in the United States.

In 2001 the committee formed the ATSC Forum for the purpose of promoting the adoption of the ATSC digital standard throughout the Western Hemisphere and Asia. Additionally, the ATSC works to promote common DTV services, including digital cable interoperability, program and system information protocols (PSIP), Internet protocol (IP) multicasting for data broadcasting, closed captioning, and digital application software and hardware specifications to support interactive television and enhancements to the vestigial sideband (VSB) aspects of the U.S. DTV standard.

FRITZ MESSERE

Further Reading

"HDTV Production: The Future Is Almost Now," *Broadcasting* (October 17, 1988)

"High Definition in High Gear in '88," *Broadcasting* (January 4, 1988)

Rice, John F., editor, *HDTV,* New York: Union Square Press, 1990

Rosenthal, Edmond, "Broadcasters Find It Easy to Get Rid of Their Ghosts," *Electronic Media* (April 5, 1993)

Schreiber, William F., "HDTV Technology: Advanced Television Systems and Public Policy Options," *Telecommunications* (November 1987)

"Step by Step to HDTV Standard," *Broadcasting* (February 1, 1988)

"Tres Grand Alliance: World Standard?" *Broadcasting & Cable* (June 21, 1993)

U.S. House of Representatives, Committee on Energy and Commerce, *Public Policy Implications of Advanced Television Systems,* Washington, D.C.: U.S. Government Printing Office, 1989

Adventures of Ozzie and Harriet, The

U.S. Domestic Comedy

The Adventures of Ozzie and Harriet was one of the most enduring family based situation comedies in American television. Ozzie and Harriet Nelson and their sons David and Ricky (ages 16 and 13, respectively, at the time of the program's debut) portrayed fictional versions of themselves on the program. The Nelsons embodied wholesome, "normal" American existence so conscientiously (if blandly) that their name epitomized upright, happy family life for decades.

Ozzie and Harriet started out on radio, a medium to which bandleader Ozzie Nelson and his singer/actor wife Harriet Hilliard Nelson had gravitated in the late 1930s, hoping to spend more time together than their conflicting careers would permit. In 1941 they found a permanent spot providing music for Red Skelton's program, a position that foundered when Skelton was drafted in 1944. In that year, the energetic Ozzie Nelson proposed a show of his own to network CBS and sponsor International Silver: a show in which the Nelsons would play themselves. Early in its run, the radio *Adventures of Ozzie and Harriet* jettisoned music for situation comedy. Nelson himself directed and co-wrote all the episodes, as he would most of the video shows.

The Nelsons signed a long-term contract with ABC in 1949 that gave that network the option to move their program to television. The struggling network needed proven talent that was not about to defect to the more established—and wealthier—CBS or NBC.

The television program premiered in 1952. Like its radio predecessor, it focused on the Nelson family at home, chronicling the growing pains of the boys and their parents and dealing with mundane issues like hobbies, rivalries, schoolwork, club membership, and girlfriends. Eventually, the on-screen David and Ricky (although never the off-screen David and Ricky) graduated from college and became lawyers. When the real David and Rick got married (to June Blair and Kristin Harmon, respectively) their wives joined the cast of *Ozzie and Harriet* on television as well as in real life.

Ozzie and Harriet lasted 14 years on American television, remaining on the air until 1966. Although never in the top ten of rated programs, it did well throughout its run, appealing to the family viewing base targeted by ABC. The program picked up additional fans in April 1957, when Rick sang Fats Domino's "I'm Walkin" on an episode titled "Ricky the Drummer."

As soon as the Nelsons realized how popular their singing son was going to be, the telegenic Rick was given every opportunity to croon over the airwaves by his father/director/manager. Sometimes his songs fitted

The Adventures of Ozzie and Harriet, Ozzie Nelson, David Nelson, Ricky Nelson, Harriet Nelson (seated), 1952–66. *Courtesy of the Everett Collection*

into the narrative of an episode. Sometimes they were just tacked onto the end: essentially, early music videos of Rick Nelson in performance.

Despite this emphasis on Rick's vocal performances, and despite the legion of young fans the program picked up because of its teenage emphasis, the character of Ozzie dominated the program. The genial, bumbling Ozzie was the narrative linchpin of *Ozzie and Harriet,* attempting to steer his young sons toward the proper paths (usually rather ineffectually) and attempting to assert his ego in a household in which he was often ill at ease.

That ego, and that household, were held together by wise homemaker Harriet. Although she may have seemed something of a cipher to many viewers, clad in the elegant dresses that defined the housewife on 1950s television, Harriet represented the voice of reason on *Ozzie and Harriet,* rescuing Ozzie, and occasionally David and Rick, from the consequences of impulsive behavior.

Ironically, in view of the weakness of paterfamilias Ozzie's character, the program was (and still is) considered, during its lengthy run, as an idealized portrait of the American nuclear family of the postwar years. The Nelsons eventually shifted their program into color and into the 1960s. Nevertheless, in spirit, and in the popular imagination, they remained black-and-white denizens of the 1950s.

TINKY "DAKOTA" WEISBLAT

Cast

Ozzie Nelson	Himself
Harriet Nelson	Herself
David Nelson	Himself
Eric Ricky Nelson	Himself
Thorny Thornberry (1952–59)	Don DeFore
Darby (1955–61)	Parley Baer
Joe Randolph (1956–66)	Lyle Talbot
Clara Randolph (1956–66)	Mary Jane Croft
Doc Williams (1954–65)	Frank Cady
Wally (1957–66)	Skip Jones
Butch Barton (1958–60)	Gordon Jones
June (Mrs. David) Nelson (1961–66)	June Blair
Kris (Mrs. Rick) Nelson (1964–66)	Kristin Harmon
Fred (1958–64)	James Stacy
Mr. Kelley (1960–62)	Joe Flynn
Connie Edwards (1960–66)	Constance Harper
Jack (1961–66)	Jack Wagner
Ginger (1962–65)	Charlene Salerno
Dean Hopkins (1964–66)	Ivan Bonar
Greg (1965–66)	Greg Dawson
Sean (1965–66)	Sean Morgan

Producers

Ozzie Nelson, Robert Angus, Bill Lewis, Leo Penn

Programming History

435 episodes

ABC

October 1952–June 1956	Friday 8:00–8:30
October 1956–September 1958	Wednesday 9:00–9:30
September 1958–September 1961	Wednesday 8:30–9:00
September 1961–September 1963	Thursday 7:30–8:00
September 1963–January 1966	Wednesday 7:30–8:00
January 1966–September 1966	Saturday 7:30–8:00

Further Reading

Barringer, Felicity, "Dialogue That Lingers: 'Hi, Mom,' 'Hi, Pop,' 'Hi, David,' 'Hi, Rick,'" *New York Times* (October 9, 1994)

Holmes, John R., "The Wizardry of Ozzie: Breaking Character in Early Television," *Journal of Popular Culture* (Fall 1989)

Weisblat, Tinky "Dakota," "Will the Real George and Gracie and Ozzie and Harriet and Desi and Lucy Please Stand Up?: The Functions of Popular Biography in 1950s Television," Ph.D. diss., University of Texas at Austin, 1991

Advertising

In late November 2001, the FOX network announced that it had already sold 70 percent of the 58 commercial slots for the upcoming Super Bowl on February 3, 2002. The going rate was estimated at $2 million for 30 seconds. FOX expected to generate over $200 million, about the same as CBS had earned the previous year, despite a general decline in advertising, occasioned by a recession and the terrorist assault on the United States on September 11, 2001. Regular advertisers such as Anheuser-Busch (with ten spots), PepsiCo, Levi Strauss, and Pizza Hut accounted for most of the sales. The investment was justified because executives expected the Super Bowl to fulfill its objective: to attract the largest television audience of the year. This example is merely one indication of advertising's continuing and central role in the story of television.

In the beginning of television history, the advertising numbers were hardly so extraordinary. In 1941, for example, Bulova Watches spent $9 to buy time on the first advertising spot offered by NBC's fledgling New York station. Soon, however, success stories such as the case of Hazel Bishop cosmetics, whose jump into TV produced a sales explosion, convinced advertisers that it was worthwhile to pay much more to reach the expanding TV audience. Ad revenue fueled the television boom in the United States during the 1950s, and by 1960 TV had become the chief medium of national advertising, earning $1.5 billion as a result. Rating agencies, notably A.C. Nielsen Company, played a crucial role by measuring the audience size and estimating the audience composition of particular shows. Advertising shaped both programming and the schedule to maximize hits—at that time, largely sports and entertainment offerings. Indeed, ad agencies controlled the actual production of many shows, securing writers, technical personnel, and talent and overseeing scripts and production design. It was not until the quiz show scandals at the end of the 1950s led the networks to take control of their programming that the advertising agencies focused their work primarily on brokering airtime and producing commercial spots.

The success of commercial television as a medium linked to the selling of products provoked an outcry. Vance Packard's 1957 exposé, *The Hidden Persuaders,* identified television as one of the chief villains in the effort to manipulate the American consumer. In 1961 the new chair of the Federal Communications Commission (FCC), Newton Minow, told a stunned audience of broadcast executives that television was "a vast wasteland," funded by a seemingly endless supply of commercials.

Initially, few countries followed the U.S. example of supporting their new broadcast media with a commercial, advertiser-supported financial base. Britain, Canada, and much of Western Europe organized television as public service systems. Program development and production, as well as the technical aspects of broadcasting, were funded in part by taxes. However, the expenses of television broadcasting were so high and the private demand for commercial airtime so great that some services accommodated advertising: the Canadian Broadcasting Corporation (CBC), for example, used ad revenues to finance indigenous programming. Both Japan and Australia launched separate commercial and public services in 1953. A year later, ad agencies, now fully international in scope and influence (notably the U.S.-based J. Walter Thompson agency), played a part in convincing the British government to end the BBC monopoly and allow a new channel, a commercial service, to be placed on the air.

Even so, television commercials, the visible artifacts of advertising in their familiar 30- or 60-second versions (and, later, in a 15-second length), long retained the imprint of their American birth. Canadian advertisers hired U.S.-based talent in New York. Young and Rubicam, an American agency, created "Ice Mountain" for Gibbs toothpaste, the first British television commercial ever aired (September 1955). The prevalent strategy of American advertising in the 1950s was the 60-second "hard sell": hit the viewer with bits of information, explain how the product is unique, repeat this argument to drive home the message. The earnest enthusiasm might please the advertisers, but it disturbed its targeted audience. If American viewers were largely satisfied with their television fare, according to a 1960 survey, they were upset by the frequency, the timing, the loudness, and the style of commercials. Still, few people in the United States were ready to pay for noncommercial television through their taxes or a license fee on the television receivers that sat in their living rooms.

Television advertising grew more sophisticated and extravagant during the 1960s. The advent of color TV accentuated the visual dimension of advertising. The increasing cost of airtime fostered a move toward 30-second commercials, which relied on metaphor even

Kellogg's Tony the Tiger.
Tony the Tiger™ is a trademark of the Kellogg Company. All rights reserved. Used with permission.

Maytag's Lonely Repairman.
© Maytag Company/Courtesy of Leo Burnett USA, Inc.

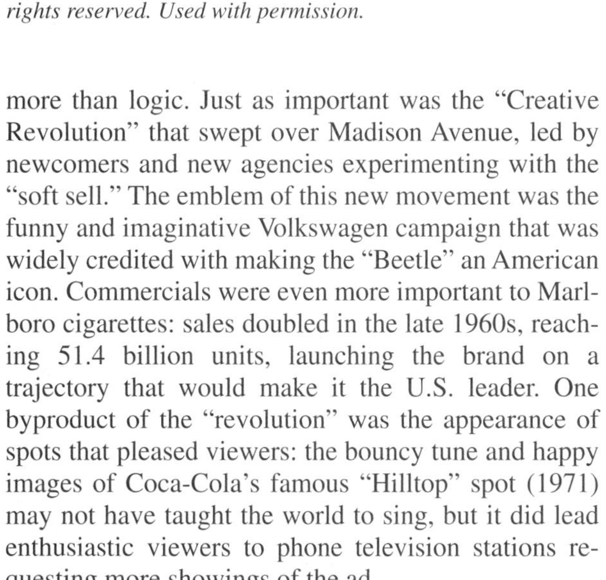

more than logic. Just as important was the "Creative Revolution" that swept over Madison Avenue, led by newcomers and new agencies experimenting with the "soft sell." The emblem of this new movement was the funny and imaginative Volkswagen campaign that was widely credited with making the "Beetle" an American icon. Commercials were even more important to Marlboro cigarettes: sales doubled in the late 1960s, reaching 51.4 billion units, launching the brand on a trajectory that would make it the U.S. leader. One byproduct of the "revolution" was the appearance of spots that pleased viewers: the bouncy tune and happy images of Coca-Cola's famous "Hilltop" spot (1971) may not have taught the world to sing, but it did lead enthusiastic viewers to phone television stations requesting more showings of the ad.

After the mid-1960s, television advertising also became a significant tool of public power. The free public service announcement (PSA) won favor as a way of convincing people to donate moneys, to stop smoking or drinking and driving, or to fight drug abuse.

Political advertising was transformed by the "Daisy" spot, a miniature horror movie that used visuals to link Republican presidential candidate Barry Goldwater (who was running against President Lyndon B. Johnson, a Democrat) to the threat of nuclear holocaust. Shown only once (on CBS, September 7, 1964), the spot featured a young girl counting to ten while pulling the petals off a daisy. When she reaches "nine," an adult voice begins counting down to zero, as the image of the girl dissolves to that of a nuclear explosion. The outcry this commercial provoked amply demonstrated how the political spot could affect viewers emotionally.

By 1988 half of the $92.1 million expended by the campaigns of Vice President George H.W. Bush (Republican) and his Democratic rival for the presidency, Massachusetts Governor Michael Dukakis, went to advertising, mostly on television. Even if these sums were much smaller than Coca-Cola or Procter and Gamble might spend in any given year, political advertising now challenged the news as the chief source of election discourse, evidenced by the attention paid to the "Willie Horton" attack ads that smeared Dukakis in 1988. By the 1994 midterm elections, not only had total ad spending in U.S. campaigns approached $1 billion but negative advertising had exploded in what a November 14 issue of *Advertising Age* called "the season of sleaze."

Maytag's Lonely Repairman.
© Maytag Company/Courtesy of Leo Burnett USA, Inc.

Meanwhile, the partial repeal of the Fairness Doctrine in 1987 had opened the airwaves to advocacy advertising. In 1993 the Health Insurance Association of America managed to catalyze public suspicion of the Clinton administration's health initiative, with its "Harry and Louise" spots, which eventually contributed to the defeat of health reform. In the electoral contest of 2000, the U.S. political parties and their allies practiced the equivalent of carpet bombing, running roughly 1 million spots in the country's 75 major markets. Since so many people avoid political news, television advertising is now the single most important form of political discourse in the United States.

Americans have remained the masters of political and advocacy advertising. However, in other realms, U.S. supremacy has been challenged. American inventiveness declined in part because the "Creative Revolution" waned in the 1970s, with American advertisers coming to favor once more the hard sell. Furthermore, in country after country, private television triumphed over public television, thereby creating new channels for advertising. In the Third World, ad revenues were crucial to the expansion of television, although a fear of excessive commercialism justified Indonesia's ban on television ads in 1981. First in Italy (in the mid-1970s), then in France (in the mid-1980s), and soon everywhere, the airwaves of Western Europe were opened to private television. Following the collapse of the Soviet empire at the end of the 1980s, ads swiftly appeared in Eastern Europe and Russia: the Marlboro cowboy, banned from American screens after 1970, could be found riding proudly on Russian television in the summer of 1993. The spread of satellite TV in Europe after 1990 offered even more time for marketing.

The British were the first to break free from American tutelage. In the United Kingdom, ad makers refined the ironic sell, which became a key marketing strategy in Europe and North America during the late 1980s: one of the first major successes using the ironic approach was the long-lasting Heineken "Refreshes" campaign launched in 1974. Also in the 1970s, the British government sponsored social ads to shape public behavior, an initiative that was pursued in Canada as well, where the state often proved to be the largest single advertiser. British ad makers soon developed the shock style of social advertising, which used brutal images of misery, death, and horror to jolt people out of their complacency. This too became commonplace in the late 1980s and early 1990s, during the global war against AIDS, drugs, drinking and driving, racism, hunger, and other ills.

Worldwide, the best television commercials had become works of art that reflected the tastes, the fears, and the hopes of their communities. The sums of money spent on making commercials were enormous: it has been estimated that the ads for Pepsi-Cola's "New Generation" campaign of the mid-1980s cost about $20,000 a second to produce, far more than regular TV programming. European ad makers usually eschewed the American passion for the hard sell and comparative advertising. Many ads acquired a kind of national signature: bizarre imagery (France), a humorous emphasis (Britain), gentleness (Canada), sensuality (Brazil and France), exposé (Germany), or beauty (Japan). Some trends applied to the whole industry. During the course of the 1990s, for example, advertising throughout the affluent world became increasingly erotic, often mixing sex and humor, to sell food products, diets, cosmetics, clothing (especially jeans), alcohol, and soft drinks. The sexual sell even spread into other categories, notably car advertising. Perhaps it was not surprising that a 2001 survey of Canadians discovered many viewers thought there was too much sex in advertising.

All these developments suggest that there may be some truth to the claim by Marshall McLuhan (cited once again by *Time* magazine in 1990) that advertising was "the greatest art form of the twentieth century." In fact, since 1980 television networks have offered up

Kellogg's Tony the Tiger.
Tony the Tiger™ is a trademark of the Kellogg Company. All rights reserved. Used with permission.

programs anthologizing old and new ads, movie houses have shown the world's best commercials (the Cannes award winners), and newspapers and magazines have reviewed ads and advertising trends.

It would, of course, be an exaggeration to apply McLuhan's label to every form of television advertising. Consider the infomercial, a form American ad makers pioneered during the late 1980s. Typically, the infomercial is a sponsored message, 30 minutes long, which masquerades as a regular program, often as a talk or interview show complete with commercial inserts. The form has been used to hype hair restorers, diet plans, memory expanders, real estate techniques, living aids, gym equipment, and so on. One infomercial promoting Tae-Bo exercises, shown around 2,000 times a week, was credited in 1998 with rebuilding the market for fitness videos, its product even outselling Walt Disney's movies. The earnest enthusiasm of the infomercial harks back to the ad style of the 1950s, while the element of direct response (the insistence that the viewer must phone now to purchase the brand) looks forward to the future of interactive television. The infomercial proved so successful by the mid-1990s that it had spread into Britain and Western Europe. In the United States and Canada, major national marketers such as Ford or Philips were experimenting with this long-form advertising. It was estimated in the mid-1990s that infomercials were generating around $1 billion worth of ad business a year.

That figure nevertheless remained modest by comparison with the scale of conventional television advertising. Altogether, television attracted over $59 billion of the total $244 billion of U.S. advertising volume in 2000, which put the medium nearly on a par with print. Indeed, in Japan, France, Italy, Brazil, and Spain, TV beat out all other media. In the United States, however, the rise of both independent and cable television over the previous two decades had dramatically altered the shares of this revenue. The "Big Three" networks—ABC, CBS, and NBC—now secured just over $14 billion, compared to nearly $11 billion for U.S. cable networks. Local spot-advertising stood at $13.5 billion. The television ad market had fragmented as a result of the proliferation of channels available to the viewing audience. The result was that advertisers had difficulty reaching masses of viewers at any one time, unless they were willing to pay out huge sums to cover all the main channels. One exception, of course, was the Super Bowl, which is why the network broadcasting the game could charge so much for a 30-second ad.

In fact, for roughly a decade, the future significance, and thus the prosperity, of television advertising has been in question. The record of television advertising as a marketing tool is not always spectacular: people avoid, discount, or disdain most commercials they see. The enormous clutter of ads on television has made recent campaigns much less memorable than ten or 20 years ago, or so surveys suggest. Advertisers have long been concerned by stories about viewers who use their remote controls to mute commercial messages or skip through the channels during a commercial break. The recent arrival of personal digital video recorders offered by TiVo or Microsoft's Ultimate TV have reawakened industry fears that viewers might construct their own ad-free television. Even so, no other rival has emerged to challenge the potential marketing power of TV. One of the ironies of the Internet craze of the late 1990s was that the "dot-coms" used television ads to deliver their messages to consumers: during the 1999 Super Bowl, for example, ABC charged some dot-coms as much as $3 million for a 30-second spot. So far, advertising on the Internet has not proved a threat to television ad revenues, amounting to less than 2 percent of the total advertising expenditures in 2000.

The laments of a Packard or a Minow have been echoed by an assortment of critics around the world who have blamed advertising for vulgarizing TV, degrading politics, and emphasizing materialism. Indeed, television advertising is often viewed as the most potent agent of a gospel of consumption. A central tenet of that gospel preaches that satisfaction is for sale. "What advertising has done is to seep out beyond its proper sphere," asserted media scholar Mark Crispin Miller in an NBC documentary, *Sex, Buys, and Advertising* (July 31, 1990), "and to kind of take over the culture."

Ultimately, such claims rest upon a presumption of the awesome cultural power of advertising. Advertising has conditioned the character of television programming, sometimes even inspired a program: Coca-Cola's "Mean Joe Greene" commercial (1979) was the model for a later NBC movie. The music video began life as a method for advertising rock groups, only to later become a form of entertainment and the foundation for the success of the cable network MTV and its imitators. Ad slogans have entered the common language: for example, the fast-food chain Wendy's query, "Where's the beef?" found a place in the 1984 U.S. presidential campaign. Ad critters, notably Kellogg's Tony the Tiger, have become kids' favorites. Ad stars have become famous: the appearance of Nick Kamen in a Levi's 501 ad in Britain in the mid-1980s made him a symbol of male sensuality. Since 2001 the notoriously sexy commercials for Victoria's Secret have been effectively transformed into televised fashion shows.

Such examples demonstrate that commercials are another source of popular culture, a vast collection of meanings and pleasures created by the public to understand and enrich their ordinary experience. The appropriation, creation, and manipulation of these meanings and pleasures by those who assume that they help to sell products continues to be a source of intense cultural and social scrutiny and debate. All the while, the variety of effects of TV advertising on our lives remain contested.

PAUL RUTHERFORD

See also **Cost-Per-Thousand; Demographics; Market; Narrowcasting; Pay Cable; Pay Television; Pay-Per-View; Ratings; Share; Sponsor; Zapping**

Further Reading

Arlen, Michael, *Thirty Seconds,* Markham, Ontario: Penguin, 1981

Barnouw, Erik, *The Sponsor: Notes on a Modern Potentate,* New York: Oxford University Press, 1978

Brown, Les, *Television: The Business Behind the Box,* New York: Harcourt, Brace, Jovanovich, 1971

Cook, Guy, *The Discourse of Advertising,* New York: Routledge, 1992

Davidson, Martin, *The Consumerist Manifesto: Advertising in Postmodern Times,* London: Comedia, 1992

Diamant, Lincoln, *Television's Classic Commercials: The Golden Years 1948–58,* New York: Hastings House, 1971

Diamond, Edwin, and Stephen Bates, *The Spot: The Rise of Political Advertising on Television,* Cambridge, Massachusetts: MIT Press, 1984; 3rd edition, 1992

Dunnett, Peter, *The World Television Industry: An Economic Analysis,* London: Routledge, 1990

Henry, Brian, editor, *British Television Advertising: The First 30 Years,* London: Century Benham, 1986

Jhally, Sut, *The Codes of Advertising: Fetishism and the Political Economy of Meaning in the Consumer Society,* London: Frances Pinter, 1987

Kurtz, Bruce, *Spots: The Popular Art of American Television Commercials,* New York: Arts Communication, 1977

Mattelart, Armand, *Advertising International: The Privatisation of Public Space,* London: Routledge, 1991

Miller, Mark Crispin, *Boxed In: The Culture of TV,* Evanston, Illinois: Northwestern University Press, 1988

Pope, Daniel, *The Making of Modern Advertising,* New York: Basic Books, 1983

Rutherford, Paul, *Endless Propaganda: The Advertising of Public Goods,* Toronto: University of Toronto Press, 2000

Rutherford, Paul, *The New Icons? The Art of Television Advertising,* Toronto: University of Toronto Press, 1994

Schudson, Michael, *Advertising, the Uneasy Persuasion: Its Dubious Impact on American Society,* New York: Basic Books, 1984

Sinclair, John, *Images Incorporated: Advertising as Industry and Ideology,* London: Croom Helm, 1987

Steiner, Gary, *The People Look at Television: A Study of Audience Attitudes,* New York: Alfred A. Knopf, 1963

Twitchell, James B., *Adcult USA: The Triumph of Advertising in American Culture,* New York: Columbia University Press 1996

Wilson, H.H., *Pressure Group: The Campaign for Commercial Television,* London: Secker and Warburg, 1961

Advertising Agency

In the early years of U.S. broadcasting, advertising agencies were quick to embrace new media. Fortunately for advertisers, the ability to reach a mass audience with radio intersected with an expansion of the U.S. economy in the 1920s. The techniques of mass production championed by Henry Ford, the rise of Taylorism, and an increase in disposable income in the years following World War I sustained an ideology of consumption that advertising both reflected and nurtured. NBC President Merlin H. Aylesworth proclaimed that radio was "an open gateway to national markets, to millions of consumers, and to thousands upon thousands of retailers."

The vision of eager consumers gathered around this remarkable appliance was irresistible to potential sponsors. The expansion of commercial broadcasting came with such astonishing speed that by 1931 radio was an enormous industry, accounting for $36 million in time sales on the networks alone. Larger agencies such as N.W. Ayer, BBDO, and J. Walter Thompson set up broadcasting departments and actively encouraged clients to pursue the medium.

The emergence of radio as an economic force was reflected in a crucial change regarding program development at the agency level. Through the 1920s most commercial programming originated with networks or local stations, with the agency serving as broker, casting about for clients willing to purchase the rights to a broadcaster-produced show. By the early 1930s, however, the agencies had reversed the equation—they were developing shows in-house for clients, then purchasing airtime from the broadcasters. The key function for the agency thus became to analyze a client's particular needs and design an entire program around those needs, an enormously complex and financially risky undertaking, yet one in which Madison Avenue was entirely successful. By the end of the 1930s, agencies produced more than 80 percent of all network commercial programming.

With the advent of commercial television in 1946, there was considerable sentiment within the networks that program creation and execution would best be left in their hands, although the personnel demands and expense of video production made it impossible for any network to produce all its programming in-house. Thus, as in radio, agencies assumed a major role in the evolution of the television schedule. There was not, however, a wholesale rush of sponsors begging to enter the medium, and the networks were compelled to offer time slots at bargain rates to attract customers. Companies such as Thompson, and Young and Rubicam, had already developed some television expertise, but the vast majority of agencies found themselves at the bottom of a very steep learning curve. Still, Madison Avenue produced some of the most enduring programs of the "golden age" of television, including *Texaco Star Theater, Kraft Television Theatre,* and *The Goldbergs.*

As more stations began operation—particularly after 1952—the cost of purchasing airtime on the networks and local stations increased dramatically, as did production budgets. Most agencies accepted as an economic fact that they could no longer afford to create and produce their own shows as they had in radio, and the recognition on Madison Avenue that complete control of television production was unprofitable to the agencies themselves contributed to the evolution in programming hegemony away from the agencies to the networks. Thus, agencies never assumed the kind of production control in television they enjoyed in radio; they could never put into play the same economies of scale as the networks and independent producers. The 15 percent commission that served as the source of agency revenue simply was not enough to cover the ever-increasing expenses associated with television production. Many agencies subsequently shifted their emphasis to the production of commercial spots, while others moved aggressively into syndication, forming partnerships with Hollywood producers to create filmed series that could be sold to a variety of sponsors.

As costs rose during the 1950s, the gap between agency income and expenses narrowed considerably, forcing a reconsideration of organizational structure, leading to the emergence of what was termed the "all-media strategy," which remains the dominant paradigm. Most agencies had relied on specialists in a strict division of labor such that a client's advertising might be divided up between three or four different departments. The all-media approach rejected this diffusion of responsibility, placing a single person or team in charge of a client's overall needs. By eliminating specialists and fostering cooperation between divisions, agencies could streamline personnel, coordinate functions, improve efficiency, and thereby reduce overhead.

Advertising agencies had an agenda distinct from that of their clients. Although publicly they represented the clients' interests, many Madison Avenue executives also promoted network control of programming in the trade press. Because of their concerns over the increasing costs and complexities of program production, and their frustration with mediating disputes between advertisers and networks, many hoped television would not continue the radio model of sponsor ownership of time slots. Concerned that the expense of television programming far outstripped that of radio production, agency executives sought ways to develop television as a mass advertising medium while also seeking to avoid draining agency revenues with television program costs. In this sense, the evolution of the all-media strategy is illustrative of how the economic pressures brought to bear on agencies during the 1950s changed the way Madison Avenue approached programming, from an advertising vehicle to one (albeit primary) component of a marketing plan.

Today, the advertising agency is primarily responsible for the production of commercial spots as well as the purchasing of airtime on behalf of clients. The situation has become murkier in recent years, however, as some large companies (Coca-Cola, for example) have begun producing much of their own advertising in-house, bypassing Madison Avenue. Further, the networks now frequently approach potential advertisers directly rather than going through the client's agency. In an era when even large stores are acquired by enormous multinational holding companies, the role of the agency is now focused more on using powers of persuasion in many different media than merely in creating a single great advertisement.

MICHAEL MASHON

Further Reading

Agnew, Clark M., and Neil O'Brien, *Television Advertising,* New York: McGraw-Hill, 1958

Hilmes, Michele, *Hollywood and Broadcasting: From Radio to Cable,* Urbana: University of Illinois Press, 1991

Lears, T. Jackson, *Fables of Abundance: A Cultural History of Advertising in America,* New York: Basic Books, 1994

McAllister, Matthew P., *The Commercialization of American Culture: New Advertising, Control, and Democracy,* Thousand Oaks, California: Sage, 1996

McMahan, Harry W., *The Television Commercial: How to Create and Produce Effective TV Advertising,* New York: Hastings House, 1954

Settel, Irving, and Norman Glenn, *Television Advertising and Production Handbook,* New York: Thomas Y. Cromwell, 1953

Advertising, Company Voice

Company voice advertising typically presents its sponsors as good corporate citizens; forward-thinking providers of products, jobs, and services; and active supporters of causes such as environmentalism. Historically a staple of magazines, radio, and sponsored motion pictures, company voice advertising helped shape sponsorships of dramatic anthology, spectacular, news, and documentary programs. After 1970 the practice helped shape Public Broadcasting Service program underwriting.

Alternately known as "public relations," or "institutional" or "advocacy advertising," company voice advertising seeks a favorable political climate for the expansion of its sponsors' commercial activities and interests. One of the earliest campaigns of its kind, dating to 1908, promoted the "universal service" of the AT&T Bell System telephone monopoly. By the late 1920s public-minded "progress" had become the highly advertised hallmark of General Electric (GE), General Motors, and other center firms. The practice picked up political significance during the New Deal and later during World War II, when all manner of advertising promoted companies' patriotic sacrifice and struggle on the production front.

After the war, business leaders remained suspicious of centralized government, confiscatory taxation, politically powerful labor, and what many believed to be the public's outmoded fear of big business. In bringing postwar public and employee relations to television, business invested in programs with objectives ranging from economic education to outright entertainment. Factory processes and free enterprise rhetoric appeared regularly. The National Association of Manufacturers, for example, launched *Industry on Parade,* a syndicated telefilm series that toured the nation's industrial centers. Initially produced by the NBC News film unit, the series ran from 1951 to 1958. Business and trade groups worked television into training and employee relations. Drexel Institute of Technology's *University of the Air,* for example, took advantage of marginal television time in the Philadelphia area for noon-hour panel discussions of labor-management issues. Designed for in-plant reception by audiences of supervisory trainees and managers, the scenes attracted spouses in the home viewing audience who, one publicist proudly noted, had become the new fans of industrial human relations.

Entering television for the first time, major corporations predicated their public and employee relations activities upon the experience of entertainment. GE and DuPont, both active in economic education, favored the editorial control of dramatic anthology programs. The company voice specialists of the *General Electric Theater* ruled out the sponsorship of panel discussions such as *Meet the Press* and *Youth Wants to Know* because the format posed the threat of spontaneous comments inimical to business. DuPont continued its investment in tightly controlled drama with the transfer of radio's *Cavalcade of America* to television in 1952. DuPont specialists justified their television investment with projected declining costs per thousand, which by 1954 would equal radio's peak year of 1948. Further delineating the audience for company voice messages, specialists anticipated the maturity of a generation with no firsthand knowledge of the depression—or, as GE's Chester H. Lang, put it, "no adult exposure to the violent anti-business propaganda of the 'depression' years. The opinions the young people form now, as they grow up," Lang explained, "will determine the climate in which we will operate in the decades of their maturity." DuPont's F. Lyman Dewey suggested that his company's investment in television affirmed its executives' appreciation of the fact that it was no longer a question of "shall we as DuPont representatives use these powerful tools of communication—but shall we use them well."

Recoiling from television's expense and unproved effect, other company voice advertisers hesitantly incorporated the new medium into their plans. More than a few invested in alternating-week sponsorships that further divided commercial breaks between product sales and company voice messages. U.S. Steel predicated its television plans in part upon a tax code that allowed deductions for product sales and company voice advertising as a business expense. Its first telecast (Christmas night 1952) presented Dickens's *A Christmas Carol. The U.S. Steel Hour* later apportioned commercial breaks between company voice messages read by "Voice of U.S. Steel" announcer George Hicks and industrywide product sales promotions acted out by U.S. Steel's "family team" Mary Kay and Johnny.

Spectacular programs built around light entertainment, sports, and special events presented sponsors as adjuncts of national life and culture. General Motors, reminiscent of its massive investments in wartime institutional advertising, entered television in the 1952–53 season with a weekly schedule of *NCAA Football,* followed by the Eisenhower Inauguration and the coronation of Queen Elizabeth II. Ford Motor Company and the electrical industry each invested in light entertainment. The success of the *Ford 50th Anniversary Show* simultaneously telecast on NBC and CBS led to similarly conceived "horizontal saturation" for the 1954 television season. *Light's Diamond Jubilee,* for example, a two-hour spectacular celebrating the 75th anniversary of Thomas Edison's invention of the electric light, appeared on four networks. The David O. Selznick production featured a filmed talk by President Eisenhower, narration by Joseph Cotten, and sketches and musical numbers with Walter Brennan, Kim Novak, Helen Hayes, Lauren Bacall, David Niven, Judith Anderson, and Eddie Fisher.

By the mid-1950s nearly every major American corporation had entered television to build audiences for company voice advertising. The Aluminum Company of America sponsored Edward R. Murrow's *See It Now* to boost its name recognition with the public and with manufacturers using aluminum. Reynolds Aluminum sponsored *Mr. Peepers,* while the Aluminum Company of Canada with others sponsored *Omnibus.* Underwritten by the Ford Foundation as a demonstration of "television at its best," the Sunday afternoon series presented diverse entertainments hosted by Alistair Cooke. Not averse to commercial sponsorship, *Omnibus* anticipated the "making possible" program environment of the Public Broadcasting Service.

While politically active corporations embraced the prestigious possibilities of drama, light entertainment, and special events, by 1960 many had become willing sponsors of science, news, and documentary programs. The promotion of scientific and technological competence took on special urgency after the Soviet launch of the Sputnik spacecraft in 1958. The corporate-cool television presence of the Bell System exemplified the trend. In 1956 Bell entered television with half-hour dramas entitled *Telephone Time.* One hundred and ten episodes ran until 1958, dramatizing the success stories of "little people." In 1959 Bell returned to the air with four musical specials that evolved into the *Bell Telephone Hour.* Light orchestral music, musical numbers, and ballet sequences accompanied "Of time and space" company voice messages. Bell also developed preemptive documentary programs on weather, genetics, circulation of the blood, and cosmic rays, and the *Threshold* series treating the American space program. Bell also purchased related CBS documentaries such as *Why Man in Space?* Adopting a similar strategy, Texaco, Gulf, and Westinghouse each televised network news and special events laden with scientific and technological news value. Texaco became an early sponsor of NBC's *Huntley-Brinkley Report.* The "unassuming authenticity and easy informality" of coanchors Chet Huntley and David Brinkley were thought to complement Texaco's "dependability" message. Gulf raised its institutional profile with "instant specials" featuring NBC correspondent Frank McGee, who covered the events of the 1960 presidential campaign and the U.S. space program. Documentary films such as *The Tunnel* rounded out the schedule. *Westinghouse Presents* featured documentary specials "Our Man in Vienna" with David Brinkley, "The Land" with Chet Huntley, and "The Wacky World of Jerry Lewis." Company voice messages promoted Westinghouse's "scientific achievements, dedication and sincere interest in people," qualities thought to mitigate the negative public relations impact of 641 civil damage suits stemming from charges of price-fixing.

The multinational aspirations of Xerox Corporation sought complementary qualities of excellence. Not unlike the program strategies pursued by steel, automotive, and electrical producers, Xerox embarked upon an aggressive public relations campaign by purchasing programs that "get talked about": *Huntley-Brinkley Reports* treating the Kremlin, Communism, Jimmy Hoffa, Cuba, and Korea; the making of the president,

1960 and 1964; and a series of 90-minute specials dramatizing the work of United Nations (UN) social agencies. Broadcast without commercial interruption on NBC and ABC, the UN series targeted the international community identified as key to the expansion of the office copier market. A model of corporate underwriting, Xerox's UN dramas won critical acclaim that helped justify the series' $4 million expense to stockholders who questioned its value. The series' most celebrated program, "Carol for Another Christmas," featured a Rod Serling script that revisited the horrors of Hiroshima, the millions unavailable to Western abundance, and the bleakest of futures prefigured by the hydrogen bomb. Xerox later sponsored *Civilisation* with Kenneth Clark. Thirteen one-hour programs presented "leading social issues and advanced art forms" reviewing "1600 years of Western man's great art and ideas... man at his finest on television at its finest."

While company voice advertisers of the early 1950s anticipated the maturity of a television generation with no direct knowledge of the depression, the company voice advertisers of the early 1960s bemoaned that generation's expectation that business extend its interests beyond the balance sheet to include social goals in the areas of minority employment, consumer protection, and environmentalism. Public opinion pollster Louis Harris described the public image of U.S. business as "bright, but flawed." Specialists set out to narrow the distance between corporate claim and performance said to be as great as the so-called generation gap. Not only had society become more impersonal and complex, they argued, but increasingly polarized and problematic. Hoping to erase lingering doubts about advertising's impact and effect, specialists sharpened claims for advocacy advertising as "the one remaining tool with which business can apply counter pressure in an adversary society."

John E. O'Toole, the thoughtful president of the Madison Avenue agency Foote, Cone and Belding, suggested that business leaders learn to emulate the "adversary culture" of intellectual and academic pursuits, political activists, and consumer groups "who seek basic changes in the system." O'Toole noted that while each "culture" had necessary and legitimate functions, the adversary culture dominated the media. In complex times, O'Toole argued, business should make certain that its unique claims of social leadership rose above the dissident clutter.

Led by the oil industry, the 1970s witnessed significant investment in company voice television. Reeling from the public relations fallout of rising energy prices, American-based petroleum producers became a presence on the Public Broadcasting Service. Mobil's *Masterpiece Theatre* with one-time *Omnibus* host Alistair Cooke debuted in January 1971. As historian Laurence Jarvik notes, Mobil soon displaced the Ford Foundation as the single largest contributor to public television, raising its initial program grant of $390,000 to $12 million by 1990. *Masterpiece Theatre, Mystery!,* and *Upstairs, Downstairs* provided cultural cover for a heavy schedule of combative advocacy ads published in the op-ed sections of the *New York Times* and the *Washington Post.* In the late 1970s the ad campaign came to television: elaborately costumed "A Fable for Now" spots featuring mimes Shields and Yarnell, the Pilobolus Dance Theatre, the Louis Falco Dance Company, the Richard Morris Dance Theatre, and members of the American Ballet Theatre enlivened Mobil's antiregulatory rhetoric in parables of scarcity and abundance drawn from the animal kingdom. "Mobil Information Center" spots aired locally before network newscasts employed an anchorman-correspondent simulation to tout "the freedom of the press," along with the progrowth logic of offshore drilling, nuclear power plant construction, deregulation of natural gas, and the restriction of environmental regulation.

While sympathetic critics wondered if Mobil could have carried out its advocacy campaign without the expense of television drama, others suggested that big oil's enthusiastic underwriting of public television had turned PBS into the "Petroleum Broadcasting Service." PBS president Lawrence K. Grossman urged perspective on the funding issue. In 1977 Grossman explained that though oil company funding had increased tenfold since the early 1970s, oil company moneys represented less than 3 percent of system income. "What conclusion," asked Grossman, "do we in public television draw from these numbers? Not that oil companies should contribute *less* but rather that corporations of all other types should be asked to contribute more!"

By 1983 corporate support for PBS had flattened out at $38 million for the two previous years, presaging a decade of declining federal appropriations that left PBS ever more dependent upon the market for support. In 1981 network officials won congressional approval for an 18-month experiment in "enhanced underwriting." Two-minute credits at the beginning and conclusion of programs telecast by nine PBS affiliates allowed mention of brand names, slogans, and institutional messages beyond previously restricted verbal mentions and static displays of logos. The discussion of corporate mascots, animated logos, product demonstrations and superlatives to tap a new class of advertising revenue alarmed established underwriters. In an effort to conserve PBS's uncluttered institutional character, national program underwriters Mobil, the Chubb Group of Insurance Companies, Chevron, AT&T, Exxon, Ford, GE, IBM, GTE, JC Penney, Morgan Guaranty Trust, Owens-Corning, and others formed the Corporations in Support of Public Television

(CSPT). The CSPT promoted the concept of "quality demographics" among potential corporate underwriters who desired to advertise "excellence," social cause identification, and the occasional product.

AT&T, for example, had recently provided $9 million for expanded one-hour coverage of the *MacNeil/Lehrer Report* (later *News Hour).* Emphasizing performance and communication, specialists expected the buy to enhance AT&T's image as an information provider after its breakup into regional "Baby Bells" by the U.S. Justice Department.

Reviewing their company voice accounts, specialists themselves perhaps wondered just what effect their long-term advertising campaigns had bought. Increasingly business found itself the subject of critical television news stories treating the environment, the OPEC oil shock, inflation, and recession. Corporate critics charged that public television had become a prime example of what Alan Wolfe described as "logo America," in which "the only price a company will charge for its public service activities is the right to display its logo." Near the opposite end of the political spectrum, critic David Horowitz described PBS's broadcast schedule as a "monotonous diet of left-wing politics," though it would have been hard to find such programs equaling the possibilities, much less access, available to the company voice advertiser. Mobil, for example, financed an hour-long PBS documentary program criticizing the antibusiness thrust of prime-time network television drama. Hosted by writer Benjamin Stein, *Hollywood's Favorite Heavy: Businessmen on Prime Time TV* used clips from *Dallas, Dynasty,* and *Falcon Crest* to contend that television had destroyed youth's outlook upon business and business ethics. A peculiar assumption, wrote critic Jay Rosen in *Channels* magazine, since television itself was a business, and advertisements had made consumption "the nearest thing to religion for most Americans." Mobil, however, had decided that it could not countenance Blake Carrington, J.R. Ewing, and other stereotypes of rapacious businessman in prime time. Interestingly, GE declined to join Mobil as a *Hollywood's Favorite Heavy* underwriter, preferring instead to stick with its "We Bring Good Things to Life" spot campaign. Having rethought its aversion to panel discussions, GE aired its "Good Things" campaign on ABC's *This Week with David Brinkley* and *The McLaughlin Group.* The latter appeared commercially on NBC's five owned and operated stations and publicly on a 230-station PBS network.

As the century draws to a close and funding for all forms of television continues to be squeezed by new outlets and new technologies such as computer access to the Internet, corporations continue to seek new connections to media. The trend that began with the origins of mass media shows no sign of abating.

W.L. BIRD

See also **Advertising;** ***Alcoa Hour, The***

Further Reading

"Answer for a Giant," *Television Age* (December 25, 1961)
Barnet, Sylvan M., Jr., "A Global Look at Advocacy," *Public Relations Journal* (November 1975)
Barnouw, Erik, *The Sponsor: Notes on a Modern Potentate,* New York: Oxford University Press, 1978
Brown, Les, *Television: The Business Behind the Box,* New York: Harcourt Brace Jovanovich, 1971
"Business Thinks TV Distorts Its Image," *Business Week* (October 18, 1982)
Chew, Fiona, "The Advertising Value of *Making Possible* a Public Television Program," *Journal of Advertising Research* (November–December 1992)
"8 Advertisers Examine Their Radio and TV Problems," *Sponsor* (April 20, 1953)
Fones-Wolf, Elizabeth, *Selling Free Enterprise: The Business Assault on Labor and Liberalism, 1945–1960,* Urbana: University of Illinois Press, 1994
Gladstone, Brooke, and Steve Behrens, "And That's Why I Underwrite PTV (Just Between Us Corporations)," *Current* (July 12, 1983)
Griese, Noel L., "AT&T: 1908 Origins of the Nation's Oldest Continuous Institutional Advertising Campaign," *Journal of Advertising* (1977)
Harrison, S.L., "Prime Time Pabulum: How Politicos and Corporate Influence Keep Public TV Harmless," *Washington Monthly* (January 1986)
Horowitz, David, "The Politics of Public Television," *Commentary* (December 1991)
"How AT&T May Help Bankroll PBS News," *Business Week* (August 16, 1982)
Howlet, Robert Michael, and Rebecca Raglon, "Constructing the Environmental Spectacle: Green Advertisements and the Greening of the Corporate Image, 1910–1990," *Environmental History Review* (Winter 1992)
"Instant News," *Television Age* (August 5, 1963)
Marchand, Roland, "The Fitful Career of Advocacy Advertising: Political Protection, Client Cultivation, and Corporate Morale," *California Management Review* (Winter 1987)
Mareth, Paul, "Public Visions: Private Voices," *Sight and Sound* (Winter 1976–77)
Murphy, M.J., "TV: Newest Way to Get Your Story into the Home," *Factory Management and Maintenance* (May 1952)
Nader, Ralph, "Challenging the Corporate Ad," *Advertising Age* (January 24, 1983)
Northart, Leo J., "Editor's Notebook," *Public Relations Journal* (November 1975)
O'Toole, John E., "Advocacy Advertising Shows the Flag," *Public Relations Journal* (November 1975)
Rosen, Jay, "Chatter from the Right," *Progressive* (March 1988)
Rosen, Jay, "Giving Them the Business," *Channels* (February 1987)
Schudson, Michael, *Advertising the Uneasy Persuasion: Its Dubious Impact on American Society,* New York: Basic Books, 1984
Schutnann, David W., Jan M. Hathcote, and Susan West, "Corporate Advertising in America: A Review of Published Studies on Use, Measurement, and Effectiveness," *Journal of Advertising* (September 1991)
Shayon, Robert Lewis, "They Sang Along with Mitch," *Saturday Review* (May 30, 1964)
Shayon, Robert Lewis, "Warm Scrooge, Cold Grudge," *Saturday Review* (January 16, 1965)

"TV's Quiet Marketer," *Television Age* (April 30, 1962)
"What Americans Really Think of Business" and "The Disenchanted Campus," *Newsweek* (May 2, 1966)
Wolfe, Alan, "The Rise of Logo America," *Nation* (May 26, 1984)
Yore, J.J., "Enhanced Underwriting: A Corporate Perspective," *Current* (March 11, 1986)

Advocacy Groups

Advocacy groups—also called public interest groups, citizen groups, consumer activist groups, and media reform groups—have existed in the United States since the 1930s as consumer checks on a broadcast industry where decisions quite often have been based not on public interest standards but rather on economic incentives and regulatory mandates. Advocacy groups have carved a niche for themselves in the broadcast industry's policy-making apparatus by first defining key public interest issues and then by advocating ways by which broadcasters may address these issues.

Advocacy group characteristics have varied widely. Some have operated nationally, with or without local chapters, and some have operated only locally. Some have remained active for many years, whereas the lifespan of others has been brief. Some advocacy groups have been well financed, often receiving substantial foundation funding, while others have operated with little financial support. Practically all advocacy groups have relied on newsletter subscriptions, video purchases, and lectures as means of raising money. Finally, some advocacy groups have devoted exclusive attention to the broadcast industry, whereas other groups with a more varied menu of concerns have developed subsidiary units to deal with broadcast-related issues.

The total number of advocacy groups, past or present, is difficult to determine, given their ephemeral nature. What is more, many such groups are smaller components of larger organizations with a mixture of agendas. Some of the more prominent advocacy groups through the years have included the National Association for Better Broadcasting, the National Citizens Committee for Broadcasting, Action for Children's Television, Accuracy in Media, the National Black Media Coalition, and the Coalition for Better Television. Besides these, the Office of Communication of the United Church of Christ has been a particularly effective advocacy group, as have the Media Task Force of the National Organization for Women and the National Parent Teachers Association (PTA). Assisting these groups through the years in legal, regulatory, and legislative matters have been pro bono public interest law firms such as the Citizens Communication Center.

Early advocacy groups, such as the Radio Council on Children's Programming and the Women's National Radio Committee, both formed in the 1930s, were concerned with program content. Group members monitored radio programs, reported their opinions on acceptable and unacceptable content in newsletters, and gave awards to radio stations and networks airing exceptional programs. That practice and mode of consumer/broadcaster interaction continued until the 1960s, when the broadcast industry became caught up in a sweeping consumers' movement. During the latter part of the 1960s, advocacy groups, led most effectively by the United Church of Christ, began challenging television station license renewals through a legal instrument called a "petition to deny." Such petitions were aimed at denying license renewal for television stations whose programming or employment practices were considered discriminatory. Advocacy groups also were successful in forcing broadcasters to accede to programming and minority-employment demands contained in "citizen agreements." When such unprecedented public access into the regulatory and station decision-making process won approval of both the federal courts and the Federal Communications Commission (FCC), advocacy groups blossomed.

The most common targets of advocacy groups during the 1970s continued to be minority programming and employment practices. However, violent program content, children's programming, and general public access to the airwaves also took on significance. Advocacy group tactics during this period included the petitions to deny and citizens agreements noted previously as well as participation in FCC rule-making and congressional hearings, actual or threatened program sponsor boycotts, and publicity. Advocacy group achievements during the 1970s usually came in small doses, but major successes included the improvement in broadcast station employment opportunities for women and minorities, greater public participation in the broadcast regulatory process, improvement in children's programming, and the banishment of cigarette advertising from the airwaves.

The nature of advocacy groups began to change during the 1980s. A more conservative political agenda derailed the consumers' movement that had bolstered the more liberal-minded advocacy groups of the 1970s. Moreover, public interest law firms and foundations that had funded many of the more prominent advocacy groups during the 1970s began either disappearing or turning their attention elsewhere. Changes in the broadcast industry itself—deregulation, the rise of cable television, and changing station/network ownership patterns—also reversed many of the early advocacy group achievements and left the leadership as well as membership of many of the groups in disarray.

However, advocacy groups did not disappear; rather, their issue emphasis took a decidedly conservative turn. Groups such as Accuracy in Media and the Coalition for Better Television gained momentum in the 1980s with a large constituency, substantial funding, and a focus on ridding the airwaves of programs that either were biased in news reporting or contained an excess of sex and violence. Extensive mailing lists also helped these groups to quickly galvanize public support for their causes.

In the 1990s there also began to appear liberal advocacy groups that set their sights on molding public opinion on a more tightly focused set of special interests than in the past. These interests included gun control, AIDS awareness and prevention, abortion rights, world hunger, and the environment. Led by Amnesty International, the Environmental Media Association, and the Center for Population Options, these advocacy groups succeeded to some extent by convincing a number of television network producers to insert messages in prime-time entertainment programs that addressed the advocacy groups' concerns.

As television entered the 21st century, the role of advocacy groups had diminished somewhat. Many of the issues on which these groups focused so much of their attention had not disappeared, but interest among members of the public in addressing the issues had waned. A plethora of new program channel outlets via cable television and direct broadcast satellite also meant that advocacy groups had opportunities never before available to them to deliver messages of their own design and choosing to television viewers nationwide.

This is not to say that advocacy groups ceased functioning. To the contrary, such groups continued their efforts. The National PTA proceeded with its annual "Take Charge of Your TV Week" campaign. The National Association for the Advancement of Colored People (NAACP) and the National Hispanic Media Coalition both threatened boycotts against the broadcast television networks during the late 1990s because of the networks' failure to include more African Americans and Hispanics in prime-time television programming. And such organizations as the Parents Television Council, the Center for Media Education, the Media Research Center, and the American Family Association continued to push for improvement in television programming, especially in programming directed toward children and young adults.

Such groups as these appeared less vocal and less visible than in the past, but a closer examination suggests that they simply employed more sophisticated means of spreading their messages. The World Wide Web had become a particularly valuable information tool that, by 2001, many advocacy groups had incorporated into their public educational tool chest. Websites also were an efficient means of providing programming "action alerts," viewers' guides, information clearinghouses, and instant calls for letter-writing campaigns and/or boycotts.

The role of advocacy groups through the years has engendered a mixture of praise and criticism. While the objectives, methods, and zealotry of some groups have met with scorn, the efforts of others have been viewed as beneficial for, at the very least, making the broadcast industry sensitive to public needs and concerns.

RONALD GARAY

See also **Action for Children's Television; Experimental Video; Public Access Television**

Further Reading

Bittner, John R., *Law and Regulation of Electronic Media,* Englewood Cliffs, New Jersey: Prentice Hall, 1982; 2nd edition, 1994

Branscomb, Anne W., and Maria Savage, *Broadcast Reform at the Crossroads,* Cambridge, Massachusetts: Kalba Bowen Associates, 1987

Brown, Les, "Is the Public Interested in the Public Interest?" *Television Quarterly* (Fall 1979)

Cole, Barry G., and Mal Oettinger, *Reluctant Regulators: The FCC and the Broadcast Audience,* Reading, Massachusetts: Addison-Wesley, 1978

Friedman, Mel, "Will TV Networks Yield to New Pressure Groups?," *Television/Radio Age* (May 4, 1981)

Garay, Ronald, "Access: Evolution of the Citizen Agreement," *Journal of Broadcasting* (Winter 1978)

Guimary, Donald L., *Citizens' Groups and Broadcasting,* New York: Praeger, 1975

Hodges, Ann, "Pressure Group Crusade Seen as Top Problem by Networks, Producers," *Houston Chronicle* (19 May 1981)

Krasnow, Erwin, Laurence D. Longley, and Herbert A. Terry, *The Politics of Broadcast Regulation,* New York: St. Martin's Press, 1978; 3rd edition, 1982

Leddy, Craig, "Probing a Pressure Group," *Electronic Media* (April 26, 1984)

Mahler, Richard, "How the Crusades Became Prime for TV," *Los Angeles Times* (April 14, 1991)

Montgomery, Kathryn C., *Target: Prime Time: Advocacy Groups and the Struggle Over Entertainment Television,* New York and Oxford: Oxford University Press, 1989

National Citizens Committee for Broadcasting, *Citizens Media Directory, 1980 Update,* Washington, D.C.: National Citizens Committee for Broadcasting, 1980

Rowe, Chip, "Watchdog Watch," *American Journalism Review* (April 1993)
Shapiro, Andrew O., *Media Access,* Boston: Little, Brown, 1976
Smith, F. Leslie, Milan D. Meeske, and John W. Wright, III, *Electronic Media and Government,* White Plains, New York: Longman, 1995

Aesthetics, Television

Aesthetics—that branch of philosophy concerned with the arts, and definitions of artistic experience and artistic value—has always been a contested category in discussions of popular culture. Suspicion of the term, and of the elitist values and assumptions it was thought to imply, was widespread among reviewers and scholars of film, popular music, and (later) television long before academic literary and cultural theory in the 1970s and beyond dismissed aesthetic arguments as the mystifications of high culture and of society's dominant ideologies.

As we entered the 21st century, the political and ideological perspectives that prevailed for a generation and more in the American academy began to yield to a new synthesis. On this emerging view, the commercial and ideological forces that shape popular entertainments are acknowledged as central but are no longer thought to exclude aesthetic questions. This return to the aesthetic has great importance for the nascent scholarship on television, which was born in the era of high theory, of deconstruction and materialist forms of cultural studies.

It is helpful to recognize that the term "aesthetic" may be understood first in a descriptive, anthropological sense. From this angle, to identify certain cultural items as aesthetic is not to praise their beauty or excellence but merely to describe their chief defining feature: their membership in a class of experiences understood to be fictional or imaginary, understood to occur in a symbolic, culturally agreed-upon imaginative space—a theater; the intimate, privatized spaces of our experience of television; the vast ritual amphitheaters of the ancient world; the dark communal space of the movie house—where "real" experience is re-presented, re-created, symbolically displayed. We watch television fiction, that is to say, in a realm of leisure and "play," a territory or environment licensed as make-believe—an aesthetic space.

In estimating the importance of aesthetic perspectives for understanding television, it is instructive to compare prevailing American attitudes toward the medium with the attitudes held a generation ago toward our homegrown movies and moviemakers. Many film scholars have pointed to the irony that the U.S.'s recognition of her own achievement in the art of film lagged far behind that of Europe. Hollywood's genre movies came finally to seem valuable to Americans, the film critics have shown, only after the French nouvelle vague directors had popularized for educated Americans the myths and conventions of those ancestors of today's police and detective series, the films of Bogart and Cagney and Edward G. Robinson.

This change in American attitudes toward the movies—or, more accurately, this change in the attitudes of the educated classes—is the more instructive, and grows more ironic, when we consider how its emergence is tied to the decline of the movies as a form of popular art. Through the 1950s and the 1960s, as critics of the American film lost their defensiveness and began to speak with the same confidence as the literary critics, the American film itself was being supplanted by television as the U.S.'s principal medium of popular narrative. (In 1951, in the early dawn of the television age, 90 million Americans attended the movies each week; by 1959 weekly attendance had fallen to 43 million; today the vast majority of Americans attend the movies only two or three times per year.) As the Hollywood studios and their vast machinery for star making and film manufacturing receded into history and as there emerged a generation of reviewers, critics, and, finally, university professors whose deepest experience of art had occurred in the movie houses of their childhoods, the American film came to be detached or liberated from its identity as a consumer item, a mere commercial product, and to be located instead within an aesthetic field.

This recognition of the essential *artistic* dimension of the Hollywood commercial movie was and remains an intellectual achievement of great magnitude, for it permitted new perspectives on the cultural history of the United States, profoundly complicating our understanding of the workings of our economic system and altering our understanding of the nature and possibilities of art itself. The most significant implication of this recognition, an implication explored by such scholars as Thomas Schatz and Leo Braudy among others, is this: capitalist greed, the crassest of alliances between commerce and modern technology, may constitute the enabling conditions of a complex narrative art.

But this recognition, which was the work of years and many scholars, was in certain respects a belated one. By the time it had been fully lodged in the educated consciousness, in museums and universities, the American film itself was no longer a habitual experience for the mass of the American population, having yielded to television not only its ability to incite contempt for manufactured entertainment but also its status as the nation's central institution for storytelling.

It seems probable, then (as the case of the movies as well as such ancestor systems as the novel and even the theater suggest), that cultures can perceive the artistic character of their primary entertainment systems only when such systems have become historical artifacts, when they are no longer experienced as habitual and common, no longer central.

In the first years of the 21st century, American television itself underwent such a transformation. The broadcast system offering a limited range of consensus stories aimed at a mass audience was undermined and will surely be supplanted by a system of narrowcasting to niche audiences and subcultures. And there were many signs that the old television, like the movies of the studio era, was ready to enter our museums and our school curricula. (This encyclopedia is itself a measure of the transition of television to an object of study and historical interest.)

The era of broadcast television parallels, and, in many respects may be seen to reenact, the history and aesthetic evolution of the movies and, in less precise ways, of such earlier instances of consensus narrative as the novel and the public theater of the Elizabethans.

What is crucial in all these instances is the intersection of historical, political, technological, economic, and aesthetic factors. In such a historicized understanding, aesthetic features appear in response to technical or ideological or cultural constraints. Human agents (writers, directors, producers, actors, audiences) may play a role, of course, but the narrative or dramatic field alters as well in obedience to what Thomas Schatz, echoing Andre Bazin, calls "the genius of the system."

These systems of storytelling and entertainment appear to follow a similar pattern of development, which cannot be accurately described without a partly aesthetic and evaluative vocabulary. Most simply, this pattern is one of self-discovery, in which the new medium begins by repeating and imitating the forms and strategies of its ancestor systems and gradually, through accident and experiment, discovers more and more thoroughly its own special resources. The novel, for example, is born as an amalgam of older forms: the romance, the picaresque tale, certain forms of religious narrative such as puritan autobiography, various forms of journalism and historical writing. At first it combines these elements haphazardly and crudely. Then, nourished by a large and eager audience that makes novel writing a highly profitable enterprise, the novel begins to distinguish itself clearly from these earlier forms, to combine its inherited elements more harmoniously and judiciously, and to exploit the possibilities for narrative that are uniquely available to fictional stories printed in books.

As many have argued, something of the same principle can be seen in the history of the movies, which begin in a borrowing and restaging of styles, formats, and performances taken from such older media as theater, still photography, visual art, and prose fiction and then evolving methods that exploit with greater and greater subtlety the unique properties of the motion-picture camera and the environment of the movie house.

Public attractions such as carnivals, the circus, and amusement parks were another source for early cinema. Some scholars have claimed that the defining attribute of the birth of the movies in the United States was the struggle between a populist "cinema of attractions" and a middle-class preference for narrative as inspired by theater and books. Such perspectives remind us that the forms achieved by a "mature" medium do not comprise some perfect fulfillment of its intrinsic potential but represent instead a narrowed range of possible outcomes as well as promises unexplored, roads not taken.

The evolution of such systems of entertainment and communication is always immensely complicated by the rivalry of competing systems, by the economic structures and political regimes that shape and support such systems and that are in turn altered themselves as the new media root themselves in people's lives. Improvements in technology and in methods of distribution and access further complicate the development of such media. In the case of film, for instance, decisive changes follow upon the advent of sound and the development of lighter, more mobile cameras and of more sensitive film stock; and seismic shifts in the very nature of film, in its relation to its audience and its society, occur with the birth of television.

Perhaps most significant of all, media systems and institutions for storytelling alter and extend their possibilities as their audiences grow more comfortable with them, learning the special codes and conventions such institutions generate and rely upon. The distance between *Fred*

Ott's Sneeze (circa 1893)—only seconds long, produced in East Orange, New Jersey, in the world's first movie studio—and Chaplin's *Modern Times* (1936) is a rich, decisive emblem for these interacting processes, these enabling conditions of popular art.

American television during the broadcast era (roughly from the medium's inception in 1946 through the decade of the 1990s) enacts a similar history. It is not a history of unremitting refinement and improvement, of course, but it is a history impossible to understand without an awareness of the aesthetics of media transition, a recognition of the complex, ongoing ways in which the medium learned to use and then to exploit more subtly such defining constraints as the commercial interruptions; the reduced visual scale of the screen; the formulas, genres, performing styles, and actors it inherited from radio, theater, and the movies; the 30- or (somewhat later) the 60-minute time slot, the domestic environment in which TV is experienced.

In its first or imitative phase, American television recycled its ancestors—radio, theater formats, and movies, though an early boycott of TV by the Hollywood studios kept most American feature films off the screen during the medium's first decade. One way to understand the misnamed "golden age of live television" is to recognize that 1950s taste hierarchies, which assumed theater's inherent superiority to movies, underpinned many journalistic and scholarly accounts of the shift of prime-time production from live dramas made in New York to filmed series made in Los Angeles. But the popularity of early series such as *I Love Lucy* (1951–61, CBS) and *Dragnet* (1952–59; revived, 1967–70, NBC; and yet again 2003, ABC), deplored by many at the time as "boob-tube" fare, now seems sensible, even aesthetically enlightened. For these pioneering programs embraced the new medium's inherent friendliness toward episodic series, and their visual styles emphasized close-ups and domestic, enclosed spaces in ways that respected the modest dimensions of the TV screen. (In its strategy of filming before an audience, *Lucy,* that timeless hybrid, also found a way to mobilize some of the energies of live performance.) Moreover, their reliance on film was not only a sensible business practice that preserved the product for repeat broadcasts, it was also a recognition that the movies were, and had been for half a century, a central aesthetic experience for most Americans.

Both *Dragnet* and *Lucy* were deeply rooted in older media but also displayed a powerful if partial awareness of the resources of television. Those resources were a function of the medium's presence in the home, easily incorporated into the daily routines of domestic life, and its audiovisual limitations. The small screen, whose images were of marginal quality even when the unsteady broadcast signal was at its strongest, was unfit for panoramas or a crowded mise-en-scène; its primary theater was, and still remains (even in our era of digital signals and high-definition television), the human face and voice.

The physical realities of the TV environment, then, help to explain its fundamental genres of sitcom, family drama, courtroom drama, soap opera, medical show, all of which rely on dialogue and argument, psychological interaction, interior, intimate settings, close encounters. Even the crime series, with its emphasis on confining urban spaces, may be said to have an affinity for the small screen as the western or other forms of action/adventure do not. (And even most TV westerns, a secondary form of the medium in any event, domesticate their genre, emphasizing interior scenes and talking heads over cattle drives and sage brush.)

An aesthetic history of the medium, and of its complex, sometimes reluctant and evasive mirroring of aspects of American social history, can be traced in part through the evolution of its primary genres. Needless to say, not every new program in a given genre is an advance. The advertising regime that requires commercial interruptions, inflexible timetables, and audience ratings also encourages trivial imitation and replication of popular formulas. But even in a rigidly formulaic system variation and technical refinements are inevitable.

In its second phase (that of a systemic technical advance, approximately the decade of the 1960s) the dominant genres of the medium become increasingly televisual, writers adapt to the enforced commercial interruptions, directors and directors of photography master the nuances of the small screen, which is hostile to excessive movement horizontally, across its confining frame, but more hospitable to motion in depth, toward and away from the camera's eye; and performers and performance styles emerge that aim for quiet, minimalist effects suited to a medium dependent on close-ups and more friendly to ordinary faces than the mythic enlargements of the movie screen or the stylized flamboyance of the theater.

During this decade of technical advance the power of this domestic appliance to establish enduring, habitual connections with its audience is fortified and extended. Although most series episodes during the 1960s were self-contained and although characters rarely remembered their previous adventures, a drama of growth and aging often played out in the faces and bodies of performers who appeared week after week for years. This brute, inherent power of television is one key to the popularity of the soap opera as well as such prime-time programs as *The Andy Griffith Show* (1960–68, CBS) and *Gunsmoke* (1955–75, CBS). The former series, notable for its leisurely pace and conversational comedy, made its debut when Andy's son Opie (Ron Howard) was a six year old and carried its audience through the heart of his childhood. In *Gunsmoke* Marshall Matt Dillon (James Arness) and his woman friend Kitty (Amanda Blake) ripen into senior citizens during the series' 20-year run. By the end of the 1960s the medium's prior history, a narrative field more widely shared by Americans than any earlier form of fiction or drama, establishes in the viewing audience a deep familiarity with story conventions and performers, and this intimate, accreting literacy itself becomes a resource on which programs can rely.

In its final phase—just before cable and satellite systems and new digital technologies threaten and then supercede the network monopolies of the broadcast era—the technical complications and refinements developed over two decades are joined to a more complex subject matter, and television fiction at its best becomes a genuine art form. The progression, for example, from *Lucy* to the *Dick Van Dyke Show* (1961–66, CBS) to the *Mary Tyler Moore Show* (1970–77, CBS), *All in the Family* (1971–79, CBS), and *M*A*S*H* (1972–83, CBS) is more than an instructive social history of American society, though it is such a chronicle. It is also an aesthetic progression, in which the situation comedy becomes perhaps the signature American art form of its era.

One measure of the relative maturity TV fiction had achieved by the 1970s is the emergence of distinctive subgenres or strains of situation comedy, an analogue to the movie era when screwball comedy, Lubitsch-style worldly comedy, and the anarchic comedy of the Marx Brothers signaled something of the diversity of the Hollywood system. In the television equivalent of such a ripening, Garry Marshall's escapist comedies—*The Odd Couple* (1970–83, ABC), *Happy Days* (1974–84, ABC), *Laverne and Shirley* (1976–83, ABC), *Mork and Mindy* (1978–82, ABC), among others—emphasized vivid star turns and slapstick situations that drew upon and updated the tone and feel of *I Love Lucy,* on whose successor, *The Lucy Show,* Marshall had worked as a writer. A second strain of comedy developed from the more character-oriented and visually restrained style of the *Mary Tyler Moore Show,* which like the early Marshall shows engendered a range of similar series produced by the MTM company through the 1970s: *Rhoda* (1974–78, CBS), *The Bob Newhart Show* (1972–78, CBS), *The Tony Randall Show* (1976–78, ABC, CBS), among others. A third flavor of comedy was created by Norman Lear, the visionary writer-creator of *All in the Family* and then a series of similar shows that included *Maude* (1972–78, CBS), *The Jeffersons* (1975–85, CBS), and *One Day at a Time* (1975–84, CBS). Produced on videotape instead of film and aiming for social relevance and an invasive, vulgar intimacy, the Lear shows were loud, harsh, and overtly political, radically unlike the witty, visually decorous MTM series or the clownish escapism of the Marshall programs.

*M*A*S*H* offered yet a fourth variation in style and substance, for this classic series, one of network television's most memorable achievements, was filmed with one camera, on movie principles, and eschewed the live audiences of the other comedy factories. Developed by Larry Gelbart from the Robert Altman film (1970), *M*A*S*H* was ostensibly set during the Korean War but spoke directly to the ambivalence and anxiety generated by the war in Vietnam. In *M*A*S*H,* as in all the strongest series of the 1970s and beyond, the experience of the characters was cumulative, their rivalries and affections developed and shifted over time, and the program explored psychology and human relationships in ways that were uniquely enabled by the format of the weekly series.

As the foregoing implies, the 1970s and 1980s are the true "golden age" of broadcast television. The medium's defining genres achieve culminating incarnations in this period, exploiting their weekly installments to dramatize character development and multiple, entwined plots with compelling complexity and authority. The MTM factory shifts away from sitcoms toward the end of the 1970s, producing hour-long dramas, some of which reach new levels of psychological and social seriousness. Examples include *Lou Grant* (1977–82, CBS), about an urban newspaper; *The White Shadow* (1978–81, CBS), set in a city high school; *St. Elsewhere* (1982–88, NBC), a hospital series, and, most notably, *Hill Street Blues* (1981–87, NBC), a landmark *policier,* marked by jittery, rapid camera work and editing and morally complex stories and characters that influenced all subsequent TV drama and established its cocreator and executive producer, Steven Bochco, as one of the primary auteur-producers in American television.

This late period of the broadcast era is distinguished as well by made-for-television movies and miniseries that move beyond the limits of the weekly series to explore political and historical topics that had never before reached the TV screen. The emergence of these longer forms is a sign of television's maturity and enlarging ambition as a narrative medium. The format of the miniseries implicitly exposes how arbitrary and relatively inflexible is the length of theatrical movies. Television, in contrast, is theoretically free to allow stories to unfold according to the needs of the material, for its audience can easily tune in to chapters or episodes running across several days or even weeks. Some of the defining programs of the 1970s and early 1980s exploit this distinctive attribute of the medium. The following are representative instances of a much larger group of such texts: *QB VII* (six hours, 30 minutes, 1974, ABC), about a libel action that becomes a story of the concentration camps; *Rich Man, Poor Man* (12 hours, 1976, ABC), an ambitious social history of the post-World War II United States; *Roots* (12 hours, 1977, ABC), an adaptation of Alex Haley's epic of the African-American experience; *Holocaust* (seven hours, 35 minutes, 1978, NBC); *The Awakening Land* (seven hours, 1978, NBC), an epic of American pioneers; and *King* (six hours, 1978, NBC), about the life and death of Martin Luther King.

Many of the television movies of this era are also thematically ambitious and visually complex. Some of these films exploit the performance history of the medium by casting actors who refine or play against personae they had established in TV series. As before, the following examples are drawn from a much larger range of texts. Elizabeth Montgomery, wholesome star of the escapist sitcom *Bewitched* (1964–72, ABC), appears in several thoughtful and disturbing films during the 1970s that deal with violence against women, including *A Case of Rape* (1974), *A Killing Affair* (1977), and *Act of Violence* (1979). Montgomery is also memorably cast against her subservient helpmeet series identity in the miniseries about frontier pioneers mentioned above, *The Awakening Land,* based on Conrad Richter's trilogy of novels. Mary Tyler Moore draws on and complicates the audience's affection for her sitcom character in a candid film about breast cancer, *First You Cry* (1978). Carol Burnett, beloved star of the variety show that bears her name (1967–77, CBS), plays a bereaved mother demanding answers from an unresponsive military in the antiwar film *Friendly Fire* (1979). David Janssen re-creates and deepens the wincing vulnerability of his roles in *The Fugitive* (1963–67, ABC) and *Harry-O* (1974–76, ABC) in such films as *A Sensitive, Passionate Man* (1977) and *City in Fear* (1980). As the titles just cited suggest, TV movies have frequently engaged painful and ambiguous material, often with a modest clarity rarely found in theatrical movies of recent decades. Both the series and longer-form programs of the 1970s through the 1990s deserve and will repay the sort of systematic cataloguing and close interpretation that is routinely granted to the movies of the studio era.

Though we are still too close to the broadcast era for a definitive verdict, it is probable that American television of the second half of the twentieth century will be recognized as a significant aesthetic achievement, the result of a never-to-be-repeated confluence of social, technological, and historical forces, a unique precursor to the digital entertainment future. It would not be the first time that popular diversions scarcely valued by the society that produced them were judged by the future to be works of art.

David Thorburn

Further Reading

Barthes, Roland, *Mythologies,* London: Vintage, 1993
Beardsley, Monroe, *Aesthetics from Classical Greece to the Present,* New York: Macmillan, 1966
Braudy, Leo, *The World in a Frame: What We See in Films,* Chicago: University of Chicago Press, 2002
Cawelti, John, *Adventure, Mystery and Romance: Formula Stories as Art and Popular Culture,* Chicago: University of Chicago Press, 1976
Danto, Arthur C., *The Transfiguration of the Commonplace: A Philosophy of Art,* Cambridge, Massachusetts: Harvard University Press, 1981
Donoghue, Denis, *Speaking of Beauty,* New Haven: Yale University Press, 2003
Feuer, Jane, Paul Kerr, and Tise Vahimagi, editors, *MTM: "Quality Television,"* London: BFI Books, 1984
Goodman, Nelson, *Languages of Art,* Indianapolis: Hackett, 1976
Greenblatt, Stephen, *Shakespearean Negotiations,* Berkeley: University of California Press, 1988
Gunning, Tom, "The Cinema of Attractions: Early Film...and the Avant Garde," in *Early Cinema: Space, Frame, Narrative,* edited by Thomas Elsaesser and Adam Barker, London: BFI, 1990
Hall, Stuart, and Paddy Whannel, *The Popular Arts,* London, Hutchinson, 1964
Marc, David, *Comic Visions* Malden, Massachusetts: Blackwell Books, 1997
Marc, David, *Demographic Vistas: Television in American Culture,* Philadelphia: University of Pennsylvania Press, 1996
Marc, David, and Robert J. Thompson, *Prime Time, Prime Movers:...America's Greatest TV Shows....,* Boston: Little, Brown, 1992
Newcomb, Horace, *TV, The Most Popular Art,* New York: Anchor Books, 1974
Newcomb, Horace, editor, *Television: The Critical View,* New York: Oxford University Press, 2000
Schatz, Thomas, *The Genius of the System: Hollywood Filmmaking in the Studio Era,* New York: Pantheon Books, 1990
Thompson, Robert J., *Television's Second Golden Age,* New York: Continuum Books, 1996
Thorburn, David, "Television as an Aesthetic Medium," *Critical Studies in Mass Communication* 4 (1987)
Thorburn, David, "Television Melodrama," in *Television: The Critical View,* edited by Horace Newcomb, New York: Oxford University Press, 2000
Thorburn, David, and Henry Jenkins, "Toward an Aesthetics of Transition," in *Rethinking Media Change,* edited by David Thorburn and Henry Jenkins, Cambridge, Massachusetts: MIT Press, 2003
Warshow, Robert, *The Immediate Experience,* New York: Doubleday, 1962
Wollheim, Richard, *Art and Its Objects,* 2nd edition, Cambridge: Cambridge University Press, 1980

Africa, Sub-Saharan

Television broadcasting in sub-Saharan Africa displays two distinct patterns. On the one hand, there is the success story reproducing itself in countries that undertook bold and substantive liberalization of the airwaves over the past decade. The flipside is the pitiable state of impeded growth, inefficiency, and decadence. While the goings-on of the early 21st century suggest a hopeful outlook for the region, a lack of succinct national/regional media policies could frustrate growth of local production capability and push the subcontinent deeper into dependence on TV output from Western countries.

In many African countries, TV broadcasting was introduced in the 1950s and 1960s by former colonial settlers. While the colonial edifices only endeavored to service the information and entertainment needs of the settlers, the first black African governments used broadcasting as a tool both to entrench themselves politically and to repress their own societies. Between the 1960s (Africa's independence decade) and the late 1980s, television broadcasting in sub-Saharan Africa was heavily controlled by the government, with virtually no private sector participation. With little (at times no) independently produced local content and weak signals limited to major urban centers, viewership grew sluggishly in many countries.

Television broadcasting changed during the late 1980s and early 1990s, as a wind of democratic reform consumed much of the continent. In almost all countries that embraced political change, television business has flourished, creating a fast-growing broadcasting sector. Such countries boast multiple private TV stations alongside revamped state broadcasters. The lure of cheap reruns of Western sitcoms and soap operas, spiced with persuasive local content from nascent but independent production houses, is winning audiences for the new African TV-owning households. Local content hardly matches the cheap foreign imports, but the emergence of regional content—from regional sporting events and from such broadcasting centers as South Africa and Nigeria—is helping maintain an African idea on the television screen.

Kenya and Nigeria were the first sub-Saharan countries to allow private broadcasting. While Kenya issued one private license in 1990 and thereafter stymied further liberalization for six years, Nigeria opened the door to private broadcasters in 1991 and kept it open. The result was the creation of Africa's most competitive TV market, with over 80 private and state-owned stations jostling for audiences and a portion of the nearly $1 billion in annual advertising spending. A vibrant local production industry flourishes alongside imported content. Indeed, these indigenous productions form Nigeria's biggest contribution to the continent's TV broadcasting. The country is home to some of Africa's most successful sitcoms, such as *Ikebe Super* and *Papa Ajasco* produced by Wale Adenuga. *Papa Ajasco* is the most-watched sitcom in West Africa, with audiences in eight countries. Since 1999, a number of Nigerian sitcoms have been on air in East Africa, with moderate success. Audience research conducted in Lagos in 1999 indicated that African Independent Television (AIT) was the most-watched station in the city, followed by Channels, MITV, and Degue Broadcasting Network (DBN). AIT and Minaj are licensed as satellite TV stations.

Nigeria has 40 government-owned TV stations, of which 29 stations were established by state governments. There are 16 private free-to-air stations, two satellite stations with global licenses, and 37 private cable and satellite rebroadcast stations. Five of the free-to-air TV licenses were issued in March 2002 by the regulating authority, Nigeria Broadcasting Commission (NBC). The NBC was established in 1992 with a primary function to regulate and supervise the industry. Over 40 government-owned stations operate under the ambit of the Nigerian Television Authority (NTA), making NTA one of the largest broadcasting operators in Africa. The NTA stations broadcast in most of Nigeria's major local languages. Communications Trends Ltd. (CTL), an indigenous satellite cable television and Internet provider, is the second largest TV network in the country, with operations in 13 of Nigeria's 30 constitutional states.

Senegal and Ghana stand out as two other showcases of rapid growth and promise in television. Both countries have a history of relatively robust and independent media. Senegal allowed private TV operators from 1991 and currently boasts one national public broadcaster (Radiodiffusion Television Senegalaise) and two subscription TV services (Canal1 Horizons Senegal and EXCAF). RTS signal covers three-quarters of the country with broadcasts in French, English, and several local languages. Canal1 Horizons is generally a sports and entertainment service that is available on the French bouquet channel, Le Sat, together with EXCAF pay TV. Ghana, on the other hand, began licensing private broadcasters in 1995 and has four TV stations. Ghana TV is state owned, while Metro TV is a joint venture between the state broadcaster and Lebanese investors. TV3, the first free-to-air station, is a joint venture between local media practitioners and Malaysian investors. Both Metro TV and TV3 broadcast one channel each to Accra and its environs. The fourth operator, Fontom TV, commenced operations in 1999 with news, sports, and entertainment broadcasts around Kumasi.

Some newcomers on the continental broadcasting scene are quickly establishing themselves as leaders. Tanzania is a case in point. After three decades of no television service, Tanzania liberalized the airwaves in the early 1990s. Since then, seven stations—Independent Television (ITV), Dar es Salaam Television (DTV), Central Television Network (CTN), Cable Entertainment Network (CEN), Star Television (STV), Television Zanzibar (TVZ), and Television of Tanzania (TVT)—have commenced operations. Alongside these are dozens of small, intermittent broadcasters licensed to operate in nearly all sizeable urban centers throughout the country. Many of these run cable networks, avoiding the costs of free-to-air transmission. Notably, only TVT is state owned. Local content is scant, as most stations relay CNN, BBC, and Deutsche Welle TV, breaking away only for a few hours nightly for local news and a handful of local productions. ITV is the only Tanzanian station available to the rest of the continent via satellite and terrestrially to five regions within the country.

Uganda has also made considerable progress over the past four years. More than a dozen licenses have been issued, although only half of these have commenced operations. Uganda Television (UTV) is the national broadcaster, with WBS-TV, Channels, STV, MultiChoice, and TV Africa as the main contenders. In the Democratic Republic of Congo (former Zaïre), Radio-Television Nationale Congolaise (RTNC) is state owned and the sole national broadcaster in the vast country. RTNC covers nearly three-quarters of this vast country via four channels, previously privately owned but nationalized by the government after civil war broke out in 1997. A number of small private subscription broadcasters have emerged in major urban centers over the past two years. These include Tropicana TV, RAGA, and Antenne A in Kinshasa, and Solar Energy in Lubumbashi.

Nevertheless, television broadcasting is still highly controlled in at least a quarter of sub-Sahara African countries. In such countries, only state-owned television stations operate on free-to-air licenses. For example, Ethiopia TV is the only television station in the country, broadcasting primarily in Amharic and minimally in English. Similarly, the Zambia National Broadcasting Corporation (ZNBC) is the only TV broadcaster in Zambia, with its signal available in major urban areas. The corporation is also the local partner in the two pay-TV services run by South Africa's MultiChoice and the African Broadcast Network (ABN). Swaziland's Television Authority (STVA) broadcasts one television channel with nationwide repeaters. In Malawi the first public TV service, Television Malawi (TVM), was opened by the government in 2000. South Africa's MultiChoice subscription service is the only substitute via satellite in Malawi's main urban centers.

In Seychelles and Mauritius, the state-owned broadcasters are the sole TV operators. The Seychelles Broadcasting Corporation offers a single channel covering the entire island, while the Mauritius Broadcasting Corporation runs three free-to-air stations and two subscription channels. Lesotho's National Broadcasting Service and Botswana's BTV operate on a very small scale, respectively, within the two land-locked countries. South Africa's MultiChoice runs subscription TV services comprising mainly sports and entertainment in the two countries.

In Rwanda, Televisiondiffusion de Rwanda (TVR) remains the only major broadcaster, with a signal covering about half the country. Over the past three years, two small stations, Tele10 and STV, have commenced operations around the capital city of Kigali. A similar story is evident in Madagascar's TV Malagasy, the state broadcaster. The recent launching of three private subscription operatiors (MaTV, TVF, and RTA) in Antananarivo has had little impact on the broadcasting scene. In Burundi, Television Nationale du Burundi is the sole broadcaster, reaching only a small section of the country.

In Zimbabwe the Zimbabwe Broadcasting Corporation runs ZBC-TV1 as the only national television service. It operates as a commercial TV station and transmits nationally. Since 1997, Joy TV has been licensed as the first independent TV service in the country. It leases ZBC-TV2's studios and transmitters, and its signal is available within a 120-kilometer radius of Harare. TV audience research shows ZBC-TV1 controlling about 52 percent of the audience, with Joy-TV accounting for 37 percent.

In Mozambique, Televisao de Moçambique (TVM), the only national station, is state owned and serves major urban areas. Plans are afoot to have the transmission available countrywide via satellite. Three private local stations, Radio Televisao Klint (RTK), TV Miramar, and Greenland Television operate around Maputo. TV Miramar is owned by the Brazilian Church Reino Universal de Assembleia do Deus (Universal Church of God), while RTK is owned by a political personality. In Angola, the government operates Televisao Popular de Angola (TPA), which has transmitters in most provincal capitals and major towns. A second station, TPA 2, operates around the capital city of Luanda.

In Namibia, the Namibian Broadcasting Corporation is a monopoly, with one television service that offers regional programming during various times of the day. Two subscription TV services, Deukom TV and MultiChoice, have operations in major urban centers. Deukom TV offers several four German-language channels (RTL, Sat1, DW, and ARD) while MultiChoice offers several English-language entertainment and sports channels beamed from South Africa.

Throughout the rest of the subcontinent (Botswana, Chad, Congo, Cote d'Ivoire [Ivory Coast], Djibouti, Equatorial Guinea, Eritrea, Gambia, Guinea-Bissau, Mali, and Sudan) the state remains the sole broadcaster. In a few other countries, like Burkina Faso, Benin, and Gabon, a multiplicity of problems have frustrated any substantive growth in television broadcasting. Yet others, such as Cameroon and Kenya, have a fledgling TV industry whose growth has been stunted, if not permanently maimed, by years of government interference.

Some notable players on the continent's broadcasting scene include MultiChoice, Le Sat, and TV Africa. MultiChoice is the largest channel bouquet operator on the continent, offering up to 50 channels to 1.2 million subscribers in 15 countries. Sub-Saharan Africa accounts for 187,000 subscribers, or one-sixth of the total, but boasts a 5 percent annual growth. Le Sat is a Francophone bouquet that is beamed to MDDS operators. TV Africa operates as a content provider to many African television broadcasters. CFI Pro and RTPi are Europe-based content providers for Francophone and Luzophone broadcasters, respectively. African Broadcast Network (ABN), a continentwide broadcaster, was founded in January 2001. It attempts to procure quality entertainment programming for affiliates and partner broadcasters in Africa.

Backhauling and downlinking of pan-African programming has improved considerably as more satellites with an African footprint have been launched in the past five years. At least a dozen satellites are currently overflying Africa, lowering the cost of transponder hosting and satellite transmission costs. For instance, MultiChoice uses transponder space on PanAmSat 4, PanAmSat 7, and EutelSat W4 satellites to beam its bouquet of channels into sub-Saharan Africa.

One of the drawbacks to the development of TV broadcasting in sub-Saharan Africa is a lack of succinct media policies. With the exception of Nigeria, no country on the subcontinent has a substantive media policy, much less an established institutional framework to administer such policy. Numerous pertinent policy issues (for example, local content regulation, ownership and control, and public service broadcasting) are yet to be addressed, creating chaotic scenarios. For example, in Tanzania, Uganda, Kenya, and Cameroon, a lack of clarity on many policy issues has set back developments in the TV broadcasting sub-sector or led to a misallocation of much-needed resources. While authorities in these countries have pledged to review the relevant media policies, their nascent TV operations are striving to stand firm in tough trading conditions.

NIXON K. KARIITHI

Further Reading

Bourgault, Louise, *Mass Media in Sub-Saharan Africa,* Bloomington: Indiana University Press, 1995

Domatob, Jerry, Abubakar Jika, and Ikechukwu Nwosu, editors, *Mass Media and the African Society,* Nairobi, Kenya: African Council on Communication Education, 1986

Paterson, Chris, "Reform or Re-colonisation? The Overhaul of African Television," *Review of African Political Economy,* Vol. 25, Issue 78 (1998)

Salama, Girgis, "Broadcasting in Africa: Past, Present and Future," *Media Development,* Vol. 36, No. 3 (1989)

Wedell, George, editor, *Making Broadcasting Useful: The Development of Radio and Television in Africa in the 1980s,* Manchester, United Kingdom, and Dover, New Hampshire: Manchester University Press in association with the European Institute for the Media.

Ailes, Roger (1940–)

U.S. Media Consultant, Producer, Executive

Roger Eugene Ailes is one of television's most versatile, outspoken, and successful producers and consultants. He has been described as "the amusingly ferocious Republican media genius" and a "pit-bull Republican media strategist turned television tycoon." He has had a variety of careers, including producer of television shows, Shakespeare, and off-Broadway plays; and president of the cable television channels CNBC, America's Talking, and FOX News.

Ailes's career in television began in Cleveland,

Roger Ailes.
Courtesy of CNBC

Ohio, where he was a producer and director at KYW-TV, for what was then a locally produced talk-variety show, *The Mike Douglas Show.* He later became executive producer for that program, which syndicated nationally, and won two Emmy Awards for his work, in 1967 and 1968. It was in this position, in 1967, that Ailes had a spirited discussion about television in politics with one of the show's guests, Richard Nixon, who took the view that television was a gimmick. Later, while campaigning for the U.S. presidency, Nixon called on Ailes to serve as his executive producer of TV. Nixon's election victory in 1968 was only Ailes's first venture into presidential television.

After founding Ailes Communications, Inc., in 1969, Ailes worked as consultant for various businesses and politicians, including WCBS-TV in New York. In the 1970s he tried his hand at theater production with the Broadway musical *Mother Earth* (1972) and the off-Broadway hit play *Hot-l Baltimore* (1973–76), for which Ailes received four Obie Awards. He was executive producer for a television special, *The Last Frontier,* in 1974, and he produced and directed a television special, *Fellini: Wizards, Clowns, and Honest Liars,* for which he received an Emmy Award nomination in 1977.

During the 1970s and 1980s, Ailes carried out political consulting for many candidates, and he returned to presidential campaigning as a consultant to President Ronald Reagan in 1984. Ailes is widely credited with having coached Reagan to victory in the second presidential debate with Walter Mondale, after Reagan had disappointed his partisans with a lackluster effort in the first debate. In 1984 Ailes won an Emmy Award as executive producer and director of a television special, *Television and the Presidency.* In 1987 he wrote a book with Jon Kraushar, *You Are the Message: Secrets of the Master Communicators,* in which Ailes discusses some of his philosophies and strategies for successful performance in the eye of the public media.

Ailes also won acclaim for his work in the 1988 presidential election, in which he helped guide Republican George Bush to a come-from-behind victory over Democrat Michael Dukakis. (Ailes did not work on the losing 1992 Bush campaign against Bill Clinton.)

In 1991 Ailes convinced a syndicator to bring Rush Limbaugh from radio to television and became executive producer of Limbaugh's late-night show. Ailes announced his withdrawal from political consulting in 1992.

In 1993 Ailes became president of NBC's cable channel CNBC and began planning another NBC cable channel, America's Talking (now called MSNBC), which debuted on July 4, 1994. After Ailes took over at CNBC, ratings increased 50 percent and profits tripled. He has had impressive success in his latest position as chairman and chief executive officer of FOX News. Since assuming this position in 1996, Ailes has overseen the launch of the FOX News Channel on cable, boosting FOX programming to a leadership position in the cable news industry. In 2000 Ailes signed a contract to continue to serve as chairman and chief executive officer of FOX News through January 2004.

LYNDA LEE KAID

Roger (Eugene) Ailes. Born in Warren, Ohio, May 15, 1940. Educated at Ohio University, Athens, B.A., 1962. Began television career as property assistant, *The Mike Douglas Show,* KYW-TV, Cleveland, Ohio, 1962, producer, 1965, executive producer, 1967–68; media adviser to Richard M. Nixon's presidential campaign, 1968; founder and owner, Ailes Communications, a media production and consulting firm, 1969–92; producer of plays *Mother Earth,* 1972, and *The Hot-l Baltimore,* 1973–76; producer, various television specials, from 1974; media consultant, Ronald Reagan's presidential campaign, 1984, and George Bush's presidential campaign, 1988, also various senatorial and congressional campaigns; president CNBC, cable television network, 1993–96; president and program host, America's Talking (MSNBC), an all-talk cable television network, 1994–96; chairman and CEO of FOX News and the FOX News Channel, since January 1996. Honorary Doctorate, Ohio University. Recipient: Obie Award, Best Off-Broadway Show, 1973, for *Hot-l Baltimore;* Emmy Awards, 1967, 1968, 1984; Silver Circle Award, National Academy of Television Arts and Sciences, 1999.

Television Series (selected)

1962–68 *The Mike Douglas Show*
1970 *The Real Tom Kennedy Show*
1981 *Tomorrow: Coast to Coast*
1992–96 *Rush Limbaugh*

Television Specials (selected)

1974 *Last Frontier*
1976 *Fellini: Wizards, Clowns, and Honest Liars*
1991 *An All-Star Tribute to Our Troops*

Stage

Mother Earth, 1972; *Hot-l Baltimore,* 1973–76.

Publications

"Attorney Style: Charisma in a Court Counts," *The National Law Journal* (July 21, 1986)
"Campaign Strategy," *Time* (May 11, 1992)
"A Few Kind Words for Presenter Tip O'Neill," *Advertising Age* (January 8, 1990)
"How to Make a Good Impression," *Reader's Digest* (September 1989)
"How to Make an Audience Love You," *Working Woman* (November 1990)
"The Importance of Being Likeable," *Reader's Digest* (May 1988)
"Lighten Up! Stuffed Shirts Have Short Careers," *Newsweek* (May 18, 1992)
"Sam and Diane: Give 'em Time," *Advertising Age* (August 21, 1989)
"They Told the Truth... Occasionally," *Adweek's Marketing Week* (January 29, 1990)
You Are the Message: Secrets of the Master Communicators, with John Kraushar, 1987

Further Reading

Barnes, Fred, "Pulling the Strings," *New Republic* (February 22, 1988)
Devlin, Patrick L., "Contrasts in Presidential Campaign Commercials of 1988," *American Behavioral Scientist* (March–April 1989)
Hass, Nancy, "Roger Ailes: Embracing the Enemy," *New York Times Magazine* (January 8, 1995)
Miller, Stuart, "Roger Ailes Hits TV with a Rush," *Variety* (June 21, 1991)
Oneal, Michael, "Roger Ailes Fixed CNBC, but Now Ted Turner Looms," *Business Week* (July 3, 1995)
Wolinsky, Leo C., "Refereeing the TV Campaign," *Washington Journalism Review* (January–February 1991)

Alcoa Hour, The

U.S. Anthology Drama

The Alcoa Hour was a 60-minute live anthology drama that replaced *The Philco Television Playhouse* and began alternating broadcasts with *The Goodyear Theatre* in the fall of 1955. (For a few months *Philco, Alcoa,* and *Goodyear* all alternated in the Sunday 9:00 to 10:00 P.M. slot on NBC. Philco withdrew sponsorship in early 1956.) *The Alcoa Hour* was sponsored by the Aluminum Company of America and was produced by Herbert Brodkin, formerly of ABC TV. Among the program's directors, many of whom went on to distinguished careers in television and film, were Dan Petrie, Robert Mulligan, Sidney Lumet, and Ralph Nelson. Coming near the end of the "golden age" of live television anthology drama, *The Alcoa Hour* had a relatively short run of just under two years, despite generally high-quality programs and mostly favorable reviews.

The first broadcast of *The Alcoa Hour* was on October 16, 1955. An original teleplay by Joseph Schull entitled "The Black Wings," the production starred Wendell Corey and Ann Todd and was directed by Norman Felton. Both *Variety* and the *New York Times* praised the high quality of acting and the attractive sets but criticized the script. *New York Times* reviewer J.P. Shanley went so far as to say that the story was "melodramatic hogwash." Schull's narrative focused on a German physician (Corey) who had been a Luftwaffe pilot during World War II. He secretly endows a clinic for the treatment of victims of a bombing raid he led over England, then falls in love with an English girl (Todd) who was crippled by the bombing. In spite of the script's weaknesses, the program was deemed a success because of the excellent performances and fine directing, and critics felt that *The Alcoa Hour* would become a worthy successor to the famous *Philco Television Playhouse.*

During its two years, *The Alcoa Hour* broadcast a wide variety of dramas, including the sixth consecu-

The *Alcoa Hour*, Bob Watson, John Hoyt, Lamont Johnson, David Wayne, 1957–60; "Operation Spark," 1959.
Courtesy of the Everett Collection

tive Christmas season airing of Gian Carlo Menotti's television opera *Amahl and the Night Visitors* on December 25, 1955. During the Christmas season of 1956, *The Alcoa Hour* broadcast a musical version of Charles Dickens's *A Christmas Carol* entitled "The Stingiest Man in Town." The adaptation featured Basil Rathbone in a singing role, crooner Vic Damone, songwriter Johnny Desmond, opera singer Patrice Munsel, and the Four Lads, a popular singing group.

Typical programs on *The Alcoa Hour* included "Thunder in Washington" (November 27, 1955) and "Mrs. Gilling and the Skyscraper" (June 9, 1957). "Thunder in Washington" was an original script by David Davidson, directed by Robert Mulligan. The broadcast featured Melvyn Douglas and Ed Begley in a story about a highly competent business executive, Charles Turner, who answers a call from the president of the United States to come to Washington to introduce efficiency into numerous sprawling governmental agencies. Soon Turner's efforts at reform offend almost everyone, and he finds himself defending his actions before a House Appropriations Committee. The program ends with Turner vowing to continue his crusade to clean up Washington and the committee chair promising to stop him. *New York Times* reviewer Jack Gould praised the broadcast by saying that it was "a play of uncommon timeliness, power, and controversy. With one more scene, it could have been a genuine tour de force of contemporary political drama." An interesting footnote to the production is that actor Luis van Rooten, hired to play the part of the president of the United States, spent hours studying the voice and mannerisms of then President Dwight D. Eisenhower to make sure his performance was authentic, even though the president was to be seen only in a head-and-shoulders shot from behind.

"Mrs. Gilling and the Skyscraper" was a very different sort of play. An original script by Sumner Locke Elliot, it was a vehicle for distinguished actor Helen Hayes, who played the part of an elderly lady trying to save her apartment from the owners of her building who intend to demolish it to make way for a skyscraper. Both the superb acting and sensitive script were praised. The script in particular was noted for how it dealt with the generational clashes between the old lady and new tenants in her building. During the 1950s, confrontations between the old and new were becoming increasingly common as large stretches of turn-of-the-century dwellings were leveled to make way for modern buildings, and the plight of Mrs. Gillings was a familiar one for many older Americans and their families.

Perhaps the most noteworthy *Alcoa Hour* was the broadcast of February 19, 1956, entitled "Tragedy in a Temporary Town." The script by Reginald Rose told the story of a vigilante group formed after a girl is assaulted at a construction camp. According to Gould, "Mr. Rose's final scene—the mob descending on an innocent Puerto Rican victim—did make the viewer's flesh creep. And the raw vigor of the hero's denunciation of the mob—the man's language had uncommon pungency—was extraordinarily vivid video drama." Directed by Sidney Lumet and starring Lloyd Bridges as the man who opposed the mob, "Tragedy in a Temporary Town" won a Robert E. Sherwood Television Award and a citation from the Anti Defamation League of B'nai B'rith as the best dramatic program of the year dealing with interethnic group relations.

The 1956–57 season saw the networks shifting away from live broadcasts and turning more to the use of film. Faced with this change and competition from a new crop of popular programs, *The Alcoa Hour* went off the air after its September 22, 1957, broadcast of "Night" starring Franchot Tone, Jason Robards, Jr., and E.G. Marshall. As of September 30, 1957, both *The Alcoa Hour* and its companion program *The Goodyear Theatre* became 30-minute filmed programs and were moved to Monday nights at 9:30.

HENRY B. ALDRIDGE

Programming History

NBC

October 1955–September 1957   Sunday 9:00–10:00

Producer

Herbert Brodkin

Further Reading

Hawes, William, *The American Television Drama: The Experimental Years,* University: University of Alabama Press, 1986

Kindem, Gorham, editor, *The Live Television Generation of Hollywood Film Directors: Interviews with Seven Directors,* Jefferson, North Carolina: McFarland, 1994
MacDonald, J. Fred, *One Nation Under Television: The Rise and Decline of Network TV,* New York: Pantheon, 1990
Skutch, Ira, *Ira Skutch: I Remember Television: A Memoir,* Metuchen, New Jersey: Scarecrow Press, 1989
Stempel, Tom, *Storytellers to the Nation: A History of American Television Writing,* New York: Continuum, 1992
Sturcken, Frank, *Live Television: The Golden Age of 1946–1958 in New York,* Jefferson, North Carolina: McFarland, 1990
Wicking, Christopher, and Tise Vahimagi, *The American Vein: Directors and Directions in Television,* New York: Dutton, 1979
Wilk, Max, *The Golden Age of Television: Notes from the Survivors,* New York: Delacorte Press, 1976

Alda, Alan (1936–)

U.S. Actor

Alan Alda is a television and film star best known for his work in the long-running CBS television series *M*A*S*H.* He has been well honored for that role, having won 28 Emmy nominations, two Writers Guild Awards, three Directors Guild Awards, six Golden Globes from the Hollywood Foreign Press Association, and seven People's Choice Awards. Alda is the only person to have been honored by the Television Academy as top performer, writer, and director.

The son of actor Robert Alda, Alan traveled with his father on the vaudeville circuit and began performing in summer stock theater as a teenager. During his junior year at Fordham University, he studied in Europe, where he performed on the stage in Rome and on television in Amsterdam with his father. After college he acted at the Cleveland Playhouse on a Ford Foundation grant. Upon returning to New York, Alda worked on and off Broadway, and on television. He later acquired improvisational training with Chicago's Second City comedy troupe and with Compass in Hyannis Port, Massachusetts, and that background in political and social satire led to his work as a regular on television's *That Was the Week That Was.*

Alda found fame on *M*A*S*H,* where his depiction of sensitive surgeon Hawkeye Pierce won him five Emmy Awards. Set in the Korean War of the 1950s, and broadcast in part during the Vietnam War in the 1970s, *M*A*S*H* won acclaim for its broad and irreverent humor, its ability to effectively combine drama with comedy, and its overall liberal humanist stance. In adapting the show from the 1970 Robert Altman film of the same name, producer and director Gene Reynolds and writer Larry Gelbart used distinctive telefilm aesthetics and a complex narrative structure that set the show apart from the proscenium-style series that dominated television in the 1960s. The show's influence was broad, traceable perhaps most directly in the large number of 1980s multicharacter dramas and "dramedies" (such as *Hill Street Blues* and *St. Elsewhere*) whose narratives also centered around a tightly knit workplace group who became like family to one another.

Alda, who also wrote and directed many episodes of the show, has become indelibly associated with *M*A*S*H,* which continues to be watched as one of the most successful comedies in syndication. His "sensitive male" persona, derived in large part from his characterization on *M*A*S*H,* continues to be sustained by public awareness of his efforts on behalf of women's rights and other causes. An ardent feminist, Alda campaigned extensively for ten years for the passage of the Equal Rights Amendment, and, in 1976, he was appointed by President Ford to serve on the National Commission for the Observance of International Women's Year. Alda's status as a feminist led a writer in the *Boston Globe* to dub him "the quintessential Honorary Woman: a feminist icon."

Despite such associations, one of Alda's most acclaimed performances was his portrayal of a conniving producer in the 1989 Woody Allen film *Crimes and Misdemeanors.* Alda won the D.W. Griffith Award and the New York Film Critics Award, and he was nominated for a British Academy Award as Best Supporting Actor for his work in the film.

Following this success, Alda added other dimensions to his "character type." For example, he continued his exploration of a "darker side" with his portrayal of a driven corporate executive in the HBO original produc-

Alan Alda.
©20th Century Fox/Courtesy of the Everett Collection

tion *White Mile* (1994). In another notable role, Alda returned to network television in 1999 as a guest star in several episodes of NBC's medical drama *E.R.;* once again, he played a doctor, but, in contrast to *M*A*S*H*'s brash, youthful Hawkeye Pierce, *E.R.*'s Dr. Gabriel Lawrence was an aging figure in tragic decline, losing his mind and his ability to practice medicine due to Alzheimer's disease. The more familiar, inquisitive, humorous Alda is currently host of the series *Scientific American Frontiers* on PBS.

DIANE NEGRA

See also **M*A*S*H**

Alan Alda. Born Alphonso D'Abruzzo in New York City, January 28, 1936. Married: Arlene Weiss, 1957; children: Eve, Elizabeth, and Beatrice. Graduated from Fordham University, Bronx, New York, 1956; studied acting at the Cleveland Playhouse, Ohio, 1956–59. Appeared in off-Broadway productions and television guest roles through 1960s; worked with improvisational groups Second City, Chicago, and Compass, Hyannis Port, Massachusetts; appeared in movies, 1960s and 1970s; began role as "Hawkeye" Pierce in the television series *M*A*S*H,* 1972, also wrote and directed episodes of the series; actor, writer, and director of films since 1983. Presidential appointee, National Commission for the Observance of International Women's Year, 1976; cochair, National Equal Rights Amendment Countdown Campaign, 1982. Trustee: Museum of Television and Radio, 1985; Rockefeller Foundation, 1989. Member: American Federation of Television and Radio Artists; Directors Guild of America; Writers Guild of America; Actors Equity Association. Recipient: five Emmy Awards; five Golden Globe Awards; Humanitas Award for Writing; D.W. Griffith Award; New York Film Critics Award; seven People's Choice Awards.

Television Series

1964–65	*That Was the Week That Was*
1972–83	*M*A*S*H*
1974	*We'll Get By* (producer and writer)
1984	*The Four Seasons* (producer)
1990–	*Scientific American Frontiers* (host)

Made-for-Television Movies

1972	*Playmates*
1972	*The Glass House*
1973	*Isn't It Shocking?*
1974	*6 Rms Riv Vu*
1977	*Kill Me if You Can*
1984	*The Four Seasons*
1993	*And the Band Played On*
1994	*White Mile*
1996	*Jake's Women*
2001	*The Killing Yard*
2001	*Club Land*

Films

Gone Are the Days, 1963; *Paper Lion,* 1968; *Jenny,* 1969; *The Extraordinary Seaman,* 1969; *The Moonshine War,* 1970; *Catch-22,* 1970; *The Mephisto Waltz,* 1971; *To Kill a Clown,* 1972; *Same Time, Next Year,* 1978; *California Suite,* 1978; *The Seduction of Joe Tynan* (also writer), 1979; *The Four Seasons* (also director and writer), 1981; *Sweet Liberty* (also director and writer), 1986; *A New Life* (also director and writer), 1988; *Crimes and Misdemeanors,* 1989; *Betsy's Wedding* (also director and writer), 1990; *Whispers in the Dark,* 1992; *Manhattan Murder Mystery,* 1993; *Canadian Bacon,* 1994; *Flirting with Disaster,* 1996; *Everyone Says I Love You,* 1996; *Mad City,* 1997; *Murder at 1600,* 1997; *The Object of My Affection,* 1998; *What Women Want,* 2000.

Stage (selected)

Owl and the Pussycat; Purlie Victorious; Fair Game for Lover; The Apple Tree; Jake's Women; Art; Our Town.

Further Reading

Alda, Arlene, *The Last Days of M*A*S*H: Photographs and Notes,* Verona, New Jersey: Unicorn, 1983

Bennetts, Leslie, "Alda Stars in *M*A*S*H* Seminar," *New York Times* (October 18, 1986)
Clauss, Jed, *M*A*S*H: The First Five Years, 1973–77: A Show by Show Arrangement,* Mattituck, New York: Aeonian, 1977
Kalter, Suzy, *The Complete Book of M*A*S*H,* New York: H.N. Abrams, 1984
Kolbert, Elizabeth, "Hawkeye Turns Mean, Sensitively," *New York Times* (May 19, 1994)
O'Connor, John J., "Hawkeye and Company in a *M*A*S*H* Salute," *New York Times* (November 25, 1991)
Reiss, David S., *M*A*S*H: The Exclusive, Inside Story of TV's Most Popular Show,* Indianapolis, Indiana: Bobbs-Merrill, 1983
Schatz, Thomas, "*St. Elsewhere* and the Evolution of the Ensemble Series," in *Television: The Critical View,* edited by Horace Newcomb, New York: Oxford University Press, 1976; 4th edition, 1987
Straut, Raymond, *Alan Alda: A Biography,* New York: St. Martin's Press, 1983

Alfred Hitchcock Presents

U.S. Suspense Anthology

Of all film directors during the 1950s, Alfred Hitchcock was probably the best known to the general public not only by name but also by appearance and through his specialist area of the suspense genre. In some part this was due to the cameo appearances he made in his feature films, but mainly it was due to the remarkable anthology mystery series he produced and hosted for television from 1955 to 1965. For its time, it was unprecedented that such a top-rank feature director would undertake what many considered a demeaning role in television. The resulting effect, however, was quite the opposite.

The half-hour-long *Alfred Hitchcock Presents* series, and later *The Alfred Hitchcock Hour,* were extraordinary collections of dark, cynical tales of crime, mystery, and suspense, with an occasional excursion into the supernatural. The series' emphasis was on ironic or twist endings, usually in which the villain appeared to go unpunished. Each episode would begin with the musical arrangement of Charles Gounod's "Funeral March of a Marionette" while on screen Hitchcock would be seen stepping into his own silhouette trademark profile.

The idea for a Hitchcock television series came from his former agent, Lew Wasserman (then president of MCA), in early 1955 and was intended to be an extension of Hitchcock's own appearances in his features. Though wary of the new medium, Hitchcock was soon persuaded that television would be the perfect showcase for all the stories he had wanted to do but which had been excluded from feature projects due to length or peculiarity. The prospect of enormous financial benefits to be accrued from a weekly television series was also persuasive.

He formed Shamley Productions (named after his summer home in England) to produce the series at Revue Studios, the television arm of Universal. The agreement with CBS and sponsor Bristol-Myers was for Hitchcock to act as host, executive producer ("An Alfred Hitchcock Production"), and occasional director. To run the television operation he brought on board longtime friend and associate Joan Harrison as producer, later joined by Norman Lloyd, and, for the hour-long series, Gordon Hessler. Although Hitchcock was head of the company his involvement was only peripheral and it was Joan Harrison who was ultimately responsible for selecting the stories for the series as well as hiring the writers and directors.

The anthology adapted stories by virtually every modern mystery writer in the genre, presenting macabre tales about ordinary people in extraordinary situations that usually resulted in an O. Henry type twist ending. The series was dark yet humorous, sometimes grim, often ironic, but never gruesome visually. The episodes were "situation tragedies," as Hitchcock quipped. His preference for published material over "developed" stories brought in many source authors who were household names, including Eric Ambler, Robert Bloch, Roald Dahl, Evan Hunter, Ellery Queen, and Henry Slesar. What made these half-hour playlets so different from the other suspense anthology programs of the time (*The Web, Suspense, Danger, Climax, The Vise, Rebound*) was the offbeat quality of the individual productions, often exploring unusual camera angles and employing low-key lighting to enhance the mood of menace and danger. Among the notable directors with a penchant for the suspenseful were

Robert Stevens, Herschel Daugherty, John Brahm, Robert Florey, and actor-turned-director Paul Henreid. Hitchcock himself directed 20 episodes in which he ghoulishly and irreverently parodied the conventions of the murder mystery. The suitably atmospheric black-and-white cinematography, mainly by John L. Russell, and the expedient film editing of Edward W. Williams and Richard G. Wray firmly established a production team working together with admirable precision.

Curiously enough, one of the most popular elements to surface from the series was Hitchcock's own tongue-in-cheek introductions and closing comments as well as his sometimes mordant segues into the commercial breaks. At first the series' sponsor Bristol-Myers was outraged at this irreverent attitude toward its product, but Hitchcock soon convinced them that "a knock is as good as a boost" when they noticed the positive commercial effects his subtle digs generated.

The writer responsible for these little on-camera comments by Hitchcock was screenwriter and playwright James B. Allardice, who was shown a rough cut of *The Trouble with Harry* (then in production) to get an idea of the cynical tone required. Allardice grasped the offbeat black comedy immediately and went on to write all of Hitchcock's prologues and epilogues for the series' ten-year run.

Alfred Hitchcock Presents received the Emmy nomination for Best Dramatic Anthology Series for 1957 and for 1958–59.

In 1957, prompted by the success of the CBS series, NBC developed its own mystery anthology, *Suspicion* (1957–58), consisting of 20 live episodes from New York and 20 episodes filmed in Hollywood, ten of the latter produced by Shamley. Joan Harrison served as associate producer, with Hitchcock credited as executive producer. *Suspicion* premiered with the Hitchcock-directed episode "Four O'Clock" (a Francis Cockrell teleplay from a Cornell Woolrich story).

Psycho (1960) has certain relevance here, produced and released midway through the series run. The film was financed by Hitchcock himself and produced through the facilities of Shamley. *Psycho* is a film that could only have come out of Hitchcock's experience with filmed television (including the "stories they wouldn't let me do on TV" factor). It was filmed at Revue with Hitchcock using his television crew (including cinematographer John L. Russell and assistant director Hilton A. Green) and applying the shortcut methods of his weekly television production. The famous *Psycho* Victorian house on the Universal backlot would also be seen in various episodes of *The Alfred Hitchcock Hour* (notably in the episode "An Unlocked Window").

After moving from CBS to NBC for one season (1960–61), the series returned to CBS to end its run in June 1962, to be replaced by an hour-long format from 1962 to 1965. When the decision was made to expand the series, *The Alfred Hitchcock Hour* continued the familiar *Presents* format, only longer. Unfortunately, in expanding the type of stories that had characterized *Alfred Hitchcock Presents,* the programs developed a rather sedate quality, provoking the criticism of "padding-out." As mystery author and series regular contributor Henry Slesar observed: "More was told about the same thing."

In September 1985 *Alfred Hitchcock Presents* returned to network television. It had been two decades since the original had left the air, and five years since the death of Hitchcock. Films of his original monochrome introductions were computer colorized and reused to introduce the new episodes. Some episodes of the 1985 revival series presented new stories, while others were remakes of original episodes. Following a one-year network run, additional episodes were filmed for the USA Cable Network in 1987. The last of the additional episodes had its cable premiere early in 1988.

TISE VAHIMAGI

Host
Alfred Hitchcock

Producer
Joan Harrison (1957)

Associate Producers
Joan Harrison (1955–57), Norman Lloyd (1957)

Writers (selected)
James B. Allardice, Francis Cockrell, Marian Cockrell, James P. Cavanagh, Bernard C. Schoenfeld, Henry Slesar, Robert Bloch.

Programming History

1955–62	265 half-hour episodes
CBS	
October 1955–June 1960	Sunday 9:30–10:00
NBC	
September 1960–June 1962	Tuesday 8:30–9:00

The Alfred Hitchcock Hour

Host
Alfred Hitchcock

Executive Producers
Joan Harrison, Norman Lloyd

Associate Producer
Gordon Hessler (1962–64)

Writers (selected)
Alfred Hayes, Henry Slesar, James Bridges, Robert Bloch, Leigh Brackett.

Programming History
1962–65 93 one-hour episodes
CBS
September 1962–December 1962 Thursday 10:00–11:00
January 1963–May 1963 Friday 9:30–10:30
September 1963–June 1964 Friday 10:00–11:00
NBC
October 1964–May 1965 Monday 10:00–11:00

Alfred Hitchcock Presents (1985–89)

Executive Producers
Christopher Crowe (1985–86), David Levinson (1987), Jon Slan (1987–89), Michael Sloan (1988–89)

Programming History
1985–86 22 Half-hour episodes
1987–89 57 half-hour episodes
NBC
September 1985–July 1986 Sunday 8:30–9:00
USA Cable Network
January 1987–April 1987
February 1988–August 1988
October 1988–July 1989

Further Reading

"Alfred Hitchcock Discusses Horror, Humor and McGuffins," *TV Guide* (October 27, 1956)
"Alfred Hitchcock Talks," *TV Guide* (February 14, 1959)
Grams Jr., Martin, and Patrik Wikstrom, *The Alfred Hitchcock Presents Companion,* Churchville, Maryland: OTR Publishing, 2001
"Hitchcock, the Great Shocker," *TV Guide* (March 25, 1961)
"Joan Harrison's Speciality: Murder!," *TV Guide* (March 8, 1958)
McCarty, John, and Brian Kelleher, *Alfred Hitchcock Presents,* New York: St Martin's Press, 1985
Taylor, John Russell, "Hitchcock Video Noir," *Emmy Magazine* (Summer 1979)
"TV Poses No Problem for Alfred Hitchcock," *TV Guide* (November 30, 1957)

Alice

U.S. Comedy Series

Based on Warner Bros.'s Oscar-winning movie *Alice Doesn't Live Here Anymore, Alice* debuted August 31, 1976, on CBS. The 1975 film, however, was not a comedy. Ellen Burstyn won an Academy Award in the title role of the film, which centered on a serious exploration of women's issues. In the series, Linda Lavin plays Alice Hyatt, a recently widowed mother of 12-year-old son Tommy Hyatt (Philip McKeon). After her husband's death, Alice left New Jersey and headed toward Hollywood to pursue her dream of becoming a professional singer. Her car broke down in Phoenix, where she took a temporary waitress job at Mel's Diner to make ends meet—a "temporary" job that lasted nine years. Although she dates occasionally and sometimes has a steady beau, Alice refuses to be dependent on a man. She is willing to make her own way, raising her son the best she can. As the most practical of Mel's waitresses, she is the one others call on for help, and her apartment is second to the diner as the most popular location for friends to gather.

Mel's Diner is central to both film and series, and Vic Tayback was the only cast member to re-create his character in the television series, as Brooklyn native Mel Sharples, the gruff, cheap diner owner. A former Navy cook, Mel is famous for both his chili and his stories. Boisterous and stingy, much of the humor of the series revolves around how little he pays his employees. They include the other waitresses who worked with Alice, Vera Louise Gorman (Beth Howland) and Florence Jean Castleberry—better known as Flo (Polly

Holliday). Flo relishes being the resident flirt of the diner. This wily veteran has seen it all, and demonstrates an aggressive, often crude approach to life, which merely conceals a soft heart. Flo is famous for her catch phrases of "Kiss my grits!" and "When donkeys fly!" She and Mel's Famous Chili are the diner's main attractions. The character left the diner and the show in 1980, moving to Houston to manage her own restaurant in the short-lived spin-off series *Flo.*

In contrast to Flo, New England native Vera is young, impressionable, and shy. She is the scatterbrained character—"dingy," in Mel's vocabulary. Vera typically serves as foil and participant in the zany antics created by others. Belle Dupree (Diane Ladd), a character introduced as Mel's "first" waitress when the diner opened, replaced Flo. (Ironically, Ladd had played Flo in the movie.) Belle and Flo share many similarities, and the diner's regulars readily accept her. Even more brash and aggressive than Flo, she is a Mississippian who writes and sings country-and-western songs. After a year her dream of a music career was realized, and again she left Mel's Diner.

Truck driver Jolene Hunnicutt (Celia Weston) was frustrated with her partner, Burt, and the two had a fight at the diner. After heaving numerous dinner plates at Burt, Jolene hid in the restroom. When the entire diner staff entered to console her, Burt barricaded them inside. After their release, Mel hired the sarcastic Jolene to work off the damage from the fight. Jolene's "temporary" job lasts four and a half years.

Television icon Martha Raye joined the cast from 1982 to 1984 playing Mel's mother, Carrie Sharples, the only character who could intimidate Mel. Most other characters were regular diner patrons. Among them are Henry Beesmyer (Marvin Kaplan), a phone company repairman, and Earl Hicks (Dave Madden), a high school basketball coach. An exception was Marie (Victoria Carroll), Mel's off-and-on girlfriend from 1978 to 1980. *Alice,* and Mel's Diner, were stops for an array of outstanding guest actors throughout the series. In addition to George Burns, such notables as Art Carney, Desi Arnaz, Telly Savalis, Joel Grey, Debbie Reynolds, Robert Goulet, Dinah Shore, Donald O'Conner, Forrest Tucker, Frank Nelson, Adam West, Eve Arden, Carl Ballantine, Jerry Reed, and numerous others appeared. Doris Roberts (since 1996, *Everybody Loves Raymond*'s Marie Barone) guest starred in 1981–82 as Alice's mother, Mona Spivak.

CBS aired weekday reruns from June 1980 to September 1982 and *Alice* has sporadically appeared in syndication. *Alice,* cast members, and staff were nominated for numerous Golden Globes and Emmys, winning many. Despite its cast changes, *Alice* was consistently popular throughout its entire nine-year run. The series was in the top 25 of the Nielsen ratings from 1977 to 1982, peaking at number four during 1979–80.

W.A. Kelly Huff

See also **Comedy, Workplace**

Cast

Alice Hyatt	Linda Lavin
Tommy Hyatt	Philip McKeon
Mel Sharples	Vic Tayback
Vera Louise Gorman	Beth Howland
Florence Jean Castleberry ("Flo") (1976–80)	Polly Holliday
Earl Hicks (1978–85)	Dave Madden
Henry Beesmyer (1978–85)	Marvin Kaplan
Chuck (1978–85)	Duane R. Campbell
Belle Dupree (1980–81)	Diane Ladd
Jolene Hunnicutt (1981–85)	Celia Weston
Steve Marsh (1981–83)	Kip Niven
Carrie Sharples (1982–84)	Martha Raye
Elliot Novak (1983–85)	Charles Levin
Nicholas Stone (1984–85)	Michael Durrell
Andy (1976–78)	Pat Cranshaw
Jason (1978–79)	Patrick J. Cronin
Cecil (1978–79)	Bob McClurg
Marie (1978–80)	Victoria Carroll
Mike (1979–80)	Michael Ballard
Brian (1979–80)	Alan Haufrect
Charlie (1979–81)	Ted Gehring
Ralph (1979–81)	Michael Alldredge
Raleigh (1979–81)	Raleigh Bond
Mitch Aames (1981–82)	Phillip R. Allen
Jerry (1981–82)	Jerry Potter
Artie (1982–85)	Tony Longo
Danny (1984–85)	Jonathan Prince
Doug (1984–85)	Doug Robinson

Producers

Bruce Johnson, Madelyn David, Bob Carroll Jr.

Programming History

1976–85	202 episodes
CBS	
August 1976	Monday 9:30–10:00
September 1976–October 1976	Wednesday 9:30–10:00
November 1976–September 1977	Saturday 9:30–10:00
October 1977–October 1978	Sunday 9:30–10:00
October 1978–February 1979	Sunday 8:30–9:00

March 1979–September 1982	Sunday 9:00–9:30
October 1982–November 1982	Wednesday 9:00–9:30
March 1983–April 1983	Monday 9:00–9:30
April 1983–May 1983	Sunday 9:30–10:00
June 1983–January 1984	Sunday 8:00–8:30
January 1984–December 1984	Sunday 9:30–10:00
January 1985–March 1985	Tuesday 8:30–9:00
June 1985–July 1985	Tuesday 8:30–9:00

Further Reading

Brooks, Tim, and Marsh, Earle, *TV's Greatest Hits: The 150 Most Popular TV Shows of All Time,* New York: Ballantine Books, 1985

Brown, Les, *Les Brown's Encyclopedia of Television,* New York: Zoetrope, 1982

McNeil, Alex, *Total Television: A Comprehensive Guide to Programming from 1948 to the Present,* 3rd edition, New York: Penguin Books, 1991

Sackett, Susan, *Prime-Time Hits: Television's Most Popular Network Programs 1950 to the Present,* New York: Billboard Books, 1993

All-Channel Legislation

U.S. Communications Policy Legislation

In July 1962 President John F. Kennedy signed into law legislation that required all television receiving sets shipped across state lines to be able to adequately receive all UHF as well as VHF frequencies. The goal of this law was to put UHF channels (channels 14 through 83) on a more equal technological footing with the VHF channels (2 through 13). Until this time, virtually all sets manufactured in or imported into the United States were equipped to receive the VHF channels only. Viewers interested in watching UHF channels were required to purchase a cumbersome UHF converter and attach it to their sets. These converters, which resembled metal bow ties and sat atop the receiver, did not allow viewers to "click in" the desired channel. The tuning dial operated fluidly, like a radio tuning knob, and viewers had to literally "tune in" the desired channel. With the commercial networks occupying the VHF channels and viewers disadvantaged in receiving the UHF frequencies, UHF channels (primarily independent commercial and educational or noncommercial stations) were in danger of extinction. The immediate goal, then, of all-channel legislation was the preservation of these channels. The longer-term goal was the encouragement of diversity (or the creation of "a multitude of tongues"), which was a guiding force behind much Federal Communications Commission (FCC) rule making at the time.

Therefore, on September 12, 1962, the commission proposed that any set manufactured in or imported into the United States after April 30, 1964, be all-channel equipped. The proposal became an official FCC order on November 21, 1962. Later amendments to FCC rules and regulations specified performance standards for the UHF circuit in the new receivers relating to sound and picture quality.

KIMBERLY MASSEY

Further Reading

Barnouw, Erik, *A History of Broadcasting in the United States,* volume 3, *The Image Empire,* New York: Oxford University Press, 1970

All in the Family

U.S. Situation Comedy

For five years, *All in the Family,* which aired on CBS from 1971 to 1983 (in its last four seasons under the title *Archie Bunker's Place*), was the top-rated show on American television and the winner of four consecutive Emmy Awards as Outstanding Comedy Series. *All in the Family* was not only one of the most successful sitcoms in history, it was also one of the most important and influential series ever to air, for it ushered in a new era in American television characterized by programs that did not shy away from addressing controversial or socially relevant subject matters.

All in the Family's storylines centered on the domestic concerns of the Bunker household in Queens, New York. Family patriarch and breadwinner Archie Bunker (Carroll O'Connor) was a bigoted loading-dock worker disturbed by the changes occurring in American society. To Archie, gains by the "Spades," "Spics," or "Hebes" of the United States (as he referred to blacks, Hispanics, and Jews, respectively) came at his expense and that of other lower-middle-class whites. Countering Archie's harsh demeanor was his sweet but flighty "dingbat" wife, Edith. Played by Jean Stapleton, Edith usually endured Archie's tirades in a manner meant to avoid confrontation. But that was hardly the case with Archie's live-in son-in-law Mike Stivic (Rob Reiner), a liberal college student who was married to the Bunkers' daughter, Gloria (Sally Struthers). The confrontations between Archie and Mike ("Meathead") served as the basis for much of *All in the Family*'s comedy. As surely as Archie could be counted upon to be politically conservative and socially misguided, Mike was equally liberal and sensitive to the concerns of minorities and the oppressed, and, because both characters were extremely vocal in their viewpoints, heated conflict between the two was assured.

Producers Norman Lear and Alan (Bud) Yorkin brought *All in the Family* into being by obtaining the U.S. rights to the hit British comedy series *Till Death Us Do Part,* which aired on the BBC in the mid-1960s and featured the character of bigoted dock worker Alf Garnett. Lear developed two pilots based on the concept for ABC, with O'Connor (Mickey Rooney had been Lear's first choice to play Archie) and Stapleton in the lead roles. But when ABC turned down the series, then known as *Those Were the Days,* it appeared that it would never get off the ground. Luckily for Lear and Yorkin, CBS President Robert D. Wood was in the market for new shows that would appeal to the more affluent, urban audience the network's entrenched lineup of top-rated but aging series failed to attract. As a result, CBS jettisoned such highly rated programs as *The Red Skelton Show* and *Green Acres* in an effort to improve the demographic profile of its audiences, and *All in the Family* seemed a perfect, though risky, vehicle to put in their place. CBS therefore made a 13-episode commitment to air the series beginning in January 1971, as a midseason replacement.

The network had good reason to be wary of reaction to its new show. *All in the Family* seemed to revel in breaking prime time's previously unbreakable taboos. Archie's frequent diatribes laced with degrading racial and ethnic epithets, Mike and Gloria's obviously active sex life, the sounds of Archie's belching and of flushing toilets—all broke with sitcom convention. These controversial touches also made people sit up and take notice of the new CBS series. In fact, its unconventionality caused *All in the Family*'s pilot episode to consistently rate below average in research tests conducted by both ABC and CBS. Nevertheless, CBS went ahead and debuted the show on January 12, 1971, although with relatively little fanfare or network promotion.

Viewer response to *All in the Family* was at first tepid. CBS's switchboards were prepared for an avalanche of calls in response to the show's initial airing, but this onslaught never materialized, in part because of the poor 15 percent audience share garnered by the first episode, which put it a distant third in its time period, behind movies on NBC and ABC. But while the show continued to languish in the Nielsen ratings in its first few months, TV critics began to take notice. Despite the negative reviews of a small number of critics, such as *Life*'s John Leonard ("a wretched program"), the critical response was generally positive. Combined with strong word of mouth among viewers, these evaluations helped the show's audience gradually grow. The May 1971 Emmy Awards helped to cap *All in the Family*'s climb. The midseason replacement was featured in the opening skit of the Emmy telecast and earned awards in three categories, including Outstanding Comedy Series. Shortly thereafter, *All in the Family* became the top-rated show in prime time, and the show held onto that position for each of the following five seasons.

The program was able to keep an especially sharp edge over its first half-dozen years thanks to the evolving character development of the series' primary cast members and the infusion of strong supporting characters. Both the Bunkers' African-American next-door neighbors, the Jeffersons, and Edith's visiting cousin, Maude Findlay, eventually went on to star in successful spin-off series of their own. *All in the Family* also benefited from occasional one-shot guest appearances, the most memorable of which featured entertainer Sammy Davis Jr.

All in the Family's impact went beyond the world of television. The show became the focus of a heated national debate on whether comedy was an appropriate means by which to combat prejudice and social inequality. In addition, the character of Archie Bunker became nothing short of an American icon. While *Till Death Us Do Part*'s Alf Garnett was generally unlikable, producer Lear chose to soften the character for American television, patterning Bunker in many ways after his own father. As a result, Carroll O'Connor's characterization of Archie contained notable sympathetic qualities, allowing many viewers to see Archie in a favorable light despite his obvious flaws.

By the late 1970s, however, it was becoming clear that the show had lost much of its earlier spark. Major cast changes occurred in 1978, when Struthers and Reiner left the series, and again in 1980, when Stapleton departed. (The fact that this contractual arrangement was written into the show as Edith's death allowed Lear and company to show once again what had made this series truly memorable.) Archie quit his job in 1977 to buy and run a neighborhood tavern, and the series was retitled *Archie Bunker's Place* in 1979 to reflect the changed nature of the program. By that point, however, though still highly rated, the show no longer stood out as unique and had become what seemed to many a rather conventional sitcom.

All in the Family's lasting impact on American television is difficult to overestimate. It helped to usher in a new generation of comedic programs that abandoned the light domestic plotlines of television's early years in favor of topical themes with important social significance. In this sense, its influence on prime-time programming continues to be felt decades later.

David Gunzerath

See also **Comedy, Domestic Settings; Lear, Norman; O'Connor, Carroll**

Cast

Archie Bunker	Carroll O'Connor
Edith Bunker (1971–80)	Jean Stapleton
Gloria Bunker Stivic (1971–78)	Sally Struthers
Mike Stivic ("Meathead") (1971–78)	Rob Reiner
Lionel Jefferson (1971–75)	Mike Evans
Louise Jefferson (1971–75)	Isabel Sanford
Henry Jefferson (1971–73)	Mel Stewart
George Jefferson (1973–75)	Sherman Hemsley
Irene Lorenzo (1973–75)	Betty Garrett
Frank Lorenzo (1973–74)	Vincent Gardenia
Bert Munson (1972–77)	Billy Halop
Tommy Kelsey (1972–73)	Brendon Dillon
Tommy Kelsey (1973–77)	Bob Hastings
Justin Quigley (1973–76)	Burt Mustin
Barney Hefner (1973–83)	Allan Melvin
Jo Nelson (1973–75)	Ruth McDevitt
Stretch Cunningham (1974)	James Cromwell
Teresa Betancourt (1976–77)	Liz Torres
Stephanie Mills (1978–83)	Danielle Brisebois
Harry Snowden (1977–83)	Jason Wingreen
Hank Pivnik (1977–81)	Danny Dayton
Murray Klein (1979–81)	Martin Balsam
Mr. Van Ranseleer (1978–83)	Bill Quinn
Veronica Rooney (1979–82)	Anne Meara
Jose (1979–83)	Abraham Alvarez
Linda (1980–81)	Heidi Hagman
Raoul (1980–83)	Joe Rosario
Ellen Canby (1980–82)	Barbara Meek
Polly Swanson (1980–81)	Janet MacLachlan
Ed Swanson (1980–81)	Mel Bryant
Billie Bunker (1981–83)	Denise Miller
Gary Rabinowitz (1981–83)	Barry Gordon
Bruce (1982–83)	Bob Okazaki
Marsha (1982–83)	Jessica Nelson

Producers

Norman Lear, Woody Kling, Hal Kanter, Mort Lachman, Don Nicholl, Lou Derman, Brigit Jensen Drake, John Rich, Milt Josefberg, Michael Ross, Bernie West, Bill Danoff

Programming History

204 episodes
CBS

January 1971–July 1971	Tuesday 9:30–10:00
September 1971–September 1975	Saturday 8:00–8:30

September 1975–September 1976	Monday 9:00–9:30
September 1976–October 1976	Wednesday 9:00–9:30
November 1976–September 1977	Saturday 9:00–9:30
October 1977–October 1978	Sunday 9:00–9:30
October 1978–March 1983	Sunday 8:00–8:30
March 1983–May 1983	Monday 8:00–8:30
May 1983	Sunday 8:00–8:30
June 1983	Monday 9:30–10:00
June 1983–September 1983	Wednesday 8:00–8:30
June 1991	Sunday 8:30–9:00
June 1991–July 1991	Sunday 8:00–8:30
September 1991	Friday 8:30–9:00

Further Reading

Arlen, Michael, *The View from Highway 1,* New York: Farrar, Straus, and Giroux, 1976

Barnouw, Erik, *Tube of Plenty: The Evolution of American Television,* New York: Oxford University Press, 1975; 3rd edition, 1990

Bedell, Sally, *Up the Tube: Prime-Time TV and the Silverman Years,* New York: Viking, 1981

Brooks, Tim, and Earle Marsh, *The Complete Directory to Prime Time Network TV Shows, 1946-Present,* 4th edition, New York: Ballantine, 1988

"CBS Sked Shake; Shift *All in Family* to Lead Sat," *Variety* (August 18, 1971)

"CBS TV's Bigot That BBC Begat Figures to Salt Up Second Season," *Variety* (July 22, 1970)

"Family Fun," *Newsweek* (March 15, 1971)

Ferretti, Fred, "Are Racism and Bigotry Funny?" *New York Times* (January 12, 1971)

Gent, George, "*All in the Family* Takes First Place in Nielsen Ratings," *New York Times* (May 25, 1971)

Gitlin, Todd, *Inside Prime Time,* New York: Pantheon, 1985; revised edition, 1994

Hano, Arnold, "Can Archie Bunker Give Bigotry a Bad Name?" *New York Times Magazine* (March 12, 1972)

Kasindorf, Martin, "Archie and Maude and Fred and Norman and Alan," *New York Times Magazine* (June 24, 1973)

Leonard, John, "Bigotry As a Dirty Joke," *Life* (March 19, 1971)

Metz, Robert, *CBS: Reflections in a Bloodshot Eye,* Chicago: Playboy, 1975

O'Neil, Thomas, *The Emmys,* New York: Penguin, 1992

Shayon, Robert Lewis, "Archie's Other Side," *Saturday Review* (January 8, 1972)

Shayon, Robert Lewis, "Love That Hate," *Saturday Review* (March 27, 1971)

Waldron, Vince, *Classic Sitcoms,* New York: Macmillan, 1987

Wander, Philip, "Counters in the Social Drama: Some Notes on *All in the Family,*" in *Television: The Critical View,* edited by Horace Newcomb, New York: Oxford University Press, 1976

Allen, Debbie (1950–)

U.S. Actor, Director, Producer, Choreographer

Debbie Allen began her show business career on Broadway in the 1970s. Her debut in the chorus of *Purlie* and her performance in *A Raisin in the Sun* were noted by stage critics, and in a 1979 production of *West Side Story,* her performance as Anita earned her a Tony Award nomination and a Drama Desk Award. Allen later returned to Broadway as a star and garnered her second Tony nomination, for a 1986–87 performance in *Sweet Charity.* In 1988 she choreographed *Carrie,* a newly composed American musical, with the Royal Shakespeare Company.

Allen's stage presence and choreography quickly moved her from the Broadway stage to the larger venue of television. Throughout the 1970s she made guest appearances on popular programs such as *Good Times, The Love Boat,* and *The Jim Stafford Show.* Her roles in the miniseries *Roots: The Next Generation* and the special *Ben Vereen—His Roots* allowed her to work with some of the most prominent African-American performers in show business and to demonstrate her dramatic and comedic acting range. She also appeared in the short-lived 1977 NBC series *3 Girls 3.*

In the early 1980s her portrayal of a dance instructor, Lydia Grant, on the hit series *Fame* brought Allen to international prominence. Although the NBC show was canceled after one season, the program went on to first-run syndication for four more years. Its popularity

Debbie Allen.
Courtesy of the Everett Collection

in Britain prompted a special cast tour there and spurred a "*Fame* mania" fan phenomena.

Allen's success as a dancer and actor allowed her to move behind the camera to direct and produce. While still a cast member of *Fame,* she became the first African-American woman hired by a television network as a director in prime time. In 1989, after directing episodes of *Fame,* she co-wrote, produced, directed, choreographed, and starred in *The Debbie Allen Special* for ABC. She received two Emmy nominations, for direction and choreography, of this variety show.

In 1988 Allen solidified her reputation as a television director and producer by turning a flawed television series, *A Different World,* into a long-running popular program. Under her leadership the program addressed political issues such as apartheid, date rape, the war in the Persian Gulf, economic discrimination, and the 1992 Los Angeles riots. The highest-rated episode focused on sexual maturity and AIDS and guest starred Whoopi Goldberg, who was nominated for an Emmy Award. Allen was awarded the first Responsibility in Television award from the Los Angeles Film Teachers Association for consistently representing important social issues on *A Different World.*

In 1989 Allen made her debut as a director of made-for-television movies with a remake of the 1960 film *Pollyanna.* The telefilm, titled *Polly,* starred two players from *The Cosby Show,* Phylicia Rashad and Keshia Knight Pullman. Set in 1955, *Polly* is a musical tale of an orphan who brings happiness to a tyrannical aunt and a small Alabama town. The film was produced by Disney and NBC. Television critics hailed the display of Allen's keen sense of innovative camera work, stemming from her ability to choreograph. The film is also notable for its all-black cast and for succeeding in a genre, the musical film, rarely popular on television. Allen followed *Polly* with a sequel, which aired in November 1990.

In the 1990–91 season, Allen directed the pilot and debut episode of *Fresh Prince of Bel-Air,* a series that had high ratings on NBC. That same season, she directed a highly rated episode of *Quantum Leap* in which she costarred. In October 1991, Allen received her star on the Hollywood Walk of Fame for her achievements in television.

In 1992 Allen directed *Stompin' at the Savoy* for the CBS network. This program included a cast of prominent African-American performers: Lynn Whitfield, Vanessa Williams, Jasmine Guy, Vanessa Bell Calloway, and Mario Van Peebles. Her most recent television series was the NBC situation comedy *In the House.* In this series, which first aired in April 1995, Allen played a newly divorced mother of two who shares her house with a former football star, played by rap artist L.L. Cool J.

Complementing Allen's versatility as a television actor and director is a repertoire of critically acclaimed film roles. In 1986 she played Richard Pryor's feisty wife in his semiautobiographical film *Jo Jo Dancer, Your Life Is Calling,* and she costarred with Howard E. Rollins and James Cagney in Milos Foreman's *Ragtime* in 1981. Allen's debut as a feature film director came in 1995, with *Out of Sync,* starring L.L. Cool J, Victoria Dillard, and Yaphet Kotto. Among the other films bearing Allen's name in the credits is *Amistad* (1997), a project she tried to produce for ten years before finally finding a collaborator in director and coproducer Steven Spielberg.

Allen is one of the few African-American women currently working as a director and producer in television and film. Her success in TV and film production has not deterred her from her love of dance, and she continues to dazzle television viewers with her choreography. In 1982 she choreographed the dance numbers for the Academy Awards, and for five consecutive years in the 1990s, her unique style of choreography was featured on the worldwide broadcast of the award ceremony. In 2003 she hosted a series on NBC titled *Fame,* in which she recruited and trained talented young dancers and singers, a show capitalizing on both the popularity of "reality television" and Allen's own celebrity. For three decades, Allen's contributions to television, on the three major U.S. networks and in syndicated programming, have highlighted the maturity of a performer and artistic producer with an impressive spectrum of talents in the performing arts.

MARLA SHELTON

See also ***Different World, A***

Debbie Allen. Born Deborah Kaye Allen in Houston, Texas, January 16, 1950. Married: 1) Wim Wilford (divorced); 2) Norm Nixon; children: Vivian Nicole and Norm Jr. Educated at Howard University, Washington, D.C., BFA (with honors) 1971; studied with Ballet Nacional and Ballet Folklorico (Mexico); Houston Ballet Foundation, Houston, Texas; New York School of Ballet. Began career as dancer with George Faison Universal Dance Experience; AMAS Repertory Theatre; taught dance, Duke Ellington School of Performing Arts; actor in television, from 1973; actor/producer/director/choreographer of various television shows, miniseries, and specials. Recipient: three Emmy Awards; one Golden Globe Award; Ford Foundation Grant; two Essence Awards; Black Filmmakers Hall of Fame Clarence Muse Youth Award, 1978; Drama Desk Award, 1979; Out Critics Circle Award, 1980; American Women in Radio and Television Lifetime Award, 2000.

Television Series

1977 *3 Girls 3*
1982 *Fame*
1987 *Bronx Zoo* (director)
1987–93 *A Different World* (producer, director)
1990–96 *Fresh Prince of Bel-Air* (director)
1990 *Quantum Leap* (also director)
1995–96 *In the House* (also director)
1996 *Jamie Foxx Show* (director)
2003 *Fame*

Television Miniseries

1979 *Roots: The Next Generation*
1984 *Celebrity*

Made-for-Television Movies

1977 *The Greatest Thing That Almost H appened*
1980 *Ebony, Ivory and Jade*
1983 *Women of San Quentin*
1989 *Polly* (director and choreographer)
1990 *Polly Comin' Home!*

Television Specials

1982, 1991–95 *The Academy Awards* (choreographer)
1983 *The Kids from Fame*
1989 *The Debbie Allen Special* (co-writer, producer, director, choreographer)
1992 *Stompin' at the Savoy* (director)

Films

The Fish That Saved Pittsburgh, 1979; *Ragtime,* 1981; *Jo Jo Dancer, Your Life Is Calling,* 1986; *Mona Must Die,* 1994; *Blank Check,* 1994; *Forget Paris* (choreographer), 1995; *Out-of-Sync* (director), 1995; *Amistad* (coproducer), 1997.

Stage (selected)

Purlie, 1971; *Ti-Jean and His Brothers,* 1972; *Raisin in the Sun,* 1973; *Ain't Misbehavin',* 1978; *The Illusion and Holiday,* 1979; *West Side Story,* 1979; *Louis,* 1981; *The Song Is Kern!,* 1981; *Parade of Stars at the Palace,* 1983; *Sweet Charity,* 1986; *Carrie* (choreographer), 1988; *Pepito's Story* (choreographer), 1995; *Soul Possessed* (writer, director, choreographer), 2000.

Publications

Brothers of the Knight, 1999
Dancing in the Wings, 2000

Further Reading

"Doing It All—Her Way! Versatility Reaps Multiple Successes for This Exciting Entertainer," *Ebony* (November 1989)
Dunning, Jennifer, "Debbie Allen Chips Away at the Glass Ceiling," *New York Times* (March 29, 1992)
Randolph, Laura B., "Debbie Allen on Power, Pain, Passion, and Prime Time," *Ebony* (March 1991)

Allen, Fred (1894–1956)

U.S. Comedian

Fred Allen hated television. Allen was a radio comedian for nearly two decades who, as early as 1936, had a weekly radio audience of about 20 million. When he visited *The Jack Benny Show* to continue their long-running comedy feud, they had the largest audience in the history of radio, only to be later outdone by President Franklin Roosevelt during a *Fireside Chat.* The writer Herman Wouk said that Allen was the best comic writer in radio. His humor was literate, urbane, intelligent, and contemporary. Allen came to radio from vaudeville, where he performed as a juggler. He was primarily self-educated and was extraordinarily well read.

Allen began his network radio career in 1932, after working vaudeville and Broadway with such comedy icons as Al Jolson, Ed Wynn, George Jessel, and Jack Benny. This was a time when the United States was in a deep economic depression, and radio in its infancy. In his autobiography *Treadmill to Oblivion,* Allen wrote that he thought radio should provide complete stories, series of episodes, and comedy situations instead of the monotonous, unrelated jokes then popular on vaudeville. With this idea in hand, he began his first radio program on NBC, called *The Linit Bath Club Review* (named after the sponsor).

Allen's world of radio was highly competitive and commercial, just as TV would be many years later. He wrote most of the material for his weekly shows himself, usually working 12-hour days, six days a week. Most comedians, like Bob Hope, had an office filled with writers, but Allen used only a few assistants when writing his comedy. Some of these assistants went on to have successful careers in literature and comedy, such as Herman Wouk, author of *The Caine Mutiny* and *The Winds of War,* and Nat Hiken, who created Phil Silver's *The Phil Silvers Show* for TV. Allen's program was imbued with literate, verbal slapstick. He had ethnic comedy routines in *Allen's Alley,* appearances by celebrities such as Alfred Hitchcock, musical numbers with talent from the likes of Richard Rodgers and Oscar Hammerstein, and social commentaries on every conceivable subject, especially criticisms of the advertising and radio industry. His radio producer, Sylvester "Pat" Weaver (later to become head of NBC TV programming), observed that Allen's humor was so popular that three out of four homes in the country were listening to Allen at the zenith of his popularity. To inform the writing of his comedy scripts, Allen compiled a personal library of more than 4,000 books of humor and read nine newspapers (plus magazines) daily. According to the scholar Alan Havig, Allen's style of comedy had more in common with such literary giants as Robert Benchley and James Thurber than with media comedians such as Jack Benny and Bob Hope.

In the 1946–47 season, Allen's program was ranked the number one show on network radio. World War II was over, Americans were beginning a new era of consumerism, and a very few consumers had recently purchased a new entertainment device called television. When Fred Allen was asked what he thought of television, he said he did not like furniture that talked. He also said television was called a medium because "nothing on it is ever well done." Allen dismissed TV as permitting "people who haven't anything to do to watch people who can't do anything." But, after nearly two decades on radio, he fell in the ratings from number one to number 38 in just a few months. Such a sudden loss of audience was due to a new ABC radio giveaway show called *Name That Tune,* starring Bert Parks, as well as a general decline in listeners for all of radio. Listeners of radio were rapidly becoming viewers of TV. And where the audience went, so went the advertisers. In a few short years the bottom fell out of radio. Fred Allen quickly, but not quietly, left radio in 1949.

Allen was first to leave radio, but Bob Hope, Jack Benny, George Burns, and Gracie Allen soon followed. They all went on to star in their own TV shows—all but Fred Allen. He made a few attempts at TV, but nothing more. He first appeared on the *Colgate Comedy Theater,* where he attempted to bring to TV his *Allen's Alley* from radio. For example, the characters of the Alley were performed with puppets.

Fred Allen, 1947.
Courtesy of the Everett Collection

Such attempts seldom successfully made the transition to the new medium. On the quiz show *Judge for Yourself* (1953–54), he was supposed to carry on witty ad-libbed conversations with guests. But as Havig states, Allen's "ad-libbing was lost in the confusion of a half hour filled with too many people and too much activity." In short, Allen's humor needed more time and more language than TV allowed. He then was on the short-lived *Fred Allen's Sketchbook* (1954) and finally a became a panelist on *What's My Line?* from 1955 until his death in 1956.

Fred Allen's contributions to TV were in two forms. First, he became one of the true critics of TV. He has remained, many decades after his death, the intellectual conscience of TV. His barbs at network TV censorship still hit at the heart of contemporary media ("Heck... is a place invented by [NBC]. NBC does not recognize hell or [CBS]"). Second, his comedy style has become part of the institution of TV comedy. His *Allen's Alley* created the character Titus Moody, who turned up on TV as the Pepperidge Farm cookie man. His Senator Claghorn, also of the *Alley,* was transfigured into Warner Bros. TV cartoon character Foghorn Leghorn the rooster. And later, the "Senator" appeared on the Kentucky Fried Chicken TV commercial. A variety of TV comedians have done direct takeoffs of Allen's performances. For example, Red Skelton's "Gussler's Gin" routine and Johnny Carson's "Mighty Carson Art Players" can be traced back to Fred Allen. Allen's "People You Didn't Expect to Meet" is an idea that has worked for David Letterman. Finally, Garrison Keillor's tales "Lake Wobegon" (as heard on National Public Radio's *A Prairie Home Companion*) are a throwback to Allen's comedic style.

Allen wrote in *Treadmill to Oblivion,*

> Ability, merit and talent were not requirements of writers and actors working in the industry. Audiences had to be attracted, for advertising purposes, at any cost and by any artifice. Standards were gradually lowered. A medium that demands entertainment eighteen hours a day, seven days every week, has to exhaust the conscientious craftsman and performer.

He was talking about radio, but his remarks could apply just as well to television many decades later.

CLAY WAITE

Fred Allen (Fred St. James, Fred James, Freddie James). Born John Florence Sullivan in Cambridge, Massachusetts, May 31, 1894. Married: Portland Hoffa, 1928. Served in U.S. Army, World War I. Began performing on stage as an amateur teenage juggler, eventually adding patter and turning pro with the billing of the "World's Worst Juggler"; for ten years as humorist toured the vaudeville circuit, including 14 months in Australia, Tasmania, New Zealand, and Honolulu, 1914–15; dropped juggling, settled on the professional name of "Fred Allen," and moved up from vaudeville to Broadway revues, early 1920s; worked on radio, notably *Allen's Alley* and *Texaco Star Theatre,* from 1932; a panel regular on the television quiz show *What's My Line?,* 1955–56. Died in New York City, March 17, 1956.

Television Series

1953	*Fred Allen's Sketchbook*
1953–54	*Judge for Yourself*
1955–56	*What's My Line?*

Films

Some film shorts, 1920s; *Thanks a Million,* 1935; *Sally, Irene and Mary,* 1938; *Love Thy Neighbor,*

1940; *It's in the Bag,* 1945; *We're Not Married,* 1952; *Full House,* 1953.

Radio

The Linit Bath Club Revue, 1932; *Allen's Alley,* 1932–49; *The Salad Bowl Revue,* 1933; *Town Hall Tonight,* 1934; *Texaco Star Theatre,* 1940–41.

Publications

Treadmill to Oblivion, 1954
Much Ado About Me, 1956
Fred Allen's Letters, edited by Joe McCarthy, 1965

Further Reading

Havig, A., *Fred Allen's Radio Comedy,* Philadelphia, Pennsylvania: Temple University Press, 1990
Taylor, R., *Fred Allen: His Life and Wit,* New York: International Polygonics, 1989

Allen, Gracie (1895–1964)

U.S. Comedian

Gracie Allen transferred her popular fictional persona from vaudeville, film, and radio to American television in the 1950s. Allen had performed with her husband and partner, George Burns, for nearly 30 years when the pair debuted in *The George Burns and Gracie Allen Show* on CBS in October 1950. They had enjoyed particular success in radio, popularizing their audio program with a series of stunts that involved Allen in fictitious manhunts, art exhibits, and even a candidacy for the presidency of the United States. The transfer of their program to the small screen both extended their career (the couple were becoming too expensive for radio) and helped to legitimate the new medium.

The Burns and Allen act, a classic vaudeville routine involving a "Dumb Dora" and a straight man, proved infinitely malleable. Initially a flirtation act, by the time it was transferred to television, it was housed in a standard situation-comedy frame: Burns and Allen played themselves, a celebrity couple, enduring various matrimonial mix-ups.

The impetus to comedy within the program was the character portrayed by Allen. Her humor was almost entirely linguistic. Often an entire episode hinged on her confusion of antecedents in a sentence, as when the couple's announcer (who also took part in the program's narrative) informed her that Burns had worked with another performer until he (meaning the other performer) had married, moved to San Diego, California, and had two sons—at which point she concluded that her husband was a bigamist.

The on-screen Gracie's reinterpretations of the world proved extremely disruptive to people and events around her, although the disruptions were generally playful rather than serious and were quickly settled (usually by her husband the straight man) at the end of each episode. Allen's character thus challenged the rational order of things without ever actually threatening it.

The character's success on the program, and popularity with the viewing public, depended in large part on her total unawareness of the comic effects of her "zaniness." The on-screen Gracie was a sweet soul who on the surface embodied many of the feminine norms of the day (domesticity, reliance on her man, gentleness) even as she took symbolic potshots at the gender order by subverting her husband's logical, masculine world.

The program, and Allen's character, were always framed by audience knowledge about the "real" George Burns and Gracie Allen. Audience members were aware, partly from well-orchestrated publicity for the show and partly from observation, that only a talented and intelligent actor could manage to seem as dumb as Allen did on-screen.

The off-screen Burns and Allen were sometimes also invoked explicitly within episodes, as when characters reminded the fictional George that he was finan-

Gracie Allen.
Courtesy of the Everett Collection

cially dependent upon his costar/spouse, who had always been the greater star of the two.

The strongest link between on- and off-screen Burns and Allen, however, was the marital bond both pairs shared—and the affection they displayed as actors and as people. Burns's first autobiography, *I Love Her, That's Why!,* placed the couple's relationship at the center of his life, reflecting its centrality to the program in which the two starred.

The George Burns and Gracie Allen Show went off the air upon Allen's retirement in 1958. Burns tried for a number of years to sustain programs and acts of his own, but it took him almost a decade to emerge as a performer in his own right. Much of his stage act for the rest of his life featured numerous jokes and stories about his wife, perpetuating the memory of her comedic energy even for those who had never seen her perform.

TINKY "DAKOTA" WEISBLAT

Gracie Allen. Born in San Francisco, California, July 26, 1895. Married: George Burns, 1926; children: Sandra Jean and Ronald John. Attended Star of the Sea Convent School. Joined sister Bessie in vaudeville act, Chicago, 1909; played vaudeville as "single" act, from 1911; teamed with George Burns, 1922; toured Orpheum vaudeville circuit; toured United States and Europe in the Keith theater circuit, from 1926; played BBC radio for 20 weeks, 1926; first U.S. radio appearance, with Burns, on *The Rudy Vallee Show,* 1930; premiered as star of *The Adventures of Gracie* on CBS radio, February 15, 1932; starred, with Burns, in *The Burns and Allen Show* on NBC radio, 1945–50; performed in movies, 1930s; starred, with Burns, in *The George Burns and Gracie Allen Show,* CBS Television, 1950–58; retired from show business in 1958. Died in Los Angeles, August 27, 1964.

Television Series

1950–58 *The George Burns and Gracie Allen Show*

Films

100 Percent Service, 1931; *The Antique Shop,* 1931; *Fit to Be Tied,* 1931; *Once Over, Light,* 1931; *Pulling a Bone,* 1931; *Oh, My Operation,* 1932; *The Big Broadcast,* 1932; *International House,* 1933; *We're Not Dressing,* 1934; *Six of a Kind,* 1934; *Many Happy Returns,* 1934; *The Big Broadcast of 1936,* 1935; *College Holiday,* 1936; *The Big Broadcast of 1937,* 1936; *A Damsel in Distress,* 1937; *College Swing,* 1938; *Honolulu,* 1939; *Gracie Allen Murder Case,* 1939; *Mr. and Mrs. North,* 1941; *Two Girls and a Sailor,* 1944.

Publication

"Inside Me," as told to Jane Kesner Morris, *Woman's Home Companion* (March 1953)

Further Reading

Blythe, Cheryl, and Susan Sackett, *Say Goodnight Gracie! The Story of Burns and Allen,* New York: Dutton, 1986
Burns, George, *Gracie: A Love Story,* New York: Putnam, 1988
Burns, George, with Cynthia Hobart, *I Love Her, That's Why! An Autobiography,* New York: Simon and Schuster, 1955
"... Burns and Allen ...," *Newsweek* (June 24, 1957)
"How Gracie Gets That Way," *TV Guide* (October 8, 1955)
Hubbard, Kim, "George Burns Writes a Final Loving Tribute to Gracie Allen ...," *People Weekly* (October 31, 1988)

Allen, Steve (1921–2000)

U.S. Comedian, Host, Composer, Writer

Steve Allen has appropriately been termed television's renaissance man. He hosted numerous television programs, appeared in several motion pictures, wrote more than 50 books, and composed several thousand songs. He once won a $1,000 bet that he could not compose 50 songs a day for a week.

Allen began his career as a radio announcer in 1942. In 1946 he joined the Mutual Broadcasting System as a comedian and two years later signed with CBS as a late-night disc jockey on KNX in Hollywood. He first gained national attention during the summer of 1950, when his program was booked as a 13-week substitute for *Our Miss Brooks.* This break led to his first television program, *The Steve Allen Show,* which debuted on Christmas Day 1950 on CBS. The show was later moved to Thursday nights, where it alternated with the popular *Amos 'n' Andy Show.*

In 1954 Allen began hosting a daily late-night show on NBC, *The Tonight Show.* During the next three years, he introduced many television innovations that have since been continued by his successors. Most of these inventions involved his audience. Using a hand microphone, he went into the audience to talk with individuals; he answered questions submitted by the audience; members of the audience would attempt to "stump the band" by requesting songs the band could not play. Allen involved his announcer, Gene Rayburn, in nightly chitchat, and he spoke with the band leaders, Skitch Henderson and Bobby Byrne. These techniques epitomized Allen's belief that "people will laugh at things that happen before their eyes much more readily than they will at incidents they're merely told about."

In 1956 Allen became a part-time host on *Tonight* because he was appearing in a new version of *The Steve Allen Show.* Still on NBC, he was now scheduled on Sunday nights, opposite *The Ed Sullivan Show* on CBS. Thus began one of the most famous ratings wars in television history. Allen and Sullivan were perhaps as distinct from one another as two men could be. Allen was a witty, innovative performer, willing to try virtually anything. Sullivan was a stiff master of ceremonies, who compelled his guests to conform to rigid standards of decorum. Although Allen occasionally received higher ratings, Sullivan eventually won the war, and after the 1960 season NBC moved *The Steve Allen Show* to Mondays. A year later, Allen took the show into syndication and continued for three more years. From 1964 to 1967, he hosted the highly successful game show *I've Got a Secret* on CBS.

Steve Allen's most innovative television offering was *Meeting of Minds.* The format was an hour-long dramatized discussion of social issues. Allen would act as the moderator accompanied in this imaginative exercise by his "guests": historical characters such as Galileo, Attila the Hun, Charles Darwin, Aristotle, Hegel, or Dostoevski. The idea for this program came in 1960, following Allen's reading of Mortimer Adler's *The Syntopicon.* Rejected by the major networks, the series was accepted by PBS in 1977 and ran until 1981.

During his long career as an entertainer, Allen developed a reputation as a social activist. He considered running for Congress as a Democrat from California, he actively opposed capital punishment, and he openly supported the controversial comedian Lenny Bruce. He wrote about the plight of migrant farm workers in *The Ground Is Our Table* (1966), discussed what he considered the collapse of ethics in the United States in *Ripoff: The Corruption That Plagues America* (1979), and, in a book finished just before his death, evaluated the state of popular culture in *Vulgarians at the Gate: Raising the Standards of Popular Culture* (2001). In the last years of his life Allen appeared only occasionally on television, spending a larger portion of his time operating Meadowlane Music and Rosemeadow Publishing, located in Van Nuys, California. Allen died in October 2000.

LINDSAY E. PACK

See also ***Steve Allen Show, The;*** **Talk Show;** ***Tonight Show, The***

Stephen (Valentine Patrick William) Allen. Born in New York City, December 26, 1921. Married: 1) Dorothy Goodman, 1943 (divorced, 1952); children: Stephen, Brian, and David; 2) Jayne Meadows, 1954;

Steve Allen.
Courtesy of the Everett Collection

child: William Christopher. Attended Drake University, 1941; Arizona State Teacher's College, 1942. Worked as radio announcer at stations KOY, Phoenix, Arizona, 1942; KFAC and KMTR, Los Angeles, 1944; entertainer-comedian, Mutual Network, 1946–47; entertainer-comedian and disc jockey, CBS television, 1948–50; created and hosted *The Tonight Show,* NBC Television, 1954–56; created and hosted *Meeting of Minds,* Public Broadcasting Service, 1977–81; continued television guest appearances, 1970s-90s; composed more than 8,500 songs, several musicals; author of more than 50 books; vocalist, pianist, more than 40 albums/CDs. Recipient: Grammy Award, 1964; Emmy Award, 1981; named to Academy of Television Arts and Sciences Hall of Fame, 1986. Died in Encino, California, October 30, 2000.

Television Series

1950 *The Steve Allen Show*
1950–52 *Songs for Sale*
1953–55 *Talent Patrol*
1954–56 *The Tonight Show*
1956–61 *The Steve Allen Show*
1964–67 *I've Got a Secret*
1967 *The Steve Allen Comedy Hour*
1977–81 *Meeting of Minds*
1980–81 *The Steve Allen Comedy Hour*
1984–85 *Inside Your Schools* (host)
1985–86 *The Start of Something Big* (host)
1989–91 *Host-to-Host*

Television Miniseries

1976 *Rich Man, Poor Man*

Made-for-Television Movies

1972 *Now You See It, Now You Don't*
1979 *Stone*
1979 *The Gossip Columnist*
1984 *The Ratings Game*
1985 *Alice in Wonderland*
1996 *James Dean: A Portrait*

Television Specials

1954 *Fanfare*
1954 *The Follies of Suzy*
1954 *Sunday in Town* (cohost)
1955 *Good Times* (host)
1957 *The Timex All-Star Jazz Show I* (host)
1966 *The Hollywood Deb Stars of 1966* (cohost)
1976 *The Good Old Days of Radio* (host)
1981 *I've Had It Up to Here* (host)
1982 *Boop Oop a Doop* (narrator)
1983–86 *Life's Most Embarrassing Moments* (host)
1984 *Stooge Snapshots*
1984–86 *Steve Allen's Music Room*

Films

Down Memory Lane, 1949; *The Benny Goodman Story,* 1955; *College Confidential,* 1960; *Warning Shot,* 1967; *Where Were You When the Lights Went Out?,* 1968; *The Funny Farm,* 1982; *Amazon Women on the Moon,* 1987; *Great Balls of Fire!,* 1989; *The Player,* 1992; *Casino,* 1995.

Publications (selected)

Mark It and Strike It: An Autobiography, 1960
Dialogues in Americanism, with William F. Buckley, Robert Maynard Hutchins, Brent L. Bozell, and James MacGregor Burns, 1964
The Ground Is Our Table, 1966
Meeting of Minds, 1978–89
Ripoff: The Corruption That Plagues America, with Roslyn Bernstein and Donald H. Dunn, 1979
Funny People, 1981

More Funny People, 1982
The Passionate Non-smokers Bill of Rights: The First Guide to Enacting Non-smoking Legislation, with Bill Adler, Jr., 1989
Dumbth: And 81 Ways to Make Americans Smarter, 1989
Hi-ho, Steverino!: My Adventures in the Wonderful Wacky World of TV, 1992
Reflections, 1994
But Seriously... Steve Allen Speaks His Mind, 1996
Steve Allen's Songs: 100 Song Lyrics, 1999
Steve Allen's Private Joke File, 2000
Vulgarians at the Gate: Raising the Standards of Popular Culture, 2001

Further Reading

Carter, Bill, "Steve Allen: The Father of All Talk Show Hosts," *New York Times* (April 14, 1994)
Gould, Jack, "TV Comedians on Serious Side," *New York Times* (February 3, 1960)
"Steve Allen's Nonsense Is Pure Gold on NBC Radio," *Television-Radio Age* (March 7, 1988)

Alliance Atlantis Communications

Two of the most successful programs in the 1997 Canadian television season represented the economic and creative maturity of the domestic industry. *Traders,* a professional drama following the emotional and financial escapades of financiers at a Toronto merchant bank, was produced by Atlantis Communications. *Due South,* a comic adventure about a Mountie relocated to Chicago, was produced by Alliance Communications. Reaching over a million viewers each with these programs, Alliance and Atlantis drew on 25 years of experience gained from competing in many of the same markets and skillfully exploiting Canadian television regulations and subsidy programs. When they announced their merger in 1998, these companies were two of the key participants in building an infrastructure for television production in Canada.

The July 1998 merger was a friendly reverse takeover of the larger company (Alliance) by the smaller. The strategic goals were clear; combining the strengths of two central players and collating their substantial libraries of television and film would allow the new company to compete more successfully with larger American entertainment conglomerates. The newly created Alliance Atlantis Communications (AAC) marked an important evolution toward a major studio-style operation in Canada. The new company anticipated a shift away from in-house production of television series and films toward greater concentration on distribution and deals with independent producers. The merger was the first in a wave of corporate convergence in the Canadian media, motivated by the desire to acquire more channels for guaranteed distribution of content, gain better access to advertising revenue, and create various possibilities for cross promotion. The Alliance Atlantis merger was a direct response to global trends of technological expansion in content delivery, privatization and deregulation in international television markets, and audience fragmentation.

This focus on building "market muscle" and establishing sure access to broadcast shelf space was presented by the new CEO Michael MacMillan as beneficial for Canadian television, and a reflection of the continuing need for strong Canadian content. Critics wondered if the creation of such a large, vertically integrated enterprise would work against smaller independents and raised the possibility that such mergers should be approved only with some restrictions on access to public financing.

The new company became the largest television and film producer and distributor in Canada, and one of the top 12 entertainment companies in the world, with a combined revenue of $700 million. Because the Canadian television market is small, more than half of this income was earned in export sales. A full 89 percent of AAC license fees come from outside Canada. Atlantis operated two cable specialty channels, the Life Network and Home and Garden Television, and distributed the U.S. Food Network in Canada. Alliance brought two more successful specialty channels, Showcase and History TV, to the marriage. In its application to the Canadian Radio-television and Telecommunications Commission (CRTC) to approve the merger and keep all four specialty channels, AAC said it would spend $8 million on new Canadian drama and documentary programs.

While AAC posted some restructuring losses in

1998, it quickly implemented a comprehensive acquisitions strategy in various areas. In March 1999 the company acquired an interest in Headline Sports (now the Score), maintaining its focus on nonfiction theme channels with tie-ins to Internet sites, radio, and magazines. In January 2000 AAC, in partnership with Montreal-based Astral Communications, launched two French-language specialty channels, Series1 and Historia.

In early 2000, AAC created a New Media Division and bought into U8TV, an Internet television station. The U8TV concept features eight young people living in a Toronto loft equipped with webcams streaming live images to the Internet 24 hours a day. Each resident also produces a short daily Internet TV segment, from which highlights are carried on Life Network's nightly half-hour top-rated program *The Lofters.* Aimed at the 18-to-30 demographic, U8TV moved into its second season in 2002 by relying on multiple revenue sources including banner ads on the website, product placement and corporate sponsorship on the webcasts, and ad sales on the Life Network.

AAC consolidated its television production activities in 2000 by purchasing Canadian documentary producer Great North Communications and its 675-hour nonfiction library, responding to demand for reality TV and fact-based programming. In 2001 AAC acquired Salter Street Films, its library of 1,100 half-hours of comedy and nonfiction, plus the company's newly granted Independent Film Channel license. Salter Street productions include *This Hour Has 22 Minutes, Lexx,* and *The Industry/Made in Canada.* Analysts accused AAC of trafficking in licences, but CRTC approved the purchase requiring that the Independent Film Channel remain in Halifax and that AAC spend a $1.25 million benefits package on developing the broadcast industry in Atlantic Canada.

Continuing its diversification into specialty broadcasting, AAC made 32 applications to the CRTC for digital licenses in 2000 and launched its new digital offerings in September 2001. The Discovery Health Channel and the Independent Film Channel are Category 1 digital services requiring mandatory carriage by the cable and satellite companies. Of its successful Category 2 license bids, AAC has also negotiated optional carriage agreements for BBC Canada, BBC Kids, National Geographic Canada, Showcase Diva, and Showcase Action. Digital channels in which AAC has part interest include PrideVision, Scream TV, and One: the Body, Mind and Spirit Channel.

In television's currently uncertain economic environment, AAC carries a relatively large debt load, a raft of unproven "developing channels," and the continuing pressure of low profit margins in production. The company has retreated from production of drama into lower-cost, more exportable children's and documentary programs, while enlarging its more profitable, well-branded broadcast operations. Focusing on the U.S. market, it has had recent successes with *CSI: Crime Scene Investigation,* CBS's third-rated program in the 2001 season, and with TV movies like *Joan of Arc, Nuremberg,* and *Life with Judy Garland.*

From its Los Angeles and international offices, AAC is applying its valuable Canadian experience in packaging financing deals and international distribution to changing global television markets. However, the company still dominates Canadian drama production, with annual access to over $100 million in public funds and tax credits for programs like *DaVinci's Inquest, Cold-Squad,* and *The Associates.* Critics point out that CRTC Canadian content regulations make broadcasters a captive market for AAC's programs, while the broadcasters themselves may not apply directly for subsidies. As a vertically integrated production company with 18 specialty channels, AAC is seen as unfairly "self-dealing" its publicly funded products to its own outlets. AAC is solid evidence that Canadian television policy has achieved the desired result of establishing a viable domestic industry. But what remains to be seen is whether the company can remain accountable to Canada's public broadcasting objectives while becoming so heavily involved in global film and television exports.

MARIAN BREDIN

Further Reading

Chidley, Joe, "Birth of a Powerhouse: Alliance plus Atlantis Equals Film-TV Clout," *Maclean's* (August 3, 1998)

Fraser, Matthew, "Our Culture Assured Through Alliance Atlantis," *National Post* (March 4, 2002)

Gray, John, "You Are What You Webcast," *Canadian Business* (February 10, 2000)

MacMillan, Michael, "Canadian TV for the World and for Canada," *Canadian Speeches* (January 1999)

O'Brien, Greg, "Get on With It: Michael MacMillan, the Head of Alliance Atlantis, Understands the Stock Market's Trepidation Towards His Company, Post-merger," *Cablecaster* (November 1999)

Scott, Sarah, "The Accidental Moguls," *Globe and Mail* (November 24, 2000)

Weinraub, Bernard, "From Shoestring to Champagne," *New York Times* (September 4, 2001)

Allison, Fran (1907–1989)

U.S. Television Personality

Fran Allison is perhaps best known for playing the warm-hearted human foil to the Kuklapolitan Players, a troupe of puppets familiar to almost every viewer in the early days of U.S. television. Allison appeared with the puppets on the children's program *Kukla, Fran and Ollie,* which aired regularly from 1948 to 1957, and in subsequent reunions in the late 1960s and mid-1970s.

Born in Iowa, Allison began working as a songstress on local Waterloo, Iowa, radio programs and eventually moved to Chicago in 1937, where she was hired as a staff singer and personality on NBC Radio. Audiences became familiar with her from numerous radio appearances, first as a singer on such programs as *Smile Parade* and *Uncle Ezra's Radio Station* (also known as *Station EZRA*), and later on *The Breakfast Club* as the gossipy spinster Aunt Fanny, who loved to dish gossip about such fictitious townsfolk as Bert Beerbower, Orphie Hackett, and Ott Ort and was based on a character she first created for a local Iowa radio program. Allison appeared on both the radio and television versions of *Don McNeill's The Breakfast Club* for more than 25 years. The Aunt Fanny character was briefly spun off on her own 30-minute radio program in 1939, *Sunday Dinner at Aunt Fanny's*. But it was on *Kukla, Fran and Ollie* that Allison became the "First Lady of Chicago Broadcasting."

While her husband, Archie Levington, was serving in the army, Allison worked on bond-selling tours, during which she met and became good friends with puppeteer Burr Tillstrom. When the time came to choose an appropriate sidekick for his new television series, Tillstrom wanted to work with "a pretty girl, someone who preferably could sing," someone who could improvise along with Tillstrom and with the show's informal structure. According to Tillstrom, when he and Allison met four days later, she was so enthusiastic about the show and working with her friend that she never asked how much the job paid. With only a handshake, they went on the air live for the first time that very afternoon.

Shortly before his death in 1985, Tillstrom tried to capture the nature of the unique relationship that Allison had with his puppets: "She laughed, she sympathized, loved them, sang songs to them. She became their big sister, favorite teacher, babysitter, girlfriend, mother." More than just the "girl who talks to Burr [Tillstrom]'s puppets," Allison treated each character as an individual personality, considered each her friend, and, by expressing genuine warmth and affection for them, made the audience feel the same way. She once remarked that she believed in them so implicitly that it would take a few days to become accustomed to a new version of one of the puppets.

It was through Allison that the Kuklapolitans came to life as individual personalities with life histories. Each show was entirely improvised. The only prior planning was a basic storyline. Characters discussed their backgrounds, where they attended school, and their relatives. Allison was the first to mention Ollie's mother Olivia and niece Dolores, and Tillstrom added them to their growing number of Kuklapolitans. In addition to prompting the characters to talk about themselves, Allison herself invented some of the characters' histories, such as announcing that Buelah Witch's alma mater was Witch Normal.

Allison's radio and television work continued after the initial run of *Kukla, Fran and Ollie.* In the late 1950s, Allison hosted *The Fran Allison Show,* a panel discussion program on local Chicago television, telecast in color and considered at that time to be "the most ambitious show in Chicago's decade of television." She also continued to appear on television musical specials over the years, including *Many Moons* (1954), *Pinocchio* (with Mickey Rooney, 1957), *Damn Yankees* (1967), and *Miss Pickerell* (1972). Allison was reunited with Tillstrom and the Kuklapolitans for the series' return in 1969 on PBS and as the hosts of the *CBS Children's Film Festival* on Saturday afternoons from 1971 to 1979. In the 1980s Allison hosted a local Los Angeles (KHJ-TV) program, *Prime Time,* a show for senior citizens.

In 1949 Allison was nominated for an Emmy Award

Fran Allison.
Courtesy of the Everett Collection

as Most Outstanding Kinescope Personality but lost to Milton Berle. In 1988 she was inducted into Miami Children's Hospital's Ambassador David M. Walters International Pediatrics Hall of Fame, which honors men and women of medicine and laypersons who have made a significant contribution to the health and happiness of children everywhere.

SUSAN R. GIBBERMAN

See also **Chicago School of Television; Children and Television; *Kukla, Fran and Ollie;* Tillstrom, Burr**

Fran Allison. Born in La Porte City, Iowa, November 20, 1907. Married: Archie Levington, 1940. Attended Coe College, Cedar Rapids, Iowa. Began career as radio singer, Waterloo, Iowa; staff singer, various shows on NBC Radio, Chicago, from 1937; star of radio show, *Sunday Dinner at Aunt Fanny's,* 1939; regular guest, *Don McNeill's Breakfast Club,* radio and television program, through 1940s and 1950s; joined Burr Tillstrom, puppeteer, with *Kukla, Fran and Ollie* television program, Chicago, 1947; host, with Tillstrom's puppets, *Children's Film Festival,* PBS, 1971–79; in local radio and television from 1970s. Died in Sherman Oaks, California, June 13, 1989.

Television Series (selected)

1948–52, 1954–57, 1961–62, 1969–71, 1976	*Kukla, Fran, and Ollie* (host)
1950–51	*Don McNeill's TV Club*

Television Specials (selected)

1953	*The Ford 50th Anniversary Show*
1953	*St. George and the Dragon*
1954	*The Kukla, Fran and Ollie Mikado*
1954	*Many Moons*
1955	*The Kuklapolitan Easter Show*
1957	*Pinocchio*
1967	*Damn Yankees*
1972	*Miss Pickerell*

Further Reading

Adams, Rosemary K., "Here We Are Again: *Kukla, Fran and Ollie,*" *Chicago History* (Fall 1997)
Anderson, Susan Heller, "Fran Allison, 81, the Human Side of 'Kukla, Fran and Ollie' Show, Dies," *New York Times* (June 14, 1989)
Fay, B., "Allison in Wonderland," *Colliers* (March 4, 1950)
"Fran Allison," *Variety* (June 21, 1989)
Hughes, C., "Kukla and Ollie's Real-Life Heroine," *Coronet* (October 1951)
Kogan, Rick, "Fran Allison, of 'Kukla, Fran and Ollie,'" *Chicago Tribune* (June 14, 1987)
Long, J., "Dragon's Girlfriend," *American Magazine* (March 1950)
Mitchard, Jacquelyn, "Kukla, Fran, Ollie, and Me," *TV Guide* (November 16, 1996)
Stover, Carol, "'Kukla, Fran and Ollie': A Show for All Time," *Antiques and Collecting Magazine* (May 1997)
"Triple Life of Fran Allison," *McCall's* (March 1953)

Allocation

U.S. Broadcast Policy

The Federal Communications Commission's (FCC) methods of allocating broadcasting frequencies in the United States have long been a subject of debate and controversy. The key issues have been: first, whether television should be controlled by the few strongest networks; second, whether the FCC is responsible for setting aside frequencies for noncommercial or educational broadcasters, even though the media operate within a privately held system; and third, whether spectrum allocations should change when new technologies, requiring use of the airwaves, are introduced. The Communication Act of 1934 provides for a way to maintain federal control over all channels of interstate and foreign radio transmission, and to provide for the use of such channels, but not their ownership.

The act outlines a four-step process for allocating frequencies. An entity that applies for a construction permit (the right to build a broadcast station) must seek a specific channel, antenna location, coverage area, times of operation, and power level of preference. If that applicant is selected for an allocation, the FCC then issues the construction permit. When the station is built, the owners must prove their transmitter and antenna can perform to FCC standards. The aspirant can then apply for a station license. Usually, applicants must also prove U.S. citizenship, good character free of criminal records, sufficient financial resources, and proof of expert technical abilities.

When a few experimenters first put voice over wireless telegraphy at the turn of the century, there was no immediate need for a system of allocation. Many "broadcasters" were amateurs working with low-power systems. Even so, other uses were apparent and growth of radio use was rapid. It was interrupted, however, by World War I, when the government chose to take over all domestic frequencies to ensure control of airwave communication. After the war, when the British government chose to retain political power of its broadcast frequencies and form a public broadcasting system, the U.S. government instead decided to rely upon the entrepreneurial spirit and allow private profit from broadcasting. The technology and the industry were regulated under the provisions of the Radio Act of 1912, which placed control in the U.S. Department of Commerce, then administered by Secretary Herbert Hoover.

The Second National Radio Conference, March 20, 1923, addressed problems associated with increasing the number of signals on the broadcast spectrum. The conference recommendations included the equitable distribution of frequencies to local areas and discussed wavelengths, power, time of operation, and apparatus. More importantly, the conference suggested three concepts that have not changed with time and technology. The first recognized that broadcasting usually covers a limited area and sanctioned local community involvement in the licensing process. The second concept acknowledged the limited amount of frequency space in the electromagnetic spectrum and supported the assignment of one consistent wavelength to broadcasters. The third concept proposed that once a broadcasting organization was assigned a certain frequency, it should not have to move that placement due to new regulation.

These recommendations died in the U.S. House Committee on the Merchant Marine and Fisheries and in Senate committee. No action was taken. Commerce Secretary Hoover believed government control had no place in American broadcasting; those using the airwaves should join together and regulate themselves.

Congress reflected the conflicting views. Though litigation against the government rendered the Radio Act of 1912 virtually inoperable, 50 separate bills failed in Congress before the federal legislature passed the Radio Act of 1927. Cases such as *Hoover v. Intercity Radio* (1923) held that the government could not refuse a license to an interested party but could designate a frequency and police interferences. In the next major case, *United States v. Zenith Radio Corporation* (1926), a federal judge ruled the Commerce Department had no jurisdiction to regulate radio. Other rulings by the U.S. Attorney General completely nullified Department of Commerce control.

Yet more radio broadcasters wanted frequencies and with 716 radio stations on the air, national regulation was more and more necessary. With the Radio Act of 1927, the federal government decided to retain ownership of the airwaves but allow private interests to hold continuing licenses. The licenses were renewable after three years, depending on the holder's ability to serve the "public interest, convenience, and necessity."

Networks had grown substantially after 1926. Religious, educational, cultural, civil liberties, and labor organizations also sought a voice amid the privately held, commercially supported licensees. Yet the 1927 act did not successfully regulate the system. It was replaced seven years later by the Communications Act of 1934.

The two acts had many similarities and neither altered the allocations already in place for the burgeoning broadcast networks CBS and NBC. Among existing nonprofit broadcasters, many educational institutions were still forced to share frequencies and in the end most educators dropped their partial licenses and chose to be silent. Yet the lobbying efforts of Paulist priest John B. Harney made Congress realize the airwaves could be used for social good by nonprofit interests and the 1934 act included a provision to study such allocations. Still, the conflict was not resolved until 1945 when 20 FM channels between 88 and 92 megahertz were reserved for noncommercial and educational broadcasting. These frequencies represented 20 percent of the broadcast band.

Among the commercial networks, each had considerable power over its affiliate stations until an FCC ruling limited the degree of contractual control over affiliate operations. But practical authority over the dependent affiliates persisted since networks supplied most programming.

By 1938 NBC and CBS commanded the great majority of licensed wattage through owned stations or affiliates. In 1941 the FCC's Report on Chain Broadcasting was accepted by the Supreme Court in *NBC v. U.S.* (1943). The ruling led to a separation of NBC into two radio networks, one of which was later sold and became ABC. Four-way network competition began in the radio marketplace among Mutual, the fledgling ABC, and the dominators, CBS and NBC.

As of 1941, six television stations had been approved and two were in operation; CBS and RCA stepped in early to receive construction permits and licenses. The major networks were joined by receiver maker Alan B. DuMont and each ventured into television as network programmers in the 1940s. The three networks divided the week, each programming two or three nights without competition.

The FCC settled the placement of the radio bandwidth in 1945, but allocation problems did not end. Television's impending maturity created more spectrum confusion. As it had done with radio, the government had issued experimental and early frequency allocations for television on the VHF and UHF spectrums. Large broadcasting corporations obtained early signal assignments both to monopolize the new medium and to sell a new product, television receivers.

The problem with television allocations was the limited amount of bandwidth compared to radio signal space. The FCC had planned 18 channels, each six megacycles wide between 50 and 294 megacycles. In the VHF spectrum space, only 13 channels existed that could support television signals. Cities 150 miles apart could share a channel; towns 75 miles apart could have consecutively placed station signals. When the commission considered rules in September of 1945, it was decided that 140 metropolitan districts would be allocated VHF broadcasting channels.

The Television Broadcast Association supported shorter distances between localities using the same spectrum space for signal transmission. ABC and CBS believed the future of television existed in the more generous UHF spectrum space. Several network leaders argued either to transfer all television delivery to the more capacious UHF or to allow existing stations to slowly move to UHF. Instead, the FCC approved a VHF delivery plan in November 1945. Five hundred stations would be allocated to the 140 communities, with no allocations planned for channel 1. The FCC plan did not move any previously granted station frequencies. It did, however, allow shorter distances between eastern U.S. station assignments. New York City was given seven channels; smaller towns were allocated limited coverage and lower powered television signals.

By 1948 the FCC realized the November 1945 plan would not work and advocated moving all television to UHF. By then 15 stations were on the air. While a final plan could be developed, the FCC added some VHF signal restrictions and completely eliminated use of channel 1. Also that year, the FCC again held further allocation hearings. The resulting ruling increased the number of stations but questioned the use of UHF for television delivery. The new plan now placed 900 stations in more than 500 communities, still utilizing only the VHF band. Confusion, conflict, and controversy continued and on September 29, 1948, the FCC halted further allocation of station licenses. Only 108 stations were on the air. This action became known as The Freeze of 1948.

Construction of the stations previously approved, but not built, continued and more VHF stations did begin broadcasting between 1948 and the end of the freeze in April 1952. Many television industry interests still supported UHF utilization, but manufacturers had not yet developed transmission equipment for UHF. Television sets were not being built to receive the higher signals. Potential problems with UHF included signal strength and interference. Nevertheless, the FCC decided to begin UHF television without additional testing.

With regard to station allocations, the FCC's Sixth Report and Order was a most salient document. There the commission decided to maintain placement of the existing VHF stations, though a few were ordered to change bandwidth within the VHF spectrum. The new plan created 2,053 allotments in 1,291 communities.

The FCC aggressively assigned UHF stations to smaller towns and left VHF for large cities. The number of stations per community depended upon population. For example, a community with 250,000 to 1 million people received four to six stations. Except for Los Angeles and New York, which secured seven stations in the VHF spectrum, the FCC allocated no more than four VHF stations per locality. Spacing of the same channel between communities depended on such factors as geographical location, population density, and tropospheric interference. Cities at least 170 miles apart could have received allotment of the same channel.

The FCC made a historically significant ruling when it chose to enter UHF broadcasting without materially altering existing allocations. Since many sets had no UHF equipment, the stations with VHF station assignments had the upper hand over new UHF stations. It would be years before any large population could receive UHF. More importantly, the decision created a situation of the early bird catching the worm. The companies with the first granted allocations, namely NBC and CBS, also had the best signal positions. The FCC chose to maintain network dominance of television and essentially gave the large networks control over the future of the new medium. For most viewers, it was easier to tune to the broadcasting giants than to new networks or independent stations.

Allocation of noncommercial stations was another important provision of the Sixth Report and Order. FCC Commissioner Frieda Hennock, a New York attorney, argued for spectrum space for educational television. She established her place in broadcasting history when the FCC decided to make 252 noncommercial assignments, including 68 VHF and 174 UHF stations. This was one-tenth of all stations assigned. Any community with one or two VHF stations in operation won a VHF educational television frequency. The first noncommercial station reached the airwaves in 1954.

Television station allocations moved slowly until the middle 1970s. ABC, operating largely on UHF stations, jockeyed for positioning against the stronger networks, CBS and NBC. In 1975, in a period of government deregulation, the FCC liberalized both frequency allocations and methods of television delivery. The large fees required for satellite receiving stations had diminished, enhancing the possibilities for both satellite and cable delivery of television to homes and businesses.

The FCC again began an aggressive period of television station allocations between 1975 and 1988, primarily assigning UHF spectrum licenses. During this period, more than 300 stations began telecasting. In 1975, 513 VHF and 198 UHF stations were on the air. By 1988, 543 VHF and 501 UHF stations broadcasted shows. The advent of cable somewhat leveled the competitive lead of lower-numbered VHF stations; the reception of each station was equal when provided through the wire and many homes now subscribed to cable systems. The added popularity of remote controlled, hundred-plus channel, cable-ready receivers made any signal a finger press away.

Deregulation also created still more television signal competition, all governed through FCC allocations. Low power television (LPTV), or short range signals serving communities within cities and smaller towns in rural areas, grew as additional licenses were granted in the 1980s. Though these stations were originally expected to handle either home shopping or community access programs, many low power stations became competitive with other television stations by becoming cable carriers.

Because the major networks already held affiliate contracts in most markets, these new UHF and LPTV stations were largely independently owned. The existence of more and more unaffiliated stations opened a door for the creation of new television networks and new program providers. In 1985 the FOX Broadcasting Network was created as a fourth network by linking a number of the new, largely independent stations. Specialty networks, such as the Spanish-language Univision and Telemundo networks, and broadcast-cable hybrid networks, such as Home Shopping Network and Trinity Broadcast Network (religious), developed in the late 1980s. In 1994 Paramount and Warner Bros. Studios entered the arena with networks of broadcast stations airing new programming. The shows presented on these alternative networks have most often been outside the scope of the large networks. Some have challenged traditional network notions of "taste" or programming standards and have presented new types of shows. Others have focused on a selected audience such as Spanish speakers or home shoppers.

In 1994 FOX Broadcasting Company became concerned with the signal power, and resulting audience reach, of its affiliates. The network made a series of contract changes, in essence trading several of its UHF outlets for stronger VHF stations. In those deals, many independent broadcasters were pushed aside for stations owned by broadcast groups such as New World Entertainment. The end result was an increase in VHF placements for FOX shows without resort to issues or problems related to allocation.

The future of station allocation is unclear. In the early 1990s, when high-definition television (HDTV) was expected to overtake U.S. television, skeptics pointed to the history of U.S. television allocations. HDTV could have required more extensive bandwidth, and, therefore, the reordering of spectrum allocations. But in the past, except for the shifting of some VHF stations required by the Sixth Report and Order, the FCC has not changed a previously granted allocation no matter how compelling or leveling the reason. The dominance of the major networks has always been preserved. The channel positions have never changed materially, and audiences have remained comfortable with familiar placements. It is unlikely that the FCC will dabble with allocations in the future. Yet as viewers grow increasingly dependent on cable as their television provider, the role of station placement may decrease in importance. Future station assignments and changes will hardly affect either cable channel placement or the social routines of the television viewer.

JOAN GIGLIONE

See also **Communications Act of 1934; Educational Television; Federal Communications Commission; "Freeze" of 1948; Hennock, Frieda B.; Networks: United States**

Further Reading

Barrows, Roscoe L., with others, "Development of Television: FCC Allocations and Standards," in *American Broadcasting: A Sourcebook of Radio and Television*, edited by Lawrence W. Lichty and Malachi C. Topping, New York: Hastings House, 1975

Brown, James A., "Struggle Against Commercialism: The 1934 'Harney Lobby' for Nonprofit Frequency Allocations," *Journal of Broadcasting and Electronic Media* (1984)

Head, Sydney W., and Christopher H. Sterling, *Broadcasting in America,* 6th edition, Boston, Massachusetts: Houghton Mifflin, 1990

Krasnow, Erwin G., "Public Airwave Ownership Was Always a Myth," *Legal Times* (August 6 1984)

Lichty, Lawrence W., "The Impact of FRC and FCC Commissioners' Background on the Regulation of Broadcasting," in *American Broadcasting: A Sourcebook of Radio and Television,* edited by Lawrence W. Lichty and Malachi C. Topping, New York: Hastings House, 1975

Mayes, Thorn, "History of the American Marconi Company," in *American Broadcasting: A Sourcebook of Radio and Television,* edited by Lawrence W. Lichty and Malachi C. Topping, New York: Hastings House, 1975

Obuchowski, Janice, "The Unfinished Task of Spectrum Policy Reform" (Special Issue on the Sixtieth Anniversary of the Communications Act of 1934), *Federal Communications Law Journal* (December 1994)

Pepper, Robert, "The Pre-Freeze Television Stations," in *American Broadcasting: A Sourcebook of Radio and Television,* edited by Lawrence W. Lichty and Malachi C. Topping, New York: Hastings House, 1975

Rivkin, Steven R., "FCC to Electrics: Move, Use, or Lose!," *Public Utilities Fortnightly* (May 1, 1992)

Sterling, Christopher H., "WTMJ-FM: A Case Study in the Development of FM Broadcasting," in *American Broadcasting: A Sourcebook of Radio and Television,* edited by Lawrence W. Lichty and Malachi C. Topping, New York: Hastings House, 1975

Sterling, Christopher H., and John M. Kittross, *Stay Tuned: A Concise History of American Broadcasting,* Belmont, California: Wadsworth, 1990; 3rd edition, Mahwah, New Jersey: Lawrence Erlbaum, 2002

Stern, Robert H., "Television in the Thirties," in *American Broadcasting: A Sourcebook of Radio and Television,* edited by Lawrence W. Lichty and Malachi C. Topping, New York: Hastings House, 1975

Turow, Joseph, *Media Systems in Society: Understanding Industries, Strategies, and Power,* White Plains, New York: Longman, 1992

Ally McBeal

U.S. Dramedy

The FOX series *Ally McBeal* catapulted into the center of cultural discussion shortly after its launch in 1997. The series' form and narrative were distinctive, marked by the use of eccentric characters, digital graphics, and the incorporation of song and dance scenes reminiscent of variety-comedies and film musicals. Significantly, however, the series' title character also sparked sometimes heated cultural debates about the status of feminism, femininity, and womanhood. The show raised many of the dilemmas faced by the post-baby boom, post–second-wave feminist generation of women. Original plans at FOX, however,

Ally McBeal, Thorne-Smith, Bellows, Germann, Flockhart, Krakowski, Carson, MacNicol.
©20th Century Fox/Courtesy of the Everett Collection

merely called for a series that would provide an audience matching the demographic makeup of the canceled *Melrose Place,* which was popular among young women and competed well against *Monday Night Football.* The network sought out writer/producer David E. Kelley (*L.A. Law, Picket Fences, The Practice*) to create such a series.

Ally McBeal follows in the television tradition of workplace series, such as *The Mary Tyler Moore Show,* in which the workplace ensemble forms a tight-knit family relationship encompassing both work and the personal, social aspects of characters' lives. Set in the Boston law firm of Cage/Fish and Associates, the series explores relationships among the various lawyers, often as they relate to specific gender issues raised in court cases. Individual episodes focus mainly on professional activities, often beginning with conference meetings, then following with the cases in which the firm members serve as counsel. As well, however, almost every episode offers intricate plots based on personal romantic relationships. At the conclusion of many episodes, the ensemble retires for drinks and dancing in the bar located in the same building as the office. The bar is the venue for the series' signature incorporation of music. Regular cast member/musician Vonda Shepard often performs, sometimes with one of the cast members or a guest star (Elton John, Sting), offering a number that frequently provides a thematic commentary on events in the episode.

The series began when Ally's law school acquaintance, Richard Fish, invited her to join Cage/Fish following her sexual harassment by a partner at her current firm. An intelligent, competent lawyer, Ally is given to fits of whimsy and struggles throughout the series to establish boundaries between the "real world" and the fantasy worlds she constructs. Accepting the offer, she finds herself in the midst of a somewhat odd assortment of colleagues.

Richard is defined by his pursuit of financial success without adherence to a politically correct moral code. Frequently characterized as boyish and immature, his superficiality is at times over the top, given to explicitly politically incorrect, sexist, and homophobic comments. But his perspective is presented in an unthreatening manner, neutralized by the overall tone of the series. John Cage (the name itself is telling) is the most eccentric character, often described by others as a "funny little man." Despite the fact that he stutters and that his nose whistles at inopportune moments, he is the master of a range of gadgets and often appears the most competent of the lawyers. In many ways he functions as the moral center of the show.

The series fluctuates considerably season to season, as the narrative emphases shift and the cast changes. The initial cast (present in most of the first three seasons) includes Ally's childhood sweetheart Billy Thomas, whom she dated from adolescence through her first year of law school, Billy's wife and fellow lawyer, Georgia, and secretary Elaine Vassal. Billy begins the series as a "sensitive" male, a proponent of gender equity. He undergoes a transformation in the third season and becomes a rather virulent male chauvinist. The character then dies suddenly at the end of the season due to complications from a brain tumor that may have contributed to his erratic behavior. Georgia has joined Fish/Cage after experiencing sex-based discrimination at another firm and exhibits none of the eccentricity defining many of the other characters. Rather, she is characterized primarily by her struggle to keep her marriage together while recognizing Billy's continuing infatuation with Ally. Elaine, the ever-present office busybody, is perhaps the most comical of characters, given to public presentation of her outrageous inventions, such as the face bra. Her hyper-sexualized demeanor is an effort to be included among the lawyers, but over the course of the series she reveals elements of her past explaining some of her eccentricities and more overt sexual behaviors.

The first season cast also included Ally's roommate, Renee, a deputy district attorney, and Judge Jennifer "Whipper" Cone, Richard Fish's girlfriend in the first two seasons. In the second season, the series added attorney Nelle Porter, whose stunningly attractive appearance masked a cutthroat legal style. When she developed a relationship with the shy and retiring John Cage, their interaction revealed unexpected complexities in both characters. Nelle also introduced her excessively litigious client, Ling Woo, who eventually joined the firm and dated Richard. Ling's character was frequently used to examine fundamental ambiguities in matters related to gender definitions and topics.

Billy, Georgia, Whipper, and Renee exited by the series' fourth year, and a budding romance between Ally and new character Larry Paul (Robert Downey Jr.) dominated the season. The series broke from a number of its conventions, going so far as to present many episodes that completely excluded any courtroom scenes. Attention focused instead on the complicated romantic relationships between Ally and Larry, John Cage and an autistic woman, Melanie West, and a romantic triangle among Ling, Richard, and another new character, Jackson Duper. The fifth season again offered more radical variation with the departure of Larry Paul (an arrest on drug charges threatened Downey's availability), Jackson, and Ling. John Cage became a part-time cast member. Several young lawyers were introduced into the firm. The series again emphasized episodic court cases. Ally displayed considerable new maturity as a mentor to youthful doppelganger Jenny. She was promoted to firm partner in John's absence, purchased a house, and became the mother of a 10-year-old girl conceived from an egg Ally had donated during law school.

As this description indicates, *Ally McBeal* is primarily a character-driven series, incorporating some serial features along with the "case-driven" episodic style of most courtroom dramas. Clearly, however, the eccentric nature of many of the characters and their constant, substantive redevelopment contributes to the series' hazy interplay of the serious and the absurd. This, in turn, fueled much of the show's debate and consideration of cultural issues. Narratives often slip unpredictably from realistic melodrama to comedy and fantasy sequences, making varied interpretations freely possible. Indeed, the slippage included the possibility that the dramatic and comedic depictions of characters are parodic, critical of the very topics they explore. These topics ranged over charged social and cultural matters such as sexual behavior, sexual harassment, gender definition, professional ethics, and racialized social structures. Public discussion of these topics was sometimes stimulated by episodes of the television series, and general commentary often made reference to *Ally McBeal.* But the series also dealt with love, truth, honesty, commitment, and honor, common elements of television produced and written by Kelley. Yet despite the titular focus on Ally, the series, particularly in early seasons, lacked a dependable central character through which the audience could gauge message and ideology. *Ally McBeal* did maintain what creator Kelley termed a "fundamental idealism" personified in Ally and John throughout its variations, as well as a "belief in love and human spirit," and concluded with Ally leaving the firm to move to New York in response to the needs of her daughter.

AMANDA LOTZ

See also **Comedy, Workplace; Dramedy; FOX Broadcasting Company; Gender and Television**

Cast

Ally McBeal	Calista Flockhart
Richard Fish	Greg Germann
Elaine Vassal	Jane Krakowski
John Cage	Peter MacNicol
Vonda Shepard	Herself
Renee Raddick (1997–2001)	Lisa Nicole Carson
Billy Alan Thomas (1997–2000)	Gil Bellows
Georgia Thomas (1997–2000)	Courtney Thorne-Smith
Jennifer "Whipper" Cone (1997–2000)	Dyan Cannon
Nelle Porter (1998–2002)	Portia de Rossi
Ling Woo (1998–2001)	Lucy Liu
Dr. Greg Butters (1998)	Jesse L. Martin
Larry Paul (2000–01)	Robert Downey, Jr.
Jackson Duper (2000–01)	Taye Diggs
Mark Albert (2000–01)	James LeGros
Melanie West (2001)	Anne Heche
Coretta Lipp (2001–02)	Regina Hall
Jenny Shaw (2001–02)	Julianne Nicholson
Glenn Foy (2001–02)	James Marsden
Raymond Milbury (2001–02)	Josh Hopkins
Maddie Harrington (2001–02)	Hayden Panettiere

Producers

David E. Kelley, Bill D'Elia

Programming History

FOX

September 1997–May 2002	Monday 9:00–10:00

Further Reading

Cooper, Brenda, "Unapologetic Women, Comic Men and Feminine Spectatorship in David E. Kelley's *Ally McBeal*" *Critical Studies in Media Communication,* Vol. 18, No. 4 (2001)

Nochimson, Martha P., "*Ally McBeal:* Brightness Falls from the Air" *Film Quarterly,* Vol. 53 (2000)

Wild, David, "David E. Kelley: The Prolific Producer-Writer Testifies to the Enduring Success of *Ally McBeal,*" *Hollywood Reporter* (18 January 2000)

Wild, David, "She Fought the Laws of TV (and Won)," *Hollywood Reporter* (18 January 2000)

Almond, Paul (1931–)

Canadian Producer, Director

Paul Almond produced and directed more than 100 television dramas in Toronto, London, and Los Angeles between 1954 and 1967. Almond has produced and directed dramas for such Canadian Broadcasting Corporation (CBC) shows as *Folio, The Unforeseen,* and *Wojeck.*

Among his many accomplishments in "live" or "live-to-tape" television are the early experimental religious drama *The Hill,* which used simple wooden platforms, a cyclorama, and improvisation; Arthur Hailey's realistic early drama about the threats of nuclear technology, *Seeds of Power;* the fascinating, televisual adaptation of Dylan Thomas's radio piece *Under Milk Wood,* which alternated between stylized shots of elements of the set with realistic shots of the actors; Harold Pinter's controversial *Birthday Party; A Close Prisoner,* the self-reflexive and chilling satire by Clive Exton; and television versions of Christopher Fry's *Sleep of Prisoners, Venus Observed,* and *A Phoenix Too Frequent* and Jean Anouilh's *Antigone.* He also produced and directed a chilling adaptation of *Crime and Punishment,* called *The Murderer;* the dark, antiwar comedy *The Neutron and the Olive;* and his creative partner, designer Rudy Dorn's, drama about World War II from the point of view of a German soldier, *The Broken Sky.* Other successful adaptations included *Macbeth,* with Sean Connery and Zoe Caldwell, using only a flight of steps and a huge throne, and *Julius Caesar,* using one 12-foot decorative column. At the time of these "experimental" productions, Dorn and Almond shared a theory that the "only real thing was the emotion expressed on the face of a really good actor."

Almond directed for the most successful series in CBC television history, *Wojeck,* including the prescient episode on drug abuse ("All Aboard for Candyland"), at a time when such subjects were rarely seen on television.

Two of his 1960s dramas were censored by the CBC: Anouilh's *Point of Departure,* which showed two unmarried people in bed together, and *Shadow of a Pale Horse,* a vivid antiwar drama that depicted, according to the broadcaster, a too-explicit hanging in one scene. In instances such as these, when the CBC management threatened to cancel a program (which became easier when tape came into use), the corporation, under pressure from its creative staff, sometimes compromised by scheduling the drama at 11:30 P.M., when it was hoped that everyone likely to complain was in bed. In the case of Michael Tait's *Fellowship,* the CBC canceled the show altogether but relented and broadcast it at a later date. In a rare return to television in 1978, Almond directed the award-winning docudrama *Every Person Is Guilty,* on the anthology *For the Record.*

Television critics and colleagues said of Almond that he was "the mystic," "the romantic," "the man with an eye for symbolic levels of meaning," an "actor's director." Cameraman and well-known television writer Grahame Woods said, "he's very responsive and creates a lot of energy. He had a passion for what he was doing and it's infectious." The actor and director David Gardner characterized Almond's work as "moody.... The camera moved a great deal. He was a very volatile director. But once you got to know Paul it was terrific."

Almond himself has said that in some ways he preferred live television to any other form, because it had not only an excitement but a flow of action. In his view, live television allowed both the cameraperson and the director more freedom to respond to the performance itself and literally "call the shots" in unforeseen patterns and rhythms. Early television did not require three people to run a camera. Almond was one of the most influential of the generation of producers and directors in the 1950s and 1960s who were discovering what could be done with the huge, clumsy, and unreliable cameras of live television. He and his coconspirators took "live-to-tape" drama, which was supposed to be taped with minimum interruption because it was very difficult to edit, into territory that demanded many pauses for change of scene, costume, or special effects. From those early experiments and the eventual discovery of cleaner, easier ways to edit tape came true electronic drama.

With limited CBC experience of filmed TV drama, Almond adapted to film so well that his first full-length feature film *Isabel* in 1968 (shown on the CBC in 1969) was a critical success and was followed by such films as *The Act of the Heart, Final Assignment,* and *Captive Hearts.* In 1999 Almond's first two books, *High Hopes: Coming of Age in the Mid-Century* and *La Vengeance des Dieux* were published by ECW Press and Art Global, respectively.

MARY JANE MILLER

See also **Wojeck**

Paul Almond. Born in Montreal, Quebec, 1931. Married: Geneviève Bujold, 1967. Attended Bishop's College School, Lennoxville, Quebec; McGill University, Montreal, B.A.; Balliol College Oxford, M.A. Director for a Shakespearean repertory company, England; returned to join the CBC in Toronto, 1954; directed or produced various drama, action, comedy, and horror series and specials for TV until 1967; independent producer since 1967. Recipient: Bronze Prize, Houston Film Festival, 1981.

Television Series (selected)

1955–67 *Folio*
1958–60 *The Unforeseen*
1959–67 *Festival*
1960–61 *R.C.M.P.*
1960–61 *First Person* (producer)
1961–64 *Playdate*
1963–66 *The Forest Rangers*
1966 *Wojeck* (director)

Made-for-Television Movies (selected)

1963 *The Rose Tattoo* (producer)
1956 *The Queen of Spades* (producer)
1957 *Who Destroyed the Earth*
1967 *La Roulotte aux Poupées* (director)
1979 *Every Person Is Guilty*

Films (selected)

Isabel, 1968; *The Act of the Heart,* 1969; *Journey,* 1971; *Final Assignment,* 1979; *Ups and Downs,* 1981; *Kiss Me Better,* 1981; *Eye of the Falcon,* 1985; *Captive Hearts,* 1987; *The Dance Goes On,* 1991; *Freedom Had a Price* (narrator), 1994.

Publications

High Hopes: Coming of Age in the Mid-Century, 1999
La Vengeance des Dieux, 1999

Further Reading

Arsenault, Andre G., "On Location: Paul Almond's Fate of a Hunter," *Cinema Canada* (February 1987)
"Director Almond Misses Prep Bandwagon," *Calgary Herald* (December 11, 1983)
Drainie, Bronwyn, *Living the Part: John Drainie and the Dilemma of Canadian Stardom,* Toronto: Macmillan, 1988
Rutherford, Paul, *When Television Was Young: Prime Time Canada 1952–1967,* Toronto: University of Toronto Press, 1990

Altman, Robert (1925–)

U.S. Director, Producer, Writer

One of the most unique of modern directors, with a film and television career that has experienced more peaks and valleys than most, Robert Altman's long journey to feature acclaim took over ten years of apprenticeship toiling in the television fields. This experience accumulated a richly diverse body of work that, along the way, helped change certain staid production perceptions and, later, introduce an innovative style to small-screen drama presentation.

His first work for television came in the early 1950s, during a period when he was engaged in directing short films for Calvin Industries, in his hometown of Kansas City. Unfortunately, this television work, a limited crime anthology called *Pulse of the City* (broadcast via the DuMont stations in late 1953), remains something of an obscurity in the program details of television history.

Following a move to Los Angeles in the mid-1950s, Altman codirected (with George W. George) the compilation documentary *The James Dean Story,* released by Warner Bros. in 1957. The documentary came to the notice of Alfred Hitchcock, who had recently launched his mystery series *Alfred Hitchcock Presents* (CBS/NBC, 1955–62) and who was immediately impressed by its expedient style of camerawork and editing. On the strength of this he invited Altman to direct two episodes of his half-hour series for the 1957–58 season. It marked the beginning of Altman's television apprenticeship.

For the next two years Altman learned the art and craft of the weekly grind of episodic television making, turning out multiple segments of the action/adventure series *The Whirlybirds, United States Marshal,* and *The Troubleshooters.* Among the more interesting moments to emerge from this period were the often-exceptional episodes he directed for *The Millionaire* series, a collection of compact, self-contained stories about the diverse types who find themselves the improbable recipients of a $1,000,000 bank draft. Altman's episodes ranged in genre from skittish comedy to gripping film noir.

From this period on, Altman began exploring the method and style of genre television, experimenting and innovating his way through the then-popular Western, private eye, and crime drama genres, mainly under contract to Warner Bros. Television.

While his work for the Warner TV westerns *Sugarfoot, Bronco, Maverick,* and *Lawman* was restricted somewhat by that studio's tight rein over their money-making properties, Altman managed somehow to invert some of the series' formal standards and conventions and celebrate his sense of offbeat adventure. Given a slightly freer hand, the eight episodes of *Bonanza* that he directed for NBC during the 1960–61 season reveal a certain flair for extracting colorful characterizations from an otherwise mundane frontier family saga.

During his period with Warner, Altman was also put to work on their private eye capers *Hawaiian Eye* and *Surfside 6,* but the studio's formula production method offered few opportunities for experimentation. However, Altman was able to fashion a few episodes with a difference from their period mobster drama *The Roaring 20's,* managing to create some surprisingly literate studies amid the screeching tires and machine gun fire.

Robert Altman.
Courtesy of the Everett Collection

In 1961 he joined his friend and the series' producer Robert Blees at Twentieth Century Fox Television to work on the character-driven drama series *Bus Stop.* This program gave Altman the opportunity to explore new dimensions without the usual restrictions of series' character and format conventions. Unfortunately, *Bus Stop* reached its terminus prematurely when the ABC network—defying objections from its affiliate stations—decided to air the controversial (Altman-directed) episode "A Lion Walks Among Us" (a disturbing study of a teenage psychopath). The episode caused a national outcry and its powerful content contributed to the ongoing Senate Subcommittee on Juvenile Delinquency hearings on television violence in 1961. *Bus Stop* was abruptly cancelled thereafter.

Altman was reunited with Blees when he was offered the director-producer assignment on the new men-at-war drama *Combat!.* This period, 1962–63, marked the peak of Altman's creative power during his years in filmed television. As director, producer, and sometimes writer (the latter often uncredited) for most of *Combat!*'s first season, he set the series' visual style and structure as well as introducing innovative production values for the television form (the handheld camera, low-key lighting, overlapping dialogue). When Altman went ahead with production on a particular episode ("Survival") that had been denied the approval of executive producer Selig Seligman, Altman was fired. (*Combat!*'s costar Vic Morrow went on to receive his only Emmy nomination for Best Actor for his work in this episode.)

He then followed Robert Blees to Universal Television, where they worked on the studio's *Kraft Suspense Theatre* anthology until, once again, Altman got himself fired for his well-publicized remark that the Kraft-sponsored series was "as bland as its cheese" (due to Altman having ten of his scripts rejected by the company). One of Altman's *Kraft Suspense Theatre* episodes, the crime thriller "Once Upon a Savage Night" (actually a backdoor pilot for a projected series), was later reedited and made available as the TV movie *Nightmare in Chicago;* it was also released to European cinemas in 1969 under that title.

For the next few years Altman pursued various personal TV pilot projects while at the same time trying to get a foothold in feature work. When, in 1970, critics discovered *M*A*S*H,* it seemed that his feature career was assured. But it was just the beginning of a new series of peaks and valleys in feature production (the high of *Nashville* and the low of *Popeye*).

Throughout most of the 1980s, Altman moved between his intermittent feature work (*Streamers, Fool for Love*) and a form of videotaped theater production for television: *The Laundromat* for HBO, *The Dumb Waiter* and *The Room* for ABC.

Then, in 1988, he introduced a captivating narrative form and style new to television drama: *Tanner '88.* This remarkable miniseries (written by Garry Trudeau) was a superb fusion of flamboyant U.S. politicking and television verité (reminiscent of the John Drew-Richard Leacock 1960 Kennedy documentary *Primary*) and featured Michael Murphy's fictional candidate Jack Tanner during the 1988 presidential campaign. The continuously active project and its irregular screenings spanned some six months (paralleling the real-life U.S. campaign). *Tanner '88* became a cult hit and was only limited in reaching a wider audience due to its presentation via cable TV. Nevertheless, Altman won the 1988–89 Emmy Award for Outstanding Directing in a Drama Series.

The 1997 dramatic anthology *The Gun,* about the effect a pearl-handled, semiautomatic pistol has on its various owners, appeared to mark a return to mainstream television for Altman, this time as executive producer (and director of one episode).

While he continues to traverse the peaks and valleys of feature film work, television eagerly awaits Altman's next visit.

TISE VAHIMAGI

See also ***Alfred Hitchcock Presents; Bonanza; M*A*S*H***

Robert Altman. Born in Kansas City, Missouri, February 20, 1925. Married: 1) La Vonne Elmer, 1946; 2) Lotus Corelli, 1954 (divorced, 1957); 3) Kathryn Reed. Studied mathematical engineering at the University of Missouri. Bomber pilot USAF, 1943–47. Coauthored (with George W. George) film treatments for *Christmas Eve* (UA, 1947) and *The Bodyguard* (RKO, 1948). Writer for magazines, radio, and TV commercials. Produced, wrote, and directed low-budget feature *The Delinquents,* 1955. Founder: Lion's Gate production company, 1970; Westwood Editorial Services, 1974; Sandcastle 5 Productions. Academy Award nominations for *M*A*S*H* (Best Film and Director), 1970; *Nashville* (Best Film and Director), 1975; *The Player* (Best Director), 1992; *Short Cuts* (Best Director), 1993; *Gosford Park* (Best Director), 2002.

Television Series (selected)

1953–54 *Pulse of the City* (cocreator, coproducer, alternating director)
1957 *Alfred Hitchcock Presents,* "The Young One"
Alfred Hitchcock Presents, "Together"
1958–59 *The Whirlybirds*
The Millionaire
1959 *Hawaiian Eye,* "Three Tickets to Lani"
Sugarfoot, "Apollo with a Gun"
1959–60 *United States Marshal*
Troubleshooters
1960 *Bronco,* "The Mustangers"
Maverick, "Bolt from the Blue"
1960–61 *The Roaring 20's*
Bonanza
1961 *Lawman,* "The Robbery"
Surfside 6, "Thieves Among Honor"
1961–62 *Bus Stop*
Bus Stop, "A Lion Walks Among Us"
1962–63 *Kraft Mystery Theatre* (and producer)
Combat! (and producer)
Combat!, "Survival"
1963–64 *Kraft Suspense Theatre*
Kraft Suspense Theatre, "Once Upon a Savage Night" (and producer)
1988 *Tanner '88* (and coproducer)
1997 *Gun* (executive producer)
Gun, "All the President's Women" (and executive producer)

Television Specials

1982 *Precious Blood* (and producer)
Rattlesnake in a Cooler (and producer)
1985 *The Laundromat*
1987 *The Dumb Waiter* (and producer)
The Room (and producer)

1988 *The Caine Mutiny Court-Martial* (and coproducer)
1993 *Black and Blue*
The Real McTeague

Films (selected)

The James Dean Story, 1957; *Countdown,* 1967; *M*A*S*H, Brewster McCloud,* 1970; *McCabe and Mrs. Miller,* 1971; *Images,* 1972; *The Long Goodbye,* 1973; *Nashville,* 1975; *Three Women,* 1977; *A Wedding,* 1978; *Popeye,* 1980; *Streamers,* 1983; *Fool for Love,* 1986; *The Player,* 1992; *Short Cuts,* 1993; *Kansas City,* 1996; *Dr. T. & the Women,* 2000; *Gosford Park,* 2001; *The Company,* 2003.

Further Reading

McGilligan, Patrick, *Jumping Off the Cliff: A Biography of the Great American Director,* New York: St Martin's Press, 1989; 2nd edition, 1991

Amen

U.S. Situation Comedy

From 1986 to 1991, *Amen* aired on NBC. Set around a Philadelphia parish, this was the first hit situation comedy to focus upon religion, an African-American church in particular, depicting, as a *Jet* magazine article put it, "the political as well as humorous side of [this] centuries-old institution." Emphasizing the relationship between the church's virtuous minister, played by Clifton Davis, and its shrewd, quick-witted deacon, played by Sherman Hemsley, this comedy highlighted the continuous conflicts between these contrasting principals. By centralizing these characters' comedic struggles, *Amen* proved a successful parody, satirizing as well as exploring the everyday workings of their church, from service to choir to congregation. Produced by Carson Productions, *Amen* gained top ratings throughout much of its prime-time life.

Focusing primarily on the apparently endless conflict between Deacon Ernest Frye and the Reverend Reuben Gregory, *Amen* was able to capitalize on the humorous dissimilarities separating these perpetually arguing characters. Frye, played expertly by Hemsley, was not unlike George Jefferson, Hemsley's arrogant, determined character for 11 seasons on *The Jeffersons.* The deacon was stubborn, aggressive, and extremely vocal. He had taken over the church from his father, the founder of the First Community Church of Philadelphia, and resisted giving up his control and decision-making power, especially to Reverend Gregory. Ironically, however, Deacon Frye's melodramatic antics usually caused more problems than they fixed, leaving a situation Reverend Gregory was often forced to resolve and opening Frye to the sarcastic ridicule of the congregation.

Gregory, on the other hand, was a kind-hearted, ethical pastor with the church's best interests at heart. Mild mannered in action and even toned in voice, Reverend Gregory was a distinct contrast to the boisterous, authoritarian Deacon Frye. Played by Davis (star of the 1974 series *That's My Mama*), who was an established real-life minister, Reverend Reuben Gregory slowly and patiently established an influence over the church, the deacon, of course, fighting him throughout. A rational voice amid the deacon's fiery outbursts, Reverend Gregory helped to temper Frye's melodramatic excitement, aiding in the resolution of the program's various episodes.

Thelma Frye (Anna Maria Horsford), the deacon's adult, socially awkward daughter, also played an important role in many episodes of *Amen.* Thelma, a romantically distraught 30 year old who still lived with her "daddy," provided a constant source of humor, her own childlike naïveté a comical contrast to the clever, often scheming Deacon Frye. Later episodes focused on the developing romantic relationship and eventual marriage between Thelma and the Reverend Gregory, a marriage that signaled Thelma's coming into adulthood while lessening the distance between the reverend and Deacon Frye. Additional characters included

Amen, Jester Hairston, Anna Maria Horsford, Roz Ryan, Sherman Hemsley, Barbara Montgomery, Clifton Davis, 1986–91. ©*NBC/Courtesy of the Everett Collection*

Rolly Forbes (Jester Hairston), the church's spunky elder church board member, and sisters Casietta and Amelia Hetebrink (Barbara Montgomery and Roz Ryan), all adult church members who frequently made humorous and sarcastic contributions to the show, most often at the expense of Deacon Frye.

Throughout its five years, *Amen* offered a lighthearted look at an African-American church, playfully satirizing its day-to-day activities. Focusing humorously on the everyday conflict between Reverend Gregory and Deacon Frye, as well as these other familiar characters, *Amen* proved a satiric, yet human, portrait of ordinary church life and people.

BRENT MALIN

See also **Hemsley, Sherman; *Jeffersons, The***

Cast

Deacon Ernest Frye	Sherman Hemsley
Reverend Reuben Gregory	Clifton Davis
Thelma Frye	Anna Maria Horsford
Casietta Hetebrink (1986–90)	Barbara Montgomery
Amelia Hetebrink	Roz Ryan
Rolly Forbes	Jester Hairston
Lorenzo Hollingsworth (1986–87)	Franklyn Seales
Leola Forbes (1987–89)	Rosetta LeNoire
Inga (1988–90)	Elsa Raven
Chris (1988–90)	Tony T. Johnson
Clarence (1990–91)	Bumper Robinson

Producers

Ed Weinberger, Michael Leeson, Marcia Govons, Reuben Cannon, Kim Johnston, Arthur Julian, Lloyd David, James Stein, Robert Illes

Programming History

110 episodes
NBC

September 1986–April 1987	Saturday 9:30–10:00
June 1987–September 1988	Saturday 9:30–10:00
October 1988–July 1989	Saturday 8:30–9:00
August 1989	Saturday 8:00–8:30
September 1989–July 1990	Saturday 8:30–9:00
August 1990	Saturday 8:00–8:30
December 1990–July 1991	Saturday 8:00–8:30

Further Reading

Collier, Aldore, "Update: Jester Harrison," *Ebony* (March 1988)

Dates, Jannette, and William Barlow, editors, *Split Images: African Americans in the Mass Media,* Washington, D.C.: Howard University Press, 1990

MacDonald, J. Fred, *Blacks and White TV: Afro-Americans in Television Since 1948,* Chicago: Nelson-Hall Publishers, 1983; 2nd edition, 1992

Stoddard, Maynard Good, "*Amen*'s Clifton Davis: A Reverend for Real," *Saturday Evening Post* (July–August 1990)

American Bandstand

U.S. Music Program

Like the soap opera, *American Bandstand* represents the transference of a successful radio format to the burgeoning arena of American television. Unlike the soap opera, however, the radio broadcast format of playing recorded music developed as popular entertainers from radio migrated to the newer medium of television. Initially located at the margins of broadcast schedules, the format of a live disk jockey spinning records targeted toward and embraced by teenagers soon evolved into the economic salvation of many radio stations. For one thing, the programs were relatively inexpensive to produce. In addition, the increased spending power of American teenagers in the 1950s attracted advertisers and companies marketing products specifically targeting that social group. Among the marketing forces were the recording companies that supplied their records without cost to stations, often including economic incentives to disk jockeys to play the companies' products. In effect, the recorded music was a commercial for itself. Given the convergence of these factors, the teen record party became entrenched as a radio format during the 1950s and throughout the 1960s, eventually developing into Top 40 Radio.

For these same reasons, this format also became highly lucrative for local television stations to produce. While the three networks provided the majority of prime-time programming and some early afternoon soap operas, local television stations had to fill marginal broadcast periods themselves. Since the primary audience for television viewing in the late afternoons included teenagers just out of school for the day, the teen record party apparently made sense to station managers as a way to generate advertising revenue during that broadcast period. As a result, a number of teen dance party programs found their way into television schedules during the early 1950s.

Bandstand, one of these, appeared on WFIL-TV in Philadelphia during September 1952. Hosted by Bob Horn, a popular local disk jockey, the show was presented "live" and included teenagers dancing to the records that were played. As the success of the televised *Bandstand* grew, Dick Clark took over the disk jockey duties of the radio program while Bob Horn was broadcasting in front of the cameras. In 1956 Horn was arrested for driving under the influence of alcohol, in the middle of an anti-drunk-driving campaign by WFIL. Soon thereafter, Dick Clark replaced him as the host of the televised program. Clark's clean-cut, boy-next-door image seemed to offset any unsavory fallout from Horn's arrest, and the show's popularity increased. By the fall of 1957, Clark, who had been shepherding kinescopes of the show to New York, convinced the programmers at ABC to include the show in its network lineup.

Adapting the name of the program to its new stature (and the network identity), *American Bandstand* first aired on the ABC network on Monday, August 5, 1957, becoming one of a handful of locally originating programs to broadcast nationally. Initially, the program ran Monday through Friday from 3:00 to 4:30 P.M., eastern standard time. Almost immediately, the show became a hit for the struggling network. In retrospect, *American Bandstand* fit in nicely with the programming strategy that evolved at ABC during the 1950s. As the third television network, ABC could not afford the high-priced radio-celebrity talent or live dramatic programming that generated the predominantly adult viewership of NBC and CBS. Therefore, ABC counterprogrammed its schedule with shows that appealed to a younger audience. Along with programs such as *The Mickey Mouse Club,* ABC used *American Bandstand* in the 1950s to build a loyal audience base that would catapult the network to the top of the prime-time ratings in the mid-1970s.

From a cultural and social standpoint, the impact of *American Bandstand* should not be underrated. Even if the show diffused some of the more raucous elements of rock 'n' roll music, it helped to solidify the growing youth culture that centered around this phenomenon. The show was important in another way as well. Once Clark took over the helm of *Bandstand* in 1956, he insisted on racially integrating the show, since much of the music was performed by black recording artists. When the show moved to the network schedule, it maintained its racially mixed image, thus providing American television broadcasting with its most visible ongoing image of ethnic diversity until the 1970s.

Dick Clark.
Photo courtesy of Dick Clark Productions, Inc.

In 1964 Clark moved the production of *American Bandstand* to California, cutting broadcasts to once a week. In part, the move was made to facilitate Clark's expansion into other program production. Additionally, it became easier to tap into the American recording industry, the center of which had shifted to Los Angeles by that time. The show's popularity with teenagers continued until the late 1960s.

At that point, white, middle-class American youth culture moved away from the rock 'n' roll dance music that had become the staple of *American Bandstand,* opting instead for the drug-influenced psychedelia of the Vietnam War era. As a response to the specialized tastes of perceived diverse target audiences, radio formats began to fragment at this time, segregating popular music into distinct categories. While *American Bandstand* attempted to integrate many of these styles into its format throughout the 1970s, the show relied heavily on disco, the emerging alternative to psychedelic art rock. Though often denigrated at the time because of disco's emergence in working-class and ethnic communities, the musical style was the logical focus for the show, given its historic reliance on presenting teenagers dancing. Consequently, *American Bandstand* became even more ethnically mixed at a time when the predominant face of the aging "youth" culture in the United States acquired a social pallor.

The foundation of *American Bandstand*'s success rested with its ability to adapt to shifting musical trends while maintaining the basic format developed in the 1950s. As a result, Dick Clark helmed the longest-running broadcast program aimed at mainstream youth to air on American network broadcast television. After 30 years of broadcasting, ABC finally dropped the show from its network schedule in 1987. In its later years, *American Bandstand* was often preempted by various sporting events. Given the commercial profits generated from sports presentations, apparently it was only a matter of time before the network replaced the dance party entirely. Additionally, the rise of MTV and other music video channels in the 1980s also helped to seal *American Bandstand*'s fate. The show began to look like an anachronism when compared to the slick production values of expensively produced music videos. Nevertheless, the music video channels owe a debt of gratitude to *American Bandstand,* the network prototype that shaped the format they have exploited so well. As a testament to *American Bandstand*'s enduring cultural influence, Dick Clark Productions and ABC aired a celebration of the program's 50th anniversary in 2002.

RODNEY BUXTON

See also **Clark, Dick; Music on Television**

Host
Dick Clark (1956–89)
David Hirsch (1989)

Producer
Dick Clark

Programming History
ABC
August 5–September 5, 1957
Syndicated

1957–63	daily, various local non-prime-time hours
1963–69	Saturday, various local non-prime-time hours

USA Cable

April 8–October 7, 1989	Saturday, non-prime-time hours

Further Reading

Clark, Dick, and Richard Robinson, *Rock, Roll and Remember,* New York: Popular Library, 1976
Shore, Michael, with Dick Clark, *The History of American Bandstand,* New York: Ballantine, 1985

American Broadcasting Company

U.S. Network

The American Broadcasting Company (ABC) came under the control of the Walt Disney Co. in August 1995 when Disney acquired the network's parent company, Capital Cities/ABC, for $19 billion. Disney's merger of a major studio with a broadcast network figured to be the model for the television industry of the future. The enticement of media synergy drove Disney to acquire ABC, and the Disney-ABC alliance has served as a model for the subsequent consolidation of networks and studios throughout the television industry.

As a result of its absorption into the Disney empire, ABC is now a highly diversified corporation with extensive U.S. and international interests in broadcasting and cable. The ABC Broadcasting group consists of ten television and 55 radio stations that are owned and operated by ABC, a television network with 225 affiliate stations, a basic radio network that provides programming for 4,600 affiliate stations, and two specialized radio program services—ESPN Radio and Radio Disney. The ABC Cable Networks group oversees a number of cable networks that are either wholly or partially owned by Disney: ABC Family, A&E Television Networks (which include A&E, Biography, and the History Channel), E! Entertainment Television, ESPN Networks (including ESPN International, which reaches 119 million households outside the United States), Lifetime and Lifetime Movies, the Soap Network, Toon Disney, and the Disney Channel and its international versions (seen in 56 countries). In addition to its own sports and news production, ABC now oversees all network and syndicated television production at Disney.

ABC was the first-place network at the time of the merger, but its ratings soon began a downward slide. In just two seasons, ABC fell from first to third in the ratings, losing 23 percent of its target 18- to 49-year-old adult viewers, 35 percent of teens, and 45 percent of children ages two to 11. Unable to deliver its promised ratings, ABC has been forced to compensate advertisers with extra airtime, which cuts deeply into network profits. Operating income dropped from $400 million to $100 million in the first two years of Disney ownership, and the network has posted significant losses in subsequent years. Except for the improbable success of 1999–2000, when *Who Wants to Be a Millionaire?* (aired as many as four times a week) carried the network into first place, ABC's prime-time ratings have never recovered—in part because the network has failed to use opportunities like the fluke success of *Millionaire* to develop new hits. As ABC has dropped into fourth place in the ratings, industry analysts have begun talking about the return to a two-network television universe, in which only NBC and CBS are actually capable of winning the race for prime time.

ABC was created by the U.S. government to address the inequities of a very real two-network universe that monopolized commercial broadcasting in the 1930s. Strictly speaking, there were three dominant radio networks in those days, but while one belonged to CBS the other two belonged to a single company, RCA, which operated both NBC-Red and NBC-Blue. RCA's dominance of the broadcasting industry led to government scrutiny in the late 1930s when the Federal Communications Commission (FCC) investigated the legitimacy of networks—referred to as "chain broadcasting"—that linked together hundreds of local, ostensibly independent stations in national chains commanded by a single owner. The three-year investigation resulted in the 1941 publication of the FCC's Report on Chain Broadcasting, which assailed RCA's influence over a majority of high-powered stations and called for the divorcement of the two NBC networks. RCA challenged the decision in court but failed to overturn the FCC's findings. In October 1943 RCA sold its Blue network for $8 million to Lifesavers candy tycoon Edward J. Noble, and he christened it the American Broadcasting Company.

Unable to match the financial resources of NBC and CBS, ABC could not compete in acquiring programs or attracting affiliates and advertisers. Into this dismal state of affairs relief came as a result of another government intervention into the media industries: the U.S. Supreme Court's 1948 *Paramount* decision. Bringing to conclusion government antitrust proceedings against the major studios of the motion picture industry, the decision ended the industry's vertical integration by requiring the studios to sell their theaters. Along with the other studios, Paramount Pictures was ordered to divest its theater chain and reduce the chain from 1,400 to 650 theaters within five years. In 1951 United Paramount Theaters (UPT), the newly independent theater company led by chairman Leonard Goldenson, offered Edward Noble $25 million for the ABC network.

When the FCC finally approved the merger in 1953, American Broadcasting-Paramount Theaters immediately committed $22 million to develop programming. Instead of competing directly with its rivals, ABC made an unprecedented decision to acquire filmed programs produced in Hollywood. NBC and CBS had a firm grip on TV's big stars and the major corporate sponsors of its live broadcasts. Besides, ABC had a very specific idea of its target market: the "youthful families" of the postwar baby boom who were able to afford staple products and small items at the supermarket but not necessarily costly big-ticket items like a new car or a major appliance.

ABC gambled first on independent producer Walt Disney by committing $2 million a year over seven years for a Disney television series to debut in October 1954. ABC also spent $500,000 to purchase a 35-percent share of Disney's ambitious theme park then under construction. With Disney's name recognition, the television series *Disneyland* attracted nearly half of ABC's advertising billings in 1954–55. The series was an immediate hit. The following season, ABC established its most profitable relationship of the 1950s with Warner Bros., whose initial series, *Warner Bros. Presents,* premiered in 1955 and launched the network's first hit drama, the western *Cheyenne.*

In spite of this taste of success, Leonard Goldenson had never been satisfied with Robert Kintner's leadership as president of the network. In October 1956 Goldenson brought in Oliver Treyz and James Aubrey to replace Kintner, who landed at the more prestigious NBC, where he served as president for another decade. Goldenson himself moved from an office at United Paramount to one at ABC, where he began to oversee the network's day-to-day operations. (He would remain in the network's top position until the Capital Cities merger in 1985.)

With Goldenson's support, Aubrey and Treyz planned for ABC to get big fast, to attract large audiences as quickly as possible in order to establish credibility with advertisers and prospective affiliates. They had no interest in gradually building an audience or in balancing popular hits with prestigious offerings. Without the luxury of time or money for experimentation, their programming philosophy was to exploit proven strengths in an attempt to repeat success. Warner Bros. was happy to oblige. Following the success of *Cheyenne,* the studio delivered the westerns *Maverick, Bronco, Sugarfoot,* and *Colt .45.* In 1958 Warner Bros. introduced *77 Sunset Strip,* a private detective series based in Los Angeles that featured an ensemble of young, attractive stars. ABC responded to the popularity of *77 Sunset Strip* by ordering three nearly identical series that differed only in their sun-drenched locales: *Bourbon Street Beat, Hawaiian Eye,* and *Surfside Six.* ABC's programming strategy became so narrowly focused that, of the 33 series in its 1959–60 schedule, 12 were westerns and seven were crime series.

With the Kennedy-era FCC scrutinizing network television for failing to fulfill its utopian promise—this was the era of FCC chairman Newton Minow's "vast wasteland" speech—and a Senate subcommittee investigating the influence of TV violence on children, ABC came under attack as the network most responsible for the shift to formulaic action series. ABC faced criticism not only for its own programs—the Warner Bros. series and the equally popular *The Untouchables*—but for its perceived influence on programming at NBC and CBS. To compete with the hard-charging ABC, the other networks had abandoned the New York–based, live formats of the 1950s and embraced filmed series made in Hollywood. Since both NBC President Robert Kintner and CBS President James Aubrey had supervised programming at ABC in the 1950s, critics argued that the ABC programming philosophy literally had taken over the airwaves.

The public relations crisis alone would have been a challenge for a network seeking greater credibility to go along with its growing audience, but the trouble was magnified by the near-simultaneous collapse of ABC's ratings. By gambling so heavily on dramas, ABC lacked experience developing situation comedies and was utterly unprepared when public taste swung back toward comedy in the early 1960s. Goldenson fired network chief Oliver Treyz, the architect of ABC's rapid rise, and replaced him with Tom Moore, but it was too late. Except for a few scattered hits over the coming years (*Marcus Welby, M.D.*, *The F.B.I.*, *The Mod Squad*), ABC posed no serious competition to NBC and CBS for more than a decade.

Several factors kept ABC from realizing its potential in the 1960s: its dismal ratings, which limited advertising income; the costly transition to color broadcasting, being driven by RCA, which stood to sell color TV sets, and CBS, which could not afford to fall behind; and the steep rise in programming costs. The network showed a net loss every year between 1963 and 1971 (although these losses were offset at the corporate level by income from AB-PT's theaters, owned-and-operated stations, and other interests).

Given its unrealized potential, ABC was vulnerable to takeover attempts and spent much of the 1960s either fighting off or courting potential suitors. In order to defend against hostile takeovers, Goldenson turned to the International Telephone and Telegraph Corporation (ITT). ITT was a huge conglomerate with interests in international telecommunications, defense and space contracts, publishing, insurance, and car rentals. With nearly 200,000 employees in 52 countries, 60 percent of its revenues from outside the United States, and nearly 10 percent of its shares owned by foreign interests, ITT was one of the first truly transnational conglomerates based in the United States. ITT's president, Harold S. Geneen, wanted to acquire ABC in order to raise his company's profile—and therefore its stock price—in the United States, where ITT had only a murky corporate identity. In December 1965 the two companies announced plans for a merger. Over the next two years the FCC and the Justice Department scrutinized the deal in what became for ABC an excruciatingly protracted series of hearings and investigations. After the long delay imposed by the investigations, ITT withdrew its offer on January 1, 1968.

Considering its history in the 1960s, ABC's resurrection in the 1970s seems nearly miraculous. When Fred Pierce was named ABC president in 1974, he presided over a perennial third-place network that hadn't turned a profit for most of the past decade, a network that had once set the pace of programming innovation but had grown used to haphazard imitation of its network rivals. Under Pierce's leadership, however, ABC rode an unprecedented wave of popular success that carried the network from third place to first in just three years. In 1979, 14 of the top 20 programs on television belonged to ABC. With advertisers and affiliates clamoring to ride the bandwagon, ABC's network profits rocketed upward: $29 million in 1975, $75 million in 1976, $165 million in 1977, and $200 million in 1979. For one year after Pierce assumed his role as president in 1974, Michael Eisner was responsible for ABC's prime-time schedule. Essentially giving up on the schedule left behind by the network's most recent program chiefs, Barry Diller and Martin Starger, Eisner and Pierce introduced six series as midseason replacements in January 1975. Amazingly, three became hits: *Baretta, S.W.A.T.,* and *Barney Miller.* Eisner is also given credit for the decision to transform the moderately successful *Happy Days* by upgrading Henry Winkler's character "Fonzie" to the lead role, a decision that eventually made *Happy Days* the number one series on television.

In spite of Eisner's accomplishments, Pierce sought a more experienced programmer to take the reins at ABC. In May 1975 he won a pubic relations coup by convincing Fred Silverman to leave CBS, where he had been responsible for scheduling many of that network's groundbreaking early 1970s comedies, and take over programming at ABC. After being identified with sophisticated character-based comedy at CBS, Silverman aimed ABC's programming squarely at younger viewers and families: warm family comedy (*Eight is Enough, Happy Days*), wacky farce (*Laverne and Shirley, Three's Company, Soap*), high-concept action (*Charlie's Angels, Six Million Dollar Man*), and escapist fantasy (*The Love Boat, Fantasy Island).*

Sports and news played a central role in ABC's reemergence during the 1970s, particularly in attracting new affiliates and contributing to the network's profile as a national institution, and Roone Arledge is the central figure in the history of both. As the producer of ABC's flagship sports program, *Wide World of Sports,* and then as president of ABC Sports beginning in 1968, Arledge revolutionized television sports coverage. He made sports competition meaningful for television by creating a narrative framework for sporting events, giving each game a storyline and developing ABC's trademark "up close and personal" style that brought out the character and personality of an athlete. He was also a showman, unafraid to burnish the spectacle of sports television with multiple camera angles and flashy graphics or to use outlandish personalities, like Howard Cosell, who often overshadowed the sports they covered.

Arledge was largely responsible for creating *Monday Night Football* in 1970, and it is difficult to exaggerate that program's importance in the history of television or professional sports. In 1977 Pierce appointed Roone Arledge as president of ABC News. Arledge's appointment was surprising, since he had no journalistic training, but his impact was profound. As president of ABC News he presided over the creation of *World News Tonight* in 1978 and *Nightline* in 1979. Later he introduced the prime-time news series, *20/20* and *Primetime,* and the Sunday morning program, *This Week with David Brinkley.* Arledge recruited the on-air talent and behind-the-scenes staff that would make ABC News the most respected news organization in television during the 1980s and early 1990s.

ABC's most innovative and influential programming achievement in the 1970s was the development of the miniseries. Martin Starger, ABC's programming chief in the early 1970s, had a hunch that American audiences might be ready for British-style, limited-episode series and introduced the concept of "novels for television." The milestone in the miniseries format was ABC's broadcast of *Roots,* the powerful adaptation of Alex Haley's multigenerational saga of an African-American family's historical journey through slavery. Because miniseries have a clear beginning and end, they do not require weekly installments and lend themselves to innovative forms of scheduling. This was the case with *Roots,* a 12-hour series that Fred Silverman chose to show in eight consecutive frigid nights in January 1977. In an age of hundred-channel digital cable and TiVo, it is almost impossible to imagine, but 130 million viewers—half the U.S. population—tuned in on the eighth night for the finale of this historical epic.

ABC settled back into the pack during the early 1980s, shortly after Fred Silverman departed for NBC. Under new entertainment president Brandon Stoddard, ABC presented several miniseries that eclipsed its earlier efforts in production cost and running time: *The Day After* (1983), *Winds of War* (1983), *The Thorn Birds* (1983), *War and Remembrance* (1988). The dominant producer at ABC during the 1980s was Aaron Spelling. He had been responsible for such 1970s hits as *Charlie's Angels* and *Fantasy Island,* but the peak of his influence at ABC came in the 1984–85 season, when his drama *Dynasty* was the top-rated series on television.

The new era of corporate mergers and acquisitions dawned at ABC when it was acquired by Capital Cities Communications in 1985 for $3.5 billion. Although CEO and chairman Thomas Murphy and president Dan Burke instituted severe cost-cutting measures throughout ABC following the merger, they kept most of the network management in place and allowed the company's divisions to operate with a considerable degree of autonomy. Murphy and Burke also made farsighted investments in cable networks A&E, the History Channel, Lifetime, and ESPN (which ABC had purchased in 1984).

In 1989 Burke and Murphy unexpectedly chose Robert Iger to succeed Brandon Stoddard as the president of ABC Entertainment. Largely unknown to the creative community in Hollywood because he had come up through ABC Sports, Iger made a strong immediate impression by making series commitments for two of the most radical dramas in television history, both developed by Brandon Stoddard: *Twin Peaks,* produced by David Lynch and Mark Frost, and the musical police drama *Cop Rock,* produced by Stephen Bochco. In doing so, Iger sent a message to the Hollywood creative community that ABC was prepared to take risks and grant creative freedom, without the smothering network oversight so typical of television production.

Iger's four years at the head of ABC Entertainment kicked off the network's last great period of ratings dominance. Iger inherited *thirtysomething* and *Roseanne* from the regime of Brandon Stoddard and added several other series that became long-running hits: *Doogie Howser, NYPD Blue, America's Funniest Home Videos, Home Improvement,* and the highly successful Friday night "TGIF" block of family oriented situation comedies, *Family Matters, Full House,* and *Perfect Strangers.* In the target market of 18- to 49-year-old adults ABC won the prime-time ratings race three times during Iger's tenure. When Disney purchased ABC in 1995 it inherited a prime-time schedule that was second in the 18- to 49-year-old demographic and first in total ratings.

Many factors have contributed to the network's sharp decline in the subsequent years, but Disney's management strategies must bear a large share of the blame. The demand for synergy has skewed network practices, distorting the most fundamental goals of identifying talented writers, producers, and performers in order to develop programs that appeal to viewers. The goal of supplying ABC with Disney-produced series has been an unmitigated disaster. No Disney series since *Home Improvement* has survived long enough to make it into syndication, and it debuted before the merger. ABC has alienated many loyal producers by giving favorable attention to Disney. Disney has failed to assure the Hollywood community that it has sorted out the potential conflicts of interest arising from the alliance of a network and a studio. Some producers are reluctant to bring ideas to Disney for fear that the studio will negotiate below-market-value deals to place its programs on ABC. Other producers worry that Disney will evaluate a project based solely on its perceived benefit to ABC. By the same token, rival networks have grown wary of projects that originate at Disney, assuming that any Disney series available on the open market must already have been rejected by ABC. In 1999 Disney tried to solve some of these problems by consolidating the network and studio under the ABC Entertainment Television Group, which formally united Disney's television production subsidiaries under the management of ABC's prime-time division. Since that time Disney has regained a bit of credibility by placing *Scrubs* on NBC, where it appears to be an emerging hit.

ABC's management of prime time has been equally disastrous, characterized by confusion and an almost ritualistic semiannual sacrifice of programming chiefs. The chaos began when Iger hired (and later fired) Jamie Tarses as head of programming after she had helped to develop comedies such as *Friends* at NBC. Without a clear leader, ABC showed the worst signs of being programmed by committee, with no clear sense of the network's identity and every uncertain decision being second guessed. Tarses alienated some of ABC's most loyal producers, who left the network for production deals elsewhere; Eisner tried to replace Tarses by recruiting Marcy Carsey, the producer of *Roseanne* and *The Cosby Show;* Iger made an expensive, two-year commitment to *Lois and Clark* just before its ratings collapsed; Eisner vetoed development deals negotiated by Iger.

Amid the turmoil, ABC failed to develop new series to replace its fading hits of the early 1990s or to capitalize on small successes like *Ellen.* Even the fleeting success of *Who Wants to Be a Millionaire?,* which some analysts estimate generated $750 million in revenue during its time on the network, led nowhere. When ABC's *Millionaire*-inflated ratings crashed, another programmer, longtime ABC executive Stuart Bloomberg, was fired and replaced by Susan Lyne. Only time will tell how long she survives. ABC finished the 2002–3 season fourth in the coveted 18- to 49-year-old demographic; without the boost provided by the Super Bowl, the ratings would have been worse. Only *Monday Night Football* and several reality series (*The Bachelor, The Bachelorette, Celebrity Mole,* and *Extreme Makeover*) broke into the Nielsen top 30. The average cost of a 30-second spot on ABC is now $50,000 less than its equivalent on NBC.

While prime-time ratings have dropped and the network has floundered, the larger ABC organization has achieved some notable success. The owned-and-operated TV and radio stations are profitable for ABC, as they are for all broadcast networks. Synergy has worked in children's programming, at least, where Disney series fill ABC's Saturday morning schedule and promote the entire range of Disney products. These programs are then distributed to the international Disney channels. The most obvious successes are in Disney's cable television group. While broadcast networks have only a single revenue source—advertising sales—cable networks earn money from advertising and from charging transmission fees to cable and satellite delivery systems, which are passed along to viewers as higher service rates. For the most successful networks, such as Disney's ESPN, these transmission fees can be raised by as much as 20 percent annually. As a result, ESPN has become the world's most valuable network, generating more than $500 million per year and establishing a brand name that Disney has successfully exploited by creating additional ESPN cable channels, an ESPN magazine, and ESPN Zone restaurants. Several of ABC's other cable networks, including the Disney Channel, A&E, and Lifetime (often the most-watched cable network in prime time), have seen steady growth in revenues and profits.

Disney executives will have to make key strategic decisions about how ABC will compete in the world of digital television: how to develop new revenue streams and new digital services; how to use multiple channels and define each channel's identity; how best to create or acquire programming; and how to redefine the network's partnership with affiliate stations. With its unrivaled brand identity and a vast library of titles, Disney certainly will play a role in drawing consumers to new digital program services available on cable, satellites, or the Internet. But what role will the ABC network play, especially if it continues along its current path? Disney president Robert Iger believes that a broadcast network has a synergistic value for a diversified media company that far outweighs its cost.

CHRISTOPHER ANDERSON

See also **Disney, Walt; Eisner, Michael; Iger, Robert; Mergers and Acquisitions; Spelling, Aaron**

Further Reading

Auletta, Ken, *Three Blind Mice: How the TV Networks Lost Their Way,* New York: Random House, 1991

Beddell, Sally, *Up the Tube: Prime-Time TV in the Silverman Years,* New York: Viking Press, 1981

Goldblatt, Henry, "American Broadcasting Crackup," *Fortune* (June 10, 2002)

Goldenson, Leonard H., *Beating the Odds: The Untold Story Behind the Rise of ABC,* New York: Scribner, 1991

Masters, Kim, *Keys to the Kingdom: How Michael Eisner Lost His Grip,* New York: William Morrow, 2000

Quinlan, Sterling, *Inside ABC: American Broadcasting Company's Rise to Power,* New York: Hastings House, 1979

Siklos, Richard, "What ABC Needs Is Home Improvement," *Business Week* (December 14, 1998)

Williams, Huntington, *Beyond Control: ABC and the Fate of the Networks,* New York: Athenaeum, 1989

American Forces Radio and Television Service

American Forces Radio and Television Service (AFRTS) comprises the primary communication media of the American Forces Information Service (AFIS), an agency of the U.S. Department of Defense (DoD). AFRTS provides radio and television news, information, sports, and entertainment programming to U.S. military personnel and their families stationed at U.S. military installations overseas and to U.S. Navy ships at sea.

AFRTS programming, acquired and distributed by the AFRTS Broadcast Center at March Air Reserve Base near Riverside, California, is selected from popular commercial and public programming found in the United States (although commercials are replaced by DoD information and spot announcements). Most AFRTS programming is acquired with little or no charge (for performance rights or residual fees), thanks to industry cooperation dating back to AFRTS beginnings during World War II. AFRTS does not produce its own entertainment shows for television. The entertainment programming includes over 90 percent of the top-rated programs in the United States.

The AFRTS Satellite Network (SATNET) broadcasts 13 radio services and ten television channels containing entertainment, news, information, and sports, which are uplinked from the Broadcast Center. AFRTS provides four television services, including the primary service, American Forces Network (AFN). Additional programming includes AFN News, AFN Sports, and AFN Spectrum (a service that includes programming from PBS and cable networks such as A&E, Discovery, and the History Channel).

To provide service to DoD personnel in more than 177 countries and U.S. territories worldwide, AFRTS uses eight satellites, reaching more than 800,000 U.S. service members and their families. More than 120 U.S. Navy ships at sea also receive live television and radio channels via the Navy's "Direct to Sailor" (DTS) initiative (created in 1997 to serve sailors and Marines specifically). The Naval Media Center participates with AFRTS in inserting unique Navy Department information programming via the DTS transmissions.

In 1996 AFRTS replaced its worldwide circuiting of videotaped programming with live satellite broadcasts of multiple radio and television channels. For many years, AFRTS broadcasts also reached a substantial "shadow" audience of U.S. citizens living abroad and citizens of host nations who viewed or listened to the programming. Although no official figures exist for the size of this shadow audience worldwide, one study of the audience in Japan found that 21 percent of the local population (approximately 25 million people) listened to AFRTS radio at least once a week. However, the shadow audience is diminishing as AFRTS has reduced its dependence on low-power, over-the-air broadcast transmissions and instead expanded its direct-to-home satellite service (where military personnel lease or purchase the service from the base exchange) and cable distribution within military installations. Nevertheless, one could safely conclude that the formerly enormous presence of AFRTS broadcasts worldwide probably played an important role in informal English-language instruction and in fostering a general acceptance of U.S. cultural products worldwide.

AFRTS's history can be traced to several small radio stations established by servicemen in Panama, Alaska, and the Philippines near the start of World War II. Following the success and popularity of these small operations, the Armed Forces Radio Service (AFRS) was established by the U.S. War Department on May 26, 1942, with the intent of improving troop morale by giving service members a "touch of home." The military also sought to provide a source of information to U.S. servicemen that would counter enemy propaganda (such as that found in the broadcasts of Axis Sally and Tokyo Rose), although officials denied the move was an attempt at counterpropaganda.

During the war, AFRS programs proved enormously popular with the troops and were made financially possible largely through the contributions of radio and film stars, who donated their time regularly without charge. Two of the more popular programs were *Command Performance* and *Mail Call,* which presented such stars as Bob Hope, Jack Benny, Clark Gable, Red Skelton, Bing Crosby, Dinah Shore, and the Andrews Sisters, among many others. Although these stars unselfishly gave of their time to contribute to the patriotic war effort, their careers most certainly did not suffer from the exposure of a somewhat captive audience. By the end of the war, there were nearly 300 AFRS radio stations operating worldwide (however, that number decreased to only 60 some four years later). Since that time, the number of stations continues to increase and decrease, depending on the level of U.S. military commitments worldwide.

Television came relatively late to the AFRS, considering the enormous impact the medium was having on American society. The impetus to introduce television, in fact, came from the need to address serious morale problems in the Strategic Air Command. Armed Forces Television (AFT) got its start at Limestone Air Force Base, Maine, in 1953, and after much success in helping to reduce absences without leave, court martials, and the divorce rate at this military installation, AFT was officially joined with the AFRS in 1954 to become AFRTS. AFRTS introduced color television in the early 1970s and was one of the first broadcasters to begin using satellites for live news and sports, doing so as early as 1968.

The AFRTS maintains that its programming is provided "without censorship, propagandizing, or manipulation." The first notable exceptions to that claim surfaced during the Vietnam War period. From 1963 to 1967, AFRTS was instructed by Defense Secretary Robert McNamara to broadcast news-analysis programs produced by the United States Information Agency (USIA)—material that was widely recognized as propaganda. The more serious challenge to AFRTS's noninterference claims came from broadcast outlets and journalists in Vietnam itself. Although AFRTS and various military policymakers maintained that censorship of programming was prohibited, numerous controversies arose (both public and internal) over news, quotes, and specific words and phrases that were kept off the air due to AFRTS guidelines. According to a history of the AFRTS commissioned by the service for its 50th anniversary, such restrictions even included "the editing of President Johnson's comments that the command believed were inaccurate." Justifications for such restrictions most often included the desire to avoid injuring troop morale, helping the enemy, or offending the host nation's sensitivities.

Although the broadcasting arm of AFRTS still maintains its claim to no censorship, it admits that local AFN stations have the right to "change the schedule to avoid broadcast of the offending programming" in some host nations. The direct broadcasting of American news programming via SATNET created problems for AFRTS broadcasters in nations particularly sensitive to criticism (such as Korea and the Philippines), but AFRTS contends that the move to new distribution systems to military households has alleviated this problem.

JEFFREY P. JONES

Further Reading

American Forces Information Service and Armed Forces Radio and Television Service, *History of AFRTS: The First 50 Years,* Washington, D.C.: U.S. Department of Defense, 1992

American Movie Classics

U.S. Cable Network

Near the close of the 20th century, the cable channel American Movie Classics (AMC) quietly became one of the fastest-growing television networks in the United States and one of the great success stories of the emergence of cable TV in the United States. Film fans loved AMC for showing classic, uncut, uncolorized Hollywood films of the 1930s, 1940s, and 1950s, with no interruptions from advertisements. However, at the beginning of the 21st century, AMC allowed a growing number of advertisements between screenings.

Over-the-air television had already served as the principal second-run showcase for Hollywood films from the mid-1950s, 1960s, and 1970s. However, the number of over-the-air TV stations in any one market limited the possible showcases for classic Hollywood films. Film buffs in major markets could watch independent television stations that frequently counterprogrammed with Hollywood movies, but they were generally displeased with the ways in which stations sanitized the presentations of theatrical films, cut them to fit them into prescribed time slots, and interrupted moving moments with blaring advertisements. With the emergence of cable television in the 1980s, AMC offered a niche for these fans, who sometimes referred

Courtesy of the Everett Collection

to the channel as the "Metropolitan Museum of classic movies." Indeed, AMC created a "repertory" cinema operable by remote control.

AMC began in October 1984 as a pay service but switched onto cable's "basic tier" in 1987, when the network had grown to 7 million subscribers in 1,000 systems across the United States. This growth curve continued, and by the end of 1989 AMC had doubled its subscriber base. Two years later it could count 39 million subscribers. As of January 2002, AMC's parent company, Rainbow Media Holdings (itself a subsidiary of Cablevision System and NBC), reported that the number of American households with access to AMC had reached more than 82 million.

No cable service in the United States has received more favorable reviews. Critics applaud AMC's around-the-clock presentation of Hollywood favorites and undiscovered gems. AMC also has created first-run documentaries that focus on various aspects of the movie business, such as a corporate profile of Republic Studios, a compilation history entitled *Stars and Stripes: Hollywood and World War II,* and a history of boxing movies labeled *Knockout: Hollywood's Love Affair with Boxing.* As of 2002 AMC also featured three original series about films and the film industry: *Backstory,* a weekly program about the making of specific Hollywood pictures; *Hollywood Lives and Legends,* which airs every weeknight and presents documentaries about movie studios, themes such as "Hollywood interpretations of the Bible," and on- and off-screen film personalities; and the weekly series *Cinema Secrets,* which explores how special effects are used in various film projects. Other programming on AMC includes comedy shorts featuring such performers as the Three Stooges or the Little Rascals.

AMC has sometimes filled slots between films with old Twentieth Century Fox Movietone Newsreels, allowing fans to watch once again as a bored John Barrymore puts his profile into the cement in front of Grauman's Chinese Theater or Shirley Temple accepts her special Oscar, then asks her mother if it is time to go home.

In other ways, too, AMC has unabashedly promoted its nostalgia-as-escapism. Consider a late 1980s marketing device by AMC and the local cable system in Wichita Falls, Texas, designed to launch AMC in that market. More than 200 couples dance in a room, painted black and white, while the sound of Gordy Kilgore's big band playing Glenn Miller's "In the Mood" fills the air.

By June 1988 AMC was successful enough to begin publishing a magazine. An old-time classic star graces the cover of each issue of *AMC Magazine;* the first featured Katharine Hepburn, later came James Stewart, Marilyn Monroe, Gregory Peck, John Wayne, and Henry Fonda, among others. Articles typically discuss the stars of the "golden age" of Hollywood (keyed to AMC showings). The magazine also includes listings of that month's AMC offerings, highlighting festivals constructed around stars, series (such as the Charlie Chan films), and themes ("Super Sleuths," for example).

However, there are limitations to the successes and benefits of AMC. Unless a new preservation print has been made (as was the case with the silent 1927 classic *Wings*), AMC runs television prints. These versions of the films are often incomplete, having been edited during the 1950s and 1960s to eliminate possibly offensive languages and images. Often TV prints have been cut to run a standard 88 minutes, timed to fit into two-hour time slots, with time allotted for advertisements. AMC runs these incomplete prints, deciding not to spend the necessary moneys to create a complete version.

Fans rarely complain about the TV prints, however, and cable operators herald AMC as what is best about cable television. The channel has replaced the repertory cinemas that used to dot the United States's largest cities and college towns and serves as a fine example of specialized niche programming in cable TV of the 1990s. As the 21st century commenced, its only serious rival was Turner Classic Movies.

DOUGLAS GOMERY

See also **Cable Networks; Movies on Television**

Further Reading

Alexander, Ron, "AMC: Where the Movie Never Ends," *New York Times* (November 17, 1991)

Brown, Rich, "Cablevision Pays $170 Million for AMC," *Broadcasting & Cable* (September 20, 1993)

Dempsey, John, "Profitable AMC Turns 10; Sets for Some Classic Competition," *Variety* (September 26, 1994)

Moshavi, Sharon D., "AMC Buys Universal Packaging," *Broadcasting* (20 May 1991)

American Women in Radio and Television

American Women in Radio and Television (AWRT) is a nonprofit organization headquartered in Washington, D.C. Originally conceived as the women's division of the National Association of Broadcasters, AWRT became an independent entity in 1950. At its first convention, AWRT had 282 women members. Today, the group maintains approximately 2,300 men and women members, largely employed by television and radio stations nationwide.

Although people of both genders can join and serve as officers, the organization's mission is to advance the impact of women in broadcasting and related fields. The group furthers community service, member employment, and education. The organization also has a definite social consciousness. AWRT produces an award-winning series of public service announcements, which have focused upon subjects such as outstanding American women preventing sexual harassment in the workplace. Its agenda has also included, as an issue for study, a concern for indecency in broadcast content.

The organization serves many functions for its members. Its nearly 30 local chapters provide a place for social and professional networking. Some chapters are an important force in their local broadcast communities; others are merely meeting places for people in similar professions. Local activities vary, but often include "Soaring Spirits" benefits to help children's hospitals, scholarship fund-raising for area college students, awards for local media professionals, educational seminars, career development, and job listing dispersal. Local chapter members also mentor meetings of the affiliated College Students in Broadcasting, a club composed of dues-paying students organized at university campus chapters.

On the national level, the organization provides many services. The main office is helmed by full-time employees and directed by both nationally elected officers and an advisory board. Within the organization, the most essential activity is an annual convention held each spring. In the past, convention activities included lobbying in Washington, recreation in Phoenix, Arizona, and education in Florida. As of 2002, however, the organization has chosen to curtail its annual meetings and instead host a yearly training seminar. This policy has been dictated by a decline in the number of members.

The organization also houses the AWRT Foundation, which is designed to help fund research, publication, institutes, lectures, and the general advancement of the electronic media and allied fields. Since 1975 the foundation has been awarding its Gracie Allen

Courtesy of the American Women in Radio and Television, Inc. (AWRT)

Awards, to honor quality programming by women, for women, and about women in broadcasting, cable, and new media.

AWRT's Washington office sponsors the annual Star Awards, which recognize media professionals or companies facilitating women's issues and concerns, whereas the Silver Satellite and the Achievement Awards commend success or advancements in electronic media fields.

The chapters differ greatly from each other. For example, the Austin, Texas, chapter's monthly luncheon serves as the primary local meeting place for executives and managers in cable, broadcasting, and advertising. Its activities include speakers with the latest news on industry developments, a preview night for each network's new fall programs in September, a Soaring Spirits five-kilometer run, sponsorship of student scholarships, and the definitive Austin media Christmas party.

In contrast, the southern California chapter has a large sampling of television producers, on-air talent, network executives, educators, screenwriters, and actors in its ranks. Its main annual fundraising event is the Genii Awards luncheon, which honors an outstanding broadcast executive and a performer. Past winners have included producers Marian Rees and Linda Bloodworth Thomason and actors Tyne Daly and Candace Bergen. Other activities include a "Meeting of the Minds" seminar updating the legal and technical knowledge in communication operations, a "Boot Camp" night, where teams wearing military gear attempt to rearrange network programming schedules to maximize competition, and the more typical social gatherings and guest speakers. The chapter gives more than five scholarships annually, each awarded to a College Students in Broadcasting member.

Although different in membership, clout, and structure, each local chapter uses the services of the national office to disseminate industry knowledge and job information. AWRT helps keep its members up to date in a rapidly changing industrial setting.

JOAN STULLER GIGLIONE

Further Reading

American Women in Radio and Television, Inc., *AWRT 1992 Resource Directory,* Washington, D.C.: American Women in Radio and Television, 1992

"AWRT Prepares for the 21st Century," *Broadcasting* (May 6, 1985)

Duncan, Jacci, editor, *Making Waves: The 50 Greatest Women in Radio and Television, As Selected by American Women in Radio and Television,* Kansas City, Missouri: Andrews McNeel, 2001

"Patricia Niekamp: Raising the Visibility of AWRT," *Broadcasting* (May 14, 1990)

Rathbun, Elizabeth, "AWRT Looks Ahead to Take Place on Superhighway," *Broadcasting & Cable* (May 30, 1994)

Sheridan, Patrick J., "AWRT Panel Addresses Indecency Issue," *Broadcasting* (May 28, 1990)

Americanization

During a nightly newscast of the Canadian Broadcasting Corporation's *CBC Prime Time News,* the anchorman, in the last news item before the public affairs portion of the program, presented words to this effect: How would you like to have a house that would cost next to nothing to build and to maintain, with no electrical or heating bills? Viewers were then shown four young Inuit adults building an igloo. They were born in the Arctic region, said the spokeswoman of the group, but had not learned the ancestral skills of carving (literally) a human shelter out of this harsh environment (-35° Celsius at night). It was a broad hint that the spin on this story would be "Young aboriginals in search of their past." The real twist, however, was that their instructors, a middle-aged man and woman, were Caucasian and that the man was born in Detroit, Michigan. The American had studied environmental architecture and was teaching this particular technique to the young Inuits.

When asked if they were embarrassed by this arrangement, the spokeswoman answered, "No. If he teaches us what we need to know, then that's all right." When asked if he found the situation a bit strange, the Detroit-born man also answered in the negative, "I was born in Detroit, but I do not know how to build a car." In fact, it was one of the Inuit hunters who had taught him how to repair his snowmobile. So why shouldn't he teach young Inuits to build igloos? In the last scene the igloo builders lay out their seal rugs and light a small fire using seal oil, enabling the heat to ice the inside walls, thus insulating the dwelling from the outside cold and creating warmth within. A final shot shows the lighted igloos against the black night sky.

Many things can be read into this short narrative. First, the typical, white, Canadian anchorman, by referring to concerns of southern Canadians (low building and maintenance costs, no taxes, clear air, and quiet neighborhoods), trivializes a technology that, over thousands of years, has allowed populations to survive and create specific societies and cultures in this particular environment. Second, we are made aware of the benefits of international trade: an Inuit teaches a Detroit-born American how to repair a motor vehicle and, in return, learns how to build an igloo. Third, we are led to understand that what the students expect from the teacher is basic working skills.

The temptation to build a case denouncing cultural imperialism, bemoaning the alienation of aboriginal cultures and the shredding of their social fabric, is strong here. On the basis of this one example, however, the argument would at best be flawed, at worst biased. However, for students of popular culture, national identity, and cultural industries, this is but one of the many thousand daily occurrences that exemplify the dynamic complexity of the concept of "Americanization."

Embedded within that term are at least two notions: the American presence and the presence of an American. In this news story, both notions are at work. On the one hand, the viewer is made aware of the American presence, and the influence of American technology on this remote society, through the reference to the snowmobile. (Although the Quebec-born inventor of the snowmobile founded what later became the internationally renowned Canadian Bombardier industries, the fact that the Detroit-born American puts the snowmobile on the same footing as the automobile implicitly makes it seem to be an American invention.) On the other hand, the viewer sees and hears the American instructor.

It is the first form of presence that usually defines the concept of Americanization. The term usually refers to the presence of American products and technology, and it is against this presence that most critics argue. Surprisingly, few argue against the presence of Americans themselves. It is perhaps this distinction that has become most significant in light of the worldwide conglomeration of media industries. Rupert Murdoch's forays into Asian and European national contexts via satellite broadcasting, the purchase of Universal Studios, first by Japanese and later by French owners, and the success of Hong Kong action cinema throughout the world all complicate notions of Americanization. Has Universal Television become Japanese, or French? Has Indian television become American (or Australian) in light of Murdoch's incursions? These questions suggest the complicated nature of intersections of identity, culture, and technology.

One is led to believe that one will become an American, will be Americanized, not by interacting with citizens of the United States but by using American products, eating American (fast) food, and enjoying American cultural artifacts. One can go so far as to live and work in the United States while remaining staunchly Canadian or Australian or British, as many artists who have succeeded in the American music and film industries remind us. The danger of becoming Americanized seems greater, however, if one remains within the comfort of one's home enjoying American cultural products such as magazines, novels, movies, music, comics, television shows and news, or computer software and games.

While these two embedded notions, the presence of Americans and the American presence, make for a fascinating debate, the concept of Americanization conceals the parallel dual notion of "the host." Hosting the American presence seems to be more prevalent and more Americanizing than hosting Americans themselves. To be a host is to make the visitor feel welcome, to make the visitor seem familiar, nonthreatening, at home. In one case, the Canadian host makes the American visitor feel welcome, "at home away from home"; in the second case, the Canadian host is "at home" in the presence of American artifacts that are part of her or his everyday way of life. To become Americanized, it is not only presumed that one consumes a steady diet of readily accessible made-in-the-U.S. products but also that one consumes these cultural products with ease: that is, as would any American.

American products are distributed internationally but are not made for international markets: they are made for the U.S. market, by, for, and about Americans. Thus, one can conclude, to enjoy these easily accessible products, one must be or become American and the more one consumes, the more one becomes American, thereby enabling increasing pleasure and ease in this consumption. Americanization is a case in point of a basic process of acculturation. It results in sounding the alarms of cultural imperialism and cultural alienation: you become what you consume, because in order to consume, you must become the targeted consumer. This is the equivalent of saying, because science (as we believe we know it) is a product of Western European civilization, then to become a scientist one must become Westernized: that is, adopt Western mores, values, and ways of thinking.

In most host countries in the world, there is an overwhelming presence of American products. The pull and pressure of those products must not be underestimated. Still, the news story of the Inuit mechanic and the Detroit igloo builder serves as a reminder that culture, or at least certain types of culture, are less bound by the economics of their technological environment and modes of production than was once assumed and theorized.

The fact that the Inuit travel on snowmobiles, live in suburban dwellings, watch a great deal of television, and have forgotten how to build igloos does not necessarily make them more Americanized when compared with the Detroit-born teacher, who is made no less American by his ability to build an igloo. Skills, products, and ideas take root in historically given contexts: they bear witness to their times. When they travel, they bring with them elements of their place of origin. To use these ideas and products, one must have an understanding of their historical background or context, of their original intent, and of their mode of operation. If the invention and the corresponding mode of production of goods and ideas are context bound, so too are their uses, and, in many cases, these have an impact on the very nature of products and ideas. This perspective leads to a better understanding of Americanization.

American composers, playwrights, and various other artists have undoubtedly affected the popular arts of the world. With the same degree of certitude, one can proclaim that American entrepreneurs and American entrepreneurship have affected the cultural industries the world over. But perhaps the most profound impact of this particular historical culture and its modes of production is found in the social uses American society has made of these cultural products. If one wishes to speak of Americanization in the realm of popular (or mass) culture, one must focus on the social uses of industrially produced and commercially distributed sounds and images. To show American-made movies in local theaters, to watch American sitcoms on the television set, to listen to American music on the radio—or to use copycat versions of any of these materials—is not, necessarily, to become Americanized. To build into the local social fabric of a non-American society the kind of social uses that Americans have made of industrially produced cultural products *is* to become Americanized but not necessarily to become an American.

To live and work and play in a permanent kaleidoscope world of industrially produced images and sounds (for example, television sets turned on all day; ads overflowing in print, on buses, on T-shirts, talk radio, Walkmans, etc.) means to share a mediated worldview. This, it can be argued, is to become Americanized, and such results are among those most often cited when the reach of newer technologies and the concentration of media ownership are examined as global forces. Yet this, too, it can also be argued, does not mean one necessarily shares an American worldview.

The *Dallas* imperialism syndrome, and its legitimate heir, the O.J. Simpson trial, are good illustrations of this distinction. The debate surrounding the reception by viewers worldwide of the U.S. serial *Dallas* rekindles the debate that greeted the American penny press and Hollywood cinema. Its central question: Is communication technology a threat to basic (Western) values, local cultures, and the human psyche? *Dallas* symbolized this ongoing debate, a debate central to Western culture. But *Dallas* also symbolized a social evolution that has not received the attention it deserves. The worldwide popularity of *Dallas* revived the paradigm of the "magic bullet" theory of direct media effects, a theory suggesting that media content and style can be "injected" into the cultural life system, infecting and contaminating the "healthy" cultural body. It also revived discussions of cultural imperialism, but in a more sophisticated fashion and on a much grander scale. And it raised the counterparadigm of the uses-and-gratifications model in communication studies.

Many researchers were eager to publish their claims that *Dallas* did not magically turn all its viewers into Americans, but that the program signified many things to many viewers. Moreover, they pointed out that, on the whole, national cultural products (including television programs) still outsold imported American ones. If they did not, they certainly enjoyed more popular support and provided more enjoyment.

Forgotten in this foray was the fact that *Dallas* symbolized the popularization and the banalization of television viewing, its normal integration within the activities of everyday life, its quiet nestling in the central foyer of the household environment. Television viewing, a remarkable new social practice in many locations, quickly and quietly became, inside and outside academia, a major source of everyday conversation, the measuring stick of many moral debates, the epitome of modern living. In so doing, television viewing displaced the boundaries of centuries-old institutions such as family, work, school, and religion. The *Dallas* syndrome symbolized the fact that in a large number of host countries, communication technology had become a permanent part of the everyday social environment, that its messages had become a permanent part of the social fabric, and that its spokespersons had joined the public club of opinion makers.

While one can debate the pros and cons of this social fact, one can also speculate that television is not the revolution that many of its critics as well as admirers had hoped or feared. It did not destroy a sacred treasure of Western values based on the technology of the written word. Rather, it revealed a blind spot among many social thinkers: the constructed centrality of the spoken word in modern societies. Television possibly revealed to the most industrialized society of the postwar era, the United States, that it was and still is, by and large, an oral society.

Communication technology did not trigger a revolution, social, moral, or sexual; it became part of the establishment in every way, shape, and form. Just as U.S. cultural industries have become an American institution, a part of the social order, and a sustainer of culture in American society, so too have cultural industries in many other societies. In this sense, other societies have become Americanized. Americanization is not to be found in the consumption of American cultural products. It lies in the establishment of a particular social formation. This formation is, to be sure, defined in part by the use of the products of national cultural industries. However, it is also defined by alterations in patterns of everyday life and by the emergence of "new" voices that take their place among existing relations and structures of power. The uses of television throughout the world are both cause and effect within these cultural and social shifts

Thus, Americanization is neither a boon nor a threat. Rather, it is a cultural and economic fact of life in most (Western) countries. The debate, therefore, should not concern whether to stop or to hasten the consumption of American cultural products. It should instead be centered on the impact of specific social uses of industrially mass-produced cultural products, whether foreign or national. For better or worse, the socialization of sounds and images, and socialization *through* sounds and images, have made more visible, and more mainstream, the oral traditions and the tradition of orality not only in American society but also in all (Western) Americanized societies.

It matters little whether television, and other technologically based cultural industries, were invented by the Americans or not. What Americans invented was a particular social use of these technologies: the massification of production, distribution, and consumption, and the commodification of industrially produced cultural products. In return, this particular social use revealed to American society, and to other industrialized societies that followed suit, the forgotten presence of traditional, nonnational, oral cultures. Cultural industries, and television in particular, revealed that print technology (the written word) had not subverted oral technology (the spoken word); the former had only partially silenced the latter by making it less "visible." Television made words and sound once again "visible" and "audible" to the eyes and ears of the mind. In doing so, it also revealed to the heavily industrialized, print-oriented, Western societies that they were blinded by their most popular visual aid, television.

In the wake of the terrorist attacks on the United States on September 11, 2001, a comparatively innocuous story that appeared in the major Canadian newspapers revealed yet another shadowy dimension to the debate about Americanization, one that perhaps indicates a willingness to downplay the notion's politics. While the event referred to here is rather anecdotal, and is presented in this vein, it does point to the reality of the imperialism of politics.

As one newspaper reported (the *Toronto Globe and Mail*), in his televised address to a joint session of the U.S. Congress on September 20, 2001, President George W. Bush thanked countries as far away as Australia and El Salvador for their support of the United States, but he "overlooked" Canada's "housing and feeding 45,000 stranded U.S. airline passengers in the days after the attacks on the World Trade Center and the Pentagon."

On the very next day, U.S. Secretary of State Colin Powell, in a joint press conference with Canada's Minister of External Affairs John Manley, put a spin on the "incident" by thanking the Canadian "brothers and sisters" for their generosity and assistance. In a later meeting with Canadian Prime Minister Jean Chrétien, on September 25, President Bush is quoted as reiterating this notion that Canada is like "a brother" to the United States, so it should not need public acknowledgment of its efforts since the terrorist strikes. While Mexico may be the United States's friend to the south, Canada is "family." Canadians need no longer to debate whether they are Americanized, or becoming American; they have been "adopted." From the status of neighbor to the north, to ally, to friend, Canada's political relation to the United States has been upgraded to consanguinity. Canada took more than a half-century to become Americanized; it took less than a week to be designated, in a politically correct fashion, as American.

ROGER DE LA GARDE

See also **Audience Research**

Further Reading

Bell, Philip, and Roger Bell, editors, *Americanization and Australia,* Sydney: University of New South Wales, 1998

Canclini, Néstor García, *Consumers and Citizens: Globalization and Multicultural Conflicts,* translated by George Yúdice, Minneapolis: University of Minnesota Press, 2001

Kroes, Rob, *If You've Seen One, You've Seen the Mall: Europeans and American Mass Culture,* Urbana: University of Illinois Press, 1996

Liebes, Tamar, and Elihu Katz, *The Export of Meaning: Cross Cultural Readings of "Dallas,"* Cambridge, England: Polity, 1990

Lull, James, *China Turned On: Television, Reform, and Resistance,* London and New York: Routledge, 1991

McKay, George, editor, *Yankee Go Home (And Take Me With U): Americanization and Popular Culture,* Sheffield, England: Sheffield Academic Press, 1997

Moores, Shaun, *Media and Everyday Life in Modern Society,* Edinburgh: Edinburgh University Press, 2000
Negrine, Ralph, and S. Papathanassopoulos, *The Internationalization of Television,* London: Pinter, 1990
Nordenstreng, Kaarle, and Tapio Varis, *Television Traffic—A One-Way Street? A Survey and Analysis of the International Flow of Television Programme Material,* Paris: UNESCO, 1974
Schiller, Herbert, *Mass Media and the American Empire,* New York: Augustus M. Kelly, 1969
Sepstrup, Preben, *Transnationalization of Television in Europe,* London: John Libbey, 1990
Silverstone, Roger, *Television and Everyday Life,* London and New York: Routledge, 1994
Smith, Anthony, *The Age of Behemoths: The Globalization of Mass Media Firms,* New York: Priority Press, 1991
Tunstall, Jeremy, *The Media Are American: Anglo-American Media in the World,* London: Constable, 1977
Varis, Tapio, *International Flow of Television Programs,* Paris: UNESCO, 1986
Wasko, Janet, *Hollywood in the Information Age: Beyond the Silver Screen,* Austin: University of Texas Press, 1994
Wells, A.F., *Picture Tube Imperialism? The Impact of U.S. Television on Latin America,* New York: Orbis, 1972

America's Funniest Home Videos

U.S. Reality-Based Comedy/Contest

A peculiar variant of reality-based television programming, *America's Funniest Home Videos* (*AFHV*) first aired as a Thanksgiving special in 1989 and later debuted on January 14, 1990, as a regular series on ABC, where it was broadcast for roughly a decade before being put on hiatus. It returned for its 11th season as a regular series in 2001. The program's simple premise—to solicit and exhibit a series of humorous video clips shot by amateurs who compete for cash prizes—has had a surprisingly enduring run on network television. *AFHV* entered into syndication in 1995.

Rooted generally in the subgenre of its comical, voyeuristic predecessors, such as *Candid Camera, TV's Bloopers and Practical Jokes,* and *Life's Most Embarrassing Moments, AFHV* more particularly owes its genesis to a weekly variety show produced by the Tokyo Broadcasting Company (TBC), *Fun with Ken and Kato Chan,* which featured a segment in which viewers were invited to mail in their home video clips. Vin Di Bona, who had earlier success with other TBC properties, eventually purchased U.S. rights to the Japanese concept. As executive producer, Di Bona expanded the segment into a half-hour hybrid of home video, variety show, stand-up comedy, and audience participation synthesized to fit the ABC profile of family viewing.

Although indebted to a prevalence of reality-based programs when it debuted, *AFHV* had a far greater and more immediate impact on weekly ratings than any of its predecessors or imitators. Cracking the Nielsen top five after only six episodes, by March 1990 it had become the highest-ranked series on Sunday evenings, temporarily unseating CBS's *60 Minutes,* a feat no other ABC program had been able to achieve in 12 years. In many instances since then, it has won its time period among children, teenagers, and women and men ages 18 to 34.

At the series' peak of popularity, producers reported receiving close to 2,000 video submissions a day. These tapes, eventually sorted out by screeners for broadcast approval, must meet criteria that render them suitable for family audiences. First and foremost, qualifying videos should portray funny, amazing, or unexpected events in everyday life, such as animal antics, blunders at birthday parties, bloopers during wedding ceremonies, and fouled plays at sporting events. Because the series emphasizes the supposed universality and spontaneity of slapstick humor, tapes that depict extreme violence, offensive conduct, and serious physical injury, or that encourage imitative behavior, are strictly forbidden. Deliberately staged videos, such as parodies of advertisements or lip-synching of popular songs, may be accepted, but, in general, events rigged to look accidental or spontaneous are disqualified (or were reserved for Di Bona's follow-up program, *America's Funniest People,* now defunct, but created especially to accommodate staged video performances).

Once a clip is approved for *AFHV,* the clip's creators and performers must sign releases for broadcast autho-

America's Funniest Home Videos, Bob Saget, 1990–97.
©ABC/ Courtesy of the Everett Collection

rization. Then follows a process during which clips are adjusted for uniform quality and matched in terms of production values, embellished with sound effects and wisecracking voice-overs by the host, organized as a montage related to a loose theme (e.g., dogs, talent shows, skiing), and finally, nestled into the format of the program. Each episode is first taped before a live studio audience, with the clips broadcast upon studio monitors so that the series' producers can gauge audience reaction. After subsequent reviews of the taping, producers pass on their recommendations to the staff, who edit out the less-successful moments before the program is broadcast nationwide. Although labor intensive, this method of television production is a relative bargain, costing less per episode than the average sitcom, and has been imitated (for example, by FOX's *Totally Hidden Video*).

Television critics have been somewhat puzzled by the continued success of *AFHV,* many having panned the series as yet another illustration of the American public's increasing willingness to broadcast their most private and embarrassing moments. Several hypotheses for the series' popularity have been cited: the desire of the viewing public to get on television in order to secure their 15 minutes of fame, the possibility of winning a $10,000 cash prize ($100,000 for "grand prize" shows), the all-expenses-paid weekend trip to Hollywood to attend studio tapings, the charisma of original host Bob Saget, the first performer since Arthur Godfrey to star in two concurrent, high-rated series (the other being the ABC family sitcom *Full House*), the universal identification with everyday life fundamental to home movies and home video, and the sheer fun of producing television about and for oneself. The series' producers, however, cite the program's humor as the key to its success. Taking the "Bullwinkle approach," which provokes different kinds of laughter from both children and their parents, *AFHV* not only seeks to attract a wide demographic but self-consciously mocks itself as insignificant, harmless fun.

Despite its overt lack of pretension, *AFHV* remains significant on several accounts, especially its international origins and appeal. Banking upon the perceived cross-cultural universality of home video productions, Di Bona had conceived of the series as international from its inception. *AFHV* has been seen in at least 70 countries and in more than a dozen languages (it is rumored to be the favorite show of the sultan of Brunei). Di Bona has subsequently sold the format rights to producers in other nations, at least 16 of which have created their own versions, while others merely replace the U.S. host with indigenous hosts. Most international affiliates also have clip trade agreements; *AFHV* itself liberally blends domestic and imported clips (blurring the title's emphasis on "America" and pointing to television's partnership in global capitalism).

Also significant is the series' premise that the typical consumers of television may become its producers, that the modes of television reception and production are more dialogic than unidirectional. This inversion, as well as the format's unique hybridization of genres, results in peculiar effects worthy of investigation: the professional's commissioning of the amateur for commercial exploitation; the home video's simultaneous status as folk art and mass media; the promise of reward through competition that reinflects the home mode of production's typical naïveté and noncommercial motivation with formal contrivance and financial incentives; the stress on comedy that excludes the banal everyday activities most typical of home video; and, finally, the format's allowance for a studio audience to vote for and reward their favorite video clip, maintaining the illusion of home video's folksy character, while the cash first prize reifies the slapstick conventions that the producers seek and that keep home viewers tuning in.

James Moran

See also **Camcorder**

Hosts

Bob Saget (1990–97)
Daisy Fuentes (1998–2000)
John Fugelsang (1998–2000)
Tom Bergeron (2001–)

Producer

Vin Di Bona

Programming History

ABC

January 1990–February 1993	Sunday 8:00–8:30
March 1993–May 1993	Sunday 7:00–7:30
May 1993–September 1993	Sunday 8:00–8:30
September 1993–December 1994	Sunday 7:00–7:30
January 1995–June 1996	Sunday 7:00–8:00
January 1997	Sunday 8:00–9:00
February 1997	Sunday 7:00–8:00
March 1997	Sunday 8:00–9:00
April 1997–May 1997	Sunday 7:00–8:00
May 1997–September 1997	Sunday 8:00–9:00
January 1998–August 1998	Monday 8:00–9:00
July 1998–December 1998	Saturday 8:00–9:00
1999–2000	various days and times
July 2001–	Friday 8:00–9:00

Further Reading

"Bob Saget, the Host with the Most on His Busy, Busy Mind," *People Weekly* (March 26, 1990)

Coe, Steve, "Home Is Where the Video Is," *Broadcasting & Cable* (April 12, 1993)

Delsohn, Steve, "The Hip, Low-Key Host of This Season's Most Surprising Hit," *TV Guide* (March 31, 1990)

Elm, Joanna, and Lisa Schwartzbaum, "Tonight's Hot Story Is Brought to You by You!: How the Camcorder Is Changing TV Newscasts," *TV Guide* (February 24, 1990)

Fore, Steve, "America, America, This Is You!: The Curious Case of *America's Funniest Home Videos,*" *Journal of Popular Film and Television* (Spring 1993)

Goldman, Kevin, "*60 Minutes* Show Beaten in Ratings by *Home Videos,*" *Wall Street Journal* (February 27, 1990)

Hiltbrand, David, "America's Funniest Home Videos," *People Weekly* (March 5, 1990)

Kaufman, Joanne, "America, Let's Go to Tape!," *People Weekly* (March 26, 1990)

Lippman, John, "ABC to Warn Viewers About Risky Videos; The Network Was Prompted by Mounting Criticism About Safety of Some Acts in Its Mega-Hit, *America's Funniest Home Videos,*" *Los Angeles Times* (April 14, 1990)

Lyons, Jeffrey, "The Best of *America's Funniest Home Videos,*" *Video Review* (August 1991)

Moran, James, *There's No Place Like Home Video,* Minneapolis: University of Minnesota Press, 2002

Rachlin, Jill, "Behind the Screens at TV's Funniest New Show," *Ladies' Home Journal* (June 1990)

Sackett, Susan, "America's Funniest Home Videos," in *Prime-Time Hits: Television's Most Popular Network Programs, 1950 to the Present,* New York, Billboard Books, 1993

Sherwood, Rick, "*The Hollywood Reporter* Salutes *America's Funniest Home Videos* on Its 100th Episode," *Hollywood Reporter* (November 19, 1991)

"That's a Wrap: *America's Funniest Home Videos:* Funniest New TV Show," *U.S. News and World Report* (July 9, 1990)

Waters, Harry F., "Revenge of the Couch Potatoes: The Outrageous Success of *America's Funniest Home Videos* Proves That Any Fool Can Be a Star," *Newsweek* (March 5, 1990)

Zoglin, Richard, "America's Funniest Home Videos," *Time* (March 5, 1990)

America's Most Wanted

U.S. Reality/Public Service Program

First aired on the seven FOX stations in February 1988, *America's Most Wanted* is a U.S. reality program featuring segments that reenact crimes committed by wanted fugitives. Two months later, the show moved to the FOX Broadcasting Corporation and its affiliates. Produced by FOX Television Stations Productions (a unit of FOX Television Stations, Inc.), *America's Most Wanted* may be cited as the first example of the "manhunt" type of reality shows. Consistently winning solid ratings throughout its history, it has also been credited as a television show that doubles as both entertainment and "public service." Through the use of a toll-free "hotline," it elicits the participation of viewers in helping to capture known suspects depicted on the program, thus garnering praise and cooperation from law enforcement officials.

As a reality program, the style and content of *America's Most Wanted* closely follows that of other program types gathered under this broad industry label (e.g., "tabloid" newsmagazines, video vérité and reenacted crime, rescue and manhunt shows, and family amateur video programs). Central to each of these genres is a visible reference to, or dramatization of, real events and occupations. Thus, while the stories told on *America's Most Wanted* stem from "real life" incidents, they are not comprised of "actual" live footage (with the exception of recorded testimony from the "real" people involved). Rather, incidents of criminality and victimization are reenacted, and in an often intense and involving manner. This dramatic component, particularly as it entails a subjective appeal, is a dominant feature of reality programs, which tend to accentuate the emotional aspects of the situation for their effectivity. Viewers are thus asked to empathize and identify with the experiences of the people represented on the show, especially insofar as these experiences involve social or moral dilemmas.

Relying upon a structure similar to that used by television newsmagazines—which move back and forth from promotional trailer to anchor to report—each episode of *America's Most Wanted* is divided into a number of segments that retell and reenact a particular crime. Beginning with an update on how many viewers' tips have thus far led to the capture of fugitives featured on the show, the program then moves to the host or "anchor," who introduces the program and the first story segment. Using both actors and live footage of the "real people" involved, these story segments are highly dramatized, making liberal use of quick edits, rock music underscoring, sophisticated camera effects, and voice-overs. In addition to supplying a narrative function, the voice-overs also include actual testimony of the event from police, victims, and the criminals involved, thus emphasizing and appealing to the subjective.

The program resembles the tabloid newsmagazine genre in its often exaggerated language, also used in promotional trailers and by the host to describe the crimes depicted on the show (e.g., "Next, a tragic tale of obsession"). Additionally, and again paralleling qualities of tabloid TV, there are noticeable efforts toward self-promotion or congratulation; the host, law enforcement officials, and even captured fugitives repeatedly hype the policing and surveillance functions of the show. And yet despite these consistencies with a denigrated tabloid TV genre, *America's Most Wanted* is distinct in its appeal to and affiliation with both "the public" and the police.

The program is hosted by John Walsh, who "anchors" *America's Most Wanted* from Washington, D.C. Given the show's cooperation with federal law agencies, such as the FBI and the U.S. Marshall Service, its broadcast from this location acts to further associate it with law enforcement institutions. Walsh, whose son was abducted and murdered in 1981, is a nationally known advocate for missing and exploited children. As part of its program format, *America's Most Wanted* airs a weekly feature on missing children, and has created "The Missing Child Alert," a series of public service bulletins that are made available to all television stations, regardless of network affiliation.

Through its toll-free hotline (1-800-CRIME-TV), which operates seven days and averages 2,500 calls a week, the program has assisted in the apprehension of hundreds of fugitives and thus has earned the appreciation of law enforcement agencies. For example, *America's Most Wanted* played a key role in the capture of the "Texas Seven," inmates who escaped from a maximum security prison in Karnes City, Texas, on December 13, 2000, and eluded police for over a month. They lived in a Colorado RV park for almost a month, claiming to be Christian missionaries. On January 21, 2001, a resident of the park informed the owner that he suspected the recent arrivals were the Texas Seven, based on an episode of *America's Most Wanted* he had seen about the fugitives. The owner then viewed the program's website, read more about the Texas Seven, and contacted the police, who apprehended the wanted men.

America's Most Wanted, John Walsh, 1988–present.
©20th Century Fox/Courtesy of the Everett Collection

America's Most Wanted sees itself as enabling a cathartic process, offering not only legal justice but psychological resolution to victims of crime. In both these respects, *America's Most Wanted* may be said to move away from much of the fixed voyeurism of reality shows, toward a more active "public" function. And yet do manhunt shows such as *America's Most Wanted* simply temper the tabloid's spectacle into a new form of "vigilante voyeurism?" Do such shows not only feed into but actively promote a public's fears regarding an ever-present criminal threat? Such questions regarding the aims, the intended audience, and the effectivity of *America's Most Wanted*'s public function must be addressed.

ELIZABETH SEATON

Host

John Walsh

Producers

Lance Heflin, Joseph Russin, Paul Sparrow

Programming History

FOX

April 1988–August 1990	Sunday 8:00–8:30
September 1990–July 1993	Friday 8:00–9:00
July 1993–January 1994	Tuesday 9:00–10:00
January 1994–	Saturday 9:00–10:00

Further Reading

Bartley, Diane, "John Walsh: Fighting Back," *Saturday Evening Post* (April 1990)

Breslin, Jack, *America's Most Wanted: How Television Catches Crooks,* New York: Harper, 1990

Cosgrove, Stuart, "Crime Can Often Become an Accessory to Fiction on TV," *New Statesman and Society* (December 7, 1990)

"F.B.I. Gives Programs Exclusives on Fugitives," *New York Times* (September 15, 1991)

Finney, Angus, "Gutter and Gore," *New Statesman and Society* (September 9, 1988)

Friedman, David, "Wanted: Lowlifes and High Ratings," *Rolling Stone* (January 12 , 1989)

Garneau, George, "FBI to Newspapers: Watch Television," *Editor and Publisher* (September 21, 1991)

Nelson, Scott A., "Crime-Time Television," *FBI Law Enforcement Bulletin* (August 1988)

Prial, Frank J., "Freeze! You're on TV," *Reader's Digest* (March 1989)

"Television: Crime Pays," *Economist* (June 10, 1989)

Thomas, Bill, "Finding Truth in the Age of 'Infotainment,'" *Editorial Research Reports* (January 19, 1990)

Walsh, John, and Philip Lerman, *Public Enemies: The Host of America's Most Wanted Targets the Nation's Most Notorious Criminals,* New York: Pocket Books, 2002

White, Daniel R., "America's Most Wanted," *ABA Journal* (October 1989)

Amerika

U.S. Miniseries

Broadcast on ABC over the course of seven nights in the middle of February 1987, *Amerika* was a controversial 14-and-1/2-hour miniseries. Tom Shales of the *Washington Post* wrote in December 1986 that Amerika "could be the hottest political potato in the history of television." It was produced by ABC Circle Films and written and directed by Donald Wrye, who was also executive producer. This series depicted life as imagined in the United States in the late 1990s, ten years after the Soviet Union took control of the United States by employing a Soviet-controlled United Nations (UN) peacekeeping force.

Some have contended that *Amerika* was produced to provide a television counter to the controversial ABC movie *The Day After,* which depicted nuclear holocaust between the United States and the Soviet Union in 1983. The ABC executive responsible for both programs denied this view. Brandon Stoddard, president of ABC Circle Films, said on October 16, 1986, at a press tour at the UN Plaza Hotel in New York City that the idea for *Amerika* "never occurred during the controversy of *The Day After,* had nothing to do with *The Day After* ...the birth of this idea happened substantially later." Stoddard went on to say that a critic of *The Day After,* Ben Stein from the *Herald Examiner,* had written something, "at a much later point, a line...that had to do with what would life be like in America in a Russian occupation." Stoddard was stuck, however, thinking about how to do such a television program without getting caught up in the actual struggle of the takeover. Sometime later, Stoddard's spouse suggested doing the project at a point in time ten years after the takeover.

Amerika.
Copyright © BBC Photo Library

At the time, *Amerika* was the most controversial television event ever broadcast by ABC. The network received more mail and phone calls about *Amerika* before it was on the air than the total pre- and postbroadcast viewer reaction of any other program in the history of ABC, including the end-of-the-world story *The Day After.*

The critics of *Amerika* came from all sides of the political spectrum. Liberals feared the program would antagonize the Kremlin, jeopardizing arms control and détente. Some on the right thought the miniseries inadequately portrayed the brutality of the USSR. The UN thought the movie would erode its image.

Despite the prebroadcast level of controversy, most of the public did not object to the miniseries. Research conducted by ABC before the broadcast indicated that 96 percent of the population over 18 years old did not object to the program. Most Americans felt strongly that they should have the right to decide for themselves whether they would watch the program.

While almost half the country watched *The Day After* (46.0 rating), *Amerika* was seen in 19 percent of all TV households. Despite lots of publicity, controversy, and viewers, research conducted by William Adams at George Washington University showed that attitudes about the things most critics thought would be influenced by *Amerika* did not change. What Americans thought about the Soviet Union, the UN, or U.S.-Soviet relations did not change in before and after surveys.

Guy Lometti

Cast

Devin Milford	Kris Kristofferson
Marion Milford	Wendy Hughes
General Samanov	Armin Mueller-Stahl
Peter Bradford	Robert Urich
Amanda Bradford	Cindy Pickett
Colonel Andrei Denisov	Sam Neill
Kimberly Ballard	Mariel Hemingway
Althea Milford	Christine Lahti
Ward Milford	Richard Bradford
Helmut Gurtman	Reiner Schoene
Herbert Lister	John Madden Towney
Will Milford	Ford Rainey

Producer
David Wrye

Programming History
ABC
February 15–February 22, 1987 9:00–11:00

Further Reading

Lometti, G.E., "Broadcast Preparations for and Consequences of *The Day After,*" in *Television and Nuclear Power: Making the Public Mind,* edited by J.M. Wober, Norwood, New Jersey: Ablex, 1992

Lometti, G.E., *Sensitive Theme Programming and the New American Mainstream,* New York: American Broadcasting Companies, 1984

Amos 'n' Andy

U.S. Domestic Comedy

Like many of its early television counterparts, the *Amos 'n' Andy* television program was a direct descendant of a radio show; the radio version originated on WMAQ in Chicago on March 19, 1928, and eventually became the longest-running radio program in broadcast history. *Amos 'n' Andy* was conceived by Freeman Gosden and Charles Correll, two white actors who portrayed the characters Amos Jones and Andy Brown by mimicking so-called Negro dialect.

The significance of *Amos 'n' Andy,* with its almost 30-year history as a highly successful radio show; its brief, contentious years on network television; its banishment from prime time and subsequent years in syndication; and its reappearance in videocassette format is difficult to summarize in a few paragraphs. The position of the *Amos 'n' Andy* show in television history is still debated by media scholars investigating the cultural history of American television.

Amos 'n' Andy was first broadcast on CBS Television in June 1951 and lasted some two years before the program was canceled in the midst of growing protest by the black community in 1953. It was the first television series with an all-black cast (the only one of its kind to appear on prime-time network television for nearly another 20 years).

The program presented the antics of Amos Jones, an Uncle Tom-like conservative; Andy Brown, his zany business associate; Kingfish Stevens, a scheming smoothie; Lawyer Calhoun, an underhanded crook whom no one trusted; Lightnin', a slow-moving janitor; Sapphire Stevens, a nosy loudmouth; Mama, a domineering mother-in-law; and the infamous Madame Queen. The basis for these characters was derived largely from the stereotypic caricatures of African Americans that had been communicated through several decades of popular American culture, most notably, motion pictures.

The program's portrayal of black life and culture was deemed by the black community of the period as an insulting return to the days of blackface and minstrelsy. Media historian Donald Bogle notes, "Neither CBS nor the programs' creators were prepared for the change in national temperament after the Second World War.... Within black America, a new political consciousness and a new awareness of the importance of image had emerged." Though hardly devoid of the cruel insults and disparaging imagery of the past, Hollywood of the post–World War II period ushered in an era of better roles and improved images for African-American performers in Hollywood. For the first time in the medium's history, American motion pictures presented glimpses of black soldiers fighting alongside their white comrades; black entertainers appeared in sequined gowns and tuxedos instead of bandanas and calico dresses. Black characters included lawyers, teachers, and other contributing members of society.

Post–World War II African Americans looked upon the new medium of television with hopeful excitement. To them, the medium could nullify the decades of offensive caricatures and ethnic stereotyping so prevalent throughout decades of motion picture history. The frequent appearance of black stars on early television variety shows was met with approval from black leadership.

African Americans were still exuberant over recent important gains in civil rights brought on by World War II. They were determined to realize improved images of themselves in popular culture. To some, the characters in *Amos 'n' Andy*—rude, aggressive women and weak black men—were offensive. Neither the Kingfish nor Sapphire Stevens could engage in a conversation without peppering their speech with faulty grammar and mispronunciations. Especially abhorred was the portrayal of black professionals. Following its 1951 summer convention, the National Association for the Advancement of Colored People (NAACP) mandated an official protest against the program. The association outlined a list of specific items it felt were objectionable: for example, "every character is either a clown or a crook," "Negro doctors are shown as quacks," and "Negro lawyers are shown as crooks." As the series appeared in June 1951, the NAACP appeared in federal court seeking an injunction against its premiere. To network executives, the show was harmless, not much different from *Life with Liugi, The Goldbergs,* or any other ethnically oriented show of the times.

Moreover, the denunciation of *Amos 'n' Andy* was not universal. With its good writing and talented cast, the show was good comedy, and it soon became a commercial success. The reaction of the black community toward this well-produced and funny program remained divided. Even the *Pittsburgh Courier,* one of the black community's most influential publications, which had earlier led in the protest against the motion picture *Gone with the Wind,* defended the show in an article appearing in June 1951.

In 1953 CBS reluctantly removed the program from the air, but not solely because of the efforts of the NAACP. As mentioned, the period featured a swiftly changing climate for race relations in the United States. Success in the southern market was important to major advertisers. In an era when African Americans were becoming increasingly vocal in the fight against racial discrimination, large advertisers were reluctant to have their products too closely associated with black people. Fear of white economic backlash was of special concern to advertisers and television producers. The idea of "organized consumer resistance" caused advertisers and television executives to avoid appearing in favor of rights for African Americans. One advertising agency executive, referring to blacks on television, noted in *Variety,* "the word has gone out, 'No Negro performers allowed.'"

Even with so much contention looming, the *Amos 'n' Andy* show remained in syndication well into the 1960s. Currently, videotape cassettes of the episodes are widely available.

PAMALA S. DEANE

See also **Racism, Ethnicity, and Television**

Cast

Amos Jones	Alvin Childress
Andrew Hogg Brown (Andy)	Spencer Williams Jr.
George "Kingfish" Stevens	Tim Moore
Lawyer Algonquin J. Calhoun	Johnny Lee
Sapphire Stevens	Ernestine Wade
Lightin'	Horace Stewart (a.k.a. Nick O'Demus)
Sapphire's Mama (Ramona Smith)	Amanda Randolph
Madame Queen	Lillian Randolph

Producers

Freeman Gosden, Charles Correll

Programming History

78 half-hour episodes
CBS
June 1951–June 1953 Thursday 8:30–9:00

Further Reading

Bogle, Donald, *Blacks, Coons, Mulattoes, Mammies, and Bucks: An Interpretive History of Blacks in American Film,* New York: Viking Press, 1973; 4th edition, New York: Continuum, 2001

Bogle, Donald, *Blacks in American Television and Film: An Encyclopedia,* New York: Garland, 1988

Campbell, Edward D.C., Jr., *The Celluloid South: Hollywood and the Southern Myth,* Knoxville: University of Tennessee Press, 1981

Ely, Melvin Patrick, *The Adventures of Amos 'n' Andy: A Social History of an American Phenomenon,* New York: Free Press, 1991

Friedman, Lester D., *Unspeakable Images: Ethnicity and the American Cinema,* Urbana: University of Illinois Press, 1991

Gray, Herman, *Watching Race: Television and the Struggle for "Blackness,"* Minneapolis: University of Minnesota Press, 1995

Hughes, Langston, *Fight for Freedom: The Story of the NAACP,* New York: Norton, 1962

MacDonald, J. Fred, *Blacks and White TV: Afro-Americans in Television Since 1948,* Chicago: Nelson-Hall Publishers, 1983; 2nd edition, 1992

Marc, David, and Robert J. Thompson, *Prime Time, Prime Movers: From I Love Lucy to L.A. Law—America's Greatest TV Shows and the People Who Created Them,* Boston: Little Brown, 1992

Nesteby, James R., *Black Images in American Films, 1896–1954: The Interplay Between Civil Rights and Film Culture,* Lanham, Maryland: University Press of America, 1982

Anchor

In U.S. television the chief news presenter(s) for network, local, cable, and satellite news programming is known as the anchor. The term distinguishes the presenter-journalist at the news desk in the television studio (or above the convention floor, etc.) from the reporter in the field. All news stories in a program are funneled through the anchor as he or she mediates between the public, the network, and/or other news reporters.

The most commonly cited source of the term "anchor" is the television news coverage of the 1952 Republican presidential conventions. The concept is not borrowed, contrary to what one might expect, from the nautical realm, but from the strongest runner of a relay team, the anchorperson, who runs the final leg of the race. In the conventional format of broadcast news, when the anchor is not personally delivering a story by directly addressing the viewing audience or speaking over symbols and visual images of the news, he or she is introducing and calling upon reporters to deliver stories from the field or announcing a commercial break. Moreover, an anchor represents the public and its need to know whenever he or she interrogates and listens to the subject of an interview. National news anchors represent their respective networks and are held accountable for the ratings success of their respective news programs in attracting viewers. In keeping with this serious representational function, the anchor's style of delivery is typically reserved and his or her appearance is designed to convey credibility. In other words, the anchor is a television host at the top of a hierarchical chain of command with special reportorial credentials and responsibilities centered around "hard" or serious news of the day—celebrity interview and tabloid news shows have hosts, not anchors, even when they are organized similarly in format to network evening news. Journalists in other television news formats without a similar division of labor between studio and field are not, strictly speaking, anchors.

Being delegated with the daily, prestigious responsibility for presenting national news has brought public exposure that has made some network television news anchors into household names. During his tenure as anchor of the *CBS Evening News,* Walter Cronkite transcended the domain of broadcast news into becoming a widely admired and "most trusted" national figure, eclipsing the fame of his cohorts, including the NBC News anchor team of Chet Huntley and David Brinkley. Network anchors since the early 1980s, ABC's Peter Jennings, CBS's Dan Rather, and NBC's Tom Brokaw, have become national celebrities and highly paid television stars. However, the role of the network anchor appears to be declining in cultural significance as the broadcast networks lose more of their audience to cable, satellite, and new-media forms of news on the Internet. The sheer number of anchors—for instance, the singles and pairs that CNN rotates over its 24 hours of news programming—dilutes the potential star power of individual personalities. On the other hand, online news has thus far developed as an interactive magazine format, so that even on network websites, anchors are decentered and reduced to a tiny image on the page. "Ananova," a female virtual web persona for 24-hour news delivery at ananova.com, represents a mouthpiece in the European "newsreader" tradition, rather than the anchor as a credible news-gathering and news-presenting subject.

Aside from abortive attempts to team Barbara Walters with Harry Reasoner and Connie Chung with Dan Rather, national news presenting has been almost exclusively the preserve of white males. However, many local stations have long represented diversity in the community by employing anchor teams of one man and one woman, with each anchor of a different race, supplemented by an ethnically diverse group of male and female reporters on the sports and weather beat and in the field. Even in the local context, however, distinctions between the ways in which male and female anchors are treated are vital. The highly publicized case of Christine Craft (who was demoted in 1981 from the anchor position at KMBC-TV in Kansas City, Kansas, because focus groups found her physically unappealing and overly aggressive) illustrates the willingness of executives to dismiss women considered "too old" or "too unattractive" to fill this highly visible role. Such judgments are rarely, if ever, made in cases involving male anchors, who are seen to develop "authority" and "gravity" as their physical glamour fades.

Corporate pressure toward expanding profit margins in broadcast and cable news divisions and increasing competition between news venues for ratings are both widely regarded as having eroded the public service orientation and journalistic standards of television news, thus diminishing the credibility and prestige of the television news anchor. The network anchors suffered great embarrassment from precipitous and inaccurate reporting of the presidential election of November 2000. During the events and the aftermath of the terrorist attacks on the United States on September 11, 2001, however, the prominence and authority accorded to anchors such as Jennings, Brokaw, and Rather showed that these figures can still personally and powerfully engage the public during a national emergency.

A secondary meaning of "anchor" comes out of semiology, or the study of signs and meaning. In "The Rhetoric of the Image," Roland Barthes uses the anchor-and-relay metaphor to describe two different functions of the caption in relation to a still image: a caption anchors the image when the former selectively elucidates the latter's meaning; when the caption sets out meanings not found in the image itself, it acts as a relay. The television news anchor may be said to function similarly as an "anchor" in this extended sense, by presenting a selection of events as news stories and by providing a framework for the interpretation of their social and cultural meaning. That "anchoring" capability has been challenged not only by the diminishing role and prestige of the network news but also by the proliferation of American-style news formats that present opposing worldviews, such as the Islamic perspectives broadcast on the Al-Jazeera network from Qatar during the war against terrorism in Afghanistan.

MARGARET MORSE

See also **Brinkley, David; Brokaw, Tom; Chung, Connie; Craft, Christine; Cronkite, Walter; Huntley, Chet; Jennings, Peter; Walters, Barbara**

Further Reading

Barnouw, Erik, *Tube of Plenty: The Evolution of American Television,* New York: Oxford University Press, 1975; 3rd edition, 1990

Barthes, Roland, "The Rhetoric of the Image," in *Image, Music, Text,* by Roland Barthes, selected and translated by Stephen Heath, New York: Hill and Wang, 1977

Cunningham, Liz, *Talking Politics: Choosing the President in the Television Age,* Westport, Connecticut: Praeger, 1995

Downie, Leonard, Jr., and Robert G. Kaiser, *The News About the News: American Journalism in Peril,* New York: Alfred A. Knopf, 2002

Engstrom, Erika, and Anthony J. Ferri, "Looking Through a Gendered Lens: Local U.S. Television News Anchors' Perceived Career Barriers," *Journal of Broadcasting and Electronic Media* 44, No. 4 (Fall 2000)

Fensch, Thomas, editor, *Television News Anchors: An Anthology of Profiles of the Major Figures and Issues in United States Network Reporting,* Jefferson, North Carolina: McFarland, 1993

Goldberg, Robert, and Gerald J. Goldberg, *Anchors: Brokaw, Jennings, Rather, and the Evening News,* Secaucus, New Jersey: Carol Publishing Group, 1990

Hallin, Dan, *We Keep America on Top of the World: Television Journalism and the Public Sphere,* London and New York: Routledge, 1994

James, Doug, *Walter Cronkite: His Life and Times,* Brentwood, Tennessee: JM Press, 1991

Marlane, Judith, *Women in Television News Revisited: Into the Twenty-First Century,* Austin: University of Texas Press, 1999

Matusow, Barbara, *The Evening Stars: The Making of the Network News Anchor,* Boston: Houghton Mifflin, 1983

Morse, Margaret, "The Television News Personality and Credibility: Reflections on the News in Transition," in *Studies in Entertainment: Critical Approaches to Mass Culture,* edited by Tania Modleski, Bloomington: Indiana University Press, 1986

Rather, Dan, and Mickey Herskowitz, *The Camera Never Blinks: Adventures of a TV Journalist,* New York: William Morrow, 1977

Rather, Dan, and Mickey Herskowitz, *The Camera Never Blinks Twice: The Further Adventures of a Television Journalist,* New York: William Morrow, 1994

Rich, Frank, "The Weight of an Anchor," *New York Times Magazine* (May 19, 2002)

Sanders, Marlene, and Marcia Rock, *Waiting for Prime Time: The Women of Television News,* Urbana: University of Illinois Press, 1988

Ancier, Garth (1957–)

U.S. Producer, Network President

Since the 1980s, Garth Ancier has shaped television programming as both a producer and creative executive. Among the milestones in his impressive career was his ability to become only the second person (after Fred Silverman) to head three networks. As both a network president and an executive producer, Ancier has been instrumental in developing shows targeted to teenagers and young adults.

Garth Ancier.
Photo courtesy of WB

He began his career in broadcasting as an intern at a public television station at the age of 12. Before Ancier turned 20, he had already worked as a radio reporter and producer at an NBC radio affiliate in New Jersey. While in high school, he created and produced a radio show that evolved into *Focus on Youth,* a program later broadcast when he attended Princeton University. The show, which continued its run at Princeton long after Ancier graduated, became one of the largest nationally syndicated public affairs radio programs in the country, broadcast weekly to more than 300 stations.

Ancier's involvement in *Focus on Youth* attracted the attention of *People* magazine, which ran a profile of him while he was still in college. He later used this article as his ticket into the office of NBC entertainment programmer Brandon Tartikoff. Ancier started in NBC's executive training program and rapidly rose up the ranks during the early 1980s, eventually becoming the network's vice president of current comedy. *The Cosby Show, The Golden Girls, Cheers,* and *Family Ties* were just a few of the shows he oversaw during his time at NBC.

Although he was quickly moving up at NBC, Ancier could not refuse the request of newly appointed FOX vice president Scott Sassa to become the fledgling network's first head of programming. Ancier initially struggled to define FOX's audience and programming strategies. However, a number of hits soon emerged, including *21 Jump Street, Married…with Children,* and *The Simpsons.* These were just a few of the programs that helped FOX solidify its image as the "alternative network"—home to edgy comedic, dramatic, and reality fare that couldn't be found on the "Big Three." In addition, these shows helped FOX attract advertisers by appealing to the highly desirable audience of viewers aged 18 to 34. Over the ensuing years, Ancier would repeatedly be praised for his success in attracting this demographic group.

Despite his accomplishments at FOX, Ancier left the network in 1989 to develop series programming for Walt Disney Television and Touchstone Television. However, his tenure at Disney was rocky and he left less than two years later amid widespread reports of power struggles between himself and upper management. Though his time at Disney was short, he was nonetheless instrumental in a number of the production company's early successes, including, most notably, *Home Improvement.*

Ancier continued to move from position to position during the early 1990s. He briefly returned to FOX before venturing into independent production. He also served as a television consultant for the Democratic National Committee during the 1992 presidential campaign, creating the 56-screen "video wall" that stood behind the podium during the party's 1992 National Convention. He then produced *Sunday's Best* and *Jane,* a couple of short-lived programs, before finding a hit in the syndicated *Rikki Lake* show.

In creating *Rikki Lake,* Ancier targeted young viewers, a strategy similar to the one he had used at FOX. Ancier identified and exploited the lack of talk shows geared to 18 to 34 year olds. *Rikki Lake* pursued this group with tremendous success, coming in behind only *The Oprah Winfrey Show* in daytime in the years following its debut in 1993. As Rikki Lake's ratings rose, Ancier's 25-percent ownership stake in the show became more valuable.

Even as *Rikki Lake* continued to ascend in the ratings, another promising opportunity arose for Ancier. His former boss at FOX, Jamie Kellner, was in the process of starting the new WB network. Ancier agreed to come on board as its first head of programming. Ancier came into the job at the WB with the mandate to pursue 12 to 34 year olds.

Upon entering into the position as the WB's programming head, Ancier initially recruited several individuals with whom he had worked at FOX. For example, *In Living Color*'s Shawn and Marlon Wayans and *Married…with Children*'s Ron Leavitt and Michael Moye developed the first WB programs, *The Wayans Bros.* and *Unhappily Ever After…* . Although the WB continued to struggle to find a comedy hit, the network found its niche with dramas targeted to teenagers and young adults. *7th Heaven, Buffy the Vampire Slayer, Dawson's*

Creek, and *Charmed* were all developed under Ancier's supervision.

At a time when the rest of the networks were suffering declines in viewership, the WB continued to grow. In addition, the network was attracting the most desirable demographic groups with advertisers. Ancier was regularly celebrated in the press for these accomplishments and for his skillful programming strategies. He reaped the fruits of his labors through his 2-percent ownership stake in the WB.

These programming achievements did not go unnoticed by the executives at NBC. Scott Sassa, in the process of moving up to the position of NBC's West Coast president, needed someone to replace him as entertainment president. In May 1999 Ancier thus teamed with Sassa once again and returned to the network where he got his start. This marked Ancier's third time as head of programming at a network. However, he now was responsible for more than just prime time. Ancier was commissioned to oversee NBC's late-night, daytime, and Saturday morning hours as well. Further, he assumed control over NBC's program development, current programming, scheduling, network promotion, and publicity.

Ancier was in his new job less than a week when NBC announced its fall 1999 schedule. Arriving at the network while it was experiencing declining ratings, and with a number of aging programs on the schedule, Ancier found himself confronted with huge expectations. Although the 1999–2000 season emerged with a few hits, including *The West Wing* and *Law & Order: Special Victims Unit,* the 2000–2001 season was a disaster.

Citing NBC's status as a quality network, Ancier refused to turn to reality programming and game shows even as ABC hit the jackpot with *Who Wants to Be a Millionaire* and CBS earned high ratings with *Survivor.* In addition, NBC was faced with a number of expensive, high-profile flops including *The Michael Richards Show* and *Titans.* Thus, after only 18 months on the job, Ancier was forced to resign.

Yet as had often proven to be the case before, Ancier quickly bounced back—once again with the help of Jamie Kellner. Kellner, who had recently become CEO of the Turner Broadcasting System, brought in Ancier to serve as executive vice president of programming. Ancier's mission in this new position was to find synergies among the various Turner and AOL Time Warner holdings, which included CNN, TNT, TBS, the Cartoon Network, and the WB. He was also charged with developing marketing and branding strategies for these divisions. The position had the biggest scope of any Ancier had occupied so far, demanding him to employ the creative and administrative skills he had developed throughout his diverse experiences in the television business.

Alisa Perren

See also **FOX Broadcasting Company; Kellner, Jamie; National Broadcasting Company; Sassa, Scott; Tartikoff, Brandon; Time Warner; Turner Broadcasting System; WB Television Network**

Garth Ancier. Born in Perth Amboy, New Jersey, September 3, 1957. B.A. in political science, Princeton University, graduated 1979. Radio reporter and producer, NBC affiliates WBUD-AM and WBJH-FM, 1972; creator and executive producer, *Focus on Youth,* 1972; participant in NBC executive training program, 1979; manager of East Coast development and assistant to NBC entertainment president Brandon Tartikoff, 1979; vice president of current comedy at NBC, 1983; senior vice president, FOX network, 1986; president of FOX network, 1987; president, network television production, Disney, 1989; television consultant, Democratic National Committee, 1991–92; executive producer, *Sunday's Best,* NBC, 1991; executive producer, *Jane,* FOX, 1992; executive producer, syndicated *Rikki Lake,* 1993; head of programming, the WB, 1994; resigned as head of programming and appointed executive consultant, the WB, 1998; entertainment president, NBC, 1999; executive vice president of programming, Turner Networks, 2001. Member, board of trustees, National Council of Families and Television; member, board of trustees, National Association of College Broadcasters; member, Hall of Fame Selection Committee, the Academy of Television Arts and Sciences; served on the Governor's Board of the Hollywood Radio and Television Society.

Further Reading

Adalian, Josef, "Ancier Rejoins Big Three," *Variety* (22 November 1999–28 November 1999)

Block, Alex Ben, *Outfoxed: Marvin Davis, Barry Diller, Rupert Murdoch, Joan Rivers, and the Inside Story of America's Fourth Television Network,* New York: St. Martin's Press, 1991

Braxton, Greg, "How FOX Broke from the Pack to Become Cutting-Edge Network," *Chicago Sun-Times* (6 April 1997)

Graham, Jefferson, "Network Whiz Ancier's Edge: 'I Love TV,'" *USA Today* (17 December 1998)

Hamilton, Kendall, "In Prime Time, and in Play," *Newsweek* (21 December 1998)

Rice, Lynette, "NBC's Stage 2: Ancier, Sassa Assume Positions," *Hollywood Reporter* (16 March 1999)

Schlosser, Joe, and John M. Higgins, "Ancier Turns to Turner; TV Veteran Will Head Programming at New Networks Division," *Broadcasting & Cable* (26 March 2001)

Schneider, Michael, "World According to Garth: Ancier Ponders NBC and More," *Electronic Media* (17 May 1999)

Ancillary Markets

Television programs have always been designed for initial exposure through local or national transmission. Once aired, some programs never run again. However, most programs are then sold in a range of subsequent, ancillary markets. As the number and variety of these "aftermarkets" has increased, and their importance as revenue sources has grown, their influence on the television industry has become more marked.

There are three major ancillary markets for television programming: international syndication, domestic rerun syndication, and home video.

International syndication—the sale of program distribution rights outside the originating national territory—has long been a lucrative source of revenue for television producers as well as a significant target of cultural criticism. Programs have been sold on this market since the 1950s, as countries began to develop and expand television service. With its fundamentally commercial media system, the United States quickly emerged as a primary exporter of programming, and its studios' slick fare was promoted as a comparably inexpensive alternative to domestic productions in many countries. As a result, many societies' primary experiences with global television have been with U.S. television, with series like *I Love Lucy* in the 1950s and *Dallas* in the 1980s being particularly influential. Some cultural critics have argued that this dominance has fostered American cultural imperialism across the planet, while others have argued that local audiences assert their own cultures and meanings over these programs.

While the United States has continued to dominate international syndication, the degree of its dominance has lessened as other countries have successfully gained reputations and market share as television exporters. Australian, Brazilian, British, and Japanese firms in particular have long sold programs to global audiences. While language and culture are certainly significant issues in international television distribution, some series have traveled quite broadly. Brazilian *telenovelas,* for example, have been a particularly successful global genre over the past two decades and have been dubbed into several different languages and dialects for runs in dozens of countries.

Rerun syndication may overlap with international syndication (e.g., after a program has already run for the first time in a foreign market) but is primarily thought of as a domestic market. Reruns are episodes of programs that are sold to local broadcast stations and cable networks after their initial transmission. The most established rerun syndication market is the United States, whose more localized broadcasting system has long relied upon the availability of extant programming. The U.S. rerun market developed in the 1950s, as the many stations coming on the air after the end of the 1948–52 license freeze all sought programs to fill their time and attract local advertisers. While first-run (i.e. "new") syndicated programs initially filled these hours, reruns of these programs, offered at a discount from their distributors, also attracted sizable audiences, contrary to expectations. The success of these programs in rerun form, and the networks' shift toward filmed programs in the latter half of the 1950s, fostered the growth of the rerun market. These "off-network" programs were sold to stations and advertisers largely on the virtue of their familiarity with audience, and by the early 1960s, they had squeezed most first-run syndicated programming out of the market entirely.

Since that time, network-originated series have generally gone into production with the hope that they eventually make it to the rerun syndication market. This has particularly been the case as production costs have increased while licensing fees—the amount paid by networks for first-run rights to series—have lagged behind. Rerun syndication generates additional revenue for series producers, often returning the first profits on the property, even after years of exposure on first-run television. Current network hits often generate enormous profits in this regard when they enter this market, as with *The Cosby Show* in the late 1980s and *Seinfeld* in the late 1990s.

Since most syndicated reruns (particularly sitcoms) are broadcast on a daily basis (i.e., five or more times a week), a series must typically have a four-season network run in order to compile enough episodes to be an attractive rerun property. Rights to series may be sold for cash, but a more common arrangement (particularly since the media recession of the late 1980s) is through barter, whereby a series is acquired for free (or at a discount) in exchange for a few minutes of advertising time in each episode. The local station still gets to attract local advertisers during its time, but the program's distributor can then sell national advertising time.

The money and broadcast time at stake in rerun syndication raised significant fears of the monopolization of television in the 1960s, and in 1970 the FCC banned the broadcast networks from the ownership and syndication of virtually all of their prime-time programming under the Financial Interest and Syndication Rules ("Fin-Syn"). Hollywood studios and independent production companies greatly benefited from these rules during the 1970s and 1980s, collecting the syndication revenues of network hits as they entered the rerun market. After a decade of relaxed regulatory limits on media ownership, however, the rules were retired in 1995, enabling networks to once again own and syndicate their own prime-time programming. In the wake of Fin-Syn's repeal, many studios, networks, station groups, and cable networks have merged, forming huge, synergistic corporations that turn network programs into lucrative off-network properties across an array of media outlets.

While domestic rerun syndication continues to be a major source of television revenue, the home video market has recently become a significant profit generator for television studios. In this market, television programs are rented or sold directly to consumers on VHS tapes or DVDs. Although the VHS rental market had been vital to the film industry since the late 1980s, it had been only marginal for television producers. Unlike a film, which can be released as one tape, a typical television series necessitates many tapes, complicating both retail and domestic storage.

The rapid consumer adoption of DVD technology at the turn of the century transformed the market for television on home video, because of the discs' high audiovisual quality and copious storage space. Series are now sold on DVD as "box sets": book-sized packages with several disks holding an entire season's worth of episodes. FOX pioneered this form with their release of the first season of *The X-Files* in early 2000; other studios soon followed, emptying their archives of older series, and, increasingly, releasing current series *before* their marketing in rerun syndication. ABC's *Alias,* CBS's *CSI,* and FOX's *24* were released as full-season DVD box sets in this manner.

Regardless of the particular form of distribution, these three markets have become anything but "ancillary" in recent years. While having an international success is still not as necessary with television as it now is with film, it has extended the market life of series for years and even decades and has helped foster a global television culture. Meanwhile, the revenue generated from rerun syndication continues to expand and usually represents the bulk of profits for most successful scripted programs. However, the sudden growth of television on home video represents perhaps the ultimate ancillary market, as programs are now sold directly to consumers as collectible cultural artifacts.

DEREK KOMPARE

See also **Financial Interest and Syndication Rules; Movies on Television; Reruns/Repeats; Syndication**

Further Reading

Ferguson, Douglas, and Susan Tyler Eastman, *Broadcast/Cable/Web Programming: Strategies and Practices,* 6th edition, Belmont, California: Wadsworth, 2001

Havens, Timothy J., "Exhibiting Global Television: On the Business and Cultural Functions of Global Television Fairs" *Journal of Broadcasting and Electronic Media,* 47 (2003)

Kompare, Derek, "Rerun Nation: The Regime of Repetition on American Television," PhD. diss., University of Wisconsin-Madison, 1999

Parks, Lisa, and Shanti Kumar, editors, *Planet TV: A Global Television Reader,* New York: New York University Press, 2003

Thussu, Daya Kishan, *International Communication: Continuity and Change,* London: Arnold, and New York: Oxford University Press, 2000

Wasser, Frederick, *Veni, Vidi, Video: The Hollywood Empire and the VCR,* Austin: University of Texas Press, 2002

Andy Griffith Show, The

U.S. Situation Comedy

The Andy Griffith Show was one of the most popular and memorable comedy series of the 1960s. In its eight years on the air, from 1960 to 1968, it never dropped below seventh place in the seasonal Nielsen rankings, and it was number one the year it ceased production. The series pilot originally aired as an episode of *Make Room For Daddy,* a popular sitcom starring Danny Thomas. Sheldon Leonard produced both shows for Danny Thomas Productions.

An early example of television's "rural revolution," *The Andy Griffith Show* was part of a programming trend that saw the development of comedies featuring

The Andy Griffith Show, Andy Griffith, Ron Howard, 1960–68. *Courtesy of the Everett Collection*

naive but noble "rubes" from deep in the American heartland. The trend began when ABC debuted *The Real McCoys* in 1957, but CBS became the network most associated with it. The success CBS achieved with *The Andy Griffith Show* provided the inspiration for a string of hits such as *The Beverly Hillbillies, Green Acres, Petticoat Junction,* and *Hee Haw.* Genial and comparatively innocuous, these shows were just right for a time when TV was under frequent attack by the Federal Communications Commission (FCC) and congressional committees for its violent content.

Sheldon Leonard and Danny Thomas designed *The Andy Griffith Show* to fit the image of its star. Griffith's homespun characterizations were already well known to audiences who had seen his hayseed interpretations of Shakespeare on *The Ed Sullivan Show* and his starring roles in the films *A Face in the Crowd* (1957) and *No Time for Sergeants* (1958). On *The Andy Griffith Show* he played Sheriff Andy Taylor, the fair-minded and easygoing head lawman of the Edenic small town of Mayberry, North Carolina. Neither sophisticated nor worldly wise, Andy drew from a deep well of unpretentious folk wisdom that allowed him to settle domestic disputes and outwit the arrogant city folk who occasionally passed through town. When he was not at the sheriff's office, Andy, a widower, was applying his old-fashioned horse sense to the raising of his young son, Opie (Ronny Howard), a task he shared with his Aunt Bee (Frances Bavier).

Mayberry was based upon Andy Griffith's real hometown, and perhaps this was partially responsible for the strong sense many viewers got that Mayberry was a real place. Over the years the writers fleshed out the geography and character of the town with a degree of detail unusual for series television. The directorial style of the series was also strikingly distinct, employing a relaxed, almost lethargic tone appropriate to the nostalgic settings of front porch, sidewalk, and barber shop. The townspeople, and the ensemble of actors who portrayed them, were crucial to the success of the show. Most of these characters were "hicks," playing comic foils to the sagacious Andy. Gomer Pyle (Jim Nabors) and his cousin Goober (George Lindsey) came right out of the "bumpkin" tradition that had been developed years ago in films, popular literature, radio, and comic strips. Town barber Floyd Lawson (Howard McNear) was a font of misinformation and the forerunner of *Cheers*' Cliff Clavin. Otis (Hal Smith), the unrepentant town drunk, was trained to let himself into his jail cell after a Saturday night bender and to let himself out on Sunday morning. Without much real police work to attend to, Andy's true job was protecting these and other citizens of Mayberry from their own hubris, intemperance, and stupidity.

Most of Andy's time, however, was spent controlling his earnest but overzealous deputy, Barney Fife. Self-important, romantic, and nearly always wrong, Barney dreamed of the day he could use the one bullet Andy had issued to him. While Barney was forever frustrated that Mayberry was too small for the delusional ideas he had of himself, viewers got the sense that he could not have survived anywhere else. Don Knotts played the comic and pathetic sides of the character with equal aplomb and was given four Emmy Awards for doing so. He left the show in 1965 and was replaced by Jack Burns in the role of Deputy Warren Furguson.

The Andy Griffith Show engendered two spin-offs. *Gomer Pyle, U.S.M.C.* was a military sitcom featuring Gomer in the Marines. *Mayberry, R.F.D.* was a reworking of *The Andy Griffith Show* made necessary by Griffith's departure in 1968. Like the parent show, the spin-offs celebrated the honesty, the strong sense of community, and the solid family values supposedly inherent in small town life.

By the late 1960s, however, many viewers, especially young ones, were rejecting these shows as irrelevant to modern times. Mayberry's total isolation from contemporary problems was part of its appeal, but more than a decade of media coverage of the civil rights movement had brought about a change in the popular image of the small Southern town. *Gomer Pyle, U.S.M.C.* was set on a U.S. Marine base between 1964 and 1969, but neither Gomer nor any of his fellow soldiers ever mentioned the war in Vietnam. CBS executives, afraid of losing the lucrative youth demographic, purged their schedule of hit shows that were drawing huge but older audiences. *Gomer Pyle, U.S.M.C.* was in second place when it was canceled in 1969. *Mayberry, R.F.D.* and the rest of the rural comedies met a similar fate within the next two seasons. They were replaced by such "relevant" new sitcoms as *All in the Family* and *M*A*S*H.*

The Andy Griffith Show remains an enduring favorite in syndicated reruns. New fan books about the program, including a cookbook of favorite dishes mentioned in specific episodes, continued to appear nearly 30 years after the end of the original network run. In 1986, a reunion show brought together most of the original cast and production team. *Return To Mayberry* was the highest-rated telefilm of the season.

ROBERT J. THOMPSON

See also **Comedy, Domestic Settings; Griffith, Andy**

Cast

Andy Taylor	Andy Griffith
Opie Taylor	Ronny Howard
Barney Fife (1960–65)	Don Knotts
Ellie Walker (1960–61)	Elinor Donahue
Aunt Bee Taylor	Frances Bavier
Clara Edwards	Hope Summers
Gomer Pyle (1963–64)	Jim Nabors
Helen Crump (1964–68)	Aneta Corsaut
Goober Pyle (1965–68)	George Lindsey
Floyd Lawson	Howard McNear
Otis Campbell (1960–67)	Hal Smith
Howard Sprague (1966–68)	Jack Dodson
Emmett Clark (1967–68)	Paul Hartman
Thelma Lou (1960–65)	Betty Lynn
Warren Ferguson (1965–66)	Jack Burns
Mayor Stoner (1962–63)	Parley Baer
Jud Crowley (1961–66)	Burt Mustin

Producers

Louis Edelman, Sheldon Leonard

Programming History

249 episodes

CBS

October 1960–July 1963	Monday 9:30–10:00
September 1963–September 1964	Monday 9:30–10:00
September 1964–June 1965	Monday 8:30–9:00
September 1965–September 1968	Monday 9:00–9:30

Further Reading

Barnouw, Erik, *Tube of Plenty: The Evolution of American Television,* New York: Oxford University Press, 1975; 3rd edition, 1990

Beck, Ken, and Jim Clark, *The Andy Griffith Show Book,* New York: St. Martin's Press, 1985

Eisner, Joel, and David Krinsky, *Television Comedy Series: An Episode Guide to 153 Sitcoms in Syndication,* Jefferson, North Carolina: McFarland, 1984

Kelly, Richard, *The Andy Griffith Show,* Winston-Salem, North Carolina: John F. Blair, 1981

Marc, David, *Comic Visions: Television Comedy and American Culture,* Boston: Unwin Hyman, 1989; 2nd edition, Malden, Massachusetts: Blackwell Publishers, 1997

Marc, David, *Demographic Vistas: Television in American Culture,* Philadelphia: University of Pennsylvania Press, 1984; 2nd edition, 1996

Watson, Mary Ann, *The Expanding Vista: American Television in the Kennedy Years,* New York: Oxford University Press, 1990

Animal Planet

U.S. Cable Network

The 1990s witnessed a wave of specialty cable networks (known in the industry as "category television"), most spun off from established networks, and most focusing on genres traditionally popular with television audiences. The more successful of these specialty networks were able to build resources and eventually redefine the boundaries of their featured genres. Discovery Networks has been an adept player

Courtesy of Discovery Networks

in this environment, and its third network, Animal Planet, has been particularly successful.

Animal Planet made its U.S. cable debut in June 1996. This basic-cable network, which features programs about both wild and domesticated animals, is particularly popular in households with children and competes with older networks such as Disney Channel and Nickelodeon. Unlike networks that target children specifically, however, Animal Planet also reaches adults. In May 2001 Animal Planet boasted 70.1 million cable and satellite subscribers, making it cable's fastest growing new network and a major competitor with more established networks.

Animal Planet represented Discovery Networks' third cable venture, following the long-standing Discovery Channel and the Learning Channel. Discovery Networks U.S. holdings now also include Travel Channel, Discovery Health Channel, Discovery Home and Leisure, Discovery Science, Discovery Kids, Discovery Wings, and Discovery Civilization. Discovery and its international partners (including the BBC) also operate versions of its networks around the world—including Animal Planet channels in Europe, India, and Latin America. While these are all distinct themed networks, Discovery is known for its efficient sharing of programs among its various networks; this helped it launch a variety of digital networks in the late 1990s.

Animal Planet launched with only the resources of Discovery and the Learning Channel to build its schedule, however. At first it featured a repertoire of classic animal show reruns, including *Lassie* and *Flipper,* as well as various documentaries. But it moved quickly into the use of original in-house productions and acquired programming. Its first original production was a children's game show called *ZooVenture* that was taped at the San Diego Zoo. Other popular Animal Planet originals have included *Emergency Vets, The Jeff Corwin Experience, Animal Precinct,* and *Lassie* (a new version of the classic series, coproduced with Canada's CINAR Productions). In spring 2002 Animal Planet announced that it would bring the classic *Mutual of Omaha's Wild Kingdom* (which ran on NBC from 1963 to 1971, then in syndication through the 1980s) back into production. Another of Animal Planet's newer programs, *The Pet Psychic,* has attained something of a cult status, particularly among the network's adult audience. Host Sonya Fitzpatrick claims to help humans better understand their animal companions.

Animal Planet programs generally focus on either domesticated or wild animals, though seldom both at the same time. *Emergency Vets* and *Animal Precinct* feature household pets in distress. Other programs, such as *Amazing Animal Videos* and *Pet Story,* echo the cute home video antics typical of *America's Funniest Home Videos. Pet Story* showcases the heartwarming drama of human-animal bonding. And *Breed All About It* targets prospective dog owners who are weighing the relative virtues of different breeds.

Wild animal–themed programs tend to have different emphases, appealing largely to the at-home viewers' taste for vicarious adventure. The popular *Jeff Corwin Experience* follows its personable host around the world as he interacts with all manner of species. *Big Cat Diary* focuses specifically on the large feline species that inhabit Kenya's Masai Mara wilderness. Similarly, on *Shark Gordon,* shark expert Ian Gordon pursues the feared but misunderstood predators throughout the world's waters.

Probably Animal Planet's best-known series is *Crocodile Hunter,* hosted by Australians Steve and Terri Irwin (owners of the Australia Zoo). Shot primarily in the Australian Outback, this program thrills viewers as Steve handles a variety of dangerous (or at least dangerous-seeming) reptiles. He frequently holds deadly vipers inches in front of his face and has been known to let a nonvenomous python sink its two-inch fangs into his forearm. The spin-off, *Crocodile Hunter's Croc Files,* is aimed at children and features such segments as "Croc Talk" (factoids), "Believe It or Nots" (nature quizzes) and "Croc Scrapbook" (home videos). *The Crocodile Hunter Diaries,* a behind-the-scenes show about Steve and Terri's life at the Australia Zoo, debuted in 2002.

Steve Irwin's exploits and bravado have earned him something of a celebrity status; he has appeared in various television commercials (notably for Pentax cameras and Federal Express) that coordinate with the themes of his programs. And he stars in *The Crocodile Hunter: Collision Course,* a feature film released in July 2002. The film is sure to enhance Discovery Networks' corporate synergies for years to come. Additionally, Universal Studios theme parks in California and Florida have added extensive Animal Planet tie-in attractions to connect with the *Crocodile Hunter* themes as well as other of the network's programs.

In fact, Animal Planet as a whole is a healthy contributor to the Discovery Networks marketing empire and its partners. Discovery Networks Stores, an international chain, sells tie-in products such as stuffed animals, themed clothing, and plastic models. More linked merchandise is available from the extensive Discovery Networks website (www.discovery.com), which includes a sub-site for Animal Planet specifically.

The colorful and animated Animal Planet website, as with many cable-related websites, tightly integrates programs, commercials, and tie-in products. It includes program directories, additional information on program content, and links to fan sites. The more popular program-related pages often feature the logos of the program's television sponsors (for example, Outback Steakhouse for *Crocodile Hunter*).

While it is clear that Animal Planet offers its corporate owners a plethora of commercial tie-ins appealing to adults as well as children, the network also achieves some public service goals. In the case of *Animal Precinct,* for example, producers have successfully linked their content to the work of the American Society for the Prevention of Cruelty to Animals (ASPCA). Other programs, including *Emergency Vets,* look in depth at veterinary medicine, encouraging young people to consider this important profession. Clearly, Animal Planet has met many of the expectations set for specialty cable networks in the early 21st century.

MEGAN MULLEN

See also **Discovery Network**

Anne of Green Gables

Canadian Family Drama

Simultaneously invoking its own homespun brand of pastoral feminism and the long-standing and often contentious debates over the role of broadcasting in Canadian national identity, *Anne of Green Gables* is widely considered one of Canada's most potent cultural icons. Filmed by Sullivan Films as a four-hour miniseries, it was first broadcast in December 1985 on the Canadian Broadcasting Corporation (CBC). This version of what Mark Twain once referred to as the "sweetest creation of childhood yet written" has become one of the most celebrated products to emerge from the Canadian tradition of subsidized coproduction to encourage distinguished programming in the competitive broadcast media marketplace created by proximity to the United States. In addition to unprecedented audience figures and multiple critical awards in Canada, its broadcast on the PBS series *Wonderworks* led the miniseries to become the first Canadian program to win the prestigious Peabody Award.

Attempts to explain the appeal of Lucy Maud Montgomery's 1908 novel have generated a paradox within literary criticism that also applies to the film version. On one hand, *Anne of Green Gables*' plot, characters, and predominant themes are considered by many scholars to be closely consistent with late 19th- and early 20th-century American literature. In Canada, however, both literary scholars and millions of children and adults have cherished Montgomery's Avonlea novels, of which *Anne of Green Gables* is the first, for their very eloquent expression of Canadian heritage, history, and culture. In the ongoing battle to define and articulate a national identity within English-speaking Canada, Anne has be-

Anne of Green Gables.
Photo courtesy of CBC Television

come a powerful force. Indeed, *Anne of Green Gables* is an icon of "Canadianness," not only within her own nation but as a global commodity that has been successfully exported to nations all over the world. The book has been translated into over 30 languages with over 35 million copies in print. Outside of Canada, Anne has enjoyed her greatest success in Japan, where theme parks have been built around the red-headed heroine's persona, and lucrative deals have been brokered to import potatoes from the island province of Prince Edward Island, where her story takes place.

Regardless of the claims made to Anne by other nations, Sullivan's affectionate and lushly filmed family drama continues to stand out in Canadian broadcasting history as one of the most successful television ventures of all time. Its original broadcast gained an audience of 4.9 million viewers on its first night and just under 6 million viewers on the following evening, some of the strongest audience figures ever recorded for a nonsports program broadcast in prime-time viewing hours. These numbers were all the more impressive considering that the CBC sold broadcast time to advertisers based on projections of 2.4 million viewers, and that the film's competition on its first evening included a National Football League (NFL) game.

In addition to its basically unprecedented popularity among viewers, *Anne of Green Gables* garnered critical acclaim for its writing, cinematography, and the performances of the principal actors. Megan Follows, a young Canadian actor, played Anne Shirley, the "scrawny, red-headed orphan" who arrives in the community of Avonlea to live with Matthew and Marrilla Cuthbert, siblings whose advancing years force them to send to a nearby orphanage for a young boy to lend a hand with the daily maintenance of their farm. Anne's gender, overactive imagination, and lack of regard for small-town social mores frame the series of minor conflicts and misadventures that complicate the Cuthberts' eventual decision to adopt her as their own. As Matthew, Richard Farnsworth lends a sweetness and vulnerability to the role of the shy, aging bachelor, while Colleen Dewhurst imbues the initially dour and judgmental Marilla with wisdom, compassion, and a growing, if grudging, affection for her young charge. Anne's eventual adoption into the Cuthbert home and her integration into the various social institutions of the small conservative town provide the backdrop for the film's exploration of the difficult terrain between girlhood and emerging adolescence. Along the way, Anne finds a "bosom friend" and "kindred spirit" in Diana Barry (Schuyler Grant), whose patrician mother's disapproval of Anne's desire to gain an education and eventually have a career foreground Anne's emerging sense of self and ambition. Once lamenting her life as "a perfect graveyard of buried hopes," Anne's love and respect for her adoptive family, acceptance by her peers, and determination suggest that adversity can be liberating when approached with compassion, filial bonds, and values that many critics suggest as basic Christian ideals.

Aesthetically, the production is almost unabashedly sentimental and Sullivan's fond rendering of the idyllic rural landscape casts Avonlea as a key supporting player in the film. Unlike the majority of productions by small independent Canadian filmmakers, Sullivan shot his film in 35 millimeter, which visually gilds the story with a warm, nostalgic glow. Coupled with the meticulously re-created sets and costumes, the lush look captured by this production of *Anne of Green Gables* later became a hallmark characterizing Sullivan's films and enchanted its audience, many of whom had grown up reading the Avonlea stories.

Sullivan's Anne was extraordinarily successful from a business perspective, as well. Shot on time and on budget, roughly 30 percent of its 2.5 million dollar price tag was provided by Telefilm Canada, a Canadian government-funded film development corporation established to support the Canadian broadcasting and film industry. Additional financial support came from the CBC, PBS, City-TV (a private Canadian network), and ZDF (a West German television network). The miniseries also won great critical acclaim. At the 1986 Gemini Awards, given out by the Academy of Canadian Cinema and Television, Anne won in ten of the 12 categories for which it was nominated, including: Best Dramatic Miniseries, Best pperformance by a Lead Actress, Best Performance by Supporting Actor and Supporting Actress, Best Writing, and Best Direction.

Jody Waters

See also **Canadian Broadcasting Corporation Newsworld; Canadian Programming in English**

Cast

Anne Shirley	Megan Follows
Marilla Cuthbert	Colleen Dewhurst
Matthew Cuthbert	Richard Farnsworth
Diana Barry	Schuyler Grant
Gilbert Blythe	Jonathan Crombie
Rachel Lynde	Patricia Hamilton

Producers
Kevin Sullivan and Ian McDougall

Programming History
CBC (Canada)
two two-hour installments
December 1–2, 1985
PBS (United States)
four one-hour episodes on *Wonderworks*
February 17–March 10, 1986

Annenberg, Walter (1908–)

U.S. Media Executive, Publisher, Diplomat

As a media magnate, Walter Annenberg controlled important properties in the newspaper, television, and magazine industries. Perhaps most significantly, he was responsible for the creation of *TV Guide,* the largest circulation weekly magazine in the world, a magazine central to understanding television in the United States. He was also very active in the arena of U.S. politics and served as U.S. ambassador to the Court of St. James. In his later life, Annenberg became renowned for his substantial philanthropic activities, which included significant donations to educational institutions and public television.

When his father was imprisoned for tax evasion in 1940, Annenberg took over the family publishing business. Triangle Publications, particularly *The Daily Racing Form,* proved to be extremely profitable, and Annenberg looked for ways to expand his company at the time television was beginning to emerge as America's communications medium of the future. Inspired by a Philadelphia-area television magazine called *TV Digest,* Annenberg conceived the idea of publishing a national television feature magazine, which he would then wrap around local television listings. The idea came to fruition when Annenberg purchased *TV Digest,* along with the similar publications *TV Forecast* from Chicago and *TV Guide* from New York. He combined their operations to form *TV Guide* in 1953 and quickly expanded the magazine by creating new regional editions and purchasing existing television listings publications in other markets.

Annenberg and his aide, Merrill Panitt (who would go on to become *TV Guide*'s editorial director), realized that in order to achieve the circulation necessary to make their publication a truly mass medium, they needed to go beyond the fan magazine approach that had been typical of most earlier television and radio periodicals. Because of this desire, they created a magazine that was both a staunch booster of the American system of television and one of the most visible critics of the medium's more egregious perceived shortcomings. *TV Guide*'s editors often encouraged the magazine's readers to support quality television programs struggling to gain an audience. In fact, *TV Guide*'s greatest accomplishment under Annenberg may have been the magazine's success in walking the fine line between encouraging and prodding the medium to achieve its full potential without becoming too far removed from the prevailing tastes of the mass viewing public. As a consequence, *TV Guide* became extremely popular, widely read, and very influential among those in the television industry. A large number of distinguished authors wrote articles for the magazine over the years, including such names as Margaret Mead, Betty Friedan, John Updike, Gore Vidal, and Arthur Schlesinger Jr. Many of these writers were attracted by the lure of reaching *TV Guide*'s huge audience; at its peak in the late 1970s, *TV Guide* had a paid circulation of nearly 20 million copies per week.

Annenberg remained supportive of conservative political causes through the years, and his efforts on behalf of Republicans were rewarded with his designation by President Richard Nixon as U.S. am-

Walter Annenberg.
Photo courtesy of Walter Annenberg

bassador to Great Britain in 1969. The appointment led Annenberg to sell his newspapers and television stations, but he retained *TV Guide* and remained active in managing the publication throughout his five-year tenure as ambassador.

Shortly after the election of his close friend Ronald Reagan as president in 1980 (he would endorse Reagan's reelection campaign in 1984 in *TV Guide,* the only such political endorsement ever to appear in the magazine), Annenberg announced a plan to provide the Corporation for Public Broadcasting with $150 million in funds over a 15-year period to produce educational television programs through which viewers could obtain college credits. Annenberg's sympathy for educational causes had already been evidenced by his financial support of the Annenberg Schools of Communication at both the University of Pennsylvania and the University of Southern California. His activities in this regard would grow even more pronounced in the years to come, particularly after his sale of *TV Guide* and Triangle Publications to Rupert Murdoch's News Corporation in 1988 for approximately $3 billion—at the time, the largest price ever commanded for a publishing property.

Annenberg continued to make news after his sale of Triangle because of his many substantial donations to educational causes. In addition, Annenberg was also one of the country's foremost collectors of art, and in 1991, he bequeathed his extensive collection—valued at more than $1 billion—to New York's Metropolitan Museum of Art. In a 1996 capstone to his storied career, Annenberg was awarded the Presidential Medal of Freedom. His post-Triangle era of charitable activities in the areas of education, art, and television further served to assure Annenberg's lasting legacy to a wide spectrum of American culture.

DAVID GUNZERATH

Walter H(ubert) Annenberg. Born in Milwaukee, Wisconsin, March 13, 1908. Married: 1) Veronica Dunkelman, 1938 (divorced, 1950); children: Wallis and Roger (deceased); 2) Leonore (Cohn) Rosentiel. Educated at the Peddie School, Highstown, New Jersey, graduated 1927; attended Wharton School of Finance, University of Pennsylvania, Philadelphia, 1927–28. Joined father, Moses Annenberg, successful publisher, as assistant in the bookkeeping office, 1928; upon father's death, 1942, assumed leadership of family business, Triangle Publications, Inc., which included the Philadelphia *Inquirer,* the *Daily Racing Form,* the *Morning Telegraph,* and other minor publications; founded *Seventeen* magazine, 1944, and *TV Guide,* 1953; acquired the Philadelphia *Daily News,* 1957; acquired WFIL-AM and FM radio, Philadelphia, 1945; expanded station to television outlet, 1947; acquired radio and television stations in Altoona and Lebanon, Pennsylvania; Binghamton, New York; New Haven, Connecticut; and Fresno, California; U.S. ambassador to Great Britain and Northern Ireland, 1968–74; sold Triangle Publications to Rupert Murdoch, 1988. Founder, Annenberg School of Communication, University of Pennsylvania; Annenberg School for Communication, University of Southern California, Los Angeles; Annenberg Washington Program in Communication Policy Studies, Washington, D.C.; Annenberg/Corporation for Public Broadcasting Math and Science Project; founder and trustee, Eisenhower Exchange Fellowships, Eisenhower Medical Center, Rancho Mirage, California. Emeritus Trustee, Metropolitan Museum of Art, New York City; Philadelphia Museum of Art; University of Pennsylvania; the Peddie School, Highstown, New Jersey; Churchill Archives Center, Cambridge College (United Kingdom). Recipient: Order of the British Empire (Honorary); Legion of Honor (France); Order of Merit (Italy); Order of the Crown (Italy); Order of the Lion (Finland); Bencher of the Middle Temple (Honorary); Old Etonian (Honorary); Freedom Medal for Pioneering Television for Educational Purposes; Gold Medal of the Pennsylvania Society; Linus Pauling Medal for Humanitarianism; George Foster Peabody

Award; Ralph Lowell Award, Corporation for Public Broadcasting; Wagner Medal for Public Service, Robert F. Wagner; Award of Greater Philadelphia Chamber of Commerce; Churchill Bell Award; Presidential Medal of Freedom.

Further Reading

Altschuler, Glenn C., and David I. Grossvogel, *Changing Channels: America in TV Guide,* Urbana: University of Illinois Press, 1992

"Annenberg Gives a Life Injection to Public Television," *New York Times* (March 1, 1981)

Blumenstyk, Goldie, "Annenberg Gives $265 Million to 3 Universities," *Chronicle of Higher Education* (June 23, 1993)

Celis, William, "Annenberg to Give Education $500 Million Over Five Years," *New York Times* (December 17, 1993)

Cooney, John, *The Annenbergs,* New York: Simon and Schuster, 1982

Fonzi, Gaeton, *Annenberg: A Biography of Power,* New York: Weybright and Talley, 1970

Grassmuck, Karen, "A $50 Million Gift Buoys Black Colleges for Ambitious Drive; Annenberg Makes Big Donation to United Negro College Fund," *Chronicle of Higher Education* (March 14, 1990)

Nicklin, Julie L., "Annenberg Shifts Priorities" (interview), *Chronicle of Higher Education* (January 12, 1994)

The Philadelphia Inquirer: The Story of the Inquirer 1829 to the Present, Philadelphia, Pennsylvania: Triangle, 1956

Russell, John, "Annenberg Picks Met for $1 Billion Gift," *New York Times* (March 12, 1991)

Anthology Drama

Anthology drama was an early American television series format or genre in which each episode was a discrete story/play rather than a weekly return to the same setting, characters, and stars. In the history of American television, the anthology dramas that were broadcast live from New York are often considered the epitome of the genre and of television's "golden age" of the 1950s. While television was otherwise maligned as lowbrow and crassly commercial, live anthology dramas represented, at least to some observers, the best of 1950s television. There were, however, several variations on the anthology drama series, and not all were critically acclaimed. A staple of late 1940s and 1950s programming, the last anthology dramas left the airwaves by the mid-1960s.

In 1946–47 a series of monthly dramas were presented on NBC's New York station as *Television Theatre.* However, its schedule was erratic, and it was NBC's *Kraft Television Theatre* that became not only the first weekly anthology drama but the first network television series in 1947. It was followed by several other series in 1948, including *The Ford Television Theater, Studio One, Philco Television Playhouse,* and *Actors' Studio.* These were hour-long dramas broadcast live from New York. Over the next several years, numerous such series appeared on the airwaves, among them, for example, *Robert Montgomery Presents, Celanese Theater,* and *The U.S. Steel Hour.* Critics praised the live, hour-long dramas for their presentations of adapted literary classics, serious dramas, and social relevance. The evocation of Broadway created prestige.

Live half-hour series appeared by 1950, such as *Colgate Theater, Lights Out, Danger,* and *Lux Video Theatre.* Some were thematic, creating continuity and programming niches. For instance, *Danger* and *Lights Out* specialized in suspense. With a few exceptions, these half-hour series were not critically acclaimed. Critics complained of dramas squeezed into half hours.

The half-hour format quickly became the province of filmed anthology dramas produced in Hollywood. Critics liked these even less. In contrast to the highbrow, Broadway-play connotations of the live New York series, critics associated filmed dramas with Hollywood, with lowbrow entertainment. But there were all kinds of filmed anthologies, just as there were all kinds of live anthologies. The first filmed anthology series was *Your Show Time* in 1949. Lasting only a few months, it was followed that same year by the first successful filmed anthology drama, *Fireside Theatre.* Other network filmed anthology dramas were *Four Star Playhouse, The Loretta Young Show,* and *Hollywood Opening Night.* Like some of the live productions, filmed anthologies sometimes also programmed for special interests. *The Loretta Young Show,* for example, was targeted at women. Some filmed anthology dramas were produced specifically for syndication. Examples include *Douglas Fairbanks Presents, Death Valley Days,* and *Crown Theatre Starring Gloria Swanson. Death Valley Days* was one of the few anthology dramas with a western theme.

In the earliest years, literary works in the public domain provided the stories for the anthology dramas.

Playhouse 90, Maria Schell, Jason Robards Jr., 1956–60; "For Whom the Bell Tolls," 1959.
Courtesy of the Everett Collection

There were no experienced television writers, and the early industry could not afford experienced writers from other fields. Television writers and original television dramas soon appeared, however, and writers as well as critics and audiences recognized the potential power of small-scale, intimate drama created for the new medium. Writers like Rod Serling and Paddy Chayefsky helped refine the form and found critical success writing anthology dramas. Serling would go on to host his own filmed anthology series, *The Twilight Zone.* By the mid-1950s, original television dramas were providing material for feature films. *Marty, 12 Angry Men, No Time for Sergeants, Requiem for a Heavyweight,* and other original television plays were made into motion pictures.

Actors and directors also found opportunities on anthology dramas. At a time when the Hollywood studio system was disappearing, television offered jobs and public exposure. Little-known actors such as Charlton Heston and Grace Kelly, as well as older Hollywood stars like Lillian Gish and Bette Davis, acted in anthology dramas. Some stars of Old Hollywood, such as Loretta Young, Douglas Fairbanks, and Barbara Stanwyck, had their own anthology series. Directors of anthology dramas who would go on to motion picture work include Sidney Lumet and Arthur Penn.

By the later 1950s, competition from the increasingly successful continuing character series filmed in Hollywood led to other innovations in the anthology drama format. *Playhouse 90* presented 90-minute plays. *Matinee Theater* presented live, color dramas five days a week. *Lux Video Theater* and some others switched from live to filmed dramas. Production moved to Hollywood. During its final season in 1957–58, *Kraft Television Theatre* was the last anthology drama broadcast live from New York.

By the end of the decade, the anthology drama was on its way out. A number of factors led to its demise. Coming up with new, quality dramas and characters every week became increasingly difficult. Some anthology dramas had presented controversial episodes, with well-publicized battles with sponsors who wanted to stick with what they considered middle-of-the-road, uncontroversial entertainment. One last attempt at a socially progressive anthology series, which never did find full sponsorship for its one season, was *East Side, West Side* (1963–64). Sponsors' attitudes, combined with their ultimate power, discouraged some writers and directors from working in the genre. The days of the glamorous Hollywood star as host were also numbered, and such anthology dramas as *The Loretta Young Show* and *The Barbara Stanwyck Show* were gone by the mid-1960s. One of the last to go was *Bob Hope Presents the Chrysler Theater,* an anthology series interspersed with variety specials, which went off the air in 1967. Filmed programming, with its possibilities for an economic afterlife in syndication, had greater profit potential than live production. With television production shifting to Hollywood, more action-oriented genres could now be cranked out. And it seemed that audiences (comprising over 90 percent of U.S. homes by the end of the 1950s) preferred them.

Few examples of the live productions from anthology dramas remain today. Most were not preserved on film, and the few that are available were preserved by filming them off of TV screens (kinescopes). Even many of the filmed programs have disappeared. Perhaps the anthology drama legacy remains today in the made-for-TV movie and in rare attempts at live dramatic productions, such as *Fail Safe* (2000) and the live 1997 season-opening episode of the medical drama series *E.R.*

MADELYN M. RITROSKY-WINSLOW

See also ***Advertising, Company Voice; Alcoa Hour, The; Armstrong Circle Theater; Brodkin, Herbert; Fireside Theater; General Electric Theater; Golden Age of Television; Hallmark Hall of Fame; Kraft***

Television Theater; Mann, Abby; Robinson, Hubbell; Rose, Reginald; Schaffner, Franklin; Playhouse 90; Studio One; Wednesday Play, The; Westinghouse-Desilu Playhouse

Further Reading

Averson, Richard, and David Manning White, editors, *Electronic Drama: Television Plays of the Sixties,* Boston: Beacon Press, 1971

Gianakos, Larry James, *Television Drama Series Programming: A Comprehensive Chronicle, 1947–1959,* Metuchen, New Jersey: Scarecrow Press, 1980

Hawes, William, *The American Television Drama: The Experimental Years,* University: University of Alabama Press, 1986

Sturcken, Frank, *Live Television: The Golden Age of 1946–1958 in New York,* Jefferson, North Carolina: McFarland, 1990

Wilk, Max, *The Golden Age of Television: Notes from the Survivors,* New York: Delacorte Press, 1976

AOL Time Warner. *See* **Time Warner**

APTN. *See* **Aboriginal People's Television Network**

Arbitron

U.S. Ratings Service

Arbitron is the name for a media research product developed by the American Research Bureau (ARB), a company that became a major institution in developing television ratings. The company's founders were Jim Seiler and Roger Cooper. Prior to 1950, when about 10 percent of U.S. homes had television, Seiler was experimenting on the East Coast to develop a satisfactory method for measuring television audiences. Around the same time, Cooper was also testing methods to develop audience data for TV station and advertiser use in the Los Angeles area.

At the time, television viewing was being measured by several different groups using varied techniques such as telephone coincidentals (calls made to viewers during television broadcasts), recalls (telephone calls made on days subsequent to broadcasts), and even door-to-door questionnaires. The common element that brought Cooper and Seiler together was that each found that distributing a viewing diary had distinct advantages in developing audience ratings for this new medium. Viewers could be measured from early morning to late night without being bothered by telephone. Moreover, audience composition, as well as household ratings, could be developed. Audiences outside normal dialing areas could be measured, and net weekly cumulative audiences could be produced.

The two researchers joined forces, incorporated, and established headquarters in Washington, D.C. At about the same time, John Landreth formed a company called Television National Audience Measurement Service. In 1951 he was directed to ARB and after a

Courtesy of Arbitron, Inc.

meeting with Seiler and Cooper became the third partner in the research endeavor.

ARB developed its own methodology for audience measurement. First, a random sample of homes was drawn from telephone directories of the area surveyed. These households were then contacted to determine whether or not a TV was present. One diary, with an explanatory letter, was mailed to the chosen respondents. Each television set in the house was monitored with a separate diary. The diary keeper in the home would record television viewing at 15-minute intervals day by day for seven days and then return the diary. It was determined that four weekly samples would be the basis for each market-research report. Diaries were tabulated manually and a simple report was prepared on a program-by-program basis during prime time. A Monday-through-Friday combination report was prepared for daytime programming.

In the early 1950s, ARB was ready to expand its operation. The Federal Communications Commission (FCC) lifted its 1948 freeze on new station license allocations in July 1952, and many new stations began telecasting. Advertising agencies needed a service to measure viewing in the increasing number of rapidly developing television markets. In 1952 ARB was measuring 15 TV markets. In order to position itself as the industry leader, the organization took a quantum leap and expanded to 35 markets. Ad agency support and usage of the company's TV market reports followed and enabled ARB to be a pioneering leader in the exciting new field of audience measurement.

By the late 1950s, it became obvious that a better way had to be found to develop the diary data. Manual tabulation of the data from diaries was impossibly slow. ARB moved its headquarters to Beltsville, Maryland, and installed a UNIVAC tabulation method and report preparation. This new system almost put the company out of business.

The first reports produced by the system were woefully late; in some markets the reports made no sense. Gradually the company worked its way out of its dilemma. By the 1961–62 television year, ARB was on a better footing and had generally solved the problems it had endured. The new computer equipment gave the company the capability to expand its market reports to include needed data on specific demographic groups, making reports invaluable tools for advertisers and their agencies seeking to buy and sell spot television time.

By the early 1960s, homes owning a TV set had increased dramatically and hundreds of additional television stations had begun telecasting. Hundreds of thousands of diaries were being placed in American homes each year. By 1967 ARB had clearly defined 225 television markets. It produced television market reports called "sweeps" twice per year for every television market, and from four to seven times a year for the larger major markets. The sweeps provided comparative cumulative data for an entire week. TV's advantage as an advertising medium was thus well documented and appreciated; hundreds of millions of dollars were pouring into station and network coffers.

At this time, as a result of demands from advertising agencies, a new and exclusive market definition called the "Area of Dominant Influence" (ADI) was introduced in ARB reports. The ADI was a collection of counties in which the viewing of particular stations in the market was dominant. Some station executives violently objected, complaining the new ratings did not reflect the true size of their station's reach. To counter this, ARB continued to report total homes viewing the station and demographic characteristics of the total audience.

From its inception, ARB's major competitor was the A.C. Nielsen Company. In the local market field, ARB was usually considered the innovative force, normally reacting quickly to what the ad agencies needed in the report. Although many advertising agencies subscribed to both rating services, ARB usually had a larger list of user agencies. In the larger TV markets, a majority of stations were subscribers to both rating services.

During the 1980s, the two services were caught up in a rapidly changing electronic media marketplace. Arbitron delivered reports on cable penetration and cable viewing within specific markets. It made a large investment in ScanAmerica, a unique service that combined viewing estimates with product purchase surveys. Additional investments were made to change methods of measurement. In larger markets, diary surveys were converted to an automated system that used a sample in which special equipment was attached to the television set. Viewing data from the meter was carried through telephone lines to an electronic data center. In the larger TV markets, metered research provided reports on a more timely basis; indeed, even overnight program ratings were now available.

These very sophisticated research methods were not only costly to install but also expensive to maintain.

This resulted in substantial increases in the cost of market reports. TV stations had always borne most of the cost for the audience research. Both Arbitron and the Nielsen Company charged agencies a token amount for the complete package of all market reports produced.

In the competition Arbitron began losing market share. By the end of the 1980s, it had 19 metered markets, to Nielsen's 29, and the number of TV stations subscribing to ARB's market reports based on the viewing diary declined.

Finally, in the fall of 1993, Arbitron president Stephen Morris declared that his company was out of the television-measuring business, contending that the marketplace would no longer support two rating services. It was revealed that approximately 275 stations subscribed to both Arbitron and Nielsen local market reports. But Arbitron's lists of exclusive station subscribers had dwindled to 180 clients while Nielsen could claim 359 exclusive subscribers. According to Morris, Arbitron would continue to provide specialized TV-audience research for television stations and advertising agencies. But for the first time in nearly 40 years, the sales offices of TV stations and the research departments of ad agencies were dependent on a single source of local market research reports.

As a company, Arbitron is still in existence. It continues to measure successfully radio-listening audiences, using the personal diary, and its research reports are widely used in the radio industry. In recent years it has developed highly successful programs of syndicated market research contracted to newspapers, cable television services, and Internet radio as well as for radio broadcasting. The most ambitious project has been the development of the Portable People Meter, a device that would record media use by individuals in any context or venue. Designed to track audiences for terrestrial, satellite, and Internet radio stations as well as broadcast, satellite, and cable television, this technology could once again alter the business of measuring media use and thereby the economics of the media industries.

C.A. Kellner

See also **Advertising; Market; Ratings; Share**

Further Reading

"Ailing Oligopoly: TV Station Rating Business: New Petry Study Confirms That More Stations Are Giving Up Either Arbitron or Nielsen," *Broadcasting* (April 23, 1990)

American Research Bureau, *Arbitron Replication: A Study of the Reliability of Broadcast Ratings,* New York: American Research Bureau, 1974

Arbitron Company, *Inside the Arbitron Television Report,* New York: American Research Bureau, 1977

Beville, Hugh Malcolm, *Audience Ratings: Radio, Television, and Cable,* Hillsdale, New Jersey: Erlbaum, 1988

Broadcast Ratings Council, Inc., *Standard Errors and Effective Sample Sizes As Reported for Broadcast Audience Measurement Surveys,* New York: Broadcast Ratings Council, 1970

Carter, Bill. "Arbitron Is Closing Down National Ratings Service," *New York Times* (September 3, 1992)

Webster, James G., and Lawrence W. Lichty, *Ratings Analysis: Theory and Practice,* Hillsdale, New Jersey: Erlbaum, 1991

Archives for Television Materials

The history of the archiving of television productions has some remarkable similarities with that of the archiving of films made for the cinema. Most striking is the parallel loss of the bulk of early production, which demonstrated the need for archiving to be formalized. Just as the majority of silent cinema failed to survive, so the bulk of television's output from the 1940s to the middle of the 1970s is similarly absent. This can partly be ascribed to the failure in the case of both media to be taken seriously as either an art form or a medium of record in their earliest years. Indeed, both were regarded as ephemeral and insignificant and the retention of their output suffered accordingly. It also took time for both to become the subject of academic study and thus for historic materials to be demanded.

However, there were also some specific factors at work in the television field which mitigated against archiving. The most important were technical: the earliest television transmissions were all live and the technology to record them did not exist. Thus, all that remains of the BBC's television service from before the World War II are some specially shot films made to illustrate the service. Indeed, the earliest remaining television materials are items shot on film and the first archives of television materials were company film li-

The archives of the Museum of Broadcast Communications (MBC).
Photo courtesy of the Museum of Broadcast Communications (MBC)

braries. In the late 1940s the technique of telerecording, also known as kinescoping, allowed the recording of transmissions on film. In the United States, this allowed the delayed transmission of programs in different time zones, and thus substantial amounts of material survive. Elsewhere, particularly in Britain, the expense meant that only the most prestigious productions and events were recorded. There was still also the feeling that the bulk of output was not worth preserving, combined with the fact that, being originally a medium developed to transmit moving pictures over a distance as the action happened, there was no such tradition anyway. In addition, the early lack of any possibility that materials would be repeated, partly because of agreements with entertainment unions, mitigated against archiving. The material being kept was mostly factual, especially news reports, which had a clear reuse and historic value.

Again, it is the output of the U.S. networks in the 1950s which has survived the best, another reason being the policy of selling programming to other countries developing their own television services. The fact that Lucille Ball and Phil Silvers still regularly appear on cable channels throughout the world has a lot to do with this fact.

At the end of the 1950s, the development of videotape gave the possibility of archiving on a larger scale, while its expense and the fact that it could be wiped and reused kept the situation uncertain. Every country has its favorite examples of material that has been lost. In the United States it is the first Super Bowl. In Britain the cult science fiction series *Dr. Who* has almost 100 lost episodes. Nevertheless, more material survives from the 1960s than from before and the growing academic interest in the medium attracted the attention of some of the major public archives already dealing with film.

By the mid-1970s, television archiving was becoming firmly established, and the foundation of an International Federation of Television Archives (FIAT/IFTA) in 1977 testifies to its spread. The most significant archives were those owned by the companies producing the programs. In the United States, these ranged from the news and sports archives of the three main networks to the Hollywood and other production houses that made the rest of the programming. In Europe, where the initial model was single state broadcasters producing all their own programming, followed by the spasmodic introduction of similar commercial broadcasters, company archiving became more centralized. Nevertheless, the commercial nature of the business meant that cultural archives of television programs, and the public access that follows, had to be provided elsewhere.

It is still the case that most countries do not have publicly funded archives of television programs in the way that they do have such archives of film productions. In those countries where such archives do exist, they have often been provided by the same organizations that already ran the film archives. This is certainly the case in Britain, where the National Film Archive, run by the British Film Institute (BFI), began collecting television material at the end of the 1950s and expanded its operation to such an extent that, in 1993, it changed its name to the National Film and Television Archive. This also reflected the fact that legislation and regulation had made it the central national archive for the output of the three main commercial channels, which came either from regional companies in the case of ITV or independent producers in the cases of Channels 4 and 5. The archive's responsibilities are preservation and public access and most material is acquired by recording transmissions, thus ensuring that the complete flow of images, including commercial breaks and promotions, is captured and preserved. A separate agreement with the BBC, which has had its own archival responsibilities imposed by government since 1979, allows for public access to the corporation's output through the BFI.

In the United States the situation is considerably more fragmented and a national survey by the Library of Congress in 1997 identified hundreds of collections of television programs, reflecting the enormous national production and highlighting the need for the coordination of preservation and access. The most significant public collections are those of the Library itself, the UCLA Film and Television Archive, and the Museum of Broadcasting, though, in the absence of federal legislation, acquisition has of necessity been spasmodic and opportunistic. Academic institutions often end up with significant specialist collections, such as the Political Commercial Archive at the University of Oklahoma.

In some other countries, especially in Scandinavia, there are laws of legal deposit for television programs, though in most there is nothing other than the company archives, most of which remain available for commercial use only. Probably the most interesting solution is in France, where the Institut National de l'Audiovisuel (INA) has the right of legal deposit of all television production and assumes the exploitation rights to much of the material it acquires after a number of years, thus making it a significant production house as well as a comprehensive national resource and study center. In the Netherlands the National Audiovisual Archive (NAA) has combined the resources of the main broadcasters and public archives.

At the end of the 1980s all television archives, company and public, woke up to the biggest problem they now face: the obsolescence of video formats. The first dominant video format, two-inch Quadruplex, which had been standard from the late 1950s to the early 1980s, had been superseded by one-inch formats and the technology was no longer being supported by the companies that had manufactured it. Since then, newer formats have followed at dizzying speeds, the latest being small gauge, highly compressed digital videocassettes, which themselves are being supplanted by disc and file formats. The only way to preserve the images in these circumstances is to transfer them to a current format, though the choices involved are difficult and the likelihood of having to do the transfer again as newer formats emerge is high. The scale of the problem is enormous and a large amount of the world's two-inch recordings still remain to be transferred.

One factor in the archives' favor is the explosion in television delivery methods, causing a massive rise in the number of channels requiring product to fill them, at the same time as there is a seemingly insatiable appetite for programming from the past. In these circumstances, the reuse of archival material is a massive operation, though the danger that only the material that is regarded as commercially viable will be transferred and preserved is a very real one. Public funding will be required on a large scale if the cultural archives' collections are to survive.

Digital technology is also bringing major changes to television archive operations. Traditional cataloging methods are being supplanted by metadata attached to the digital images themselves, requiring the archive's documentalists to become involved at the production stage, rather than, as traditionally, after transmission. News in particular is becoming a fully digital operation and it is no surprise that the first archive to implement a full digitization policy and make its catalog available on the Internet is that of CNN. Of course, the technology needed to support such operations is notoriously even more unreliable than videotape in terms of its longevity and future compatibility with currently operating models.

Having fought hard to establish themselves and their operations, television archives thus face an uncertain future. At least it is now realized that, for both commercial and cultural reasons, the preservation and continuing accessibility of archival television material is a necessity.

STEVE BRYANT

Further Reading

Ballantyne, James, editor, *The Researcher's Guide to British Film and Television Collections,* London: British Film and Video Council, 1993

Davies, Brenda, editor, *International Directory of Film and TV Documentation Sources,* New York: FIAF, 1980

Godfrey, Donald G., *Reruns on File: A Guide to Electronic Media Archives,* Hillsdale, New Jersey: Erlbaum, 1992

Mehr, Linda Harris, editor, *Motion Pictures, Television and Radio: A Union Catalogue of Manuscript and Special Collections in the Western United States,* New York: FIAF, 1977

Rowan, Bonnie G., *Scholars Guide to Washington, D.C. Film and Video Collections,* Washington, D.C.: Smithsonian Institution Press, 1980

Argentina

Argentina is one of the most important television and cable markets in Latin America. After Brazil and Mexico, it has the largest number of television receivers in the region (7,165,000 receivers/4.6 persons per receiver, according to the *Britannica Book of the Year,* 1994). Its cable penetration is the highest in Latin America (52 percent, according to *Produccíon and Distribucíon,* 1995). Domestic programs actively compete with foreign productions, and popular genres include variety shows, sitcoms, *telenovelas,* and sports and children's programs. The history of television in this country is characterized by cyclical patterns of state and private media ownership that parallel the changes occurring in the political and economic arena.

Argentine television began its transmissions in 1951 through channel 7, during the presidency of Juan Domigo Perón. Jaime Yankelevitch, a pioneer of the medium in the country, was a local radio entrepreneur who traveled to the United States to buy the equipment needed for television broadcasting. Initially, the transmitters were operated by the Ministry of Public Works, and the legal framework established the state as the owner of the broadcasting service. During this time, the government had absolute control over television, even though advertising spots were sold to commercial advertisers from its inception.

The military government of Pedro Eugenio Aramburu that overthrew Perón instituted private television in 1957 through the enactment of the decree 15,460. With the intention of controlling the dissemination of messages, this decree-law also prohibited the existence of broadcasting networks in the country. The stations in Buenos Aires could not send signals to the rest of the country, and as a result many independent stations with limited coverage emerged throughout the country. The first pay-TV systems were founded in 1962–63. They used community antenna television (CATV) technology, coaxial cables, and inexpensive equipment and bought most of their programming from the broadcast stations in Buenos Aires. Ironically, the pay-TV stations that resulted from the 1957 prohibition stand at the root of the high cable penetration and the economic boom in the Argentine cable business today.

The first private channels in the capital city of Buenos Aires started operating in 1960—channels 9, 13, and 11. Though Argentine law prohibited foreign ownership of TV channels, at first the American networks managed to make "backdoor" deals with the local stations by creating parallel production companies. Foreign investment could flow to these companies because they were not limited in terms of ownership. Thus the American television corporation NBC invested in channel 9 through the production company Telecenter, ABC invested in channel 11 through Telerama, and CBS and Time-Life invested in channel 13 through Proartel. In this way the American networks became partners of the private Argentine channels.

The founder of channel 13 was Goar Mestre, a famous Cuban broadcasting entrepreneur who left Cuba when Fidel Castro came to power in 1959 and emigrated to Argentina. Because Mestre was married to an Argentine, his wife was able to become the owner of the license for channel 13. At the same time, Mestre established a financial arrangement with CBS and Time-Life in which he owned 60 percent of Proartel (Producciones Argentinas de Televisión), channel 13's production company. As Elizabeth Fox argues in *Media and Politics in Latin America* (1988), the entrance of foreign capital had a strong impact on national broadcasting, by exposing Argentina to large investments in advertising and driving the development of mass consumption markets.

In the mid-1960s national entrepreneurs invested in the majority stocks of the three private channels, and the American networks withdrew from the market. In 1965, Alejandro Romay bought channel 9. In the early 1970s, the Vigil family, owner of the publisher Editorial Atlántida, invested in channel 13, and Héctor Ricardo García, from the publisher Editorial Sarmiento, invested in channel 11. In *Quien te ha visto y quién TV* (1988), Argentine television expert Pablo Sirvén considers the 1960s the best years of private television, a period characterized by the high competition between the stations and the success of their programming.

Yet this golden period came to an end in 1974 when the third Peronist government decided that the private licenses should return to the state and expropriated the major television stations. Silvio Waisbord indicates that the rationale for deciding not to renew their commercial licenses was based on the defense of the national interest, the elimination of commercialism, and the advancement of cultural goals. However, the state's appropriation of private channels brought no major changes because the stations continued to be supported by advertising and the programming was produced by the same production companies as before.

The government did not fulfill its promise to support the national industry and no cultural programming was produced. As reruns of old programs and movies became commonplace, both audiences and advertising declined and the stations needed additional state support to continue operating.

The fact that all television channels were state owned played directly into the hands of the military dictatorship during the period from 1976 to 1983. The military exercised tight ideological control over the content of all programming, and there were "black lists" with the names of prestigious producers, scriptwriters, and actors who could not work in television. The 22,285 broadcasting law enacted during this period dealt extensively with the content of the programming. Any appeal to violence, eroticism, vice, or crime was prohibited as well as any content that challenged the ethical, social, or political norms of the country. During this period, in 1980, the first color transmissions began for the national market.

During the dictatorship, all state units, including all television stations, were allocated one-third to the army, one-third to the navy, and one-third to the air force. Channel 9 went to the army, channel 11 to the air force, channel 13 to the navy, and channel 7 to the presidency. While the military government managed to keep an intense ideological control over the content of the programs, their poor administration of the stations indebted them to the point of bankruptcy. For instance, in order to compete with each other, each of the three branches of the armed forces paid enormous sums of money to hire famous stars. Yet the revenues generated by advertising were not enough to cover these expenses.

The military regime was in principle against any kind of state intervention in the economy. Unlike previous governments that had tried to promote the national industry, the last military government eliminated all tariffs and protectionistic measures impeding the free flow of goods in the marketplace. However, in the area of communication their free-market policies were not so clear. Oscar Landi writes in *Devórame Otra Vez* (1988) that the military intended to privatize the channels while keeping them under their ideological control at the same time. Given this ambivalence, the process of privatization undertaken during this period with the enactment of the 1980 Broadcasting Law was intentionally slow and started with the smaller stations in the provinces. Only in 1984, during the democratically elected government of Raúl Alfonsón, did the wave of privatization reach Buenos Aires. It was at this point that channel 9 returned to its previous owner, Alejandro Romay.

Notwithstanding the elimination of all censorship and "black lists," the communication sector inherited by Alfonsón still operated under the legal legacy of the military regime and was highly inefficient. As a result, cable television, particularly in the interior of the country, developed without regulation, and television channels continued to violate the legal limit of advertising time. Despite many attempts, the Alfonsón administration did not succeed in reforming the broadcast sector. This failure is generally attributed to the gridlock resulting from the strong economic and political pressures that operated during the transition to democracy.

President Menem learned his lesson from Alfonsón's experience, and early in his administration implemented by decree the "Law of State Reform" that included, among other state enterprises, the privatization of channel 11 and channel 13 in December 1989. At this point the deregulation of broadcasting acquired full force. Today there are five superstations in Buenos Aires; four of them are privately owned (channels 2, 9, 11, and 13) and one remains public (channel 7/ Argentina Televisora Color).

The loosening of cross-media ownership allowed for the emergence of national media conglomerates. Publishers had extensively lobbied for this measure. Channel 13 was licensed to the conglomerate Clarón, the owner of the largest circulation newspaper in the country; ARTEAR, a film and television production company; two radio stations, Radio Mitre and FM100; a publishing company, Editorial Aguilar; an expanding multiple service operator (MSO), Multicanal (400,000 subscribers); three satellite-delivered channels; and one of the partners of a newsprint factory, Papel Prensa, and the national news agency, Diarios y Noticias (DyN). Channel 11 was licensed to Telefé, a consortium integrated by the publisher Editorial Atlántida that also owns Produfé, a program production and distribution company, and at present controls 15 cable systems (200,000 subscribers). ARTEAR and Telefé are the channels that dominate the broadcast landscape and fiercely compete for top ratings.

Toward the end of the 1980s, the number of cable operators in the country reached about 2000. The main players were Video Cable Comunicación (VCC) and CableVisión. In the early 1990s new operators linked to Clar'n and Telefé entered the market and gradually began to buy up cable franchises from smaller operators across the country. At present cable ownership is concentrated in the following four groups: VCC, CableVisión, Clarón, and Telefé. These companies are also investing in fiber optic cable and are implementing Multichannel Multipoint Distribution Services (MMDS) to distribute their signals across areas that cannot be reached by cable. Another player in the cable business is Imagen Satelital, a company that supplies Argentine cable systems with five in-house channels (Space, I-Sat, Infinito, Universo, and Jupiter) and distributes nine additional signals, among them

Televisa's Eco Noticias, Bandeirantes from Brazil, and Much Music from Canada. Argentine signal distributors and programmers have grown rapidly since the launching of the domestic satellite Nahuel in 1992. This satellite's footprint covers the northern part of Argentina, the western part of Brazil, and most of the territory of Chile, Paraguay, and Uruguay.

During the years following the privatization of television channels, advertising expenditures have more than quadrupled. Television and cable operators pay an 8-percent tax on advertising revenues to the National Broadcasting Committee (COMFER), which supports the government channel 7/Argentina Televisora Color. Currently the COMFER also directs 25 percent of this income to the National Film Institute for the subsidy of local film production.

Further trends toward deregulation of communications resulted in the signing of a bilateral accord between Argentina and the United States in September 1994 that allows for American investment in Argentine broadcast and cable operations. American capital entered the market soon afterward, when TCI Inc. and Continental Cable invested in the two largest cable system operators in Argentina, CableVisión and VCC, respectively.

For about $35 a month, cable subscribers in Argentina receive a varied menu of about 65 channels, which includes (in addition to the domestic superstations): European channels (e.g., RAI from Italy, TV5 from France, TVE from Spain, and Deutsche Welle from Germany); Latin American channels (e.g., Globo TV, Manchete, and Bandeirantes from Brazil, Inravisión from Colombia, ECO from Mexico, and Venevisión from Venezuela); and American channels (FOX, USA, CNN, ESPN, the Discovery Channel, Cartoon Network, MTV, Nickelodeon, HBO Olé, etc.). At present no premium cable channels are offered in Argentina, and all the services are included in the basic subscription package.

Variety shows are among the most popular programs. They are scheduled at different times throughout the day, often in the early afternoon (1:00 to 2:00 P.M.) or during the peak of prime time (8:00 to 9:00 p.m.). The Argentine version of a variety show features a combination of musicals, interviews, comic skits, and games in which the audience participates by calling the host of the program, who frequently is a famous national actor. An example of a daily variety show that has reached top ratings since 1984 is *Hola Susana,* hosted by actor Susana Giménez. Another popular variety show is *Videomatch,* hosted by Marcelo Tinelli. His program starts at midnight, targets a young, 15- to 30-year-old audience, and includes video clips, bloopers, and sports.

In general, *telenovelas* are shown from Monday through Fridays in the afternoon (1:00 to 4:00 p.m., depending on the channel) and early prime time (6:00 to 8:00 p.m.). The former are targeted at women, while the latter are targeted at a young adult audience. Weekly drama series broadcast after 10:00 p.m. are also popular. These attempt to reach an adult audience by dealing with socially controversial themes such as corruption, drugs, homosexuality, and so on.

A typical TV prime-time evening starts at 6:00 p.m. with light *telenovelas,* variety shows, or game shows. These programs precede the one-hour newscasts that are scheduled in different time slots in each channel. Channel 11 and ATC/channel 7 broadcast their evening news programs at 7:00 p.m., channel 2 at 9:00 p.m., and channel 9 and channel 13 compete on the news front at 8:00 p.m. From 10:00 p.m. to midnight viewers may opt for movies (which are usually imported), weekly drama series, or public affairs programs led by well-known national journalists and political pundits.

Sports programs are generally scheduled during weekends. They cover different matches and report on the result of national, regional, or world championships. Soccer is the sport followed by the largest audience; the broadcast of a soccer cup final never fails to reach top ratings. But popular sports programs also include tennis, boxing, motoring, and rugby.

Unfortunately, there is no recent data on the proportion of imported programs available in this country. Early studies on the world flow of television programs conducted by Tapio Varis (1974) show that in 1971 channel 9 and channel 11 respectively imported 10 percent and 30 percent of their programming. A decade later, Varis (1984) found that channel 9 imported 49 percent of its programming. Considering the changes in the Argentine television landscape since 1989 (i.e., privatization, liberalization, the growth of cable, etc.), those partial figures cannot be considered a reliable estimate of the proportion of the current imported/domestic programming. Nevertheless, rating figures show that in general the Argentine audience prefers domestic productions. For instance, in August 1994, according to data from the market research company IBOPE (TV International, 1994), the five programs with the highest ratings were: soccer championship *Copa Libertadores* (13.0 of rating); variety show *Hola Susana* (12.6); family sitcom *¡Grande Pá!* (12.6); movie cycle *Cine ATP* (11.3); and *The Simpsons* (11.2).

JAQUI CHMIELEWSKI FALKENHEIM

Further Reading

Fox, E., "Nationalism, Censorship, and Transnational Control," in *Media and Politics in Latin America,* edited by E. Fox, London: Sage, 1988

Morgan, Michael, "Television and the Cultivation of Political Attitudes in Argentina," *Journal of Communication* (Winter 1991)
Muraro, H., "Dictatorship and Transition to Democracy: Argentina 1973–86," in *Media and Politics in Latin America,* edited by E. Fox, London: Sage, 1988
Salwen, M.B., and B. Garrison, *Latin American Journalism,* Hillsdale, New Jersey: Erlbaum, 1991
"Shining Star of South America's Southern Cone Lures New Investors," *TV International* (October 24, 1994)
Varis, T., "Global Traffic in Television," *Journal of Communication* (1974)
Varis, T., "The International Flow of Television Programs," *Journal of Communication* (1984)
Zuleta-Puceiro, E., "The Argentine Case: Television in the 1989 Presidential Election," in *Television, Politics, and the Transition to Democracy in Latin America,* edited by Thomas E. Skidmore, Washington, D.C., and London: Woodrow Wilson Center Press, 1993.

Arledge, Roone (1931–2002)

U.S. Media Producer, Executive

Roone Arledge, former president of ABC News, had a more profound impact on the development of television news and sports programming and presentation than any other individual. In fact, a 1994 *Sports Illustrated* magazine ranking placed Arledge third, behind Muhammad Ali and Michael Jordan, in a list of 40 individuals who have had the greatest impact on the world of sports in the previous four decades. In addition, a 1990 *Life* magazine poll listed Arledge as among the "100 Most Important Americans of the 20th Century."

In 1960 Arledge defected from NBC to join a struggling ABC. Later, in his role as vice president of ABC Sports, Arledge created what would become the longest-running and most successful sports program ever, *ABC's Wide World Sports.* He brought his production specialty to ABC and overhauled sports programming, including introduction of such techniques as slow motion and instant replays. These production techniques enabled Arledge to create a more exciting and dramatic sports event. He combined his production skills with "up close and personal" athlete features, which changed the way the world viewed competing athletes. He was one of the first users of the Atlantic satellite, enabling him to produce live sporting events from around the world.

Arledge's success in sports resulted in his promotion to sports division president in 1968, where he served until 1986. Shortly after his promotion, he again elevated ABC's sports prominence with *NFL Monday Night Football.* This prime-time sports program gave ABC the lock on ratings during its time slot and earned Arledge even greater respect.

Under Arledge's lead, ABC Sports became the unchallenged leader in network sports programming. Arledge's innovations on *Wide World* were also successful for the ten Olympic games he produced. Inducted into the Olympic Hall of Fame for his commitment to excellence, Arledge was later awarded the Medal of Olympic Order by the International Olympic Committee, making him the first television executive and one of a select group of Americans to receive this prestigious award.

Despite his successful transformation of ABC Sports, his promotion to president of ABC News came as a surprise to many individuals because Arledge had no formal journalistic training. He was president of ABC Sports and ABC News for nearly ten years.

With the development of shows such as *20/20, World News Tonight,* and *Nightline,* ABC was soon on the top of the network news battle. Among his greatest skills was identification of potential stars. Arledge successfully recruited the strongest and most promising journalists for his news team, including *World News Tonight* star Peter Jennings. Arledge recognized Jennings's talent and cast this once-defeated *ABC Evening News* anchor in the spotlight, and it worked. Arledge's team included David Brinkley, Diane Sawyer, Sam Donaldson, Ted Koppel, Barbara Walters, and Hugh Downs.

Arledge put news on the air in nontraditional formats and at nontraditional times and received high ratings. In its more than 20 years, *Nightline* has battled entertainment personalities such as Johnny Carson, David Letterman, and Jay Leno for ratings and in 1995

Roone Arledge, President of ABC News and ABC Sports, 11/20/84.
Courtesy of the Everett Collection

was the highest rated late-night program. From its first show with Ali Agah, Iranian affairs leader, and Dorothea Morefield, wife of American hostage Richard Morefield, *Nightline* has been a leader in international affairs reporting.

Arledge's other news show creations include *Primetime,* with Diane Sawyer and Sam Donaldson; *This Week with David Brinkley; World News Now,* a 2:00–6:00 A.M. Monday through Friday overnight news program; and numerous *ABC News Presents* specials, such as *Turning Point* and *Viewpoint.* Arledge also designed inventive news broadcasts such as *Capital to Capital,* the first satellite news series to promote discussion between U.S. and Soviet legislators.

His shows have received virtually every broadcasting honor possible. In 1995 ABC News was the first news organization to receive the Alfred I. du Pont-Columbia University Award, given for the network's overall commitment to excellence. Interestingly, Arledge won his first of 37 Emmy Awards for producing the puppet show featuring Lambchop and Shari Lewis.

In a speech following his appointment at ABC, Arledge declared, "We (ABC) will be setting the standards that everyone will be talking about and that others in the industry will spend years trying to equal." It is clear, based on the success of ABC Sports and ABC News, that Arledge lived up to his immodest words.

Arledge died December 5, 2002, due to complications from cancer. He was 71. Arledge served as a trustee of Columbia College from 1999 until his death. He was benefactor of the Roone Arledge Auditorium and Cinema at Columbia and 1998 recipient of the Alexander Hamilton Medal, the alumni association's highest award.

JOHN TEDESCO

See also **American Broadcasting Company; News, Network; Olympics and Television; Sports on Television; Sportscasters**

Roone Arledge. Born in Forest Hills, New York, July 8, 1931. Married: Joan Heise, 1953 (divorced, 1971); children: Elizabeth Ann, Susan Lee, Patricia Lu, and Roone Pinckney. Educated at Mepham High School, Merrick, New York; Columbia College, New York, B.A. 1952. Served in United States Army, 1953–55. Production assistant, DuMont Television Network, 1952; producer-director, radio public relations spots for U.S. Army, 1953–55; stage manager, director, and producer, NBC Television, 1955–60; joined ABC Television, field producer, NCAA Television, 1960; producer, *ABC's Wide World of Sports,* 1961; vice president, ABC Sports, 1965; president, ABC Sports, 1968–86; created *NFL Monday Night Football,* 1969; president ABC News, 1977; group president, ABC News and Sports, 1985–90; president ABC News, 1990–98. Recipient: 37 Emmy Awards; four George Foster Peabody Awards; two Christopher Awards; Broadcast Pioneers Award; Gold Medal, International Radio and Television Society; Distinguished Service to Journalism Honor Medal, University of Missouri; John Jay Distinguished Professional Service Award, Columbia University; Distinguished Achievement Award, University of Southern California Journalism Association; Founders Award, Academy of Television Arts and Sciences; Grand Prix, Montreaux Television Festival; Medal of Olympic Order, International Olympic Committee; Grand Prize, Cannes Film Festival; Man of the Year, National Association of Television Program Executives; Academy of Television Arts and Sciences Hall of Fame, 1990; U.S. Olympic Hall of Fame, 1990; du Pont-Columbia Award, 1995; Lifetime Achievement Award, National Academy of Television Arts and Sciences, 2002. Died December 5, 2002.

Further Reading

Arledge, Roone, *Roone: A Memoir,* New York : HarperCollins, 2003

Flander, Judy, "Rooneglow," *Washington Journalism Review* (July–August 1990)
Goldenson, Leonard, *Beating the Odds,* New York: Scribner, 1991
Gunther, Marc, "Blue Roone," *American Journalism Review* (April 1994)
Gunther, Marc, *The House That Roone Built: The Inside Story of ABC News,* Boston: Little, Brown, 1994
Gunther, Marc, and B. Carter, *Monday Night Mayhem: The Inside Story of ABC's Monday Night Football,* New York: William Morrow, 1988
O'Neil, Terry, *The Game Behind the Game: High Pressure, High Stakes in Television Sports,* New York: Harper and Row, 1989
Patton, Phil, *Razzle Dazzle: The Curious Marriage of Television and Professional Football,* Garden City, New York: Dial Press, 1984
Powers, John, "Roone Arledge," *Sport* (December 1986)
Rader, Benjamin G., *In Its Own Image: How Television Has Transformed Sports,* New York: Free Press, 1984
Roberts, Randy, "Roone Arledge and the Rise of Televised Sports," *USA Today* (January 1992)
"Roone Arledge on ABC's Wide World of News" (interview), *Broadcasting & Cable* (October 10, 1994)
Rushin, Steve, "Roone Arledge (Forty for the Ages)," *Sports Illustrated* (September 19, 1994)
Spence, Jim, with Dave Giles, *Up Close and Personal: The Inside Story of Network Television Sports,* New York: Athaneum, 1988
Sugar, Bert Randolph, *The Thrill of Victory: The Inside Story of ABC Sports,* New York: Hawthorne, 1978
Waters, Harry F., "A Relish for Risks; The Ups and Downs of ABC's Roone Arledge," *Newsweek* (June 15, 1987)

Armed Forces Radio and Television Service.

See **American Forces Radio and Television Service**

Armstrong Circle Theatre

U.S. Dramatic Anthology

Armstrong Circle Theatre premiered in the summer of 1950, joining 13 other anthology programs already on the air, and went on to become one of the longest-running anthology series in television history. It aired for 14 seasons, first in a 30-minute format and later expanding to one hour. *Armstrong Circle Theatre* was produced by Talent Associates, Ltd., the agency formed by David Susskind and Alfred Levy, which also produced the *Kaiser Aluminum Hour* and individual productions for the *DuPont Show of the Month, Kraft Television Theatre,* and the *Philco Television Playhouse.*

What differentiated the *Armstrong Circle Theatre* from other anthology series was the show's change in focus after its first few seasons. Initially, *Armstrong Circle Theatre* presented typical, formula dramas, with little to distinguish it from other anthologies. In 1952 producers decided to change their approach. An advertising agency gathered scripts from all sources, including first-time writers (such as Rod Serling, whose early story "Acquittal" aired in 1952 as "The Sergeant"), and with this agency's assistance, the producers opted for "quality dramas" that emphasized characterization over pure plot devices. The new stories presented on *Armstrong Circle* attempted a continuity of mood, theme, and style from production to production without presenting the same type of protagonist in varying situations. Some critics described the stories as sentimental, with a "pleasantly related moral" as their thematic approach. One example of this "family type" dramatic style was "The Rocking Horse" (July 25, 1950), a tender story about a reunion between mother and son.

In 1955, when *Armstrong Circle Theatre* expanded to one hour, the series continued its emphasis on the

Armstrong Circle Theatre: "Battle of Hearts."
Photo courtesy of Wisconsin Center for Film and Theater Research

story and presented the earliest form of the docudrama (fact-based dramatizations). Executive producer David Susskind and producer Robert Costello de-emphasized the role of actors and made the story the "star." According to Costello, their aim was "to combine fact and drama—to arouse interest, even controversy, on important and topical subjects." Using a news story or idea was not enough: the series also had to "be able to present some potential solution, some hope for your citizens to consider, to think about." Examples of these fact-based dramas include "S.O.S. from the Andrea Doria" (October 16, 1956) and "Lost: $2,000,000" (October 11, 1955), a drama about the effect of Hurricane Diane on the small town of Winsted, Connecticut.

The docudrama format was enhanced by having a news anchor serve as the host/narrator for the program, and for this task, NBC hired news anchorman John Cameron Swayze. When the series switched from NBC to CBS in 1957, Swayze was replaced by CBS news anchor Douglas Edwards. Edwards was subsequently removed by CBS when network executives felt his credibility as a news anchor would be diminished by hosting a non-news program. He was replaced by reporter Ron Cochran, formerly of ABC.

At the time that its format was lengthened to one hour, *Armstrong Circle Theatre* alternated with *Playwrights '56*. Problems arose between the two series because each was sponsored by a different company with different advertising aims. Pontiac, sponsor of *Playwrights '56,* wanted a very distinct sales message aimed at a large audience. *Armstrong Circle* desired strong sponsor identification with its special type of programming. Although *Playwrights '56* produced a number of distinctive dramas, they were not as critically successful as other anthologies. Pontiac considered the ratings for the show too low and withdrew its sponsorship at the end of the season. The next season, *Armstrong Circle* alternated with *The Kaiser Aluminum Hour,* also produced by David Susskind's Talent Associates, Ltd. In 1957 *Armstrong Circle Theatre* switched to CBS and alternated with *The U.S. Steel Hour* until the end of its television run.

SUSAN R. GIBBERMAN

See also **Advertising, Company Voice; Anthology Drama; "Golden Age" of Television**

Hosts/Narrators

Nelson Case (1950–51)
Joe Ripley (1952–53)
Bob Sherry (1953–54)
Sandy Becker (1954–55)
John Cameron Swayze (1955–57)
Douglas Edwards (1957–61)
Ron Cochran (1961–62)
Henry Hamilton (1962–63)

Producers

Robert Costello, Jacqueline Babbin, George Simpson, Selig Alkon, Ralph Nelson

Programming History

NBC

June 1950–June 1955	Tuesday 9:30–10:00
September 1955–June 1957	Tuesday 9:30–10:30

CBS

October 1957–August 1963	Wednesday 10:00–11:00

Further Reading

Adams, Val, "An Original Approach to TV Drama," *New York Times* (November 16, 1952)
"Armstrong Executive Craig W. Moodie, Helped Create Armstrong Broadcasts," *Intelligencer Journal* (July 21, 1999)
Gast, Harold, *Full Disclosure, As Presented on the Armstrong Circle Theatre,* Larchmont, New York: Argonaut, 1961

Gianakos, Larry James, *Television Drama Series Programming: A Comprehensive Chronicle, 1959–1975,* Metuchen, New Jersey: Scarecrow, 1978
Gianakos, Larry James, *Television Drama Series Programming: A Comprehensive Chronicle, 1947–1959,* Metuchen, New Jersey: Scarecrow, 1980
Schowalter, Alice Boter, "A Study of the Creative Development and Production of the 'Armstrong Circle Theatre' Television Documentary Drama," master's thesis, Kent State University, 1968
Settel, Trudy S., and Irving Settel, *The Best of Armstrong Circle Theatre,* New York: Citadel, 1959
Shaw, Myron Berkley, "A Descriptive Analysis of the Documentary Drama Television Program, 'The Armstrong Circle Theatre' 1955–1961," Ph.D. diss., University of Michigan, 1962

Army-McCarthy Hearings

U.S. Congressional Inquiry

Broadcast "gavel to gavel" on the ABC and DuMont networks from April 22 to June 17, 1954, the Army-McCarthy hearings were the first nationally televised congressional inquiry and a landmark in the emergent nexus between television and U.S. politics. Although the Kefauver Crime Committee hearings of March 1951 can claim priority as a congressional TV show, and subsequent political spectacles (the Watergate hearings, the Iran Contra hearings, the Clarence Thomas-Anita Hill hearings, President Clinton's impeachment proceedings) would rivet the attention of later generations of television viewers, the Army-McCarthy hearings remain the genre prototype for sheer theatricality and narrative unity.

Ostensibly, the Army-McCarthy hearings convened to investigate a convoluted series of charges leveled by the junior Republican senator from Wisconsin, Joseph R. McCarthy, at the U.S. Army and vice versa. In November 1953 a consultant on McCarthy's staff named G. David Schine was drafted into the Army. Even before Schine's formal induction, Roy M. Cohn, McCarthy's chief counsel, had begun a personal campaign to pressure military officials—from the secretary of the Army on down to Schine's company commander—into giving Private Schine special privileges. When on March 11, 1954, the Army issued a detailed chronology documenting Cohn's improper intrusions into Schine's military career, McCarthy responded by claiming the Army was holding Schine "hostage" to deter his committee from exposing communists within the military ranks. To resolve the dispute, the Senate Permanent Subcommittee on Investigations, of which McCarthy was chair, voted to investigate and to allow live television coverage of the inquiry. McCarthy relinquished the chairmanship to Karl Mundt (Republican, South Dakota) in order to become, with Cohn, contestant and witness in a widely anticipated live television drama.

Throughout the 36 days of hearings, 188 hours of broadcast time were given over to telecasts originating from the Senate Caucus Room. The network "feed" came courtesy of the facilities of ABC's Washington, D.C., affiliate, WMAL-TV. Initially, all four networks were expected to carry the complete hearings live, but NBC and CBS balked at the loss of revenues from commercial programming. With an eye to its profitable daytime soap opera lineup, CBS opted out before the hearings began, leaving NBC, ABC, and DuMont formally committed to coverage. On the second day of hearings, however, after a particularly tedious afternoon session, NBC announced it was bailing out. Henceforth NBC, like CBS, broadcast nightly roundups edited from kinescopes of the daytime ABC telecasts. CBS broadcast from 11:30 p.m. to 12:15 A.M., so when NBC followed suit, it counterprogrammed its recaps from 11:15 p.m. to 12:00 midnight. Looking for a way to put his third-string news division on the map, ABC's president Robert E. Vintner stuck with his decision to broadcast the entire event live, jettisoning the network's daytime programming for continuous coverage, gavel to gavel. Even so, some major markets in the United States (Los Angeles for one) were deprived of live coverage when local affiliates chose not to take the network feed.

In televisual terms, the hearings pitted a boorish McCarthy and a bleary-eyed Cohn against a coolly avuncular Joseph N. Welch of the Boston law firm of Hale and Dorr, whom the Army had hired as its special

Roy Cohn, Senator Joseph McCarthy, at Senate Committee, 1950s.
Courtesy of the Everett Collection/CSU Archives

counsel. Welch's calm patrician manner served as an appealing contrast to Cohn's unctuous posturing and McCarthy's rude outbursts (the senator's nasal interjection "Point of order!" became a national catchphrase). Senators, military men, and obscure staffers on the McCarthy Committee became household names and faces, among them chain-smoking committee counsel Ray H. Jenkins, Secretary of the Army Robert T. Stevens, and, hovering in the background, a young lawyer for the committee Democrats named Robert F. Kennedy. Along with an often partisan gallery in the packed, smoke-filled hearing room, an audience of some 20 million Americans watched the complicated testimony, a crossfire of mutual recriminations over monitored telephone conversations, doctored photographs, and fabricated memoranda.

The afternoon of June 9, 1954, brought the emotional climax of the hearings, an exchange replayed in myriad cold war documentaries. Ignoring a prehearing agreement between Welch and Cohn, McCarthy insinuated that Fred Fisher, a young lawyer at Hale and Dorr, harbored communist sympathies. Welch responded with a righteous outburst that hit all the hot buttons: "Until this moment, senator, I think I never gauged your cruelty or recklessness.... Have you no sense of decency, sir, at long last? Have you left no sense of decency?" When McCarthy tried to strike back, Welch cut him off and demanded the chair "call the next witness." Pausing just a beat, the hushed gallery erupted in applause. The uncomprehending McCarthy turned to Cohn and stammered, "What happened?"

What happened was that television, whose coverage of McCarthy's news conferences and addresses to the nation had earlier lent him legitimacy and power, had now precipitated his downfall. Prolonged exposure to McCarthy's odious character and ill-mannered interruptions was a textbook demonstration of how a hot personality wilted under the glare of a cool medium. Toward the close of the hearings, Senator Stuart Symington (Democrat, Missouri) underscored the lesson in media politics during a sharp exchange with McCarthy: "The American people have had a look at you for six weeks. You are not fooling anyone."

The Army-McCarthy hearings were a television milestone not only because of the inherent significance of the event covered but also because television coverage itself was crucial to the meaning, and unfolding, of events. Moreover, unlike many historic television moments from the 1950s, the hearings have remained alive in popular memory, mainly due to filmmaker Emile de Antonio, who in 1963 culled from extant kinescopes the landmark compilation film *Point of Order!,* the definitive documentary record of the U.S.'s first great made-for-TV political spectacle.

THOMAS DOHERTY

Further Reading

de Antonio, Emile, and Daniel Talbot, *Point of Order! A Documentary of the Army-McCarthy Hearings,* New York: Norton, 1964

Straight, Michael, *Trial by Television,* Boston: Beacon, 1954

Arnaz, Desi (1917–1986)

U.S. Actor, Media Executive

Desi Arnaz is best known for his role as Ricky Ricardo in the early television situation comedy *I Love Lucy.* The series, which starred his wife, Lucille Ball, as his fictional wife, Lucy Ricardo, appeared weekly on CBS. The show originally ran from the fall of 1951 through the 1957 season, and during this time it ranked consistently among the top three national programs. In addition to being a perfect comic straight man for Ball's genius, Arnaz was one of Hollywood's most perceptive and powerful producers in television's early years. His shrewd business skills and his realization of particular combinations of the television's technological and cultural connections enabled him to develop aspects of the medium that remain central to its economic and cultural force.

Arnaz began his show business career in 1935. After singing and playing guitar with the Xavier Cugat orchestra, Desi toured with his own rumba band, but his big break was being cast in the Broadway show *Too Many Girls* in 1939. He met Lucille Ball in Hollywood the next year, when both had roles in the movie version of the play. They were married in 1940 and continued their careers, Ball in motion pictures and radio, and Arnaz in music.

Ball had gained success with her CBS radio program, *My Favorite Husband,* in which she starred as the wife of a banker, played by Richard Denning. CBS was interested in creating a television version of the show, but when Ball insisted that Arnaz play her husband, the network felt that viewers would not be attracted to a show not easily related to their own lives. Executives at CBS were skeptical about whether Arnaz, a Cuban bandleader, would be believable and readily accepted by viewers as Ball's husband. In order to prove the network wrong, the couple set out on a nationwide stage tour designed to gauge public reaction to their working together in a comedy act. CBS was impressed with the positive public response to the couple as well as with a sample script for a TV series developed by the writers from *My Favorite Husband.*

The basics were there, including Arnaz as Ricky Ricardo, a struggling bandleader, and Ball as Lucy, a housewife with little talent but a giant yearning to break into show business. This homey battle-of-the-sexes premise for the show convinced the network that viewers could relate, and a pilot version of the program impressed the Philip Morris Company, which agreed to sponsor 39 episodes for the 1951–52 season on the CBS network Monday nights at 9:00 p.m. Arnaz and Ball insisted on producing the show in California so they could work together and live at home; such an arrangement had been impossible with Ball acting in films and on radio while Arnaz toured with his band, and the separation had strained their marriage. The idea of recording *I Love Lucy* on film was directly related to the couple's desire to work together in show business as a family and to live in their home in California.

In 1951, before the perfection of videotape, nearly all television shows were live productions, fed from the East Coast because of time-zone differences. Philip Morris approved the idea of filming *I Love Lucy,* but the sponsor wanted a live audience, which had been effective on radio. Arnaz and cinematographer Karl Freund, a veteran of pre–World War II German expressionist cinema working in Hollywood, devised a plan for staging the show as a play, performing each act before an audience and simultaneously filming with three or four cameras stationed in different locations. Because this technique increased network production costs, CBS asked that Arnaz and Ball take a cut in salary to compensate for the expense. In negotiation Arnaz agreed, providing Desilu, a company he and Ball had created, would then own the shows after the broadcasts. A few years later the couple sold the films back to CBS for more than $4 million, a sum that provided the economic base for building what became the Desilu empire. The practice of filming television episodes also paved the way to TV reruns and syndication. After *I Love Lucy* was established as a hit, Desilu applied its multicamera film technique to the production of other shows, such as *Our Miss Brooks, December Bride,* and *The Lineup.* By 1957 Desilu was so successful that additional facilities were needed and it bought RKO Studios from the General Tire and Rubber Company.

Desilu had become the world's largest studio. But as the business grew ever larger, Arnaz and Ball drifted

I Love Lucy, Lucille Ball, Desi Arnaz, 1951–57.
Courtesy of the Everett Collection

apart, ending their 20-year marriage in 1960 and splitting their interests in Desilu. In 1962 Ball bought Arnaz's share in the company, and he retired for a short time to his horse-breeding farm. Both later married others, and Arnaz returned to television, forming an independent production company and making occasional guest appearances. Desilu was purchased by Gulf Western Industries in 1967. Arnaz died in 1986 and Lucille Ball in 1989. *I Love Lucy* is still popular with television audiences today, thanks to the pioneering production techniques of Desilu.

B.R. Smith

See also ***Ball, Lucille; I Love Lucy***

Desi (Desiderio Alberto, III) Arnaz (Y De Acha). Born in Santiago, Cuba, March 2, 1917. Married: Lucille Ball, 1940 (divorced, 1960); children: Lucie Désirée and Desiderio Alberto, IV (Desi Jr.). Attended Colegio Delores, Jesuit Preparatory School, Santiago, Cuba. Moved with family to the United States, 1930s. U.S. Medical Corps., 1943–45. Began entertainment career as singer, with Xavier Cugat Band, 1935–36; formed own band at the Conga Club, Miami, Florida, 1938, height of the "conga craze"; Broadway musical debut, *Too Many Girls,* 1939; RKO film version of the musical, 1940; music director, the Bob Hope radio show, 1946–47; performed with Ball in radio show, *My Favorite Husband,* 1947–50; produced pilot for *I Love Lucy* with own funds, 1951; performed as Ricky Ricardo, *I Love Lucy,* 1951–57; president and cofounder, Desilu Productions, 1951–62. Recipient: Best Performance of the Month, *Photoplay Magazine,* 1943. Died in Del Mar, California, December 2, 1986.

Television Series

1951–57	*I Love Lucy* (actor, producer)
1958–60	*Westinghouse Playhouse* (producer)
1962–65, 1967	*The Lucy-Desi Comedy Hour* (actor, producer)

Films

Too Many Girls, 1940; *Father Takes a Wife,* 1941; *The Navy Comes Through,* 1942; *Four Jacks and a Jill,* 1942; *Bataan,* 1943; *Holiday in Havana,* 1949; *Cuban Pete,* 1950; *The Long, Long Trailer,* 1954; *Forever Darling,* 1956; *The Escape Artist,* 1982.

Publication

A Book by Desi Arnaz, 1976

Further Reading

Anderson, Christopher, *Hollywood TV: The Studio System in the Fifties,* Austin: University of Texas Press, 1994
Andrews, Bart, *The "I Love Lucy" Book,* New York: Doubleday, 1985
Andrews, Bart, and Thomas J. Watson, *Loving Lucy,* New York: St. Martin's Press, 1980
Brady, Kathleen, *Lucille: The Life of Lucille Ball,* New York: Hyperion, 1994
Firmat, Gustavo Perez, *Life on the Hyphen: The Cuban-American Way,* Austin: University of Texas Press, 1994
Harris, Warren G., *Lucy and Desi: The Legendary Love Story of Television's Most Famous Couple,* New York: Simon and Schuster, 1991
Higham, Charles, *Lucy: The Life of Lucille Ball,* New York: St. Martin's Press, 1986
Sanders, Coyne Steven, and Tom Gilbert, *Desilu: The Story of Lucille Ball and Desi Arnaz,* New York: Morrow, 1993
Schatz, Thomas, "Desilu, I Love Lucy, and the Rise of Network TV," in *Making Television: Authorship and the Production Process,* edited by Robert J. Thompson and Gary Burns, New York: Praeger, 1990

Arsenio Hall Show, The

U.S. Talk Show

The Arsenio Hall Show, a syndicated late-night talk show starring African-American stand-up comedian Arsenio Hall, ran from January 1989 to May 1994. Paramount Domestic Television's syndicated division produced and distributed the show, which aired primarily on stations affiliated with FOX Broadcasting. During its five-year run, the show peaked at a 3.9 national rating in February 1990, an amazing feat for a syndicated show that had access to fewer TV stations than network programs and did not have a specific airing time across the nation (though it usually aired sometime between 11:00 p.m. and 1:00 A.M.). During its run, the show received six Emmy nominations, including two for Outstanding Variety, Music, or Comedy Program in 1989 and 1990.

Hall had his first break in late-night television when he became a guest host on FOX's *The Late Show with Joan Rivers.* After Rivers departed in May 1987, the show had a rotating series of guest hosts, including Hall. After fronting the show for several nights, Hall was invited to stay for 13 weeks. That time permitted Hall to develop as a talk show host while solidifying his position as a well-known popular entertainer. Although both Hall and the show were doing moderately well, FOX decided to cancel *The Late Show,* replacing it with *The Wilton North Report.* During that time, when Hall was without a regular television job, Paramount approached him with a multifilm deal, a deal eventually renegotiated to include a talk show. Yet Hall was still under contract with FOX. In order to prevent a legal suit against both Hall and Paramount, FOX affiliates were used as the main venue for Hall's talk show.

The format of *The Arsenio Hall Show* followed traditional structures set by other late-night talk shows: entrance and rapport with the band (known on Hall's program as "the posse") and the studio audience, the host's initial monologue at the center of the stage, interviews with guests (usually two to three) in the sitting area, and a musical number by an invited artist. Hall nevertheless brought some changes (sometimes quite subtle), in order to provide a more informal mood for his show. There was no desk in the sitting area where interviews were conducted, so he could be closer to his guests. Hall did not have a sidekick on the show. The set had an area at the stage left of the band designated as the "dog pound" where a group of guests would sit and cheer Hall with barks ("Woof," "Woof," "Woof!") while moving their right fists in circles above their heads. These more informal elements of the show were attuned to Hall's agenda of providing an alternative kind of entertainment to the traditional late-night scene.

From the outset, *The Arsenio Hall Show* distinguished itself by targeting audiences that have been largely ignored by other late-night talk shows: urban African Americans and Latinos as well as younger viewers whom he identified on several occasions as the "MTV generation." Hall reached these audiences through a hip and casual approach to the show, strongly informed by his talent as a stand-up comedian as well as by tales of his childhood experiences in a Cleveland, Ohio, lower-middle-class community. In fact, Hall constantly invoked stories about being someone who left the ghetto for another type of life but who was still emotionally and politically connected to it. The strategy kept his television persona grounded at a level closer to urban audiences.

Another technique Hall used to reach a multiethnic younger audience was showcasing a wide variety of artists, comedians, and performers who were less mainstream and thus not usually invited to participate on other talk shows (for example, Dea DeLaria, Tupac Shakur, Snoop Doggy Dog). In terms of entertainment, some of *The Arsenio Hall Show*'s highlights included a whole night dedicated exclusively to musical performances by the reclusive artist Prince, a surprise visit in 1992 by presidential candidate Bill Clinton (who performed two songs on the saxophone), and the taping of the series' 1,000th show at the Hollywood Bowl, starring Madonna.

Although entertainment was a priority for Hall, he also conceived of his show as a space where audiences, especially youth, could be educated. For example, he had a special show with Jesse Jackson as well as a night dedicated to commemorating Martin Luther King Jr. Furthermore, Hall became a spokesperson for

Arsenio Hall.
Courtesy of the Everett Collection

safer sex/AIDS awareness, mainly owing to his close friendship with basketball star Magic Johnson, who chose *The Arsenio Hall Show* as the venue for his first public discussion about AIDS after announcing that he was HIV positive.

The Arsenio Hall Show also had its moments of controversy. Twice, for example, Hall invited the infamous comedian Andrew Dice Clay, notorious for his sexist, racist, and homophobic jokes. On the second visit, members of the gay- and lesbian-rights groups Queer Nation and ACT UP showed up on the program in order to voice their disapproval of the guest as well as of Hall for having him. These organizations had already confronted Hall during an earlier show, both for not having gay or lesbian guests and for ridiculing homosexuals through one of his recurring impersonations. The visit of Nation of Islam leader Louis Farrakahn created another controversial moment for the show, and Hall was severely criticized for not being aggressive in his interview. More generally, Hall's laudatory attitude toward most of his guests was constantly criticized by the popular press.

The Arsenio Hall Show can be regarded as an example of a syndicated show that was able to succeed temporarily by targeting an audience largely ignored by other late-night shows, the nonwhite, urban multiethnic youth. In fact, in its most popular days, *The Arsenio Hall Show* was able to rank second in the late-night rating race, just behind *The Tonight Show with Johnny Carson.*

GILBERT BLASINI

See also **Race, Ethnicity and Television; Talk Shows**

Host
Arsenio Hall

Producers
Arsenio Hall, Marla Kell Brown

Music
The Michael Wolff Band

Programming History
1,248 episodes
Syndicated, 1989–94

Further Reading

Freeman, Michael, "Rivals Circle *Arsenio* Slot," *MediaWeek* (April 26, 1994)
King, Norman, *Arsenio Hall,* New York: William Morrow, 1993

Arthur, Beatrice (1926–)

U.S. Actor

Bea Arthur stands five foot nine and a half inches tall and has a voice that one reviewer characterized as "deep as a pothole." Her formidable stature and booming vocal register made her an unlikely leading lady in an industry driven by a narrow regime of feminine beauty. But as character traits for Maude Findlay, they proved to be the perfect foil for the sexist bravado of Archie Bunker in Norman Lear's 1970s sitcom, *All in the Family,* in which Arthur first appeared in the role. The spin-off series *Maude* was created for her virtually overnight. As opinionated and caustic in her own way as Archie, Maude Findlay was a crusader for women's liberation. And in the nascent gender consciousness of the 1970s, the women's movement's fictional spokeswoman had to be big and booming.

Television viewers' love affair with the character Arthur created in Maude resulted in a struggle with the actors' nemesis: typecasting. Arthur was a recognized actor on Broadway before making the move to television, appearing in, among others, *Fiddler on the Roof, The Threepenny Opera,* and *Mame* (for which she won a Tony Award), but she is nevertheless most remembered as the bombastic caricature of a liberated woman on the small screen. Upon leaving *Maude* in 1978, Arthur took a four-year hiatus before accepting another television series, in hopes the Findlay character would fade from the public mind. When she reappeared on the short-lived *Amanda's* in 1983, playing the owner of a seaside hotel, it was as a physically thinner person. Yet despite Arthur's attempt at transformation, audiences and reviewers alike found it hard to shake their favorite character. "Bea has shed so many pounds she is scarcely recognizable as the imposing, flotilla-like Maude," wrote one reviewer. Arthur responded to the evocation of her prior character, "what can you do? I'm still five feet nine and my voice is still deep. But I'm not going to cut off my legs or change my voice." Arthur's typecasting continued on the hit series *Golden Girls,* which first aired in 1985. Playing alongside well-established actors Rue McClanahan, Betty White, and Estelle Getty, only Arthur seemed rooted in a past performance. Her character, Dorothy Zbornak, was a continuation of the Maude character: loud, worldly, and flippant, she was Maude, approaching old age.

Whether as Maude, breaking television's mold of female beauty, or as Dorothy, challenging the omnipotent image of youth, Arthur's roles on the two hit series were instrumental in broadening television representation. She has been recognized for her work in television with two Emmys, for *Maude* and *Golden Girls.* In 2000, a guest appearance on the series *Malcolm in the Middle* garnered her another Emmy nomination and an American Comedy Award for Funniest Guest Appearance in a TV Series. She has been nominated five times for an American Comedy Award's Lifetime Achievement Award. In 2002, she returned to the stage in her one-woman show, *Bea Arthur on Broadway: Just Between Friends.*

Lisa A. Lewis

See also ***All in the Family; Golden Girls; Lear, Norman; Maude***

Beatrice Arthur.
Courtesy of the Everett Collection

Beatrice Arthur. Born Bernice Frankel in New York City, May 13, 1926. Married: actor and theater director Gene Saks, 1950 (divorced); children: Matthew and Daniel. Attended Blackstone College, Blackstone, Virginia; Franklin Institute of Science and Arts, Philadelphia, Pennsylvania, degree in medical technology; studied acting with Erwin Piscator at the Dramatic Workshop, New School for Social Research, New York. Began career in theater and nightclub performance, New York City, 1947, and thereafter appeared frequently in summer stock, 1951–53; on the New York stage, 1947–66; guest appearance as Maude Findlay in *All in the Family,* September 1971; starring role in the series *Maude,* 1972–78; costar, *The Golden Girls,* 1985–92. Recipient: Tony Award, *Mame,* 1966; Emmy Award, 1977 and 1988; American Comedy Award, 2000.

Television Series

1971	*All in the Family*
1972–78	*Maude*
1983	*Amanda's*
1985–92	*The Golden Girls*

Television Specials

1980	*The Beatrice Arthur Special*
1986	*Walt Disney World's 15th Birthday Celebration* (host)
1987	*All Star Gala at Ford's Theater* (host)

Stage (selected)

Lysistrata, 1947; *The Dog Beneath the Skin,* 1947; *Yerma,* 1947; *No Exit,* 1948; *The Taming of the Shrew,* 1948; *Six Characters in Search of an Author,* 1948; *The Owl and the Pussycat,* 1948; *Le Bourgeois Gentilhomme,* 1949; *The Creditors,* 1949; *Yes Is for a Very Young Man,* 1949; *Heartbreak House,* 1949; *Personal Appearance, Candle Light, Love or Money, The Voice of the Turtle* (summer stock), 1951; *The New Moon, Gentlemen Prefer Blondes* (summer stock), 1953; *The Threepenny Opera,* 1954; *Shoestring Revue,* 1955; *Seventh Heaven,* 1955; *What's the Rush* (touring), 1955; *Mistress of the Inn* (stock), 1956; *Nature's Way,* 1957; *Ulysses in Nighttown,* 1958; *Fiddler on the Roof,* 1964; *Mame,* 1966; *The Floating Light Bulb,* 1981; *Bea Arthur on Broadway: Just Between Friends,* 2002.

Further Reading

"Bea Arthur's Having a Ball at the Opera," *Chicago Tribune* (March 21, 1994)
"Maude Is Getting Comfortable in Her Own Skin," *South Florida Sun-Sentinel* (August 10, 2001)
Rose, Linda, "Actresses' Roles Continue to Evolve," *Daily Variety* (June 6, 1996)

Arthur Godfrey Shows (Various)

U.S. Variety/Talent/Talk Show

Arthur Godfrey's shows helped define the first decade and a half of TV history in the United States. While there were a number of television shows on which Godfrey appeared, his fame, fortune, and pioneering activities centered on two variety shows presented on the CBS TV network: *Arthur Godfrey's Talent Scouts* and *Arthur Godfrey and His Friends.* These two proved so popular that during the 1950s they served as a cornerstone of the CBS TV's programming strategies.

In December 1948, after more than a decade on radio, principally for CBS, Arthur Godfrey ventured onto prime-time TV by simply permitting the televising of his radio hit *Arthur Godfrey's Talent Scouts.* On TV *Arthur Godfrey's Talent Scouts* ran until July 1958 on Monday nights at 8:30 for a half hour and proved Godfrey's best venue on television. Fans embraced this amateur showcase, and during the 1951–52 TV season it reached number one in the ratings. Next season *I Love Lucy* vaulted into first place, but through most of the 1950s *Arthur Godfrey's Talent Scouts* regularly finished in TV's prime-time top ten.

The formula for *Arthur Godfrey's Talent Scouts* was simple enough. "Scouts" brought on their discoveries to a converted New York theater to perform before a live studio audience. Most of these "discoveries" were in fact struggling professionals looking for a break, and so the quality of the talent was quite high. At the program's conclusion, the studio audience selected the winner by way of an applause meter.

Godfrey significantly assisted the careers of Pat Boone, Tony Bennett, Eddie Fisher, Connie Francis, Leslie Uggams, Lenny Bruce, Steve Lawrence, Connie Francis, Roy Clark, and Patsy Cline. His "discovery" of Patsy Cline on January 21, 1957, was typical. Her scout, actually her mother Hilda Hensley, presented Patsy, who sang her recent recording "Walkin' After Midnight." Though this was heralded as a country song, and recorded in Nashville, Tennessee, Godfrey's staff insisted Cline not wear one of her mother's handcrafted cowgirl outfits but appear in a cocktail dress. The audience's ovations stopped the meter at its apex, and for a couple of months thereafter Cline appeared regularly on Godfrey's radio program. In short, although Cline had been performing for nearly a decade, and had been recording and appearing on local Washington, D.C., TV for more than two years, it is Godfrey who is heralded as making Patsy Cline a star through his highly rated program. Yet Godfrey proved fallible. He turned down both Elvis Presley and Buddy Holly!

Arthur Godfrey and His Friends, Haleloke, Arthur Godfrey, The Mariners, 1949–57.
Courtesy of the Everett Collection

Godfrey's other top-ten TV hit was *Arthur Godfrey and His Friends,* which premiered in January 1949. On Wednesday nights Godfrey hosted this traditional variety show, employing a resident cast of singers, which over the years included Julius La Rosa, Frank Parker, Lu Ann Simms, Pat Boone, and the Cordettes. Reprising his role on *Arthur Godfrey's Talent Scouts,* Tony Marvin served as both announcer and Godfrey's "second banana." The appeal of the hour-long *Arthur Godfrey and His Friends* rested on the popularity of the assembled company of singers, all clean-cut young people, and guest stars. Godfrey played host and pitchman.

Indeed, to industry insiders, Godfrey ranked as television's first great salesman. He blended a Southern folksiness with enough sophistication to sell almost anything. As he had long done on radio, Godfrey frequently kidded his sponsors but always "sold from the heart," only hawking products he had actually tried and/or regularly used. Godfrey made it sound as if he were confiding to you and to you alone, and early television viewers listened to his rich, warm, resonant descriptions and went out and purchased what he endorsed.

During the early 1950s Godfrey seemed unable to do anything wrong, despite a press that could find little reason for his vast popularity. He began a fall from grace in October 1953, when he fired the then-popular La Rosa—on the air. Because of the negative fallout, Godfrey thereafter regularly feuded with a host of powerful newspaper columnists including Dorothy Kilgallen and John Crosby.

By the end of the 1950s Godfrey's ratings were falling and his brand of variety show was giving way to action and comedy series made in Hollywood. Still, through the 1960s, CBS unsuccessfully sought new ways to showcase Godfrey. He flopped on *Candid Camera* but appeared on regular specials: *Arthur Godfrey in Hollywood,* which aired on October 11, 1963; *Arthur Godfrey Loves Animals* on March 18, 1963; and so on, once or twice a season. His final television special came on March 28, 1973.

Television in the United States is most dependent on the star system, and Arthur Godfrey, despite commonsense declarations that he had "no talent," must be counted as one of television's greatest stars. Prior to 1959 there was no bigger TV draw than this freckle-faced, ukulele-playing host. There was something about Godfrey's wide grin, his infectious chuckle, his unruly shock of red hair that made millions tune in not just once, but again and again.

DOUGLAS GOMERY

See also **Godfrey, Arthur**

Arthur Godfrey and His Friends

Host
Arthur Godfrey

Regular Guests
Tony Marvin
The Chordettes (Virginia Osborn, Dorothy Schwartz, Carol Hagedorn, Janet Ertel) (1949–53)
Janette Davis (1949–57)
Bill Lawrence (1949–50)
The Mariners (Jim Lewis, Tom Lockard, Nat Dickerson, Martin Karl) (1949–55)
Haleloke (1950–55)
Frank Parker (1950–58)
Marion Marlowe (1950–55)
Julius LaRosa (1952–53)
Lu Ann Simms (1952–55)
The McGuire Sisters (Christine, Dorothy, Phyllis) (1952–57)
Carmel Quinn (1954–57)
Pat Boone (1955–57)
The Toppers (1955–57)
Miyoshi Umeki (1955)
Frank Westbrook Dancers (1959)

Orchestra
Archie Bleyer (1949–54)
Jerry Bresler (1954–55)
Will Roland and Bert Farber (1955–57)
Bernie Green (1958–59)

Programming History
CBS

January 1949–June 1957	Wednesday 8:00–9:00
September 1958–April 1959	Tuesday 9:00–9:30

Arthur Godfrey's Talent Scouts

Host
Arthur Godfrey

Announcer
Tony Marvin

Orchestra
Archie Bleyer (1948–54)
Jerry Bresler (1954–55)
Will Roland and Bert Farber (1955–58)

Programming History
CBS

December 1948–July 1958	Monday 8:30–9:00

Further Reading

Castleman, Harry, and Walter Podrazik, *Watching TV: Four Decades of American Television,* New York: McGraw-Hill, 1982

Arts and Entertainment

The Arts and Entertainment (A&E) Network is the tenth-largest cable programmer in the United States, boasting about 86 million subscribers. Since its launch in February 1984, the network has spawned smaller cable networks (the History Channel and the Biography Channel), magazines, websites, and many other media products. Through its A&E Television Networks (AETN) subsidiary, it publishes *Biography Magazine* and sells videotapes and DVD copies of its cable airings, though published reports show that AETN has tried to sell *Biography Magazine.* A&E has purchased services to add to the viewing experience such as genealogy.com and a travel company to help the audience plan excursions based on the channel's shows; these services, along with the company's lucrative video/DVD sales subsidiary, are successful auxiliary lines of business for the cablecaster.

As AETN is the parent corporation of several smaller cable channels, its ownership is shared by three larger media conglomerates. A&E is owned 37.5 percent by the Hearst Corporation, 37.5 percent by ABC, and 25 percent by NBC. Though Hearst has recently downsized its television operations, its interest in A&E has remained unchanged.

Since the channel's initial telecast, Nickolas Davatzes has held the title of president and CEO, A&E Television Networks. Davatzes received the NCTA's Vanguard Award for distinguished leadership in June 2003 for his many years of cable industry service.

Over the years, A&E programming has garnered many awards. Most honors have been Emmys from the Academy of Television Arts and Sciences, but other organizations have acknowledged A&E's quality as well. The programs *The Crossing* and *Pride and Prejudice* were recognized with Peabody trophies. The 23rd Annual Banff Television Festival gave its outstanding achievement award to the A&E Channel as a whole. In 2003, A&E Network's *Biography* won the Producer's Guild Award for reality/game/informational series. During the years that the National Academy of Cable Programming awarded CableAce Awards, A&E won 88 times.

Since its first nomination in 1990 for best children's program for *All Creatures Big and Small,* the channel has been selected to vie for 65 Emmy Awards (20 in 1999 alone) and has won the golden statue 12 times. A&E's shows competing for awards included *The House of Elliott, Napoleon, Pride and Prejudice, Jane Austen's Emma, Investigative Reports' The Farm: Life Inside Angola Prison, Dash and Lilly, PT Barnum,* and *Peter Pan Starring Cathy Rigby.* The long-running *Biography* series collected 11 Emmy nominations with two wins (for Judy Garland and the Rat Pack); the drama *Horatio Hornblower* had 11 nominations and two wins. In 2000, the channel won the academy's Governor's Award for its Biography Project for Schools.

Although A&E has had a strong success record within the cable industry, the past few years have been the most difficult in terms of corporate management. As compared to the majority of cable networks, A&E had stellar performance under former general manager Brooke Bailey Johnson. When she resigned in 2000 after ten years with the company, viewers saw a difference. Audiences declined dramatically during the 2000–2001 season. In the earlier years, A&E provided an eclectic mix of off-network crime dramas, BBC mysteries, dramedy such as *Northern Exposure,* and original series aimed at a target audience of mature women. Those shows centered around A&E signature programming such as *Biography* and *Investigative Reports.*

Of its shows, the highest ratings routinely came from the *Biography* series and off-network reruns such as *Law & Order.* In 1999, the *Hollywood Reporter* listed those two shows within the top five cable programs in terms of advertising revenue, with no other A&E series placing within the top 50. A&E showed the Dick Wolf-produced crime drama at least twice during the day, airing a more recent episode weekly at night, and often had multihour marathons during the weekend. In 1999, A&E did not choose to renew *Law & Order;* the domestic syndication rights were purchased by TNT. The asking price rose from A&E's $150,000 per episode to the $800,000 per episode ultimately paid by the AOL Time Warner–owned channel. Similarly, Hallmark bought the license to rerun *Northern Exposure.*

Biography seemingly lost some of its singularity as cablers such as VH1, E!, and Court TV replicated *Biography*'s core formula to fit their own programming needs. In addition, A&E created separate cable channels for both the History Channel and the Biography Channel, giving fans another location, around the clock, to see favorite shows. A&E placed its development dollars into first-run drama that impressed Emmy voters but did not draw the steady, large numbers reminiscent of *Law & Order.* After a nearly 10-percent increase in viewers from 1998 to 1999, A&E suffered a 33-percent decline in viewers from 2000 to 2001, primarily in the 25-to-54 demographic.

While A&E's cable audience numbers declined, its video and DVD sales climbed at warehouse mass market stores and through Internet sales. In July 2001 sales spikes were reported for double disc sets of special interest "Collector's Choice" selling at $19.95 and running about three and one half hours each. Titles included "The Wonders of Ancient Egypt," "The Civil War Journal," and the award-winning "The Rat Pack." Through the DVD sales, the company sells segments of A&E's original productions, *Dr. Quinn Medicine Woman* with extras such as a *Biography* segment on Jane Seymour, and imports such as *The Avengers, Monty Python's Flying Circus,* and *The Prisoner.* In 2002 A&E earned fourth place in market share of TV DVDs behind HBO Home Video, FOX Home Entertainment, and Paramount Home Entertainment.

To try to improve viewership levels on cable, the channel brought in new teams of programmers to reshape and rebrand the channel. Throughout this period, A&E remained a top-ten cable network. Alan Sabinson, formerly of TNT and Showtime, attempted to create quality programming including the series *Nero Wolfe* and *100 Centre Street,* and A&E licensed a daily "repurposed" showing of ABC's daytime talk show *The View.* During his year-and-a-half tenure, working with an annual programming budget of about $200 million, he succeeded with critics but failed with the channel's general audience. The budget allowed Sabinson to try new quality shows at the expense of outbidding TNT for *Law & Order.*

Courtesy of the Everett Collection

In late 2002 Abbe Raven, a 16-year veteran of the company, took over as general manager. Her answers to the problems include spending money for film rights, first-run movies for television, artful reality programming (*Makeover Mamas* and *The Well Seasoned Traveler*), new dramas (*MI-5*), off-network shows (*Third Watch, Crossing Jordan,* and *Columbo*), and A&E's signature shows. The company purchased 45 "art house" films geared toward its primary audience.

Programming planned for the 2003–4 season, according to Nancy Dubuc, vice president of documentary programming at A&E, includes a biographical movie about Senator Hillary Clinton and a reality show, *House of Dreams,* where several couples will compete "to plan, design, build and decorate their dream house." These shows will be delivered to affiliates through digital feeds, unlike past seasons where the channel utilized analog technology.

A&E often utilizes well-respected news personalities, past and present, to host its signature programming. This includes ABC's Harry Smith for *Biography* and Joan Lunden for *Behind Closed Doors,* CBS's Bill Kurtis anchors *Cold Case Files* and *American Justice,* and Mark McEwen hosts *Live by Request.* Former *Northern Exposure* and *Sex in the City* star John Corbett gave his voice to *The Love Chronicles,* an A&E documentary attempt that lasted one season. Actor Paul Winfield provides the narration for the ongoing *City Confidential;* classical radio personality Elliott Forrest has conducted interviews for the channel's *Breakfast with the Arts* for more than a decade. In addition, Forrest licensed radio rights for *Biography* from A&E; he produces a weekly *Biography* radiocast aired to over 100 U.S. stations.

A&E answers to three masters, and it is still in the midst of rebranding itself after a viewership decline in the late 1990s. By changing its programming personnel, taking time to understand the new TV viewer, updating its operational technology, tightening its corporate spending, and embracing reality TV, the channel is showing viewer improvement. Alhough some programmers and branch sales offices are gone, the core offerings of the channel—*Biography,* original dramas, British imports, top-named concerts, prestigious award shows such as the annual George Foster Peabody Awards, and similar accessible yet highbrow programs—remain, letting viewers know their dial is set to the same old A&E, now streamlined for the new millennium.

JOAN GIGLIONE

Further Reading

Cable Program Investor (February 28, 2003)
Friedman, Wayne, "A&E to Get a Little Less Stuffy," *Television World* (June 6, 2003)
"Nickolas Davatzes," *Broadcasting & Cable* (November 8, 1999)
Roman, Allison, "Davatzes works to bring A&E back to where it once belonged," *Broadcasting & Cable* (June 9, 2003)
TV Guide Fall Preview, Vol. 32, No. 36 (September 8, 1984)

Ascent of Man, The

British Documentary Series

Born in Poland in 1908, Jacob Bronowski belongs as much to the scattering of central Europe in the wake of pogroms, revolutions, and Nazism as he did to the easy learning and liberal and humane socialism of the postwar consensus in Britain. A mathematician turned biologist, with several literary critical works to his name, he was a clear choice to provide David Attenborough's BBC 2 with the follow-up to the international success of Kenneth Clarke's *Civilisation.*

By Bronowski's testimony, work began on the program in 1969, though the 13-part series only arrived on screen in 1974. Intended as a digest of the history of science for general viewers, and to match the claims of the Clarke series, it actually ranged further afield than the Eurocentric *Civilisation,* although Bronowski retained a rather odd dismissal of pre-Colombian science and technology in the New World. The series faced, however, perhaps a greater challenge than its predecessor, in that the conceptual apparatus of science is less obviously telegenic than the achievements of culture. Nonetheless, the device of the "personal view" that underpinned BBC 2's series of televisual essays gave the ostensibly dry materials a human warmth that allied them successfully with the presenter-led documentaries already familiar on British screens.

The Ascent of Man covers, not in strict chronological order but according to the strongly evolutionary model suggested in the title, the emergence of humanity, the agricultural revolution, architecture and engineering, metallurgy and chemistry, mathematics, astronomy, Newtonian and relativistic mechanics, the industrial revolution, Darwinism, atomic physics, quantum physics, DNA, and, in the final program, what we would now call neurobiology and cognitive science and artificial intelligence. As well as a generous use of locations, the series boasted what were then extremely advanced computer graphics, largely refilmed from computer monitors, and an appropriate delight in the most recent as well as the most ancient tools, skills, crafts, and technologies.

Bronowski's scripts, reprinted almost verbatim as the chapters of the eponymous book accompanying the series, display his gift for inspired and visual analogies. Few have managed to communicate the essence of the special theory of relativity with such eloquence as Bronowski aboard a tram in Berne, or of Pythagorean geometry by means of the mosaics in the Alhambra. A decision made early in the filming process, to use sites that the presenter was unfamiliar with, perhaps explains some of the air of spontaneity and freshness that other presenter-led blockbuster documentaries buried beneath the modulated accents of expertise. Though sometimes gratuitous, the use of locations assured more than the visual interest of the series: it at least began the process of drawing great links between the apparently disparate cultures contributing to the development of the modern worldview, from hominid skulls in the Olduvai Gorge, by way of Japanese swordsmiths and Inca buildings to the splitting of the atom and the unraveling of DNA.

That profound belief in progress that informs the series, its humanism, and its faith in the future seem now to date it. But Bronowski's facility in moving among social, technological, and scientific history makes his case compelling even now. His account of the industrialization of the West, for example, centers on the contributions of artisans and inventors, emphasizing the emergence of a new mutuality in society as it emerges from the rural past. On the other hand, the attempt to give scientific advance a human face has a double drawback. First, it privileges the role of individuals, despite Bronowski's attempts to tie his account to the greater impact of social trends. And second, as a result, the series title is again accurate in its gendering: not even Marie Curie breaks into the pantheon.

But it is also the case that *The Ascent of Man,* in some of its most moving and most intellectually satisfying moments, confronts the possibility that there is something profoundly amiss with the technocratic society. For many viewers, the most vivid memory of the series is of Bronowski at Auschwitz, where several members of his family had died. For Bronowski, this is not the apogee of the destructive bent of a dehumanizing secularism but its opposite, the triumph of dogma over the modesty and even awe with which true science confronts the oceanic spaces of the unknown.

In some ways, *The Ascent of Man* stands diametrically opposed to the patrician elegance of Clarke's *Civilisation.* The elegy to Josiah Wedgewood, for example, is based not on his aristocratic commissions but on the simple creamware that transformed the kitchens of the emergent working classes. For all his praise of genius, from Galileo to von Neuman, Bronowski remains committed to what he calls a democracy of the intellect, the responsibility that knowledge brings and that cannot be assigned unmonitored into the hands of the rich and powerful. Such a commitment, and such a faith in the future, may today ring hollow, especially given Bronowski's time-bound blindness to the contributions of women and land-based cultures. Yet it still offers, in the accents of joy and decency, an inspiration that a less optimistic and more authoritarian society needs perhaps more than ever.

SEAN CUBITT

Presenter
Jacob Bronowski

Programming History
BBC 2
May 5–July 28, 1973

Further Reading

Bronowski, Jacob, *The Ascent of Man,* Boston: Little, Brown, 1974

Asner, Ed (1929–)

U.S. Actor

Ed Asner is one of U.S. television's most acclaimed and most controversial actors. Through the miracle of the spin-off, Asner became the only actor to win Emmy Awards for playing the same character in both a comedy and dramatic series. A former president of the Screen Actors Guild (SAG), Asner's mix of politics and acting have not always set well with network executives, corporate sponsors, or the viewing public.

Ed Asner.
Courtesy of the Everett Collection

While Asner is best known for his *Mary Tyler Moore Show* supporting character Lou Grant, the role was a departure from his dramatic roots. Asner began his professional career with the Chicago Playwright's Theatre Company, graduating later to off-Broadway productions. Asner came to Hollywood in 1961, where he received a steady stream of roles, including his first episodic work in the series *Slattery's People,* which ran on CBS in the 1964–65 season.

Asner's big break came when he was spotted by MTM Enterprises cofounder Grant Tinker in an ABC made-for-TV movie; Tinker asked *Mary Tyler Moore Show* creators James L. Brooks and Alan Burns to consider Asner for the role of Mary Richards's boss, the gruff-yet-lovable Lou Grant. According to Brooks, Asner gave a terrible first reading; however, Brooks agreed that Asner had a special quality that made him the clear choice for the role.

Although Asner had previously shied away from comedy, he felt that *The Mary Tyler Moore Show* script was the finest piece of writing he had ever seen. The series paid off for Asner, MTM, and the audience. Lou Grant not only became one of the most successful supporting roles in a comedy series but the prototype for such characters as *Taxi*'s Louie DePalma, whose comedy depends on superb timing in the delivery of well-crafted, trick-expectancy dialogue.

After *The Mary Tyler Moore Show* voluntarily retired, Asner became part of another historic TV event when he starred as Captain Davies, a brutal slave trader, in the epic miniseries *Roots.* Meanwhile, James L. Brooks, Allan Burns, and *M*A*S*H* executive producer Gene Reynolds began adapting the Lou Grant character to become the lead dramatic role in a CBS series, in which Asner would star as the crusading editor of the fictional *L.A. Tribune.* Despite a shaky start, the beloved comic character gradually became accepted in this new venue. More than just moving to the big city and losing his sense of humor, however, Asner's more serious Grant become a fictional spokesperson for issues ignored by other mass media venues, including the mainstream press. At the same time, the dramatic narrative offered opportunities for exploring the character more deeply, revealing his strained domestic relationships and his own complex emotional struggles. These revelations, in turn, complicated the professional persona of Lou Grant, the editor.

Like his character, Asner could be outspoken. His first brush with politics occurred when he became a labor rights activist during SAG's 1980 strike, which delayed the 1980–81 TV season. Asner's work on behalf of the actors helped make him a viable candidate for the SAG presidency, to which he was elected in 1981. His political agenda widened, and, in the face of a growing right-wing national sentiment highlighted by the 1980 presidential election of Ronald Reagan, Asner became increasingly vocal against U.S. public policy, including that affecting U.S. involvement in Latin America.

Through *Lou Grant,* Asner's own popularity was growing, leading to appearances in the 1980 film *Fort Apache, The Bronx,* and the 1981 TV movie *A Small Killing.* This level of success was soon to crumble, however, when Asner took part in a fund-raiser to send medical aid to El Salvadoran rebels who were fighting against the Reagan-supported regime. Most disturbing to conservative minds was Asner's direct-mail letter on behalf of the aid organization, which began with, "My name is Ed Asner. I play Lou Grant on television." Conservative SAG members, including Charlton Heston, rose up in arms over Asner using his character to support his own political agenda (of course, one can argue that Heston is so closely associated with his own on-screen persona that his links to conservative causes are just as manipulative).

In his essay on MTM drama, Paul Kerr quoted Allan Burns's assessment of the ensuing anti-Asner onslaught: "I've never seen anybody transformed so quickly from being everyone's favorite uncle to a communist swine." Within weeks, *Lou Grant* was canceled. While CBS maintains the cancellation was based on dwindling ratings, Asner, and others on the *Lou Grant* production team, feel this was swift punishment for Asner's political beliefs. Interestingly enough, Howard Hesseman, star of *WKRP in Cincinnati,* was also involved with the Asner-supported El Salvador rally; *WKRP* and *Lou Grant* were canceled the same day.

It was not until 1985—the year he resigned as SAG president—that Asner obtained another episodic role on TV, this time playing the grouchy co-owner of an L.A. garment factory in the ABC series *Off the Rack.* After 12 years of quality scripts from his MTM days, Asner's *Off the Rack* experience can be viewed as paying penance for his perceived crimes. In 1988, however, he was back in a more serious role, in the short-lived NBC series *The Bronx Zoo,* which focused on the problems faced by an inner-city high school. In a departure from his own personal views, Asner later landed the role of a conservative ex-cop who often confronted the liberal heroine in *The Trials of Rosie O'Neil,* which starred Sharon Gless as a crusading public defender. Asner has continued to be active as an actor, appearing in made-for-television and feature films and various sitcoms. None of these roles, however, have been as weighty or as important as *Lou Grant.*

MICHAEL B. KASSEL

See also ***Lou Grant; Mary Tyler Moore Show***

Edward Asner. Born in Kansas City, Missouri, November 15, 1929. Married: Nancy Lou Sikes, 1959; children: Matthew, Liza, Kathryn, and Charles. Attended University of Chicago, Illinois, 1947–49. U.S. Army Signal Corps, 1951–53. Professional debut, Playwright's Theatre, Chicago, 1953; Broadway and off-Broadway productions and television guest appearances, 1950s and 1960s; prominent as Lou Grant in *The Mary Tyler Moore Show,* 1970–77, and as the title character in *Lou Grant,* 1977–82. President, Screen Actors Guild, 1981–85. Recipient: five Golden Globe Awards; seven Emmy Awards; Fund for Higher Education Flame of Truth Award, 1981; Screen Actors Guild Lifetime Achievement Award, 2002.

Television Series

1964–65 *Slattery's People*
1970–77 *The Mary Tyler Moore Show*
1977–82 *Lou Grant*
1985 *Off the Rack*
1987–88 *The Bronx Zoo*
1991–92 *The Trials of Rosie O'Neill*
1992–93 *Hearts Afire*
1994–95 *Thunder Alley*

Television Miniseries

1976 *Rich Man, Poor Man*
1977 *Roots*

Made-for-Television Movies (selected)

1966 *The Doomsday Flight*
1969 *Doug Selby, D.A.*
1969 *Daughter of the Mind*
1969 *The House on Greenapple Road*
1970 *The Old Man Who Cried Wolf*
1971 *They Call It Murder*
1971 *The Last Child*
1971 *Haunts of the Very Rich*
1973 *The Police Story*
1973 *The Girl Most Likely to…*
1975 *Twigs*
1975 *The Imposter*
1975 *Hey, I'm Alive!*
1975 *Death Scream*
1977 *The Life and Assassination of the Kingfish*
1977 *The Gathering*
1979 *The Family Man*
1981 *A Small Killing*
1981 *The Marva Collins Story* (narrator)
1983 *A Case of Libel*
1984 *Anatomy of an Illness*
1985 *Vital Signs*
1985 *Tender Is the Night*
1986 *Kate's Secret*
1986 *The Christmas Star*
1987 *Cracked*
1988 *A Friendship in Vienna*
1990 *Not a Penny More, Not a Penny Less*
1990 *Happily Ever After* (voice)
1990 *Good Cops, Bad Cops*
1991 *Yes Virginia, There Is a Santa Claus*
1991 *Switched at Birth*
1991 *Silent Motive*
1992 *Cruel Doubt*
1993 *Gypsy*
1994 *Heads*
1996 *Gone in the Night*
1996 *The Story of Santa Claus*
1997 *Dog's Best Friend*
1997 *Payback*
1999 *Olive, the Other Reindeer* (voice)
2000 *Common Ground*
2000 *Becoming Dick*

Films

The Slender Thread, 1965; *The Satan Bug,* 1965; *Peter Gunn,* 1967; *El Dorado,* 1967; *The Venetian Affair,* 1967; *The Todd Killings,* 1970; *Halls of Anger,* 1970; *Change of Habit,* 1969; *They Call Me Mister Tibbs,* 1970; *Skin Game,* 1971; *Gus,* 1976; *Fort Apache, The Bronx,* 1980; *O'Hara's Wife,* 1982; *Daniel,* 1983; *Pinocchio and the Emperor of the Night* (voice), 1987; *Moon Over Parador,* 1988; *JFK,* 1991; *Earth and the American Dream* (voice), 1993; *The Long Way Home,* 1997; *Hard Rain,* 1998; *Love and Action in Chicago,* 1999; *The Bachelor,* 1999; *Bring Him Home,* 2000; *Above Suspicion,* 2000; *The Animal,* 2001; *The Confidence Game,* 2001.

Further Reading

Dane, Clark, "The State vs. Asner in the Killing of *Lou Grant,*" *Journal of Communication Inquiry* (1987)

Daniel, Douglass K., *Lou Grant: The Making of TV's Top Newspaper Drama,* Syracuse, New York: Syracuse University Press

Feuer, Jane, Paul Kerr, and Tise Vahimagi, editors, *MTM: "Quality Television,"* London: British Film Institute, 1984

Gitlin, Todd, *Inside Prime Time,* New York: Pantheon, 1985; revised edition, 1994

Asper, Izzy (1932–)

Canadian Media Executive

Izzy Asper is executive chairman of CanWest Global Communications, a multimedia company based in Winnipeg, Manitoba, which controls the Global Television Network as well as interests in production, distribution, international television, and newspaper publishing.

Asper's career began in law and politics. In 1964 he was called to the Manitoba bar and established himself as an expert on tax law. From 1966 to 1977, Asper wrote a nationally syndicated newspaper column on taxation, and in 1970 he authored a book critical of the federal government's tax reform proposals. He was named queen's counsel in 1975. Asper also pursued a political career. From 1970 to 1975, he was leader of the Manitoba Liberal Party and from 1972 to 1975 sat in opposition as a member of the Manitoba Legislative Assembly.

In the early 1970s, Asper turned to broadcasting, as he and partner Paul Morton set up Winnipeg independent television station CKND. In 1974 Asper became involved in a financial package to salvage a Toronto-based station, Global Television. Global Television, located in the Toronto-Hamilton corridor, Canada's richest media market, soon became the flagship of a new programming service that supplied Asper's other stations, mostly located in western Canada, with a mixture of Canadian-originated content and top-rated U.S. shows. Throughout the 1980s and 1990s, Asper continued to acquire other broadcasting assets in an attempt to construct a national television network.

By 1986, however, disputes had erupted between Asper and his partners. The disputes were resolved in 1989, when the Manitoba Court of Queen's Bench ordered that the contentious partnerships be dissolved and the assets auctioned to the former partners. Asper emerged victorious from this "corporate shoot-out" as head of a new entity called CanWest Global Communications Corporation.

Upon assuming control of CanWest Global, Asper was able to pursue his goal of creating Canada's third national television network (after the Canadian Broadcasting Corporation [CBC] and Canadian Television [CTV]). He achieved this goal in 2000 with the acquisition of the over-the-air assets of WIC Western International Communication. This effectively transformed Global Television into a full-fledged national network consisting of 11 stations reaching 88 percent of the Canadian population.

Asper, however, has not confined his vision to television or limited his ambitions to Canada only. Under his direction, CanWest has assumed an international profile. As of 2001, it owned TV3 and TV4 in New Zealand as well as 57.5 percent of Australia's Ten Network. In 2001 it also held a 45-percent equity stake in the Republic of Ireland's TV3 and a 29.9-percent equity stake in UTV (Ulster, Northern Ireland). In 1998 CanWest also acquired Fireworks Entertainment (producer of such programs as *Relic Hunter, Queen of*

Swords, and *Gene Roddenberry's Andromeda*), and in 2000 it acquired the assets of Endemol International Distribution. These moves supply CanWest with Canadian content that can also be sold on the international market. In 1999 Asper became executive chairman of CanWest Global while his son Leonard became president and chief executive officer.

Asper's broadcasting career has been characterized by an evolving vision and a willingness to seize opportunities. He has shifted the broadcasting system away from central Canada (Toronto and Montreal) toward the west and even to other parts of the world. He has been pragmatic in producing content that can both meet Canadian regulatory requirements and reach an international audience, and he has positioned CanWest not just as a broadcaster but also as a producer and distributor able to seek synergies across platforms.

PAUL ATTALLAH

Izzy Asper (Israel Harold Asper). Born in Minnedosa, Manitoba, August 11, 1932. Married: Ruth Bernstein, 1956; children: David, Leonard, and Gail. Educated at the University of Manitoba, B.A. 1953; LL.B. 1957, LL.M. 1964. Newspaper columnist on taxation, 1966–77; leader of the Liberal Party in Manitoba, 1970–75; sat in Manitoba Legislative Assembly, 1972–75; named Queen's Counsel, 1975; acquired ownership of a string of independent stations, 1970s; partner, Global Television programming service; head of CanWest Global Communications Corporation and CanWest Capital Group Inc., from 1989, executive chairman, since 1999. Officer, Order of Canada, 1995; CAB Broadcast Hall of Fame, 1995. Recipient: Honorary LL.D., University of Manitoba, 1998; Honorary Ph.D., Hebrew University, 1999.

Association of Independent Television Stations/ Association of Local Television Stations

The Association of Independent Television Stations, known as INTV, began November 10, 1972. Its purpose was to promote the needs of local telecasters throughout the United States that had no network affiliation. At first, the organization served about 70 stations, mostly located in large markets, and worked primarily to solve the economic problems encountered by small stations trying to buy costly shows to fill their programming schedules. One special effort involved attempts to both lower the cost and simplify transmission of programs to nonnetwork stations by means of AT&T's "longlines." When the Federal Communications Commission (FCC) deregulated satellite access to national programming in 1975, this problem was eliminated, and much of the recent increase in the profitability of independent television stations can be attributed to reliance on satellite technology. In this same period the FCC also began to allow more station licenses and frequencies per market.

One area of FCC regulation supported by INTV involved the financial interest and syndication rules. These rules restricted network ownership and future syndication rights to the programs networks broadcast and gave those rights to the shows' producers. The restrictions created an aftermarket for network shows that could not be controlled by ABC, CBS, or NBC. With access to satellite distribution, independent stations had easier ways to purchase and receive shows and to reach new markets. Due to these changes, INTV's number of member stations—and its power—grew.

In the context of U.S. broadcasting, largely defined by networked stations, independent stations had three obstacles to overcome. The first was the ability to obtain programming at a reasonable cost and in spite of competition from richer affiliate stations in the same local market. INTV eventually advocated support of the Primetime Access Rule (PTAR), which strengthened the syndication industry and made more shows available for independent stations. The PTAR required an hour each day for local programming and succeeded partially because of INTV lobbying efforts. With the implementation of this rule, every type of station, whether network affiliate or independent, had a scheduling space in which independent producers could place shows.

The second obstacle was related to advertising, lifeblood of the U.S. broadcasting industries. Independent stations generally provided advertisers with a "spot" market based on demographics rather than on audience size. However, the advertisers had routinely placed national commercials with the national programmers that delivered the huge mass audience. Sponsors were unaware, in some ways, of the profit available from wooing audience segments defined by shared age, wealth, or product-purchasing characteristics. This obstacle was exacerbated in 1970, when Congress banned cigarette advertising on television. This move greatly reduced the advertising revenue available to electronic media, and remaining dollars were keenly sought by all operating stations.

The third obstacle was the audience itself. Independent stations had to provide viewers with shows as compelling as network programs. In addition, UHF stations had to make audiences aware of their very existence and their program schedules. In 1978 only 91 independent stations aired programming, but this mushroomed to 321 by the close of 1988. Most of these stations telecast on newly allocated UHF frequencies with less signal strength and poorer picture quality than the network affiliates, making their identity problems even more difficult. At first, many independent's schedules followed a similar format: movies each night during prime time, network reruns during the day, strong news hours during prime-time access, and religious programming on weekends.

By 1980 INTV's members looked toward the burgeoning cable television industry as a way to increase both viewership reach and advertising revenues. Instead, however, cable providers offered new options for the viewer and actually hurt independent stations in local markets. Independent stations began legal battles, seeking to require local cable operators to carry their signal on local systems, an issue not resolved until 1992.

The entire landscape for independent television stations in the United States changed in 1985, when Rupert Murdoch purchased Twentieth Century Fox Studios from Marvin Davis. Murdoch appointed Barry Diller, formerly of ABC Television and Paramount Studios, to head the venture. Diller believed enough unaffiliated stations existed to support a fourth television network. Murdoch then purchased the Metromedia Corporation, which owned independent stations in the largest U.S. cities, and these acquired stations provided a foundation that allowed Diller and Murdoch to begin the FOX Broadcasting Company.

The new FOX network satisfied INTV stations' needs for regular access to relatively inexpensive programming from Hollywood suppliers. This programming also attracted national advertisements and appealed to the local audience. In signing its new affiliates, FOX recruited heavily from INTV member stations, and for the next few years, INTV held its annual conventions in tandem with FOX-affiliate meetings in Los Angeles. These meetings had a profound impact upon the burgeoning fourth network. At the 1988 meeting, the INTV/FOX affiliates made FOX change its operations strategy. Instead of seeking the best producers, who would design programs according to their own tastes and interests, the network now sought to satisfy its member stations. The first result was the cancellation of FOX's short-lived late-night replacement show, *The Wilton North Report.* INTV's leader, Preston Padden, worked closely with FOX executives to institute the pro-affiliate change.

However, INTV made a philosophical break from FOX and began focusing its service on non-FOX members. As FOX's original a-few-days-a-week schedule expanded, the organization showed signs of becoming a network as defined by the FCC, rather than a conglomeration of truly independent stations. In 1990, when 30 percent fewer station members attended the annual INTV meeting, syndicators began curtailing their presence at the organization's conventions. As a result, INTV began holding its conventions in conjunction with the National Association of Television Programming Executives (NATPE), a meeting that attracted far more syndicators than did the FOX affiliates' meeting. FOX hired Padden away from INTV to become its senior vice president for affiliate relations (later, Disney wooed him away from FOX).

INTV welcomed the advent of still more new-network-start-up programming services from Warner Bros. and Paramount Studios. The new arrangements have once again provided greater advertising revenue and easier program acquisition for the INTV members affiliated with the new networks, WB (Warner Bros.) and UPN (United Paramount). However, these affiliations have not lessened the power or interests of INTV. At that time, association leaders were looking toward telephone companies for video dial-tone possibilities and as a means for greater audience access to television programming.

As of March 1995, only 84 stations in the United States had no program provider affiliation, according to David Donovan, vice president of legal and legislative affairs for INTV. Of the other 301 stations considered independent, FOX Broadcasting Company had 150 as affiliates, UPN had 96, WB had 45, and ten stations had combined alliances with both FOX and UPN.

A year later, INTV became the Association of Local Television Stations (ALTV), reflecting the need for advocacy for broadcasters affiliated with nascent networks FOX, UPN, WB, and PaxNet. Over the next six years, the organization focused on issues such as digital must-carry, satellite carriers, the cable exclusivity rule, and also the repeal of the newspaper/broadcast cross-ownership rule.

ALTV canceled its plans for the January 2002 convention in Las Vegas, Nevada, and reconsidered its role as an advocate for local television stations. On February 5, 2002, the association's board voted to cease its existence. The *Hollywood Reporter* suggested that media consolidation and the weakness in the marketplace for television advertising were the chief reasons for the ALTV's disbandment.

ALTV board chairman Ray Rajewski, executive vice president of Viacom Television Stations Group, said his industry became "far more concentrated, with firms becoming more vertically integrated and expanding into competitive media businesses as well. The end result is that companies are more inwardly focused, and that, combined with a prolonged recession in sales, doomed our association." At the end, ALTV had 130 member stations.

JOAN GIGLIONE

Further Reading

Dempsey, John, "Syndex, Must-Carry, Show Costs Are Issues Confronting INTV," in *Variety Broadcast-Video Sourcebook I, 1989–1990,* edited by Marilyn J. Matelski and David O. Thomas, Boston: Focal Press, 1990

Harris, Paul, "Campaign to Ballyhoo Free TV Launched at NAB Confab," in *Variety Broadcast-Video Sourcebook I, 1989–1990,* edited by Marilyn J. Matelski and David O. Thomas, Boston: Focal Press, 1990

McClellan, Stephen, "Indie Group ALTV Signing Off," *Hollywood Reporter* (February 6, 2002)

McClellan, Stephen, "Raining on INTV's parade," *Broadcasting* (January 7, 1991)

McClellan, Stephen, "Some Syndicators Cutting Back on INTV Presence," *Broadcasting* (September 3, 1990)

ASTRA. *See* **European Commercial Broadcasting Satellite**

Atkinson, Rowan (1955–)

British Actor

By the mid-1990s, Rowan Atkinson had achieved a certain ubiquity in British popular culture, with comedy series (and their reruns) on television, character roles in leading films, and even life-size cutouts placed in branches of a major bank (a consequence of his advertisements for that bank). Yet despite Atkinson's high profile, his career has been one of cautious progressions, refining and modestly extending his repertoire of comic personae. As one of his regular writers, Ben Elton, has commented, Atkinson is content to await the roles and vehicles that will suit him rather than constantly seek the limelight.

After revue work at the Edinburgh Fringe Festival and London's Hampstead Theatre in the 1970s, Atkinson first achieved prominence as one-quarter of the team in the BBC's satirical review *Not the Nine O'Clock News* (broadcast on BBC 2 while the *Nine O'Clock News* occupied BBC 1). After a decade in which British satire had diminished, in the wake of the expiration of the *Monty Python* series, a "second wave" was thereby ushered in as a new conservative government took power in 1979. The four performers (also including Mel Smith and Griff Rhys Jones, who later formed a successful production company together, and talented comedian Pamela Stephenson) had similar university backgrounds to those of the earlier generations of British television satire since *Beyond the Fringe*. But the show's rapid-sketch format, often accompanied by a driving soundtrack, was less concerned with elaborate deflations of British political and

Rowan Atkinson.
Courtesy of the Everett Collection

social institutions or *Python*esque surreal narratives; instead, it was a combination of guerilla sniping and playful parody, loosely held together by fake news announcements (the most political and topical segments of the program). Though the quality of the writing varied hugely, Atkinson succeeded most clearly in developing an individual presence through what were to become his comic trademarks—gawky physicality, an abundance of comic facial expressions from sneering distaste to sublime idiocy, shifting mood changes and vocal registers from nerdish obsequiousness to bombast, and his ability to create bizarre characterizations, such as his ranting audience member (planted among the show's actual studio audience) or his nonsense-speaker of biblical passages.

From being the "first among equals" in *Not the Nine O'Clock News,* Atkinson moved to center stage to play Edmund Blackadder in the highly innovative *Blackadder* (also for the BBC), co-written by Elton and Richard Curtis, the latter a writer of Atkinson's stage shows. The first series was set in a medieval English court, with Edmund Blackadder as a hapless prince in waiting; subsequent series traveled forward in time to portray successive generations of Blackadders, in which Edmund became courtier in Elizabethan England, then courtier during the Regency period, and finally Captain Blackadder in the trenches of World War I. With a regular core cast, who constantly refined their performances as the writers honed their scripts, the series combined, with increasing success, a sharpening satirical thrust with an escapist sense of the absurd. The format served Atkinson extremely well in allowing him to play out variations on a character theme, balancing consistency with change. While all the incarnations of Edmund Blackadder pitted the rational, frustrated, and much put-upon—though intellectually superior—individual against environments in which the insane, tyrannical, and psychopathic vied for dominance, the youthful, gawky prince of the first series evolved through the wishful, self-aggrandizing courtier of the 1800s, to the older, world-weary soldier attempting merely to stay alive amid the mayhem of war. While the *Blackadder* series undoubtedly took time to find its feet, the attention to detail in all matters, from script to opening credits and period pastiche music, produced in the World War I series a highly successful blend of brilliantly conceived and executed characterizations, a situation combining historical absurdity and tragedy, and a poignant narrative trajectory toward final disaster: in the last episode, Blackadder and his entourage finally did go "over the top" into no man's land and to their deaths, as in one last trick of time the trenches dissolved into the eerily silent fields that they are today.

If *Blackadder* exploited Atkinson's skills at very English forms of witty verbal comedy and one-upmanship, his persona in the *Mr. Bean* series linked him with another tradition—that of silent film comics, notably Buster Keaton. Though silent-comedy "specials" have made occasional appearances on British television, this was an innovative attempt to pursue the mode throughout a string of episodes. Inevitably, Atkinson also became, to a much greater extent than previously, conceiver and creator of a character, though Curtis again had writing credits. In *Mr. Bean* Atkinson portrays a kind of small-minded, nerdish bachelor, simultaneously appallingly innocent of the ways of the world, yet, in his solipsistic lifestyle, deeply selfish and mean spirited: the pathetic and the contemptible are here closely allied. It is a comedy of ineptitude, as Bean's attempts to meet women, decorate his flat, host a New Year's Eve party, and so on all become calamitous, his incapabilities compounded by a seemingly malevolent fate. With its sources in some of his earlier characterizations, Atkinson has been able to exploit his physical gawkiness and plunder his repertoire of expressions in the role. While *Blackadder*'s wit achieved popularity with mainly younger audiences, the *Mr. Bean* format of eccentric protagonist in perpetual conflict with his intractable world took Atkinson fully into the mainstream, with its appeal to all ages. A feature film version, released in 1997, was hugely successful, though it garnered mixed reviews.

Atkinson's most recent television role–Inspector Fowler in *The Thin Blue Line*–has been a kind of merging of the otherworldliness of *Mr. Bean* with the witty barbs of *Blackadder.* He plays a middle-ranking, idealistic, uniformed policeman with an absolute respect for the values of the law and the job, often ridiculed by his more cynical colleagues. This new series, widely seen as writer Ben Elton's attempt to create a character-based comedy in a similar vein to the classic *Dad's Army,* received mixed reviews. This bold attempt to reinvigorate an older format has remained a minority taste, regularly revived in the later-evening schedules of BBC 2 but never emerging into the limelight. Its mixed-genre approach, combining character-comedy gentility with an often baroque verbal structure (such as elaborate unintentional double entendres) has tended to mystify viewers. For Atkinson, though, it is something of a logical progression—a variation as opposed to a revolution, and a further integration into the comic mainstream.

So far Atkinson has given no sign of any desire to break out of the character portrayals for which he is renowned. Though his film work has included some strongly defined subsidiary roles (such as his bumbling vicar in *Four Weddings and a Funeral*), he has not attempted to make the move into serious drama and has never had call to portray genuine and serious emotions. Indeed, almost all of his comic characters exude a separateness from other human beings; Blackadder is generally uninterested in women, Bean cannot make contact with prospective partners or friends, and Fowler prefers a hot mug of cocoa to sexual relations with his permanently frustrated female partner. This apparent avoidance of roles demanding emotional display may indicate limitations in his acting range. But Atkinson himself may well regard it more as a choice to concentrate on a steady perfection and crafting of the kind of comic characterization now so closely identified with him.

It seems that the films of *Mr. Bean* and lately Atkinson's Bond-spoof *Johnny English* (from the character created for his Barclaycard advertisements) signal a move away from television. There are still occasional cameo appearances and contributions to charity specials, but it remains to be seen whether Atkinson will return to the medium that established his career.

MARK HAWKINS-DADY

See also **Not the Nine O' Clock News**

Rowan (Sebastian) Atkinson. Born in Newcastle-upon-Tyne, England, January 6, 1955. Married: Sunetra Sastry, 1990; one son. Attended Durham Cathedral Choristers' School; St. Bees School; Newcastle University; Queen's College, Oxford, BSc, MSc. Launched career as professional comedian, actor, and writer after experience in university revues; established reputation in *Not the Nine O'Clock News* alternative comedy series and later acclaimed as the characters Blackadder and Mr. Bean; youngest person to have a one-man show in London's West End, 1981; runs Tiger Television production company. Recipient: Variety Club BBC Personality of the Year Award, 1980; BAFTA Best Light Entertainment Performance Award, 1989.

Television Series

1979 *Canned Laughter*
1979–82 *Not the Nine O'Clock News* (also co-writer)
1983 *The Blackadder*
1985 *Blackadder II*
1987 *Blackadder the Third*
1989 *Blackadder Goes Forth*
1990–91 *Mr. Bean* (also co-writer)
1991–94 *The Return of Mr. Bean* (also co-writer)
1991–94 *The Curse of Mr. Bean* (also co-writer)
1995–96 *The Thin Blue Line*

Television Specials

1987 *Just for Laughs II*
1989 *Blackadder's Christmas Carol*
1991 *Merry Christmas Mr. Bean*
1995 *Full Throttle*
1997 *Blackadder Back & Forth*
1999 *Comic Relief: Doctor Who and the Curse of Fatal Death*

Films

The Secret Policeman's Ball (also co-writer), 1981; *The Secret Policeman's Other Ball,* 1982; *Never Say Never Again,* 1983; *The Tall Guy,* 1989; *The Appointment of Dennis Jennings,* 1989; *The Witches,* 1990; *Camden Town Boy,* 1991; *Hot Shots! Part Deux,* 1993; *The Lion King* (voice only), 1994; *Four Weddings and a Funeral,* 1994; *Bean (Bean: The Movie,* U.S. title), 1997; *Maybe Baby,* 2000; *Rat Race,* 2001; *Scooby Doo,* 2002; *Johnny English,* 2003; *Love Actually,* 2003.

Stage

Beyond a Joke, 1978; *Rowan Atkinson,* 1981; *The Nerd,* 1984; *The New Revue,* 1986; *The Sneeze,* 1988.

Further Reading

Dessau, Bruce, *Rowan Atkinson,* London: Trafalgar Square, 2000
O'Connor, John J., "Mr. Bean," *New York Times* (April 2, 1992)
O'Steen, Kathleen, "Mr. Bean," *Variety* (April 6, 1992)
Schine, Cathleen, "Blackadder," *Vogue* (February 1990)

Attenborough, David (1926–)

British Producer, Host, Media Executive

David Attenborough joined the BBC's fledgling television service in 1952, fronting *Zoo Quest,* the breakthrough wildlife series that established the international reputation of the BBC Natural History Unit at Bristol. The first of these, *Zoo Quest for a Dragon,* established Attenborough as an intuitive performer, so prepossessed by his fascination with the subject at hand and unconcerned for his own dignity in front of the camera that he seemed to sweat integrity. A sense of daring has always surrounded him with a glamorous aura: even in this early outing, the massive Komodo dragon, object of the quest through Borneo, looked as ferocious as its name portends, and Attenborough's presence seemed to prove not only the reality and size of his specimens but a kind of guarantee that we too, as viewers, were part of this far-flung scientific endeavor, the last credible adventure in the period that witnessed the demise of the British Empire. Moreover, *Zoo Quest* engaged, albeit in an entertainment format, a far higher level of scientific seriousness than more child-oriented and anthropomorphic competitors from Europe and the United States. Perhaps only Jacques Cousteau was so resistant to the temptation of cuteness.

Despite this rare skill, shared only by a handful of his fellow scientists (mainly in weather reporting), Attenborough was promoted to senior management at the BBC, where he served for 15 years. As controller of BBC 2, he oversaw (and introduced on screen) the arrival of color on British screens on July 1, 1967, and is credited with turning BBC 2 around from an elite ghetto to an attractive, varied, and increasingly popular alternative to the main channels. His skill as scheduler was evidenced in the "common junctions" scheduling policy, which allowed announcers on the two BBC channels to introduce a choice of viewing, a practice that opened the corporation up to charges of unfair advantage from the commercial broadcasters and contributed indirectly to the pressure for a fourth, commercial channel. Attenborough introduced popular sports like snooker as well as *The Forsyte Saga,* and he pioneered the blockbuster, personality-presenter documentaries like Kenneth Clark's *Civilisation,* Jacob Bronowski's *The Ascent of Man,* Alistair Cooke's *America,* J.K. Galbraith's *The Age of Uncertainty,* and his own *Life on Earth.* Common to these expensive—and to that extent, risky—projects was a faith in television as a medium for quite complex historical, cultural, and scientific ideas. Even those series that were less popular achieved the talismanic status of the kind of programs license fees should be used to make. Promoted to deputy controller of programs for the whole network, third in the BBC's hierarchy, he was hotly tipped for the post of director general but abandoned management because, he said, "I haven't even seen the Galapagos Islands." However, he continued to speak passionately in defense of the public service ethos in many public forums.

Life on Earth, for which over 1.25 million feet of film were exposed in over 30 countries, subsequently sold in 100 territories and was seen by an estimated 500 million people worldwide. Though he has always claimed modestly that photographing animals will always bring in an audience, the accumulated skills of naturalists and wildlife cinematographers, as well as enormous planning, are required to reach remote places just in time for the great wildebeest migration, the laying of turtle eggs, or the blooming of desert cacti, scenes that have achieved almost mythic status in the popular history of British television. The multimillion pound sequels to *Life, The Living Planet* and *The Trials of Life,* the former concentrating on environments and ecologies, created, through a blend of accessible scholarship and schoolboyish enthusiasm, the archetypal middlebrow mix of entertainment and education that marked the public service ethos of the mature BBC. Throughout the trilogy, the developing techniques of nature photography, allied with a sensitive use of computer-generated simulations, produced a spectacular intellectual montage, driven by the desire to communicate scientific theories as well as a sense of awe in the face of natural complexity and diversity. Though it is possible to be irritated by the lack of concern for the human populations of exotic countries, symbolized by the absence of local musics from the soundtrack, Attenborough's combination of charm and amazement has been profoundly influential on a generation of ecologically aware viewers.

David Attenborough.
Photo Courtesy of David Attenborough

The Private Life of Plants, devoted to the evolution and adaptation of flora worldwide, was another spectacular success in the old mold. It has been followed by further focused series on *The Life of Birds, The Life of Mammals,* and the scientific and aesthetic triumph of *The Blue Planet.* From dangling in the rainforest canopy to revealing unseen wonders of the deep oceans, Attenborough, now in his 70s, retains his drawing power and credibility. 2000's *State of the Planet* summarized a generation's ecological commitment. Approaching 80, the age he has announced for his retirement, Sir David is said to be preparing another blockbuster on the *Life of Insects.* Honored by the academy, respected by his peers, and loved by audiences, Attenborough's imminent retirement leaves the BBC with a major problem in finding a replacement. Competitors have largely dispensed with on-screen presentation. Attenborough may be not only the first but the last of a disappearing species.

SEAN CUBITT

See also ***Ascent of Man; Civilisation; Life on Earth***

David (Frederick) Attenborough. Born in London, England, May 8, 1926, brother of actor Sir Richard Attenborough. Married: Jane Elizabeth Ebsworth Oriel, 1950; one son and one daughter. Attended Wyggeston Grammar School for Boys, Leicester; Clare College, Cambridge. Served in Royal Navy, 1947–49. Worked for educational publishers, 1949–52, joined BBC as trainee producer, 1952; host, long-running *Zoo Quest,* 1954–64; controller, BBC 2, 1965–68; director of programmes, BBC, 1969–72; returned to documentary making in 1979 with *Life on Earth* wildlife series; has since made several more similarly acclaimed nature series. D.Litt.: University of Leicester, 1970; City University, 1972; University of London, 1980; University of Birmingham, 1982. D.Sc.: University of Liverpool, 1974; Heriot-Watt University, 1978; Sussex University, 1979; Bath University, 1981; University of Ulster, 1982; Durham University, 1982; Keele University, 1986; Oxford University, 1988; Plymouth University, 1992. LLD: Bristol University, 1977; Glasgow University, 1980. D.Univ.: Open University, 1980; Essex University, 1987; Antwerp University, 1993. Sc.D.: Cambridge University, 1984. D.Vet.Med.: Edinburgh University, 1994. Honorary Fellow: Manchester Polytechnic, 1976; University of Manchester Institute of Science and Technology, 1980; Clare College, Cambridge, 1980. Fellow: British Academy of Film and Television Arts, 1980; Royal Society, 1983; Royal College of Physicians, 1991. Honorary Freeman, City of Leicester, 1990. Commander of the British Empire, 1974; Commander of the Golden Ark (Netherlands), 1983; knighted, 1985; Commander of the Royal Victorian Order, 1991. Member: Nature Conservancy Council, 1973–82; corresponding member, American Museum of Natural History, 1985; president, British Association for the Advancement of Science, 1990–91; president, Royal Society for Nature Conservation, since 1991. Trustee: Worldwide Fund for Nature U.K., 1965–69, 1972–82, 1984–90; Worldwide Fund for Nature International, 1979–86; British Museum, since 1980; Science Museum, 1984–87; Royal Botanic Gardens at Kew, 1986–92. Recipient: Society of Film and Television Arts Special Award, 1961; Royal Television Society Silver Medal, 1966; Zoological Society of London Silver Medal, 1966; Society of Film and Television Arts Desmond Davis Award, 1970; Royal Geographical Society Cherry Kearton Medal, 1972; UNESCO Kalinga Prize, 1981; Boston Museum of Science Washburn Award, 1983; Philadelphia Academy of Natural Science Hopper Day Medal, 1983; Royal Geographical Society Founder's Gold Medal, 1985; Encyclopedia Britannica Award, 1987; International Emmy Award, 1985; Royal Scottish Geographical Society Livingstone Medal, 1990; Royal Society of Arts Franklin Medal, 1990; Folden Kamera Award, Berlin, 1993.

Television (writer, presenter)

1954–64	*Zoo Quest*
1975	*The Explorers*
1976	*The Tribal Eye*
1977–	*Wildlife on One*
1979	*Life on Earth*
1984	*The Living Planet*
1987	*The First Eden*
1989	*Lost Worlds, Vanished Lives*
1990	*The Trials of Life*
1993	*Wildlife 100*
1993	*Life in the Freezer*
1995	*The Private Life of Plants*
2000	*State of the Planet*
2002	*The Blue Planet*

Publications

Zoo Quest to Guiana, 1956
Zoo Quest for a Dragon, 1957
Zoo Quest in Paraguay, 1959
Quest in Paradise, 1960
Zoo Quest to Madagascar, 1961
Quest Under Capricorn, 1963
The Tribal Eye, 1976
Life on Earth, 1979
The Living Planet, 1984
The First Eden, 1987
The Trials of Life, 1990
The Private Life of Plants, 1994

Aubrey, James T. (1918–1994)

U.S. Media Executive

James T. Aubrey was president of CBS from 1959 until 1965. He later headed MGM Studios, from 1969 to 1973, under studio owner Kirk Kerkorian, and then finished his career as an independent producer. While he is remembered in some circles as the man who oversaw the dismantling of much of MGM's heritage in an effort to save the failing studio from financial ruin, it was his tenure at CBS that earned him his place in the annals of entertainment history.

Aubrey began his broadcasting career as a salesman for CBS's Los Angeles radio station, KNX, in 1948. Aubrey also worked with CBS's new television station, KNXT, and soon advanced into the ranks of the network's West Coast programmers, where he was largely responsible for the development of the offbeat western series *Have Gun, Will Travel.* Aubrey left CBS in 1956 to join ABC, where he was made head of programming, and while there he was responsible for scheduling such shows as *77 Sunset Strip, The Real McCoys, The Rifleman, Maverick,* and *The Donna Reed Show.* He was lured back to CBS in 1958, and shortly thereafter he was named president of the network, succeeding Lou Cowan.

In this position Aubrey's star shined. He assumed complete control over the network's programming decisions and added shows to the CBS schedule that would become staples for the next decade, including CBS's famed lineup of "rural comedies." Among the programs for which Aubrey can be credited as the overseer of development are *The Beverly Hillbillies, The Andy Griffith Show, The Dick Van Dyke Show, Mr. Ed, Petticoat Junction,* and *The Munsters.* He also unsuccessfully urged CBS chairman William S. Paley to purchase a Paramount Pictures package of theatrical films to air on the network; the decision to stay away from theatricals returned to haunt CBS, for it allowed NBC to enjoy a substantial advantage in programming feature films throughout the 1960s.

While many critics saw Aubrey's lowbrow programming tastes as tarnish on CBS's "Tiffany" reputation for quality programs, no one could question his knack for finding shows that met with enormous commercial success. By the 1963–64 season, CBS had 14 of the 15 highest-rated programs in prime time and dominated the daytime ratings in a similar fashion. CBS's net profits doubled in kind during Aubrey's tenure, from $25 million a year in 1959 to $49 million in 1964.

Aubrey's downfall at CBS came quickly and for a number of reasons. CBS started the 1964–65 season slowly, and its once seemingly insurmountable lead

James T. Aubrey, 1962.
Courtesy of the Everett Collection/ CSU Archives

over NBC and ABC was in danger. Aubrey likely would have been given more time to correct the situation had it not been for other factors weighing against him in the minds of Paley and his right-hand man, Frank Stanton. For one, Aubrey's brusque and sometimes ruthless style often alienated his allies as well as his foes, earning him the nickname "The Smiling Cobra." His abrupt and arrogant manner in dealing with people proved especially troublesome when he treated CBS talent in the same way. At various times, he had run-ins with stars such as Jack Benny (whose long-running program was cancelled by Aubrey), Lucille Ball, Garry Moore, and others. Also contributing to Aubrey's demise at CBS were questions of improprieties in the handling of his business and personal affairs, including allegations that he gave special consideration to certain program producers in exchange for personal favors and gifts. These factors combined with the downturn in CBS's programming fortunes and led Paley and Stanton to fire Aubrey from his post in February 1965. Evidence of Aubrey's impact on CBS, at least in the minds of Wall Street financial executives, came in the immediate nine-point drop in CBS's stock price that followed his dismissal.

Aubrey's reputation as a hard-fighting, hard-living executive would follow him for the rest of his life, thanks in part to his immortalization as a leading character in a number of nonfiction and fiction books. He was featured prominently and unflatteringly in Merle Miller's best seller about the television industry, *Only You, Dick Daring!,* while Jacqueline Susann acknowledged patterning the ruthless character of Robin Stone after Aubrey in her 1969 novel, *The Love Machine.* Among Aubrey's credits in his later career as an independent producer was that of co-executive producer of the highly rated and critically panned 1979 ABC made-for-television movie *The Dallas Cowboys Cheerleaders.*

David Gunzerath

See also **Columbia Broadcasting System**

James T(homas) Aubrey Jr. Born in La Salle, Illinois, December 14, 1918. Married: Phyllis Thaxter, 1944 (divorced, 1963); children: Schuyler and James Watson. Graduated from Princeton, New Jersey, B.A. cum laude 1941. Served in U.S. Air Force as test pilot, 1941–45. Started postwar career selling advertising space, Street and Smith and Condé Nast publications, 1946–48; account executive, CBS affiliate KNX, Los Angeles, 1948, and KNXT, 1951; sales manager, then general manager, KNXT and CTPN, 1952–55; manager, CBS television's West Coast network programming (where he and Hunt Stromberg Jr., wrote the outline, based on an idea by other writers, originating the hit television series *Have Gun, Will Travel*), 1956; vice president in charge of programs and talent, ABC, 1956–58; with ABC president Oliver Treyz, initiated *The Real McCoys, Maverick, The Donna Reed Show, 77 Sunset Strip,* and *The Rifleman;* vice president in charge of creative services, CBS television, 1958; appointed executive vice president of the CBS television network, 1959; CBS network president, December 1959; launched many successful series, notably *The Beverly Hillbillies, Mr. Ed, Gomer Pyle, The Munsters, My Favorite Martian, Route 66, The Defenders,* and *The Dick Van Dyke Show;* abruptly dismissed by Frank Stanton, president of CBS, Inc., and William S. Paley, chair of the board, February 27, 1965; headed Aubrey Productions, 1965–69; president, MGM, 1969–73; independent producer, from 1973 to 1994. Died in Los Angeles, September 3, 1994.

Television Series

1956 *Have Gun, Will Travel*

Made-for-Television Movies

1979 *The Dallas Cowboys Cheerleaders*

Films

Futureworld, 1976; *The Hunger*, 1983.

Further Reading

Bart, Peter, *Fade Out: The Calamitous Final Days of MGM,* New York: William Morrow, 1990

Hay, Peter, *MGM: When the Lion Roars,* Atlanta, Georgia: Turner Publishing, 1991

Metz, Robert, *CBS: Reflections in a Bloodshot Eye,* Chicago: Playboy Press, 1975
Miller, Merle, and Evan Rhodes, *Only You, Dick Daring!: Or How to Write One Television Script and Make $50,000,000,* New York: William Sloane, 1964
"No. 1 Supplier of TV Viewers," *Business Week* (April 25, 1964)
"Only You, Jim Aubrey," *Newsweek* (March 15, 1965)
Oulahan, Richard, and William Lambert, "The Tyrant's Fall That Rocked the TV World," *Life* (September 10, 1965)
Pace, Eric, "James Aubrey Jr., 75, TV and Film Executive," *New York Times* (September 12, 1994)
Paley, William S., *As It Happened: A Memoir,* Garden City, New York: Doubleday, 1979
Paper, Lewis J., *Empire: William S. Paley and the Making of CBS,* New York: St. Martin's Press, 1987
Rosenfield, Paul, "Aubrey: A Lion in Winter," *Los Angeles Times* (April 27, 1986)
Shales, Tom, "The Hazzards of James Aubrey: Barefooted Slob Heroes Running on TV," *Washington Post* (January 21, 1979)
Smith, Sally Bedell, *In All His Glory: The Life of William S. Paley, the Legendary Tycoon and His Brilliant Circle,* New York: Simon and Schuster, 1990

Audience Research: Cultivation Analysis

A culture's stories reflect and cultivate its most basic and fundamental assumptions, ideologies, and values. Mass communication is the mass production, distribution, and consumption of cultural stories. Cultivation analysis, developed by George Gerbner and his colleagues, explores the extent to which television viewers' beliefs about the "real world" are shaped by heavy exposure to the most stable, repetitive, and pervasive patterns that television presents, especially in its dramatic entertainment programs.

Cultivation analysis is one component of a long-term, ongoing research program, called "cultural indicators," which follows a three-pronged research strategy. The first, called "institutional process analysis," investigates the pressures and constraints that affect how media messages are selected, produced, and distributed. The second, called "message system analysis," quantifies and tracks the most common and recurrent images in television content. The third, cultivation analysis, studies whether and how television contributes to viewers' conceptions of social reality.

The cultural indicators project was first implemented in the late 1960s, and by the mid-1990s the bibliography of studies relating to it included more than 300 scholarly publications. Although early cultivation research was especially concerned with the issue of television violence, over the years the investigation has been expanded to include sex roles, images of aging, political orientations, environmental attitudes, science, health, religion, minorities, occupations, and other topics. Replications have been carried out in Argentina, Australia, Brazil, Canada, England, Germany, Hungary, Israel, the Netherlands, Russia, South Korea, Sweden, Taiwan, and other countries.

The methods and assumptions of cultivation analysis were designed to correct for certain blind spots in traditional mass-communication research. Most earlier studies looked at whether individual messages or genres could produce some kind of change in audience attitudes and behaviors; in contrast, cultivation sees the totality of television's programs as a coherent *system* of messages and asks whether that system might promote stability (or generational shifts), rather than immediate change in individuals. Whereas most research and debate on, for example, television violence has been concerned with whether violent portrayals make viewers more aggressive, Gerbner and his colleagues claimed that heavy exposure to television was associated with exaggerated beliefs about the amount of violence in society.

Cultivation analysis is not concerned with the impact of any particular program, genre, or episode. It does not address questions of style, artistic quality, aesthetic categories, high versus low culture, or specific, selective "readings" or interpretations of media messages. Rather, cultivation researchers are interested in the aggregate patterns of images and representations to which entire communities are exposed—and which they absorb—over long periods of time.

Cultivation does not deny the importance of selective viewing, individual programs, or differences in viewers' interpretations; it just sees these as different research questions. It focuses on what is most broadly shared, in common, across program types and among large groups of otherwise heterogeneous viewers. No matter what impact exposure to genre X may have on attitude Y, the cultivation perspective argues that the consequences of *television* cannot be found in terms of isolated fragments of the whole. The project is an attempt to say something about the more broad-based ideological consequences of a commercially supported cultural industry celebrating consumption, materialism, individualism, power, and the status quo along lines of gender, race, class, and age. None of this denies the fact that some programs may contain some messages more than others, that not all viewers watch the same programs, or that the messages may change somewhat over time.

The theory of cultivation emphasizes the role that storytelling plays in human society. The basic difference between human beings and other species is that we live in a world that is created by the stories we tell. Great portions of what we know, or think we know, come not from personal or direct experience but from many forms and modes of storytelling. Stories—from myths and legends to sitcoms and cop shows—tend to express, define, and maintain a culture's dominant assumptions, expectations, and interpretations of social reality.

Television has transformed the cultural process of storytelling into a centralized, market-driven, advertiser-sponsored system. In earlier times, the stories of a culture were told face-to-face by members of a community, such as parents, teachers, or the clergy. Today, television tells most of the stories to most of the people, most of the time. Storytelling is now in the hands of global commercial conglomerates that have something to sell. Most of the stories we now consume are not handcrafted works of individual expressive artists but mass produced by bureaucracies according to strict market specifications. To be acceptable to enormous audiences, the stories must fit into and reflect—and thereby sustain and cultivate—the "facts" of life that most people take for granted.

For the cultural indicators project, each year since 1967, weeklong samples of U.S. network television drama have been recorded and content analyzed in order to delineate selected features and trends in the overall world that television presents to its viewers. In the 1990s the analysis has been extended to include the FOX network, "reality" programs, and various new cable channels. Through the years, message system analysis has focused on the most pervasive content patterns that are common to many different types of programs but characteristic of the system of programming as a whole, because these hold the most significant potential lessons television cultivates.

Findings from the analyses of television's content are then used to formulate questions about people's conceptions of social reality, often contrasting television's "reality" with some other real-world criterion. Using standard techniques of survey methodology, the questions are posed to samples of children, adolescents, or adults, and the differences (if any) in the beliefs of light, medium, and heavy viewers, other things held constant, are assessed. The questions do not mention television, and respondents' awareness of the source of their information is seen as irrelevant.

The prominent and stable overrepresentation of well-off white males in the prime of life pervades prime time. On prime-time TV, women are outnumbered by men at a rate of three to one and allowed a narrower range of activities and opportunities. The dominant white males are more likely to commit violence, while old, young, female, and minority characters are more likely to be victims. Crime in prime time is at least ten times as rampant as in the real world, and an average of five to six acts of overt physical violence per hour involve well over half of all major characters.

Cultivation researchers have argued that these messages of power, dominance, segregation, and victimization cultivate relatively restrictive and intolerant views regarding personal morality and freedoms, women's roles, and minority rights. Cultivation theory contends that heavy exposure to television violence does not stimulate aggression, but it does cultivate insecurity, mistrust, alienation, and a willingness to accept potentially repressive measures in the name of security, all of which strengthens and helps maintain the prevailing hierarchy of social power.

Cultivation is not a linear, unidirectional, mechanical "effect" but part of a continual, dynamic, ongoing process of interaction among messages and contexts. Television viewing usually relates in different ways to different groups' life situations and worldviews. For example, personal interaction with family and peers makes a difference, as do real-world experiences. A wide variety of sociodemographic and individual factors produce sharp variations in cultivation patterns.

These differences often illustrate a phenomenon called "mainstreaming," which is based on the idea that television has become the primary common source of everyday culture of an otherwise heterogeneous population. From the perspective of cultivation analysis, television provides a relatively restricted set of choices for a virtually unrestricted variety of interests and publics; its programs eliminate boundaries of age, class, and region and are designed by commercial necessity to be watched by nearly everyone.

Mainstreaming means that heavy television viewing may erode the differences in people's perspectives that stem from other factors and influences. Mainstreaming thus represents a relative homogenization and absorption of divergent views and a convergence of disparate viewers. Cultivation researchers argue that television contributes to a blurring of cultural, political, social, regional, and class-based distinctions; the blending of attitudes into the television mainstream; and the bending of the direction of that mainstream to the political and economic tasks of the medium and its client institutions.

Cultivation has been a highly controversial and provocative approach; the results of cultivation research have been many, varied, and sometimes counterintuitive. The assumptions and procedures of cultivation analysis have been vigorously critiqued on theoretical, methodological, and epistemological grounds; extensive debates and colloquies (sometimes lively, sometimes heated) continue to engage the scholarly community and have led to some refinements and enhancements.

Some researchers have looked inward, seeking cognitive explanations for how television's images find their way into viewers' heads, and some have examined additional intervening variables and processes (e.g., perceived reality, active versus passive viewing). Some have questioned the assumption of relative stability in program content over time and across genres and emphasized differential impacts of exposure to different programs and types. The spread of alternative delivery systems such as cable and VCRs has been taken into account, as has the family and social context of exposure. Increasingly complex and demanding statistical tests have been applied. The paradigm has been implemented in at least a dozen countries besides the United States.

The literature contains numerous failures to replicate the cultivation analysis project's findings as well as numerous independent confirmations of its conclusions. The most common conclusion, supported by meta-analysis, is that television makes a small but significant contribution to heavy viewers' beliefs about the world. Given the pervasiveness of television and even light viewers' cumulative exposure, finding any observable evidence of effects at all is remarkable. Therefore, the discovery of a systematic pattern of small but consistent differences between light and heavy viewers may indicate far-reaching consequences.

Cultivation theory was developed when television viewing in the United States was dominated by three broadcast networks. Yet in the early 21st century, six broadcast networks barely attract 60 percent of prime-time viewers. With cable and satellite, the audience is divided among many dozens of specialized channels devoted to news, sports, movies, fashion, cooking, music, health, and more. With the spread of VCRs, the newer personal video recorders, and multichannel digital broadcasting, audiences now seem to choose from an extraordinary range of diverse content, contradicting the assumptions of cultivation.

However, the mere existence of new delivery systems does not fundamentally change the dynamics that drive program production and distribution. There has been little reduction in exposure to "network-type" programming; many new channels mainly offer more of the same types of programs. Concentration of media ownership is increasing as the traditional barriers among networks, stations, studios, syndicators, cable operators, cable networks, and advertisers dissolve.

Furthermore, key aspects of the earlier media system are amplified; for example, premium cable channels have much higher levels of violence than do broadcast networks. Available evidence indicates that new technologies intensify cultivation; for heavy viewers, new media mean even greater exposure to more of the same messages. Thus, technological developments will not diminish cultivation if the messages do not change.

In sum, cultivation research is concerned with the most general consequences of long-term exposure to centrally produced, commercially supported systems of stories. Cultivation analysis concentrates on the enduring and common consequences of growing up and living with television: the cultivation of stable, resistant, and widely shared assumptions and conceptions reflecting the institutional characteristics and interests of both the medium itself and the larger society. Understanding the dynamics of cultivation can help develop and maintain a sense of alternatives essential for self-direction and self-government in the television age. The cultivation perspective will become even more important as we face the vast institutional, technological, and policy-related changes in television the 21st century is sure to bring.

MICHAEL MORGAN

See also **Americanization; Children and Television; Demographics; Market; Ratings; Share; Violence and Television**

Further Reading

Bryant, Jennings, "The Road Most Traveled: Yet Another Cultivation Critique," *Journal of Broadcasting and Electronic Media* (1986)

Carlson, James M., *Prime Time Law Enforcement: Crime Show Viewing and Attitudes Toward the Criminal Justice System,* New York: Praeger, 1985

Gerbner, George, "Communication and Social Environment," *Scientific American* (1972)

Gerbner, George, "Cultural Indicators: The Third Voice," in *Communications Technology and Social Policy,* edited by George Gerbner, Larry Gross, and W.H. Melody, New York: John Wiley, 1973

Gerbner, George, "Toward 'Cultural Indicators': The Analysis of Mass-Mediated Message Systems," *Audio Visual Communication Review* (1969)

Gerbner, George, and Larry Gross, "Editorial Response: A Reply to Newcomb's 'Humanistic Critique,'" *Communication Research* (1979)
Gerbner, George, and Larry Gross, "Living with Television: The Violence Profile," *Journal of Communication* (1976)
Gerbner, George, Larry Gross, Michael Morgan, and Nancy Signorielli, "Charting the Mainstream: Television's Contributions to Political Orientations," *Journal of Communication* (1982)
Gerbner, George, Larry Gross, Michael Morgan, and Nancy Signorielli, "A Curious Journey into the Scary World of Paul Hirsch," *Communication Research* (1981)
Gerbner, George, Larry Gross, Michael Morgan, and Nancy Signorielli, "Growing Up with Television: The Cultivation Perspective," in *Media Effects: Advances in Theory and Research,* edited by J. Bryant and D. Zillmann, Hillsdale, New Jersey: Erlbaum, 1994
Gerbner, George, Larry Gross, Michael Morgan, and Nancy Signorielli, "The 'Mainstreaming' of America: Violence Profile No. 11," *Journal of Communication* (1980)
Hawkins, Robert P., and Suzanne Pingree, "Television's Influence on Social Reality," in *Television and Behavior: Ten Years of Scientific Progress and Implications for the 80s,* volume 2, *Technical Reviews,* edited by D. Pearl, L. Bouthilet, and J. Lazar, Rockville, Maryland: National Institute of Mental Health, 1982
Hirsch, Paul, "The 'Scary World' of the Nonviewer and Other Anomalies: A Re-analysis of Gerbner et al.'s Findings of Cultivation Analysis," *Communication Research* (1980)
Melischek, Gabriele, Karl Erik Rosengren, and James Stappers, editors, *Cultural Indicators: An International Symposium,* Vienna: Verlag der Osterreichischen Akademie der Wissenschaften, 1984
Newcomb, Horace, "Assessing the Violence Profile of Gerbner and Gross: A Humanistic Critique and Suggestion," *Communication Research* (1978)
Morgan, Michael, and James Shanahan, *Democracy Tango: Television, Adolescents, and Authoritarian Tensions in Argentina,* Cresskill, New Jersey: Hampton Press, 1995
Ogles, Robert M., "Cultivation Analysis: Theory, Methodology, and Current Research on Television-Influenced Constructions of Social Reality," *Mass Comm Review* (1987)
Potter, W. James, "Cultivation Theory and Research: A Conceptual Critique," *Human Communication Research* (1993)
Potter, W. James, "Cultivation Theory and Research: A Methodological Critique," *Journalism Monographs* (1994)
Shanahan, James, and Michael Morgan, *Television and Its Viewers: Cultivation Theory and Research,* Cambridge and New York: Cambridge University Press, 1999
Signorielli, Nancy, and Michael Morgan, editors, *Cultivation Analysis: New Directions in Media Effects Research,* Newbury Park, California: Sage, 1990

Audience Research: Effects Analysis

Within the field of television studies, effects studies have been both tendentious and critical. Their relative importance is reflected in the following from a 1948 paper by Harold Laswell: "A convenient way to describe an act of communication is to answer the following questions: "*Who* Says *What* in *Which Channel* to *Whom* with *What Effect?*"

The question as it is applied to television typically becomes either, How is society different because television is part of it? or, How are individuals or specific groups of people different because they live in a world in which television is available? The first of these questions may be thought of as a matter of media effect upon society, while the second is a matter of media effect upon the development or status of individual people.

Effects of television, then, may be social or psychological and developmental. They may also be short term or long term. Walter Weiss, writing in the second edition of the *Handbook of Social Psychology* (1969), discussed effects literature under ten headings: (1) cognition, (2) comprehension, (3) emotional arousal, (4) identification, (5) attitude, (6) overt behavior, (7) interests and interest-related behavior, (8) public taste, (9) outlook and values, and (10) family life.

For the most part, such effects, however they are characterized, have been studied in a haphazard fashion characterized by the funding priorities of governments and nonprofit foundations. For example, there have been many efforts to assess the effect of the availability of television upon the developmental processes in children. A case in point concerns the British Home Office, which in 1963 established its Television Research Committee with sociologist J.D. Halloran as its secretary. The effects of television were to be studied as both immediate and cumulative, with separate attention paid to perceptions of TV, its content, and its function for viewers.

One area that has been heavily studied and produced an extensive research literature addresses the specific issue of violence, especially the connection between television treatment of violence and its manifestation in society. This work addresses whether portrayals of violent behaviors result in members of the viewing audience becoming more violent in their relationships with others. This issue is often related to other presumed connections between the models projected by television and various modes of perception and behavior. Thus, the manner in which women and minorities are presented in various television programs may be connected by some researchers to the ways these groups are perceived by viewers in other groups and by the group members themselves.

Just as the presence or absence of a medium or some particular of program content (e.g., violence) can be considered capable of producing effects in an audience, so can such technological innovations as pay-per-view, satellite delivery, three-dimensional presentation, stereo sound, interactive television, the Internet, or streaming. Any of these technological innovations may be linked in a research question with special viewing populations and special samples of program materials in attempts to determine whether or not the shift in technology has an effect on subsequent behavior or attitude.

Effects research is grounded in various forms of social scientific analysis and often depends on such techniques as controlled experiments, surveys, and observations. Challenges to methods, design, or sample size are used to call results into question, and clear, incontrovertible conclusions are difficult to establish. Particularly with regard to research focused on children or on the role of televised violence, these philosophical and scientific difficulties have made it almost impossible to develop broadcasting policies based on research findings.

JAMES FLETCHER

Further Reading

Alexander, Alison, James Owers, and Rod Carveth, editors, *Media Economics: Theory and Practice,* Hillsdale, New Jersey: Erlbaum, 1993

Baran, Stanley J., and Dennis K. Davis, *Mass Communication Theory: Foundations, Ferment, and Future,* Belmont, California: Wadsworth, 1995

Beville, Hugh Malcolm, Jr., *Audience Ratings: Radio, Television, Cable,* Hillsdale, New Jersey: Erlbaum, 1988

Brooks, Tim, and Earle Marsh, editors, *The Complete Directory to Prime Time Network TV Shows—1948–Present,* New York, Ballantine, 1981

Dominick, Joseph R., and James E. Fletcher, editors, *Broadcasting Research Methods,* Newton, Massachusetts: Allyn and Bacon, 1985

Dominick, Joseph R., and James E. Fletcher, editors, *Handbook of Radio and TV Broadcasting: Research Procedures in Audience, Program and Revenues,* New York: Van Nostrand Reinhold, 1981

Fletcher, James E., editor, *Broadcast Research Definitions,* Washington, D.C.: National Association of Broadcasters, 1988

Lindzey, Gardner, and Elliot Aronson, editors, *The Handbook of Social Psychology,* volume 5, *Applied Social Psychology,* Reading, Massachusetts: Addison-Wesley, 1969

Schramm, Wilbur, and Donald F. Roberts, editors, *The Process and Effects of Mass Communication,* Chicago: University of Chicago Press, 1971

Audience Research: Industry and Market Analysis

The television audience is the commodity that stations and networks sell to advertisers. Television audiences are bought and sold, and audience research is the currency, so to speak, that the industry relies upon to make these transactions. From the television side of the business, the goal is to sell as many ads as possible while at the same time charging as much as advertisers are willing to pay. From the advertiser's perspective, the goal is to buy time in programs whose audience contains as many people as possible with the demographic characteristics most desired by the advertiser. Advertisers want to buy these audiences as efficiently as possible. In order to accomplish this task, the industry usually describes audiences and their prices in terms of costs per thousand. This is simply the cost to purchase one or more ads divided by an estimate of the number of people in thousands. For example, if the cost for one advertisement is $300,000 and the program audience estimate is 40 million women, 18 to 49 years old, then the cost per thousand is $300,000 / 40,000 = $7.50. There are 40,000 1,000s in 40 million. In this example, an advertiser will spend $7.50 for every 1,000 women 18 to 49 years old who watch the program in which the ad will be placed. Audience research provides the estimates of the size and characteristics of the audience that the industry buys and sells.

In the United States, the A.C. Nielsen Company provides the audience estimates to stations, networks, program producers, advertisers, and advertising agencies. Employing probability sample survey research methodology, ACNielsen identifies which programs people watch and how long they watch them. Printed reports and online computer access allow Nielsen's clients to examine a detailed picture of television audiences. Internet audience estimates are provided by Nielsen/Net Ratings.

Advertisers use this research information to locate the programs, stations, and networks that have large numbers of viewers with demographic characteristics they desire. These characteristics are based upon other market research that indicates such factors as age, sex, income, household size, and geographic location of people who are most likely to purchase and use their products or services. As they identify the significant users and purchasers of their products, advertisers look for television viewers with similar characteristics. These target audiences become the focus of the deals that buyers and sellers make. The audience research data helps identify the size and characteristics of the audience as well as the efficiency of a particular advertising buy.

Television stations and networks approach this equation from the other side. They use market research to identify the characteristics of users and purchasers of products and services to whom they hope to sell advertising. TV sales executives then employ Nielsen audience research to find the programs these target audiences watch. They will then do competitive analyses to compare the size and composition of other station and or network program audiences. They will use this data to convince advertisers that they can deliver more of the target audience at a better price than their competition.

Audience research is an integral part of this business ritual. It is the starting point for the negotiations in which buyers and sellers engage. As in any business transaction, there are many other factors that will determine price. Supply and demand, personal relationships, and other intangibles affect prices, but in the television industry, audience research plays an important role in how business is conducted.

Audience research has become more complicated with the extraordinary growth in the use of VCRs, cable and satellite delivery, video games, personal video recorders, and digital technology. The audience ratings for a given TV show must be measured in a way that takes into account each of the many ways we use television. In order to obtain accurate audience research, all viewing devices connected to the TV set must be metered and monitored to account for the viewing of television programs delivered over the air, via cable or satellite, playing a video game, playing a tape or DVD, employing a digital personal video recorder, or using a computer in conjunction with the TV. These audience research methods will become even more complex as TV stations and cable systems deliver digital television to a wider audience. This technology will allow for the delivery of either more traditional TV programs or higher audio and video quality.

GUY E. LOMETTI

Further Reading

Lometti, Guy E., "Measuring Children's Television Viewing," in *Children's Research,* New York: Advertising Research Foundation, 1988

Stipp, H., and Schiavone, N., "Research at a Commercial Television Network: NBC 1990," *Marketing Research* (September 1990)

Audience Research: Overview

The history of media audience studies can be seen as a series of oscillations between perspectives that have stressed the power of the text (or message) over its audiences and perspectives that have stressed the barriers "protecting" the audience from the potential effects of the message. The first position is most obviously represented by the whole tradition of effects studies, mobilizing a "hypodermic" model of media influence, in which the media are seen to have the power to "inject" their audiences with particular "messages," which will cause those audiences to behave in particular ways. This has involved, from the right, perspectives that see the media as causing the breakdown of "traditional values" and, from the left, perspectives that see the media causing their audiences to remain quiescent in political terms, with the media inculcating consumerist values or causing the audience to inhabit some form of false consciousness.

One of the most influential versions of this kind of "hypodermic" theory of media effects was that advanced by Theodor Adorno and Max Horkheimer, along with other members of the Frankfurt School of Social Research. Their "pessimistic mass-society thesis" reflected the authors' experience of the breakdown of modern Germany into fascism during the 1930s, a breakdown that was attributed, in part, to the loosening of traditional ties and structures, a disintegration regarded as leaving people more "atomized" and exposed to external influences and especially to the pressure of the mass propaganda of powerful leaders, the most effective agency of which was the mass media. This "pessimistic mass-society thesis" stressed the conservative and reconciliatory role of "mass culture" for the audience. Mass culture was seen to suppress "potentialities" and to deny awareness of contradictions in a "one-dimensional world"; only art, in fictional and dramatic form, could preserve the qualities of negation and transcendence. Implicit in this theory was a "hypodermic" model of the media, which were seen as having the power to "inject" a repressive ideology directly into the consciousness of the masses.

However, against this overly pessimistic backdrop, the emigration of the leading members of the Frankfurt School (Adorno, Horkheimer, Herbert Marcuse) to the United States during the 1930s led to the development of a specifically "American" school of research in the 1940s and 1950s. The Frankfurt School's "pessimistic" thesis proved unacceptable to American researchers. According to these researchers, the "pessimistic" thesis proposed too direct and unmediated an impact by the media on audiences; it took too far the thesis that all intermediary social structures between leaders/media and the masses had broken down; it did not accurately reflect the pluralistic nature of American society; it was sociologically naive. Clearly, the media had social effects; these must be examined and researched, but, equally clearly, these effects were neither all-powerful, simple, nor even necessarily direct. The nature of this complexity and indirectness also needed to be demonstrated and researched. Thus, in reaction to the Frankfurt School's predilection for critical social theory and qualitative and philosophical analysis, American researchers, such as Herta Herzog, Robert Merton, Paul Lazarsfeld, and, later, Elihu Katz began to develop a quantitative and positivist methodology for empirical audience research into the "sociology of mass persuasion."

Throughout the 1950s and 1960s, the overall effect of this empirically grounded "sociology of mass persuasion" was to produce a much more qualified notion of "media power," in which media consumers were increasingly recognized to not be completely passive "victims" of the culture industry.

Among the major landmarks here were Merton's *Mass Persuasion* and Katz and Lazarsfeld's *Personal Influence,* in which they developed the concept of "two-step flow" communication, where the influence of the media was seen as crucially mediated by "gatekeepers" and "opinion leaders" within the audience community.

Looking back at these developments from the perspective of the 1970s, Counihan noted the increasing significance of a new perspective on media consumption: the "uses-and-gratifications" approach, largely associated in the United States with the work of Katz and, in Britain, with the work of Jay Blumler and James Halloran as well as the studies of the Leicester Centre for Mass Communications Research, during the 1960s. Within that perspective, the viewer came to be credited with an active role, so that there was then a question, as Halloran put it, of looking at what people do with the media, rather than what the media do to them (see Halloran). This argument was obviously of great significance in moving the debate forward: to begin to look to the active engagement of the audience with the medium and with the particular television programs that they might be watching. A key advance developed by the uses-and-gratifications perspective was that of the variability of response and interpretation. From this perspective, one can no longer talk about the "effect" of a message on a homogenous mass audience, who are all expected to be affected in the same way. Clearly, uses-and-gratifications did represent a significant advance on effects theory, insofar as it opens up the question of differential interpretations. However, critics argue that the theory is limited because the perspective remains individualistic, insofar as differences of response or interpretation are ultimately attributed solely to individual differences of personality or psychology. From this point of view the approach remains severely limited by its insufficiently sociological or cultural perspective.

It was against this background that Stuart Hall, working at the Centre for Contemporary Cultural Studies at the University of Birmingham, England, developed the "encoding/decoding" model of communication as an attempt to take forward insights that had emerged within each of these other perspectives. In subsequent years, this model has come to be widely influential in audience studies. It took from the effects theorists the notion that mass communication is a structured activity, in which the institutions that produce the messages do have the power to set agendas and to define issues. This model moves away from the idea that the medium has the power to make a person behave in a certain way (as a direct effect, which is caused by a simple stimulus, provided by the medium), but it holds onto a notion of the role of the media in setting agendas (see the work of Bachrach and Baratz on the media's agenda-setting functions) and providing cultural categories and frameworks within which members of the culture will tend to operate.

Hall's paradigm also attempts to incorporate from the uses-and-gratifications perspective the idea of the active viewer, making meaning from the signs and symbols that the media provide. However, the model was also designed to take on board concerns with the ways in which responses and interpretations are socially structured and culturally patterned at a level beyond that of individual psychologies. The model was also, critically, informed by semiological perspectives, focusing on the question of how communication works and drawing on Umberto Eco's early work on the decoding of TV as a form of "semiological guerrilla warfare." The key focus was on the realization that we are, of course, dealing with signs and symbols, which only have meaning within the terms of reference supplied by codes (of one sort or another) that the audience shares, to some greater or lesser extent, with the producers of messages. In this respect, Hall's model was also influenced by Roland Barthes's attempts to update Ferdinand de Saussure's ideas of semiology—as "a science of signs at the heart of social life"—by developing an analysis of the role of "mythologies" in contemporary cultures.

The premises of Hall's encoding/decoding model are (1) the same event can be encoded in more than one way; (2) the message always contains more than one potential "reading"—messages propose and "prefer" certain readings over others, but they can never become wholly closed around one reading: they remain polysemic (i.e., capable, in principle, of a variety of interpretations); (3) understanding the message is also a problematic practice, however transparent and "natural" it may seem. Messages encoded one way can always be decoded in a different way.

The television message is treated here as a complex sign, in which a "preferred reading" has been inscribed but retains the potential, if decoded in a manner different from the way in which it has been encoded, of communicating a different meaning. The message is thus a structured polysemy. It is central to Hall's argument that all meanings do not exist "equally" in the message, which is seen to have been structured in dominance, despite the impossibility of a "total closure" of meaning. Further, the "preferred reading" is itself part of the message and can be identified within its linguistic and communicative structure. Thus, when analysis shifts to the "moment" of the encoded message itself, the communicative form and structure can be analyzed in terms of what the mechanisms are that prefer one, dominant reading over the other readings; that is, the means the encoder uses to try to "win the assent of the audience" to one's preferred reading of the message.

Hall assumes that there will be no necessary "fit," or transparency, between the encoding and decoding ends of the communication chain. It is precisely this lack of transparency, and its consequences for communication, that must be investigated, Hall claims. Having established that there is always a possibility of disjunction between the codes of those sending and those receiving through the circuit of mass communications, the problem of the "effects" of communication could now be reformulated, as that of the *extent* to which decodings take place within the limits of the preferred (or dominant) manner in which the message has been initially encoded. However, the complementary aspect of this problem is that of the extent to which these interpretations, or decodings, also reflect, and are inflected by, the code and discourses that different sections of the audience inhabit and the ways in which this reflection or deflection is determined by the socially governed distribution of cultural codes between and across different sections of the audience: that is, the range of different decoding strategies and competencies in the audience. In this connection, the model draws both on Frank Parkin's work on "meaning systems" and on Pierre Bourdieu's work on the social distribution of forms of cultural competence.

During the 1970s, at around the same time that Hall was developing the encoding/decoding model, the growing influence of feminism led to a revitalization of interest in psychoanalytic theory, in which concern for issues of gender take a central place. Within media studies, this interest in psychoanalytic theories of the construction of gendered identities, within the field of language and representation, was one of the informing principles behind the development of the particular approach to the analysis of the media (predominantly the cinema) and its effects on the spectator, developed by the journal *Screen* (for a time in the late 1970s, heavily influential in this field, particularly in British film studies).

Screen theory emphasized the analysis of the effects of cinema (and especially, the regressive effects of mainstream, commercial Hollywood cinema) in "positioning" the spectator (or subject) of the film, through the way in which the text (by means of camera placement, editing, and other formal characteristics) "fixed" the spectator into a particular kind of "subject-position," which, it was argued, "guaranteed" the transmission of a certain kind of "bourgeois ideology" of naturalism, realism, and verisimilitude.

Screen theory was largely constituted by a mixing of Jacques Lacan's rereading of Sigmund Freud, stressing the importance of language in the unconscious, and

Louis Althusser's early formulation of the "media" as an "Ideological State Apparatus" (even if operating in the private sphere), which had the principal function of securing the reproduction of the conditions of production by "interpellating" its subjects (spectators, audiences) within the terms of the "dominant ideology." Part of the appeal of this approach for media scholars rested in the weight the theory gave to ("relatively autonomous") language and "texts" (such as films and media products) as having real effects in society. To this extent, the approach was argued to represent a significant advance on previous theories of the media (including traditional Marxism), which had stressed the determination of all superstructural phenomena (such as the media) by the "real" economic "base" of the society, thus allowing no space for the conceptualization of the media themselves as having independent (or at least, in Althusser's terms, "relatively autonomous") effects of their own.

Undoubtedly one of screen theory's great achievements, drawing as it did on psychoanalysis, Marxism, and the formal semiotics of Christian Metz, was to restore an emphasis on the analysis of texts that had been absent in much previous work. In particular, the insights of psychoanalysis were extremely influential in the development of later feminist work on the role of the media in the construction of gendered identities and gendered forms of spectatorship.

Proponents of screen theory argued that previous approaches had neglected the analysis of the textual forms and patterns of media products, concentrating instead on the analysis of patterns of ownership and control—on the assumption, crudely put, that once the capitalist ownership of the industry was demonstrated, there was no real need to examine the texts (programs or films) themselves in detail, as they would only display minor variations within the narrow limits dictated by their capitalist owners. Conversely, screen theory focused precisely on the text and emphasized the need for close analysis of textual/formal patterns: hardly surprisingly, given the background of its major figures in English and literary studies. However, these theorists' arguments, in effect, merely inverted the terms of the sociological/economic forms of determinist theory that they critiqued. In screen theory, it was the text itself that was the central (if not exclusive) focus of the analysis, on the assumption that, since the text "positioned" the spectator, all that was necessary was the close analysis of texts, from which their "effects" on spectators could be automatically deduced, as spectators were bound to take up the "positions" constructed for them by the text (film).

The textual determination of screen theory, with its constant emphasis on the "suturing" (see Heath) of the spectator into the predetermined subject position constructed for him or her by the text, thus allocated a central place in media analysis to the analysis of the text. As Moores puts it, "the aim was to uncover the symbolic mechanisms through which cinematic texts confer subjectivity upon readers, sewing them into the film narrative, through the production of subject positions" on the assumption that the spectator (or reading subject) is left with no other option but, as Heath suggests, to "make...the meanings the film makes for him/her."

Although film studies remains influenced by the psychoanalytic model (which has been usefully developed by Valerie Walkerdine in a way that attempts to make the paradigm less universalist/determinist), within communication and media studies it was Hall's encoding/decoding model that set the basic conceptual framework for the notable boom in studies of media consumption and the media audiences that occurred during the 1980s. To take only the best-known examples, the body of work produced in that period included David Morley's study of the *Nationwide* audience, Dorothy Hobson's study of *Crossroads* viewers, Tania Modleski's work on women viewers of soap opera, Janice Radway's study of readers of romance fiction, Ien Ang's study of *Dallas* viewers, John Fiske's study entitled *Television Culture,* Greg Philo and Justin Lewis's studies of the audience for television news, Sut Jhally and Lewis's study of American audiences for *The Cosby Show,* and the work of K. Schroder and Tamar Liebes and Elihu Katz on the consumption of American television fiction in other cultures. Toward the end of the 1980s, much of the most important new material on media consumption was collected together in the published proceedings of two major conferences on audience studies—Phillip Drummond and Richard Paterson's collection *Television and Its Audience,* bringing together work on audiences presented at the International Television Studies Conference in London in 1986, and Ellen Seiter's collection *Remote Control: Television, Audiences, and Cultural Power,* based on the influential conference of that name held in Tubingen, Germany, in 1987.

During the late 1980s, a new strand of research developed in audience studies, focusing on the domestic context of television's reception within the household, often using a broadly ethnographic methodology and characteristically focusing on gender differences in TV viewing habits within the household or family. The major studies in this respect are Morley's *Family Television,* James Lull's *Inside Family Viewing,* Ann Gray's *Video Playtime,* Roger Silverstone's *Television and Everyday Life,* and, from a historical perspective, Lynn Spigel's *Make Room for TV.*

In recent years, a number of technological and market developments have transformed the terrain of media consumption. The rise of home video, with its capacity for "time shifting," has meant that viewers are no longer compelled to watch programs when they are broadcast but can integrate the shows more readily into their personal schedules. The remote control enables viewers to "graze" the broadcast schedules without rising from their armchairs, making audience members capable of "cannibalizing" what the broadcasters offer into their own customized/personalized viewing selections. At the same time, the development of cable and satellite services in many countries has led to the growth of multichannel viewing environments, where TV viewers now have a far wider range of choices.

Some observers have argued that these developments lead to the greater empowerment of the viewer/consumer in relation to the broadcasters. In combination with the dominant consumerist ideologies of the 1980s and 1990s, these technological and institutional changes have strengthened the development of what has come to be known as "active audience" theory. However, more recently some critics have urged caution, warning that audience activity should not be conflated with audience power, insofar as the media institutions continue to set the agenda (even if it is now broader and more readily time shifted and cannibalized by the viewer) from which audiences have to make their viewing choices.

One of the most significant issues that arises in this new technological and institutional context is that of the cultural consequences of the fragmentation of broadcast audiences. In this new situation, fewer people share a common broadcast experience as provided by a national broadcast channel. National broadcasting systems can no longer encourage social or cultural integration to the same extent that they did in the past. This trend continues with the rise of satellite broadcasting systems, which often bring together diasporic audiences across wide geographical territories, which transcend and cut across national communities and boundaries.

David Morley

See also **Americanization; Children and Television; Demographics; Market; Ratings; Share; Violence and Television**

Further Reading

Adorno, Theodor, and Max Horkheimer, "The Culture Industry: Enlightenment As Mass Deception," in *Mass Communication and Society,* edited by James Curran et al., London: Edward Arnold, 1977; Beverly Hills, California: Sage, 1979

Althusser, Louis, "Ideological State Apparatuses," in *Lenin and Philosophy, and Other Essays,* by Louis Althusser, translated by Ben Brewster, London: New Left Books, 1971; New York: Monthly Review Press, 1972

Ang, Ien, *Watching "Dallas": Soap Opera and the Melodramatic Imagination,* translated by Della Cuiling, London and New York: Methuen, 1985

Blumler, Jay, et al., "Reaching Out: A Future for Gratifications Research," in *Media Gratification Research,* edited by K. Rosengren, et al., Beverly Hills, California: Sage, 1985

Bourdieu, Pierre, *Distinction: A Social Critique of the Judgment of Taste,* translated by Richard Nice, London: Routledge, and Cambridge, Massachusetts: Harvard University Press, 1984

Brunsdon, Charlotte, "*Crossroads:* Notes on a Soap Opera," *Screen* (1981)

Budd, Michael, et al., "The Affirmative Character of American Cultural Studies," *Critical Studies in Mass Communication* (1990)

Byars, Jackie, *All That Hollywood Allows: Re-reading Gender in 1950s Melodrama,* Chapel Hill: University of North Carolina Press, and London: Routledge, 1991

Certeau, Michel de, *The Practice of Everyday Life,* translated by Steven Rendall, Berkeley: University of California Press, 1984

Condit, Celeste, "The Rhetorical Limits of Polysemy," *Critical Studies in Mass Communication* (1989)

Corner, J., "Meaning, Genre, and Context," in *Mass Media and Society,* edited by James Curran and Michael Gurevitch, London: Edward Arnold, 1977; Beverly Hills, California: Sage, 1979

Curran, James, "The 'New Revisionism' in Mass Communication Research," *European Journal of Communication* (1990)

Drummond, Phillip, and Richard Paterson, editors, *Television and Its Audiences: International Research Perspectives,* London: British Film Institute, 1988

Evans, W., "The Interpretive Turn in Media Research," *Critical Studies in Mass Communication* (1990)

Fish, Stanley, *Is There a Text in This Class? The Authority of Interpretive Communities,* Cambridge, Massachusetts: Harvard University Press, 1980

Fiske, John, *Television Culture,* New York and London: Methuen, 1987

Gledhill, C., "Pleasurable Negotiations," in *Female Spectators: Looking at Film and Television,* edited by E. Deidre Pribram, London and New York: Verso, 1988

Gray, Ann, *Video Playtime: The Gendering of a Leisure Technology,* London and New York: Routledge, 1992

Gripsrud, Jostein, *The Dynasty Years: Hollywood Television and Critical Media Studies,* London and New York: Routledge, 1995

Hall, Stuart, "Encoding and Decoding in the TV Discourse," in *Culture, Media, Language: Working Papers in Cultural Studies, 1972–97,* edited by Stuart Hall et al., London: Hutchinson, 1981

Halloran, James D., editor, *The Effects of Television,* London: Panther, 1970

Hay, James, Lawrence Grossberg, and Ellen Wartella, editors, *The Audience and Its Landscape,* Boulder, Colorado: Westview Press, 1996

Heath, S., "Notes on Suture," *Screen* (1977–78)

Hobson, Dorothy, *Crossroads: The Drama of a Soap Opera,* London: Methuen, 1982

Iser, Wolfgang, *The Act of Reading: A Theory of Aesthetic Response,* Baltimore, Maryland: Johns Hopkins University Press, 1976

Iser, Wolfgang, *The Implied Reader: Patterns in Communication from Bunyon to Beckett,* Baltimore, Maryland: Johns Hopkins University Press, 1974
Jauss, H.R., "Literary History As a Challenge to Literary Theory," *New Literary History* (Autumn 1970)
Jensen, K.B., "Qualitative Audience Research," *Critical Studies in Mass Communication* (1987)
Jensen, K.B., and K.E. Rosengren, "Five Traditions in Search of an Audience," *European Journal of Communication* (1990)
Jhally, Sut, and Justin Lewis, *Enlightened Racism: The Cosby Show, Audiences, and the Myth of the American Dream,* Boulder, Colorado: Westview Press, 1992
Katz, Elihu, and Paul F. Lazarsfeld, *Personal Influence: The Part Played by People in the Flow of Mass Communications,* Glencoe, Illinois: Free Press, 1955
Kuhn, Annette, *Women's Pictures: Feminism and Cinema,* London and Boston: Routledge, 1982; 2nd edition, London and New York: Verso, 1994
Lewis, Justin, *The Ideological Octopus: An Exploration of Television and Its Audience,* London and New York: Routledge, 1991
Liebes, Tamar, and Elihu Katz, *The Export of Meaning: Cross-Cultural Readings of Dallas,* Oxford and New York: Oxford University Press, 1991
Lull, James, *Inside Family Viewing: Ethnographic Research on Television's Audiences,* London and New York: Routledge, 1991
MacCabe, C., "Days of Hope," in *Popular TV and Film,* edited by T. Bennet et al., London: British Film Institute, 1981
MacCabe, C., "Realism and the Cinema," *Screen* (1974)
Mattelart, M. *Women, Media, Crisis: Femininity and Disorder,* London: Comedia, 1984
Merton, Robert K., *Mass Persuasion: The Social Psychology of a War Bond Drive,* New York: Free Press, 1946
Metz, C., "The Imaginary Signifier," *Screen* (1975)
Modleski, Tania, *Loving with a Vengeance: Mass-Produced Fantasies for Women,* Hamden, Connecticut: Archon Books, 1982; London: Methuen, 1984
Moores, Shaun, *Interpreting Audiences: An Ethnography of Media Consumption,* Thousand Oaks, California, and London: Sage, 1993
Morley, David, *Family Television: Cultural Power and Domestic Leisure,* London: Comedia, 1986
Morley, David, *The Nationwide Audience,* London: British Film Institute, 1980
Morley, David, *Television, Audience, and Cultural Studies,* London: Routledge, 1992
Parkin, Frank, *Class Inequality and Political Order: Social Stratification in Capitalist and Communist Societies,* London: MacGibbon and Kee, and New York: Praeger, 1971
Radway, Janice A., *Reading the Romance: Women, Patriarchy, and Popular Literature,* Chapel Hill: University of North Carolina Press, 1984
Rosengren, K.E., "Growth of a Research Tradition," in *Media Gratifications Research,* edited by K.E. Rosengren et al., Beverly Hills, California: Sage, 1985
Schroder, K., "Convergence of Antagonistic Traditions?," *European Journal of Communications* (1987)
Seaman, William, "Active Audience Theory: Pointless Populism," *Media, Culture, and Society* (1992)
Seiter, Ellen, et al., editors, *Remote Control: Television, Audiences, and Cultural Power,* London and New York: Routledge, 1989
Silverstone, Roger, *Television and Everyday Life,* London and New York: Routledge, 1994
Spigel, Lynn, *Make Room for TV: Television and the Family Ideal in Postwar America,* Chicago: University of Chicago Press, 1992
Tomkins, Jane P., editor, *Reader Response Criticism: From Formalism to Poststructuralism,* Baltimore, Maryland: Johns Hopkins University Press, 1980
Tulloch, John, *Watching Television Audiences: Cultural Theories and Methods,* London: Arnold, and New York: Oxford University Press, 2000
Turnoch, Robert, *Interpreting Diana: Television Audiences and the Death of a Princess,* London: British Film Institute, 2000
Walkerdine, V., "Video Replay," in *Formations of Fantasy,* edited by Victor Burgin et al., New York and London: Methuen, 1986

Audience Research: Reception Analysis

Despite the (implicit) nominal link of "reception analysis," as defined in media studies, to the work on what is called "reception theory" within the field of literary studies, the body of recent work on media audiences commonly referred to by this name has, on the whole, a different origin than the work in literary theory—although there are some theoretical links between the two fields (see, for example, the work of Stanley Fish). In practice, the term "reception analysis" has come to be widely used as a way of characterizing the wave of audience research that occurred within communications and cultural studies during the 1980s and 1990s. On the whole, this work has adopted a "culturalist" perspective, has tended to use qualitative (and often ethnographic) methods of research, and has been concerned primarily with exploring the active choices, uses, and interpretations made of media materials by their consumers.

The single most important point of origin for this work lies with the development of cultural studies in the writings of Stuart Hall at the Centre for Contemporary Cultural Studies at the University of Birmingham,

England, in the early 1970s, and, in particular, Hall's widely influential "encoding/decoding" model of communications. Hall's model provided the inspiration, and much of the conceptual framework, for a number of the center's explorations of the process of media consumption, notably David Morley's widely cited study of the cultural patterning of differential interpretations of media messages among *The Nationwide*'s audience and Dorothy Hobson's work on women viewers of the soap opera *Crossroads.* These works were the forerunners of a blossoming, throughout the 1980s and 1990s, of cultural studies analyses focusing on the media audience, including the influential feminist studies of Tania Modleski and Janice Radway on women consumers of soap opera and romance, and the work of Ien Ang, Tamar Liebes and Elihu Katz, Kim Schroder, and Jostein Gripsrud on international, cross-cultural consumption of American drama series such as *Dallas* and *Dynasty.*

Much of this work has been effectively summarized and popularized, especially in the United States, by John Fiske, who has drawn on the theoretical work of Michel de Certeau to develop a particular emphasis on the "active audience," operating within what Fiske terms the "semiotic democracy" of postmodern pluralistic culture. Fiske's work has subsequently been the object of some critique, in which a number of authors, among them B. Budd, Celeste Condit, W. Evans, Jostein Gripsrud, and William Seaman, have argued that reception analysts' emphasis on the openness (or "polysemy") of the message and on the activity (and the implied "empowerment") of the audience has been taken too far, to the extent that the original issue—the extent of media power—has been lost sight of, as if the "text" had been theoretically "dissolved" into the audience's (supposedly) multiple "readings" of (and "resistances" to) it.

In the late 1980s, many called for scholars to recognize a possible "convergence" of previously disparate approaches under the general banner of "reception analysis" (see, for example, Jensen and Rosengren), whereas Jay Blumler and his coauthors claimed that the work of a scholar such as Radway is little more than a "re-invention" of the "uses and gratifications" tradition—a claim hotly contested by K. Schroder. More recently, both James Curran and J. Corner have offered substantial critiques of "reception analysis"—the former accusing many reception analysts of ignorance of the earlier traditions of media audience research, and the latter accusing them of retreating away from important issues of macropolitics and power into inconsequential microethnographies of domestic television consumption. For a reply to these criticisms, see Morley, 1992.

David Morley

Further Reading

See under **"Audience Research: Overview."**

Auf Wiedersehen, Pet

Auf Wiedersehen, Pet was a critically acclaimed and popular drama series from 1983 about an ill-assorted group of British builders working on a German construction site. Perhaps one of the earliest examples of the comedy-drama genre in Britain, *Auf Wiedersehen, Pet* fused gritty realism with wry humor to play out the personal tensions between the groups and the historical and football rivalries between England and Germany. Penned by the comedy writing team Ian La Frenais and Dick Clement, it produced a rogue's gallery of recognizable and lovable characters that resurfaced in two more series, one in 1986 and the other 16 years later in 2002.

The program was created by film director Franc Roddam after he visited his home village in the northeast of England in the late 1970s, only to discover that many of the people he had grown up with were working as builders in Germany. He took the idea to La Frenais and Clement, who were particularly known for their working-class sitcom set in the northeast, *The Likely Lads* (1964–66), and its follow-up, *Whatever Happened to the Likely Lads* (1973–74). The original aim was to make a two-hour film, but Central Television persuaded them to expand it into 13 hour-long episodes.

A cast of unknowns was gathered, many coming from the northeast region after producer Martin McKeand and his directors Roger Bamford and Baz Taylor went to Newcastle to review people from local bands and theater groups. Once recruited, the mixed group of actors practiced building crafts on set for a month before shooting began. Shooting took place over 18 months at Elstree Studios and on location in Frankfurt. The series was the first British drama to be shot abroad, and at the time this use of location video gave the program a visually distinctive and dynamic edge.

The series follows the exploits of the seven builders, who came from all over Britain to find work. They live in a squalid hut on the building site and have to brave rain and mud to get to the temporary ablutions hut. The camp mentality is ironically reminiscent of World War II prisoner-of-war films like *The Great Escape* (1963) and *The Colditz Story* (1955) as the characters squirm under German management, and much of the humor derives from the inevitable cultural misunderstandings that occur between the British and their hosts.

The humor is also derived from the relationships among a disparate group of people thrown together. Sharply observed with a witty script, the drama is also underscored by the regional differences between the characters. One of the most striking aspects of *Auf Wiedersehen, Pet* is the use of language, especially working-class vernacular and regional dialects. The seven characters all conform to different types, such as Barry Taylor (Timothy Spall), the sensible but irritating bore from Birmingham, and Wayne Norris (Gary Holton), the Cockney "wide-boy" philandering his way through the young German women. Yet it is three "Geordies" who provide the lynchpin for the action ("Geordie" is a term for the working-class accent of the northeast of England and the people who live there). Dennis Patterson (Tim Healey) is the mature voice of reason; Neville Hope (Kevin Whately), whiny and homesick; and "Oz" Osbourne (Jimmy Nail), the large, loud, loutish oaf.

Although *Auf Wiedersehen, Pet* can now be regarded as a comedy drama it was, at the time and at heart, a serious drama. Transmitted in 1983, it reflected a period of growing unemployment and economic depression in areas such as the northeast of England. Described in the press as *Boys from the Blackstuff* (1982) with jobs, the series looked at what happened to those who left home to find work to feed their wives and families. The colloquialism of the title suggests this sequestration from home and community. The word "pet," a Geordie endearment, is appended to the German phrase for "goodbye," and thus alludes to the women left behind in Britain, and also perhaps in Germany. The lyricism of the language and regional affinity thus celebrates a sense of community, and thereby more powerfully evokes its loss.

Most of the cast members were propelled to success in their respective acting careers. Nail went on to take the lead role in *Spender* (1991–93) and *Crocodile Shoes* (1994). Whately went on to play in a number of dramas but will perhaps be best remembered for playing Sergeant Lewis, the sidekick to John Thaw, in *Inspector Morse.* Timothy Spall went on to a career in film and television, notably turning up in works by Stephen Poliakoff such as *Shooting the Past* (1999) and *Perfect Strangers* (2001), and in films by Mike Leigh such as *Secrets and Lies* (1996)

The program returned in two more incarnations. The second 13-part series follows the group as they work on a villa in Spain owned by a gangster played by Bill Paterson. The production was tragically marked by the premature death of Gary Holton in 1985 from a heroin overdose. Production was sufficiently advanced, however, that there was enough footage of Holton to ensure the completion of the series.

After a break of 16 years, the third series came about by chance and was aired by the BBC. Whately, Nail, and Healey had reprised their characters for a charity stage show (for which La Frenais and Clement had written scenes) and news reached Roddam, who held the rights to the series. Roddam lived next door to BBC 1 Controller Alan Yentob, and a deal was made over the garden fence.

In the new six-episode series, the old gang is reunited by Oz to help move the Middlesborough transporter bridge to Arizona. La Frenais and Clement cleverly show how the characters have fared over the years, and Wayne is replaced in the series by his fictional long-lost son, played by Noel Clarke. The comeback was a critical success and a ratings triumph for the BBC. In May 2002 discussion was under way regarding a fourth series.

ROB TURNOCK

See also ***Boys from the Blackstuff;*** **La Frenais, Ian;** ***Likely Lads, The***

Cast

Dennis Patterson	Tim Healey
Leonard "Oz" Osbourne	Jimmy Nail
Neville Hope	Kevin Whately
Brian "Bomber" Busbridge	Pat Roach
Wayne Norris	Gary Holton (1983, 1986)
Barry Taylor	Timothy Spall
Albert Moxey	Christopher Fairbank
Herr Grunwald	Michael Sheard (1983)
Dagmar	Brigiette Kahn (1983)
Ally Frazer	Bill Paterson (1986)
Wyman	Noel Clark (2002)
Jeffrey Granger	Bill Nighy (2002)

Creator
Franc Roddam

Producers
Martin McKeand (1983, 1986)
Joy Spink (2002)

Writers
Ian La Frenais
Dick Clement
Stan Hey (1983, 1986)

Programming History

ITV	
1984–85	13 episodes
November 1984–January 1985	Friday 9:00–10:00
1986	13 episodes
February–May 1986	Friday 9:00–10:00
BBC	
2002	6 episodes
April–June 2002	Sunday 9:00–10:00

Australia

Before the recent shift away from oligopoly, Australian television showed a pattern of "historical modernity." The key features of this were as follows: a dual or mixed system consisting of private, commercial television broadcast networks as well as a public service sector; heavy reliance on American-style programming practices and, initially at least, equally heavy reliance on imported programs from the United States to fill the television schedule; the start-up of local programs on the commercial networks that, when coupled with imported programs, guaranteed the overall viewing popularity of this sector; a relatively weak public service sector, perpetually caught in the dilemma of attempting to hold its traditional minority audiences with innovative, local programs and attracting larger, entertainment-oriented audiences with more mainstream programs, often imported from the international paradigm of public broadcasters, the BBC. While this pattern has been generally true for local television, it has not, however, been a static one. In particular Australian television has followed a classic economic tendency of "import substitution" whereby, after an initial flood of U.S. programs, locally produced popular television programs soon appeared that displaced imported programs in the schedule. In other words, imports played an important role in the development of a local television production industry. However, in the present post-oligopoly era, broadcasters again find themselves heavily reliant on imports, this time in the shape of TV program formats.

These broad features—vigorous private commercial networks, weakened public service sector; ongoing substitution of locally produced programs for imports—are part of a more general international and historical pattern that is repeated elsewhere in the past and the present. Hence there is a good deal of interest for television scholars generally in the historic trajectory of Australian television, both for its own sake and because of the comparative insights it offers. McLuhan once claimed that Canadian media developments were an "early warning system" for trends that would later appear elsewhere and Richard Collins has echoed this claim, warning pessimistically of the possible "Canadianization" of television in Europe and elsewhere. However, the Australian experience has been at once more complex, more interesting, and more positive. Given the linguistic and cultural barriers at work in countries in Europe and in other parts of the world, there are strong grounds for believing that "*Dallas*-ization" of international television, so much feared in the 1980s and early 1990s, was in fact a passing phase. Instead, the Australian experience of television, most especially that of "import substitution," is likely to be repeated elsewhere.

Structure

Television broadcasting began in the 1950s (Sydney and Melbourne in 1956 and Brisbane and Adelaide in 1959), a time that links it with television start-ups in other "major minor" territories including Canada, Italy, and the Netherlands. In fact, however, the structure of the Australian system was set in place in 1950 when a newly elected conservative federal government reversed the decision of a postwar socialist government that television was to be a monopoly in the hands of a public service broadcaster. Instead, the new government decided that television was to be a dual system comprising a private, commercial sector and a public service one. This decision could be justified on the structural grounds that Australian radio had been a dual system since 1932 when the Australian Broadcasting Commission (ABC) had been established. (In point of fact the 1932 development had been intended to create a unitary, public service broadcasting system along the lines of the BBC, an outcome thwarted when private broadcasters bought out community radio licenses after surrendering their own to the government.)

This dual system of Australian television remained in place from 1956 until the licensing of community television stations in 1994 and the advent of a cable subscription service in 1995. This is not, however, to suggest that the channel choice of viewers remained the same over this period. In 1956 viewers in the larger cities had two commercial and one public service channel to choose from. By 1965 there were three commercial services available. In 1980 a second public service channel went on the air while the community channels of 1994 signaled both the advent of a third sector as well as the sixth channel in the system. In deciding on the shape of the commercial services the initial consideration was technical: how many transmitting frequencies could be made available in each center of population? The answer generally was one, although in larger centers it was two.

Commercial television licenses were awarded to two operators in the state capitals of Sydney, Melbourne, Brisbane, and Adelaide, and one in Canberra, Perth, and Hobart. One commercial license was awarded in smaller cities and towns. This development occurred in several stages but by 1965 nearly 80 percent of the country came within the reach of television.

The granting of two licenses in the four most populous cities facilitated the development of networking arrangements across the east coast capital cities. Between 1956 and 1987, this system meant a combining together of local interests for the purposes of cost sharing for program buying and program production. With newspaper companies securing major shares in several of these stations, the first metropolitan networking arrangements built on long-term associations between different capital city press proprietors. Hence, for example, Frank Packer's TCN Channel 9 Sydney soon had links with HSV Channel 7 Melbourne. However, Packer had ambitions to establish a television network chain, applying unsuccessfully for commercial licenses in Brisbane and in country areas of New South Wales. In 1960 he bought GTV Channel 9 in Melbourne and the Nine Network was born. With some 35 percent of the national population, Sydney and Melbourne formed the hub of the network while Brisbane and Adelaide became satellites. The commercial stations with the designation "7" were forced into partnership but, lacking a common owner, the Seven Network (which emerged later in the decade) was always a looser association.

The Packer buyout was permitted under a two-station ownership rule contained in the 1956 Broadcasting and Television Act and the Melbourne purchase highlighted the dominance of newspaper interests in Australian commercial television. Until the rule was changed in 1987, the Packer Consolidated Press group controlled TCN 9 and GTV 9, and the Herald & Weekly Times group operated HSV 7 while John Fairfax and Sons controlled ATN 7. The other notable press entrant was the young Rupert Murdoch, owner of the afternoon *Adelaide News,* who in 1958 gained the license for one of the first two commercial Adelaide television stations, NWS Channel 9.

In 1953 a Royal Commission had recommended that the ABC run the public service television service. The government accepted this advice and allocated one channel to the ABC. Single ABC television stations began in Sydney and Melbourne in 1956–57 and other ABC stations rippled out across the country over the next nine years. Under its long-serving general manager, Sir Charles Moses, the ABC gave little thought to the new medium. Instead it regarded television as an extension of radio, an attitude it shared with its great parent and model, the BBC. Thus by 1964, when Moses retired, the ABC's audience share was below 10 percent and badly in need of a shake-up.

Programs

Early television owners and executives did not give a great deal of thought to program supply, concerned as they were with the capital cost of establishing and operating stations. Although several would-be licensees expressed commitment to the idea of locally produced programs both during the hearings of the 1954 Royal Commission on Television and the subsequent License Inquiries (1955–59), their initial practice did not encourage local production. Fortunately for them, the early 1950s had seen American television switch from the live production of network programs, including variety and drama, in New York and Chicago, to filmed-series production of fiction in Hollywood. Hence when television actually began in Australia, there was already a plentiful supply of high-quality fiction and other U.S. programming available and these soon dominated the prime-time schedule on the commercial stations. Owners and operators took advantage of this low-cost supply and quickly offset initial establishment capital costs of the system. Meanwhile, the ABC also achieved the same end through programs derived from the BBC.

Additionally these imports subsidized the production of local programs in several different genres. Variety/ light entertainment programs represented an important investment in the early years of Australian television and programs such as *The Johnny O'Keefe Show, In Melbourne Tonight,* and *The Bobby Limb Late Show* rated extremely well in prime time. Other genres of local production included news, game shows, and sporting broadcasts. There was also a small amount of "live" fiction produced in this period although, generally, it did not rate sufficiently well to justify the costs involved.

The most interesting area of local production was, however, that of television commercials. In 1960 the federal government issued a requirement that 100 percent of all commercials be locally produced. Even more than the indigenizing of formats and formulas, already under way in game shows and light entertainment, this protectionist measure signaled that import substitution was under way. Shortly, it would spread to higher-cost genres, including fiction.

The initial functions of Australian television stations lay both in distribution/exhibition and in program production. Hollywood in the studio era with its vertically integrated structure offered an appropriate blueprint. In the Australian situation, the creation of television production soundstages was necessary because the fragile feature film production industry of the 1950s mostly lacked such infrastructure. In addition, owning these facilities would give television operators control over programs, deemed to be necessary given the often dictatorial practices advertisers had already demonstrated in radio.

The most notable stations for in-house production in this early period were ATN Channel 7 in Sydney, GTV Channel 9 in Melbourne, and the ABC in those two cities. GTV Channel 9's highly successful *In Melbourne Tonight* ran until 1975. Meanwhile, ATN persisted with in-house production until 1970, while the ABC only opened its doors to outside independent packagers in 1986.

Development of the System

Australian television history can be divided into four periods, covering the years from 1956 to the present. These can be designated as eras of Live Television, Filmed-Series Television, "Quality" Television and New Television. Some of their features have been touched upon already but they can be outlined as follows.

Live Television

In the phase up to 1965, the period of Live Television, the institution was bounded in part by its technology. Programs were either imported and therefore available on film, put live to air, or kinescoped as a filmed record of a live broadcast. The first video recorder was imported by Channel 7 Sydney in 1958, but, until around 1965, when other stations and production companies had video playback and editing facilities, the early machines made little difference to the practice of "live" television. A second technical feature was the local or regional character of the institution. Until 1964 there were no cable facilities that allowed the transmission of television signals from one capital city to another. Thus the continent consisted of a series of discrete, isolated television markets that often saw different local programs, regional schedules, and frequently geographically distinct commercials.

News programs, soap operas, and some early teenage music programs were a quarter-hour in length, although most programs ran for half an hour. A few imported fiction series, plays, and variety programs were longer, running 60 or 90 minutes. Schedules were dominated by half-hour programs such as *The Mickey Mouse Club, The Lone Ranger, Sergeant Bilko, Hancock's Half Hour, I Love Lucy,* and others. Dominant fiction genres included westerns, action and crime, and situation comedy. This period of live television was also marked by a minority popularity of the one-off television play. This came in two forms; the first, emanating from the BBC, was dominated by a West End conception of drama and theater. It favored the stage plays of famous British playwrights such as Shakespeare, Shaw, and, in the modern period, Noel Coward and Terence Rattigan. This model was the one adopted by ABC television. From the late 1950s it combined BBC imports with television versions of some famous Australian plays, generally adapting preexisting theatrical materials to television. The other kind came from US live television in programs such as *The U.S. Steel Hour* and *Playhouse 90.* The latter was adopted by ATN Channel 7 and its partner stations and led to several notable productions including *Other People's Houses, Tragedy in a Temporary Town,* and *Thunder of Silence.*

Meanwhile, the ascent of current affairs still mostly lay in the future, although there were two notable pioneers. *Four Corners,* modeled on the BBC's *Panorama,* did not begin on the ABC until 1961. In its earliest form it was more of a newsreel or news digest program, with miscellaneous items in each episode, rather than the hard-hitting investigative program it would later become. Its first producer left the ABC in 1963 and began a spinoff, *Project 63,* on TCN Channel 9, which ran for two years. Meanwhile, there was also little in the way of locally oriented documentary films.

The ABC did not establish a production facility (teams of cameramen available to news, documentary, and drama) until 1959. Instead, especially in news, there was an enormous reliance on overseas filmed material.

Any "Australian content" in this era occurred in lower-cost production genres such as variety and quiz shows. Indeed there was a boom in local variety shows. Programs such as *In Melbourne Tonight, In Sydney Tonight, Revue 60/61, Bandstand,* and *Six O'Clock Rock* were important landmarks. In the more peripheral cities of Brisbane and Adelaide, local "tonight shows" were hosted by figures such as George Wallace Junior, Gerry Gibson, and Ernie Sigley. Early successful local quiz shows included the imported *Concentration* and *Tic-Tac Dough,* all adapted for TCN Channel 9 by Reg Grundy.

A final feature of these years was the practice of switching various formats, programs, and personalities from radio. Local examples of this kind of adaptation included *Consider Your Verdict, Pick a Box,* and *Wheel of Fortune,* which all made successful transitions to the small screen. There was also an unsuccessful attempt to move soap opera from radio to television between 1958 and 1960 when ATN Channel 7 produced, first, *Autumn Affair* and, then, *The Story of Peter Gray.* The same pattern of success and failure was repeated with radio personalities. Bob Dyer, Graham Kennedy, and others all made triumphant moves to television although one notable casualty of the new medium was famous radio personality Jack Davey.

These local successes in variety, game shows, and more occasionally drama meant that, despite the overwhelming presence of imported material, Australian programs had a distinct place in the television schedule. Indeed, it was through the variety program, the paradigmatic form of this early live period, that Australian television was given a local look or flavor. The genre also played its part in the emergence of a scheduling practice, still with us in the present, that mixed imported high-cost programs with lower-cost local content. But in the case of the variety show cycle, these often had international guests. Therefore, although they qualified under local content rules as Australian, they had, nevertheless, a distinctly international flavor.

However, various developments were afoot in the television system. By 1965 it was clear that Australian television had changed markedly. The task of popularizing the new medium had been immensely successful. Advertisers and audiences had seemingly signed an apparently permanent contract with television that installed them both as continuing subjects at, as it were, different ends of the system. The overall result, so far as the commercial broadcasters were concerned, was that owning a television station was akin to having a license to print money. However, influenced as always by the example of both U.S. and United Kingdom broadcasting, station owners came to wonder whether they might indeed follow the overseas lead and, as it were, print even more money. To do so, they needed to overhaul the existing system.

Filmed-Series Television

Two major changes in the institution at this time would bring about such an increase in profitability. First, an outsourcing of most production, particularly in the area of fiction, became a cost-stabilizing measure as stations farmed out production responsibility, especially labor budgeting, to independent producers. Thus, it is from around this time that we date the beginnings or consolidation of independent production companies. It is also no coincidence that at approximately the same time, ABC television drama was reorganized by the splitting of a composite radio and television department and the establishment of a separate TV drama division. Profitability was further boosted by a new form of routinization that revolved around the filmed series. For despite the drive toward financial rationality in the establishment period, the live television/magazine format had been financially unstable, capable of varying considerably so far as cost and quality were concerned. By contrast, the filmed-series use of recurring actors, sets and costume, stock footage, fictional formulas, and continuing characters helped establish this form as a more reliable guarantee of predictable costs and quality and, thus, the preferred form of Australian television programming. Consequently, the expensive, attention-grabbing variety shows and television plays of the early phase were less and less necessary as their "signature" function in the television schedule was increasingly usurped by filmed series.

At the level of corporate capital, television markets continued to be tightly controlled, mostly closed affairs although there was some negotiation of existing oligopolies when a third commercial station came on the air in the east coast capital cities and a second commercial station appeared in Perth. These new stations were partly brought about by the federal government's desire to introduce new players into the field of commercial television station ownership. Ansett, a major transportation group, secured the licenses of ATV 0 Melbourne and TVQ Brisbane while amalgamated wireless Australasia, a telecommunications manufacturing group, obtained the license of Ten 10 Sydney. The new stations formed themselves into the 0-10 Network, so that east coast Australia now had three commercial networks. The newcomer was the weakest in terms of audience ratings—so much so that in 1973 a new federal labour government briefly contemplated revoking these licenses.

Apart from these difficulties, it was business as usual. The broadcasting stations endured as a modified vertically integrated business operation, deriving their program product both by making in-house and by buying-in from independent producers, retaining the core and most lucrative part of the business by distributing programs and commercials to the same wide and mostly captive audience that they had constituted in the earlier phase. Full program sponsorship declined as a broadcaster/advertiser practice in favor of magazine-type commercial "spotting" with the slots in question being increasingly filled by filmed rather than live commercials.

Meanwhile, the decision of stations to farm out program production to outside independent producers was an indication of just how confident in their own power they were in dealing with advertisers. In any case, the conditions of television production of filmed series favored them both in relation to advertisers but also in relation to the independent producers themselves. Not only did they continue to control finance but they also remained in charge of station facilities that constituted the below-the-line resources on most filmed series.

Like the establishment of a permanent coaxial cable between Sydney and Melbourne in 1964, the advent of the filmed series also helped reconfigure the size of television audiences. Now, as even smaller regional stations acquired videotape machines, regular program recording on videotape occurred, most especially with the more expensive forms of programs being produced in Sydney and Melbourne. In turn, two-inch tapes of these could be "bicycled" from one place to another across the country, thereby altering and improving production economies. Increasingly, the television market was not just that of one region but rather Australia wide.

With the exception of the Nine Network, there was no common ownership of Sydney and Melbourne stations. Nevertheless, loose networking arrangements remained in play so far as production cost sharing was concerned. Independent producers, led by Crawfords Productions, developed a production method that guaranteed to broadcasters the delivery of a standard-length half-hour or one-hour program episode each week. Producers set about their task by preshooting a certain amount of outside location film scenes and marrying this to station-produced indoor scenes. Some weeks later in the television station's studios, this film material was integrated with program segments staged in the studios with a composite being recorded on videotape. Although film was later to replace video for outside recording, this integrated system became a standard in Australian television fiction production from this point on, easily surviving the introduction of color in 1975.

This shift in the method of program output changed both the production system and the look of Australian television. Live television had drawn heavily on vaudeville, stage, and theatrical traditions. By contrast, the filmed series was based on the example of Hollywood. Under this new order, there was a change in the preferred style and subject matter of Australian television. Host, studio audience, and soundstage space were banished. Instead, the filmed series tied its segments together by dint of a continuous fictional space wherein its dramatic characters moved and acted. The form also offered greater generic variety. Hence the Australian television fiction output in this period included such types as the thriller, the action/adventure form including the Australian western, situation comedy, and children's fiction. But the popularity and success of these genres and some individual programs were as nothing compared with that of the police crime series. Indeed, there is no better index of the enormous stability of Australian television at this time than the remarkable durability of this genre across the period and the fact that one company, Crawford, could turn out programs (*Homicide, Division 4,* and *Matlock Police*) for each of the commercial networks. These were sufficiently alike for programmers and viewers to be sure of what they were getting and sufficiently different for them to keep coming back for more.

Meanwhile the development of a "vernacular literature" in filmed series was not confined to fiction but also occurred in current affairs and documentary. After a shaky start, the weekly *Four Corners* settled down to a new kind of investigative journalism. In 1967 the ABC began a daily current affairs show, *This Day Tonight (TDT),* modeled on the BBC series *Today Tonight.* The program had a hard-hitting journalistic drive that examined political and social issues in ways never imagined by earlier programs. It was a very big success for the ABC and markedly improved its ratings performance. These two programs were enormously influential in extending the range of current affairs television, on the ABC and commercial stations. Documentary series also brought the life of the nation within their scope. The ABC's *Chequerboard* introduced cinema verité to Australian television, significantly expanding the range of social concerns and issues that could be examined. Meanwhile a second documentary series, *A Big Country,* also enlarged the audience's sense of what constituted the nation.

However, the cancellation of the Crawford police series by the three networks within months of each other in 1975–76 indicated a crucial transformation overtaking the Australian television institution. The service was almost 20 years old and no longer an oddity or a newcomer but a permanent feature of the economic and social landscape. However, if television had become commonplace and taken for granted, this changed in 1975 with the advent of color. These changes (the end of the police cycle and the introduction of color transmission) signal a decisive shift in the Australian television institution.

"Quality" Television

The new technology reinvented television's novelty and allure for broadcasters, advertisers, and viewers. Color led to a new boom in television advertising and in the sales of domestic receivers. A new drama serial, Crawfords *The Sullivans,* which began on the Nine Network in 1976, nightly reminded its viewers of this institutional shift. The program's opening credit sequence juxtaposed its fictional family frozen ineluctably in a black-and-white past as against their spontaneous movement and activity in the "living color" of the present. Indeed, the show's negotiation of a dramatic space between entertainment and quality marks the years between 1975 and around 1991 as a third period in the development of Australian television.

Without major disruption to the existing oligopoly, viewer choice was extended between 1976 and 1986 with the advent of new services and technologies. A new network, the Special Broadcasting Services (SBS), came on the air in 1980, at first serving only Sydney and Melbourne but gradually spreading to the other capital cities. SBS Television was designed to increase the media services available to ethnic Australians and it did this with multilingual programming. But SBS, with developing strengths in the areas of news, current affairs, documentary, and foreign films, also appealed to English-language viewers. As a second public service television broadcaster, it extended the range of choice of the traditional ABC audience, giving it an alternative to the ABC just as commercial viewers had gained an alternative to the Nine and Seven Networks in the mid-1960s.

Meanwhile, commercial television was booming. A major move had been the reinvigoration of the Ten Network thanks to Rupert Murdoch's News Limited purchase of ATV Channel 0 Melbourne in 1978, and Ten Channel 10 Sydney in 1979. Determined to increase the network's ratings, Murdoch strengthened Ten's program budget. The network scheduled heavily in the area of miniseries and feature films and these helped push the network ahead of Nine and Seven in the ratings.

Television networking arrangements continued and consolidated. Networking still meant cost sharing between partners but now, with common Sydney and Melbourne ownership in the case of two of the three, it also came to mean an increasing centralization of administrative, financial, and program power in these two capitals, most especially Sydney. And, in turn, this also meant a diminution of local autonomy in the other state capital stations. The public service networks were national in their agency and reach. Indeed, the newcomer, SBS TV, went further in centralizing its network in Sydney with a schedule and a content that was entirely national.

Seven, Nine, and Ten continued to service the east coast state capital cities although in 1987, as a sweetener to major changes in cross-media ownership rules, the federal government allowed them to spread their operations across regional television catchments. The upshot of these changes was the gradual emergence toward the end of this period of a single, unified, Australia-wide television market. And, in turn, this structural shift underwrote a rationalization of television production facilities among the state capital city members. The chief of these was television studio spaces. Network partners used these and related facilities in a systematic way invariably locating the production of higher-budget programs such as fiction series in Sydney and Melbourne. Other types of lower-cost content including game shows and children's television were usually allocated to studios in the outer state capital cities.

Advertising remained as the crucial element in the institution. As always, the fundamental and unchanging intention was to constantly maximize audience size to ensure that purchase rates for advertisers were as high as possible. Consistently too, networks needed to keep the frequency and volume of ads down in order to keep ad prices and audiences' patience up. Advertisers on the other hand continued to want to run as many commercials as possible, keeping them short, cheap, and distanced from each other. Shifting from sponsorship to "spotting" had facilitated a general increase in advertising revenue.

On the face of it, however, such revenue could not rise beyond a certain point so that a new strategy was necessary to generate additional financial returns. How then to print more money? The answer that the Australian networks derived from their U.S. counterparts was demographics. By the early to mid-1970s, moving away from programming designed to aggregate a mass undifferentiated television audience, the broadcasters began developing finer demographic targeting, a strategy that could make some shows more expensive than the prevailing norm. The consequence was a new emphasis on programming that would attract varying demographics and thus generate further revenues within the system. Accordingly, as always, there were moves to vary repetition with difference, standardization with distinction, innocuousness with active attraction. The era of "quality" television had arrived.

"Stripping" became a major scheduling strategy on commercial networks. As vehicles for this kind of scheduling, three important programming forms emerged in 1971–72. These were the nightly current affairs program, the early evening game show shown five evenings a week, and the half-hour continuing soap opera. From a network programming point of view, each of these "stripped" forms was a variant of each other, performing the same task of offering viewers the regularities and the pleasures of a steady feed of routine and, within limits, novel pieces of content of various kinds. Of the three, the most original was the continuous soap opera. Although produced in the first place for a domestic Australian audience, the cycle of drama serials that runs from *Number 96* in 1972 to *Neighbors* and *Home and Away* achieved remarkable international sales success, particularly in the 1980s and 1990s.

Meanwhile, with these "bread and butter" forms in place, it became possible for the Australian television institution to develop a more complex hierarchy of programming types and reputations. Several fiction programs ceased to be anonymous industrial commodities. Hence, for example, some scriptwriters and producers became recognized names even outside the television industry. And, in turn, television series such as the ABC's *Scales of Justice* also became objects of sustained critical attention not only as entertainingly informative viewing but also as auteur-based dramatic investigations of serious social subjects and issues.

Indeed, with a convergence of sorts between an Australian art cinema and a kind of Australian (art) television, notable writers and directors were joined by other noted feature film producers including Hal and Jim McElroy and Anthony Buckley. But the most famous name above the title was to be that of Kennedy-Miller, responsible for the popular and critical international success of the *Mad Max* feature film trilogy. In the 1980s, this group turned its attention to television and the result was a cycle of five historical miniseries beginning with *The Dismissal* (1983) and ending with *Bangkok Hilton* (1989), which garnered both popular and critical success. Significantly, for this general project of a "quality" television, a Kennedy-Miller auteur television "style" was soon identified.

However, this moment was not to last, as changes to cross-media ownership rules in 1987 brought about, first, the sale of networks and, shortly thereafter, their bankruptcy. These disturbances only heralded more ongoing reconfigurations of the institutional field. Australian television is undergoing a sustained shift, away from an oligopolistic-based scarcity associated with broadcasting toward a more differentiated abundance associated with the present period of post-oligopoly. Thus, it is necessary to recognize that television has shifted into a fourth phase and needs to be labeled accordingly.

New Television

With a proliferation of new and old television services, technologies, and providers, Australian television is rapidly becoming a multichannel environment. As the system becomes more differentiated, new institutional players are coming from within and without. Thus, a sixth free-to-air channel, presently dedicated to community use, came on the air in 1994–95 while a fourth commercial network has been scheduled to begin in 2007. That same year of 1995 also saw the commencement of cable television and a pay-TV service. Hence, the present field not only includes the older network interests but also several newcomers including FOX, Telstra, Optus, and AUSTAR. At the same time, in the wings and looking to extend their newspaper interests into broadcasting are other groups such as News Corporation and Fairfax. Meantime, new trade agreements are likely to encourage other groups, both local and international, to enter the television arena.

The new multichannel environment is served and stimulated by new distribution technologies such as satellite, cable, and microwave and new computer software including the Internet. Television is also characterized by a multiplying nonexclusivity of content, which is now becoming available through other modes including marketing and the World Wide Web Additionally, the convergence with computers and mobile phones yields new forms of interactivity including electronic commerce, online education, and teleworking. Meantime, digital TV, Web TV, and personal video recorders may further strengthen a tendency toward niche and specialized programming.

Transfers, recycling, and franchising are rapidly becoming central features of the new Australian television landscape. At the same time, behind this proliferation of transfers is a set of new economic arrangements designed to secure a degree of financial and cultural insurance not easily available through other sources. Adapting already successful materials and content offers some chance of duplicating past and existing successes. Consequently, in Australian television over the past decade, like television elsewhere, there has been an explosion in the number of locally produced programs whose format or basic blueprint was first developed elsewhere. Among the favored modes are reality programs, game shows, and lifestyle and talk shows.

Some of the circumstances surrounding two reality productions can be cited as examples of this trend. First, the fact that a local production company, Southern Star, signed a joint venture agreement in 2000 with the Dutch format giant, Endemol. In turn, this arrangement led to several seasons of the global television program *Big Brother* being made for Australian television from 2001 onward. Meanwhile, a locally based production and distribution company, Screentime, recognized the format possibility of a New Zealand documentary series that traced the making of a local pop band. Remade with a variety of multimedia spinoffs and revenue streams, *Pop Stars* was a popular success in Australia. Screentime then introduced it in over 30 other countries, forming United Kingdom, Ireland, and New Zealand chapters in the process.

However, despite these local developments, the popular and industrial success of particular genres including those of reality television comes at a price. Thus, it has been noted that there has been a significant downturn in the production of more expensive genres of content. Chief among these have been current affairs and fiction television. Thus, whereas previously Australian television achieved a distinctive place for itself in the area of international fiction exports, this is no longer the case. Instead, the industry in its most recent phase is a net importer of formats for the production of new series.

In summary then, certain key features in the structure and trajectory of Australian television are worth reiterating. Australia has in the past been relatively slow to innovate various technologies associated with television including the broadcast service itself, color transmission, and multichannel pay services. Nevertheless, despite these time lags, the system has exhibited a "historical modernity" in terms of its dual sections, weak public service, and strong independent commercial. In the years of the broadcasting oligopoly, substantial import substitution occurred leading to a vigorous television production industry that by the 1980s became a significant export earner. In the process the system spawned a number of successful companies and groups such as Murdoch's News Limited, Packer, and the Grundy Organization that have been important players both locally and internationally. However, in recent years Australian television has been increasingly globalized in new ways including those of ownership, program content, and technology. This has also been a period of upheaval and transition and is still without an end in sight.

ALBERT MORAN

See also **Australian Production Companies; Australian Programming**

Further Reading

Agardy, Susanna, and David Bednall, *Television and the Public: National Television Standards Survey,* Melbourne: Australian Broadcasting Tribunal, 1982

Beck, Christopher, editor, *On Air: 25 Years of TV in Queensland,* Brisbane, Australia: One Tree Hill Publishing, 1984

Beilby, Peter, editor, *Australian TV: The First 25 Years,* Melbourne: Nelson, 1981

Bell, Philip, with others, *Programmed Politics: A Study of Australian Television,* Sydney: Sable, 1982

Brown, Allan, "The Economics of Television Regulation: A Survey with Application to Australia," *Economic Record* (December 1992)

Collins, Richard, "National Broadcasting and the International Market: Developments in Australian Broadcasting Policy," *Media, Culture and Society* (January 1994)

Cunningham, Stuart, and Toby Miller, with David Rowe, *Contemporary Australian Television,* Sydney: University of New South Wales Press, 1994

Hall, Sandra, *Supertoy: 20 Years of Australian Television,* Melbourne: Sun Books, 1976

An Inquiry into Australian Content on Commercial Television, Sydney: Australian Broadcasting Tribunal, 1991–92

Jacka, Elizabeth, *The ABC of Television Drama,* Sydney, Australia: Australian Film, Television and Radio School, 1991

Johnson, Nicholas, and Mark Armstrong, *Two Reflections on Australian Broadcasting,* Bundoora, Victoria, Australia: Centre for the Study of Educational Communication and Media, La Trobe University, 1977

MacCallum, Mungo, editor, *Ten Years of Television,* Melbourne: Sun Books, 1968

Moran, Albert, *Images and Industry: Television Drama Production in Australia,* Sydney: Currency Press, 1985

Moran, Albert, *Moran's Guide to Australian TV Series,* Sydney: Australian Film, Television and Radio School, 1993

O'Regan, Tom, *Australian Television Culture,* St. Leonards, New South Wales: Allen and Unwin, 1993

O'Regan, Tom, with others, *The Moving Image: Film and Television in Western Australia, 1896–1985,* Perth: History and Film Association of Australia, 1985

Seymour-Ure, Collin, "Prime Ministers' Reactions to Television: Britain, Australia, and Canada," *Media, Culture and Society* (July 1989)

Tulloch, John, and Graeme Turner, editors, *Australian Television: Programs, Pleasures, and Politics,* Sydney and Boston, Massachusetts: Allen and Unwin, 1989

TV 2000: Choices and Challenges: Report of the Proceedings of the Australian Broadcasting Tribunal Conference Held at the Hilton Hotel, Sydney, 16–17 November 1989, Sydney: ABC Tribunal Conference, 1990

Australian Production Companies

The Australian Broadcasting Corporation

As Australia's main public service broadcaster, the Australian Broadcasting Corporation (ABC) has always played a leading role in local program production, and it is arguably the single most significant force in Australia in one-off television drama, documentary, nature programming, and perhaps children's programming.

The ABC was virtually unrivaled in any category of drama until the mid-1970s. The period from 1968 until 1975 is often referred to as the "Golden Era" of the ABC, the time of long-running and popular series or acclaimed miniseries such as *Bellbird, Contrabandits, Certain Women, Rush, Marion, Ben Hall,* and *Power Without Glory.* Until the late 1980s, the ABC, like other public broadcasters around the world, was a vertically integrated producer-broadcaster. With the exception of a few coproductions (mainly with the BBC), all of the ABC's production was initiated, financed, and produced in-house. In the 1980s *Patrol Boat, 1915, Spring and Fall, Scales of Justice, Palace of Dreams,* and *Sweet and Sour* broke new ground in Australian television drama and provided an arena for trying out new writers and attempts at formal or conceptual innovation. Innovative comedy, such as *Mother and Son,* strong investigative journalism, such as the weekly current affairs program *Four Corners* (in production since 1961), and quality drama continue to attract critical and audience approval.

In the early 1980s a period of confusion and demoralization followed in the wake of a major review, the *Dix Report.* Then, in 1986, the ABC head of drama, Sandra Levy, initiated a "revival" in network drama content, the aim of which was to increase output to at least 100 hours a year. A decision was made to move ABC productions more toward the "popular" end of the drama spectrum and away from programming regarded as more esoteric, eccentric, or specialized. At the same time, it was decided that the way to get quantity, quality, and spread was by concentrating on a mixture of long-running series and miniseries and by eschewing one-offs, which are usually deemed too expensive relative to the rather limited audience they are likely to attract. Finally, it was also decided that the only way to increase drama hours was by entering into coproduction arrangements with local producers who could raise cash from the "10BA" tax-relief scheme and other government assistance schemes and from overseas presales, with the ABC contributing facilities and technical staff and as little cash as possible.

This strategy was immediately successful, at least in quantity and audience terms. Close to 100 hours of programming was achieved by 1988, and there was an immediate improvement in the ratings for miniseries and series, notably, in the latter category, the prime-time medical soap *GP.*

In the period 1988–91, the ABC coproduced and broadcast a large number of prestigious miniseries, all with local and overseas partners. Titles from this period include *Act of Betrayal* (with TVS), *A Dangerous Life* (with HBO in the United States and Zenith in the United Kingdom), *Eden's Lost* (with Central TV), *The Leaving of Liverpool* (with the BBC), *The Paper Man* (with Granada). Also during this period, *GP* began to be sold to a number of overseas buyers, although the series has never achieved a large success in foreign markets. The ABC's most successful situation comedy, both domestically and overseas, *Mother and Son,* was also sold during this period.

From 1992, the possibilities for financing programs in the British market diminished, and the ABC began to swing back toward the production of programs fully financed in-house. Examples are *Phoenix I* and *II, Seven Deadly Sins, The Damnation of Harvey McHugh, Heartland,* and *Janus.* In-house miniseries included *Come in Spinner, True Believers, Secret Men's Business* (with Southern Star), *Time and Tide, Marriage Acts* (with Beyond Reilly Pty. Ltd.); other parties hold the major rights to around 20 titles, including *Bodysurfer, Brides of Christ, Children of the Dragon, Frankie's House,* and *The Leaving of Liverpool,* most of which were coproduced with United Kingdom partners.

The success of ABC drama in the 1990s was in part due to the role of commissioning editor Sue Masters. Most notable productions were the 13-episode *RAW FM* in 1997 (with Generation Films Pty. Ltd.), *Fallen Angels* (1997), *A Difficult Woman* (1998, with Southern Star), *Grassroots* (1999), and the 2000 in-house production *Love Is a Four Letter Word,* about the lives of "twenty-somethings" in an inner-city pub environment. Masters's attempts to make ABC drama more innovative and relevant to a younger demographic were derailed when she departed for Ten Network in 2001, following the appointment of Jonathan Shier as managing director of the national broadcaster. The ABC has continued to produce in-house drama, the most expensive recent outlay being *Changi* (2001), a story of prisoners-of-war internment at the hands of the Japanese in World War II, handled with a comedic touch. The move to outsourcing production saw the ABC link up in 2002 with Southern Star (*Bad Cop, Bad Cop*). Recent comedy series successes for the ABC were *The Games* (2000; produced with Beyond Productions), which benefited from the art-imitates-life antics of Sydney's Olympic Games management, and *The Micallef Pogram,* a coproduction with Red Heart Productions Pty. Ltd. (1998–2000).

The Grundy Organization

Although it was bought in 1995 by the United Kingdom publishing and media conglomerate Pearsons, the history of the Grundy Organization is predominantly Australian, and its Australian operations remain the single biggest national contribution to its overall activities. The history of Grundy is of a radio game show producer in the 1950s that transformed into a television game show producer for the local market during the 1960s. In the 1970s the Grundy Organization expanded considerably as a local drama producer and consolidated its reputation as a leader in light entertainment.

Without maintaining any particular link to any one network, Grundy has built up a substantial catalog of game shows such as *Celebrity Squares, Wheel of Fortune, Family Feud, The Price Is Right, Blankety Blanks,* and *Sale of the Century* as well as such highly successful drama programs as *Young Doctors, Number 96, The Restless Years, Prisoner, Sons and Daughters,* and its flagship soap, *Neighbours,* which began production in 1984.

Grundy experienced a breakthrough success with *Neighbours* both in Australia and in Britain. While that platform was the base on which a number of serials and series produced by Grundy and other Australian companies were sold into the British market, it also was the impetus to develop the key globalizing strategy that Reg Grundy, founder and chairman, dubbed "parochial internationalism." Under this strategy, Grundy set up wholly owned local production companies to make programs that feature local people and are made by local Grundy staff who are nationals of the country in which the program is made.

By the mid-1990s, Grundy was producing about 50 hours of television a week worldwide. It sold in more than 70 countries worldwide, employed around 1,200 people in production and administration functions, and claimed to be the second-largest producer of light entertainment for television in the world until its takeover in 1995 by Pearsons, which was itself incorporated into the RTL Group and renamed Freemantle-Media in 2001. With Grundy now operating as Grundy Worldwide Ltd., Europe generates more production throughput for the organization than does Australia. In collaboration with the Producers Group, Grundy Australia was responsible for the children's miniseries *Escape of the Artful Dodger* in 2000.

Criticisms leveled at Grundy include the charge that the producers remained committed to innocuous formats (game and quiz shows) and safe drama renditions. However, programs such as *Prisoner* and the New Zealand soap opera *Shortland Street* were risky and innovative for their time and places of production, while a program like *Man O Man* represents an equally risky strategy in light entertainment.

Village Roadshow and Roadshow, Coote, and Carroll

The Village Roadshow group of companies has been unique in Australia. First established in the 1950s as a drive-in theater operator, it is now the only completely integrated audiovisual entertainment company, involved in studio management, production of both film and television, film distribution and exhibition, television distribution, video distribution, and movie theme park management. The conglomerate is also moving into multimedia development and exhibition holdings in southeast Asia. Its approach to internationalization is also unique in that the main thrust of its strategy is to attract offshore productions to its Warner Roadshow Movieworld Studios, near the Gold Coast in southeast Queensland.

The studios were founded in 1988–89 by housing two offshore television productions for the Hollywood studio Paramount. These were *Dolphin Bay* and *Mission Impossible.* It is estimated that an hour of series drama can be made offshore at a cost about 30 percent lower than a comparable hour made in Hollywood.

Since 1989 the studio has attracted partial or whole production of several feature films, a mixture of Australian and overseas productions including *The Delinquents, Blood Oath, Until the End of the World,* and *Fortress.* It has also hosted a number of U.S. series, most of which have not been shown in Australia, including *Animal Park, Savage Sea,* and a new production of *Skippy.* In 1992–93 it housed the major U.S. series *Time Trax,* which, unlike *Mission Impossible,* used a considerable number of Australian creative personnel, including directors and postproduction people.

However, *Time Trax* was conceived in, scripted in, and entirely controlled from Hollywood.

Until 1995 Village Roadshow had a satellite production company, Roadshow, Coote, and Carroll (RCC), an outstanding boutique producer of midrange budget television such as *GP* and *Brides of Christ.* RCC was critically and culturally successful both locally and internationally, but it was not economically significant in the context of the whole conglomerate. This is because the huge investment in the studios depends totally on the success of Village Roadshow Pictures in attracting production to them. RCC is a very small organization with very little fixed infrastructure, and it finally broke away from the parent company in 1995 so that its principal, Matt Carroll, could pursue wholly independent projects.

The strategy, scale, and philosophy of RCC were at the opposite end of the spectrum from its parent company. Founded in 1984, RCC has chalked up an impressive list of television drama: *True Believers, Barlow and Chambers: A Long Way from Home, The Paper Man, Brides of Christ,* and *Frankie's House* as well as the long-running ABC series *GP.* Many of its projects have been coproduced with the ABC. It is a marriage made in heaven: the expertise of RCC combined with the reputation of the facilities-rich ABC.

RCC's bigger-budget productions, which cost about $1.2 million (Australian) an hour, were typically financed one-quarter through Australian presale (usually to the ABC), one-quarter Film Finance Corp. (FFC) investment, one-third United Kingdom presale, and about one-sixth other investors (including the ABC).

Brides of Christ exemplified big-budget RCC productions. It rated 30 in Australia, making it, in ratings terms, the most successful drama ever broadcast by the ABC. The repeats did almost as well (it had a third run on the Ten Network), and it sold well on video. It also received uniform critical approval. In the United Kingdom, it also rated extremely well on Channel 4, gaining an audience of 6 million. Apart from Brenda Fricker (and an Irish orchestra playing the soundtrack music), all other aspects of the program were Australian. While its theme and mode of telling remained unambiguously Australian and the idiom and cultural feel of it were very local, its story of moral upheavals in the Catholic Church in the 1960s, set against the wider changes that were occurring during that era, was recognizable enough in other places for the program to gain wide acceptance internationally.

Brides of Christ, however, was an expensive miniseries, set up when the European television market was still buoyant. Changes in the European television environment since then have meant that RCC now orients itself toward cheaper 13-, 26-, and 39-part series. While continuing with *GP,* they also developed *Law of the Land* for the Nine Network.

Crawfords

Having been in existence more than 50 years, Crawfords is one of the oldest and most respected production companies in Australia. Before starting to produce television in 1954, it was Australia's most important producer of radio serials.

In the first 30 years of its existence as a television production company, Crawfords occupied a central place in Australian television. It pioneered popular police shows such as *Homicide, Division 4,* and *Matlock Police* in the 1960s and early 1970s; it made an early entry into soap opera with the long-running serial *The Box* (1974); in 1976 it innovated again with the World War II serial *The Sullivans,* which ran for 520 episodes and raised long-form drama to new heights of production values and cultural authenticity; and Crawfords was one of the earliest production companies to see the potential of 10BA as a vehicle for high-quality miniseries, with *All The Rivers Run* (1982). The company sailed through the early to mid-1980s on the back of productions like the glamorous *Carson's Law* and *Cop Shop,* another successful police serial, and further 10BA miniseries. Much of the Crawfords catalog has had great staying power; for example, both *The Sullivans* and *All the Rivers Run* continue to perform well around the world.

The company has always had its own extensive production facilities, unlike many newer production companies. In the late 1980s, keeping the facilities occupied became more difficult for Crawfords, and recent further investment in new studios may have been ill-advised given the constant pressure of keeping the existing facilities occupied. This was the height of the company's prosperity of recent times; *The Flying Doctors* was making excellent overseas sales (it was voted most popular drama in the Netherlands in 1992), and the Crawfords catalog had been sold to the Kirch Group and to other territories with a view to the company diversifying into coproductions with overseas partners, game shows, sitcoms, and made-for-television movies.

The results of this strategy include the popular and ground-breaking multicultural sitcom, *Acropolis Now;* the game show *Cluedo,* produced in association with Zenith Productions of the United Kingdom; a coproduced package of six television movies, called *The Feds,* with presales to the Nine Network, TVNZ, and a United Kingdom distribution guarantee; and the children's series *Halfway Across the Galaxy and Turn Left,* a 1991 coproduction with one of the Kirch subsidiaries, Beta-Taurus. The series became one of the most popular children's television programs on British television.

Despite the success of some of these programs, the cancellation of *The Flying Doctors* by the Nine Network in 1992, when it was still doing well in overseas markets, was a severe blow. It had a temporary stay of execution in 1993, when Crawfords were given a chance to revamp it as *RFDS* (for Royal Flying Doctor Service). The changes, although thorough, were not enough to save the program, and without the fallback of "volume television" such as that produced by Grundy, the viability of Crawfords has been questioned of late. Crawfords only real drama success in the late 1990s was *State Coroner* (1997). Other output of note from that era included the George Miller–directed miniseries *Tribe* and the children's series *The Saddle Club,* an Australian-Canadian coproduction with Protocol Entertainment, produced for the ABC.

The Beyond International Group

A young company among leading Australian television producers, the Beyond International Group (BIG) began in 1984 when the public service broadcaster, the ABC, axed *Towards 2000,* a four-year-old popular science and technology program, because it was be coming too expensive. An independent production company was set up, and the new program, *Beyond 2000,* was sold to the Seven Network in 1984 and then the Ten Network in 1993.

BIG has progressed to become a highly focused boutique production and distribution house, whose corporate portfolio also includes merchandising, music publishing, corporate video, and separate media production groups in the United States and New Zealand. Since its inception BIG has produced and/or coproduced more than 1,800 hours of programming, including information and documentary programs, magazine and lifestyle series, dramas, children's shows, light entertainment, variety programs, comedies, and miniseries. The group's operating divisions include Beyond Productions Pty. Ltd. (television production), Beyond Distribution/Beyond Films Limited (feature film sales and international distribution), Beyond Online Pty. Ltd. (CD-ROM and Internet), and Beyond Entertainment Ltd. (feature film development and support). From the mid-1980s, what became Beyond International produced in differing formats, participated in international coproductions, and became involved in distribution domestically and internationally, but its resounding success was the *Beyond 2000* format, which has been sold in more than 90 countries, been dubbed in ten languages, and attracted an international audience of 50 million.

BIG has also involved itself in predominantly European coproduction partnerships. In 1989 BIG and the BBC embarked upon the coproduced *Climate in Crisis* and then the four-part series *Great Wall of Iron,* a documentary about the Chinese military. BIG has also ventured into the production of drama series, miniseries, and children's programming, with somewhat less success. The children's series *Bright Sparks* typifies the Beyond International strategy—animated robots take journeys around the world exploring science and technology. *Chances,* an adult drama series featuring nudity and outlandish storylines, was a failure. BIG's forays into local feature filmmaking virtually began and ceased with *The Crossing* in 1989. The failure of this film led the company to emphasize the more stable activity of distribution, and the distribution arm that began operation in 1990 became, along with Southern Star Distribution, one of two significant Australian-owned independent international distributors.

Beyond International has also moved into joint-venture relationships with leading Australian-content creators. In 1995 Beyond Simpson le Mesurier Pty. Ltd was formed, drawing on the creative expertise of Roger Simpson and Roger le Mesurier. The venture's primary output was police investigation, prime-time commercial television dramas including *Halifax f.p., Good Guys Bad Guys,* and *Stingers* as well as the early evening serial *Something in the Air* for the ABC.

Liberty and Beyond, which began in 1995, saw Liberty Films come under the Beyond International banner. This company was created to make high-quality commercial film and television drama. Likewise Mullion Creek and Beyond was formed in 1998 to develop a wide variety of productions including television series, feature documentaries, and large-format films. Another company in the joint-venture production suite is Beyond Reilly Pty. Ltd, which has as its target commercial television ventures, building on the success of Gary Reilly Productions experience with sitcoms such as *The Naked Vicar Show* and *Kingswood Country.*

Southern Star

Southern Star is a lean, diversified operation with an integrated approach to production and distribution through film, television and video, and merchandising. Like most front-running independents, this diversity enables Southern Star to balance higher-risk and lower-risk ventures. After a management buyout of the Taft-Hardie Group (whose major shareholders included the Great American Broadcasting Company and James Hardie Industries) in 1988 by Neil Balnaves, Southern Star reorganized into six operating units, including a distribution arm; a Los Angeles–based animation unit responsible for programs such as *Berenstein Bears* and *Peter Pan and the Pirates,* made for the FOX Network; a video- and audiotape duplication division; a merchandising arm handling the BBC, Columbia TriStar, and Paramount material; and a home-video division.

Southern Star Entertainment is a broad corporate umbrella for established independent producers: Errol Sullivan/Southern Star Sullivan, Hal McElroy/Southern Star McElroy, and Sandra Levy and John Edwards/Southern Star Xanadu. The production arms run as partnerships with Southern Star meeting all running costs, producer and staff salaries, and finance and administration as well as publicity. McElroy and McElroy's *Last Frontier* (1986) was a model for programs that traveled internationally and promoted growth across the company through video release and a 22-hour series spin-off.

Many of Southern Star's major coproductions have been with the ABC and the BBC, including *Four Minute Mile* (1988), *Children of the Dragon* (1991), and *Police Rescue* (1990–96). The *Police Rescue* pilot was originally made for the BBC. The program was a coproduction between Southern Star Xanadu and the ABC, with presale to the BBC, which made a substantial contribution to the $7 million budget. For their initial financial contribution to the series in 1990, the BBC maintained script, director, and cast control. The program was driven by its ongoing success in Australia, and its success was built on a recognized format, a variation of the cop show, but with a 1990s balance between action and personal storylines that showcased the natural and built environment of Sydney and the star profile of Gary Sweet. Southern Star has also been involved in a successful coproduction with China Central Television (CCTV), a 52-episode children's television series called *Magic Mountain.* This was sold to 60 countries. In all, 50 percent of Southern Star's TV sales revenues derive from cable and satellite channels outside Australia.

In 1993 the Southern Star Group was responsible for a new successful long-running series, *Blue Heelers,* set around a country police station in Victoria. The general feel of the program is very much *A Country Practice* revisited, and this seems to appeal to audiences. In 1994 it was the highest-rating Australian drama across all channels.

The most successful international product to emerge from the Southern Star stable to date has been the McElroy/Southern Star police/action drama *Water Rats* (1996–), set on Sydney Harbor, with the landmark Harbor Bridge heavily featured. The program achieved the honor of being the most internationally distributed Australian television drama, sold to 168 countries. In 2001 Southern Star, in collaboration with John Edwards, Ten Network, and Channel 4 (United Kingdom), produced *The Secret Life of Us,* a "twenty-something" series set in a Melbourne apartment block. In 2000 Hal McElroy and Di McElroy, operating as McElroy TV, produced the innovative series *Going Home* for the Special Broadcasting Service (SBS). Scripted and produced on a day-by-day schedule, and featuring an ensemble cast, this highly acclaimed short series allowed viewers to contribute to narrative development through a linked website.

Film Australia

Currently a government-owned enterprise that is expected to generate up to two-thirds of its own revenue, Film Australia started life in 1911 as a production unit within the federal government, before becoming a government-owned film production company in 1945. In the period after 1945, it nurtured the documentary tradition, and a significant number of filmmakers who went on to play important roles in the film and television industries were trained there. In 1976 the Commonwealth Film Unit became a branch of the Australian Film Commission and took on its present name, Film Australia. In 1987 it was made a government-owned business enterprise working under the stricture to become partly self-sufficient from government.

The mission to produce films and programs "in the national interest" continues, and this is represented by the government's continuing to fund Film Australia under the so-called National Interest Program (NIP). This program is the core of Film Australia's business and the reason for it being a government-owned company. Both *Mini-Dragons* and *The Race to Save the Planet* used NIP money.

Outside of NIP projects, *The Girl from Tomorrow,* a fantasy/science fiction children's series, is one of Film Australia's most successful exports, and many countries that bought it also bought the sequel, *Tomorrow's End.* The preschool children's series *Johnson and Friends* has sold exceptionally well and in addition has become an international marketing phenomenon. Film Australia also does well with nature programs such as *Koalas: The Bare Facts* and the series *Great National Parks.* Other good sales have come from documentaries with an environmental or scientific angle, such as *After the Warming, The Loneliest Mountain, Mini-Dragons,* and *Roads to Xanadu.*

Teachers of the World was a 1992 seven-part documentary series that dealt with the life of a teacher in each of the contributing countries (Australia, Canada, the United States, Korea, and Poland). As a result of the *Teachers of the World* coproduction, some of the partners came together again to produce a special documentary series called *Family* to celebrate the Year of the Family in 1994.

Film Australia's success lies in part in its specialization in those program categories with greatest international currency (nature, environmental, and science documentaries, and children's programming) and it has had the foresight to focus on the burgeoning markets of Asia with product that does not confront too many cultural hurdles. In addition, it is blessed with good facilities and the safety net of government funding.

Granada Australia/Red Heart

In 1998 Granada Media assumed a prominent place on the Australian production landscape when it acquired a 9.1-percent stake in Channel 7, making it the second-largest individual shareholder behind Kerry Stokes. Following this, Granada bought a 50-percent stake in Artist Services Pty. Ltd, which was later rebranded as Red Heart Productions. Artist Services had initially specialized in sketch comedy in the early 1990s (*Fast Forward, Full Frontal*). Founded by Steve Vizard and Andrew Knight, it achieved wider brand recognition with its productions for the ABC: the miniseries *Simone de Beauvoir's Babies* (1997) and the popular television serial *Sea Change* (1998). It also produced feature films such as *Siam Sunset, Dead Letter Office,* and *The Sound of One Hand Clapping.*

By bringing together the resources of Granada, the rebranded Red Heart was intended to act as a conduit for the distribution of both British and Australian concepts and formats. However, the partnership with the Seven Network failed to deliver the benefits to both Granada and Red Heart, despite the successful Seven Network drama series *Always Greener,* a spin-off of the *Sea Change* concept.

The Seven Network

The Seven and Nine Networks were the two original commercial broadcasters in Australia and until the late 1980s enjoyed stable ownership and management, which allowed them to build up a high degree of programming expertise and audience loyalty. One of Seven's greatest strengths has been its commitment to drama, whereas the Nine Network has been stronger in news and current affairs and sport, which are far less internationally tradable.

With its traditional emphasis on drama, the Seven Network was well positioned to take advantage of 10BA, and during the 1980s it produced a number of high-quality miniseries with local and overseas partners. Series and serials sold by Seven on behalf of itself and the independent producers involved include *Rafferty's Rules, Skirts,* and *A Country Practice.* Some of the programs from the 1980s that were sold that way (and which still sell today) were *Land of Hope* and *The Fremantle Conspiracy, Jackaroo, Sword of Honour,* and *Melba.*

Two of the most successful programs of the early 1990s were *Home and Away* (which began in 1988 and still airs as of 2003) and *Hey Dad* (which ran for seven years, until 1994). The first is produced in-house by the Seven Network; the second was produced by Gary Reilly and Associates and sold jointly by them and the network through RPTA.

Home and Away, produced by Seven Network subsidiary Amalgamated Television Services Pty. Ltd., was developed in-house as an immediate response to the success of *Neighbours* on the Ten Network. Ironically, the latter had originally begun on Seven in 1985, but after indifferent ratings that network let it go. When *Neighbours* achieved such success on Ten, Seven realized the potential for youth-oriented soaps. *Home and Away* has gone on to achieve great popularity in both Australia, where it outrates its rival *Neighbours,* and in the United Kingdom, where in the late 1990s it was achieving audiences of 8 million for ITV (it was sold to Channel 5 in 2000).

By the mid-1990s, the Seven Network seemed well positioned to continue its strong record in commissioning and producing programs with strong export potential. The free-to-air service is flourishing, and Seven is exploring new markets in Asia and Eastern Europe, which, while not lucrative in the short term, have great potential in the future. Through its association with Granada Media, the Seven Network acquired international distribution for its local content and a stream of United Kingdom content. Seven has also invested in docu-soap coproductions (*Popstars, Temptation Island*). Seven is exploring pay television and other broadband services and it is safe to predict that it will remain a force in the Australian entertainment industry in the years to come.

Children's Television Producers

Australia is a significant player in world children's television. Most major children's programs made in Australia recently have enjoyed international sales success, and critical acclaim for Australian programs is a regular occurrence.

The structure of regulation and production in Australia for children has strengths that, in some respects, are unmatched elsewhere in the world. Within the general liberalization of broadcasting regulation seen in the Broadcasting Services Act 1992, the only mandated regulations that continued from the old Australian Broadcasting Tribunal (ABT) were those for Australian content and for children, so that in the new regime the most-detailed imposed regulations pertain to children.

The Australian Children's Television Foundation (ACTF) dominates the field of Australian children's television. A body established as a result of both federal and Victorian government support and incorporated in 1982, the ACTF produces, commissions, and distributes children's television programming as well as acting as a kind of think tank and clearinghouse for children's television advocacy. ACTF has produced more than 150 hours of programming, which has been screened in more than 90 countries, and it has received many international awards. *Lift Off, Round the Twist,* and *Round the Twist 2* were all high-profile ACTF series that were very popular in the United Kingdom, and *Sky Traders* has sold into a diverse range of territories. In 1998 a third series of *Round the Twist* was made as well as a cyberspace, live-action drama called *The Crash Zone,* commissioned by Buena International and produced in association with the Seven Network.

Western Australia-based Barron Films concentrates on quality children's/family television series as well as social realist films and adult television drama, having made *Falcon Island, Clowning Around,* and *Ship to Shore.* Yoram Gross Film Studios, an established specialist producer of animated children's films, crossed successfully to television with the production and distribution of a 26-part television series based on its *Blinky Bill* films. Yoram Gross merged with the German-based EM-TV in 1999. The new company has consolidated its international distribution and coproductions in Europe, Canada, and the United States. International successes include *Flipper and Lopaka* (1999). Jonathan Shiff/Westbridge has specialized in children's television since 1988, its biggest production being the $3 million series *Ocean Girl,* which sold to Disney in the United States and to the BBC for a record sum for a children's series in the United Kingdom. Roger Mirams/Pacific Productions, a Sydney-based producer of children's programming since the 1950s, shot the $8 million *Mission Top Secret* in seven countries. Pacific Productions made *South Pacific Adventures* in 1990, and Media World Features, another company involved in animated features, made a miniseries based on its animated film *The Silver Brumby.*

Beyond International produced *Deepwater Haven,* a children's drama series with a curious mix of French and New Zealand actors, in Auckland. Millennium Productions made *Miraculous Mellops,* a fantasy/science fiction family series, and Warner Roadshow has produced *The Adventures of Skippy* and *Animal Park.*

Other Production Companies

JNP Productions established its reputation almost solely on its long-running and well-regarded series *A Country Practice.* The program ran as one of the major Seven Network dramas from 1981 to 1993, before being bought by the Ten Network in 1994. Despite a reworked format and setting, the new series on Ten failed; JNP has yet to produce anything as remotely successful.

Like JNP, Gannon Television/View Films has built its name on one major television product, *Heartbreak High,* a youth-oriented series noted for its high production values and its treatment of youth issues. The series suffered from scheduling changes imposed by the Ten Network but picked up important sales in the lucrative markets of the United Kingdom, France, and Germany to the extent that the series was produced on the basis of these sales, without any Australian network deal. In addition to several feature films, View Films has also produced two television miniseries: *Shout! The Story of Johnny O'Keefe* (1985), for the Seven Network; and *Shadow of the Cobra* (1988), for Zenith in the United Kingdom, the BBC, and the Seven Network. Gannon Television has collaborated with Foxtel, France 2, and Carlton International on a drama for the ABC called *Head Start.* Ben Gannon also teamed with Michael Jenkins to produce the acclaimed ABC police drama *Wildside* in 1997–98.

Working Dog Pty. Ltd., a company that evolved out of the 1988 *D-Generation* and 1992 *Late Show* skit comedies, went on to produce successful feature films *The Castle* and *The Dish.* Working Dog's most successful television programs include the television news satire *Frontline;* a late-night talk format featuring selected guests (*The Panel*); and a fishing docuformat, *A River Somewhere.*

The Special Broadcasting Service produces occasional innovative short series, such as *Going Home* (with McElroy TV) and risky cult comedy (*Pizza*). Through SBS Independent (SBSI), the service commissions documentaries from local filmmakers. One of the most successful productions has been the *Mary G Show,* an indigenous-affairs magazine produced in the town of Broome in Western Australia.

STUART CUNNINGHAM

See also **Crawford, Hector; Grundy, Reg; Gyngell, Bruce; Murdoch, Rupert**

Further Reading

Carmichael, Helen, *The Australian Film and Television Industry: An Overview, 1999,* http://www.aftrs.edu.au/Reports/industry_overview.html
"Film Funder (Film Finance Corp.) Under Review, Oz Edgy," *Variety* (April 27, 1992)
Groves, Don, "Aussies Target U.S. for Partners, Growth," *Variety* (January 16, 1995)
Harris, Mike, "Lean Times for Drama Down Under," *Variety* (March 23, 1992)
Harris, Mike, "Local Programs Give Aussie Nine Its Shine," *Variety* (April 27, 1992)
Harris, Mike, "TV Traveling Well to Europe," *Variety* (October 31, 1994)
Margolis, Irwin, "Crocodile Dundee's Aussie Pack Invades British Television," *Television-Radio Age* (November 23, 1987)
Murdoch, Blake, "Looking Up Down Under," *Variety* (April 26, 1993)
"The New Global Order: Site Purchase Instills Faith in Global TV's Future," *Variety* (October 31, 1994)

Australian Programming

The peculiarly Australian television program is still in the minority on Australian television screens, which remain dominated by the Hollywood product. Yet compared with the situation of the 1980s, Australian television programs today vie with Australian films in the search for markets worldwide. Australian soap operas such as *Neighbours* and *Home and Away* have achieved high ratings in such countries as England and Ireland, and while the Grundy Organization, Australia's largest producer of television shows in the late 20th century before being absorbed in 1995 into the United Kingdom-based conglomerate Pearsons (which, as of 2002, was itself a part of FreemantleMedia), began by "borrowing" concepts and formats from U.S. game shows, it progressed to making a profitable business by selling recycled and rejuvenated American shows back to the country of their origin. *Sale of the Century* and *Wheel of Fortune* typified this genre. In Australia, the so-called reality shows of the *Survivor* and *Big Brother* genre, in their Australian derivatives, have attracted high ratings, as did *The Weakest Link,* a United Kingdom-derived quiz show. While the ultimate ownership of the Australian companies is today increasingly in the hands of multinational corporations, the Australian character of their television programs now seems established and production resides in Australia.

To outline the origin of this national character, however, one must examine the antecedent media. As in any other national context, television programming in Australia can be understood only by examining its origins in radio and film. As in the U.S. context, and unlike the British, the major impetus to radio programming in Australia came from the commercial sector with the explosive growth of commercial radio in the 1930s. From the soap opera to the singing commercial, the Australian experience mimicked the American. While, as the American critic Norman Corwin has observed, Australia is one of the few places on the globe where radio drama was considered as an art form, the vast bulk of commercial radio dramatic product was of the soap opera variety. In its heyday, Australian radio succeeded brilliantly by its own commercial standards, meeting not only a domestic niche but also providing a steady stream of programs for export. It employed a small army of professional writers and production people who formed the nucleus of writers, actors, and producers for the infant Australian television industry when the new medium began in the mid-1950s.

Unlike the American, and like the British experience, however, since the beginning of the 1930s, Australia has also had a powerful national, publicly owned noncommercial broadcasting entity, the Australian Broadcasting Commission (ABC). (After 1983, "Commission" became "Corporation.") This corporation is recognized as the primary culture-making force in Australian national life. The ABC has, in fact, sponsored many nonbroadcasting aspects of public culture, from the establishment of symphony orchestras in all states, involvement in children's clubs, sporting activities, and advice to farmers, through specialized agricultural service and comment on markets and weather, to the explorations of the culture of the rural environment.

Still, it must be pointed out that despite the widespread misconception by commentators, the Australian Broadcasting Commission did not owe its origins to a simple amalgamation of the "good points" of American and British thinking. Rather, it arose from the exigencies of the indigenous experience—an Australian response to an Australian requirement. Given its origins and its mandate, the programming from the ABC provided a contrast to the commercial television stations.

The early British broadcasting experience, was, however, very important in the formative years of the ABC. The impact on the ABC of the BBC's "Reithian ethic" of high moral purpose, nation building, and elevating popular tastes, can, in hindsight, hardly be overestimated. The ABC encouraged high culture through classical music programs and community building through popular music programs, which often featured Australian musicians performing the latest popular songs from overseas. Sporting programs, such as the dominant national pastime of horse racing and test cricket (in the early days especially with England), have been a broadcasting staple from the 1930s to the present time. These broadcasts set the pattern of national participation by the time television arrived in Australia in 1956, and the various programming categories and genres can be seen to derive from them.

Local programming by independent stations reached its heyday in the decade of the 1980s and exhibited patterns similar to that in other countries. It was relatively common for local stations to do a program on a local event or a car-club rally, but local stations became "aggregated" by government policy into networks not unlike the U.S. commercial system. Local programming then found it necessary to appeal to a geographically wider-spread audience, and by the 1990s began to fade away.

The generalization that the British programming on Australian television tends to be mostly on the ABC is valid. On the other hand, commercial stations sometimes take British programs, which have proven to be popular from ABC exposure, and rebroadcast them to achieve higher ratings. A range of programs, from the ubiquitous *Yes, Minister* series to the more vulgar *Are You Being Served?* type, vie with David Attenborough nature documentaries and similar British fare as might appear on PBS in the United States.

In sum, Australian television programming bears the marks of several systems that preceded it. Like many other systems, however, Australian TV continues to mold those influences in its own ways. Whether the specifically "Australian" character of television can withstand an onslaught from new economic configurations and new technologies that transcend national boundaries remains to be seen.

Nonfiction Programming

Talk shows, music, morning programs, sports, news, and current affairs programs are all represented in the Australian television lineup, and again, all derived from radio antecedents. As far as television is concerned, little about them is specifically Australian.

In the light entertainment talk shows, for example, the programming is decidedly derivative. *Tonight Live* with Steve Vizard in the early 1990s betrayed its lineage to David Letterman and Johnny Carson. Admittedly, there was an Australian strain of boyish irreverence inherited from the Australian stars such as Graham Kennedy and Bert Newton, but the sets, presentation, and overall style would be easily recognized by an American viewer. Most importantly, in the commercial medium, Vizard's success was due to the economic fact that his popularity allowed the Seven Network to extend prime time and charge premium rates for what was, comparatively, an inexpensively produced program.

Music

High culture is typically provided on television through opera or symphony concerts simulcast on Sunday night by the ABC. At the other end of the scale, the ABC provided, in early morning hours, a simulcast of Triple J, the youth national radio network, which broadcast rock music accompanied by exceptionally raunchy dialogue. Music videos are broadcast at various times on both commercial and national television. For example, on the ABC, *Rage* can go from 6 to 10:30 on Saturday mornings and reappear on Sunday morning for an hour or so.

Morning Television

In the very early morning hours, the ABC provides high-quality instructional television, which can be correlated with written instruction and tutorial interaction and taken for college credit. Language, biology, business, and other Open Learning subjects provide the casual viewer with exceptional, totally involving informational programming, most often of American origin.

Predictably, since the 1980s Channel 9 has aired the Australian *Today* show, with one male and one female host and providing a mixture of news, interviews, sports, and weather in a well-tested format. Variations of this theme have come and gone on competing networks. By the mid-1990s, for example, in the 9:00 A.M. slot, morning television featured *Good Morning Australia* with Bert Newton, another reference to an American programming format. Again, the interview is the feature of choice, with perhaps a lighter vein to vary the flavor. At least one station usually counterprograms these shows with cartoons for children.

Sports

While watching sports on television had long been a favorite Australian pastime, the connection between sports and advertising was traditionally not as strong in Australia as in the United States. However, the televised presentation of sporting events is increasingly influenced by American programming strategies. The Australian broadcasting industry had long been poised for intensive activity surrounding the business of sports on television, and media moguls Kerry Packer and Rupert Murdoch vied for (and collaborated with on occasion) various contracts with players, licenses, and outlets for the advertising dollars and pay-TV subscriptions.

For example, the tradition of cricket had been inherited from the British Empire, where white-suited cricketers (divided into "gentlemen," who were amateurs, and "professionals," who were paid) took days to play a "test" match. By the 1970s, Packer was credited with promoting a game more suited to television coverage: played in one day, with colorful costumes, showbiz accoutrements, and players exhibiting enthusiasm rather than the old British "stiff upper lip." Similar transformations occurred in tennis, football, hockey, soccer, netball, and other sports. The trend toward Americanization was markedly increased with the introduction of Rupert Murdoch's Superleague, an entirely new combination of Rugby League teams, and with pay-TV sports programs, which were becoming more prevalent by the mid-1990s.

Through all these changes, the scheduling strategies have remained quite the same. A typical week's viewing would begin with the traditional Saturday afternoon when all channels present one sport or another. The same pattern holds for Sunday afternoon, with one commercial channel starting sports programming at 9:00 A.M. (The ABC has counterprogrammed a high-culture arts ghetto on Sunday afternoons, and the Special Broadcasting Service [SBS] also tends to eschew sports on Sunday afternoon.) The regular television news on Sunday nights tends to increase its sports coverage beyond the acceptable 30 percent for Australian television newscasts, and there are also irregular sports specials programmed in various primetime slots.

While special football games of various codes are broadcast during one or two weeknights in Australia, American football tends to be consigned to late-night taped presentations on the ABC, except for the Super Bowl, which is broadcast live. Basketball is the fastest-growing sport in Australia, and, thanks to television, in one celebrated 1994 survey 11-year-old Australians considered Michael Jordan to be the best sportsman.

The television sporting scene is also affected by the specialized narrowcasting of events to pubs and clubs across Australia by satellite transmission. Horse racing is perhaps the sport most associated with gambling, but with the advent of new technologies, and especially with the advent of sports on pay TV, the ubiquitous TABs (gambling shops) will undoubtedly evolve to exploit the new media.

With the Olympic Games in Sydney in 2000, the influence of commercial sponsorship of sport increased and the influence of television on the world of sports in Australia gathered more impetus.

News

Australian radio news was available in the early days in a prototypal form with the stories taken from the newspapers. The newspaper proprietors, having already demonstrated their political clout by keeping the ABC from commercial taint (and revenues), were able to stifle radio news until the war years (1939–45). During World War II, a coalition government, pressured by the imminence of a Japanese invasion, decided that ABC Radio was crucial to the war effort. Once established, ABC News became one of the world's most professional news broadcasting services with bureaus worldwide.

Typically, ABC Television's nightly news is of half-hour duration, presented from each individual state with common stories from overseas feeds, and followed by a current affairs program. The presenter is of the BBC "Newsreader" variety and is not typically a practicing journalist. Richard Morecroft, who fronts the ABC TV 7:00 P.M. news in New South Wales (the state with the largest population), is perhaps the best exemplar of the ABC style.

The ABC format is boilerplate: local, state, national, and international news, plus sports and weather. The commercial stations tend to have similar formats, with quicker pacing and a more lurid selection of topics. Australian newscasts typically devote six or seven minutes of a 30-minute slot to sport, a proportion far greater than typical in the United States. Brian Henderson, the anchor of the Channel 9 (commercial) news, is the longtime champion in the news ratings and provides his network with the coveted high-rated lead-in position for the rest of the night.

The SBS, often admired for the quality of its television news, has an unmatched foreign coverage and tends to longer and more comprehensive stories. Besides the nightly news, there are shorter programs throughout SBS's broadcast day, some being short updates.

Documentary and Current Affairs

The prototypal Australian television documentary (or current affairs) program is the long-running *Four Corners* program (ABC), which is an institution in its Monday night slot at 8:30. Perhaps the finest hour in Australian television was the *Four Corners*' broadcast of "The Moonlight State" on May 11, 1987, when Australia's premier investigative journalist, Chris Masters, demonstrated on film existence of the illegal speakeasies, the prostitution, and the gambling dens that had all been long denied by the self-righteous government of the state of Queensland. Senior police officers went to jail and a government was overthrown following the subsequent inquiry triggered by the program.

Channel 9 presents a prestigious current affairs program, *Sunday,* on Sunday morning, and from time to time other commercial concerns have attempted to match 9 and the ABC with serious public affairs programming, but their efforts seem to vanish as management turns to more profitable programming.

SBS and the ABC both program several high-quality documentaries in any broadcasting week. Typical titles, chosen at random for illustration only, are *The Big Picture, That Was Our War, Documentary, Australian Biography, Great Books,* and *A Most Remarkable Planet.*

While a number of these presentations move toward television that is distinctively Australian, it is in fictional programming that the clearest and most powerful explorations of a national character and mode of representation have been established.

Fictional Programming

Although the Gorton Liberal (conservative) government in the early 1970s initiated the process, Australia's great renaissance in motion picture and television programming really began with the free-spending Whitlam Labour government of 1973–75. Because the same people worked in film as worked in television, it is hard to separate out the histories of the different media. The technical infrastructure for movies was aided by the fact that, since 1960, imported commercials were banned from Australian TV. This meant that in the capital cities, especially in Sydney and Melbourne, motion picture laboratories developed a steady business and the technical expertise required to provide high-quality professional product in the advertising arena. Until the advent of electronic newsgathering (ENG) in the 1970s (when tape began to be used instead of film), television news shot on 16-millimeter film also provided a steady source of supplementary business for the film labs.

The topics of television programming echoed those covered in the motion pictures. Australia, before the 1930s, had an economically viable silent film industry, which did not survive the advent of sound and the economic depression of the 1930s. Hollywood (and, to a lesser extent, British) product then dominated Australian cinema screens. Because film is a cultural artifact as well as being a salable commodity, the Australian audiences became saturated with American culture. Almost ten years after the advent of television in Australia, the American authority Wilson Dizard could make his famous statement: "The daily schedule of a typical Australian television station, particularly in prime listening hours, is virtually indistinguishable from that of a station in Iowa or New Jersey." And as late as 1967, the Australian Broadcasting Control Board required that only two hours of Australian drama be broadcast per month in prime time.

Thus deprived of Australian stories on the screen, when the 1970s renaissance occurred, the subject of the programming tended to be the indigenous classics as well as contemporary themes that imparted a distinctly Australian flavor. In 1976 the government decreed (with a "points system") that there be 50-percent Australian content between the hours of 4:00 P.M. and 10:00 P.M., and demanded compliance of commercial licensees. Despite their early protests, the commercial stations found that the Australian programs were very popular with Australian audiences.

Available for television a year or so after cinema release, Australian films became an important part of the indigenous programming, but the epitome of television programming art was seen to be in the miniseries.

Miniseries

The miniseries brought important national myths and icons to the television screen. The quintessential Australian nation-building myth is that of the Australian and New Zealand Army Corps (ANZAC). The ANZAC story is one of volunteer soldiers, who, in 1915, on behalf of the British war effort against Germany, invaded Turkish territory on the Gallipoli peninsula. The campaign was a defeat, but the valor of the soldiers, celebrated in a national day of commemoration (ANZAC Day, April 25), became a central theme of the Australian nation, representing a cause worth any sacrifice. The television miniseries *Anzacs* thus complemented the major motion picture *Gallipoli* to tell the ANZAC story. The popularity of this story has proved robust. In the latter half of 2001, the ABC reran the 1982 miniseries *1915,* starring Sigrid Thornton. The nostalgic beginning lured the viewers into expecting a conventional love story. The ending, however, left the viewers confronting death, betrayal, and the facial and mental scarring of the protagonists. The concluding sets portrayed a prosperous and genteel Sydney harbor-side lifestyle and made no concessions to any romantic vision of warfare.

Similarly, following the nationalistic, nostalgic (and essentially mythic) impetus, another miniseries, *The Last Outlaw,* told the story of arguably the most famous Australian folk hero, Ned Kelly. He is (literally) an Australian icon; in his self-made steel body armor, he looked like a medieval knight, with six guns. Like his American contemporary, Jesse James, Kelly was a highway robber, but, unlike James, his behavior elicited considerable public sympathy, with large crowds protesting his hanging in 1880. Today his story is all-pervasive in Australian culture, with the Ned Kelly icon appearing in the high culture of Sidney Nolan paintings in the National Gallery in Canberra, and the armor and six guns featured as a logo for a brand of sliced bread. Yet beyond the Australian version of the Robin Hood image lies a historical reality. Because Kelly epitomizes for Australia the rebellious Irishman persecuted by British rule, his story ties in neatly with a long tradition of republicanism, which despite its recent repudiation by referendum still lurks in the wings.

The television miniseries *Against the Wind* (1978) depicts another important facet of Australian history that had been ignored while American stories had dominated the Australian television screens. This program, too, harks back to mythic origins, as Australia's convict past is evoked by the story of a spirited Irish girl who was transported to Australia as a political prisoner. She falls in love with a fine upstanding convict unjustly treated by a vicious system. The settings of the program resemble more the production values of Disney studios than the squalor portrayed by recent historical accounts of the 18th-century settlement, but the program fulfilled the requirements of standard founding myths requisite in all cultures.

A depiction of a 19th-century family saga, *Seven Little Australians* (ABC, 1973) provided a local version of the American *Little House on the Prairie* or Canadian *Anne of Green Gables* genre. Other miniseries covered well-known Australian legends, such as those relating to the sporting stories between the wars. *Bodyline* (1984) portrayed unsportsmanlike Englishmen attacking stalwart and long-suffering Australians when playing the extremely popular sport of cricket. The title, *Bodyline,* made reference to a tactic of aiming at the batsman's body, rather than at the wicket (a tactic that worked). The English won the test series in 1936 and a number of Australians were, in fact, injured. The other casualty was Australian good feeling for the British, although the Australians took the high moral ground and did not reciprocate with the "bodyline" tactic. This material, clearly restricted in commercial terms to the "old empire" of cricket players, is the stuff of myth and legend, and as such proved popular with its intended market.

Similarly, the mythic imperative of coming to grips with former enemies was handled with the miniseries *Cowra Breakout* (1984). In 1944 Japanese prisoners of war (POWs) "broke out" of a POW camp in the remote Australian town of Cowra. By the early 1980s, when the program was made, Japan and Australia had experienced a quarter-century of mutual economic interest as trading partners, and Japan was the most important Australian market by far. The deaths of the brave but culturally incomprehensible Japanese were treated in this series in a way not unlike that of the pacifist film of the 1930s, *All Quiet on the Western Front.* By the end of 2001, the Australian wartime experience with the Japanese was crystallized in the six-part miniseries *Changi.* Much more sophisticated in style, than, for example, *1915,* the POW epic *Changi* is a narrative that travels from the bucolic to the brutal, with the Australian edition of *Time* magazine describing it in terms of Marcel Proust's *Remembrance of Things Past. Changi* was about the power of sense memory. Its title comes from the prison in Singapore where 130,000 Allied troops were housed for three and a half years. These soldiers were not defeated in battle but ordered to surrender, a fate not appreciated by their Japanese captors. The Australian POWs who survived maintained their spirits by presenting a carefree character, singing and joking their sufferings away. The story is told through the prism of the 60-year-old memories of six Australian veterans.

Clearly the initial outpouring of depictions of Australian history and culture resulted in part because of government production subsidies, provided as partial support for the requirement that holders of the lucrative television licenses broadcast Australian content. Then, when the ratings for the earliest of these miniseries demonstrated that such Australian stories were very popular with Australian audiences, it seemed tangible proof that a cultural imperative was also inherent in their acceptance by the indigenous audience.

By the 1980s, however, the economic climate changed. Broadcasting seemed dominated by takeovers of the major television networks. Furthermore, deregulation and privatization, rather than activist nationalistic initiatives, seemed to capture the governmental imagination. Thus, by the end of the decade, the traditional mythical Australian themes of the tragic losers (Ned Kelly, the ANZACS, the bodyline cricketers, Les Darcy the boxer, and even Phar Lap the racehorse) were being superseded by a new type of Australian story. The audiences, satisfied by the availability of their indigenous stories, began to demand a change of programming, and the program makers began to look beyond the most obvious indigenous themes.

By the 1990s, the motion picture industry was tackling contemporary themes presented with high production values. For example, *The Heartbreak Kid* (1993) concerned an affair between a high school student and his young teacher. The milieu of Greek culture in Melbourne provided a conflict intermingling male dominance (the teacher's fiancé resorts to violence, and her father's role is stereotypical) and a depiction of conflicting loyalties. The television serial spin-off was called *Heartbreak High* (1994–99), with the same young male lead and an approximation of the cinematic verisimilitude in the sets. Produced around the same time was *Paradise Beach* (1993–94), in the tradition of *Baywatch,* with Surfers Paradise in Queensland standing for the California coast.

Traditional themes, however, remained a staple. For example, *The Man from Snowy River,* a 1982 motion picture derived from a poem by Banjo Patterson, the author of "Waltzing Matilda" (the Australian national song), had been a success in the 1980s. By 1994 a 13-part television miniseries entitled *Banjo Patterson's The Man from Snowy River* continued the genre. It is perhaps a sign of the maturity of the industry in Australia that the subjects and formats that secured the initial popularity for Australian programs with Australian viewers now are merely one type of program among many. By 2000 the national broadcaster captured a large audience with *Sea Change,* a story of a workaholic professional woman who, with the breakup of her marriage, quits her city job and relocates her family to a seaside village. Starring Sigrid Thornton, this highly rated program went for two seasons on Sunday night. It provided evidence for a sea change in Australian tastes. Former miniseries had a rousing, romantic, or uplifting message, yet *Sea Change* portrayed a rather rueful recognition of contemporary life.

Soap Operas

As in the United States, soap operas are programmed in Australia during the day, and the typical commercial offering has a mixture of U.S. programming (*Days of Our Lives, The Bold and the Beautiful, The Young and the Restless*) interspersed with Australian soap operas such as *Home and Away* and *Neighbours.* The basic rules of the daytime serials that were established in the 1930s radio era still apply, regardless of the racier themes and more topical situations. Perceptions of the "Australianness" of the indigenous soap operas vary and provide interesting perspectives on cultural productions. The general Australian opinion is that the lives of the protagonists in Australian soaps are mostly ordinary, everyday, and working class. Yet to European observers, the Australian soap opera is characterized by relatively healthy, happy beings who endure their endless travails in a fortunate sun-drenched situation. Regardless of these "Australian" traits, the Australian soap opera remains true to type, exhibiting, most significantly, the "endless narrative" that characterizes the genre worldwide.

Comedy

Much of Australia's television comedy is derivative. For example, for several years the Channel 9's *Australia's Funniest Home Video Show* used the standard U.S. formula established in *America's Funniest Home Videos.*

Perhaps with a more indigenous flavor, the family situation comedy *Hey Dad!* (1986–94; in daytime reruns by the mid-1990s) followed the U.S.-sitcom formula but focused on the same everyday working-class context presented in the Australian soap operas. *Acropolis Now* (1989–92), a politically incorrect sitcom, made gentle fun of Australia's ethnic communities placed within a dominant Anglo culture.

On the ABC from 1983 to 1994, *Mother and Son* presented a genuinely challenging comic world. Veteran actors Ruth Cracknell and Gary Macdonald explored the tribulations of a man taking care of his mother, who is afflicted with Alzheimer's disease. The cult comedy *Frontline* (1994–97) starred Rob Sitch as Mike More, an unhinged, venal, television talking head. A send-up of a television current affairs program, this show was generally considered to be thinly disguised social commentary.

Police Procedurals

The police serial in Australia began with Crawfords, a major production company in Melbourne. Crawfords came to prominence with *Homicide* (1964–75) and established a format with *Cop Shop* (1977–84). More recently the Australian police show genre has been exemplified by two programs, *Police Rescue* (1990–96) and *Blue Heelers* (1994–). *Police Rescue,* with its star Gary Sweet as the lead Mickey, took place in an urban setting. With high production values (as befitted its ABC origins and overseas coproducers), *Police Rescue*'s storylines dealt with tensions of contemporary life in a city that was not necessarily recognizably Australian.

Blue Heelers, on the other hand, is set in mythical, bucolic, small-town Australia. Produced for Channel 7, *Blue Heelers* is constrained by a modest budget monitored by the creative guiding hand of leading Australian writer Tony Morphett. The program is clearly indigenous, and it is thus not as accessible to overseas audiences as *Police Rescue.* The very name, *Blue Heelers,* plays a word game recognizable to Australian audiences, yet which would escape viewers unaware of Australian nuances. It refers simultaneously to the standard blue uniforms that identify police in most of the English-speaking world and to a breed of cattle dog, the Queensland blue, notorious for sneaking behind unsuspecting people and nipping at their ankles. The star, John Wood, is positively avuncular, although the show has elements of action drama. While Australians are among the most urbanized people on Earth, the call of the small town, as exemplified by the long-running program *A Country Practice* (1981–94), seems to provide an appeal in national escapism as provided by television.

Both *Blue Heelers* and *Police Rescue* have been aimed at a family audience at 8:30 P.M. Both present continuing characters who constitute a "family" in the workplace. Both offer the usual recipe of conflict, violence, sexual attraction, and humor. Nevertheless the program set in the country is much more clearly mythical, Australian, and designed to reassure its audience. While Australian viewers, as the ratings attest, have enjoyed the restless camera and edgy performances of the American offerings *NYPD Blue* and *Law & Order,* just as they enjoyed *Hill Street Blues,* Australian producers have generally stayed with less gritty serials. On the other hand, police-based short series such as *Janus* (1994–95), produced by the ABC from its Melbourne studios, have explored a much darker vision for the policing profession than that exemplified by the prototypal *Blue Heelers* and *Police Rescue.*

MYLES BREEN

See also **Country Practice; Four Corners; Heartbreak High; Hey Hey It's Saturday; Homicide; Neighbours; Power Without Glory; Prisoner; Sale of the Century; Sex; Sylvania Waters**

Further Reading

Agardy, Susanna, and David Bednall, *Television and the Public: National Television Standards Survey,* Melbourne: Australian Broadcasting Tribunal, 1982

Bell, Philip, with others, *Programmed Politics: A Study of Australian Television,* Sydney: Sable, 1982

Breen, Myles, "National Mythology on Film and Television: The Australian Experience," *Communication* (1989)

Breen, Myles, "Television News Is Drama," *Media Information Australia* (1983)

Brown, Allan, "The Economics of Television Regulation: A Survey with Application to Australia," *Economic Record* (December 1992)

Burke, Jacinta, Helen Wilson, and Susanna Agardy, *"A Country Practice" and the Child Audience: A Case Study,* Melbourne: Australian Broadcasting Tribunal, 1983

Collins, Richard, "National Broadcasting and the International Market: Developments in Australian Broadcasting Policy," *Media, Culture, and Society* (January 1994)

Cunningham, Stuart, and Toby Miller, with David Rowe, *Contemporary Australian Television,* Sydney: University of New South Wales Press, 1994

Hall, Sandra, *Supertoy: Twenty Years of Australian Television,* Melbourne: Sun Books, 1976

Henningham, John, *Looking at Television News,* Melbourne: Longman Cheschire, 1988

Inglis, Kenneth S., *This Is the ABC: The Australian Broadcasting Commission, 1932–1983,* Melbourne: Melbourne University Press, 1983

An Inquiry into Australian Content on Commercial Television, Sydney: Australian Broadcasting Tribunal, 1991–92

Johnson, Nicholas, and Mark Armstrong, *Two Reflections on Australian Broadcasting,* Bundoora, Victoria: Centre for the Study of Educational Communication and Media, La Trobe University, 1977

MacCallum, Mungo, editor, *Ten Years of Television,* Melbourne: Sun Books, 1968

McKee, Alan, *Australian Television: A Genealogy of Great Moments,* Melbourne: Oxford University Press, 2001

Mitchell, Tony, "Treaty Now! Indigenous Music and Music Television in Australia," *Media, Culture, and Society* (April 1993)

Mitchell, Tony, "Wogs Still Out of Work: Australian Television Comedy As Colonial Discourse," *Australasian Drama Studies* (April 1992)

Moran, Albert, *Images and Industry: Television Drama Production in Australia,* Sydney: Currency Press, 1985

Moran, Albert, "Interview: Writing Television Comedy," *Australasian Drama Studies* (October 1983)

O'Regan, Tom, *Australian Television Culture,* St. Leonards, New South Wales: Allen and Unwin 1993

O'Regan, Tom, with others, *The Moving Image: Film and Television in Western Australia, 1896–1985,* Perth: History and Film Association of Australia, 1985

Rowe, David, and Geoff Laurence, editors, *Sport and Leisure: Trends in Australian Popular Culture,* Sydney: Harcourt Brace Jovanovich, 1990

Seymour-Ure, Collin, "Prime Ministers' Reactions to Television: Britain, Australia, and Canada," *Media, Culture and Society* (July 1989)

Tulloch, John, and Graeme Turner, editors, *Australian Television: Programs, Pleasures, and Politics,* Sydney and Boston, Massachusetts: Allen and Unwin, 1989

Turner, Graham, and Stuart Cunningham, *The Australian TV Book,* St. Leonards, New South Wales: Allen and Unwin, 2000

TV 2000: Choices and Challenges: Report of the Proceedings of the Australian Broadcasting Tribunal Conference Held at the Hilton Hotel, Sydney, 16–17 November, 1989, Sydney: ABC Tribunal, 1990

Williams, Kerry L., "The Cure for Women in Comedy: History As TV Talk Show Therapy," *Australasian Drama Studies* (April 1993)

Australian Programming: Indigenous

Indigenous Australians have been very important to Australian television. As with many areas of Australian culture, the indigenous inhabitants have been co-opted in television's formation of an Australian sense of identity. Although less than 2 percent of the Australia population identifies itself as indigenous, it is unusual to watch an evening's television without encountering some representation of Aboriginality: in an advertisement for the Mitsubishi Pajero, a trailer for a Yothu Yindi concert, or a news item on the refusal of the prime minister to apologize for injuries done to indigenous populations. Aboriginal characters and issues have appeared in most genres of Australian television. Soap operas such as *Neighbours* and *Home and Away* have featured Aboriginal characters, as have children's programs like *Dolphin Cove* and *Kideo,* cop shows like *Wildside* and *Water Rats,* game shows such as *Wheel of Fortune* and *Family Feud,* and lifestyle programs such as *Australia's Funniest Home Videos*—with *The Great Outdoors* even featuring an Aboriginal presenter, Ernie Dingo.

In addition to these insistent, unsystematic images of Aboriginality, some parts of Australian television feature a greater amount of indigenous representation. This is true both in Aboriginal-produced and -circulated programming and in the arena of the broadcast mainstream.

In "mainstream" free-to-air broadcast television, there is a fairly consistent representation of indigenous Australians and issues on Australia's news and other nonfiction forms of programming (documentaries and current affairs). The greatest number of television news stories focus on issues of governance and the relations between imported and indigenous forms of social and political organization. In the early 1990s, many stories were about land rights and native title, indigenous attempts to gain some recognition that they owned the land of Australia before it was stolen by European invaders. In the second half of the 1990s, most public debate took place around the "Stolen Generations": that group of indigenous Australians who were removed from their families during the 20th century (up to the 1970s) as part of official and deliberate government policy aimed at "breeding out" indigenous Australians. The fact that, even after this policy had been subjected to public scrutiny, the prime minister at the time (John Howard) refused even to say "sorry" to these people (many of whom now testified to having severe emotional difficulties due to the abuse associated with this process) became a matter of public concern. Most recently, media debate has focused upon the continuing poor health of indigenous communities, and the forms of governance best suited to addressing this problem.

There have also been avowedly indigenous programs on mainstream broadcast television. *First in Line* (Special Broadcasting Services [SBS], 1989) and *Blackout* (Australian Broadcasting Corporation [ABC], 1989) were both Aboriginal-produced and -presented magazine-style programs. *From Sand to Celluloid* (1995) was a series of short films by indigenous filmmakers, co-funded and broadcast by TV station SBS. *Bush Mechanics* (1998), a four part "whimsical" documentary, was produced by the Warlpiri Media Association and broadcast on the ABC. Perhaps most revolutionary in form was *The Mary G Show* (2001), which eschewed the magazine and art formats to produce "banal" indigenous Australian culture: a chat show presented by an indigenous drag queen. Despite their historical importance, none of these programs have been ratings successes.

The ABC miniseries *Heartland* (1994) retains its importance in the history of Australian television and remains worthy of a category of its own. This 13-hour-long drama presented a series of Aboriginal communities, rural and urban, and a wide range of characters, all contributing to a vastly increased range of available discourses on Aborigines. An entertaining, watchable piece of television, *Heartland* is truly distinctive in the history of Australian programming.

Ernie Dingo is a key figure in the history of indigenous televisual representation in Australia. He was responsible for a large amount of the Aboriginal representation on Australian television in the early 1990s. In addition to starring in *Heartland* and presenting *The Great Outdoors,* he has appeared on programs such as *Dolphin Cove, Clowning Around, Wheel of Fortune, GP, The Flying Doctors, Heartbreak High,* and many others. Recently, however, Dingo seems to have settled into his lifestyle work, while Aaron Pedersen—who first came to public attention as a host of the game show *Gladiators*—has become more visible. Deborah Mailman (star of the youth series *The Secret Life of Us*) is becoming a popular indigenous female presence on television.

Any consideration of indigenous programming must also cover the material that is made and distributed by Aboriginal groups and communities. Anybody interested in finding out about indigenous broadcasting is encouraged to visit, in the first instance, the website of the National Indigenous Media Association of Australia (www.nimaa.org.au), which represents most indigenous broadcasting groups.

Broadcasting for Remote Areas Community Scheme (BRACS) is one of a series of projects set up by Australia's federal government to ensure that Aboriginal communities at a distance from the continent's urban centers can have access to broadcast television. BRACS is the successor of such projects as Remote Area Television Scheme (RATS), Self-Help Television Reception Scheme (STRS), Remote and Underserved Communities Scheme (RUCS), and the Self-Help Broadcasting Reception Scheme (SHBRS). Initially funded by the 1987–88 budget of the (then) Federal Department of Aboriginal Affairs, the purpose of BRACS was slightly different from that which had gone before. Rather than simply ensuring reception of broadcast television, BRACS would provide rebroadcasting and production facilities to allow Aboriginal communities to decide for themselves how much of the material received should actually be shown in their communities and to make their own material to replace that which they did not want. In order to make this possible, BRACS supplies the community with satellite reception equipment, a domestic quality video camera, two domestic video recorders (to allow for basic editing), and the equipment to rebroadcast to the community. The initial idea was that this would allow broadcast in little-used languages (some Aboriginal languages have less than 100 speakers) and allow deletion of offensive material.

The scheme has had varying degrees of success. Difficulties have included the lack of well-trained personnel to look after the equipment, the built-in obsolescence of domestic equipment, and equipment incompatibility with desert settings; a lack of consultation with Aboriginal communities as to whether they wanted the equipment; the limited-range capability of the rebroadcast equipment; and, underlying many of these other problems, the lack of recurrent national funding for the project. However, it seems that the scheme (available to over 110 indigenous communities by 2001) has at least taken into consideration the ways in which communities might want to use television.

Perhaps the most active examples of such local television production have been the indigenous communities in Ernabella and Yuendumu. Both of these towns preempted the government's BRACS scheme, establishing their own pirate television broadcasting well before BRACS legitimized the idea of Aboriginal TV production. In the latter community, the Warlpiri Media Association has produced hundreds of hours of programming: records of community life, travel tapes, the *Bush Mechanics* documentary noted previously, and *Manyu Wana,* an indigenous version of *Sesame Street* designed to teach local children the Warlpiri language. This community also takes part in the Tanami Network, which offers a state-of-the-art video conferencing facility privately run by four Aboriginal communities.

Aboriginal video and radio programs are also produced by some indigenous media groups, including Central Australian Aboriginal Media Association (CAAMA), Townsville and Aboriginal Islander Media Association (TAIMA), Top End Aboriginal Bush Broadcasting Association (TEABBA), Western Australian Aboriginal Media Association (WAAMA), Mount Isa Aboriginal Media Association (MIAMA), and Torres Strait Islander and Aboriginal Media Association (TSIAMA). The radio programs are often carried on the networks of the Australian Broadcasting Corporation. Larger organizations than the media producers in the BRACS communities, these groups make material that is less locally oriented and that has an address wider than a single community.

Remote and rural areas of Australia receive their commercial television broadcasts on the AUSSAT satellite. Several Remote Commercial Television Service (RCTS) licenses were sold on this satellite; one is held by the CAAMA group. All of the bidders for these satellites were required to guarantee that their services would include material specifically commissioned for the Aboriginal people, who formed a relatively high proportion of their audiences (up to 27 percent in some cases). All did so, but none has done particularly well in keeping to those promises. The Golden West Network has one Aboriginal magazine program, *Milbindi.* Queensland Satellite Television broadcasts material provided by the governmental Aboriginal and Torres Strait Islander Commission and the Queensland State government—programs that present carefully positive images of Aboriginality.

Imparja, the station owned by CAAMA, has found constraints of economy have made it difficult to produce broadcast-quality Aboriginal material. The amount of indigenous programming on the channel has varied. When it started broadcasting in 1988, Imparja featured an Aboriginal magazine-style program, *Nganampa Anwernekenhe.* By contrast, by the 1990s, the station's Aboriginal broadcasting consisted only of community service announcements.

In Australia there is a vast range of material encompassed by the term "indigenous broadcasting": mainstream television on indigenous issues; indigenous programs broadcast on the mainstream; and indigenous-produced and -controlled broadcasting, which allows Aboriginal groups in Australia to interact assertively with new technologies, negotiating the places these will hold in their communities.

ALAN MCKEE

Further Reading

Hartley, John, and Alan McKee, *The Indigenous Public Sphere,* Oxford: Oxford University Press, 2000

Hartley, John, and Alan McKee, editors, *Telling Both Stories: Indigenous Australia and the Media,* Perth, West Australia: Edith Cowan University Arts Enterprise, 1996

Turner, Neil, *National Report on the Broadcasting for Remote Aboriginal Communities Scheme,* Prepared for the National Indigenous Media Association of Australia, 1998

Avengers, The

British Thriller

Possibly Britain's most successful television export, *The Avengers* (1961–69) was the last English-made television show to find a prime-time slot on U.S. network television. Originally *The Avengers* was designed to showcase the breakout star of *Police Surgeon* (1960), Ian Hendry, in the role of a doctor who, after the murder of his fiancée, joins forces with mysterious secret agent John Steed (Patrick Macnee). Six episodes were initially scheduled; 26 were made (three were videotaped) before Hendry left. Macnee continued to star in *The Avengers* for another eight years (136 episodes), finally resuming his role in 1976 in *New Avengers* (produced by Fennell and Clemens). During the subsequent five seasons, he was teamed with three female sidekicks: Cathy Gale (Honor Blackman), a widowed, leather-clad, martial arts expert with a Ph.D.; Mrs. Emma Peel (Diana Rigg), an aristocratic young widow, successful industrialist, psychologist, and skilled fighter; and, finally, Tara King (Linda Thorson), a young professional secret agent with less charisma or self-reliance than her amateur predecessors.

Once Macnee was teamed with Blackman, the show started to develop its characteristic flavor. Steed became more upper-class, dressed in increasingly dandified Edwardian fashion, while Gale represented a new vision of the strong, intelligent, active, and equal woman. Shot on multiple-camera video, these episodes did not display the same flair for the fantastic as the later filmed series (indeed, they look very much like the period's realistic "kitchen sink" dramas), but the narratives did start to flirt with the bizarre and unexpected.

During this same period (1962–64), there was increasing American interest in *The Avengers,* culminating in 1964 when ABC bought the series for the fall 1965 season. The network wanted a filmed series, so the show went on hiatus for nearly a year, reappearing on ITV in 1965 with new star Rigg. ABC chose to wait until 1967, when color episodes would be available rather than risk showing an imported black-and-white series while the U.S. networks were converting to all-color TV. After two seasons, Rigg left and was replaced by Thorson (1968–69). ABC canceled the show in 1969 because audiences sharply declined after it was scheduled against the new hit *Rowan and Martin's Laugh-In.* Although *The Avengers* continued to garner top ratings in Britain and throughout Europe, production stopped (it was never officially canceled) because the production company, Associated British, now relied on U.S. money.

While *The Avengers* is often considered part of the James Bond/cold war cycle of espionage thrillers, it actually dealt less with international issues and more with changes in modern Britain. Narratives explicitly engaged with issues of colonialism, national heritage, and questions of imperial British history, often parodying the nation's past, its institutions, and its stock stereotypes such as the English gentleman and the retired army major. This humorous reflection on national identity was combined with a fascination with space-age technology and an emphasis on modern femininity, a juxtaposition that recalled Britain's own long emergence out of postwar deprivation into the new, trendsetting world represented by Carnaby Street and the Beatles.

MOYA LUCKETT

The Avengers, 1961–69; Patrick Macnee, Diana Rigg, 1966–69.
Courtesy of the Everett Collection

See also **Lumley, Joanna; Rigg, Diana; Spy Programs**

Cast

John Steed	Patrick Macnee
Dr. David Keel	Ian Hendry
Carol Wilson	Ingrid Hafner
One Ten	Douglas Muir
Cathy Gale	Honor Blackman
Venus Smith	Julie Stevens
Dr. Martin King	Jon Rollason
Emma Peel	Diana Rigg
Tara King	Linda Thorson
"Mother"	Patrick Newell
Rhonda	Rhonda Parker

Producers

Leonard White, John Bryce, Julian Wintle, Albert Fennell, Brian Clemens

British Programming History

161 50-minute episodes
ITV
January 7, 1961–December 30, 1961
September 29, 1962–March 23, 1963
September 28, 1963–March 21, 1964
October 2, 1965–March 26, 1966
January 14, 1967–May 6, 1967
September 30, 1967–November 18, 1967
September 25, 1968–May 21, 1969

U.S. Programming History

ABC

March 1966–July 1966	Monday 10:00–11:00
July 1966–September 1966	Thursday 10:00–11:00
January 1967–September 1967	Friday 10:00–11:00
January 1968–September 1968	Wednesday 7:30–8:30
September 1968–September 1969	Monday 7:30–8:30

Further Reading

Buxton, David, *From The Avengers to Miami Vice: Form and Ideology in Television Series*, Manchester: Manchester University Press, 1990

Miller, Toby, *The Avengers*, London: British Film Institute, 1996

Rogers, Dave, *The Complete Avengers*, New York: St. Martin's Press, 1989

Azcarraga, Emilio Vidaurreta (d. 1972)

Azcarraga, Emilio Milmo (1930–1997)

Mexican Media Moguls

There were two Emilio Azcarragas, both equally significant in the history of television in Mexico: Emilio Azcarraga Vidaurreta, the William Paley of Mexican broadcasting, and his son and heir, Emilio Azcarraga Milmo, the principal owner of the Mexican entertainment conglomerate Televisa. The elder Azcarraga created the first Mexican radio station in 1930 and soon took on a leading role in the development of Latin American broadcasting. He convened meetings of fledgling Latin American broadcasting entrepreneurs where it was decided that the region would follow the U.S. commercial model and not the noncommercial, government-supported, public service British model.

Azcarraga, already the sole Mexican agent for Victor/RCA Records and a successful theater owner, promoted Mexican artists (who were under exclusive contract to him) through his growing chain of radio stations, which included several along the U.S.-Mexican border. In 1950 he created Mexico's first television station, and, a decade later, he established the first U.S. Spanish-language television stations. The Televisa radio and television networks have, since their inception, been characterized by their close association with the Mexican ruling party, known by its Spanish initials, PRI. Televisa produces conservative, nationalistic entertainment programming and fawning, uncritical news coverage of the Mexican government. Partly as a result of this comfortable relationship, broadcasting in Mexico is virtually unregulated.

This situation continued through the stewardship of the second Emilio Azcarraga, known in Mexico as *El Tigre* (The Tiger), as much for the white streak in his hair as for his reputedly ferocious manner. Azcarraga expanded Televisa's monopolistic hold on Mexican broadcasting by buying media properties in other Latin American countries and selling Televisa programming throughout the world. For example, a Televisa *telenovela* (soap opera) was a huge hit in Moscow in the early 1990s. In 1993 Azcarraga acquired controlling interest of PanAmSat, a hemispheric communications satellite, further consolidating Televisa's position as the world's largest producer of Spanish-language television programming.

In 1986 Azcarraga was forced to sell Televisa's U.S. subsidiary when it was found to be in violation of U.S. laws restricting foreign ownership. Just six years later, Azcarraga bought 25 percent of the U.S. network while continuing to provide the majority of its programming. In Mexico, Azcarraga diversified his holdings to include the largest stadium in the hemisphere, sports teams, publishing and recording companies, and even Mexico City real estate. Azcarraga maintained offices and homes in New York and Los Angeles as well as Mexico City and was featured on the cover of *Fortune*'s 1994 issue on the world's richest men.

In the early 1990s, Televisa began to downplay its relationship with the PRI, presenting fairer political coverage. This trend coincided with a reduction of Televisa's market dominance, when a second broadcast network, TV Azteca, was launched in 1993 and MVS Multivision challenged Televisa's leading role in the satellite television and cable markets.

A month before his death in April 1997, Azcarraga relinquished control of Televisa to his 29-year-old son, Emilio Azcarraga Jean.

America Rodriguez

See also **Mexico; Spanish International Network; Univision**

Emilio Azcarraga Vidaurreta. Married: Laura; children: Emilio, Laura, Carmela. Representative for Victoria/RCA Records; began radio station XEW, Mexico City, 1930; built Churrubusco Studios, 1940s; creator and owner of Channel 2, 1950; became the first president of Telesistema Mexicano, 1955; involved in 92 different businesses by 1969; established Televisa, a production company for his stations. Died 1972.

Emilio Azcarraga Milmo. Born August 1930. Married four times; fourth wife: Paula Cusi; children include: Emilio Azcarraga Jean. Educated at Culver

Military Academy, graduated 1948. Worked in various positions in television; owner, Univision, a 12-station Spanish-language U.S. network, 1960s and 1970s; controlling shareholder of Televisa, S.A.; owner of *The National* U.S. sports daily, 1990–91; owner of major Mexican television stations; chair, Galavision; also involved in publishing, video, and real estate ventures. Died in Miami, Florida, April 16, 1997.

Further Reading

Andrews, Edmund L., "FCC Clears Hallmark Sale of Univision TV Network," *New York Times* (October 1, 1992)

Besas, Peter, "Dynastic Quarrels Undo Mex Media Mix," *Variety* (December 24, 1990)

Deutschman, Alan, "Reclusive Tiger," *Fortune* (February 12, 1990)

Fisher, Christy, "Azcarraga Again Prowls U.S. Media," *Advertising Age* (February 1, 1993)

Malkin, Elisabeth, "The Rupert Murdoch of Mexico? Televisa's Azcarraga Wants to Crash the Global Major Leagues," *Business Week* (December 11, 1995)

Millman, Joel, "El Tigre Pounces Again," *Forbes* (January 6, 1992)

Stilson, Janet, "Hispanic Stations in Jeopardy: Staving Off Loss of TV Licenses," *Variety* (January 15, 1986)

B

Baird, John Logie (1888–1946)

Scottish Inventor

John Logie Baird pioneered early television with the mechanical scanning system he developed from 1923 to the late 1930s. He is remembered today as an inventor (178 patents) with considerable insight, who was in many ways ahead of his time. Among his pioneering ideas were early versions of color television, the video disc, large-screen television, stereo television, televised sports, and pay television by closed circuit. But he is also a tragic figure who often worked alone for lack of financial backing and lived to see his technical ideas superseded. He was forgotten by the time he died at the age of 58.

Baird did not select television as a field of endeavor so much as he backed into it. As a teen, he had toyed with the notion of pictures by wireless, as had others fascinated with the new technology. Later, having unsuccessfully tried innovation in several more mundane fields (socks, jams, glass razors, shoe soles), Baird traveled to Hastings (on England's south coast) in 1923 to see if the sea air would aid his always marginal health. During a series of long walks there, his mind returned to his earlier notions of how to send wireless images. But he was not well trained in electronics, and this lack of basic knowledge often limited his thinking and experiments.

Beginning in 1923 and continuing until 1939, Baird produced a series of mechanical video systems that could scan (and thus transmit and receive) moving images. These offered a crude picture (about 30 lines of definition from 1929 to 1935, improving to about 240 before he broke off development) by means of a cumbersome system of large rotating discs fitted with lenses. Baird promoted initial public interest in television with the first public demonstrations (one in a London department store window) in 1925 and 1926, and long-distance transmissions by wire (between London and Glasgow in 1926) and short-wave (transatlantic from London to New York in 1927). By 1928 he was experimenting with "phonovision," a means of recording his crude images on a phonograph-like disc. His efforts at promotion and sale of "televisor" devices created considerable controversy among experts as to whether television was sufficiently developed to promote public viewing and purchase of receivers.

For many years the British Broadcasting Corporation (BBC) resisted his efforts to utilize its frequencies and studio facilities in his work. Under pressure from the British Post Office (then in charge of all wire and wireless transmission), the BBC reluctantly began to work with Baird in 1930. Several years of experiments culminated in a regular daily broadcast comparison of his 240-line system with an RCA-like, all-electronic 405-line system developed by Marconi-EMI in 1936–37. Baird's now outmoded approach was soon dropped in favor of the latter's vastly superior electronic system.

Baird continued developmental work on color television, now making use of cathode-ray technology, and achieved 600-line experimental color telecasts by 1940. He continued his effort to perfect large-screen projection color television during World War II, along with some apparent work for the British military. But his health, never strong, gave out and he died in 1946.

Did Baird "fail"? He ignored or denied the growing value of the cathode-ray tube for too long (until the late 1930s) and held on to hopes for his mechanical alternative. His companies did not develop sufficient engineering depth and research capability beyond Baird himself. He kept no regular laboratory notes or records, making support for some of his claims difficult to find. And—perhaps most important as an indicator of impact—he achieved little commercial success. Still, there is growing appreciation of his pioneering if limited role among scholars of British television.

CHRISTOPHER H. STERLING

See also **Television Technology**

John Logie Baird. Born in Helensburgh, Dumbartonshire, Scotland, August 13, 1888. Attended Royal Technical College, Glasgow, and Glasgow University. Served as superintendent, Clyde Valley Electric Power Company; helped pioneer television transmission, successfully transmitting image of a Maltese cross several feet, 1924; gave scientists a demonstration of "Noctovision," a form of infrared television imaging, January 26 1926; succeeded with world's first transatlantic television transmission from London to New York and produced first television images in natural color, 1928; experimented with stereoscopic television; the BBC adopted his 30-line, mechanically scanned system, 1929, used for the first televising of the Derby from Epsom, 1931. Recipient: first Gold Medal of the International Faculty of Science given to an Englishman, 1937. Died in Bexhill, Sussex, England, June 14, 1946.

Publication

Sermons, Soap, and Television: Autobiographical Notes, 1988

Further Reading

Baird, Margaret, *Television Baird,* Cape Town, South Africa: Haum, 1973

Burns, R.W., *British Television: The Formative Years,* London: Peter Peregrinus, 1986

Exwood, Maurice, *John Logie Baird: 50 Years of Television,* London: Institution of Electronic and Radio Engineers History of Technology Monograph, 1976

Hallett, Michael, *John Logie Baird and Television,* Hove, England: Priory, 1978

McArthur, Tom, and Peter Wedell, *Vision Warrior: The Hidden Achievement of John Logie Baird,* Glasgow: Scottish Falcon Books, 1990

Moseley, Sydney, *John Baird: The Romance and Tragedy of the Pioneer of Television,* London: Odhams, 1953

Percy, J.D., *John L. Baird: The Founder of British Television,* London: Royal Television Society, 1950; revised edition, 1952

Rowland, John, *The Television Man: The Story of John L. Baird,* New York: Roy Publishers, 1966

Tiltman, Ronald F., *Baird of Television: The Life Story of John Logie Baird,* London: Seeley Service, 1933; reprinted, New York: Arno Press, 1974

Bakewell, Joan (1933–)

British Broadcast Journalist

Joan Bakewell is one of the most respected presenters and commentators on British radio and television, with a career that spans more than 30 years. At the start of her career in the 1960s, she was one of the first women to establish a professional reputation in what had previously been an almost exclusively male preserve. She has since consolidated her status as one of the more serious-minded and thoughtful of television's "talking heads," making regular appearances both with the BBC and the independent companies and also becoming a regular writer for leading British broadsheet newspapers such as *The Times* and *The Sunday Times.*

Early appearances on such programs as BBC 2's *Late Night Line Up* provided evidence of her understanding of a range of subjects and her ability to extract from complex arguments the crucial issues underlying them. She also profited by her youthful good looks, which earned her the unwanted tag (initially bestowed by humorist Frank Muir) "the thinking man's crumpet." Gradually, however, Bakewell shook herself free of the limitations of her physical description and went on to present a wide range of programs from current affairs, discussions of the arts, and questions of public and private morality (notably in her long-running series *The Heart of the Matter*) to the less intellectual territory inhabited by, for instance, *Film 73* and *Holiday*.

Always calm, Bakewell has sometimes been accused of having a somewhat "dour" and even cold personality; viewers have complained that only rarely has she been seen to smile with any conviction. Intent on getting to the bottom of a particular issue, she is never distracted by opportunities for light relief or lured into exploring the possibilities of a colorful tangential course. Even when presenting holiday reports from various exotic parts of the globe, she never gave the impression she was ready to abandon herself to anything resembling relaxed frivolity or other conventional "holiday-making" (she was consequently usually dispatched to report back from destinations with obvious cultural and artistic links).

This seriousness of purpose is, however, arguably dictated largely by the material Bakewell is usually associated with: weighty matters of relevance to consumers, voters, enthusiasts of the arts, and so on. Her unflurried, concerned tone of voice enables the viewer to concentrate upon the intellectual questions being raised during discussions of such emotional topics as providing funds for the treatment of terminally ill children—questions that in less-practiced hands could otherwise all too easily be swamped by sentimentality. There is nonetheless a lighter side to Bakewell's character, amply demonstrated by her contributions to the jovial BBC radio program *Newsquiz*, among other humorous productions.

DAVID PICKERING

Joan (Dawson) Bakewell. Born in Stockport, Cheshire, England, April 16, 1933. Attended Stockport High School for Girls, Stockport, Cheshire; Newnham College, Cambridge, B.A. Married: 1) Michael Bakewell, 1955 (divorced, 1972); children: Matthew and Harriet; 2) Jack Emery, 1975. Joined BBC radio as studio manager; subsequently hosted numerous arts, travel, and current affairs programs; television critic, *The Times*, 1978–81; associate, 1980–81, associate fellow, 1984–87, Newnham College, Cambridge; columnist, *Sunday Times*, since 1988; BBC television arts correspondent, 1981–87; has also written for *Punch* and *Radio Times;* president, Society of Arts Publicists, 1984–90; member, governing body, British Film Institute, since 1994; board member, Royal National Theatre, since 1996. Commander of the Order of the British Empire, 1999. Recipient: Richard Dimbledy Award, 1994.

Television Series

1962	*Sunday Break*
1964	*Home at 4.30*
1964	*Meeting Point*
1964	*The Second Sex*
1965–72	*Late Night Line Up*
1968	*The Youthful Eye*
1971	*Moviemakers at the National Film Theatre*
1972	*Film 72*
1973	*Film 73*
1973	*For the Sake of Appearance*
1973	*Where Is Your God?*
1973	*Who Cares?*
1973	*The Affirmative Way*
1974–78	*Holiday*
1974	*What's It All About?*
1974	*Time Running Out*
1974	*Thank You, Ron* (producer, writer)
1974	*Fairest Fortune*
1974	*Edinburgh Festival Report*
1976	*Generation to Generation*
1976	*The Shakespeare Business*
1976	*The Brontë Business*
1976–78	*Reports Action*
1977	*My Day with the Children*
1979	*The Moving Line*
1980	*Arts UK: OK?*
1988–2000	*The Heart of the Matter*
1998	*Travels with Pevsner: Derbyshire*
2000	*My Generation*

Radio

Away from It All, 1978–79; *PM*, 1979–81; *Newsquiz; There and Back* (play; writer); *Parish Magazine* (play; writer); *Artist of the Week*, 1998– ; *The Brains Trust*, 1998– .

Stage

Brontës: The Private Faces (writer), 1979.

Publications

The New Priesthood: British Television Today (with Nicholas Garnham), 1970

A Fine and Private Place (with John Drummond), 1977

The Complete Traveller, 1977

The Heart of "The Heart of the Matter," 1996

Ball, Lucille (1911–1989)

U.S. Actor, Comedian

Lucille Ball was one of television's foremost pioneers and a preeminent woman in the history of television. As a young contract player for MGM, Ball began her career as a Goldwyn Girl, eventually moving up to become a moderately respected star of "B" movies. She came to television after nearly 20 years in motion pictures, having undergone a gradual transformation from a platinum blonde sex symbol to a wise-cracking redhead.

Her first television program, *I Love Lucy,* premiered October 15, 1951, and for the next 25 years Lucille Ball virtually ruled the airwaves in a series of situation comedies designed to exploit her elastic expressions, slapstick abilities, and distinct verbal talents. A five-time Emmy Award winner, the first woman inducted into the Television Academy's Hall of Fame, recipient of a Genii Award and a Kennedy Center Honor, Lucille Ball was perhaps the most beloved of all television stars, and certainly the most recognizable.

In all of her television series, the protagonist she played was at once beautiful, zany, inept, and talented. Her comedic skills were grounded in the style of the silent comics, and Buster Keaton, with whom she once shared an office at MGM, seems to have been particularly influential in the development of Ball's daring exploits, hang-dog expressions, and direct looks at the audience. Although she personally fueled the myth that much of her performance was ad-libbed, in actuality, every move was choreographed. An accomplished perfectionist, she spent days practicing a particular routine before incorporating it into her programs. So distinct were her rubbery facial expressions that scriptwriters for *I Love Lucy* referred to them with specific code word notations. For example, the cue "puddling up" directed the star to pause momentarily with huge tear-filled eyes and then burst into a loud wail. "Light bulb" was an indication to portray a sudden idea, while "credentials" directed the star to gape in astonished indignation. Her importance for future comedians such as Mary Tyler Moore, Candice Bergen, and Cybill Shepard was paramount; Ball demonstrated that a woman could be beautiful and silly, and that she could perform the most outrageous of slapstick routines and still be feminine. Ball's unusual use of props and her imaginative escapes from the most implausible of situations influenced future sitcom stars such as Penny Marshall, Bronson Pinchot, Ellen Degeneres, and Robin Williams, whose comedic styles and series' storylines echoed her own.

But while her acting contributions are singularly laudable, it was Ball's role in redefining the very structure of television programming that makes her noteworthy. Her independence, popularity, and determination, coupled with her husband's technical and financial savvy, resulted in their co-ownership and control of one of the most successful television production studios in history.

I Love Lucy was one of the first television series to be produced live on film, using a multiple-camera technique in front of a studio audience. The filmed nature of the program granted it a permanency that allowed Ball and her husband, Desi Arnaz, to profit from reruns, syndication, and foreign distribution. The program was incomparably successful, reaching the number one position by February of its first season and remaining number one for four of its six years on the air, averaging a 67 share. Aired in more than 100 countries, the series quite literally financed the creation of Desilu Studios, where Ball and her husband reigned as vice president and president, respectively. Desilu went on to become the production headquarters for many of the greatest TV hits of the 1950s and 1960s, including *Our Miss Brooks, Make Room for Daddy, The Dick Van Dyke Show, The Untouchables, Mission Impossible, Mannix,* and *Star Trek.* Indeed, it was Ball's clout with the CBS network that convinced its executives to pick up the latter three pilots.

Ball's first success with *I Love Lucy* allowed her a power denied most entertainers. She was one of the few 1950s television stars to successfully fight the Communist witch-hunts of the House Un-American Activities Committee (HUAC), when a 1953 Walter Winchell program attempted to derail her career. Established film stars, such as Orson Welles, William Holden, and Joan Crawford, who had previously shunned television, made guest appearances on Ball's program for the sake of appearing with the queen of prime time. Ball's popularity with the press and her fans forced CBS executives to acquiesce to her decision to reveal her real-life pregnancy during the show's

Lucille Ball.
Courtesy of the Everett Collection

second season. This television first was monitored carefully by a trio of clergy who oversaw each script. While timid CBS executives insisted the word "expectant" be substituted for "pregnant," seven episodes detailed the fictional Lucy's pregnancy in near symmetry with the actress's own physical condition. Backlogging five episodes for use while she convalesced from delivery, the program worked around Ball's due date, so that her real-life Caesarean delivery coincided with the airing of her television delivery. The episode set a rating record of 71.1, with more viewers tuning in to witness the fictional Lucy Ricardo give birth than had seen Eisenhower's inauguration.

With her 1962 buyout of Desilu from her by then ex-husband Desi Arnaz, Ball became the first woman to head a major television production studio. Through the mid-1970s she starred in three additional series for CBS, with her third series, *The Lucy Show,* earning the highest initial price ever paid for a 30-minute series ($2.3 million for 30 episodes). In the mid-1960s, she sold Desilu to Gulf and Western for $17 million, and she went on to form Lucille Ball Productions with her second husband, Gary Morton, as vice president. Her final CBS series, *Here's Lucy,* while not as critically acclaimed as her previous ventures, was responsible for launching the careers of her children Lucie Arnaz and Desi Arnaz Jr., and for bringing Elizabeth Taylor and Richard Burton into situation comedy.

By the mid-1970s, diffused lighting, surgical tape "face lifts," skilled makeup, and a bright wig could not hide her diminishing physical flexibility or her increasing reliance on cue cards. A 1986 ABC series, *Life with Lucy,* seemed forced and stodgy and lasted a mere 13 weeks. But even in her decline there were flashes of brilliance. In 1985 she surprised critics and fans with her appearance as a homeless woman in the CBS made-for-TV movie *Stone Pillow.* With her death in 1989, she was eulogized by fans, network executives, and even the president of the United States, as "the first woman of television."

For all her impact upon the very nature of television production, Ball is most vividly recalled as a series of black-and-white images. To remember Lucille Ball is to recall a profusion of universal images of magical mayhem—a losing battle with a candy conveyor belt, a flaming nose, a slippery vat of grapes—images that, unlike most American situation comedy, transcend nationalities and generations, in an absolute paradigm of side-splitting laughter.

Nina C. Leibman

See also **Arnaz, Desi; Comedy, Domestic Settings; *I Love Lucy;* Gender and Television; Independent Production Companies**

Lucille (Désirée) Ball (Lucy Montana, Diane Belmont). Born in Jamestown, New York, August 6, 1911. Attended John Murray Anderson-Robert Milton Dramatic School, New York City. Married: 1) Desi Arnaz, 1940 (divorced, 1960); children: Lucie Désirée and Desi Jr.; 2) Gary Morton, 1961. Began her performing career in the 1920s under the name Diane Belmont, being hired for, then quickly fired from, Earl Carroll's *Vanities* and the Schuberts' *Stepping Stones;* had a walk-on role in *Broadway Thru a Keyhole,* 1933; selected as a Goldwyn Girl for film *Roman Scandals,* 1933; signed with Columbia, 1934; under contract to RKO, from 1935; moved to MGM 1943–46; played role on CBS radio program *My Favorite Husband,* 1947–50; co-starred with Bob Hope in *Sorrowful Jones,* 1949, and *Fancy Pants,* 1950; with husband Desi Arnaz established Desilu Productions, which began producing the *I Love Lucy* television series, 1951–57, and later series such as *The Ann Sothern Show* and *The Untouchables;* with Arnaz, bought RKO studios and lot in 1957; debuted on Broadway in *Wild-*

cat, 1960; bought Arnaz's share of Desilu, 1962, which she managed until 1967; sold Desilu to Gulf and Western Industries, 1967; formed and managed Lucille Ball Productions, 1968; starred in film *Mame,* 1974; played a Manhattan bag lady in made-for-television movie *Stone Pillow,* 1985; starred in series *Life with Lucy,* 1986. Recipient: five Emmy Awards; Golden Apple Award, 1973; Ruby Award, 1974; Entertainer of the Year, 1975; Television Academy Hall of Fame, 1984. Died in Los Angeles, California, April 26, 1989.

Television Series

1951–57	*I Love Lucy*
1957–60	*The Lucille Ball and Desi Arnaz Show*
1962–65, 1967	*The Lucy-Desi Comedy Hour*
1962–68	*The Lucy Show*
1968–74	*Here's Lucy*
1986	*Life with Lucy*

Made-for-Television Movies

1974	*Happy Anniversary and Goodbye*
1976	*What Now, Catherine Curtis?*
1985	*Stone Pillow*

Television Specials

1975	*The Lucille Ball Special Starring Lucille Ball and Dean Martin*
1975	*The Lucille Ball Special Starring Lucille Ball and Jackie Gleason*
1977	*Bob Hope's All-Star Tribute to Vaudeville*

Films

Bulldog Drummond, 1929; *Broadway Thru a Keyhole,* 1933; *Blood Money,* 1933; *Roman Scandals,* 1933; *The Bowery,* 1933; *Moulin Rouge,* 1934; *Nana,* 1934; *Bottoms Up,* 1934; *Hold That Girl,* 1934; *Bulldog Drummond Strikes Back,* 1934; *The Affairs of Cellini,* 1934; *Kid Millions,* 1934; *Broadway Bill,* 1934; *Jealousy,* 1934; *Men of the Night,* 1934; *Fugitive Lady,* 1934; *The Whole Town's Talking,* 1934; *Carnival,* 1935; *Roberta,* 1935; *Old Man Rhythm,* 1935; *The Three Musketeers,* 1935; *Top Hat,* 1935; *I Dream Too Much,* 1935; *The Farmer in the Dell,* 1936; *Chatterbox,* 1936; *Follow the Fleet,* 1936; *Bunker Bean,* 1936; *That Girl from Paris,* 1936; *Winterset,* 1936; *Don't Tell the Wife,* 1937; *Stage Door,* 1937; *Go Chase Yourself,* 1938; *Joy of Living,* 1938; *Having Wonderful Time,* 1938; *The Affairs of Annabel,* 1938; *Room Service,* 1938; *The Next Time I Marry,* 1938; *Annabel Takes a Tour,* 1939; *Beauty for the Asking,* 1939; *Twelve Crowded Hours,* 1939; *Panama Lady,* 1939; *Five Came Back,* 1939; *That's Right, You're Wrong,* 1939; *The Marines Fly High,* 1940; *You Can't Fool Your Wife,* 1940; *Dance, Girl, Dance,* 1940; *Too Many Girls,* 1940; *A Girl, a Guy, and a Gob,* 1941; *Look Who's Laughing,* 1941; *Valley of the Sun,* 1942; *The Big Street,* 1942; *Seven Days' Leave,* 1942; *Dubarry Was a Lady,* 1943; *Best Foot Forward,* 1943; *Thousands Cheer,* 1943; *Meet the People,* 1944; *Ziegfeld Follies,* 1944 (released 1946); *Without Love,* 1945; *Bud Abbott and Lou Costello in Hollywood,* 1945; *The Dark Corner,* 1946; *Easy to Wed,* 1946; *Two Smart People,* 1946; *Lover Come Back,* 1946; *Lured,* 1947; *Her Husband's Affairs,* 1947; *Sorrowful Jones,* 1949; *Easy Living,* 1949; *Miss Grant Takes Richmond,* 1949; *A Woman of Distinction,* 1950; *Fancy Pants,* 1950; *The Fuller Brush Girl,* 1950; *The Magic Carpet,* 1951; *The Long, Long Trailer,* 1954; *Forever, Darling,* 1956; *Critic's Choice,* 1963; *A Guide for the Married Man,* 1967; *Yours, Mine and Ours,* 1968; *Mame,* 1974.

Radio

Phil Baker's show, 1938; Jack Haley's *Wonder Bread Show,* 1938; *Lux Radio Theatre; Suspense; Screen Guild Playhouse; My Favorite Husband,* 1947–50.

Stage

Dream Girl, 1947–48; vaudeville tour with Desi Arnaz, 1950; *Wildcat,* 1960.

Publication

Love Lucy, with Betty Hannah Hoffman, 1996

Further Reading

Anderson, Christopher, *Hollywood TV: The Studio System in the Fifties,* Austin: University of Texas Press, 1994

Andrews, Bart, *Lucy and Ricky and Fred and Ethel,* New York: Dutton, 1976

Andrews, Bart, *The "I Love Lucy" Book,* Garden City, New York: Doubleday, 1985

Andrews, Bart, and Thomas Watson, *Loving Lucy: An Illustrated Tribute to Lucille Ball,* New York: St. Martin's Press, 1980

Arnaz, Desi, *A Book by Desi Arnaz,* New York: Morrow, 1976

Brady, Kathleen, *Lucille: The Life of Lucille Ball,* New York: Hyperion, 1994

Brochu, Jim, *Lucy in the Afternoon: An Intimate Memoir of Lucille Ball,* New York: William Morrow, 1990

Dinter, Charlotte, "I Just Couldn't Take Any More," *Photoplay* (June 1960)

Doty, Alexander, "The Cabinet of Lucy Ricardo: Lucille Ball's Star Image," *Cinema Journal* (1990)

Harris, Warren G., *Lucy and Desi: The Legendary Love Story of Television's Most Famous Couple,* New York: Simon and Schuster, 1991

Higham, Charles, *Lucy: The Life of Lucille Ball,* New York: St. Martin's Press, 1986
Kanfer, Stefan. *Ball of Fire: The Tumultuous Life and Comic Art of Lucille Ball.* New York: Knopf, 2003
"Lucille Ball" (interview), *Dialogue on Film* (May–June 1974)
Mellencamp, Patricia, "Situation Comedy, Feminism and Freud: Discourses of Gracie and Lucy," *Studies in Entertainment,* edited by Tania Modleski, Bloomington: Indiana University Press, 1986
Morella, Joe, and Edward Epstein, *Forever Lucy: The Life of Lucille Ball,* Secaucus, New Jersey: L. Stuart, 1986
Nugent, Frank, "The Bouncing Ball," *Photoplay* (September 1946)
Sanders, Coyne Steven, and Tom Gilbert, *Desilu: The Story of Lucille Ball and Desi Arnaz,* New York: Morrow 1993
Schatz, Thomas, "Desilu, I Love Lucy, and the Rise of Network TV," *Making Television: Authorship and the Production Process,* edited by Robert J. Thompson and Gary Burns, New York: Praeger, 1990
Shipman, David, *The Great Movie Stars: The Golden Years,* New York: Crown, 1970

Barbera, Joseph. *See* **Hanna, William and Joseph Barbera**

Barney Miller

U.S. Comedy/Variety Program

Barney Miller, a gentle and witty comedy, was one of the most successful ensemble comedy series of all time. Co-created (with Theodore J. Flicker) and produced by Danny Arnold, who wrote other popular programs (*The Real McCoys, That Girl,* and *Bewitched*), the show was originally conceived as the story about a compassionate police officer. The pilot, *The Life and Times of Captain Barney Miller,* aired as part of the summer anthology series *Just For Laughs* (ABC, 1974), and the action was divided between the police captain's workplace and his home life with wife Elizabeth (Abby Dalton) and children Rachel and David (Anne Wyndham and Michael Tessier).

When the series premiered as a mid-season replacement (January 23, 1975), the action focused on the work environment. Earlier series such as *The Dick Van Dyke Show* (CBS, 1961–66) and *The Mary Tyler Moore Show* (CBS, 1970–77) depicted the workplace "family" in addition to the characters' home lives, but *Barney Miller* was the first domestic comedy to focus on the workplace and the activities taking place in the dingy 12th precinct station house in New York's Greenwich Village. Barney's family life was relegated to a much smaller role and, although Barbara Barrie succeeded Dalton as wife Elizabeth, the children were soon written out completely.

Few series before or since have achieved the ethnic and racial diversity featured in *Barney Miller.* The title character was a middle-aged Jewish man (played by Broadway veteran Hal Linden) with a paternal concern for the detectives serving under him. The detectives included the fiery Puerto Rican Chano Amenguale (Gregory Sierra), Nick Yemana (Jack Soo), a contemplative middle-aged Asian-American with a weakness for gambling and an inability to make a decent pot of coffee, Ron Harris (Ron Glass), a stylish African-American with grand ambitions to publish his detective novel (*Blood on the Badge*), Stanley Wojciehowicz (Max Gail), a Polish Catholic with a passion for fighting injustices, and sexagenarian Phil Fish (Abe Vigoda). The squad room also had its token female officer in the outspoken Janice Wentworth (Linda Lavin). Rounding out the cast were Fish's wife Bernice (Florence Stanley), the tough yet sentimental Frank Luger (James Gregory), and Scanlon of Internal Affairs (George Murdock). And, parading through each episode, were the "crazies, crooks, con men, hookers, juvenile muggers, and other street denizens" of the precinct, including one of television's first recurring gay characters, Marty (Jack DeLeon).

Barney Miller.
Photo courtesy of ABC Photo Archives

Sierra and Lavin both left after the first season, and Vigoda's character was "retired" after the second to star in his own spinoff, *Fish* (ABC, 1977–78). Amenguale and Wentworth were replaced by the droll intellectual Arthur Dietrich (Steve Landesberg) and Carl Levitt (Ron Carey), a diminutive beat officer with aspirations to plainclothes duty. June Gable briefly joined the cast in the second season as Maria Baptista.

The use of the nontraditional extended family as the basis for this comedy is exemplified in the show's opening credits. In the style of many domestic comedies (e.g., *The Donna Reed Show*), each "family member" is introduced in the credits, acting in a way that reflects their individual personalities, for example, Barney stopping to listen to an officer, Harris working at his writing. The sense of family and ensemble extended to the actors themselves, and audiences felt that special bond. When actor Jack Soo died in January 1979, a special episode was aired the following May and featured the late actor in clips from past shows and included reminiscences from the other cast members. At the end of the episode, the entire cast raised their coffee cups in heartfelt salute.

Unlike many comedy series, each episode featured two or three storylines, allowing the action to shift from one story to the other, similar to a one-act play. But the key to the success of the series was its low-key dialogue and underplayed reactions to the mayhem occurring around them. There are no car chases, no shoot-outs. The characters react like real police detectives. They take their time, they listen to the people who come in to file a complaint, and they deal with the mounds of paperwork. More importantly, the officers always exhibit their affection and understanding for human beings in trouble.

At a time when most comedy series emphasized being filmed in front of a live audience, *Barney Miller* was one of the few comedy series that was not, due mainly to long filming hours that often lasted well into the night (and very early into the following morning).

According to the actors, writer/producer Arnold was a perfectionist and constantly honed lines of dialogue. Linden said Arnold "did not want to put anything on the screen that wasn't as perfect as he could make it, and it kept us up until six o'clock in the morning very often."

After a dispute with the network, the series came to an end in 1982. Like *The Mary Tyler Moore Show, Barney Miller*'s ending three-part episode dealt with the break-up of the familial unit. It is discovered that the station house was once Theodore Roosevelt's headquarters, when he served as New York Police Board president in the 1890s. Thus the building is declared a historic landmark, forcing the precinct to vacate the premises. And, even though Barney is finally promoted to Deputy Inspector and Officer Levitt finally achieves the rank of sergeant, the detectives of the "ole One-Two" are all reassigned to other precincts throughout the city.

Throughout its eight seasons on the air, the series never made the top ten in the Nielsen ratings, but it garnered multiple honors, including a total of 32 Emmy nominations, seven Golden Globe nominations, and an award from the Directors Guild of America.

The series continues in syndication and remains a cultural icon. Eleven pieces from the series are now part of the popular culture collection at the Smithsonian's Museum of American History: the squad room assignment board, the cell door and key, as well as the police badges of Miller, Luger, Harris, Wojciehowicz, Dietrich, Levitt, and Yemana, along with the latter's name plate and coffee cup.

SUSAN R. GIBBERMAN

See also **Police Programs**

Cast

Captain Barney Miller	Hal Linden
Det. Ron Harris	Ron Glass
Det. Stanley "Wojo" Wojciehowicz	Max Gail
Inspector Frank Luger	James Gregory
Elizabeth Miller	Barbara Barrie
Det. Sgt. Chano Amenguale	Gregory Sierra (1975–76)
Det. Phil Fish	Abe Vigoda (1975–77)
Det. Nick Yemana	Jack Soo (1975–78)
Det. Arthur Dietrich	Steve Landesberg (1976–82)
Officer Carl Levitt	Ron Carey (1976–82)
Bernice Fish	Florence Stanley (1975–77)
Det. Janice Wentworth	Linda Lavin (1975–76)
Det. Maria Baptista	June Gable (1976–77)
Lt. Ben Scanlon	George Murdock (1976–82)

Producers

Danny Arnold, Chris Hayward, Arne Sultan

Programming History

169 episodes

ABC

January 1975–January 1976	Thursday 8:00–8:30
January 1976–December 1976	Thursday 8:30–9:00
December 1976–March 1982	Thursday 9:00–9:30
March 1982–April 1982	Friday 8:30–9:00
April 1982–September 1982	Thursday 9:00–9:30

Further Reading

Adelson, Suzanne, "Amid Hugs and Tears, TV's *Barney Miller* Heads for Its Final Lock-up—and Reruns," *People Weekly* (May 10, 1982)

Andrews, Peter, "*Barney Miller*," *Saturday Review* (April 12, 1980)

Ben, Pesta, "Cross Lou Costello with a Trappist Monk, Put Him in Blues," *TV Guide* (May 23, 1981)

Eisner, Joel, and David Krinsky, *Television Comedy Series: An Episode Guide to 153 TV Sitcoms in Syndication,* Jefferson, North Carolina: McFarland, 1984

Emerson, Gloria, "Why *Barney Miller* Lasted So Long," *Vogue* (July 1982)

Fejes, Fred, and Rita J. Simon, "Real Police on Television Supercops," *Society* (September–October 1980)

Handelman, Jay, "*Barney Miller* and His Detectives Solve a Case of Missing Comedy," *Sarasota Herald Tribune* (November 26, 2000)

Knoedelseder, William K., Jr., "You Have To Care About Your Character," *TV Guide* (October 25, 1980)

Mitchell, Janis L., "*Barney Miller*": *A Psychoanalytic and Formulaic Analysis of an Episode,* Masters Thesis, San Francisco State University, 1983

Yuknes, John J., "A Cop's-Eye View of *Barney Miller:* This Real-Life Manhattan Detective Says that the Squad-room Comedy Is More Realistic Than We Might Think, *TV Guide* (March 21, 1981)

Barnouw, Erik (1908–2001)

Historian

Erik Barnouw, the preeminent historian of broadcasting in the United States, belongs to the New Deal generation of American progressive intellectuals whose coming of age in the Depression, wartime experience, and postwar work in public service influenced and inspired generations of students and activists after them. Born in 1908 in the Netherlands, Barnouw emigrated with his family to the United States in 1919. His father, Adriaan Barnouw, took a faculty position at Columbia University and Erik experienced the heady days of 1920s New York as a student at the Horace Mann School. While an undergraduate at Princeton, he became a member of the exclusive Triangle Club, and wrote a series of popular campus musicals, including *Zuider Zee* in collaboration with Joshua Logan. After brief stints as a theatrical stage manager, a writer for the fledgling *Fortune* magazine, and a world traveler funded by a Princeton fellowship, Barnouw returned in 1931 to a United States greatly changed by the Depression. He found himself among the ranks of the unemployed, until an encounter with a Princeton classmate in a speakeasy led to an offer of employment at the Erwin, Wasey advertising agency, working on the Camel cigarette account as director of *The Camel Quarter-Hour* on CBS.

The early, experimental years of sponsored network radio presented the equally inexperienced, experimental Barnouw with ample opportunity to flex his dramatic skills. He produced and directed series such as *The True Story Court of Human Relations* and *Bobby Benson of the H-Bar-O Ranch.* But, several years later, when offered a position of vice president in charge of programming at the agency, Barnouw resigned, and accepted an offer from Columbia University to teach a radio writing sequence.

The move to academe led to a growing reputation as a "serious" writer just as the networks moved into their first New Deal-era efforts at program uplift. This led to assignments to work on prestige programs such as *Cavalcade of America* and *Theater Guild of the Air.* In 1942 he moved to NBC as script editor of public service programs, an increasingly important area during the war, which led to an appointment as educational director with the Armed Forces Radio Service in 1944–45. In 1946 Barnouw resumed his faculty post at Columbia, now adding television to the curriculum in cooperation with NBC. During this period Barnouw became the president of the Radio Writers Guild, a labor union organized to stabilize and protect the rights of the often unacknowledged writers behind radio's frenetic production.

Over the next 20 years, Barnouw's career exhibited a stunning variety of accomplishments, including a barrier-breaking VD awareness campaign for the Public Health Service, co-founding the Writers Guild of America, producing and writing the film series *Decision: The Constitution in Action* as well as the groundbreaking documentary *Hiroshima-Nagasaki, August 1945,* and founding the Center for Mass Communication at Columbia. In 1959 he was commissioned by Oxford University Press to write a three-volume history of U.S. broadcasting. Barnouw produced the first volume, *A Tower in Babel,* in 1966, followed by *The Golden Web* in 1968 and *The Image Empire* in 1970.

It is hard to imagine the situation of broadcasting history in this country without the presence of Erik Barnouw's overarching yet accessible account of the industry he knew so well. With access to many of the key players from the still-recent early days of radio, Barnouw's project drew on, but also crucially added to, the Oral History Collection at Columbia, an invaluable resource. His compilation of documents, photographs, and recordings from stations, producers, writers, journalists, industry personnel, and his interpretation and analysis in such a lively and engaging narrative, has made the American broadcasting heritage accessible to generations of students and scholars.

As the one-volume condensation of the larger work, *Tube of Plenty,* as well as his more pointed summary *The Sponsor: Notes on a Modern Potentate,* demonstrate, Barnouw's primary allegiance is to the New Deal reformer's philosophy that broadcasting's problems lie primarily in its commercial basis. Though more open-minded than many, he reserves his approval—and in later volumes, most of his attention—for the "serious" side of public affairs, documentary and news broadcasting, reflecting his own background and experience as well as the unquestioned cultural hierarchy of the New Deal Ivy League left, posing patrician public service squarely in opposition to vulgar commercialism. No populist, yet not entirely comfortable with the elite disdain for popular culture found in much of the criticism of his contemporaries, a levity and wit run though his writings that often manages to insult all sides equally.

Erik Barnouw's long career includes over a dozen books, numerous scripts and film and video productions, and numerous articles. He served as Chief of the Motion Picture, Broadcasting, and Recorded Sound Division of the Library of Congress from 1978 until 1981, won numerous grants and awards for his work, was extremely active in unions, organizations, and scholarly activities throughout his life, publishing his last book, *Conglomerates and the Media,* in 1997 at the age of 89. He died on July 19, 2001, at the age of 93.

MICHELE HILMES

Erik Barnouw. Born in The Netherlands, June 23, 1908; moved to United States, 1919, naturalized citizen, 1928. Married: Dorothy Maybelle Beache June 3, 1939; children Jeffrey, Susanna, Karen. Education: Princeton University, A.B., 1929, University of Vienna, Reinhardt Seminar, 1930. Worked as program director and writer for Erwin, Wasey and Company, 1930–35; Arthur Kudner, Inc, advertising, 1935–37. Joined Columbia University faculty in 1937. Served as script editor at NBC 1942–44, and as educational director of the Armed Forces Radio Service 1944–45. Returned to Columbia University 1946; worked on *Calvacade of America* and *The Theatre Guild of the Air* 1946–49. President, Radio Writers Guild, 1947–49; Secretary of Authors League of America 1949–53; Co-founder, Writers Guild of America, 1954. Wrote "VD: The Conspiracy of Silence" campaign, 1948; producer-writer *Decision: The Constitution in Action* television series, 1957–59; producer *Hiroshima-Nagasaki, August 1945,* 1970; writer-producer *Fable Safe,* 1972, with Robert Osborn. Library of Congress, Chief of Motion Picture, Broadcasting and Recorded Sound Division, 1971–81. Married Elizabeth Prince Allen, 1989. Died in Fair Haven, Vermont, July 19, 2001.

Awards

American Bar Association Gavel Award, 1959, for *Decision;* Fulbright Award, India, 1961; Guggenheim Fellowship, 1969; Bancroft Prize, 1971, for *The Image Empire;* John D. Rockefeller III Fund grant for research in Asia, 1972; Silver Dragon Award, Cracow Film Festival, for *Fable Safe;* Woodrow Wilson Fellow, Smithsonian Institution, 1976; Indo-American Fellowship, 1978; Eastman Kodak Gold Medal for Service to Film and Television, 1982; Litt. D. Columbia University, 1984; Vermont Peace Festival Award, 1985, for *Hiroshima-Nagasaki;* International Documentary Association scholarship and preservation award, 1985.

Publications (selected)

Handbook of Radio Writing: An Outline of Techniques and Markets in Radio Writing in the United States, 1928
Radio Drama in Action (editor), 1945
Mass Communication: Television, Radio, Film, Press: The Media and Their Practice in the United States of America, 1956
The Television Writer, 1962
Indian Film (with S. Krishnaswamy), 1963
A Tower in Babel, Vol. 1, *A History of Broadcasting in the United States,* 1966
The Golden Web, Vol. 2, *A History of Broadcasting in the United States,* 1968
The Image Empire, Vol. 3, *A History of Broadcasting in the United States,* 1970
Documentary: A History of the Non-Fiction Film, 1974
Tube of Plenty: The Evolution of American Television, 1975
The Sponsor: Notes on a Modern Potentate, 1978
The Magician and the Cinema, 1981
International Encyclopedia of Communications (editor-in-chief), 1989
Media Marathon: A Twentieth-Century Memoir, 1996
Conglomerates and the Media, 1997

Further Reading

Kitross, John M., "The Barnouw Trilogy: History As We Know It?" *Journal of Broadcasting and Electronic Media,* 40 no. 4 (1996)
Lichty, Lawrence L., editor, "A Conversation With Erik Barnouw," *Film and History,* Vol., nos. 2 and 3 (1991)
Sterling, Christopher H., "An Appreciation of Erik Barnouw's *A History of Broadcasting in the United States,*" *Film and History,* 21, nos. 2-3 (1991)

Bassett, John (1915–1998)

Canadian Media Executive

Few individuals in the history of Canadian television have inspired as much controversy as John Bassett, a founder of Toronto station CFTO and key figure in the formation of the CTV network, Canada's first privately owned television network. Bassett parlayed a career in journalism and his financial connections into a major ownership role in Canadian commercial television. Media historian Paul Rutherford identifies him as one of the architects of Canadian television. Bassett also was a player in national politics, and in the 1980s he was named chair of the Canadian Security Intelligence Review Commission and appointed to the Privy Council of Canada, an appointment that carried with it the title Honourable.

When in 1959 the Board of Broadcast Governors (BBG), reflecting the views of the recently elected Conservative government of John Diefenbaker, decided to allow an expansion of private telecasting in Canada, the most coveted market was Toronto, seen correctly as a potential gold mine. Many prominent business groups wanted the license and nine eventually applied. Bassett joined the Eaton family, owners of a large department store chain, and others in an enterprise known as BATON Broadcasting, which was awarded the Toronto rights. When the winner was announced, the decision was roundly criticized. Some critics alleged that Bassett, a party insider and (unsuccessful) candidate for the Progressive Conservative party, had capitalized on his political connections and personal relationship with the prime minister. The new licensee also owned the Toronto *Telegram,* an unashamedly right-wing supporter of the party. (The newspaper closed its doors in 1971.) This connection also aroused concerns about cross-media ownership. Bassett may have had some influence on the Diefenbaker government's decision to weaken the television monopoly held by the public network. However, historians report no evidence that the prime minister personally intervened in the BBG decision to award the license to BATON.

Conflict of interest was also suspected when the rights to televise Canadian professional football games went to BATON, rather than to the publicly owned Canadian Broadcasting Corporation (CBC) with its national audience. Bassett also owned the Toronto club in the league at the time. Initially cool to Spence Caldwell's CTV network, Bassett was forced to come to an agreement with CTV—and the CBC—to reach a national audience for the then highly popular Canadian Football League telecasts. The national championship, known as the Grey Cup game, was a major national event, important to viewers and profitable for broadcasters with a national audience. Once in the fold, Bassett came to dominate the private network.

With its prime-time schedule filled with U.S. imports, CFTO was soon accused of reneging on promises it made during the license hearings to promote Canadian content. Similar allegations were leveled at the entire CTV network, and the BBG was seen as either gullible or politically motivated in failing to enforce promises made during application hearings. During the BBG hearings, the BATON group had promised to fight the "battle of Buffalo," appealing to Canadian cultural concerns about U.S. domination. Bassett's promise was to compete with Buffalo, New York, television stations for Toronto viewers, many of whom had been watching U.S. programming for some years before Canadian stations came on the air.

Making matters worse, BATON agreed to sell stock to the U.S. network ABC, a move endorsed by the BBG in 1961. Condemnation of the sale was fierce and sustained. The BBG retracted its decision, but Bassett engineered a different arrangement whereby ABC would make a substantial loan to CFTO in return for a contract to provide "management services" and personnel. This issue arose from concerns about undue U.S. influence in the operation and development of Canadian television.

CFTO went on the air on January 1, 1961, and by the early 1970s it was extremely profitable. BATON was clearly the key force behind CTV and provided production services through Glen Warren Productions. Toronto was the center for CTV's limited Canadian production activities, and Bassett and his partners began to purchase other media assets, including shares in other CTV affiliates. At times, BATON's ambitions have collided with other partners in the network, producing friction with other ambitious owners. BATON finally gained full control of CTV in 1997, just four months before Bassett's death. (The network was sub-

John Bassett.
Photo courtesy of National Archives of Canada/CBC Collection

sequently sold to BCE, Inc., and became part of Bell Globemedia, which also owns the Toronto *Globe and Mail* newspaper.)

Bassett ran BATON from its inception until 1979, when he turned the day-to-day operations over to his son, Douglas, who has overseen further expansion of BATON's activities. Well over six feet tall and projecting a "tough, arrogant" image, John Bassett was a major player in the development of commercial television in Canada and the erosion of the dominance of the CBC. Perhaps not surprisingly, given his newspaper background, Bassett's stations made their greatest contributions in news and public affairs programming.

FREDERICK J. FLETCHER AND ROBERT EVERETT

John White Hughes Bassett. Born in Ottawa, Canada, 1915. Began career in journalism; owner of CFTO-TV, Toronto, and the Toronto *Telegram;* significant leader in CTV, Canadian commercial television network cooperative from 1966; chairman of the Toronto Argonauts football team. Head of Canadian Security Intelligence Review, 1989–92. Commission Made an Officer of the Order of Canada in 1985; elevated to Companion of the Order of Canada, 1992. Member, Order of Ontario, 1988. Inducted posthumously into Canadian Association of Broadcasters Hall of Fame as a pioneer, November 2000. Died in Toronto, April 17, 1998.

Further Reading

Desbarats, Peter, *Guide to Canadian News Media,* Toronto: Harcourt Brace Jovanovich, 1990

Levine, Allen, *Scrum Wars: The Prime Ministers and the Media,* Toronto: Dundurn, 1993

Rayboy, Marc, *Missed Opportunities: The Story of Canada's Broadcasting Policy,* Montreal: McGill-Queen's University Press, 1990

Siggins, Maggie, *Bassett,* Toronto: Lorimer, 1979

Batman

U.S. Action-Adventure Parody

Batman was created by Bob Kane in 1939 as a comic book hero. During his long career, the character was featured in the *Superman* radio series and in two movie serials produced during World War II. In 1966 the ABC network decided to produce the first *Batman* television series, and it became an immediate hit. Initially, the show aired twice a week. On Wednesdays Batman and his sidekick Robin would confront one of their archenemies and would end the episode in horrible danger, only to save themselves at the beginning of the next episode on Thursdays. These cliff-hangers closely followed the tradition created by Kane in the comic books.

The television series also followed the comic books' plot. Bruce Wayne (played by Adam West) was orphaned in his teens when criminals killed his parents. He inherited a huge fortune and, obsessed with fighting the evil-doers who plagued Gotham City, became

Batman, Burt Ward, Adam West, 1966–68.
©20th Century Fox/Courtesy of the Everett Collection

Batman, the Caped Crusader. Under his mansion, Batman constructed the Batcave, an elaborate laboratory used to fight crime. His young ward, Dick Grayson (played by Burt Ward), also orphaned due to evildoers, became Robin, the Boy Wonder, under Batman/Wayne's tutelage. Together they defended the city against the sick-minded criminals that populated the underworld. The only person who knew their identity was Alfred (Alan Napier), Wayne's butler, who raised Bruce after his parents were killed. In the Batlab and at the Batcave, Batman and Robin were helped by the most advanced technology to fight their enemies. Police Commissioner Gordon (Neil Hamilton) could ask Batman for help either through the use of a searchlight, the Batsignal, or the Batphone, a direct line between the police station and Bruce Wayne's mansion. To defeat their enemies, Batman and Robin also used the Batmobile, their utility belts, and other Bat-devices.

The success of the series attracted several famous actors and actresses to play the villains. Among the most famous enemies were the Riddler (played first by Frank Gorshin and then John Astin), the Penguin (Burgess Meredith), the Joker (Cesar Romero), King Tut (Victor Buono), Egghead (Vincent Price), and Catwoman (played at different times by Julie Newmar, Lee Ann Meriwether, and Eartha Kitt).

Batman incorporated the expressive art and fashion of the period in its sets and costumes. It also relied excessively on technological gadgetry, transforming the show into a parody of contemporary life. It was this self-reflexive parody/camp of the comic character that boosted the ratings of the program to the top ten during its first season. The show was not to be taken seriously. The acting was intentionally overdone and the situations extremely contrived. In the fight scenes, animated "Bangs," "Pows," and "Bops" would fill the screen every time a blow was struck. However, these characteristics, besides displeasing many fans of the superhero, were not enough to save the show.

Batman came to television supported by a massive advertising campaign followed by heavy merchandising placement. Directed toward adults and children, this campaign cost millions of dollars. Originally scheduled to start in the fall of 1966, the show debuted earlier, in the middle of the spring season. ABC aired *Batman* in prime time from January 12, 1966, to March 14, 1968. By the fall of 1966, ratings were already falling. To offset this trend, in the fall season of 1967, the show was cut to once a week and Batgirl (Yvonne Craig) was introduced. This time, she came to save the show from falling ratings and not to protect Batman and Robin against accusations of a homoerotic relationship, as was the case for her creation by the comic book writers in the mid-1950s. Batgirl, the daughter of Commissioner Gordon and a librarian, fought crime on her own and was many times paired with the Dynamic Duo. Her debut, however, was not enough to save the series. The producers tried to enliven the plots with the new sexy heroine, but it did not work, and *Batman* went off the air in midseason in the spring of 1968.

In September 1968 CBS produced an animated version of *Batman* in which the super duo shared one hour with Superman (in separated segments). Even though the program introduced a less camp version of Batman and Robin, possibly in response to fan criticisms to the prime-time serial, the program lasted only two seasons. Between February and September 1977, CBS broadcast an animated version with the voices of Adam West and Burt Ward. In September of that year, CBS changed the *New Adventures of Batman* to *The Batman/Tarzan Hour,* in which Batman and Tarzan shared one hour back to back, in separate segments.

In the fall of 1992, FOX television released a new animated series capitalizing on publicity for the movie *Batman Returns.* This new series followed the stylistic changes in the comic book hero. The FOX series earned critical and popular acclaim for its high-quality graphics and action-packed storylines. Interestingly, as in two of the Batman movies released in the 1990s, this new animated series erased Robin from the scene, possibly responding to criticism of the homoerotic subtext between the two heroes. Originally shown every afternoon, the FOX series moved to the Saturday-morning FOX line-up in the spring of 1994. At the same time the series also brought Robin back, possibly responding to the word that a new Batman film (*Batman and Robin,* 1997) would again include Robin in its plot.

ANTONIO C. LA PASTINA

Cast

Bruce Wayne (Batman)	Adam West
Dick Grayson (Robin)	Burt Ward
Alfred Pennyworth	Alan Napier
Aunt Harriet Cooper	Madge Blake
Police Commissioner Gordon	Neil Hamilton
Chief O'Hara	Stafford Repp
Barbara Gordon (Batgirl) (1967–68)	Yvonne Craig

Producers

William Dozier, Howie Horwitz

Programming History

120 episodes

ABC

January 1966–August 1967	Wednesday and Thursday 7:30–8:00
September 1967–March 1968	Thursday 7:30–8:00

Further Reading

Brooker, Will, *Batman Unmasked,* New York: Continuum, 2000

Grossman, G., *Saturday Morning TV,* New York: Arlington House, 1987

Pearson, R., and W. Uricchio, editors, *The Many Lives of Batman: Critical Approaches to a Superhero and His Media,* New York: Routledge, 1991

Reynolds, R., *Super Heroes: A Modern Mythology,* London: Batsford, 1992

BBC. *See* **British Television**

BBM Canada

BBM Canada is a cooperative, nonprofit Canadian audience research organization, which has at times struggled to survive in the face of increasing competition from the U.S.-based A.C. Nielsen Company (now known as ACNielsen), advances in electronic systems of audience measurement, and ambivalent support from the major Canadian broadcasters. BBM was created on May 11, 1944, on the recommendation of the Canadian Association of Broadcasters, and granted a government charter a year later. Originally called the Bureau of Broadcast Measurement (BBM), its first president was Lew Phenner of Canadian Cellucotton Products. It had no paid staff initially but received administrative assistance from the Association of Canadian Advertisers and technical support from the Canadian Broadcasting Corporation (CBC). The bureau's primary purpose in the beginning was to provide radio stations with reliable coverage estimates so that they could compete with the print media for advertising. The first BBM survey, released in October 1944, was conducted by the private ratings company Elliott-Haynes, using the unaided mail-ballot technique developed by CBS; instead of checking stations from a prepared list, participants compiled their own lists of stations to which they had listened.

Although financed largely by broadcasters, BBM was controlled for many years by advertising interests; of the nine positions on the original board of directors, three were filled by advertisers, three by advertising agencies, and three by broadcasters. Shortly after the creation of BBM, a similar organization called the Broadcast Measurement Bureau (BMB) was established in the United States. As a result of the efforts of Horace Stovin, chairman of BBM's technical committee, the two organizations worked in concert for a few years, using the same mail-ballot technique and running their surveys simultaneously. This enabled advertisers to operate on either side of the border with equal facility. However, BMB was criticized for its methods, plagued by high costs, and thrown into disarray by the resignation of its president, Rugh M. Feltis. In 1950 it threw in the towel and left the U.S. station coverage field to the A.C. Nielsen Company, which used an interview-aided recall method.

By the end of Phenner's presidency in 1951, BBM had increased the number of areas surveyed, introduced bilingual ballots in some areas, and more than doubled its broadcasting membership. However, a number of stations still refused to join, and in 1956 the CBC withdrew because of dissatisfaction with BBM's surveys. The same year, BBM began producing time-period ratings for radio and television using a panel-diary method pioneered in Canada by International Surveys Limited (ISL). The new surveys were initially conducted every spring and fall, with each member of participating households keeping a week-long diary of listening and viewing by half-hour periods. At the same time, the circulation surveys were increased from every other year to twice a year. However, the CBC remained critical of BBM operations and subscribed instead to the A.C. Nielsen Company, ISL, and McDonald Research. A 1962 CBC report criticized BBM's surveys for their "non-coverage, biased selection procedure, low response and poor quality of response." By then BBM was also coming under strong criticism from both advertisers and private broadcasters, and there was a danger that it might collapse.

Under Bill Hawkins of CFOS Owen Sound, BBM began to put its house in order. It revised its constitution so as to increase the representation of broadcasters, and in 1964 the bureau became the first ratings service in the world to introduce computerized sample selection. It also increased the number of surveys, redesigned the bilingual household diary, and switched its premium from a card of safety pins to a 50-cent coin. In terms of winning back confidence in the validity of its surveys, the most important step was taken in 1967, when BBM decided to switch from household diaries, which had usually been kept by the harried homemaker, to personal diaries sent to selected members of households—including children, although their diaries were filled out by an adult. This change increased the response rate for mailed diaries to almost 50 percent and facilitated the acquisition of demographic data. Within a few years, BBM became the only audience measurement service for radio in Canada, and in television the competition was reduced to Nielsen. Between 1963 and 1968, BBM increased its membership from 357 to 534, or about 90 percent of the broadcasting industry, including the CBC.

Unlike the original household diary, the new personal diary was used for both radio and television, largely for reasons of cost. In theory, however, the most reliable diary is the single-medium personal diary. In addition, the use of dual-media diaries irritated radio broadcasters, who argued that they provided BBM with twice as much revenue as television broadcasters but only received the same benefits. In 1975, therefore, following several studies and considerable debate, BBM adopted separate diaries for each medium, including different samples and survey dates. This move greatly increased survey costs, however, so that in the mid-1980s BBM implemented household flooding or saturation sampling for both radio and television. Ironically, this development brought BBM almost full-circle back to its original household diary technique and illustrated the fact that audience measurement methods generally are determined as much by economic considerations as by the requirements for scientific validity.

In the mid-1970s, BBM began investigating electronic measuring systems. A committee was set up to develop a proposal for a meter-based system for television, and a contract was signed with Torpey Controls Ltd. for a prototype using existing circuitry and the vertical blanking interval. Despite successful test results, however, the cost of switching from diaries to meters was considered prohibitive, especially since diaries would still be required for radio and to supplement the data gathered for television. It was not until the advent of "electronic diaries," or Peoplemeters, by the A.C. Nielsen Company and others in the early 1980s that BBM gave serious consideration to replacing its traditional diary system for television. Unlike the original Nielsen Audimeter, the Peoplemeter measured viewing rather than mere tuning and could track audience flow much more precisely.

In 1984, while still testing its new meter technology in the United States, Nielsen announced its intention to launch a Peoplemeter service in Canada. In response, BBM turned initially to Audits of Great Britain for help but then decided to invite bids from other companies as well, including Nielsen. In November 1985, A.C. Nielsen Company and BBM reached a tentative agreement by which Nielsen would provide BBM with Peoplemeter data from 1,800 Canadian households, which BBM could then market as it saw fit. The agreement later fell through, however, and in September 1989 Nielsen launched on its own a Peoplemeter service for network television in Canada. BBM tried to develop its own electronic television audience measurement (TAM) system in conjunction with Les Entreprise Videoway, but the tests results were unsatisfactory. Late in 1990, BBM and Nielsen resumed talks for a joint venture to extend Peoplemeters from the national network level to local and regional broadcasting. The following year, however, a proposed deal again fell apart, because of the concerns of local and regional broadcasters about costs and various technical matters. In 1996 BBM created a New Media division to measure interactive media, and in 1998 the bureau launched an advanced TV Peoplemeter service in Vancouver with plans to expand nationally. In 1999, ComQUEST Research Inc., a subsidiary of BBM formed a decade earlier, joined with Media Metrix Inc. to form Media Metrix Canada.

ROSS A. EAMAN

Further Reading

Blankenship, A.B., C. Chakrapani, and W.H. Poole, *A History of Marketing Research in Canada,* Toronto: Professional Marketing Research Society, 1985

Eaman, Ross A., *Channels of Influence: CBC Audience Research and the Canadian Public,* Toronto: University of Toronto Press, 1994

Beachcombers, The

Canadian Family Drama Series

The Beachcombers, in production for 19 years, was the longest running series drama in Canadian television history. Developed by Marc Strange, producer Phil Keatley, and a string of very good West Coast writers, this family series turned on the adventures of an ensemble of characters. Nick Adonidas (Bruno Gerussi) was a licensed beachcomber on the northwest coast of British Columbia. He was primarily involved with his young Native partner Jesse (Pat Johns) and his unscrupulous adversary and rival beachcomber Relic (Robert Clothier). Working out of the port of Gibson's Landing, Nick ran the *Persephone* into the inlets of the Sunshine coast, a setting filled with rugged individuals. The combination of characters, locations, and events strongly appealed to audiences abroad and was a driving force of the show's plot.

The format focused on physical action—boat chases, storms, rising tides, various rites of passage, a long-distance swim, taming a wild dog, a vision quest—but violence was largely confined to physical objects that break up or blow up or somehow threaten the characters. Comedy was part of almost every episode, and there was often a documentary flavor to the scenes of fishing, logging, and beachcombing. The show also used Canada's multicultural diversity. Germans, Italians, Japanese, Dutch, East Indians, Swedes, and even a Colonel Blimp from England, all provided opportunities for new plot developments.

Well-loved characters from the early seasons included the two children, Margaret and her older brother Hughie, and their "gran" who owned "Molly's Reach." As Jesse matured, he was joined by a younger sister, Sara, who also grew up on the show. He then married a widow, Laurel, whose son, Tommy, became the series' resident child. In *Beachcombers,* children of both sexes were respected as human beings who had much to learn and to share. Other running characters were Gus McLoskey, Captain Joe, and teenage homeless lad, Pat O'Gorman. Constable John, the well-meaning, slightly klutzy member of the Royal Canadian Mounted Police (RCMP) was one of the most popular of the continuing characters. He very seldom pulled a gun or even made an arrest.

The basic premise of *The Beachcombers* demanded that Nick remain a volatile Greek, unattached and available for many interesting women. Relic was his clever and unscrupulous antagonist for 19 years. Early on, his misanthropy was given a context in one of the best episodes, "Runt o' the Litter," written by Merv Campone. Born to a loveless Welsh coal-mining family, Relic is despised by his father—the father for whom he has nevertheless built fantasies of wealth in letters home. In this episode, Relic's "Da" is present, and in some sort of doomed attempt to win back the family's honor, he challenges Nick, 30 years younger, to an anchor pull. Others look on in horror as "Da" collapses in the sand, humiliated by yet another "failure." Relic, full of hatred and contempt, yet disappointed (every emotion to be read on the actor's face) grabs the rope, hauls the anchor across the line, and says bitterly to his father "go home." The old man weeps. The episode is a miniature tragedy. Such ambiguity and ambivalence appeared regularly in the show's early years, and writers and producers occasionally used noncomedic endings, resisting genre conventions.

The best episodes of the later years used two narrative strategies. The first was to continue the introduction of topical issues: the recurring issue of the confiscation of Japanese fishing boats during World War II, clear-cutting logging practices, or First Nations' land claims. This last topic was treated primarily in stories involving "The Reach," enabling writers to focus the issue in familiar terms using Laurel and Jesse, characters whom viewers knew well. Nick's fictional surrogate family and the show's viewers were disturbed—and informed. The second narrative strategy of the series' later period continued to revolve around conflicts between Relic and various other characters. As the 1980s brought increasing awareness of cultural appropriation and rising political tensions, however, this distinctive thread almost disappeared.

In a late attempt to boost ratings, a displaced urban mom, Dana, and her son, Sam, took over "The Reach." But conflicts constructed around urban vs. small-town, or capable Westerner vs. effete Easterner seemed not to interest the audience. The writing became tired, and the plots heavily reliant on action sequences. The series ended with an elegiac but rather lifeless one-hour special. To this day, however, the reruns and worldwide syndication of *Beachcombers* represent Canada and Canadians to millions of viewers around the world.

MARY JANE MILLER

See also **Gerussi, Bruno**

Cast

Nick Adonidas	Bruno Gerussi
Molly	Rae Brown
Hughie	Bob Park
Margaret	Nancy Chapple
Jesse	Pat Johns
Relic	Robert Clothier
Constable John	Jackson Davies

Producers

Philip Keatley, Elie Savoie, Hugh Beard, Bob Fredericks, Don S. Williams, Brian McKeown, Gordon Mark, Derek Gardner

Programming History

324 episodes
CBC

November 1972–October 1983	Sunday 7:00–7:30
November 1983–October 1989	Sunday 7:30–8:00
November 1989–April 1990	Wednesday 7:00–7:30

Further Reading

Miller, Mary Jane, *Turn Up the Contrast: CBC Television Drama Since 1952,* Vancouver: University of British Columbia Press, 1987
Miller, Mary Jane, *Rewind and Search: Conversations with the Makers and Decision-Makers of CBC Television,* Montreal: McGill-Queen's University Press, 1996

Beaton, Norman (1934–1994)

British Actor

Norman Beaton was one of those unique actors who managed to stand out in classical roles, yet excel in light comedies. From 1989 to 1994 he enjoyed nationwide popularity on British television with Channel 4's highly successful situation comedy series *Desmond's.* This show was described as an African-Caribbean equivalent of America's *The Cosby Show.* With sharp scripts by young black writer Trix Worrell, Beaton gave a brilliant performance as the manic owner of a South London barbershop.

Born in Guyana (then British Guiana), Beaton came to Britain in 1960. His reputation as an actor grew steadily. He progressed from regional theater to leading roles at the Old Vic, the National Theatre (where he played Angelo in a black-cast version of Shakespeare's *Measure for Measure* in 1981), and the Royal Court Theatre. Apart from Shakespeare, his theater roles also encompassed Pinter, Beckett, Gilbert and Sullivan, Brecht, Moliere, and pantomime. In 1974 he established the Black Theatre of Brixton, which was instrumental in developing black theatre in Britain. During this period he also became one of Britain's leading television actors. Among his biggest successes were dramatic roles in *Afternoon Dancing* (1974); *Black Christmas* (1977); *Empire Road* (1978–79), Britain's first all-black soap opera; *Play for Today's* "Easy Money" (1981); *Nice* (1984); *Dead Head* (1986); *Playing Away* (1986); *Big George Is Dead* (1987); *When Love Dies* (1990); and *Little Napoleons* (1993). He was also interviewed in the documentary

Black and White in Colour (1992), a history of black people in British television.

Alongside Lenny Henry, Norman Beaton was the star of British television's first black situation comedy series, *The Fosters,* which ran for two seasons in 1976–77. But the actor will be best remembered for *Desmond's.* As a result of its popularity, African-American television star Bill Cosby invited him in 1991 to make a couple of guest appearances in *The Cosby Show.* Beaton readily accepted a role as a cricket-loving doctor, and Cosby was so taken by the actor that he wore Beaton's gift of a *Desmond's* baseball cap in the show. Shortly after he died in 1994 at the age of 60, Channel 4 aired *Shooting Stars* in the series *Black Christmas,* with a memorable appearance by Beaton reading a sonnet by Shakespeare.

STEPHEN BOURNE

Norman (Lugard) Beaton. Born in Georgetown, British Guiana (now Guyana), October 31, 1934. Attended local schools in Georgetown. Married and divorced three times; children: Jeremy, Norman, Jayme, and Kim. Made debut as actor while at teacher training college, 1956; enjoyed success as singer and recording artist, becoming Guyana Calypso Champion, 1956; settled in Britain, 1960, and worked as teacher, Liverpool; appeared in repertory theatre, Liverpool, Bristol, and Worthing, late 1960s, made television debut, 1966; subsequently stage, television, and radio performer; chair: Black Theatre of Brixton, 1975; events subcommittee (U.K.), World Black and African Festival of Arts and Culture, 1976; Minorities Arts Advisory Service, 1979; artistic director, Ira Aldridge Memorial Theatre Company, 1983. Member: Consultative Committee for the Arts Britain Ignores, 1975; Afro-Asian subcommittee, British Actors Equity, 1979; West Midlands Arts and Drama Advisory Panel, 1979. Recipient: Variety Club of Great Britain Film Actor of the Year Award, 1978; *Caribbean Post* Golden Sunshine Award, 1978. Died December 13, 1994.

Television Series

1976–77	*The Fosters*
1978–79	*Empire Road*
1985	*Dead Head*
1989–94	*Desmond's*
1994	*Little Napoleons*

Television Plays

1977	*A Black Christmas*
1980	*Growing Pains*
1986	*Playing Away*

Films (selected)

Two for a Birdie; Pressure, 1975; *Black Joy,* 1977; *Barbados* (narrator), 1978; *Eureka,* 1982; *Real Life,* 1983.

Radio

I Come from the Sun, 1966; *Blues for Mister Charlie,* 1974; *Finding Manbee,* 1974; *Home Again,* 1975; *Carnival in Trinidad,* 1975; *Margie,* 1975; *Pantomime,* 1978; *Play Mas,* 1979; *Alterations,* 1980; *The Fast Lane,* 1980; *Remembrance,* 1981; *The British Empire Part 2,* 1982; *The Comedians,* 1984; *No Get Out Clause,* 1985; *Ascension Ritual,* 1985; *Still Life,* 1985; *Cricket's a Mug's Game,* 1985.

Recording (selected)

Come Back Melvina, 1959.

Stage

Le Bourgeois Gentilhomme (composer), 1956; *Jack of Spades,* 1965; *Cleo* (composer and narrator), 1965; *Bristol Fashion* (composer and narrator), 1966; *A Tale of Two Cities* (composer and narrator), 1966; *The Ticket-of-Leave Man,* 1968; *Richard Three* (composer and narrator), 1968; *The Merchant of Venice,* 1968; *Shylock X,* 1968; *Sit Down Banna* (writer); *The Country Wife* (also composer and narrator), 1968; *Bakerloo to Paradise,* 1968; *So You Think You're One of Us,* 1968; *The Tempest,* 1970; *Prometheus Bound,* 1971; *Arrest,* 1971; *Murderous Angels,* 1971; *Pirates,* 1971; *Tyger,* 1971; *The National Health,* 1971; *Cato Street,* 1971; *Two for a Birdie,* 1971; *The Threepenny Opera,* 1972; *Up the Chastity Belt,* 1972; *Signs of the Times,* 1973; *Talk Shop,* 1973; *Mind Your Head,* 1973; *Larry and Marian,* 1973; *Play Mas,* 1974; *Anansi and the Strawberry Queen* (director), 1974; *Jumbee Street March* (director), 1974; *The Black Mikado,* 1975; *Rum and Coca-Cola,* 1976; *Seduced* (director), 1978; *Sergeant Ola and His Followers,* 1979; *Nice,* 1980; *Samba,* 1980; *Measure for Measure,* 1981; *The Caretaker,* 1981; *The Night of the Day of the Imprisoned Writer,* 1981; *In the Mood,* 1981; *The Miser,* 1982; *The Sol Raye Variety Gala* (also director), 1982; *You Can't Take It With You,* 1983; *Cargo Kings,* 1983; *Jackanory,* 1983; *Blues for Railton,* 1985; *The Black Jacobins,* 1986.

Publication

Beaton but Unbowed (autobiography), 1986

Further Reading

Bourne, Stephen, *Black in the British Frame: Black People in British Film and Television 1896–1996,* London and Washington, D.C.: Cassell, 1996; second edition, as *Black in the British Frame: The Black Experience in British Film and Television,* London: Continuum, 2001

Pines, Jim, editor, *Black and White in Colour: Black People in British Television since 1936,* London: British Film Institute, 1992

Beavis and Butt-head

U.S. Animated Series

In March 1993 *Beavis and Butt-head* first aired on the U.S. cable network MTV. This show, which combined animation and music videos, was an example of the unique programming that MTV has consistently provided for its youthful demographics. The half-hour program alternated between a simple narrative, which focused on the exploits of two low-life adolescents, and clips from music videos, which the two teens commented on. Creator Mike Judge had penned the aimless duo for a festival of animation, and Abby Turkuhle, MTV's senior vice president picked up an episode for the network's animated compendium *Liquid Television.* MTV immediately contracted for 65 episodes from Judge, with Turkuhle as producer, and placed *Beavis and Butt-head* in the 7:00 and 11:00 P.M. weekday time slots.

The characters Beavis and Butt-head are rude, crude, and stupid and can be placed in the "dumb comedy" tradition, which includes Abbott and Costello, the Three Stooges, Cheech and Chong, *Saturday Night Live*'s Wayne and Garth, and FOX's *The Simpsons.* When *Beavis and Butt-head* debuted, television critics differed in their opinions, with some praising the show for daring to present the stupidity of male "metalheads" who watch too much television (effectively satirizing the core MTV audience), but others categorizing *Beavis and Butt-head* as another example of television's declining quality. *Beavis and Butt-head* did find an audience and began pulling in MTV's highest ratings, but the show was also quite controversial, instigating heated public debate on the interconnected issues of representations of violence in the media and generational politics surrounding youth subcultures.

In October 1993, a two-year-old Ohio girl was killed in a fire lit by her five-year-old brother. The children's mother said that her son was inspired by the pyromaniac proclivities of *Beavis and Butt-head.* This real-life event sparked the ire of media watchdog groups, who claimed that there was a direct link between the television show and the violent act of this impressionable child. One psychiatrist proclaimed *Beavis and Butt-head* a "*Sesame Street* for psychopaths." Concurrent Senate hearings on television violence placed these issues at the forefront of American cultural politics. Because of this incident, and given the cultural climate, MTV eliminated all references to fire, pulled four episodes off the air, and moved the cartoon to 10:30 P.M. only. MTV executives insisted that they changed the time slot not because they believed the show was directly responsible for the incident, but because they felt that it was designed for an older audience, and that a different time slot would allow them to target that audience more effectively. Claiming that 90 percent of the program's audience was over 12 years of age, MTV attempted to move the discussion away from the children's television debate.

Beavis and Butt-head was especially popular with people in their 20s. Many observers found it bothersome that young people enjoyed the show and laughed at its two imbecilic boys, even if these fans were much more intelligent than Beavis and Butt-head. In this sense, *Beavis and Butt-head* raised the issue of generational taste cultures. Definitions of "taste," Pierre Bourdieu argues,

> unite and separate, uniting those who are the product of similar conditions but only by distinguishing them from all others. And taste distinguishes in an essential way, since it is the basis of all that one has—people and things—and of all that one is for others, whereby one classifies oneself and is classified by others.

To the degree that taste cultures agree, they are brought together into a subcultural formation; but to this degree they are also separated from those with whom they differ. It was the "bad taste" of *Beavis and Butt-head*'s audience that bothered many, and this brings to the

Beavis and Butthead, Beavis, Butthead, 1993–97.
Courtesy of the Everett Collection

surface another one of the reasons why *Beavis and Butt-head* was so controversial.

Cultural critics, educators, and concerned parents gathered skeptically, sternly, and anxiously in front of the television set and passed judgment upon the "tasteless" *Beavis and Butt-head* show. Meanwhile, in an ironic reversal, *Beavis and Butt-head* countered by ascending the cultural hierarchy. The two youths channel-surfed, looking for videos that did not "suck" (i.e., those with heavy metal or hardcore rap, those that contained violence or encouraged genital response). In becoming the self-proclaimed Siskel and Ebert of music video, they served to evaluate pop culture with an unencumbered bottom line: does a music video "suck" or is it "cool"? As a television show, *Beavis and Butt-head* was certainly toward the lower end of traditional scales of cultural "quality," but these two animated "slackers" evaluated other media, and so pronounced their own critical opinions and erected their own taste hierarchies. Beavis and Butt-head had their own particular brand of "taste": they determined acceptability and unacceptability, invoking, while simultaneously upending, notions of "high" and "low" culture. In this manner, they entered that hallowed sphere of criticism, where they competed with others in overseeing the public good and preserving the place and status of artistic evaluation. They disregarded other accepted forms of authority, refusing to acknowledge their own limited perspectives. As with other critics, this attitude was an important part of their appeal. After all, critics are sought out for straightforward opinion, not muddled oscillation.

In this recuperation of the critical discourse, Beavis and Butt-head joined with their audience, approximating the contradictory impulses of contemporary cynical youth, who mixed their self-delusion with self-awareness. In the case of fans of *Beavis and Butt-head,* these lines of demarcation indicated both a generational unity and the generation-based barriers between the "baby boomers" and the "baby busters." The reputed cynicism of the "twentynothings" was on view as *Beavis and Butt-head* evoked both a stunted adolescence that was long past and an unsure and seemingly inaccessible future.

PAUL J. TORRE

Voices

Beavis, Butt-head Mike Judge

Producers

Abby Turkuhle, Mike Judge

Programming History

MTV
1993–97 Various times

Further Reading

Barrett, Wayne M., "*Beavis and Butt-Head:* Social Critics or the End of Civilization As We Know It?" *USA Today Magazine* (September 1994)

Gardner, James, "Beavis and Butt-head," *National Review* (May 2, 1994)

Hudis, Mark, "Heh-Heh. Heh-Heh. That's Cool. So You Thought *Ren and Stimpy* Was Tasteless: MTV's *Beavis and Butt-head* Go Beyond Tasteless and Crude," *MediaWeek* (August 2, 1993)

Hulktrans, Andrew, "MTV Rules (for a Bunch of Wussies)," *Artforum* (February 1994)

Katz, Jon, "Animated Arguments: Why the Show's Critics Just Don't Get It," *Rolling Stone* (March 24, 1994)

Leland, John, "Battle for Your Brain," *Newsweek* (October 11, 1993)

Mandese, Joe, "Job Is All Fun and Games for MTV New Media Exec: Del Sesto Interacts with *Beavis and Butt-head,*" *Advertising Age* (February 7, 1994)

Young, Charles M., "Meet the Beavis! The Last Word From America's Phenomenal Pop Combo," *Rolling Stone* (March 24, 1994)

Zagano, Phyllis, "*Beavis and Butt-head,* Free Your Minds!" *America* (March 5, 1994)

Belgium

Belgium is not the easiest media landscape to explain. The broadcasting market reflects the structure of the Belgian state and society, which has long been based on the segmentation in various sociopolitical and linguistic pillars. Each politico-ideological opinion organized itself as a separate microcosmos. The Flemish or Dutch-speaking Flanders and the Francophone Wallonia constitute two primary linguistic regions in Belgium. Within these regions, most of the early radio stations in the 1920s were directly linked to political parties representing the four main political tendencies. Catholic, Socialist, Liberal-conservative and Nationalist parties each had private radio stations. In 1930 a national, bilingual public corporation body, the INR-NIR (Institut National de Radiodiffusion—Nationaal Instituut voor Radio-omroep), was set up, fully funded and controlled by the government. After World War II, the INR-NIR was granted a monopoly and the private, ideological radio stations were incorporated within the structure of the national broadcasting corporation. Under the form of "guest" programs, the major political parties, management and trade unions, and religious factions were allocated airtime.

In 1960 the unified INR-NIR was split into two sections: the Flemish BRT (Belgische Radio en Televisie), later renamed VRT (Vlaamse Radio en Televisie), and the Francophone RTB (Radiodiffusion-Télévision Belge), later renamed RTBf. However, instead of giving each sociopolitical pillar its own channel (as was done in the Netherlands), the decision was made to create a system of so-called "internal plurality." Belgian public broadcasting was supposed to provide for a proportionate representation of all political and philosophical opinions within one institute. Within such a setting the influence exerted by the political powers remained high. Political control was maintained as all top functions were prearranged and allocated, while the other jobs were also more accessible for party members or for people who had party support. This Belgian custom of preferring party loyalty over the qualities needed to do a job well is called politicization. While this system is gradually disappearing, it is not yet completely dispensed with. In critical moments, for instance on the eve of elections, most media still show their partisan colors.

Belgium can moreover be described as a country that is gradually evolving to a federalized structure. Simplifying Belgium's complicated structure, one could say that there are two main linguistic groups: a Flemish/Dutch-speaking majority (about 60 percent of the population) and a Walloon/French-speaking minority (about 40 percent of the population). The so-called "regionalization" Law of February 2, 1977, not only reinforced the differences between these "language" communities, but also complicated the Belgian media policy. The control of broadcasting, for instance, is in the hands of the Flemish and Walloon Ministers of culture or the media, who are part of the regional governments, while technical issues remain national matters. The two communities have also grown apart in the field of media policy. In part this results from their different political structures: in the Walloon region predominantly socialist and humanistic, in Flanders predominantly liberal-conservative and Catholic. The media policies also differ, however, because of external factors; for instance, the influence of the commercial Luxembourg-based TV station RTL on French-speaking Belgium forces the RTBf to different policy options than the Flemish stations. Therefore, one cannot speak of Belgian media, except with reference to the official law gazette (Belgisch Staatsblad/Moniteur Belge) and the national press agency Belga. All major newspapers, magazines, radio and television stations are either Flemish/Dutch or Walloon/Francophone, though some media in one community have links with media in the other linguistic community. Some media also cater to the other language communities living and working in Belgium.

As a consequence, the Francophone and Flemish television programs show a different visual culture. The presentation of the news broadcasts is different, as are entertainment programs, shows, and comedies. The distinction is even obvious in commercials. Moreover, the two linguistic communities have little interest in one another's television programs. Flemish people hardly ever watch the Francophone RTBf or RTL-TVi, while Walloons watch the Flemish VRT or VTM even less. The ratings clearly show that viewing habits are predominantly linked with culture and language.

Furthermore, Belgium is the most densely cabled country in the world (94 percent of all households are connected to a cable network). In the beginning the cable companies only distributed the national programs, but very soon the programs of foreign television stations were also distributed. Therefore, the factual monopoly of the public broadcasters was indirectly undermined by the cable networks, which offered an increasing number of television stations (at least 25, often more than 50 channels). RTBf was losing viewers to RTL and the French channels, BRT to the Netherlands and to a certain degree to UK and international channels.

The major part of the Flemish population predominantly watches Dutch-language programs (including those of The Netherlands), with the BBC producing the second-most-watched programming. The Walloons almost exclusively tune in on the RTBf and other Francophone channels (including those of Luxembourg and France). Exception has to be made for popular sport programs, especially soccer, and to lesser degree for films. In those cases the more educated segments of the population also look beyond the language borders.

Another noteworthy shift, which took place in most European countries during the 1980s and 1990s, was of a commercial nature. Deregulation, commercialization, internationalization, privatization, and commodification changed the face of broadcasting (a "boom" of new channels and program genres and a crisis within the public broadcasting sector) but not its fundamental existing practices. In other words, this shift has to be seen in connection with the already mentioned politicization of the Belgian society. Politics have always been prominently present in the discussion on television, and the establishment of commercial television in Flanders was not the result of strictly economic but rather political pressure.

Already in the 1960s, public broadcasting was seen as vulnerable when traditional parties complained about the supposed lack of objectivity of the news on the public broadcasting corporation BRT. While extensive research showed little or no systematic distortion, politicians emphatically tried to meddle with the contents of media products. Gradually a direct censorship of broadcasting was replaced by more subtle forms of influencing and self-censorship.

The undermining of the public broadcasting monopoly was first begun by illegal local radio stations ("radio pirates"), which emerged in the late 1970s. In September 1981 these radio stations were legalized in Wallonia, and in May 1982 the same happened in Flanders. Advertising remained illegal at first, but under political and commercial pressure, the ban on radio advertising was lifted in December 1985.

In 1981 the coalition agreement between the Christian-democrats and conservative-liberals proposed a commercial television channel that would be placed in the hands of the press. The Flemish business world was reluctant about the proposal, which was initially met with extremely negative reactions from advertising companies and advertisers as well as from press companies. The first group preferred commercials on the BRT to a commercial channel that still had to be established. They argued that the BRT already reached the viewing public and that a new channel would not only be confronted with growing pains but would also have to compete with foreign channels. The press was divided. They were afraid that a commercial channel would drain away even more money from the press sector. They demanded guarantees from the government: a majority share of control for the Flemish publishers and an advertising monopoly for the commercial station VTM (Vlaamse TV Maatschappij).

Notwithstanding the fact that the European Commission objected to the Flemish broadcasting decree because of its advertising monopoly, the obligated majority participation of the press, and the obligated share of Flemish productions, the commercial station VTM started broadcasting on February 1, 1989. Contrary to all expectations, it was a success from the start.

In 1997 the government finally accepted the objections by the European Commission and promised to adapt its legislation. As a result VT4, a Britain-based affiliate of the American-Scandinavian media group SBS that transmits its Dutch-language programs through the Flemish cable network, had to become "Flemish."

The immense success of VTM forced the public broadcaster to reinvent itself, a process that took many years and put public television through a number of crises. Gradually, it regained most of the market share it lost to the commercial stations. Today the two public television channels seem to have a stable and even slightly growing audience share, even though they are now facing many commercial channels. Three of those channels belong to the Flemish VTM; another is VT4. Ten local commercial television stations, a handful of specialized channels (business, life style, travel, and music) and a few commercial radio networks complete the picture.

Consequently, channel proliferation has also led to viewer diversification and segmentation. The competition for highly specialized audience segments is becoming very sophisticated. As a result, market strategies have taken over the programming of most channels, including the public service providers. The situation in Wallonia is similar. Two public channels, two main private channels, and about a dozen local stations are competing on the television market. A particular feature of that market is the presence of French stations.

The newest digital "revolution," by which television converges with computer functions and multimedia features, may change broadcasting itself. An interactive, multi-usable medium will replace one-way television and promises users the ability to communicate with each other, companies, and governments. Television won't just be for watching anymore, but it will also become a tool for shopping, working, and maybe even voting. Still, many legal, technological, financial, and content-related questions need to be answered, making any precise prediction about the future highly speculative.

With no clear view of who is authorized to lay down a digital policy, no legal framework concerning digital broadcasting and hardly any public debate about the issue, digital broadcasting in Belgium is somewhat of a non-event. So far, the VRT offers one digital audio package (using the DAB Eureka147-standard) with seven radio stations: the five national stations, the international service, and a brand new, digital-only channel called DAB Klassiek (round-the-clock classical music). Since almost no one in Flanders has a digital receiver yet, this is no more than an experiment.

Belgium faces its own kind of digital divide: one between Flanders and Wallonia. Indicators show that computer and Internet use in Flanders is more established than in Wallonia. Within each region the digital divide is threefold: an age gap, a gender gap, and an education gap. In short, older people, women, and less-educated people are lagging behind. The Flemish government, as part of its digital policies, has awarded the VRT the role of "bridge builder" to correct the digital divide. Therefore, the VRT is seen as a major player and ally in the Flemish government's plan to take the region into the digital future.

In sum, culture and media policies have never received priority treatment by the Belgian lawmakers. Many media laws have only confirmed situations that were already in existence. In other words, Belgium has followed a media policy of laissez-faire. Therefore, many media laws are ambiguous and can be interpreted in different ways. In recent years media policies have been strongly oriented toward deregulation and liberalization of the TV market: new private initiatives have been supported such as commercial radio, pay television, and new commercial television networks.

No measures have been taken against the increasing concentration of the media. International and national business interests get an increasing grip on the Belgian media landscape. The government policy is regularly dictated by economic and financial interests. That is why the government is often confronted with faits accomplis. As a result, Belgium is drifting toward a commercially dictated political and media reality.

JAN SERVAES

Further Reading

d'Haenens, Leen, and Frieda Saeys, "Media Politics in Dutch-speaking Belgium: The Reluctant Mutation from a Monopoly to a Multi-channel Landscape," in *Media Dynamics and Regulatory Concerns in the Digital Age,* edited by d'Haenens and Saeys, Berlin: Quintessenz Verlag, 1998

Servaes, Jan, "Media and Politics in Belgium," in *Changing Media and Communications: Concepts, Technologies and Ethics in Global and National Perspectives,* edited by Yassen Zassoursky and Elena Vartanova, Moscow: ICAR, Moscow State University Press, 1998

Bell Canada

Canadian Telecommunications Company

Bell Canada, a subsidiary of BCE Inc. of Montreal, is the largest of Canada's telecommunications companies. It provides telephone service to about 9 million customers in the provinces of Ontario and Quebec, and in portions of the Northwest Territories. Bell was created by federal act of Parliament in 1880 and since 1906 has been subject to regulation by a succession of federal regulatory agencies, currently by the Canadian Radio-television and Telecommunications Commission (CRTC).

Bell Canada's involvement in broadcasting type services dates back to the earliest years of telephony in Canada. Bell's predecessor companies, controlled by Alexander Melville Bell (father of Alexander Graham Bell), offered point-to-mass content services over telephone lines as early as 1877: songs, duets, glees, and sermons, for example, were transmitted for reception by subscribers using ordinary telephone instruments as receivers. As in other jurisdictions, these experimental closed-circuit content services dwindled within a few years, to re-emerge in the 1950s with the advent of cable television.

Bell entered Canadian broadcasting in 1922 by securing licenses for radio stations in Toronto and Montreal. These one-year licenses were allowed to lapse in 1923, however, when Bell signed a patent-sharing agreement with radio set manufacturers (Canadian Westinghouse, International Western Electric, and Canadian General Electric) and with a radio telegraph company (Marconi) whereby the signatories agreed to split the fields into exclusive domains: Bell henceforth was not to engage in broadcasting or in radio telegraphy, while the other parties agreed not to compete with Bell in telephony.

Resulting from this 1923 contract bifurcating communication into distinct broadcasting and telephone (telecommunication) sectors, unique regulatory frameworks arose for each. Broadcasting companies came to be regulated under the provisions of a succession of broadcasting acts, requiring that licensed broadcasting undertakings contribute to the Canadian cultural and political identity. Broadcasting undertakings, furthermore, were to retain full responsibility for all programming carried; as a practical matter this meant that broadcasting organizations or their affiliates produced themselves a large portion of their Canadian content.

The legal/regulatory paradigm governing the telephone industry differed markedly from that for broadcasting. Telephone companies, as common carriers, came to be precluded from influencing message content; their mandate, rather, was simply to relay any and all messages on a nondiscriminatory basis upon the request of clients and upon payment of government-approved tariffs. As well, telephony, unlike broadcasting, was presumed to be a "natural monopoly," whose prices and profits needed to be subject to regulatory supervision and approval.

Although precluded from engaging directly in broadcasting, telephone companies nonetheless figured prominently in the provisioning indirectly of broadcasting services. With the advent of network broadcasting, for example, telephone companies such as Bell Canada provided inter-urban transmission facilities interlinking stations regionally, nationally, and internationally. Telephone companies also served the cable television industry by providing independent cable firms with poles, ducts, rights-of-way, and with certain essential equipment such as coaxial cables. Initially telephone companies forced upon cable firms highly restrictive contracts intended to foreclose all possibility of competition in the provisioning of two-way, point-to-point telecommunication services. By the late 1970s, the CRTC had overturned most of these restrictive contractual provisions, however, requiring telephone companies under its jurisdiction to provide reasonable access to telco poles and rights-of-way.

Courtesy of Bell Canada

Under Canadian law, cable TV constitutes a component of the broadcasting system, and the CRTC as of the mid-1990s had been unable and unwilling to license telephone companies to provide cable-type services. Bell Canada and other Canadian telephone companies for many years argued, however, that they should be permitted to own exclusively any and all communication wires into the home or office, including the cable TV connection. Telephone companies proposed leasing portions of the bandwidth of their (to be acquired) broadband facilities to licensed cable entities that would thereby provide cable TV service in the mode of a value-added carrier. These proposals have never met with government approval.

More recently Canadian telephone companies led by Bell, as part of an "information highway" initiative, have argued that the technological convergence of broadcasting, telecommunications, and computer communications not only erodes previously distinct industry demarcations, but as well makes anachronous regulatory policies premised on such distinctions. Bell has argued further that telephone companies should now be permitted to enter directly the cable television industry, whether by leasing bandwidth from cable companies or by interconnecting their own coaxial or fiber optic facilities with those of cable companies, in order to receive signals for retransmission from cable headends. Telephone companies have argued further that cable systems, if they should choose so to do, should be permitted to enter the domain of the telephone companies in the provisioning of two-way, point-to-point telecommunications services. Telephone companies wish also to engage in video program creation, distribution, storage, and related activities, for example the sale of advertising, long associated with broadcasting, and as well to enter emerging interactive, multimedia services.

Allowing telephone companies to enter cable TV and other content services would appear to be the likely next step in the CRTC's "pro-competitive" policy stance toward telecommunications. Indeed in

September 1994 the commission published its "Review of Regulatory Framework" decision, wherein it announced its intention to promote "open entry and open access" to the greatest extent possible for "all telecommunications services." In March 1995, in response to a request from the Canadian federal government, the CRTC held public hearings concerning, in part, the terms under which telephone companies should be allowed to enter cable and content services.

As competition increasingly penetrates more and more areas of communication, venerable regulatory techniques, principles, and goals are threatened. The principle of common carriage and the separation of content from carriage, for example, will be undermined if and when telephone companies are allowed to enter cable TV and other content creation markets. Likewise, the historical goal of safeguarding and promoting Canadian culture through broadcasting will prove to be increasingly elusive as internationally interconnected information highways are put in place. Information highway is the apotheosis of convergence, and hence of deregulation, but in Canada market forces historically have militated against indigenous program production and distribution. A deregulated information highway, whether controlled or not by erstwhile telephone companies enhances the power of those who would further commoditize information, as opposed to formulating information policy for social, political, and cultural purposes.

ROBERT BABE

Further Reading

Babe, Robert E., *Telecommunications in Canada: Technology, Industry, and Government,* Toronto and Buffalo, New York: University of Toronto Press, 1990

Babe, Robert E., *Communication and the Transformation of Economics: Essays in Information, Public Policy, and Political Economy,* Boulder, Colorado: Westview, 1995

Bell Globemedia

Bell Globemedia was created in January 2001 when BCE Enterprises, one of Canada's wealthiest publicly traded companies, finalized an agreement with the Thomson Corporation to establish a communications conglomerate of impressive size and scope. Headquartered in Toronto, the firm's communications assets include the country's principal private television network, CTV, an assortment of specialty analog and digital channels, the *Globe and Mail* (Canada's self-styled "national newspaper"), the direct-to-home content provider Bell ExpressVu, interests in Internet provider Sympatico and other interactive services, and Telesat, a satellite broadcast distribution service.

The empire built by BCE Enterprises grew on the foundation of Bell Canada, which held the local and long-distance telephone monopoly in much of the country before telecommunications were deregulated. BCE was transformed into a diversified entity, and has a robust investment arm, but remains focused on communications. Telephone utilities are prominent among its core assets.

BCE controls just over 70 percent of the shares in Bell Globemedia, with the remaining stock held by one-time newspaper giant Thomson Corporation and the personal investment company of Ken Thomson (who continues to chair the board of the *Globe and Mail*). Convergence opportunities drove the deal, but Thomson also wanted to preserve the *Globe and Mail* after divesting other newspapers in a global chain founded by his father. He invested $385 million (Canadian) in the joint venture, a significant amount that is nonetheless dwarfed by BCE's stake.

In a move that came to have profound consequences for the entire broadcasting system, BCE acquired CTV for $2.3 billion early in the year of 2000. Thanks to a series of acquisitions and structural changes, CTV no longer resembled the loose network of its founding era of the 1960s. Eighteen of the network's 28 stations had been brought under a single corporate umbrella, along with six network-owned affiliates of the Canadian Broadcasting Corporation. At the time of the merger CTV also owned a number of cable channels and had purchased a majority of specialty channel player Netstar.

The takeover of CTV was but one in a string of such transactions during what was to become Canada's year of media convergence. A frenzy of mergers and acquisitions resulted in the consolidation of several media conglomerates. Bell Globemedia's fiercest challenger for private sector paramountcy, CanWest Global, emerged at roughly the same point in time and with a similarly diverse communications portfolio. Lesser companies followed suit and entered into deals that resulted in a major reshaping of the broadcast industry in 2000.

The flurry of transactions alarmed critics. It was feared that Bell Globemedia and other exponents of convergence would seek to maximize profits at the expense of content and reduce workforces through the sort of rationalization that often follows on the heels of integrations. CTV had attracted criticism over the years for relying too heavily on imported American fare in prime time, and investing too meanly in quality domestic programming. The network's nightly national newscast had long dominated ratings, and its supper-hour news programming has tended to eclipse the offerings of competitors in local markets. Did the merger herald an erosion of news and other fare on the broadcast side?

In December 2000 the Canadian Radio-television and Telecommunications Commission (CRTC) formally approved the takeover of CTV by the budding Bell Globemedia partnership. The CRTC did attach a number of conditions to its decision that it claimed would result in a significant infusion of funds for Canadian programming. The CRTC ruling required that Bell Globemedia invest some $230 million (roughly 10 percent of the transaction) in its broadcast holdings. Approximately 60 percent of the total was to be funneled into programming, the vast majority commissioned from domestic independent production companies. Bell Globemedia was also obliged to auction off Sportsnet, one of Canada's two main specialty sports channels available on cable, after CTV had purchased arch-rival The Sports Network.

There was another important, albeit indirect, outcome to the merger. BCE owned and operated Bell ExpressVu, one of two digital, direct-to-home satellite services in Canada. With the addition of CTV, the new Bell Globemedia would be in the position of both providing content and distributing it. Conventional analog cable operators argued that they, too, should be allowed to own channels as well. Advocacy groups such as the Friends of Canadian Broadcasting opposed this on the grounds that it would pave the way for greater concentration of ownership. Fearing that they would be disadvantaged when it came to favorable channel placement and marketing, specialty channel licensees not in the cable business also spoke out against this prospect.

In June 2001 the CRTC agreed with the cable companies. In its ruling the CRTC did say that all channels should receive fair and equitable treatment and identified a number of concrete steps that should be taken to embody this principle. Critics were not mollified. To them, further concentration seemed inevitable and the CRTC had effectively blessed the entanglements that increasingly characterize broadcast media ownership in Canada.

Another controversial aspect of the creation of Bell Globemedia involved the propriety of uniting a prestigious newspaper with a major television network. Historically, cross-ownership of media enterprises has been frowned upon by media regulators in Canada. Sensitivities about the *Globe and Mail* have been especially acute given the newspaper's national reach and its influence on policymakers and other news media. Until the convergence boom, newspaper chains and broadcasting enterprises partnerships were generally kept apart or participated in informal ownership and content-sharing relationships. In August 2001 the CRTC agreed to extend CTV's license for a further seven years. In doing so it cited promising "journalistic synergies" between the newsrooms of CTV and the *Globe and Mail,* while insisting that editorial control was divided.

As of January 2002, the Bell Globemedia stable included its CTV network properties and CBC affiliates, together with interests in 13 specialty and pay channels and five digital specialty channels. Although primarily serving English-speaking audiences, Bell Globemedia has branched out to hold a stake in six French-language specialty and digital services. On a variety of indices, this roster makes Bell Globemedia the largest private-sector player in Canadian broadcasting.

ROBERT EVERETT

See also **Canadian Broadcasting Corporation Newsworld; Canadian Television Network**

Further Reading

BCE Enterprises, Montreal, *Annual Report 2000*

Canada, Canadian Radio-television and Telecommunications Commission, *Annual Report 2001,* Ottawa, 2002

Damsell, Keith, and Gordon Pitts, "Round 2 Bell Rings in Convergence Fight, Toronto, *Globe and Mail* (April 13, 2002)

Fraser, Matthew, "Media Merger Frenzy Will Go On in 2001," *National Post* (January 2, 2001)

Hutchinson, George, "Media 'Convergence' Is Bad News," *Toronto Star* (June 8, 2001)

Scoffield, Heather, "CRTC Okays Newsroom Convergence, *Globe and Mail* (August 3, 2001)

Bellamy, Ralph (1904–1991)

U.S. Actor

Ralph Bellamy, the character actor of stage and film, began his career in 1922, when he joined a traveling troupe of Shakespearean players. Later that same year, Bellamy performed in stock and repertory theaters with the Chautauqua Road Company. In 1929 he made his Broadway debut in *Town Boy,* followed by a screen debut in 1931 in *The Secret Six.* In 1948 he made his television debut in the *Philco Television Playhouse.* He then went on to star in one of the medium's first crime series, *Man against Crime,* from 1949 to 1955.

In a career that spanned six decades on stage and screen, Bellamy played roles that fell into three broad categories: (1) the rich, reliable, but dull figure who is jilted by the leading lady; (2) the detective who always finds his prey; and (3) the slightly sinister but stylish villain. Usually appearing in supporting roles, Bellamy acted in more than 100 films. He starred in several "B" movies, notably four in which he portrayed the detective Ellery Queen. Bellamy often said he never regarded himself as a leading man, so no one else did either. He is best remembered on film and television as the "dull other man." It was on the stage that Bellamy made his mark as a strong actor, in plays such as *Tomorrow the World, State of the Union,* and, most notably, *Sunrise at Campobello.* It was in the latter play that Bellamy built his reputation as an actor, by portraying Franklin Delano Roosevelt. By delving into the history of Roosevelt the man and the politician, Bellamy came to an understanding of the personality and psyche of the character. He then spent weeks at a rehabilitation center learning how to manage braces, crutches, and a wheelchair so that his portrayal of Roosevelt after he was stricken with polio would be realistic and accurate. Character acting was defined and perfected by Ralph Bellamy. He won the Tony and New York's Critics Circle Award as best actor in *Sunrise at Campobella* and starred in the subsequent film version in 1960.

Bellamy appeared in several television series during the 1960s and 1970s, including *The Eleventh Hour* (1963–64), *The Survivors* (1969), *The Mostly Deadly Game* (1970), and *Hunter* (1976). He returned true to his roles as detective, villain, and other man in each of these series. It was in 1969 that Bellamy made a radical character shift by playing a diabolist in *Rosemary's Baby.* More recently, he played a benevolent shipping magnate in the 1990 movie *Pretty Woman* and a millionaire in *Trading Places* (1983). He again played Roosevelt in the television miniseries *The Winds of War* (1983) and *War and Remembrance* (1988).

A champion of actors' rights, Bellamy founded the Screen Actors Guild and served four terms as president of the American Actors' Equity between 1952 and 1964. He doubled the equity's assets within six years and established the first actors' pension fund. Bellamy guided the Actors' Equity through the political blacklisting of the McCarthy era by forming a panel that established ground rules to protect members against unproved charges of being members of or sympathiz-

Ralph Bellamy.
Courtesy of the Everett Collection

ers with the Communist Party. He also actively lobbied for the repeal of theater admission taxes and for income averaging in computing taxes for performers.

"B" movie actor, the Ellery Queen of the 1940s, champion of actors' rights, a well-known name in the film and television industries, a portrayer of Franklin Delano Roosevelt in the 1950s and 1980s, Bellamy was most noted as an actor for his roles as the "nice but bland other man." No one played love's loser better than Bellamy. "I never got the girl," he once recalled.

GAYLE M. POHL

See also **Detective Programs**

Ralph Bellamy. Born in Chicago, Illinois, June 17, 1904. Attended New Trier High School, Wilmette, Illinois. Married: 1) Alice Delbridge, 1922 (divorced, 1931); 2) Catherine Willard, 1931 (divorced, 1945); children: Lynn and Willard; 3) Ethel Smith, 1945 (divorced); 4) Alice Murphy, 1949. Formed acting troupe, North Shore Players, 1922; stage manager, Madison Stock Company, 1922–24; formed Ralph Bellamy Players, stock company, Des Moines, Iowa (later moved to Nashville, Tennessee), 1927; appeared on Broadway in *Town Boy,* 1929; founding member and member, first Board of Directors, Screen Actors Guild; president for 12 years of Actors' Equity; appeared in film, theater, and radio, 1940s; began television career in *Man against Crime,* live production, 1949–54. Presidential appointee, National Board of the United Service Organization (USO), 1958–60; chair, New York Regional National Council of Christians and Jews Brotherhood Week, 1963; Member: Presidential Commission on the 50th Anniversary of the Department of Labor, 1962; founding member, California Arts Commission; member, board of directors, People to People, Project Hope, Theatervision, 1972–73; Board of Governors, Academy of Motion Picture Arts and Sciences, 1982. Recipient: New York Drama Critics Award, 1958; Tony Award, 1959; Honorary Academy Award, 1986. Died in Santa Monica, California, November 29, 1991.

Television Series

1949–54	*Man against Crime*
1957–59	*To Tell the Truth* (quiz show panelist)
1961	*Frontier Justice* (host)
1963–64	*The Eleventh Hour*
1969–70	*The Survivors*
1970–71	*The Most Deadly Game*
1977	*Hunter*
1985–86	*Hotel*
1989	*Christine Cromwell*

Television Miniseries

1976	*Once an Eagle*
1976	*Arthur Hailey's The Moneychangers*
1977	*Testimony of Two Men*
1978	*Wheels*
1983	*The Winds of War*
1985	*Space*
1989	*War and Remembrance*

Made-for-Television Movies

1967	*Wings of Fire*
1969	*The Immortal*
1970	*The Most Deadly Game*
1972	*Something Evil*
1974	*The Missiles of October*
1975	*Search for the Gods*
1975	*Murder on Flight 502*
1975	*The Log of the Black Pearl*
1975	*Adventures of the Queen*
1976	*Return to Earth*
1976	*Nightmare in Badham County*
1976	*McNaughton's Daughter*
1976	*The Boy in the Plastic Bubble*
1977	*Charlie Cobb: Nice Night for a Hanging*
1978	*The Millionaire*
1978	*The Clone Master*
1979	*The Billion Dollar Threat*
1980	*Power*
1980	*The Memory of Eva Ryker*
1980	*Condominium*
1984	*Love Leads the Way*
1985	*The Fourth Wise Man*
1989	*Christine Cromwell: Things That Go Bump in the Night*

Television Specials

1961	*Brief Encounter*
1962	*Saturday's Children*
1975	*The Devil's Web*

Films (selected)

The Narrow Corner, 1933; *Hands across the Table,* 1935; *His Girl Friday,* 1940; *Dance Girl Dance,* 1940; *Sunrise at Campobello,* 1960; *Rosemary's Baby,* 1968; *Oh, God!,* 1977; *Trading Places,* 1983; *Coming to America,* 1988; *Pretty Woman,* 1990.

Stage (selected)

Town Boy, 1929; *Tomorrow the World; State of the Union; Sunrise at Campobello,* 1958–59.

Publication

When the Smoke Hit the Fan, 1979

Further Reading

"Bellamy, Ralph," *Current Biography* (January 1992)
Clarke, Gerald, "The $40 Million Gamble," *Time* (February 7, 1983)
Novak, Ralph, "Pretty Woman," *People Weekly* (April 9, 1990)
"Sundown for a Pro," *People Weekly* (December 16, 1991)
"The Talk of the Town," *The New Yorker* (April 9, 1990)

Ben Casey

U.S. Medical Drama

Ben Casey, a medical drama about the "new breed" of doctors, ran on ABC from October 1961 to May 1966. James Moser, who also created the Richard Boone series *Medic,* created *Ben Casey,* and Matthew Rapf produced the program for Bing Crosby Productions. The show was very successful for ABC and broke into the top 20 shows for its first two years. A 1988 made-for-TV movie, *The Return of Ben Casey,* enjoyed only moderate success.

Ben Casey was one of two prominent medical dramas broadcast during the early 1960s. In *The Expanding Vista,* Mary Ann Watson characterizes this show as a "New Frontier character drama." Indeed, the title character often stood as a metaphor for the best and the brightest of his generation. Often the ills to which Casey attended were stand-ins for the ills of contemporary society. Symbolism was the stock-in-trade of *Ben Casey,* as evidenced by its stylized opening: a hand writing symbols on a chalk board as Sam Jaffe intoned, "Man, woman, birth, death, infinity."

County General Hospital was the setting for the practice of its most prominent resident in neurosurgery, Ben Casey, played by Vince Edwards. Edwards had been discovered by Bing Crosby, who saw to it that his protégé had a suitable vehicle for his talents. As Casey, Edwards was gruff, demanding, and decisive. Casey did not suffer fools lightly and apparently had unqualified respect only for the chief of neurosurgery, Dr. David Zorba (Sam Jaffe). The only other colleagues from whom he would seek counsel were anesthesiologist Dr. Maggie Graham (Bettye Ackerman) and Dr. Ted Hoffman (Harry Landers). Both Hoffman and Graham provided counterpoints of emotion and compassion to the stolid Casey. Virtually every episode in the entire first season of *Ben Casey* involved a patient with a brain tumor. But the nature of the malady was merely a device that allowed Casey to interact with a panoply of individuals with unique problems, only one of which was their illness. Like many shows of its era (*Route 66, The Fugitive*), the core of *Ben Casey* could be found in the development and growth of the characters in any given episode. It was what Casey brought to a person's life as a whole that really drove the show.

Patients were not the only ones with problems. In *Ben Casey* the limits of medicine, the ethics of physicians, and the role of medicine in society were examined. The hospital functioned as a microcosm of the larger society it served. The professionals presented in *Ben Casey* were a tight group sworn to an oath of altruistic service. The majority of physicians in the employ of County General were not terribly inflated with self-importance. Their world was not so far removed from the world inhabited by those they helped. The problems that plagued the world outside the walls of County General could often be found within as well. During their work at County General, Casey and his colleagues came into contact with representatives from every level of society. Part of that contact was learning about and making judgments on certain societal issues and problems. Racial tension, drug addiction, the plight of immigrants, child abuse, and euthanasia were a few of the issues treated in *Ben Casey.*

The series followed an episodic format for its first four years. The final season saw Dr. Zorba replaced by Dr. Freeland (Franchot Tone) and a move to a serial, soap opera-like story structure. In so doing, *Ben Casey* moved away from the examination and possible correction of society's problems and toward a more conventional, character-driven drama. Vince Edwards, hoping to flex his creative muscles, directed several of the episodes of the last two seasons. Chiefly in these

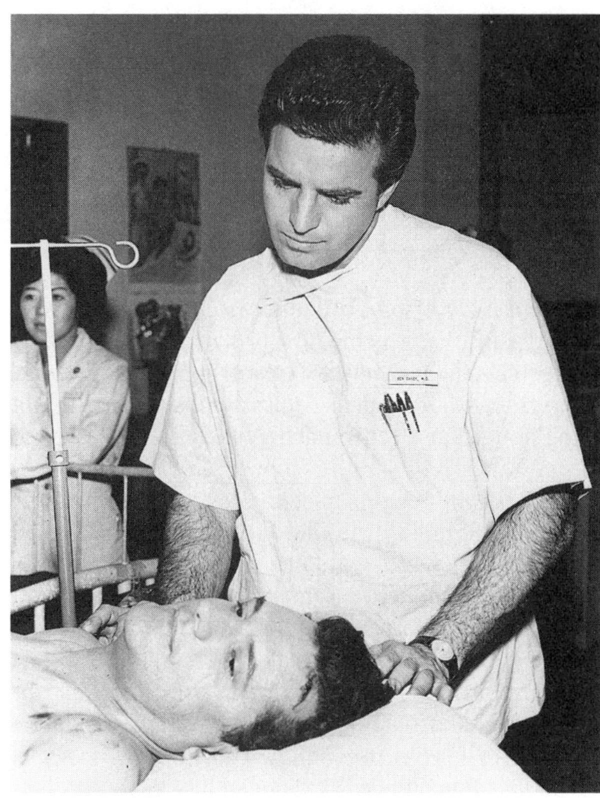

Ben Casey, Steven Hill, Vince Edwards, 1961–66; "Legacy from a Stranger."
Courtesy of the Everett Collection

ways, *Ben Casey* departed from the characteristics of the "New Frontier character drama" and more closely resembled an ordinary medical melodrama. In March 1966, ABC canceled the show.

The real value of *Ben Casey* was in its presentation of maladies of the body and mind as representative of larger problems that existed in society. The show was one of Hollywood's reactions to Federal Communications Commission Chairman Newton Minnow's plea for better television. With the character of Ben Casey at the center of each episode, the show presented (often quite skillfully) the interrelationship of mental, physical, and societal health.

JOHN COOPER

See also **Workplace Programs**

Cast

Dr. Ben Casey	Vince Edwards
Dr. David Zorba (1961–65)	Sam Jaffe
Dr. Maggie Graham	Bettye Ackerman
Dr. Ted Hoffman	Harry Landers
Nick Kanavaras	Nick Dennis
Nurse Wills	Jeanne Bates
Jane Hancock (1965)	Stella Stevens
Dr. Mike Fagers (1965)	Ben Piazza
Dr. Daniel Niles Freeland (1965–66)	Franchot Tone
Dr. Terry McDaniel (1965–66)	Jim McMullan
Sally Welden (1965–66)	Marlyn Mason

Producers

James E. Moser, John E. Pommer, Matthew Rapf, Wilton Schiller, Jack Laird, Irving Elman

Programming History

153 episodes
ABC

October 1961–September 1963	Monday 10:00–11:00
September 1963–September 1964	Wednesday 9:00–10:00
September 1964–March 1966	Monday 10:00–11:00

Further Reading

Alley, Robert S., "Media, Medicine, and Morality," in *Understanding Television: Essays on Television as a Social and Cultural Force,* edited by Richard P. Adler, New York: Praeger, 1981

Turow, Joseph, *Playing Doctor: Television, Storytelling, and Medical Power,* New York: Oxford University Press, 1989

Watson, Mary Ann, *The Expanding Vista: American Television in the Kennedy Years,* New York: Oxford University Press, 1990

Bennett, Alan (1934–)

British Actor

Alan Bennett has been a household name in British theatre ever since he starred in and coauthored the satirical review *Beyond the Fringe* with Dudley Moore, Peter Cooke, and Jonathan Miller, in 1960 at the Edinburgh Festival. Later, the same show played to packed houses in London's West End and in New York. Although Bennett started by writing and acting for the stage, he very soon turned his attention to writing plays for television.

Bennett's career, though less spectacular than those of his *Fringe* companions, has displayed great diversity and solid achievement. To many he is regarded as perhaps the premiere English dramatist of his generation. This is all the more surprising given the low-key themes and understated expression of the "ordinary people" who populate his dramatic world. Like the poetry of Philip Larkin (another Northerner whose writings he admires), his work frequently focuses on the everyday and the mundane: seaside holidays, lower-middle-class pretensions, obsessions with class, cleanliness, propriety, and sexual repression. Like Larkin, Bennett casts a loving but critical eye on the objects of his irony, revealing what underlies the apparently trivial language of his protagonists. In "Say Something Happened," the clichéd expression of Dad is shown to be more constructive than the social work jargon of his interviewer June, since it functions to set at ease his gauche interlocutor. While June clings to lexical propriety, Dad attends to the much more important level of the speech act. In *Kafka's Dick* and *Me—I'm Afraid of Virginia Woolf,* Bennett pokes mischievous fun at Wittgenstein and the ordinary language philosophy of Austin, but his ear for telling dialogue reveals that he shares with those philosophers an awareness that language is a series of games, operating at different levels, whose rules can only be inferred from within. We cannot assume that we know what people mean by reference to our own usage.

Bennett's dramas are easier to enjoy than to categorize, and the writer himself is a dubious guide. In the introduction to the five teleplays written for London Weekend Television in 1978–79, *The Writer in Disguise,* Bennett identifies the silent central character in three of them as "the writer in disguise." To the five plays written for the BBC in 1982 Bennett supplies a title *Objects of Affection,* but immediately disclaims he felt any such theme at the time of writing. The writer is not the center of attention: Trevor in *Me—I'm Afraid of Virginia Woolf* is pathologically obsessed with not being noticed and yet somehow becomes the center of others' attentions. He becomes an absent center through whom other characters seek to make sense of their lives. Similarly, the Chinese waiter Lee, sent on a wild goose chase in search of a female admirer by a cruel fellow-worker, is a device to exhibit the casual xenophobia and fear of intimacy of the English lower-middle classes.

The occasion for a Bennett play is often a holiday, or at least a break from routine: these are suggested in the titles of *All Day on the Sands, One Fine Day, Afternoon Off,* "Our Winnie," *A Day Out,* and even "Rolling Home." The break serves to highlight the peculiar nature of ordinary living by providing a distanced view of it: in extreme instances the distance indicates a near breakdown, as the estate agent Phillips in *One Fine Day* takes to living in a tower block he is unable to let, overwhelmed by the inauthenticity of the language and values of his employment. Hospitals figure in "Rolling Home", "Intensive Care" and "A Woman of No Importance": here too, it is the intrusion of death that leads to a search for the significance of life, though frequently it is the lives of the visitors, not the patient, that are subjected to scrutiny, and Bennett's irony militates against any portentousness about life.

"A Woman of No Importance" marks an important step in Bennett's development: It is the first play featuring a single actress (Patricia Routledge), speaking directly to the camera with minimal scene changes, thus anticipating the format adopted for the six monologues of *Talking Heads.* The play is essentially a character study of a boring woman whose life revolves around the minutiae of precedence and status of canteen groupings. Peggy sees herself as creating happiness, order, and elegance in a shabby world, but the audience sees her as bossy, insensitive, and narrow-minded. Bennett's critique is subtle and sensitive as the gap between her and our vision of the world progressively narrows. Peggy is half-aware of the futility of her life, which endows her struggle to make significance out of trivia with a heroic pathos. A more blink-

Alan Bennett, 1965.
Courtesy of the Everett Collection

ered version of this character is to be found in Muriel in "Soldiering On" in *Talking Heads,* who refuses to acknowledge her son's embezzlement and husband's incest. Here, our sympathy for her gradual social and economic privation is offset by the damage to the family of her collusive blindness to its shortcomings. The most successful of *Talking Heads* is probably "Bed Among the Lentils," the narrative of an alcoholic vicar's wife (brilliantly played by Maggie Smith) who is restored to some sense of self-worth by an affair with an Asian shopkeeper. Possessed of greater intelligence and insight than her husband and his adoring camp-followers, she is, despite her wit and perceptiveness, a figure of pathos: marooned in a marriage and a social role she despises, but lacking the courage to abandon them or the belief that real change is possible. In Bennett's world those who succeed do so by unselfconscious egoism, energy, and lack of imagination, but are marginal to our attention; conversely, the failures exhibit insight and wit, but a crippling self-awareness that inhibits action.

While Bennett's "Englishness" and "Northerness" (terms by no means synonymous) are evident, they are no more nationalistic nor restricting than Chekhov's "Russianness." The characters he writes about are rooted in a particular social environment, but the issues they highlight are of universal appeal: the essential isolation of human beings within the protective social roles they have adopted or have had thrust upon them, the gap between self-awareness and the capacity to change, the crippling power of propriety. All of these themes are relayed through a tone that is simultaneously ironic and tender.

BRENDAN KENNY

Alan Bennett. Born in Leeds, Yorkshire, England, May 9, 1934. Attended Leeds Modern School, 1946–52; Exeter College, Oxford, 1954–57, B.A. 1957. National service with Joint Services School for Linguists, Cambridge and Bodmin, 1957–59. Temporary junior lecturer in history, Magdalen College, Oxford, 1960–62. Stage debut at Edinburgh Festival, 1959; subsequently wrote and appeared in acclaimed comedy revue *Beyond the Fringe,* 1960; has since worked as writer, actor, director, and broadcaster for stage, television, radio, and films. D.Litt.: University of Leeds, 1990. Honorary Fellow, Exeter College, Oxford, 1987. Trustee, National Gallery, since 1994. Recipient: *Evening Standard* Awards, 1961, 1968, 1971, and 1985; Tony Award, 1963; Guild of Television Producers Award, 1967; Broadcasting Press Guild Awards, 1984 and 1991; Royal Television Society Awards, 1984 and 1986; Hawthornden Prize, 1989; Olivier Award, 1990.

Television Series

1966–67 *On the Margin* (also writer)
1987 *Fortunes of War*

Television Specials

1965 *My Father Knew Lloyd George* (also writer)
1965 *Famous Gossips*
1965 *Plato—The Drinking Party*
1966 *Alice in Wonderland*
1972 *A Day Out* (also writer)
1975 *Sunset Across the Bay* (also writer)
1975 *A Little Outing* (also writer)
1978 *A Visit from Miss Prothero* (writer)
1978 *Me—I'm Afraid of Virginia Woolf* (writer)
1978 *Doris and Doreen* (*Green Forms*) (writer)
1979 *The Old Crowd* (writer)
1979 *Afternoon Off* (writer)
1979 *One Fine Day* (writer)
1979 *All Day On the Sands* (writer)

1982 *Objects of Affection* ("Our Winnie," "A Woman of No Importance," "Rolling Home," "Marks," "Say Something Happened," "Intensive Care") (also writer)
1982 *The Merry Wives of Windsor*
1983 *An Englishman Abroad* (writer)
1986 *The Insurance Man* (writer)
1986 *Breaking Up*
1986 *Man and Music* (narrator)
1987 *Talking Heads* ("A Chip in the Sugar," "Bed Among the Lentils," "A Lady of Letters," "Her Big Chance," "Soldiering On," "A Cream Cracker Under the Settee") (also writer)
1987 *Down Cemetery Road: The Landscape of Philip Larkin* (presenter)
1988 *Dinner at Noon* (narrator)
1990 *Poetry in Motion* (presenter)
1990 *102 Boulevard Haussmann* (writer)
1991 *A Question of Attribution* (writer)
1991 *Selling Hitler*
1992 *Poetry in Motion 2* (presenter)
1994 *Portrait or Bust* (presenter)
1995 *The Abbey* (presenter)
1998 *Talking Heads 2*
2000 *Telling Tales*

Films

Long Shot, 1980; *A Private Function* (writer), 1984; *Dreamchild* (voice only), 1985; *The Secret Policeman's Ball,* 1986; *The Secret Policeman's Other Ball,* 1982; *Pleasure at Her Majesty's; Prick Up Your Ears* (writer), 1987; *Little Dorrit,* 1987; *Parson's Pleasure* (writer); *The Madness of King George* (writer), 1995.

Radio

The Great Jowett, 1980; *Dragon,* 1982; *Uncle Clarence* (writer), 1986; *Better Halves* (narrator), 1988; *The Lady in the Van* (writer, narrator), 1990; *Winnie-the-Pooh* (narrator).

Stage

Better Late, 1959; *Beyond the Fringe* (also co-writer), 1960; *The Blood of the Bambergs,* 1962; *A Cuckoo in the Nest,* 1964; *Forty Years On* (also writer), 1968; *Sing a Rude Song* (co-writer), 1969; *Getting On* (writer), 1971; *Habeas Corpus* (also writer), 1973; *The Old Country* (writer), 1977; *Enjoy* (writer), 1980; *Kafka's Dick* (writer), 1986; *A Visit from Miss Prothero* (writer), 1987; *Single Spies* (*An Englishman Abroad* and *A Question of Attribution*) (also writer and director), 1988; *The Wind in the Willows* (writer), 1990; *The Madness of George III* (writer), 1991; *Talking Heads* ("A Chip in the Sugar," "Bed Among the Lentils," "A Lady of Letters," "Her Big Chance," "Soldiering On," "A Cream Cracker Under the Settee") (also writer), 1992.

Publications (selected)

Beyond the Fringe (with Peter Cook, Jonathan Miller, and Dudley Moore), 1962, 1963
Forty Years On, 1969
Getting On, 1972
Habeas Corpus, 1973
The Old Country, 1978
Enjoy, 1980
Office Suite, 1981
Objects of Affection (five teleplays), 1982
A Private Function, 1984
The Writer in Disguise (five teleplays and introduction), 1985
Prick Up Your Ears, 1987
Two Kafka Plays, 1987
Single Spies, 1989
Talking Heads (collection of six monologues), 1988, 1990
The Wind in the Willows, 1991
Forty Years On and Other Plays (collection), 1991
The Madness of George III, 1992
Writing Home, 1994
The Laying on of Hands, 2001
The Clothes They Stood Up In, 2001

Further Reading

Bergan, Roland. *Beyond the Fringe... and Beyond: A Critical Biography of Alan Bennett, Peter Cook, Jonathan Miller, and Dudley Moore.* London, 1990
Kendle, Burton S. "Alan Bennett," *Contemporary Dramatists,* edited by K.A. Berney, London and Detroit, Michigan: St. James, 1973; 5th edition, 1993
Wu, Duncan. *Six Contemporary Dramatists: Bennett, Potter, Gray, Brenton, Hare, Ayckbourn.* London: St. Martin's Press, 1995

Benny, Jack (1894–1974)

U.S. Comedian

Jack Benny was among the most beloved American entertainers of the 20th century. He brought a relationship-oriented, humorously vain persona honed in vaudeville, radio, and film to television in 1950, starring in his own television series from that year until 1965.

Benny grew up in Waukegan, Illinois, and went on the vaudeville stage in his early teens playing the violin. The instrument quickly turned into a mere prop, and his lack of musicianship became one of the staples of his act. Benny's first major success was on the radio. He starred in a regular radio program from 1932 to 1955, establishing the format and personality he would transfer almost intact to television. Most of his films capitalized on his radio fame (e.g., *The Big Broadcast of 1937*), although a couple of pictures, *Charley's Aunt* (1941) and *To Be or Not to Be* (1942), showed that he could play more than one character.

Benny's radio program spent most of its run on NBC. In 1948 the entertainer, who had just signed a deal with the Music Corporation of American (MCA) that allowed him to form a company to produce the program and thereby make more money on it, was lured to CBS, where he stayed through the remainder of his radio career and most of his television years.

His television program evolved slowly. Benny made only four television shows in his first season. By the 1954–55 season, he was up to 20, and by 1960–61, 39. The format of *The Jack Benny Show* was flexible. Although each week's episode usually had a theme or starting premise, the actual playing out of that premise often devolved into a loose collection of skits.

Benny played a fictional version of himself, Jack Benny the television star, and the program often revolved around preparation for the next week's show—involving interactions between Benny and a regular stable of characters, which included the program's announcer, Don Wilson, and its resident crooner, Dennis Day. Until her retirement in 1958, Benny's wife, Mary Livingstone, portrayed what her husband termed in his memoirs "a kind of heckler-secretary," a wisecracking friend of the family and of the television program.

The main point of these interactions was to show off Benny's onscreen character. The Jack Benny with whom viewers were familiar was a cheap, vain, insecure, untalented braggart who would never willingly enter his fifth decade. Despite his conceit and braggadocio, however, Jack Benny's video persona was uniquely endearing and even in many ways admirable. He possessed a vulnerability and a flexibility few male fictional characters have achieved.

His myriad shortcomings were mercilessly exposed every week by his supporting cast, yet those characters always forgave him. They knew that "Jack" was never violent and never intentionally cruel, and that he wanted nothing (not even money) so much as love. The interaction between this protagonist and his fellow cast members turned *The Jack Benny Show* into a forum for human absurdity and human affection.

"Human" is a key word, for the Benny persona defied categorization. Benny had shed his Jewish identity along with his Jewish name on his way from vaudeville to radio. The character he and his writers sustained on the airwaves for four decades had no ethnicity or religion.

He had no strongly defined sexuality either, despite his boasts about mythical romantic success with glamorous female movie stars and his occasional brief dates with working-class women. In minimizing his ethnicity and sexuality, the Benny character managed to transcend those categories rather than deny them. Beneath his quickly lifted arrogant facade lurked an American Everyperson.

The Jack Benny Show further crossed boundaries by being the only program for decades that consistently portrayed Americans of different races living and working side by side. Jack Benny's ever-present butler/valet/nanny, Rochester (portrayed by Eddie Anderson), had first appeared on the Benny radio program as a Pullman porter but had pleased audiences so universally that he moved into Benny's fictional household. Unlike the popular African-American radio characters Amos and Andy, Rochester was portrayed by a black actor, Eddie Anderson, rather than a white actor in blackface.

Rochester's characterization was not devoid of racism. As Benny's employee, he was, after all, always in a nominally subservient position. Nevertheless, neither Rochester nor his relationship with his employer

Jack Benny.
Courtesy of the Everett Collection

was defined or limited by race. Like the other characters on the program, Rochester viewed Benny with slightly condescending affection, and frequently got the better of his employer in arguments that were obviously battles between peers. Rochester was, in fact, the closest thing the Benny character had to either a spouse or a best friend.

The complex relationship between the two was typical of the Benny persona and its fictional formula, which relied on character rather than jokes. Benny sustained the persona and the formula in his regular half-hour program and in a series of one-hour specials, until both wore out in the mid-1960s. He returned to television from time to time thereafter to star in additional specials but never dominated American ratings as he had in the 1950s, when he spent several years in the Nielsen top 20s and garnered Emmy Awards year after year.

Off screen, Benny was apparently ambivalent about television. In his memoirs, *Sunday Nights at Seven,* posthumously published with his daughter as coauthor in 1990, he wrote, "By my second year in television, I saw that the camera was a man-eating monster. It gave a performer close-up exposure that, week after week, threatened his existence as an interesting entertainer." Despite this concern, Jack Benny and American television clearly did well by each other.

TINKY "DAKOTA" WEISBLAT

See also ***Jack Benny Show, The***

Jack Benny. Born Benjamin Kubelsky in Waukegan, Illinois, February 14, 1894. Married: Mary Livingstone (Sadie Marks), 1927. Served in U.S. Navy, World War I. Worked in vaudeville as violinist in orchestra pit, 1909–14; after military service in World War I, returned to vaudeville, touring as comic and dancer under name Ben K. Benny; small-part actor in Broadway musicals during the 1920s; first film appearance, *Bright Moments* (short), 1928; role as the emcee in feature film *The Hollywood Revue of 1929,* 1929; worked on Broadway in successful *The Earl Carroll Vanities,* 1930; radio debut, *The Ed Sullivan Show,* 1932; own radio series, *The Jack Benny Show,* 1933–41; starring film roles in *Buck Benny Rides Again,* 1940, *Love Thy Neighbor,* 1940, and *Charley's Aunt,* 1941; notable performance in film *To Be or Not to Be,* 1942; had own television series *The Jack Benny Show,* 1950–64 (CBS), 1964–65 (NBC); later guest roles in films. Died in Beverly Hills, California, December 26, 1974.

Television Series

1950–64	*The Jack Benny Show*
1964–65	*The Jack Benny Show*

Films

Bright Moments (short), 1928; *The Hollywood Revue of 1929,* 1929; *Chasing Rainbows,* 1930; *Medicine Man,* 1930; *Mr. Broadway,* 1933; *Transatlantic Merry-Go-Round,* 1934; *Broadway Melody of 1936,* 1935; *It's in the Air,* 1935; *The Big Broadcast of 1937,* 1936; *College Holiday,* 1936; *Artists and Models,* 1937; *Manhattan Merry-Go-Round,* 1937; *Artists and Models Abroad,* 1938; *Man about Town,* 1939; *Buck Benny Rides Again,* 1940; *Love Thy Neighbor,* 1940; *Charley's Aunt,* 1941; *To Be or Not to Be,* 1942; *George Washington Slept Here,* 1942; *The Meanest Man in the World,* 1943; *Hollywood Canteen,* 1944; *It's in the Bag,* 1945; *The Horn Blows at Midnight,* 1945; *Without Reservations,* 1946; *The Lucky Stiff,* 1949; *Somebody Loves Me,* 1952; *Who Was That Lady?,* 1962; *It's a Mad, Mad, Mad, Mad World,* 1963; *A Guide for the Married Man,* 1967; *The Man,* 1972.

Radio

The Jack Benny Show, 1933–41.

Stage

The Earl Carroll Vanities, 1930.

Publication

Sunday Nights at Seven: The Jack Benny Story (with Joan Benny), 1990

Further Reading

Fein, Irving, *Jack Benny: An Intimate Biography,* New York: Putnam, 1976

Jack Benny: The Radio and Television Work, New York: Harper, 1991

Josefberg, Milt, *The Jack Benny Show,* New Rochelle, New York: Arlington House, 1977

Benson

U.S. Situation Comedy

Benson premiered in August 1979 on ABC, a spin-off of the popular program *Soap,* which ran from 1977 to 1981. Robert Guillaume took the title role in the new series, joining a new cast of characters and moving from the home of a wealthy (if utterly absurd) family to a butler's position in a governor's mansion. The series ran for seven consecutive seasons, with a few minor cast changes and with Benson's promotions from his first assignment to state budget director and, finally, to lieutenant governor.

Although the storylines and the character of Benson poke fun at the incompetence of those in positions of wealth and power, the portrayal of an African-American man as a butler remained a strong stereotype that served to uphold racial power relations and reinforce social values in the neoconservative United States of the 1970s and 1980s. Despite conscious efforts of writers and actors, the main character's role remains problematic: why in contemporary television was an African-American man still portrayed as a servant? However lighthearted and fictitious *Benson* might have been, its significance in television history is both serious and real.

Comedy has long been a means of representing characters of color in both American film and television. Hollywood film picked up where minstrel shows left off, using stereotypes (and often white actors in blackface makeup) to portray African-American characters. One stereotype in particular that became nearly omnipresent in many classic Hollywood films is the figure of the black servant, a remnant of the antebellum American south. This stereotypical trope of the servant is seen time and time again, subtly suggesting the superior status of whites and simultaneously dictating to the viewing audience the position of African Americans in society. The persistence of such representation in contemporary television demonstrates the continuing use of characters of color for racial demarcation and for comic relief.

As a source of humor, *Benson* is historically significant in television. Few American programs featuring characters of color have been dramas. Instead, beginning with *Beulah* and *Amos 'n' Andy* in the 1950s and continuing into the present, most programs with minority characters have fallen into the genre of situation comedy. Issues of race are to be addressed, it seems, through laughter. Although the character of Benson was indeed allowed to rise along the occupational ladder, this advancement was carefully contained within the realm of comedy. It was also controlled by the narrative, as evidenced in a 1983 episode in which the ghost of *Soap* character Jessica Tate (Benson's former, white employer) haunts Benson and reminds him of how far he has come.

The premise in the half-hour sitcom *Benson* is that the title character has been "loaned" by Jessica to her cousin, Governor James Gatling, after his wife passes away. This loan becomes permanent as Benson's utility becomes indispensable to the governor. Through his service in the governor's mansion—saving the governor from political blunders, managing both the political and domestic staff, and helping to raise the governor's daughter, Katie—Benson is seen as the source of not only composure and wisdom but also of warmth. At the same time, he is known for his sharp wit, often expressed at the expense of other characters on the show.

The critical view of *Benson* has generally been positive and, moreover, addresses the issue of Benson as a butler by arguing his is a "dignified" portrayal. Never-

Benson, Robert Guillaume, 1979–86.
Courtesy of the Everett Collection

theless, the limitations of the role are clearly set in the way in which he is characterized. For example, the headlines of some reviews instruct their readers in specific ways: "*Benson* Moves Out and Up," "Benson Butlers His Way into a Sensational Spin-off," "ABC May Clean Up with *Benson.*" One critic describes Benson as the "smug, cocky and perennially bored black butler." These descriptions and plays on words only emphasize the position that Benson is expected to occupy; his rise "out and up" is deemed unusual, irreverent, and ultimately funny. In this light, a "cocky" servant who is smarter than his masters is not a subversive portrayal, as some may wish to believe; it is exactly the opposite. The often overdetermined praise of Benson's independence and sophistication perhaps reveals the effort on the part of critics to compensate for the fact that Benson is a servant. Unfortunately, arguing that these characteristics of an African-American man/butler are exceptional only further dictates what his place is supposed to be. To be "uppity" or insolent, as Benson is sometimes described, implies that he must somehow be put back down where he belongs.

This contradiction—Benson as the defiant, yet also stereotypical, character—seemed to have confused audiences. Although *Benson* was not among the top 10 shows (it was in the top 25 in its first year only), the program lasted for seven seasons. And although Robert Guillaume was nominated several times for an Emmy Award for Best Leading Actor during his years on *Benson,* he won only in the category of Best Supporting Actor for his work in *Soap.* While the producers and writers of the show worked consciously to make Benson's character reflect the strides in civil rights that were made in the previous decades, they still chose to use the stereotype of the black servant. Hence, though far lower rated, the fact that *Benson* far outlasted such programs as *Taxi* and even its parent program, *Soap,* might suggest that American television audiences were ultimately sustaining and supporting the status quo.

Guillaume has taken a critical stance toward his own role, saying variously, "I will not go back to 1936"; "This is not going to be one of those plantation-darky roles"; "It was employer-employee, not master-servant." Still, despite Guillaume's talent and his determined attempts to bring substance and accuracy to his role, the long-standing cultural connotations of an African-American servant predominated the program. *Benson* is not derogatory or inflammatory and, in fact, can be quite entertaining. Nevertheless, the program stands as part of an ongoing practice of representing people of color in subordinate positions. Though liberal, the television industry is by no means revolutionary. Accordingly, *Benson* attempts to portray the life of an African American in a progressive and "dignified" manner, yet cannot escape the trappings of a deeply embedded cultural classification.

LAHN S. KIM

See also **Racism, Ethnicity, and Television; *Soap***

Cast

Benson DuBois	Robert Guillaume
Gov. James Gatling	James Noble
Katie Gatling	Missy Gold
Gretchen Kraus	Inga Swenson
Marcy Hill (1979–81)	Caroline McWilliams
John Taylor (1979–80)	Lewis J. Stadlen
Clayton Endicott III (1980–88)	Rene Auberjonois
Pete Downey (1980–85)	Ethan Phillips
Frankie (1980–81)	Jerry Seinfeld
Denise Stevens Downey (1981–85)	Didi Conn
Mrs. Cassidy (1984–88)	Billie Bird
Sen. Diane Hartford (1985–88)	Donna Laurie

Producers

Paul Junger Witt, Tony Thomas, Susan Harris, Don Richetta

Programming History

158 episodes
ABC

September 1979–July 1980	Thursday 8:30–9:00
August 1980–March 1983	Friday 8:00–8:30
March 1983–April 1983	Thursday 8:00–8:30
May 1983–March 1985	Friday 8:00–8:30
March 1985–September 1985	Friday 9:00–9:30
October 1985–January 1986	Friday 9:30–10:00
January 1986–August 1986	Saturday 8:30–9:00

Further Reading

Bretz, Mark, "Robert Guillaume Keeps Rolling Along as TV's Smug, Cocky Benson," *St. Louis Globe-Democrat* (July 24–25, 1982)
Gelman, Steve, "*Benson* Soft-Soaps No One," *TV Guide* (September 15, 1979)
Holsopple, Barbara, "*Benson* Moves Out and Up," *Pittsburgh Press* (July 22, 1979)
Krupnick, Jerry, "Benson Butlers His Way into a Sensational Spin-off," Newark *Star-Ledger* (September 13, 1979)
Miller, Ron, "Benson," *San Jose Mercury News* (January 24, 1985)
Torrez, Frank, "ABC May Clean Up with *Benson,*" *Los Angeles Herald Examiner* (September 13, 1979)

Berg, Gertrude (1899–1966)

U.S. Actor, Writer, Producer

Gertrude Berg was perhaps the only woman to attain authorial control of a prime-time network television series during the 1950s, serving as the creator, principal writer, and star of her own weekly situation comedy, *The Goldbergs.* When the show came to television, she was already thoroughly identified in the public mind with her lifelong dramatic persona, Molly Goldberg, a Jewish-American mother she had developed into a quintessential stereotype on a long-running radio series. Public familiarity with the Molly character tended to obscure her career as a remarkably prolific writer.

Berg began writing and performing skits at her father's resort hotel in the Catskill Mountains, later studying playwriting at Columbia University. After selling several dramatic scripts to radio, her big break came in 1929 with the debut of her own series on NBC, *The Rise of Goldbergs* (later shortened to *The Goldbergs*). It was among the most popular programs of the radio era, often rivaling *Amos 'n' Andy,* another NBC series based on racial stereotypes, at the top of the national ratings. Fifteen-minute episodes of *The Goldbergs* aired Monday through Friday, placing the form of the program somewhere between the contemporary parameters of situation comedy and daytime soap opera. Berg wrote most of the episodes, which, after a 20-year production run, numbered more than 5,000. A pioneer in product tie-in concepts, the writer-performer capitalized on the Molly Goldberg phenomenon with short stories, stage plays, a feature film, and even a cookbook.

The Goldbergs premiered on television as a CBS sitcom in 1949. During its five-season production run, the show would move around the dial to NBC, DuMont, and first-run syndication. A sentimentalized vision of melting-pot assimilation, *The Goldbergs* was "pure schmaltz," a mythic idealization of the American dreams and aspirations of a lower-class Jewish family in the Bronx. The differences between traditional shtetl values and middle-American values are consistently exposed as merely stylistic. The older members of the family, including Molly, her husband Jake, and Uncle David, all speak with thick Yiddish accents, while Molly's children, Rosalie and Sammy, sound more like the voices heard on *Ozzie and Harriet.* When it was becoming clear in the mid-1950s that ethnic sitcoms of this type were on the way out, Berg revamped the show by moving the family to the suburbs, renaming the series *Molly* (1954–55), and offering it in first-run syndication. These changes, however, could not save it.

For the next five years Berg was a frequent guest on comedy-variety shows, appearing with Perry Como, Kate Smith, Ed Sullivan, and others. She also played several dramatic roles on anthology showcases, such as *The U.S. Steel Hour* and *The Alcoa Hour.* In 1961

Gertrude Berg.
Courtesy of the Everett Collection

Berg attempted to return to situation comedy with *Mrs. G Goes to College* (also called *The Gertrude Berg Show*) on CBS. It was the first time she had appeared on series television as any character other than Molly Goldberg. The old assimilationist themes remained at the heart of Berg's work; she played Sarah Green, an elderly widow pursuing the education denied her by a poverty-stricken youth. Once again, Jewish values and American values were portrayed as distinguishable only in matters of style.

Berg's autobiography, *Molly and Me,* was published in 1961. Her papers, including many of her radio and television scripts, are collected at the George Arents Research Library at Syracuse University. It is worth noting that Berg took a stand against the blacklist in 1951, refusing to fire her long-time costar Philip Loeb (he resigned to prevent the show's cancellation and later committed suicide).

David Marc

See also **Goldbergs, The**

Gertrude Berg. Born Gertrude Edelstein in New York City, October 3, 1899. Extension courses in playwriting at Columbia University. Married: Lewis W. Berg, 1918; children: Harriet and Cherney Robert. First radio script, *Effie and Laura,* 1927; wrote, starred in, and produced the NBC radio series situation comedy, *The Rise of the Goldbergs,* starting 1929; *The Rise of the Goldbergs* cast and Goldberg toured vaudeville, 1934–36; half-hour radio serial *The House of Glass,* 1935; first film, *Make a Wish,* 1937; wrote and starred in Broadway reworking of the Goldberg saga, titled *Me and Molly,* 1948; wrote and starred in *The Goldbergs,* CBS television, 1949–54; with N. Richard Nash co-wrote the movie version, *Molly,* starring in the title role, 1951; starred in *The Goldbergs,* NBC-TV, 1952 and the summer of 1953, then locally on WABD (Channel 5), 1954; appeared in MGM's *Main Street to Broadway,* 1953; acted in non-Molly Goldberg roles in stage plays, from 1956; starred in television series *Mrs. G Goes to College,* later retitled *The Gertrude Berg Show,* 1961–62. Recipient: Federation of Jewish Philanthropies of New York Award, 1949; Emmy Award, 1950; Girls Clubs of America Radio and TV Mother of the Year; Antoinette Perry Award, 1959. Died in New York City, September 14, 1966.

Television Series (as writer, star, and producer)

1949–54 *The Goldbergs* (*The Rise of the Goldbergs*)
1954–55 *Molly*
1961–62 *The Gertrude Berg Show* (originally titled *Mrs. G Goes to College*)

Films

Make a Wish (writer), 1937; *Molly,* 1951; *Main Street to Broadway,* 1953.

Radio

Effie and Laura (writer only), 1927; *The Rise of the Goldbergs* (star, producer), 1929–45; *The House of Glass* (star, producer), 1935.

Stage

Me and Molly, 1948; *The Solid Gold Cadillac,* 1956; *The Matchmaker,* 1957; *A Majority of One,* 1959; *Dear Me, The Sky Is Falling,* 1963.

Publications

The Molly Goldberg Cookbook, 1955
Molly and Me, 1961

Berle, Milton (1908–2002)

U.S. Comedian, Actor

Milton Berle's career was one of the longest and most varied in show business, spanning silent film, vaudeville, radio, motion pictures, and television. He started in show business at the age of five, appearing as a child in *The Perils of Pauline* and *Tillie's Punctured Romance*. Through the 1920s Berle moved up through the vaudeville circuit, finding his niche in the role of a brash comic known for stealing the material of fellow comedians. He also became a popular master of ceremonies in vaudeville, achieving top billing in the largest cities and theaters. During the 1930s Berle appeared in a variety of Hollywood films and further polished his comedy routines in night clubs and on radio.

Berle is best known for his role as host of *Texaco Star Theater,* television's most popular program during its early years. The show had begun on the ABC radio network in the spring of 1948, and Berle took part in a television test version for Texaco and NBC in June of that year. He was selected as host, and the first east coast broadcast of the TV series began in September. Within two months Berle became television's first superstar, with the highest ratings ever attained and was soon referred to as "Mr. Television," "Mr. Tuesday Night," and "Uncle Miltie." Restaurants, theaters, and nightclubs adjusted their schedules so patrons would not miss Berle's program at 8:00 P.M. on Tuesdays. Berle is said to have stimulated television sales and audience size in the same way *Amos 'n' Andy* had sparked the growth of radio.

Although the budget for each program was a modest $15,000, many well-known entertainers were eager to appear on *Texaco Star Theater* for the public exposure it afforded, providing further viewer appeal and popularity for the program. The one-hour, live shows typically included visual vaudeville routines, music, comedy, and sketches. Other regular features included the singing Texaco station attendants and the pitchman commercials by Sid Stone. Berle was noted for interjecting himself into the acts of his guests, which, along with his opening appearance in outlandish costumes, became a regular feature. His use of sight gags, props, and visual style seemed well suited for the TV medium. In 1951 Berle signed a contract with NBC granting him $200,000 a year for 30 years, providing he appear on NBC exclusively.

His was one of the first television shows to be promoted through merchandising, including Uncle Miltie T-shirts, comic books, and chewing gum. When other programs evolved to compete with Berle's popularity, his dominance of the television audience began to wane, and Texaco ended its sponsorship. In the 1953–54 season, the *Buick-Berle Show,* as it was retitled, was set into the 8:00 P.M. Tuesday time slot. Facing greater competition and sensing the need for more determined effort to compensate for the dwindling novelty of both the program and the medium, Berle's staff and writers changed focus from the zany qualities of the show's early days to a more structured format.

Milton Berle.
Courtesy of the Everett Collection

Berle continued to attract a substantial audience, but he was dropped by the sponsor Buick at the end of the season in 1955. Hour-long variety shows had become more difficult to orchestrate due to higher costs, increasing salary demands, and union complications. Also, Berle's persona had shifted from the impetuous and aggressive style of the *Texaco Star Theater* days to a more cultivated, but less-distinctive personality, leaving many fans somehow unsatisfied. The show was produced in California for the 1955–56 season, but it failed to capture either the spirit or the audience of Uncle Miltie in his prime.

Berle was featured on *Kraft Music Hall* in the late 1950s and *Jackpot Bowling,* a 1960s game show. In 1965 he renegotiated his 30-year contract with NBC, allowing him to appear on any network. He later made guest appearances in dramas as well as comedy programs, earning an Emmy nomination for one of his last TV roles, a dramatic part on *Beverly Hills 90210,* when he was 87 years old. In addition to television, Berle's career in the later years included film, night club acts, and benefit shows. He was the subject of nearly every show business tribute and award, including an Emmy and TV specials devoted to his contributions and legacy in broadcasting. Because of declining health, Berle's television appearances in the final years of his life were limited to brief interviews. He died in his home in Los Angeles in March 2002.

B.R. Smith

See also ***Milton Berle Show;*** **Variety Programs**

Milton Berle. Born Mendel Berlinger in New York City, July 12, 1908. Attended Professional Children's School. Married: 1) Joyce Mathews (twice; divorced twice); two children; 2) Ruth Gosgrove Rosenthal, 1953 (died, 1989); children: Vicki and Billy; 3) Lorna Adams. Began career by winning contest for Charlie Chaplin imitators, 1913; children's roles in Biograph silent film productions; cast member E.W. Wolf's vaudeville children's acts; in theater since *Floradora,* Atlantic City, New Jersey, 1920, debuted in New York City with *Floradora,* 1920; in radio, 1930s; toured with Ziegfeld Follies, 1936; television series and specials from 1948; lyricist of more than 300 songs; contributor to *Variety* magazine. Honorary H.H.D., McKendree College, Lebanon, Illinois, 1984. Recipient: Yiddish Theatrical Alliance Humanitarian Award, 1951; *Look* magazine TV Award, 1951; National Academy of Arts and Sciences Award, Man of the Year, 1959; AGVA Golden Award, 1977; Special Emmy Award for Lifetime Achievement, 1978–79. Died in Los Angeles, California, March 27, 2002.

Television Series

1948–56 *Texaco Star Theater* (later called *The Milton Berle Show* and *Buick-Berle Show*)
1958–59 *Milton Berle Starring in the Kraft Music Hall*
1960–61 *Jackpot Bowling*
1966–67 *The Milton Berle Show*

Made-for-Television Movies

1969 *Seven in Darkness*
1972 *Evil Roy Slade*
1975 *The Legend of Valentino*
1988 *Side by Side*

Television Specials

1950 *Uncle Miltie's Christmas Party*
1950 *Show of the Year* (host)
1951 *Uncle Miltie's Easter Party*
1955 *The Big Time* (cohost)
1959 *The Milton Berle Special*
1961 *The Chrysler Television Special*
1962 *The Milton Berle Special*
1972 *Opening Night: U.S.A.*
1973 *A Show Business Salute to Milton Berle*
1975 *Milton Berle's Mad Mad Mad World of Comedy*
1976 *The First 50 Years* (cohost)
1978 *A Tribute to "Mr. Television" Milton Berle*
1986 *NBC's 60th Anniversary Celebration* (cohost)

Films (selected)

Various Biograph silent productions; *New Faces of 1937; Radio City Revels,* 1938; *Tall, Dark, and Handsome,* 1941; *Sun Valley Serenade,* 1941; *Rise and Shine,* 1941; *A Gentleman at Heart,* 1942; *Over My Dead Body,* 1942; *Whispering Ghosts,* 1942; *Margin for Error,* 1943; *Always Leave Them Laughing,* 1949; *Let's Make Love,* 1960; *It's a Mad, Mad, Mad, Mad World,* 1963; *The Loved One,* 1965; *The Oscar,* 1966; *The Happening,* 1967; *Who's Minding the Mint?,* 1967; *Where Angels Go, Trouble Follows,* 1968; *For Singles Only,* 1968; *Can Hieronymous Merkin Ever Forget Mercy Humppe and Find True Happiness?,* 1969; *Lepke,* 1975; *The Muppet Movie,* 1979; *Broadway Danny Rose,* 1984; *Driving Me Crazy,* 1992; *Storybook,* 1995.

Radio (selected)

Texaco Star Theater, 1939–48; *The Milton Berle Show,* 1939; *Stop Me if You've Heard This One* (cohost); *Let Yourself Go,* 1944; *Kiss and Make Up,* 1946.

Stage

Floradora, 1920; *Earl Carroll Vanities,* 1932; *Saluta,* 1934; *Life Begins at 8:40,* 1935; *See My Lawyer,* 1939; *I'll Take the High Road,* 1943; *Spring in Brazil,* 1945; *Seventeen,* 1951; *Top Banana,* 1963; *The Goodbye People,* 1968; *Two by Two,* 1971; *The Milton Berle Show,* 1971; *Last of the Red Hot Lovers,* 1970–71; *Norman, Is That You?,* 1973–75; *The Best of Everybody,* 1975; *The Sunshine Boys,* 1976.

Publications

Laughingly Yours, 1939
Out of My Trunk, 1945
Earthquake, 1959
Milton Berle: An Autobiography (with Haskel Frankel), 1974
B.S. I Love You, 1987
Milton Berle's Private Joke File, 1989
More of the Best of Milton Berle's Private Joke File, 1993

Further Reading

Allen, Steve, *The Funny Men,* New York: Simon and Schuster, 1956
Berle, William, and Bradley Lewis, *My Father, Uncle Miltie,* Fort Lee, New Jersey: Barricade Books, 1999
Bester, Alfred, "The Good Old Days of Mr. Television," *Holiday* (February 1958)
"The Child Wonder," *Time* (May 16, 1949)
Clark, Champ, "Still Smokin'," *People Weekly* (October 27, 1997)
Glut, Donald F., and Jim Harmon, *The Great Television Heroes,* New York: Doubleday, 1975
Johnson, Ted, "Berles of Wisdom," *TV Guide* (July 21–27, 2001)
"Milton Berle: Television's Whirling Dervish," *Newsweek* (May 16, 1949)
Sylvester, Robert, "The Strange Career of Milton Berle," *Saturday Evening Post* (March 19, 1949)
"TV's First Star and Favorite Uncle," *Broadcasting & Cable* (October 28, 1996)
Van Gelder, Lawrence, "Milton Berle, TV's First Star As Uncle Miltie, Dies at 93," *New York Times* (March 28, 2002)

Berlusconi, Silvio (1936–)

Italian Media Mogul, Prime Minister

While still a student, Silvio Berlusconi, the son of a Milan bank official, displayed two of the main qualities that marked his later career as a media tycoon: business acumen and a penchant for performing. While preparing a dissertation on "The Newspaper Advertising Contract" for his honors degree in law from Milan University, he helped finance his studies by working as a singer on cruise ships.

Upon graduating, he was quick to recognize the entrepreneurial opportunities opened up by the wave of postwar affluence that rolled across Italy in the 1960s. He moved into the booming construction sector, and in 1969 borrowed 3 billion lire to build a prestigious dormitory suburb, Milano 2, on the edge of the city. His decision to install a cable network in the complex in 1974 was his first entry into a television marketplace that was about to undergo a massive expansion.

The historic monopoly over national broadcasting enjoyed by the public sector organization, RAI (Radio Televisione Italiana) had been confirmed by Law 103, passed in 1975. But the following year, the Constitutional Court ruled that it did not extend to the local level. This decision legitimated the mushrooming "pirate" television operators and attracted new investors with around 700 commercial stations springing up around the country. Berlusconi was quick to see the enormous potential in this explosion of activity, and in 1975 he set up a holding company, Fininvest, to manage his expanding interests. In 1979 he established a major film library, renting titles to stations on the condition that they carried advertising purchased through his Publitalia subsidiary. He rapidly became the dominant force in a market that saw television increase its share of national advertising from 15 percent in 1976 to nearly 50 percent, ten years later. By 1983, Publitalia's advertising revenues had overtaken those of RAI, and by the end of the decade they accounted for around 70 percent of all television advertising expenditure.

His power within the new commercial television marketplace was further cemented by his own moves into station ownership. Between 1977 and 1980, he created a nationwide network, Canale 5, creating the illusion of a single channel by dispatching video tapes by courier for simultaneous transmission. Programming was unashamedly populist, relying heavily on imported films and soap operas and home produced game shows. In 1981 the Constitutional Court revised its earlier decision and ruled in favor of national private networks providing there were strong antitrust provisions. Berlusconi took full advantage of this opening, buying out one of his main competitors, Italia 1, in 1982, and acquiring his only other serious challenger, Rete 4, in 1984. These moves confirmed his domination of commercial television, earning him the nickname *Su' Emittenza* ("His Transmitter-ship," a pun on the traditional title for a cardinal).

His power did not go unopposed, however. In October 1984, magistrates ruled that his channels breached RAI's monopoly right to broadcast a simultaneous national service and shut them down. But he had powerful political friends, including the prime minister, Bettino Craxi, who returned from overseas early to sign a decree reopening them. Even in a climate of growing enthusiasm for deregulation, no other European government had allowed a single individual to accumulate such concentrated control over terrestrial television. This political support established an effective duopoly in national television for the rest of the decade, giving Fininvest's three commercial networks and RAI's three public channels an overall share of between 40 to 45 percent each.

Reviewing this situation in 1988, the Constitutional Court sent a warning to parliament urging them to introduce strong antitrust provisions at the earliest opportunity. Parliament's response, the Broadcasting Act of 1990 (known as the "Mammi Act" after the Post and Telecommunications Minister who presented it) fell way short of this. The parliamentary debate was bitter, with the former chair of the Constitutional Court arguing that the Act disregarded the Court's antitrust instructions and was far too sympathetic to private television power. The new law legitimated the status quo. Berlusconi was allowed to keep his three broadcasting networks, and Publitalia's domination of the television advertising market remained untouched. However, new cross-ownership rules did require him to sell 90 percent of his shares in the country's first pay-TV venture, Telepiu, and to divest his majority stake in the Milan daily newspaper, *Il Giornale Nuovo,* which passed to his brother Paolo. Critics of his communicative power were unimpressed, and in 1992 media workers mounted a strike to protest against Finivest's domination of the advertising market.

Renewed pressure for tougher antitrust legislation coincided with a worsening financial situation within Finivest, as the group absorbed the costs of recent acquisitions. In 1986 Berlusconi bought the soccer (football) club AC Milan and spent substantial sums on making it into the most successful Italian club of all time. In 1988 he acquired the La Standa department store chain, one of the largest in Italy. And, after an expensive and bitterly fought contest with Carlo de Benedetti of the computer company Olivetti, in 1990, he had made a major move into newspaper, magazine, and book publishing, with the purchase of the Mondadori group, giving him control of 20 percent of the domestic publishing market. These outlays led to a 12-fold increase in the group's debt, which stood at $2 billion by 1994.

Faced with continuing demands for the break-up of his television empire, he seized the political initiative and, at the beginning of 1994, announced that he would contest the forthcoming general election. Luciano Benetton, head of the clothing group, spoke for many when he wryly observed that, "Silvio Berlusconi's love of politics is motivated by fear of losing his television interests." His vehicle was an entirely new party, *Forza Italia* (named after the football chant "Go Italy") in coalition with the federalist Northern League and the remnants of the neo-fascist MSI movement, renamed the National Alliance. During the campaign he relied heavily on orchestrated support from his press and television interests, leading the distinguished journalist, Indro Montanelli, to resign the editorship of *Il Giornale* in protest. He projected an image of a man untouched by the old corruption, in touch with the aspirations of young Italy, and in favor of low taxation, free markets, and personal choice.

His coalition of the right won 43 percent of the popular vote in the March 1994 election and formed a government with Berlusconi as prime minister. There were immediate allegations of conflicts of interest. He had tried to forestall these at the start of his election campaign by resigning from all managerial positions and handing chairmanship of his major company to his old piano accompanist, Fidele Confalonieri. But since he and his family still held 51 percent of the group's shares, critics were unconvinced. These suspicions, coupled with the defection of the Northern League, led to the fall of his administration after nine months.

His exit from office coincided with other shifts in his personal circumstances. In July 1995, he announced that he had sold a 20 percent stake in his new subsidiary, Mediaset (covering his television, advertising, film, and record interests) to three outside investors (including the German media magnate, Leo Kirch) for $1.1 billion. More shares were sold later to banks and other institutions, reducing his holding to 72 percent. Then, two days before the April 1996 election, he announced a public flotation that would eliminate his majority control.

His political standing was also under threat. His carefully cultivated image of a man outside the corrupt old guard had been dented by revelations that in 1978 he had joined the secretive Masonic lodge, P2 (Propoganda 2) that had formed a powerful state within a state with connections to the armed forces, secret services, banks, and government. Then, in January 1996, he was called before magistrates in Milan to answer charges that he had bribed financial police to present a favorable tax audit of his corporate accounts.

This helped to sour his return to politics in the general election in April 1996. Although he was elected as a member of parliament, his right-wing bloc was forced to concede control of government to the Olive Tree Alliance, Italy's first successful center-left coalition since World War II.

Having spent the late 1990s reorganizing his party, he was once again elected prime minister on May 13, 2001. Berlusconi is the prime minister of Italy, leader of the *Forza Italia* party, head of the center-right coalition known as the House of Liberties, and the wealthiest man in Italy, with an estimated net worth of $10.3 billion.

Whether he remains a central figure in Italian politics and business in the future, Berlusconi will be remembered as the man who in the space of just 25 years built a conglomerate that rose to dominate Italian commercial television and become Europe's second largest media empire (after Bertelsmann of Germany) and Italy's third biggest private company, and the man who used his communicative power and his flair for showmanship to launch a new political party that gathered enough votes to secure his election as prime minister in just four months. Overall, his career over the last 30 years stands as an impressive illustration and warning of the power of concentrated media ownership in a lightly regulated marketplace.

GRAHAM MURDOCK

See also **Italy**

Silvio Berlusconi. Born in Milan, Italy, September 29, 1936. Educated at Milan University, degree in law 1971. Married: 1) Carla Dall'Oglio (divorced), children: Marina and Pier; 2) Veronica Lario, 1990. Founded real estate development companies Cantieri Riuniti Milanesi, 1962, and Edilnord, 1963; financed construction of suburbs Milano 2, 1969, and Milano 3, 1976; created Telemilano cable television system, 1974; established Canale 5 television network 1977–80; purchased television networks Italia 1, 1982, Rete 4, 1984; purchased movie theater chain, 1985; purchased Milan AC soccer club, 1986; acquired the La Standa department store chain, 1988; acquired interests in publishing conglomerate Arnoldo Mondadori Editore S.p.A., 1990; formed political party Forza Italia, 1994; Prime Minister of Italy, 1994. Member: Masonic lodge Propoganda 2, 1978 (disbanded, 1981); Confindustria (Italian Manufacturers' Association). Honorary degree in managerial engineering from Calabria University, 1991. Recipient: Cavalliere del Lavoro, 1977; named Man of the Year by the International Film and Programme Market of Television, Cable, and Satellite, 1991.

Further Reading

"Blind Trust—In Berlusconi: Italy," *The Economist* (April 30, 1994)

Fisher, William, and Mark Shapiro, "An InterNation Story: Four Titans Carve Up European TV," *The Nation* (January 9, 1989)

Ginsborg, Paul. *Silvio Berlusconi: Television, Power, and Patrimony,* London and New York: Verso Books, 2004

"Playing Silvio's Song: Italian Television," *The Economist* (July 29, 1995)

Walter, David, "Winner Takes All," *Index on Censorship* (September–October 1994)

"The Way Things Are in Italy," *The Economist* (June 17, 1995)

Zucconi, Vittorio, "White Stallion of TV," *New Perspectives Quarterly* (Summer 1994)

Bernstein, Sidney (1899–1993)

British Media Executive

Sidney Bernstein was one of Britain's first television "barons," the least flamboyant but probably the most enduringly influential of a select number of show business entrepreneurs who won the first independent commercial television franchises in the 1950s. As founding chair of the London-based Granada Group, and later of its famous subsidiary the Granada Television Network Ltd., Bernstein earned a considerable reputation as a man sensitive to the frequently contradictory ideals of popular entertainment and public service. Today, Granada Television continues to thrive, nearly 50 years after its creation, reconciling its twin roles as a powerful purveyor of regional culture and a majority participant in a vigorous national network. It is one of the most profitable and highly respected television companies in Europe and the only British Channel 3 contractor still surviving in anything like its original form. In 1956, the first year of Granada's transmissions, the Granada Group posted pretax profits of $364,930 (£218,204); by 1980 that figure had grown to over $72 million (£43 million), while the operating profit for 2001 was around $334 million (£200 million). Sidney Bernstein, socialist millionaire and "benevolent despot," is the visionary who brought this empire into being. As a consequence of TV ownership deregulation, Granada had, by 2001, acquired control of seven major British independent television (ITV) licenses, covering 35.7 million viewers in over 60 percent of homes.

Bernstein had developed a considerable show business organization long before his controversial entry into television. Inheriting from his father a modest interest in a handful of small London cinemas while in his early 20s, he went on to build, with his brother Cecil, a successful circuit of some 60 cinemas and theaters on the way to creating a diversified leisure group with interests in publishing, property, motorway services, retail shops, and bowling alleys, as well as the hugely profitable business of television rentals. It is said he chose the name Granada for his cinema chain, and later for his television company, because its Spanish reference connoted sun-drenched gaiety and flamboyance, the qualities he sought to have associated with his entertainment establishments, which tended in the early days of cinema to be decorated in the Spanish baroque style. Another story suggests that Bernstein, rambling in Andalusia while looking for a name for his company, visited the city of Granada and its exotic splendor suggested the name. Always considering himself first and foremost an unashamed showman (an attitude underlined by his unqualified admiration for Phineas T. Barnum, whose portrait hung symbolically in various parts of the Granada empire), Bernstein nevertheless possessed a seriousness of purpose. He introduced serious foreign films into his cinemas at a time when distribution outlets for them were scarce and was a founder of the British Film Society. More significantly for the future of independent television, he fought a crusade to equate popularity and accessibility with quality and depth.

Bernstein had been aware of the commercial potential of television from an early stage but his socialist principles prevented him from questioning the BBC's monopoly. From 1948 he had been lobbying the government to give the cinema industry the right to produce and transmit television programs, not to individual homes as the BBC did, but to collective audiences in cinemas and theaters. Indeed, the evidence of Granada Theatres Ltd. to the Beveridge Committee of Enquiry into Broadcasting (report published 1951) fully acknowledged the sanctity of the public monopoly principle with respect to domestic broadcasting. All the same, Granada and Bernstein were quick to overcome their reservations when the resulting Television Act of 1954 signaled the end of the BBC's monopoly and permitted private companies to apply for the first regional commercial franchises.

The London-based Granada group surprised the establishment by bidding, not for a lucrative contract in the affluent southeast, but for the northern weekday license centered on Manchester in the industrial north and embracing an area which then extended geographically right across the north of England and Wales. Granada's evidence to the Pilkington Committee of Enquiry into Broadcasting in 1961 justified this decision thus: "The North and London were the two biggest regions. Granada preferred the North because of its tradition of home-grown culture, and because it offered a chance to start a new creative industry away from the metropolitan atmosphere of London." Bernstein himself shrewdly put it another way:

> the North is a closely knit, indigenous, industrial society; a homogeneous cultural group with a good record for music, theatre, literature and newspapers, not found elsewhere in this island, except perhaps in Scotland. Compare this with London and its suburbs—full of displaced persons. And, of course, if you look at a map of the concentration of population in the North and a rainfall map, you will see that the North is an ideal place for television.

Despite certain objections to a commercial franchise being awarded to a company with overtly left-wing leanings, Granada commenced broadcasting from Manchester in May 1956, proudly proclaiming its origins with the slogan "From the North" and labeling its new constituency "Granadaland." The first night's programming began, at Bernstein's insistence, with a homage to the BBC, whose public broadcasting pedigree he had always admired, and closed with a worthy, public-spirited statement of advertising policy that suggested an initial ambivalence surrounding the commercial imperative. Already by January 1957, Granada was responsible for all the top-ten rated programs receivable in its region, and, in 1962, it became the first station to screen the Beatles to the British television audience. Bernstein's company soon came to be regarded as one of the most progressive of the independent television contractors and more consistently identifiable than most with the aspirations of its region. Its reputation for quality popular drama in the long-running serial *Coronation Street* and for high-profile current affairs and documentary in programs such as *World in Action* and *What the Papers Say* gave it early prestige and aligned it unmistakably with the ideals of its founder.

In the 1970s, Lord Bernstein finally relinquished stewardship of the television company and moved over to the business side of the Granada Group. He retired, after a long career, in 1979, and died in 1993, aged 94.

TONY PEARSON

See also **British Program Production Companies**

Sidney Lewis Bernstein. Born in Ilford, Essex, England, January 30, 1899. Married: Sandra Malone (died, 1991); children: one son and two daughters. Inherited control of cinema chain from his father, 1921; founding member, British Film Society, 1924; introduced Saturday morning film matinees for children, 1927; acquired control of some 30 cinemas by late 1930s; chair, Granada Group, encompassing films, television, and publishing, 1934–79; film adviser to British Ministry of Information, 1940–45; posted to British Embassy, Washington, D.C., 1942; chief of film section, allied forces in North Africa, 1942–43, allied forces in Europe, 1943–45; collaborated as producer with film director Alfred Hitchcock, 1948–52; founder, with his brother Cecil, of Granada Television, part of Granada Entertainment Group, 1956; governor, Sevenoaks School, 1964–74; lecturer on film and international affairs, New York University and Nuffield Foundation, 1965–72; president, Granada Group, 1979–93; chair, Royal Exchange Theatre, Manchester, 1983–93. Fellow, British Film Institute, 1984. Created Baron Bernstein of Leigh, 1969. Recipient: International Emmy Directorate Award, 1984. Died February 5, 1993.

Films (producer)

Rope, 1948; *Under Capricorn,* 1949; *I Confess,* 1952.

Further Reading

Black, Peter, *The Mirror in the Corner: People's Television,* London: Hutchinson, 1971

British Film Institute, *Granada: The First 25 Years* (BFI Dossier No. 9), London: British Film Institute, 1981

Tinker, Jack, *Television Barons,* London: Quartet Books, 1980

Year One: The Story of the First Year of Granada TV Network, Manchester, England: Granada, 1958

Bertelsmann AG

Bertelsmann AG is one of the largest media corporations in the world (fourth as of 2002). Headquartered in Gutersloh, Germany, Bertelsmann is an international media conglomerate with major investments in book, magazine, and newspaper publishing, recordings and music publishing, broadcasting, online services, and other allied entertainment and information products. Bertelsmann operates in 56 countries, employs more than 80,000 people, and had revenues of over $20 billion in 2001.

A privately owned corporation dating back to 1835, Bertelsmann was revived after World War II by Reinhard Mohn, a fifth-generation member of the founding family. In the 1950s, Bertelsmann established itself as a major publisher through its book clubs. The company's publishing interests were enhanced in the 1970s with the purchase of majority interest in Gruner + Jahr, a publisher of German newspapers and magazines including such titles as *Stern* and *Geo,* and the 1986 purchase of Bantam Doubleday Dell, the second-largest trade publisher in the United States. The publishing division still contributes the majority of Bertelsmann's revenues and includes additional imprints such as Random House, Knopf, Vintage, and the Modern Library. Bertelsmann's book clubs include the Book of the Month Club, the Literary Guild, and Quality Paperback Book Club.

The primary corporate divisions of Bertelsmann include the RTL Group, with 23 television and 17 radio stations in Europe, the United States, South Africa, and Australia; Random House, the world's leading trade book publisher; Gruner + Jahr, Europe's largest magazine publisher; Bertelsmann Music Group (BMG), record labels and music publishing; Bertelsmann-

BERTELSMANN
media worldwide

Courtesy of Bertelsmann, Inc.

Springer, professional media specializing in science, technology, and medicine; Arvato, a media services provider; and DirectGroup, a direct-to-customer e-commerce company for Bertelsmann's book and music clubs.

The RTL Group was created in 2000 as a merger of CLT-UFA and Pearson TV, and is Europe's largest broadcaster. RTL Group properties include four stations in Germany (RTL, RTL II, SuperRTL, and VOX), as well as M6 in France, Channel 5 in the United Kingdom, RTL Klub in Hungary, Antena 3 in Spain, RTL TVI in Belgium, and RTL 4 and Yorin in the Netherlands. RTL is also Europe's largest television content producer, including FremantleMedia and UFA Film and TV Production companies.

Ever since the German television market opened its previously public-based system to commercial competition in 1985, Bertelsmann's strong financial position in the media marketplace has allowed it to become one of the dominant forces in the commercial television market. Bertelsmann's pan-European approach has also led the company to pursue horizontal and vertical integration strategies in relation to content production, broadcasting, and the Internet. The RTL Group houses a New Media division that runs websites and Internet advertising in Germany, France, and the Netherlands.

With the rise of the Internet and e-commerce in the mid- to late-1990s, Bertelsmann sought to exploit its various book, music, and e-commerce divisions by creating DirectGroup in 2000 to handle online distribution of its book and music properties. DirectGroup, which includes BMG Music Service and CDNOW, also purchased a 52 percent option in Napster, the online file-sharing service, that same year. In April 2002, Bertelsmann offered to take control of Napster with an estimated $20 million buyout of the company (despite the fact that Napster was at that time embroiled in lawsuits with much of the music industry over copyright disputes). Although Bertelsmann had maintained a joint-ownership stake in AOL Europe, it divested those interests in early 2002 by selling to AOL Time Warner. Bertelsmann's corporate strategy nevertheless continues to emphasize the potential for online marketing and distribution of its enormous media holdings.

JEFFREY P. JONES

Further Reading

Kleinsteuber, Hans J., and Bettina Peters, "Media Moguls in Germany," in *Media Moguls,* edited by Jeremy Tunstall and Michael Palmer, New York: Routledge, 1991

Smith, Anthony, *The Age of Behemoths: The Globalization of Mass Media Firms,* New York: Priority Press, 1991

Thussu, Daya Kishan, editor, *Electronic Empires: Global Media and Local Resistance,* London and New York: Arnold Publishers, 1998

Berton, Pierre (1920–)

Canadian Journalist, Broadcast Personality

Pierre Berton is one of Canada's best-known personalities and arguably Canada's best-known living writer. He has also been an important television presence since the earliest days of Canadian television. For more than 30 years, he was rarely absent from the nation's television screens, and by the 1970s he was correctly described as "clearly Canada's best-known and most respected TV public affairs personality" by Warner Troyer in *The Sound and the Fury: An Anecdotal History of Canadian Broadcasting.* Berton was also one of most highly paid personalities. During his career as a columnist and commentator, he has been a tireless defender of public broadcasting and the importance of Canadian content. In all of his many public roles, he has been a prodigious popularizer of the Canadian experience. He may be remembered most for his many books, mostly popular histories, but he has long had an arresting television presence.

Berton's first TV appearance was probably in 1952, as a panelist on *Court of Opinion,* soon after he arrived in Toronto from Vancouver, where he got his start as a student newspaper editor (*The Ubyssey*) and daily newspaper writer. Always well informed and opinionated, he provided a strong journalistic thrust to various CBC public affairs programs. In 1957 he became the host of the interview show *Close-Up* and joined the panel of *Front Page Challenge,* a long-running program that featured "mystery guests." The guests were connected with stories in the news, and the task of the panel was to identify them by asking questions and then to conduct a brief interview with the guest. After many years on the air, the program was finally canceled in 1995. In 1963, on the newly formed private network CTV, Berton premiered *The Pierre Berton Show* (also known as the *Pierre Berton Hour*), another talk show, which ran until 1973.

Berton's commitment to popular history led in 1974 to *My Canada* on a new, private television service, Global. The program made use of his formidable talents as a storyteller in order to present Canadian history to viewers. The program had few props and relied on Berton's ability to hold an audience with the story. Later, from 1986 to 1987, he was host of CBC Television's *Heritage Theatre,* a series of dramatizations of true Canadian stories.

Among Berton's major television triumphs was the 1974 CBC production of *The National Dream.* Based on his books, *The National Dream* and *The Last Spike,* the drama-documentary series consisted of eight hour-long programs on the opening of the Canadian west and the building of the Canadian Pacific Railway. Berton wrote the series outline and served as on-air guide to the documentary and drama segments. The series premiered at 9:00 P.M., Sunday, March 3, 1974, and had 3.6 million viewers, a very large audience in English-speaking Canada, where, at that time, the average audience was 3.1 million. More recently, Berton's popular histories were an important resource for the monumental TV series *Canada: A People's History,* broadcast by the CBC (2000–2002). Two of Berton's titles, *The Invasion of Canada, 1812–13* and *Flames Across the Border, 1813–14,* are cited on the website for the series.

Over the course of his career, Berton has made a major contribution to Canadian television. Not surprisingly, he has been an ardent champion of public broadcasting and the CBC. Closely involved with the Canadian Radio and Television League, he helped found a successor organization, the Friends of Canadian Broadcasting, which has been a critical supporter of the CBC and Canadian production. As a Canadian cultural nationalist, Berton has played a most notable role in the development of a distinctly Canadian approach to television.

FREDERICK J. FLETCHER AND ROBERT EVERETT

Pierre Berton.
Photo courtesy of Pierre Berton

See also ***Canada: A Peoples' History***

Pierre Berton. Born in Whitehorse, Yukon Territory, Canada, July 12, 1920. Married: Janet; six children. Began career as reporter for the *Vancouver News Herald,* from 1942, and *Vancouver Sun,* 1945–47; managing editor, *Maclean's* magazine, 1947; editor/columnist, *Toronto Star* newspaper, 1958–62; writer of documentaries and plays for TV, film, and radio, as well as revue sketches and musical comedy for theater; author of more than 40 books. Member: Canadian News Hall of Fame. Recipient: Companion of the Order of Canada, three Governor General Awards for Creative Nonfiction; two National Newspaper Awards; two ACTRA Awards for broadcasting.

Television Series (selected)

1957–95	*Front Page Challenge* (weekly panelist)
1957–63	*Close-Up* (host)
1963–73	*The Pierre Berton Show* (host)
1974	*The National Dream* (writer/narrator)
1976	*Greenfell*
1979	*The Dionne Quintuplets* (writer)
1984–87	*Heritage Theatre* (story editor/host)

1985 *Spirit of Batoche*
1988 *The Secret of My Success* (writer/interviewer)

Film

Klondike (writer), 1960.

Publications (selected)

"Make Way for the One-Eyed Monster," *Maclean's* (June 1, 1949)
"Everybody Boos the CBC," *Maclean's* (December 1, 1950)
The Mysterious North, 1956
The Klondike Fever: The Life and Death of the Last Great Gold Rush, 1958; revised edition, as *Adventures of a Columnist,* 1960
The Secret World of Og (juvenile fiction), 1961
The Big Sell: An Introduction to the Black Arts of Door-to-Door Salesmanship and Other Techniques, 1963
The Comfortable Pew: A Critical Look at Christianity and the Religious Establishment in the New Age, 1965
The Cool, Crazy, Committed World of the Sixties: Twenty-one Television Encounters, 1965
Historic Headlines: A Century of Canadian News Dramas (editor), 1967
The Smug Minority, 1968
The Last Spike: The Great Railway, 1881–1885, 1971
The Great Railway, Illustrated, 1972
Klondike Fever: The Last Great Gold Rush, 1972
Drifting Home, 1973
The National Dream: The Great Railway, 1871–1881, 1974
Canadian Food Guide, 1974
Hollywood's Canada: The Americanization of Our National Image, 1975
My Country: The Remarkable Past, 1976
The Dionne Years: A Thirties Melodrama, 1977
The Wild Frontier: More Tales from the Remarkable Past, 1978
The Invasion of Canada, 1812–1813, 1980
Flames across the Border: 1813–1814, 1981
Why We Act Like Canadians: A Personal Exploration of Our National Character, 1982
The Klondike Quest: A Photographic Essay, 1897–1899, 1983
The Promised Land: Settling the West, 1896–1914, 1984
The Impossible Railway: The Building of the Canadian Pacific, 1984
Starting Out: 1920–1947, 1987
The Arctic Grail: The Quest for the North West Passage and the North Pole, 1818–1909, 1988
The Great Depression, 1929–1939, 1990
Niagara: A History of the Falls, 1992
My Times: Living with History, 1947–1995, 1995
Farewell to the Twentieth Century, 1996
1967: The Last Good Year, 1997
Worth Repeating: Literary Resurrections, 1948–1994, 1998
Pierre Berton's Canada: The Land and the People, 1999
Marching As to War: Canada's Turbulent Years, 1899 to 1953, 2002

Further Reading

Gould, Terry, "Front Page Challenged: Aging Panelists Were One Thing, then They Got Grumpy," *Saturday Night* (July/August 1995)
"A Star Is Born: In His New Memoirs, Pierre Berton Describes How TV Brought Him Fame and Fortune," *Maclean's* (September 11, 1995)
Stewart, Sandy, *Here's Looking at Us: A Personal History of Television in Canada,* Toronto: CBC Enterprises, 1986
Troyer, Warner, *The Sound and the Fury: An Anecdotal History of Canadian Broadcasting,* Toronto: Wiley, 1980

Betacam

The rise and fall of Sony's Betacam as a dominant technology worldwide for more than two decades provides an opportunity to consider a range of technologies, industrial practices, and cultural factors in the development of television. Faced with the widespread adoption of new digital formats, Sony finally discontinued manufacturing Betacam SP camcorders in the fall of 2001, but only after having sold 450,000 of these high-end units internationally. This market reach and longevity stand as anomalies in an industry defined by technical incompatibilities and rapid obsolescence.

After its introduction in 1981, Betacam became the standard professional field camera for location video work. Its adoption on a wide scale was no small accomplishment, given the brutal competition that characterized the "format wars" in television equipment manufacturing—a high-stakes, capital-intensive struggle that produced scores of competing and incompatible high-end recording formats in less than a decade. The Panasonic Recam, Bosch QuarterCam, and RCA Hawkeye "alternatives" all proved costly losers to Sony in the race for the first successful broadcast-quality "camcorder," a single unit containing both camera and videocassette recorder.

Before Betacam, electronic news-gathering (ENG) utilized the ¾″ U-matic cassette format introduced in 1973. While ¾″ tape economies made 16mm news-film obsolete in the late 1970s, the video format was actually a step backward in terms of portability and ease of use. Whereas 16mm news-film cameras such as the CP16R combined a magnetic sound-recording head within the camera head, ¾″ videotape shooting required a separate video cameraperson, sound recordist, and videocassette recorder (VCR) operator—all tethered together by multipin camera/sound cables in a cumbersome relationship that made moving shots extremely difficult. The 20- to 30-pound weight of each loaded VCR and camera in the tethered system of the late 1970s made logistics and transportation crucial in any location news assignment. Add to this the fact that ¾″ videotape was only marginally "broadcastable," and the system's limitations are apparent. While Ampex marketed a true broadcast-quality portable 1″ system in the early 1980s (the 53-pound VPR-20) and producers had used AC-powered 1″ type-C VTRs housed in trucks in the field, neither proved adequate solutions for those who sought to cover fast-breaking, spontaneous stories without being intrusive. At a mere 17.7 pounds, and in a configuration that combined both ½″ VCR and camera in an integrated unit on the shoulder of a single camera operator, the BVW-1 Betacam was widely hailed as a revolution.

Betacam's significance came in three areas: in new technologies that the format introduced; in broader technical improvements that Betacam simply incorporated; and in a number of new practices that developed alongside widespread adoption of the format. First, Betacam's defining edge resulted from rejecting the dominant system of "composite" recording—whereby electronic information is recorded as part of *one* combined signal. Betacam was engineered around "component" recording. By recording and manipulating luminance (brightness) and chrominance (color) information separately throughout the production process, component recording aimed to solve one of the built-in flaws of the U.S. NTSC broadcast standard. Historically, NTSC was standardized for black-and-white recording and was more than adequate for live transmission. However, as approved by the Federal Communications Commission (FCC) in the late 1940s, color was a troubling afterthought for the NTSC system. Engineers struggled to fit color information onto its existing and very limited black-and-white composite signal. The resulting compromise meant that interference between chroma and luminance, and color instability due to multiple generations or amplifications, became synonymous with the NTSC standard. Component engineers argued that the production process should not remain hostage to the limited bandwidth of broadcasters but could take advantage of superior—even if incompatible—alternatives, as long as the end product was compressed back to NTSC before broadcasting. Component recording, then, emerged as a production, rather than transmission, format. By maintaining the integrity of signal components throughout production, Betacam eliminated the cross-interference that degrades NTSC composite image quality, even as Sony hyped a "field look" that rivaled 1″ or 2″ "studio quality."

Apart from logistical benefits that came with Betacam's size and portability, and the enhancements that came with its shift to component processing, the camcorders that followed the BVW-1 and BVW-3 became, in the next 15 years, a veritable index of historical improvements in video technology. In 1983, for example, NEC first introduced charged coupled device (CCD) camera sensors. These solid-state chips eliminated the aberrations of traditional camera pick-up "tubes": blooming, burning, image variability, bulkiness, and high light levels. It was Sony, however, that quickly exploited the breakthrough. Upgraded with CCDs, Betacams became even smaller, yet allowed videographers film-quality contrast at extremely low light levels. Sony made the format "dockable" with high-end Ikegami cameras, added metal tape and the processing designation "SP" (for superior performance), and increased the camera resolution to 700+ lines. Betacam SP's visual sophistication made it the dominant rental camera in commercial production in the 1990s. The format was widely used in the field, in multicamera shoots, and in microwave uplinks for live news coverage.

Betacam also led to important changes in video postproduction. First, the advantages of component recording were only fully realized in editing systems that were also entirely component. While the shift was expensive, the 1980s saw widespread changeover to all-component processing in editing suites across the United States. Second, the emergence of Betacam encouraged the development of "interformat" editing systems as well. Before Betacam, system source decks and master recorders typically utilized the same format. After the arrival of Betacam source tapes that equaled the quality of 1″ online systems, however, "bumping" tapes up to 1″ made no sense, given the inevitable loss in quality that resulted from copying. Third-party engineers quickly customized interformat suites that could exploit first-generation Betacam quality for 1″ program masters. In 1994 Sony introduced Digital Betacam in order to compete with Panasonic's D-3 and D-5 digital tape formats, and analysts speculated that Sony's existing market share and Betacam "branding" would ensure the format's future.

While Betacam can be seen as a barometer of technical developments, the unit is also symptomatic of aesthetic changes in the medium. Betacam emerged along with a number of new genres in the late 1980s. Its accessible "broadcast quality" gave half-hour "infomercials" the affordable wall-to-wall quality control that the form needed. Its extreme low-light capability provided the gritty street look of the new "reality" shows that emerged from 1988 to 1990 (*COPS, Rescue 911, America's Most Wanted*). Its portability and collapsed crew size provided ample fragmentary fodder for the new tabloid shows (*Hard Copy, A Current Affair*). Even "higher" journalistic forms that disdained the tabloids—such as the prime-time news magazines that experienced explosive growth in the early to mid-1990s (*First Person, 20/20, Dateline*)—made Betacam a bottom-line workhorse to fill prime-time hours. When several Betacams were stolen from the frenzied corps that covered the O.J. Simpson trial in 1995, police quickly theorized that the gear—essentially low-cost studios-in-a-package—was probably already being used in the pornographic video industry that flourished in the San Fernando Valley area near Los Angeles. Technologies do not "cause" changes in narrative or genre, but Betacam's proliferation in the 1980s and 1990s, alongside economic and institutional shifts, suggests that the system helped comprise the technical preconditions for one of television's most volatile stylistic periods.

The fate and decline of analog Betacam was tied to the development of three new and alternative imaging systems, and to new industrial practices that accompanied each: "DV" formats, digital television, and "24p." From 1996 to 2001, DV, DVCAM, and DVCPro emerged as the first widely successful digital recording formats for consumer and industrial use, although DV was never intended (by Sony) as a replacement for Betacam. DV's 4:1:1 compression scheme created more electronic "artifacts," or image errors, than Betacam's 4:2:2 compression and superior bandwidth. However, television stations worldwide immediately began adopting DVCAM and DVCPro as replacements for their workhorse Betacam systems. At first, deployment of the new, small, digital formats was met with the standard benchmark expectations: were these technologies "as good as" or "better than Beta SP?" But such questions (like the earlier network "broadcast quality" barrier) proved irrelevant in the highly competitive, contemporary television marketplace. The performance-to-cost ratio of the new digital formats was simply impossible for Betacam's costly but proven quality to match.

Sony had weathered challenges from small-format alternatives before—with the use of Hi8mm by network news divisions in the 1991 Gulf War and after; and the use of small-format DV in the second coming of "reality" television that began in the late 1990s. However, the death knell may have finally come when the cable news channel CNN announced in May 2001 that it would no longer purchase $35,000 Betacam SX camcorders for its ENG crews. In opting instead for Sony's $3,500 "industrial" (prosumer) DSR150 DVCAM format cameras, CNN boasted of its plans to shift to two-person, rather than three-person, crews, helmed by new "multitalented" journalists who would somehow be able to shoot images first-person as well as report. Cynics of the stunt pointed out that the mini-camcorders brought with them immense cost savings; something much-needed at CNN in the fiscal crisis following the AOL Time Warner merger, after which CNN laid off 400 employees. Advocating for their professional constituencies, the National Association of Broadcast Employees and Technicians (NABET) and other labor representatives condemned the move, but it was clear that the DV technologies had a compelling logic in television's new industrial-economic order.

Whereas news operations opted for "lower" digital alternatives, prime-time dramas went to higher-resolution alternatives—to HDCAM and "1080i" (1,080 lines interlaced) to meet the new standards mandated for "digital television" by the FCC. Complicating matters further still, television's film origination community in Hollywood argued for its almost centuries-old frame rate (24fps) and began shifting productions from film to digital "24pHD" in 2000 and 2001. If HDTV eclipses Betacam's lower resolution, the current groundswell of support for the 24fps digital format will arguably complete the obsolescence of 30fps Betacam.

In retrospect, Betacam has played an important role

in the history of television technologies, in no small measure because of the integral role it played in altering and standardizing production methods and aesthetic practices over a 20-year period.

JOHN THORNTON CALDWELL

Further Reading

Denison, D.C., *As Seen on TV: An Inside Look at the Television Industry,* New York: Simon and Schuster, 1992

Gross, Lynne, and Larry Ward, *Electronic Moviemaking,* Belmont, California: Wadsworth, 1994

Grotticelli, Michael, "CNN Moves to Small Format ENG," *Broadcasting & Cable* (May 14, 2001)

Grotticelli, Michael, "Sony Retires Analog Camcorder," *Broadcasting & Cable* (October 29, 2001)

Jennings, Robert, "DV vs. Betacam SP: 4:1:1 vs. 4:2:2, Artifacts, and Other Controversies" (1997), http://www.dvcentral.org/DV-Beta.html

Matthias, Harry, and Richard Patterson, *Electronic Cinematography,* Belmont, California: Wadsworth, 1985

Patterson, Richard, and Dana White, editors, *Electronic Production Techniques,* Los Angeles: American Society of Cinematographers, n.d.

Ward, Peter, *Basic Betacam Camerawork,* Boston: Focal Press, 1994

Betamax Case

U.S. Legal Decision

Universal City Studios, Inc. et al. v. Sony Corporation of America Inc. et al., commonly known as the Betamax case, was the first concerted legal response of the U.S. film industry to the home video revolution. After nearly a decade of announcements and false starts by one U.S. company or another, Sony, the Japanese electronics manufacturing giant, introduced its Betamax video tape recorder to the U.S. consumer market in early 1976 at an affordable price. In its marketing strategy Sony promoted the machine's ability to "time shift" programming—that is, to record a television program off the air even while watching another show on a different channel.

The plaintiffs, Universal and Walt Disney Productions on behalf of the Hollywood majors, charged that the ability of the Betamax to copy programming off air was an infringement of copyright and sought to halt the sale of the machines. The studios were ostensibly trying to protect film and television producers from the economic consequences of unauthorized mass duplication and distribution. However, Universal might have also wanted to prevent Betamax from capturing a significant segment of the fledgling home video market before Universal's parent company, MCA, could introduce its DiscoVision laserdisc system, which was to scheduled for test marketing in the fall of 1977.

The Betamax case was filed in the U.S. Federal District Court of Los Angeles in November 1976 and went to trial on January 30, 1979. In its defense, Sony asserted that a consumer had the absolute right to record programs at home for private use. It drew an analogy to the audio cassette recorder, which was introduced in the 1960s and had made music tapers out of millions of American teenagers. Although the practice had not been tested in the courts, Sony believed a tradition had been established.

Handing down its decision in October 1979, the U.S. District Court ruled in favor of Sony, stating that taping off air for entertainment or time shifting constituted fair use; that copying an entire program also qualified as fair use; that set manufacturers could profit from the sale of VCRs; and that the plaintiffs did not prove that any of the above practices constituted economic harm to the motion picture industry.

These rulings pertained to the court's interpretation of the fair use doctrine as it applied to consumers. Addressing the matter of retailing of videocassettes, the court let stand the First Sale Doctrine of the 1976 Copyright Act, which stated that the first purchaser of a copyrighted work (e.g., a motion picture on videocassette) could use it in any way the purchaser saw fit as long as copyright was not violated by illegal duplication, etc. This right extended to the rental of videocassettes purchased from Hollywood studios. Until the arrival of the VCR, film companies had received a portion of the box office or a fee each time one of their films was shown. As holders of copyright on their pictures, the studios were legally entitled to these forms of remuneration. Since the court's interpretation of the First Sale Doctrine threatened to undermine Hollywood's control over the use of its product, Universal appealed the decision.

Although the U.S. Court of Appeals reversed the lower court's decision in October 1981, the decision, if it were to stand, would have been impossible to enforce. The home video market had expanded enormously since the start of the case; annual VCR sales had increased from 30,000 sets in 1976 to 1.4 million in 1981. Meanwhile, Sony lost the lead to its Japanese rival Matsushita, which introduced a competing format—VHS (for "video home system")—recorder in 1977. Normally, Sony and Matsushita cross-licensed recording and playback equipment, but for the home video market, the two Japanese companies went their separate ways by marketing systems that were incompatible with one another. (The VHS cassette was larger than the Beta and had a longer recording capability.) VHS overtook Beta as the preferred format for home video, and by 1981 more than six Japanese manufacturers had entered the business both in their own names and as suppliers of VHS machines to U.S. firms. Starting out at around $1,300, the price of the machine had been dropping steadily, enabling it to become a standard appliance for most middle-class Americans.

The Betamax case went all the way to the U.S. Supreme Court, which reversed the appeals court decision on January 17, 1984. By 1986 VCRs had been installed in 50 percent of American homes, and annual videocassettes sales surpassed the theatrical box office. At first, the major studios believed that the only logical way to market videocassettes was direct sales, reasoning that consumers wanted to buy cassettes and create "libraries" in much the same way as they acquired record albums. However, people preferred renting to buying, and as the situation stood, retailers and not film producers initially wrung most of the profits from the market. After purchasing a cassette for around $40 wholesale, a retailer could rent it over and over at a nominal charge. In contrast, the film company's profit would be small, less than a few dollars after materials, duplication, and distribution costs had been covered.

In their struggle with retailers to capture a dominant share of the home video market, the major Hollywood companies formulated a two-tiered pricing policy. For the first six months after a new movie went on sale, it would be priced relatively high on the assumption that the overwhelming majority of transactions would consist of sales to video stores for rental purposes. Then as demand began to ebb, the same movie would be reissued at a much lower price to stimulate home sales. The majors used similar strategies overseas and soon became the principal beneficiaries of the new distribution technology.

Tino Balio

See also **Time Shifting; Videocassette; Videotape**

Further Reading

Harris, Paul, "Supreme Court O.K.'s Home Taping: Approve 'Time Shifting' for Personal Use," *Variety* (June 18, 1984)

Lardner, James, "Annals of Law; The Betamax Case: Part 1," *The New Yorker* (April 6, 1987)

Lardner, James, "Annals of Law; The Betamax Case: Part 2," *The New Yorker* (April 13, 1987)

Beulah

U.S. Situation Comedy

Beulah, the first nationally broadcast weekly television series starring an African American in the leading role, ran on ABC from 1950 to 1953. The role had originally been created by white male actor Marlin Hurt for the *Fibber McGee and Molly* radio program, and the character was spun off onto "her" own radio show in 1945. After Hurt's untimely death in 1946, Hattie McDaniel played the role on radio until her death in 1953. Ethel Waters played the character on television during its first two seasons and Louise Beavers in its third year.

A half-hour situation comedy, the program revolved around the whimsical antics of a middle-aged black domestic, Beulah, the so-called queen of the kitchen, and the white family for whom she worked—Harry and Alice Henderson and their young son, Donnie. Beulah's boyfriend Bill Jackson ran a fix-it shop but managed to spend most of his time hanging around Beulah's kitchen. Beulah's other black companion was Oriole, a feather-brained maid who worked for the white family next door. Storylines tended to involve Beulah coming

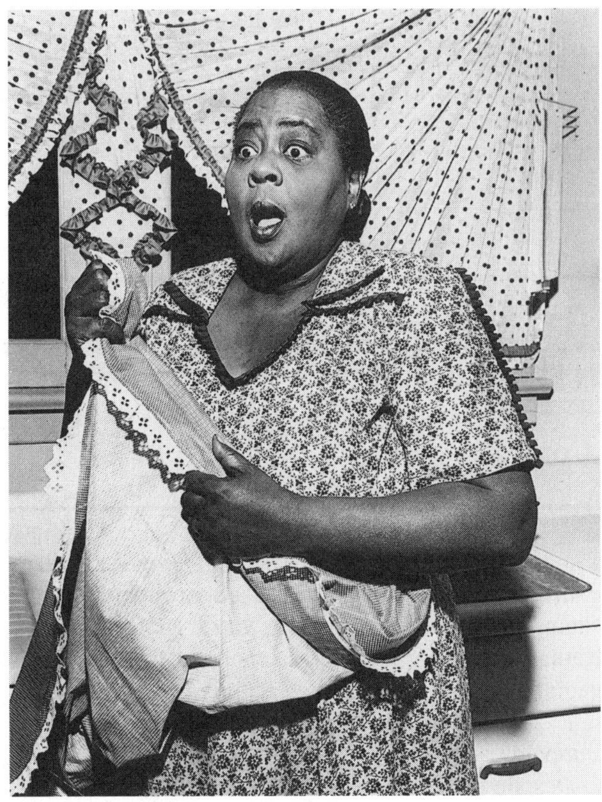

Beulah, Louise Beavers, 1950–53.
Courtesy of the Everett Collection

to the rescue of her employers, by providing a great spread of Southern cuisine to impress Mr. Henderson's business clients, teaching the awkward Donnie how to dance jive and impress the girls, or saving the Hendersons' stale marriage. Beulah's other major obsession was trying to get Bill to agree to marry her. A regular comedic feature of the show involved Bill hyperbolically proclaiming his devotion to Beulah, while always finding a reason why the two could not wed just yet.

As one of the very few images of African Americans on prime-time television in this period, the program came in for a certain amount of criticism for perpetuating comic black stereotypes. The show was panned in the *New York Times* and condemned by widely syndicated television critic John Crosby, who singled out Ethel Waters for censure. Waters achieved great renown as a vocalist, an actress (particularly for her work in the Broadway production, *A Member of the Wedding*), and the author of a brutally honest rags-to-riches autobiography. Yet her work in *Beulah* was considered by Crosby, and some critics in the black press, as a betrayal of her other exemplary accomplishments. Actor Bud Harris, who had been contracted to play the role of Bill, quit the series a few months into its run, complaining that the show's writers were forcing him to play the character as an "Uncle Tom" and engage in comic activity he found degrading to his race.

Despite these examples of controversy, *Beulah* never generated the amount of heated debate that *Amos 'n' Andy* provoked. The latter series joined the television airways a year after *Beulah* and became a flashpoint for organized protest. At its June 1951 annual convention, the National Association for the Advancement of Colored People condemned both shows for depicting black people in a derogatory manner that "tends to strengthen the conclusion among uninformed or prejudiced peoples that Negroes and other minorities are inferior, lazy, dumb, and dishonest." The organization, however, chose to engage in a consumer boycott only of *Amos 'n' Andy*'s sponsor, and not Procter and Gamble, the sponsor of *Beulah.*

Beulah is significant in that it was part of a phenomenon in early entertainment television programming that saw more diversity in ethnic and racial depictions than would be seen again at any time until the late 1960s. The portrayals may have been stereotyped—as they were in other early 1950s ethnic sitcoms such as *The Goldbergs* and *Life with Luigi*—but at least African Americans were visible in prime-time hours. After *Beulah* left the air in September 1953, no program would star a black woman again until 15 years later in 1968, when *Julia* appeared.

ANIKO BODROGHKOZY

See also **Waters, Ethel**

Cast

Beulah (1950–52)	Ethel Waters
Beulah (1952–53)	Louise Beavers
Harry Henderson (1950–52)	William Post, Jr.
Harry Henderson (1952–53)	David Bruce
Alice Henderson (1950–52)	Ginger Jones
Alice Henderson (1952–53)	Jane Frazee
Donnie Henderson (1950–52)	Clifford Sales
Donnie Henderson (1952–53)	Stuffy Singer
Oriole (1950–52)	Butterfly McQueen
Oriole (1952–53)	Ruby Dandridge
Bill Jackson (1950–51)	Percy (Bud) Harris
Bill Jackson (1951–52)	Dooley Wilson
Bill Jackson (1952–53)	Ernest Whitman
Alice's Mother	Madge Blake
Harry's Mother	Ruth Robinson

Producer
Roland Reed

Programming History
ABC
October 1950–September 1953   Tuesday 7:30–8:00

Further Reading

Dates, Jannette L., and William Barlow, editors, *Split Image: African Americans in the Mass Media,* Washington, D.C.: Howard University Press, 1990

Kolbert, Elizabeth, "From Beulah to Oprah: The Evolution of Black Images on TV," *New York Times,* January 15, 1993

MacDonald, J. Fred, *Blacks and White TV: Afro-Americans in Television Since 1948,* Chicago: Nelson-Hall Publishers, 1983; 2nd edition, 1992

Steenland, Sally, *The Unequal Picture: Black, Hispanic, Asian, and Native American Characters on Television,* Washington, D.C.: National Commission on Working Women, 1989

Beverly Hillbillies, The

U.S. Situation Comedy

The Beverly Hillbillies (1962–71, CBS) was the brainchild of Paul Henning, the cracker-barrel surrealist also responsible for *Petticoat Junction, The Real McCoys,* and, notably, *Green Acres.* Certainly the most popular sitcom in television history, and quite possibly the most successful network series ever, *The Beverly Hillbillies* ran more than 200 episodes, clocking in as the top-rated show of its premier season and remaining in the top ten throughout its nine-year tenure. Individual episodes almost always placed in the Nielsen Top 20 and, on occasion, rivaled the ratings of Super Bowls.

As explained in the opening montage and cadenced theme song, Jed Clampett (Buddy Ebsen) is an Ozarks mountaineer who, through epic fortuity and sheer ineptitude rather than the Protestant work ethic, falls into unfathomable wealth with the discovery of oil beneath his worthless Arcadian scrub oak. When a roving petrochemical concern gets wind, they buy him out for $25 million, whereupon town sophisticate Cousin Pearl (Bea Benaderet) convinces him fabled Beverly Hills might provide a suitable beau for his daughter Elly May (Donna Douglas) and career opportunities for his wayward nephew Jethro Bodine (Max Baer Jr.). Taking their cue from *The Grapes of Wrath* (John Steinbeck via John Ford), they load up the truck and move to Beverly Hills, California—replete with a rocking chair up top to house Granny (Irene Ryan), the family's reluctant matriarch.

Despite his mystification at the newfangled trappings of luxury, and the craven depths to which almost everyone around him sinks, Jed remains a bastion of homespun wisdom—very much the Lincolnesque backroads scholar. Virtually recycling his George Russel character, the sidekick in Disney's *Davy Crockett* series from the mid-1950s, Ebsen eventually carried the Lincoln conceit over into his private life, authoring a stage play in 1966 titled *The Champagne Generation,* in which he starred as the late president. (When Nancy Kulp, the birdwatching Vassar grad Miss Jane Hathaway, ran for a Congressional seat from Pennsylvania in the early 1980s, she lost only when Buddy Ebsen, a lifelong Republican, stepped in to actively campaign against her.)

Despite the silliness of much of its humor, *The Beverly Hillbillies* managed to bolster its credibility among its core audience with a kind of hillbilly authenticism. Bluegrass avatars Lester Flatt and Earl Scruggs were enlisted for the theme song, which quickly became a number one hit on country-western charts, and they frequently appeared on the show as themselves (long before their music was appropriated for its native exoticism by the film *Bonnie and Clyde*). Cousin Pearl was a textbook recreation of Grand Ol' Opry mainstay Minnie Pearl, and Roy Clarke was an occasional guest before inheriting the show's constituency with his 20-year stint as host of *Hee Haw.* Even the series name was taken from a bluegrass band of the 1930s. And, of course, the characters of Jethro, Elly Mae, and Granny seemed to borrow more than casually from Li'l Abner, Daisy May, and Mammy Yokum, respectively.

Yet, turning up in the fall of 1962 as they did, the paradigmatic arrivistes, the Clampetts seemed to mirror almost perfectly another eccentric clan of uninvited backwoods arrivals, one which was thrust into the national spotlight—decisively and distastefully—with the Kennedy assassination. Suddenly, instead of glamorous Brahmins dictating the national agenda, the United States was headed by Texas crackers straight off the farm (whose political fortunes could be traced back to Texas Tea of their own). And long before Lyndon Johnson was known for his consummate political savvy and rattlesnake ruthlessness, he entered the pop-

The Beverly Hillbillies, Buddy Ebsen, Donna Douglas, Irene Ryan, Max Baer Jr., 1962–71.
Courtesy of the Everett Collection

ular culture as a national embarrassment, remembered and endlessly ridiculed for turning off the lights in the White House to save electricity, or showing an incredulous nation his gallbladder scar.

By extension, the show became in certain quarters something of a public embarrassment as well, emblematic of the nation's having slipped another notch into pandering anti-intellectualism, a pervasive "bubbling crude" that stained all in its wake. By the time television had caught up with the changing times—the fall of 1971—youth culture and its built-in consumer demographic looked far more appealing to advertisers on the professional rut, and *The Beverly Hillbillies,* while still vastly successful, was caught in the same network purge that claimed Jackie Gleason, Red Skelton, and rural mainstays such as *Mayberry RFD* and Henning's own *Green Acres.* This was the same changing of the guard that ushered in *The Mary Tyler Moore Show, All in the Family, M*A*S*H,* and, ostensibly, social realism and the death of the 1960s. A made-for-television movie about *The Beverly Hillbillies* appeared on CBS in 1981, without Baer, and the series was later remade as a feature film in 1993 by the makers of *Wayne's World,* but neither did justice to the original.

PAUL CULLUM

See also **Comedy, Domestic Settings**

Cast

Jed Clampett	Buddy Ebsen
Daisy Moses (Granny)	Irene Ryan
Elly May Clampett	Donna Douglas
Jethro Bodine	Max Baer Jr.
Milburn Drysdale	Raymond Bailey
Jane Hathaway	Nancy Kulp
Cousin Pearl Bodine (1962–63)	Bea Benaderet
Mrs. Margaret Drysdale (1962–69)	Harriet MacGibbon
Jethrene Bodine (1962–63)	Max Baer Jr.
John Brewster (1962–66)	Frank Wilcox
Edythe Brewster (1965–66)	Lisa Seagram
Jasper DePew (1962–63)	Phil Gordon
Ravenswood, the butler (1962–65)	Arthur Gould Porter
Marie, the maid (1962–63)	Sirry Steffen
Sonny Drysdale (1962)	Louis Nye
Janet Trego (1963–65)	Sharon Tate
Lawrence Chapman (1964–67)	Milton Frome
Studio Guard (1964–66)	Ray Kellogg
John Cushing (1964–67)	Roy Roberts
Dash Riprock (nee Homer Noodleman)(1965–69)	Larry Pennell
Homer Cratchit (1968–71)	Percy Helton
Elverna Bradshaw (1969–71)	Elvia Allman
Shorty Kellems (1969–71)	George "Shug" Fisher
Miss Switzer (1969–70)	Judy Jordan
Helen Thompson (1969–71)	Danielle Mardi
Miss Leeds (1969)	Judy McConnell
Susan Graham (1969–71)	Mady Maguire
Gloria Buckles (1969–71)	Bettina Brenna
Shifty Shafer (1969–71)	Phil Silvers
Flo Shafer (1969–71)	Kathleen Freeman
Joy Devine (1970–71)	Diana Bartlett
Mark Templeton (1970–71)	Roger Torrey

Producers

Paul Henning, Al Simon, Joseph DePew, Mark Tuttle

Programming History

216 episodes
CBS

September 1962–September 1964	Wednesday 9:00–9:30
September 1964–September 1968	Wednesday 8:30–9:00
September 1968–September 1969	Wednesday 9:00–9:30
September 1969–September 1970	Wednesday 8:30–9:00
September 1970–September 1971	Tuesday 7:30–8:00

Further Reading

Marc, David, *Demographic Vistas: Television in American Culture,* Philadelphia: University of Pennsylvania Press, 1984; 2nd edition, 1996

Marc, David, *Comic Visions: Television Comedy and American Culture,* Boston: Unwin Hyman, 1989; 2nd edition, Malden, Massachusetts: Blackwell Publishers, 1997

Marc, David, and Robert J. Thompson, *Prime Time, Prime Movers: From I Love Lucy to L.A. Law—America's Greatest TV Shows and the People Who Created Them,* Boston: Little, Brown, 1992

Story, David, *America on the Rerun: TV Shows That Never Die,* Secaucus, New Jersey: Carol, 1993

Beverly Hills 90210

U.S. Serial Drama

Despite a slow start in its inaugural season on FOX in fall 1990, *Beverly Hills 90210* quickly became an important fixture on the network and in the popular discourse of adolescents and young adults. In that first season the show's main characters (Dylan, Kelly, Donna, Steve, David, Andrea, and twins Brandon and Brenda) all attended West Beverly Hills High School (zip code 90210). Transplants from Minneapolis, Minnesota, Brandon and Brenda Walsh and their parents were a stable nuclear family with strong values; their home was a safe haven for the whole gang and the center of much of the drama during the early years of the program. By its third season, the show's popularity had soared, and in 1993 it became available in syndication both in the United States and internationally. By 1996 the teenage characters in this highly rated show had graduated from high school; in subsequent seasons some went on to attend, and then graduate from, fictional California University. Over the history of the program, a number of original cast members left the program and new characters were introduced. Despite such changes, *Beverly Hills 90210* continually attracted a loyal viewership for ten seasons.

Produced by Aaron Spelling, who has seemed to have his finger on the pulse of popular television taste since the 1960s, *Beverly Hills 90210* was the first in a string of programs on FOX geared toward adolescent and young adult audiences. As fans were attracted to the show's glamour and attention to certain issues, *90210*'s popularity soared. Cast members were interviewed regularly on other television programs and in such magazines as *TV Guide, Seventeen, Rolling Stone,* and *Ladies' Home Journal.* Soon, *Beverly Hills 90210* dolls, books, and fan clubs were everywhere. The show set clothing and hairstyle trends for both male and female youth. Young women regularly sent letters to the character Brenda, asking her advice on their dating and other personal problems. Addressing topics of concern to adolescents in a way unlike any other teen drama to date, the series was soon taken seriously by parents, educators, and scholars as well. Plots involved learning disabilities, prejudice, divorce, date rape, sexuality, alcoholism, and drug use. In the first season it was revealed that one of the main characters, Dylan, had recurring drug and alcohol problems, while another, Kelly, had a drug- and alcohol-abusing mother in recovery. Donna overcame a learning disability, and several others struggled through parental divorce and remarriage. Many of the show's adolescent characters were sexually active, and issues concerning safe sex and contraception were openly discussed on the program.

However, not everyone considered *90210* realistic. Some critics charged that the show offered unreal or stereotypical representations. The characters were almost all white and upper class. Nonwhites appeared almost exclusively in episodes dealing with prejudice or difference. They were also almost always lower income, from a zip code outside Beverly Hills. Of the main characters, Andrea was the only Jewish female, and she was portrayed as the brainy, less-attractive female, whereas Kelly, Donna, and Brenda were sexier and less intellectual. Most viewers could not identify with the high-income, mostly WASP background of the Beverly Hills teens. Yet in spite of criticisms and differences, *Beverly Hills 90210* retained a diverse youth audience.

Hoping to capitalize on the early success of *90210,* other FOX-Spelling collaborations followed. The first, *The Heights,* which was less glamorous but featured the same age group, did not last. Neither did the later *Models, Inc.,* set in the fashion industry, nor *Malibu Shores,* another show about rich adolescents, which lasted only nine episodes in 1996. However, *90201* spin-off *Melrose Place,* did become a hit. That program, also set in southern California, featured a cast in their 20s, working on careers and later-life issues such as marriage and divorce. *Melrose Place* differed from *Beverly Hills 90210* by being far less sincere or moralistic in treating issues. *Melrose Place* relationships and plots were more sensationalized, in a manner reminiscent of early 1980s prime-time serials, *Dynasty* and *Dallas.*

The rise of *Beverly Hills 90210* and its ilk coincided with changes in broadcast network television in an era of increased competition from cable television. Network program "narrowcasting" to the youth market represented an attempt to remain competitive with other television distribution outlets. It also signaled a renewed effort to take seriously issues of importance to young people, a large and lucrative niche market.

KATHERINE FRY

Beverly Hills, 90210, 1990–2000; Shannen Doherty, Luke Perry, Tori Spelling, Brian Austin Green, Jennie Garth, Jason Priestley, Gabrielle Carteris, Ian Ziering, 1991.
Courtesy of the Everett Collection

Cast

Brandon Walsh (1990–98)	Jason Priestley
Brenda Walsh (1990–94)	Shannen Doherty
Kelly Taylor	Jennie Garth
Donna Martin	Tori Spelling
Dylan McKay (1990–95, 1998–2000)	Luke Perry
Steve Sanders	Ian Ziering
Andrea Zuckermann (1990–95)	Gabrielle Carteris
David Silver	Brian Austin Green
Scott Scanlon (1990–91)	Douglas Emerson
Jim Walsh (1990–95)	James Eckhouse
Cindy Walsh (1990–95)	Carol Potter
Nataniel "Nat" Buccigio	Joe E. Tata
Clare Arnold (1993–97)	Kathleen Robertson
Valerie Malone (1994–98)	Tiffani-Amber Thiessen
Jesse Vasquez (1994–95)	Mark D. Espinoza
Ray Pruit (1994–96)	Jamie Walters
Jackie Taylor	Ann Gillespie
Mel Silver	Matthew Laurance
Felice Martin (1991–2000)	Katherine Cannon
Carly Molloy (1997)	Hilary Swank
Noah Hunter (1998–2000)	Vincent Young
Janet Sosna (1998–2000)	Lindsay Price
Matt Durning (1998–2000)	Daniel Cosgrove
Gina Kincaid (1998–99)	Vanessa Marcil

Producers

Jessica Klein, Larry Mollin, Jason Priestley, Aaron Spelling, E. Duke Vincent, Paul Waigner, Steve Wasserman

Programming History

FOX

October 1990–August 1992	Thursday 9:00–10:00
July 1992–May 1993	Wednesday 8:00–9:00
June 1993–August 1993	Tuesday 8:00–9:00
September 1993–May 2000	Wednesday 8:00–9:00

Further Reading

Fitzgerald, Kate, "*90210* Promo ZIP: Marketers Hitch a Ride as Show Goes Worldwide," *Advertising Age* (September 6, 1993)

Freeman, Mike, "Worldvision Pitches Reps on Strength of *90210*," *Broadcasting & Cable* (March 22, 1993)

Rapping, Elayne, "The Year of the Young," *The Progressive* (February 1993)

Roberts, Donald F., "Adolescents and the Mass Media: From *Leave It to Beaver* to *Beverly Hills 90210*," *Teachers College Record* (Spring 1993)

Simonetti, Marie-Claire, "*Degrassi Junior High* and *Beverly Hills 90210*," *Journal of Popular Film and Television* (Spring 1994)

Bewitched

U.S. Situation Comedy

Bewitched, a fantasy situation comedy featuring the suburban life of a witch housewife married to a mortal, aired on ABC from 1964 to 1972. In its first season, it was the highest-rated new series, and for its first five seasons, the program found itself consistently in Nielsen's top 12. By 1968 its reruns had sold to ABC for $9 million.

Set in Westport, Connecticut, *Bewitched* chronicles the difficulties Samantha (Elizabeth Montgomery) has negotiating between her supernatural powers and her role as the suburban housewife of advertising executive Darrin Stevens (Dick York, replaced by Dick Sargent after the fifth season). Other major characters include Samantha's mother, Endora (Agnes Moorehead), who enjoys employing meddling witchcraft to complicate her daughter's marriage; a suspicious neighbor named Gladys Kravitz (Alice Pearce, later replaced by Sandra Gould); and Darrin's neurotic boss, Larry Tate (David White). Sporadically, Elizabeth Montgomery would appear as her cousin, Serena, embodied as a "teeny-bopper," counterculture type, with a knack for free-spirited and manipulative sorcery. Eventually, Samantha and Darrin have a daughter, Tabitha, and a son, Adam, both of whom display witchly powers. (In 1977 ABC attempted a spin-off called *Tabitha,* in which the now grown witch [Lisa Hartman] worked as assistant producer for a California news program, with Robert Urich as the anchorman. The spin-off failed before season's end.)

Bewitched's formula typically involves a disruption created by either Samantha's or Darrin's family, or by Darrin's boss, Larry. Samantha's responsibility for maintaining family harmony comes into conflict with her vow not to exercise witchcraft. Usually, the resolution does come about through witchcraft, but Samantha's role as a "good" wife undergoes re-inscription because she has performed her spells for the sake of her family.

Samantha generally exercises her witchcraft by twitching her nose and mouth (known at the time of the show as the "witch twitch"), or by casting verbal spells. Either method may result in making objects and people disappear or appear; or Samantha may grant unearthly powers to herself or others, or turn herself or others into various kinds of animals. Samantha constantly subordinates her supernatural powers at the request of her husband—he is particularly adamant that she not cheat her domestic duties. Samantha could easily have the entire house cleaned and dinner on the table with a single "witch twitch" but, for Darrin's sake, she chooses to perform the labor of housework herself.

At the same time, Samantha takes a keen interest in Darrin's job and gets him out of many a campaign jam with her "imagination" and "intuition"—sometimes attributed to her witchcraft, sometimes not. She often saves Darrin's job by producing sales concepts on the spot for his clients, sometimes even going to the extent of turning his clients into animals to prove a point or buy him time. Her mastery in this area includes shoring up Darrin's ego and making him feel that it is *his* ideas that saves the day. In this way, *Bewitched* addressed a host of pressing concerns for mid-1960s middle-class American culture, such as anxieties about women's place in the public and private spheres and general mistrust between the sexes: What is the appropriate woman's role? How should a woman exercise her own agency to the best of her abilities? What do we do with female power, since it has been relegated to a place outside of culture for so long? Toward the end of the run of *Bewitched,* Samantha often traveled to far away places and times or interacted with historical figures, somewhat displacing the centrality of the home and middle-class suburban life.

Bewitched, Elizabeth Montgomery, Agnes Moorehead, Dick York, 1964–72.
Courtesy of the Everett Collection

Notably, Elizabeth Montgomery's real-life husband was William Asher, the director of the series (who also directed *I Love Lucy, The Danny Thomas Show,* and *The Patty Duke Show*). Asher and Montgomery owned a percentage of profits of *Bewitched* as well as a percentage of the merchandising rights, which involved the conception of a Samantha doll, jewelry, cosmetics, and a *Bewitched* ice cream flavor. The couple's first child was born three weeks before the production of the first episode, leading much of the popular press at the time to refer to the initiation of the show as a "birthing process."

That series premier remains one of *Bewitched*'s most memorable episodes in many ways. When Samantha reveals to Darrin that she is a witch, he seeks the advice of others (best friend, doctor, bartender), each of whom refuses to take him seriously. So he returns home, resolving, "So my wife's a witch. Every married man has to make some adjustments." His conclusion rings true and continues to define much of the series—marriage may not be what it appears on the surface, and the commitment to marriage and family, certainly for late 20th-century Americans, meant confronting male fears about women's sexuality and otherness, women's power, and the changing social and cultural significance of domestic institutions.

CHRISTINA LANE

Cast

Samantha Stephens/Serena	Elizabeth Montgomery
Darrin Stephens (1964–69)	Dick York
Darrin Stephens (1969–72)	Dick Sargent
Endora	Agnes Moorehead
Maurice	Maurice Evans
Larry Tate	David White
Louise Tate (1964–65)	Irene Vernon
Louise Tate (1965–72)	Kasey Rogers
Tabitha Stephens (1966–72)	Erin and Diane Murphy
Adam Stephens (1971–72)	David and Greg Lawrence
Abner Kravitz	George Tobias
Gladys Kravitz (1964–66)	Alice Pearce
Gladys Kravitz (1966–72)	Sandra Gould
Aunt Clara (1964–68)	Marion Lorne
Uncle Arthur (1965–72)	Paul Lynde
Esmerelda (1969–72)	Alice Ghostley
Dr. Bombay (1967–72)	Bernard Fox

Producers

Harry Ackerman, William Froug, Danny Arnold, Jerry Davis, Bill Asher

Programming History

306 episodes
ABC

September 1964–January 1967	Thursday 9:00–9:30
January 1967–September 1971	Thursday 8:30–9:00
September 1971–January 1972	Wednesday 8:00–8:30
January 1972–July 1972	Saturday 8:00–8:30

Further Reading

Marc, David, "Every Witch Way but Loose," *Village Voice* (August 20, 1985)
Marc, David, *Comic Visions: Television Comedy and American Culture,* Boston: Unwin Hyman, 1989; 2nd edition, Malden, Massachusetts: Blackwell Publishers, 1997
Pilato, Herbie J., *The Bewitched Book: The Cosmic Companion to TV's Most Magical Supernatural Situation Comedy,* New York: Dell, 1992
Spigel, Lynn, "From Domestic Space to Outer Space: The 1960s Fantastic Family Sit-Com," in *Close Encounters: Film, Feminism, and Science Fiction,* edited by Constance Penley, Elisabeth Lyon, Lynn Spigel, and Janet Bergstrom, Minneapolis: University of Minnesota Press, 1991

Big Brother

International Reality Program Format

Big Brother was a hugely popular international phenomenon that swept across Europe, North and South America, Africa, and Australia during the "reality" programming boom that began in the Netherlands in late 1999, with subsequent distinct culture-specific manifestations airing in about 20 different countries over the following two years. All of the various permutations have followed the same basic formula. Described by the Dutch production company Endemol, as a "real life soap," *Big Brother* is a hybrid genre: part verité documentary and part game show, with the ongoing daily rhythm of the soap opera, yet married in a new and different way to the webcasting capabilities of the Internet.

Based upon the Orwellian concept of a group of people subject to an all-seeing, all-knowing, and all-controlling power (in this case, the producers) the premise is simple. Select ten participants who agree to be isolated together as a group in a fabricated "house" lined with not-so-hidden television cameras rolling around the clock for 12 weeks. Deprive them of contact with the outside world, and create opportunities for them to bond—or not—as they form a community. Present them with tasks and challenges that will either encourage teamwork or create competition. Create a way for contestants (euphemistically called "houseguests") to nominate their peers for "banishment," but in which the viewing audience actually gets the final vote as to which contestant is removed each week. Allow a special room in which the contestants can talk "privately" to the cameras and the producers to express their "feelings, frustrations, thoughts and nominations," all the while being filmed. Broadcast highlights from the daily lives and mundane interactions of the contestants on television in prime time multiple nights of the week, while also creating a website with live streaming video feed from multiple cameras that interested fans can access 24 hours a day. Each week, have a studio-based show in which the "host" of the program talks to the contestants, announces who has been voted off, and then removes the banished contestant and interviews him or her as well as family and friends of the contestants in front of a studio audience. In this way, the number of contestants is slowly whittled down to the winner of the sizeable grand prize (250,000 Dutch guilders in the original version; $500,000 in the first U.S. version, broadcast on CBS television network in the summer of 2000).

The first attempts at the Endemol reality formula in Europe were received with phenomenal popular success, both economically and in terms of stirring up a public discourse about cultural values, ethics, privacy, and the human condition. The popular press covered the "new reality TV" extensively, focusing on its potential to radically change the notion of television in our society. As they had in Europe, the upcoming U.S. adaptations of the reality television formulas in the summer of 2000 (notably *Survivor* and *Big Brother*) received extraordinarily heavy promotion.

The narrative "action" and interpersonal drama that take place in the *Big Brother* house are supposed to be naturally occurring, although the producers affect the drama through their casting of the "characters" and their structuring of the daily activities of the houseguests around a series of programmed tasks ("challenges"). A high degree of self-consciousness also curtails the spontaneity of the contestants' behavior, owing to their knowledge that everything they do or say is subject to national broadcast via web feed or television. On the viewing end, the experience is one that *Maclean's* contributor Robert Sheppard calls "orchestrated voyeurism."

The first U.S. version of Endemol Production Company's *Big Brother* was broadcast on CBS television with concurrent live online feeds in partnership with America Online (AOL). Unlike its European predecessors, it was described as a "ratings disappointment" for CBS despite its fairly consistent weekly placement in the Nielsen top 20; however, the most notable aspect of the *Big Brother* phenomenon was its remarkable crossover Internet presence and the strong and loyal online audience it created and maintained. It gained acclaim as an unprecedented, momentous hit on the Internet. America Online, which partnered with CBS and Endemol to provide the streaming web feed of the voyeuristic cameras, as well as setting up the program's official website, boasted about the overwhelming success of the online ratings. In fact, this became the most remarkable aspect of the entire U.S. *Big Brother* venture. Journalist David Kronke reported that *Big Brother* "has changed the way television and new media can interact," while popular culture scholar Robert Thompson was quoted as saying that, because of this unprecedented convergence, "When the final history of TV is written, *Big Brother* will be considered more important than the better and more highly rated *Survivor*." News reports indicated that the AOL-sponsored site was the most visited new Internet site in July of 2000, the month the program premiered, with more than 4.2 million visitors. AOL's publicity articles touted the "unprecedented convergence between television and the Internet" achieved by the CBS-AOL *Big Brother* alliance as the "largest ongoing webcast in history," and claimed a "tenfold increase in participants [of] the streaming webcast during peak usage time in the first week."

Big Brother broke new ground in establishing a multiplicity of ways that a television program could reach its audience. In fact, one could argue that what we call *Big Brother* actually consists of several different programs, several distinct audiences, and multiple versions of its narrative. The *Big Brother* production, in its multimedia entirety, provides opportunities for viewers to engage with the narrative situation engendered by the program's premise in a variety of ways: all mediated, but to varying degrees and through different media discourses and structures. Moreover, the complexity of the phenomenon makes it difficult to even find the language to talk about it. Is it a television "show," a webcast, a form of performance art, a cultural phenomenon, an unfolding news event? In many important ways, it is all of these—and that will, ultimately, be *Big Brother*'s lasting contribution to television history.

PAMELA WILSON

See also **Reality Programming; *Survivor***

Further Reading

August, Melissa et al., "Reality Bites Back," *Time* (September 14, 2000)

Carter, Bill, "Television's New Voyeurism Pictures Real-Life Intimacy," *New York Times* (January 30, 2000)

Charski, Mindy, "TV Companion Site Creates Buzz," *Inter@ctive Week* (July 17, 2000)

Johnson, Brian D., "We Like To Watch," *Maclean's* (January 29, 2001)

Knight, Brooke A., "Watch Me! Webcams and the Public Exposure of Private Lives," *Art Journal* (Winter 2000)

Miller, Edward D., "Fantasies of Reality: Surviving Reality-Based Programming," *Social Policy* (Fall 2000)

Podhoretz, John, "*Survivor* and the End of Television," *Commentary* (November 2000)

Poniewozik, James et al., "We Like To Watch," *Time* (June 26, 2000)
Rosenbaum, Steven, "Peeping Tom TV: The Beginning of the End or the Birth of Meaningful Media?" *Television Quarterly* (Summer 2000)
Rothstein, Edward, "TV Shows in Which the Real Is Fake and the Fake Is Real," *New York Times* (August 5, 2000)
Sardar, Ziauddin, "The Rise of the Voyeur," *New Statesman* (November 6, 2000)
Sheffield, Rob, "Reality," *Rolling Stone* (September 14, 2000)
Sheppard, Robert, "Peeping Tom Television," *Maclean's* (April 10, 2000)
Wolcott, James, "Now Voyeur," *Vanity Fair* (September 2000)

Billy Graham Crusades

U.S. Religious Program

Billy Graham is often at pains to distinguish himself from the band of preachers known as "televangelists," and his programs have typically been formulaic in the extreme. Still, no other evangelist has used television as efficiently, effectively, and, ultimately, as creatively as has Billy Graham.

The legendary preacher's initial experiment with television occurred in 1951, when he attempted to take his phenomenally successful radio program, *The Hour of Decision,* to the new medium. Some programs featured filmed segments from live crusades, where Graham was at his best, but most were studio productions that showed him in a study or living-room setting. They often included obviously rehearsed interviews and did not allow him to preach with the kind of intensity and effectiveness he could manifest before a large crowd. The program ran for nearly three years on the fledgling ABC network, but neither Graham nor his associates have ever regarded it as a particularly memorable effort. Years later he told an interviewer, "They are interesting films, but I can't find anyone who ever saw one! Prime time on Sunday nights on network TV, and no one remembers."

Graham's next attempt to fulfill the Great Commission via the cathode ray tube came in 1957, during his summer-long crusade at Madison Square Garden in New York City. At ABC's invitation, and with J. Howard Pew's financial guarantees, Graham began airing his Saturday-night services live from the Garden. The first broadcast, on June 1, posted an 8.1 Trendex rating, which translated into approximately 6.4 million viewers, more than enough to convince the evangelist of television's great promise as a vehicle for the gospel. A Gallup poll taken that summer revealed that 85 percent of Americans could correctly identify Billy Graham, and three-quarters of that number regarded him positively. In an innocent masterpiece of understatement, *Christian Life* magazine cautiously observed, "Undoubtedly, this fact will affect Graham's ministry."

Those first telecasts were quite simple. Cliff Barrows led a huge chorus in familiar hymns. George Beverly Shea sang "How Great Thou Art"; a celebrity or two gave a testimony of the power of Christ in his or her life; Graham preached; and hundreds of people streamed toward him when he offered the invitation at the conclusion of his sermon. Remarkably, Graham has stuck to that same prosaic formula for more than 40 years. To be sure, production values have improved dramatically, viewers are sometimes treated to a brief tour of the host city, Graham has adjusted his speaking style and bodily movements to the smaller screen, and the programs are aired weeks after the crusades end rather than live—but the basic elements remain the same.

One key to Graham's success in using television was an early decision not to attempt a weekly Sunday morning program. As years of Nielsen and Arbitron ratings have demonstrated, his programs, usually aired in prime time in groups of three on a quarterly basis, draw audiences far larger than those for the syndicated Sunday programs of other religious broadcasters. This larger audience also appears to contain far more unchurched people than do the Sunday shows. No less important, 12 programs a year, filmed while he is doing what he would be doing anyway, cost less than a weekly studio program, minimize the risk of overexposure, and cause far less drain on the evangelist's time and energy. In recent years, the production team has filmed all services in a crusade and then blended the best segments into three composite programs.

In addition to reaching for a mass audience with an edited product, Graham has long used the television medium to carry crusade services live to audiences in locations far from the central arena. In 1954, during a 12-week effort that packed London's Harringay Arena, the sound from the crusade was carried to various sites by landline relay. Twelve years later, during his 1966 visit to London, Graham used Eidophor projection equipment to supply a television feed to beam his message into auditoriums and stadiums in British cities where the ground had been prepared as if he were going to be present for a full-scale live crusade. A similar effort, also in London, followed in 1967. In 1970 he used an ambitious and innovative television relay system to transmit a crusade in Dortmund, Germany, to theaters, arenas, and stadiums throughout western Europe and into Yugoslavia—"unscrambling Babel," as one aide put it—to reach speakers of eight different languages in ten nations.

In recent years, many of Graham's crusades, especially those outside the United States, have used satellite technology to elaborate on this means of multiplying the effectiveness of his crusades. Interestingly, the number of "inquirers" responding to Graham's invitation almost always match or exceed those registered at the central site. Encouraged by such results, the Billy Graham Evangelistic Association launched an ambitious effort to reach virtually the entire world in a series of transmissions collectively known as *Mission World.* In 1989 Graham preached from London to more than 800,000 people gathered at 247 "live-link" centers throughout the United Kingdom and the Republic of Ireland, and to an astonishing 16,000 sites in 13 nations of Africa. In most cases, the down-link was effected by means of low-cost portable satellite dishes. Another 20 African nations received the program by videotape a week or two later, usually after translation into one of nine different languages. The aggregate attendance at the African sites exceeded 8 million. In 1990 similar technology was used to beam Graham's sermons from Hong Kong to an estimated 100 million persons assembled at 70,000 locations in 26 countries of Asia. In 1991 a Buenos Aires satellite mission reached 5 million people at 850 locations in 20 countries. The European edition of *Mission World,* dubbed "ProChrist '93," transmitted services from Essen, Germany, to 386 remote sites in Germany, Austria, and Switzerland and beyond these to more than 1,000 venues in 56 countries or territories in 16 time zones.

The climax to these efforts and, in all probability, to Billy Graham's ministry, came in March 1995, when the 76-year-old evangelist's distinctive voice and familiar message soared upward from his pulpit in Puerto Rico to a network of 30 satellites that bounced it back to receiving dishes in 185 countries in all 29 time zones, to be viewed at appropriate hours. With the possible exception of the Olympics, this may well have been the most technologically complex example of worldwide communication ever attempted. Plausible estimates indicate that, when network television telecasts and delayed videotape presentations were included, as many as 1 billion people heard at least one of Graham's sermons during this campaign, aptly titled *Global Mission.* In 1996 the Graham organization produced two World Television Series, in which approximately 1 million churches worldwide helped set up video house parties to which church members could invite their friends and neighbors.

Billy Graham.
Photo courtesy of the Billy Graham Evangelistic Association

Graham sees no contradiction between "the old, old story" and the newest means to transmit it. "It is time," he observed, "for the church to use the technology to make a statement that in the midst of chaos, emptiness and despair, there is hope in the person of Jesus Christ."

William Martin

See also **Religion on Television**

Further Reading

Frady, Marshall, *Billy Graham: A Parable of American Righteousness,* Boston: Little, Brown, 1979

Martin, William, *A Prophet with Honor: The Billy Graham Story,* New York: William Morrow, 1991

Morgan, Timothy C., "From One City to the World," *Christianity Today* (April 24, 1995)

Muck, Terry, and Harold L. Myra, "William Franklin Graham: Seventy Exceptional Years" (interview), *Christianity Today* (November 18, 1988)

Neff, David, "Personal Evangelism on a Mass Scale," *Christianity Today* (March 8, 1993)

Pollock, John Charles, *To All the Nations: The Billy Graham Story,* Cambridge, Massachusetts: Harper and Row, 1985

Rosell, Garth M., "Grace Under Fire," *Christianity Today* (November 13, 1995)

Streiker, Lowell D., and Gerald S. Strober, *Religion and the New Majority: Billy Graham, Middle America, and the Politics of the 70s,* New York: Association Press, 1972

Thomas, William, *An Assessment of Mass Meetings as a Method of Evangelism: Case Study of Eurofest '75 and the Billy Graham Crusade in Brussels,* Amsterdam: Redopi, 1977

Birt, John

British Television Executive

John Birt is certainly the most controversial and quite possibly the most significant director general of the BBC of the first 80 years of existence. A Tony Blair and Labour party supporter, he was appointed to clean up what was considered by the Conservative party to be a bureaucratically bloated quasi-governmental organization with a bias against right-wing policies. Birt's tenure at the helm of the world's largest broadcasting organization was supposed to bring about a slimmed down organization with ever greater creative control for its producers and directors. But critics now argue that Birt listened too much to management consultants who knew little about the principles and practices of what is arguably the greatest public service broadcasting organization in the world. Among the older generation of BBC producers, Birt's policies are considered to have led to a permanent weakening of the BBC. His short-term employment policies destroyed that sense of security that can lead to the best of creative work. While some BBC staff who left created successful new independent production companies, others whose commercial abilities did not match their creative ones were lost to broadcasting permanently.

Birt's successor, Greg Dyke, struggles to repair the damage and to eliminate all traces of "Birtism," but in fact the BBC of the 21st century is a less happy and less confident organization than the BBC that flourished in the great days of Directors General Hugh Carleton Green and Ian Trethowan.

John Birt received an engineering degree from Oxford University, joined Granada Television and then London Weekend television and is partly credited with the success of LWT's political program "Weekend World." Birt's name first came to public attention when he coauthored an article in the *Times* that suggested that the treatment of politics on television created a "bias against understanding," and that political broadcasting needed to change.

Prime Minister Margaret Thatcher, long critical of the BBC and its director general Alasdair Milne, appointed the right-wing former editor of the *Sunday Times,* Marmaduke Hussey, as chairman of the BBC. Hussey fired Milne and in 1987 employed Birt as head of news, with the understanding that Birt would replace the interim director general, Michael Checkland, in due course. For 60 years the chairmen of the BBC had not interfered with BBC management; it was argued that constitutionally, their role was to represent the interests of the public, not to manage. Hussey ignored tradition, and worked closely with Birt to remove most of the top management. Hussey and Birt used the U.S. management consultants McKinsey to introduce vast and ultimately wastefully bureaucratic plans like "producer choice," and fired or gave early retirement to all who objected. The average age of BBC employees fell from 40 to 28; almost the entire cadre of seasoned producers and directors were removed.

In defense of Birt, it was claimed that the BBC was too large and too expensive when Birt became director general in 1993. In 1996 Birt reorganized the BBC into six divisions. BBC Broadcast scheduled channels and commission services, BBC Production developed BBC in-house radio and television, and BBC News was responsible for an integrated national and international news organization. BBC Worldwide was responsible for generating commercial income at home and abroad, and for the World Service. BBC Resources provided the facilities and expertise to serve and support BBC program-makers. And the BBC Corporate Center provided strategic services. Key executives like Jenny Abramsky, director of BBC Radio and Music, considered the changes disastrous; the money, and therefore the power, had been transferred to the broadcast division, and producers in the vast new production division (which included both radio and television) were mere suppliers, competing with the independent sector for work within the BBC. Suddenly BBC producers and their departments were forced to declare war on each other as they battled for commissions in order to keep their jobs. Departmental priorities were eroded; science producers could suggest programs on religion and vice versa. All producers felt undervalued and some felt they were being treated with contempt; radio producers suffered more than most. As cost cutting was the purpose of this whole vast reorganization, program editors were dismissed and production teams amalgamated. With many producers on short-term contracts, they abandoned adventurous new ideas, relying instead on the formulaic programming that could guarantee their jobs for the next six months. Their desperation to earn commissions led departments, especially in radio, to submit a host of underdeveloped ideas for every available slot, rather than concentrate on producing two or three quality proposals. One head of radio claimed that each producer in the drama department spent an average of 14 weeks of the year working up proposals, 90 percent of which were never commissioned.

Birt's introduction of "producer choice," while controversial, made BBC producers more financially accountable. His vision of the BBC as a 21st-century "information provider" was promising; he foresaw scores of new cable channels for many offshoots of BBC programming, a digital future similar to that envisaged by the AOL-Time Warner or Disney-ABC conglomerates. However, the BBC is not a truly commercial organization; its principal income came from its license fee, not commercial operations.

Little of Birt's BBC structure survived his departure. The new director general, Greg Dyke, was appointed in the year 2000 and dismantled and reorganized most of Birt's bureaucracy. Birt's concept of "bi-media" was swept away, and radio and television news were reinstated as separate production departments. Dyke believed that collaboration, not destructive internal competition, was needed to make a creative organization like the BBC thrive.

ANDREW QUICKE

See also **British Programming; British Television; Dyke, Greg**

Black Entertainment Television

U.S. Cable Network

Black Entertainment Television (BET) is the first and only television network in the United States primarily devoted to African-American viewers. Launched with a paltry $15,000 investment in 1980, the black-owned, basic-cable franchise had grown into a diversified, $61 million media enterprise by the mid-1990s. Despite this rather phenomenal growth, however, BET's audience reach continues to be overshadowed by larger cable-industry players (e.g., Home Box Office [HBO] and ESPN).

Based in Washington, D.C., BET has added about 2 million subscriber homes per year since 1984, reaching more than 40 million cable households in 2,500 markets by 1995. Moreover, the network has more than tripled revenues since 1985; it reported profits for the first time in 1986, when it finally hit Nielsen ratings charts and attracted major advertisers. In 1991 BET Holdings, Inc. (BET's parent company) became the first black-owned company to be traded on the New York Stock Exchange.

From the very beginning, the heart and soul of BET programming was the music video. Predating MTV by a year, BET has offered as much as 18 hours of music videos a day, prompting many to perceive the 24-

Courtesy of BET

hour network as essentially a black-oriented music video service. Thus, while MTV was being criticized in 1983 for excluding black artists from its playlist (Tina Turner and the interracial group English Beat excepted), many viewers were tuning into BET for such offerings. Indeed, the network's flagship program, *VideoSoul,* has become a household name in many black communities.

As BET grew, however, the network began to diversify its program offerings and image. By its tenth anniversary in 1990, the network had initiated several original programs and projects, including *For the Record,* featuring members of the Congressional Black Caucus; *Teen Summit,* a Saturday afternoon show for youth; *Black Agenda 2000,* a series of forums on issues of interest to the black community; *Conversation with Ed Gordon,* an interview program with contemporary newsmakers; *Inside Studio A,* concerts and interviews taped before a live audience; *Personal Diary,* one-on-one interviews with prominent blacks; *On Stage,* plays written and performed by blacks; and *Our Voices,* a daily talk show.

More recent BET program schedules have included *ComicView,* a stand-up comedy review; *Screen Scene,* a black-oriented entertainment journal; *Jazz Central,* a jazz music program; and *Rap City,* a rap video program. From time to time, BET also airs sporting events featuring teams from historically black colleges and universities, and rounds out its schedule with reruns of popular black-oriented shows such as *Sanford and Son, What's Happening, Frank's Place,* and *Roc.* News and public affairs programs tend to be relegated to the weekends.

BET was the brainchild of Robert L. Johnson, who developed the idea for the network in 1979 while serving as vice president for governmental relations at the National Cable Television Association. Johnson, an African American, noted in 1989 that BET "should be for black media what Disney is to the general media or what Motown was to music." Industry observers have applauded Johnson's efficient management style and his aggressive plans to expand the company's product base and consumers.

Johnson argued in 1989 that industry racism had stunted BET's growth. In particular, he noted that many cable operators had been slow to carry BET (it was carried on only 1,825 of the nation's 7,500 systems in 1989), and that BET had been saddled with some of the lowest subscriber fees in the industry (e.g., BET earned only about 5 cents per subscriber in 1989, while other cable services typically earned between 15 and 20 cents per subscriber). Some analysts agreed with Johnson's charges of industry racism, but noted that many of BET's problems were due to the network's lack of resources and Johnson's corresponding inability to adequately market it.

Nonetheless, since its humble beginnings BET has become much more than just a basic-cable network. By 1995 BET Holdings owned and operated a broad array of black-oriented media products, including *Black Entertainment Television,* the basic-cable network; *YSB* (*Young Sisters and Brothers*), a magazine targeted at black youths; *Emerge,* a magazine offering analysis and commentary on contemporary issues facing black America; Action Pay-Per-View, a national, satellite-delivered, pay-per-view movie channel based in Santa Monica, California; BET International, a provider of BET programming throughout Africa and other foreign markets; Identity Television, a London-based cable service targeting Afro-Caribbean viewers; BET Productions, a subsidiary providing technical and production services to outside companies; BET Radio Network, a radio service providing news and entertainment packages to affiliated stations across the United States; and BET Pictures, a joint venture with Blockbuster Entertainment Corporation to produce and distribute black, family-oriented films.

After successfully reverting BET back to private ownership in 1998, Johnson in late 2000 moved to merge his 20-year-old company with industry powerhouse Viacom. At the time of the proposed merger, Viacom owned MTV, VH1, CMT, the Box, MTV2, and dozens of radio stations. Critics in the African-American community bemoaned the loss of black control over what had become the largest African-American media company. Viacom and Johnson countered that BET would retain its African-American focus, adding that Johnson had agreed to a five-year contract with Viacom to run BET. Johnson became the second-largest individual stockholder in Viacom.

DARNELL M. HUNT

See also **Johnson, Robert**

Further Reading

Brown, Joe, "Toasting a Sure BET: Black Network Links to New Satellite," *Washington Post* (August 16, 1982)

Hall, Carla, "Birth of a Network: Salesman and Stars at a Kick-off for BET," *Washington Post* (January 25, 1980)
Hay, Carla, and Frank Saxe, "BET, Viacom Solidify Merger," *Billboard* (November 18, 2000)
Little, Benilde, "Robert Johnson: The Eyes Behind BET," *Essence* (November 1990)
Margulies, Lee, "Black Cable TV Network Grows," *Los Angeles Times* (December 8, 1981)
Osborne, Karen, "BET: Tuning into Viewers," *Black Enterprise* (April 1989)
Shales, Tom, "Beyond *Benson:* Black-Oriented Channel from a Cable Pioneer," *Washington Post* (November 30,1979)
Stein, Lisa, "Getting BETter: After 10 Years, TV's Black Network Comes of Age," *TV Guide* (June 16, 1990)
Sturgis, Ingrid, "The BE 100s: BET Expands into Pay-Per-View," *Black Enterprise* (September 1993)
Watson, John G., "Black Network Debuts on Cable," *Los Angeles Times* (January 29, 1980)
Williams, Christopher C., "A Black Network Makes Its Move: Cable's BET Puts Plenty of Ambition into Its Fall Schedule," *New York Times* (September 17, 1989)

Black and White in Colour

British Documentary

In 1992 BBC Television broadcast a season of programs celebrating the contributions black and Asian people have made to British television. Prior to the five consecutive evenings' special screenings, BBC 2 broadcast *Black and White in Colour* (June 26 and July 3, 1992), a two-part documentary tracing black participation in British television. The programs resulted, in part, from the British Film Institute (BFI) Race and Ethnicity Project. This project began in 1985 and aimed, through archival research, to examine black people's involvement in British television, both on and off the screen. The research emerged at a time when the debate about race and cultural representation was at its peak, and when there was increasing criticism of images of blackness on British television.

Black and White in Colour is a British Film Institute production, directed by the black British filmmaker, Isaac Julien. It examines both the sociopolitical context and on-screen developments, and in so doing, it effectively traces the shifts and contours of black British television history. The documentary, which uses rare archive footage, is narrated by the scholar Stuart Hall and includes interviews with actors, actresses, cultural critics, directors, and other key players in the making of black British television history.

The first part of *Black and White in Colour* begins by noting black American performers' contribution to British variety in the 1930s and 1940s. American entertainers such as Adelaide Hall, Buck and Bubbles, and Elisabeth Welch were some of the first images on TV that British people saw of black people. Compared to other genres, light entertainment was significantly advanced in celebrating black performers such as Harry Belafonte and Shirley Bassey. *Black and White in Colour* goes on to discuss how the image of black person as social problem was developed in the postwar years, particularly in news and documentary programming. The late 1950s saw the emergence of some innovative drama focused on race and the black British experience—for example, John Elliot's *A Man from the Sun* (1956) and John Hopkin's *Fable* (1965). What *Black and White in Colour* highlights is that most pre-1970s programming quite clearly spoke about and referred to black people but this population was not directly addressed.

The second part of *Black and White in Colour* concentrates on black representation on British television from 1962 to 1992. It begins by describing how Enoch Powell and his 1968 "Rivers of Blood" speech influenced perceptions of black British people. The most popular program on British television at this time was Johnny Speight's sitcom *Till Death Us Do Part,* which, although it rarely featured black characters, gave space to the blatantly racist views of Alf Garnett (often described as Powell's alter-ego). *Black and White in Colour* points out that, generally speaking, the first part of the 1970s was an uncreative time in terms of images of blackness. A number of situation comedies during the 1970s, such as *Love Thy Neighbour, Mind Your Language,* and *Mixed Blessings,* claimed that they were diffusing racial tension by laughing at racism, but in fact these shows developed their own set of racist stereotypes. During the same period, the first programs that featured predominantly black casts began to emerge. *Empire Road* (1978–79) was the first black soap opera to be made for British television screens. *Black and White in Colour* also examines off-screen developments at this time, when many black artists were beginning to complain and campaign for better roles on television. For example, the Equity's Coloured Artists Committee was established in 1974. In 1979 the Campaign against Racism in the Media critically assessed television's representation of race in *It Ain't Half Racist Mum.*

Black and White in Colour examines the impact of Channel 4 and the black British independent film movement on black cultural representation during the 1980s. Black programming was built into the structure of Channel 4, which began in 1982. Subsequently, black audiences were offered their own magazine programs, such as *Eastern Eye* and *Black on Black* and comedies such as *No Problem!, Tandoori Nights,* and *Desmond's.* The specifically black programs of the 1980s spurred a number of debates about black audiences, race, and television.

Although *Black and White in Colour* traces a history that reveals an improvement in images of blackness on British television since 1936, the analysis makes it clear that representations of black people remained far from perfect and that many of the early patterns were still apparent. In that sense, the two-part documentary is more a retrospective than a celebration. Most importantly perhaps, *Black and White in Colour* manages to illustrate how much black artists and practitioners have had to struggle to gain access to the British television institution.

SARITA MALIK

Programming History

Documentary aired in two parts
BBC
June 26, and July 3, 1992

Further Reading

Dhondy, Farrukh, "*Black and White in Colour* in the U.K," *Intermedia* (August 1992)

Pines, Jim, editor, *Black and White in Colour: Black People in British Television since 1936,* London: British Film Institute, 1992

Black and White Minstrel Show, The

British Music/Variety/Minstrel Show

One hundred years after the "nigger minstrel" entertainment tradition had begun in London's music halls, the convention was revived on television in the form of *The Black and White Minstrel Show.* This variety series was first screened on BBC Television on June 14, 1958, and it was to stay on air for the next two decades. *The Black and White Minstrel Show* evolved from the "Swannee River" type minstrel radio shows. One year before it was first broadcast on television, George Inns produced the *1957 Television Minstrels* (BBC TV 2; September 1957) as part of the National Radio Show in London.

The occasional television specials soon developed into a regular series with a 45-minute nonstop format of Mississippi tunes and country-and-western songs. The series was devised and produced by Inns and featured music conducted by George Mitchell and the Television Toppers Dance Troupe. The series showcased the Mitchell Minstrels as well as solo performances from entertainers such as Tony Mercer, John Boulter, and Dai Francis. During the early years, various comedians such as Lesley Crowther, Stan Stennett, and George Chisholm acted as "fillers" between the slick song-and-dance routines.

The Black and White Minstrel Show won the 1961 Golden Rose of Montreux. The variety series could almost always guarantee an audience of at least 16 million and frequently managed to top 18 million viewers. At a time when the variety show was a popular television genre for the whole family, *The Black and White Minstrel Show* established itself as one of the world's greatest musical programs on television. The music from the show broke sales records, and the stage show was equally popular. Robert Luff's production opened at the Victoria Palace Theatre in 1969 and established itself in *The Guinness Book of Records* as the stage show seen by the largest number of people. At this time, the creation had gained considerable international respect and kudos. *The Black and White Minstrel Show*'s success was marked by its regular

Saturday night transmissions over a vast period. The program managed to maintain its freshness, its manic pace, and its nostalgic premise on a weekly basis.

What accounts for such immense popularity? Part of the explanation was undoubtedly the pleasure many received from the program, with its meticulously choreographed dance routines and popular songs and melodies. Inns combined white dancers with black-faced singers, and this was believed to be visually striking, particularly when color television was introduced in 1967. *The Black and White Minstrel Show* harked back to a specific period and location—the deep American South, where coy white women could be seen being wooed by docile, smiling black slaves. The black men were, in fact, white artists "blacked-up." The racist implications of the premise of the program were yet to be widely acknowledged or publicly discussed, but it was this aspect that contributed significantly to the program's eventual demise.

Many believed that a large part of "minstrel humor" is based on caricaturing black people and depicting them as being both stupid and credulous. This image was thought to be insensitive and inappropriate in an increasingly multiracial and multicultural Britain. *The Black and White Minstrel Show* is important in the context of British television because it outlines how racist representations became part of public debate and how performance is linked to social context. The program revealed tensions between the television controllers, critics, and audience. Many were angry because during this time there were very few other representations of black people on British television. On May 18, 1967, the Campaign against Racial Discrimination delivered to the BBC a petition signed by both black and white people, which requested that the program be taken off television. Despite the controversy, the program continued until July 1, 1978. Ultimately, its removal from the air coincided with the demise of the popularity of the variety genre on British television.

SARITA MALIK

Regular Performers
Leslie Crowther
George Chisholm
Stan Stennett

Singers
The Mitchell Minstrels

Solo Performers
Tony Mercer
Dai Francis
John Boulter

Dancers
The Television Toppers

Producer
George Inns

Programming History
BBC
June 1958–July 1978

Blackadder. *See* **Atkinson, Rowan**

Blacklisting

Blacklisting is the practice of refusing to hire or terminating from employment an individual whose opinions or associations are deemed politically inconvenient or commercially troublesome. In the U.S. tradition, the term is forever linked to the fervent anticommunism of the cold war era, a time when government agencies, private newsletters, and patriotic organizations branded selected members of the entertainment indus-

The Report of
COMMUNIST INFLUENCE IN RADIO AND TELEVISION

Published June, 1950

By AMERICAN BUSINESS CONSULTANTS
Publishers of
COUNTERATTACK
THE NEWSLETTER OF FACTS TO COMBAT COMMUNISM
55 West 42 Street, New York 18, N. Y.

Cover of *Red Channels.*
Photo courtesy of Wisconsin Center for Film and Theater Research

try as (variously) card-carrying Communists, fellow travelers, pinkos, or unwitting dupes of Moscow. The rubric "McCarthyism" is often used as shorthand for the reckless accusations and limitations on free expression during the cold war, but from a media perspective, the term is something of a misnomer. The period of the blacklist predated and postdated the reign of the junior senator from Wisconsin, and Joseph R. McCarthy himself evinced little interest in the entertainment industry: his targets of choice were the Department of State and the U.S. Army. The blacklisting of directors, writers, and performers in film, radio, and television was the project of a much wider coalition of anticommunist forces, a web of interlocking agents that included government investigators (the Federal Bureau of Investigation, or FBI), legislative committees (the House Un-American Activities Committee [HUAC] and the Senate Internal Security Subcommittee), private interest groups (American Business Consultants, AWARE, Inc.), and patriotic organizations (the American Legion, the Veterans of Foreign Wars). These forces applied pressure on, and worked in concert with, fearful and compliant studio heads, network executives, sponsors, and advertising agencies to curtail the employment opportunities and civil rights of targeted undesirables.

The convergence of two cultural historical factors abetted the blacklist. One of the legacies of World War II was a heightened sensitivity to the political impact of the popular media; one of the coincidences of history was that television's early days paralleled precisely the escalating intensity of the cold war in the years from 1946 to 1954. The contest between East and West, Soviet Communism and American democracy, found its domestic expression in impassioned debates over the subversive influence of the mass media. In June 1950, the atmosphere reached fever pitch with the arrest of the atomic spies Julius and Ethel Rosenberg and the outbreak of the Korean War. That same month the editors of *Counterattack,* a four-page "newsletter of facts on communism," issued a special report titled *Red Channels, The Report of Communist Influence in Radio and Television,* a listing of 151 names of performers deemed to be Communist party members or to have like-minded opinions and associations (called "fellow travelers" in the argot of the day). The *Red Channels* report formalized an informal practice in effect since at least November 1947, when representatives from the major Hollywood studios pledged they would "not knowingly employ a communist" and "take positive action" on "disloyal elements." Though the scholarship of *Red Channels* was slipshod—the actors listed ranged from unapologetic Communist party members to mainstream liberals to bewildered innocents—its impact was immediate and long-lasting. CBS instituted in-house loyalty oaths; the advertising firm of Batten, Barton, Durstine, and Osborn recruited executives to serve as security officers. A study on blacklisting in the entertainment industry published by the Fund for the Republic in 1956 concluded that *Red Channels* put in black-and-white what was previously an ad hoc practice and thus "marked the formal beginning of blacklisting in the radio-TV industry."

As an emergent medium subject to government oversight by the Federal Communications Commission, television was the most timorous of the mass media when confronted by state power. The scrutiny of legislative bodies concentrated the minds of network executives powerfully, notably the hearings held by the House Un-American Activities Committee in October 1947 and throughout the early 1950s and a kindred set of hearings on the "Subversive Influence of Radio, Television, and the Entertainment Industry" held by Senator McCarran's Internal Investigatory

Subcommittee in 1951. Moreover, as an advertiser-supported medium still in embryonic development, television was especially susceptible to protests from special interest groups threatening product boycotts, pickets, or public censure. Casting the widest commercial net possible, the networks aimed for "100 percent acceptability" and assiduously avoided alienating any group of potential viewers.

Though the effect of the blacklist was punitive, its rationale was preemptive. From the perspective of the networks, its purpose was less to rid the medium of subversive content than to avoid the controversy that ensued upon the appearance of a suspect individual. Rather than canceling the appearance of announced performers or firing known talent, the blacklist tended to operate off-camera, behind the scenes, by deleting or clearing talent in advance. Though the list in *Red Channels* was the founding document, other lists and publications (not to say rumors and innuendo) might also render an individual politically radioactive in the eyes of any one of the networks, sponsors, or advertising agencies.

For talent tainted with the Communist brush, the path to vindication was tortuous. Once accused, actors might suffer in silence, defy the accusations, or engage in rituals of public recantation or denial ("clearance") either before Congress, in the public press, or at the offices of *Counterattack* itself. Given the difficulty of proving a negative, the total number of people burned by the blacklist—careers permanently derailed, jobs lost, or energies squandered—is difficult to gauge, but hundreds were listed and investigated and thousands were singed by paranoia. Even allowing for the vagaries of memory and self-romanticization, the blacklist traumatized a generation of artists in the entertainment industry. One particularly tragic case may stand for many. Listed in *Red Channels,* Philip Loeb, who played the warm Jewish patriarch on *The Goldbergs* during the show's first television season in 1950–51, was replaced in the show's second season after General Foods withdrew its sponsorship. An embittered and unemployed Loeb committed suicide in 1955.

In the wake of the TV-inspired downfall of McCarthy in 1954, some of the pressure to purge alleged subversive from the airwaves lifted, but the blacklist—both as a formal, institutionalized procedure and as an informal gentleman's agreement—endured well into the next decade. The motion picture industry began gingerly defying the blacklist in the late 1950s and by 1960 was giving screen credit to once-blacklisted writers. By contrast, television, ever cautious, kept well back in the ranks of defiance. Not until the fall of 1967, on *The Smothers Brothers Comedy Hour,* was blacklisted folk singer Pete Seeger finally "cleared" for a return to network television.

THOMAS DOHERTY

See also **Censorship; *Smothers Brothers Comedy Hour, The***

Further Reading

Bentley, Eric, *Are You Now or Have You Ever Been: The Investigation of Show Business by the Un-American Activities Committee, 1947–1958,* New York: Harper and Row, 1972

Burton, Michael C., *John Henry Faulk: The Making of a Liberated Mind,* Austin, Texas: Eakin Press, 1993

Ceplair, Larry, *The Inquisition in Hollywood: Politics in the Film Community, 1930–1960,* Garden City, New York: Anchor Press/Doubleday, 1980

Cogley, John, *Report on Blacklisting,* New York: Fund for the Republic, 1956

Faulk, John Henry, *Fear on Trial,* New York: Simon and Schuster, 1964

Foley, Karen Sue, *The Political Blacklist in the Broadcast Industry: The Decade of the 1950s,* New York: Arno Press, 1979

Navasky, Victor S., *Naming Names,* New York: Viking, 1980

Red Channels: The Report of Communist Influence in Radio and Television, New York: American Business Consultants, 1950

Vaughn, Robert, *Only Victims: A Study of Show Business Blacklisting,* New York: Putnam, 1972

Bleasdale, Alan (1946–)

British Writer

Alan Bleasdale is one of the most successful and influential writers working in British television today. Drawing on the traditions of realist television drama, he established his reputation with several powerful but darkly comic screenplays set in the depressed cities of northern England.

Bleasdale's first success as a writer came with the development of the character of Scully, a Liverpool youth whose anarchic adventures challenge the authority of those responsible for the impoverished society in which he lives. A series of stories about Scully was broadcast on BBC Radio Merseyside in 1971, while Bleasdale was still earning his living as a teacher. From 1974 to 1979, Bleasdale presented the *Franny Scully Show* on Radio City Liverpool; the character also appeared in a touring theater show, a television play called *Scully's New Year's Eve,* broadcast by the BBC in 1978; and two novels that became the basis of a Granada television series in 1984.

The ability to create characters who capture the popular imagination was also apparent in *Boys from the Blackstuff,* the series that firmly established Bleasdale as a key figure in British television in the 1980s. This project had its roots in a single play called *The Black Stuff,* broadcast by the BBC in 1980, dealing with the disastrous money-making efforts of a gang of road workers from Liverpool. With the support of producer Michael Wearing, Bleasdale was able to create a five-part series dealing with the effects of unemployment on the "boys" and their families after their return to Liverpool.

Boys from the Blackstuff was first shown in a late-night time slot on BBC 2 in 1982 but proved so popular that it was quickly repeated in prime time on BBC 1 in January 1983. Each episode centers on a different character, but their paths frequently cross and the action builds toward the final episode in which they all come together at the funeral of an old worker whose socialist ideals no longer inspire the men of Margaret Thatcher's Britain. The impact of the series grew out of its commitment to showing the experience of unemployment from the point of view of the unemployed. It drew on the conventions of northern working-class realism prevalent in British cinema and television since the 1960s but also included elements of black comedy (derived from Liverpool's traditional "scouse" humor) and grotesque nightmare images that expressed the psychological pressures of unemployment. This mixture of elements created an unsettling effect, but, despite its bleak vision, *Boys from the Blackstuff* promoted a sense of solidarity in viewers who faced similar problems. Catchphrases from the series were incorporated into chants by the supporters of the Liverpool soccer team.

Bleasdale has continued to write for television, as well as for film and theater, but the closest he has come to repeating the success of *Boys from the Blackstuff* has been with *GBH,* a seven-part serial broadcast on Channel 4 in 1991. Dealing with the takeover of a northern English city by a fascist organization, *GBH* was related to earlier serials, such as Troy Kennedy Martin's *Edge of Darkness* (1985) and Alan Plater's *A Very British Coup* (1988), which blended science fiction and political thriller to address growing fears that the British democratic system was threatened with collapse. Bleasdale's political message was more explicitly stated here than in *Boys from the Blackstuff,* but the fiction was once again enriched by grotesque comedy, largely associated with the casting of Michael Palin, a member of the Monty Python troupe, as an unassuming school teacher who inadvertently becomes a symbol of resistance to the new order.

In 1994 Bleasdale took on a new role as producer of a series on Channel 4 called *Alan Bleasdale Presents,* using the influence made possible by the popular success of his work to give young writers a chance to demonstrate their talents. While the dramas presented in this series have adopted a variety of approaches, they owe much to Bleasdale's own achievement, grounded in the tradition of "naturalism" in British television drama but creating compelling fictions by gradually introducing disruptive elements drawn from popular genres.

In his two most substantial screenplays of the mid- to late 1990s, Bleasdale moved away from the northern working-class environments of his earlier work. *Jake's Progress* (Channel 4, 1995) was a six-part serial dealing with a crisis in a middle-class family, while *Oliver Twist* (ITV, 1999) was an eight-hour adaptation of Charles Dickens's novel. Both continued Bleasdale's efforts to push the boundaries of realism, filtering reality through the perceptions of a child for whom the adult world becomes a nightmare and often challenging viewers with highly disturbing images.

JIM LEACH

See also ***Boys from the Blackstuff***

Alan Bleasdale. Born in Liverpool, England, March 23, 1946. Attended St. Aloysius Roman Catholic Infant and Junior Schools, Huyton, Lancashire, 1951–57; Wade Deacon Grammar School, Widnes, Lancashire, 1957–64; Padgate Teachers Training College (Teacher's Certificate), 1967. Married Julia Moses, 1970; children: two sons and one daughter. Teacher, St. Columbus Secondary Modern School, Huyton, Lancashire, 1967–71, King George V School, Gilbert and Ellice Islands, 1971–74, and Halewood Grange Comprehensive School, Lancashire, 1974–75; resident playwright, Liverpool Playhouse, 1975–76, Contact Theatre, Manchester, 1976–78; joint artistic director, 1981–84, and associate director, 1984–86, Liverpool Playhouse. Liverpool Polytechnic, D.Litt. 1991. Recipient: Broadcasting Press Guild Television Award for Best Series, 1982; British Academy of Film and Television Arts Writers' Award, 1982; Royal Television Society Writer of the Year, 1982; Pye Television Award, 1983; Toronto Film Festival Critics' Award, 1984; *London Standard* Best Musical Award, 1985; ITV Best British TV Drama of the Decade Award, 1989; Broadcasting Press Guild Television and Radio Award, 1991.

Television Series

1982 *Boys from the Blackstuff*
1984 *Scully*
1991 *GBH*
1994 *Alan Bleasdale Presents* (producer)
1995 *Jake's Progress*
1997 *Melissa* (also executive producer)
1999 *Oliver Twist* (also producer)

Television Specials

1975 *Early to Bed*
1976 *Dangerous Ambition*
1978 *Scully's New Year's Eve*
1980 *The Black Stuff*
1981 *The Muscle Market*
1986 *The Monocled Mutineer*
1991 *Julie Walters and Friends* (co-writer)

Film

No Surrender, 1986.

Stage

Fat Harold and the Last 26, 1975; *The Party's Over,* 1975; *Scully* (with others), 1975; *Franny Scully's Christmas Stories* (with Kenneth Alan Taylor), 1976; *Down the Dock Road,* 1976; *It's a Madhouse,* 1976; *Should Auld Acquaintance,* 1976; *No More Sitting on the Old School Bench,* 1977; *Crackers,* 1978; *Pimples,* 1978; *Having a Ball,* 1981; *Young People Today,* 1983; *Are You Lonesome Tonight?,* 1985; *Love Is a Many Splendoured Thing,* 1986; *On the Ledge,* 1993.

Publications

Scully (novel), 1975
Who's Been Sleeping in My Bed? (novel), 1977
No More Sitting on the Old School Bench (play), 1979
Love Is a Many Splendoured Thing (play), 1979
Scully (play), with others, 1984
Scully and Mooey (revised version of *Who's Been Sleeping in My Bed?*), 1984
Boys from the Blackstuff (television play), 1985
Are You Lonesome Tonight? (musical), 1985
It's a Madhouse / Having a Ball (plays), 1986
The Monocled Mutineer (television play), 1986
No Surrender: A Deadpan Farce (screenplay), 1986

Further Reading

Millington, Bob, "Boys from the Blackstuff," in *British Television Drama in the 1980s,* edited by George W. Brandt, Cambridge: Cambridge University Press, 1993
Millington, Bob, and Robin Nelson, *Boys from the Blackstuff: The Making of TV Drama,* London: Comedia, 1986
Paterson, Richard, "Restyling Masculinity: The Impact of *Boys from the Blackstuff,*" in *Impacts and Influences: Essays on Media Power in the Twentieth Century,* edited by James Curran, Anthony Smith, and Pauline Wingate, London: Methuen, 1987
Paterson, Richard, editor, *Boys from the Blackstuff,* London: British Film Institute, 1984
Saynor, James, "Clogging Corruption," *Sight and Sound* (July 1991)
Tulloch, John, *Television Drama: Agency, Audience, and Myth,* London: Routledge, 1990

Blue Peter

British Children's Program

Blue Peter is one of British television's longest-running programs, regularly reaching 5 to 6 million children and teenagers. It takes its name from the blue-and-white flag hoisted by a ship leaving port on a voyage. The originator of the program wanted this to suggest the voyage of discovery that the show would provide for its young viewers. The programming has a magazine format that involves a combination of studio presentation, interview, and demonstration with additional film report items. It is transmitted live from the

BBC's Television Centre after hectic rehearsal. The program was launched with its catchy "Barnacle Bill" signature tune in 1958 as a 15-minute slot, involving two presenters, described by Barnes and Baxter as "Chris Trace playing with trains and Lelia Williams playing with dolls." It became a twice-weekly, 30-minute program in 1963. A third presenter was later introduced, and its Monday/Thursday slots were changed to thrice-weekly transmission (Monday/Wednesday/Friday) in 1965. *Blue Peter* runs for a 40-week season from autumn to early summer with a 10-week break in which special overseas items are filmed. The program is broadcast between 17:05 and 17:35 hours, a bridging slot taking teenagers into an Australian soap opera and into "adult" early evening news. It has won more than 20 major television awards, including from BAFTA, the Sun Television, and the National Viewers and Listeners Association for excellence in children's programming.

Blue Peter is successful as a program because it has remained true to the basic format of its original creator, John Hunter Blair, but has accommodated itself to the social changes that have taken place over two generations of television viewing. Editorial continuity was achieved through the singular influence of long-standing editor Biddy Baxter, who worked on *Blue Peter* between 1962 and 1988. Baxter was a liberal, inventive, but demanding leader of the program team, with a very shrewd sense of how the developing medium could best be harnessed for a young audience. In the best tradition of British public service broadcasting, *Blue Peter* aims to inform, educate, and stimulate its target viewers with entertaining content, and it remains one TV program that parents encourage their children to watch.

In the 1960s many of the program's innovations were quickly imitated by rivals or adapted in later programs, such as ITV's *Magpie,* which aired from 1968 to 1980. In 1965, for instance, *Blue Peter* introduced a puppy to the program and then asked its viewers to send in suggestions for its name. Petra became the nation's first TV pet. Phenomenally popular, other pets, including cats and tortoises, were added to the program so that respect for animals and pet care tips could be passed on. The program actively encouraged the participation of its viewers by instituting a *Blue Peter* badge scheme (awarded for appearances on the program or special achievements), regular competitions, and an annual Christmas appeal to raise money for charity.

The studio items very often involve presenters trying new hobbies, cooking, making homemade toys from household rubbish (washing-up liquid bottles, wire coat hangers, and "sticky-backed plastic" being favored materials), or bringing talented youngsters into the studio to make their achievements more widely known. The overall ethos of the program encourages children by the example of the adult presenters to "have a go," to try something new and be inquisitive about the world around them. *Blue Peter* presenters with strong personalities involved in unforgettable exploits have impressed themselves on the popular memory of television viewers. The phrases of their scripted cookery demonstrations ("here's one I made earlier") and idiosyncratic expressions ("get down, Shep!") have become clichés and are parodied in pop songs. The show remains "live," which means that unplanned incidents occur, much to the delight of the viewers. One such moment has gone down in British television lore. It involved a baby elephant ("Lulu") departing from the script by defecating in the studio and running amok with its elderly zookeeper as the transmission came to a close.

Today's presenters follow in a long line of enthusiastic personalities who have played no small part in shaping the views of generations of viewers. Critics of the program suggest that *Blue Peter*'s format, content, and presentation epitomize a "safe" agenda of middle-class attitudes, that it is patronizing toward young people, replicating a dominant ideology. The program's own audience research would suggest that on the whole its target audience do not feel patronized. Given the centrality of *Blue Peter* to its scheduling area, it is not surprising that it tends to reflect the values and aspirations of the institution from which it originates. It is more accurate to see *Blue Peter* as a barometer of social values and cultural change in Britain over the extended period of its existence. Like all successful programs, *Blue Peter* has had to deal with change and be flexible to a degree, but this has been uneven. Lewis Bronze, who succeeded Baxter in 1988, introduced Diane-Louisi Jordan, a black presenter, in 1990. The editorial team was quietly accepting and supportive of the unmarried status of Janet Ellis, who became pregnant, but shaken to find out that one of its ex-presenters, Michael Sundin, turned out to be gay. The significance of *Blue Peter* within British television history resides in its longevity, continued popularity, and institutional centrality. Within Children's BBC, *Blue Peter* is still, in the words of Anna Home, head of Children's Television, "very deliberately chosen as one of the foundation stones upon which the rest of the schedule can be built."

LANCE PETTITT

Presenters

Christopher Trace, Leila Williams, Valerie Singleton, Peter Purves, John Noakes, Diane Louisi-Jordan, Janet Ellis, Michael Sundin, and others

Producer
John Hunter Blair

Programming History
BBC
Various times, from 1958

Further Reading

Baxter, B., and E. Barnes, *Blue Peter: The Inside Story,* London: BBC Books, 1989
The Blue Peter Annual, London: BBC, 1964–
Ferguson, Robert, "Black Blue Peter," in *Television Mythologies: Stars, Shows, and Signs,* edited by Len Masterman, London: Comedia, 1984

Bob Newhart Show, The/Newhart

U.S. Situation Comedies

The Bob Newhart Show and *Newhart* are both prime examples of the ensemble comedy that came into vogue in U.S. television during the 1970s and enjoyed continued popularity in the 1980s and 1990s. The two shows had much else in common (in addition to their star, Bob Newhart); both had sharp writing, well-drawn characters, and a distinctive style of humor that was intelligent and sophisticated, yet just a bit off-the-wall.

As with many 1970s ensemble sitcoms, such as *The Mary Tyler Moore Show, The Bob Newhart Show* focused on career-oriented adults, mostly single, related by circumstance rather than blood. Newhart played Dr. Bob Hartley, a psychologist practicing in Chicago. He treated a variety of patients whose problems, no matter how eccentric, were played for laughs; the star among them was the misanthropic Elliott Carlin (Jack Riley). Bob's office mate was Dr. Jerry Robinson (Peter Bonerz), an orthodontist and typical 1970s "swinging single"; they shared the services of a quick-witted secretary-receptionist, Carol Kester (Marcia Wallace). Bob's wife, Emily—smart, funny, and sexy—was played by Suzanne Pleshette. The couple's neighbor and closest friend in their high-rise apartment building was Howard Borden (Bill Daily), a childlike airline navigator who ate most of his meals with the Hartleys and had them water his plants even when he was home; he was, in effect, the offspring they did not have. "That guy could lose an argument with a fern," was the caustic Carlin's comment on Howard.

A few lines and situations illustrate the show's deft and daft humor: Bob and Emily have a bicentennial party in 1976 and invite Carlin because, according to Bob, "He says he gets lonely every bicentennial"; Howard explains how spilling salt could be fatal—after Bob nearly falls down an elevator shaft and becomes obsessed with death; the Hartleys send Howard to a psychologist so he can become independent and responsible—but then want the old Howard back; Jerry comes into money, gives up his practice, and turns into "the village coot," who wants to do nothing but whittle and watch the sunrise.

These characters, even if defined by their specific quirks, developed and grew throughout the show's long run. Emily began as a substitute teacher, became a full-time teacher, and moved up to vice principal; Carol married a travel agent and also tried out some other careers, but always came back to Bob and Jerry; Howard was engaged for a time to Bob's sister Ellen, a newspaper reporter, but she went out of his life and off the show when she moved to Cleveland, Ohio, for a better job (and after she had a flirtation with Howard's visiting brother, game warden Gordon Borden). The show made creative use of running gags such as Bob's one-sided telephone conversations, which had been a popular part of Newhart's standup act; his habit of trying to explain situations by using analogies no one understood; and his bedtime conversations with Emily, when each would turn back on the light and make one more comment.

When Newhart retired the show, by choice, he expressed misgivings about the direction of situation comedy as the 1970s gave way to the 1980s. Broad physical comedy and obvious jokes seemed to be pushing out wit and sophistication. The subsequent success of *Newhart,* however, showed there was still a place for intelligent, eccentric comedy. In this series Newhart played Dick Loudon, a writer of how-to books who moved from New York to Vermont to realize his dream of running a country inn. His wife, again smart, funny, and sexy, was named Joanna and was played by Mary Frann. Again there were numerous

The Bob Newhart Show, B. Dailey, B. Newhart, M. Wallace, S. Pleshette, P. Bonerz, 1972–78.
Courtesy of the Everett Collection

Newhart, Peter Scolari, Julia Duffy, Tom Poston, Bob Newhart, Mary Frann, 1982–90.
©CBS/ Courtesy of the Everett Collection

quirky supporting characters. Tom Poston, who had frequently guest starred on the earlier show, portrayed the inn's unhandy handyman, George Utley. Julia Duffy played the hilariously vain and spoiled Stephanie Vanderkellen, an heiress working as a maid at the inn (Stephanie replaced her less interesting cousin, Leslie, after the first season). Stephanie's boyfriend, Michael Harris (Peter Scolari), was an insufferable yuppie and producer of a local TV show, *Vermont Today,* which Dick began hosting a few years into *Newhart*'s run. Perhaps the most memorable, and certainly the most unusual, characters were three bizarre back-woodsmen, of whom only one ever spoke (until the final episode). "I'm Larry, this is my brother Darryl, and this is my other brother Darryl," was their stock introduction. They could always be counted upon to enjoy any activity that would disgust most people. The show, like Newhart's earlier sitcom, weeded out weak characters and developed the strong ones as it went along.

Newhart closed its successful eight-year run with one of the best final episodes of any series. It involved everyone in town, except the Loudons, selling their property to a Japanese corporation, included a parody of *Fiddler on the Roof,* and ended with Newhart waking up in bed with Suzanne Pleshette, the woman who portrayed his wife on his previous show, and explaining that he had had a very strange dream (a parodic reference to the famous 1986–87 season of *Dallas*).

As this ending indicates, *The Bob Newhart Show* of the 1970s is especially fondly remembered, and there have been several other tributes to its enduring popularity. Marcia Wallace made a guest appearance on *Taxi* as the dream date of cabby Jim Ignatowski, who had nearly memorized every episode of *The Bob Newhart Show.* (Many members of the creative staff of *Taxi* had begun their careers at MTM Entertainment, the company that produced *The Bob Newhart Show.*) Newhart reprised Dr. Bob Hartley on a *Saturday Night Live* segment in the 1990s, with Hartley being the only voice of reason on a talk show panel. And when TV character Murphy Brown (as part of a continuing joke on the show of the same name) was finally assigned a competent secretary, it was again Marcia Wallace, playing Carol. At the end of the episode, however, Newhart showed up as Bob Hartley and, after reducing himself to begging, won Carol back from Murphy.

TRUDY RING

See also **Newhart, Bob**

The Bob Newhart Show

Cast

Robert (Bob) Hartley	Bob Newhart
Emily Hartley	Suzanne Pleshette
Howard Borden	Bill Daily
Jerry Robinson	Peter Bonerz
Carol Kester Bondurant	Marcia Wallace
Margaret Hoover (1972–73)	Patricia Smith
Dr. Bernie Tupperman (1972–76)	Larry Gelman
Ellen Hartley (1974–76)	Pat Finley
Larry Bondurant (1975–77)	Will McKenzie
Eliot Carlin	Jack Riley
Mrs. Bakerman	Florida Friebus
Miss Larson (1972–73)	Penny Marshall
Michelle Nardo (1973–76)	Renee Lippin
Mr. Peterson (1973–78)	John Fiedler
Mr. Gianelli (1972–73)	Noam Pitlik
Mr. Vickers (1974–75)	Lucien Scott
Mr. Herd (1976–77)	Oliver Clark

Producers

Tom Patchett, Jay Tarses, David Davis, Lorenzo Music, Michael Zinberg

Programming History

138 episodes

CBS

September 1972–October 1976	Saturday 9:30–10:00
November 1976–September 1977	Saturday 8:30–9:00
September 1977–April 1978	Saturday 8:00–8:30
June 1978–August 1978	Saturday 8:00–8:30

Newhart

Cast

Dick Loudon	Bob Newhart
Joanna Loudon	Mary Frann
Kirk Devane (1982–84)	Steven Kampmann
George Utley	Tom Poston
Leslie Vanderkellen (1982–83)	Jennifer Holmes
Stephanie Vanderkellen (1983–90)	Julia Duffy
Larry	William Sanderson
First Darryl	Tony Papenfuss
Second Darryl	John Voldstad
Jim Dixo	Thomas Hill
Chester Wanamaker	William Lanteau
Cindy Parker Devane (1984)	Rebecca York
Michael Harris (1984–90)	Peter Scolari
Harley Estin (1984–88)	Jeff Doucette
Elliot Gabler (1984–85)	Lee Wilkof
Bev Dutton (1984–88)	Linda Carlson
Constable Shifflett (1985–89)	Todd Susman
J.J. (1985–87)	Fred Applegate
Bud (1985–90)	Ralph Manza
Paul (1988–90)	Cliff Bemis
Prudence Goddard (1989–90)	Kathy Kinney
Art Rusnak (1989–90)	David Pressman

Producers

Barry Kemp, Sheldon Bull

Programming History

182 episodes

CBS

October 1982–February 1983	Monday 9:30–10:00
March 1983–April 1983	Sunday 9:30–10:00
April 1983–May 1983	Sunday 8:30–9:00
June 1983–August 1983	Sunday 9:30–10:00
August 1983–September 1986	Monday 9:30–10:00
September 1986–August 1988	Monday 9:00–9:30
August 1988–March 1989	Monday 8:00–8:30
March 1989–August 1989	Monday 10:00–10:30
August 1989–October 1989	Monday 10:30–11:00
November 1989–April 1990	Monday 10:00–10:30
April 1990–May 1990	Monday 8:30–9:00
May 1990–July 1990	Monday 10:00–10:30
July 1990–August 1990	Friday 9:00–9:30
September 1990	Saturday 9:00–9:30

Further Reading

Hamamoto, Darrell Y., *Nervous Laughter: Television Situation Comedy and Liberal Democratic Ideology,* New York: Praeger, 1989

Marc, David, *Demographic Vistas: Television in American Culture,* Philadelphia: University of Pennsylvania Press, 1984; 2nd edition, 1996

Marc, David, *Comic Visions: Television Comedy and American Culture,* Boston: Unwin Hyman, 1989; 2nd edition, Malden, Massachusetts: Blackwell Publishers, 1997

Mayerle, Judine, "The Most Inconspicuous Hit on Television: A Case Study of *Newhart,*" *Journal of Popular Film and Television* (fall 1989)

"*Newhart* Gets Early Airing on Some Stations in 'Surprise' Option Plan," *Television-Radio Age* (June 27, 1988)

Sorenson, Jeff, *Bob Newhart,* New York: St. Martin's Press, 1988

Bochco, Steven (1943–)

U.S. Writer-Producer

Steven Bochco has created and produced some of the most acclaimed and successful American television drama series since the 1980s, and with series like *Hill Street Blues, L.A. Law,* and *NYPD Blue* has managed to make highly innovative yet popular programs.

In January 1980, Steven Bochco and Michael Kozoll pitched NBC an idea for an ensemble show set in a busy city hotel. But NBC wanted a cop show. This resulted in the series that would make Bochco's name: *Hill Street Blues* (1981–87). *HSB* was different from any American television dramatic series of its time. Its visual style, influenced by documentary police tapes, was dark, grainy and dense, and it was filmed with handheld cameras to provide a documentary-like feel, a feel further enhanced by the overlapping dialogues. The storytelling was also groundbreaking, with a large ensemble cast, characters with complex personal lives, several subplots and ongoing storylines: a form of storytelling that up to that point in American television was typical only of soap operas.

Following a first season in which the series performed badly in ratings terms it seemed that only the luck of circumstances saved the show from being canceled. However, a positive critical response worked in the show's favor. Moreover, NBC noted that the show did well among viewers who had cable television, indicating the cop drama was the type of show NBC and other networks needed to stave off the pay-TV threat. But probably the most important factor in *HSB* becoming the lowest rated show to be renewed for a second season was the fact that it picked up a record 21 Emmy nominations, and won eight. By its second season viewers finally tuned in to see what the excitement was all about and the show became, relatively speaking, a hit.

The success of *HSB* ran through television as many new drama series picked up its ensemble style—in fact, it can be argued that to this day every realistic cop show traces its dramatic roots to *HSB*—but Bochco's own follow up, *Bay City Blues* (1983), the story of a minor-league baseball team in Northern California, was short lived (nowadays it is worth noting that Sharon Stone was in the cast, and it also had TV's first full-frontal vomiting scene). The failure of this expensive series coupled with increasing costs on *HSB* was the last straw for MTM, and Bochco was fired in 1985 (*HSB* stayed on the air until May 1987).

However, the direct negotiations Bochco had with NBC resulted in a promise for a series of his own, and this commitment became the long-running legal hit drama *L.A. Law* (1986–94) which he developed for Twentieth Century Fox. There were clearly similarities between *L.A. Law* and *HSB,* most notably the ensemble acting and overlapping, ongoing storylines, but *L.A. Law* was cheerful, bright, and populated by successful people; however, it, too, dealt with stories of a moral complexity unusual in mainstream television.

In 1987 Bochco created *Hooperman* (ABC, 1987–89) a half-hour comedy/drama series focused on a San Francisco police officer who also owned an apartment building. After this series, and following negotiations with all three networks, Bochco accepted ABC's unprecedented offer of a $50 million deal, for ten series over a ten-year period, plus a $5 million signing bonus. This deal was especially important to Bochco, who wanted to start his own production company based on stability and longevity.

Steven Bochco Productions was established in 1988, and its first series under the ABC deal was *Doogie Howser, M.D.,* a half-hour comedy/drama telling the story of a 16-year-old doctor. This hit series, co-created by Bochco and David E. Kelley, ran for four seasons. Next came Bochco's biggest critical and commercial failure *Cop Rock* (1990). The episodes of *Cop Rock* included, in a Dennis Potter-like manner, dramatic scenes interrupted by singing police officers, criminals, attorneys, and crooks. Although this was a bold experiment with the genre, critics and audiences were equally unimpressed and the show lasted only a few weeks.

Bochco's next show for ABC was a prime-time cartoon series telling the story of mice living in the White House—*Capitol Critters* (1992)—that lasted just a few months. Next up was *Civil Wars* (1991–93) the story of a New York divorce attorney's office. Although this series lasted for two years, it too failed to achieve either high ratings or critical acclaim. Bochco's greatest hit was yet to come.

In the early 1990s, with so many television choices, Bochco realized that network TV drama was being hurt, so much so that the common wisdom at the time was that the one-hour format was dead. It also became clear to him that network drama could no longer compete with the more explicit violence and sex on cable and pay TV, so he set out to develop what he referred to as an "R-Rated" cop drama that became *NYPD Blue* (1993–present). This series about homicide detectives in New York City resembled *HSB* in its serialized, unstable narrative development and visual style, but if *HSB* broke new ground for the 1980s, *NYPD Blue* attempted to expand the limits of network standards even further. The show was controversial even before its appearance on the schedule since it was announced in advance it would include partial nudity and more flavorful language than was common on television at the time. Conservative groups called for a boycott, and ABC and its affiliated stations were nervous. But the audience responded overwhelmingly. In fact, apart from high ratings, over the years the show has been nominated for and won numerous awards. However, some have noted that it actually broke little new ground as far as the genre's conventions are concerned.

Murder One (1995–97), on the other hand, rewrote the rules of television by following a single murder story through an entire series. It was Bochco's response to the O.J. Simpson trial, based upon his understanding that the Simpson trial changed the audience's perception of the law. *Murder One* dealt with one case, looking closely at the strategies for both the prosecution and the defense and following it to the verdict and its aftermath. The series did not do well in the United States, probably due to it being slotted against NBC's medical drama *ER* in its first season and NBC's hit sitcom *Seinfeld* in its second season. And yet, in countries like Britain this series was highly regarded and relatively successful.

In the fall of 1999, national civil rights groups complained about the lack of representation of African Americans on television on the big four networks, especially as far as leading roles in drama series are concerned. CBS was able to promise immediate change with the hospital drama Bochco was developing at the time. While Bochco included African Americans in many of his previous series, *City of Angels* (2000) was the first truly all African-American drama. The show was surrounded by debates, with some arguing that its (few) white characters were depicted as ignorant or even evil. Be that as it may, the first season did not draw audiences, and it was renewed mainly due to the campaigning of black groups. Some changes were introduced and critics wrote about it more favorably, but the ratings remained low. The show was canceled in mid-season.

Steven Bochco.
Photo courtesy of Steven Bochco

In 1999 Bochco also had some high profile battles first with Twentieth Century Fox, the distributors of his series, and then with ABC. In 2000, having left Twentieth Century Fox, he signed a five-year development deal with Paramount Television. The first show under the new contract was *Philly* (2001–2002), an irreverent fast-paced legal drama series, the story of a single mom who owns her own firm barely a year out of law school, steadily building her reputation as a tough no-nonsense defense attorney in the weathered courtrooms of Philadelphia's city hall. It did earn some respectable reviews, but hardly the ratings successes that guarantee renewal into another season.

In 2003 HBO announced the start of production for *Marriage,* a Bochco coproduced series set entirely in and around the bedroom of a young married couple. Restricting the action to the bedroom, bathroom, and closet was meant to create "an intimate, almost voyeuristic sense of how a couple deals with each other and their marriage," according to the press release, which also said the series would debut sometime in 2004. But after looking at the pilot, directed by the acclaimed Michael Apted (*The World Is Not Enough, Coal Miner's Daughter,* and the *7 Up* documentaries) and the scripts for later episodes, HBO executives dropped the project.

In 1996 Bochco became the first television writer to receive the Writers Guild Foundation Annual Career

Achievement Award. At the time of this writing, it is unknown which Bochco project will be aired next, but it is certain to be a compelling, high-quality work.

ALINA BERNSTEIN

See also ***Hill Street Blues; L.A. Law; NYPD Blue***

Steven Ronald Bochco. Born in New York City, December 16, 1943. Married: 1) divorced from first wife (daughter of Louis Blau) in 1966. 2) Barbara Bosson, actress; married in 1969; children: Jesse John and Melissa; divorced in 1999. 3) Dayna Kalins, married in 2000 (head of Steven Bochco Productions). His long list of awards includes, among others, *Emmy Awards:* in 1981, 1982, 1983, and 1984 for *Hill Street Blues;* in 1987, 1989, and 1990 for *L.A. Law;* in 1995 for *NYPD Blue. Golden Globe:* in 1981 and 1982 for *Hill Street Blues;* in 1986 and 1987 for *L.A. Law;* in 1993 for *NYPD Blue. People's Choice:* in 1994 and 1995 for *NYPD Blue;* in 1998 for *Brooklyn South. Writers Guild of America Award* in 1994 for *NYPD Blue* and in 1996 the Laurel Award (Career Achievement). In 1996 BAFTA for Best Foreign Television Program, *Murder One.* In 1997 the George Foster Peabody Award for *NYPD Blue;* Golden Satellite for *NYPD Blue.* In 1998 the David Susskind Lifetime Achievement in Television (the Producers Guild of America). In 1999 Directors Guild of America: Diversity Award.

Television Series

1967–75	*Ironside* (writer)
1968–72	*The Name of the Game* (writer)
1971	*Columbo* (story editor)
1971–76	*McMillan and Wife* (writer)
1974	*Griff* (writer-producer)
1976–77	*Delvecchio* (writer)
1978	*Richie Brockelman* (writer)
1979	*Turnabout* (writer)
1979–80	*Paris* (executive-producer, writer)
1981–87	*Hill Street Blues* (executive-producer, writer)
1983	*Bay City Blues* (executive-producer, writer)
1986–94	*L.A. Law* (executive-producer, writer)
1987–88	*Beverly Hills Buntz* (producer)
1987–89	*Hooperman* (executive-producer, writer)
1989–93	*Doogie Howser, M.D.* (executive-producer, writer)
1990	*Cop Rock* (executive-producer, writer)
1992	*Capitol Critters* (producer)
1991–93	*Civil Wars* (executive-producer, writer)
1993–	*NYPD Blue* (executive-producer, writer)
1994	*The Byrds of Paradise* (producer)
1995–97	*Murder One* (executive-producer, writer)
1996	*Public Morals* (executive producer)
1997	*Total Security* (executive producer)
1997–98	*Brooklyn South* (executive producer)
2000	*City of Angels* (executive producer)
2001–02	*Philly* (executive producer, writer)

Further Reading

Feuer, Jane, Paul Kerr, and Tise Vahimagi, editors, *MTM. Quality Television,* Bloomington: Indiana University Press, 1984

Gitlin, Todd, *Inside Prime Time,* Berkeley: University of California Press, 2000

Longworth, James L., *TV Creators: Conversations with America's Top Producers of Television Drama,* Syracuse, New York: Syracuse University Press, 2000

Marc, David, and Robert J. Thompson, *Prime Time, Prime Movers: From I Love Lucy to L.A. Law—America's Greatest TV Shows and The People Who Create Them,* 2nd edition, Syracuse, New York: Syracuse University Press, 1995

Thompson, Robert J., *Television's Second Golden Age: From Hill Street Blues to ER: Hill Street Blues, Thirtysomething, St. Elsewhere, China Beach, Cagney & Lacey, Twin Peaks,* Syracuse, New York: Syracuse University Press, 1997

Bogart, Paul (1919–)

U.S. Director

Paul Bogart has enjoyed a career as a director in almost every medium of visual communication. Bogart is one of a handful of individuals who has directed live television productions of the "Golden Age," the telefilm, the made-for-television movie, and the feature film.

Bogart's career began as a puppeteer and actor with the Berkeley Marionettes in 1946. From there he went on to be stage manager and associate director at NBC, working on such Golden Age cornerstones as *Kraft Television Theater, Goodyear Playhouse,* and *Armstrong Circle Theater.* During the 1955–56 season, when *Goodyear Playhouse* was known as the *Alcoa Hour-Goodyear Playhouse,* Bogart directed an episode entitled "The Confidence Man" and an award-winning partnership began. This was the first time Bogart had directed for producer Herbert Brodkin. Bogart would go on to direct many episodes of Brodkin's *The Defenders,* one of television's most honored series, and garner his first Emmy Award for directing "The 700-Year Old Gang," a two-part *Defenders* episode. Bogart worked almost exclusively for Brodkin series during the early to mid-1960s (*The Defenders, The Nurses, The Doctors and Nurses,* and *Coronet Blue*).

After *The Defenders* period, the larger part of Bogart's work was in long form—either television specials, television movies, or feature films. His work for *CBS Playhouse* was particularly noteworthy. Under that banner, Bogart won Emmys for his direction of "Dear Friends" (again with Brodkin producing) and "Shadow Game." During this period Bogart produced the 1966 television series *Hawk,* starring Burt Reynolds; he also directed the pilot and a handful of episodes for the series. For theatrical release he directed *Halls of Anger* (1968), *Marlowe* (1969), and *The Skin Game* (1971).

In the mid-1970s, Bogart began another long-term relationship with a single production unit. He directed scores of episodes of *All in the Family* for Norman Lear and Bud Yorkin's Tandem Productions and in 1978 earned another Emmy for his work on the series. *The Golden Girls* brought Bogart yet another Emmy in 1986. In 1986, he directed *The Canterville Ghost* for television and *Torch Song Trilogy* for theatrical release.

Bogart has said that, in an ideal world, the feature film is his form of choice because the time constraints of television production are absent. Still, he is a singular talent among television directors. He has expressed a partiality for strong characters over a strong story. This preference takes advantage of the intimacy of the television medium, and allows those characters to reveal themselves to viewers through the nuance and subtlety of staging and blocking. These qualities are at a premium in entertainment television today, but because Bogart's aesthetic sensibilities were developed early, in the theater and live television, the episodes he directs are graced by excellent staging and movement of characters. One need only carefully watch Bogart's work for *The Defenders, All in the Family,* or *Nichols* to understand that this ability to place characters for the camera is one of the strongest characteristics of his work.

Director Paul Bogart (middle) with Pamela Payton-Wright and Timothy Bottoms in *Look Homeward, Angel* rehearsals, 1972. *Courtesy of the Everett Collection*

A second characteristic is that he directs like an editor. Bogart begins a directing assignment with a very clear idea of what the program should look like. He then creates the images he needs and pays particular attention to the way those images are linked to make a program. He has stated that, in his view, one of the most important aspects of visual expression is how one image follows another and contributes to the cumulative effect of those joined images. Bogart understands that the power of emotions and ideas can be reinforced or defeated by the manner in which shots are linked. The result is a directorial style that draws on the best elements of the editor's art—the linking of carefully composed images for emotional and dramatic emphasis.

In 1991 Bogart was awarded the French Festival Internationelle Programmes Audiovisuelle at Cannes, one of the few television directors to be recognized for a remarkable body of work. Many directors working in television today are members of a generation raised on television. The better of these directors are those who paid attention to the work of Paul Bogart.

JOHN COOPER

See also ***All in the Family;*** **Anthology Drama; "Golden Age" of Television;** ***Golden Girls***

Paul Bogart. Born in New York City, November 21, 1919. Attended public schools in New York City. Married: Jane, 1941; children: Peter, Tracy, and Jennifer. Served in U.S. Army Air Force, 1944–46. Puppeteer-actor with the Berkeley Marionettes, 1946–48; TV stage manager and associate director, NBC television, 1950–52; director, installments of various live television dramas, 1950s–1960s; director, telefilm series and made-for-television movies, from 1960s. Recipient: Emmy Awards, 1965, 1968, 1970, 1978, 1986; Christopher Awards, 1955, 1973, and 1975; Golden Globe, 1977; French Festival Internationale Audiovisuelle, Cannes, 1991.

Television Series (selected)

1947–58	*Kraft Television Theater*
1949–55	*One Man's Family*
1950–63	*Armstrong Circle Theatre*
1951–60	*Goodyear Playhouse*
1953–63	*U.S. Steel Hour*
1961–65	*The Defenders*
1962–65	*The Nurses*
1966–76	*Hawk*
1971–83	*All in the Family*
1985–92	*The Golden Girls*
1990	*Baghdad Café*

Made-for-Television Movies

1966	*Evening Primrose*
1970	*In Search of America*
1972	*The House Without a Christmas Tree*
1974	*Tell Me Where It Hurts*
1975	*Winner Take All*
1980	*Fun and Games*
1986	*The Canterville Ghost*
1987	*Power, Passion and Murder*
1987	*Natica Jackson*
1992	*Broadway Bound*
1992	*The Last Mile*
1994	*The Gift of Love*
1995	*The Heidi Chronicles*

Television Specials

Ages of Man; Mark Twain Tonight; The Final War of Ollie Winter; Dear Friends; Secrets; Shadow Game; Look Homeward, Angel; The Country Girl; Double Solitaire; The War Widow; The Thanksgiving Treasure; The Adams Chronicles.

Films

Halls of Anger, 1968; *Marlowe,* 1969; *The Skin Game,* 1971; *Class of '44,* 1973; *Mr. Ricco,* 1975; *Oh, God! You Devil,* 1984; *Torch Song Trilogy,* 1988.

Further Reading

Wicking, Christopher, and Tise Vahimagi, *The American Vein: Directors and Directions in Television,* New York: Dutton, 1979

Bolam, James (1938–)

British Actor

James Bolam has proved one of the most popular and enduring character stars of British television comedy and drama, capitalizing on his northern background and on his natural, pugnacious charm in a variety of roles over four decades. Bolam had the good fortune to begin his screen career at a time when there was a tremendous vogue in British theater, film, and television for working-class northern drama. With his punchy but vulnerable Geordie persona and undisguised accent, Bolam was a natural choice for such worthy though relatively plodding films as *The Kitchen,* which was based on the play by Arnold Wesker, and John Schlesinger's North Country feature *A Kind of Loving*. Subsequently, among other films, he supported fellow-northerner Tom Courtenay in *Otley* and played second lead to Alan Bates in Lindsay Anderson's *In Celebration* (a David Storey play set in the mining towns of Nottinghamshire in which he and Bates had already appeared on the Royal Court stage).

It was as a favorite of television comedy and period drama audiences, however, that Bolam (a former trainee chartered accountant) was destined to make his mark. Cast as the girl-chasing, anti-establishment cynic Terry Collier opposite Rodney Bewes's diffident and socially aspiring Bob Ferris in the long-running and warmly realistic comedy series *The Likely Lads* (1964–66), written by Ian La Frenais and Dick Clement, Bolam cut a fine line between pathos and brash northern cockiness. In his scorn for Bob's middle-class pretensions, Bolam's work-shy proletarian Terry typified northern prejudice and aggression, but in his overt sensitivity to any rejection by his aspiring childhood friend and drinking partner, he became both endearing and sympathetic, as much a victim of a hostile class system as Bob's soul companion. The friendship between the two characters was in many situations their only defense, coupled with a shared nostalgia for time-honored northern ways. The series, which relied heavily on the writing of Le Frenais and Clements as well as upon the innate charm of Bolam and Bewes, was significant in that it raised issues of greater relevance to the viewing public than was attempted by virtually any other sitcom of the time (and, indeed, by many in succeeding decades).

The underlying theme of nostalgia for the values of the old north, and the comedy inherent in two northern lads trying to keep their friendship alive while coming to terms with the realities of life, was underlined in the even better later series, *Whatever Happened to the Likely Lads?* (1973–74), in which the pathos was strengthened by an awareness of time passing. This revival, which took up the lives of the two friends after Terry's return from four years in the army and Bob's assumption of bourgeois respectability (and engagement to the self-willed Thelma, played by Bridgit Forsyth), proved as well written and as pointed as the first series, the friendship tottering and swaying as the two men argued heatedly about their conflicting views on such issues as class, sexual equality, and self-advancement.

Though identified primarily with northern working-class characters, Bolam has managed to vary his diet by escaping from the straitjacket of television comedy on several occasions. Particularly notable was his success as the indomitable entrepreneur Jack Ford in the long-running between-the-wars period drama set in South Shields, *When the Boat Comes In,* which extended to four series and finally ended with Ford's death in the Spanish Civil War. Jessie Seaton, women's campaigner and Ford's love interest in the series, was played by Bolam's off-stage wife, Susan Jameson.

To underline Bolam's versatility, he also appeared with success in a BBC production of William Shakespeare's *As You Like It* and in the 1980s forged a new variation on the sympathetic but single-minded northerner theme as Trevor Chaplain, the inquisitive, jazz-loving schoolteacher investigating corruption in Alan Plater's *The Beiderbecke Affair* and its sequels.

A long-established favorite of low-brow television comedy, since the days of *The Likely Lads,* Bolam has continued to enjoy success in such unchallenging fare as *Only When I Laugh,* an unexceptional hospital sitcom that nevertheless lasted four series, *Room at the Bottom, Andy Capp, Executive Stress, Sticky Wickets, Eleven Men against Eleven* (a comedy thriller in which Bolam played the beleaguered manager of an ailing Premier Division football team, under crooked chairman Timothy West), and *Pay and Display.* In 1996 his chilling performance as the evil Mr. Peters in the film *Stella Does Tricks* provided audiences with fresh evidence of his range as a performer.

DAVID PICKERING

See also ***The Likely Lads***

James Bolam. Born in Sunderland, Tyne and Wear, England, June 16, 1938. Attended Bede Grammar School, Sunderland; Bemrose School, Derby. Married: Susan Jameson; one child: Lucy. Trained as actor at Central School of Speech and Drama, London; stage debut, Royal Court Theatre, London, 1959; established reputation as television star in the long-running series *The Likely Lads,* 1964–66, and the sequel *Whatever Happened to the Likely Lads?,* 1973–74; subsequently consolidated reputation as popular star of situation comedy as well as playing straight roles and acting in films.

Television Series

1964–66	*The Likely Lads*
1973–74	*Whatever Happened to the Likely Lads?*
1976–81	*When the Boat Comes In*
1979	*The Limbo Connection*
1979–83	*Only When I Laugh*
1985	*The Beiderbecke Affair*
1986	*Executive Stress*
1987	*The Beiderbecke Tapes*
1987	*Room at the Bottom*
1987	*Father Matthew's Daughter*
1988	*The Beiderbecke Connection*
1988	*Andy Capp*
1991–93	*Second Thoughts*
1994	*Sticky Wickets*
1995	*Eleven Men Against Eleven*
1997	*Have Your Cake*
1997	*The Missing Postman*
2000	*Pay and Display*

Films

The Kitchen, 1961; *A Kind of Loving,* 1962; *The Loneliness of the Long Distance Runner,* 1962; *HMS Defiant,* 1962; *Murder Most Foul,* 1965; *Half a Sixpence,* 1967; *Otley,* 1969; *Crucible of Terror,* 1971; *Straight on Till Morning,* 1972; *O Lucky Man!,* 1973; *In Celebration,* 1974; *The Likely Lads,* 1976; *The Great Question,* 1982; *The Plague Dogs* (voice only), 1982; *Clash of Loyalties,* 1983;

Clockwork Mice, 1995; *Stella Does Tricks,* 1996; *End of the Affair,* 1999; *It Was an Accident,* 2000.

Radio
Second Thoughts, 1988.

Stage (selected)
The Kitchen, 1959; *Events while Guarding the Bofors Gun,* 1966; *In Celebration,* 1969; *Veterans,* 1972; *Treats,* 1976; *Who Killed 'Agatha' Christie?,* 1978; *King Lear,* 1981; *Run For Your Wife!,* 1983; *Arms and the Man,* 1989; *Who's Afraid of Virginia Woolf?,* 1989; *Victory,* 1989; *Jeffrey Bernard Is Unwell,* 1990; *Glengarry Glen Ross,* 1994; *Wild Oats,* 1995; *Endgame,* 1999; *Semi-Detached,* 1999; *Sick Dictators* (director), 2001.

Further Reading

Grant, Linda, "The Lad Most Likely to..." *The Guardian* (August 12, 1995)
Ross, Deborah, "What Really Happened to the Likely Lads?" *Daily Mail* (July 17, 1993)

Bonanza

U.S. Western

Bonanza, the first western televised in color, premiered on a Saturday night in the fall of 1959. After *Gunsmoke, Bonanza* was the longest-running and most successful western in U.S. television, airing for 14 seasons. The series related the story of Ben Cartwright (Lorne Greene) and his three sons, Adam (Pernell Roberts), Hoss (Dan Blocker), and Little Joe (Michael Landon), prosperous ranchers in the vicinity of Virginia City, Nevada, in the mid-19th century, during the Civil War years and the discovery of the Comstock Silver Lode. The show was designed to appeal to a broad audience, crossing age and gender groups. The action elements catered to a more traditional audience for westerns, while dramatic issues and family values expanded the show's popularity to a more general audience. The careful photography presented beautiful scenery, and interiors resembled movies more than other contemporary television shows.

The Cartwrights were not a traditional nuclear family. The patriarch was a three-time widower, with a son from each wife. In the first few seasons, personality differences between the sons motivated most of the plot conflicts. Two years after its debut, *Bonanza* moved to Sunday night and its popularity soared. By this time, the three sons had worked out most of their differences and the show was about the dealings of a well-integrated all-male family as well as their problems with mining and ranch interests. Other characters would wander into the community and cause conflict, leading the members of the family individually or communally as a group to restore the order. The oldest son, Adam, was the most serious of the three brothers, the potential patriarch. The middle son, Hoss, was the buffoon type, big and friendly, naive yet explosive. Little Joe was the impulsive and romantic member of the family.

Bonanza differed from other westerns in its relatively limited use of violence and "shoot-outs." Conflicts were resolved through dialogue between the main characters and guest stars. Generally, this one-hour show tackled topical issues (i.e., racial discrimination, voting, religion). Famous guest stars such as Yvonne De Carlo, Ida Lupino, Barry Sullivan, Ricardo Cortez, and Jack Carson added to the show's popularity. *Bonanza* was also the first show to introduce the ranch, in this case the thousand-acre Ponderosa, as an important element in the narrative, the fifth character, as producers referred to it. Brauer and Brauer argue that this emphasis on the "piece of land" was symbolic of a shift from emphasizing mobility, the lone wanderer with his gun and horse, to a focus on the settled landowner (see Brauer and Brauer). These changes also led to a restructuring of the leading characters' role in the community.

The cook at Ponderosa was Hop Sing (Victor Sen Yung), a Chinese immigrant. He was presented in the traditional subservient role reserved for minorities in the period the show was produced. He spoke with a heavy accent, wore generic Asian clothes, had long, braided hair, and always delivered words of wisdom.

Bonanza, Pernell Roberts, Michael Landon, Lorne Greene, Dan Blocker, 1959–73.
Courtesy of the Everett Collection

In several episodes the family engaged in various conflicts with outsiders to protect Hop Sing against discrimination. In doing so, the show foregrounded racial discrimination of the historical period as well as the ongoing racial conflicts of the 1960s.

Between September 12, 1959, and January 16, 1973, a total of 440 episodes were produced. Those years witnessed several cast changes. Pernell Roberts left the series at the end of 1964–65 season, calling it "junk TV" and complaining about the glorified portrayal of wealthy ranchers. His character was eliminated from the series. Dan Blocker died before the beginning of the 1972–73 season. After his death, the show's ratings started to fall, and it was canceled in 1973. A change from the traditional slot on Sunday to Tuesday evening, after 11 years on the air, might also have caused the demise of the show. Even before the show was canceled, it was already being rerun, under the name *Ponderosa,* by NBC on Tuesday evenings. *Bonanza* was exported throughout the world and has aired in syndication in the United States.

In the mid-1980s there was an attempt to revive the series with a made-for-television movie entitled *Bonanza: The Next Generation.* None of the original cast of the series appeared in the show. Greene's death forced the producer to cast another actor in the role of Ponderosa's patriarch; in the movie John Ireland played Ben Cartwright's brother. He could not control the ranch and it was almost taken over by miners and oil speculators. It was only when the sons of Little Joe and Hoss returned that the ranch experienced a new Bonanza.

ANTONIO C. LA PASTINA

See also **Western**

Cast

Ben Cartwright	Lorne Greene
Little Joe Cartwright	Michael Landon
Eric "Hoss" Cartwright (1959–72)	Dan Blocker
Adam Cartwright (1959–65)	Pernell Roberts
Hop Sing	Victor Sen Yung
Sheriff Roy Caffee (1960–72)	Ray Teal
Candy (1967–70, 1972–73)	David Canary
Dusty Rhoades (1970–72)	Lou Frizzel
Jamie Hunter (1970–73)	Mitch Vogel
Griff King (1972–73)	Tim Matheson
Deputy Clem (1961–73)	Bing Russell

Producers

Richard Collins, David Dortort, Robert Blees

Programming History

440 episodes

NBC

September 1959–September 1961	Saturday 7:30–8:30
September 1961–September 1972	Sunday 9:00–10:00
May 1972–August 1972	Tuesday 7:30–8:30
September 1972–January 1973	Tuesday 8:00–9:00

Further Reading

Brauer, R., and D. Brauer, *The Horse, the Gun and the Piece of Property: Changing Images of the TV Western,* Bowling Green, Ohio: Bowling Green University Popular Press, 1975

Jackson, R., *Classic TV Westerns,* New York: Citadel, 1994

Kirkley, D., *A Descriptive Study of the Network Television Western During the Seasons 1955–56 Through 1962–63,* New York: Arno Press, 1979

MacDonald, J. Fred, *Who Shot the Sheriff? The Rise and Fall of the TV Western,* New York: Praeger, 1987

Boone, Richard (1917–1981)

U.S. Actor

Richard Boone was one of the television acting profession's gladiators, a craggy, determined, and almost menacing figure among the actors and directors who worked with him. His uncompromising commitment to his work often brought him into conflict with his fellow players and was also a constant source of frustration to the directors and producers who tried to control him. That his work for television eventually brought him critical acclaim and viewer popularity while he simultaneously alienated certain sections of the industry may be, perhaps, the hallmark of his genius.

In 1947 he traveled to New York and joined the well-known Actor's Studio (where his classmates included such then-unknowns as Marlon Brando, Karl Malden, Eva Marie Saint, and Julie Harris). He got his growth, he claimed, as an actor in some 150 live TV shows in New York between 1948 and 1950, after which he returned home to California. He was also reportedly a regular on the CBS children's program *Mr. I. Magination* in 1949 (when the program was a local New York show) and appeared as one of the reporters in *The Front Page* series (1949–50) during its early days. Back in Los Angeles, he was put under contract to Twentieth Century Fox and his first feature film was *Halls of Montezuma,* directed by Lewis Milestone in 1950 (Milestone would later be invited to direct episodes of *Have Gun—Will Travel* and *The Richard Boone Show*). While at Fox, he was working for Jack Webb in his radio *Dragnet* when, still as an unknown bit player, around the summer of 1950, he did a single radio drama called *The Doctor* (written by *Dragnet* writer James Moser). This radio show turned out to be the forerunner of Boone's first starring TV role, *Medic.*

By 1954 the role of Dr. Konrad Styner, *Medic*'s host and narrator and a frequent participant in its stories made Boone a household name. Created and written by Moser, *Medic* (1954–56) employed a dramatic-documentary style, factual and educational in content but with a dramatic impact that few if any physician-centered programs achieved until the advent of *Ben Casey* in 1961. With Moser writing and generally steering the series, *Medic* developed a highly effective semidocumentary technique similar to TV's popular *Dragnet.* The program took its stories from the files of the Los Angeles County Medical Association, real medical case histories showing inherent drama. Boone's stolid underplaying heightened the dramatic force of the series; however, there were critics and viewers at the time who thought his character too dour and gruff. When *Medic* came to an end, Boone found other parts elusive; although this had been his first real doctor role, casting directors had come to see him as a "doctor" character, and his strong screen association with the role of Dr. Styner left him typecast in the "he always plays doctors" file.

Boone's most memorable TV role, however, was set in a completely different genre, as he was featured as an 1870s San Francisco gentleman-adventurer who hired himself out as a mercenary gunslinger. As the impassive troubleshooter Paladin in the post–Civil War West of *Have Gun—Will Travel* (1957–63), Boone helped push the series to top-ten positions in the Nielsen ratings (numbers 3 and 4) during its first four seasons. The part was originally offered to Randolph Scott, who at the time had other commitments. After first turning down Boone for the role, CBS made a five-minute test film for New York executives still prepared to typecast him as a physician—and then signed him to a five-year contract. While *Have Gun—Will Travel* and Boone's popularity rose in the ratings and in the esteem of fans, his standing among people in the industry dropped significantly. His strict dedication to his work, which he also demanded of everyone around him, saw him all but legally take over the CBS production: scripts, actors, directors, even costumes, all had to receive his personal approval. From 1960 onward, Boone was particularly active in the series' director's chair, directing almost one in four episodes himself. "When I direct a show, I'm pretty arbitrary," he commented to *TV Guide* in early 1961. "If I have a fault, it's that I see an end and go for it with all my energy; and if I'm bugged with people who don't see it or won't go for it, it looks as though I'm riding all over them."

During this time, he continued appearing in multiple TV plays. Notable performances during this period came with David Shaw's acclaimed "The Tunnel" (1959; for *Playhouse 90*); in *The Right Man* (1960), for which he delivered a fine performance as Abraham Lincoln; and with his work as narrator for Stephen Vincent Benet's Pulitzer Prize-winning poem *John Brown's Body* (1962).

The repertory theater concept of *The Richard Boone Show* was first proposed by Boone in 1960 to CBS. When CBS executives suggested that they might find a slot for such a program on their Sunday afternoon schedule, Boone put the idea on a back burner until he had acquired his "go-to-hell money" (as he put it) from the millions of dollars he made during his years with *Have Gun—Will Travel* and, to a lesser extent, from *Medic.* It was not until his idea received the enthusiasm and support of the distinguished playwright Clifford Odets, the Goodson-Todman production company, and NBC president Robert Kintner that the television repertory company series started becoming a reality. *The Richard Boone Show* (1963–64) featured a workshop of ten actors whom Boone considered the best in the business: Robert Blake, Lloyd Bochner, Laura Devon, June Harding, Bethel Leslie, Harry Morgan, Jeanette Nolan, Ford Rainey, Warren Stevens, and Guy Stockwell. Boone himself starred at times and served as the regular host. With Odets as the program's script editor, the series' prestige was almost guaranteed. Unfortunately, after completing much of the preliminary work for the series, Odets died in August 1963. Before the 24 episodes had completed their run (and despite having just been voted "the best dramatic program on the air" in the 15th Annual Motion Picture Daily poll), the program was canceled in January 1964. Boone took the news hard. It had been a very personal project for him, and—as a result of a premature NBC press office re-

Richard Boone, 1963.
Courtesy of the Everett Collection

lease—he learned of his program's demise in a morning trade paper. Still, his anger was tempered by the knowledge that he was by that time already receiving $50,000 a year for 20 years after selling out his interest in *Have Gun—Will Travel;* he was also to receive a reported $20,000 a week for his now-defunct show, also on a deferred payment basis.

From 1964 to 1971 Boone lived a very comfortable life with his family in Honolulu, Hawaii, traveling to the mainland United States only for the occasional movie such as *Hombre* (1966) and *The Kremlin Letter* (1969). He also helped induce producer Leonard Freeman to film *Hawaii Five-O* in Honolulu instead of the intended San Pedro; Freeman even offered him the leading part of McGarrett, but Boone declined.

In 1971 Boone was offered the lead role in Universal TV/Mark VII's *Hec Ramsey* (1972–74) series (two seasons as one of four rotating 90-minute TV movies). The program, about a grizzled, turn-of-the-century lawman with a fascination for the new science of criminology, was in its way, perhaps, a gentle monument to Boone's earlier TV performances: Hec Ramsey was Paladin grown older, with an accumulation of artfulness and astuteness along with a stockpile of barely contained impatience.

The latter part of Boone's career was taken up with such diverse made-for-TV movie plots and themes as the elaborate murder set-up of *In Broad Daylight* (1971), the espionage tale of *Deadly Harvest* (1972), the period private-eye spoof *Goodnight, My Love* (1972), the Depression-era drama *The Great Niagra* (1974), and the rather sorry fantasy adventure *The Last Dinosaur* (1977).

With his dedication to his work in television, Boone always gave an extraordinarily commanding performance, always straightforward, always the center of interest.

TISE VAHIMAGI

See also ***Have Gun—Will Travel***

Richard (Allen) Boone. Born in Los Angeles, California, June 18, 1917. Attended military school; Stanford University, 1934–37. Married: 1) Jane Hopper, 1937 (divorced, 1940); 2) Mimi Kelly, 1949 (divorced, 1950); 3) Claire McAloon, 1951; child: Peter. Served in U.S. Navy, 1941–45. Oilfield worker, 1930s; painter and short-story writer, 1930s; after World War II studied acting at the Neighborhood Playhouse and Actors Studio; studied modern dance with Martha Graham; stage debut as soldier and as understudy to John Gielgud's Jason, in Broadway staging of *Medea,* 1947; acted in radio drama *The Halls of Montezuma,* 1950; led to role in the movie version, 1951; film actor, 1951–79; starred in television series *Medic,* 1954–56; starred in CBS Television's *Have Gun—Will Travel,* 1957–63; developed and directed repertory theater-style television series, *The Richard Boone Show* (also host and often the lead), 1963–64; in Hawaii, after *The Richard Boone Show* canceled, established movie company Pioneer Productions, and taught acting; starred in NBC Television's *Hec Ramsey,* one of four rotating series comprising the *Sunday Night Mystery Shows,* 1972–73; lectured on acting at Flagler College. Member: Academy of Television Arts and Sciences; Academy of Motion Picture Arts and Sciences. Recipient: Three American Television Critics Best Actor Awards. Died in St. Augustine, Florida, January 10, 1981.

Television Series

1949	*Mr. I. Magination*
1949	*The Front Page*
1954–56	*Medic*
1957–63	*Have Gun—Will Travel* (also director)
1963–64	*The Richard Boone Show* (host; also director)
1972–74	*Hec Ramsey*

Made-for-Television Movies

1971	*In Broad Daylight*
1971	*A Tattered Web*
1972	*Goodnight, My Love*
1972	*Deadly Harvest*
1974	*The Great Niagra*
1977	*The Last Dinosaur*
1977	*The Hobbit* (voice only)

Television Specials

1960	*The Right Man*
1960	*The Spirit of the Alamo*
1962	*John Brown's Body* (narrator)

Films

The Halls of Montezuma, 1950; *Call Me Mister,* 1951; *Rommel, Desert Fox,* 1951; *Kangaroo,* 1952; *Return of the Texan,* 1952; *Red Skies of Montana,* 1952; *Way of a Gaucho,* 1952; *Man on a Tightrope,* 1953; *City of Bad Men,* 1953; *Vicki,* 1953; *The Robe,* 1953; *Beneath the 12-Mile Reef,* 1953; *The Siege at Red River,* 1954; *Dragnet,* 1954; *The Raid,* 1954; *Man without a Star,* 1955; *Ten Wanted Men,* 1955; *Robbers' Roost,* 1955; *Battle Stations,* 1956; *Star in the Dust,* 1956; *Away All Boats,* 1956; *Lizzie,* 1957; *The Garment Jungle,* 1957; *The Tall T,* 1957; *I Bury the Living,* 1958; *The Alamo,* 1960; *A Thunder of Drums,* 1961; *Rio Conchos,* 1964; *The War Lord,* 1965; *Hombre,* 1967; *Kona Coast,*

1968; *The Night of the Following Day,* 1968; *The Arrangement,* 1969; *The Kremlin Letter,* 1969; *Madron,* 1970; *Big Jake,* 1971; *The Shootist,* 1976; *The Big Sleep,* 1978; *Winter Kills,* 1979; *The Bushido Blade,* 1979.

Radio

Dragnet, 1949; *The Halls of Montezuma,* 1950; *The Doctor,* 1950.

Stage

Medea, 1947; *Macbeth,* 1948; *The Man,* 1950; on tour, *The Hasty Heart,* 1959; *The Rivalry,* 1959.

Further Reading

Grams, Martin, and Les Rayburn, *The Have Gun—Will Travel Companion,* n.p.: OTR Publishing, 2000

Rothel, David, *Richard Boone: A Knight Without Armor in a Savage Land,* Madison, North Carolina: Empire Publishing, 2000

Borrowers, The

British Children's Series

The Borrowers, an award-winning children's period drama fantasy series about a family of little people living undetected beneath the floorboards of a large English house, was produced for the BBC by Working Title Television and first screened in the United Kingdom as six half-hour episodes in November and December, 1992. A second series of six half-hour episodes followed toward the end of 1993. Based on a series of established classics of children's literature, it remains a faithful and loved screen adaptation, and is often included on lists of the best television series made for children.

The children's novel *The Borrowers* was published in 1952 by Mary Norton (who also authored *Bedknobs and Broomsticks*) and has remained enduringly popular ever since, winning the Library Association's Carnegie Medal, among other accolades. Mary Norton had spent her childhood in a large family house in Leighton Buzzard, Bedfordshire, England, and conceived the notion of miniature people living their own parallel secret lives in the house from the games she played on the floor with small dolls. She called these six-inch-tall folk "Borrowers" because they relied upon salvaging discarded oddments from the "human beans" with whom they shared the house, to refashion as furniture and tools.

The Borrowers introduces the diminutive Clock family. Pod, Homily, and their daughter Arrietty live behind the kitchen clock, out of sight of the full-sized humans who occupy the house, entirely oblivious of the Clocks' existence. Trouble ensues after Arrietty befriends the human boy who lives upstairs. The adventures are continued in *The Borrowers Afield* (1955), in which Pod and his family face the perils of the great outdoors after being obliged to leave their home, and in *The Borrowers Afloat* (1959), in which the Borrowers are made homeless once again until rescued by their equally tiny friend Spiller and installed in a new home by the river (a kettle). In *The Borrowers Aloft* (1961) the family think their troubles are over when they move into a new home in a model village, only to find themselves pursued by the wicked Mr. Platter, who wants live inhabitants for his own rival model village. The series ends with *The Borrowers Avenged* (1982), in which, after further adventures, the Borrowers have their revenge on the Platters and finally settle down in their perfect home.

As adapted for the small screen by Richard Carpenter, the first series followed the adventures of the Borrowers after they are first detected and, narrowly escaping the destruction of their home as well as death by rat poison and other threats, are forced to leave their home. The second series, shot on location at Chawton House in Hampshire and at Pinewood Studios, saw them end up at the model village. As in the original books, the underlying theme was the trust that develops between the various characters as they face the challenge of the unfamiliar dangers of the outside world together. The relationships between Arrietty and her parents and between Arrietty and the human boy lie at the heart of the story, which is essentially a fable about the process of growing up and facing the challenges of an alien adult world.

Transforming Mary Norton's books into a live-action television serial presented obvious technical difficulties, particularly as the makers did not have access to the kind of computer technology that would have offered them more alternatives a few years later. The necessary miniaturization, achieved partly through superimposition of "reduced" live actors against full-sized backgrounds and through the judicial use of oversized props such as needles and matchboxes, was not perhaps always as convincing as it might have been with computer-enhanced technology, but what the series lacked in special effects (a problem exacerbated by the limited budget available) it made up for in the quality of the acting and the careful preservation of the charm and humor of Norton's writing. Norton's characters were colorful and complex, and the casting of the respected actors Ian Holm (as the pessimistic patriarch Pod) and his real-life wife Penelope Wilton (as the shrewish Homily) was crucial to the success of the series. The acting by the rest of the cast, which included Rebecca Callard (as Arrietty) and Sian Phillips (as Mrs. Driver), was equally assured. Some expressed doubts about the role of Richard Lewis, however, who acted as a sort of host, popping up somewhat incongruously at various points to comment upon the action.

The series was widely screened internationally and remains one of the most acclaimed of children's fantasy dramas for children, maintaining the BBC's reputation for quality period drama based on established literary classics. It was particularly admired for its visual qualities, being shot largely in a warm, misty glow which created an evocative, nostalgic atmosphere. The quality of the camerawork was formally recognized when the first series won BAFTA and Agfa awards for best television photography. The second series was again nominated for the same BAFTA award.

An earlier U.S. version of Mary Norton's books, starring Eddie Albert, Tammy Grimes, Judith Anderson, Beatrice Straight, and Barnard Hughes and also titled *The Borrowers,* was reasonably successful when screened by Twentieth Century Fox in 1973. The story was given the Hollywood movie treatment, with the release of *The Borrowers* in 1997. Starring John Goodman, Jim Broadbent, Mark Williams, Hugh Laurie, Celia Imrie, and others and publicized under the slogan "Small is awesome," this latest transatlantic incarnation of Norton's adventures took full advantage of the special effects made possible by a budget of $30 million and was received well enough by family audiences.

David Pickering

See also **Adaptations; British Programming; Children and Television**

Cast

Pod	Ian Holm
Homily	Penelope Wilton
Arriety	Rebecca Callard
Mrs. Driver	Sian Phillips
Mildeye	Tony Haygarth
Uncle Hendreary	Stanley Lebor

Additional cast for second series

Paul Cross, Ross McCall, Pamela Cundell, Victoria Donovan, Bay White, John Tordoff.

Director

John Henderson

Producers

Grainne Marmion, Angela Beeching (executive producer, second series)

Programming History

BBC
November 8–December 13, 1992
November 14–December 19, 1993

Boyle, Harry (1915–)

Canadian Writer, Media Executive

Harry Boyle made his career in broadcasting, but, given the ephemeral nature of radio and television productions, he may be remembered more as an author and humorist. Television historians, however, will likely see his accomplishments as a broadcast regulator as the most significant aspects of his long career. Boyle started his career on a radio station in Wingham, Ontario, and after a brief detour into the newspaper business, he joined the Canadian Broadcasting Corporation (CBC) in 1943 as a farm commentator. He advanced rapidly into executive ranks and joined the television service in the 1960s, serving as program director and executive producer. In both radio and television, he established a reputation as a creative programmer who launched the careers of many talented broadcasters, such as the comedy team of Wayne and Shuster, and the eclectic Max Ferguson. He was known for defending the independence of producers against management restrictions.

Boyle's career as a regulator began in 1967. While serving as program supervisor at CBC-Toronto, he was appointed by the Board of Broadcast Governors (BBG) to an 11-member consultative committee on program policy, the only member from the CBC. The committee issued its report in 1968, just as the BBG was abolished by the 1968 Broadcasting Act, to be replaced by a new, more powerful regulatory body, the Canadian Radio-television Commission (CRTC), later called the Canadian Radio-television and Telecommunications Commission.

Boyle was appointed vice chair of the commission, led by the formidable Pierre Juneau. He served with Juneau until Juneau resigned in 1975. Boyle was named acting head and then confirmed in the role in 1976, but he left after a year, by some accounts disenchanted with his limited influence on programming.

Throughout his career, Boyle promoted a vision of Canadian identity as an expression of a sense of place, best realized in specific communities. He argued that in pursuing national audiences, the CBC, and Canadian broadcasting generally, neglected local, regional, and multicultural programming. Boyle once commented that he agreed to the CRTC appointment in the hope of pushing the CBC into providing such coverage.

The team of Juneau, dapper and precise, and Boyle, rumpled and disorganized, accomplished much more than anyone expected in carrying forward the ambitious goals of the 1968 Broadcasting Act. They safeguarded domestic ownership of Canada's broadcasting industry, produced a strong set of Canadian-content quotas for television (regulations that contributed significantly to the development of Canada's independent television production industry), supported the extension of the private network CTV, and formulated the first rules for the cable TV industry. Although rendered increasingly obsolete by new broadcast technologies, these initiatives provided important opportunities for Canadian expression.

Boyle's most controversial legacy was a report tabled by the Committee of Inquiry into the National Broadcasting Service in 1977. Boyle presided over the inquiry, which was launched shortly after the 1976

Harry Boyle.
Photo courtesy of National Archives of Canada/CBC Collection

Quebec election, in which a party dedicated to a sovereign Quebec received a majority in the provincial government. Not surprisingly, the event added to concerns about Canadian unity and led to accusations that the French-language news services of the CBC were biased in favor of Quebec independence. It has been suggested that Boyle accepted the task to forestall a more politically motivated investigation. He may also have been motivated by the fact that the committee's mandate reflected his much-quoted view that Canada "exists by reason of communication." The report expressed concern about the centralization of the Canadian television system, the lack of programming from regions outside central Canada, and, in particular, the gulf between French and English audiences. Although supportive of the CBC, Boyle also expressed the hope that new communications technologies, formats, and programming would bridge the divisions in Canadian society. One example was the multichannel possibilities presented by cable television and pay-per-view programming. The report, with others, helped to lay the foundation for the expansion of cable services.

With respect to content, the report characterized the CBC as "biased to the point of subversiveness" for its failure, in the committee's view, to promote communication among the country's regional and linguistic communities. The report was not received favorably by CBC journalists—who contended that it was inaccurate and unfair—but it was successful in turning attention away from accusations of "separatist bias" to the extent to which the English and French networks reflected Canada as a whole. Debate about the latter issue has continued. In the politically charged atmosphere of 1977, however, the tack taken by Boyle helped to defuse French-English tensions a little.

Boyle's substantial personal archives have been deposited with York University in Toronto and will attract scholars interested in making sense of a crucial time in the development of Canadian television.

FREDERICK J. FLETCHER AND ROBERT EVERETT

Harry Boyle. Born in St. Augustine, Ontario, Canada, October 7, 1915. Attended St. Jerome's College in Kitchener, Ontario. Married: Marion McCaffery, 1937; children: Patricia and Michael. Worked for radio station CKNX, Wingham, Ontario, 1936–41; writer, *Beacon-Herald,* Stratford, Ontario, 1941–42; farm broadcaster, CBC, Toronto, Ontario, 1943; supervisor of farm broadcasts, 1943–45; program director, Trans-Canada Network, 1946–52; regional program director, radio and television, 1952–55; supervisor of radio features, from 1955; television executive producer, from 1963; weekly columnist, *Toronto Telegram,* 1956–68; author of numerous books, from 1961; vice chair, Canadian Radio-television Commission, 1968–75; chair, 1976–77; columnist, *Montreal Star,* from 1978. Recipient: Stephen Leacock Medal for Humour, 1964; John Drainie Award, Association of Canadian Television and Radio Artists, 1970; named to Canadian Newspaper Hall of Fame, 1979; Jack Chisholm Award, Canadian Film and TV Directors' Association, 1980.

Publications (selected)

With a Pinch of Sin, 1966
Memories of a Catholic Boyhood, 1973

Further Reading

Peers, Frank W., *The Public Eye: Television and the Politics of Canadian Broadcasting, 1952–68,* Toronto: University of Toronto Press, 1979
Raboy, Marc, *Missed Opportunities: The Story of Canada's Broadcasting Policy,* Montreal: McGill-Queen's University Press, 1990

Boys from the Blackstuff

British Drama Series

Boys from the Blackstuff, the first television series by Liverpool playwright Alan Bleasdale, was a technical and topical triumph for BBC English Regions Drama, capturing the public mood in 1982, at a time of economic recession and anxiety about unemployment. Set in a grimly recognizable Liverpool, it chronicled the disparate and sometimes dissolute attempts of five former members of a tarmac gang to find work in a city hit hard by mounting unemployment and depression. As an outwardly realist intervention into a serious social problem, its impact, sustained through its dramatic power and emotional truth, was comparable to that of *Cathy Come Home* 15 years earlier. With its ostensibly somber subject matter leavened by passionate direction and flashes of ironic Scouse wit, *Boys from the Blackstuff* overcame its regional setting and minority channel scheduling (on BBC 2) to receive instant critical acclaim, winning an unprecedented repeat run only nine weeks later on BBC 1 and a BAFTA award for best drama series of 1982.

Bleasdale (who described it as "an absurd, mad, black farce") originally conceived *Boys from the Blackstuff* in 1978 during filming for *The Black Stuff* (directed by Jim Goddard), his single play introducing the Boys as a tarmac gang (hence the title) and culminating in their sacking for "doing a foreigner" (non-contract job). But while technically a sequel, *Boys from the Blackstuff* was a deeper and darker investigation of character and circumstance consisting of five linked plays of varying lengths (from 55 to 70 minutes). As such, it proved difficult to fit into the production and budgetary system of English Regions Drama.

However, the delay to the production that this caused contributed significantly to the strength and originality of the final work, as well as providing a timely conjunction between its transmission and the apex of British unemployment.

To cut costs, the production was budgeted across two financial years, using newly available lightweight video equipment, except for one episode ("Yosser's Story") made on film with the unit's annual film budget. Unusually for the time, the video episodes were edited in postproduction, and the series' filmic qualities were further enhanced by Ilona Sekacz's specially composed music and by the replacement of Goddard (no longer available) with Philip Saville, through whose elegant and inventive shooting style Liverpool's dereliction took on a crumbling grandeur.

Of the five central characters, Chrissie (Michael Angelis) is the most ordinary (standing, perhaps, for Bleasdale himself), desperate for legitimate work and increasingly soured by the indignity and insecurity of life on the dole. Loggo (Alan Igbon), more defiant, stands as an ironic observer least affected by the experience. Dixie (Tom Georgeson), once the gang's foreman, has become embittered and unforgiving, his pride as a working man shattered. George (Peter Kerrigan), much the oldest, represented the dignity of labor, wise and greatly respected as a trade union official, refusing to give up hope even on the remarkable wheelchair ride through the decaying Albert Dock that precedes his death—a scene that includes an emotional speech based partly on Kerrigan's own experiences as a docker. But it was Bernard Hill's maniacally self-destructive Yosser, a colossal performance of incoherence, savagery, and pathos, who captured the public imagination. Deprived of his dignity and eventually of his children, he is reduced to butting authority figures with the bewildered declaration: "I'm Yosser Hughes!" Yosser's head-butts and his woeful "gizza job" became totems in the popular press.

The delay in production also benefited the series in enabling the script to develop through ruthless changes initiated by producer Michael Wearing. In the most extreme case, lamenting the absence of female and domestic perspectives on unemployment, Wearing returned the original episode 3 with an instruction to "write Angie." In the rewrite, Angie (Julie Walters), Chrissie's wife, emerged as a pivotal character. In an emotionally charged performance, she utters the lines that seem to sum up the series' message about Liverpool and the dole: "It's not funny, it's not friggin' funny. I've had enough of that 'if you don't laugh you'll cry.' I've heard it for years. This stupid soddin' city's full of it.... Why don't you fight back, you bastard. Fight back."

As well as pricking the national conscience (helping to dissolve the popular characterization of the unemployed as "scroungers"), *Boys from the Blackstuff* confirmed Bleasdale as one of the nation's leading writers for stage and television, although his subsequent television work might have benefited from the editorial influence of Wearing. Equally important, it helped to put Liverpool on the map as a dramatic location of special significance, where brutality, decay, and poverty could serve as a backdrop for the expression, through darkly defiant wit, of the resilience and spirit of ordinary people. Its indirect influence is detectable in the proliferation of Liverpool-based television and film drama of the 1980s, including the sitcom *Bread,* resembling a travestied *Boys from the Blackstuff* stripped of its social conscience, and the long-running soap *Brookside,* which inherited its shooting style (single-camera shooting on lightweight video) as well as part of its milieu. Capitalizing on the success of such series and aided by the city's thriving Film Office, Liverpool's range of locations and local production expertise has brought it an international reputation as a location for the making of film and television drama.

PETER GODDARD

See also **Bleasdale, Alan**

Cast

Chrissie Todd	Michael Angelis
Loggo	Alan Igbon
Dixie Deans	Tom Georgeson
George Malone	Peter Kerrigan
Yosser Hughes	Bernard Hill
Angie Todd	Julie Walters

Producers

Alan Bleasdale, Michael Wearing

Programming History

Five episodes of varying length
BBC
October 10, 1982–November 7, 1982

Further Reading

Millington, Bob, and Robin Nelson, "*Boys from the Blackstuff*": *The Making of TV Drama,* London: Comedia, 1986

Paterson, Richard, editor, *BFI Dossier 20: "Boys from the Blackstuff,"* London: British Film Institute, 1983

Boys of St. Vincent, The

Canadian Docudrama

The Boys of St. Vincent (1993), directed by John N. Smith for the National Film Board of Canada, is a two-part docudrama that caused considerable controversy when it first appeared. At the time of its broadcast, the criminal trials of several Canadian priests accused of child molestation were in progress. The Canadian Broadcasting Corporation (CBC) was not allowed to broadcast the film in Ontario or western Quebec, in case it should in some way interfere with fairness of the trials—even though a disclaimer, saying that the film is loosely based upon several different events and not any real individuals, was added. Part 1 of *The Boys of St. Vincent* deals with the brutalization and sexual molestation of several orphans under the care of a group of priests headed by brother Peter Lavin (Henry Czerny). Part 2, which takes place 15 years later, concerns the events surrounding Lavin's trial and the lives of the boys, who are now adults. *The Boys of St. Vincent* is a powerful, adult docudrama about a painful and largely repressed part of Canadian history.

The critic John Caughie locates the specificity of docudrama in the integration of two distinct discourses: the realist narrative drama (which I would in this case call *melodrama*), and the Griersonian documentary, from which the docudrama adopts two aspects—a strong desire for social education presented in a palatable form, and the need to reveal repressed histories. The melodramatic aspect attracts an audience and the documentary aspect serves to keep the narrative truthful. In effect, the documentary acts to "detrivialize" the melodrama—an essential function if the work's moral point is to be taken seriously. Some critics, such as Elaine Rapping, have taken the made-for-television movie seriously, but it is still widely castigated for its overly emotional representation of domestic disasters.

Unlike most American-made telefeatures, *The Boys of St. Vincent* does not have a hero. The two main characters, Kevin Reeny, who is one of the abused children, and Peter Lavin, the head of the orphanage, are not really figures with whom the audience can identify easily. In Part 1 Reeny is a badly abused child who barely speaks. Smith builds up tremendous sympathy for Reeny in Part 1, showing the child's desperate attempts to avoid the priest and escape from the orphanage. His youthfulness makes him an object of our compassion, particularly as he struggles to free himself and stand up to the predatory Lavin. Audience identification is much stronger with him in this part of the film. In Part 2 Reeny becomes a troubled man, unable to deal with his past. A loner given to bouts of violence, and clearly troubled in his relationship with his girlfriend, he is a closed and emotionally withdrawn character with whom it is possible to sympathize, but not really identify.

Peter Lavin is certainly the center of both the film's controversy and its insightful and troubling depiction of child molestation. The fact that Lavin is a handsome, intelligent, and charismatic man, as well as a brutal and overbearing pedophile is part of what makes *The Boys of St. Vincent* such a complex experience. In many child molestation films, the child molester is a villain, pure and simple. This is never the case with the Smith film. The film in fact asks the audience to understand Lavin, and even gives the audience his point of view as he molests Kevin. This is a shocking moment in the narrative. As the first scene of molestation begins, the camera is placed in an observer's position. But as the sequence develops, the camera moves close to Lavin's point of view as he fondles Kevin's body. When Kevin refuses the priest's advances, he is severely beaten and a statue of a wounded Jesus juts into the frame as if to comment upon what is taking place. The next morning as Brother Lavin watches the boys shower, the camera shows an aesthetically pleasing and sensuous depiction of their naked bodies. How is the spectator expected to respond to those pictures of desire—when the object of that desire is a beautiful, nude ten-year-old boy seen through the eyes of a pedophile? This highly charged and controversial sequence was cut when *The Boys of St. Vincent* was shown on the Arts and Entertainment (A&E) channel in the United States. This excision, however, undermines Smith's attempt to ask the audience to understand a pedophile rather than merely condemning him or turning him into a melodramatic villain.

Of further significance in *The Boys of St. Vincent* is Smith's critique of patriarchy as a whole, with its patterns of dominance and submission worked throughout the educational system and the religious and governmental orders. We are shown boys literally owned by the church, brutalized not only physically but intellectually through the fear and guilt instilled in them in both church and classroom. Lessons are taught by hypocritical and tedious rote, and the boys are harshly disciplined for seemingly minor infractions. *Boys* is nothing if not a thorough critique of middle-class, patriarchal capitalism in its most brutalizing form. Interestingly, Smith shows that both the boys and the priests are all victims of this system, that in fact this kind of behavior is institutionalized and even traditional in orphanages.

Except for one of the older boys, the janitor, and one policeman, no one is much outraged by what has gone on. Through *The Boys of St. Vincent* we are kept thoroughly off balance, not only by Smith's style, which tends to throw us into situations with few establishing shots, but also by the difficulty of identifying with any of the damaged characters in the fiction. Nor does the ending of the film bring any relief. Although the priests are brought to trial, Brother Lavin is neither healed nor forgiven; ironically, he is only able to confess his sins in the confessional, where he may in fact be confessing to another child molester, and his confession never becomes public. We are never shown whether he has confessed his problems to his psychiatrist, and because the film ends before the verdict is given, we do not have the satisfaction of knowing what will happen to him. The film ends with Lavin's wife demanding to know if he has molested his own sons—and no answer is forthcoming here either. Kevin Reeny, who has resisted all attempts to speak up at the trial, finally manages to testify, but we are left with no sense of either triumph or revenge. One of the other boys, who has become a prostitute and a drug addict, overdoses and dies before the trial is complete. This film does not offer us any comfortable assurances about the future, and by avoiding closure, it implies that this kind of crime does not go away. In a film that consistently violates convention, this may be the most difficult of all to face, since no morally reassuring note is sounded at the film's conclusion.

The Boys of St. Vincent fully develops the potential of the made-for-television movie. Although it has a high-concept plot and is based upon a sensational news story, it violates many of the conventions of the U.S. telefeature. *Boys* mounts a damning condemnation of both the Catholic Church and the government of Newfoundland. It asks the audience to consider a child molester as a human being, not merely a depraved monster. By controlling the worst excesses of the melodrama and adopting documentary techniques, it manages to become a believable and powerful depiction of a serious social problem, proving that the simplicity of the made-for-television movie does not have to equal simplemindedness, and that made-for-television movies can become sites for significant, but accessible social critique.

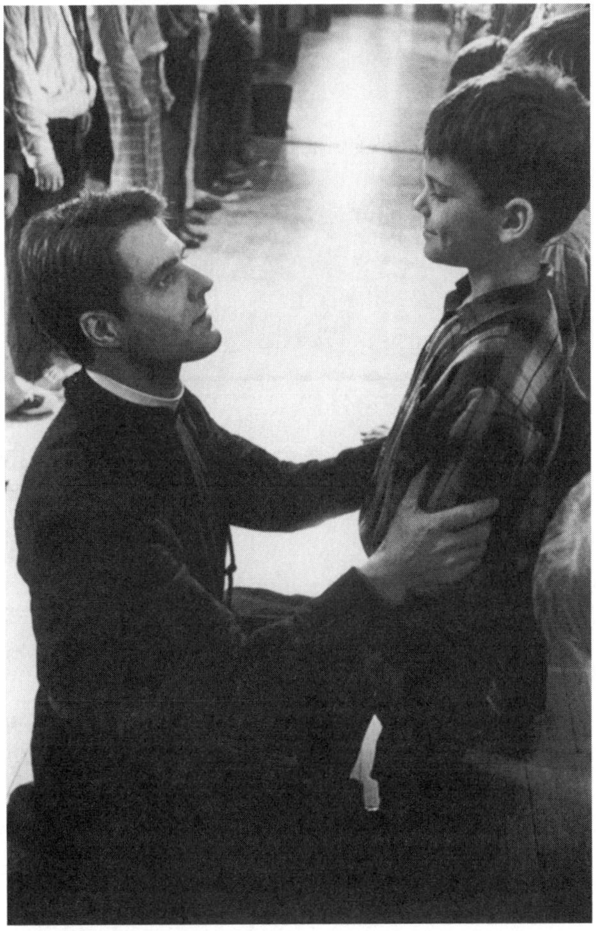

The Boys of St. Vincent.
Photo courtesy of Tele-Action

JEANNETTE SLONIOWSKI

See also **Canadian Programming in English; Docudrama**

Cast

Peter Lavin	Henry Czerny
Kevin Reeny	Johnny Morina
Kevin Reeny (at age 25)	Sebastian Spence
Brian Lunny	Ashley Billard
Brian Lunny (at age 30)	Timothy Webber
Billy Lunny	Jonathon Hoddinott
Steven Lunny	Brian Dodd
Steven Lunny (at age 25)	David Hewlett
Sheilah	Kristine Demers
Detective Noseworthy	Brian Dooley
Commission Lawyer	Sheena Larkin

Chantal	Lise Roy
Lenora	Mary Walsh

Producers
Sam Grana, Claudio Luca

Programming History
CBC
1993

Further Reading

Caughie, John, "Progressive Television and Documentary Drama," in *Popular Film and Television,* edited by Tony Bennett et al., London: British Film Institute, 1981
Goodwin, Andrew, et al., *Drama-Documentary,* London: British Film Institute, 1983
Rapping, Elaine, *The Movie of the Week: Private Stories, Public Events,* Minneapolis: University of Minnesota Press, 1992

Brady Bunch, The

U.S. Situation Comedy

When it premiered on ABC in 1969, *The Brady Bunch* garnered mostly negative reviews. From that date until 1974, its entire network run, the series never reached the top-ten ranks of the Nielsen ratings. Yet, the program stands as one of the most important sitcoms of American 1970s television programming, spawning numerous other series on all three major networks, as well as records, lunch boxes, a cookbook, and even a stage show and two feature films.

In an era in which situation comedies emphasized how social climes were changing, *The Brady Bunch* was one of the few series that hearkened back to the traditional family values seen in such sitcoms as *Leave It to Beaver* and *Father Knows Best.* Executive producer Sherwood Schwartz conceived of the premise: a widower, father of three boys, marries a widow, mother of three girls. The concept worked as a springboard for dramatizations of an array of childhood and adolescent traumas. The cluster of children—Greg (Barry Williams), Marcia (Maureen McCormick), Peter (Christopher Knight), Jan (Eve Plumb), Bobby (Mike Lookinland), and Cindy (Susan Olsen)—provided male and female versions for three separate stages of youth. With this group, the show managed to portray the typical crises of orthodontia, first crushes, neighborhood bullies, and school plays, as well as such home-bound issues as sibling rivalry and problems with parental restrictions. Father Mike Brady (Robert Reed) was always there with a weekly homily that would explain to the children the lessons they had learned. Although mother Carol Brady (Florence Henderson) was initially written as a divorcée, and episodes of the first season did deal with the problems of children getting used to a new mother or father, the half-hour show repeatedly and firmly upheld the family as a tight unit of support, love, and understanding.

Unlike *All in the Family* or even *Julia, The Brady Bunch* tried to steer clear of the political and social issues of the day. Rarely were nonwhite characters introduced into the series. Women's liberation and gender equality were boiled down to brother-sister in-fighting. The counterculture of the 1960s was represented in random minor characters portrayed as buffoons—or in the scene of Greg trying to impress a girl with hippie jargon.

The series' representation of childhood as a time of blissful innocence was in marked contrast to what was happening off camera. Many of the boys and girls playing the Brady children dated each other secretly, making out in their trailers or in the doghouse of the Brady's pet, Tiger. The oldest boy, Williams, attempted to date Henderson and filmed at least one episode while high on marijuana. All these incidents (as well as Reed's homosexuality) were obscured behind closed doors, coming to light only in the years after the series originally aired.

The decided emphasis of the series on the Brady children made it very popular among younger audiences. ABC capitalized on this appeal, programming the show early on Friday evenings. This popularity also resulted in various attempts to create other prof-

The Brady Brunch.
Courtesy of the Everett Collection

itable spin-off products: The Brady Kids, a pop rock group (patterned on the Archies and the Partridge Family), a Saturday morning cartoon called *The Brady Kids* (1972–74), and regular appearances of the young actors and actresses (particularly McCormick and Knight), in teen fan magazines.

Following its initial network run, *The Brady Bunch* became inordinately popular in rerun syndication. This success can be attributed in part to children's afternoon-viewing patterns. Often programmed as a daily "strip" in after-school time periods, the show found new viewers who had not previously seen the series. The age distribution of the cast may have created appeal among a range of young viewers, and as those viewers aged, they were able to take a more ironic viewing stance toward the entertainment of their childhood.

The ongoing success of the Brady characters has continually brought them back to television. *The Brady Bunch Hour,* produced by Sid and Marty Krofft from 1976 to 1977 on ABC, had the family hosting a vividly colored, disco-oriented variety series. *The Brady Brides,* on NBC in 1981, was a half-hour sitcom about Marcia and Jan as they dealt with their new husbands and the trials of being married. In December 1988, CBS aired the TV-movie *A Very Brady Christmas,* which became the network's highest-rated made-for-TV movie that season. This led in 1990 to a short-lived hour-long dramatic series called simply *The Bradys.*

Although the dramatic series faded quickly, a live-stage parody of the original series quickly became a national sensation after its debut in Chicago in 1990. Playing the original scripts as camp performance, *The Real Live Brady Bunch* seemed to tap into viewers' simultaneous love for and cynicism toward the values presented by the series. The stage show and the subsequent films *The Brady Bunch Movie* (1995) and *A Very Brady Sequel* (1996) reveled in the kitsch taste of 1970s culture, complete with "groovy" bell bottoms and day-glo orange and lime-green color schemes. Yet, although the stage production and the films gleefully deconstructed the absurdity of the wholesomeness of the Brady family, an admiration remained. Many children who grew up with the show came from families of divorce, or were "latch-key" children with both parents working. Consequently, some of those amused at the naiveté of the series also admittedly envy the ideal nuclear family that they never had and that the Bradys represent.

Much like *Star Trek,* another Paramount-produced television series of the late 1960s, *The Brady Bunch* was underappreciated by critics and network executives, but fan loyalty has made the series a franchise for book deals, memorabilia, and feature films. A cultural throwback even in its time, the family led by "a lovely lady" and "a man named Brady" has become celebrated in part precisely for its steadfast obliviousness to societal change.

Sean Griffin

See also **Comedy, Domestic Settings**

Cast

Mike Brady	Robert Reed
Carol Brady	Florence Henderson
Alice Nelson	Ann B. Davis
Marcia Brady	Maureen McCormick
Jan Brady	Eve Plumb
Cindy Brady	Susan Olsen
Greg Brady	Berry Williams
Peter Brady	Christopher Knight
Bobby Brady	Mike Lookinland

Producers

Sherwood Schwartz, Lloyd J. Schwartz, Howard Leeds

Programming History

117 episodes
ABC

September 1969–September 1970	Friday 8:00–8:30
September 1970–September 1971	Friday 7:30–8:00
September 1971–August 1974	Friday 8:00–8:30

Further Reading

Bellafante, Gina, "The Inventor of Bad TV: What Would the '70s Have Been Without Sherwood Schwartz?" (interview), *Time* (March 13, 1995)

Briller, Bert, "Will the Real Live Brady Bunch Stand Up?" *Television Quarterly* (Spring 1992)

Williams, Barry, with Chris Kreski, *Growing Up Brady: I Was a Teenage Greg,* New York: Harper Perennial, 1992

g, Melvyn (1939–)

ledia Executive, Personality, Author

sman for the (ITV). Pre- since 1978, on Weekend ion since 1990, he is now president of the National Campaign for the Arts and has arguably done more to advance the cause of arts programming on television and radio than anyone else.

Bragg was a working-class boy who won a scholarship to Wadham College, Oxford, before joining the BBC in 1961 as a radio and, later, television producer. Bragg has never forgotten his origins; he shares with his viewers his genuine delight in new artistic discoveries, and readers of his novels delight in his portraits of northern England. Bragg worked for the BBC Television flagship arts program, *Monitor,* under its brilliant editor Huw Wheldon, and in 1967 he became producer and editor of BBC 2's first arts program, *New Release,* as well as the program *Writers' World.* Interviewed in 1970, he explained that when he worked for the BBC in the 1960s, he had wanted to make arts programs current; he added that he wanted to put on the arts because

> I think it's the only way that People, with a capital P, are going to find out about the things that I particularly like. Missionary is too strong a word for it and propaganda is the wrong word—but it's certainly to do with the fact that the people I was born and brought up among very rarely read books, but all of them look at television.

Bragg's tenure as the anchor of the BBC Radio 4 program *Start the Week,* as well as his editorship of *The South Bank Show,* have led to his being known as the "Arts Tsar" or "Arts Supremo." Critics have suggested that "any traffic between high art and mass taste had to pass through Bragg's custom post," as Henry Porter wrote in the *Guardian.* Bragg replied that in England if people get too big for their boots, they get cut off at the knees.

Bragg's long tenure as presenter of *The South Bank Show* has kept the flag flying for the arts on ITV, and Bragg claims that ITV shows more arts programming than the BBC does. Among the outstanding episodes of *The South Bank Show* that will go down in history are Bragg's portrait of the English film director David Lean, and Bragg's moving 70-minute interview with the dying screenwriter Dennis Potter.

In the 1990s Bragg became the most articulate contributor to the "two cultures" debate since the late Lord Snow, and he proved himself equally at ease in the worlds of science and social science. In 1998 Bragg presented the BBC Radio 4 series on the history of science, *On Giant's Shoulders,* with his own book to accompany the series, and in 2001 he chaired the televised *Darwin Debate,* which examined the significance of evolution theory for human society on BBC 2. His 20-part television series on the history of Christianity, *Two Thousand Years* (ITV, 1999), demonstrates the breadth of his intellectual interests; he wrote two books to accompany the series. Bragg has also written screenplays for such dramas as *Isadora, Jesus Christ Superstar,* and, with Ken Russell, *Clouds of Glory.* Of his 19 novels, *A Time to Dance* was televised in 1992, and his novel *The Soldier's Return* won the W.H. Smith Writer's Award in 2000.

Bragg profited from his support of London Weekend Television's franchise-renewal application to the tune of several million pounds, and he also became chair of the ITV program contractor, Border Television, in 1990. Without his skills and dedication, it is possible that arts programs on ITV might have been marginalized in the same way that ITV religious programs have been. His presence and his promotional skills have ensured good time slots and good ratings for *The South Bank Show.* His clear-sighted integrity has endeared him to television makers, artists, and politicians alike. Bragg became chancellor of the University of Leeds in 1998, a well-deserved recognition from a university that has encouraged the interaction of the worlds of academia and television for many years. He currently hosts two programs on BBC Radio 4: *In Our Time,* in which he discusses key cultural and scientific topics with his guests, and *The Routes of English,* which traces the evolution and development of the language.

Established as an outstanding arts presenter, Bragg is also seen as a wise elder statesman commenting on the future of British television. In the 1990s he warned the government that British television was being

Melvyn Bragg with Dame Edna Everage, *The South Bank Show.*
Courtesy of the Everett Collection

turned into a two-tier system, "telly for nobs and telly for slobs" and that the medium was being destroyed by a "class and cash" system whereby satellite and cable systems were able to siphon off prime material. Every newspaper reported his speech, and the *Daily Telegraph* devoted an editorial to the subject. Such leadership, all too rare in the independent sector, suggests that Melvyn Bragg will be remembered as one of the greatest of the ITV leaders in the 1980s and 1990s, and at the dawn of the 21st century.

ANDREW QUICKE

Melvyn Bragg. Born in Carlisle, Cumberland, England, October 6, 1939. Educated at Nelson-Thomlinson Grammar School, Wigton, Cumberland, 1950–58; Wadham College, Oxford, 1958–61, M.A. honors, 1961. Married: 1) Marie-Elisabeth Roche, 1961 (died, 1971); one daughter; 2) Catherine Mary Haste, 1973; one daughter and one son. General trainee, BBC, 1961; producer and presenter numerous arts programs, 1963–67; writer and broadcaster, 1967–78; editor and presenter of *The South Bank Show,* since 1978; head of arts, London Weekend Television, 1982–90; deputy chair, Border Television, 1985–90; presenter, BBC Radio's *Start the Week,* since 1988; controller of arts, London Weekend Television, from 1990; chair, Border Television, Carlisle, from 1990; chancellor, University of Leeds, since 1998; host, *In Our Time* and *The Routes of English,* BBC Radio 4. D.Litt.: University of Liverpool, 1986; University of Lancaster, 1990; Council for National Academic Awards, 1990; D.Univ.: Open University, Milton Keynes, Buckinghamshire, 1987; LL.D., University of St. Andrew's, 1993; D.CL., University of Northumbria, 1994. Fellow: Royal Society of Literature, 1970; Royal Television Society; Lancashire Polytechnic, 1987; St. Catherine's College, Oxford, 1990. Member: Arts Council (chair, Arts Council Literature Panel, 1977–80); Cumbrians for Peace (president, since 1982); Northern Arts (chair, 1983–87); National Campaign for the Arts (chair, since 1986). Recipient: Writers Guild Screenplay Award, 1966; Rhys Memorial Prize, 1968; Northern Arts Association Prose Award, 1970; Silver Pen Award, 1970; Broadcasting Guild Award, 1984; Ivor Novello Musical Award, 1985; British Academy of Film and Television Arts Dimbleby Award, 1986; W.H. Smith Writer's Award, 2000. Named Lord Bragg of Wigton, 1998.

Television Series

1963–65	*Monitor* (producer)
1964–70	*New Release/Review/Arena* (editor)
1967–70	*Writers' World* (editor)
1964–70	*Take It or Leave It* (editor)
1971	*In the Picture* (presenter)
1973–77	*Second House* (presenter)
1976–77	*Read All about It* (editor and presenter)
1978–	*The South Bank Show* (editor and presenter)
1983	*Melvyn Bragg's Cumbria*
1989–	*The Late Show* (presenter)
1995	*Johnny and the Dead* (executive producer)
1998	*The Sundays* (presenter)
1999	*Two Thousand Years*
2000	*Who's Afraid of the Ten Commandments*

Television Specials (selected)

1965	*The Debussy Film* (writer, with Ken Russell)
1970	*Charity Begins at Home* (writer)

1972	*Zinotchka* (writer)
1978	*Clouds of Glory* (writer, with Ken Howard)
1979	*Orion* (writer, with Ken Howard and Alan Blaikley)
1982	*Laurence Olivier: A Life* (editor, presenter, and writer)
1989	*Norbert Smith: A Life*
1989	*A British Picture*
1991	*A Time to Dance* (writer)

Films (writer)

Play Dirty, with Lotte Colin, 1968; *Isadora,* with Clive Exton and Margaret Drabble, 1969; *The Music Lovers,* 1970; *Jesus Christ Superstar,* with Norman Jewison, 1973; *Clouds of Glory* (with Ken Russell), 1978; *The Tall Guy* (actor only), 1989; *Marathon: The Flames of Peace,* 1992.

Radio (selected)

Robin Hood (writer), 1971; *Start the Week* (presenter), from 1988; *On Giants' Shoulders,* 1998; *In Our Time; The Routes of English.*

Stage (writer)

Mardi Gras, with Alan Blaikley and Ken Howard, 1976; *The Hired Man,* with Howard Goodall, 1984; *King Lear in New York,* 1992.

Publications (selected)

For Want of a Nail (novel), 1965
The Second Inheritance (novel), 1966
Without a City Wall (novel), 1968
The Hired Man (novel), 1969
A Place in England (novel), 1970
The Nerve (novel), 1971
The Hunt (novel), 1972
Josh Lawton (novel), 1972
The Silken Net (novel), 1974
A Place in England, 1975
Speak for England: An Essay on England, 1900–1975, 1976
A Christmas Child (children's fiction), 1976
Autumn Manoeuvres (novel), 1978
Kingdom Come (novel), 1980
My Favourite Stories of Lakeland, editor, 1981
Love and Glory (novel), 1983
Land of the Lakes, 1983
The Cumbrian Trilogy (collection), 1984
Laurence Olivier, 1984
Cumbria in Verse, editor, 1984
The Hired Man (play), 1986
The Maid of Buttermere (novel), 1987
Rich: The Life of Richard Burton, 1988
A Time to Dance (novel), 1990
Crystal Rooms (novel), 1992
Credo (novel), 1996
Giants' Stories: Great Scientists and Their Discoveries from Archimedes to DNA, 1998
Two Thousand Years, 1999
The Soldier's Return (fiction), 1999
The Adventure of English: The Biography of a Language, 2004

Further Reading

Field, Michele, "Melvyn Bragg: The Author of a Biography of Richard Burton Finds That His Own Background Has Much in Common with That of His Subject," *Publishers Weekly* (February 3, 1989)

Brambell, Wilfrid (1912–1985)

British Actor

British character actor Wilfrid Brambell gained national fame late in his career as Albert Steptoe in the BBC's most popular and successful sitcom, *Steptoe and Son,* although the character he played was considerably older than he was. He was never one for starring roles but supplied reliable support in a variety of stage, screen, and television roles before Albert Steptoe thrust him into the limelight. Television appearances included a variety of parts in adaptations of classic texts, including *The Government Inspector* (1958), *Bleak House* (1959), and *Our Mutual Friend* (1959), all for the BBC.

Writers Ray Galton and Alan Simpson wanted to use straight actors, rather than comedians, when cast-

Wilfrid Brambell.
Courtesy of the Everett Collection

ing the leads for their new BBC comedy *Steptoe and Son* in 1962. Harry H. Corbett was cast as Harold Steptoe, and Brambell given the role of his father Albert. Over the years to follow, the actors and writers together were to develop characters that found their way into the national consciousness.

Albert Steptoe is an old-time rag-and-bone man who inherited the family business of the title from his father and now runs it with his son Harold. Harold goes out on the cart to collect the junk, while Albert remains at home, ostensibly to run the administrative side of the business, but, in reality, to take it easy or go out to the cinema. Albert is a widower. He still has an eye for the ladies, and for the main chance, though generally espousing an old-fashioned morality. He is a veteran of the Great War and bemoans declining standards, but his own behavior is often gross and earthy in the extreme. He rarely washes and, when he does, is liable to eat his evening meal in the bath. His language and behavior are, in Harold's eyes in particular, uncouth, prompting the description, "You dirty old man!," the series' only catchphrase.

Brambell played Albert Steptoe as a grumpy old curmudgeon, capable of resorting to the most pathetic pleading to get his own way. The role of the scruffy old man could not have been further from the rather suave and cultured person Brambell was in real life.

Steptoe and Son ran for four seasons between 1962 and 1965. It regularly attracted audiences of over 20 million, from all sectors of society, and in 1963 a *Steptoe and Son* sketch was performed by Brambell and Corbett as part of that year's Royal Variety Performance. Between series and after Galton and Simpson brought it to an end, both Brambell and Corbett were in demand for movie parts because of their great popularity. Among Brambell's roles were those of Paul McCartney's grandfather in the Beatles film *A Hard Day's Night* and the White Rabbit in Jonathan Miller's 1966 television version of *Alice in Wonderland.*

Steptoe and Son was revived, in color, by the BBC in 1970 and ran for another four series between then and 1974. There were also two spin-off feature films. The characters and situations had not changed—nor had the quality of writing and performance or the popularity of the show.

STEVE BRYANT

See also **Steptoe and Son**

Wilfrid Brambell. Born in Dublin, Ireland, March 22, 1912. Attended schools in Dublin. Married: Molly (divorced, 1955). Stage debut as a child, entertaining troops during World War I, 1914; began professional acting career as an adult at the Gate Theatre, Dublin; toured with ENSA during World War II; first appearance on London stage, 1950; single appearance on Broadway, 1965; played character parts in theater and films before achieving fame as Albert Steptoe in long-running *Steptoe and Son* comedy series, 1962–74. Died in London, England, January 18, 1985.

Television Series

1962–65, 1970–74 *Steptoe and Son*

Films

The 39 Steps, 1935; *Odd Man Out,* 1946; *Another Shore,* 1948; *Dry Rot,* 1956; *The Story of Esther Costello,* 1957; *The Salvage Gang,* 1958; *The Long Hot Summer,* 1958; *Serious Charge,* 1959; *Urge to Kill,* 1960; *The Sinister Man,* 1961; *Jack's Horrible Luck,* 1961; *Flame in the Streets,* 1961; *What a Whopper!,* 1961; *The Grand Junction Case,* 1961; *In Search of the Castaways,* 1962; *The Boys,* 1962; *The Fast Lady,* 1962; *The Small World of Sammy Lee,* 1963; *Crooks in Cloisters,* 1963; *The Three Lives of Thomasina,* 1963; *Go Kart Go!,* 1963; *A*

Hard Day's Night, 1964; *San Ferry Ann,* 1965; *Alice in Wonderland,* 1966; *Where the Bullets Fly,* 1966; *Mano di Velluto,* 1966; *Witchfinder-General,* 1968; *Lionheart,* 1968; *Cry Wolf,* 1968; *The Undertakers,* 1969; *Carry On Again, Doctor,* 1969; *Some Will, Some Won't,* 1970; *Steptoe and Son,* 1972; *Steptoe and Son Ride Again,* 1973; *Holiday on the Buses,* 1973; *The Adventures of Picasso,* 1978; *High Rise Donkey,* 1980; *Island of Adventure,* 1981; *Death and Transfiguration,* 1983; *Sword of the Valiant,* 1983; *The Terence Davies Trilogy,* 1984.

Radio
Steptoe and Son.

Stage (selected)
Blind Man's Buff; Stop It, Whoever You Are; The Canterbury Tales; The Ghost Train; Kelly; A Christmas Carol.

Publication

All Above Board (autobiography), 1976

Further Reading

Burke, Michael, "You Dirty Old Man!" *The People* (January 9, 1994)
"How We Met: Ray Galton and Alan Simpson," *The Independent* (June 11, 1995)

Branding

"Branding" has emerged as a central concern of the television industry in the age of digital convergence. Referring not simply to product or company names, titles, or the trademark designations created by marketers and advertisers, the ideal brand expresses a more holistic identity to viewers and consumers. "Brand-builders," as they are now called, aspire to bring to client corporations a set of recurrent goals and market ideals: a widely and easily recognizable image, a distinct personality among competitors, a consistency wherever the brand is encountered, and a confidence in the quality of the branded product. In what some term the "old economy" (which utilized market research to characterize its "average" customer), industry created brands by providing a level of quality and uniqueness for goods and services that would attract buyers to a product. Once a brand like Coca-Cola or Ford was established it could be efficiently "franchised" across a large market in order to exploit "economies of scale." The current mediascape no longer follows the once-trusted laws or "rationality" of Fordist-era industry, where appropriate pricing and (sometimes) heavy-handed advertising simply persuaded mass market buyers to use a product by changing their minds. Instead, producers of both consumer goods and media content today face more highly competitive and "flexible" post-Fordist markets and a culture defined by narrower "economies of scope." These economies are comprised of distinctive niche consumer taste-cultures, whose demographically-based consumption practices (which include spending and viewing habits) form the basis for the kind of narrowcasting favored in the new world of cable and digital media. Given this change in context, a number of brand-builders now enjoin corporations in the digital age of information economies to shift from an older emphasis on product and pricing, to carefully targeted emotional, therapeutic and "relationship" branding strategies. For example, some argue (Gobe) that branding is no longer "about market share when it is really about mind and emotions share," while others (D'Alessandro) propose branding models based on intimate, interpersonal paradigms of "co-dependency." These general economic and marketing shifts—and the branding discourses attending them—have had a marked impact on cable and television as well.

Television and cable networks deploy branding (NBC's "peacock" in the 1960s), rebranding (NBC's "must see TV" in the 1990s and early 2000s), and co-branding (NBC and Microsoft's current cable news network MSNBC) strategies to differentiate their programming fare from competitors. Television/cable branding typically includes three components (Mullen, Turow): (1) the consistent use of logos and other on-screen components, (2) signature shows, and (3) "compatible" reruns. The programming and marketing departments of cable and television networks today typically have formal branding policies and preferences in each of these three areas. But this was not always the case. In stark contrast to the early years of television, for example, a far greater share of the average programming hour today is comprised of "self-promotions" produced and aired by the network or channel brand. This increasing promotional reflexivity is partly due to broad-based efforts to raise a network's programming above the clutter, and partly due to a fundamental shift in the ways that brands were talked about in relation to television.

During the postwar era, marketing departments and ad agencies spent considerable energy designing, developing, and promoting brands for their clients, who were mostly large manufacturers (Procter and Gamble, Colgate-Palmolive, Goodyear, GM, and other Fortune 500 companies) that successfully promoted their products by advertising on network television. In a few cases, such as DuMont, companies operated both as manufactured brands (of television sets) and as broadcasters (of programs), but this soon changed. The television networks that survived and prospered during this period, on the other hand (NBC, CBS, ABC), did so in part by promoting themselves to governmental policymakers and audiences not as manufacturers of proprietary, branded consumer products, but as enlightened stewards and caretakers of the airwaves. This successful promotion of the networks as trustees (rather than brands) protecting a vast public resource, helped legitimize and sanction a network "oligarchy" during the 1950s (one controlled by only three corporations who were referred to officially in abbreviated three-initial short-hand). But even as caretakers of the public trust, the same networks were always producers of content as well, and any time this reality surfaced in public discussions, tensions emerged among policymakers and industry management. These tensions typically resulted in the application of constraints to the television industry (such as limitations on syndication rights allowed the networks when they acted as producers). Such constraints were intended to ensure the free and open flow of trade and speech on the airwaves. But this situation slowly changed, as the major television networks (and then the federal government starting in the Reagan era) began to acknowledge the original networks less as public trustees than as corporations (and the branded manufacturers of content) fighting for market share. Early on the networks exploited one side of their dualistic identity (lobbying for trusteeship with regulators), even though they effectively and simultaneously sold themselves to viewers (as branded providers of entertainment). This tension between branding and trusteeship has existed in American network television from the start, but shifts in industry emphasis became even more dramatic in the 1980s and 1990s.

With the current proliferation of programming choices and the expansion of channel competition during the digital era, branding has shifted from its status as an off-screen concern of marketing personnel and ad agency research, to a self-conscious form of promotional reflexivity that has also altered the very look and sound of contemporary television. The venerable "eye" of CBS and the once proud "peacock" of NBC easily ruled the roost of public consciousness as corporate symbols that stood above all sorts of lesser fare in the 1960s and 1970s.

Yet, by the mid-1990s, a large array of multichannel competitors had taken away the very viewership base that made the eye and the peacock almost universally recognized symbols in households across America. A few years earlier this decline in viewership and brand identity forced a boardroom shakeup at CBS, a takeover by GE of NBC, and a takeover by Capital Cities of ABC. A few years after that a second wave of takeovers and mergers followed when the same networks were the takeover targets of Viacom (CBS) and Disney (ABC). With upstarts like HBO, MTV, CNN, ESPN, FOX, WB, and UPN "cluttering" up corporate identities along with program choices in viewer living rooms, the major TV networks all embarked on public campaigns to "rebrand" themselves. CBS's and NBC's simple, stable, historic marquees of "quality" no longer seemed (to use Brandon Tartikoff's terms) to bring acceptable numbers of viewers "into the network tent."

Branding has been an obligatory marketing staple of corporate business strategies outside of broadcasting for many years. And while NBC once had the brand identity and loyalty of, say a Coca-Cola, it no longer did by the early 1990s. ABC garnered the lion's share of critical and public attention for branding in its "yellow campaign" starting in 1997. No longer even an issue of typography and logo, ABC simply plastered the color yellow on every promo in print, broadcast, or billboard, along with ironic and knowing tag lines that mocked everything from the uncool tastes of parents ("this is not your father's TV") to the exaggerated claims of mental decline (that TV is mind-numbing and lowers literacy) and physical decline (programs for couch-potatoes) attributed to television by concerned consumer advocates and liberal watchdogs. True postmodern irony might be the well-earned reputation of actual programs on and by MTV, for example, but even if it did not have comparably hip programs, the ABC corporation could still front itself as postmodern by making irony and pastiche a part of every institutional and promotional self-reference. ABC put itself front-and-center by making the network packagers (rather than the production community) the authoring source of irony, and it signaled this new and very visible ever-presence with a branded promotional hue.

While ABC's yellow campaign scored notoriety and

endless news-hits for rebranding—in everything from the *Wall Street Journal* and *New York Times* to *Entertainment Tonight* and the tabloids—a comparably comprehensive on-screen overhaul of a network began in 1994 by NBC with its "NBC-2000" campaign (a campaign that set the standard for the subsequent rebranding initiatives at both CBS and ABC). NBC's campaign involved far more than color and ironic tag lines. The smug confidence of the networks about their initial prowess in the multichannel flow had eroded to the point of crisis by the mid-1990s. With drastic loss in market share, the three major networks now needed a way to make not just audiences but also industry members aware of the power and benefits that came with the network "family." The networks, that is, were in a state of crisis, with prognostications of demise or merger forming a steady rhetorical flow in the trades.

In 1995 and 1996, NBC counterattacked by borrowing former President Bush's much maligned "thousand points of light" mythos. Research showed that the traditional four-letter station call-letters were simply too complicated for most viewers to remember. The response? Local stations *owned* by the national network were to drop the "K's" and "W's" nationally (as in "KNBC, Burbank"), and adopt the NBC plus channel number ("NBC-4, Burbank") as a simpler, substitute designation and common logo. These nationally aired station/network IDs that focused on local *affiliate* stations, however, show the full extent to which anxiety about the network's future ruled the corporate enterprise. As the camera scans a graphic map of the country in one set of NBC's spots, hundreds of points of light mark the network's "214 affiliates nationwide, including KJRH-2 Tulsa, Oklahoma." This campaign, not illogically, followed soon after the much publicized "abandonment" of CBS by a number of long-time affiliate stations, which opted for the rising fortunes and hipper programming of the newer fourth network, FOX.

NBC's celebration and symbolic construction of a network "family," can be seen as a kind of preemptive corporate strike. It was, in essence, industry damage control aimed at vigorously reasserting the aura of network authority and quality. Not since the 1950s had the networks had to work this hard to teach viewers and stations about the *benefits* of national network affiliation. These kinds of mediating video texts also function as shorthand corporate reports for anxious affiliate stations that may have considered jumping ship. The top-down model of prestige programming (which includes Hollywood television and network news) has always promised to guarantee the welfare of the affiliate family members, broadcasting in the provinces.

The kind of aggressive, and heavy-handed, damage control evident in these spots came as part of a broader range of marketing "innovations." NBC had also induced consent on the part of program producers to include the NBC logo "inside" scenes from aired programs themselves. This gambit amounted to a very clever sort of blackmail, since program producers for years have complained that license fees from networks were never fair (that is, never paid for the actual cost of program production). These costs were ultimately only covered through later syndication revenues that went directly to the producers' companies. NBC here was subtly coercing its partners to erect televised billboards inside episodes that NBC had not fully paid for. Apparently, the long-term financial prospects of NBC were both significant and enough in jeopardy that program providers realized that their fates were ultimately affected by the "health" of the network that first launched them. By eliminating commercial breaks between shows, and by asking for network IDs within diegetic scenes, the network could promise greater viewer carry-over from show to show. Program providers could certainly appreciate this, if the networks "hammocked" them between strong, proven shows. But the real lesson of these programming moves lies in public consciousness that the fates of program producers, the network, and the affiliate stations were all very much intertwined. Both the network "family-of-stations" ID campaign and the tactic of intra-diegetic branding with logos stand as very public ways that television mediates and negotiates changes, even as it mollifies insecurities in the industry.

In a moment of feigned nonpartisanship, *Today Show* host Katie Couric announced that viewers were about to see the network's "most dramatic make-over ever." Visual evidence that something had changed in the aesthetic ways that the major networks did business came in the segment that followed, which summarized NBC's 1994 campaign to overhaul its corporate logo and identity. The makeover also initiated a proliferation of intermediary video forms, all designed to drive home and publicly "manage" the overhaul in the audience's mind. NBC's marketing machine, that is, simultaneously flooded the programming world with intermediary texts that both legitimized and analyzed their "new" look and "attitude." The once staid and venerable NBC "commissioned" cutting-edge "post-modern" artists (who they described as "the baddest" and "biggest names in design and animation") to draft, engineer, sculpt, and animate the avant-garde look that expressed its newfound attitude. In essence, NBC had finally stopped ignoring its cable competitors, and now earnestly emulated Viacom/MTV's house style—an approach that featured its ever-mutating brand-logo as a persistent part of each day's programming.

The majors (NBC, ABC, and then CBS), thus consented not to the old goal of a stable corporate "brand," but to the importance of something more volatile and lucrative—of "rebranding" as an evolving genre of "content," as a defining index of a network's personality, and as a media event in its own right. The imperative to rebrand was fueled in great measure by the growing sense that there now was simply not enough of an audience to go around; that is, not enough to share (profitably) with all of the competition. Although some critics (Lowry) counter that quality content (rather than a preoccupation with brands) will ultimately bring audiences back to the TV networks, the ratings and profits of those majors continue to decline. Others argue (Lindstrom and Andersen, Marrioti) that new digital technologies will endlessly splinter audiences and that innovative approaches to brand-building must necessarily be a central focus. Interactive-TV and dot-com startups continue to compete not just for viewers lost in the clutter, but for discrete "eye-balls" and "click-throughs" on the Internet as well. With no credible indicator of what will survive as the dominant economic model for profitability in interactive media (advertising, sponsorship, membership, or subscriptions), several other related trends have worked to counter the splintering. Corporate reconglomeration, content multipurposing, and the possibilities of endless syndication have created new corporate aggregates (like Time-Warner-HBO-Turner-CNN, and Viacom-CBS-Paramount-UPN). These groups have essentially become "super-brands." Such entities no longer attempt to standardize viewer-user taste into a mass demographic brand, but rather work to reaggregate potentially endless niche-tastes into branded "tiers" within the same conglomerate. In what some have wrongly termed the "post-network" age of television, innovative rebranding strategies stand at the center of current attempts to profitably "re-network" through mergers. These new networks intend to maintain (and capitalize on) heterogeneous audiences, but only within a single, newly branded conglomerate.

JOHN CALDWELL

Further Reading

Battaglio, Stephen. "ABC Campaign to Get Bad Reaction," *New York Times* (August 18, 1997)

D'Alessandro, David F., *Brand Warfare: 10 Rules for Building the Killer Brand,* New York: McGraw-Hill, 2001

Dupree, Scott, "Building Better Brands," *Adweek* (February 12, 1996)

Gobe, Mark, *Emotional Branding: The New Paradigm for Connecting Brands to People,* New York: Allworth Press, 2001

Lindstrom, Martin, and Tim Frank Andersen, *Brand Building on the Internet,* Copenhagen: Kogan, Page, 1997

Lowry, Brian, "On TV, It's the Show, Not the Network, That Keeps Viewers Watching," *Los Angeles Times* (July 27, 1999)

Marrioti, John, *Smart Things To Know About Brands and Branding,* Milford, Connecticut: Capstone, 1999

Mullen, Megan, "Chapter 6: Framing and Video Bites," *The Revolution Now in Sight: Cable Television Programming in the United States, 1948–1995,* Austin: University of Texas Press, forthcoming

Turow, Joseph, *Breaking Up America: Advertisers and the New Media World,* Chicago: University of Chicago Press, 1997

Bravo

U.S. Cable Network

Among cable's most long-established networks, Bravo's history stands as both typical and exceptional—typical because, like most early networks, it had to adjust its programming plans to meet the expectations of audiences; exceptional because it did this without abandoning its founding mission. Launched in December 1980, Bravo was at the forefront of a wave of arts and culture networks that began largely in response to the utopian visions set for cable a decade earlier, during the medium's "Blue Sky" years. One of these networks—CBS-Cable—failed at the outset. Two others—ABC-ARTS and The Entertainment Channel—redeveloped their respective goals and merged to form A&E (Arts & Entertainment), an advertising-supported, general interest "culture" channel. Bravo, however, managed to maintain its intended emphasis by broadening its definition of arts programming to include forms new to U.S. television. It also retained its commercial-free cachet.

Bravo was founded by Charles Dolan, who had brought cable service to Manhattan in the 1960s and gone on to launch Home Box Office in the 1970s. In 1973, after leaving HBO, Dolan founded Cablevision Corporation. Rainbow Media Group (RMG), a Cablevision programming subdivision, was formed in 1980, with Bravo as its first network. It should be noted that current RMG CEO Joshua Sapan had served as Bravo's president for a number of years. RMG went on to launch American Movie Classics, MuchMusic, Independent Film Channel, Romance Classics (which became WE: Women's Entertainment in 2001), and several regional SportsChannel networks. As of 2002, Bravo was RMG's second largest network (after American Movie Classics), reaching more than 60,000 cable households. RMG (along with its international partners) also operates Bravo channels in Canada and Brazil. Bravo's extensive website, www.bravotv.com, provides complete, annotated program schedules, as well as arts news and links to related merchandise such as VHS and DVD versions of the network's featured programming.

Bravo has been acclaimed within both arts and business circles for staying close to its original programming mission. Its ability to accomplish this, as well as to remain commercial-free, is due in large part to a gradual move from cable's premium tier to its less risky basic tier during the 1980s and early 1990s. Basic cable's per-subscriber (or "sub") fees offer a guaranteed income source for Bravo, since all basic tier subscribers of systems carrying the network must pay for the channel regardless of whether or not they actually watch it.

Bravo has also successfully tapped into public television-style corporate sponsorship. In 1992 Bravo signed an underwriting deal with Texaco that increased its performing arts budget by 20 percent. For Texaco, basic cable sponsorship held a similar appeal to PBS sponsorship: conveying an image of populist support for the arts. The first Texaco Showcase presentation, *Romeos and Juliets,* billed as a "modern interpretation of the Prokofiev ballet score," was aired less than a month after the sponsorship deal was signed. Other corporate underwriters, including Kodak and Mercedes-Benz, were to follow.

Initially committed to a schedule of costly live arts performances (notably theater, opera, ballet, classical music, and jazz), Bravo began early on to add foreign and independent films to its schedule, reaching a balance of 50 percent arts programming and 50 percent film by the mid-1990s. It began to develop shorter in-house studio programs, including the highly popular *Inside the Actors Studio,* as well as *Champlin on Film* and *Bravo Profiles* to complement its longer film and arts offerings. Clearly this was a successful programming mix—and it no doubt brought many viewers to cable who otherwise would have seen little reason to subscribe. Bravo's programmers and marketers were aware that few parts of the United States outside of larger metropolitan areas offer regular access to arts events or even films other than mainstream Hollywood fare.

Courtesy of the Everett Collection

Indeed, so popular was this programming mix that in 1994, RMG launched a Bravo spin-off network, the Independent Film Channel (IFC), which is offered on both the expanded basic and premium tiers, as well as direct satellite. IFC focuses exclusively on films (including short films rarely seen on television) and film-related programs (such as *At the Angelika* and *Dinner for Five,* which feature interviews, chat, and previews). IFC's schedule and productions are guided by a Filmmakers Advisory Board made up of notable film industry figures Martin Scorsese, Robert Altman, Tim Robbins, Joel and Ethan Coen, Martha Coolidge, Jim Jarmusch, Spike Lee, Ed Saxon, Steven Soderbergh, and Jodie Foster.

In the tradition of more established premium cable networks such as HBO and Showtime, IFC began to invest in film production almost immediately so as to guarantee first television rights to new productions. IFC Entertainment has funded numerous independent theatrical films. The first, *Gray's Anatomy,* was released in theaters in 1997, and was shown on the television network a year later. More recent notable IFC productions have included Kimberly Peirce's Oscar-winning *Boys Don't Cry* and Karyn Kusama's *Girlfight.* Another division of IFC Entertainment, Next Wave Films, was established to provide finishing funds and other support to emerging filmmakers from the United States and abroad working on low-budget, feature-length films. IFC Entertainment also produces live coverage of film festivals and other special events.

As IFC continues to build its reputation as a home for foreign and independent films, Bravo has expanded farther into genres traditionally described as "quality television." Over the years, Bravo has featured critically acclaimed off-network dramas such as *Max Headroom, Twin Peaks, thirtysomething, Hill Street Blues, St. Elsewhere,* and *Moonlighting.* In summer 2002, Bravo debuted the first-run series, *Breaking News,* an ensemble drama about a 24-hour news network. Another addition to Bravo's schedule is the popular British antique appraisal show, *Antiques Roadshow.*

Bravo also has provided a home for programming considered too risky or eclectic for more mainstream channels. For example, in June 1997, it aired productions of iconoclastic British playwright Dennis Potter's last two plays, *Karaoke* and *Cold Lazarus.* In summer 1999, it began airing episodes of controversial filmmaker and telejournalist Michael Moore's series, *The Awful Truth.* And in summer 2003, Bravo drew a great amount of attention from the broad television audience by introducing the comical and somewhat controversial program, *Queer Eye for the Straight Guy. Queer Eye* features the antics of a team of gay men helping a hapless straight man get his life together (and hopefully win a woman's affections) through instruction in fashion, hairstyle, home decorating, and gourmet cooking.

Bravo also has been involved in public service initiatives. Its annual program, *Unfinished Stories,* has been a fundraiser for AIDS caregiving organizations. Bravo in the Classroom provides a combination of arts programming and resource materials for secondary schools. It was one of the founding members of Cable in the Classroom, educational programming provided free of charge to schools by local cable companies. Bravo's On with the Show (theater), Bravo for Books (reading), and Public Art Works (visual art) campaigns have offered support to various youth organizations. Bravo has supported local arts groups through its ArtsBreak, Community Cinema, and Arts Partnership programs, which give airtime to local arts and media productions.

In November 2002, in a $1.2 billion transaction, NBC acquired Bravo from Cablevision Corp.—augmenting cable holdings that already included CNBC and MSNBC (IFC was not part of this transaction and remained part of Rainbow Media Holdings, a division of Cablevision). The merger facilitated the showing of shortened episodes of *Queer Eye for the Straight Guy* during NBC prime time.

Bravo represents an extraordinary success story dating back to the early days of satellite cable. It quickly identified its programming goals and has strived resourcefully to adhere to those goals. While it can be said the contemporary version of this cable network represents a more broadly focused programming mix than the one initially envisioned, it must also be said that a large portion of this programming still is unlikely to be found elsewhere on U.S. television. Bravo, along with its sister channel, IFC, appears poised to hold its ground in the competitive multichannel cable/satellite television environment of the early 21st century.

MEGAN MULLEN

Further Reading

Barchak, Leonard J., "Bravo," in *The Cable Networks Handbook,* edited by Robert G. Picard, Riverside, California: Carpelan, 1993

Flinn, John, "Almost Invisible Support," *Cablevision* (February 10, 1992)

McConville, Jim, "Bravo Broadens Its Reach," *Broadcasting & Cable* (September 16, 1996)

Waterman, David, "The Failure of Cultural Programming on Cable TV: An Economic Interpretation," *Journal of Communication* (Summer 1986)

Bravo! Canada

Canadian Cable Network

Bravo! Canada debuted in 1995 along with seven other services as part of the third wave of specialty channels to emerge in the country. Like its predecessor U.S. namesake, Bravo! Canada ranges over a broad spectrum of performing arts content. When it granted a license to Bravo! Canada in 1994, the federal regulator, the Canadian Radio-television and Telecommunications Commission expected that the channel would expose audiences in smaller Canadian communities to the performing arts while stimulating the independent production industry across the country. It is widely available to cable subscribers and has found a stable and profitable niche within the expanding constellation of specialty and pay services in Canada. While Bravo!'s audience share is surpassed by many other specialty channels, it has exploited the advantage that comes from having no direct domestic competitors for its unique brand of programming.

Bravo! is fully owned by CHUM Limited of Toronto. CHUM's media properties, once confined to a handful of radio holdings until the early 1970s, began to expand when it acquired Toronto's CityTV. The company has grown to encompass 28 radio stations, 8 local television stations, and an additional 16 specialty channels. Although it shares a name and programming orientation with the American channel, there are no ownership ties between the two services. Some content is imported from the American channel. However, a condition of Bravo!'s original license, granted in 1994, stipulates that no more than 25 percent of its programming can originate with its U.S. counterpart. Bravo! is also required to broadcast at least 60 percent Canadian content during the broadcast year, with a minimum threshold of 50 percent domestically produced programming airing in prime time.

As with so many other enterprises under the CHUM banner, the genesis of Bravo! is generally traced to the fertile mind of the founding visionary behind CityTV, Moses Znaimer. Znaimer has been the guiding light behind a number of successful (and not infrequently controversial) innovations in Canadian and international broadcasting. Although financial struggles forced him to sell his shares in CityTV to CHUM, he continued to preside over the fortunes of the media company that coalesced and expanded around the station. One of his pet projects in the early 1990s was Bravo!, and he is billed as the executive producer of a number of the channel's offerings.

CHUM's television headquarters, located in a trendy neighborhood of Toronto, feature open "environments" where personalities and crews working for various channels are encouraged to roam about unhindered by traditional studio constraints, and even take to the streets. To make room for Bravo!, the building was renovated to include a small but acoustically sophisticated studio where, in this particular environment, artists' performances and reflections are recorded for various shows.

Bravo! bills itself as "Canada's 24-hour NewStyleArtsChannel" and, according to press releases issued by CHUM, is "dedicated to entertaining, stimulating and enlightening viewers who have a taste for a more complex television." The lineup has included Canadian-produced programs such as "Live at the Rehearsal Hall" (performance and interviews), "Culture Warriors" (interview), "Bravo!News," "Bravo! Bulletin Board," and "Arts and Minds," a show dedicated to an examination of the creative process. Over the years (and especially at the outset) the independent Toronto production company Sleeping Giant has been responsible for developing programs for Bravo! Canada. The weekly schedule is organized around the themes of dance, music, drama, literature, cinema, great performances, and the visual arts.

One unique facet of the channel's license is the requirement that Bravo! must invest in Canadian content through a foundation now known as Bravo!FACT (originally the Foundation to Assist Canadian Talent in the Arts, or ArtsFACT). The idea had its origins in a similar initiative, called VideoFACT, that helped support the making of Canadian music videos for CHUM's MuchMusic channel. Film and video makers are eligible to apply to Bravo!FACT for a maximum of $25,000 (Canadian) to defray up to half of the costs of a project. Bravo! also provides other assistance to successful grant applicants. The mandate is to "stimulate public interest in Canadian excellence in the arts, encourage the creation of new ways of presenting the arts on television, increase public recognition of Canadian artists and their works, and provide professional opportunities for film and video-makers."

As of 2002, the foundation had provided some $4.5 million to more than 400 shorts aired on Bravo! Projects have also been screened, and earned awards, at film festivals and special events around the world. Although the investments seem impressive, and certainly make up one of the largest pools of funding for short works on serious topics in Canada, Bravo!'s support for independent film- and videomakers was the subject of some controversy when the channel's license was renewed in 2000. According to the Canadian Radio-television and Telecommunications Commission, Bravo! had fallen behind in its payments to the foundation. For this reason the Commissions' renewal was conditional upon Bravo! adding to the fund and meeting its future commitments (an annual expenditure of the greater part of $600,000, or five percent of the previous fiscal year's gross revenues).

It is a rare feat for a Canadian specialty channel to claim a place among the top ten shows. Bravo! was able to accomplish this thanks to the popularity of its late-night American import *Sex and the City.* The program's devotees have boosted Bravo!'s subscriptions. According to Matthew Fraser of the *National Post,* the success of *Sex and the City* may be part of a wider phenomenon that has seen Canadian viewers seek out high-quality drama on specialty channels such as Bravo! while deserting the poorer nightly fare offered up by conventional networks in the United States and simulcast in Canada. Fraser speculates that this trend, if it continues, may result in private Canadian networks diversifying their sources of content and even moving toward more in-house production after relying so heavily on American shows to fill prime-time slots. It would be ironic if an American show on a specialty channel accelerated the restructuring of Canada's television industry, but the history of the country's broadcasting system is full of contradictions and complications.

ROBERT EVERETT

See also **Citytv; MuchMusic; *Sex and the City;* Znaimer, Moses**

Further Reading

Canada, Canadian Radio-television and Telecommunications Commission, Decision CRTC 94–281 [Bravo!], Ottawa, June 6, 1994

Canada, Canadian Radio-television and Telecommunications Commission, Decision CRTC 2001–231 [Bravo!], Ottawa, April 25, 2001

Fraser, Matthew, "Southern Exposure May Sting Networks, *National Post* (May 20, 2002)

Lacey, Liam, "Moses Disposes," *Globe and Mail* (March 28, 1995)

Morrison, Ian, "Analysis of Canadian Association of Broadcasters' Submissions to Commons Heritage Committee," Friends of Canadian Broadcasting (March 18, 2002)

Brazil

Brazil has one of the world's largest and most productive commercial television systems. Its biggest television network, TV Globo, is the fourth largest commercial network in the world. Brazil is also one of the largest television exporters within Latin America and around the world, particularly of *telenovelas,* the characteristic Latin American prime-time serials that have become popular in many countries.

Though Brazilian television began in 1950, it remained urban and elitist. Sets were expensive, programs were broadcast live, and transmitters covered only major centers. As in many other settings, that era of early television produced quite a bit of classic drama, and during this period local traditions in variety, news, drama, and *telenovelas* were established. The advent of videotape around 1960 opened Brazil to imported programs. Again, typical of countries then developing their television systems, the imports dominated programming for much of the decade, but their presence also stimulated some efforts at creating local networks. Two major early networks, TV Tupi and TV Excelsior, operated at that time.

Television became a truly mass medium in Brazil earlier than in most developing countries. The military governments that took power in 1964 saw televisual communication as a potential tool for creating a stronger national identity, creating a broader consumer economy, and controlling political information. The military pushed television deeper into the population by subsidizing credit for set sales, building national microwave and satellite distribution systems, and promoting the growth of one network they chose as a privileged partner. TV Globo, which also started in 1964, created the first true national network by the late 1960s. Censorship of news was extensive under the military governments between 1966 and 1978, but they also encouraged national television program production. In the early 1970s, several government ministers pushed the commercial networks hard to develop more Brazilian programming and reduce reliance on imported programs, particularly those that contained violence.

The 1960s represented a formative period for genre development. Brazilian *telenovelas* had largely been patterned after those in other Latin American countries, even using imported scripts, but during these years they were developed into a considerably more sophisticated genre by TV Excelsior in São Paulo and TV Globo in Rio de Janeiro. A key turning point was the 1968 *telenovela, Beto Rockefeller,* a well-produced story reflecting a singular Brazilian personality, the Rio good-lifer or *boa vida.* By the 1970s, *telenovelas* were the most popular programs and dominated prime time on the major networks, TV Globo and TV Tupi. TV Globo, in particular, began to attract major writers and actors from both film and theater to also work in *telenovelas.* The Brazilian *telenovelas* became good enough, as commercial television entertainment, to be exported throughout Latin America and into Europe, Asia, and Africa.

Another major genre of the 1960s was the *show de auditório,* a live variety show mixing games, quizzes, amateur and professional entertainers, comedy, and discussion. The *shows de auditório* have been extremely popular with the lower-middle and lower classes, and, according to analyses such as Sérgio Miceli's 1972 *A Noite da Madrinha* (*Evening with the Godmother*), played an extremely important role in drawing them into television viewing.

The years 1968 to 1985 constitute Brazilian television's second phase. In this period TV Globo dominated both the audience and the development of television programming. It tended to have a 60 to 80 percent share of the viewers in the major cities at any given time. TV Globo was accused during this period of representing the view of the government, of being its mouthpiece. Other broadcast television networks found themselves pursuing smaller, more specific audience segments largely defined by social class. SBS (Sílvio Santos) targeted a lower-middle-class, working-class, and poor audience, mostly with variety and game shows. The strategy gained it a consistent second place in ratings in most of the 1980s and 1990s. TV Manchete targeted a more elite audience initially, with news, high budget *telenovelas,* and imported programs, but found the segment too small to gain adequate advertiser support. TV Bandeirantes tended to emphasize news, public affairs, and sports. All three ultimately wished to pursue a general audience with general appeal programming, such as *telenovelas,* but generally discovered that such efforts still did not gain an audience sufficient to pay for the increased programming costs.

Brazilian television since 1985 has gone through a third phase, marked by its role in the transition to a new civilian republic. In 1984 TV Globo initially supported the military government against a campaign for direct election of a civilian government, while other media, including other television networks, many radio stations, and most of the major newspapers supported the change. Perceiving that it might literally lose its audience to the competition, Globo switched sides and supported transition to a civilian regime, which was indirectly elected in a compromise situation. The new political circumstances immediately reduced political censorship and pressure on broadcasters.

The fourth phase of Brazilian television has been its internationalization. The importation of television programs into Brazil declined from the 1970s through the 1980s, as Brazilian networks produced more of their own material. TV Globo often filled 12–14 hours a day with indigenous productions. TV Globo and other networks also began to export programs, particularly *telenovelas,* and Brazilian exports of programming to the rest of the world and soon became economically and culturally significant. Brazilian exports reached over 100 countries, and the programs have often proved great international successes. This is particularly the case with historical *telenovelas* such as *A Escrava Isaura* (*Isaura the Slave*), about the abolition of slavery in Brazil, a hit in countries as diverse as Poland, China, Cuba, and most of Latin America.

The fifth phase of Brazilian television is marked by the appearance of some new video distribution systems. The first new technology to diffuse widely in Brazil was the home videocassette recorder (VCR), which largely gave the middle and upper classes greater access to imported feature films. The new technology with the most effect on Brazilian electronic media, however, is the satellite distribution of television to small repeaters throughout the country. In the 1980s, thousands of small towns in rural Brazil purchased satellite dishes and low-power repeaters to bring in Brazilian television networks, effectively extending television to 99 percent of the population. Studies show that over 90 percent of the population probably has television sets. New video technologies entered the Brazilian television market in the 1990s, offering focused or segmented programming through additional advertising-supported UHF (ultra high frequency) channels or pay-TV systems such as subscription television (STV), cable TV systems, multichannel multipoint distribution systems (MMDS), and direct satellite broadcasting (DBS).

In this period three main approaches have so far been used to support programming and distribution: advertising-supported UHF, exemplified by the Brazilian adaptation of MTV, which features about 10–20 percent Brazilian music; over-the-air pay-TV systems, which usually rely on imported channels like CNN, ESPN, and HBO; and DBS (direct broadcast satellite) systems, which require subscription. So far only MTV has gained even a small share of the audience. Studies to date indicate that most satellite dishes and many cable connections are being used to secure better reception of Brazilian channels.

Even though the new technologies seem to threaten to bring in a new wave of largely U.S. programming, then, the audience studies so far do not indicate a strong audience response to them, except perhaps among a globalized elite and upper middle class. The dominant characteristic of Brazilian television still seems to be that of a strong national system with a distinct set of genres very popular with its own audience and in export.

Joseph Straubhaar

See also **Telenovela**

Further Reading

Fachel Leal O., "Popular Taste and Erudite Repertoire: The Place and Space of Television in Brazil," *Cultural Studies* (1990)

Kottak, C.P., *Prime Time Society—An Anthropological Analysis of Television and Culture,* Belmont, California: Wadsworth, 1990

Lima, V.A., "Television and the Brazilian Elections of 1989," in *Television, Politics and the Transition to Democracy in Latin America,* edited by Thomas Skidmore, Washington, D.C.: Woodrow Wilson Center/Smithsonian Institution Press, 1993

Lins da Silva, C.E., "Transnational Communication and Brazilian Culture," in *Communication and Latin American Society—Trends in Critical Research, 1960–1985,* edited by R. Atwood and E.G. McAnany, Madison: University of Wisconsin Press, 1986

Mattelart, M., and A. Mattelart, *The Carnival of Images: Brazilian Television Fiction,* New York: Bergin and Garvey, 1990

Mattos, S., "Advertising and Government Influences on Brazilian Television," *Communication Research* (1984)

McAnany, E.G., "The Logic of Cultural Industries in Latin America: The Television Industry in Brazil," in *Critical Communications Review,* edited by V. Mosco and J. Wasco, Norwood, New Jersey: Ablex, 1984

Oliveira, O.S., "Brazilian Soaps Outshine Hollywood: Is Cultural Imperialism Fading Out?" in *Beyond National Sovereignty: International Communication in the 1990s,* edited by Kaarle Nordenstreng and Herbert Schiller, Norwood, New Jersey: Ablex, 1993

Sarti, I., "Communication and Cultural Dependency: A Misconception," in *Communication and Social Structure,* edited by V. Mosco and J. Wasco, New York: Praeger, 1981

Straubhaar, J., "The Development of the Telenovela as the Paramount Form of Popular Culture in Brazil," *Studies in Latin American Popular Culture* (1982)

Straubhaar, J., "The Decline of American Influence on Brazilian Television," *Communication Research* (1984)

Straubhaar, J., "The Reflection of the Brazilian Political Opening in the Telenovela, 1974–1985," *Studies in Latin American Popular Culture* (1988)

Straubhaar, J., "Beyond Media Imperialism: Asymmetrical Interdependence and Cultural Proximity," *Critical Studies in Mass Communication* (1991)

Vink, N., *The Telenovela and Emancipation—A Study on TV and Social Change in Brazil,* Amsterdam: Royal Tropical Institute, 1988

Brideshead Revisited

British Miniseries

Brideshead Revisited was made by Granada television, scripted by John Mortimer, and originally shown on ITV in October 1981. The 11-episode adaptation of Evelyn Waugh's novel of the same name helped set the tone of a number of subsequent screen presentations of heritage England, such as *Chariots of Fire* (1981), *The Jewel in the Crown* (1982), *A Passage to India* (1984), and *A Room with a View* (1986). These "white flannel" dramas, both on television and on the big screen, represented a yearning for an England that was no more, or never was. *Brideshead Revisited* opens in England on the eve of the World War II. Charles Ryder (played by Jeremy Irons), the main character and narrator, is presented as a rather incompetent officer in the British Army. He stumbles upon an English country house, which he had visited more than 20 years before. Upon seeing the house, Charles begins to tell the story of his years at Oxford, his meeting with Sebastian Flyte (Anthony Andrews), and his love for Julia (Diana Quick). This retrospective narrative is nostalgic in two senses. It is concerned with Charles's nostalgia for his affairs in the interwar period, but it is also concerned with a nostalgia for a time before World War I—a longing for a lost way of life, for an Edwardian England.

The first five episodes focus on Charles's relationship with Sebastian, dealing candidly with homosexual passion. Parts six through eight portray Charles's "dead years," his ties to the Flyte family apparently severed. His growing love for Julia returns him to Brideshead. The final three parts follow the development and decline of this relationship and the death of Lord Marchmain.

The locations are centrally important in the drama. In the early episodes of the serial, Charles recounts his years at university in Oxford. Establishing shots of "dreaming spires" and college courtyards paint a picture of opulent, languid, summer days. Likewise, Brideshead Castle, the home of Sebastian and Julia, presents in stark symbolic form the once commanding heights of a now declining aristocracy. The stately home was actually Castle Howard in Yorkshire, the home of the then BBC chair, George Howard. These were deliberate signs of "quality." *Brideshead Revisited* visually displayed all the hallmarks of "quality

Brideshead Revisited, Anthony Andrews, Laurence Olivier, Jeremy Irons, 1982.
Courtesy of the Everett Collection

television." The cost of the serial, which lasted over 12 hours in total, was officially given by Granada television at £4.5 million, but other estimates put the figure closer to £11 million. Granada was committed to capturing an accurate atmosphere of Waugh's original novel, and the high production values signaled a desire for authenticity. For example, filming on board the ocean liner the *Queen Elizabeth II* cost £50,000 per eight minutes of film. Other rich backdrops were provided by expensive location filming in Venice, Malta, and the island of Gozo. The large budget was justified by artful creation: "every frame a Rembrandt," as Mike Scott put it. Viewers, taken with the obvious prestigious connotations of the production, frequently mistook the serial as originating from the British Broadcasting Corporation.

The visual lushness of the serial is matched by the excessive decadence of Sebastian and his various friends. Waugh's misogyny is revealed, and we are delivered a gathering of aristocratic men accustomed to each other's company rather than to women. The myth of Edwardian England is fashioned through their clothes and manners. Sebastian is styled in cricket whites, Charles in tweed. The foppishness of their characters is matched by the flow of their loose-fitting wardrobes. All together, we are presented with a 1920s version of the Edwardian dandy—"tastefully" homoerotic. Sebastian's teddy bear, Aloysius, which Sebastian clutches closely in the early episodes, became a popular icon in the early 1980s of a new breed of white-flannelled men. As the drama unfolds, Charles is caught within a more engulfing family romance. As Charles comes to know the family and comes to love Julia, Sebastian grows more melancholy and the idyllic images of Oxford and Brideshead Castle give way to a more disturbing ambience of loss and mourning.

The elegance and nostalgia, the longing for a bygone "Englishness" of empire and perceived stability led to *Brideshead* being widely attacked in cultural criticism. It was seen as a "Thatcherite text," part of a resurgence of regressive nationalism. It was criticized for its slow, reverential pace, for wallowing in inherited wealth, for being a glorified "soap." Nevertheless, the production is seen internationally as an example of what the British do best, a large-scale "quality" production of television drama.

DAVID OSWELL AND GUY JOWETT

See also **Adaptations; British Programming; Miniseries**

Cast

Charles Ryder	Jeremy Irons
Lady Julia Flyte	Diana Quick
Sebastian Flyte	Anthony Andrews
Edward Ryder	John Gielgud
Anthony Blanche	Nikolas Grace
Nancy Hawkins	Mona Washbourne
Boy Mulcaster	Jeremy Sinden
Jasper	Stephen Moore
Sergeant Block	Kenneth Graham
Barber	John Welsh
Commanding Officer	John Nettleton
Lord Marchmain	Laurence Olivier
Cara	Stephane Audran
Lady Marchmain	Claire Bloom
Brideshead	Simon Jones
Cordelia	Phoebe Nicholls
Samgrass	John Grillo
Wilcox	Roger Milner
Hayter	Michael Bilton
Rex Mottram	Charles Keating
Nurse	Mary McLeod
Hooper	Richard Hope
Dr. Grant	Michael Gough

Producers

Michael Lindsay-Hogg, Derek Granger

Programming History

11 episodes
Granada Television
October 12–December 22, 1981

Further Reading

Brunsdon, Charlotte, "Problems with Quality," *Screen* (Spring 1990)

Wollen, Tana, "Over Our Shoulders: Nostalgic Screen Fictions for the 1980s," in *Enterprise and Heritage: Crosscurrents of National Culture,* edited by John Corner and Sylvia Harvey, London: Routledge, 1991

Briggs, Asa (1921–)

British Historian

Asa Briggs is the most important broadcasting historian in Britain. By writing about broadcasting as part of modern British social history, he has become a powerful advocate for the continuation of the British Broadcasting Corporation (BBC).

A Victorian historian of considerable note, Asa Briggs began his great work, *The History of Broadcasting in the United Kingdom,* in the 1960s. The first volume, entitled *The Birth of Broadcasting,* was published in 1961 and contained a marvelously evocative description of the birth of the BBC, and its founder John Reith, through 1927. The second volume, *The Golden Age of Wireless,* published in 1965, covered the period from 1927 to 1939 and received very favorable reviews. Volume three, *The War of Words,* covered the war years, 1939 to 1945. The fourth volume, entitled *Sound and Vision,* covered the period from 1945 to 1955, and the final volume, *Competition,* from the end of the BBC monopoly in 1955 to the mid-1970s.

Because independent television was not created in Britain until 1955, Briggs is primarily a historian of the BBC. However, in 1985 Briggs was commissioned by the independent British companies to write with Joanna Spicer an account of the way the Independent Broadcasting Authority organized the awarding of franchises in 1980. In this book, *The Franchise Affair,* Briggs's normal Olympian detachment from the poli-

Asa Briggs.
Photo courtesy of Asa Briggs

tics of broadcasting was dropped in a fascinating and often critical account of the development of independent TV. Cynics pointed out that Briggs had been a director of Southern Television, one of only two companies whose franchise was arbitrarily removed in 1980. *The Franchise Affair* was published by Hutchinson, a wholly owned subsidiary of London Weekend Television, which was re-awarded its franchise.

Made Baron Briggs of Lewes in 1976, Briggs is often seen as an establishment figure keen on preserving the status of the BBC. However, readers of his 1985 compilation volume, *The BBC: The First 50 Years,* were delighted to find that Briggs was not uncritical of the organization that sponsored his mammoth *History of Broadcasting in the United Kingdom* and paid for his offices in London.

Perhaps Briggs's greatest contribution to British broadcasting may not be his history books; it could be his role from 1978 to 1994 as chancellor of the Open University, a nonresidential institution that provides primary contacts with its students through radio and television broadcasts. The Open University has grown to become a major educational institution, awarding degrees for low fees, while maintaining high intellectual standards. Briggs has spent some of his prodigious energies fostering the growth of similar Open Universities of the Air in countries of the British Commonwealth.

As a member of the Campaign for Quality Television, Briggs has been a great defender of the BBC's charter, which came up for renewal in 1996. Thanks to the many defenders of the BBC's position in British society, not least to the Campaign for Quality Television, the BBC had its charter renewed for a further 15 years. Briggs was well satisfied with the result. Thanks to his influence, perhaps in the future some historian will be able to write a history of the first hundred years of the BBC. Briggs's contribution to broadcasting is that of historian and advocate. He has skillfully narrated the story of the most important of all British media enterprises.

ANDREW QUICKE

Asa Briggs. Born in Keighley, Yorkshire, England, May 7, 1921. Attended Keighley Grammar School; Sidney Sussex College, Cambridge, 1941; University of London, first-class B.S. in Economics, 1941. Married: Susan Anne Banwell, 1955; children: Katharine, Daniel, Judith, and Matthew. Served in Intelligence Corps, 1942–45. Fellow, Worcester College, Oxford, 1945–55; professor of history, Leeds University, 1955–61; professor of history, later vice chancellor, Sussex University, 1961–66; provost, Worcester College, Oxford, 1976–91; chancellor, Open University, Milton Keynes, 1979–94. Made Baron Briggs of Lewes, East Sussex, 1976. President: Social History Society, from 1976; Victorian Society, from 1983; Ephemera Society, from 1984; British Association for Local History, 1984–86; Association of Research Associations, 1986–88. Chair: Standing Conference for Study of Local History, 1969–76; European Institute of Education and Social Policy, Paris, 1975–90; Commonwealth of Learning, Vancouver, 1988–93; Advisory Board for Redundant Churches, 1983–89. Governor: British Film Institute, 1970–77. Trustee: Glyndebourne Arts Trust, 1966–91; International Broadcasting Institute, 1968–87; Heritage Education Group, 1976–86; Civic Trust, 1976–86. Member: American Academy of Arts and Sciences, 1970. Fellow: Sidney Sussex College, Cambridge, 1968; Worcester College, Oxford, 1969; Saint Catherine's College, Cambridge, 1977; British Academy, 1980. Numerous honorary degrees. Recipient: Marconi Medal for Communication History, 1975; Médaille de Vermeil de la Formation, Fondation de l'Académie d'Architecture, 1979; Royal College of Anaesthetists Snow Medal, 1991.

Publications (selected)

The History of Broadcasting in the United Kingdom, 5 volumes, 1961–95
Governing the BBC, 1979
The BBC: The First Fifty Years (with Joanna Spicer), 1985
The Franchise Affair: Creating Fortunes and Failures in Independent Television, 1986

Brinkley, David (1920–2003)

U.S. Broadcast Journalist

David Brinkley and Chet Huntley debuted NBC's *The Huntley-Brinkley Report* in October 1956. A few months earlier, NBC producer Reuven Frank had put them together as a team to anchor the network's television coverage of the Democratic and Republican presidential nominating conventions. Network news would never be the same. Nor would Sunday mornings a quarter of a century later, when Brinkley introduced on ABC, *This Week with David Brinkley,* which ran from 1981 until shortly before Brinkley's retirement from television in 1997 (the program continues, but without Brinkley as moderator and without his name in the title). From the mid-1950s on, Brinkley not only reported the news, he also helped to shape the industry of television news. His renowned wit, his singular delivery, and his superb TV news writing style made him an institution in broadcast journalism.

However, Brinkley was no star when he first went to NBC Radio in 1943. His talent for strong and clear writing became evident as he continually struggled to write for announcers who read only the words and seemed to miss the meaning. He also began to gain experience as a newscaster when he did ten-minute newscasts for the network. He was not yet famous when he became the Washington, D.C., reporter for John Cameron Swayze's *Camel News Caravan,* NBC's early TV news effort. However, as the 1956 political conventions came into focus for the U.S. TV audience, viewers came to see, hear, and to know Brinkley as a new breed of TV journalist.

Brinkley was one of the first journalists to be absolutely comfortable with this new medium of TV. As his boss at NBC, Reuven Frank, often said, Brinkley had wit, style, intelligence, and perhaps most importantly, a lean writing style filled with powerful declarative sentences that is very effective in TV news. Brinkley was aware that TV was made up of pictures and corresponding sounds. He understood that the reporter has to stop talking and let the news footage tell the story. "Brinkley writes silence better than anyone else I know," said Frank, and when this natural TV journalist was teamed with the California reporter Huntley, it proved to be a winning formula.

TV news before Huntley and Brinkley was a combination of dull film reports, similar to movie newsreels of the 1940s, and a radio reporting style similar to that of the World War II era. Huntley and Brinkley took TV news into a new age of electronic journalism. According to one of their main competitors, Don Hewitt of CBS, who produced Walter Cronkite and, later, *60 Minutes,* "They came at us like an express train." When Huntley spoke, it was clear the story was a global story. When Brinkley spoke, it was clear it was a story about Washington. They began with a 15-minute newscast, and in 1963 the program increased to 30 minutes per night. Audiences now take for granted the sight of different journalists in different cities talking to each other on TV, but it was *The Huntley-Brinkley Report* that began such techniques. The switching back and forth between Huntley in New York and Brinkley in Washington created the now famous final exchange from every newscast: "Good night, David"... "Good night, Chet." The order of the exchange alternated night by night—until their last newscast together in 1970, when Huntley's "Good night, David" brought the response, "Good-bye, Chet."

In that year, Huntley retired to a Montana ranch, and Brinkley became increasingly restless at NBC. His important role in *The Huntley-Brinkley Report* could not be matched, and he did not continue producing the excellent documentaries on *David Brinkley's Journal.* He became known as the grumpy older newsman in the NBC family. He did a series of programs for NBC, including *NBC Nightly News* and *NBC Magazine with David Brinkley.* However, he hated to go to New York to do the news, since he wanted Washington to be his news beat. Finally, in 1981, Roone Arledge hired Brinkley for ABC. All those years working on *The Huntley-Brinkley Report* had made Brinkley into the absolute Washington insider. When ABC gave him the Sunday program *This Week with David Brinkley,* he and his guests could talk among themselves and with all the other Washington insiders about the week's news event.

Brinkley asked his friend George Will to join him

on *This Week with David Brinkley.* ABC reporter Sam Donaldson joined as the resident "liberal" to confront Will's avowed "conservative" stance. Besides the guests who were interviewed every week, other reporters such as National Public Radio's Cokie Roberts joined Brinkley, Will, and Donaldson. (Roberts was later to become a permanent fixture on ABC's Sunday morning news program, sharing the moderating duties with Donaldson for a period after Brinkley's retirement.) Some critics deemed the program to be very opinionated; it could be cynically referred to as ABC's op-ed page. However, there had traditionally been very little interpretation of news on U.S. TV, and *This Week with David Brinkley* seemed to fill the void at least partially. Because of Brinkley's strong Washington ties, the show at times appeared to consist of one group of Washingtonians talking to another. Criticisms aside, with ABC's *This Week with David Brinkley,* Brinkley's enormous talents and his many decades of TV news experience were given free reign.

Following his retirement, some criticism was leveled at Brinkley for appearing in commercials for Archer-Daniels-Midland, the giant agribusiness company. The primary point of the criticism was the fact that ADM was a key sponsor for *This Week.* But Brinkley's presence was also seen by some as blurring the boundaries between journalistic responsibility and commercialization of news and information.

Brinkley received many awards, most notably the Presidential Medal of Freedom from President George H.W. Bush. Also among Brinkley's awards were ten Emmys and four Peabodys, including one in 1992 for reporting on the fiftieth anniversary of the Japanese attack on Pearl Harbor. When asked what he thought his legacy to TV news would be, however, Brinkley told *Broadcasting* magazine, "Every news program on the air looks essentially as we started it [with *The Huntley-Brinkley Report*]. We more or less set the form for broadcasting news on television which is still used. No one has been able to think of a better way to do it." David Brinkley passed away on June 11, 2003.

CLAYLAND H. WAITE

See also **Anchor; Huntley, Chet; News (Network)**

David Brinkley.
Courtesy of the Everett Collection

David Brinkley. Born in Wilmington, North Carolina, July 10, 1920. Educated at New Hanover High School, Wilmington; special student in English, University of North Carolina, Chapel Hill, 1939–40; special student in English, Emory and Vanderbilt universities, 1941–43. Married: 1) Ann Fischer, 1946 (divorced); children: Alan, Joel, and John; 2) Susan Melanie Benfer, 1972; child: Alexis. Served in U.S. Army, 1941–43. Reporter at Wilmington, North Carolina, *Star-News,* 1938–41; reporter, bureau manager, United Press news service (later United Press International), various southern cities, 1941–43; radio news writer and nonbroadcast reporter, NBC, Washington, D.C., 1943; NBC-TV, from 1946; Washington correspondent, NBC, 1951–81; co-anchor, with Chet Huntley, *The Huntley-Brinkley Report,* 1956–70; correspondent, commentator, *NBC Nightly News,* 1971–76; co-anchor, *NBC Nightly News,* 1976–79; anchor, ABC's *This Week with David Brinkley,* 1981–97. Member: Cosmos Club, Washington; National Press Club, Washington; trustee, Colonial Williamsburg. Recipient: DuPont Award, 1958; Golden Key Award, 1964; four Peabody Awards; ten

Emmy Awards; Scholastic Bell Award; Presidential Medal of Freedom, 1992. Died from complications due to a fall, June 11, 2003.

Television Series

1951–56	*Camel News Caravan* (correspondent)
1956–70	*The Huntley-Brinkley Report*
1961–63	*David Brinkley's Journal*
1971–76	*NBC Nightly News* (commentator only)
1976–79	*NBC Nightly News* (co-anchor)
1980–81	*NBC Magazine with David Brinkley*
1981–97	*This Week with David Brinkley*
1981–97	*ABC's World News Tonight* (commentator)

Publications

David Brinkley: A Memoir, 1995
David Brinkley's Homilies, 1996
Everyone Is Entitled to My Opinions, 1997
Washington Goes to War, 1999

Further Reading

Carter, Bill, "Don't Call It Gravitas; David Brinkley Was a Brand Unto Himself," *New York Times* (June 15, 2003)
Cook, P., D. Gomery, and L. Lichty, editors, *The Future of News: Television-Newspapers-Wire Services-Newsmagazines,* Washington, D.C.: Woodrow Wilson Center Press, 1992
Frank, Reuven, *Out of Thin Air: The Brief Wonderful Life of Network News,* New York: Simon and Schuster, 1991
Gunther, M., *The House That Roone Built: The Inside Story of ABC News,* Boston: Little, Brown, 1994

British Academy of Film and Television Arts

The British Academy of Film and Television Arts (BAFTA) developed from the British Film Academy (founded 1947) and the Guild of Television Producers and Directors (founded 1953). The two organizations amalgamated as the Society of Film and Television Arts in 1958; the Society assumed its present identity as BAFTA in 1976. BAFTA has over 5,000 members and is located in London, with branches in Scotland, North England, Wales, Los Angeles, and New York. Any person working within the film and television industries in Britain is eligible to join.

One of the Guild's stated aims was to provide awards of merit for outstanding work in television. The first of the Guild award ceremonies was held at the Television Ball of the Savoy Hotel in October 1954. The awards on this occasion were six in number, presented to actors (two awards), a writer, a producer, a designer, and a "personality." In 1957 the number of awards was expanded to nine to accommodate entries from Independent television, including one for "Light Entertainment Artist" which went to Tony Hancock. In 1960 the Desmond Davis award for "outstanding service to television" was added to commemorate a founding member and past chairman. The first recipient was the broadcaster Richard Dimbleby. The number and the categories covered increased and varied over the years, and by 1967 there were 17 Guild awards and three additional awards presented under the aegis of the Guild by Mullard Ltd., Shell International, and the National Institute of Adult Education. The total currently stands at 39 television awards and 23 film awards (or BAFTAs).

In 1998 the film and television awards ceremonies were separated. Since then, *Radio Times* has acted as sponsor of the television awards (the official name of the event is now The British Academy Television Awards sponsored by Radio Times). Orange (a mobile phone company) has sponsored the film awards since 1998, which are now formally known as The Orange British Academy Film Awards. BAFTA hosts five awards ceremonies annually. The film awards are held in February. Television production is honored in April, and television craft in May. In October the interactive entertainment awards ceremony is held (in 2003, this was split into two separate awards categories, interactive and games). Finally, the children's film and television awards are presented late in the year (November/December).

Nominations for awards are initially determined by suggestions from members, broadcasters, and producers. Before the announcement of nominations, voting members are responsible for determining the television nominations. After nominations are announced, the voting membership is asked to vote again, this time for the winners in the categories of actor, actress, entertainment performance, and comedy performance. All other awards are determined by a jury of industry-based individuals.

The BAFTA awards enjoy a high degree of credibility and prestige. Although not as influential as the American Academy Awards, the BAFTA awards are increasingly seen as enhancing the subsequent commercial success of films and programs. Televising of the awards ceremony in Britain is a media event second only to the Oscars, and keeps BAFTA awards in the public eye. Despite the benefits of awards, there has been little evidence in Britain of any lobbying to influence panel decisions.

Television awards are primarily devoted to British television. New categories of award are constantly emerging in response to developments within the media. A recent addition has been the Lew Grade Audience Award (the People's Vote).

Film awards are international, although there is one reserved for best British film, the Alexander Korda Award. This category is increasingly difficult to determine given the prevalence of co-production arrangements, films made for television with prior release to cinema audiences (e.g. *FilmFour* by Channel 4), and films made in Britain with American backing.

Distinguished contributors to the shaping of the organization include Richard Cawston, Lord Attenborough, Sir Sydney Samuelson, and Sir David Puttnam.

BRENDAN KENNY

Further Reading

www.bafta.org

BRITISH
ACADEMY
OF FILM AND
TELEVISION
ARTS

British Academy of Film and Television Arts.
The British Academy Award is based on a design by Mitzi Cunliffe

British Programming

The BBC provided the world's first public high-definition regular domestic television service from 3:00 P.M. on November 2, 1936. After the initial introductory speeches, the first program began with a cinema newsreel, followed by an international variety show involving British, U.S., and Chinese performers. After closing down at 4:00 P.M., the service resumed for another hour at 9:00 P.M., when a short documentary and a magazine program were screened; the newsreel was then repeated. In the three years until the closedown of British television on September 1, 1939 (due to the announcement of Britain entering World War II), a complete range of television programs had been transmitted on the fledgling service. These included newsreels, documentaries, dramas, magazine shows, light entertainment, and children's programs. Drama productions were almost solely theatrical productions of classics; on March 28, 1938, Cecil Madden established the Sunday night TV drama, beginning with the transmission of Pirandello's *Henry IV.*

From the earliest days, a mobile broadcast unit was used. The coronation of King George VI was covered in 1937, with a viewing audience of more than 10,000 people. The unit also covered other public occasions such as the Lord Mayor's Show, the Armistice Day Service, and a range of sporting events such as Wimbledon (tennis) and the FA Cup Final (association football). Undoubtedly the most popular offering was the twice-weekly one-hour magazine program of topical and general interest, *Picture Page,* which ran from 1936 to 1939 and then returned in 1946 for a further 300 editions until 1954.

The high cost of television reception equipment, and the fact that the service could only be received in the London area, meant that the programming was aimed at the well-to-do elements of society. Apart from a couple of documentary films about the service, no moving-image record of the programs from the prewar service exists.

The immediate postwar years saw the continuation of *Picture Page* and the broadcast of events such as the Victory Parade (June 8, 1946), and royal and sporting events such as tennis and test cricket. The largest such coverage of the 1940s was the televising of the XIVth Olympiad held in London in 1948.

Many plays were transmitted (including some written especially for television) although very few films and filmed newsreels were broadcast, due to industry fears of supporting the competition. The few films that were shown were recognized classics such as D.W. Griffiths' *The Birth of a Nation* (1915), Josef von Sternberg's *Der Blaue Engel* (*The Blue Angel,* 1930), Sergei Eisenstein's *Alexander Nevsky* (1938), and Marcel Carne's *Les enfants du paradis* (1945).

The early 1950s saw a rapid expansion of TV-set ownership, with the broadcast of the 1953 coronation of Queen Elizabeth II often cited as one of the driving causes. More than 2 million licenses were registered in 1953 (approximately 20 percent of all households). Licenses rose to over 10 million by the end of the decade. The coronation was broadcast for seven hours; it is estimated that 20 million people in the United Kingdom saw it before it was shipped for screenings in Europe, North America, and across the Commonwealth.

In the 1950s, the BBC's monopoly of television broadcasting ended. The government ushered in television funding through the sale of advertising revenue at the end of July 1954, with transmissions starting on September 22, 1955. Commercial television transformed the safe, traditional, and cozy world depicted in many programs produced by the BBC. The commercial news service, ITN, also challenged the BBC's establishment-oriented approach, and the Suez Crisis of 1956 saw an end to the deferential attitude of television toward government and politicians.

The early 1950s saw the production of the United Kingdom's longest running police series, *Dixon of Dock Green* (BBC, 1955–76), created by Ted Willis, one of the world's most prolific creators of television series. *The Good Old Days* (BBC), an Edwardian-style variety show, ran from 1953 to 1983. *What's My Line?* (BBC, 1951–62, 1973–74; Thames, 1984–90) could be characterized as a quiz show but belongs to a typically British radio and TV genre that continues to this day. This genre is best described as a parlor game show played by guest celebrities. Other examples include *Face the Music* (BBC 1967–84), *A Question of Sport* (BBC, 1970–), *Celebrity Squares* (ATV/Central, 1975–79; 1993–97), *Call My Bluff* (BBC 1965–88), and *Give Us a Clue* (Thames 1979–91).

Commercial television introduced new ideas and many new areas of programming. British television drama, for instance, was transformed by *Armchair Theatre* (ABC, 1956–69, Thames, 1970–74), which served as an umbrella program for different productions by new writing talent (particularly under Canadian producer Sidney Newman) and introduced more working-class characters to the screen.. A more North American-style of entertainment was also produced, such as the variety show *Sunday Night at the London Palladium* (ATV, 1955–67, 1973–74), and game shows such as *Double Your Money* (A-R, 1955–68) and *Take Your Pick* (A-R 1955–68). One example of the BBC buying an American format was *This Is Your Life* (BBC, 1955–64), although Thames took it over from 1969, though it returned to the BBC in 1995.

A very popular production was the science fiction/horror serial *The Quatermass Experiment* (BBC, 1953) from which there have been a number of spin-offs. It was the half-hour filmed period action series that became the most popular drama. These included *The Adventures of Robin Hood* (ABC/ Sapphire/ITP, 1955–59), *The Adventures of Sir Lancelot* (Sapphire, 1956–57), *The Adventures of William Tell* (ITC-NTA, 1958–59), *The Count of Monte Cristo* (Vision Productions, 1958), *Ivanhoe* (Sydney Box Prods.-Screen Gems/ITC, 1958).

In comedy, the first edition of *The Benny Hill Show* was produced by the BBC in 1955. The BBC continued to produce it, with a one-year gap in 1967, until 1968. Thames (ITV) took it over in 1969 and ran it for the next 20 years. *Hancock's Half Hour* (1956–60) showcased the talents of Britain's best-loved radio comic, Tony Hancock, and Alfie Bass and Bill Fraser, the two main characters of the situation comedy *The Army Game* (Granada, 1957–61), featured in the spin-off *Bootsie and Snudge* (Granada, 1960–63). The American shows *The Phil Silvers Show* and *I Love Lucy* were very popular.

In the 1950s, ITV established the practice of buying American shows to supplement its own production. The most popular purchases were traditionally American genres: westerns such as *Gunsmoke/Gun Law, Wagon Train, Cheyenne, The Lone Ranger, Rawhide,* or fast-moving police series such as *Highway Patrol* and *Dragnet.* Gradually British TV began to imitate such police series and the first of these was *No Hiding Place* (A-R, 1959–67). *The Alfred Hitchcock* shows were also popular (*Alfred Hitchcock Presents* and *The Alfred Hitchcock Hour*). In light entertainment, *The Black and White Minstrel Show* (BBC 1958–78) ran for 20 years until eventually the offensiveness of white performers "blacking up" was finally acknowledged. *Opportunity Knocks!* (A-R, 1956; ABC, 1964–67; Thames, 1968–78) was a talent show—a genre that has continued in many guises since.

Popular music shows began with *Six-Five Special* (BBC, 1957–58) and was followed by *Oh Boy!* (ABC, 1958–59), *Juke Box Jury* (BBC, 1959–67; 1979; 1989–90), *Thank Your Lucky Stars* (ABC, 1958–59). The notorious *Eurovision Song Contest* began in 1956, and the United Kingdom has broadcast it from 1957 to the present day.

The first twice-weekly soap opera was set in a hospital (*Emergency Ward 10,* ATV, 1957–65) and was soon followed by the popular American import *Dr. Kildare.*

Current affairs began to develop as a key area of television broadcasting in the 1950s with the introduction of an early evening five-nights-a-week program *Tonight* (BBC, 1957–65). General arts programs were launched with *Monitor* (BBC, 1958–65). The 1950s also saw the introduction of a number of programs that still ran 40 years later. These include *Grandstand* (BBC, 1958–), the longest running live sports series on TV; *The Sky at Night* (BBC, 1957–), which is an astronomy program presented by Patrick Moore; and the range of programs with many titles fronted by Alan Whicker offering his idiosyncratic travelogues of the world. The children's program *Blue Peter* (BBC) also enjoyed surprising longevity, running from 1958 until the present day.

On April 21, 1964, the BBC launched its second channel, BBC 2. To the annoyance of the commercial TV companies (who were not allocated their second channel, Channel 4, for nearly two decades), the BBC could schedule some of its more specialist programming to this "minority" channel and therefore compete more directly with ITV by running the most popular programming on BBC 1.

To further restrict the commercial companies, in August 1965 the ITA instructed that from 8:00 to 8:55 P.M. Monday through Friday no more than two of five programs could be from the United States, and no more than three could be crime or western series. This was followed by the rule whereby only 14 percent of output could be originated in the United States with a further 2 percent allowed from the Commonwealth and 1.5 percent from Europe. These proportions were not changed until the development of cable and satellite in the 1980s, and still pertain to broadcast television.

On December 2, 1967, color TV was officially introduced on BBC 2. The 1960s saw some of the most innovative and imaginative programming in the history of broadcasting in Britain, reflecting the turbulent nature of that particular decade and causing a backlash in Mary Whitehouses's "clean up television" campaign. In the field of drama, the BBC introduced *The Wednesday Play* (BBC, 1964–70), which, like *Armchair Theatre,* was innovative and commissioned a number of controversial and subsequently famous plays. These included Jeremy Sandford's *Cathy Come Home* (1966), Nell Dunn's *Up the Junction* (1965), and Dennis Potter's *Vote, Vote, Vote for Nigel Barton* (1965). Peter Watkins' *Culloden* (1964) covered an important battle in Scottish history, and *The War Game* (1966) dealt with the devastating results of nuclear war. *The War Game* was not transmitted for 25 years because it was considered too distressing. On the popular drama front, one of the most enduring shows was the espionage series *The Avengers* (ABC, 1961–69). Popular too was the BBC's production of the French novelist George Simenon's *Maigret* (BBC, 1960–63) and the medical series set in rural Scotland *Dr. Finlay's Casebook* (BBC, 1962–71), which STV revived as a new series in 1993.

The BBC also introduced a new form of gritty realism with the creation of *Z Cars* (BBC, 1962–78), a police show, which was supported with the spin-off *Softly, Softly* (BBC, 1966–70). Another highly successful espionage series was *Danger Man* (ATV/ITC, 1960–61; 1964–67), starring Patrick McGoohan. As a result of this success, McGoohan was allowed to produce the enigmatic *The Prisoner* (Everyman/ATV, 1967–68), which, although only 17 episodes long, became one of the great cult series. Roger Moore starred in two "mid-Atlantic" thrillers, *The Saint* (ATV, 1962–69), which was followed in the 1970s by the unsuccessful series, *The Persuaders!* (Tribune/ITC, 1971–72), co-starring Tony Curtis.

BBC's most successful series, *Doctor Who* (1963–89), a science fiction program about a time lord who travels through time, was designed for children but developed a cult status enjoyed by a huge and faithful adult audience. This was also the decade in which some major soap operas were created. In 1960 Granada TV launched *Coronation Street,* a representation of daily life in a northern working-class community, in the northwest but it was soon networked across the country. It still remains at the top of the audience ratings after over 35 years, and transmissions have been increased from twice to four times a week.

In 1964 ATV introduced the highly popular *Crossroads,* a soap set in a Midlands motel, which ran for 24 years and was revived in 2001. Until 1985, when the BBC introduced the highly successful *EastEnders,* the BBC did not fare well with its soaps. Two were experimented with: *Compact* (1962–65) was set in the offices of a magazine, and *The Newcomers* (1965–69) presented the story of a London family that moved to a country town.

In the 1960s *Comedy Playhouse* (BBC, 1961–74) was created. This was a premiere comedy showcase in which pilots written by writers such as Alan Simpson and Ray Galton were televised. A number of the pilots went on to become some of the best loved comedy series on British TV. They included *Steptoe and Son* (BBC, 1962–65; 1970; 1972, 1974), and *Till Death Us Do Part* (BBC, 1966–68; 1972; 1974–75, which later became *In Sickness and in Health,* BBC 1985–1990). In the 1960s, there was a rise of satirical comedy shows such as *That Was the Week That Was* (BBC, 1962–63) and *Not Only—But Also...* (BBC, 1965–66; 1970), innovative shows such as *Monty Python's Flying Circus* (BBC, 1969–70; 1972–73), and the enduring favorite *Dad's Army* (BBC, 1968–77), a sitcom about a partially geriatric Home Guard in the early days of World War II. A number of Gerry Anderson's puppet productions were also produced: *Supercar* (ATV/AP/ITC, 1961–62), *Fireball XL5* (AP/ATV/ITC, 1962–63), Stingray (AP/ATV/ITC, 1964–65), *Thunderbirds* (ATV/AP/ITC, 1965–66), and *Captain Scarlett* and *The Mysterons* (ITC/Century 21 TV Prod, 1967–68).

Eric Morecambe and Ernie Wise grew in popularity until they were a national institution. Their show, under different titles, ran from 1961 to 1983, regularly changing channels. In the pop music field, *Thank Your Lucky Stars* (ABC, 1961–66), *Ready, Steady Go!* (A-R, 1963–66) and the BBC's *Top of the Pops* was launched in 1964 and continues to the present day.

In the nonfiction field, a number of notable series were broadcast. In 1967 the BBC initiated David Attenborough's long-running *The World About Us* (BBC, 1967–86), a natural history series that resulted in the creation of the BBC's natural history unit at its Bristol studios. Sir Kenneth Clark's renowned *Civilization* (BBC, 1969) charted the history of western culture from the collapse of Greece and Rome to the 20th century.

In the area of news and topical journalism, ITN created the first half-hour evening news bulletin, *News at Ten,* in 1967. Granada TV's groundbreaking current affairs series *World in Action* (Granada, 1963–98) brought a fresh and campaigning approach to the coverage of domestic politics and overseas issues like Vietnam, while the BBC's contemporary documentary series *Man Alive* (BBC, 1965–82) tackled pressing issues of social concern.

Television in the 1970s moved away from the experiments of the 1960s into safer territory. For example, apart from *Play for Today* (BBC, 1970–84), original TV drama was replaced with period- and novel-based serials. These included such series as *The Six Wives of Henry VIII* (BBC, 1970) and *Upstairs Downstairs* (LWT, 1971–75). It was also the decade of the major, solemn documentary series such as *The World at War* (Thames, 1973–74), *The Ascent of Man* (BBC, 1973), and *Life on Earth* (BBC, 1979).

Comedy moved more into the fairly bland with *Are You Being Served?* (BBC, 1973–83). There were, however, some notable exceptions such as *Fawlty Towers* (BBC, 1975; 1979), *Porridge* (BBC, 1974–77), *Some Mothers Do 'Ave 'Em* (BBC, 1973–75; 1978), *Rising Damp* (YTV, 1974–78), *The Fall and Rise of Reginald Perrin* (BBC, 1976–79), *The Liver Birds* (BBC 1969–79), and *The Last of the Summer Wine* (BBC, 1973–). There was also the zany *The Goodies* (BBC, 1970–77; 1980) and the perennially popular *The Two Ronnies* (BBC, 1971–86).

American westerns virtually disappeared in the 1980s, and American crime series were in ascendance. However, programs such as *Kojak* were influential, and indirectly encouraged the development of more action-oriented British crime series. One company in particular, Euston Films Limited (a subsidiary of Thames TV), developed a portfolio of such programs for the ITV network. These included *Van der Valk* (Thames, 1972–73; Euston, 1977; Thames, 1991–92), *The Sweeney* (Euston, 1975–78), *Minder* (Euston, 1979–85; 1988–94), *Widows* (Euston, 1983; *Widows II,* 1985), *Reilly—Ace of Spies* (Euston, 1983). Series from other commercial companies included *The Professionals* (LWT, 1977–83) and two grittily realistic and much applauded serials made by the BBC, *Gangsters* (1976; 1978) and G.F. Newman's four-part *Law and Order* (1978).

There were also a number of highly successful drama series, two of which focused on courtroom situations—the daytime (three days a week) *Crown Court* (Granada, 1972–84), and the immensely popular *Rumpole of the Bailey* (Thames, 1978–79; 1983; 1987–88; 1991). There was also a highly successful serial set in a secondary school, *Grange Hill* (BBC, 1978–), devised by the ex-teacher Phil Redmond (who went on to found Mersey Productions and to produce Channel 4's equally successful soap *Brookside).*

On the soap front, Yorkshire TV produced a rural daytime serial, *Emmerdale Farm,* which began in 1972 and became increasingly popular as *Emmerdale.* The BBC also experimented with an all-black soap (written by a black author), *Empire Road* (1978–79).

In light entertainment, there was Bruce Forsyth's *Generation Game* (BBC, 1971–77), a very popular format that has continued on and off (with Larry Grayson taking over his role); the chat show *Parkinson* (BBC, 1971–82; 1996–) featuring Michael Parkinson; the long-running *That's Life* (BBC, 1973–94); *The Muppet Show* (ATV/Central, 1976–81); *Blankety Blank* (BBC, 1979–89). There were quiz shows ranging from *Mastermind* (BBC, 1972–), where contestants compete for a title by answering complex general-knowledge questions and obscure questions about specialist areas of knowledge they possess, through *Sale of the Century* (Anglia, 1972–83), to the banal *Mr. and Mrs.* (ATV/Border, 1972–88).

There was a great deal of television activity in the 1980s. The commercial second channel, Channel 4, was launched on November 2, 1982, with a funding formula that freed it from commercial concern and gave it a remit to innovate. Breakfast television was introduced on three of the four channels. There was a massive growth in video recorder ownership. Cable and satellite networks were established. American soaps such as *Dallas* and *Dynasty* dominated the ratings, media coverage, and popular debate. Possibly the most disastrous attempt to compete with the United States head on was the production of *Chateauvallon* (1985), where five European networks attempted to produce a competitive equivalent to *Dallas.*

In programming terms, the 1980s represented a period when some very expensive classic drama was produced. This included *Death of a Princess* (ATV, 1980), which gained notoriety because it was about the public beheading of a Saudi princess and her lover. The Saudi government tried to stop its transmission and banned its importation to Saudi Arabia. Because of video technology, it was being clandestinely viewed in Saudi Arabia within 24 hours of first transmission in the United Kingdom. Almost as controversial was the BBC's *Boys from the Blackstuff* (BBC, 1982) about unemployment in Liverpool. Granada TV produced two hugely expensive, highly successful 13-part series: *Brideshead Revisited* (1981), from the Evelyn Waugh novel, and *The Jewel in the Crown* (1984), which was shot almost entirely in India. The BBC also produced the film-noir-style six-part drama, *Edge of Darkness* (1985), about the attempt to sabotage a nuclear power station, and Dennis Potter's complex masterpiece *The Singing Detective* (1986). The most significant development in television drama, however, was the decision by Channel 4 to make feature films, many of which played theatrically before being seen on television, rather than single plays. The success of this venture and the decision of other broadcasters to follow suit signaled the death of the single play, shot on video in the studio, on British television.

Police dramas proliferated in the 1980s. Both the BBC and ITV had female detectives, *Juliet Bravo* (BBC, 1980–85) and *The Gentle Touch* (LWT, 1980–84), respectively; there was a black detective, *Wolcott* (ATV 1981); a local radio detective, *Shoestring* (BBC, 1979–80); a Chinese detective, *The Chinese Detective* (BBC, 1981–82); a Scottish detective, *Taggart* (STV, 1983–); the long-running series set on the island of Jersey, *Bergerac* (BBC, 1981–91); the highly acclaimed series set in Oxford starring John

Thaw, *Inspector Morse* (Central, 1987–92); and literary private detectives: *The Adventures of Sherlock Holmes* (Granada, 1984–85; *The Return of Sherlock Holmes,* 1986–88; *The Casebook of Sherlock Holmes,* 1991; *Sherlock Holmes,* 1993) with Jeremy Brett offering what is currently considered to be the definitive performance of the great detective; and two famous Agatha Christie detectives, the BBC-produced *Miss Marple* (1984–92) and ITV's *Poirot* (LWT/Carnival 1989–).

Popular noncrime series included the BBC's *A Very Peculiar Practice* (1986 and 1988), set in a university health center; and two highly realistic long-running series, one based in a fire station, *London's Burning* (LWT, 1988–), and the other an equally long-running hospital series, *Casualty* (BBC, 1986–).

A number of new soap operas started in the 1980s. First there was Scottish TV's daytime soap *Take the High Road* (1980–); Channel 4's *Brookside* (Mersey, 1982–2003); the BBC's first successful soap that rivaled *Coronation Street* in the audience ratings *EastEnders* (1985–); and a police soap, *The Bill* (Thames, 1984–).

In the 1980s a range of highly successful and, in some cases long-running, sitcoms developed. There was Carla Lane's long-running *Bread* (BBC, 1986–91) and *Yes, Minister* (BBC, 1980, 1982) was successful enough for Paul Eddington (the minister) to return as the prime minister in *Yes, Prime Minister* in 1986 and 1988. *Hi-De-Hi!* (BBC, 1981–88), *'Allo, 'Allo* (BBC, 1984–92, and *Only Fools and Horses* (BBC, 1981–) are long-running series that, like *Dad's Army* and *Fawlty Towers,* continue to be regularly repeated. Over the decades the BBC has always been more successful with sitcoms than the ITV companies, but in the 1980s ITV enjoyed significant success in this field with Rik Mayall's *The New Statesman* (Yorkshire, 1987–92).

In the 1980s U.K. television produced its first all-black sitcom, *No Problem!* (C4, 1983–85), Rowan Atkinson in *Blackadder* (BBC, 1983–89), and Peter Fluck and Roger Law's award-winning satirical puppet show *Spitting Image* (Central, 1984–96). This last show has enjoyed significant international format sales.

In the area of light entertainment, the BBC's *The Lenny Henry Show* (BBC, 1984–85; 1987–88) and *French and Saunders* (BBC, 1987–88) were very successful, and Channel 4 enjoyed success with the innovative pop music show *The Tube* (Tyne, Tees 1982–87) and the even more original *Max Headroom* (Chrysalis, 1985).

A number of new game shows were introduced in the 1980s. *Bulleseye* (ATV, 1981–94), a show based on the game of darts, and Channel 4's *Countdown* (Yorkshire, 1982–), a word game with which C4 opened transmissions. Two American formats were hugely successful: *The Price Is Right* (Central, 1984–88) and *Blind Date* (LWT, 1985–). In current affairs, the BBC introduced *Newsnight* (1980–), and LWT made the first ethnic minority current affairs programs for Channel 4, *Black on Black* (1982–85) and *Eastern Eye* (1982–85).

In the 1980s programs about cooking—for example, *Food and Drink* (BBC/Bazal, 1982–)—and holidays—for example, *Holiday* (BBC, 1969–), which has a number of rivals including ITV's *Wish You Were Here... ?* (Thames, 1976–)—proliferated and became hugely popular.

The 1980s saw a large increase in channel output hours, and Channel 4's approach, combined with the introduction of cheaper, lightweight video equipment, gave a much rougher edge to the look of programs. At first this was regarded as unprofessional but later became the standard. The growth of the independent production sector during the years of the Thatcher government also allowed many more people, with a more businesslike approach, to enter the previously closed world of television production, as did the breaking down of old union restrictions.

The 1990s saw the increasing commercialization of British television after the 1990 Broadcasting Act, plus the development of satellite companies and the financial battle over the rights to major world sporting events, with Rupert Murdoch's BSkyB seeming to win most of the battles. It was also the decade that the Australian soaps such as *Neighbours* and *Home and Away* dominated the U.K. daytime schedules and the fifth terrestrial channel, Channel 5, began.

Although satellite and cable channels were a well-established part of the British television landscape by the early years of the 21st century, their impact on original programming is difficult to assess. The most successful channels were the ones that carried first-run movies or sports, and the latter, especially Sky Sports, with its exclusive live coverage of Premier League soccer and events like the Ryder Cup golf, certainly revolutionized sports coverage. Sky News also had a big impact, inspiring the creation of 24-hour news channels by the BBC and ITN. The BBC's channel was in place for the biggest domestic news story of all: the death and funeral of Diana, Princess of Wales, which replaced the published schedules on all channels for over a week in 1997. However, the satellite entertainment channels contained mostly imported or repeat material, and few original programs made an impact, with the exception of Sky One's *Ibiza Uncovered* (LWT for BSkyB, 1997), which led to a rash of programs exploring the racy behavior of young vacationers.

Back on the established channels, the major drama successes were *Prime Suspect* (Granada, 1991–2003), *The Darling Buds of May* (Yorkshire, 1991), *Oranges Are Not the Only Fruit* (BBC, 1990), *Between the Lines* (BBC, 1992–94), *Cracker* (Granada, 1993–95), *Our Friends in the North* (BBC, 1996) and *Holding On* (BBC, 1997). Although many of these were critical and/or ratings successes, it was not a time amenable to original writing for television, and most channels concentrated their resources on expensive classic period dramas, such as the BBC's highly successful *Pride and Prejudice* (1995). However, the end of the decade saw a spate of contemporary comedy-dramas, inspired by the enormous success of Granada's *Cold Feet* (1997–2002).

Successful sitcoms included *One Foot in the Grave* (BBC, 1990–2000), Channel 4's set in a TV newsroom *Drop the Dead Donkey* (Hat Trick, 1990–98), *Absolutely Fabulous* (BBC, 1992–), and *The Royle Family* (BBC, 1998–2000). However, probably the most acclaimed comedy show of the decade was the wickedly funny *Have I Got News For You* (Hat Trick, 1990–), which is a panel game recorded the day before transmission to ensure its biting satire is completely topical. Experimental comedy also thrived, with a number of forays into the world of the surreal such as *Vic Reeves' Big Night Out* (Channel 4, 1990–91) (followed by the BBC's *The Smell of Reeves and Mortimer, 1993–95*), *Father Ted* (Channel 4, 1995–98), *The League of Gentlemen* (BBC, 1999–), and Chris Morris's *Jam* (Channel 4, 2000). *The Fast Show* (BBC, 1994–2000) took the sketch show in a new direction, while *The Office* (BBC, 2001–03) provided a sitcom in the style of a documentary.

The two most significant programming developments of this period, however, were the docusoap, such as the BBC's *Driving School* (1997), and the worldwide phenomenon of reality television, which dominated schedules in the early years of the 21st century. Possibly the biggest success, and the first in the field, was a format that came from Holland, *Big Brother* (Channel 4, 2000–), but British TV soon gave its own formats to the world, including *I'm a Celebrity, Get Me Out of Here* (2002–), which was a major success for ITV. Probably the biggest format exported from Britain, though, was the ITV prize quiz *Who Wants To Be a Millionaire?* (1998–), which in Britain transformed ITV's fortunes through strip scheduling and was the most significant new game show in over a decade. It went on to worldwide success with exactly the same set, style, and music as used in Britain, thus providing the template for success in program format export for the subsequent years.

The beginning of the 21st century also saw the spread of widescreen digital terrestrial television in Britain, and with it an expansion of the BBC's service to seven channels, including two for children. BBC 3 provided youth entertainment programming from 2003, while BBC 4 was on air a year earlier with an outstanding mix of serious arts, documentary, and discussion programs. Many saw this as confirmation of the decline of BBC 2 and Channel 4, both of which had formerly provided such programming, but had moved away from it in the search for ratings.

STEVE BRYANT AND MANUEL ALVARADO

See also ***Absolutely Fabulous; Avengers, The; Big Brother; Blackadder; Boys from the Blackstuff; Brideshead Revisited; Brookside; Civilization; Coronation Street; Cracker; Dad's Army; EastEnders; Fall and Rise of Reginald Perrin, The; Fawlty Towers; Grange Hill; Have I Got News for You; Man Alive; Monty Python's Flying Circus; Not Only–But Also . . . ; One Foot in the Grave; Only Fools and Horses; Our Friends in the North; Parkinson; Porridge;*** **Princess Diana: Death and Funeral Coverage;** ***Quatermass; Ready, Steady, Go!; Rising Damp; Rumplole of the Bailey; Singing Detective, The; Some Mothers Do 'Ave 'Em; Spitting Image; Steptoe and Son; That Was the Week That Was; Till Death Us Do Part; Top of the Pops; Upstairs Downstairs; World at War; World in Action; Yes, Minister***

Further Reading

Alvarado, Manuel, and John Stewart, *Made for Television: Euston Films Limited,* London: British Film Institute, 1985

Davis, Anthony, *Television: The First Forty Years,* London: Severn House, 1976

Halliwell, Leslie, with Philip Purser, *Halliwell's Teleguide,* London: Granada Publishing, 1979

Halliwell's Television Companion, 3rd edition, London: Grafton, 1986

Kingsley, Hilary, and Geoff Tibbals, *Box of Delights: The Golden Years of Television,* London: Macmillan, 1989

Vahimagi, Tise, editor, *British Television: An Illustrated Guide,* Oxford: Oxford University Press, 1994

British Sky Broadcasting

International Satellite Broadcasting Service

British Sky Broadcasting (BSkyB) is the first entrepreneurial venture of any significance to have challenged the hitherto closely regulated, four-channel, public service character of British television. As part of the international media empire that includes the Fox Network and Star TV, BSkyB has rapidly become a major player in the world broadcasting marketplace. It is a large commercial satellite network, available principally to viewers in the British Isles, although audiences anywhere within the European ASTRA satellite system footprint can receive it.

Owned 36.3 percent by News Corporation and successfully floated on the U.K. and U.S. stock exchanges at the end of 1994, BSkyB is immediately associated with the name of media tycoon Rupert Murdoch, who invested heavily in the venture from 1983, accepting enormous initial losses while awaiting the profit potential of satellite television in Britain. Initially with a purely analog service, and subsequently with a dual-illuminated digital/analog service, BSkyB has become the primary nonterrestrial broadcaster in the United Kingdom and is regarded by the terrestrial sector as the true commercial competition. In just a decade and a half of wide consumer access, the network has firmly established itself as the third force in British broadcasting.

The inauspicious origins of BSkyB can be traced to Murdoch's purchase in 1983 of a 65 percent share (subsequently increased to 82 percent) in a fledgling, London-based operation called Satellite Television Ltd., which, as the first European satellite television channel, had been transmitting programs for about a year to small audiences in western Europe over one of the earliest EUTELSAT satellites. Murdoch, who once famously described satellite television as "the most important single advance since Caxton invented the printing press," relaunched the company as the Sky Channel and commenced broadcasting a new programming mix in January 1984, receivable in Britain by cable households only (at that time no more than about 10,000). By 1987 Sky had achieved an 11.3 percent share of viewing in those homes capable of receiving it and had raised some £28 million in rights issues to fund its planned expansion into direct-to-home delivery.

Sky's expansion, widely criticized at the time as irresponsibly risky, began in February 1989, when the company's new three-channel package went on air over the first Luxembourg-owned ASTRA satellite. Indeed, since U.K. broadcasting legislation did not then permit a satellite undertaking to uplink signals from British soil, Sky was only legally able to do so by virtue of its non-British transmission source. At first available unscrambled and free-of-charge, the original Sky package consisted of a premium film channel (Sky Movies), a 24-hour news channel (Sky News), and a general entertainment/family channel (Sky One). This package, however, experienced a very slow initial take-up by the British public for a number of reasons, the main one being that many potential customers were holding back in anticipation of the heavily advertised launch of a rival satellite service, British Satellite Broadcasting (BSB), which promised subscribers an attractive range of alternative benefits with a distinctly British cultural emphasis.

The rise and fall of BSB represents something of a fiasco in broadcasting deregulation, but in retrospect it can be seen as an unprecedented opportunity for the entrepreneurship of Murdoch's Sky. BSB, specially provided for in the British government's Broadcasting Act of 1990, was licensed as the official Direct Broadcast by Satellite (DBS) provider, legally enabled to uplink from British soil and established as the direct competitor of Sky. BSB was claimed to possess an enormous technological advantage over its rival in that BSB would use a much higher powered satellite, with the more technically sophisticated D-MAC transmission standard delivering a higher fidelity TV picture than Sky's inferior (but more affordable) PAL standard. BSB's two Marco Polo satellites (at an astronomical cost of some £500 million each) were duly launched from Cape Kennedy by space shuttles between August 1989 and early 1990, by which time Sky had been consolidating its audience for over a year. After several embarrassing delays, BSB launched on April 29, 1990. Its five-channel service competed uneasily with Sky throughout the summer and autumn of 1990 but was even slower than Sky to attract consumer interest. On November 2, 1990 (ironically, the day after the Broadcasting Act was finally passed), BSB suddenly collapsed, recognizing that the market could not sustain two such capital-intensive satellite operations in competition. Without the permission of the Independent Broadcasting Authority, Sky immediately announced a merger with BSB to form the BSkyB network. Although this was, in effect, a serious breach of BSB's contract, the merger (in effect, a takeover) was allowed to proceed in the best interests of viewers, and transitional arrangements were put in hand to compensate dispossessed BSB subscribers so that a five-channel service, now provided by the new BSkyB organization, would continue to be available to them via Marco Polo until the end of 1992.

Freed from nonterrestrial competition, BSkyB was now in a position to rationalize its activities, especially in the area of subscription services. It immediately relaunched BSB's Movie Channel, having acquired the rights to an expanded cartel of Hollywood feature films, thus giving itself greater flexibility and market domination in movie scheduling. In October 1992, the company replaced a short-lived Comedy Channel experiment with a third movie channel, Sky Movies Gold, dedicated to classic films. Then, in September 1993, BSkyB introduced its most aggressive market move to date when it announced the "Sky Multichannels" subscription package, with various price options to suit viewer preference. By this point, a Sports Channel had been added to the network, later to be followed by Sky Sports 2, Sky Travel, and Sky Soaps. Interestingly, the Multichannels package also included a number of competing English-language ASTRA channels, such as Discovery, Bravo, Children's Channel, Nickelodeon, and QVC, which paid BSkyB a premium for the use of its patented Videocrypt decoding technology. Hence, BSkyB was cleverly generating revenue not only from its own programs but also from those of its immediate competitors.

Murdoch initially regarded the Sky satellite venture as a five-year risk to profitability from 1988. After gigantic early losses that would have deterred more timid investors, the company had already begun to move into profit by early 1992 and went on to build itself into an extremely valuable and powerful business, with an ever growing slate of channels and a steadily rising customer base. In 1998 BSkyB launched Sky Digital, the first digital TV proposition in the United Kingdom and the fastest, most successful rollout of any European digital service. By September 2001, Sky Digital had attracted 5.5 million direct-to-home subscribers out of BSkyB's total subscription population of 10.2 million.

The network's rise to its current preeminence has not been entirely without setbacks; management changes and the capital intensive roll-out of the digital service contributed to temporary downturns in profitability in the late 1990s. Nevertheless, by 1999, the company had entered the list of the world's top 250 companies. In the six months ending December 31, 2001, revenue increased on the preceding half-year by 22 percent to £1.32 million ($2.24 million) and operating profit by 39 percent to £70 million ($119 million). This growth was achieved in the face of competition in the United Kingdom from both digital terrestrial and digital cable ventures. With more than 250 digital TV and radio channels (including some 75 pay-per-view options) available in 2001, BSkyB's Sky Digital offered an unparalleled choice of entertainment and information programming supported by a range of interactive services such as e-mail, home shopping and banking, online games, camera-angle selection, and over-the-air voting and betting. Subscribers could select from more than 90 different package options ranging from £10 to £37 per month. A new service, Sky +, was launched in September 2001, offering viewers the added facility of an integrated Personal Television Recorder and delivering new levels of control over the TV viewing experience.

Undoubtedly the leading digital player in the United Kingdom, BSkyB remains well positioned to respond to future technological and regulatory change. It has become so well established as part of an enormous vertically integrated international media empire that it is likely to maintain its market advantage unless cross-media ownership rules eventually place debilitating constraints on its potential.

TONY PEARSON

See also **Murdoch, Rupert; Satellite**

Further Reading

Chippindale, Peter, *Dished: The Rise and Fall of British Satellite Broadcasting,* London: Simon and Schuster, 1991

Collins, Richard, "The Language of Advantage: Satellite Television in Western Europe," in *Television: Policy and Culture,* edited by Richard Collins, London: Unwin Hyman, 1990

Collins, Richard, "The Prognosis for Satellite Television in the U.K," in *Television: Policy and Culture,* edited by Richard Collins, London: Unwin Hyman, 1990

Collins, Richard, *Satellite Television in Western Europe,* London: John Libbey, 1990

Collins, Richard, *The Second Generation: The Lessons of Satellite Television in Western Europe,* PICT Policy Research Paper, no. 12, London: Economic and Social Research Council, 1991

Collins, Richard, *Direct Broadcasting by Satellite in the U.K.: From Sky to BSkyB,* PICT Policy Research Paper, no. 15, London: Economic and Social Research Council, 1991

Crouch, Colin, "The Perversity of Television Markets (Monopoly and Regulation in British Broadcasting)," *Political Quarterly* (January–March 1994)

Horsman, Mathew, *Sky High: The Inside Story of BSkyB,* London: Orion Business, 1997

"In a Hole," *The Economist* (June 17, 1995)

"The Nimbleness of Murdoch," *The Economist* (May 20, 1995)

British Television

The Public Service Concept

Throughout much of its post–World War II history, British television has formed a recognizable if evolving system: principled, realistic, capacious, and flexible. Its goals, structures, and production practices have periodically been retuned to chime with shifting social needs, cultural tastes, and more pragmatic imperatives, including government policy requirements. Yet, amid its numerous adaptations to change, significant continuities of principle and approach have hitherto endured.

Can the same element of principled continuity be discerned today, when the pressures of change on British broadcasting are unprecedentedly far-reaching, challenging, and continuous? Is what is emerging from the present vortex of pressure, rethinking, and adaptation a system revamped but in fundamental respects still true to itself? Or is a quite different television system being born in Britain?

The crux of the answers to these questions lies in the fate of the public service idea in new and less-congenial conditions. Although until recently the British notion of "public service" was nowhere explicitly defined, it was widely understood to embrace purposes of programming range, quality, and popularity with the general viewing audience. Other emphases included universality of reception; reflection of national identity and community; provision of a civic forum, enabling debate and informing audiences on the key issues of the day; due impartiality in coverage of such issues; the editorial independence of program makers within the overall regulatory framework; respect for children's entire personality and development needs; special regard for minorities; avoiding offense to law and order, taste and decency; and, latterly, the promotion of intercultural awareness and understanding.

The sway of this idea of public service helps to explain many past programming strengths of British television:

- investment in news and current affairs programming, including treatment of election campaigns as transforming civic events
- an impressive tradition of children's television, including a wide range of entertainment, information, drama, and animation, not only on Saturday and Sunday mornings but also on midafternoon weekdays on the two most popular channels;
- provision of drama in a very wide range of formats, subject matter, and cultural levels;
- reading soap operas frequently laced with explorations of significant social issues and moral dilemmas;
- vigorous documentary strands;
- the cultural patronage role of arts coverage, including funding of a chorus and five large orchestras by the British Broadcasting Corporation (BBC);
- well-resourced programming in natural history, popular science, and technology;
- investment in a wide range of educational television (for schools, further and adult education, the Open University, and prime-time public awareness campaigns), social access programs, public access programs, and programs for immigrant communities.

The traditional role and influence of "public service," however, can no longer be taken for granted. Some broadcasting executives and knowledgeable commentators are even suggesting that it has reached its "sell-by date," although others still believe that it can be revised for meaningful application in current conditions.

Be that as it may, many of the props that used to support the classical version of public service broadcasting have been undermined by sociocultural and technological forces. On the one hand, audience tastes have shifted. Didacticism is less acceptable. Deference to cultural and political elites has evaporated. Interest in conventional politics has diminished. Audiences specifically for television news have declined, especially among younger viewers and listeners. Under these conditions, past ways of fulfilling the civic function of broadcasting appear less viable. On the other hand, advances in technology have given audience members more opportunities to choose programming in line with their tastes.

The Structure of British Television

Until relatively recently, British television was a limited-channel, highly regulated, public service system that periodically admitted, while striving to contain, commercially competitive impulses. Three of its five terrestrial analog channels still have public service remits (BBC 1, BBC 2, and Channel 4); the fourth

(Channel 3 of Independent Television ([ITV], a federal grouping of 15 regionally based services, plus national companies of breakfast television and Independent Television News) has significant public service requirements; whereas the fifth (Channel 5, which was launched in 1997 and covers approximately two-02.31 thirds of the country) has more notional ones. Competition for larger audiences is principally waged between BBC 1 and ITV's Channel 3 (with the former overtaking the latter in 2001, after lagging behind in previous years).

The opening of Channel 4 in 1982 as an advertising-financed but nonprofit publisher (not a producer) of programs changed the prevailing television system in two ways. Legally required to be innovative, Channel 4 did pioneer new forms and styles of both factual and fictional programming. Structurally, it encouraged the growth of a large sector of some 900 independent program-making companies of diverse sizes and production specialties. This growth was strengthened by the Broadcasting Act of 1990, which obliged all terrestrial broadcasters to commission at least 25 percent of their output from such sources. As a consequence, the production arms of the ITV companies were scaled back, and a process whereby network controllers entertain or solicit program pitches from other companies became more common.

After an initially slow diffusion of cable and satellite offerings, British television is fast becoming a fully fledged multichannel system. Forty percent of the country's households can receive numerous channels via one of three methods: through locally based cable systems (mostly provided by Telewest and NTL, serving about 3 million subscribers in 2002); through a nationally distributed digital satellite system provided by BSkyB (which is 36 percent owned by Rupert Murdoch's News International Corporation and serves over 5 million subscribers); or through a terrestrial digital system provided by ITV Digital (owned by Carlton Communications and Granada Television, now the dominant companies of the ITV network, having acquired most of the others in successive takeovers and mergers; ITV Digital offers to just over 1 million subscribers somewhat fewer channels than its competitors).

At the end of 2001, channels other than the five terrestrial networks attracted a one-fifth share of total viewing. The main loser was ITV's Channel 3, the advertising revenue of which was squeezed as its share fell to 25 percent of the total audience. The BBC's share was nearly 40 percent (over 25 percent for BBC 1 and nearly 13 percent for BBC 2), while Channel 4 attracted 10 percent of the viewing audience (slightly down on previous years) and Channel 5 was watched by 6 percent (on a slight upward trend). A significant slice of the nonterrestrial audience gravitates to BSkyB's premium sports and movie channels. Nevertheless, even in multichannel homes, the mainstream networks combined held almost 60 percent of the total viewing audience, and for the commissioning and financing of original fictional or factual programming, British television is still predominantly dependent on the BBC, ITV, and Channel 4.

Governance

Three organizations have been central in the governance of British television. First, government responsibility for broadcasting is lodged with the Department of Culture, Media, and Sport (previously termed the Department of National Heritage, succeeding the Home Office in 1992, which had taken over from the Postmaster General some years earlier). This department appoints the members of all regulatory bodies, oversees policy development (increasingly in collaboration with the Department of Trade and Industry), and initiates legislation and debates in Parliament.

Second, a board of 12 governors is appointed by the Queen in Council (in practice the government of the day) to direct the British Broadcasting Corporation in the public interest. The BBC is a large organization of approximately 24,000 employees and a £2.4 billion annual income, the bulk of which comes from an annual license fee (£104 in 2000–01) levied on every household with a television set. Fixed by negotiation between the BBC and the government, the level of the fee tended in the past to keep pace with the retail price index, but it is due to exceed that by 1.5 percent annually until 2006.

The BBC's obligations are outlined in a Royal Charter and Agreement, the present terms of which run until 2006. These spell out in some detail both the BBC's public service programming role and the governors' supervisory duties, and the charter also authorizes BBC involvement in commercial activities (which earned the corporation £100 million in 2000–2001). The governors appoint the BBC director general and, in consultation with him or her, an executive committee of 17 directors, including four individuals responsible for programming (drama, entertainment, and children's; factual and learning; sport; and news) plus a "new media" director, who is in charge of the BBC's increasingly entrepreneurial interactive and online services. Traditionally, senior management decided most matters of BBC policy and programming, with the governors serving more as a sounding board and ultimate authorizer, commenting only after the fact on individual broadcasts of which they approved or disapproved. From the 1970s, however, the governors became increasingly active, and in the late 1980s they were a spur for fundamental organizational reform. More recently, they have come under pressure to demonstrate their independent ability to oversee the BBC in the "public interest," rather than its corporate interests.

The third governing body is the Independent Television Commission (ITC, known in previous incarnations as the Independent Broadcasting Authority and the Independent Television Authority), which holds jurisdiction over all advertising-financed television. The ITC's writ has run over Independent Television's Channel 3; Channel 4, which is legally required to be innovative and to cater to different interests and tastes from those served by Channel 3; Channel 5; cable and satellite services originating in Britain; and, since 1997, a multiplex of digital terrestrial television.

The ITC's duties are set out in the Broadcasting Act of 1990, and its 12 members are appointed by the government. Its main tasks have been to franchise the commercial television companies by a process of first tendering for and then auctioning the licenses, and to enforce the license conditions thereafter. The Broadcasting Act posited a "quality threshold," which all applying companies had to cross before being admitted to the auction itself, at which the highest bidder would normally be the winner. From 1993, when the new Channel 3 licensees took over, the ITC was a relatively resolute regulator, holding the companies to their obligations (through directives, warnings, and fines as necessary), and annually reporting, sometimes critically, on their programming performances. As of late 2001, however, this system was poised to depend more heavily on self-regulation by the companies themselves.

Two other features of the system of governance should also be mentioned. First, elaborate codes of practice have been evolved to cover a wide range of matters on which programs could cause offense. The ITC has drawn up four such codes—on program sponsorship; advertising standards and practices; advertising breaks; and a so-called Program Code—and the ITV companies are required to introduce effective compliance procedures. The BBC has developed a 300-page booklet of Producers' Guidelines, oversight of which is vested in a separate Editorial Policy Unit. In addition, for the specific areas of violence, sexual display, taste, decency, and bad language, the government established in 1988 a Broadcasting Standards Council (now Commission) to issue a Code of Practice, which all broadcasters must take into account and in light of which viewers may submit complaints for Commission findings.

Second, public expectations of broadcasting and options for its future development have been shaped in the past by a series of comprehensive reviews by independent committees of inquiry appointed by the government. (The committees' main reports are listed in the Further Reading section of this entry.)

The History of the British Television System

Thus, Britain hosts a complex and thoroughly mixed television system. From its inception, British television has progressed through five overlapping phases.

First, up to 1955, development of the medium was subordinated to the needs of radio. Having provided sound broadcasting since 1922, the BBC inaugurated the world's first television service in 1936, shut it down during World War II, and reopened it in 1946. In the early postwar years, however, television enthusiasts waged an uphill battle against those in higher BBC echelons who saw the medium as a cultural Trojan horse—committed predominantly to entertainment, brash and childish, not very civilized, and conducive to audience passivity. The balance began to shift in 1952, first, after the appointment as director general of Sir Ian Jacob, who realized that television had to be taken more seriously, and, second, with the striking success in June of that year of the televising of the coronation of Queen Elizabeth—a spectacle with great symbolic impact, audience reach, and appeal.

This phase came to an end through a characteristic political development, one that aimed to reconcile a cultural mission for broadcasting with chances to exploit the advertising potential of television and to upgrade the claims of popular taste. The Television Act of 1954 authorized creation of a new advertising-financed service, to be called Independent Television (purposely not "Commercial Television"), in competition with the BBC. Although the Beveridge Committee enquiry of 1951 had recommended renewal of the BBC's monopoly, the incoming Conservative government in that year adopted a minority report that proposed "some element of competition" in television. Bitterly challenged inside and outside Parliament, the government had to concede crucial safeguards against rampant commercialism: no sponsorship; only time spots of controlled length and frequency would be sold to advertisers who would have no say in program content; and creation of a new public corporation, an Independent Television Authority, to appoint the companies and supervise their performance in light of requirements specified in the act.

From the mid-1950s to the early 1960s, there followed a second phase, one of vigorous but creative competition between an insurgent ITV and a threatened BBC. Although it aroused doubts, fear, and dismay among some at the time, that competition is now widely regarded as having advanced the medium's programming powers and viewers' all-round enjoyment. From the outset, ITV set its cap at neglected mass tastes, especially for entertainment, while cultivating a more informal and accessible presentation style and celebrating what one executive termed "people's television." After experiencing a dramatic loss of viewers (down to a 28 percent share at the nadir), the BBC fought back hard all across the programming board.

Many achievements ensued. Since ITV was based on separate companies in London and other parts of the country, British television catered for the first time to diverse regional interests in addition to metropolitan ones. Television news was transformed—with named news readers, pace, incisiveness, and eye-catching pictures. Inhibitions on political and election coverage were shed. Saturday afternoons were devoted to coverage of top sporting events. A host of memorable children's programs were developed. New forms of television drama were pioneered. New comedy stars (for example, Tony Hancock, Jimmy Edwards, Charlie Drake) emerged, served by high-profile writers. The BBC created an early evening topical magazine, *Tonight,* the sprightliness and irreverence of which broke sharply with the corporation's traditions. Yet the flag of authoritativeness was also flown in its weekly current affairs program, *Panorama;* a new arts magazine, *Monitor;* and an in-depth interview program, *Face to Face.*

In this phase, the British concern for blending potentially opposed impulses in its television system remained strong. For its part, the BBC had to become more competitive and seek a larger audience share to sustain its claim to license-fee funding and its status as Britain's national broadcaster. However, this was not to be its sole aim and was to be achieved through high standards of quality across a broad range of programming. Endorsing its record, the Pilkington Committee enquiry (1962) recommended that the BBC be awarded a second channel (BBC 2, which opened in 1966). Finding that ITV programming had become too commercial, trivial, and undemanding, the committee proposed stronger regulatory powers and duties for the ITA. The next television act accordingly instructed the Independent Television Authority to ensure a "proper balance and wide range of subject matter having regard both to the programmes as a whole and also to the day of the week on which, and the times of day at which, the programmes are broadcast," as well as "a wide showing of programmes of merit." The ITV companies were also obliged to submit their program schedules for advance approval to the ITA, which could direct the exclusion of any items from them.

In much of the 1960s and early 1970s, a third phase ensued, as hierarchical and consensual ties loosened and traditional institutions were criticized more often in the name of modernization. Broadcasters became concerned to portray the different sectors of a pluralist society realistically in both fictional and factual programs, and to be more probingly critical themselves. For Hugh Greene, BBC director general from 1960 to 1969, public service implied putting an honest mirror before society, reflecting what was there, whether it was "bigotry...and intolerance or accomplishment and inspiring achievement." He also believed broadcasters had a duty to take account of changes in society, the challenges and options such changes posed, and where they might lead. He even regarded impudence as an acceptable broadcasting quality (a far cry from founding father John Reith's stress on dignity). Illustrative of this spirit were hard-hitting satire (*That Was the Week That Was*), anarchic comedy (*Monty Python's Flying Circus*), more forceful political interviewing, series set in northern towns (*Coronation Street, The Likely Lads*), realistic police series (*Z Cars*), social-issue drama (*Cathy Come Home*), and socially conscious comedy (*Till Death Us Do Part,* featuring a Cockney racist, and *Steptoe and Son,* featuring a rag-and-bone man and his son).

In a fourth phase, throughout much of the 1970s, British television increasingly acquired the image of an overmighty subject, attracting unprecedentedly sharp criticism and pressure to mend its ways. On balance, more of the fire was directed at factual than fictional programming. In 1971 politicians of all parties had been outraged by a BBC program about Labour in opposition, *Yesterday's Men,* deploring its flippant tone, lack of openness when interviewees were briefed about the intended approach, and questions put to former Prime Minister Harold Wilson that seemed beyond the pale (e.g., about earnings from his memoirs). Thereafter, the political establishment became more assertive of its interests, more organized in its pursuit and more vocal in its complaints. Spokespersons of other groups also voiced dissatisfaction over stereotypical portrayals and limited access. Traditional moralists (like the members of Mary Whitehouse's Viewers' and Listeners' Association) were deeply unhappy about what they regarded as increasingly permissive depictions of sex and violence in programs. Media sociologists chipped in with a series of studies purporting to undermine the pretensions of broadcasters to impartiality and objectivity, and to demonstrate how news coverage of social conflicts supported the ideological status quo. Other critics perceived a middle-ground convergence in BBC and ITV output that excluded unconventional perspectives and opinions. Behind these otherwise different reactions, there was a shared concern over the difficulties of holding broadcasters to account for their policies and performance.

Structural responses to this chorus of criticism included some tightening of editorial controls; creation by the BBC of a Community Programming Unit to help groups to present their ideas on their own terms in a new strand of access broadcasting; and establishment of a Programme Complaints Board by the BBC to consider complaints against producers of unfair representation and invasions of privacy. The most important outcome, however, was the creation in 1982 of Channel 4 with its brief to be different, experimental, and heterodox. Although commercials would be sold on the channel, pains were taken to avoid competition for advertising with ITV. Channel 4's budget was therefore fixed by the IBA on the basis of funds it levied from the ITV companies, which were allowed to sell (and keep the revenues from) its advertising. Thus, a viable source of funding would be tapped, Channel 4 would be guaranteed sufficient resources for its tasks, and its innovative efforts would be insulated from advertisers' conformist pressures.

Beginning in the mid-1980s, the fifth phase of British television has been dominated by issues of structure and finance, plus probing of the contemporary meaning of public service. This period has witnessed a more interventionist role for government, which apparently has felt obliged to pronounce more often upon wide-ranging policy questions.

The era has hosted two main waves of development. One, up to the mid-1990s (during the Conservative administrations of Margaret Thatcher and John Major), unleashed a tide of radically revisionist commercialism, which effected major changes but was also resisted and curbed at key points. The other (from 1996 to the present) has promoted the development and diffusion of digital terrestrial television, aiming to position the United Kingdom as a "world leader" in this new communications technology.

The curtain-raiser was appointment in 1985 of the Peacock Committee on Financing the BBC to consider alternative sources of revenue to the license fee, including advertising and sponsorship. Its 1986 report condemned the existing system as a cozy and overly "comfortable duopoly," lacking financial disciplines to keep costs down in both the BBC and ITV; it defined the fundamental aim of broadcasting as increasing through competition "the freedom of choice of the consumer and the opportunities available to offer alternative wares to the public"; and it proposed that "public service" in British television be scaled down from a full-blown to a market-supplementing model. Yet the committee also counseled against the sale of commercials by the BBC, since competition for advertising would narrow its range of programming. Although the government accepted this last recommendation, it drew heavily on the committee's rationale for its policies to overhaul British television.

The government acted directly on the advertising-financed sector through three significant features of the 1990 Broadcasting Act. One was the introduction of competition for advertising by requiring Channel 4 to sell its own commercials and authorizing a fifth commercial channel. Another was the new franchising system of auctioning licenses to the highest bidder among qualified applicants. A third was a change in status of the regulator, whereby the new ITC lost the old IBA's broad powers to preview programs and schedules in advance; hereafter it could only enforce company compliance to specific obligations defined in law and licenses after the fact.

Even so, a full-scale commercialism was avoided. Channel 4 was given a safety net, whereby it would be subsidized by the Channel 3 companies should its advertising income fall below 14 percent of the total advertising and sponsorship income of Channels 3 and 4. Also, in a period of intense debate while the act was passing through Parliament, the "quality threshold" for franchise applicants was much strengthened. Companies would have to give a "sufficient amount of time" to a series of mandated programs, including national and regional news, current affairs, religion and children's television; cater to a variety of tastes; and give a "sufficient amount of time" to "programmes that are of high quality." Moreover, the ITC fleshed out some of these requirements in precise quantitative terms, specifying, for example, that companies would have to offer 90 minutes of high-quality current affairs programs weekly, at least two hours of religious programs, and 10 hours a week of children's television, including a range of entertainment, drama, and information.

The government promoted change at the BBC by conveying its expectation of far-reaching reforms, appointing a forceful chair of the Board of Governors (Marmaduke Hussey) who shared its priorities, and implying that the terms of the next BBC Charter (to take effect in 1996) were at stake in the process. Led by directors general Michael Checkland (from 1987) and John Birt (from 1991), the BBC's managerial structure was overhauled. Overheads were cut, axing more than 2,000 jobs. Most important from the government's standpoint were two steps: an internal market (known as Producers' Choice) was introduced in relations between program producers and providers of technical facilities, and an aggressive policy was adopted of BBC entry into international markets of multichannel television, program sales, and coproduction. Nevertheless, the BBC also undertook a fundamental review of the meaning and implications of "public service" in multichannel conditions, the results of which appeared in *Extending Choice* (1992) and *People and Programmes* (1995). Concentrating mainly on future directions and roles, the former proposed three priority purposes: "informing the national debate"; "expressing British culture and entertainment"; and "creating opportunities for education." More attuned to the modern choosy audience member, the latter stressed themes of relevance and accessibility and the need for program makers in all fields to take greater account of popular interests, tastes, and attitudes.

A commitment to promote digital technology was announced in a 1995 White Paper (*Digital Television Broadcasting: The Government's Proposals*) and embodied in the Broadcasting Act of 1996. The presumed advantages of digital technology included massive expansion of channel capacity; improved picture and sound quality; release of analog spectrum for other uses; early entry of British producers into the global market of digital programming; and readier access of British households to the "information society" via interactivity, home shopping, home banking, e-mail, and the Internet. This last advantage appealed especially to the Labour government, which came into power in 1997 under Prime Minister Tony Blair, who set a target of making Internet access available to all Britons wanting it by 2005. The 1996 Act required the ITC to license a multiplex for provision of digital terrestrial television, which it awarded in 1997 to a consortium of the two largest ITV companies under the name of Ondigital (now ITV Digital).

This push for digital television has required fresh policy thinking in three areas. First, how quickly can digital replace analog transmission? Specifying two tests by which the shift to digital would be guided, availability (all receivers of analog television should be able to receive the same channels digitally) and affordability (consumers should not have to face unacceptably large costs), the government hopes that switchover will be possible by no later than 2010.

The second area of policy reevaluation concerns the role and financing of the BBC. In 1998 the Secretary of State for Culture, Media, and Sport declared that public service broadcasting remained essential in the digital age. He defined public service television as neither a niche nor a safety net for that which commercial TV would not deliver, but as a broad approach to programming of interest to the community. It followed that the BBC should maintain its role as a "high quality comprehensive public service broadcaster," with the place of its services being guaranteed on all multichannel systems, "with due prominence." Also, the BBC should develop a portfolio of new digital terrestrial channels, additional to its existing BBC 1 and BBC 2 services, subject to approval by the Secretary of State as conforming to public service criteria.

The BBC's response coincided with the 2000 appointment of Greg Dyke, a former ITV executive with a track record for policies of realistic pragmatism, as director general. Overall, he seeks to ride two policy horses simultaneously: to justify a universally imposed license fee by demonstrating the BBC's programming popularity with the viewing audience and to offer programming sufficiently different from commercial provision to legitimate the BBC's public status.

Five particular aims have characterized Dyke's regime at the BBC: to cut sharply its administrative costs (from 24 percent to 15 percent of its income by 2003), channeling the savings into programming; to compete more vigorously for the mass audience against ITV, especially by scheduling more popular programming on BBC 1 (to clear the way for such shows, BBC 1's half-hour news at 9:00 P.M. was moved to 10:00 P.M.); to press program makers in all genres, particularly news, current affairs, and politics, to address audiences more accessibly; to focus a significant part of the BBC's public service contribution on the large-scale production of so-called landmark factual events (e.g., such series as *Walking with Dinosaurs, Walking with Beasts,* and *The Blue Planet,* and a day-long coverage of the country's National Health Service in February 2002, culminating in an interview with the prime minister); and, finally, to carve out a significant place for the BBC in the multichannel future of digital television.

Pursuit of this last aim has been shaped by the assumption that to appeal to increasingly choosy and diverse audiences, channels must have clear profiles. As digital television diffuses more widely, more singular identities will gradually be sought for the mixed-genre channels of BBC 1 and BBC 2. In addition, the BBC intends to create five new free-to-air digital channels: a 24-hour news service (News 24, already in operation); a channel geared to the tastes of younger audiences (to be named BBC 3); an "unashamedly intellectual" channel, based on the arts, music, ideas, and in-depth discussion (BBC 4); and two daytime channels of children's programming. To finance all this, the government awarded the BBC a uniquely generous increase in the license fee of 1.5 percent above inflation annually until 2006 (rejecting a 1999 proposal by the Davies Committee on the Future Financing of the BBC for owners of digital sets to pay a supplement to the license fee, as likely to deter investment in new sets by consumers).

The third main item on the government's media policy agenda was the regulatory framework. Anticipating greater cross-media convergence via digital technology, the government proposed in its 2000 White Paper (*A New Future for Communications*) a radical overhaul of the regulatory system, which had hitherto relied on separate authorities for specific services. The five existing regulatory agencies (the Independent Television Commission, the Broadcasting Standards Commission, the Radio Authority, the Radio Communications Agency, and the Office for Telecommunications) will be merged into a single body, the Office for Communications (OFCOM)—modeled, some contend, on the U.S. Federal Communications Commission (FCC).

As of early 2002, implementing legislation had not been introduced into Parliament. However, two features of the government's ideas are noteworthy and controversial. One is relaxation of the public service obligations of advertising-financed television. These would be overseen through a system of monitored self-regulation, depending heavily on annual statements by providers of how they intended to realize—and subsequently how they had fulfilled—those obligations. The second feature is retention of the Board of Governors as a separate regulator of the BBC, which would not be placed under OFCOM (although the BBC would possibly be open to sanctions by OFCOM for failure to uphold the corporation's public service remit).

Looking to the Future

British television has thus been extensively revamped since the 1980s. The resulting system is very difficult to define. It conforms neither to classic public-service models nor to a U.S.-style fully commercial paradigm (merely allowing a market-supplementing public sector at the margin). Multichannel expansion plus digitally based new media seem to be spawning new kinds of television systems, which may prove more nationally idiosyncratic than previously.

In early 21st-century Britain, three differences from the past stand out. First, the competition for viewers is far less restrained, and it matters far more than it ever did to all big players in the system. Second, British broadcasting is becoming less closely regulated than it used to be. Third, different programming balances are being struck. For example:

- The early evening soap operas have been conscripted into heavy competitive service, appearing three to five nights a week on BBC 1, ITV, and Channel 4 (instead of only once or twice as in the past).
- Analytic documentaries on social and political issues have largely been displaced by historical, nature, and slice-of-life documentaries, as well as various "docudramas."
- The diversity of children's television has narrowed, with increased reliance on animation, entertainment, and imported programs from the United States.
- Certain "old-fashioned" public-service standbys of arts, current affairs, and religious programming have been moved out of prime-time into late-night, weekend, or minority-channel slots.
- Political programming is continually being reviewed and revised in the cause of popular accessibility.
- Certain program genres, which previously would have been regarded as unacceptable, now flourish, such as quizzes with huge rewards for winners, dating shows, confessional programming (even *Jerry Springer*), and a host of "reality" programs, featuring ordinary people in extraordinary, testing, or sensational situations.

Amid all these developments, the public service tradition remains influential in important ways. First, it continues to operate at the level of "high policy," in the government's commitment to a capacious, community-serving notion of public service and to the BBC as its keystone provider. This was reflected in the appointment in 2001 of Gavyn Davies, a staunch supporter of public service broadcasting, as chairman of the BBC Board of Governors. Second, the BBC demonstrates its commitment to the public service tradition in its decision to extend its public service presence into multichannel and multimedia settings. However, its multichannel portfolio is edging television provision toward a radio model, offering relatively bounded bodies of content to relatively segmented audiences. Third, the BBC, ITV, and Channel 4 continue to invest significant resources in a broad range of programming (including educational television and high-quality news), not concentrating them only on entertainment. Finally, the public service tradition is expressed in the abiding values and sources of creative motivation among many working producers, directors, and writers.

From such evidence, it may be concluded that a serious effort is being made in Britain to adapt public service principles to multichannel expansion, competitive exigencies, and the onset of a more selective, consumer-minded, less-deferential, and more skeptical viewing public. In this sense, British television is straining to be true to its past self.

Nevertheless, the role of "public service" in the British system is being appreciably modified. From an overarching creed that applied across the board of all genres, it has become a more singular one, jostling for influence amid the impact of many other imperatives (such as the need to beat the competition, the need to be accessible, the need to be eye-catching, and the need to be exportable, as well as the need to fill time slots inexpensively with repeats or old movies). From a principle that shaped all channels similarly, the public service concept is being applied more unevenly (less present on the majority channels than on those serving minorities). As a consequence, "diversity," once a core value of British broadcasting, appears destined to become less a vertical and more a horizontal feature as the system evolves in coming years.

JAY G. BLUMLER

Further Reading

Barnett, Steven, and Andrew Curry, *The Battle for the BBC: A British Broadcasting Conspiracy?* London: Aurum Press, 1994

Blumler, Jay G., "The British Approach to Public Service Broadcasting: From Confidence to Uncertainty," *Public Service Broadcasting in a Multichannel Environment,* edited by Robert K. Avery, New York and London: Longman, 1993

Blumler, Jay G., "United Kingdom," in *Television Requires Responsibility,* edited by Bertelsmann Foundation and European Institute for the Media, Gutersloh, Germany: Bertelsmann Foundation Publishers, 1994

Bonner, Paul, *Independent Television in Britain,* vols. 5–6, London: Macmillan, 1998–2002

Born, Georgina, and Prosser, Tony, "Culture and Consumerism: Citizenship, Public Service Broadcasting and the BBC's Fair Trading Obligations," *Modern Law Review* 64, no. 5 (2001)

Briggs, Asa, *The History of Broadcasting in the United Kingdom,* 5 vols., Oxford and New York: Oxford University Press, 1961–95

Briggs, Asa, *Governing the BBC,* London: British Broadcasting Corporation, 1979

Briggs, Asa, *The BBC: The First Fifty Years,* Oxford and New York: Oxford University Press, 1985

Burns, Tom, *The BBC: Public Institution, Private World,* London: Macmillan, 1977

Buscombe, Edward, *British Television: A Reader,* Oxford: Oxford University Press, 2000

Extending Choice: The BBC's Role in the New Broadcasting Age, London: British Broadcasting Corporation, 1992

Franklin, Bob, editor, *British Television Policy: A Reader,* London and New York: Routledge, 2001

Goodwin, Peter, *Television Under the Tories: Broadcasting Policy 1979–1997,* London: British Film Institute, 1998

Hearst, Stephen, "Broadcasting Regulation in Britain," *Television and the Public Interest: Vulnerable Values in West European Broadcasting,* edited by Jay G. Blumler, London: Newbury Park, 1992

Nossiter, T.J., "British Television: A Mixed Economy," *Broadcasting Finance in Transition: A Comparative Handbook,* edited by Jay G. Blumler and T.J. Nossiter, Oxford and New York: Oxford University Press, 1991

Paulu, Burton, *British Broadcasting in Transition,* London: Macmillan, 1961

People and Programmes: BBC Radio and Television for an Age of Choice, London: British Broadcasting Corporation, 1995

Potter, Jeremy, *Independent Television in Britain,* vols. 3–4, London: Macmillan, 1989–90

Scott, Peter Graham, *British Television: An Insider's History,* Jefferson, North Carolina: McFarland, 2000

Sendall, Bernard, *Independent Television in Britain,* vols. 1–2, London: Macmillan, 1982–83

Wilson, H.H., *Pressure Group: The Campaign for Commercial Television,* London: Secker and Warburg, 1961

Official Inquiry Committee Reports

The Sykes Report, Cmnd. 1951, London: His Majesty's Stationery Office: 1923

The Crawford Report, Cmnd. 2599, London: His Majesty's Stationery Office, 1926

The Selsdon Report, Cmnd. 4793, London: His Majesty's Stationery Office, 1935

The Ullswater Report, Cmnd. 5091, London: His Majesty's Stationery Office, 1936

The Beveridge Report, Cmnd. 8116, London: His Majesty's Stationery Office, 1951

The Pilkington Report, Cmnd. 1753, London: Her Majesty's Stationery Office, 1962

The Annan Report, Cmnd. 6753, London: Her Majesty's Stationery Office, 1977

The Peacock Report, Cmnd. 9824, London: Her Majesty's Stationery Office, 1986

Brittain, Donald (1928–1989)

Canadian Documentary Filmmaker

Donald Brittain is well known for his National Film Board documentaries, all shown on Canadian Broadcasting Corporation (CBC) television. In the 1980s, Donald Brittain directed *Running Man,* an early exploration of homosexuality in the CBC's topical anthology *For the Record.* He then created two biographical docudramas: one about mobster and union boss Hal Banks, the two-hour docudrama special *Canada's Sweetheart: The Saga of Hal C. Banks* (1985); the other about Prime Minister William Lyon MacKenzie King, a six-hour miniseries, *The King Chronicles* (1987).

Donald Brittain.
Photo courtesy of National Archives of Canada/CBC Collection

In *Canada's Sweetheart,* Brittain shows us, through the lens of the Seafarers' International Union, the primitive state of labor-management relations in Canada from the late 1940s to early 1960s. In *The King Chronicles,* he explores Canadian political culture from the days following World War I to the wrenching changes in society in the aftermath of World War II. Brittain spells out Canadian complicity in the activities of both men—an imported thug who controlled Great Lakes shipping and a prime minister who, to quote Brittain's narrative, was "a creature who cast no shadow though he ruled the land of the midnight sun."

Canada's Sweetheart incorporated interviews with survivors from those years, stills, newsreels, and dramatization. Brittain uses full color for the dramatized Royal Commission hearings, the interviews with real people, and some of the flashbacks. Black-and-white scenes include Banks's quiet entrance into Canada and his equally surreptitious exit, and union leader Jim Todd's futile challenge to an executive in a packed meeting hall. Some scenes that are particularly violent or menacing are given a specifically film noir treatment.

The film is also quite self-reflexive. Todd recalls how Banks's bully-boys came to his house one night while his wife was in the kitchen. The camera then discloses the hitherto silent Mrs. Todd, who tells us that "Friday is fish and chips night" and that when she heard a commotion she went into the living room with a full pan of boiling fat in her hand. At her firm word "that dinner was ready," the thug left. Her understated telling of the situation is far more effective than a dramatization would be, a strong illustration of what happened when ordinary seamen and lock masters had finally had enough. In another sequence, Jack Pickersgill, a cabinet minister in St. Laurent's government, is filmed with a pet dog in his lap—a nicely ironic touch. He damns himself without knowing it. The episodic narrative then turns into one of the oldest forms of dramatic confrontation—the trial. However, in typically Canadian fashion, the drama ends not with the damning report of the Royal Commission but with Banks slipping out of the country with the implicit cooperation of cabinet ministers.

In *The King Chronicles,* Brittain dramatizes both the public records and the private diaries of Prime Minister King. As with Hal Banks, the public King is represented by news footage intercut with drama, often with ironic effect. For the private life of King (who was discovered, after his death, to have been a spiritualist who talked to his dead mother and his dead dog), Brittain uses recurring, visually lyrical motifs. Less successfully, he also uses grotesque fantasy sequences for King's visions.

The primary focus in each film is on power: how it is used for a variety of purposes, and how it changes the men who use it. Throughout both films, Brittain shows his viewers how Hal Banks and Willie King grappled with the necessity of maintaining an acceptable public face and how they managed to hide both their goals and methods and their eccentric and dangerous private personae.

Of course, he shows us King the manipulator, the obsessively vain and insecure politician, object of a hundred political cartoons, editorials, and sardonic poems. Yet there are enough glimpses of the man's ability to surprise us throughout the miniseries. Maury Chaykin as Banks and Sean McCann as King gave superb performances full of subtextual nuance covering a wide range of emotions. Each actor was physically brilliant in his gestures and body language.

Brittain has said he enjoyed "the tone of someone's voice combined with a certain visual setup against something that went before," an effect achieved in postproduction. Editorial decisions such as splicing are crucial to his work. Brittain includes a sense of scale and of social context, a feel for curious juxtapositions, a sense of ironic detachment and black humor, and what has been called his signature, a "tart historical narrative."

In both these films, Brittain provides almost continuous voice-over, counterpointing the images on the screen with a highly personal interpretation of events.

This ironic inflection of the "voice of god" convention of early National Film Board of Canada documentaries was intended to signify an objective, omniscient perspective. These two films also stand within a tradition of docudrama at the CBC, one that included the very controversial modern adaptation of the Easter story told in the style of direct cinema, *The Open Grave* (1964), as well as massive 1970s projects such as the six-hour *The National Dream* and the critical look at Canada's *October Crisis.* Brittain was one of the few who used television to tell memorable tales that redefined the life and times of the viewers.

MARY JANE MILLER

Donald Brittain. Born in Ottawa, Ontario, in 1928. Attended Queen's University, Kingston, Ontario. Journalist for the *Ottawa Journal;* member, National Film Board of Canada, 1954–68; worked for the Fuji Group, Japan, 1968; independent producer, from 1970; director, producer, and writer of theatrical and TV films of documentary and dramatic nature. Recipient: 15 Genie and CFA awards; ACTRA Awards, 1981 and 1983; two Geminis, 1985 and 1986. Died in Montreal, Quebec, September 11, 1989.

Films and Made-for-Television Movies (selected; as writer, director, and producer)

1963 *Bethune* (writer and coproducer)
1965 *Ladies and Gentlemen... Mr. Leonard Cohen* (writer and codirector)
1975 *His Worship, Mr. Montréal*
1976 *Henry Ford's America*
1978 *The Dionne Quintuplets* (director and producer)
1979 *Paperland: The Bureaucrat Observed*
1981 *The Most Dangerous Spy*
1981 *A Blanket of Ice*
1983 *The Accident* (director)
1983 *Something to Celebrate*
1984 *The Children's Crusade*
1985 *Canada's Sweetheart: The Saga of Hal C. Banks*
1986 *The Final Battle* (also narrator)
1987 *The King Chronicles*
1988 *Family: A Loving Look at CBC Radio*
1991 *Brittain on Brittain*

Further Reading

Boone, Mike, "Great Brittain: Witness Series Focuses on Documentary Film Genius," *Montreal Gazette* (December 12, 1992)
"Donald Brittain: Green Stripe and Common Sense," *Canadian Film Reader,* edited by Seth Feldman and Joyce Nelson, Toronto: Peter Martin, 1977
Dwyer, Victor, "A Fond Farewell: Donald Brittain's Last Film Eyes CBC Radio," *Maclean's* (June 10, 1991)
Johnson, Brian D., "A Chronicler for a Nation *(The King Chronicles),*" *Maclean's* (March 28, 1988)
Kolomeychuk, Terry, editor, *Brittain: Never the Ordinary Way,* Toronto: National Film Board Publication, 1990

Broadband

Broadband refers to any high-capacity communications network capable of sustaining multiple independent channels for the simultaneous transmission of voice, data, and video signals. At present, the U.S. Federal Communications Commission defines broadband as a service with a two-way carrying capacity exceeding 200 kilobits per second (commercial ultra-high-speed networks have the carrying capacity of 100 megabits per second). Most media consumers today, however, associate broadband technology with the high-speed Internet connectivity offered through traditional copper telephone lines (via digital subscriber line [DSL] service), cable (both wired and wireless), satellite, and other wireless platforms. Broadband is significantly faster than the conventional "narrowband" Internet access obtained through the dialup modem, which currently offers transmission speeds up to 56 kilobits per second. Narrowband continues to function as a medium for the transmission of noninteractive text (affectionately known as "brochureware") and audio content, hence the tremendous popularity of Internet "radio." However, with its increased carrying capacity and access speeds, broadband is more capable of handling the complex mix of audio and visual data traditionally associated with the everyday television experience. In addition, because of the bidirectional capacity of broadband networks, media programming can acquire the kind of personal customization hitherto unavailable to the home television viewer. The sheer "girth" of broadband's pipeline—its

Courtesy of Comcast

high speed and prodigious carrying capacity—opens up possibilities for the transmission of multichannel digital programming, as well as new interactive media forms resulting from the convergence of the television and the personal computer.

The creation of hybrid multimedia content makes sense for the television industries in an age of competing media forms. The convergence of television and PC technologies, with the attendant promises of interactivity, has spurred the development of multimedia programming, particularly in statistics-heavy categories such as news, sports, and financial investment. Many major television and cable news networks around the world have a strong presence on the web, using streaming video and complementary programming to extend their brand recognition. Television network websites are increasingly designed as portals into a more general online experience, offering program guides, search engines, stock quotes, news, sports, and interactive game, chat, and e-mail functions. In addition, broadband offers multiple venues for existing programming content, whether a single program is broadcast across multiple outlets from television to the Internet or whether it is "repurposed" for online interactive engagement. Through the use of set-top boxes and various subscription schemes, the television viewer gains access to an array of additional programming services that build upon and enhance the primary broadcast. At the same time, there is a significant opportunity for the development of original programming for broadband distribution, including "parallel programming" that spins off from original broadcast content, and original programming like animated short films or the increasingly popular web soaps and reality-based webcam programs. Internet game shows, spun off from TV standards such as *Wheel of Fortune* and *Jeopardy,* take advantage of "incomplete content," where the user is prompted to fill in missing content such as the answer to a question. Here, the traditional back-and-forth of the game show (which dictates the textual parameters of the established television genre) can be maintained in a familiar, demarcated form of interactivity. At the same time, a company like Sony (which owns both game shows) can enter into alliances with interactive television companies to produce set-top boxes designed to facilitate game interaction. While it offers possibilities for engagement with broader forms of electronic commerce—including video-on-demand, gambling, and multiplayer interactive gaming—broadband technology also affords the creation of new digital formats for television.

Programming designed for broadband delivery blurs traditional generic distinctions between the web page, the newspaper, and the television program. At the same time, because broadband operates at the effective conjuncture of the telephone, cable television and satellite, and computer software and hardware industries, its technology permeates traditional industrial boundaries. With business models garnered from a number of communication technologies—including traditional telephony service, pay television, Internet service providers, and hardware and software development—broadband involves the synergy of a vast array of network services. Not surprisingly, cable companies that also provide consumer broadband access are now developing set-top boxes, which bundle a number of these services together, providing digital video, high-speed data and Internet connectivity and, most recently, cable residential telephony.

Television broadcasters in many Western countries are updating to digital transmission (in the United States, they are mandated by law to do so). However, advertisers, broadcasting's traditional source of revenue, are unwilling to subsidize the cost of modernization by paying higher rates. Instead, media corporations have focused on developing a "walled garden" of proprietary content with access based on subscription services, contributing to the gradual erosion of free-to-air broadcasting on a large scale. The commercial control of delivery conduits is the most crucial issue here, and content industries (like film and television studios) have entered into mergers with companies that have access to the pipelines of digital delivery. Coupling programming and delivery under the same corporate umbrella, so the commercial logic goes, subsidizes the unending task of technology development by using content that has already been tested in another media. The massive technological investment in broadband infrastructure is therefore supported by the use of established content providers in order to minimize risk and maximize subscriptions.

The worldwide climate of industrial deregulation, which allows for cross-ownership and vertical integration, has facilitated the "merger mania" that dominates the media trade today. For example, the merger of America Online (AOL) and Time Warner attests to the powerful presence of vertically integrated new media firms, merging AOL's Internet portal services with access to both original content and Time Warner's extensive library of programming. AOL Time Warner also has an exclusive contract with RoadRunner, the second largest provider of residential broadband service in the United States. While broadband platforms for content distribution and exhibition might offer independent producers greater opportunities to showcase their product, smaller production companies have no way to deal with the tremendous leveraging power available to the newly merged new media conglomerate. In addition, the gradual shifting of the computer industry away from hardware manufacture and software development, and toward Internet service provider and multimedia content developer, is indicative of the synergistic logic of commercialized new media. In 1997, for example, Microsoft acquired a significant stake in Comcast, the third largest cable system operator in the United States. The same year, Microsoft also purchased the WebTV networks, a move clearly designed to bolster the penetration of web-based services into non-PC equipped households by providing Internet access to ordinary television sets via preexisting telephone connections.

Traditional television broadcasters in the United States and other countries have often viewed the streaming of television signals over computer networks with considerable skepticism, lobbying against the adoption of technological standards to make convergence a practical reality. Nevertheless, many in the industrial and regulatory community agree that a combination of compelling multimedia content and high-speed data connectivity will drive broadband subscriptions (many broadband developers insist that it is easier to design information services rather than produce entertainment programs). While the traditional television industries' ambivalent relationship to distributing over broadband networks is partly a function of intellectual property concerns, the Internet is increasingly important as a programming venue, especially when enabled by broadband connectivity. For the first time, Internet rights were negotiated separately from broadcast rights for the 2004 Olympics, which testifies to their centrality in the new media landscape.

The Internet is simultaneously a transmitter technology and a delivery conduit, an exhibition and point-of-purchase site, a distribution philosophy, a content gathering and talent differentiating device, an advertising platform, and a globally linked network of copying machines. These multiple (and sometimes divergent) forms of address signal the array of possibilities that the Internet makes available to the traditional television industries. Even the single act of viewing either parallel or repurposed programming can attach a number of different profitable schemes for the television industry: from being a sale (the Internet as a point-of-purchase), to a broadcast (the Internet as transmitter technology), to a mechanical copy (the Internet as a copy clearance center) (see Mann, 2000). It is inevitable that the television networks will become even more interested in the "value-added" opportunities afforded by the Internet. Television and cable broadcasters can take advantage of a number of opportunities from the positioning of content delivered via broadband networks: tracking services (providing instant audience feedback and consumer mining capability), information management tools like electronic programming guides (EPGs), video-on-demand (built from preexisting audiovisual libraries), and personal video recording services (like TiVo). As digital television continues to fragment audiences in the multichannel environment, electronic program guides and other navigation aids become crucial sites for the recruitment and influence of audience preference.

However, the possibilities for ownership abuse are clear, and telecommunications regulators in Europe are on the watch for equal access to EPGs and other "conditional access" systems. Indeed, for all the techno-futurist proclamations of radical technological and programming possibility, broadband invites the perennial issues that have accompanied the emergence of communications networks from the telegraph to the cable television: intellectual property, technological standards (particularly compression standards and backward compatibility), content regulation, and regulatory issues around the preservation of the public access versus the commercial logic of media ownership and delivery. Government intervention in the administration of broadband service is commonplace around the world, including the production of cultural heritage content for Canadian new media, the European Union's extension of "must carry" rules requiring that digital cable and satellite operators reserve space for consumers to access public service broadcasting, and calls for the Australian government's support of subsidies for universal broadband access and the facilitation of export opportunity.

Of course, any export of new media technology takes place on a terrain defined by uneven development on a global scale. Certainly, world PC sales were estimated at well over 80 million units in 1997, approaching the 120 million color TV sets sold the same year. Yet, of over 3.5 million homes with broadband connection worldwide in early 2000, over 2.5 million were in the United States, 500,000 in the Asia Pacific region, 340,000 in Western Europe (concentrated in the Netherlands and Austria), and 25,000 in Latin America. New research suggests that broadband users in the United States will surpass dialup users by

2007, with numbers growing from 10.8 million broadband users in 2001 to 41.7 million in 2007. Although 45 million U.S. households were online with dialup connections at the turn of the 21st century, with less than 5 million possessing either DSL or cable modem hookup, an estimated half of American television households were broadband-ready by mid-2004. Korea has the highest broadband penetration in the world, at around 10 percent, with adult entertainment and gaming offering the most common programming choices. Canada ranks second in broadband connectivity.

At the same time, there are tremendous and systemic inequalities in basic telecommunications access. For example, Africa is home to 12 percent of the world's population, but has only 2 percent of its telephone lines, and telephone penetration in India is .7 per 1,000 people. Clearly, there is a need for installation of noncommercial and nonhierarchical community infrastructures, the continued use of narrowband technologies that power tactical media networks and free and open-source software movements around the world, and even the social benefits of pirated hardware and software technologies (see Sundaram, 2000).

Convergence technologies are nothing new in the history of television. Television pictures were sent over telephone wires as early as 1927, and fiber optic technology has existed since the 1950s. By the mid-1990s, low-resolution video became available to dial-up modem users using new video software. Now, compressed audiovisual (AV) data could be sent from an encoding site (e.g., an Internet server) to the consumer in real-time in buffered form. In this way, AV data can be played before the entire file is received, a close approximation of the traditional broadcasting experience. Rather than waiting for enormous files to be fully downloaded, the PC user equipped with the proper decoding software can now interact with the media as it "streams" onto their desktop, with enough material stored in a temporary buffer to allow smooth playback.

With broadband's capacity for greater data transmission rates, the corporate owners of intellectual property are also fond of the streaming format, since it does not involve the downloading of the full file onto a consumer's computer, which would make it more susceptible to piracy and retransmission. The fidelity and inexhaustible reproductive quality of the digital image have pushed the commercial media into a lobbying frenzy for the circumscription of viewer's rights, especially the strict maintenance of the bar between creators and users of new media. However, the televisual future of broadband will be defined by three interrelated factors that have traditionally shaped the private consumption of image media: quality, cost, and malleability. This means that all the familiar issues are still in play: the development of genres and programming forms suited to the emergent technology and the fidelity of the transmitted image; the price of procuring the image, including transmission speed and the carrying capacity of its network; and, most importantly, the options available for the consumer to engage the image across a variety of delivery platforms and viewing occasions.

NITIN GOVIL

See also **Mergers and Acquisitions; Streaming; Time Warner**

Further Reading

"A Citizen's Guide to Broadband," Center for Digital Democracy, 2002, available online at www.democraticmedia.org

Anderson, Lessley, and Jason Krause, "I'll Take Broadband for $200, Alex," *Industry Standard* (July 1, 1999)

Benner, Jeffrey, "Getting the Lock on Broadband" 2002, available at www.salon.com/tech/feature/2002/06/07/broadband/index.html

Brinkley, Joel, *Defining Vision: The Battle for the Future of Television,* New York: Harcourt Brace, 1997

Burgelman, Jean-Claude, "Regulating Access in the Information Society: The Need for Rethinking Public and Universal Service," *New Media and Society,* 2, no. 1 (2000)

Castells, Manuel, *The Rise of the Network Society,* Oxford: Blackwell, 1996

Filling the Pipe: Stimulating Canada's Broadband Content Industry through R&D, CANARIE/Delvinia, 2001, available online at www.canarie.ca/press/publications/pdf/broadband_report.pdf

Jacka, Marion, *Broadband Media in Australia—Tales from the Frontier,* Australian Film Commission, 2001, available online at www.afc.gov.au/resources/online/pdfs/broadband.pdf

Mann, Charles C., "The Heavenly Jukebox: Efforts To Obtain Control Access to Sound Recordings from the Internet," *Atlantic Monthly* (September 1, 2000)

Papathanassopoulos, Stylianos, *European Television in the Digital Age,* Cambridge: Polity Press, 2002

Schiller, Dan, *Digital Capitalism: Networking the Global Market System,* Cambridge, Massachusetts: MIT Press, 1999

Spá, Miquel de Moregas, Carmelo Garitaonandía, and Bernat López, editors, *Television on Your Doorstep: Decentralization Experiences in the European Union,* Luton: University of Luton Press, 1999

"Special Report: New Media," *Television Business International* (October 2000)

Streeter, Thomas, "Notes Towards a Political History of the Internet 1950–1983," *Media International Australia Incorporating Culture and Policy,* No. 95 (2000)

Sundaram, Ravi, "Beyond the Nationalist Panopticon: The Experience of Cyberpublics in India," *Electronic Media and Technoculture,* edited by John T. Caldwell, New Brunswick, New Jersey: Rutgers University Press, 2000

Van Tessel, Joan, *Digital TV Over Broadband: Harvesting Bandwidth,* Boston: Focal Press, 2001

Broadcasting

Broadcasting is a means of distributing audio- and video-based information and entertainment to large audiences through systems that rely at least in part on the electromagnetic spectrum. Although cablecasting, satcasting (satellite broadcasting), narrowcasting, and other competing terms have been used over the years as alternative multichannel distribution technologies emerged, broadcasting remains a generally accepted expression for the process of transmitting sound and images from a centralized point for mass consumption.

Despite the encroachment of cable and satellite, owners of terrestrial broadcast stations remain a powerful force in the radio and television industries. By 2000 almost 80 percent of households in the United States subscribed to cable or satellite television, but broadcast stations are still highly valued commodities in a media marketplace defined by station ownership groups and media conglomerates. As of 2002, there were 1,712 broadcast television stations and 13,296 radio stations in the United States. These stations have been the focus of intense rounds of merger and consolidation struggles since the mid-1980s. Broadcasting has arguably maintained an even more dominant role in the United Kingdom, where five national public-service and commercial channels are distributed by terrestrial broadcast, supplemented by a relatively weak cable television industry (with 30 percent penetration), a more robust satellite broadcast sector, and a growing presence for digital multichannel broadcasting.

In the U.S. and U.K. contexts alike, the continued strength of terrestrial broadcast is largely the result of its ability to attract a mass audience more effectively than other means. Federal policies have ensured this advantage by requiring all cable and satellite systems to carry local broadcast channels, thereby giving broadcast-based national networks a higher "cumulative," or potential, audience than any single cable channel, which may not be featured on all cable systems. The cumulative audience for the NBC television network, for example, was 81 percent of U.S. television households in 2000; this large audience is an expression of NBC's combined reach as a broadcast and cable network. By contrast, one of the highest-rated cable networks, TBS Superstation, could be seen in only 43 percent of U.S. households in that year. These differences in reach are one basis for the contemporary distinction between broadcasting and narrowcasting; still, since even a low-rated cable network attracts a national audience in the hundreds of thousands, the qualifiers "narrow" and "broad" should be taken as the relative terms they are. As a history of the term "broadcasting" further reveals, it is a complicated concept not fully explained by the generally accepted technological and industrial definitions.

Invention

Not long after Guglielmo Marconi developed his wireless telegraph system in 1896, the term "broadcasting" entered the language. The U.S. Navy, an early adopter of Marconi's wireless, popularized the term as the method by which it sent instructions to ships at sea, "broadcasting" orders across miles of open ocean to the entire fleet at once. The expression was borrowed from agriculture, after a method of sowing seeds in which farmers walked their fields throwing—or casting—seed over a large area with wide sweeps of the arm. It neatly captured the nature of wireless signaling, wherein an antenna sends signals in all directions, enabling instantaneous communication over long distances.

The promiscuous nature of the broadcast signal was a problem, though, for those who wanted to use the wireless for its commercial, public safety, or military applications. Security, privacy, and reliability are highly valued by businesspeople, public safety officials, and military strategists, but wireless offered none of these in its early incarnations. These failings were exacerbated when a new group of wireless users emerged: the amateurs. Using cheaply made crystal set detectors, wireless hobbyists constructed transmitters and began communicating informally with each other, creating a social network of listeners and talkers that was the forerunner of today's ham radio. Amateurs eavesdropped on official communications and some broadcast their own signals to "jam" the original senders' messages and promulgate hoaxes. Although disorganized and only loosely institutionalized by wireless clubs and the like, this subculture prefigured radio and television in important ways by using broadcasting, as Susan Douglas has written, "not by necessity, but for fun."

The need to reduce interference and establish rules for using "the ether" led to the first government regulation of wireless, the Radio Act of 1912. World War I (1917–19) interrupted the public uses of radio in the United States, but within a year of the end of hostilities a convergence of popular interest, cheap and readily available radio equipment, and institutional promotion led to the "broadcast boom" of 1920–22. Hundreds of radio stations went on the air with regular program schedules in this period. The most famous of these, KDKA, was funded by Westinghouse Corporation, an electric equipment manufacturer, and operated by Frank Conrad, a war veteran, Westinghouse engineer, and avid radio amateur.

Following the "broadcast boom," broadcasters struggled to find a means to finance regular radio service. Early broadcasting was characterized by the diversity of its practitioners, which included churches, municipalities, educational institutions, small businesses, large industrial concerns, and many others. Within a few years, though, many found the high costs of maintaining radio equipment, hiring a staff, and paying for radio content to be prohibitive. American Telephone and Telegraph (AT&T) found an early solution in "toll broadcasting," charging all comers for time on its stations, and this scheme quickly demonstrated radio's potential as a mass marketer. Soon the expanding advertising and marketing industry, led by firms such as J. Walter Thompson and N.W. Ayer, joined emerging broadcasters in exploiting the AT&T solution. This marked the beginning of the so-called "American model" of broadcasting, an advertiser-supported system in which networks and stations provided listeners with free content while selling commercial time to advertising agencies and sponsors. In other nations broadcasting was typically organized to allow a larger role for government agencies. Many European nations adopted the "public service model" wherein semi-independent or independent broadcasting agencies (such as the British Broadcasting Corporation) were funded by fees or taxes paid by the public. In contrast with the U.S. and public service models, nations with authoritarian governments often took firm control of broadcasting in this era, in some cases discouraging broadcasting within their borders entirely.

In the United States, the Radio Corporation of America (RCA), General Electric, and the Westinghouse Corporation created two advertiser-supported radio networks in 1926 and 1927 under the banner of the National Broadcasting Company (NBC-Red and NBC-Blue). A competing network, the Columbia Broadcasting System (CBS) was formed in 1927. The Radio Act of 1927 and its successor, the Communications Act of 1934, codified the American model of broadcasting and created the Federal Communications Commission (FCC), the government agency that still regulates broadcasting. The FCC forced RCA to sell NBC-Blue in 1943, and the network was renamed the American Broadcasting Corporation (ABC). Each of these radio networks would successfully make the transition to television after World War II.

Television Broadcasting

Inventors and corporate laboratories pursued a method of television broadcasting through the 1920s and 1930s, resulting in numerous competing and incompatible systems. In 1938 inventor Allen B. DuMont founded the DuMont network to compete with NBC's and CBS's nascent television operations. The DuMont television network had difficulty competing with the better established networks and went out of business in 1955. NBC unveiled its system with a historic telecast of President Franklin D. Roosevelt opening the New York World's Fair in 1939. World War II interrupted the networks' plans for the introduction of television, but 1940 to 1952 was nonetheless a crucial period in the technological and institutional development of broadcast television. The National Television System Committee (1940) was founded to resolve competing technological standards, and the FCC produced numerous decisions that shaped the future television industry. For instance, the FCC suddenly stopped issuing television licenses from 1948 to 1952 to resolve persistent signal interference problems, among other issues. At the time of the so-called television freeze, 106 television stations had been licensed around the country and, although impeded considerably, the industry did not halt its development. Indeed, television underwent what Erik Barnouw called a crucial "laboratory period" in the freeze years, during which NBC and CBS solidified their advantage in the field of broadcasting and networks and stations experimented with adapting radio's staple genres—variety, situation comedy, and drama—to the new medium.

Rise of the Network Era

When the FCC's *Sixth Report and Order* lifted the freeze in 1952, television quickly became a phenomenal success. The percentage of U.S. households with televisions rose from less than 1 percent in 1948, to 9 percent in 1950, to 87 percent by 1960, and in the process created what William Boddy has called "the world's largest advertising medium." By the end of the 1950s, the three broadcast networks dominated the television industry and, arguably, reshaped the economics and aesthetics of the film, radio, and music industries as well. The networks commanded about half of television's total revenues after 1953, using their profitability and powerful influence on popular culture to assume a commanding position in American culture and the entertainment economy for the next three decades.

For critics, programming in the network era represented the best and worst of television. Critics hailed live and telefilm dramas, public affairs programming, and comedies such as *I Love Lucy* and *All in the Family.* However, they assailed game shows, soap operas, and violent action thrillers such as *The Untouchables* and sensational made-for-TV movies. The astonishing omnipresence of the medium troubled many, and the critics asked, as they had with radio before: Does television reflect society, or does society reflect television? As network programmers converged on the "Least Objectionable Programming" strategies of the 1960s, Newton Minow famously called the television schedule a "vast wasteland." Minow and others cited Edward R. Murrow's unflinching social critiques on *CBS Reports* as the model for quality television. Yet this was also the period of inspired weirdness in the *Twilight Zone,* crime dramas with the trashy glamour of *77 Sunset Strip* and the downtown cool of *Peter Gunn,* peripatetic Americana along *Route 66,* and law and order melodrama on *Gunsmoke.* A great deal of television programming was uninteresting, or worse. Still, as many critics have noted, the relentless invention and reinvention of television programming through the years of network dominance in the 1950s, 1960s, and 1970s only underscored the medium's seeming imperviousness to definitive conclusions about its social significance.

Contemporary Television

Prior to 1980 the television sets that had come to occupy 98 percent of U.S. households could be seen as mere extensions of the broadcast networks. The "big three" distributed nearly all of the programming, news, and commercial announcements seen on television. In the late 1970s, television began a profound transformation. Cable networks offered original programming and drew more subscribers. Independent television stations proliferated. People began to use their televisions differently, as monitors for video game consoles and videocassette recorders (VCRs). In 1986 Australian media mogul Rupert Murdoch launched FOX, a fourth broadcast television network. The WB and United Paramount Network followed in 1995. As new sources of programming and new uses for the television set multiplied, the economic power of broadcast networks eroded and they were swept up in the waves of consolidation that dramatically reconfigured the media industries between 1985 and 2000.

The multiplication of channels and networks has resulted in a new conception of the television audience. Cable networks such as Lifetime, Nickelodeon, and Spike increasingly attempt to create brand identities to better market themselves to niche audiences, and appeals to particular demographics have become a key element in programming strategies. For some observers, the fragmentation of the audience resulting from these changes is an alarming development that threatens to exacerbate social conflict in populations already divided by race, class, gender, and generational difference. Others see the multiplication of stories and characters on television as a fitting expression of modern, pluralistic society, one long-denied by the technological and economic limitations of the three-channel broadcast universe. Still other critics are more equivocal about the effects of such fragmentation, suggesting that television, even as it splinters, will do no better or worse than it ever has at reflecting the concerns and controversies of its national audiences.

Terrestrial broadcast may no longer be the dominant technological means of distributing television, but the advertiser-supported economic basis of television has remained largely the same. Cable and satellite companies have benefited from their ability to collect revenue through both subscription and advertising, and other business models have emerged over the years, such as those that underlie premium cable and pay-per-view events. New business models will develop to account for technologies such as personal video recorders and video-on-demand. Nonetheless, the advertiser-supported model continues to finance the vast majority of television in the United States, whether it is seen on broadcast, cable, or satellite. Since the Independent Television Authority (ITV) was established in the United Kingdom in 1955, commercial television has become increasingly prominent in that nation, and has been adopted in many other nations as well.

The continued presence of the commercial model links the early days of broadcasting with today's multichannel universe. Today, even as programming and the audience seemingly fragment into hundreds of niches, most channels still interrupt programming periodically to hail the audience from the marketplace. Advertising on television generated $54 billion in revenue in the United States alone in 2002, compared with $44 billion in newspaper advertising and $18 billion in radio. The consumerist "evangelism" of television, as David Marc has called it, is neither the whole of television's message nor an insignificant aspect of that message. However, it may represent our best contemporary definition of broadcasting, one that avoids the simplicities of the technological definition. That is, the broadcast media today are any that cast a signal for maximum dispersion to permit sponsors to better sell their wares and spread their ideas.

From terrestrial broadcast's heyday as the dominant entertainment medium, to the complex mix of broadcast, cable, and satellite in today's industry, broadcast television has remained the most widely viewed form of television. The persistence of broadcasting helps explain programmer's continuing search, in an age of supposed specialization, for television programs with broad popular appeal such as *Survivor, Law and Order,* and *Friends.* Even in nations where the public service model remains influential, the significance of reaching a broad audience still plays a role in programming decisions, due, at least in part, to institutional mandates to represent the public and its diversity of perspectives rather than, as in the U.S. model, responding to the marketplace and a range of consumer products. Audiences may never again rival the masses assembled by programs such as *I Love Lucy* or *Gunsmoke,* but in many ways the creators and managers of television still imagine it as a broadcast medium and its viewers as a mass audience.

CHRIS LUCAS

See also **American Broadcasting Company; Columbia Broadcasting System; Narrowcasting; National Broadcasting Company**

Further Reading

Anderson, Chris, *Hollywood TV: The Studio System in the Fifties,* Austin: University of Texas Press, 1994

Balio, Tino, *Hollywood in the Age of Television,* Boston: Unwin Hyman, 1990

Barnouw, Erik, *Tube of Plenty: The Evolution of American Television,* 3rd edition, New York: Oxford University Press, 1990

Bergreen, Laurence, *Look Now, Pay Later: The Rise of Network Broadcasting,* Garden City, New York: Doubleday, 1980

Boddy, William, *Fifties Television: The Industry and Its Critics,* Urbana: University of Illinois Press, 1990

Browne, Nick, *American Television: New Directions in History and Theory,* London: Routledge, 1993

Douglas, Susan, *Inventing American Broadcasting: 1899–1922,* Baltimore: John Hopkins University Press, 1987

Hilmes, Michele, *Hollywood and Broadcasting: From Radio to Cable,* Urbana: University of Illinois Press, 1990

Hood, Stuart, and Thalia Tabary-Peterssen, *On Television,* Chicago: Pluto Press, 1997

Marc, David, *Demographic Vistas: Television in American Culture,* revised edition, Philadelphia: University of Pennsylvania Press, 1984

Newcomb, Horace, *TV: The Most Popular Art,* Garden City, New York: Anchor Books, 1974

Smulyan, Susan, *Selling Radio: The Commercialization of American Broadcasting, 1920–1934,* Washington, D.C.: Smithsonian Institution Press, 1994

Walker, James, and Douglas Ferguson, *The Broadcast Television Industry,* Boston: Allyn and Bacon, 1998

Broadcasting Standards Commission

British Regulatory Commission

Television has been described as a battleground for rival sets of moral perspectives and disputed assessments of the medium's power to influence its audiences. It enters the home, may trade in vivid and unexpected images, and appeals greatly to children. It presents both reassuring and disturbing impressions of values and behaviors prevalent in society. The propriety of its program standards is therefore continually debated in many countries.

In Britain the government responded to perceived public concerns of this kind by establishing a Broadcasting Standards Council, on a prestatutory basis in 1988 and as a statutory body under the Broadcasting Act of 1990. Its remit covered the portrayal in television and radio programs and in advertising of violence, sexual conduct, and matters of taste and decency. This was broadened when the Broadcasting Act of 1996 merged the Council with a Broadcasting Complaints Commission, which, since its statutory establishment in 1982, had considered complaints arising from alleged unfairness toward people appearing in or dealt with in programs, or from alleged invasions of privacy. The new body was called the Broadcasting Standards Commission (BSC).

The Broadcasting Act of 1996 confers three main tasks on the BSC: (1) to draw up, and from time to time review, codes giving guidance on the principles to be observed, and practices to be followed, relating to standards, fairness, and privacy, which it is the duty of all broadcasting organizations and other regulatory bodies to "reflect" (not adopt) in their own codes and program guidelines; the most recent version of the commission's codes was published in 1998; (2) to consider and adjudicate upon complaints about programs for violation of the principles concerned; (3) to monitor programs, commission research, and issue reports in the areas of its remit.

The BSC is not an instrument of censorship, for it has no authority to consider programs before transmission. Since its findings are essentially subjective judgments (not determinations of fact within a framework of law), neither is it a judicial body. Any viewer or listener may make a complaint about the portrayal of violence, sex, or other issues of taste and decency (including bad language), but only those individuals with a direct interest in a broadcast may complain of unfair treatment or an unwarranted invasion of privacy. For the latter, the commissioners always study written exchanges of evidence and may hold a hearing with both the complainant and broadcaster present.

The BSC's powers are relatively limited. It may require broadcasters to supply tapes of programs and statements in response to complaints about them. It publishes its findings in a monthly Complaints Bulletin (which is widely reported in the press), and in serious cases it may require the offending broadcaster to do so on air or in print as well. The BSC is made up of 13 members, including a chair and deputy chair, appointed by the Secretary of State for Culture, Media, and Sport. It is served by a staff of 21 full-time posts, including a director, deputy director, and research director, and had a budget of £1.9 million in 2000–01.

The Broadcasting Standards Commission's role and approach may be summarized in five features. First, its remit is more wide-ranging than might be supposed. Although its Codes of Guidance cover the main areas of violence, sexuality, bad language, fairness, and privacy, they also deal with the stereotyping of women, men, the elderly, and ethnic minorities; disparaging treatments of the disabled and mentally ill; depictions of death, grief, bereavement, suicide, and disasters; and responsible presentations of alcohol, drugs, and smoking.

Second, the BSC's "philosophy" of standards is not one-sidedly illiberal. It aims to balance the claims of creativity, investigative journalism, and explorations of contemporary reality against those of respect for audience sensitivities.

Third, the commission does not apply the simple precepts of a black-and-white morality. Its Codes of Guidance read more like standards for editorial responsibility than a set of proscriptions. Very little is ruled out per se, and most code provisions and complaints findings are couched in a spirit of context-sensitivity. Conditioning factors when standards are at issue may include the channel and the time of scheduling, the program genre and viewers' expectations about what works in that genre tend to present, likely audience composition at the time of broadcast, whether advance warnings of sensitive material have been given, and the role of such material in the overall flow of the story or report. Among the contextual influences, much weight is given to a 9:00 P.M. "watershed," before which nothing that is unsuitable for children should be shown and after which it is acceptable to move to a more adult type of material. But even after 9:00 P.M., carte blanche is not envisaged, and broadcasters are expected to move only gradually into more challenging waters. The main conditioning factor when an infringement of privacy is considered is whether such an invasion was justified by an overriding public interest in disclosure of the information concerned.

Fourth, although the BSC has had to deal with an increasing volume of complaints (rising in the case of standards from 512 in 1990–91 to 1,473 in 1993–94; 2,032 in 1994–95; and 3,123 in 2000–01, plus 80 complaints in that last year about fairness and privacy), its approach has not been draconian. In 2000–01, for example, 21 percent of fairness and privacy complaints and only 10 percent of standards complaints were upheld (compared with about 20 percent in the mid-1990s).

Fifth, aware that community standards are not fixed, the Broadcasting Standards Commission has largely based its work on an understanding of the broad limits and tolerances of British public opinion, including how these are evolving. To that end, it consulted a large number of organizations when drawing up its Codes of Guidance. Its members periodically travel on "road shows" to meet diverse groups in different parts of the country, exchanging views on broadcasting standards. Above all, it has commissioned and published the results of a great deal of high-quality, often-cited, and well-regarded research.

This research has included broad surveys over time of both program content and audience attitudes in the key remit areas. The results have drawn attention to the diversity of public opinion about the boundaries between acceptable and unacceptable treatments of violence, sex, and other matters and have done justice to the complexity of people's views. This has supported the commission's emphasis on "context" when dealing with complaints. Other projects have included a review of research findings on violence and pornography effects; an inquiry into the future of children's television; an international review of approaches to media education; a study of delinquents' media-use patterns; in-depth studies of interpretations of screened violence by women, men, and victims of actual violence, the portrayal of ethnic minorities, perspectives on the portrayal of disabilities by both disabled and able-bodied viewers, and public attitudes to broadcasting regulation; as well as a several-sided examination of how the producers of "reality" programs and talk shows secure consent from and treat "ordinary" members of the public appearing in them. In recent years, much of the BSC's research has been cosponsored with other regulators, including a large-scale investigation of children's uses of the television screen in the new media environment. It also commissioned an independent analysis of the representativeness of those who submit complaints to it, suggesting that the complainants came from a relatively broad spectrum of the audience.

In its early days, critics objected to the role of this body on one of three grounds: for inducing caution among broadcasters; for imposing "fuddy-duddy" restrictions on a medium of expanding diversity and choice; and for a confusing overlap of jurisdiction with other regulators, particularly the Independent Television Commission (ITC), which has its own codes and procedures for handling complaints. The first two objections are rarely voiced nowadays, however, and the third will be met when both the BSC and the ITC are incorporated into the government's proposed new, integrated broadcasting and communications regulator, Office for Communications (OFCOM), along with the other three regulatory bodies (Oftel, the Radio Authority, and the Radiocommunications Agency). OFCOM was scheduled to be operational by the end of 2003.

JAY G. BLUMLER

See also **British Television**

Further Reading

Broadcasting Standards Commission, *Annual Reports* (1997–98 to 2000–01)
Broadcasting Standards Commission, *Briefing Updates* 1–9 (1998–2001)
Broadcasting Standards Commission, *Codes of Guidance,* London: Broadcasting Standards Commission, 1998
Broadcasting Standards Council, *Annual Reports* (1990–91 to 1996–97)
Broadcasting Standards Council, *Annual Research Reviews* 1–7 (1990–97)
Coleman, Francis, "All in the Best Possible Taste: The Broadcasting Standards Council, 1989–92," *Public Law* (Autumn 1993)
Gauntlett, David, *A Profile of Complainants and Their Complaints,* Research Working Paper 10, London: Broadcasting Standards Council, 1995
Hibberd, Matthew, et al., *Consenting Adults?* London: Broadcasting Standards Commission, 2000
Livingstone, Sonia, *Young People and New Media: Childhood and the Changing Media Environment,* London: Sage, 2002
Shaw, Colin, "Taste, Decency, and Standards in Television," in *Television: An International History,* edited by Anthony Smith, Oxford and New York: Oxford University Press, 1995
Shaw, Colin, *Deciding What We Watch: Taste, Decency, and Media Ethics in the UK and the USA,* Oxford and New York: Clarendon Press, 1999

Brodkin, Herbert (1912–1991)

U.S. Producer

Herb Brodkin enjoyed a singular career in television because of his insistence on quality, his uncompromising standards, and his longevity. Brodkin, who served as executive producer or producer on some of television's finest moments, began his television career producing live television in its "golden age," and produced until his death in 1991.

Brodkin came to television with a background in theater and scenic design. He began working as a set designer for CBS in 1950. After three years, he was handling the production chores for no less than three anthology dramas. Brodkin continued to work in the anthology format during what has been generally termed the "golden years of television." These dramas, such as *Playhouse 90* and *Studio One,* were splendid vehicles for Brodkin's broad and varied theatrical experience. One telecast in particular would prove fortuitous for Brodkin and others. "The Defender" (February 28 and March 4, 1957), starring Ralph Bellamy and William Shatner, would serve as a model for one of Brodkin's cornerstone filmed series.

When the telefilm began to flourish in the 1950s and most filmed production came from Hollywood, Brodkin remained in New York, although he, too, changed from the live format to film. Brodkin brought a great deal of technical expertise to telefilm production, for he had made dozens of films for the Army Signal Corps. His first series, *Brenner,* focused on a father-son team of cops and was scheduled sporadically by CBS. Brodkin's next series was the landmark *The Defenders.* The series was based on the *Studio One* show and featured E.G. Marshall and Robert Reed as a father-son team of lawyers. The "Brodkin approach" of treating controversial issues with intelligence and dispassion, developed during the live years, translated well to the filmed medium of television. Brodkin had always held the script in the highest esteem and consistently used writers of excellence—Ernest Kinoy, Robert Crean, and Reginald Rose. Though television was and is a medium that appeals largely to the emotions, Brodkin's productions consistently asked the viewer to think, to consider, and to weigh. Issues considered taboo, such as abortion, euthanasia, racial prejudice, and blacklisting, were familiar ground to Brodkin. CBS constantly battled affiliates that refused to clear *The Defenders,* and the network endured some financial hardship caused by advertisers pulling out from the series. Nevertheless, the hallmark of every Brodkin production was a thoughtful and even-handed examination of an issue in a dramatic context. *The Defenders* enjoyed a four-year run in which it garnered every major award for television drama.

Brodkin's filmed series work often used the settings of the legal and medical profession to explore a variety of very contemporary controversies. The series also used the convention of the mentor-student relationship. In *The Defenders* as well as *Brenner,* the protagonists are father and son. In the unsold pilot *The Firm,* written by long-time Brodkin associate Ernest Kinoy, the protagonists are father and daughter. Brodkin, and those who wrote for him, proved especially adept at balancing the maturity of the mentor and the intellectual enthusiasm of the student as a framework for examining the issues of the day.

In 1965 Brodkin shifted his attention from his Plautus Productions to his newly created Titus Productions (formed with Robert Berger), under whose banner some of his most memorable dramatic specials were produced. This was also the year of one of Brodkin's more metaphorical productions. *Coronet Blue* was a short series run by CBS in the summer of 1967. It chronicled amnesiac Michael Alden's search for his identity while being pursued by a shadowy band of assailants. The only clue to Alden's identity was the cryptic phrase, "coronet blue." The character of Alden can be seen as a metaphor for the angst-ridden youth of the 1960s. His search mirrored the search of the "counterculture" for its identity, its place in the world. The series was fairly well-received but could not be revived for regular production because Frank Converse, who played Michael Alden, was already signed for another series.

In 1981 Titus Productions was acquired by the Taft Entertainment Company. Both Brodkin and Berger remained to produce dramatic specials for Taft. Notable among those specials was *Skokie,* starring Danny Kaye as a Holocaust survivor who fights to keep a group of neo-Nazis from marching in Skokie, Illinois, and the HBO special *Sakharov,* which featured Jason Robards and Glenda Jackson as Soviet dissident Andrei Sakharov and his wife Elena Bonner. In 1985 the Museum of Broadcasting in New York mounted a retrospective of Herbert Brodkin's career. In the words of television curator Ronald Simon, "the ouevre of Herb Brodkin is an impressive collection of socially significant dramas." Herb Brodkin died in 1991, leaving a legacy of creative and intellectual integrity unparalleled in the annals of television.

Herbert Brodkin.
Courtesy of the Everett Collection/CSU Archives

JOHN COOPER

See also **Defenders, The**

Herbert Brodkin. Born in New York City, November 9, 1912. University of Michigan, B.A. 1934, Yale Drama School, M.A. 1941. Served in U.S. Army, 1943–46. Began career in theater as scene designer, Bucks County Playhouse, Pennsylvania, 1946–48; production manager, director, scenery designer, Westport Country Playhouse, Connecticut, 1946–50; set designer, City Center and Theatre Guild, New York, 1946–50; opera set designer, City Center, New York, 1946–50; began television career as producer and designer, *Charlie Wild, Private Detective,* 1950–52; producer of numerous live television productions; *The Defenders,* 1961–64; producer of made-for-television movies, from 1970s. Died 1991.

Television Series

1950–52	*Charlie Wild, Private Detective*
1953–55	*ABC Album*
1953–55	*The TV Hour*
1953–55	*The Motorola TV Hour*
1953–55	*Center Stage*
1953–55	*The Elgin Hour*
1955–56	*The Alcoa Hour*
1955–56	*Goodyear Playhouse*
1957	*Studio One*
1958–60	*Playhouse 90*
1959–64	*Brenner*
1961–64	*The Defenders*
1962–65	*The Nurses*
1966	*Shane*
1967	*Coronet Blue*

Television Miniseries

1978	*Holocaust*

Made-for-Television Movies

1970	*The People Next Door*
1981	*Skokie*
1982	*My Body, My Child*
1983	*Ghost Dancing*
1984	*Sakharov*
1985	*Mandela*
1988	*Stones for Ibarra*
1990	*Murder Times Seven*

Further Reading

Barnouw, Erik, *Tube of Plenty: The Evolution of American Television,* New York: Oxford University Press, 1975; 3rd edition, 1990

Produced by... Herb Brodkin, New York: Museum of Broadcasting, 1985

Watson, Mary Ann, *The Expanding Vista: American Television in the Kennedy Years,* New York: Oxford University Press, 1990

Brokaw, Tom (1940–)

U.S. Broadcast Journalist

Tom Brokaw serves as anchor and managing editor of *NBC Nightly News,* a position he is contracted to hold until the end of 2004. Sole anchor of the program since 1983, he had previously been anchor of NBC News' *Today Show* from 1976 to 1982 and had worked in a series of increasingly prominent assignments for NBC News. Brokaw's distinctively smooth style and boyish charm have made him a well-recognized star through the shifting stakes in television news in the 1980s and 1990s.

After an early position in Sioux City, Iowa, Brokaw's career in broadcast news began in earnest in 1962 when he worked in Omaha, Nebraska. He moved to Atlanta, Georgia, in 1965 to report on the civil rights movement, then joined NBC in Los Angeles as a reporter and anchor in 1966. From the west coast, Brokaw moved to Washington, D.C., eventually becoming NBC's White House correspondent during the Watergate era. In 1976 and 1980, he was a member of the NBC News team of floor reporters for the Democratic and Republican conventions. Since 1984 he has served as anchor of all NBC News coverage of the primaries, national conventions, and presidential election nights. In the fall of 1987, Brokaw scored a number of high-profile successes, interviewing Mikhail Gorbachev in the Kremlin, Ronald Reagan in the White House, and in December 1987 moderating a live, televised debate from Washington among all declared candidates for the presidential nomination from both parties. He also moderated the first debate among the declared Democratic candidates for president in December 1991.

Brokaw's opportunity to serve as anchor arose when, after being courted by ABC, NBC countered by teaming him with Roger Mudd (apparently attempting to replicate the Chet Huntley/David Brinkley pairing), and the two went on the air as co-anchors in April 1982. Mudd was soon dropped by NBC, and Brokaw took over as sole anchor in August 1983. At CBS Dan Rather had replaced Walter Cronkite in 1981; at ABC Peter Jennings, who had anchored from 1965 to 1968, returned to that position in 1983; and thus a three-man race was put in place that continues to structure the national nightly news.

When each of the networks was bought by a large conglomerate in the mid-1980s (ABC by Capital Cities, CBS by Laurence Tisch's Loews Corporation, and NBC by General Electric), network news divisions became cost-accountable in new ways that also impinged on the importance of the anchor. While budgets and staffs were cut, promotional campaigns were expanded, and, increasingly, the center of those campaigns was the persona of the news anchor, who became a virtual corporate symbol.

Brokaw has been one of the most well-recognized participants in the trend toward expanding the role of the news reader into a prominent position of creative control and celebrity. Along with Rather and Jennings, Brokaw emerged in the 1990s as a kind of living logo, the image taken to be representative of an entire news organization. A number of critics have raised questions about the quality and integrity of news presentation in this increasingly star-driven climate, charging that on the national news broadcasts, journalism has become subordinate to entertainment. Brokaw was reportedly the model for William Hurt's Tom Grunick, the protagonist in James L. Brooks's 1987 film *Broadcast News.*

As an anchor, Brokaw is renowned for his globetrotting, and he has provided live coverage of such important events as the dismantling of the Berlin Wall, North Atlantic Treaty Organization attacks in Yugoslavia, and the events following the bombing of the Murrah Federal Building in Oklahoma City and the terrorist attacks on the United States on September 11, 2001. In addition to *NBC Nightly News,* Brokaw anchored, with Katie Couric, the nighttime program. *Now with Tom Brokaw and Katie Couric* (1993–94) as well as the short-lived *Exposé,* a news magazine show on the order of *60 Minutes.*

He has also anchored a number of prime-time specials, including a January 1999 special on the "Greatest Generation." That program profiled some of the same people discussed by Brokaw in his books *The Greatest Generation* (1998), *The Greatest Generation Speaks* (1999), and *An Album of Memories* (2001). Each of these projects reflects Brokaw's abiding interest in the stories of Americans who grew up in the Depression, served in World War II, and participated prominently in shaping postwar U.S. society.

In May 2002, NBC announced that Brokaw will end his term as anchor of *NBC Nightly News* at the end of 2004, to be succeeded by CNBC's Brian Williams. Brokaw intends to continue as a contributor to NBC News after he leaves the anchor desk.

DIANE M. NEGRA

See also **Anchor; *Dateline NBC***

Tom Brokaw, Anchorman for the *NBC Nightly News,* 1998.
©NBC/Courtesy of theEverett Collection

Tom (Thomas John) Brokaw. Born in Webster, South Dakota, February 6, 1940. Educated at University of South Dakota, B.A. in political science, 1962. Married: Meredith Lynn Auld, 1962; children: Jennifer Jean, Andrea Brooks, and Sarah Auld. Began career as newscaster, weatherman, and staff announcer KTIV, Sioux City, Iowa, 1960–62; morning news editor KMTV, Omaha, Nebraska, 1962–65; editor for 11:00 P.M. news, WSB-TV, Atlanta, Georgia, 1965–66; joined NBC news as anchor, KNBC-TV, Los Angeles, California, 1966; reporter and anchor, NBC, since 1966. Honorary degrees: University of South Dakota; Washington University; Syracuse University; Hofstra University; Boston College; Emerson College; Simpson College; Duke University, 1991; Notre Dame University, 1993; Fairfield College. Recipient: Seven Emmy Awards; two duPont Awards; Peabody Award, 1988; Honor Medal for Distinguished Service in Journalism, University of Missouri-Columbia School of Journalism, 1997; Fred Friendly First Amendment Award, 1998. Inducted into Broadcasting and Cable's Television Hall of Fame, 1997.

Television Series

1973–76 *NBC Saturday Night News* (anchor)
1976–82 *Today Show* (host)
1982–2004 *NBC Nightly News* (anchor)

1991	*Exposé* (anchor)
1992–	*Dateline NBC* (co-anchor)
1993–94	*Now with Tom Brokaw and Katie Couric* (co-anchor)

Television Specials (selected)

1987	*To Be a Teacher*
1987	*Wall Street: Money, Greed, and Power*
1987	*A Conversation with Mikhail S. Gorbachev*
1988	*Home Street Home*
1988	*To Be an American*
1999	*The Greatest Generation*

Publications

The Greatest Generation, 1998
The Greatest Generation Speaks, 1999
An Album of Memories, 2001

Further Reading

Corliss, Richard, "Broadcast Blues," *Film Comment* (March–April 1988)

Goldberg, Robert, and Gerald Jay Goldberg, *Anchors: Brokaw, Jennings, Rather and the Evening News,* New York: Birch Lane, 1990

Jones, Alex S., "The Anchors: Who They Are, What They Do: The Tests They Face," *New York Times* (July 27, 1986)

Kaplan, James, "Tom Brokaw: NBC's Air Apparent," *Vogue* (April 1988)

Westin, Av, *Newswatch: How TV Decides the News,* New York: Simon and Schuster, 1982

Brooke-Taylor, Tim (1940–)

British Comedian, Writer

Tim Brooke-Taylor has established himself as a familiar face on British television since making his first appearances in the early 1960s, when he was one of a celebrated generation of young new comedians and comedy writers to emerge from the famous Cambridge University Footlights Revue.

Brooke-Taylor began his television career working for *On the Braden Beat,* which was one of a flood of innovative new comedy shows to be created around 1962 to 1964. Subsequently he teamed up as a writer with star Eric Idle on *The Frost Report* and also contributed as writer and performer to the spin-off series *At Last the 1948 Show,* on which his collaborators were John Cleese, Marty Feldman, Graham Chapman, and Aimi Macdonald, under the leadership of David Frost as producer. This last show was a significant step in British television comedy, having a distinctly surreal air with its unconnected sketches and eccentric, often slapstick humor, which paved the way for the *Monty Python* series, among other successors.

After teaming up as straight man to Marty Feldman on *Marty,* Brooke-Taylor entered upon the most successful collaboration of his television career to date, completing a highly popular comedy trio with Graeme Garden and Bill Oddie in *The Goodies.* Oddie, Garden, and Brooke-Taylor had in fact already worked together once before with some success, first developing their sparky three-man act in the series *Twice a Fortnight* in 1967. Anarchic, weird, and often hilarious, *The Goodies* sought to save the world from such bizarre threats as a marauding giant kitten and a plague of Rolf Harrises. Pedaling into action on a beflagged three-seater bicycle, the trio were purveyors of a more slapstick, light-hearted brand of comedy than their counterparts in *Monty Python* and consequently appealed to a wider age range, with many fans in their teens or even younger.

Much of the humor in *The Goodies* evolved from the contrasting, and ludicrous, personalities of the three heroes. While Graeme Garden was the obsessive scientist who dreamt up all manner of wacky schemes to save the world and Bill Oddie was a short, scruffy hippy with a strong cynical streak, Tim Brooke-Taylor was the clean-cut patriot in Union Jack waistcoat, always ready with a rousing Churchillian speech when things looked bleak but first to bolt when danger reared its head. Targets of the humor included a range of contemporary fads and issues, from satirical swipes at the science fiction adventure serial *Dr. Who* to takeoffs of the Hollywood western.

The series was hugely successful, but ultimately it fell victim to the BBC's indecision about whether it should be scheduled for adult or younger audiences

Tim Brooke-Taylor.
Photo courtesy of Jill Foster Ltd.

(despite pleas from the performers themselves, it was broadcast relatively early in the evening, thus restricting the adult content of the material). The team switched to London Weekend Television in 1981 in the hope that they might fare better there, but there was no real improvement and no more programs were made after 1982.

After *The Goodies,* the three stars went their more or less separate ways, Tim Brooke-Taylor managing to maintain the highest profile in subsequent years. As well as establishing himself as a prominent panelist on such long-running radio programs as *I'm Sorry, I Haven't a Clue,* he also developed a second television career in situation comedy, starring in several efficient but fairly unremarkable series in the 1980s and early 1990s. Perhaps the most successful of these latter efforts was *Me and My Girl,* in which Brooke-Taylor gave support as best friend Derek Yates to Richard Sullivan, an advertising executive struggling to bring up a teenage daughter on his own. Typical of other series that were greeted with only lukewarm praise was *You Must Be the Husband,* in which Brooke-Taylor was the startled uptight husband of a woman newly revealed as the best-selling author of salacious romantic novels.

David Pickering

See also **Cleese, John**

Tim(othy Julian) Brooke-Taylor. Born in Buxton, Derbyshire, England, July 17, 1940. Attended Cambridge University. Married: Christine Wheadon, 1968; children: Ben and Edward. Actor, Cambridge Footlights Revue while at university; writer, various 1960s comedy series, costar, *The Goodies,* 1970–80, 1981–82; later appeared in situation comedies and consolidated reputation as radio performer.

Television Series (selected)

1962–67	*On the Braden Beat*
1966–67	*The Frost Report* (co-writer)
1966–67	*At Last the 1948 Show* (also producer)
1968	*Marty*
1970–80, 1981–82	*The Goodies*
1970–72	*His and Hers*
1984–88	*Me and My Girl*
1987–88	*You Must Be the Husband*

Films

Twelve Plus One; The Statue; Willy Wonka and the Chocolate Factory.

Radio

I'm Sorry, I'll Read That Again; I'm Sorry, I Haven't a Clue; Hello Cheeky; Does the Team Think?; Loose Ends; The Fame Game; Hoax.

Recordings

Funky Gibbon; The New Goodies LP; The Goodies' Beastly Record; The Least Worst of Hello Cheeky; The Seedy Sounds of Hello Cheeky.

Stage (selected)

The Unvarnished Truth, 1978; *Run for Your Wife; Not Now Darling; The Philanthropist; The Ladykillers,* 1999; *Why Me?,* 2001; *Bedside Manners,* 2001.

Publications

Rule Britannia, 1983
Tim Brooke-Taylor's Cricket Box, 1986
Tim Brooke-Taylor's Golf Bag, 1988
I'm Sorry, I Haven't a Clue (with Barry Cryer, Graeme Garden, Willie Rushton, and Humphrey Littleton), 1999

Brooks, James L. (1940–)

U.S. Writer, Producer, Director

James L. Brooks is one of television's most outstanding and successful writer-producers. He is also one of the few to have become a highly successful screenwriter and director of feature films. His work in both media has been recognized with numerous awards from peers and critics, and both television programs and films have been acclaimed by audiences.

Although Brooks's career in television began as a writer for series such as *My Three Sons, The Andy Griffith Show,* and *My Mother the Car,* he also worked in a very different arena. He was a writer for CBS News in New York from 1964 to 1966. In 1966, he moved to Los Angeles and became a writer and producer of documentaries for David Wolper at Wolper Productions. By 1968, however, Brooks and his partner, Allan Burns, had created the hit television show *Room 222,* where they served as executive story editors. This program broke new ground for television by focusing on the career of a black high school teacher, Pete Dixon (Lloyd Haynes). The show tackled tough issues such as drug use and racial conflict in a concerned, humane manner and won an Emmy as Outstanding New Series in 1969.

Much of the same style and tone carried over into Brooks's and Burns's next success, *The Mary Tyler Moore Show.* At MTM Entertainment, Brooks and Burns were among the first members of a large group of extremely talented individuals, all working in a creatively charged atmosphere established by executive producer Grant Tinker. Tinker's philosophy was to acquire the services of creative individuals and then assist them in every way possible to become even more productive. Brooks and Burns thrived under the system, working first on *The Mary Tyler Moore Show,* then creating or co-creating, *Rhoda, Paul Sand in Friends and Lovers, Taxi, The Associates,* and *Lou Grant.* On the basis of these successes, the team of Brooks and Burns became known as members of a new group of Hollywood television producers, often referred to as the "auteur" producers. They were the creative force behind their shows, imparting a recognizable, distinctive style and tone. Indeed, programs created at MTM have been referred to as the defining examples of "quality television."

The programs were noted not only for their wit and quick jokes, but for establishing a focus on character. Most were built around groups of characters related by circumstance or profession rather than by family relations. They were quickly recognized by critics as something different from the earlier forms of television comedy focused either on zany "situations" or on domestic settings. These new programs were among the first and strongest of the "ensemble comedies" that were to dominate television for decades to come. Human frailty and the comfort of friends, professional limitations and the joy of co-workers, a readiness to take one's self too seriously at times, matched by a willingness to puncture excessive ego: these are the hallmarks of the Brooks style of ensemble comedy. While social issues might come to the foreground in any given episode, they were always subordinate to the comedy of human manners, and to character. In this way, the MTM shows were distinguished from the more overtly issue-oriented style of Norman Lear. This focus on character and ensemble has been passed down through professional and industrial relationships into the work of other producer-writers in shows as diverse as *ER* and *Hill Street Blues,* and programs such as *Cheers, Murphy Brown,* or *Seinfeld* are clear descendants of the work of Brooks and his various partners.

In 1978 Brooks began to shift his work toward feature films. He worked as writer and coproducer on the film *Starting Over* and in 1983 he wrote, produced, and directed *Terms of Endearment,* a highly successful film in terms of both box office and critical response. As writer, producer, or director he has continued his involvement with a string of box office successes, including *Jerry Maguire* (1996) and *As Good As It Gets* (1997). He has also been instrumental as a mentor to young writer-directors in film, most notably Wes Anderson, who paid "Special Thanks" to Brooks in the credits for his films *Rushmore* (1998) and *The Royal Tenenbaums* (2001).

In 1984 Brooks founded Gracie Films, his own production company, to oversee work on film and television projects. To date, the best known television programs developed at Gracie Films have been *The Tracey Ullman Show* and its immensely popular spinoff, *The Simpsons.* With some degree of irony, given

James L. Brooks.
Photo courtesy of James L. Brooks

Brooks's career, these two shows are marvelously skewed views of television comedy. *The Tracey Ullman Show* was replete with send-ups of American TV "types" such as the housewife-mother, the bored "pink collar" worker, and the prime-time vamp. *The Simpsons,* using all the techniques of animation at its disposal, pokes fun at the idealized version of domestic comedy that has long been a television staple and, at the same time, serves as the site of some of television's sharpest commentary on contemporary social and cultural life. While Brooks's involvement with these shows remains primarily at the level of executive producer, the style and attitude he developed throughout his years in television comedy is clearly at work. In some ways he might be said to have inherited the mantle of Grant Tinker, discovering new talent, making a space for creative individuals, and changing the face of television in the process.

HORACE NEWCOMB

See also ***Mary Tyler Moore Show; Room 222; Simpsons, The***

James L. Brooks. Born in Brooklyn, New York, May 9, 1940. Attended New York University, New York City, 1958–60. Married: 1) Marianne Katherine Morrissey, 1964 (divorced), child: Amy Lorriane; 2) Holly Beth Holmberg. Began career at CBS television sports division; writer/producer, David Wolper Productions, 1966; co-creator, with Alan Burns, *Room 222;* writer/producer, MTM; founder, Gracie Films, 1984; film writer, producer, and director. Recipient: numerous Emmy Awards; Golden Globe Awards; Peabody Awards; Humanitas Awards; Directors Guild Awards; Writers Guild of America Awards.

Television

1960	*My Three Sons* (writer, two episodes)
1960	*The Andy Griffith Show* (writer, two episodes)
1965	*My Mother the Car* (writer, two episodes)
1968–69	*Room 222*
1970–77	*The Mary Tyler Moore Show*
1974	*Paul Sands in Friends and Lovers*
1974–75	*Rhoda*
1976	*The New Lorenzo Music Show*
1977–82	*Lou Grant*
1978–83	*Taxi*
1978	*Cindy*
1979	*The Associates*
1986–90	*The Tracey Ullman Show*
1990	*The Simpsons*
1993	*Phenom*
1994 and 2000	*The Critic*
2001	*What About Joan*

Made-for-Television Movie

1974	*Thursday's Game* (writer-producer)

Films

Starting Over (writer, producer), 1979; *Modern Romance* (actor), 1981; *Terms of Endearment* (director, writer, producer), 1983; *Broadcast News* (director, writer, producer), 1987; *Big* (producer), 1988; *The War of the Roses* (producer), 1989; *Say Anything...* (executive producer), 1989; *I'll Do Anything* (director, writer), 1994; *Bottle Rocket* (executive producer), 1996; *Jerry Maguire,* 1996 (producer); *As Good As It Gets,* 1997 (producer); *Riding in Cars With Boys,* 2001 (producer).

Further Reading

Alley, Robert S., and Irby B. Brown, *Love Is All Around: The Making of The Mary Tyler Moore Show,* New York: Delta, 1989

Corliss, Richard, "Still Lucky Jim? Comedy Czar James L. Brooks Tries To Fix the Movie That Used To Be A Musical," *Time* (January 31, 1994)

Feuer, Jane, Paul Kerr, and Tise Vahimagi, *MTM: "Quality Television,"* London: British Film Institute, 1985

Lovece, Frank, *Hailing Taxi,* New York: Prentice Hall, 1988
Mitchell, Sean, "James L. Brooks (Don't Worry Be Unhappy)," *American Film* (May 1989)
Newcomb, Horace, and Robert S. Alley, *The Producer's Medium: Conversations with Creators of American TV,* New York: Oxford University Press, 1983
Orth, Maureen, "Talking To...James Brooks" (interview). *Vogue* (April 1988)
Tinker, Grant, *Tinker in Television: From General Sarnoff to General Electric,* New York: Simon and Schuster, 1994
Zehme, Bill, "The Only Real People On T.V. (The Simpsons)," *Rolling Stone* (June 28, 1990)

Brookside

British Soap Opera

Brookside, produced independently by Mersey Television, was inextricably linked to the history of the British independent publishing channel, Channel Four. Founded in 1982, Channel Four's remit was to attract audiences to which other channels did not cater, and to innovate in form and style. In particular, *Brookside* attracted a young audience, who were essential to the serial's success.

Unlike earlier serial dramas, *Brookside* avoided the traditional television studio; the show was filmed on a small housing estate, built as part of a Liverpool housing redevelopment. The structure of the close itself, with small "two up, two down" working-class accommodations next to large detached houses for wealthier occupants, set the stage for confrontation between classes, with politically contentious issues dealt with in an upfront manner.

Whereas its competitor soaps were perceived to be "character-based," *Brookside*'s initial aim was a realism that directly tackled the social and political problems apparent in the Britain of the 1980s. This approach has been followed by the BBC's *Eastenders,* which also copied *Brookside*'s "weekend omnibus repeat" format. More recently, the pressing concerns of audience maximization led to a more sensationalist approach to social issues, with *Brookside* offering British television's first "on-screen" lesbian kiss, while late storylines focused on incest, rape, murder, and drug abuse. These developments led to suggestions that *Brookside,* in particular its Saturday omnibus edition, was unsuitable for "family audiences."

One crucial difference between the *Brookside* of the 1980s and other British soaps was the lack of a central community meeting point, such as a pub or corner shop, forcing characters to interact either on the close itself, or in scenes shot on location in and around Liverpool. However, the addition of a shopping development to the set in later seasons led to more traditional interactions over the counter of a pizza parlor, or in the nearby hair salon, medical center, petrol station, bar, or nightclub.

Many of the main changes in *Brookside* were symbolized by the fate of the Grant family. Moving onto the close at the start of the program, the Grants symbolized the expansion in working-class property ownership encouraged by the Conservative governments of the 1980s. Bobby Grant, a trade unionist with a fierce attachment to socialist rhetoric, suffered unemployment; Damon Grant was murdered in London (with the death filmed as part of a *Brookside* spin-off titled *Damon and Debbie,* a format copied by Granada's *Coronation Street*); Karen Grant left home to study at university; and Sheila Grant left Bobby, symbolizing the breakdown of the traditional post–World War II family unit. Barry Grant gradually developed the role of a ruthlessly competitive young entrepreneur, encouraged by the boom-bust cycle of the British economy during the 1980s and 1990s. He continued with the series into the 1990s but gradually disappeared after murdering the wife and child of his lifelong best friend, Terry Sullivan. Murder and violence were no strangers to *Brookside,* which suffered numerous murders, several armed sieges, several violent rapes, and a fatal, cocaine-fueled car accident.

Channel Four broadcast three episodes a week of the soap, and *Brookside* was invariably the channel's most popular program, giving it a greater scope for minority-oriented programming elsewhere in the schedule. Over the course of *Brookside*'s history, gritty social realism gradually has given way to a more populist approach: whereas early episodes did their best to reflect the specific concerns of the northwest of England, more recently Brookside rarely referred to its

Brookside.
Photo courtesy of Mersey Television

Liverpudlian roots. In 2000 Phil Redmond, executive producer and creator of *Brookside,* suggested that Brookside required a major shake-up. However, despite rumors of a "back to basics" return to social realism, Redmond promised, "another mutation and another fresh intake of talent and ideas, and especially really interesting ones about terribly interesting people leading terribly interesting lives—but still occasionally raping, killing and betraying each other!"

In June 2003, Channel 4 announced that *Brookside* would cease production at the end of that year. After 21 years on the air, the program's place in the history of the soap opera genre is assured.

STUART BORTHWICK

See also **British Programming; *Coronation Street; EastEnders;* Soap Opera**

Cast

Carl Banks	Stephen Donald
Eddie Banks	Paul Broughton
Rosie Banks	Susan Twist
Sarah Banks	Andrea Marshall
Anabelle Collins	Doreen Sloane
Gordon Collins	Nigel Crowley
Lucy Collins	Katrin Cartlidge
Paul Collins	Jim Wiggins
Jackie Corkhill	Sue Jenkins
Jimmy Corkhill (1986–)	Dean Sullivan
David Crosbie	John Burgess
Jean Crosbie	Marcia Ashton
D.D. Dixon	Irene Morot
Mike Dixon (1990–)	Paul Byatt
Ron Dixon (1990–)	Vince Earl
Max Farnham (1990–)	Steven Pinder
Jacqui Farnham (1990–)	Alex Fletcher
Patricia Farnham	Gabrielle Glaister
Ali Gordon (2002–)	Kris Mocherri
Kirsty Gordon (2002–)	Jessica Noon
Stuart Gordon (2002–)	David Lyon
Barry Grant	Paul Usher
Bobby Grant	Ricky Tomlinson
Damon Grant	Simon O'Brien
Karen Grant	Shelagh O'Hara
Sheila Grant	Sue Johnston
Heather Huntingdon	Amanda Burton
Roger Huntingdon	Rob Spendlove
Mick Johnson	Louis Emerick
Beth Jordache (1993–)	Anna Friel
Mandy Jordache (1993–)	Sandra Maitland
Rachel Jordache/Dixon (1993–)	Tiffany Chapman
Audrey Manners	Judith Barker
Mo McGee	Tina Malone
Bev McLoughlin (1993–)	Sarah White
Adele Murray (2000)	Katy Lamont
Anthony Murray (2000)	Raymond Quinn
Jan Murray (2002)	Helen Sheals
Marty Murray (2000)	Neil Caple
Steve Murray (2000)	Steven Fletcher
Debbie McGrath	Gillian Kearney
Tim O' Leary (1996)	Philip Olivier
Emma Piper	Paula Belle
Lance Powell (2000)	Mickey Poppins
Katie Rogers (1987)	Diane Burke
Sammy Rogers (1987–)	Rachael Lindsay
Sinbad	Michael Starke
Nikki Shadwick (1998–)	Suzanne Collins
Ruth Smith (2002–)	Lynsey McCaffrey
Sean Smith (2002–)	Barry Sloane
Gavin Taylor	Daniel Webb
Petra Taylor	Alexandra Pigg
Viv	Kerrie Thomas

Producers

Mel Young, Paul Marquess

Programming History

Channel Four (Brookside Productions)
1982–2003

Further Reading

Brown, Mary Ellen, *Soap Opera and Women's Talk: The Pleasure of Resistance,* Thousand Oaks, California: Sage, 1994

Geraghty, Christine, *Women and Soap Opera: A Study of Prime Time Soaps,* Cambridge: Polity Press, 1991

Kilbourn, R.W., *Television Soaps,* London: Batsford, 1992

Buffy the Vampire Slayer

U.S. Drama

The original opening voice-over for the television drama series *Buffy the Vampire Slayer* at once signifies what makes this show unique even as it disguises what makes the series a hit with its fans. "In every generation, there is a chosen one. She alone will stand against the vampires, the demons, and the forces of darkness. She is the Slayer." Buffy Summers (Sarah Michelle Gellar), a 16-year-old girl living in Sunnydale, California, goes to high school during the day and fights demons and vampires by night. She is a superhero, and she is female. In March 1997, when *Buffy* (based on the 1992 movie *Buffy the Vampire Slayer*) first aired as a mid-season replacement on the new WB television network, shows featuring a physically and intellectually strong female were rare. The series quickly became a hit for this reason, but a major element of what kept the show a hit is the fact that Buffy does not work alone. Buffy's interesting (and constantly evolving) group of friends has made this series a largely female-oriented ensemble success.

Willow Rosenberg (Alyson Hannigan) and Xander Harris (Nicholas Brendon) are Buffy's best high school friends, privy to her "secret identity." Rupert Giles (Anthony Stewart Head) is Buffy's Watcher, a member of the Watcher's Council, educated to train and assist Slayers across time. As the series developed and the characters moved through high school and into college, other key allies (affectionately known as members of the "Scooby Gang") emerged, many of them played by women. Sunnydale High's lead cheerleader became unwillingly involved with Buffy's inner circle (Cordelia Chase, played by Charisma Carpenter); Buffy's mother found out that her daughter is the Slayer while she was still in high school (Joyce Summers, played by Kristine Sutherland); and another Slayer emerged in the third season (Faith, played by Eliza Dushku). In college, Willow began to date a female witch (Tara, played by Amber Benson); Xander became engaged to a former demon (Anya Emerson, played by Emma Caulfield); and Buffy suddenly had a younger sister (Dawn Summers, played by Michelle Trachtenberg). Other key characters included male romantic interests in high school for Willow (Oz, a werewolf played by Seth Green) and Buffy (Angel, a vampire with a soul played by David Boreanaz), and male romantic interests for Buffy in her college years (Riley Finn, a government soldier played by Marc Blucas, and Spike, a vampire and former enemy played by James Marsters).

The show also became a hit because of its blend of generic modes. While technically classified as a drama by the Academy of Television Arts and Sciences, *Buffy* defies genre conventions. To begin with, Buffy Summers repeatedly holds her own in the most formidable of well-choreographed fight scenes. *Buffy* also incorporates aspects of fantasy/science-fiction with its use of demons, vampires, prophetic dreams, multiple realities, and magic. (For example, Buffy's sister was created by religious monks; "she" was originally pure cosmic energy of great power.) The show also has a strong comic streak. Relying heavily on verbal witticisms ("When the apocalypse comes... beep me") and creating humor out of situations as diverse as dating in high school and battling fashion-savvy evil goddesses in college, *Buffy* is rife with smart humor even as it develops intensely melodramatic and serious plotlines.

Buffy has pushed the television format to its limit in a number of unusual episodes. An especially notable episode was "Hush" (in the fourth season), which was conducted purely in silence for 28 minutes. The sixth season featured "Once More With Feeling," a musical episode, which featured the cast members singing and dancing.

This combination of a strong female hero, a stalwart ensemble cast, and a defiant blend of genre characteristics helped make *Buffy* an industrial and critical success as well as a cult favorite. Critics praised the acting (Sarah Michelle Gellar was nominated for a Golden Globe in 1999) and the writing (the show's creator and initial head writer, Joss Whedon, earned an Emmy nomination in 2000). Joss Whedon in particular has been singled out for creating a "teen show" that is distinguishable from other teen shows on the WB because of the intelligence with which it addresses topics relevant not only to teenagers but to adults as well. (The median age for *Buffy* viewers is 29.) The show has addressed how divorce affects children ("Nightmares"), date rape ("Reptile Boy"), relationship violence against women ("Beauty and the Beasts"), men stalking women ("Passion"), the ramifications of sexual intercourse ("Innocence"), high school violence ("Earshot"), and the death of a parent ("The Body").

Buffy has also been praised by lesbian, gay, and bisexual organizations for its representation of a lesbian relationship, which began in the show's fourth season. While the series had already addressed teen female sexuality through the sexual relationship between Buffy and Angel (and to a lesser degree between Willow and Oz), when the Scooby Gang broke down and reformed in the first year after high school, the writers introduced Tara. After Willow and Oz broke up, Willow became involved with Tara through a Wicca group on their college campus. By the fifth season the writers were finally allowed by the WB network to depict an on-screen kiss ("The Body"); and when the series moved to another network (UPN) for its sixth season, Willow and Tara were clearly a sexually active couple ("Once More, With Feeling"). Without ever becoming a show that was "about" lesbians, *Buffy* nevertheless became the first prime-time series to feature a lead lesbian character in an open and committed relationship since ABC's *Ellen.*

Buffy's move to UPN in the fall of 2001 and the furor it caused indicates how much of a cultural phenomenon the show had become by its sixth season. *Buffy's* strong WB ratings and marketing ties (Sarah Michelle Gellar, Alyson Hannigan, and Seth Green have been in financially successful films since *Buffy* began, and the series has spawned comic books and novels) prompted the WB to use the series as an anchor show for many of its subsequent hits, such as *Dawson's Creek* and *Felicity.* As the show began its fourth season on the WB, it anchored a spin-off featuring Angel and Cordelia (*Angel*). *Buffy* and *Angel* remained together on the WB through *Buffy's* fifth season; and then suddenly, in early spring of 2001, a bidding war erupted between the WB and UPN for rights to *Buffy* (which is produced by FOX).

The "issues" were largely financial, although "loyalty" was often bandied about in the press as a factor as well. *Buffy,* after all, had helped to solidify the WB as a viable network both critically and financially. The show had struggled with a tiny budget for its first five years, even as its stars and writers were becoming increasingly marketable both on television and in the movie industry. However, the WB network would not match UPN's bid. *Buffy* was forced to move to UPN amid rumors that star Sarah Michelle Gellar would break her contract if this shift occurred (a rumor helped in no small way when, in the WB finale of the series, Buffy Summers died). More importantly, UPN was a smaller network than the WB, reaching fewer major markets and available in some major cities only via cable or satellite. This move also

Buffy the Vampire Slayer, David Boreanaz, Anthony Stewart Head, Seth Green, Alyson Hannigan, Sarah Michelle Gellar, Nicholas Brendon, Charisma Carpenter.

split *Buffy* from its spin-off, *Angel,* putting an end to crossover promotions. In spite of the move, both shows did well at their respective networks.

During *Buffy*'s seventh season, the producers and cast announced that they the show would conclude production at the end of the television season (spring 2003). Fans anticipated eagerly "the big finish" and watched throughout the season as Buffy and her friends dealt with the return of an ancient enemy known as "The First," a pentultimate form of evil that sought to end the world. Potential Slayers throughout the world were dying as The First sought to end the Slayer line, and Giles began bringing those who were still alive to Sunnydale, where Buffy began to train them for a final battle. Viewers learned more about how Slayers were created (unwillingly, through the force of men too cowardly to fight evil themselves) and had a full season to ponder the ramifications of Spike the vampire now having a soul, like Angel did. Willow struggled to recuperate from having murdered the killer of her lover, Tara (in the sixth season), frightened to use her magic skills for fear that she would become murderous again. Xander struggled to come to terms with having broken off his engagement with Anya the year before. With the Scooby Gang in such disarray, the apocalypse seemed imminent. Indeed, when Faith returned to Sunnydale to help the potential Slayers, Buffy's friends and family turned on Buffy, and she left them to face The First on their own.

In the end, however, Buffy discovered the way in which to best The First—a strategy that fit the history of the series as a TV show about female empowerment. With Willow's Wicca skills and the collective force of the potential Slayers on hand, Buffy defied the rules of her lineage and Willow cast a spell that allowed Buffy to share her Slayer powers and strength; all the potential Slayers became actual Slayers (and Willow became a goddess). "Every one of you, and girls we've never known, and generations to come...they will have strength they never dreamed of, and more than that, they will have each other. Slayers. Every one of us," Buffy explained in the finale ("Chosen").

SHARON MARIE ROSS

Cast

Buffy Summers	Sarah Michelle Gellar
Willow Rosenberg	Alyson Hannigan
Xander Harris	Nicholas Brendon
Spike	James Marsters
Rupert Giles	Anthony Stewart Head (1997–2001; recurring thereafter)
Cordelia Chase	Charisma Carpenter (1997–99)
Angel	David Boreanaz (1997–99)
Oz/Daniel Osbourne	Seth Green (1998–99)
Faith	Eliza Dushku (1998–99)
Riley Finn	Marc Blucas (1999–2000)
Joyce Summers	Kristine Sutherland (1997–2001)
Dawn Summers	Michelle Trachtenberg (2000–03)
Anya Emerson	Emma Caulfield (1999–2003)
Tara	Amber Benson (1999–2002)

Producers

Joss Whedon, Marti Noxon, David Solomon, David Fury, David Greenwalt, Gail Berman, Sandy Gallin

Programming History

144 episodes
WB

March 1997–December 1997	Monday 9:00–10:00
January 1998–May 2001	Tuesday 8:00–9:00

UPN

October 2001–May 2003	Tuesday 8:00–9:00

Further Reading

Golden, Christopher, and Nancy Holder, *The Watcher's Guide,* New York: Pocket Books, 1998

Holder, Nancy, *The Watcher's Guide,* Vol. 2, New York: Pocket Books, 2000

Kaveney, Roz, editor, *Reading the Vampire Slayer: An Unofficial Critical Companion to Buffy and Angel,* New York: Tauris Parke Paperbacks, 2002

Parks, Lisa, *Red Noise: Television Studies and Buffy the Vampire Slayer,* Durham, North Carolina: Duke University Press, forthcoming 2005.

Ross, Sharon, "Super(Natural) Women: Female Heroes, Their Friends, and Their Fans," Ph.D. dissertation, University of Texas at Austin, 2002

Ross, Sharon, "'Tough Enough': Female Friendship and Heroism in *Xena* and *Buffy,*" in *Action Chicks,* edited by Sherrie A. Inness. New York: Palgrave Macmillan, forthcoming.

Slayage: The OnLine International Journal of Buffy Studies; available at http://www.slayage.tv/ the on-line international journal of Buffy studies

South, James B., editor, *Buffy the Vampire Slayer and Philosophy: Fear and Trembling in Sunnydale,* New York: Open Court Publishing, 2003

Wilcox, Rhonda V., and David Lavery, editors, *Fighting the Forces: What's at Stake in Buffy the Vampire Slayer,* Lanham, Maryland: Rowman and Littlefield, 2002

Bulman. *See XYY Man*

Bureau of Measurement

The Bureau of Measurement is a cooperative, nonprofit Canadian audience research organization that has struggled to survive in the face of increasing competition from the U.S.-based A.C. Nielsen company, advances in electronic systems of audience measurement, and ambivalent support from the major Canadian broadcasters. It was created on May 11, 1944, on the recommendation of the Canadian Association of Broadcasters, and granted a government charter a year later. Originally called the Bureau of Broadcast Measurement (BBM), its first president was Lew Phenner of Canadian Cellucotton Products. It had no paid staff initially but received administrative assistance from the Association of Canadian Advertisers and technical support from the Canadian Broadcasting Corporation. Its primary purpose in the beginning was to provide radio stations with reliable coverage estimates so that they could compete with the print media for advertising. The first BBM survey, released in October 1944, was conducted by the private ratings company Elliott-Haynes using the unaided mail ballot technique developed by CBS; instead of checking stations from a prepared list, participants compiled their own lists of stations to which they had listened.

Although financed largely by broadcasters, BBM was controlled for many years by advertising interests; of the nine positions on the original board of directors, three were filled by advertisers, three by advertising agencies, and three by broadcasters. Shortly after the creation of BBM, a similar organization called the Broadcast Measurement Bureau (BMB) was established in the United States. As a result of the efforts of Horace Stovin, chairman of BBM's technical committee, the two organizations worked in concert for a few years, using the same mail ballot technique and running their surveys simultaneously. This enabled advertisers to operate on either side of the border with equal facility. However, BMB was criticized for its methods, plagued by high costs, and thrown into disarray by the resignation of its president, Rugh M. Feltis. In 1950 it threw in the towel and left the U.S. station coverage field to A.C. Nielsen, which used an interview-aided recall method.

By the end of Phenner's presidency in 1951, BBM had increased the number of areas surveyed, introduced bilingual ballots in some areas, and more than doubled its broadcasting membership. But a number of stations still refused to join, and in 1956 the CBC withdrew because of dissatisfaction with BBM's surveys. The same year, BBM began producing time-period ratings for radio and television using a panel-diary method pioneered in Canada by International Surveys Limited. The new surveys were initially conducted every spring and fall with each member of participating households keeping a week-long diary of listening and viewing by half-hour periods. At the same time, the circulation surveys were increased from every other year to twice a year. However, the CBC remained critical of BBM operations and subscribed instead to Nielsen, ISL, and McDonald Research. A 1962 CBC report criticized BBM's surveys for their "non-coverage, biased selection procedure, low response and poor quality of response." By then BBM was also coming under strong criticism from both advertisers and private broadcasters, and there was a danger that it might collapse.

Under Bill Hawkins of CFOS Owen Sound, BBM began to put its house in order. It revised its constitution so as to increase the representation of broadcasters, and in 1964 became the first ratings service in the world to introduce computerized sample selection. It also increased the number of surveys, redesigned the bilingual household diary, and switched its premium from a card of safety pins to a 50-cent coin. In terms of winning back confidence in the validity of its surveys, the most important step was taken in 1967, when BBM decided to switch from household diaries, which had usually been kept by the harried homemaker, to personal diaries sent to selected members of households—including children, although their diaries were filled out by an adult. This change increased the response rate for mailed diaries to almost 50 percent and facilitated the acquisition of demographic data. Within a few years, BBM became the only audience measurement service for radio in Canada, and in television the competition was reduced to Nielsen. Between 1963 and 1968, BBM increased its membership from 357 to 534 or about 90 percent of the broadcasting industry, including the CBC.

Unlike the original household diary, the new per-

BBM Bureau of Measurement.
Courtesy of BBM Bureau of Measurement

sonal diary was used for both radio and television, largely for reasons of cost. In theory, however, the most reliable diary is the single-medium personal diary. In addition, the use of dual-media diaries irritated radio broadcasters, who argued that they provided BBM with twice as much revenue as television broadcasters, but only received the same benefits. In 1975, therefore, following several studies and considerable debate, BBM adopted separate diaries for each medium, including different samples and survey dates. This move greatly increased survey costs, however, so that in the mid-1980s BBM implemented household flooding or saturation sampling for both radio and television. Ironically, this development brought BBM almost full-circle back to its original household diary technique and illustrated the fact that audience measurement methods generally are determined as much by economic considerations as by the requirements for scientific validity.

In the mid-1970s, BBM began investigating electronic measuring systems. A committee was set up to develop a proposal for a meter-based system for television, and a contract was signed with Torpey Controls Ltd. for a prototype using existing circuitry and the vertical blanking interval. Despite successful test results, however, the cost of switching from diaries to meters was considered prohibitive, especially since diaries would still be required for radio and to supplement the data gathered for television. It was not until the advent of "electronic diaries" or Peoplemeters by Nielsen and others in the early 1980s that BBM gave serious consideration to replacing its traditional diary system for television. Unlike the original Nielsen audimeter, the Peoplemeter measured viewing rather than mere tuning and could track audience flow much more precisely.

In 1984, while still testing its new meter technology in the United States, Nielsen announced its intention to launch a Peoplemeter service in Canada. In response, BBM turned initially to Audits of Great Britain for help, but then decided to invite bids from other companies as well, including Nielsen. In November 1985, Nielsen and BBM reached a tentative agreement by which Nielsen would provide BBM with Peoplemeter data from 1,800 Canadian households, which it could then market as it saw fit. The agreement later fell through, however, and in September 1989 Nielsen launched a Peoplemeter service for network television in Canada on its own. BBM tried to develop its own electronic television audience measurement system in conjunction with Les Entreprise Videoway, but the tests results were unsatisfactory. Late in 1990, BBM and Nielsen resumed talks for a joint venture to extend Peoplemeters from the national network level to local and regional broadcasting. But the following year, a proposed deal again fell apart because of the concerns of local and regional broadcasters about costs and various technical matters. Since then, BBM has continued to use its diary method of audience measurement for both radio and television.

The BBM continues to expand its staff and its services. Its website (http://www.bbm.ca) provides information on the full array of services provided by BBM.

Ross A. Eaman

Further Reading

Blankenship, A.B., C. Chakrapani, and W.H. Poole, *A History of Marketing Research in Canada,* Toronto: Professional Marketing Research Society, 1985

Eaman, Ross A., *Channels of Influence: CBC Audience Research and the Canadian Public,* Toronto: University of Toronto Press, 1994

Burnett, Carol (1933–)

U.S. Comedian, Actor

The many honors awarded Carol Burnett attest to the approbation of her peers and the love of her public. Burnett has been Outstanding Comedienne for the American Guild of Variety Artists five times and the recipient of six Emmys. She received *TV Guide*'s award as Favorite Female Performer for three consecutive years in the early 1960s, and a Peabody award in 1963. The Academy of Television Arts and Sciences proclaimed her Woman of the Year; a Gallup Poll found her to be one of America's 20 Most Admired Women in 1977. She received the first National TV Critics Circle Award for Outstanding Performance, the first Ace Award for Best Actress, and the Horatio Alger Award, conferred by the Horatio Alger Association of Distinguished Americans. The latter is, in many ways, most significant, as Burnett's personal style and endearing "everywoman" qualities resulted from a life filled with emotional abuse and the ravages of poverty. She was inducted into the Television Hall of Fame in 1985.

Her grandmother wanted her to go to secretarial school, with the objective of marrying a rich executive. Burnett wanted college and a degree in journalism. The odds were slim against her finding tuition and carfare of more than $50, at a time when the family's rent was $35 per month. When an anonymous donor placed a $50 bill in the mailbox, she enrolled at the University of California, Los Angeles, quickly switching from journalism to theater arts. Eventually, she joined a musical comedy/opera workshop where she honed her skills in characterization, comic music, and acting. She became a campus star. But her family's poverty made her dreams of moving to New York City and playing on Broadway seem unattainable. A performance at a professor's home in a skit from the musical *Annie Get Your Gun* in 1954 offered her an unexpected break. A party guest gave Burnett and her boyfriend, Don Saroyan, each a grant of $1,000 designed to jump-start their careers. The benefactor attached four stipulations to the money: Burnett must never reveal his identity, she must move to New York City to try her luck; she had to repay the loan within five years; and she was honor-bound to help other young people attain careers in the entertainment business. Within 18 months, she managed to fulfill two of these criteria. While living at New York's Rehearsal Club, the hotel haven for aspiring actresses that had inspired the movie *Stage Door,* she made her own break by organizing the First Annual Rehearsal Club Revue, which showcased the myriad talents of her housemates. While others gained varying opportunities from the program, Burnett signed with the William Morris Agency and rapidly found outlets for her comedic and singing talents.

The Winchell-Mahoney Show, Paul Winchell's children's program, was Burnett's first break in television; for 13 weeks in 1955 she played comic foil for his ventriloquist dummies, where she sang but did little comedy. She played Buddy Hackett's girlfriend in NBC's short-lived 1956 sitcom, *Stanley.* A comedic nightclub act and her collaboration with writer/composer Ken Welch gave her more opportunities for exposure to television audiences. Welch wrote a song spoofing the Elvis Presley craze; Burnett's rendition of "I Made a Fool of Myself over John Foster Dulles" led to appearances on *The Tonight Show* with Jack Paar, *Toast of the Town* with Ed Sullivan, and an amazing amount of publicity as the dour secretary of state fielded questions regarding his "relationship" with Burnett. In 1956 she appeared on CBS-TV's morning show with Garry Moore, and from 1959 to 1962 was a regular on Moore's eponymous prime-time program. Critical and popular praise followed, as Burnett portrayed as many as five or six characters an hour in each show; ranked as America's Favorite Female Performer of 1961–62 by *TV Guide,* that season she received her first Emmy. She also made a television special based on her successful 1959–61 portrayal of Princess Winifred, the gangly, sensitive heroine of the off- then on-Broadway musical, *Once upon a Mattress.* She and Julie Andrews made an Emmy-winning special, *Julie and Carol at Carnegie Hall.* Burnett's popularity amply confirmed, CBS negotiated a ten-year contract which required her to perform in specials and guest appearances for the first five years. During the remaining five, Burnett was to dedicate herself to her own show.

The Carol Burnett Show debuted on September 11, 1967, and ran for 11 seasons. It gave Burnett the opportunity to integrate a vaudeville-inspired mélange of guest stars, music, and various comedic styles with her own unique blend of sophistication and folksiness. By filming the show live, with an in-studio audience and a

The Carol Burnett Show, Carol Burnett, circa late 1970's.
Courtesy of the Everett Collection

recurring ensemble cast, *The Carol Burnett Show* fused the aura of live performance with the benefits of filmed production. Burnett's opening question-and-answer session with audience members showcased her congenial, unpretentious persona and illustrated her astonishing spontaneity in dealing with the unexpected. Bits and pieces of her life experience found their way into the show: her signature ear-tug, originally a signal to her grandmother; the working-class grace of her Charwoman character; her childhood fascination with movies and stars; and the painfully funny relationship between Burnett's Eunice character and Vicki Laurence's Mama in "Family" sketches. The show reached its ratings peak in 1972 but remained popular enough to carry it through 1978, when Burnett terminated the program before it became too stale.

After *The Carol Burnett Show,* Burnett continued to perform in all aspects of the entertainment industry, from television to Broadway. Highlights of her television career include the made-for-television movie, *Friendly Fire* (1979), which examined issues confronting families with sons in Vietnam, the miniseries *Fresno* (1986), which lampooned such popular nighttime soap operas as *Dallas* by presenting comedic elements as if they were serious drama, and musical/opera specials with stars as diverse as Beverly Sills and Dolly Parton. In 1997 she received yet another Emmy for guest appearances in the NBC sitcom *Mad About You.* Burnett added playwright to her list when she and daughter Carrie Hamilton co-wrote *Hollywood Arms,* based on Burnett's memoirs and scheduled for debut during the 2002–03 season at Chicago's Goodman Theatre.

Burnett-as-performer is also known as Burnett-the-Crusader: in 1981, she won a lawsuit against *The National Enquirer* tabloid, which had slandered her in 1976 with an article suggesting that she was drunk and rowdy at a gathering of celebrities and international political figures. Burnett's diverse list of credits continue to grow, and even after a lifetime of success, this consummate professional remains true to the pledge she made to her anonymous benefactor—she continues to help others find their way into television, motion pictures, and legitimate theater.

KATHRYN C. D'ALESSANDRO

See also ***Carol Burnett Show;*** **Variety Programs**

Carol Burnett. Born in San Antonio, Texas, April 26, 1933. Attended the University of California, Los Angeles (UCLA), 1951–54. Married: 1) Don Saroyan, 1955 (divorced, 1962); 2) Joe Hamilton, 1963 (divorced, 1984); children: Carrie Louise, Jody Ann, and Erin Kate; 3) Brian Miller, 2001. UCLA summer stock, summer 1952 and 1953; moved to New York, 1954; hat-check girl, 1954–55; signed with William Morris Agency, 1955; in television from 1955; debuted on Broadway as lead in *Once upon a Mattress,* 1959; recorded first solo record album, 1961; toured Midwest in concert, summer 1962; signed with CBS-TV, 1962; in film, from 1963, debut, *Who's Been Sleeping in My Bed?,* 1963. Recipient: six Emmy Awards, 1962–97; five American Guild of Variety Artists Awards; TV Guide Award, 1961, 1962, and 1963; Peabody Award, 1963; National Television Critics Circle Award, 1977; San Sebastian Film Festival Award for Best Actress, 1978; 12 People's Choice Awards; two Photoplay Gold Medals; eight Golden Globe Awards; Academy of Television Arts and Sciences Woman of the Year; Ace Award, 1983; Television Hall of Fame induction, 1985; Horatio Alger Award, 1988.

Television Series

1950–63 *Pantomime Quiz*
1953–64 *The Garry Moore Show*

1955 *The Winchell-Mahoney Show*
1956 *Stanley*
1964–65 *The Entertainers*
1967–78 *The Carol Burnett Show*
1990–91 *Carol and Company*
1991 *The Carol Burnett Show*
1995–99 *Mad About You*

Television Miniseries

1986 *Fresno*

Made-for-Television Movies

1974 *6 RMS RIV VU*
1975 *Twigs*
1978 *The Grass Is Always Greener Over the Septic Tank*
1979 *Friendly Fire*
1979 *The Tenth Month*
1982 *Life of the Party: The Story of Beatrice*
1983 *Between Friends*
1985 *Laundromat*
1988 *Hostage*
1994 *Seasons of the Heart*
1998 *The Marriage Fool*

Television Specials

1962 *Julie and Carol at Carnegie Hall*
1963 *Calamity Jane*
1963 *An Evening with Carol Burnett*
1964 *Once upon a Mattress*
1966 *Carol and Company*
1967 *Carol + 2*
1969 *Bing Crosby and Carol Burnett—Together Again for the First Time*
1971 *Julie and Carol at the Lincoln Center*
1972 *Once upon a Mattress*
1975 *Twigs*
1976 *Sills and Burnett at the Met*
1978 *A Special Carol Burnett*
1979 *Dolly and Carol in Nashville*
1982 *Eunice*
1982 *Hollywood: The Gift of Laughter* (cohost)
1984 *Burnett "Discovers" Domingo*
1985 *Here's TV Entertainment* (cohost)
1987 *Plaza Suite*
1987 *Carol, Carl, Whoopi, and Robin*
1987 *Superstars and Their Moms*
1988 *Superstars and Their Moms*
1989 *Julie and Carol—Together Again*
1991 *The Funny Women of Television*
1991 *The Very Best of the Ed Sullivan Show* (host)
1993 *The Carol Burnett Show: A Reunion*
1994 *A Century of Women*
1994 *Men, Movies, and Carol*
1998 *CBS: The First 50 years*
2001 *The Carol Burnett Show: Show Stoppers*

Films

Who's Been Sleeping In My Bed?, 1963; *Pete 'n' Tillie,* 1972; *The Front Page,* 1974; *A Wedding,* 1978; *Four Seasons,* 1981; *Chu Chu and the Philly Flash,* 1981; *H.E.A.L.T.H.,* 1982; *Annie,* 1982; *Noises Off,* 1992; *Trumpet of the Swan* (voice), 2000.

Stage

Once upon a Mattress, 1959; *Fade Out—Fade In,* 1964; *Plaza Suite,* 1971; *I Do! I Do!,* 1973; *Same Time Next Year,* 1977; *Love Letters,* 1990; *Moon Over Buffalo,* 1995; *Putting It Together,* 1999.

Publication

One More Time: A Memoir, 1986

Further Reading

Marc, David, "Carol Burnett: The Last of the Big-time Comedy-Variety Stars," *Quarterly Review of Film Studies* (July 1992)

O'Connor, John J., "Funny Women of Television: A Museum of Television and Radio Tribute," *New York Times* (October 24, 1991)

"The Serious Business of Being Funny" (interview), *The New Yorker* (August 21, 1995)

Taraborrelli, J. Randy, *Laughing Till It Hurts: The Complete Life and Career of Carol Burnett,* New York: Morrow, 1988

Burns, Allan (1935–)

U.S. Writer, Producer

Allan Burns moved to Los Angeles in 1956 intending to pursue a career as a cartoonist or commercial artist. After being laid off from his job as a page at NBC, he did begin earning a living as a cartoonist for greeting cards. He soon moved to television, employed in 1962 by Jay Ward on the cartoon series *Rocky and His Friends* and *The Bullwinkle Show.* Burns then formed a partnership with Chris Hayward, and they created *The Munsters,* perhaps an obvious next step for a cartoonist. Burns then moved on to the comedy series *He and She,* where he won the first of six Emmy Awards for his writing. Of that series Burns says, "That was my first great experience, creating character rather than gimmicks." On *He and She,* he met Jay Sandrich, who was directing the show.

Hayward and Burns then became story editors for *Get Smart,* where they worked with Mel Brooks and Buck Henry and where Sandrich also worked for a time as a producer. Following that experience, the Burns-Hayward partnership dissolved, and in 1969 Burns saw the pilot of *Room 222* (created by James L. Brooks), liked it, and began to write for the show. When Brooks took a leave to do a movie, Grant Tinker, the executive in charge of programming, asked Burns to produce *Room 222.*

At about this same time, Tinker received a 13-week commitment from CBS for an undeveloped series starring Mary Tyler Moore, to whom he was then married. CBS agreed that the project was to be under the complete control of Tinker and Moore; Tinker approached Burns and Brooks and asked them to collaborate to develop a show. As Burns remembers, "We had this remarkable situation where we had an office and an on-air commitment and nothing else."

The group rejected the idea of a domestic comedy and determined to portray a woman who was 30 years old, unmarried, and employed "somewhere." Burns recalls that they had to explain "30 and unmarried" to the network, so "We thought, 'Ah! here is our chance to do a divorce.'" CBS would have no part of that idea, however, and the executives in New York sent word to Tinker, "Get rid of those guys." He refused. Instead, the creators changed the plot to begin with Mary having just ended a failed love affair. The pilot was made, with Sandrich directing, and one of television's landmark series, *The Mary Tyler Moore Show,* was on its way.

In 1977, when the show concluded after 168 episodes, most of the writing staff moved to Paramount with long-term contracts. Burns, however, decided to stay with Tinker and joined with Gene Reynolds to create *Lou Grant.* Despite the fact that it essentially reinvented the Lou Grant character, the series was a major success, and soon became part of the CBS Monday-night response to ABC football.

Burns also directed his talent to the writing of feature films, one being the highly praised *A Little Romance,* starring Laurence Olivier, for which Burns received an Oscar nomination for Best Screenplay Adaptation. Burns left MTM in 1991 after developing several other TV series.

Calm and persuasive, Allan Burns combines outstanding talent with an ability to work extremely well with a variety of competing personalities. Observing him on the set of a series in production, one senses that he quickly commands both trust and respect from those with whom he collaborates. Director Sandrich sums it up well, "Allan is the best."

Robert S. Alley

See also ***Lou Grant; Mary Tyler Moore Show, The***

Writer/director Allan Burns with Christine Lahti.
Courtesy of the Everett Collection

Allan Burns. Born in Baltimore, Maryland, May 18, 1935. Attended University of Oregon, 1953–56. Married: Joan Bailey, 1964, children: Eric C. and Matthew M. Screen and television writer from 1964. Recipient: Emmy Awards, 1968, 1971, 1977, 1974, 1976, 1977; Writers Guild Award, 1970.

Television Series

1964–66	*The Munsters* (co-creator)
1965–70	*Get Smart* (head writer)
1967–68	*He and She* (head writer)
1969–74	*Room 222* (also director and producer)
1970–77	*The Mary Tyler Moore Show* (also creator)
1974–75	*Paul Sand in Friends and Lovers* (creator and producer)
1974–78	*Rhoda* (also creator)
1977–82	*Lou Grant* (also creator)
1984	*The Duck Factory* (also creator)
1988	*Eisenhower and Lutz* (also creator)

Films

Butch and Sundance: The Early Days, 1979; *A Little Romance,* 1979; *I Won't Dance,* 1983; *Just the Way You Are,* 1984; *Just Between Friends* (also director and coproducer), 1986.

Further Reading

Newcomb, Horace, and Robert S. Alley, *The Producer's Medium: Conversations with Creators of American TV,* New York: Oxford University Press, 1983

Burns, George (1896–1996)

U.S. Comedian, Actor

Over the course of his lengthy career, George Burns moved from serving as a vaudeville straight man to being one of the grand old men of American show business and an expert on the history of entertainment in the United States. The television program he shared with his wife, comedienne Gracie Allen, for eight years (1950 to 1958 on CBS) was central to Burns's professional life, chronologically and symbolically.

According to accounts of his early life (all of which originate from Burns himself), he was drawn to show business as a small child, singing on street corners with friends for pennies, and never seriously considered any other calling. Burns floundered in vaudeville for years, changing his act with great frequency, until he met Allen in 1922 (or 1923; accounts vary), and the couple inaugurated the straight-man/"Dumb Dora" pairing they would enact for more than four decades. The team moved successfully into film and radio in the early 1930s and finally into television in October 1950.

In *The George Burns and Gracie Allen Show,* Burns and Allen played versions of themselves, a show-business couple living in Beverly Hills, California. As she had throughout their joint career, Allen acted as the comedian of the two, creating chaos through her misunderstandings of the world about her, while Burns served as her straight man. He helped establish her elaborate humorous situations, set the timing for their conversations, and lovingly extricated his partner and wife from the fictional consequences of her "zany" personality—all the while maintaining a deadpan stance.

The pair were supported by Bea Benaderet playing their neighbor Blanche Morton, by a series of actors portraying Blanche's husband Harry, by their announcer (first Bill Goodwin, later Harry von Zell) playing himself, and eventually by their son Ronnie. The program was playful and sophisticated, relying more on linguistic than on physical humor. Although the character of Gracie was dumb in many ways, she never lost the respect and affection of her fellow cast members, particularly not of her husband. Her mistakes were never unkind, and her dumbness was in its own way brilliant. Perhaps more than any other couple-oriented situation comedy of its day, *Burns and Allen* presented an egalitarian marriage, in large part because George Burns as straight man was always dependent on his partner's comic abilities.

Burns used the new medium of television to expand his straight-man role, however. In *Gracie: A Love Story,* his 1988 biography of Allen, he jokingly explained his function in planning the show:

George Burns.
Courtesy of the Everett Collection

> My major contribution to the format was to suggest that I be able to step out of the plot and speak directly to the audience, and then be able to go right back into the action. That was an original idea of mine; I know it was because I originally stole it from Thornton Wilder's play *Our Town*.

Burns thus moved from merely setting up his partner's jokes to interpreting them, and indeed the entire action of the program, to the audience. Eventually, the program's writers (of whom Burns himself served as the head) gave the character George-as-narrator additional omniscience by placing a magic television set in his den. This device enabled him to monitor and comment on the plot even when he was not directly involved in it.

Television gave additional responsibilities to the off-screen George Burns as well as to his on-screen counterpart. Like many video stars of the 1950s, Burns owned the program in which he starred. His production company, McCadden, also produced or coproduced a number of advertisements and two other situation comedies: *The Bob Cummings Show* (1955–59) and *The People's Choice* (1955–58).

The ever-busy Burns also used the *Burns and Allen* years to become an author. He produced his first volume of memoirs, *I Love Her, That's Why!,* with Cynthia Hobart Lindsay in 1955. The book enhanced Burns's reputation as a raconteur and staked his claim to authorship of the Burns and Allen team.

Unfortunately for Burns, he was soon to discover that he was still not the star of that team. When Allen retired from their act and from show business in 1958, he immediately reassembled his writers and his cast to churn out *The George Burns Show,* a situation comedy featuring all of *The George Burns and Gracie Allen Show*'s characters except Allen. The show foundered after one season.

Burns persevered, trying nightclub work alone and with other actresses. In the fall of 1964, attempting to recover from Allen's death earlier that year, he returned to television, costarring in *Wendy and Me* with Connie Stevens and producing *No Time for Sergeants.* Neither program lasted beyond the first season. The following year, he was back producing another short-lived program, *Mona McCluskey.*

Burns continued to move along on the edges of American show business until 1975, when, after the death of his close friend Jack Benny, he was given Benny's part in the film version of Neil Simon's comedy *The Sunshine Boys.* His success in this role led to other film work (including portrayal of the almighty in three *Oh, God!* pictures), television specials, and contracts for several more books—mostly memoirs.

His final book, *100 Years, 100 Stories,* was published in 1996. In many ways, this small and entertaining volume summed up the life and career of George Burns. It consisted of a number of often retold, highly repolished jokes. Its origins, like Burns's own ethnic roots, were obscured but oddly irrelevant-seeming. (Burns himself was in such poor health during the book's production that he clearly played little part in writing it; nevertheless, the stories were ones he had told for years and years.) Years after Allen's death, the book's content still depended heavily on Burns's relationship with his wife, who figured prominently in many of the stories. And coming out as it did in the weeks between its author's 100th birthday in January of 1996 and his death in March, this final volume exhibited the sort of timing for which George Burns was justly renowned.

TINKY "DAKOTA" WEISBLAT

See also **Allen, Gracie; *George Burns and Gracie Allen Show, The***

George Burns. Born Nathan Birnbaum, in New York City, January 20, 1896. Married: Gracie Allen, 1926 (died, 1964); children: Sandra Jean and Ronald Jon. Early career in vaudeville as singer in children's quartet, then as dancer, roller skater, and comedian; formed comedy partnership with Gracie Allen, 1923; costarred with Allen in radio program, 1932–50; partnership moved to television in *The George Burns and Gracie Allen Show,* 1950–58; continued as star of *The George Burns Show,* 1958–59; after death of Allen in 1964, continued to work in film, notably in *The Sunshine Boys,* 1976. Honorary degree: University of Hartford, 1988. Recipient: Academy Award, 1976; Kennedy Center Honor, 1988. Died in Beverly Hills, California, March 9, 1996.

Television Series

1950–58	*The George Burns and Gracie Allen Show*
1958–59	*The George Burns Show*
1964–65	*Wendy and Me*
1964	*No Time for Sergeants* (producer)
1965	*Mona McCluskey* (producer)
1985	*George Burns Comedy Week*

Television Specials (selected)

1959	*George Burns in the Big Time*
1976	*The George Burns Special*
1977	*The George Burns One-Man Show*
1981	*George Burns in Nashville*
1981	*George Burns' Early, Early, Early Christmas Show*
1982	*George Burns' 100th Birthday Party*
1982	*George Burns and Other Sex Symbols*
1983	*George Burns Celebrates 80 Years in Show Business*
1983	*Grandpa, Will You Run with Me?*
1984	*George Burns: An Hour of Jokes and Songs*
1984	*George Burns' How to Live to Be 100*
1986	*George Burns' 90th Birthday Party: A Very Special Special*
1988	*Disney's Magic in the Kingdom* (host)
1991	*George Burns' 95th Birthday Party*

Films

Lamb Chops, 1929; *Fit to Be Tied,* 1930; *Pulling a Bone,* 1930; *The Antique Shop,* 1931; *Once Over, Light,* 1931; *One Hundred Per Cent Service,* 1931; *The Big Broadcast of 1932,* 1932; *Oh My Operation,* 1932; *The Babbling Book,* 1932; *Hollywood on Parade A-2,* 1932; *International House,* 1933; *Love in Bloom,* 1933; *College Humor,* 1933; *Patents Pending,* 1933; *Let's Dance,* 1933; *Walking the Baby,* 1933; *Six of a Kind,* 1934; *We're Not Dressing,* 1934; *Many Happy Returns,* 1934; *Here Comes Cookie,* 1935; *Love in Bloom,* 1935; *The Big Broadcast of 1936,* 1936; *College Holiday,* 1936; *The Big Broadcast of 1937,* 1937; *A Damsel in Distress,* 1937; *College Swing,* 1938; *Many Happy Returns,* 1939; *Honolulu,* 1939; *Two Girls and a Sailor,* 1944; *Screen Snapshots No. 224,* 1954; *The Solid Gold Cadillac* (narrator only), 1956; *The Sunshine Boys,* 1975; *Oh God!,* 1977; *Sgt. Pepper's Lonely Hearts Club Band,* 1978; *Going in Style,* 1979; *Just You and Me, Kid,* 1979; *Two of a Kind,* 1979; *Oh God! Book Two,* 1980; *Oh God, You Devil!,* 1984; *Eighteen Again,* 1988; *Radioland Murders,* 1994.

Recordings

I Wish I Was Young Again, 1981; *George Burns in Nashville,* 1981; *George Burns—Young at Heart,* 1982; *As Time Goes By* (with Bobby Vinton), 1993.

Publications

I Love Her, That's Why! (with Cynthia Hobart Lindsay), 1955
Living It Up, or, They Still Love Me in Altoona, 1976
How to Live to Be 100: Or More! The Ultimate Diet, Sex and Exercise Book, 1983
Dear George: Advice and Answers from America's Leading Expert on Everything from A to Z, 1985
Gracie: A Love Story, 1988
All My Best Friends (with David Fisher), 1989
Wisdom of the 90s (with Hal Goldman), 1991
100 Years, 100 Stories, 1996

Further Reading

Blythe, Cheryl, and Susan Sackett, *Say Goodnight Gracie! The Story of Burns and Allen,* New York: Dutton, 1986

Burns, Ken (1953–)

U.S. Documentary Filmmaker

Ken Burns is one of public television's most celebrated and prolific producers. He has already fashioned a record of 16 major Public Broadcasting System (PBS) specials, addressing a wide range of topics from U.S. history, such as *Brooklyn Bridge* (1982), *The Shakers: Hands to Work, Hearts to God* (1985), *The Statue of Liberty* (1985), *Huey Long* (1986), *Thomas Hart Benton* (1989), *The Congress* (1989), *The Civil War* (1990), *Empire of the Air: The Men Who Made Radio* (1992), *Baseball* (1994), *The West* (1996), *Thomas Jefferson* (1997), *Lewis and Clark: The Journey of the Corps of Discovery* (1997), *Frank Lloyd Wright* (1998), *Not For Ourselves Alone: The Story of Elizabeth Cady Stanton and Susan B. Anthony* (1999), *Jazz* (2001), and *Mark Twain* (2002), all of which have won various awards and recognitions from both professional and scholarly organizations and at international film festivals.

Burns is a 1975 graduate of Hampshire College in Amherst, Massachusetts, where he studied under the photographers Jerome Liebling and Elaine Mayes, and received a degree in film studies and design. Upon graduation, he and two of his college friends started Florentine Films and struggled for a number of years doing freelance assignments, finishing a few short documentaries before beginning work in 1977 on a film based on David McCullough's book, *The Great Bridge* (1972). Four years later, they completed *Brooklyn Bridge,* which won several honors, including an Academy Award nomination, thus ushering Burns into the ambit of public television. While editing *Brooklyn Bridge* in 1979, Burns moved Florentine Films to Walpole, New Hampshire, surviving on as little as "$2,500 one year to stay independent."

Much about Burns's career defies conventional wisdom. He operates his own independent company in a small New England village more than four hours north of New York City, hardly a crossroads in the highly competitive and often insular world of corporate-funded, PBS-sponsored productions. His television career is a popular and critical success story, beginning at a time when the historical documentary generally holds little interest for most Americans. His PBS specials so far are also strikingly out of step with the visual pyrotechnics and frenetic pacing of most reality-based TV programming, relying instead on techniques that are literally decades old, although Burns reintegrates these constituent elements into a wholly new and highly complex textual arrangement.

Beginning with *Brooklyn Bridge* and continuing through *Mark Twain,* Burns has intricately blended narration with what he calls his "chorus of voices," meaning readings from personal papers, diaries, and letters; interpretive commentaries from on-screen experts, usually historians; his "rephotographing" technique, which closely examines photographs, paintings, drawings, daguerreotypes, and other artifacts with a movie camera; all backed with a musical track that features period compositions and folk music. The effect of this collage of techniques is to create the illusion that the viewer is being transported back in time, literally finding an emotional connection with the people and events of America's past.

At first, it may appear that Burns has embraced a wide assortment of subjects—a bridge, a 19th-century religious sect, a statue, a demagogue, a painter, Congress, the Civil War, radio, the national pastime, the United States' westward expansion, a founding father, two early explorers, an architect, two seminal feminists, a musical genre, and a writer—but several underlying common denominators bind this medley of Americana together. Burns's body of work casts an image of America that is built on consensus and is celebratory in nature, highlighting the nation's ideals and achievements. He suggests, moreover, that "television can become a new Homeric mode," drawing narrative parameters that are epic and heroic in scope. The epic form tends to celebrate a people's shared tradition in sweeping terms, while recounting the lives of national heroes is the classical way of imparting values by erecting edifying examples for present and future generations.

In this way, Burns's chronicles are populated with seemingly ordinary men and women who rise up from the ranks of the citizenry to become paragons of national (and occasionally transcendent) achievement, always persisting against great odds. The Brooklyn Bridge, for example, described by the "chorus of voices" in Burns's first film as "a work of art" and "the greatest feat of civil engineering in the world," is the "inspiration" of a kind of "Renaissance man," John A.

Roebling, who died as the building of the bridge was beginning, and his son, Washington Roebling, who finished the monument 14 years later through his own dogged perseverance and courage, despite being bedridden in the process.

Along with being an outstanding documentarian and popular historian, Burns, like all important cultural voices, is also a moralist. Taken as a whole, his series of films stand as morality tales, drawing upon epic events, landmarks, and institutions of historical significance. They are populated by heroes and villains who allegorically personify certain virtues and vices in the national character as understood through the popular mythology of modern memory. At the beginning of *Empire of the Air,* for instance, Jason Robards's narration explains how Lee DeForest, David Sarnoff, and Edwin H. Armstrong "were driven to create [radio] by ancient qualities, idealism and imagination, greed and envy, ambition and determination, and genius." Burns himself describes Huey Long as "a tragic, almost Shakespearean story of a man who started off good, went bad, and got killed for it."

Burns is best known of course, for his 11-hour documentary series *The Civil War.* The overwhelming popularity of this program, aired in September 1990, made him a household name. Much of the success of the series must be attributed to Burns's ability to make this 130-year-old conflict immediate and comprehensible to a contemporary audience. He adopted a similar strategy with *Baseball.* That documentary, he has stated, "is as much about American social history as it is about the game," as it examines such issues as immigration, assimilation, labor and management conflicts, and, most importantly, race relations. Burns explains that "Jackie Robinson and his story are sort of the center of gravity for the film, the Gettysburg Address and Emancipation Proclamation rolled into one." This 18.5-hour history of the sport debuted over nine evenings in September 1994, lasting nearly twice as long and costing twice the budget ($7 million) of *The Civil War.*

Most remarkably, 70 million Americans have now seen *The Civil War,* while 50 million have watched *Baseball;* and all of Burns's other documentaries from the mid-1990s on have averaged an estimated 15 million viewers during their debut telecasts. "I've been working in two parallel tracks," Burns describes, "One has been a trilogy of three major series—*The Civil War, Baseball,* and *Jazz*—and in a parallel track, I've been working on a series of biographical portraits."

The cumulative popularity of Burns's biographical or quasi-biographical histories is striking by virtually any measure, and these films have over time redefined the place of documentaries on prime-time television.

Ken Burns.
Photo courtesy of Lisa Berg/General Motors/ Florentine Films

Jazz, specifically, is fully representative of Burns's work at midcareer. This ambitious, multipart documentary confirms certain aesthetic and ideological priorities, honed by Burns over a quarter-century of producing and directing television specials for PBS. Approaching 19 hours (and more than 150 years of American history), the miniseries exhibits an epic storyline overflowing with historical people, places, and events.

Nielsen averages put *Jazz* at a 3.6 household rating and a 6 percent share of the national audience for the run of the ten episodes during four successive weeks in January 2001. These percentages are double the customary public television averages, translating into approximately 23 million viewers when calculated over the entire length of the miniseries. Given the aggregate numbers eventually amassed by both *The Civil War* and *Baseball, Jazz*'s U.S. audience is likely to double in the first decade of the 21st century and then expand.

Despite his long-standing and highly successful affiliation with noncommercial television in the United States, Burns still remembers his boyhood dream of becoming the next John Ford. It is likely that noone has ever done a better job of probing and revivifying the past for more Americans through the power and reach of prime-time television than Ken Burns.

GARY R. EDGERTON

See also ***Civil War, The***

Ken Burns. Born in Brooklyn, New York, July 29, 1953. Educated at Hampshire College, B.A. in film studies and design, 1975. Married: Amy Stechler, 1982, children: Sarah and Lily. Cinematographer, BBC, Italian television, and others; president and owner, Florentine Films, since 1975; producer, cinematographer, and director of documentaries, since 1977. Member: Academy of Motion Picture Arts and Sciences; Society of American Historians; American Antiquarian Society; Massachusetts Historical Society; Walpole Society for Bringing to Justice Horse Thieves and Pilferers. Honorary degrees (selection): University of New Hampshire, L.H.D., Notre Dame College, Litt.D., Amherst College, Litt.D., 1991, Pace University, L.H.D., Bowdoin College, L.H.D., 1991, and CUNY, Ph.D. Recipient: Christopher Awards, 1973, 1987, 1990; two Erik Barnouw Awards; eight CINE Golden Eagle Awards; Producer's Guild of America's Producer of the Year Award, 1990; two Emmy Awards, 1991; People's Choice Award, 1991.

Television Documentaries (producer, director, cinematographer)

1982 *Brooklyn Bridge*
1985 *The Shakers: Hands to Work, Hearts to God* (also co-writer)
1985 *The Statue of Liberty*
1986 *Huey Long* (also co-writer)
1989 *The Congress*
1989 *Thomas Hart Benton*
1990 *Lindbergh* (executive producer only)
1990 *The Civil War* (also co-writer)
1991 *The Songs of the Civil War*
1992 *Empire of the Air: The Men Who Made Radio*
1994 *Baseball*
1996 *The West*
1997 *Thomas Jefferson*
1997 *Lewis and Clark: The Journey of the Corps of Discovery*
1998 *Frank Lloyd Wright*
1999 *Not For Ourselves Alone: The Story of Elizabeth Cady Stanton and Susan B. Anthony*
2001 *Jazz*
2002 *Mark Twain*

Publications

The Shakers: Hands to Work, Hearts to God (with Amy Stechler Burns), 1987
The Civil War: An Illustrated History (with Ric Burns and Geoffrey C. Ward), 1990
Baseball: An Illustrated History (with Geoffrey C. Ward), 1994
"Preface" (with Stephen Ives), *The West: An Illustrated History,* 1996
"Preface," *Jazz: A History of America's Music,* by Geoffrey C. Ward, 2000

Further Reading

Cripps, Thomas, "Historical Truth: An Interview with Ken Burns," *American Historical Review* (June 1995)
Edgerton, Gary, "Ken Burns's America: Style, Authorship, and Cultural Memory," *Journal of Popular Film and Television* (Summer 1993)
Edgerton, Gary, "Ken Burns's American Dream: Histories-for-TV from Walpole, New Hampshire," *Television Quarterly* (Winter 1994)
Edgerton, Gary, *Ken Burns's America,* New York: Palgrave/St. Martin's Press, 2001
Thelen, David, "The Movie Maker As Historian: Conversations with Ken Burns," *Journal of American History* (December 1994)
Thomson, David, "History Composed with Film," *Film Comment* (September–October 1990)
Tibbetts, John C., "The Incredible Stillness of Being: Motionless Pictures in the Films of Ken Burns," *American Studies* (Spring 1996)

Burr, Raymond (1917–1993)

U.S. Actor

Raymond Burr is so associated with his characterization of television lawyer/detective *Perry Mason* that his rich and varied career in film, radio, and television is often ignored. His face, in the words of *Perry Mason* creator Erle Stanley Gardner, was cow-eyed. He was broad-shouldered, heavy, robust, but excelled at playing introverted rather than extroverted characters. This may be, in part, why Burr accomplished the rare television feat in which actor becomes almost thoroughly identified with character, the performer inseparable from the role. Just as William Shatner is James Kirk, Peter Falk is Columbo, and Carroll O'Connor is Archie Bunker, Burr is Perry Mason.

Burr began as a stage actor who performed small roles in radio. His early film work was remarkable only in the sense that he rarely played anything other than the villain in such films as *Raw Deal* (1948). Burr even managed to play the "heavy" in comedies, such as the Marx Brothers' *Love Happy* (1949). When he was in the courtroom drama *A Place in the Sun* (1951), he assumed the role of the relentless district attorney. During these movie years Burr continued to work in several radio series such as *Pat Novak for Hire* (1949) and *Dragnet* (1949–50). In 1954 he confirmed his villainous persona with his appearance as the menacing wife-killer Lars Thorwald in Alfred Hitchcock's *Rear Window* (1954).

In 1955, when he learned that the lawyer/detective drama *Perry Mason* was being cast for television, Burr was requested to audition—but for the part of district attorney Hamilton Burger, another "villain." As the story goes, the producers at Paisano Productions (the *Perry Mason* production company) allowed Burr to try for the title role simply to secure his audition for Burger. Erle Stanley Gardner, author of the original Mason novels and co-creator of the television series, is said to have taken a look at Burr during the audition and declared "He's Perry Mason." This was the role Burr played from 1957 to 1966 and reprised in a successful series of made-for-television movies from 1985 until his death in 1993.

At the time of *Perry Mason*'s popularity, Burr was one of the highest paid actors in series television, commanding a yearly salary of $1 million. Yet he was well known for his philanthropy. Between television production seasons, he would take the time to journey to Vietnam on his own—not to perform but to meet and visit with those serving on the front lines. Burr was comfortable with self-deprecating humor and appeared in numerous television send-ups of his own career and characters on shows such as *The Jack Benny Show* and *The Red Skelton Show.*

What happened to Burr was a classic case of an actor being blended with a character he or she successfully plays. During his time on *Perry Mason,* Burr and his character gradually merged so much that when the series was recast in 1973, with Monte Markham in the title role, the audience refused to accept anyone else as Mason. The Markham version was canceled after 15 unsuccessful episodes. The Burr-Mason association was so strong that Burr even received an honorary law doctorate from the McGeorge School of Law in Sacramento, California.

Raymond Burr.
Courtesy of the Everett Collection

This connection between character and actor was a burden to Burr. He continued to be associated with Mason, even when he starred as a wheelchair-bound policeman in another successful series, *Ironside* (1967–75). In this series, Burr portrayed Chief of Detectives Robert Ironside, crippled by an assassin's bullet in the pilot episode. Although urged to retire, Ironside worked to ferret out criminals—this time from the prosecution's side. The show was pure crime drama common to the late 1960s, mixed with "hip" dialogue and situations relevant to the time. As Richard Meyers argues in *TV Detectives* (1988), Ironside was the perfect "armchair detective." It was still rational detection, in the *Perry Mason* mode, that was Burr's strongest asset.

Burr tried several other series, but after the twin successes of *Perry Mason* and *Ironside* he was unable to capture the unity of character that a television series needs. In 1976, he had the title role of a lawyer in *Mallory: Circumstantial Evidence,* a pilot that never went to series. Next he played an investigative reporter in *Kingston,* which aired as a series for less than a season 1977, and another lawyer in *The Jordan Chance* (1978), also a failed pilot. Through the early to mid-1980s Burr was a pitchman for a number of products such as the Independent Insurance Agents association.

Only when he revisited the role of Mason in the made-for-television movie *Perry Mason Returns* (1985) was he able to renew his success in American television. He also reprised his role as Chief Ironside in *The Return of Ironside* in 1993. The original cast returned for what was planned to be a new series of made-for-television movies, but only the first movie was completed. Burr finally succumbed to cancer on September 12, 1993.

To every character, Burr brought a cool calculation and intensity. In his three most notable roles—as Lars Thorwald in Hitchcock's *Rear Window,* Perry Mason, and Robert Ironside—his acting is introspective and low-key. He portrayed Thorwald as stony-faced and deliberate, thoroughly menacing. That same focus was present in his Mason and Ironside characters, but in those roles it transformed Burr into the hero rather than the villain. While his Thorwald could level a stare across a courtyard to frighten voyeurs looking out their rear window, his Mason could stare down a witness and bring a quick and heartfelt confession. Burr's stare still reveals more than the ranting and pacing of most other actors.

J. Dennis Bounds

See also ***Perry Mason***

Raymond Burr. Born in New Westminster, British Columbia, Canada, May 21, 1917. Attended Stanford University, University of California, Columbia University, and University of Chungking. Married: 1) Annette Sutherland, 1941 (died, 1943); children: Michael and Evan (died, 1953); 2) Isabella Ward, 1947 (divorced); 3) Laura Andrina Morgan, 1953 (died, 1955). Served in California Conservation Corp and Forestry Service. Began stage career as teenager, eventually performing on Broadway in *Crazy with the Heat,* 1941, and *The Duke in Darkness,* 1944; director, Pasadena Community Playhouse, 1943; started film career in 1946; cast often as villain, notably in *A Place in the Sun,* 1951, and *Rear Window,* 1954; television actor, appearing as title character in *Perry Mason,* CBS, 1957–66, and *Ironside,* NBC, 1967–75; returned to television as Perry Mason in 1985–86 made-for-television movie, which led to 25 subsequent Perry Mason made-for-television movies on NBC; started Royal Blue Ltd., television production company with business partner Robert Benevides, 1988. Recipient: Emmy Awards, 1959 and 1961. Died in Dry Creek, California, September 12, 1993.

Television Series

1957–66	*Perry Mason*
1967–75	*Ironside*
1977	*Kingston: Confidential*

Television Miniseries

1977–79	*Park Ave*
1978	*Centennial*
1978	*The Bastard*

Made-for-Television Movies

1967	*Ironside: Split Second to an Epitaph*
1971	*The Priest Killer*
1976	*Mallory: Circumstantial Evidence*
1977	*Kingston* (pilot)
1978	*The Bastard* (narrator)
1978	*The Jordan Chance*
1979	*Love's Savage Fury*
1979	*Disaster on the Coastliner*
1980	*Curse of King Tut's Tomb*
1980	*The Night the City Screamed*
1981	*Peter and Paul*
1985	*Perry Mason Returns*
1986	*Perry Mason: The Case of the Notorious Nun*
1986	*Perry Mason: The Case of the Shooting Star*
1987	*Perry Mason: The Case of the Lost Love*
1987	*Perry Mason: The Case of the Murdered Madam*
1987	*Perry Mason: The Case of the Scandalous Scoundrel*
1987	*Perry Mason: The Case of the Sinister Spirit*
1988	*Perry Mason: The Case of the Avenging Ace*
1988	*Perry Mason: The Case of the Lady in the Lake*
1989	*Perry Mason: The Case of the All-Star Assassin*
1989	*Perry Mason: The Case of the Lethal Lesson*
1989	*Perry Mason: The Case of the Musical Murder*
1990	*Perry Mason: The Case of the Desperate Deception*
1990	*Perry Mason: The Case of the Poisoned Pen*
1990	*Perry Mason: The Case of the Silenced Singer*
1990	*Perry Mason: The Case of the Defiant Daughter*
1991	*Perry Mason: The Case of the Maligned Mobster*
1991	*Perry Mason: The Case of the Ruthless Reporter*
1991	*Perry Mason: The Case of the Glass Coffin*
1991	*Perry Mason: The Case of the Fatal Fashion*

1992	*Perry Mason: The Case of the Fatal Framing Grass Roots*
1992	*Perry Mason: The Case of the Reckless Romeo*
1992	*Perry Mason: The Case of the Heartbroken Bride*
1993	*The Return of Ironside*
1993	*Perry Mason: The Case of the Telltale Talk Show Host*
1993	*Perry Mason: The Case of the Skin-Deep Scandal*
1993	*Perry Mason: The Case of the Killer Kiss*

Films

Without Reservations, 1946; *San Quentin,* 1947; *Code of the West,* 1947; *Desperate,* 1947; *I Love Trouble,* 1947; *Fighting Father Dunne,* 1948; *Pitfall,* 1948; *Raw Deal,* 1948; *Ruthless,* 1948; *Sleep My Love,* 1948; *Station West,* 1948; *Walk a Crooked Mile,* 1948; *The Adventures of Don Juan,* 1948; *Abandoned,* 1949; *Black Magic,* 1949; *Bride of Vengeance,* 1949; *Love Happy,* 1949; *Red Light,* 1949; *Borderline,* 1950; *Key to the City,* 1950; *Unmasked,* 1950; *Bride of the Gorilla,* 1951; *His Kind of Woman,* 1951; *M,* 1951; *The Magic Carpet,* 1951; *New Mexico,* 1951; *A Place in the Sun,* 1951; *The Whip Hand,* 1951; *Horizons West,* 1952; *Mara Maru,* 1952; *Meet Danny Wilson,* 1952; *Bandits of Corsica,* 1953; *The Blue Gardenia,* 1953; *Fort Algiers,* 1953; *Serpent of the Nile,* 1953; *Tarzan and the She-Devil,* 1953; *Casanova's Big Night,* 1954; *Gorilla at Large,* 1954; *Khyber Patrol,* 1954; *Passion,* 1954; *Rear Window,* 1954; *Thunder Pass,* 1954; *Count Three and Pray,* 1955; *A Man Alone,* 1955; *They Were So Young,* 1954; *You're Never Too Young,* 1955; *The Brass Legend,* 1956; *A Cry in the Night,* 1956; *Godzilla: King of the Monsters,* 1956; *Great Day in the Morning,* 1956; *Please Murder Me,* 1956; *Ride the High Iron,* 1956; *Secret of Treasure Mountain,* 1956; *Affair in Havana,* 1957; *Crime of Passion,* 1957; *Desire in the Dust,* 1960; *P.J.,* 1968; *Tomorrow Never Comes,* 1977; *The Return,* 1980; *Out of the Blue,* 1980; *Airplane II: The Sequel,* 1982; *Godzilla 1985,* 1985; *Delirious,* 1985.

Stage

Night Must Fall; Mandarin; Crazy with the Heat, 1941; *The Duke in Darkness,* 1944.

Further Reading

Hill, Ona L., *Raymond Burr: A Film, Radio, and Television Biography,* Jefferson, North Carolina: McFarland, 1994

Kelleher, Brian, and Diana Merrill, *The Perry Mason Show Book,* New York: St. Martin's Press, 1987

Margolick, David, "Raymond Burr's Perry Mason Was Fictional, but He Surely Was Relevant and, Oh, So Competent," *New York Times* (September 24, 1993)

Martindale, David, *The Perry Mason Casebook,* New York: Pioneer, 1991

Meyers, Richard, *TV Detectives,* San Diego, California: A.S. Barnes, 1988

Burrows, James (1940–)

U.S. Director, Producer

James Burrows is one of the few television directors who has made the successful transition to producer. He became one of the top sitcom directors at MTM Productions, the company founded by Mary Tyler Moore and Grant Tinker. Later, while working as the resident director for *Taxi,* Burrows helped form the independent production company responsible for the long-running NBC series *Cheers.* His critically acclaimed directing and production talents have won numerous awards, including nine Emmys.

One of Burrows's first goals was to establish an identity separate from that of his famous father, Abe, who had written the books for a number of successful musicals, including *Guys and Dolls* and *How To Succeed in Business Without Really Trying.* Interestingly, the senior Burrows had also written for the popular 1930s radio series *Duffy's Tavern,* which, like *Cheers,* was set in a bar. While this did not inspire the younger Burrows to duplicate that situation in *Cheers,* his father's work on a stage adaptation of Truman Capote's *Breakfast at Tiffany's,* which starred Mary Tyler Moore, did lead James Burrows to an informal meeting with MTM President Grant Tinker. At that time, the younger Burrows was known simply as "Abe's kid."

In 1974, while directing theater in Florida, Burrows asked Tinker for a job at MTM. Tinker hired him to observe other MTM sitcom directors, with his first assignment being *The Bob Newhart Show.* Tinker recounts in his autobiography, *Tinker in Television,* that as Burrows became more comfortable with his role as observer, he began drawing closer to the action on the *Bob Newhart* set, causing Newhart to turn to his producer and demand, "Get that guy out of here. He makes me nervous."

This incident marked a significant turning point in Burrows's career, for Tinker responded by teaming Burrows with MTM's veteran director Jay Sandrich. The two hit it off immediately, and Burrows proved a quick study. Today he is considered as accomplished a director as Sandrich himself. Like Sandrich, he developed a directing style sensitive to the specific needs of the weekly sitcom format, which includes actors who already have a deep understanding of the characters they portray. Burrows's goal is to make his actors "director proof," so that subsequent directors do not erode the developed, established personae.

Burrows stayed with MTM until 1977, gaining directing experience on every sitcom they produced, including *The Bob Newhart Show.* He then joined MTM alumni James L. Brooks, Stan Daniels, David Davis, and Ed Weinberger on the series *Taxi,* for which he directed 76 episodes. Because *Taxi* had such a large set, Burrows became one of the first directors to use four cameras simultaneously, an adaptation of the three-camera system that had been a staple of sitcom production since *I Love Lucy.* A testament to his talent, Burrows won Emmys in both 1980 and 1981 for his *Taxi* efforts.

In 1982 Burrows, along with Glen Charles and Les Charles, formed the Charles-Burrows-Charles Company and then created and produced *Cheers.* Lasting into the 1990s, *Cheers* allowed Burrows, now in the role of producer, to carry on the tradition of quality television established two decades earlier at MTM. Although the Charles-Burrows-Charles Company disbanded after *Cheers* voluntarily retired, Burrows has continued working as a director for such comedies as *Wings, Friends, News Radio, Third Rock from the Sun, The Tracey Ullman Show,* and *Frasier.* He is executive producer of the NBC sitcom *Will & Grace,* and directed every episode of the first three seasons.

MICHAEL KASSEL

See also ***Bob Newhart Show, The/Newhart; Cheers; Mary Tyler Moore Show, The; Taxi***

James Burrows. Born in Los Angeles, California, December 30, 1940. Educated at Oberlin College, B.A.; Yale University, M.F.A. Director, some off-Broadway productions; worked at MTM Productions, 1974–77, directed episodes of *The Mary Tyler Moore Show, The Bob Newhart Show, Rhoda, Phyllis, Taxi,* and *Lou Grant* for MTM; with Glen and Les Charles, formed Charles-Burrows-Charles Company, 1982; co-creator and co-executive producer, as well as director of *Cheers;* other directing credits include *Dear John* (pilot), *Night Court, Wings* (pilot), as well as episodes of *Friends, News Radio, The Tracey Ullman Show, Third Rock from the Sun, Frasier,* and *Will & Grace.* Recipient: three Directors Guild of America awards for comedy direction; nine Emmy Awards; American Comedy Award for Lifetime Achievement, 1996.

Television Series (as director of various episodes)

1970–71	*The Mary Tyler Moore Show*
1972–78	*The Bob Newhart Show*
1974–78	*Rhoda*
1975	*Fay*
1975–77	*Phyllis*
1976–83	*Laverne and Shirley*
1977	*Busting Loose*
1977–78	*The Betty White Show*
1977–82	*Lou Grant*
1978	*Husbands, Wives, and Lovers*
1978	*Free Country*
1978–83	*Taxi*
1979–80	*A New Kind of Family*
1979–80	*The Associates*
1980	*Good Time Harry*
1981–82	*Best of the West*
1982–93	*Cheers* (also co-creator, co-executive producer)
1984–92	*Night Court*
1986–88	*Valerie*
1986	*All Is Forgiven*
1987	*The Tortellis*
1987–90	*The Tracey Ullman Show*
1988	*Dear John* (pilot)
1990	*Wings* (pilot)
1990	*The Marshall Chronicles*
1990	*The Simpsons*
1991	*Flesh 'n' Blood*
1992–93	*Flying Blind*
1993–97	*Frasier*
1994–2004	*Friends*
1995–99	*Caroline in the City*
1995–99	*News Radio*
1995	*Partners*
1995	*Hudson Street*

1996–2001	*Third Rock from the Sun*
1996	*Pearl*
1996–97	*Men Behaving Badly*
1997	*Chicago Sons*
1997	*Fired Up* (pilot)
1997–98	*George and Leo*
1997–2002	*Dharma and Greg*
1997–2000	*Veronica's Closet*
1997	*Union Square*
1998–2001	*Will & Grace* (also executive producer)
1998	*Conrad Bloom*
1998–2000	*Jesse*
1999	*Ladies' Man*
1999–2000	*Stark Raving Mad*
2000	*Madigan Men*
2000–01	*Cursed (The Weber Show)*
2002	*Good Morning, Miami* (pilot)
2002	*Bram and Alice* (pilot)
2003	*Two and a Half Men* (pilot)
2003	*The Stones*

Made-for-Television Movies

1978	*More than Friends*
1981	*Every Stray Dog and Kid*
2002	*Dexter Prep Pilot*

Film (director)

Partners, 1982.

Further Reading

Lovece, Frank, and Jules Franco, *Hailing Taxi,* New York: Prentice Hall, 1988

Sackett, Susan, *Prime Time Hits,* New York: Billboard, 1993

Sorensen, Jeff, *The Taxi Book,* New York: St. Martin's Press, 1987

Tinker, Grant, with Bud Rukeyser, *Tinker in Television,* New York: Simon and Schuster, 1994

Van Hise, James, *Cheers: Where Everybody Knows Your Name,* Las Vegas, Nevada: Pioneer, 1993

C

Cable Modem

Cable modem systems deliver broadband connectivity, providing constant high-speed Internet access to small businesses and residential users. In the 1990s, major community antennae television (CATV) vendors improved their networks using fiber-optic cable to provide greater bandwidth and allocating channels to allow upstream capability. These renovations and others allowed millions of subscribers to receive broadband Internet connectivity over their traditional regional cable system. The first cable modems were tested in 1995 and commercially deployed in late 1996. By 1998 half a million subscribers received interactive broadband service via their local cable networks. As of the December 2001, cable companies claimed 7.2 million modem subscribers. Cable modem manufacturers include Cisco Systems, Motorola, Toshiba, and Sony.

Early cable modem systems in the 1990s did not use hybrid fiber-coaxial networks, and they often had to rely on traditional telephone modems for upstream capability. Users could download media at speeds of up to 2 megabits per second—much faster than the dominant 28.8 kilobit telephone modem connections, but much slower than contemporary systems, which have potential download speeds of 10 or more megabits per second. Because customers share the cables in their local neighborhoods, speeds can vary according to the number and activities of other people in the customer's neighborhood.

Cable modem technology allows service providers to use a 6 megahertz slice of bandwidth, the same size as a television channel, for downstream data. Up to a thousand users can use this 6 megahertz connection with the Internet, and this one channel is capable of throughput speeds of 30 to 40 megabits per second—very high speed indeed, although this bandwidth is shared among the system's users. Online content comes over an Internet connection to the cable system's head end and is routed through the cable modem termination system (CMTS). The CMTS sends downstream data to all cable modem users in the system, whose individual networks act as gatekeepers, recognizing whether or not the data is meant for them. On the customer's premises, the cable is connected to the actual cable modem, which modulates and demodulates the signal. The cable modem can be internal or external to the user's computer, and it can also be part of a digital system's set-top box. Incoming data is demodulated, changed from a radio frequency signal to the binary format of digitized data, which is then sent to the user's computer. When the cable modem customer sends information upstream, the data is remodulated and converted from the computer's digital format to radio frequency signals.

Cable modems generally provide asymmetrical access, allowing only a 2 megahertz channel of bandwidth for upstream use, assuming that customers are likely to need most of the bandwidth for downloads.

Users sending data upstream send it in small bursts to the CMTS, where it is then uploaded to the Internet. Since most of these bursts of upstream data consist of mouse clicks and other small pieces of information, the narrow upstream channel is usually sufficient.

One of the earliest challenges for cable modem service was standardization. CableLabs, a nonprofit research and development consortium, established Data Over Cable Service Interface Specification (DOCSIS), as an internationally recognized standard in 1998. The adoption of DOCSIS1.0 smoothed the way for multiple vendors to enter the cable modem market, defining standard interfaces among cable modems and promoting interoperability for multiple system operators (MSOs) offering cable modem service. Currently, the industry is studying a new version, DOCSIS 1.1, which will allow cable modem service providers to offer tiered services and greater security.

Security has been a primary concern for cable modem customers, due to the shared nature of the local network nodes. Cable modem users in the same neighborhood share the local node, which can accommodate up to 500 customers. Because of this, subscribers with active file-sharing capability risk having their files viewed by other subscribers. The constant connectivity of cable modem technology compounds this risk, making it easier for others to access a customer's computer, and also making the customer's system more vulnerable to deliberate online attacks. While DOCSIS standard modems use data encryption to prevent other network users from reading private transmissions, other basic precautions include shutting off file-sharing capability and installing firewalls.

In 2001 the primary players in cable modem service included the largest cable MSOs, such as Time Warner, Comcast, AT&T, and Cox Cable. These systems offer broadband access via proprietary Internet service providers (ISPs) such as Time Warner's Roadrunner system. Increasingly, however, competing ISPs are being allowed to enter these previously exclusive markets.

Originally, MSOs offered cable modem service with no choice of ISP. This meant that customers of AT&T's system had to do business with @Home, AT&T's broadband network, and customers of Time Warner had to do business with Roadrunner, Time Warner's cable ISP. Other ISP companies protested this arrangement, arguing that cable modem networks should allow for competitive ISPs, allowing "open access" to the established cable networks. This suggestion was initially met with much resistance from traditional cable operators, who referred to the issue as one of "forced access" and argued that it was unfair for regulators to allow external ISPs to take advantage of MSOs' hardware investments. The Federal Communications Commission (FCC) and Federal Trade Commission (FTC) mandated open access requirements in December 2000 and insisted that AOL and Time Warner agree to these regulations in order to receive approval for the companies' 2001 merger. Since then, other large cable systems including AT&T and Comcast have agreed to participate in "managed access" agreements, providing a choice of ISPs to their customers while avoiding potential common carrier status. One of the most visible ISPs involved in such managed access contracts is EarthLink, formerly known as MindSpring, a national ISP.

In March 2002, however, the FCC announced that cable modem service would be classified as an interstate information service, subject to FCC regulation but distinct from telecommunications service and exempt from common carrier regulation. The National Cable and Telecommunications Association (NCTA) responded favorably to this announcement, suggesting that this classification, combined with the current competition in broadband services, will result in an atmosphere of regulatory restraint.

Traditionally, MSOs offer a standard package of broadband Internet access and cable modem rental for $30 to $50 per month. About 30 percent of this revenue goes to proprietary ISP partners, such as Roadrunner, but this billing system will change as multiple ISP choices are offered to the customer.

KAREN GUSTAFSON

See also **Broadband**

Further Reading

Abe, George, and Alicia Buckley, *Residential Broadband,* Indianapolis: Cisco Press, 1999; 2nd edition, 2000

Azzam, Albert A., *Broadband Access Technologies: ADSL/VDSL, Cable Modems, Fiber, LMDS,* New York: McGraw-Hill, 1999

Bates, Regis J., *Broadband Telecommunications Handbook,* Boston: McGraw-Hill, 1999; 2nd edition, 2002

Farmer, James, David Large, and Walter S. Ciciora, *Modern Cable Television Technology: Video, Voice, and Data Communications,* San Francisco: Morgan Kaufmann, 1999

Laubach, Mark, Stephen Dukes, and David Farber, *Breaking the Access Barrier: Delivering Internet Connections over Cable,* New York: Wiley, 2001

Ovadia, Shlomo, and Bernard Goodman, editors, *Broadband Cable TV Access Networks: From Technologies to Applications,* Upper Saddle River, New Jersey: Prentice Hall, 2001

Smith, Roderick W., *Broadband Internet Connections: A User's Guide to DSL and Cable,* Boston: Addison-Wesley, 2002

Stockman, Mike, and Derek Ferguson, *Broadband Internet Access for Dummies,* Foster City, California: IDG Books Worldwide, 2001

Wolf, Jason, Natalie Zee, and Norman Meyrowitz, *The Last Mile: Broadband and the Next Internet Revolution,* New York: McGraw-Hill, 2000

Cable Networks

Cable networks are programming services that deliver packages of information or entertainment by satellite to local cable television systems. The cable systems then redistribute the network programs, through wires, to individual residences in their local franchise areas. The number of cable networks carried by any particular cable system varies and is based on the channel capacity of the system. Older cable systems may have as few as 20 channels whereas newer ones may have more than 300 channels. Local cable-system managers or executives at large corporations that own many cable systems decide which cable networks will be carried. They base such decisions on local and national government regulations, the cable system's own economic needs, and local audience preferences. One way to divide cable networks is into basic, pay, and pay-per-view networks.

Basic Networks

The majority of channels on most cable systems are devoted to basic cable networks. These are termed "basic" because the subscriber can obtain a large number of them for a relatively low price. The following are some of the most popular basic cable networks in the United States:

Arts and Entertainment (A&E): cultural fiction and nonfiction.

Black Entertainment Television (BET): talk shows, children's programs, game shows, and other fare particularly aimed at people of color.

Bravo: cultural programming.

Cable News Network (CNN): 24 hours a day of news and information.

Comedy Central: situation comedies, stand-up comedians, comedy movies, and similar fare.

Consumer News and Business Channel (CNBC): primarily business news.

Courtroom Television: coverage of cases being tried in the courts and other programming related to the justice system.

C-SPAN: coverage of Congress and other political bodies and events.

The Discovery Channel: documentaries and informational programming.

E! Entertainment Television: programming by and about the entertainment industry.

ESPN: 24-hour sports programming.

The Family Channel: wholesome programming including reruns of older commercial TV series.

The Food Channel: cooking shows and other information about food.

The Learning Channel (TLC): formal college credit courses and general education material.

Lifetime Television: information and entertainment shows aimed primarily at women.

MTV: music videos and music-related material aimed at teenagers.

Nickelodeon: children's and family programming.

QVC Network: a home shopping service.

Turner Network TV (TNT): old movies and some original programming.

TVLand: reruns of previous network television shows.

USA Network: a general service that includes network reruns, children's programs, and originally produced material.

VH-1: primarily music videos and music shows aimed at postadolescent viewers.

The Weather Channel: 24 hours a day of weather information.

Most basic cable networks charge the cable systems for their service. The fee is based on the number of subscribers the cable system has. A typical basic network charges a cable system an amount between 3 and 25 cents per month per subscriber, depending on its popularity. ESPN, for example, can charge more than TVLand.

The systems must recoup their expenses, and potentially garner some profit, by selling the cable TV service to consumer households. Most cable systems offer a "basic service" as a package to their subscribers. This includes all local origination and public access channels, all local broadcast stations, and all basic networks for a cost of about $20 a month. Some cable systems divide this basic package into two or more "tiers." They offer local origination, public access, local broadcast stations, and some of the public service and less glamorous basic networks (C-SPAN, The Learning Channel) for a very inexpensive price, about $5. The second, and more expensive, tier may include MTV, ESPN, USA, A&E, and other more entertainment-oriented basic networks.

Most basic networks sell advertising. As a result they have two sources of income: cable system sub-

Courtesy of the Everett Collection

scriber fees and fees paid by advertisers. Cable advertising rates are not as high as those for commercial U.S. networks such as NBC, ABC, or CBS because cable audiences are not as large. Most cable networks are delighted if they obtain a rating of 4, whereas commercial network program ratings tend to be in the 11-to-15 range. One reason cable network audiences are smaller is that many cable networks program for relatively specific audiences: Lifetime to women, ESPN to sports fans, Nickelodeon to children.

Among the basic networks, there is considerable variation in operating procedure. C-SPAN, which features the proceedings of the U.S. House and Senate, is noncommercial. All revenue comes from money paid to it by the cable systems. The home shopping networks, which make their money because viewers call in and buy the products shown, are usually provided to cable systems free of charge. As an initial enticement to try their material, networks sometimes pay systems to carry their programming. If the system later decides to carry the network on a regular basis, the system must start paying the network.

In addition to "moving picture" networks, other services are offered to cable systems as part of the basic package. These include digital sound services such as Music Choice and electronic text services such as news bulletins from Associated Press and Reuters.

Some basic channels produce most of their own programming. ESPN, for example, provides its own coverage of sporting events, and CNN produces its own newscasts. The same applies to C-SPAN, Courtroom Television, the Weather Channel, and the home shopping channels. Many networks, however, acquire programming from other sources. Lifetime, the Family Channel, Nickelodeon, and others often contract with independent producers to develop movies or series for them, a practice that has become more common as channels seek to provide original programming. Even sports, music, and court channels now sometimes offer original movies and series. Other channels obtain movies from the major motion picture studios. A&E and Discovery buy some of their programming from the British Broadcasting Corporation (BBC). Many

Courtesy of Discovery Networks

channels program old commercial network series. USA Network, for example, has programmed *Murder, She Wrote* and Lifetime has used *Cagney and Lacey* in addition to programming an expanding array of original movies and series. In a few instances, cable networks have picked up commercial series canceled by the major broadcast networks (*Paper Chase, The Days and Nights of Molly Dodd*), produced new episodes, and aired them as a series.

Pay Networks

Pay-cable networks, such as HBO, the Movie Channel, Showtime, and Cinemax, do not sell advertising. They derive all income from the cable systems that carry them. The systems, in turn, charge consumers subscription fees for each pay network, usually at a rate of $10 to $20 per month per pay service. In other words, the pay services are on a more expensive tier than basic services. The systems and the networks divide the consumer fee, usually about 50-50, but this ratio is subject to negotiation. Consumers who do not subscribe to the pay services receive scrambled signals on channels occupied by those services. To justify their additional monthly fees, pay channels must offer subscribers programming or services they cannot receive for free. Most of these channels present feature films. The pay networks purchase rights from motion picture studios that allow these channels to show feature films shortly after their theatrical runs and prior to their

Courtesy of Cartoon Network

availability to broadcast networks. Such networks show the films uncut and without commercial interruptions. To many viewers, this programming policy is worth the extra dollars they pay each month. Some pay channels also offer commercial-free specials such as sporting events, documentaries, miniseries, comedy specials, music concerts, and original movies created for the pay service. Some of the channels, primarily HBO and Showtime, cablecast their own television series, either by producing them in-house or by obtaining them from outside production companies. Such programs usually contain language or themes that commercial networks do not present to their larger, general audiences. Notable among these series are *The Sopranos, Sex in the City,* and *Six Feet Under,* all on HBO.

Pay-per-View Networks

Of all forms of cable networks, pay-per-view networks are the newest, and therefore the most unsettled. With these systems, subscribers pay only for those programs they actually watch. If they have not paid for a particular program, a scrambled signal appears on the pay-per-view channel. The network and the system divide the subscriber fees, based on a negotiated percentage. The subscriber pays what the market will bear. Movies can be seen for a few dollars, while major sports events may have a price tag in the $20-to-$50 range.

Courtesy of Comedy Central

Courtesy of Discovery Networks

Most cable systems that offer pay-per-view programming employ addressable technology that allows for interaction. Viewers who want to see a particular program can press a button on a remote control device that sends a signal back through the wire to the cable system. The program is then unscrambled or otherwise made viewable by the consumer. A computer also notes that the subscriber should be billed for the program, and the cost is added to the monthly amount the subscriber must pay. Systems without addressable technology can operate pay-per-view options by having subscribers call a toll-free number to order a particular program, but the instant access provided by the remote control works better.

Some pay-per-view services program 24 hours a day. They mainly show newly released hit movies, but they also present sports and entertainment specials. Other pay-per-view networks cablecast on an as-needed basis. For example, VideoSeat Pay-Per-View shows only football games from some of the top universities. Playboy at Night cablecasts each evening and is the oldest of the services that are now pay-per-view. It was originally a pay-cable service, but many community groups objected to the "adult entertainment" content of the material. They pointed out that if parents subscribed to the Playboy Channel on a monthly basis, unsupervised children could easily tune in—accidentally or on purpose. As a pay-per-view option, each Playboy program must be specifically requested.

By the early 21st century, many pay-per-view networks were turning into near-video-on-demand (NVOD) services. These networks occupy a number of cable system channels, so they can show the same moves at different times, usually 15 minutes apart. That way a viewer who wants to see the movie but misses the 8:00 P.M. starting time on channel 48 can catch it on channel 49 starting at 8:15.

An even tighter programming form, video-on-demand (VOD), is in the experimental stages. With

Courtesy of the Everett Collection

this service, individual viewers can watch programs precisely when they want to. As of 2002, a large number of video-on-demand experiments were under way, most of which involved a large server at the cable system that contains an enormous amount of information: movies, TV programs, video games, and so on. When a consumer asks for a particular movie (or anything else), it is downloaded on one of the cable system channels into a digital box on top of the consumer's TV set. (The movie, of course, also remains in the cable server so that another customer can request and receive it.) The consumer can then play the movie, stop it, rewind, and fast-forward at will.

Regional Networks

Regional networks that supply programming to a limited geographic area are fairly numerous in the cable world. Almost all of them are sports- or news-oriented (e.g., Home Team Sports, Madison Square Garden Network, and New York 1 News). Regional sports networks are active only when games are in progress, but most of the news services provide 24 hours a day of regional news information. Some of these news services are operated in conjunction with a local newspaper or local TV station.

Even though they contain advertisements, some regional sports networks are considered pay or pay-per-view services. The placement of such sports channels in the "basic" or "pay" category usually depends on the particular system. Some systems juggle regional sports networks between basic and pay. If the system can obtain greater revenue by offering a pay service, it may do so. If there is little interest among consumers, the network is placed in the basic tier.

History

The first cable network was Home Box Office (HBO). This service was established in 1972 by Time, Inc., as a movie/special service for Time's local cable system in New York City. The company then decided to expand the service to other cable systems and set up a traditional broadcast-style microwave link to a cable system in Wilkes-Barre, Pennsylvania. In November 1972, HBO sent its first programming from New York to Wilkes-Barre. During the next several years, HBO expanded its microwave system to include about 14 cable companies The venture was not overly successful, nor was it profitable for Time.

In 1975, however, shortly after domestic satellites were launched, Time used satellite transmission from Manila to program the Muhammad Ali–Joe Frazier heavyweight championship match for two of its U.S. cable systems. The experiment was technically and financially successful, and HBO decided to distribute all its programming by satellite. The satellite distribution system was easier and cheaper than the microwave system. It also made it possible for HBO signals to be received throughout the United States by any cable system willing and able to buy an Earth station satellite-receiving dish.

HBO began marketing its service to cable systems across the United States, but this effort initially was not very successful. Few local systems were willing to pay the almost $150,000 required for the technology required to receive the signal. However, satellite technology changed quickly, and by 1977 dishes sold for less than $10,000. Other pricing and programming problems had to be overcome as well, but once the service reached consumers, it was readily accepted. Viewers were willing to pay to watch uncut movies without commercial interruptions. By October 1977, Time was able to announce that HBO had turned its first profit.

Shortly after HBO beamed onto the satellite, Ted Turner, who owned WTBS, a low-rated UHF station in Atlanta, Georgia, decided to put his station's signal on the same satellite as HBO. Cable operators who had installed a receiving dish for HBO could now also place Turner's station, complete with network reruns and the Atlanta Braves baseball games, on one of their channels. A company transmitting the station charged cable operators 10 cents a month per subscriber for the signal, but the systems provided WTBS free to their subscribers. The rationale for presenting the station in this manner was that the extra program service would entice more subscribers. The charge to the cable companies did not cover WTBS's own costs, but the station was now able to set higher advertising rates because its audience was spread over the entire United States.

Courtesy of E! Entertainment Television

SHOWTIME®

Courtesy of the Everett Collection

With two successful programming services on the satellite, the floodgates opened, and many other companies set up cable networks. Viacom launched a pay-cable service, Showtime, to compete with HBO. Like Time, Viacom owned various cable systems throughout the United States and had been feeding them movies and special events through a network that involved shipping the tapes by mail for microwave relay. Following the launch of Showtime, Warner Amex began the Movie Channel, a pay service that provided movies 24 hours a day. Not to be outdone, Time established a second network, Cinemax, a service that consisted mostly of movies, programmed at times complementary to HBO. Other pay services that sprung up were Galavision, a Spanish-language movie service; Spotlight, a Times Mirror movie service; Bravo and the Entertainment Channel, both cultural programming services; and Playboy, an adult service that entered the cable business by joining forces with an already established network, Escapade.

Services that accepted commercials (later to be known as basic services) also exploded in number. ESPN was an early entry, and its sports programming was much in demand. Other basic services that appeared by the early 1980s were CNN (also owned by Turner), the Christian Broadcasting Network (CBN), USA, MTV, and C-SPAN. Two basic cultural services were formed: one, owned by ABC, was called ARTS; the other was CBS Cable, a service very expensive for its broadcast-network owner because it featured a great deal of originally produced material. Satellite News Channel (SNC), a 24-hour news joint venture between Westinghouse and ABC, was established to compete with CNN. Daytime was a service geared toward women, and Cable Health Network programmed material dealing with physical and mental health.

For several years in the early 1980s, new pay and basic networks were announced at a rapid rate—sometimes several in one day. Some of these never materialized and some existed only for short periods, but many showed signs of longevity. The entire cable TV industry was growing. Revenues and profits increased by more than 100 percent a year.

Of course, this could not last forever. In the mid-1980s, cable growth began to decline and the entire cable industry went through a period of retrenchment. Many cable networks consolidated or went out of business. Both Galavision and Bravo converted from pay services to basic services. Spotlight went out of business. The Entertainment Channel turned its pay programming over to the basic network ARTS, which then became A&E. The Playboy Channel shifted programming between hard-core and soft pornography, caught between angry citizens who objected to televised nudity and a small but loyal group of viewers who wanted access to it. This shifting strategy angered its partner, Escapade, and the two parted company, with Playboy paying Escapade $3 million. MTV's ownership changed from Warner Amex to Viacom, as did Nickelodeon's. Getty Oil, which owned ESPN, was purchased by Texaco. The new owner had no interest in the sports network and sold it to ABC. CBN changed from a strictly religious format to a broader, family-oriented format and became the Family Channel. Daytime and Cable Health Network joined to form Lifetime.

The most highly touted failure was that of the CBS-owned cultural channel, CBS Cable, which ended programming in 1983 after losing $50 million. The service did not receive sufficient financial support from either subscribers or advertisers. Its demise was almost applauded by some cable companies that resented the encroachment of the broadcast networks into their business. Another well-publicized coup occurred when Ted Turner's CNN bought out the Westinghouse/ABC Satellite News Channel. This transaction meant less competition for CNN, which proceeded on less tenuous financial footing. The Turner organization then established CNN2, a headline service that used the same writers and reporters as the original CNN.

Very few new U.S. cable networks were introduced in the mid- to late 1980s, in part because many cable systems had filled all their channels and had no room for newcomers. One notable exception was the Discovery Channel, launched in 1985, which became quite successful.

The U.S. cable network landscape changed somewhat in the 1990s. The downsizing of the late 1980s allowed for moderate growth in the next decade. In addition, in 1992 Congress passed a bill requiring cable networks to sell their programming to services in competition with cable, such as direct broadcast satellite (DBS) and multichannel multipoint distribution service (MMDS). Prior to this time, cable systems had tried to keep cable network programming to themselves. In fact, many cable system owners also owned all or part of cable networks, making it convenient and financially rewarding to make sure their cable networks provided content for their own cable systems. For example, TCI (Telecommunications, Inc.), at that time the largest cable system owner, had a financial stake in American Movie Classics, Black Entertainment Television, CNN, the Discovery Channel, the Family Channel, QVC Home Shopping, Turner Network TV, and WTBS.

Technology also improved in the 1990s and 2000s. A digitally based technology called "compression" allows video and audio to be squeezed into a much smaller space than previously possible. When compressed video is delivered over fiber optics, many more channels can be brought into the home, upwards of 500. Although not many cable systems have 500 channels, many have rebuilt their systems so that they have more than 100. The systems must find some way to fill all those channels, and with new markets and new technologies in mind, a number of companies launched new networks.

Although a few of the newer channels, such as the Military Channel, come from companies with no experience in the cable TV business, most of the channels are run by well-established companies that operate other channels. These companies have the infrastructure to develop and sell channels that will have only small numbers of interested viewers. For example, a new Do-It-Yourself channel that programs primarily information about remodeling homes was started by the same company that owns the Food Channel. Noggin, an educational channel, comes from Viacom, which also has Nickelodeon.

Often, the channels are just repackaged programs of another channel. For example, Discovery has reorganized the material it has broadcast over the years into channels dealing with such subjects as science, health, animals, and children—each of which is a new channel. Lifetime created an offspring, Lifetime Movies, which shows various made-for-television movies previously shown on the parent channel.

Another way cable systems are looking to utilize their expanded channels is through video-on-demand and near-video-on-demand. Some pay-per-view channels, such as HBO, have a form of NVOD in that they distribute multiple versions of their programming over different channels. Some of this variation is to accommodate different time zones, but it also gives viewers flexibility as to when they watch the program material. True VOD is not widespread as yet, but it is on the horizon.

The changes in both technology and policy will continue to keep cable television services at the center of issues surrounding television. Just as early cable networks transformed the meaning and experience of television programming and viewing, the newer practices will undoubtedly continue to alter our understanding and use of the television medium.

LYNN SCHAFER GROSS

See also **American Movie Classics; Black Entertainment Television; Cable Networks; Canadian Cable Television Association; Cable News Network; Direct Broadcast Satellite; Distant Signal; Federal Communications Commission; Geography and Television; Home Box Office; Association of Independent Television Stations; Levin, Gerald; Mergers and Acquisitions; Midwest Video Corporation Case; Music Television; Must-Carry Rules; Narrowcasting; National Cable Television Association; National Telecommunications and Information Administration; News Corporation; Pay Cable; Pay Television; Pay-Per-View Cable; Prime Time Access Rule; Public Access Television; Satellite; Scrambled Signals; Star-TV (Hong Kong); Super Station; Telcos; Time Warner; Translator; Turner, Ted; Turner Broadcasting Systems**

Further Reading

Brooks, Tim, and Earle Marsh, *The Complete Directory to Prime Time Network and Cable TV Shows, 1946–Present,* 7th edition, New York: Ballantine Books, 1999

Eastman, Susan Tyler, and Douglas A. Ferguson, *Broadcast/Cable Programming: Strategies and Practices,* 5th edition, Belmont, California: Wadsworth, 1996

Goldberg, Robert, and Gerald Jay Goldberg, *Citizen Turner: The Wild Rise of an American Tycoon,* New York: Harcourt Brace, 1995
Howard, Herbert H., Michael S. Kievman, and Barbara A. Moore, *Radio, TV, and Cable Programming,* 2nd edition, Ames: University of Iowa Press, 1994
Johnston, Carla Brooks, *Winning the Global TV News Game,* Boston: Focal Press, 1995
Jones, Felecia G., "The Black Audience and the BET Channel," *Journal of Broadcasting and Electronic Media* (Fall 1990)
Lamb, Brian, et al., *C-SPAN: America's Town Hall,* Washington, D.C.: Acropolis, 1988
Mair, George, *Inside HBO: The Billion Dollar War Between HBO, Hollywood, and the Home Video Revolution,* New York: Dodd, Mead, 1988
O'Daniel, Michael, "Basic-Cable Programming: New Land of Opportunity," *Emmy* (Summer 1980)
Pendelton, Jennifer, "Surf City," *Emmy* (December 1998)
Vane, Edwin T., and Lynne S. Gross, *Programming for TV, Radio, and Cable,* Boston: Focal Press, 1994
Whitmore, Hank, *CNN, The Inside Story,* Boston: Little, Brown, 1990

Cable News Network

U.S. Cable Network

Cable News Network (CNN) ranks as one of the most important—perhaps the most important—innovations in cable television during the final quarter of the 20th century. In 1984 CNN first began to earn widespread recognition and praise for its nearly around-the-clock coverage of the Democratic and Republican presidential nominating conventions. By 1990 Ted Turner's 24-hour-a-day creation had become the major source for breaking news. Praise became so routine that few were surprised when a mid-1990s Roper survey found that viewers ranked CNN as the "most fair" among all TV outlets, and the Times Mirror's Center for the People and the Press found that viewers trusted CNN more than any television news organization.

However, success did not come overnight. Launched in June 1980 by the then-tiny Turner Broadcasting of Atlanta, Georgia, in the beginning CNN (mocked as the "Chicken Noodle Network") accumulated losses at the rate of $2 million a month. Ted Turner transferred earnings from his highly profitable superstation TBS and slowly built a first-rate news organization. CNN set up bureaus across the United States and then around the world, beginning with Rome and London. Yet, at first Turner and his executives were not positive they would survive the stiff competition from rival Satellite News Channel (SNC), a joint venture of Group W Westinghouse and ABC. In January 1982, Turner let Satellite News Channel know he was serious and initiated a second CNN service, "Headline News." Through 1982 and most of 1983, CNN battled SNC. In October 1983, ABC and Westinghouse gave up and sold their news venture to Turner for $25 million, ending for a time effective competition for CNN in the United States.

CNN then took off. By 1985 it was reaching in excess of 30 million homes in the United States and had claimed its first profit. Turner added bureaus in Bonn, Moscow, Cairo, and Tel Aviv. Also, in the years before Court TV, CNN was the sole channel to televise celebrated trials such as the murder case against Claus von Bulow. In 1987, when President Ronald Reagan met Soviet premier Mikhail S. Gorbachev at a summit that would signal the end of the Cold War, CNN was on the air continuously with some 17 correspondents on-site. By 1989 CNN had 1,600 employees and an annual budget of about $150 million, and the channel was available in 65 countries with such specialized segments as a daily entertainment report, *Show Biz Today,* and a nightly evening newscast, *The World Today.* Larry King had moved his interview show to CNN and become famous for attracting ambitious politicians and infamous celebrities. In 1991, as the only TV network in the world operating live from the very beginning of Operation Desert Storm, CNN reported everything the military permitted—from the first bombing of Baghdad to the tank blitz that ended the conflict. Indeed, at a press conference after the initial air bombing runs by the U.S. Air Force, Defense Secretary Richard B. Cheney and General Colin L. Powell, chairman of the Joint Chiefs of Staff, admitted that they were getting much of their war information from CNN.

However, the fame of CNN's Gulf War coverage did not translate into corporate fortune, for the cost of cov-

Courtesy of the Everett Collection

ering a wide-ranging set of battles had risen faster than advertising revenues. The peak in viewership came on the night of the invasion of Kuwait by Iraq, when CNN captured 11 percent of the audience, as compared with the channel's usual 1 to 2 percent audience shares. Advertising time had already been sold.

As the late 1980s and early 1990s provided regular disasters, wars, and "media events," CNN enjoyed surges in interest and ratings. Viewers turned to the station to watch the confrontations at Tiananmen Square, the calamities of the San Francisco earthquake, and the long-awaited announcement of the verdict in O.J. Simpson's "trial of the century."

Whatever the news mix, CNN's prestige continued to grow. It became a basic component of how the new global village communicated. When U.S. troops invaded Panama in 1989, the Soviet foreign ministry's first call did not go to its counterpart in the U.S. diplomatic corps, but to the Moscow bureau of CNN, offering a statement condemning the action that could be read on camera. Turner proudly told anyone who would listen that Margaret Thatcher, François Mitterrand, Nancy Reagan, and Fidel Castro had all declared themselves faithful viewers of CNN.

However, as CNN moved well past 50 million households reached in the United States (and millions more abroad), all was not calm inside the organization. Staff members began to grumble about low wages and pressure not to unionize. Furthermore, by the early 1990s, Turner seemed to lose his innovative magic. In 1992 he heralded and launched an "Airport Channel" and a "Supermarket Channel," but neither added much in the way of new audience or profits. Also, as CNN reached more of the world, indigenous local news organizations began to publicly label Turner a "cultural imperialist."

Yet there was no doubt that, as CNN turned 15 in June 1995, it had surely become a prosperous and important part of the new world of cable television. CNN's yearly revenues neared $1 billion, but growth stalled as advertisers concluded that the CNN audience was "too old" and "not as affluent" as could be found elsewhere.

The year 1995 was an especially eventful one. First, Turner sold his complete operation, including CNN, to media giant Time Warner, leading skeptics to grumble that a serious news organization would have difficulty functioning as part of such a corporate colossus. At the end of the year, Microsoft announced it would ally with NBC to form MSNBC to challenge CNN directly. Rupert Murdoch's News Corporation, Inc., and Capital Cities/ABC also promised future 24-hour news services to contest CNN around the world.

In the late 1990s, the competitors MSNBC and FOX News (the latter owned by News Corporation) began to affect the fortunes at CNN. It stalled and seemed less innovative than its younger competitors. Thus, as Time Warner merged with America Online to form AOL Time Warner (the merger was announced in January 2000 but not formally approved and executed until January 2001), CNN began a series of radical changes. In March 2001, AOL Time Warner hired Hollywood veteran Jamie Kellner to supervise all Turner networks, including CNN's various editions. Kellner fired 400 employees, including the longtime symbol of CNN Headline News, Lynn Russell, bringing in actress Andrea Thompson, formerly of *NYPD Blue,* to replace her. Headline News's image suddenly came to look more like an Internet screen than a traditional anchored news service. Walter Isaacson, former managing editor of Time magazine, replaced longtime CNN president Rick Kaplan as head of the CNN division with its two U.S. news services, 14 other international and satellite news services, and a dozen CNN-related Internet sites. The executive shuffle continued at CNN with Isaacson's departure in early 2003 to head the Aspen Institute. Kellner soon followed, returning to Los Angeles and the WB television network, where he announced a retirement to be effective early in 2004. Isaacson's replacement, Jim Walton, former head of the CNN News Group, a veteran in the organization, oversaw cancellation of the *Connie Chung Show* and the creation of *Anderson Cooper 360°,* a news and commentary program that continues to draw viewers in 2004. In late 2003, Walton replaced Teya Ryan, executive vice president and general manager of CNN/U.S., with Princell Hair, a former vice president for Viacom Television's television station group, with primary responsibility for local news.

All these shifts and changes occurred in the context of continuing competition among 24-hour news services in which FOX News regularly drew more viewers than CNN. A new era had begun, with all three of the all-news cable networks battling for preeminence. Even though each of the competitors was backed by a wealthy media corporation, it was not clear that all three would survive.

DOUGLAS GOMERY

See also **Cable Networks; Kellner, Jamie; News, Network; Superstation; Turner Broadcasting Systems; Turner, Ted**

Further Reading

Bibb, Porter, *It Ain't as Easy as It Looks: Ted Turner's Amazing Story,* New York: Crown, 1993
Picard, Robert G., editor, *The Cable Networks Handbook,* Riverside, California: Carpelan, 1993
Whittemore, Hank, *CNN: The Inside Story,* Boston: Little Brown, 1990

Cable Television: United States

In its short history, cable television has redefined television in many ways. It became a cultural force that profoundly altered news, sports, entertainment, and music programming with services such as CNN (Cable News Network), HBO (Home Box Office), ESPN (Entertainment and Sports Network), and MTV (Music Television). It spawned a huge variety of "narrowcast" programming services, as well as new services with broad appeal. By 2002 national programming services numbered 308, according to the Federal Communications Commission (FCC) and the industry's main professional association, the National Cable Television Association (NCTA). About 85 regional programming services also are available. The cable television industry has altered the structure of the programming industry by developing new markets for both very old and very new program types. It has become an entertainment service that has contributed to changed viewing practices, suggested by the now widespread use of remote controls to "surf" along the now extensive channel lineup, the onset of digital services, and a viewing environment of hundreds of "on-demand" services facilitated by personal video recorders (PVRs) such as TiVo. As of 2003, cable was the most widespread provider of household broadband Internet connections in the United States. Cable television also has inspired an important debate concerning the ability of citizens to control and contribute to local media. Cable's organizational development, economic relationships, and regulatory status have profoundly altered the video landscape in ways entirely unforeseen, and in the course of its growth and development many accepted notions about First Amendment rights of speakers and listeners/viewers, and about the functions and obligations of communication industries, have been challenged. The first of many communication systems to stretch the meanings and boundaries established in the U.S. Communications Act of 1934, cable television has had a pivotal role in altering conceptions about television.

In the United States, the cable television industry eclipsed broadcasting's asset and revenue values in the late 1980s and passed broadcast TV's prime-time-viewer market-share levels in 2002. Now the dominant multichannel provider in the United States, cable television has contributed to a substantial drop in broadcast network viewing. From 1983 to 1994, weekly broadcast audience shares dropped from 69 to 52 while basic-cable networks' shares rose from 9 to 26, according to ACNielsen in 1995. By 2003, cable programming attracted an average prime-time audience share of 56.5 and a total day share of 58.3 as it continued to erode the networks' hold on television viewing.

Cable television service is available to 97 percent of all television households in the United States, and about 65.3 percent of all television households (68.8 million) subscribed to it as of the end of 2002, according to FCC data. More than 36 million households subscribe to premium cable services on top of their basic subscriptions. FCC statistics indicate that average cable system capacity was 666 megahertz as of July 2001, and two-thirds had facilities for 750 megahertz or above. This translates, approximately, into more than 80 channels delivered in a mix of analog and digital signals. Even with this number of channels, however, broadcast fare carried over cable is still heavily viewed.

Cable service comprises a collection of several industries. Primary among them are the distributors of video product, which are called either "operators" or, sometimes, "multiple system operators" (MSOs). Cable operators establish and own the physical system that delivers television signals to homes using coaxial cable or optical fiber. Operators also have become Internet service providers (ISPs), offering cable-modem connections to the Internet. Programming services produce or compile programming and sell their services to cable as well as to direct broadcast satellite (DBS) and other multiple video program distributors. Other entities and institutions connected to the cable industry include investors underwriting distribution or production efforts, the creative community, and loosely coupled groups such as advertisers, local community access groups and producers, recording companies, equipment suppliers, satellite and terrestrial microwave relay companies, Internet companies, software companies designing interactive interfaces, and telephone companies (telcos).

Cable television service relies on three fundamental operations. The first is signal reception, using satellite, broadcast, microwave, and other receivers, at a "head end," where signals are processed and combined. Second, signals are distributed from that head end to the home, using coaxial cable or optical fiber (or a blend of the two) or microwave relays, abetted by amplifiers and other electronic devices that ensure signal quality. Third, components at or near the home are necessary, including converters (now generally already in television sets) that change cable signals into tunable television images; descramblers that decode encrypted programming; modems to allow computers to communicate with the cable network; and still other equipment that allows for delivery or control of services on demand through a process called "addressability." Cable television's traditional tree-and-branch-system network design typifies one-way delivery services, although in the late 1990s system modifications, particularly the installation of more optical fiber throughout the network and intelligent devices at the head end, began to support two-way delivery services such as broadband Internet connections and digital video, including video-on-demand (VOD) programming. Cable television's huge and always-growing channel capacity, or bandwidth, enables it to support a variety of programming services and leaves it favorably positioned to expand into other service areas, such as high-definition television (HDTV), compressed video, pay-per-view channels, Internet-based content, and even telephony.

Programming on cable television began with retransmitted broadcast fare but evolved to include services unique to cable, some targeted at specialized audience groups such as children, teenagers, women, or specific ethnic groups, and some providing only one type of programming, such as weather, news, or sports. Such "narrowcast" programming appeals to specific demographic groups, rather than to broadcast television's wide audience. Therefore, it attracts advertisers who require more targeted approaches.

Traditionally, cable operators have organized their programming into "tiers," with different subscriber charges accruing at different levels. The least expensive option is "basic tier," which includes retransmitted broadcast channels and public access channels. Moving up the price ladder, next comes special cable-only packages of channels, often called "expanded basic." On a more expensive tier are single-channel premium services such as HBO, Showtime, Cinemax, or Playboy, with separate fees for each premium service. Digital video and VOD programming occupy still another tier, one that requires that the household subscribe to digital services. As of 2002, some VOD services, such as reruns of older HBO movies, were available for a small monthly fee (about $5), while contemporary movies could be available for one-off charges that rival those of video rental firms.

Since the early 1970s, cable television's surplus of channel space and low costs have helped to spawn several new formats, including infomercials, 24-hour news and weather services, music video services, home shopping channels, arts channels, children's channels, and a host of other narrowly targeted programming. Federal regulations of the 1970s that required cable operators to support community access channels dedicated to public, educational, and governmental programming likewise led in many cases to distinctive public service programming, even if that requirement has since lapsed. (As of 2002, only about 15 percent of cable systems carry public, educational or government access programming.) Upgrading to a digital plant has enabled systems to offer VOD and Internet connectivity.

Cable systems must lay cable in the ground or string it along telephone or electric poles; therefore, they must negotiate for the use of poles and rights-of-way. This is the crux of cable television's dependence on municipalities, since many states, cities, and towns control their own rights-of-way and sometimes also own the utility poles used by cable companies. Cable operators must negotiate franchises with municipalities that entitle them to use rights-of-way in exchange for fees (capped at 5 percent of revenues). A conventional franchise lasts 15 years. Because it uses public rights-of-way and deploys a capital-intensive network, conveys but does not create content, and bills subscribers on a monthly basis, cable television's utility-like aspects initially encouraged communities to treat it as they do other utilities. Generally, only one cable company would be franchised in a single municipality, effectively rendering that company a monopoly. Thus, rates charged to subscribers (and sometimes even companies' rates of return) were regulated by cities in the industry's early years, a practice largely eliminated by this point in time. One source of long-standing friction between cities and cable companies concerns which specific services a municipality may expect a cable operator to provide (e.g., specialized channels for public, educational, or government access or numbers of ISPs linked to the cable network), or the service base on which franchise fees are calculated. These controversies are attributable, in part, to cable television's common-carrier or utility characteristics, as well as the community's expectation that monopoly-like services require some regulation.

Cable television, like home video, taps viewers' willingness to pay directly for programs, a source of revenue untouched by traditional broadcasters. Subscribers pay a monthly fee for programming to the operators, and the operators in turn pay programming networks, such as ESPN or MTV, for the right to use their services. The price of the programming depends on the specific programming (for example, ESPN is usually more expensive than the Discovery Channel) and the size (subscribership) of the MSO or operator, although the very largest MSOs take advantage of their economies of scale to obtain smaller unit prices on programming. Most basic programming services carry advertisements and also allow local cable operators to insert ads (called "ad avails") during designated programming segments. Advertising revenues, both national and local, were initially slow to develop for cable programming services, as advertisers waited for significant subscriber levels and solid ratings data that could indicate viewer levels. Over time, however, ad revenues grew steadily, and commercials have proved to be an important part of programming services' revenues. Premium services such as HBO, Showtime, and the Disney Channel eschew ads and instead rely on higher, separate subscription fees assessed to subscribers. Cable-modem services likewise are assessed as separate fees.

Cable television's development was very dependent on the regulatory treatment and economic models developed for predecessor systems of telephony and broadcasting. As a hybrid communications system unanticipated in the Communications Act of 1934, cable television challenged regulators' conceptions of what it should be, how it should operate in a landscape already dominated by broadcasters, and how it might take advantage of its delivery system and capacity. The consequences of this uncertainty included some dramatic shifts in ideas of cable obligations to the public and to the communities it serves, and in the scope of cable television's First Amendment rights.

The Four Phases of Cable's Development

Since its origins, cable television in the United States has passed through four distinct phases. The first, from cable television's inception through 1965, was a slow-growth period predating any major regulatory efforts. During the second phase, from 1965 to roughly 1975, the FCC attempted to restrict cable television to nonurban markets and to mold it into a local media service. In the third phase, from 1975 to 1992, a series of judicial, legislative, and regulatory acts, including the Cable Communications Policy Act of 1984, catalyzed cable television's expansion across the United States and promoted dozens of new satellite-delivered programming services. In the fourth phase, signaled by the Telecommunications Act of 1996, most communication industries were deregulated. New competitors to cable television appeared in the form of multichannel multipoint distribution services (MMDSs), direct broadcasting satellites, new telephone company ventures into video media, and Internet-based video content. Many of the companies behind those separate services merged. Cable television infrastructure from the 1990s and into the next decade moved toward higher-capacity, fiber networks that could transmit digital signals and offer subscribers interactive services. As cable television has entered an environment in which many different delivery systems can duplicate its services, its unique identity has begun to fade. Now, very large telephone/cable/Internet/entertainment conglomerates undertake digital programming and transmission that combine voice, video, and data.

Phase One: Rural Roots and Slow Growth

Although cable television systems are now present in many regions of the globe, they began in the rural areas of North America. A product of both the geographic inaccessibility of terrestrial broadcast signals and a television-spectrum allocation scheme that favored urban markets, cable systems, also called "community antenna television" (CATV), grew out of simple amateur ingenuity. Retransmission apparatuses—such as extremely high antenna towers or microwave repeater stations, often erected by television repair shops or citizens groups—intercepted over-the-air signals and delivered them to households that could not receive them using regular VHF or UHF antennas. The earliest cable television systems, established in 1948, are usually credited to Astoria, Oregon, or Mahoney City, Pennsylvania, both mountainous, rural communities. Such retransmission systems spread across remote and rural parts of the United States throughout the 1950s and 1960s. According to *Television Factbook 1980–81,* there were 640 systems with 650,000 subscribers in 1960. By 1970 those numbers had grown to 2,490 systems with 4.5 million subscribers. The systems were generally mom-and-pop operations with 12 channels at best, although the MSO form of cable system ownership, in which one company owned several cable-distribution systems in different communities, already was spreading under the impetus of certain visionary entrepreneurs such as Bill Daniels, Monty Rifkin, Glenn Jones, and John Malone.

When cable systems began importing signals from more distant stations using microwave links, broadcasters' objections to the new service escalated. Many broadcasters had never been happy with cable service, claiming that such systems "siphoned" their programming, since cable operators had no copyright liability and therefore never paid for the programming. In 1956 broadcasters petitioned the FCC to generate a policy regarding cable television. The commission initially declined; it did not possess clear regulatory authority over CATV (originally "community antenna television," now often "community access television," but more commonly, refers to cable television) because the technology did not use the airwaves. The agency reconsidered, however, and finally asserted jurisdiction over cable television in 1962 in the *Carter Mountain Transmission Corporation v. FCC* case. The FCC's rationale for regulating CATV focused on cable's impact on broadcasters: to the extent that cable television's development proved injurious to broadcasting (an industry the FCC was obligated to sustain and promote), cable television required regulation. While this justification sustained the FCC's position throughout the second phase of cable television's development, it later crumbled under judicial scrutiny.

Phase Two: Restricted Expansion and Localism, 1965–75

While the Carter Mountain case addressed only the microwave and hence over-the-air portion of CATV service, the FCC eventually extended its authority to all aspects of cable television, and it issued two major policy statements: the "First Cable Television Report and Order" (1965) and the "Second Cable Television Report and Order" (1966). In these orders the FCC, hoping to prevent any deleterious effects on broadcasting, required cable operators to carry local broadcast signals under "must-carry" rules. With its ruling on "nonduplication," the commission required cable companies to limit imported programming that duplicated anything on local broadcast. By placing ownership prohibitions or limitations on television and telephone companies and by preventing cable television from entering the top 100 markets, a set of 1969 rules deliberately kept cable television from growing toward urban markets or from attaining the capital or benefits of entrenched industries. Federal programming mandates instituted channels for local public access and created a prohibition on showing movies less than ten years old and sporting events that had been on broadcast television within the previous five years. These rules were intended to promote cable's local identity and prevent it from obtaining programming that might interest or compete with broadcasters.

Although cable operators continued to press for limitations on the FCC's ability to impose such program obligations, the courts rebuffed their claims. For example, when Midwest Video Corporation challenged the FCC's requirement that the company originate local programming, the U.S. Supreme Court found in 1972 that such a rule was "reasonably ancillary" to the FCC's broadcasting jurisdiction (*U.S. v. Midwest Video Corp.*).

The net effect severely constrained the programming options for cable television operators, and in particular it diminished opportunities for a pay television service that would show movies or sports. During the 1960s, the FCC conceived of cable television as an alternative to broadcasting and promulgated the must-carry, nonduplication, and other rules; with such moves, the commission aimed to enhance cable television's community presence and possibilities and at the same time protect broadcasters from competition from the new delivery system. The agency positioned cable television as a hybrid common-carrier–broadcasting service, one limited to mandatory channels (the must-carry rules, local access channels, constrained nonlocal programming) with regulated rates. Such regulations fettered opportunities for networking, for national distribution, and for direct competition with broadcasters.

By the late 1960s and early 1970s, more public interest in cable television—fueled by a coalition of community groups, educators, cable industry representatives, and think tanks such as the Rand Corporation—heralded cable television's potential for creating a wide variety of social, educational, political, and entertainment services beneficial to society. These constituencies objected to the FCC's policies because they seemed to inhibit the promise of the "new technology." Ralph Lee Smith's 1972 book *Wired Nation* presented scenarios of revolutionary possibilities cable television could offer if only it were regulated in a more visionary fashion, particularly one that supported developing the two-way capabilities of cable and moving it toward more participatory applications.

In 1970 and 1971, the White House's Office of Telecommunication Policy spearheaded a series of meetings among cable, programming, and broadcast companies that culminated in the FCC revising its cable rules. This 1972 "Cable Television Report and Order" issued new rules softening some of the restrictions on cable television's expansion to new markets, particularly with respect to importing distant signals ("leapfrogging"). However, it continued several rules and standards that the industry found onerous, such as mandatory two-way cable service in certain markets and local-origination rules requiring operators to generate programs. Still more programming restrictions on movies and sporting events adopted in 1975 chafed at the cable industry's desires to offer something new and appealing to subscribers.

Phase Three: Deregulation, National Networks, Rapid Development, 1975–92

Nevertheless, in the wake of the 1972 "Report and Order," cable delivered more than just local broadcast signals to viewers by importing programs from distant markets via microwave, and its attractiveness and profitability grew. Two significant events spurred even more growth in the late 1970s. First, in 1975, HBO became a national service by using a communications satellite to distribute its signal, thereby demonstrating a way to bypass telephone companies' expensive network-carriage fees (commercial television networks depended on AT&T's lines for their national transmissions) and offering the possibility for many new program services to cost-effectively form national networks. Second, a series of judicial decisions sanctioned the cable industry's rights to program as it pleased, to enter the top television markets, and to offer new services. This third phase constituted cable television's greatest growth period.

As early as 1972, HBO had offered East Coast subscribers event programming, such as sports, on a "pay-cable" basis using a microwave relay, but with satellite feeds it could reach cable operators across the United States. HBO wanted to switch from microwave relays to the new RCA satellite Satcom I, which would take its signal across the entire country once the satellite launched in 1975. There were two major impediments to this plan. First, the FCC required each cable operator to use large, 9-meter dish antennas to receive a satellite feed, and these receiver dishes were expensive. Second, the restrictive FCC programming rules still prevented cable services from acquiring certain types of programming. HBO helped pay for the receiving dishes cable operators needed to receive its signal, and it became Satcom I's first television customer. Just two years later, 262 systems around the nation had HBO service, yet the best programming (current movies and sporting events) was still off-limits to cable programmers. HBO then took the commission to court, claiming that the FCC had exceeded its jurisdiction in limiting programming options. Supporting HBO's position in *HBO v. FCC,* the District of Columbia Court of Appeals concluded that the FCC's broadcast protectionism was unjustifiable and, perhaps more important, that cable television service resembled newspapers more than broadcasting and consequently deserved greater First Amendment protections. This reasoning paved the way for the cable industry to argue against other government rules, which fell one by one after the strong message sent by the HBO case to the FCC.

Even as the agency stripped away federal syndicated exclusivity rules, reduced the size (and consequently the cost) of allowable satellite dishes, and eliminated remaining distant-signal importation rules, the courts underscored cable television's rights to expand as it wished and to use any programming it desired. On the heels of the HBO case, the Supreme Court declared in its 1979 *FCC v. Midwest Video Corp.* decision that the FCC's rules imposed unacceptable obligations on cable operators. This verdict undermined the earlier Midwest Video decision, as the court concluded that insofar as the commission required cable operators to function as common carriers with the access channels (operators had no control over the content of access channels and they had to carry community programs on a first-come, first-served basis), and insofar as it prescribed a minimum number of channels, the FCC violated cable operators' First Amendment rights. The industry claimed the court decision affirmed its status as an electronic publisher, and it has continued its fight against regulatory obligations under this banner ever since. The electronic-publisher label underscores cable's First Amendment protections: like print publishers, cable television selects and packages materials for exhibition, and, like print, it should be under no obligation to exhibit material prescribed by regulatory powers.

With the regulatory barriers to entry now reduced, cable systems experienced huge growth from the late 1970s through the early 1980s: in 1975 there were 3,506 systems serving nearly 10 million subscribers; a decade later, 6,600 systems served nearly 40 million subscribers. Programming services likewise emerged. Ted Turner's UHF station WTCG, renamed superstation WTBS (and later just TBS), followed HBO's lead in national satellite delivery in 1976. The Showtime movie service and the sports service Spotlight followed suit in 1978. Two other superstations (local broadcasters delivering signals nationwide), New York's WOR and Chicago's WGN, began around the same time. Warner launched the children's service Nickelodeon and the Movie Channel in 1979, while

Getty Oil began the Sports Programming Network (later called ESPN). Turner's Cable News Network launched in 1980. Other programmers rushed to satellite distribution, so that by 1980 there were 28 national programming services available, according to National Cable Television Association records.

As programmers developed new channels to view, cable operators moved quickly to claim new markets in suburban and urban areas. Their systems finally had something new to offer these urban areas already used to several over-the-air broadcast signals, and cable companies sought to wire the most lucrative areas as soon as possible. MSO owners bought out many independent cable systems, even as they sought new territories to wire. The period of time between roughly 1978 and 1984, often called the "franchise war" era, saw cable companies competing head-to-head with each other in negotiating franchises with communities, often promising very high capacity, two-way cable systems in order to win contracts, only to renege on those promises later. Warner Amex's QUBE system, a highly publicized but actually very limited two-way cable service that the company promised to develop in many of its markets, was one such casualty, as were security systems, special two-way institutional networks called I-Nets, and a host of other cost-inefficient services, including public access channels. Most large, urban markets were franchised during this time, and several were promised 100-channel systems with two-way capabilities plus extensive local access facilities. Few markets, however, ended up with such amenities. Companies such as Time's American Television and Communications Corporation; Warner Amex; TelePrompTer; Jones Intercable; Times Mirror; Canada-based Rogers; Cablevision Systems; Cox; United; Viacom; Telecommunications, Inc. (TCI); and other large MSOs garnered many of these franchises. Many such companies have since been purchased by or merged with other media businesses.

Expanded markets and new programming services abetted by favorable judicial decisions contributed to the cable industry's power to lobby for more favorable treatment in other domains. The industry's pleas met favorable response within the Reagan administration, and Mark Fowler, the Reagan-appointed chair of the FCC from 1981 to 1987, supported a marketplace approach to media regulation that essentially put cable on a more equal footing with broadcasting.

The Cable Communications Policy Act of 1984 addressed the two issues that still hindered cable television's growth and profitability: rate regulation and the relative uncertainty surrounding franchise renewals. Largely the result of extensive negotiation and compromise between the National Cable Television Association (the cable industry's national organization) and the League of Cities representing municipalities franchising cable systems, the act provided substantial insurance regarding the future of the cable industry. Its major provisions created a standard procedure for renewing franchises that gave operators relatively certain renewal, and it deregulated rates so that operators could charge what they wanted for different service tiers as long as there was "effective competition" to the service. This was defined as the presence of three or more over-the-air signals, a standard that more than 90 percent of all cable markets could meet. The act also allowed cities to receive up to 5 percent of the operator's revenues in an annual franchise fee and made some minor concessions in mandating "leased access" channels to be available to groups desiring to "speak" via cable television. Other portions of the act legalized signal scrambling, required operators to provide lock boxes to subscribers who wanted to keep certain programming from children, and provided subscriber privacy protections. One year after the passage of the Cable Communications Policy Act, must-carry rules were overturned in *Quincy Cable TV v. FCC* (1985), and the cable industry's freedom from most obligations and regulatory restraints seemed final.

With rate deregulation and franchise renewal assured, the cable industry's value soared, and its organization, investments, and strategies changed. MSOs consolidated, purchasing more independent systems or merging, even as they expanded into new franchises, with large MSOs getting even bigger. The growth of TCI, shepherded by John Malone to become the largest MSO for many years, garnered a great deal of criticism. Several systems changed hands as large MSOs sought to "cluster" their systems geographically so they could reap the benefits of economies of scope by having several systems under regional management. After 1984 more finances poured into the industry, since its future seemed assured, and the industry's appetite for expansion made it a leader in the use of junk bonds and highly leveraged transactions—questionable financial apparatuses that Congress would later scrutinize. Many of the largest companies such as Time (later Time Warner), TCI, and Viacom acquired or invested in programming services, leading to a certain degree of vertical integration. The issues both of size and vertical integration became the subject of congressional inquiries in the late 1980s, but the inquiries resulted only in warnings to the industry. Investments in programming, operators argued, justified higher rates, and after 1984 rates jumped tremendously: according to Government Accounting Office surveys, an average of 25 to 30 percent from 1986 to 1988 alone, a pace far greater than the inflation rate. Subscription charges increased so quickly that a backlash among consumer groups grew. As the industry's market penetration and control over programming escalated, its growth strategies targeted new markets, predominantly in Europe and Latin America, and also focused on thwarting new domestic competitors such as direct broadcasting satellites, terrestrial point-to-multipoint distribution service (MDS) and its offspring system, called multichannel multipoint distribution service (MMDS).

In this profitable decade, many new programming services were launched and flourished. The 28 national networks in 1980 grew to 79 in 1990. New systems were built, bringing cable television to 60 million television households by 1990; channel capacity expanded, making the 54-channel system common in about 70 percent of all systems. Although pay-service subscriptions leveled off as most U.S. households purchased videocassette recorders (VCRs), and although offerings such as pay-per-view (single programs or events subscribers could order for a premium fee on a onetime basis) did not work well technologically or economically, cable services quietly grew, so that by 1992 they were in more than 60 percent of all U.S. households.

However, several controversies simmered throughout the 1980s. One concerned the rate increases, which many consumers and policymakers felt escalated too rapidly. Another involved rural viewers who wanted to access programming at reasonable prices via their own satellite dishes. After the 1984 act legalized scrambling, such newly scrambled services were unavailable to rural customers, or were only available at what they considered very high prices (higher than those paid in cities), and this situation created an especially heated exchange in Congress and even protests in Washington by satellite dish–carrying vehicles from rural regions. As well, the size and vertical integration of several MSOs worried some policymakers, who contended that the companies had undue opportunities to exercise their power over a captive market. Broadcasters continued their cry for remuneration when cable television carried the three major network channels (ABC, CBS, and NBC): even though most cable subscribers still spent much of their viewing time with network channels, operators paid nothing for that programming. Moreover, as cable operators' power grew, concerns rose about the convention of municipalities authorizing only one cable system for a given territory, thus creating a de facto monopoly. TCI, for example, was singled out for criticism because its systems served more than half of all television households in some states. Finally, the growing deregulation of telephone companies made cable television services a target of the telcos' expansion desires.

A new set of regulations then slowed the cable industry's successful expansion. With the Cable Television Consumer Protection and Competition Act of 1992, Congress attempted to reinstate some review of cable prices. The act regulated rates for basic and expanded services and required that the FCC generate a plan (called must-carry/retransmission consent) by which broadcasters would receive compensation for their channels. The retransmission-consent portion of this legislation was the culmination of years of lobbying by the broadcast industry, and it effectively forced cable operators to financially acknowledge the importance of broadcast programming on their tiers. The act called for new definitions of effective competition and for supervised costing mechanisms for other aspects of cable service, such as installation charges, and it decreed that programming services must be available to third-party distributors such as satellite systems and MMDS providers. However, portions of this legislation, the only legislation during President George H. Bush's administration to command an override of his veto, ultimately succumbed to the considerable momentum behind reducing government regulation and promoting marketplace forces in industries such as telephony and its growing family of related services. Consequently, the 1992 law's significance was minor compared with the major push for deregulation in the last four years of the 20th century.

Phase Four: Deregulation, a Maturing Industry, and Digital Services

In the 1990s and early 2000s, the cable industry matured in at least three major ways. First, much of the industry invested in system upgrades to allow the plant to deliver digital signals, which facilitated providing Internet connections as well as digital and interactive television (e.g., video-on-demand). Second, programming services continued to expand and innovate, and viewers migrated to cable programming from commercial television networks. Premium service HBO produced series such as *The Larry Sanders Show* (1992–98), *Sex in the City* (1998–2004), *The Sopranos* (1999–), and *Six Feet Under* (2001–), which received highly favorable critical and audience response. Third, major deregulation legislation opened the way for numerous mergers among cable and other communication companies, the elimination of rate regulation, and improved opportunities for cable operators to offer new services such as broadband Internet access. That legislation, however, also prompted new questions about the roles and obligations of cable operators.

In the late 1990s, personal and business use of the Internet became a powerful impetus for the evolving telephone, cable, and backbone networks crossing the United States (and, indeed, the world); it also complicated the definitions of services that various communication industries provided. The cable industry prepared its physical infrastructure for more digital and interactive services by investing extensively in hybrid fiber-coaxial cable plant in the 1990s. The goal of this upgrade was to be able to offer interactive services, including Internet connectivity and voice telephony (sometimes using Internet protocol) as well as digital television services, including video-on-demand. Compressed video allows digital cable networks to carry 4 to 12 video channels in the same channel capacity previously used to deliver just one analog channel. Transmissions from the head ends to local hubs were carried via optical fiber and then distributed in neighborhoods by cable. New set-top boxes were designed (without the benefits of an industry-wide standard) to allow digital and interactive services to be delivered to the analog televisions in most households. As the industry created more opportunities for generating revenue from existing and new programming by altering its network toward digital transmission capabilities, the entirely new service of broadband connectivity became a relatively easy service for cable television operators to provide. By 2002 about 16.8 million cable subscribers had digital plant capable of serving video, voice, and high-speed data, and a little more than seven million subscribed to cable-modem service. By 2003 cable television provided broadband Internet services to far more households than did telephone companies.

A deregulated legal and regulatory context influenced investment in new infrastructure and new programming and services. The Telecommunications Act of 1996, although primarily focused on restructuring the telephone industry, affected the cable industry and most other communication industries. The act was designed to encourage cable and telephone companies to compete in each other's markets. In that sense, it was a logical follow-up to the federally mandated breakup of AT&T's long-distance telephone monopoly 12 years earlier. Whereas that divestiture had created competition in the long-distance phone market, the 1996 act was supposed to create competition in the local calling market, as well as in other communication industries and services, particularly the provision of cable television. The 1996 act recognized the convergent capabilities of the many media systems that historically had been viewed as separate entities and consequently were regulated differently. By systematically reducing restrictions on company size, ownership, and types of services each medium could offer, the law (and judicial decisions subsequent to it) sought to encourage new providers and new services. For example, the 1996 law relaxed some of the 1992 Cable Act's rules; significantly, it determined that by 1999 rate regulation once again would be eliminated for all cable services except those in the basic tier. Rate deregulation for small cable operators went into effect immediately. A product of strong industry pressure and with scant input from citizen groups, the Telecommunications Act of 1996 was landmark deregulatory legislation.

The cable industry's move into Internet services raised new questions about where certain services, such as providing Internet access, fit within the evolving industry definitions and regulations. Providing basic Internet service (e.g., dial-up service using telephone links) had been a very competitive offering from independent ISPs during the late 1980s and early 1990s, although as that market grew, it became dominated by America Online (AOL) and Microsoft. Few ISPs owned the actual lines delivering the service, however; rather, they leased them from telephone companies. As Internet applications became more bandwidth-hungry, with music and video file sharing escalating, the desire for broadband connections with their faster line speeds made cable-provided Internet connectivity desirable.

However, having cable companies provide such connections challenged ideas about what the service actually was: was the Internet connection a cable service that would be figured in the franchise fee? Would a cable operator be an ISP, or would it allow many ISPs to use its lines, much as telephone companies had been doing for years with independent ISPs such as AOL? Would providing Internet access be deemed a phone service, a decision that might require cable services to incur certain compensation requirements common in the telephone world? Complicating matters, language in the 1996 Telecommunications Act prescribing how telephone networks would be "unbundled" in order to facilitate competitors using telephone infrastructure was held up as a model for also unbundling cable networks.

The cable industry was loath to relinquish control of its privately owned plant and anxious not to have such a common-carrier-like obligation imposed on its Internet services. This dilemma prompted lawsuits from a handful of cities that wanted competing ISPs to offer broadband services over cable. Ultimately, the FCC defined ISPs as providing "information services," which are not subject to any regulation. Under this definition, local cable networks cannot be forced to become open-access platforms for numerous broadband vendors.

Since the passage of the 1996 Telecommunications Act, the lively, competitive marketplace for video programming anticipated by the act has not materialized. Instead, cable television in the United States dominates in urban markets, although it faces some competition in suburban and rural markets from direct broadcast satellites. The FCC concluded in its 2002 Ninth Video Competition assessment that among the 33,000 U.S. cable communities, only a very small percentage have a wireline competitor to cable. Satellite competition rarely amounts to radically different programming offerings. The Satellite Home Viewer Improvement Act of 1999 prompted a growth spurt in DBS subscriptions when it enabled the satellite systems to distribute local broadcast television stations within local markets.

Telephone companies have not entered the video market as anticipated by the 1996 law. In the 1990s, major deregulation initiatives, legislative and judicial, enabled telcos to move into new home-information and home-entertainment services but largely failed to generate competitive video offerings. Instead, companies have simply purchased each other, resulting in a more consolidated market with fewer major companies. For example, phone company US West purchased Continental Cable in 1996 to become the third-largest cable operator in the United States at that time. AT&T purchased the largest cable company, TCI, in 1999, and it later purchased MediaOne, another large MSO. It then spun off its cable unit into AT&T Broadband. In 2002 this unit in turn merged with the third-largest MSO, Comcast, to create a company serving about 32 million subscribers. Major cable programmer and MSO Viacom (owner of MTV, BET, Nickelodeon, and Showtime, among other cable channels) purchased CBS. Such mergers led the FCC to characterize the cable industry as highly "horizontally integrated."

The 1990s were marked by consolidation among operators, programmers, and other entertainment companies as a dominant organizational response to regulatory and technological opportunity. In light of Disney's acquisition of Capital Cities/ABC, Viacom's purchase of CBS, and the expansion of FOX across movie making, TV, cable services, and direct broadcast satellites, the large, vertically integrated and multifaceted company with international holdings seems to be the new industry template for survival. The cable industry remade the television world of the "Big Three" networks, upsetting their hold on programming and viewers and initiating a 24-hour, tumultuous and changeable video domain. As the larger video-media industry changes, the cable industry's boundaries, roles, and influences will likewise be reshaped, but the historical legacy of its accomplishments will surely continue to be felt.

SHARON STROVER

See also **Communications Act of 1934; Federal Communications Commission; Home Box Office (HBO); Must-Carry Rules; Narrowcasting**

Further Reading

Blumler, Jay, *The Role of Public Policy in the New Television Marketplace,* Washington, D.C.: Benton Foundation, 1989

Cooper, Mark, *Cable Mergers and Monopolies: Market Power in Digital Media and Communications Networks,* Washington, D.C.: Economic Policy Institute, 2002

Fowler, M., and D. Brenner, "A Marketplace Approach to Broadcast Regulation," *Texas Law Review* (1982)

Horwitz, Robert, *The Irony of Regulatory Reform,* New York: Oxford University Press, 1989

Le Duc, Don, *Cable Television and the FCC: A Crisis in Media Control,* Philadelphia: Temple University Press, 1973

Le Duc, Don, *Beyond Broadcasting: Patterns in Policy and Law,* New York: Longman, 1987

Owen, B., and S. Wildman, *Video Economics,* Cambridge, Massachusetts: Harvard University Press, 1992

Parsons, P., and R. Friedan, *The Cable and Satellite Television Industries,* Boston: Allyn and Bacon, 1997

Smith, R.L., *The Wired Nation: The Electronic Communication Highway,* New York: Harper and Row, 1972

Streeter, T., "The Cable Fable Revisited: Discourse, Policy, and the Making of Cable Television," *Critical Studies in Mass Communication* (1987)

Whiteside, T., "Cable I," *New Yorker* (May 20, 1985)

Whiteside, T., "Cable II," *New Yorker* (May 27, 1985)

Whiteside, T., "Cable III," *New Yorker* (June 3, 1985)

Caesar, Sid (1922–)

U.S. Comedian

Son of a Yonkers restaurant owner, Sid Caesar learned firsthand the variety of dialects and accents he would later be known to mimic as a comedian. But his first performing interest was as a musician. He studied saxophone at Julliard and later played with nationally famous bands (Charlie Spivak, Claude Thornhill, Shep

Sid Caesar, c. early 1960s.
Courtesy of the Everett Collection

Fields, Art Mooney). During World War II, Caesar was assigned as a musician in the Coast Guard, taking part in the service show "Tars and Spars," where producer Max Liebman overheard him improvising comedy routines among the band members and switched him over to comedy. Caesar went on to perform his "war" routine in the stage and movie versions of the review, and he continued in Liebman's guidance after the war, appearing in theatrical reviews in the Catskills and Florida.

Liebman cast Caesar in the Broadway review *Make Mine Manhattan* in 1948, and in 1949 he brought him to star on television in the big-budget variety show *Admiral Broadway Review,* which was simultaneously broadcast on both the NBC and DuMont networks. Caesar had appeared on Milton Berle's *Texaco Star Theater* the previous fall but became an enormous success on his own program, starring with the multitalented and splendid comedian Imogene Coca (who had appeared on TV as early as 1939), Mary McCarty, Marge and Gower Champion, and Bobby Van, among others. The series, produced and directed by Liebman, adopted the format of a Broadway review, with top-name guest stars in comedy skits and big production numbers. It also introduced a savvy genre bending that would help to characterize Caesar's programs: the opening show closed with an elaborate parody of both opera and Billy Rose, called "No, No, Rigoletto." Seen in every city with television facilities in the United States (either live or by filmed kinescope), the show dominated Friday night viewing, the way Berle did on Tuesday and Ed Sullivan on Sunday. Its sponsor, Admiral, was a major manufacturer of television sets. Running an hour in length, the show lasted only 17 weeks, from January to June 1949.

Its successor, *Your Show of Shows,* was a Saturday night fixture for four years, adopting a similar format of comedy monologues, skits, and parodies of movies and plays. But this program was less a showcase for guest stars than for Caesar and Coca, ably supported by Carl Reiner (who replaced Tom Avera after the first season) and Howard Morris (who joined a season later). Writers Mel Tolkin, Lucille Kallen, and Mel Brooks, choreographer James Starbuck, set designer Frederick Fox, and conductor Charles Sanford were all *Admiral* alumni; the other writers completed a Who's Who of post–World War II American comedy—Larry Gelbart (*M*A*S*H,* TV series), Bill Persky and Sam Denoff (*The Dick Van Dyke Show*), Neil Simon, and also Joe Stein (*Fiddler on the Roof*) and Mike Stewart (*Hello, Dolly* and *Bye, Bye Birdie*). The writing sessions were reputedly raucous and sometimes even violent, splitting up into groups of two or three who competed with one another, all fighting for attention and success—with the possible exception of Simon, whispering his suggestions to Reiner, who would repeat them to the group. It has long been reported that Woody Allen worked on the show, though this has recently been suggested to be untrue.

The show included a large cast of regular singers and dancers, and it was originally the New York half of a larger overall show, NBC's *Saturday Night Revue.* (Jack Carter hosted a Chicago portion an hour earlier.) At the end of the first season, Carter and the umbrella title were dropped, and Caesar and company went on to perform some 160 telecasts—all live, original comedy. Both raucous and urbane, the show combined revue and sketch comedy with a rather sophisticated sense of satire and parody, especially for early TV: how many other programs of this era would have conceived a spoof of Italian neorealist cinema?

Caesar, notorious for his deviations from the script, was skilled at mime, dialects, monologues, foreign language double-talk, and general comic acting. Whether alone, paired with Coca, or part of the four-man repertory group, he excelled. Not a rapid-fire jokester like Berle or Fred Allen, Caesar was often compared in the press to the likes of Chaplin, Fields, or Raimu. The 90-minute show usually featured a guest host (who played a minor role), at least two production numbers, sketches between Caesar and Coca, the showcase parody of a popular film (e.g., "Aggravation Boulevard," "From Here to Obscurity"), further sketches (as many as ten per show), Caesar in monologue or pantomime (e.g., an expectant father in the waiting room, the autobiography of a gum-ball machine), and the entire company in a production number. The most famous characters included Charlie and Doris Hickenlooper, a mismatched married couple; the Professor, a Germanic expert scientist in everything and nothing; storyteller Somerset Winterset; jazz musicians Cool C's and Progress Hornsby; and the mechanical figures of the great clock of Baverhoff, Bavaria, striking one another in addition to the hour.

In the fall of 1954, Leibman went on to produce "Spectaculars" for NBC, Caesar began *Caesar's Hour* (with Reiner, Morris, and Nannette Fabray), which lasted three seasons, while Coca had her own half-hour show, lasting one season. Caesar and Coca reunited in 1958 on the short-lived *Sid Caesar Invites You.*

Building on the interest generated by a 1972 *Esquire* article about the show, Liebman compiled routines of several programs from 1950 to 1954 into a feature film, *Ten from Your Show of Shows* (1973). NBC had thrown away their copies of the program, but Caesar and Liebman had retained their kinescopes made during the show's original run. A series of 90-minute TV specials anthologized from the original shows were syndicated in 1976. By the mid-1970s, Caesar was seen only in occasional guest appearances, and later in diverse TV series and films (*Grease,* 1978). His autobiography, *Where Have I Been?,* was published in 1983. Caesar and *Your Show of Shows* served as the not-so-thinly-veiled inspiration behind the film *My Favorite Year* (1982).

MARK WILLIAMS

See also **"Golden Age" of Television; Kinescope; Variety Programs; *Your Show of Shows***

Sid Caesar. Born in Yonkers, New York, September 8, 1922. Graduated Yonkers High School, 1939. Married: Florence Levy, 1943; children: Michele, Richard, and Karen. Studied saxophone and clarinet, New York City; played in small bands, then the orchestras of Charlie Spivak, Shep Fields, and Claude Thornhill; toured theaters and nightclubs as a comedian; appeared in film, on Broadway, and on television, from 1945; starred in several TV shows; returned to Broadway as star of *Little Me,* 1962–63; appeared in such films as *It's a Mad, Mad, Mad, Mad World,* 1963, *Silent Movie,* 1975, and *Grease,* 1978; appeared in opera *Die Fledermaus,* 1987. Recipient: Best Comedian on TV Award from *Look* magazine, 1951 and 1956; Emmy Award, 1956; Sylvania Award, 1958.

Television Series

1949	*Admiral Broadway Review*
1950–54	*Your Show of Shows*
1954–57	*Caesar's Hour*
1958	*Sid Caesar Invites You*
1962–63	*As Caesar Sees It* (syndicated)

Made-for-Television Movies

1976	*Flight to Holocaust*
1977	*Curse of the Black Widow*
1981	*The Munsters' Revenge*
1983	*Found Money*
1985	*Love Is Never Silent*
1988	*Freedom Fighter*
1988	*Side by Side*
1988	*Nothing's Impossible*
1995	*The Great Mom Swap*

Television Special

1959	*The Sid Caesar Special*

Films

Tars and Spars, 1945; *The Guilt of Janet Ames,* 1947; *It's a Mad, Mad, Mad, Mad World,* 1963; *The Busy Body,* 1966; *The Spirit Is Willing,* 1966; *A Guide for the Married Man,* 1967; *Ten from Your Show of Shows,* 1973; *Airport 1975,* 1974; *Silent Movie,* 1975; *Fire Sale,* 1977; *Barnaby and Me,* 1977; *Grease,* 1978; *The Cheap Detective,* 1978; *The Fiendish Plot of Dr. Fu Manchu,* 1980; *History of the World, Part I,* 1981; *Grease 2,* 1982; *Over the Brooklyn Bridge,* 1983; *Cannonball Run II,* 1983; *Stoogemania,* 1985; *The Emperor's New Clothes,* 1987; *The South Pacific Story,* 1991; *Vegas Vacation,* 1997; *The Wonderful Ice Cream Suit,* 1998.

Stage

Make Mine Manhattan, 1948; *Little Me,* 1962–63; *Die Fledermaus* (opera), 1987; *Does Anybody Know What I'm Talking About?* 1989.

Publications

Caesar's Hours: My Life in Comedy, with Love and Laughter (with Eddy Friedfeld), 2003

"What Psychoanalysis Did for Me," *Look* (October 2, 1956)

Where Have I Been? 1983

Further Reading

Adir, Karen, *The Great Clowns of American Television,* Jefferson City, North Carolina: McFarland, 1988
Bester, Alfred, "The Two Worlds of Sid Caesar," *Holiday* (September 1956)
Davidson, Bill, "Hail Sid Caesar!" *Colliers* (November 11, 1950)
Myers, Deb, "The Funniest Couple in America," *Cosmopolitan* (January 1951)
Robbins, Jhan, and June Robbins, "Sid Caesar: 'I Grew Up Angry,'" *Redbook* (November 1956)
Sennett, Ted, *Your Show of Shows,* New York: Macmillan, 1977

Cagney and Lacey

U.S. Police Series

Cagney and Lacey, a U.S. police procedural with pervasive melodramatic overtones, is, deservedly, one of the most widely discussed programs in television history. The series aired on the CBS television network from 1982 to 1988 and presented a set of bold dramatic combinations, blending and bending genre, character, and narrative strategies. Though rated in the list of top 25 programs only once during those years, the show drew critical acclaim—and controversy—and established a substantial audience of fiercely loyal viewers who, on at least one occasion, helped save the program from cancellation by the network. As demonstrated by television scholar Julie D'Acci's outstanding study *Defining Women: Television and the Case of Cagney and Lacey,* the history of *Cagney and Lacey* provides a textbook case illustrating many issues pervasive in the U.S. television industry as well as that industry's complicated relationship to social and cultural issues.

Created in its earliest version by writer-producers Barbara Corday and Barbara Avedon in 1974, *Cagney and Lacey* was first designed as a feature film. Unable to sell the project, the women presented it to television networks as a potential series. Rebuffed again, they finally brought *Cagney and Lacey* to the screen as a 1981 made-for-television movie, coproduced by Barney Rosenzweig, then Corday's husband. The movie drew high ratings and led to the series, which premiered in 1982. The difficulties involved in the production history to this point were indicative of struggles encountered by women writers and producers in the film and television industries—especially when their work focused on women. Those difficulties, however, were merely the beginning of continuing contests.

As put by D'Acci, "the negotiation of meanings of *women, woman,* and *femininity* took place among a variety of vested interests and with considerable conflict." Throughout the run of the series the "negotiations" continued, and the interests included the creative team for the series—producers, writers, actors, directors. They also included network executives and officials at every level, television critics, special interest groups, and the unusually involved audience that actively participated in ongoing discussions of the series' meanings and directions.

While many of these controversies took place on sets, in writers' meetings, and in boardrooms, one of the earliest spilled over into public discussion in newspapers, magazines, and letters. In the made-for-television movie, the character of Christine Cagney was played by Loretta Swit and that of Mary Beth Lacey by Tyne Daly. Unavailable to take on the Cagney role in the series because of her continuing work in *M*A*S*H,* Swit was replaced by Meg Foster. Almost immediately discussion at CBS and in some public venues focused on potential homosexual overtones in the relationship between the two women. Foster, who had played a lesbian in an earlier television role, was cited as "masculine" and "aggressive," and after considerable argument CBS threatened to cancel the series and made Foster's removal and replacement a condition of continuing the show. The fall 1982 season began with Sharon Gless, presumably more conventionally feminine and heterosexual, portraying Cagney.

Similar, though not so visible, conflicts and adjustments continued throughout the history of the series. Questions of appearance—dress, body weight, hair styles—were constantly under consideration and negotiation. Story material, particularly when focused on issues of vital concern to women—rape, incest, abortion, breast cancer—often proved controversial and led to continuing battles with the network standards and practices offices. Daly reported that even in the matter of sexual relations with her fictional husband, Harvey (John Karlin), differences of opinion flared into argument over how to present domestic sexual behavior.

In the spring of 1983, CBS executives had more straightforward matters to present to the producers of *Cagney and Lacey;* pointing to low audience ratings, they canceled the program. By this time, however, the producers and the production company for the series had mounted an impressive public relations campaign and letter writers from across the country mailed their protests to the company, the network, the producers—to anyone who would read and make use of them. The National Organization for Women took a lead role in the publicity campaigns. Newspaper critics called attention to the campaign. The series won numerous awards, Daly's Emmys for Best Actress in 1982–83 and 1983–84 among them. In the fall of 1983, CBS announced it would program seven "trial episodes" beginning in March 1984. *Cagney and Lacey* was back and remained on the air four more seasons.

All these difficulties were played out as the series developed narrative strategies that took best advantage of U.S. commercial television's abilities to present serious social and personal issues in the context of genre fiction. Two factors stand out among the techniques that distinguish *Cagney and Lacey.* One strategy, evidenced in many of the conflicts described above, is the series' ability to blend three areas of concern into single dramatic productions. First, most episodes of *Cagney and Lacey* dealt with the ongoing difficulties two women encounter in a male-dominant profession. This entailed far more than simply presenting gender conflicts in the workplace, though certainly there were many of those. Rather, this dramatic structure required a reconsideration of the entire generic structure of the "cop show." As the two women dealt with issues such as violence, guns, male criminals, or the streets—all elements of police fiction—writer-producers as well as audiences were required to reflect on new resonances within the genre.

Second, each narrative usually focused on a particular crime and criminal investigation. The generic modifications were intertwined with rather conventional police matters, and the sense of strangeness caused by the gender shift was combined with the familiarity of crime drama.

Third, each story usually linked the crime drama to a social problem, the kinds of issues often explored in television drama throughout the history of the medium. Thus, the issues previously cited, often though not always definable as "women's issues," formed a third aspect of the narrative triad structuring individual episodes.

Cagney & Lacey, Sharon Gless, Tyne Daly (TV Movie/Pilot), 1981.
Courtesy of the Everett Collection

The series was at its best when these elements were "balanced," that is, when it was not overly didactic regarding the social issue, nor utterly conventional as a police drama, nor submerged in the exploration of gender-inflected genre. If, as sometimes happened, one of these aspects did take over the story, the result was often a very thin examination of the element.

The second major narrative strategy of the series militated against this imbalance. This was the establishment of *Cagney and Lacey* as a "cumulative narrative." Unlike serial dramas such as *Hill Street Blues,* or, in the more strictly melodramatic vein, *Dallas, Cagney and Lacey* did usually bring each episode to closure. Criminals were caught. Cases were solved. Sometimes, even the particular gender-related workplace issue was brought to a satisfactory solution.

But beneath these short-term narrative aspects of the series, the long-term narrative stakes were continually explored. More important, each of the closed episodes shed light on those ongoing matters. Thus, as viewers watched the Lacey children move from childhood into adolescence, they also saw strains appear in the Lacey marriage, the toll that strain took on professional commitments, the conflicts the strain caused in the interpersonal relationship of the two women, and so on. Similarly, each small development could lead to new story possibilities, new inflections of character. Elements from past episodes could be brought into play. Features of character biographies could be revealed to explain events in a particular episode, then used to develop further characteristics in future episodes.

The cumulative narrative, one of television's strongest forms, was put to near perfect use in *Cagney and Lacey.* Evidence of the utility of this strategy, and the ways in which its methods of story elaboration can appeal to viewers, came in the latter years of the series. Though some critics see the series as diminishing its stronger feminist tonality in this period, it is also possible to see the growing emphasis on the "personal" and "the domestic" as a fuller union of public and private.

One of the most significant developments in the series in this period was the exploration of Christine Cagney's alcoholism. In addition to their own focus on this topic, the writer-producers have cited viewer letters calling attention to the fact that Cagney often turned to alcohol in times of stress. In a harrowing, two-part, award-winning performance, Sharon Gless portrayed Cagney's descent into "rock bottom" alcoholic behavior. What is significant about the development is that it altered not only the series present and future, but its history as well, and simultaneously altered the "triadic" structure of social issue, personal problem, and police drama.

Cagney and Lacey left network program schedules in 1988. But it continued for some time as a staple for the Lifetime network's programming aimed at female audiences. Critical and viewer responses to the series continue to be mixed even now. Most recently the series characters have been resurrected in the form of several made-for-television movies. Older, physically changed, perhaps "wiser," these fictional characters and the narratives in which they appear continue to explore complex issues and themes, and to experiment with narrative forms.

HORACE NEWCOMB

See also **Daly, Tyne; Gender and Television; Gless, Sharon; Police Programs**

Cast

Detective Mary Beth Lacey	Tyne Daly
Detective Chris Cagney (1982)	Meg Foster
Detective Chris Cagney (1982–88)	Sharon Gless
Lieutenant Bert Samuels	Al Waxman
Detective Mark Petrie	Carl Lumbly
Detective Victor Isbecki	Martin Kove
Detective Paul La Guardia (1982–85)	Sidney Clute
Deputy Inspector Marquette (1982–83)	Jason Benhard
Desk Sergeant Ronald Coleman	Harvey Atkin
Harvey Lacey	John Karlin
Harvey Lacey, Jr.	Tony La Torre
Michael Lacey	Troy Slaten
Sergeant Dory McKenna (1984–85)	Barry Primus
Inspector Knelman (1984–88)	Michael Fairman
Detective Jonah Newman (1985–86)	Dan Shor
David Keeler (1985–88)	Stephen Macht
Alice Lacey (1985–87)	Dana and Paige Bardolph
Alice Lacey (1987–88)	Michele Sepe
Detective Manny Esposito (1986–88)	Robert Hegyes
Detective Al Corassa (1986–88)	Paul Mantee
Josie (1986–88)	Jo Corday
Kazak (1986–87)	Stewart Coss
Beverley Faverty (1986–87)	Beverley Faverty
Tom Basil (1986–88)	Barry Laws
Verna Dee Jordan (1987–88)	Merry Clayton

Producers

Barney Rosenzweig, Barbara Corday, Barbara Avedon, Richard Rosenbloom, Peter Lefcourt, Liz Coe, Ralph Singleton, Patricia Green, P.K. Knelman, April Smith, Joseph Stern, Steve Brown, Terry Louise Fisher, Georgia Jeffries, Jonathan Estrin, Shelly List

Programming History

125 episodes

CBS

March 1982–April 1982	Thursday 9:00–10:00
October 1982–September 1983	Monday 10:00–11:00
March 1984–December 1987	Monday 10:00–11:00
January 1988–April 1988	Tuesday 10:00–11:00
April 1988–June 1988	Monday 10:00–11:00
June 1988–August 1988	Thursday 10:00–11:00

Made-for-Television Movies

Cagney & Lacey: The Return, November 6, 1994
Cagney & Lacey: Together Again, May 2, 1995
Cagney & Lacey: True Convictions, January 29, 1996
Cagney & Lacey: The Glass Ceiling, September 5, 1996

Further Reading

Brower, Susan, "TV 'Trash and Treasure': Marketing *Dallas* and *Cagney and Lacey,*" *Wide Angle* (1989)

Clark, Danae, "*Cagney and Lacey:* Feminist Strategies of Detection," in *Television and Women's Culture: The Politics of the Popular,* edited by Mary Ellen Brown, Newbury Park, California: Sage, 1990

D'Acci, Julie, *Defining Women: Television and the Case of Cagney and Lacey,* Chapel Hill: University of North Carolina Press, 1994

Fiske, John, *Television Culture,* London: Methuen, 1987

Mayerle, Judine, "Character Shaping Genre in Cagney and Lacey," *Journal of Broadcasting and Electronic Media* (Spring 1987)

McHenry, Susan, "The Rise and Fall—and Rise of TV's *Cagney and Lacey,*" *Ms.* (April 1984)

Montgomery, Kathryn C., *Target Prime Time: Advocacy Groups and the Struggle over Entertainment Television,* New York: Oxford University Press, 1989

Rosen, Marjorie, "*Cagney and Lacey,*" *Ms.* (October 1981)

Call Signs/Call Letters

U.S. Broadcasting Policy

Call letters are used by television stations to identify themselves to the TV audience. The call letters usually consist of various combinations of four letters, sometimes followed by the suffix "TV": for example, WAAA-TV. Since many early television stations shared common ownership with radio stations, they often shared the same call letters. If the radio station call letters were WBBB, the TV station simply became WBBB-TV.

Federal Communications Commission (FCC) regulations require that each TV station identify itself at least once each hour by call letters and by city of license. The announcement should be made at or close to the hour during a natural break in programming and can be made either visually or aurally. Stations have the option to insert their channel numbers between the call letters and the city of license, and virtually all stations follow this practice: for example, KRON-TV, channel 4, San Francisco. In advertising and promotional announcements, stations generally promote their channel assignments more vigorously than their call letters.

Some of the more ingenious call letters actually identify the channel either by word or by Roman numeral. These include KTWO, Casper, Wyoming; KFOR, Oklahoma City; WTEN, Albany, New York; and KTEN, Ada, Oklahoma. Two Roman numeral examples include WIXT, Syracuse, New York, and KXII, Ardmore, Oklahoma. Two other stations, WPVI, Philadelphia, and KPVI, Pocatello, Idaho, both use a P for their respective cities followed by Roman numerals to indicate their channel-6 assignments.

The procedures for assigning call letters have their origin in the earliest days of radio. Blocks of initial letters were assigned to various countries following the London International Radiotelegraph Conference of 1912. The letters W, K, N, and A were assigned to the United States. W and K were used to designate commercial broadcasters, whereas N and A were allocated to military users of the radio spectrum. The initial letters C and X were assigned to Canada and Mexico, respectively, and are still used today to identify Canadian and Mexican television stations.

The first U.S. radio stations were allowed to select their own call letters beginning with either a W or a K. Also, early radio stations could select either a three-letter or a four-letter combination. Later, around 1928, the Federal Radio Commission formalized rules requiring that all stations use four-letter combinations. Further, those stations east of the Mississippi were required to use an initial W, while those stations west of the Mississippi were required to use an initial K.

Stations already on the air were allowed to keep their call letters regardless of number or location. Radio and, later, television stations such as KDKA, Pittsburgh, Pennsylvania; WGN, Chicago; WHO, Des Moines, Iowa; and WOW, Omaha, Nebraska, demonstrate their pioneer status and their unbroken ownership by being notable exceptions to the current rules. When WOR-TV, New York, was acquired by a new owner, the station was required to adhere to the four-letter requirement and became WWOR-TV.

Call letters often tell something about station ownership. New York stations WABC-TV, WCBS-TV, and WNBC-TV are each owned and operated by the respective networks contained within their call letters. So too are Los Angeles stations KABC-TV, KCBS-TV, and KNBC-TV. Ted Turner's WTBS (Turner Broadcasting System) is still another example. A change in ownership will often, but not always, bring a change in call letters. When Philadelphia TV station WTAF was sold by Taft Broadcasting to another owner, it became WTXF.

Some TV call letters trace their origins to the slogans of their radio station predecessors. Examples include WGN (World's Greatest Newspaper), the Chicago station owned by the *Chicago Tribune;* WLS (World's Largest Store), the Chicago station originally owned by Sears Roebuck; WSM (We Shelter Millions), the Nashville, Tennessee, station originally owned by an insurance company; and WSB (Welcome South, Brother), the Atlanta, Georgia, station that conveys regional boosterism in its call letters.

Public television stations have continued this tradition. Chicago's WTTW (Windows to the World) and Philadelphia's WHYY (Wider Horizons for You and Yours) are two examples. Both WQED, Pittsburgh, and KQED, San Francisco, use the abbreviation for the Latin phrase *quod erat demonstrandum* (which was to be proven) in their call letters.

The growth of cable has increased the promotional value of call letters since some cable systems retransmit TV signals "off-channel." For example, a VHF station that broadcasts on channel 10 might be carried on cable channel 5; a UHF station that broadcasts on channel 48 might be carried on cable channel 13. As a result, many TV stations continue to identify themselves by channel assignments but also promote their call letters more extensively than in the past.

When television stations broadcast a digital signal in addition to the traditional analog signal, they usually add DT to the call letters for that signal. Those stations broadcasting a high-definition signal may add an HD to their call letters.

NORMAN FELSENTHAL

See also **Networks; United States**

Further Reading

Barnouw, Erik, *A History of Broadcasting in the United States,* volume 1, *A Tower in Babel, to 1933,* New York: Oxford University Press, 1966

Inglis, Andrew F., *A History of Broadcasting: Technology and Business,* Boston: Focal Press, 1990

Sterling, Christopher H., and John M. Kittross, *Stay Tuned: A Concise History of American Broadcasting,* Belmont, California: Wadsworth, 1978; 3rd edition, Mahwah, New Jersey: Erlbaum, 2002

Camcorder

"Camcorder" is a commercial name for professional and home video cameras that combine a camera and video recorder in one unit. Since the introduction of this technology in 1981, camcorders have become the tool of choice for local and national electronic news gathering. Consumer camcorders, introduced by Sony in 1985, have rendered Super 8 film for home movies obsolete. Moreover, some critics and academic media theorists claim the camcorder has democratized the media, as well.

Professional and consumer camcorders are based on several, incompatible formats. Ed Beta and MII are popular professional formats, while VHS, compact VHS, and ultra-compact 8 millimeter dominate among consumers. The 8-millimeter format led to significantly smaller cameras that can be operated with one hand (Sony uses the trade name Handycam to describe its 8-millimeter models). Super VHS (S-VHS) and Hi-8, which are compatible with their lower-resolution counterparts, offer higher definition and color control when used with high-resolution playback equipment. S-VHS and Hi-8 are used by high-end consumers, as well as academic and industrial videographers. The camcorder has also led to a growing sophistication in ancillary equipment for the home video market, with numerous titlers, editors, and mixers available to both average and high-end users. Computer-based multimedia allows camcorder images to be incorporated in computer presentations for business and instructional use.

The camcorder came into prominence in early 1991, when Hollywood plumbing store manager George Holliday focused his camcorder on the beating of Rodney King by members of the Los Angeles Police Department. The tape, which Holliday submitted to KTLA, received international attention, and showed the power amateur video can wield over the national, indeed, world psyche. Previous to this, local stations,

A VHS camcorder.
Photo courtesy of Magnavox

as well as cable news giant CNN, had solicited and used newsworthy amateur video. The popular ABC series *America's Funniest Home Videos* and similar television programs throughout the world are based on the existence of camcorders, as well.

The camcorder has also become an icon of numerous dramas and sitcoms, which commonly frame home and family scenes within the confines of a camcorder viewfinder, replacing the very notion of "home movies" as a form of expression.

MICHAEL B. KASSEL

See also **Experimental Video; Home Video; Public Access Video; Videocassette; Videotape**

Further Reading

Aufderheide, Pat, "Vernacular Video: For the Growing Genre of Camcorder Journalism, Nothing Is Too Personal," *Columbia Journalism Review* (January–February 1995)

Berko, Lili, "Video: In Search of a Discourse," *Quarterly Review of Film Studies* (April 1989)

Brodie, John, "Hi8: Expanding the Role of TV Reporter," *Columbia Journalism Review* (September–October 1991)

Dullea, Georgia, "Camcorder! Action! Lives Become Roles," *New York Times* (August 15, 1991)

Hedgecoe, John, *John Hedgecoe's Complete Guide to Video,* New York: Sterling, 1992

Luft, Greg, "Camcorders: When Amateurs Go After the News," *Columbia Journalism Review* (September–October, 1991)

Metz, Holly, "Camcorder Commandos," *The Progressive* (April 1991)

Mouzard, Froncois, *Camcorder—Camscope,* Ottowa, Canada: Department of the Secretary of State of Canada, 1991

Oulette, Laurie, "The (Video) Revolution Will Be Televised," *Utne Reader* (March–April 1992)

Oulette, Laurie, "Will the Revolution be Televised? Camcorders, Activism, and Alternative Television in the 1990s," in *Transmission: Toward a Post-Television Culture,* edited by Peter d'Agostino and David Tafler, Thousand Oaks, California: Sage, 1995

Slouka, Mark Z., " 'Speak, Video': Life, Death, and Memory in the New Age," *Georgia Review* (Summer 1993)

Talty, Stephen, "Family Record," *Film Comment* (May–June 1991)

Warren, George, "Big News: Little Cameras," *Washington Journalism Review* (December 1990)

Weiss, Michael J., "Camcorder Consumers," *American Demographics* (September 1994)

Cameron, Earl (1915–)

Canadian Newsreader

Earl Cameron was English Canada's first noteworthy TV news anchor, once known as "Mr. CBC News." Unlike his successors, however, Cameron was a presenter in the British tradition, not a journalist in the American tradition, and he fell victim to the professionalization of television news during the 1960s.

The news service of the Canadian Broadcasting Corporation (CBC) was created in the early years of World War II and modeled on the style of the British Broadcasting Corporation (BBC). The key figure was Dan McArthur, the first chief news editor, who believed that broadcast news should be delivered in a calm, neutral fashion, free of any showmanship or editorializing. McArthur wanted the news to appear "authoritative"—meaning the news reader must act as an impersonal presenter of the news text.

Cameron was trained in this tradition. He had begun to deliver the National News Bulletin in 1944, the year he joined the CBC, and remained a top CBC radio announcer throughout the 1950s. Although he had little or no experience in television, he succeeded to the job of reading the nightly 11:00 P.M. TV news in 1959, probably because of his reputation as a top announcer.

For the next seven years, Cameron was almost unchallenged as the voice of the news, since the rival CTV News, born in 1962, lacked the resources to match the quality of CBC's *The National* (then called *CBC Television News*). He obeyed the rules laid down long ago by McArthur—he appeared solid, even bland, and spoke in measured, careful tones that avoided all hint of emotion or bias. "No matter what Earl Cameron reads," noted one critic, "he makes it sound less alarming than it sounds coming from someone else." Within a few years, *The National* had earned a reputation as more being reliable and believable than newspapers and radio.

As the 1960s progressed, however, Cameron looked increasingly outdated. He was not, in any sense of the word, a journalist: "I just read the words," he once told Knowlton Nash, who would later anchor *The National.* Such an attitude did not sit well with the new people who had entered the ranks of CBC News. First, Cameron was prohibited from narrating commercials, a task that had been common amongst staff announcers as a source of extra revenue. His participation in such a crass business as selling toothpaste apparently undermined the credibility of the news. Then Bill Cunningham, the executive producer of news and an admirer of Walter Cronkite, proposed a sweeping change in the character of the CBC news service along the lines common in the United States. He urged a longer newscast, 18 minutes instead of 13 during the week, more pictures and fewer talking heads, more coverage across Canada (rather than just Ottawa, Montreal, and Toronto), and, above all, more "pizzazz." The changes would require that *The National* be delivered by a newsperson: only a journalist could properly convey the significance of the news to the viewing audience.

The argument was not wholly specious: it was true that viewers expected the anchor to understand the news. However, the key was the performance of the anchor, his or her ability to act as a storyteller, to present the news items in a coherent and organized fashion that would serve to make clear what happened. An announcer could carry out this crucial task as well as, or better than, a journalist. Whatever the merits of Cunningham's argument, it apparently swayed CBC management. Cameron was replaced in 1966 by an actual journalist. Ironically, union regulations prevented his frustrated successor from writing or editing *The National,* a situation that was not remedied until many years later. Only a few of the recommendations of Cunningham's report were effectively implemented, and he himself was soon removed as executive producer.

Cameron did not immediately disappear from Canadian screens. He became the host of *Viewpoint,* a talking-head program that ran for about five minutes after *The National* as a vehicle for individual opinions on public issues. But, according to one of his compatriots, Cameron remained unhappy over his treatment and eventually took early retirement from the CBC, a victim of changing fashions.

PAUL RUTHERFORD

See also **National, The/The Journal**

Earl Cameron. Born in Canada, 1915. Began career as radio news announcer, 1944; moved to television as newsreader for *The National,* 1959–66; host of *Viewpoint* (a five-minute commentary).

Television Series

1959–66 *The National*

Radio (selected)

National News Bulletin; CBC News Round-Up.

Further Reading

Lochead, Richard, editor, *Beyond the Printed Word: The Evolution of Canada's Broadcast News Heritage,* Kingston, Ontario: Quarry, 1991

Nash, Knowlton, *Prime Time at Ten: Behind-the-Camera Battles of Canadian TV Journalism,* Toronto: McClelland and Stewart, 1987

Rutherford, Paul, *When Television Was Young: Prime-Time Canada, 1952–1967,* Toronto: University of Toronto Press, 1990

Trueman, Peter, *Smoke and Mirrors: The Inside Story of Television News in Canada,* Toronto: McClelland and Stewart, 1980

Canada

The story of Canadian television begins in 1952, with the launching of bilingual French-English broadcasts by the Canadian Broadcasting Corporation (CBC) in Montreal. Within a year, the CBC was well on its way to establishing two national television networks.

The CBC had been charged with setting up a public service television system following the study carried out by a wide-ranging royal commission on the arts, letters, and sciences, which reported in 1951. This procedure followed the tradition of an earlier royal commission on radio, which had recommended establishing a public broadcasting corporation along the lines of the British Broadcasting Corporation (BBC) model and had led to the creation of the CBC in 1936. However, radio in Canada developed during the 1930s and 1940s under "mixed" ownership, with public and private stations coexisting in a single system and competing for advertising. This model was to be repeated in television. While the CBC would enjoy a virtual monopoly for most of television's crucial first decade in Canada, private commercial television appeared in 1960. As of 1961, CTV, a national network linking private television stations, was on the air competing vigorously with the CBC.

The 1950s were critical in setting the tone for Canadian television, in both English and French. Distinctive Canadian news and current-affairs formats were developed, and, in French particularly, popular dramatic serials known as *téléromans* were established. *Hockey Night in Canada,* programmed in both official languages, became a national ritual that continues unto this day. In contrast, as in most other television systems, some important genres, such as live theater, remain strictly in the memory of the aging.

The basic legislation governing Canadian broadcasting was rewritten in 1958, following the election of a Conservative government friendly to the interests of the private broadcasting industry. Responding to a long-standing demand of the Canadian Association of Broadcasters (CAB), an independent regulatory authority, the Board of Broadcast Governors (BBG) was created, removing the regulation of private broadcasting from the responsibility of the CBC. Shortly thereafter, the BBG began to license private television stations.

Meanwhile, the CBC faced a series of political crises. On the English side, attempts by the government to interfere with programming led to massive resignations among current-affairs staff in 1959. In the same year, a strike by French-language Radio-Canada producers paralyzed the French television service for more than two months and became an important symbolic reference point for the emerging Quebec nationalist movement.

During the 1960s, news and information programming continued to be a source of friction both within the CBC and in the corporation's relationship with the government. The unorthodox weekly program *This Hour Has Seven Days,* which rated the highest audience "enjoyment index" of any CBC show, provoked an internal management and authority crisis that eventually toppled the CBC's senior management while redefining Canadian television journalism. During the same period, French service news programs infuriated the government by paying serious attention to Quebec separatist politicians and issues, and in 1968 the law was rewritten, albeit with little effect, obliging the CBC to "contribute to national unity."

While the CBC led the way in Canadian programming, private television was slowly and steadily carving a place for itself, building an audience by consistently offering the most popular U.S. programs, competing with the CBC for the broadcasting rights to Canadian sports classics such as professional football's annual Grey Cup Game and emulating the CBC's successes in news and current affairs. By the late 1980s, the CBC's share of the Canadian television audience was down to around 20 percent in English and 30 percent in French.

The issue of maintaining a balance between Canadian and U.S. programs was tackled by the regulatory authority early on. Beginning in 1960, Canadian television broadcasters were required to offer 55 percent Canadian programs. (In 1970 the regulation was stiffened to 60 percent in prime time.) Canadian-content regulations remain a controversial and ongoing issue in Canadian television up to the present. Aside from the philosophical question surrounding the legitimacy of intervening in audience "choice," the effectiveness of content quotas in bringing Canadian programs to the screen and getting Canadians to watch them has been a subject of continual debate. Since the 1960s, however, there has been a general consensus that without Canadian-content requirements, commercial broadcasters would have no incentive to produce Canadian programs when they could acquire U.S. exports for as little as one-tenth the cost. A more recent development has been the establishment by both the public and private sector of a number of television production funds in the 1980s and 1990s, leading to the rise of a Canadian independent production industry by increasing the pool of available capital and making it easier to get airtime. The notion of what constitutes "Canadian content" has also evolved over time.

The 1968 reform of the Broadcasting Act replaced the BBG with the Canadian Radio-Television Commission, or CRTC (which became the Canadian Radio-television and Telecommunications Commission in 1976). The CRTC spent most of the 1970s developing a regulatory framework for the rapidly expanding cable industry, which had emerged in the 1950s as community antenna television serving remote areas. By retransmitting signals picked out of the air from U.S. border-town transmitters (for which Canadian cable companies paid no license fees until 1989), the Canadian cable industry built an attractive product for the Canadian television audience, which quickly developed a taste for the best of both worlds. To paraphrase the 1929 royal commission on broadcasting, Canadians wanted Canadian programming, but they wanted U.S. programming too.

Aware that the increasingly widespread cable model was undermining its policy to support and promote Canadian content, the CRTC moved to ensure that cable, as well, contributed to the overriding policy objective of delivering Canadian television to Canadians. Must-carry provisions ensured that every available Canadian over-the-air signal in any area was offered as basic service, along with a local community channel. In exchange, cable companies were authorized to distribute the three U.S. commercial networks, ABC, NBC, and CBS, as well as the U.S. public network, PBS. This was, for many years, the basic cable package available to Canadian cable subscribers, and on this basis, cable penetration grew to 76 percent of Canadian homes by 1992.

The CRTC was also charged with putting in place Canadian ownership regulations, limiting foreign participation in Canadian broadcasting companies to 20 percent. As a result, Canadian television today is entirely Canadian owned, with only a handful of operations having any proportion of foreign ownership at all. It has not affected the rise of Canadian media conglomerates along the lines of those known elsewhere, however, and the Canadian television industry is characterized by a high degree of concentration of ownership. The trend since the mid-1980s has been toward the takeover of private television outfits by cable companies. Since the late 1990s, cross-media convergence combining press, broadcasting, and telecommunications outfits has led to the creation of multimedia conglomerates, which in some cases verge on monopoly. The best-known examples are Bell Canada Enterprises (BCE), owners of CTV and the national *Globe and Mail* newspaper as well as the country's largest telephone company; CanWest Global, owners of the Southam newspaper chain as well as the national Global Television network; Rogers Communications, Canada's largest cable company and owner of the Maclean Hunter chain of magazines; and Quebecor, owners of Vidéotron (Quebec's largest cable company), TVA (Canada's largest private French-language television network), as well as the *Sun* chain of newspapers. In 2002 all of these companies were reportedly in financial difficulty due to their ambitious recent acquisitions and attempts to establish themselves in new-media and other Internet-based activities.

An important shift in the ecology of Canadian television occurred in the 1970s, when the CRTC began to license second private stations in large metropolitan markets. Regional networks such as Global (in southern Ontario) and Quatre Saisons (in Quebec) grew out of this policy, which also saw the establishment of independent stations in many cities, including Toronto's highly successful CityTV. The resulting audience fragmentation contributed to the erosion of the CBC's audience share. Consequently, it also weakened important arguments that would legitimize the spiraling cost of public broadcasting to the public purse.

Although advertising had always been a component of CBC television, basic funding was provided by an annual grant from Parliament. By the late 1980s that grant had risen to more than $1 billion (Canadian) annually. Advertising, meanwhile, represented more than 20 percent of the budget—enough to be an important consideration in every programming decision, but not nearly enough to take the pressure off the public treasury. The CBC's dilemma, particularly for services provided in English, has been how to maintain a distinctive television profile while competing commercially, and how to respond to the vast demands of an encompassing mandate in a context of government cutbacks. It has not been an easy process.

Private television, meanwhile, after two lucrative decades in the 1960s and 1970s, also began to experience the financial doldrums of a weak market in the 1980s. As a period of stagnating advertising revenues followed the earlier licensing boom, many private television operations became ripe for takeover, especially by cable companies.

Conventional broadcasters faced a further challenge with the introduction, in 1982, of pay-TV and later, in 1987, of a series of Canadian specialty channels. The CRTC had resisted pressure from the cable industry to allow the importation of the new U.S. services such as HBO that came on the market in the mid-1970s. The commission opted instead to promote development of Canadian services along the same lines. In most cases, such as movies, sports, and rock videos, the Canadian services provide a range of programs similar to those of their American counterparts, but they are Canadian owned, subject to CRTC licensing, and they do offer at least a window for Canadian programs. In some cases, such as the CBC's 24-hour news service, Newsworld, or the international francophone channel, TV5, the first generation of Canadian specialty services licensed in 1987 represented a distinctive addition to the program offerings.

The financing of Canadian pay-TV and specialty channels provides an instructive example in the problems such entities have when competing with globally distributed television products in a small domestic market. The regulatory justification for creating Canadian pay-TV in 1982 was to provide an additional vehicle for Canadian feature films, but the actual percentage of Canadian films offered has never been statistically significant. At the same time, weak penetration of the cable market by film channels made such channels commercially unviable. Thus, when the CRTC decided to license a new series of specialty channels in 1987, it chose a different funding formula. This time, cable operators were authorized to provide the new range of services to all subscribers in their territory, and charge accordingly. The discretionary aspect was thus shifted from the consumer to the cable operator, who could calculate the economics of the deal with great precision. The cost to the consumer for each additional service was relatively low, and as rates were regulated, the market mechanism was essentially removed. At the same time, cable operators could still offer the available Canadian discretionary pay-TV channels, which the operators were by now packaging along with a range of authorized U.S. services not considered to be competitors of the Canadian offerings.

Since 1987, then, Canadian cable subscribers in most markets have received a 24-hour CBC news channel (at first in English and, since 1994, in French as well); channels featuring music videos, sports, weather, and children's programming (in either English or French); and the international francophone channel TV5. In addition, viewers could choose to subscribe to pay-TV movie channels, specialized channels in the other official language, and, depending where they lived, a range of U.S. channels including CNN (but not, for example, MTV, which was a direct competitor of the new Canadian equivalent).

By the early 1990s, combined viewing of all of these services accounted for less than 20 percent of the overall audience share. However, pressure to establish even more Canadian services continued. It was grounded in discussions of the coming "500-channel universe" and the perceived need to maintain the attractiveness of a cable subscription for Canadian viewers and forestall their defection to direct broadcast satellites. Thus, as of January 1, 1995, a cable-ready Canadian household (now up to 76 percent) could receive, in addition to everything mentioned previously, a French-language CBC news channel; arts-and-entertainment channels in English or French (depending on the market); a science channel; a women's channel; a lifestyle channel; a Canadian country music channel; and a channel featuring old programs. The specific offer and funding formulas have become extremely complicated and vary from territory to territory according to the leeway provided by the CRTC to each cable operator. The initial response from consumers has been laced with confusion and frustration, for despite the concept of "consumer sovereignty" that supposedly accompanies increased channel capacity, the consumer finds that he or she is not really the one who has the choice. In all, between 1984 and 1999, the CRTC licensed six pay-TV and 48 specialty television services and added another 283 digital pay and specialty services in 2001.

In the mid-1990s, Canadian television was struggling to adjust to the new technological and economic environment characterized by the metaphor of the "information highway." The CRTC's regulatory regime was under review, the CBC faced increasingly radical budgetary restrictions, and private broadcasters were competing for dwindling advertising revenue. As in other Western countries, the conventional model of generalist television was increasingly in a state of siege. However, Canadian distribution undertakings—still protected from U.S. dominance under the cultural industries exemption within the North American Free Trade Agreement (NAFTA)—were well positioned in the Canadian market, and, across the range of channels available, Canadian independent productions were finding an audience.

In addition, Canadian television provided some unique programming services in the form of its provincial government–supported educational broadcasters, community broadcasters, and autonomous undertakings run by northern and native broadcasters. Since 1932 broadcasting has been recognized in the Canadian Constitution as being under federal jurisdiction, but in the 1970s an exception was made for provinces seeking to establish educational broadcasters, provided that these organizations operated at arm's length from their respective provincial governments. This led to the establishment of Radio-Québec (now Télé-Québec), TVOntario, the Saskatchewan Communications Network, ACCESS Alberta (now ACCESSTV and privately owned), and British Columbia's Knowledge Network of the West (KNOW). Canadian cable and satellite services boast a number of unique not-for-profit services, including a multifaith channel, Vision TV, and the world's first network entirely owned and operated by indigenous people, the Aboriginal People's Television Network (APTN).

Issues surrounding the future of public broadcasting, concentration of ownership, the role of the CRTC, and new media have been at the heart of television policy debates in the early 2000s. Indeed, talking about television continues to be an important aspect of public discourse in Canada. In all its facets, Canadian television has constituted a complex system that, in the spirit of the Broadcasting Act, has been seen as "a public service essential to the maintenance and enhancement of national identity and cultural sovereignty."

MARC RABOY

See also **Canadian Broadcasting Corporation Newsworld; Canadian Cable Television Association; Canadian Film and Television Production Association; Canadian Production Companies; Canadian Programming in English; Canadian Programming in French; Canadian Television Network; Citytv; First People's Television Broadcasting in Canada; Telefilm Canada; Television Northern Canada**

Further Reading

Audley, Paul, *Canada's Cultural Industries: Broadcasting, Publishing, Records, and Film,* Toronto: Lorimer, 1983

Broadcasting Act, Statutes of Canada, 1991

Collins, Richard, *Culture, Communication, and National Identity: The Case of Canadian Television,* Toronto: University of Toronto Press, 1990

Lorimer, Rowland, and Mike Gasher, *Mass Communication in Canada,* 4th edition, Toronto: Oxford University Press, 2001

Miller, Mary Jane, *Turn Up the Contrast: CBC Television Drama Since 1952,* Vancouver: University of British Columbia Press, 1987

Nash, Knowlton, *The Microphone Wars: A History of Triumph and Betrayal at the CBC,* Toronto: McClelland and Stewart, 1994

Peers, Frank W., *The Public Eye: Television and the Politics of Canadian Broadcasting, 1952–1968,* Toronto: University of Toronto Press, 1979

Raboy, Marc, *Missed Opportunities: The Story of Canada's Broadcasting Policy,* Montreal: McGill-Queen's University Press, 1990

Rutherford, Paul, *When Television Was Young: Primetime Canada 1952–1967,* Toronto: University of Toronto Press, 1990

Skene, Wayne, *Fade to Black: A Requiem for the CBC,* Vancouver: Douglas and McIntyre, 1993

Smythe, Dallas W., *Dependency Road: Communications, Capitalism, Consciousness, and Canada,* Norwood, New Jersey: Ablex, 1981

Task Force on Broadcasting Policy, *Report,* Ottawa: Ministry of Supply and Services, 1986

Woodcock, George, *Strange Bedfellows: The State and the Arts in Canada,* Vancouver: Douglas and McIntyre, 1985

Canada: A People's History

Historical Documentary Series

The production statistics for *Canada: A People's History,* surely the most monumental production in the history of Canadian television, are staggering. A fully bilingual 17-part documentary on Canadian history from the prehistoric to the contemporary periods, the series was produced at a cost of $25 million (Canadian) and broadcast in French and English versions simultaneously on the Canadian Broadcasting Corporation (CBC) and its French-language arm Société Radio-Canada (SRC) in one 9-part and one 8-part series, the first beginning in autumn 2000 and the second beginning the following autumn. Broadcast on Sunday nights, and rebroadcast on the CBC's Newsworld channel, more than half of the nation's citizens (some 15 million) watched all or some of the first nine episodes, with average viewership in the neighborhood of 2.2 million per episode. These are extraordinary numbers, more the kind generated for an important hockey match than for a CBC-produced historical documentary.

In addition to the 17 hours each of French and English documentary, the program was accompanied by a two-volume book set, which used many of the archival images researchers had collected for the series; a CD recording of the series' original score; and a still-existing website addressed primarily to school children as an accompanying resource to the VHS and DVD versions of the series, which are themselves, according to the CBC, found in 80 percent of Canadian classrooms. These accompanying elements have in their own ways been as successful as the broadcast of the series itself, inasmuch as they made a significant impact on the national culture in Canada, with the book set, for example, achieving best-seller status, and—arguably due to the judgment of many historians as to the relative soundness of the version of history presented by the series, notwithstanding the numerous dissenting voices—with the educational and entertainment value of the production spurring strong sales of the VHS and DVD packages.

The chief problem posed by historical documentary, selection and omission, was especially acute for the producers of *Canada: A People's History* because of the enormity of a subject called "the history of Canada." Acknowledging this problem from the beginning of the undertaking, the series producers made much of their efforts toward inclusivity, especially as the historical treatment of Canada's native peoples, women, and ethnic minorities was concerned, and it was the issue of historical "accuracy," filtered through the lens of an inclusive "people's history," that dominated the significant discourse, both academic and in the popular press, that surrounded the series.

The history of Canada is presented in the series through means of reenactment; heavy reliance on archival images, including maps, drawings, paintings, photographs, and moving images; and narration and dialogue drawn only from words documented to have been written or spoken by actual historical figures—that is, without any "talking head" interviews or mediated commentary on the events, words, and images presented. While the narrative of the history presented is organized chronologically, a thematic organizational structure meant that there are temporal overlaps from episode to episode, whereby, for example, episode six, "The Pathfinders," covering the period 1670 to 1850, is concerned with the exploration of the continent, while episode seven, "Rebellion and Reform," covers the overlapping period 1815 to 1850 and is concerned with governance in the colonies of British North America, and especially with the rebellions that lead eventually to colonial self-rule.

Typical of historical surveys, the more distant past receives less attention than more contemporary events; thus, "When the World Began," the first episode, covers by far the largest swath of time (from the prehistory period, beginning about 15,000 B.C., up until European contact with the aboriginal peoples) while subsequent episodes generally cover much smaller time periods, with the last episode, "In an Uncertain World," covering a mere 14 years, 1976 to 1990.

The series pays significant attention to those historical moments generally held to have been formative for the nation, including the construction of the Canadian Pacific Railway through the west to British Columbia and Canada's participation in World War I, with the nation's disproportionately high casualties seen as indicative of the maturation of the new country into a full participant in world affairs. Other important historical events, such as the Winnipeg General Strike of 1919 and the conscription crisis of World War II, also receive due treatment, and some of the nation's more shameful moments are also aired, such as the virulent racism and anti-Semitism that has infected the nation.

The high profile of the series at the time of its original broadcast, and even the very fact of its existence on such a grand scale, can perhaps be attributed to an increasing sense of popular nationalism, especially as felt and expressed by young people, during the period. Canadian popular music and advertising of the period can be seen as examples of surging national pride, of which the grand production and broadcast of *Canada: A People's History* was a part.

Mark Starowicz, the series' executive producer, was a well-known figure in Canadian broadcasting and was the creator of a handful of very successful programs for the CBC including the innovative current-affairs radio program "As It Happens" and the popular and successful reorganization of the CBC television news into two connected parts, *The National,* the nightly newscast, and *The Journal,* a current-affairs segment that followed the newscast with interviews and/or news documentaries. Starowicz's reputation as a successful broadcast innovator and his devotion to the project was probably a contributing factor of the CBC management's decision to risk such a huge undertaking.

PETER URQUHART

See also **Starowicz, Mark**

Canadian Broadcasting Corporation Newsworld

Canadian News Channel

When it went on the air in August 1989, Canada's English-language all-news 24-hour channel, Canadian Broadcasting Corporation Newsworld, followed CNN as the second such network in the world. News has historically been a strong suit on Canadian television, with many innovative programs including *CBC Newsmagazine, This Hour Has Seven Days,* and *The Journal.* Canadian audiences have consistently demonstrated a taste for news produced indigenously, reflecting local concerns, as well as for Canadian perspectives on international events. Unlike other areas of television, such as drama and situation comedy, news programming has been able to draw significant and reliable audience numbers. Consequently, the availability of only the U.S.-based CNN during the 1980s sparked an interest in the formation of a similar Canadian 24-hour news network.

The Canadian Broadcasting Corporation (CBC) won the license for the all-news network in November 1987. Private broadcasters fought this decision made by the Canadian Radio-television and Telecommunications Commission (CRTC). In particular, Allarcom Ltd., whose own bid lost to CBC, contended that the national public broadcaster received undue favoritism. After a tough challenge in a Conservative parliament sympathetic to Allarcom's charges, the CRTC's decision was finally accepted, although not without delaying the network's start date for more than a year. Federal cabinet actions, however, modified the conditions of the license by insisting that CBC Newsworld involve the private sector in its operations and that it develop a similar French-language service.

The perception that CBC has a central Canadian bias, and therefore that it does not adequately reflect the diverse interests and locations of the nation as a whole, also surfaced as a criticism of the CRTC decision. In a bid to address the issue of the CBC's centralization in Toronto, CBC Newsworld began by situating its broadcast centers in Halifax, Nova Scotia; Winnipeg, Manitoba; and Calgary, Alberta.

CBC Newsworld's financing is entirely separate from that of the CBC. The cable channel's revenue comes from advertising and "pass-through" cable fees. As part of basic cable service, the pass-through fee means that all cable subscribers have to pay for the service, whether they want it or not. The monthly cost to cable subscribers was 44.5 cents (Canadian) in 1989; it increased to 63 cents in 2000. Some cable operators, particularly around Montreal, initially refused to accept the service because the pass-through fee for an English-language service made no sense to their majority francophone subscribers.

Network operations are roughly one-tenth the size of CNN's, in terms of both budget and staff. Thus, CBC Newsworld has relied on other news gatherers (e.g., local CBC reports, CBC national news, and internationally packaged programming from the BBC and CNN) as well as partnerships with independent production companies. This need for inexpensive programming led toward the news-panel and phone-in format for many of the channel's productions (e.g., *Sunday Morning Live, Petrie in Prime, On the Line with Patrick Conlon,* and *Coast to Coast*). Current programming includes *Foreign Assignment, counterSpin, Culture Shock, Fashion File, Health Matters,* and *The National. Rough Cuts* and *The Passionate Eye* are prominent windows for documentary film. As of 2000, 90 percent of CBC Newsworld programming had Canadian content.

In 1994 the CBC French-language all-news service received its license. Le Reseau de l'information (RDI) went on the air in 1995, and like CBC Newsworld, it is part of the basic cable service in Canada. Received by 8.8 million households in Canada, CBC Newsworld reaches a wider audience than any other specialty channel in the country.

In association with Power Broadcasting, CBC made a repackaged version of its services, called Newsworld International, available to U.S. audiences in 1994. It is the only 24-hour channel focusing on international news in the United States and was bought by USA Networks in 2000. Despite the change in ownership, CBC Newsworld remains the content provider of this international branch. In January 2000, the CRTC renewed CBC Newsworld's license for another seven years.

CHARLES ACLAND

Further Reading

Allen, Glen, "News Around the Clock: CBC's Newsworld Takes to the Air," *Maclean's* (August 7, 1989)
Corelli, Rae, "A Committed News Junkie: Head of Newsworld, Joan Donaldson," *Maclean's* (August 7, 1989)
Corelli, Rae, "The CBC's Future: Budget Cuts Have Plunged the CBC into the Worst Crisis of Its 52-year History," *Maclean's* (August 7, 1989)
Ellis, David, *Split Screen: Home Entertainment and the New Technologies,* Toronto: Lorimer, 1992
Jensen, Holger, "Growing Pains: Newsworld's Debut Is Shaky but Promising," *Maclean's* (August 14, 1989)

Canadian Cable Television Association

In 1957 Canada's fledgling cable operators formed the National Community Antenna Television Association of Canada to represent their collective interests to the public and various government bodies. In 1968, after the passage of the Broadcasting Act and the creation of the Canadian Radio-television and Telecommunications Commission (CRTC), the cable industry changed the name of its umbrella organization to the Canadian Cable Television Association (CCTA). Over the last three decades Canada's cable operators have dramatically altered the character of Canadian television services by extending the range of programming and services available to Canadians and opening the door to the "500-channel universe."

The first Canadian cable television system was established in London, Ontario, in 1952 (though it was preceded by a Montreal cable system that delivered audio-only service until later the same year). Cable's original purpose was simply to improve the quality of over-the-air reception from local and regional TV stations. In London, Ontario, in 1952 the cable TV system delivered the Canadian Broadcasting Corporation (CBC) signal from Toronto and the U.S. networks from border cities. In 1963, Canadian cable TV operators began using microwave technology to deliver services to rural and remote communities.

In the 1970s, cable subscriptions rose sharply. By 1977, the number of households subscribing to cable passed 50 percent. As of 2000, 95 percent of Canadian TV households were passed by cable and 74 percent of those households subscribed to cable services. Through microwave relay and satellite systems, cable TV services were available in more than 2,000 small and rural communities across Canada.

The cable business has been extremely lucrative for most CCTA members. Between 1983 and 1993, cable rates rose an average of 80 percent compared with a 31 percent increase in local telephone rates and a 47 percent increase in the consumer price index. Moreover, the CRTC only regulates the basic subscription rate charged by cable operators, but 96 percent of subscribers chose a package of channels known as extended basic, whose rate is unregulated.

Like other media industries, cable is now characterized by a significant level of corporate concentration; the six largest companies account for 90 percent of total subscribers. With just under 30 percent of all Canadian cable subscribers and close to 45 percent of all English-Canadian subscribers under its corporate banner, Rogers Communications is the dominant national firm. The other leading firms are Shaw Cablesystems, with 28 percent of total subscribers, and Vidéotron, with 18 percent of total subscribers.

The expansion of cable in Canada in the 1970s can be attributed to a number of regulatory decisions made by the CRTC. In 1969, after much public pressure and lobbying from the CCTA, the CRTC permitted cable systems operating at a distance from the U.S. border, as in Edmonton and Ottawa, to use microwave distribution technology to gather U.S. broadcast signals. Cable's success as a distribution technology was directly related to its ability to provide Canadian households with U.S. signals they either could not otherwise receive or received poorly with conventional rooftop antennas. In 1975, the CRTC declared that cable was a "chosen instrument of public policy" and developed detailed regulations concerning the signals and services that cable companies can or must provide, the rates charged subscribers, the provision of a community channel, and more.

In many respects, cable was the first of the much-ballyhooed new technologies. Aside from its early use of microwave technology, Canadian cable TV initiated the use of satellite-delivered services when, in the

1970s, it offered the House of Commons proceedings to subscribers across the country. Cable companies also developed the first alphanumeric television services in Canada. Home shopping and real estate services have been available in larger centers for several years. Some cable systems also offer travel information, electronic mail, video games, and instructional services. Cable companies are involved in a number of field trials to deliver broadband, interactive home services.

At the local level, the member companies of the CCTA have supported community channels for more than 25 years. In 1993, 225 community channels across the country provided more than 235,000 hours of programming. For all but the smallest cable companies, community channels are a condition of their license to operate. Cable companies must make available both space and equipment to community groups and individuals interested in producing television programming; the cable operators are legally responsible for all the material broadcast on the community channels. Although they were initially envisioned as a great experiment in citizen participation and democratic communication, the community channels have by and large developed into rather paternalistic institutions that avoid controversial and politically charged programming. Instead, local council meetings, local sports events, and multicultural information programming make up the bulk of the offerings on most community channels.

As Canada moves forward into the age of interactive information and entertainment services, the CCTA must contend with the looming possibility of competition from Canada's telephone companies. The CCTA has argued repeatedly that cable operators are better suited to provide Canadians with access to the information superhighway. CCTA companies are currently engaged in an elaborate project to improve the interactive, multimedia, transactional capabilities of cable systems, including a plan to establish national interconnection via cable. As of 2002, 7.9 million Canadian households subscribed to cable. The CCTA has also maintained that, unlike the telephone companies, cable operators are committed to protecting and supporting the production of Canadian material in the interests of reinforcing Canadian sovereignty and cultural identity.

TED MAGDER

See also **Canada**

Further Reading

Babe, Robert E., *Cable Television and Telecommunication in Canada: An Economic Analysis,* East Lansing: Michigan State University, 1975

Brady, Diane, "Competing Channels: Regulators Debate Television's Future," *Maclean's* (March 22, 1993)

Cable Television, Ottawa: Statistics Canada, 1971–

Cable Television in Canada, Ottawa: Canadian Radio-television Commission, 1971

Freeman, Mike, "Canada Test Angers Border Broadcasters," *Broadcasting* (June 8, 1992)

Hollins, Timothy, *Beyond Broadcasting: Into the Cable Age,* London: British Film Institute, 1984

Murray, Karen, "Canadian Co-op Combats Yank Satellite Attack," *Variety* (May 17, 1993)

Canadian Film and Television Production Association

The Canadian Film and Television Production Association (CFTPA) is a national, nonprofit association of more than 300 companies in Canada's independent production industry. The CFTPA is Canada's only national film producers' association, bringing together entrepreneurial companies engaged in film, television and video production, distribution, and the provision of facilities and services to the independent production industry. Member companies include Canada's leading independent film and television producers, such as Alliance Atlantis and Corus Entertainment.

The CFTPA promotes the interests of its members by lobbying government on policy matters; negotiating labor agreements on behalf of independent producers (including a low-budget production agreement that entitles CFTPA members to discounts on ACTRA performers); sponsoring conferences, seminars, and workshops; and publishing a variety of material to assist CFTPA members. The CFTPA is also the founding member of the Canadian Retransmission Collective, the body that claims royalties from Canadian cable companies on behalf of program creators.

The CFTPA is the latest incarnation of voluntary organizations that have represented Canada's independent film and television producers. The first such organization, the Association of Motion Picture Producers and Laboratories of Canada (AMPPLC), was established in 1948. The AMPPLC focused its lobbying efforts on reducing the role of the National Film Board of Canada (NFB) and expanding opportunities for Canada's independent producers. Throughout the 1950s and into the early 1960s, the AMPPLC challenged what it described as the NFB's "expansionist, monopolistic psychology" and repeatedly called for the contracting out of government film work. By the 1960s, the AMPPLC had also joined the growing chorus of organizations and individuals making the case for government subsidies for the production of private-sector feature films.

Since the 1960s, and especially since the establishment of the Canadian Film Development Corporation (now Telefilm Canada), the independent sector for film and television production in Canada has grown substantially. The industry employs more than 150,000 Canadians in direct and indirect positions. Total production volume reached $5 billion in 2001, a figure that includes Canadian-certified production, broadcaster in-house production, and foreign-location production. Exports of Canadian film and television productions are now valued at well over $150 million a year, more than double the value of exports in 1986.

CFTPA members benefit from a number of government programs and regulations designed to stimulate independent film and television production in Canada. Since 1968, the Canadian Film and Development Corporation has offered a combination of loans, subsidies, and grants to private-sector feature film production. In 1983, Telefilm Canada initiated the Canadian Broadcast Program Development Fund, earmarked especially for Canadian television productions. CFTPA members also make use of a wide range of provincial funding sources, the largest of which is the Ontario Film Development Corporation. As of 1993, the total annual amount of government funds available for private-sector film and television productions was $340 million.

Aside from the availability of government funds to "prime the pump" of independent film and television production, CFTPA members also benefit from the Canadian-content regulations that are a condition of license for all Canadian broadcasters. Administered by the Canadian Radio-television and Telecommunications Commission, the Canadian-content regulations ensure that Canadian broadcasters do not operate merely as conduits for foreign programming, which is much cheaper to acquire. Since the early 1980s, traditional over-the-air broadcasters, such as CTV and Global, have made much greater use of product from the independent sector to fulfill their Canadian-content responsibilities.

CFTPA members have also benefited considerably from the licensing of new specialty cable and pay-TV channels in the 1980s. Indeed, the global expansion of new outlets for television programming has greatly enhanced the fortunes of CFTPA members. CFTPA members now export their product to markets around the world, and many of the larger firms have developed effective working relationships with foreign partners. Joint ventures with U.S. firms have become a mainstay of the industry, in part because of the savings in production costs that result from the relative value of the Canadian dollar.

The CFTPA plays a crucial role in ensuring a stable business climate for its members. In the midst of political pressure to reduce the level of government spending, the CFTPA has repeatedly lobbied on behalf of the efforts of Telefilm Canada, the provincial fund agencies, and the Canadian Broadcasting Corporation (which is the major buyer of independent TV programs in Canada). The CFTPA has also been at the forefront of efforts to establish a refundable tax credit system for Canadian producers. Aside from issues related directly to the production of Canadian film and television, the CFTPA is also a vocal proponent of the need to maintain regulations that ensure a minimum level of Canadian content on new and proposed delivery systems, such as the information highway. Relatedly, the CFTPA has argued repeatedly for legislation that would enhance the role of Canadian film distributors by making it impossible for U.S. film distributors to treat Canada as part of their domestic market.

TED MAGDER

See also **Telefilm Canada**

Further Reading

Ayscough, Suzan, "Factions Fracture Pic Funds," *Variety* (November 16, 1992)

Clanfield, David, *Canadian Film,* Toronto: Oxford University Press, 1987

Johnson, Brian D., "Successes on the Screen: Canada Develops Its Film Industry," *Maclean's* (September 10, 1990)

Lyon, S. Daniel, *Public Strategy and Motion Pictures: The Choice of Instruments to Promote the Development of the Canadian Film Production Industry,* Toronto: Ontario Economic Council, 1982

Magder, Ted, *Canada's Hollywood: The Canadian State and Feature Films,* Toronto: University of Toronto Press, 1993

Pendakur, Manjunath, *Canadian Dreams and American Control: The Political Economy of the Canadian Film Industry,* Detroit, Michigan: Wayne State University Press, 1990

Posner, Michael, *Canadian Dreams: The Making and Marketing of Independent Films,* Vancouver: Douglas and McIntyre, 1993

Wallace, Bruce, Joseph Treen, and Robert Enright, "A Campaign in Support of Entertainment," *Maclean's* (March 17, 1986)

Winikoff, Kenneth, "They Always Get Their Film: The Canadian Government Has Sired a National Cinema, but Can a Film Industry Thrive When Every Taxpayer Is a Producer?" *American Film* (July 1990)

Canadian Morning Television

Canadian morning television is partially defined by the perception that audiences use television differently at that time of day. Much morning programming is designed to fit into the patterns of everyday rituals; the discrete nature of programs and content that often defines prime-time programming breaks down in the patterns of morning television.

Historically, morning TV in Canada has been the location of the marginalia of television culture. Farm reports were regular features of morning television after the sign-on of local stations in the early 1960s, and some local religious programming was part of early regional television in a rotation that covered the principal Christian denominations. After 6:00 A.M., television became the province of news or children's programming. Children's programming generally divided along the lines of syndicated U.S. situation comedies and cartoons with live hosts who catered to the local market. In commercial television the early-morning hours were the province of the local station and rarely determined by network time organization. This resulted in a great variety of programs across the country. A morning movie could be part of one television market, while the *Junior Forest Rangers* part of another. Because the Canadian Broadcasting Corporation (CBC) partially operated on a network of commercial affiliates, the early-morning hours were generally not programmed with CBC network feeds. One of the principal changes of early-morning television that moved it closer to its contemporary form was the shift away from this local focus to network programming.

In 1972 CTV, a private network established in 1960, introduced *Canada A.M.*, a program modeled on *Today,* a long-running U.S. program on NBC. *Canada A.M.* is a news and chat show—with regular bulletins of news, sports, and weather—that begins each day at 6:30 and runs until 9:00 A.M. In its live presentation and with its relatively relaxed hosts who move seamlessly into softer news stories and entertainment gossip, *Canada A.M.* attempts to be an ambient program designed to be used during other preparations for the workday. The CBC also launched *CBC Morning News,* which provides a similar diet of bulletins and easy-listening banter among hosts and guests. The rest of the CBC's early-morning schedule is designed for preschool viewers, with programs such as the British Columbia–produced *Scoop and Doozie* and the Nelvana-made computer-animated cartoon *Rolie Polie Olie.* Regional networks such as Global in Ontario have counterprogrammed against this style of "flow" television with either reruns of children's cartoons (which provides needed Canadian content) or religious programming drawn from both Canadian and U.S. sources.

The pattern of morning network television shifts quite dramatically after 9:00 A.M.; the news flow model organized for the working audience transforms into something that targets those connected neither to work nor school, and the divide between the commercial stations and the public broadcasters becomes more obvious. Public stations generally engage in children's educational programming aimed primarily at the preschool age group. The provincially funded education networks such as TVO in Ontario and the Knowledge Network in British Columbia vary this diet with programs aimed at older students within the school and university system. With its larger mandate, the CBC's programs operate commercial free, providing a series of critically acclaimed and internationally successful children's series, which have included the long-running *Mr. Dress Up, Fred Penner's Place, Under the Umbrella Tree,* and *Theodore Tugboat.* These programs have followed in the tradition of *Chez Helene* (1959–72) and the *Friendly Giant* (1958–85) as staples of childhood experience in Canada. A Canadian ver-

Canada A.M. hosts.
Photo courtesy of CTV Inc.

sion of *Sesame Street* has run on CBC since 1973, and inserts of Canadian puppets and stories (including French-language training) derived from Canadian city and country landscapes have increased from five minutes to 25 percent of the program content of this U.S. program. *Sesame Street* and the Canadian coproduction *Arthur,* an animated series about an aardvark and his family and friends, bookend the CBC's morning programming for children.

In contrast, the commercial free-to-air stations have provided almost exclusively adult-oriented programming during this same time period, with talk and game shows predominating in the schedule. *Dini,* an hour-long talk show hosted by Dini Petty in the tradition of *Oprah* and *Donahue,* has had a successful Canadian run on CTV and BBS and made a brief appearance in the U.S. market. Peppered into the schedule are imported U.S. programs such as *Regis and Kelly,* which provide talk-celebrity shows better connected to the Hollywood circuit of stars, or issue talk shows such as Barbara Walters's talkfest *The View.* Exercise programs have on occasion been successful at either the pre– or post–9:00 A.M. slot. The most successful in terms of Canadian and U.S. syndication was the 1980s Citytv production *The Twenty-minute Workout,* which featured three female models performing aerobics routines to a *Miami Vice*–like synthesized backbeat soundtrack.

Religious programming is also presented on Canadian television to some degree. The most prevalent Canadian program to compete with U.S. productions is *100 Huntley Street.* Like the "infomercials," religious programs often buy blocks of time directly from the station and use them for their own forms of promotion. Because they are often out of the general flow of morning television, such programs are also placed further to the margins of early morning.

Weekend morning television presents another principal distinction in Canadian programming. On both Saturday and Sunday mornings, the commercial stations expand their children's programming to span virtually the entire time period. This focus on cartoons and hosted programs aimed at children gradually dissolves by late morning into sports programming. Sunday morning is divided among a variety of Canadian and U.S.-based religious programs and children's television. The religious programs are further subdivided between local production and more slickly produced syndicated shows.

The expansion of Canadian television channels since the 1980s has made the temporal designations in programming—such as the category of "morning television"—less valid. The patterns of morning television have instead been expanded into actual channels, where the former marginalia of television populate the entire broadcast day. For instance, CBC Newsworld, the 24-hour news channel, does alter its content throughout the day, but the general pattern resembles breakfast television news programs that predated the channel's launch. Subtle differences can be seen in channels producing what could be described as micro-genres. MuchMusic, the nationally distributed cable music channel, organizes its morning into *Videoflow* and the retro-oriented mid-morning *ClipTrip.*

These channel orientations are complicated, however, by technological factors. Satellite distribution, unless it delays the signal—as it does for the more traditional networks of CTV and the CBC—means that programming strategies of the cable-to-satellite channels break down in their attempts to match the temporal flows of their viewers. Programming designed for morning television in Toronto would appear in its satellite feed as very early morning television in Vancouver. Partly as a result of these difficulties, one can discern a slight tendency to program for the most populous part of Canada, connected to Montreal, Ottawa, and Toronto, all in the eastern time zone.

Nevertheless, what can be identified more generally is that morning television, as it is now presented through the more than 100 channels available on Canadian television, may be slipping into programs associated with other day parts and even other generations, or "eras," from previous years of television. Past television becomes the domain of channels such as Bravo, and the distinction between morning and prime time appears to dissolve. Cable channel advertising decisions now rotate commercials through the entire day of programming. Such a strategy indicates that the newer cable channels aim to gather their target audience through cumulative reach, rather than with the purchase of a particular prime-time moment at a premium rate.

Morning television, then, does continue to provide particular categories of viewing practices and has produced associated genres connected to this marginalized part of television. The emerging reality of multichannel television in Canada has made this sense of Canadian morning television and its connection to a temporal identification less distinct, but it is nevertheless a clear and continuing pattern in both programming and production practices.

P. DAVID MARSHALL

Canadian Production Companies

Most Canadian production companies are relatively recent phenomena. Prior to 1983 and the creation of Telefilm Canada, the independent production sector was either extremely weak or virtually nonexistent. Since 1983, however, the sector has blossomed, and Canada now has a number of financially sound production companies. The largest production companies are Alliance Atlantis Communications, Astral Communications, and Corus Entertainment. Other companies include Nelvana, Barna-Alper Productions, Fireworks Entertainment, Cinar Corporation, and Sullivan Entertainment.

Production before Telefilm

From 1952 to 1982, Canadian television production was dominated by the television networks themselves. This was especially true of the Canadian Broadcasting Corporation (CBC), which produced almost entirely in-house and was, until 1961, the only network in Canada. The dominance of network production has arisen from three main factors. First, unlike U.S. networks, Canadian networks are restricted neither from owning all of their affiliates nor from producing all of their content. As the owner of its affiliates, the CBC naturally seeks to fill their airtime with content that it produces in its fully owned facilities. Second, there existed in Canada no film industry similar to Hollywood, from which the nascent television networks could draw content, expertise, or ideas. Third, CBC television adopted its operational methods from CBC radio, where in-house production was the norm.

Consequently, the CBC—and, to a lesser extent, private networks (after 1961)—filled the need for content itself. The CBC thus became Canada's first major television production company, and, until the early 1980s, it dwarfed competitors and collaborators alike in terms of both the quantity and quality of its output.

The sheer volume of CBC production is difficult to characterize fairly, but we can point to certain structural features. As a public network, the CBC's production activities necessarily occur within the framework of its parliamentary mandate, which enjoins it to "reflect Canada and its regions to national and regional audiences, while serving the special needs of those regions," and to "contribute to shared national consciousness and identity." Hence, CBC production must provide for both mass and specialized audiences, while being "distinctively Canadian." Second, as the CBC is largely independent of commercial revenues, it has traditionally enjoyed the freedom to experiment and schedule material that is either challenging or of limited audience appeal. Third, the CBC's heavy reliance on in-house production has resulted in a recognizable network style across all program categories.

Nonetheless, since its inception, the CBC has produced not only news and public affairs, for which it has earned a well-deserved reputation, but also drama (*CBC Playbill, On Camera, For the Record*), variety (Anne Murray specials), comedy (*King of Kensington, Mosquito Lake*), science (*The Nature of Things*), game shows (*Front Page Challenge, Reach for the Top*), weekly serials (*Seeing Things, Traders*), talk shows (*Take 30, 90 Minutes Live*), children's shows (*The Friendly Giant, Chez Hélène, Fred Penner's Place*), miniseries (*The Whiteoaks of Jalna, Empire Inc.*), arts programming (*Adrienne Clarkson Presents*), religious programming (*Man Alive*), cooking shows, do-it-yourself shows, numerous sports shows, and so on.

Four major aspects of CBC production stand out. The first is its stability. For example, the CBC continued to produce prime-time variety shows long after other North American broadcasters abandoned the genre. Likewise, the entrenchment of existing genres has made the CBC slow to respond to new trends, such as reality television. Additionally, many CBC shows remain in continual production for more than 20 years: *The Nature of Things* debuted in 1956 and is still in production (as of 2003); *Front Page Challenge* ran for 38 years (1957–95); comedians Wayne and Shuster appeared from 1952 until well into the 1980s; *The Beachcombers* ran uninterruptedly for 18 years (1972–90). CBC production, then, runs on a longer cycle than U.S. production, largely because the CBC is responsive to social and cultural rather than commercial and economic imperatives.

The second notable aspect of CBC production is its variety. The CBC clearly attempts to produce for a much broader range of audience tastes and interests than virtually any other North American broadcaster. As a result, its production slate is perhaps the most highly varied in North America.

The third aspect concerns the nature of in-house production. Prior to 1983, this practice effectively precluded the emergence of an independent production sector. The CBC perceived no need to call upon outside resources since everything could be done in-house. Likewise, outside resources had few opportunities to break into the business since the CBC would not buy from them. As a result, the independent sector languished and CBC production, despite its abundance and variety, acquired a recognizable look. Independent producers were forced to depend on private broadcasters, which were financially weak and slow to develop. However, the 1983 requirement that the CBC purchase dramatic content from independent producers both altered the look and feel of CBC programming and greatly assisted the independent production sector.

The fourth distinctive aspect of CBC production concerns the way in which CBC programs attempt to meet the requirements of the Broadcasting Act. Systematically, they appeal to varied and various audiences, cover topics of broad appeal and specialist interest, are set in various regions of the country, cover different types of interest, are overwhelmingly prosocial, and deal with recognizably Canadian characters and situations.

In this respect, the most typical CBC genre may be the nature/adventure drama, of which outstanding examples include *The Forest Rangers* (1963–66), *Adventures in Rainbow Country* (1970), *The Beachcombers, Ritter's Cove* (1979–91), *Danger Bay* (1984–90), and others. The genre is highly durable and usually features children or adolescents surrounded by caring adults in a nature or wilderness setting. Each week, a problem arises that the young people, often accompanied by a favorite animal, attempt to solve through their own resources and the help of authoritative others, typically parents, the local Royal Canadian Mounted Police detachment, or a native person.

The genre corresponds well to the objectives of the Broadcasting Act. By decentralizing production to nonurban locations, it shows Canada to Canadians and gives all regions a sense of representation. It also appeals to parents as nonviolent programming with potentially educational benefits. Furthermore, the genre's lower costs coincide with the resources of Canadian producers. Finally, as the child audience is both very forgiving and constantly renewed, the same programs can be reissued, thereby building up a profitable backlog of shows. For all of these reasons, independent producers have also shown a proclivity for this genre or elements of it.

The CBC's French-language network, Société Radio-Canada (SRC), shares some of the same characteristics as its English-language counterpart. The SRC was until 1961 virtually the only French-language producer in Canada and, like the CBC, produced huge quantities of programs across an enormous range of categories. The SRC was bound by budgetary constraints, due to the size of its market (approximately 6 million viewers concentrated mainly in Quebec), and by the Broadcasting Act. However, it evolved quite differently than the CBC.

Television in Quebec was immediately embraced as a tool for shaping a cultural community. As a result, French-language productions enjoy a popularity and cultural status unimaginable for English-language productions. The very rapid development of an indigenous star system and advertising culture further reinforced the French productions' appeal. They address a loyal and voracious audience and are less concerned with "showing Canada to Canadians" than with representing and affirming French Canada's own culture. There is little crossover between French- and English-language productions.

The most popular and enduring genre of French-language TV is the *téléroman.* It is highly comparable to both the South American *telenovela* and the Australian "soapie" and represents a cross between American daytime soap opera, for production values, and prime-time drama, for audience interest, cultural impact, and prestige. *Téléromans* are frequently written by leading authors or playwrights and may possess a cultural status similar to an important play or novel.

Private networks (CTV, TVA) began to go to air in 1961. Their production activities, however, were much more limited than those of the CBC and tended to resemble the patterns of American TV. They typically produced news and sports but called upon outside producers to provide game shows (*It's Your Move, The Mad Dash*), the occasional sitcom (*The Trouble with Tracy, Pardon My French, Snow Job*), and some drama (*The Littlest Hobo, The Starlost*). They heavily supplemented their schedules with U.S. imports. On the French-language side, importation was more difficult, and broadcasters soon became producers. Hence, the French-language TVA network became an important production company in its own right, duplicating much of the SRC's output although with a heavier emphasis on populist representations. TVA has also come to rely on the *téléroman.*

The market represented by private networks, however, was sufficiently small that only a very few independent production companies could coexist. As a result, the private networks tended to draw heavily on a very small number of independent producers, thereby reproducing in the private sector a situation analogous to the public sector's use of in-house production.

This entire period is characterized, therefore, by the dominance of public networks, the prevalence of in-house production or its analogue, a relatively small number of private broadcasters relying on U.S. imports, and the absence of a syndication market. Beginning in the early 1980s, the situation changed.

Production after Telefilm

In 1983 the federal government established Telefilm Canada. Telefilm, in conjunction with the private sector, administers the Canadian Television Fund (CTF), which had an annual budget of some $230 million (Canadian) in 2001. Telefilm also participates in other funding initiatives. This money is available for independent producers, and Telefilm invests in all phases of production: scriptwriting and preproduction, production, postproduction, dubbing, marketing, test-marketing, and distribution.

To receive funding, a project must satisfy Telefilm that it is financially viable by obtaining an up-front licensing agreement from a broadcaster. This draws broadcasters into Telefilm's strategies. The project must also be certified as "Canadian" according to the "point system" administered by the Canadian Audio-Visual Certification Office (CAVCO). Specifically, the rights must be owned and developed by Canadians; the project must be shot and set primarily in Canada; and the project must reflect Canadian themes and subject matter. Additionally, it must obtain ten points on the following scale: two points each for the director and screenwriter; one point for the highest-paid actor; one point for the second-highest-paid actor; and one point each for the art director, music composer, picture editor, and director of photography.

The criteria were drastically tightened in 1999–2000, when a run on the CTF emptied its coffers overnight, but satisfying them entitles producers to important tax concessions. Additionally, provincial governments have instituted parallel structures to support film and television production and attract activity to their territory. To date, Vancouver, Toronto, and Montreal have emerged as the centers of a vigorous independent film and television production industry.

Telefilm is, therefore, the funding arm of a complex web of regulatory bodies: the Canadian Radio-television and Telecommunications Commission (CRTC) sets Canadian-content quotas for broadcasters; broadcasters turn to producers for content that satisfies the quotas; the producers submit their content to CAVCO for certification and tax breaks; Telefilm funds the productions and directs money to the worthiest projects.

Telefilm's success, however, coincided with four other factors: the widening of the Canadian television industry, the emergence of a U.S. syndication market for Canadian content, the development of a system of international coproductions, and the decline of the Canadian dollar.

The television market was widened in several ways. In 1983 the CBC was ordered to acquire entertainment programming from outside sources. A majority of its entertainment content now comes from independent producers. The CBC has therefore been transformed from a producer to a purchaser of programming, thereby creating opportunities for the independent production sector.

Additionally, since 1982, the CRTC has licensed more than 30 specialty and pay-TV channels, and more than 250 digital channels. These channels frequently require highly specialized content, thereby causing diversification within production companies or the emergence of parallel specialized producers. For example, music video channels obviously require musical content, and a fund, VideoFax, has been set aside for the production of Canadian music videos. Movie channels require a certain number of Canadian movies. YTV, the youth channel, has likewise spawned shows aimed at its target audience. All of these channels also provide a second life to many older shows, thereby capitalizing the earlier investments of production companies.

The CRTC also maintained its Canadian-content quotas, thereby creating a permanent domestic market for Canadian content. U.S. cable networks have also emerged as a syndication market for Canadian content. These networks have insatiable appetites for programming but are often restricted to smaller budgets than those of the major U.S. networks. As a result, they need content that is more affordable while still possessing acceptable production values. Consequently, they have turned to Canadian production companies, and it is estimated that up to 30 percent of original programming on U.S. cable networks comes from Canadian producers.

The success of cable networks using Canadian content has convinced not only the major U.S. networks but also major U.S. production companies to begin investing in Canada, where many American shows are now produced. This trend has been accelerated by the declining Canadian dollar, which was worth approximately 65 percent of the U.S. dollar in 2001, making it financially sound for many Hollywood productions to relocate to the proximity of Canada, where they find not only highly skilled, English-speaking crews intimately conversant with American television but also significantly lower costs and potential tax breaks and government subsidies. Although the attractiveness of Canada has generated within Hollywood the perceived crisis of "runaway production," total Canadian production at the turn of the 21st century actually equaled less than 2 percent of Hollywood production.

Within Canada, the same phenomena have resulted in a "crisis" of their own. Some argue that targeting a market beyond Canada (principally the United States) results in content that is merely "industrially Canadian" (i.e., Canadian-made content), thereby damaging "genuinely Canadian" content (i.e., content reflecting/exploring Canadian cultures, history, and values). It was in response to this criticism, and to the perception that CTF funds were "industrially" used, that CAVCO criteria were tightened. Others, however, argue that the distinction is parochial and restricts the range of permissible "Canadian" topics to the most stereotypical.

Thus, several conditions have combined to transform the fortunes of Canadian production companies. On the one hand, new sources of funding have been created through the establishment of Telefilm Canada and tax deductions. Furthermore, the regulatory environment has contributed to Canadian production through the maintenance of content quotas and the CAVCO certification procedure. Finally, the market has expanded through the licensing of new channels and the emergence of a U.S. syndication market. Even the declining Canadian dollar has resulted in opportunities for Canadian producers by affording them high-profile exposure that they might not otherwise obtain. Together, these factors have given Canadian production companies two things much in demand: a track record and a backlog of marketable product.

On the other hand, the Canadian television market remains too small and too fragile to support the current scale of Canadian production. Indeed, in January 1995, Atlantis Communications reported that fully 80 percent of its license fees came from outside Canada. Hence, access to the wider North American and international markets constitutes the key to continued viability for Canadian production companies. They are therefore driven to seek additional sources of funding through international partnerships, and Canada has developed a highly elaborate system of "international coproductions."

Coproductions involve partners from Canada and another country contributing to the manufacture of a single film or television program. They occur within the framework of treaties signed by the governments of both countries and covering financial participation, mutual tax concessions, national treatment, creative control, and copyright. Canada is the world's leading coproducer.

The advantages of coproductions are higher production values, access to foreign markets, and opportunities for ongoing business relations between the production partners. Their disadvantages are that they also create opportunities for conflict over financial and creative control, can be highly complex to administer, and can result in culturally unspecific content. The success of coproductions in their various markets is, of course, extraordinarily variable, but they have served the fundamental purposes of broadening the financial base of production companies and giving them international reach.

Production Companies and Their Structures

An examination of some Canadian production companies reveals strategic differences and similarities.

Astral Media of Montreal was founded in 1961 as Angreen Photo. Its corporate name has since undergone many variations. Before becoming Astral Media in 2000, it was known principally as Astral Bellevue Pathé and Astral Communications. Until 1996, Astral was known chiefly as a service provider with some media interests. It owned a motion picture laboratory in downtown Montreal and more than 100 photographic stores, and it distributed audiovisual material and provided video duplication, postproduction, and dubbing services. It also manufactured compact discs. In fiscal 1997, media activities accounted for only 37 percent of Astral's revenue. Since then, it has become a pure-play media company, with media activity accounting for 100 percent of its revenue by the beginning of the 21st century. In television alone, Astral operates five pay and pay-per-view movie networks (TMN—The Movie Network, MOVIEPIX, Viewer's Choice, SuperEcran, Canal Indigo) and six French-language specialty channels (VRAK-TV, Canal D, Canal Vie, Historia, Séries1, Z). It owns the Family Channel, which manages the English and French Teletoon channels, and possesses 50 percent of MusiquePlus and MusiMax. With additional holdings in radio, outdoor media, and e-business, Astral's strength lies not in the content it produces, but in the distribution networks it controls and in its ability to market across media. Importantly, as with many Canadian production companies, Astral's television interests cover both the English- and French-language markets.

Alliance Atlantis Communications was formed in 1998 from the merger of two leading Canadian production companies, Alliance Communications and Atlantis Communications, both of Toronto. They bring together broadcasting assets, extensive production experience, and a catalog of film and television shows. The company is divided into a broadcast group, a television group, and a motion picture group, the latter being very active in film production and distribution. As of 2001, the Alliance Atlantis broadcast group owned wholly or in part eight specialty channels: Showcase (100 percent), Life Network (100 percent), HGTV Canada (67 percent), History Television (88 percent), Séries1 (50 percent), Historia (50 percent), Headline Sports (48 percent), and Food Network Canada (51 percent). It is also the corporate sponsor for the U.S.-based Health Network, and it has expanded its existing franchises or formed partnerships for digital channels with BBC Canada, BBC Kids, National Geographic Channel, Showcase Diva, Showcase Action, IFC, and WebMD. The television group produces for Canada, the United States, and other countries, while adhering to the rule that 80 percent of all production costs must be covered by third-party commitments. In 2001 current productions included *CSI: Crime Scene Investigation, Beastmaster, Gene Roddenberry's Conflict Earth, Nuremberg, The Associates, North of 60,* and *Joan of Arc.* Like Astral, Alliance Atlantis is involved in both film and television. Unlike Astral, it not only distributes content but also produces and coproduces, for both the English- and French-language markets. Its production slate is a classic mixture of "industrial" and "genuine" Canadian, and its funding strategy makes full use of available resources. It has had success in placing its content not only in Canada but also on CBS (e.g., *CSI,* CBS's top-rated drama in 2001–02) and U.S. cable networks.

Paragon Entertainment Corporation was formed in 1985 and filed for bankruptcy in 1997. Although the company was based in Toronto, its chief executive officer and chairman, Jan Slan, was located in Los Angeles, and Paragon's strategy was not to rely on the Canadian market but to produce for the North American and international markets. It had been relatively successful, producing *Forever Knight, Lamb Chop's Play-Along, Kratts' Creatures,* and *Zoboomafoo,* among other programs. The "Canadian" element of these programs was to be found in their financial and creative control rather than in their thematic or stylistic content.

Nelvana Ltd. of Toronto was established in 1971 and has specialized in the traditional Canadian niches of animation and children's programming. Its productions include *Babar, Franklin the Turtle, Bob and Margaret, Rolie Polie Olie, Tintin,* and numerous others. *Babar, Franklin, Pippi Longstocking, Rupert,* and *Donkey Kong* have yielded profitable marketing tie-ins (toys, posters, etc.). Nelvana also owned 20 percent of the cartoon specialty channel Teletoon. In 2000 Nelvana was purchased by Corus (owned by Shaw Communications) for $554 million (Canadian).

Cinar Films of Montreal has likewise targeted children with programs such as *Wimzie's House/La maison de Ouimzie.* It has also sold *The Busy World of Richard Scarry,* based on the popular children's book known around the world, and produced *Are You Afraid of the Dark?,* a horror/fantasy show for young people, for both Nickelodeon and YTV. It was successful in licensing merchandise based on its characters, but in 2000 it became embroiled in a government investigation and lawsuits over unaccounted-for funds. It eventually reached a settlement with the government.

Independent producer Kevin Sullivan has enjoyed enormous success, first with the two *Anne of Green Gables* miniseries, then with the weekly series *Road to Avonlea,* which ran for seven seasons, and finally with his TV movie *Butterbox Babies.* All of these ranked among the highest-rated Canadian television programs.

Interestingly, many independent production companies have attempted to locate at least some of their output in an area of traditional Canadian strength, the "family drama," which both incorporates and transforms elements of the nature/adventure genre. Like nature/adventure shows, family dramas usually involve children and families, although they possess few of the precocious or saccharine characteristics of U.S. sitcoms. They also systematically eschew violence in favor of cleverness or circumstance and foreground pro-social values. However, unlike nature/adventure shows, family dramas freely mix humor with drama, often fail to end happily, and jettison the requirement for wilderness settings and animals in favor of urban, frequently highly ironic plotlines.

The most celebrated example is probably *The Kids of Degrassi Street* (Playing with Time Productions), which spawned *Degrassi Junior High, Degrassi High,* and *Degrassi: The Next Generation.* Like nature/adventure shows, the *Degrassi* series are aimed squarely at a family audience, feature young people, and involve weekly dilemmas, but *Degrassi* casts these challenges in an urban setting with frequently unforeseen results, and these series are neither clearly drama nor comedy. Other independent productions include *Ready or Not* (Insight Productions), which followed the everyday lives of two young teenage girls; *Popstars* (Lone Eagle Entertainment), portraying the trials and tribulations of real teenagers who want to become pop singers; *The Pit Pony* (Cochran Entertainment), about a boy in turn-of-the-20th-century Cape Breton; and *Drop the Beat* (Back Alley Films/Alliance Atlantis), the story of a hip campus radio show in Toronto.

While Astral has been a publicly traded company since 1974, most other Canadian production companies only went public after 1993. Significantly, at the turn of the 21st century, they have tended toward consolidation into larger production units, as when Alliance Atlantis purchased Salter Street productions;

toward alliances with broadcasters, as when Shaw (through Corus) purchased Nelvana; and toward integration into production/distribution/broadcast units, as illustrated by the structure of Alliance Atlantis. Just as they have themselves absorbed other entities, it seems likely that many of these producers will become part of other companies, particularly broadcasters seeking production units.

In sum, Canadian production companies are relatively recent phenomena that produce for both film and television. They increasingly aim to control distribution outlets, thereby tending to make them integrated production/distribution houses on the CBC model, and they frequently attempt to acquire film libraries to feed their distribution networks and to market internationally alongside their own material. Relying heavily upon international markets but taking advantage of funding opportunities in Canada, their content is frequently "Canadian" from the point of view of creative and financial control, rather than from the perspective of thematic and stylistic content.

Paul Attallah

See also ***Degrassi; Kids in the Hall; North of 60; Road to Avonlea;*** **Telefilm Canada**

Further Reading

Attallah, Paul, "Public Broadcasting in Canada," *Gazette,* 62 (2000).

Collins, Richard, *Culture, Communication, and National Identity: The Case of Canadian Television,* Toronto: University of Toronto Press, 1990

Magder, Ted, *Canada's Hollywood: The Canadian State and Feature Films,* Toronto: University of Toronto Press, 1993

McKinsey and Company, *Public Service Broadcasters Around the World,* London: McKinsey, 1999

Rainsberry, F.B., *A History of Children's Television in English Canada, 1952–1986,* Metuchen, New Jersey: Scarecrow Press, 1988

Canadian Programming in English

The term "Canadianization" is used by some Europeans as a metonym for their fear of the audience fragmentation new satellite technologies would bring to their orderly systems of state-supported public service broadcasting. But if the presence of alternative programming choices is this powerful, how did distinctive Canadian programming survive alongside the largest and most enclosed media giant in the world? Decades before cable and satellite, the majority of Canadians could flick a dial and find ABC, NBC, and CBS, plus dozens of local U.S. stations. In the 1970s and 1980s, Canadians had a cornucopia of specialty channels on cable, although the mix was controlled by the Canadian Radio-television and Telecommunications Commission (CRTC). By the mid-1970s, parts of southern Ontario rivaled New York City for television choices, and the number of choices throughout Canada has only grown in more recent years, especially when many digital channels were added in 2001. Yet here stands Canada—its electronic frontier as permeable as the world's longest unguarded border—still a separate nation-state. Canada's response to and appropriation of other sources of television may serve more as a success story for other national contexts than as a model of dire consequences.

In 1952, when the Canadian Broadcasting Company (CBC) first went to air, thousands of Canadians along the border from coast to distant coast had already set their aerials to receive signals from the many U.S. stations within range. Even in those early days, American television genres shaped the expectations of Canadian viewers about the conventions of television. At the same time, however, these types of programs were beginning to differ significantly from the radio prototypes—variety shows, soaps, quiz and game shows—that had also been familiar beyond the northern border. Viewers were also enjoying the more televisual treatment of sports, documentaries, and dramas.

On American television, these program genres were usually clearly separated. However, the first CBC head of programming, the multitalented Mavor Moore, and his producers and directors (who were drawn from the National Film Board, the theater, radio, and off the street) were interested in experimenting with the forms of television. For example, on series such as *Horizon* and anthologies like Robert Allen's *Scope/Folio/Festival,* Daryl Duke's *Q for Quest,* and Mario Prizek's *Eyeopener,* they combined dramatization with panel discussions or documentaries or interviews.

After the early years of experimentation, the genres for the most part settled back into their self-defined places, and thus the history of Canadian broadcasting can be summarized in terms of separate compartments, reflecting not only the sharpened distinctions made for the viewers but also the developing administrative empires.

In the first 15 years of CBC TV, arts and drama producers broadcast the first full-length opera and programmed evenings of jazz, poetry, and avant-garde drama (the outlawed American play *The Brig* and scripts by Harold Pinter, Edward Albee, Samuel Beckett, and Arrabal Anouilh). They adapted George Bernard Shaw and Anton Chekhov. They broadcast live the family serial *The Family Plouffe* in both French and English, wrote and broadcast musicals for television (*Anne of Green Gables* is still performed on stage), and trained writers new to television on half-hour adaptations of Stephen Leacock's *Sketches of a Sunshine Town.* They produced ballet, Gilbert and Sullivan shows, regular classical music, and folk and jazz concerts and made a quite successful *Hamlet* under severe limitations imposed by a tiny drama studio. Until 1967 almost all of the output was in black and white (color came late to Canada), and live or live-to-tape productions dominated until the late 1960s. CBC producers stirred up a major controversy (duplicated in the United Kingdom when the BBC bought the film) with Ron Kelly's direct cinema, experimental drama, *The Open Grave.* Kelly had the nerve to treat the Resurrection as a breaking news story, full of interruptions and improvisations, using familiar reporters from CBC News and the following scenario: the previous Friday, Joshua Corbett had been hanged for alleged terrorism, although in fact he has disrupted the war industries with his pacifist ideas. Now his grave is empty, and neither Mary Morrison, a ravaged, rather vague middle-aged prostitute, nor any of his other friends know where he is. The film, intended for broadcast on Easter Sunday, made the headlines for weeks.

In the United States, series from radio (soaps, westerns, cop shows, and situation comedies) were transferred to television, but, in contrast, for many years the CBC did not make series. On American television, viewers saw 1950s television anthologies such as *Playhouse 90* and *Studio One* fade to black in the 1960s, under the tide of strippable series filmed by major studios or independent producers in Hollywood. In the 1960s, the CBC introduced *RCMP* (with the title referring to the Royal Canadian Mounted Police) and *Seaway,* two moderately successful independent productions for an adult audience. These were followed in 1966 by Ron Weyman's hugely successful and innovative in-house CBC series about a coroner, *Wojeck.* However, the CBC also kept anthology drama alive for another three decades. With neither the inclination nor the resources to succumb to the "disease of the week" or "murder of the week" staples of the popular American movies of the week, the CBC preferred to put a significant portion of its revenue into drama specials and the long-running topical drama anthology *For the Record.* This program was followed in the late 1980s and 1990s by explorations of Canada's regions with *The Way We Are* and ethnic communities with *Inside Stories.* Anthology disappeared from Canadian TV in the early 1990s, only to reappear with *Straight Up* (1997), *Twitch City* (1998), *Foolish Heart* (1999), and *Foreign Objects* (2000)—each one composed of six half-hour installments, all of which introduced experiments in structure, dramatic conventions, and cinematic techniques.

Sports

Hockey Night in Canada was a staple of Saturday night radio in the 1930s and 1940s, with the well-loved voice of Foster Hewitt shouting, "He shoots... he scores!" from the gondola in Toronto's Maple Leaf Gardens. When hockey came to television, *Hockey Night in Canada* continued as a consistent ratings winner right up to the mid-1990s. What began as the "hot stove league" (commentary occurring between playing periods) became weekly tirades by the much-loved or much-hated Don Cherry. Initially, the expert camera work and the on-air commentary of the Toronto program spoiled Canadians for coverage from the expansion teams, but the gaps have closed—although Canadian viewers are bemused by the electronic pucks, cartoons, and other "explanations" of the game used in U.S.-based telecasts. By the early 21st century, specialty channels were making it possible to see every Canadian team in every game. New digital channels cover the National Hockey League (NHL) contests, as well as women's hockey and other women's sports.

Coverage of the short season of the Canadian Football League (CFL) contests, including the Grey Cup Championship Game, began in 1952, at a time when the league was immensely popular. However, the survival of the CFL, now tied to television revenues as well as an ill-advised expansion, has been in doubt since the 1990s. The national curling bonspiels were another regular sports feature on Canadian TV. First seen on the CBC in 1955, W.O. Mitchell's much-loved drama, *The Black Bonspiel of Wullie MacRimmon,* is still played in theaters around the country more than 40 years later, reflecting the Canadian affection for this purely amateur winter sport.

Baseball came late to national Canadian television, first with the Montreal Expos and then the Toronto Blue Jays. Although in two different leagues, these teams came to echo the traditional winter-hockey rivalry between the two cities—and between the two languages those cities represent.

As the Olympic coverage has expanded, other sports receive more regular coverage: from skiing and gymnastics, which are natural fits for television, to track and field, swimming, and rowing. There are also annual events, such as the rodeo competitions at the Calgary Stampede and the Queen's Plate, the oldest horse race on the continent. Women are used as color commentators in many of these sports; and they are also authoritative voices in women-only competitions, as well as sports where both sexes appear in one field of competitors, such as horse racing, dressage, and show jumping.

In recent years, with the introduction of hemi-, demi-, and semifinals that extend the NHL season into June, many Canadian viewers have complained that sports are dominating not only Saturday afternoons and nights and Sunday afternoons but also too much weeknight CBC prime time as well. Private broadcasters repeatedly urge the CRTC and the government to force the CBC out of this lucrative field. The CBC reply is direct. Government revenues have been cut in constant dollars from 1982 onward. Professional sports programming, particularly hockey, gets ratings, makes money—and thus subsidizes the coverage of amateur sports that the private networks such as CTV and Global/CanWest will not cover. The policy of displacing all other programming for ten weeks when the hockey playoffs get under way in April continues.

Figure skating specials have represented a very successful crossover between sports and entertainment. In the early 1980s, Toller Cranston was a pioneer in this type of programming, with *Strawberry Ice.* Noted skaters such as Brian Orser, Elizabeth Manley, Kurt Browning, Elvis Stojko, and others have followed with their own specials, which offer a little narrative, a lot of music and spectacle, other international medal-winning skaters and nonskating stars, and superb special effects to complement the skating.

Religion

From the mid-1930s to 1995, both the CBC and the private networks were explicitly forbidden to sell time to radio and television evangelists. However, the CBC offers weekly a church service drawn from a variety of denominations, while individual stations program local church services or sell time to a few evangelists on late-night or early-morning television. In 1995 the CRTC did license a small evangelical station in Lethbridge, Alberta, and the regulator has more recently allowed a Christian "family viewing" channel on basic cable.

In the 1950s and early 1960s, the CBC broadcast specific words-and-music or drama programming keyed to Christmas and Easter, notably the innovative dramas *The Hill* and *The Open Grave.* In today's more ecumenical and culturally diverse times, such specific observances outside of the church or synagogue have disappeared. However, *Man Alive,* a 30-year-old program on ethical and moral issues, continues (now broadcast on both the CBC and Vision) and is widely sold abroad.

A broadcasting initiative unique to Canada is Vision, a network run by a consortium of several faiths. It is financed by sales of weekend time to all kinds of groups from Christian televangelists to Ba'hai. This "Mosaic" programming, so identified, must conform to Canadian laws regarding defamation, and a few programs have been pulled from the air. Vision's weekday and prime-time programming offers a mix of documentaries, news, commentary, controversy, films, and series from other countries, as well as programs made by the marginalized, most of which offer an ethical perspective on the issues of the day as well as addressing more permanent issues raised by the human condition. These programs usually present more questions than answers. The network is provided on basic cable and also depends on viewer donations

News and Current Affairs

Canadians take their news, news analysis, current affairs, and documentary programs very seriously. They demand the best, and they often get it. Since 1980, significant numbers have been willing to watch an hour of CBC news analysis and documentaries from 10:00 to 11:00 P.M., then switch to CTV at 11:00 P.M. for another half hour. CTV depends more on U.S. and British feed than the CBC and too often neglects the regions outside of central Canada, but on national stories the private network often does as well or better than the public one, finding fresh information or a different angle. Both newscasts attract significant numbers. However, when a national crisis such as the 1995 referendum looms, the CBC and CBC Newsworld (a separate, all-news and features network) combine forces to bring Canadians detailed and comprehensive coverage and analysis. In those circumstances, as the ratings indicate, the CBC is the first choice of Canadian viewers. In 2001 both the CBC and CTV offered 48 hours of commercial-free, round-the-clock coverage of the September 11 terrorist attacks on the United States, with the CBC simulcast with Newsworld persisting longer and having more in-depth analysis and wider coverage of reactions around the world. The efforts of Global, whose national news coverage was only a few weeks old at the time, were more sparse.

If someone from another country asks, "Who are the Canadian TV 'stars'?," the candidates are likely to appear among the ranks of reporters and anchors, rather than from the leads of a sitcom or cop show. The foreigner is also likely to be told how Knowlton Nash resigned as anchor of *The National* so that Peter Mansbridge would stay in Canada to replace him, rather than taking up a far more lucrative offer in the United States. However, no Canadian anchor or reporter has ever influenced his or her country's opinion on a national issue as profoundly as CBS anchor Walter Cronkite is said to have affected American views of the Vietnam War. Canadians accord no individual in broadcasting that kind of influence or impact, not even the late and much-lamented anchor of *The Journal,* Barbara Frum.

Throughout its history, Canadian television has emphasized news and current affairs; this is particularly true of the CBC, which is charged with that task as part of its public mandate. The nightly newscasts began in the early 1950s—with film clips rapidly gaining prominence. Anchors, many of whom were also reporters, have included Earl Cameron, Larry Henderson, Stanley Burke, Knowlton Nash, Peter Mansbridge, Lloyd Robertson (at both CBC and then CTV), Sandie Renaldo, Hana Gartner, Alison Smith, Pamela Wallin, Sheldon Turcotte, and Nancy Wilson.

From the 1970s on, the CBC has used men and women in all the hot spots and on most beats, with CTV adapting this practice at a later date. Well-known reporters include Peter Kent reporting from Cambodia; Anne Medina, an American who became an incisive Canadian voice from Lebanon; Brian Stewart from Ethiopia and Rwanda; Joe Schlosinger from all over the world; Bill Cameron; Anna-Maria Tremonti from Russia and Bosnia; senior Ottawa correspondents Jason Moscowitch and David Halton; Terry Malewski; Mary-Lou Finlay; Ian Hanomansingh; Eve Savory on social policy; and Der Ho Yen on economic policy.

Well-known CBC current-affairs and features series have included *Close-Up, Telescope Quarterly Report,* and the much-admired and feared 1960s "gotcha" journalism of *This Hour Has Seven Days,* whose cancellation in 1966 led to debate in Cabinet, a crisis in confidence between CBC management and producers, and a chilling effect on current affairs. After a hiatus in the late 1960s, the news and current-affairs department came back strongly in 1975 with *The Fifth Estate.* CTV answered with *W5.* Among the widely acclaimed 1960s documentaries were Beryl Fox's *cinéma vérité* treatment of Vietnam, *The Mills of the Gods,* and Larry Gosnell's *Air of Death,* on air pollution. For more than 30 years, the CBC has also offered a variety of analytic as well as descriptive programming about science and the natural world on the weekly series *The Nature of Things.*

In the 21st century, convergence has become an increasingly important factor in television news and information programming, with each network having ties with print media and large conglomerates. All networks now offer websites to publicize their news as well as much of their information programming.

Morning, Noon, and Night Shows

Until quite recently, CTV has had the only national "morning show" in *Canada A.M.*—where lighter fare, news, and national weather were the backdrop for incisive questioning of national and international figures. Norm Perry, Pamela Wallin, Valerie Pringle, and Keith Morrison gave a jump-start to sluggish viewers heading out for work or into the day's work at home. In the 1980s, CityTV (Toronto) and some other local stations offered a lighter version of "breakfast television." CBC Newsworld offers full news and analysis to the country, updated hourly.

The CBC, again unlike the American networks, did not leave the afternoons completely to the soap opera and the rerun. From the early 1960s, *Take 30* used the considerable journalistic talents of hosts like Adrienne Clarkson and Paul Soles to provide women at home with a daily half hour of news, current affairs, personalities, reviews, interviews, and regular features, including by far the most thorough coverage at the time of the Royal Commission on the Status of Women. The program was replaced in 1994 by *Midday,* an hour at noon for the same audience, updated to include regular gardening features, analysis of popular culture, and minidocumentaries. However, *Midday* was chopped in the 2000 round of budget cuts and replaced with drama reruns.

Tabloid was an early (1953–63) national supper-hour show featuring personalities from politics and entertainment. With a chalk-tossing weatherman, Percy Saltzman, the show was hosted by the genial Dick MacDougal and hostess Elaine Grand, and later Joyce Davidson. For the most part, however, supper-hour shows of news, weather, sports, and features have been the territory of local stations. Under severe financial constraints and in some haste, the CBC closed some local stations in the late 1980s and ordered the stations that survived to cover a wider market with their supper-hour shows—a decision that devastated morale and resulted in much lower ratings in some areas. In 2000, retrenchment at the CBC cut those news hours to half hours and added a half hour of national news originating from Vancouver. Many local stations have been bought by CHUM, and their local programming has been modified to look like City's informal presentations for a younger, more urban demographic.

Basically, all stations in Canada, whether independently or publicly owned or part of a network, provide supper-hour shows as well as news, weather, and sports at 11:00 P.M. The quality varies enormously, but Toronto stations (with a potential market of 3 million) will cover transit policy, policing in the suburbs, and "what's on" in the nightclubs, while CKNX Wingham, Ontario (population 10,000 with a market of 50,000), will cover the day's prices for cattle, the problems of the Saugeen Valley water authority, and the "snowfest" in Durham.

Children's and Youth Programming

Programming for children is specifically mentioned in the existing CBC mandate. The CBC has offered very creative, commercial-free, nonviolent programming on weekday mornings since its inception. Ed McCurdy, Raffi, Sharon Lois and Bram, and Fred Penner brought all kinds of music to kids. Puppets such as Uncle Chichimus and his friend Hollyhock, on the programs *Let's See* (1952–53) and *Uncle Chichimus Tells a Story,* were followed by somewhat more sophisticated, much-loved and very long-lived series such as *Mister Dress-Up* with his puppet friend Casey and *The Friendly Giant* with Rusty and his silent pal, the giraffe Jerome. *Romper Room* on CTV and *Polka Dot Door* on TVO (the Ontario educational network) were other popular programs for young children. Special segments in both French and English were made in Canada as inserts for *Sesame Street.* Since its inception in 1970, TVO has devised all kinds of award-winning children's series.

For older children viewing in prime time, there were 1960s adventure series on the CBC such as *Adventures in Rainbow Country* and *The Forest Rangers.* Both series were set in Canada's wilderness and structured around the usual gaggle of boys—and a girl or two—who get in and out of trouble, very little of it violent, with the help of parents or adult friends. Both programs are still shown in reruns.

The 1970s and 1980s belonged to *The Edison Twins,* who used science to solve domestic puzzles; CTV's well-written family series *The Campbells,* set just before the Rebellion of 1837; and the three CBC *Degrassi* series (*The Kids of Degrassi Street, Degrassi Junior High,* and *Degrassi High*), which followed basically the same group of young characters as they grew up. Using workshops and improvisational exercises, the series developed characters and plots reflecting the actors' own lives until the "kids" graduated from high school. In 2001 CTV launched the series *Degrassi: The Next Generation,* which includes characters from the original series, now as parents and teachers to a new group of young adolescents. The success of the original *Degrassi* series led to the more gritty *Northwood* and Global's *Madison,* as well as the excellent "tween" show *Ready or Not,* which was widely sold in international markets.

A much more complex concept for the 1990s was the CBC's *The Odyssey,* which took its viewer from the regular "Upworld" of school and work, where the protagonist, Jay, lay in a coma, into the "Downworld," an adventure-filled realm inhabited entirely by children. In the mid-1990s, the CBC addressed youth audiences with *The Rez,* set on a First Nations reservation; *Liberty Street,* about young people in their first jobs; *Straight Up,* an urban, somewhat experimental anthology; and *Drop the Beat,* the story of a hip-hop DJ and his world. *Emily of New Moon* and *Pit Pony* are period series for families.

Variety

In the 1950s and 1960s, variety shows combined singers, dancers, puppet shows, acrobats, animal acts, and comedy sketches—including recurring favorites on *The Ed Sullivan Show,* the Canadian team Wayne and Shuster. In Canada there were such copies of U.S. programs as *Cross-Canada Hit Parade* and *Show-Time;* and country-and-western shows like *Holiday Ranch* and, for 25 years, *The Tommy Hunter Show.* Light music shows starred homegrown favorites like everyone's "pet Juliette," who, on her program *Juliette,* sang pop tunes and ballads and always said good night to her mom. CTV responded to Canadian-content regulations requiring cultural diversity with an imitation English pub, *The Pig and Whistle,* and the homegrown *Ian Tyson Show.*

A special case was the much-loved down-East fiddle music of *Don Messer's Jubilee.* With Marg Osborne and Charlie Chamberlain, Messer and his Islanders flourished for years on radio and then on television—until the late 1960s music "revolution" persuaded the executives in Toronto to cancel the *Jubilee* for *Hullabaloo,* a limp imitation of similar American shows. Reedited for the 1990s, *Don Messer's Jubilee* was a surprise hit. By 2000, however, the networks did not feature regular music programs, instead airing occasional musical specials with stars such as Shania Twain.

Talk Shows and Game Shows

The nearly 40-year run of *Front Page Challenge* reflected the Canadian preference for hybrid form and an emphasis on current affairs. Part quiz, part current-affairs show, its guests included domestic and foreign prime ministers, sports and entertainment celebrities, and ordinary citizens who had made the headlines. Most other Canadian quiz shows have been "Canadian-content fillers" (produced to meet requirements for Canadian content) and merely less expensive imitations of American game shows. On CTV, *Shirley, Dini Petty,* and, in a more serious vein, *Jane Hawtin Live* were successful daytime talk shows. *Pamela Wallin Live* on Newsworld was a 1990s prime-time success story, with a very wide range of guests and subjects and a few callers. Other cross-country call-in shows on Newsworld have been oriented toward public affairs. Newsworld's nightly program *counterSpin* includes contrarian views from people who do not ordinarily appear on television. Mike Bullard's *Open Mike* (CTV and Comedy Network) is the first successful Canadian late-night talk and music show.

Comedy

For more than 50 years, Canadians have excelled in developing small companies that perform satirical, usually topical revue comedy on radio and television. The grandfather of them all was the Wayne and Shuster duo. The grandmother was the annual theatrical revue *Spring Thaw.* The proud children were *SCTV,* in the 1970s, and *The Royal Canadian Air Farce,* still going strong on television. The grandchildren are *CODCO* (and its stepchild *This Hour Has 22 Minutes*) and *Kids in the Hall.* With their gentle, literate, yet often slapstick parodies of both high and popular culture, edited reruns of *The Wayne and Shuster Hour* were popular in many countries. *SCTV* (also in reruns) was so self-reflexive that it became a cult favorite with a younger, media-literate generation, as did *Kids,* whose executive producer, Canadian Lorne Michaels, is closely connected to *Saturday Night Live.* In contrast to *Kids in the Hall, CODCO*'s much harder-hitting satire and complex, sustained characterizations were informed by the eloquence of Newfoundland speech and a more distinctly Canadian sense of values. Some of *CODCO*'s original members moved on to turn their biting wit on the week's news in *This Hour Has 22 Minutes.* Many Canadian and U.S. comic series are now rerun on the specialty Comedy Channel, which also cablecasts a few new programs, such as *Liography.* The CBC's *The Newsroom and More Tears* (Ken Finkleman's short satirical series on local and national news) and Rick Mercer's *Made in Canada* (satirizing the whole television industry) are sharply, often outrageously funny. Very different is the champion of duct tape from *Possum Lodge Green Red.*

Drama

In the absence of any strong professional theater, the general policy for the first 20 years of the CBC TV drama department was that it should entertain, inform, and reflect national and regional concerns (which it did intermittently and with significant gaps). CBC drama was expected to experiment with television as a medium, show Canadians what classical and contemporary world theater looked like, and explore the relationship of the documentary and the fictional. From the 1960s, the drama department was also expected to inflect some forms of American popular culture (cop shows, mysteries, sitcoms) and ignore others, like soaps, and continue with anthology drama. Finally, in very occasional miniseries or films, the "single" play—whether a light comedy, a theater adaptation, a docudrama, or an intensely personal vision—would find a home.

Biography

Throughout its history, the CBC has explored various dramatic forms to produce biographies. A mixture of voice-over commentary, selections from the subjects' works of fiction or paintings, sustained satire, and even musical numbers have been used to produce a nonstandard series of biographies: the mix of drama, documentary, and commentators in *The Baron of Brewery Bay,* with John Drainie playing Stephen Leacock; the lives of artists Tom Thompson and Emily Carr; Kate Reid as suffragist Nellie McLung; three versions of the life of feminist Emily Murphy; and the stories of prime ministers John A. Macdonald (several times) and William Lyon MacKenzie King (once as a satire, *Rexy,* once as a miniseries by Donald Brittain). Biographies of other, less well-known subjects included Brittain's *Canada's Sweetheart: The Saga of Hal Banks* (the imported thug who ran the waterfronts of Canada) and profiles of colorful newspaper editors and columnists like Bob Barker and "Ma" Murray. The CBC also presented the trials of the assassin of D'Arcy McGee twice and told the story of rebel/martyr Louis Riel two times, first as a two-part drama, then as a lavish, revisionist miniseries, shot in both French and English in 1979. Another telling of the latter story came in the 1990s, when Bob Rock, a Metis filmmaker, explored Riel and the Metis heritage in *The Missing Bell of Batoche,* for repeated viewing on Sasketchewan's educational network.

The lives of explorers, politicians, financiers, and engineers were treated in the hugely successful six-part adaptation of Pierre Berton's trilogy *The National Dream.* The miniseries combined contemporary narrative, shot by Berton on locations across Canada, with dramatizations of the men who made it happen. In the 1980s *Some Honourable Gentlemen* also depicted a wide variety of historical figures—not all of them heroes. In 1998, the CBC ran a miniseries on *Big Bear.*

In 2000–01 the CBC presented a massive, very costly, and very popular series, *Canada: A People's History.* Supported by videos of each episode, an excellent website, and two books, and structured for later use in the schools, this was an epic, episodic look at Canada largely from the point of view of ordinary settlers, soldiers, people of the First Nations, and fur-trading explorers. Shot in English and French and shown on the CBC and the Société Radio-Canada (SRC; the French-language network of the CBC), the series garnered huge ratings—to everyone's surprise and the CBC's relief, as it had committed much of its slender resources to the project.

Notable experiments on the private networks include *The Life and Times of Edwin Alonzo Lloyd* (with veteran actor Gordon Pinsent) and Pierre Berton's inexpensive and fascinating half-hour vignettes on *Heritage Theatre.* In the 1990s and early 2000s, CTV and Global presented dramas on Sheldon Kennedy (the story of the physical abuse of a hockey player); murderer Evelyn Dick; James Mink (a successful African Canadian in the 19th century); falsely imprisoned Davis Milgaard; and a squad of peacekeepers in Bosnia.

Docudrama

The perception that current events are raw material for the often-debased U.S. "docudrama" permeates U.S. society. Since the 1990s, in the North American context, it may be one of the most distinctive things about Canadian culture that front-page events are not yet seen as fodder for the movie-of-the-week mill, nor are Canadians, as they live their lives, perceived as featured players for next week's video releases.

In fact, Canadians still care very much about the differences between evidence, argument, reenactment, and the "make it up or leave it out, whichever makes a more entertaining television movie" approach. Canadian audiences can still distinguish between docudrama (real people are characters), topical drama (foregrounding a contemporary issue), and historical drama (a mixture of real and fictional characters set in a time when most viewers will not have firsthand knowledge of the "history" portrayed). The example of the very controversial coproduction with the National Film Board (NFB), *The Valour and the Horror,* illustrates the difference between Canadians and Americans. It is unimaginable that Americans in the United States would argue strenuously, as Canadians did, for months on end about the verisimilitude of both the documentary and dramatized segments of three programs about World War II.

Jeanine Locke, a writer-producer of period and topical dramas, made many distinctive specials. Her programs include *Chautauqua Girl* (which looks at both 1930s prairie populism and the Chautauqua circuit), *You've Come a Long Way Katie* (about alcoholism—Katie dies), and *The Greening of Ian Elliot* (which combines the debate about the ordination of homosexual ministers in the Unified Church and the fight against the Aleimeda-Rafferty Dam).

From 1976 to 1985, the CBC presented an anthology of what R.L. Thomas, the first executive producer, called "journalistic dramas." Searching, topical, often controversial, innovative in subject matter and not usually too didactic, *For the Record* attracted the best talent in Canada, in front of and behind the cameras. Some of the most notable productions were *A Far Cry from Home, Ready for Slaughter, Blind Faith, Every Person Is Guilty, I Love a Man in Uniform, Maria, One of Our Own,* and *The Winnings of Frankie Walls.* Subjects included unemployment, the economic troubles of family farms, euthanasia, aboriginal injustice, televangelism, wife abuse, and a francophone/anglophone marriage at the time of the 1980 referendum.

When the CBC made *The Scales of Justice,* a 1990s series of drama specials about notable (sometimes sensational, sometimes only half-remembered) legal cases, they hired a well-known criminal lawyer to advise on the scripts and serve as an on-camera/voice-over guide through the intricacies of the law. The parts of the script based on testimony and those based on speculation, as well as the contradictions, were explicitly pointed out. *The Scales of Justice* appeared two or three times a year, presenting Canadian judicial and social history without losing track of the ethical questions involved in docudrama.

Miniseries of the late 1980s and 1990s also presented distinctive voices, sometimes dissonant to the English-Canadian culture under scrutiny: producer Bernard Zukerman's *Love and Hate* (1982) explored the personalities involved and also the cultural context of the terrorizing and murder of the wife of a well-known Saskatchewan political family. His *Conspiracy of Silence: The Story of Helen Betty Osborne* (1991) is a searching account of the racism in a northern community. He has also made *Dieppe* (1993), the story of an ill-fated raid by Canadian forces in World War II; *Million Dollar Babies* (1994), about the Dionne quintuplets; and *The Sleep Room* (1998), about unethical experiments in the 1950s on mentally ill patients.

The 1992 TV movie *Liar, Liar* looked at the possibility that a child may lie about child abuse, whereas

Life with Billy (1994) also examined wife and child abuse. *Butter Box Babies* recreated a period tale of neglect in an orphanage. Many of these docudramas have been ratings hits on American prime time.

John Smith's *The Boys of St. Vincent,* a 1993 CBC/NFB collaboration, is the best example of the survival of a distinctive English-Canadian television voice. It is also worth noting that, like *The Valour and the Horror, The Boys of St. Vincent* eluded efforts at censorship through a court injunction in Ontario and parts of Quebec because the NFB (partnered with an independent company with a broadcast window and input from the CBC) had the conviction and the resources to put these programs on cassette for sale or loan. The miniseries had a Canada-wide airing a few months later.

No such "state" institutions exist in the United States. More important is the fact that the commercial constraints on the independent television filmmakers and the American networks would have likely ensured that such programs were not made. When shown on the U.S. cable channel A&E in 1994, some of the scenes from *The Boys of St. Vincent,* scenes that made the viewer a potentially complicit spectator—a point vital to the moral challenge of the work—were simply cut. Unfortunately, this masterwork was not shown on the CBC without commercials on the "publicly owned broadcasting system." The effect was very damaging to the integrity of the work.

Soap Opera

Some of the most popular U.S. genres have never taken hold on Canadian television. Unlike every other developed country and despite successful efforts in 1940s and 1950s radio, until the 1990s, there were no soap operas, no *téléromans* (a francophone long-serial form at which SRC excels), on English-Canadian television. There was only one brief, though seminal fling, in the 1960s, at short serials on film. There is a straightforward reason for the absence of this genre. In the early days the CBC had no interest. When CTV arrived in the early 1960s, soaps were "too expensive" because they involved a sustained commitment to TV drama. In the 1970s, CBC TV tried the longer-serial form, based on Mazo de la Roche's widely popular Whiteoaks novels. *Jalna* was shot using experimental techniques, multiple storylines and timelines—and it failed. In the same decade, the CBC also tried a twice-weekly nighttime soap called *House of Pride.* Reflecting the CBC mandate to show Canadians the five "regions" (a largely fictional, but still potent set of geopolitical myths dividing Canada into "the Atlantic provinces," Quebec, Ontario, "the West," and British Columbia), *House of Pride* was set and taped in five cities across the country. Ahead of its time (*Dallas* was five years away), logistics and problems with the storylines killed the serial.

More than ten years after *House of Pride,* two half-hour daytime soaps appeared on the private networks, Global's *A Foreign Affair* and CTV's *Family Passions,* both coproduced with several other countries. CTV also aired two seasons of steamier adult sex and social issues in *The City.* Then the CBC tried to emulate the U.K. soap *Coronation Street* in *Riverdale,* initially a twice-weekly, early-prime-time serial. *Riverdale* was addictive to some and offered some good cultural observations, but it lasted only two seasons. In 2001 the specialty channel Showcase began offering *Paradise Falls.*

Series

Most Canadian series are produced by the CBC and are inflections or sometimes hybrids of U.S. genres. Yet, in contrast to the U.S. programs of the same type, Canadian series show a different legal or medical system, different urban landscapes (no mean streets), very different ethnic mixes and attitudes, and are less violent. Canadian series are also often less confrontational, although not always, as illustrated by *Street Legal* and its mid-1980s rival, CTV's only high-quality series, *E.N.G.* In the 1990s, Global had its first adult hit with *Traders,* a high-energy, complex serial about stockbrokers, which aired in the evenings. In most of these series, we see actors who are comfortable working in ensemble, usually performing in less-extroverted ways than their U.S. cousins. The writers, producers, and executives of Canadian series have always been more comfortable than their U.S. counterparts with ambiguity in characterization, literate dialogue, sometimes-open endings, and often complex subtext.

The fact is, if Canadians created many U.S.-genre clones, such as CTV's action-adventure series *Counterstrike,* they could not compete with the production values or the stars and would not be worth watching when the originals are a channel-changer's zap away. However, it is also true that Canadians were delighted that the huge neighbor to the south broadcast in prime time—and then renewed midseason 1995–96—CTV's *Due South,* the "odd couple" comedy/cop show that featured a Mountie from the far north displaced to the streets of Chicago, and Ray, his cynical sidekick. (When coproduction partners withdrew, thus ending the program in the United States, CTV continued *Due South* for two more seasons in Canada.)

It is true that, when time and money are spent on it,

Canadian popular drama has always been competitive with "theirs." Note the success of *Wojeck, The Manipulators,* the much-loved period series *A Gift to Last, The Great Detective,* and sitcoms like *King of Kensington, Hangin' In, Max Glick,* and the wonderful hybrid mystery show *Seeing Things.* For that series, coproducers David Barlow and Louis DelGrande inflected the cop show to produce a unique protagonist, Louie Ciccone—a shortsighted newspaper reporter with glasses, who has visions of murders he would much rather ignore; does not drive or know which end of a gun is which; is rescued by a flying puck, a cake, and often by his wife, Marge. The series had a strong moral center and a lot of culturally specific topical satire, and it also worked as a good whodunit.

Canada's Exports

People

Canadians take rueful pride in the export of talent that has happened throughout their broadcast history: host Bernard Braden and many producers, including Sydney Newman, to the United Kingdom; actors Raymond Massey, Leslie Nielson, Lorne Green, William Shatner, John Colicos, Martin Short, and John Candy, producer Lorne Michaels, writers Bernard Slade, Arthur Hailey, Anna Sandor, and Bill Gough, and literally dozens of others to the United States. In the 1980s, the independently made satire *The Canadian Connection* used several expatriates to explore the theory that Canadians were involved in a conspiracy to take over Hollywood—and thus all of American culture. It has been rerun several times.

Programs

Why did Canada not simply export some of its entertainment programming to the United States instead of its talent? The answers are many. First, there was no star system in English-Canadian TV until the mid-1970s, and then only fitfully—no actor was "bankable." Since its beginning, Canadian television could not retain some of its major talent because it paid much less than competitors in other countries. When talented individuals stay—and many do—it is because of the life in Canada and the opportunities to do a very different kind of work.

Still, Canadian television has been shaped from the beginning by a steady exodus of its programming. The 19 seasons of *The Beachcombers* were among the CBC's most profitable exports. The U.S. network NBC bought the concept, writer, star, and much of the technical team of *Wojeck,* which, after being run through the network blender, aired as the barely recognizable *Quincy.* Nearly 20 years later, to garner a summer prime-time run in the United States, the fairly gritty, and not overtly Canadian, CTV cop show *Sidestreet* (which had been scheduled by CBS at midnight, although run in Canada at 10:00 P.M.) featured American stars as guests on the series, while the scripts were made more straightforward with less allusion and ambiguity. In the case of *Danger Bay,* a popular 1980s family/adventure series set in part at the Vancouver aquarium, the CBC and its independent partner had to struggle with coproducers from Disney to allow a scene and a storyline featuring the live birth of a whale. One of the CBC's most successful exports, *Road to Avonlea,* featured at least one American or British guest star in most episodes because Disney was coproducer.

Francophone and First Nations Populations and Canadian Television

The French presence in Quebec, the million Francophones outside Quebec, and the aboriginal nations scattered throughout Canada and dominant in the north have all been visible intermittently in English Canada's television drama. *La famille Plouffe* (1953–59 on CBC, 1952–59 on SRC) was broadcast live, sequentially, in both languages. There have also been a few efforts to reflect each culture to the other in the arts. *Festival* presented in English the works of a handful of Quebec playwrights, including Michel Tremblay's *Les Belles Soeurs.* In 1979 *For the Record* produced a contemporary drama on the topic of Quebec separatism, *Don't Forget: Je me souviens.* However, despite a near miss in the 1995 referendum on the issue, there has been no other drama on this subject on the CBC in the last couple of decades. This silence is notable, for television fiction can be a site where the conflicting discourses of society are made concrete, sometimes mediated, and sometimes exposed as unresolved.

As the CBC itself admitted in its 1978 submission to the CRTC, "the perception of the need to reflect the two linguistic communities to one another emerged in the CBC at about the same time as it emerged in the country—gradually over the last half of the 1960s and then early 1970s and then abruptly in the mid-1970s." In the 1980s and 1990s, the CBC presented Canada's fractious politics at length on *The Nation, The Journal, The Fifth Estate,* and in special "Town Halls."

Whereas the CBC represents English-French conflicts for its English-language audience, the SRC creates its own mythology: for example, by decontextualizing and repeating months later, over and over, the "rednecks stomp on the Quebec flag" episode during the Meech

Lake Accord fiasco of 1987. The SRC also regularly ignores the arts in the rest of Canada (as well as most Anglophone popular culture) with a nationalist fervor that creates a deafening silence.

There were a few "cross-cultural" dramas during and after the first Quebec referendum in 1980. Miniseries such as the French *Duplessis, Laurier,* and *Shehaweh,* as well as the very successful English *Empire Inc.* and the less successful *Chasing Rainbows* (all set in Montreal, all lavish period pieces), were dubbed into the other language. However, the story of hockey player Pierre Lambert, *Lance et Compte* (in English, *He Shoots! He Scores!*) (1986–88), which was shot in both languages, turned into a litmus test of both cultures. *Lance et Compte* started on the SRC with 1 million viewers and soon nearly tripled to 2.7 million, out of a total viewing population of 6 million. However, the same scripts in English, using the same actors, directors, producer, and crew drew only 750,000 viewers at its peak in a hockey-obsessed culture.

It is safe to say that at no time in its history did CBC English Television depend on a soupçon of French for a distinctive flavor to its stew. Although efforts in news and current affairs continue, if Quebec leaves Canada the opportunities for shared music, drama, news reporting, sportscasts, and documentaries on a daily basis that have been wasted over the previous five decades may be one of the clearest discernible reasons for the divorce. However, in recent years continual budget cuts have forced the CBC and the SRC to cooperate more closely.

A more consistently distinctive motif in Canadian television has been the representation of First Nations peoples. The subject was first fully explored by Philip Keately (producer/director) and Paul St. Pierre (writer), who created a 1960s anthology with recurring characters, *Cariboo Country,* a contemporary western that was as far away as it could get from the U.S. TV westerns so popular at the time. Representations of indigenous Canadians appeared sporadically in other places throughout the 1970s and 1980s: Claude Jutra's *Dreamspeaker, Where the Heart Is, A Thousand Moons, Loyalties,* many episodes of *Beachcombers,* a few episodes of *Danger Bay,* all of the short series for children *Spirit Bay,* and, most notably and controversially, *Where the Spirit Lives* (1989), a historical drama about residential schools, which was sold to PBS and around the world and rebroadcast in Canada four times.

Beginning in 1992, the CBC presented six full seasons of *North of 60,* set on a reservation in the North West Territories. *North of 60* does not use aboriginal people as an exotic backdrop. By the end of the second season, the two leads were aboriginal. A Cree partner for Michelle, the leading character who is a recovering alcoholic, single mother, and RCMP corporal, was added in the last two seasons. Outsiders—such as hunters, an archeologist, an RCMP inspector, a bank manager, European fur designers, and oil and diamond explorers—are made to feel different. Even the continuing characters who are not aboriginals—the nurse, band manager, and storekeeper—are never fully part of the community, although deep friendships are formed. The series presented complex and sustained examinations of alcoholism; the effect of residential schools and forced acculturation on individuals and families; internal feuds and band politics; interference from government, anthropologists, and ill-informed animal-rights activists; the ongoing friendships and resentments among the white band manager, the storekeeper, the nurse, various chiefs, the treatment center staff, and visiting artists; housing shortages; and the conflict between traditional consensual ways and modern life and politics. Since the series ended, there have been three made-for-TV movies based on *North of 60: In the Blue Ground, Trial by Fire,* and *Dream Storm.*

Also in the 1990s, the CBC represented First Nations peoples in the half-hour drama/comedy series *The Rez.* Notable drama specials portraying First Nations peoples have included, from the 1980s, *Isaac Littlefeathers, Hunting Mary Marsh,* and *Conspiracy of Silence: The Helen Betty Osborne Story;* and, from the 1990s, *Spirit Rider* and *Medicine River,* the latter based on a novel by aboriginal writer Thomas King. However, stereotypes can still be found in reruns of the late-1980s *Bordertown,* the CTV western about a Mountie, a U.S. marshal, and a woman doctor from France (the series was a coproduction with France), or Global's steamy *Destiny Ridge,* and in the CBC's *Trial at Fortitude Bay* (1994).

Nevertheless, since the Oka crisis of 1990 (named for the Quebec village of Oka, a three-month-long standoff sparked by land rights and other issues, pitting Mohawks against Quebec police and federal troops) and in the midst of an ongoing debate about cultural appropriation, Canadians have changed what they watch on television and how they watch it. Meanwhile, the long-running and evolving aboriginal motif has now been claimed by those whose lives it reflects, although—with the exception of four half hours in a mini-anthology called *Four Directions*—in drama the dominant culture still prevails when presenting this complete subject. Since 1999, all Canadian cable systems have carried the Aboriginal People's Television Network (APTN). It offers a variety of aboriginal perspectives on all kinds of topics, in native languages, French, and English.

The future of the CBC remains uncertain. However, despite its proximity to the biggest media giants in the world, its "mixed" structure, and its inevitable ups and downs, Canadian television (and the CBC in particular) has retained a distinctive voice, supporting, amplifying, and sometimes defining a distinctive national culture.

MARY JANE MILLER

See also ***Beachcombers; Boys of St. Vincent; Cariboo Country; CODCO; Degrassi; E.N.G.; Family Plouffe, La; Fifth Estate; For the Record; Front Page Challenge; Hockey Night in Canada; Kids in the Hall; Man Alive; Market Place; National; Nature of Things; North of 60; Quentin Durgens, M.P.; Road to Avonlea; Second City TV; Street Legal; This Hour Has Seven Days; Tommy Hunter Show; Valor and the Horror; Wayne and Shuster; Wojeck***

Further Reading

Collins, Richard, *Culture, Communication, and National Identity: The Case of Canadian Television,* Toronto: University of Toronto Press, 1990

Miller, Mary Jane, *Turn Up the Contrast: CBC Television Drama Since 1952,* Vancouver: University of British Columbia Press, 1987

Miller, Mary Jane, *Rewind and Search: Makers and Decision-makers of CBC Television Drama,* Montreal: McGill-Queens University Press, 1996

Nash, Knowlton, *The Microphone Wars: A History of Triumph and Betrayal at the CBC,* Toronto: McClelland and Stewart, 1994

Peers, Frank W., *The Public Eye: Television and the Politics of Canadian Broadcasting, 1952–68,* Toronto: University of Toronto Press, 1979

Raboy, Marc, *Missed Opportunities: The Story of Canada's Broadcasting Policy,* Montreal: McGill-Queens University Press, 1990

Rutherford, Paul, *When Television Was Young: Primetime Canada 1952–1967,* Toronto: University of Toronto Press, 1990

Canadian Programming in French

Television was embraced by French-language viewers more quickly than any other group in Canada. They bought TV sets more rapidly and watched more television than did their English-speaking counterparts. A majority of television households were concentrated among the working-class families of Montreal. From the beginning, La Societé Radio-Canada, Canada's public francophone broadcaster, was the center of French programming in Canada.

As the only francophone television broadcaster, it enjoyed a monopoly position. Because it faced no competition either inside or outside Canada, and because it had to produce more than 75 percent of its own programming, Radio-Canada was able to craft programs intended to enlighten and educate as well as entertain its captive audience. The power of television was very quickly understood by Quebec's creative community and, unlike comparable groups in anglophone Canada, television production in Quebec drew upon some of the most creative and inventive minds in French-Canadian society. Historians and commentators generally describe francophone television's early years from 1952 to 1960 as a "golden age." Leading academics, artists, and intellectuals were quick to embrace the new medium, making television a powerful force in Quebec's Quiet Revolution.

In the realm of news and information, Radio-Canada was determined to keep its public well informed—not only about the country but about the entire world. Journalists such as Gerard Pelletier and André Laurendeau argued that television could be an instrument of modernity that would not only introduce the rest of the world to Quebec but serve to improve knowledge and raise the sense of national pride. Pelletier hosted *Les idées en marche* (1955–61), a public affairs show that featured debates and interviews with prominent intellectuals on domestic and international issues. Laurendeau presided over *Pays et merveilles* (1953–61), a world-travel series that featured film footage and guests who would discuss such issues as the Middle East. Other popular news and information shows included *Carrefour* (1958–59) and *Premier Plan* (1959–60), which were interview-based. But the most critically acclaimed news and information program was *Point de Mire* (1957–59), hosted by René Lévesque, the future premier of Quebec. This show attempted to popularize international issues such as the Algerian crisis and used maps, charts, film footage, and even a blackboard to educate and inform viewers. Only occasionally did the show address Quebecois or Canadian themes.

Other shows, such as *Panoramique* (1958–59), a series of historical documentaries from the French division of the National Film Board of Canada, drew viewers' attention to Canadian and Quebec historical issues. *Le roman de la science* was a docudrama about major scientific discoveries throughout history. *Je me souviens/Dateline* was a bilingual informational program on Quebec and Canadian history. *Explorations* (1956–61) was another history series that tried to bridge the Canadian cultural and linguistic divide. One segment from the series, "Two Studies of French Canada," was run on the English-language Canadian Broadcasting Corporation (CBC). Hosted by Lévesque, this program tried to explain to anglophone Canadians the recent history and aspirations of French Canadians.

Variety and musical programs also carried an international flavor. *Music Hall* (1955–65), Quebec's alternative to *The Ed Sullivan Show,* hosted a lineup of international francophone stars that included Maurice Chevalier, Edith Piaf, Charles Aznavour, and well-known Canadian singers such as Monique Leyrac and Denise Filiatrault.

Radio-Canada provided a broad range of variety programs to suit all tastes. *Feu de joie* featured jazz; *Dans tous les cantons* ran traditional French-Canadian folk music; *Chansons vedettes* and *Chansons canadiennes* showcased contemporary popular artists. Despite this impressive lineup with extravagant costumes and lavishly produced numbers, the shows did not attract viewers. Variety programming was the least popular of all the types of television produced by Radio-Canada in the 1960s, and, unlike the CBC, the system never had a truly popular program such as those hosted on the CBC by Don Messer or Tommy Hunter. The only light-entertainment show that developed any following was the comedy-sketch series *Quelles nouvelles,* which had been a popular radio series and starred Jean Duceppe and Marjolaine Hébert.

Comedy was, however, a central feature of game shows. Cheap and easy to design and produce—particularly since they involved little prize money—quiz shows like *Le nez de Cléopâtre* (1953–57) and *Point d'interrogation* (1956–62) featured panels of well-known personalities given a limit of 20 questions in which to identify a person or object. Other shows, such as *Chacun son métier* (1954–59), were a French version of the popular American program *What's My Line?*

Radio-Canada's real strength was the novelty or fun show. Shows such as *La clef des champs* (1955–59) and *Le club des autographs* (1957–62) were popular with audiences as much for their comedy as for their contests. Both were based on simple premises: *La clef des champs* was a charades game, but the actor and comedians competed more for laughs than for prizes, while *Le club des autographs* invited celebrities to twist and shake in a comical dance contest. The audience's favorite, and the most extreme example of this kind of programming, was *La rigolade* (1955–58). Referring to itself as the "least serious broadcast on the air," it invited ordinary people to test their skills at the silliest contests the producers could invent. As the contests became zanier, critics decried it as a scandalous spectacle, and it was pulled off the air after only three seasons despite being among the top-ranked shows on Radio-Canada.

Francophone programmers were continually faced with trying to balance such popular programs with their cultural and educational mandate. Any kind of spectacle seemed to have a large audience. *La Lutte* (1952–59) and *La Boxe* (1952–55) broadcast weekly prize fights that attracted a large following (even among women). Sports were consistently in demand, especially *La soirée du hockey,* the most popular program on television. Though hockey had always been popular in Quebec, television made players like Rocket Richard, the star of the Montreal Canadiens, into national heroes. As many as 2 million fans watched each Canadiens' game. Richard had become such a cultural icon that when he was suspended from the playoffs in the spring of 1995, the city exploded into rioting. It was no accident that Richard made public television appeals to induce the crowds to end the violence.

This incident only added to the dilemma facing programmers as more and more viewers demanded more sports while the elites and the clergy condemned television for inciting and promoting violence. Television programmers tried to counteract these charges in the 1950s by scheduling most sportscasts on the weekends and by increasing television's broadcast of the performing arts.

Radio-Canada had always believed that television could stimulate and educate the viewer. Music, ballet, opera, and drama were presented several times a week in various anthologies. *L'heure du concert* (1954–66) was devoted to concerts, opera, and ballet. Initially, it offered a series of excerpts from various productions and provided brief lectures on various art forms. Theater also occupied the most prominent place in Radio-Canada's early programming, and despite the challenges, difficulties, and production costs involved with live television drama, CBFT produced as many as two dramas a week throughout the 1950s. A demand for local productions fueled an enormous expansion in the development of Quebecois literature. Initially, great classical works such as Cocteau's *Oedipe-Roi* had been presented, but these were quickly replaced with local works. Soon short stories and even novels had to be adapted for television as more traditional works were soon exhausted. Eventually, Quebecois authors were commissioned to write specifically for television.

Between 1952 and 1960, Radio-Canada aired 435 plays, 80 percent of which were originally written or adapted by popular Quebecois writers such as Marcel Dubé, Hubert Aquin, Françoise Loranger, and Felix Leclerc. The majority of teleplays were showcased on *Le Telethéâtre de Radio-Canada* (1953–66), which presented more than 160 works, and *Théâtre populaire* (1956–58), which presented more than 100 plays. Other series included *Théâtre d'été* (1954–61) and *En première* (1958–60), *Théâtre du dimanche* (1960–61), *Jeudi Théâtre* (1961–62), and *Théâtre d'une heure* (1963–66).

While the teleplays received great critical acclaim, they were far less popular than the téléromans, televised serials adapted from popular novels. Since the debut of Roger Lemelin's *La famille Plouffe* (1953–59), this television genre has been a mainstay of francophone programming. Usually broadcast in half-hour episodes in peak hours over the fall/winter schedule, the stories would generally be completed in two or three seasons, but two series lasted much longer than the norm. *Les Belles Histoires des pays d'en haut* went on for 14 years, while *Rue des Pignons* continued for 11 years. Other popular téléromans included *Quartorze, rue de Galais* (1954–57), *Le Survenant* (1954–57, 1959–60), *Cap-aux-sorciers* (1955–58), *La Pension Velder* (1957–61), *La Côte de sable* (1960–62), *De 9 à 5* (1963–66), and *Septième nord* (1963–67).

A producer's strike at CBFT in Montreal from December 1958 to March 1959 brought serious disruption to francophone programming and an end to the "golden age" of French-Canadian broadcasting. Not only did popular shows like *Point de Mire* and *La famille Plouffe* end their run, but many critically acclaimed programs were never to return to the airwaves. The strike has become part of the annals of Quebec's Quiet Revolution. Some of the province's most popular television personalities like René Lévesque abandoned careers in broadcasting, in Lévesque's case to launch himself into politics.

The strike and its aftermath reflected the changing realities that television faced. In 1960 Radio-Canada faced competition from a private broadcaster. Télé-Métropole, "le 10," promoted itself as the station for ordinary people. In 1971 it became part of the Télé-Diffuseurs Associés (TVA) network. Its programming relied heavily on foreign movies and dubbed American drama series. Quiz shows like *Quiz-O* and *Télé-poker* became mainstays on the schedule, along with hockey broadcasts and variety programs that showcased Quebec's popular comedians and singers such as Robert Charlebois and Yvon Deschamps.

"Le 10" did produce a daily serial, *Ma femme et moi,* which ran in 1961, but it was only with *Cré Basile* (1965–68) that Télé-Métropole and the TVA network found critical acclaim for its television dramas. *Cré Basile* was Quebec's first sitcom, and for the first time, comedy was to become an integral part of francophone television drama. Télé-Métropole went on to develop other popular burlesque comedies—*Lecoq et fils* (1967–68), *Symphorien* (1974–78), *Les Brillant* (1979–80)—and situation comedies—*Dominique* (1977–80) and *Peau de banane* (1982–87). Télé-Métropole's programming was immediately popular. By 1966 it had 23 out of the top 25 shows and, in turn, spurred Radio-Canada to change many of its programs.

With competition, advertising revenues and sponsorships began to play a larger role in determining the television schedule. Radio-Canada's own internal surveys taken in 1960 had shown that viewers were little affected by the interruption in programming save for the loss of the téléromans. Feature films that had occupied much of the 1959–60 schedule had drawn as large an audience as its regular lineup. American imports were now available on film and could be easily translated and dubbed for a francophone audience. Not only were they cheaper than locally made productions, they were watched by more people and generated more revenue for their broadcasters. By the mid-1960s, Radio-Canada had virtually abandoned its notion of public service in favor of a more streamlined and entertaining schedule.

Performing arts broadcasts were the first victims of this change. *L'heure du concert* was cut back to bimonthly broadcasts and presented only one performance per episode as it dropped all pretensions of educating the public. Teleplays were confined to 90 minutes per week or appeared only in summer anthologies. From a high of almost 100 broadcast hours per year, theater drama had dropped to 20 hours per year in the mid-1960s. By 1966 all music, opera, ballet, and theatrical programs were combined in the two-hour anthology *Les beaux dimanches,* which has remained as part of the Sunday lineup.

A shift to lighter programming affected all genres. Public affairs programming reflected this change with the introduction of *Appelle-moi Lise,* a late-night talk show with host Lise Payette, which became the new model for the interview format. Sports gained more prominence, and giveaway shows such as *La poule aux oeufs d'or* (1958–65), which had replaced *La rigolade,* were modeled on American quiz shows such as *The $64,000 Question.* It was later joined by *Tous pour* *un* (1963–64), which became the most watched program on Tuesday nights.

Téléromans, which had always been successes, remained as the backbone of Radio-Canada's production. They were joined by locally made comedies and sitcoms as the public broadcaster sought to win back viewers. *Moi et l'autre* (1966–71), *La p'tite semaine* (1972–76), *Du tac à tac* (1977–81), and *Poivre et sel* (1983–87) were just some of the lighter television series that competed with the private network.

When TVA launched its celebrated *Les Berger* (1970–78) series, francophone television added the new family saga genre to its drama repertoire. *Rue des Pignons* (1970–77), *Grand-Papa* (1976–85), and *Terre humaine* (1978–84) were part of the regular lineup on Radio-Canada that competed with TVA's *Le Clan Beaulieu* (1978–82), *Marisol* (1980–83), and *Les Moineau et le Pinsons* (1982–85).

A growing concern over the sharp decline in educational and cultural programming, as well as a sharp increase in dubbed American imports, prompted the Quebec provincial government to launch its own public broadcaster, Radio-Québec, in 1968. Its programming was, and still is, devoted to providing educational and cultural programs that reflect Quebecois society. Largely a community-based system, it did not begin to broadcast in the evening until the 1972–73 season. Its programming featured many documentaries and nature and science shows as well as broadcasts of the proceedings of the legislative assembly. In recent years, it too has developed its own series such as *Avec un grand A* (1985–92). It has also showcased some English-made series such as *Degrassi* but has remained committed to its educational mandate. Over half of its programming is educational, and very few of its programs are American imports.

With the development of cable systems and more private stations, fears that the airwaves would be overrun with American programming once again became an issue. Although studies had shown that foreign imports constituted only about 20 percent of all programming, they also showed that local productions were dominant only in the informational, sports, and educational genres. More alarming was the fact that over 80 percent of all drama and comedies were American-made imports.

This led to a call for a stronger commitment on the part of the province's two public broadcasters to producing more local dramas since the studies also indicated that when given a clear choice between imports and local shows, Quebecois viewers prefer to see their own artists and programs. The success of drama series such as *Lance et Compte, Les Filles du Caleb,* and the comedy hit *La Petite vie,* which have had huge followings both domestically and internationally, attest to Quebecois television's vitality and creativity.

MANON LAMONTAGNE

See also **Famille Plouffe, La; Téléroman**

Further Reading

Collins, Richard, *Television and Culture,* London: Unwin Hyman, 1990

Raboy, Marc, *Missed Opportunities: The Story of Canada's Broadcasting Policy,* Montreal: McGill-Queen's University Press, 1990

Rutherford, Paul, *When Television Was Young: Primetime Canada 1951–1967,* Toronto: University of Toronto Press, 1990

Trofimenkoff, Susan, *The Dream of Nation,* Toronto: Gage, 1983

Canadian Specialty Cable Channels

The broadcasting of specialty services in Canada began in 1984 and increased dramatically in terms of number of channels, diversity of programming, and revenue throughout the decades. For the fiscal year 2001, specialty services collectively earned just less than $1.2 billion (Canadian). Not counting pay-TV offerings, currently there are 45 analog specialty channels available to subscribers, as well as more than 50 digital specialty channels and hundreds of digital offerings that have been licensed by the Canadian Radio-television and Telecommunications Commission (CRTC) but have yet to be launched. Overall, specialty services not only have proven to be the fastest-growing sector in the Canadian media industry but have garnered praise for their innovative, eclectic programming, hefty financial support for homegrown production, and showcasing of Canadian content.

The overall growth trend of specialty channels began on the shaky foundations laid by the launch of pay-TV in 1982. While pay-TV has remained an extra-cost cable service generally offering movie channels and pay-per-view sporting events, specialty services have developed into a diverse array of themed channel destinations, with some channels included as part of the basic cable package. The first two channels to be licensed by the CRTC in 1984 were MuchMusic and The Sports Network (TSN), followed later that year by Telelatino, Chinavision, and the now defunct The Life Channel. The next spate of licenses issued by the CRTC, in 1987, included French services as well as family-, religious-, and youth-oriented options in the form of TV5, Canal Famille, Musique Plus, Réseau des Sports, MétéoMédia/Weather Now, Vision, Youth Television (YTV), and CBC Newsworld.

The 1990s saw a boom in specialty service offerings—mostly Canadian-owned channels that, by the latter end of the decade, accounted for approximately a quarter of English-language viewing and just under a fifth for the francophone sector. As of 1999, there were 43 specialty services. Overall revenue rose from 12.4 million in 1990 to $30.2 million (Canadian) by the year 2000. Moreover, due in part to strategic regulation of the industry, by 1996, audience data indicated that Canadian-owned channels were easily outperforming foreign programming offerings for both English and French-Canadian specialty channels. The high-ratings earners at the end of the decade were TSN, YTV, and Teletoon, with audience shares of 3.7, 3.2, and 1.8 respectively.

By 1996, with the addition of 22 new channels, analog channel capacity was becoming increasingly scarce. As a result, both the industry and the CRTC pushed ahead with negotiations to implement digital services. Though limited digital offerings were previously available as far back as 1997 through such systems as direct-to-home (DTH) and multipoint distribution system (MDS), the official launch of digital cable came in September 2001. This initiative, with more than 50 operating channels and 283 licensed, stands as the world's largest coordinated launch of digital channels in the history of broadcasting.

There is a strong historical belief in Canada that film and television are cultural industries and representative of a shared cultural heritage. Boasting a 72 percent cable penetration rate into Canadian homes, specialty channels are not only high-revenue earners but also a staple of the Canadian televisual environment. Therefore, a Canadian specialty channel is differentiated from its U.S. counterpart by operating in a highly regulated environment. Regulations have allowed the channels to prosper (though some may claim to struggle) in an intensely competitive cable market. Sustaining a media industry next to the United States' overwhelming entertainment infrastructure, Canada's regulatory environment is geared toward protecting homegrown interests while attempting to allow the advantages of a competitive, free-market approach. Regulations revolve around programming, packaging, and ownership concerns as well as ensuring access to the publicly owned broadcasting spectrum by licensed broadcasting services that include conventional television, radio, and specialty and pay television. Recognizing the close ties between the Canadian government and the television industry is key to understanding the successes and limitations of this complex and evolving sector.

Though they are private businesses, specialty channels and the cable and satellite companies that distribute them are primarily regulated by the Canadian government through the CRTC. Its dual role as both protector and regulator of the industry has often put it at odds with the profit-minded goals of distributors and broadcasters. To advocate for these sectors, the Canadian Cable Television Association (CCTA) represents cable companies—the distributors of specialty services—to the CRTC and cable stakeholders. The Specialty and PayTV Association (SPTV), now merged with the Canadian Association of Broadcasters (CAB), operates an advocate for specialty and pay television programmers' interests. Both the CCTA and CAB are a strong presence in the regulatory field. Among their many activities, they have helped to create a unique self-regulating system.

The CRTC's regulatory influence over content is extensive. The overarching programming standards for specialty services are expressed through three main documents. Each channel is issued a license, generally for seven years, which is a binding contract drawn up by the CRTC, thereby giving the programmer the authority to be distributed by a cable distribution company and played over Canadian airwaves. The license is issued with a document called a "condition of license" (COL), which is individually tailored to the particular content concerns for each service. For example, in the case of YTV, there are stipulations on genre, percentage of programming targeted to different ages, amount of advertising, and, since YTV is aimed at children and young adults, age of protagonists who appear in the programs. All COLs reflect the minimum amounts of Canadian content (usually between 20 and 50 percent) and the percentage amount of revenue to be spent on purchasing Canadian content, and they ensure that the channel adheres to the spirit of its original concept. COLs can be amended at the time of license renewal or through special request.

On a larger scale, the Broadcasting Act (1991) is the prime overarching legal statute for the industry that represents the general expectations for Canadian programmers and distributors. It is to the spirit of this all-encompassing act that all other regulations must conform. The 1990 Specialty Services Regulations is a key document geared to specialty service providers. Other important documents are industry-adopted codes such as the Sex Role Portrayal Code (1990) and the Voluntary Code Regarding Violence in Television Programming (1993). In general, all documents reflect, depending on their focus, a commitment to Canadian support of homegrown content, programming that is sensitive to racial and gender portrayals, and programming that upholds the general ideals of cultural diversity, enrichment, and quality.

Specialty channels are affected as well by the regulations directed at the distributors that carry them (and who may own shares in various channels). Specialty services have historically been distributed through cable, though in the mid- to late 1990s new distribution systems, such as DTH satellite and MDS, became more important in this sector, particularly with digital services. Canada has well over a hundred cable companies, serving 8 million households, though giants like Rogers, Shaw, Vidéotron, and, to a lesser extent, Cogeco dominate the market. These cable companies follow the Broadcasting Distribution Regulations as well as numerous other CRTC rulings. Of particular importance to specialty services are tiering, linkage, and ownership.

"Tiering" is the bundling of specialty (and premium) services into different consumer packages to be sold at different prices. While the companies themselves decide on the final package, broadcast regulations dictate aspects of this packaging by regulating what gets included in a basic package or as an optional, also known as a discretionary, service. In the beginning, these services were offered on a discretionary basis. The tiers have since grown to include "optional-to-basic," a term used between 1987 and 1993 to indicate that services were basic unless the service itself opted for the discretionary tier. Services such as MuchMusic and TSN vied to amend their licenses in this manner in order to have the option to negotiate their placement on either a discretionary or basic tier in any given cable market.

The terms have since evolved to incorporate flexibility for the cable company, the channel, and the varied markets in which they operate. As of 2001, depending on each particular market in which it is operating, a cable distributor must distribute items from a list that includes offerings such as CBC Newsworld, YTV, and *Le Réseau de l'information.* However, this stipulation is made on the "dual status basis," meaning that the specialty service can opt to have it placed on a discretionary tier. For the discretionary tier, or "dual modified status," the list includes offerings like The Food Network Canada, Canal Vie, The Comedy Network, and CTV Newsnet. The rule here is that the list of services can only be placed on basic with the mutual consent of the specialty programmer and the cable company. The upshot is that while being placed on the basic tier is desirable for a service, given the greater advertising reach (since more people subscribe to basic as the less expensive service), a sought-after service can potentially earn more on the higher-priced discretionary tier in terms of money charged to the cable company to pick up the channel and money earned by the cable company by selling a higher-priced service to the consumer.

"Linkage" is a term that describes the rules governing the distribution of foreign, often American, channels. Cable companies must give priority carriage to Canadian channels but can choose foreign programming from a list of eligible satellite services. Shrewdly packaging Canadian offerings with tried-and-tested American channels such as CNN, Canadian specialty services have lured audiences toward acquiring Canadian specialty services from the outset. Creating a list of "Eligible Satellite Services" from which distributors can apply for foreign programming, the CRTC originally dictated that non-Canadian channels could only be offered on a two-to-one basis per tier. This meant for every two foreign channels carried, there had to be one Canadian offering. This regulation was changed in 1993 and now the ratio is one to one. Moreover, no foreign service can overlap in content or theme with a Canadian channel. In the event that a new Canadian channel is licensed that somewhat matches an existing foreign channel's programming thrust, then the foreign service may have its license suspended. Most notably, this occurred in 1994 in the case of American-owned Country Music Television, Canada (CMT) and Canada's New Country Network (CNC), which exploded into a heated trade dispute that ended only with the last-minute partnering of the two companies.

Finally, ownership concerns affect both foreign ownership as well as Canadian cable companies, who have had a variable history in their ownership allowances. In short, the Canadian specialty landscape, unlike Canada's cinema exhibition system, is Canadian owned and operated. Foreign ownership is limited to 33.3 percent of media companies, but it generally is restricted to the 20 percent maximum shareholder allowance if the company holds a broadcast license, which it must do to operate a specialty service. A Canadian cable company, on the other hand, has had greater flexibility in ownership rules. From their inception cable companies were allowed to own specialty channels, although the regulations tightened in the mid-1990s in the wake of increasing media consolidation, whereupon only minority shareholder status was permissible. The regulations have since loosened, due somewhat to the recent CRTC ruling that allowed Bell

Canada Enterprise to own a satellite distribution company along with specialty channels through its CTV broadcasting network.

These types of regulations have met with success in creating a prosperous specialty sector. However, with the licensing of the new digital channels, also known as diginets, there have been some notable differences from their analog counterparts reflecting a more competitive, and less protected, market environment. Though Canadian content expectations are high (ranging between 35 percent and 50 percent) and Canadian ownership is essential for licensing, tiering does not follow suit in the digital environment. While the CRTC has licensed 21 Category 1 (or "must-carry") channels arranged as distinct genres, the other hundreds are a free-for-all in terms of packaging. However, all Category 1 channels have been carefully arranged not to have overlapping genres, and linkage rules remain in the one-to-one ratio with a mandate to not directly compete with Canadian offerings. Distributors, be they cable, DTH, or MDS, have no ownership restrictions for the channels. However, for every channel that they own, they are required to carry five channels in which they have no ownership claims, otherwise known as the five-to-one rule.

Within this complex regulatory environment in which distributors and programmers operate is the extremely competitive business side of specialty services. A specialty channel in Canada generates revenue through advertising and subscription fees, paid to the service by the distributor on a per-subscriber basis. Though historically deriving the approximately 70 percent of its profits from subscriber fees, advertising revenue is on the increase, reflected by the increased viability of niche marketing and the CRTC's increase for nearly all specialty channels in the latter 1990s of advertising from 8 to 12 minutes per hour.

Both the cable companies and specialty networks have obligations to fund Canadian programming through their revenues. In the case of a cable distribution, a small percentage of revenue is contributed to production funds. Of the percentage set aside for content funds, 80 percent goes toward the Canadian Television Fund (CTF). The other 20 percent is capital that the cable company may invest at its discretion toward other funding schemes. The CTF is a "public-private" fund that is dually financed by the federal government and cable industry to support Canadian production ventures. The specialty channels, however, are required to "shop Canadian," and a percentage of their revenue, outlined in their COL, is destined for purchasing Canadian programming. Since each channel is mandated to air a specified amount of Canadian programming, the system operates a consistent supply-and-demand market for Canadian content.

With an overloaded analog spectrum and a successful albeit fledgling digital distribution system, the landscape for Canadian television players has been indelibly altered. While this has resulted in broadening consumer choice, it has added further complexity to one of the world's most innovative television markets. However, the specialty landscape is one of Canada's cultural successes due in part to regulatory protection, active trade representation, and shrewd business management. The dawning digital era has been hopeful. As of March 2002, total subscribership for digital offerings stood at 2.9 million with a growth rate that is 4 percent higher than that in the United States. As an indication of Canada's commitment to establishing a digital environment, in January 2000, the CRTC ceased licensing analog channels, except in exceptional circumstances. How the sector will fare in the era of digital transmission is still uncertain though Canada's lead in this sector bodes well for the industry and consumers alike.

JULIA TAYLOR

See also **Cable Networks; Canadian Broadcasting Corporation Newsworld; Canadian Cable Television Association; Canadian Television Network; Digital Television; MuchMusic; Youth Television**

Further Reading

Aynsley, Julian, "The Development of Specialty Television Channels," pt. 1, *Broadcast Dialogue* (February 2002)

Aynsley, Julian, "The Channels Multiply," pt. 2, *Broadcast Dialogue* (March 2002)

Aynsley, Julian, "The Development of Specialty Channels," pt. 3, *Broadcast Dialogue* (April 2002)

Chen, Jennifer, and Gary Graves, "Media Ownership in Canada," *CBC News Online* (May 2001) www.cbc.ca/news/indepth/background/mediaownership.html

Chidley, Joe, "Can the Seven New Channels Survive?" *Maclean's,* 108, no. 6 (February 1995)

Coopers and Lybrand, "Specialty Services: Background and Business Analysis," report prepared for the Canadian Association of Broadcasters, June 30, 1998

Dalglish, Brenda, "New Specialty Channels Lack Space, Funds: Four Channels Will Be Added to Existing Services, the Rest Will Be Scrambling for Space," *Financial Post* (September 27, 1996)

Department of Canadian Heritage, "Pay-TV and Specialty Services: Industry Overview 1992," November 1993

Easton, Ken, *Building an Industry: A History of Cable Television and Its Development in Canada,* East Lawrencetown, Nova Scotia: Pottersfield, 2000

Edelson, Abbe, "CRTC Sets Rules for New Pay and Specialty TV Services," *ETR News: Canada's National Communications Journal* (February–March 2000)

Forrester, Chris, *The Business of Digital Television,* Boston: Focal Press, 2000

Hyatt, Laurel, "Cable Challenges BCE over Specialty Channels," *Cablecaster,* 12 (2000)

McCabe, Michael, "Specialty and Pay: The Dawn of the Digital Era," *Broadcaster,* 59, no. 9 (September 2000)

Canadian Television Network

The Canadian Television Network Ltd. (CTV) was incorporated in 1961 as Canada's first private television network. Its network structure has evolved significantly over the years.

CTV is the most popular Canadian network, attracting up to 15 percent or more of the English-speaking audience. It has been accused by cultural nationalists and regulatory agencies of airing U.S. imports in prime time and relegating its few, often inexpensive Canadian productions to off-peak hours. Although the network has produced relatively little drama or comedy, it has achieved some notable programming successes. In 1967 CTV launched the news magazine *W5,* which still enjoys excellent ratings. In 1972, it launched *Canada A.M.,* which became the prototype for ABC's *Good Morning, America.* CTV's news and sports programs have also enjoyed steady success, even at times surpassing the CBC. In the mid- to late 1980s, CTV coproduced such highly successful dramas as *Night Heat* and *E.N.G.* Ultimately, CTV's protestations that its achievements are underappreciated must be balanced against the view that it has failed to contribute fully to the development of national culture.

CTV's network structure has moved through four distinct phases. From 1961 to 1965, CTV was controlled principally by its founder, Spencer Caldwell. Having won the original license, he planned to supply affiliates with ten hours of programming per week: content acquired internationally, original content produced in the affiliates' stations, and content controlled by the affiliates but offered to the network. Caldwell hoped to increase the weekly hours until CTV rivaled the CBC.

Three factors prevented the realization of this plan. First, Caldwell underestimated the technological start-up costs and was forced to seek loans from the affiliates. Second, the affiliation agreements worked to the detriment of the network, since affiliates could demand network compensation even if the network had not managed to sell all of its airtime. Third, as CTV supplied only ten hours per week, the affiliates established a parallel acquisition service to fill another 24 hours. The ITO (Independent Television Organization) effectively competed against CTV and drove up prices.

By 1965, on the brink of bankruptcy, Caldwell sold out to the affiliates. Until 1993, CTV operated as a cooperative. As such, each affiliate became a shareholder in the network, each shareholder sat on the board of directors, and each held the power of veto over board decisions. Additionally, the network now provided 39.5 hours of programming per week, thereby obviating the need for the ITO, which was abolished in 1969. Finally, affiliates could no longer demand compensation for unsold airtime.

This structure introduced new tensions. First, the affiliates served highly differentiated markets and held correspondingly divergent views on appropriate programming. Second, as major local independents, affiliates derived as much profit from local market dominance as from network affiliation. Hence, they tended to put their own profitability before the network's health, treating it at times as a necessary evil and approving only minimal operating budgets. Third, although the larger affiliates attracted a larger share of the audience, and therefore contributed proportionally more to network profits, each of them had only one vote and could be overruled. Fourth, some shareholders acquired more than one affiliate but were nonetheless restricted to a single vote. As a result, some shareholders lobbied for changes to the network structure. Finally, some shareholders owned stations unaffiliated with CTV, thereby creating potential conflicts of interest, especially as these stations sometimes competed against CTV for both program acquisition and market share.

CTV therefore failed to develop as a powerful network. Its weakness as a network curtailed its ability to produce Canadian content and therefore to meet the expectations of the Broadcasting Act.

In 1986 CTV's corporate structure came to the attention of the Canadian Radio-television and Telecommunications Commission (CRTC), which introduced new conditions at the network's license renewal hearings. For example, between 1987 and 1994, the CRTC instructed CTV (1) to spend $403 million (Canadian) on Canadian programming; (2) to schedule 120 hours of Canadian dramatic features, miniseries, and limited series in prime time; (3) to provide 24 hours of Canadian musical programming; and (4) to provide a minimum of 1.5 hours of regularly scheduled Canadian programming in prime time, rising to 3.5 hours per week. CTV spent $417 million, scheduled 126 hours of dramatic features, and programmed 40 hours of musical content, but it requested that the minimum number of regularly scheduled dramatic hours not exceed three per week.

Courtesy of CTV Inc.

Acting under the Canadian Business Corporations Act, CTV now consisted of seven shareholders who had each invested $2 million in the network. Board decisions would be made by majority vote, with no party having a veto. Shares could be sold and transferred so long as they were first offered to the other shareholders. The network also undertook to provide 42.5 hours of programming per week and to purchase airtime from affiliates at a fixed annual sum.

This arrangement brought CTV closer to the U.S. network model although CTV still possessed no owned-and-operated stations and remained an alliance of shareholders who controlled important single stations or strings of stations throughout the country. Furthermore, beginning in 1993, a new sequence of events convulsed CTV. Between 1993 and 1996, one of the shareholders, Baton (a contraction of "Bassett" and "Eaton," the names of its two controlling families), undertook acquisitions, stock swaps, and mergers that effectively gave it control of CTV. As of 1997, therefore, CTV fully resembles a U.S.-style network, with unified management and owned-and-operated stations in key markets.

In 1996 CTV launched five specialty or cable channels: News1 (now CTV Newsnet), the Comedy Channel, the Discovery Channel, the Outdoor Life Network, and SportsNet. These gave CTV a strategic presence in the increasingly crowded broadcast and cable spectrum, diversified its income streams, multiplied its broadcast windows, and reinforced its relationship with production companies. In 1999, CTV acquired TSN, an all-sports specialty channel and the most profitable of all cable networks, and its French-language counterpart, RDS (Réseau des sports). However, with control of two sports channels—TSN and SportsNet—CTV will be required to dispose of one of them. In September 2000, CTV also launched Talk TV, a specialty channel. By 2000, CTV was the dominant Canadian television network.

In 2000 CTV was acquired by the telecommunications giant Bell Canada Enterprises (BCE) for $2.3 billion. However, in 2001, BCE also acquired the *Globe and Mail,* a widely respected and influential newspaper. This resulted in a new corporate entity, Bell GlobeMedia, and a new corporate structure: Jean C. Monty became chairman of the board of Bell GlobeMedia; Ivan Fecan is president of Bell GlobeMedia and chief executive officer of CTV; Trina McQueen is president and chief operating officer of CTV.

These events mirrored similar developments in the United States, as CTV sought both to consolidate well-known brand names and to develop synergies. In 2001 CTV's position was further strengthened by the launch of seven new specialty channels: WTSN (women's sports), CTV Travel, Info Sports, Animal Planet, Discovery Civilization, ESPN Classic Canada, and The NHL Network. In addition to the above, CTV also holds interests in ROB-TV (a spin-off of the *Globe and Mail*'s "Report on Business" section) and CTV pay-per-view sports. It holds minority interests in Viewer's Choice Canada (pay-TV movies) and History Television.

PAUL ATTALLAH

Further Reading

Building Partnerships: Television in Transition: Reports Produced Following the Television Industry Summit of December 1991, Ottawa: Supply and Services Canada, 1992

Caplan, Gerald, and Florian Sauvageau, *Report of the Task Force on Canadian Broadcasting,* Ottawa: Government of Canada, 1986

Communications Department of Telefilm Canada, *Directory: Canadian Film, Television, and Video Industry,* Ottawa: Canada Communication Group, 1994

Gittins, Susan, *CTV: The Television Wars,* Toronto: Stoddart, 1999

Nolan, Michael, *CTV: The Network That Means Business,* Calgary: University of Alberta Press, 2001

Candid Camera

U.S. Humor/Reality Program

Candid Camera, the first and longest-running reality-based comedy program, premiered on ABC August 10, 1948, under its original radio title, *Candid Microphone.* The format of the program featured footage taken by a hidden camera of everyday people caught in hoaxes devised by the show's host, Allen Funt. In the world of *Candid Camera,* mailboxes talked to passersby, cars rolled along effortlessly without engines, little boys used X-ray glasses, and secretaries were chained to their desks, all to provoke a reaction from unsuspecting mechanics, clerks, customers, and passersby. In a 1985 *Psychology Today* article, Funt explained his move to television by saying that he "wanted to go beyond what people merely said, to record what they did—their gestures, facial expressions, confusions, and delights."

The program changed its name to *Candid Camera* when it moved to NBC in 1949, but it did not gain a permanent time slot until it finally moved to CBS in 1960. For the next seven years it was consistently rated as one of television's top ten shows before it was abruptly canceled. Funt was frequently joined by guest hosts such as Arthur Godfrey, Durward Kirby, and Bess Meyerson. A syndicated version of the program containing old and new material aired from 1974 to 1978. Aided by his son Peter, Funt continued to create special theme episodes (e.g., "Smile, You're on Vacation," "Candid Camera Goes to the Doctor," etc.) for CBS until 1990, when *The New Candid Camera,* advised by Funt and hosted by Dom DeLuise, went into syndication. Low ratings finally prevented King Productions from renewing the show for the 1992–93 season. However, in 1998, the program was revived again, with Peter Funt and Suzanne Somers as cohosts. New episodes of this version continued on the cable channel PAX in the early 21st century.

The scenarios designed and recorded by Alan Funt and his crew were unique glimpses into the quirks and foibles of human nature never before deliberately captured on film. The average scenario lasted approximately five minutes and was based on one of five strategies: reversing normal or anticipated procedures, exposing basic human weaknesses such as ignorance or vanity, fulfilling fantasies, using the element of surprise, or placing something in a bizarre or inappropriate setting. As Funt noted, "You have to make lots of adjustments to create viewer believability and really involve the subject. You need the right setting, one in which the whole scenario will fit and make sense to the audience even when it doesn't to the actor." Finding the right setting and the right people for *Candid Camera* stunts was not always an easy task.

Early attempts to film *Candid Camera* were hampered by technical, logistical, and censorship difficulties. While they appeared simple, the staged scenes took many hours to prepare, and success was far from guaranteed. Approximately 50 recorded sequences were filmed for every four or five aired on the program. Funt and his crew had to contend with burdensome equipment that was difficult to conceal. The cameras were often hidden behind a screen, but the lights needed for them had to be left out in the open. Would-be victims were told that the lights were part of "renovations." Microphones were concealed in boxes, under tables, or, in a number of episodes, in a cast worn by Funt himself. In his book *Eavesdropping at Large* (1952), Funt also described his battles with network censors and sponsors who had never before confronted this type of programming and were often fickle in their decisions about what was and was not acceptable material for television at the time. Funt himself destroyed any material that was off-color or reached too deeply into people's private lives. A hotel gag designed to fool guests placed a "men's room" sign on a closet door. The funniest, but ultimately unaired, reaction came from a gentleman who ignored the obvious lack of accommodations and "used" the closet anyway.

Candid Camera's unique approach to documenting unexpected elements of human behavior was inspired in part by Funt's background as a research assistant at Cornell University. At Cornell, Funt aided psychologist Kurt Lewin in experiments on the behaviors of mothers and children. He also drew on his experiences in the Army Signal Corps, where he was responsible for recording soldiers' letters home. *Candid Camera* was different from other programming because of its focus on the everyday, and on the extraordinary things that happen in ordinary contexts. "Generations have been educated to accept the characterizations of the stage and screen," Funt noted in his chronicle of the

Candid Camera, Susan Storrs, Durward Kirby, Allen Funt, 1960–67.
Courtesy of the Everett Collection

program's history. "Our audiences have to unlearn much of this to accept candid studies, although anyone can verify our findings just by looking around and listening."

Candid Camera spawned a new genre of "reality programming" in the late 1980s, including such shows as *America's Funniest Home Videos* and *Totally Hidden Video.* Television audiences were forced to become reflexive about their own role in the production of comedy and in thinking about the practices of everyday life. "We used the medium of TV well," Funt commented. "There were close ups of people in action. The audience saw ordinary people like themselves and the reality of events as they were unfolding. Each piece was brief, self-contained, and the simple humor of the situation could be quickly understood by virtually anyone in our audience." Conceived in a less complex era free of camcorder technology, *Candid Camera* used insight and humor to explore both the potential of television and the role of the TV audience.

AMY W. LOOMIS

Original Host
Allen Funt

Cohosts
Arthur Godfrey (1960–61)
Durward Kirby (1961–66)
Bess Myerson (1966–67)
Peter Funt (1990, 1998–)
Dom DeLuise (1991)
Eva LaRue Callahan (1991)
Suzanne Somers (1998–)

Producer
Allen Funt

Programming History

ABC	
August 1948–September 1948	Sunday 8:00–8:30
October 1948	Sunday 8:30–8:45
November 1948–December 1948	Friday 8:00–8:30
NBC	
May 1949–July 1949	Sunday 7:30–8:00
July 1949–August 1949	Thursday 9:00–9:30
CBS	
September 1949–September 1950	Monday 9:00–9:30
NBC	
June 1953	Tuesday 9:30–10:00
July 1953	Wednesday 10:00–10:30
CBS	
October 1960–September 1967	Sunday 10:00–10:30
July 1990–August 1990	Friday 8:30–9:00
Syndication	
1991	various times
PAX	
1998–	various times

Further Reading

Brooks, T., and E. Marsh, *The Complete Directory to Prime Time TV Shows: 1946–present,* New York: Ballantine, 1992

Carey, P., "Catching Up with Candid Camera," *Saturday Evening Post* (1992)

Funt, Alan, *Eavesdropping at Large: Adventures in Human Nature with Candid Mike and Candid Camera,* New York: Vanguard Press, 1952

Zimbardo, P. "Laugh Where We Must, Be Candid Where We Can," *Psychology Today* (1985)

Cannell, Stephen J. (1941–)

U.S. Producer, Writer

Stephen J. Cannell emerged as one of television's most powerful producer-writers in the 1980s. A prolific writer, he would eventually also become a series creator, an executive producer, a director, a station owner, and the head of his own studio. He specializes almost exclusively in crime shows and action-adventures, and his work, by its sheer volume, has played a significant role in redefining the parameters of those genres. Early in his career, he created and produced programs with such other crime show auteurs as Jack Webb, Roy Huggins, William Link and Richard Levinson, and Steven Bochco.

Like many other aspiring television artists in the 1960s, Cannell got his start at Universal Television, where he joined the writing staff of *Adam-12* in 1970. After a few years of writing for several of the company's other series, he began to create and produce his own shows for Universal, including *Chase; Baretta; Baa Baa Blacksheep; Richie Brockelman, Private Eye; The Duke;* and *Stone. The Rockford Files,* which won an Emmy for Outstanding Drama in 1978, was by far his most commercially and critically successful series of this period. The show exhibited all the trademarks of the Cannell style: a facile blending of comedy and drama, up-to-the-minute contemporary vernacular dialogue, and a protagonist who was a likable outsider, in this case an ex-convict.

In 1979 Cannell left Universal to form Stephen J. Cannell Productions. He won a Writers Guild Award for *Tenspeed and Brownshoe* and achieved some modest ratings success for *The Greatest American Hero,* but it was *The A-Team* that established the company as a major force in Hollywood in 1983. Adding a heavy dosage of cartoonlike action to the familiar Cannell themes, *The A-Team* made Nielsen's top ten in its debut season. Three years later, Cannell had six series on the network prime-time schedule, including *Hunter, Riptide,* and *Hardcastle and McCormick.*

Many critics who had praised *The Rockford Files* rejected this latest batch of Cannell's series, complaining that they were juvenile and overly formulaic. With the debut of *Wiseguy* in 1987, however, one of Cannell's shows once again earned critical respect for its intelligent dialogue, complex characterization, and occasional treatment of timely issues. *Wiseguy* also employed an innovative new narrative structure, the "story arc," whereby the season was in effect divided into several multipart episodes.

In an effort to lower production costs, Cannell opened a major studio facility in Vancouver, British Columbia, toward the end of the 1980s. One of the first series shot there was *21 Jump Street,* the highest-rated show of the new FOX network's first season. *Scene of the Crime,* a mystery anthology series for CBS's late-night schedule, was also filmed in Vancouver and was hosted by Cannell himself.

Stephen J. Cannell.
Photo courtesy of Stephen J. Cannell Productions, Inc.

Cannell Studios, the company he had set up in the mid-1980s to incorporate his production company and his many other diversified interests, was purchased by New World Communications in 1995. That same year, Cannell turned his attentions to a new career as a novelist. *The Plan,* a political thriller, was published in 1995 and became a best-seller. Since then, Cannell has written five other novels. As of late 2001, Cannell was developing projects for both film and television, including feature-film adaptations of *The A-Team* and *The Greatest American Hero.*

ROBERT J. THOMPSON

See also **Bochco, Steven; Huggins, Roy; *Rockford Files***

Stephen J. Cannell. Born in Los Angeles, California, February 5, 1941. University of Oregon, B.A. 1964. Married: Marcia C. Finch, 1964; children: Derek (deceased), Tawnia, Chelsea, Cody. Began career as television writer in late 1960s, selling story ideas to Desilu Productions; head writer, Universal Studios, *Adam-12,* 1970; creator, writer, producer of other Universal action-adventure programs, through 1970s; founder, Stephen J. Cannell Productions, 1979. Recipient: Mystery Writers Award; four Emmy Awards; four Writers Guild of America Awards.

Television Series (writer-producer)

1970 *Adam-12*
1973 *Chase*
1973–74 *Toma*
1974–80 *The Rockford Files*
1976–78 *Baa Baa Blacksheep (The Blacksheep Squadron)*
1978 *Richie Brockleman, Private Eye*
1979 *The Duke*
1980 *Tenspeed and Brownshoe*
1980 *Stone*
1981–83 *The Greatest American Hero*
1982 *The Quest*
1983–84 *The Rousters*
1983–86 *Hardcastle and McCormick*
1983–87 *The A-Team*
1984–86 *Riptide*
1984–91 *Hunter*
1986 *The Last Precinct*
1986–87 *Stingray*
1987–88 *J.J. Starbuck*
1987–90 *21 Jump Street*
1987–89 *Wiseguy*
1988 *Sonny Spoon*
1989 *Unsub*
1989–90 *Booker*
1991–99 *Silk Stalkings*
1991 *The Commish*
1991–94 *Scene of the Crime*
1994–95 *Them*
1994–95 *Hawkeye*
1995 *Marker*
1996 *Profit*
1996 *Two*

Made-for-Television Movies

1990 *I Love You Perfect*
1991 *Always Remember I Love You*
1991 *Living a Lie*
1992 *Highway Heartbreaker*
1993 *Jonathan: The Boy Nobody Wanted*
1993 *A Place for Annie*
1993 *Firestorm: 24 Hours in Oakland*
1995 *Jake Lassiter: Justice on the Bayou* (executive producer)
1995 *The Return of Hunter: Everybody Walks in L.A.* (executive producer)
1995 *The Rockford Files: Friends and Foul Play* (writer)
1995 *The Dog Hermit*
1996 *Wiseguy*
1996 *The Rockford Files: Crime and Punishment* (supervising producer)
1997 *The Rockford Files: Murder and Misdemeanors* (supervising producer)
1999 *The Rockford Files: If It Bleeds... It Leads* (writer)

Publications

The Plan, 1995
King Con, 1997
Riding the Snake, 1998
The Devil's Workshop, 1999
The Tin Collectors, 2001
The Viking Funeral, 2002

Further Reading

Christensen, Mark, and Cameron Stauth, *The Sweeps,* New York: William Morrow, 1984
Fanning, Deirdre, "What Stuff Are Dreams Made Of?" *Forbes* (August 22, 1988)

Freeman, Mike, "Man of the Hours," interview, *Broadcasting* (January 25, 1993)
Perry, Jeb, *Universal Television: The Studio and Its Programs, 1950–1980,* Metuchen, New Jersey: Scarecrow, 1983
Shindler, Merill, "Okay, Cannell, Come Clean," *Los Angeles Magazine* (October 1983)
Thompson, Robert J., *Adventures on Prime Time: The Television Programs of Stephen J. Cannell,* New York: Praeger, 1990
Wicking, Christopher, and Tise Vahimagi, *The American Vein: Directors and Directions in Television,* New York: Dutton, 1979

CanWest Global Communications

CanWest Global Communications Corporation (CWG) is one of Canada's leading diversified media conglomerates and an international presence in the production and distribution of film, radio, and television. Comprising major holdings in print publishing, marketing, Internet portals, and film and television production and distribution in Canada, CanWest also has interests in Australia, Ireland, and New Zealand as well as offices in London and Los Angeles. As of 2001, it commanded a 30 percent market share of the Canadian conventional TV market and had a potential reach to 97 percent of Canadian homes. CWG is also the leader in Canadian newspapers, holding 37 percent of the market. Headquartered in Winnipeg, Manitoba, and until recently headed by an outspoken owner and executive chair, the late Israel "Izzy" Asper, this family-run company stands as one of Canada's media giants and its first multimedia conglomerate.

Originating as CanWest Capital, the company began its rise as an international media company with the acquisition of a single television holding, a North Dakota station called KCND. After rearranging the call letters to CKND, and headquartering it in Winnipeg, CanWest was awarded a television license in 1974 by the Canadian Radio-television and Telecommunications Commission (CRTC). In 1977 CWG purchased a 40 percent interest in Toronto-based Global Television. By 1982 it owned a further 20 percent interest, and by 1984 the company had changed its name to CanWest Communications and was almost wholly owned by Asper. Since then, CWG has continued to acquire television, publishing, and Internet holdings, pursuing an overall trend toward diversification and vertical integration.

By 1989 Global Television was under complete ownership by Asper, who then modified the company name to its current version, CanWest Global Communications. Throughout the 1980s, CWG acquired television stations piecemeal across western Canada. Starting with the purchase of a Vancouver station in 1987 (since relinquished to one of its competitors) under the subsidiary company CanWest Pacific, other stations were acquired in Saskatoon and Regina, gaining licenses around the same time under the subsidiary SaskWest Television. Next came a station servicing the Halifax and St. John region, followed by a station in Quebec.

However, it was not until the acquisition of Western International Communication Ltd. (WIC) in 2000 that CWG became a full-fledged Canadian network, the third in Canada. Its direct competitors are Bell Canada Enterprises' (BCE's) subsidiary Bell Globemedia, which houses the CTV network, and the government-supported Canadian Broadcasting Corporation (CBC). Considered one of the largest buyouts at the time, WIC's assets were divvied up between Shaw Communications Inc., CWG, and Corus (a subsidiary of Shaw). From this dissolution of WIC's assets, CWG obtained all of WIC's conventional television broadcasting undertakings, gaining nine television stations in the process (the ninth added in a separate negotiation from the other eight). CWG's gains did not happen without criticism from its competitor BCE and the lobby group Friends of Canadian Broadcasting (FSCB). The former felt that this acquisition would give CWG an unfair dominance in strong markets like Vancouver, and the latter felt that its new strength would be put to use purchasing more American pro-

Courtesy of CanWest Global Communications Corp.

gramming, thus diminishing the presence of Canadian content. CWG attempted to allay these fears with the promise of an $84.3 million (Canadian dollars) production fund package focusing on homegrown programming, cultural diversity, and media education. Though it was required by the CRTC that CWG divest itself of its then current holding CKVU in Vancouver, CWG's Global Network went from reaching 16 percent of the Canadian viewing audience in 1996 to 88 percent by the year 2000, and by 2002, it reached 97 percent of Canadian homes.

CWG's Canadian television assets now include 16 conventional television stations, 11 that make up its Global Network; three independent stations in Hamilton, Montreal, and Vancouver Island; and two CBC affiliate stations in Kelowna, British Columbia, and Red Deer, Alberta. Despite the rapid growth of Canada's specialty sector throughout the 1990s, the company holds only one analog cable interest, PRIME, which targets the 50-year-old-plus demographic with popular syndications such as *M*A*S*H* and lifestyle shows like *Canadian Travel Show.* CWG was quicker to capitalize on the digital specialty licensing wave and has managed to obtain the licenses to 47 channels, though it has launched only six services to date. These digital channels are Men TV, a men's lifestyle network; Mystery; Deja View, showcasing predominantly American syndicated classics; Lone Star, a western-themed channel; FOX Sportsworld Canada, including sporting events from around the world; and X-treme Sports.

Meanwhile, CWG had been expanding its interests in foreign markets as well as its stake in the newspaper publishing sector. In 1991 CWG acquired 20 percent of TV3 New Zealand, a widely distributed network with international programming that appeals to an 18-to-49-year-old demographic. By 1997 it owned 100 percent of this station and had, in the same year, launched TV4. CWG also has a stake in FM radio interests in New Zealand. In 1992 CWG turned its efforts toward Network Ten, Australia, holding a majority interest in the network and a 60 percent interest in Network Ten's advertising company Eye Corp, acquired in 2000. In both countries, these networks appeal to a young, hip audience with indigenously focused and imported programming. The Irish TV3 has a 45 percent CWG stake and is Ireland's first national private network. CWG also holds a 29.9 percent stake in North Ireland's UTV, as well as its subsidiary holding, UTV Internet. Despite spanning three countries, CWG's revenue from its international holdings generated only 8 percent of its sales in 2001.

Though CanWest's interests began in television and that remains its central concern, its largest acquisition to date has been Conrad Black's Hollinger's newspaper chain and Internet holdings. This development solidified CWG's place as the largest media company in Canada. It also stands as Canada's largest chain of newspapers, including a 50 percent stake (raised to 100 percent in 2002) in the fledgling national daily the *National Post.* The details of the acquisition sent shockwaves through the Canadian media industry, regulatory bodies, and the government: a $2.1 billion (Canadian) transaction for hundreds of news sources as well as the Internet portal Canada.com. This merger has been closely monitored by the CRTC, CWG's competitors, as well as special interest groups, and it has spurred a slew of criticisms. Notable among these criticisms has been the newspaper's editorial bias, sparking a provocative debate in the various competing newspapers in early 2002.

The strategic advantage gained from the Hollinger acquisition was to create news-related content for its growing distribution outlets in television. However, the CRTC limited this potential integration for both CWG and BCE (which owns CTV and the national daily newspaper *The Globe and Mail*) at the time of their 2001 license renewal. For both companies, it was expected that the print and television newsrooms were to remain separate. As a compromise with the CRTC, each media company has committed to keeping its editorial managers separate but has requested to share news-gathering resources between the print and television holdings. In return, the companies will propose and follow voluntary codes of conduct for news delivery. The CRTC has also forced a commitment by each conglomerate to financially support an independent monitoring committee.

As part of creating a synergistic news-gathering structure, CWG needed to feed its growing distribution chains with entertainment content. During its growth in the 1990s, CWG's 1998 purchase of Fireworks Entertainment Inc., a Canadian film and television production company, consolidated its position as a content producer. This company was created in 1995 and since its acquisition has expanded to become the Toronto-based headquarters for Fireworks Television, Fireworks Pictures, and Fireworks International. With this purchase, CWG also acquired Skyvision Entertainment's library, a purchase Fireworks made in 1996. The Fireworks subsidiaries focus on film and television production, distribution, and financing projects and have offices based in Los Angeles and London.

In 2000 Fireworks bought the film library of Dutch-based ENDEMOL International Distribution (EID), doubling CWG's distribution rights for more than 1,200 hours of television programming. Between Fireworks and EID, CanWest now has access to television series such as *Beastmaster* and *Relic Hunter,* made-for-TV movies such as *The Audrey Hepburn Story,* as well as feature films such as *Johnny Mnemonic, Rules of Engagement,* and *An American Rhapsody.* Moreover, the same year as the EID acquisition, CWG entered into a joint venture with Samuel Goldwyn Films and Stratosphere Releasing, forming IDP Distribution.

As of 2002, CWG boasted a strategically built diversified media empire that dominated the Canadian market and had vertically integrated its strengths into its national and international interests. However, as a Canadian media company, it is subject to Canada's stringent rules and regulations concerning content, regulated by the CRTC, and to pursuing the mandates of the 1991 Broadcasting Act. CWG's Global Television network has been criticized over the years by lobbyists and competitors alike for reneging on its Canadian-content obligations. A typical Global prime-time lineup is dominated by American first-run and syndicated shows including *The Simpsons, The X-Files,* and *Seinfeld.* Though CWG has counterargued that it has fostered some of the top-rated Canadian dramatic series, such as the show *Traders* (considered to be an underserved genre in the Canadian television landscape), FSCB has noted that CWG spends only 18 percent of its revenue buying CanCon.

However, CWG's television interests have fulfilled their obligations by servicing Canadians with local and regional news programming through CWG's stations. Moreover, in its annual report CWG announced that in the spring 2001 "sweeps" month, it was the top-rated network in Canada, averaging a 12 rating compared with a 6 rating for CTV, its closest competitor. PRIME, CWG's analog specialty channel, continues to grab audiences, showing increased ratings for 2001.

CWG has shown throughout its rise to conglomerate status that it is an ambitious, tenacious, and strategic player in the Canadian and international media landscape. Asper, who relinquished formal control in 1999 to son Leonard and passed away in October 2003, went on record stating that his goal for CanWest Global was to rival global media giants like Viacom Inc. and AOL-Time Warner Inc. It remains to be seen, given CanWest's $4 billion (Canadian) debt since its Hollinger acquisition and the economic downturn in North America, whether CWG's current toeholds in its various markets will foster Asper's vision.

JULIA TAYLOR

See also **Canadian Broadcasting Corporation Newsworld; Canadian Television Network**

Further Reading

Canadian Corporate News, "CanWest Acquires Fireworks Entertainment," *Canadian Corporate News* (May 5, 1998)

Flavelle, Dana, "Regulator Redraws TV Industry Blueprint," *Toronto Star* (July 7, 2000)

Flavelle, Dana, and Susan Pigg, "Broadcasting Moguls Await Fate," *Toronto Star* (July 6, 2000)

Hyatt, Laural, "Money for Something: Global Pledge$ Million$ to Get CRTC Approval of WIC Deal," *Broadcaster* (March 2000)

Tillson, Tamsen, "Webs Tangle for Dominance (CanWest Global and CTV)," *Variety* (April 3, 2000)

Wells, Jennifer, "Izzy's Dream," *Maclean's* (February 19, 1996)

Wilson-Smith, Anthony, "What's Going at Global?: News Anchor Peter Kent, Possibly, as the Network Revamps and Shifts Westward," *Maclean's* (February 28, 2000)

Worthington, Peter, "Under the Influence in Tackling Critics of Southam's Editorial Policies, Its Defenders Harp on CanWest Global's Limited Influence—Which Seems at Odds with the Way the Company Describes Itself," *Ottawa Sun* (April 30, 2002)

Captain Video and His Video Rangers

U.S. Children's Science Fiction Program

Captain Video and His Video Rangers, which premiered June 27, 1949, on the DuMont Network, was the first science fiction, space adventure program on television and was to inspire a spate of similar offerings. As it combined many of the early staples of children's programming, such as the inclusion of inexpensive film clips and pointed moral lessons, *Captain Video* also capitalized on the public fascination with science and space and the technical elements of the new television medium to create the longest-running science fiction show in early television.

Captain Video was the creation of James L. Caddigan, a DuMont vice president. Set in the year 2254, the show was an ambitious undertaking: it was live, technically demanding, and programmed as a continuing serial appearing every evening from 7:00 to 7:30 P.M. The show was designed to take advantage of the new technology; dissolves, superimpositions, and crude luminance key effects were utilized to place Captain Video in fanciful surroundings and allow him to travel through space and time. Without the luxury of videotape and editing, however, scripts, written by Maurice C. Brock (a veteran radio scriptwriter for *Dick Tracy* and *Gangbusters*), had to contain a great deal of exposition in order to allow time to set up for short bursts of action.

The lack of sustained action was the reason given by creator Caddigan for using clips from the DuMont film library. In a typical program, as the conflict subsided for a moment, Captain Video (played by Richard Coogan, who later portrayed U.S. Marshal Matt Wayne on *The Californians*) would turn to his Remote Tele-Carrier, or, inexplicably, the show would switch to Ranger Headquarters, to show the exploits of other rangers (often cowboys such as Bob Steele and Sunset Carson in western films). These clips always involved action-oriented sequences and helped to pick up the pace of the show and allow time for the production crew to change sets and set up special effects.

Other breaks between scenes were filled with Ranger Messages. While messages on other children's programs would focus on children's issues such as safely crossing the street, Ranger Messages dealt with more global issues such as freedom, the Golden Rule, and nondiscrimination. The sophistication of these messages seemed to anticipate an adult audience, but the shifts between space and western adventures were incomprehensible to many adults. The show was most popular with children, and by 1951 it was carried by 24 stations and seen by 3.5 million viewers, outdrawing its nearest competitor, *Kukla, Fran, and Ollie.*

As the "Master of Science," Captain Video was a technological genius, who invented a variety of devices including the Opticon Scillometer, a long-range, X-ray machine used to see through walls; the Discatron, a portable television screen that served as an intercom; and the Radio Scillograph, a palm-sized, two-way radio. With public concerns about violence in television programming, Captain Video's weapons were never lethal but were designed to capture his opponents (a Cosmic Ray Vibrator, a static beam of electricity able to paralyze its target; an Atomic Disintegrator Rifle; and the Electronic Strait Jacket, which placed captives in invisible restraints). In testimony before Senator Estes Kefauver's subcommittee probing the connection between television violence and juvenile delinquency, Al Hodge, who had previously starred in radio's *Green Hornet* and became Captain Video in 1951, noted that he did not even use the word "kill" on the show.

In addition to the futuristic inventions, the plots featured sharply drawn distinctions between good and bad science. Although Captain Video, with the 15-year-old Video Ranger (played by Don Hastings, who later appeared in *The Edge of Night* and *As the World Turns*), battled a wide array of enemies, the most clever and persistent was the deranged scientist Dr. Pauli (originally portrayed by Bram Nossem, who could not sustain the grueling live schedule and was replaced by Hal Conklin). The battles were originally Earth-bound, with Captain Video circling the globe in his X-9 jet to thwart the plans of Dr. Pauli, who joined forces with other villains, such as the evil Heng Foo Sueeng. However, in response to other newly created science fiction competitors, in 1951 Captain Video began to patrol the universe and battle aliens in the spaceship Galaxy, under the auspices of the Solar Council of the Interplanetary Alliance. He encountered

Captain Video & His Video Rangers, Al Hodge, Don Hastings, 1951–55.
Courtesy of the Everett Collection

such notable villains as clumsy McGee (played by Arnold Stang), an inept Martian; Norgola (played by Ernest Borgnine), who turned the sun's energy into magnetic forces; and television's first robot, Tobor ("robot" spelled backward), played by Dave Ballard.

The audience was exceptionally involved in the show, often writing to oppose plot developments or to suggest new inventions. For example, Tobor and Dr. Pauli were destroyed when their schemes backfired; however, the opposition of the viewers was great enough to bring them back in later episodes. Young viewers were also encouraged to join the Video Rangers Club and to buy Captain Video merchandise, including helmets, toy rockets, games, and records, although the show was not as extensively merchandised as some of its competitors. The show was supported, however, by large sponsors such as Skippy peanut butter and Post cereals. Fawcett also published six issues of *Captain Video Comics* in 1951. A 15-chapter movie serial, *Captain Video, Master of the Stratosphere* (released by Columbia Pictures in 1951, starring Judd Holdren and Larry Stewart), was the first attempt by Hollywood to capitalize on a television program. DuMont also attempted to build on the popularity of the show by developing *The Secret Files of Captain Video,* a 30-minute, weekly adventure complete within itself, which ran concurrently with the serial from September 1953 until May 1954.

However, although Captain Video was "The Guardian of the Safety of the World," he was not able to escape the economic necessities of the industry nor prevent the demise of the DuMont network. When Miles Laboratories canceled its sponsorship of the Morgan Beatty news program, *Captain Video* remained as DuMont's only sponsored program between 7:00 and 8:00 P.M. Unfortunately, the income from that program was not large enough to justify the rental of the coaxial cable, and *Captain Video* left the air on April 1, 1955, with DuMont folding that same year.

SUZANNE WILLIAMS-RAUTIOLLA

Cast

Captain Video (1949–50)	Richard Coogan
Captain Video (1951–55)	Al Hodge
The Ranger	Don Hastings
Dr. Pauli (1949)	Bran Mossen
Dr. Pauli (1950–53)	Hal Conklin

Producers

Olga Druce, Frank Telford, James L. Caddigan, Al Hodge

Programming History

DuMont

June 1949–August 1949	Tuesday, Thursday, Friday 7:00–7:30
August 1949–September 1953	Monday–Friday 7:00–7:30
September 1953–April 1955	Monday–Friday 7:00–7:15
February 1950–September 1950	Saturday 7:30–8:00
September 1950–November 1950	Saturday 7:00–7:30

Further Reading

Fischer, Stuart, *Kids TV: The First Twenty-Five Years,* New York: Facts on File, 1983

Grossman, Gary H., *Saturday Morning TV,* New York: Dell, 1981

Houston, David, "The 50s Golden Age of Science Fiction Television," *Starlog* (December 1980)

Captioning

Captioning is the display, in writing, of dialogue, narration, or other unspoken information on the screen. As an audiovisual medium, television makes extensive use of writing. Captions usually appear in two to three lines at the bottom of the screen.

Captions used for translating a foreign-language text or program are usually called "subtitles." While such "translation subtitling" is rarely used in some countries, including the United States, captioning in the same language is indispensable, especially in information programs such as news, documentaries, and weather reporting or in entertainment programs such as game shows. Captions are also used when intelligibility is reduced by poor voice quality, dialect, colloquialism, or other features of speech. Commercials make extensive use of captioning, sometimes with calligraphic expression. The written element enhances the spoken, visual, graphic, sound, or musical components of an advertisement or provides additional information.

Captions are either "open" (that is, appear on the screen without viewer control of their display) or "closed" (i.e., available for display at viewer's choice); closed captions can be "opened" with a decoder. An increasingly important use of closed captions is for making the spoken language of television available to hearing-impaired audiences. The first experiments with such captioning were initiated by PBS in the early 1970s and approved by the Federal Communications Commission (FCC) in 1976. PBS's Boston station, WGBH-TV, established a Caption Center, which set standards for captioned programming. Although a real success with hearing-impaired viewers who lobbied for more, some in the hearing audience complained about the distraction of open captions. The problem was solved when it became possible to assign line 21 of the vertical-blanking interval (VBI) for hiding captions, which could be conveniently opened up by a decoder. The nonprofit National Captioning Institute (NCI), formed in 1981, promoted the service and tried to gradually meet viewers' demands. In Britain, the 1990 Broadcasting Act stipulated the captioning of a minimum of 50 percent of all programs by 1998. In Canada, broadcasters raised public interest in this service by opening closed captions during a Captioning Awareness Week in 1995. In the United States, all television sets with screens larger than 13 inches produced after 1993 were required to be equipped with decoders.

Nonstandardized technology is an obstacle to transnational exchange of closed-caption programs in countries speaking the same language. By the mid-1990s, there were some 3,000 captioned videos in the United States. However, NCI-captioned products in Britain could be viewed only with a decoder because the VBI lines used in the two countries are not compatible.

In both film and television, captioning began as a postproduction activity. Technological advances as well as a growing demand by hearing-impaired viewers have made it possible to provide real-time captioning for live broadcasting. This is done with the aid of a courtroom stenograph or shorthand machine; a high-speed stenographer can type no less than 200 words per minute, which is adequate for keeping up with the speed of normal conversation. Stenographed texts are not readable, however, because words are abbreviated or split into consonant and vowel clusters. While the stenographer strikes the keyboard, a computer transforms the keystrokes into captions and delivers them to the transmitting station, making it possible for the viewers to read the words seconds after they are spoken. Stenocaptioning was first tried in the early 1980s in Britain and the United States. The improved system was in use in North America in the mid-1990s, although alternative technologies were being developed in Europe.

While captioning allows millions of deaf and hard-of-hearing citizens access to television, it usually involves heavy editing of the spoken language. Screen space is limited, and captions can be displayed for only a few seconds. Thus, to allow viewers enough time to read the captions and watch the pictures, the dialogue or narration must be summarized; such editing entails change of meaning or loss of information. However, refined, although not yet standardized, styles have been developed to help the viewer get a better grasp of the spoken language. When more than one speaker is present, the captions may either be placed next to each speaker or marked by different colors. Moreover, codes or brief comments are used to indicate the presence of some features of the speech, music, and sound effects.

Captioning is a useful teaching aid in second-language learning, child or adult acquisition of liter-

An example of captioning.
Photo courtesy of The Caption Center

acy, and in most types of educational programming. It also has a potential for creating new television genres and art forms. Digital broadcasting improves the production and reception of captions by, for instance, allowing viewers to adjust text size and diversifying fonts and styles.

AMIR HASSANPOUR

Further Reading

Clark, Joe, "Typography and TV Captioning," *Print* (January–February 1989)

"Closed Captioning: Between the Lines," *The Economist* (May 7, 1994)

Neuman, S.B., and P.S. Koskinen, *Using Captioned Television to Improve the Reading Proficiency of Language Minority Students,* Falls Church, Virginia: National Captioning Institute, 1990

Subtitling for the Deaf and Hard of Hearing People: Report for the Royal National Institute for Deaf People, London: RNID, 1999

U.S. Congress, House Committee on Energy and Commerce, Subcommittee on Telecommunications and Finance, *Television Closed Captioning: Hearing Before the Subcommittee on Telecommunications and Finance of the Committee on Energy and Commerce, House of Representatives, One Hundred First Congress, Second Session, on H.R. 4267, May 2, 1990,* Washington: U.S. Government Printing Office, 1990

Cariboo Country

Canadian Drama Series

Cariboo Country, one of the most imaginative, innovative, and evocative series ever broadcast by the Canadian Broadcasting Corporation (CBC), was a hybrid of anthology and series programming originating in Vancouver, British Columbia. It appeared on the CBC as a summer replacement from 1960 to 1967 and was among the first Canadian television dramas to be filmed on location. This meant that the team of producer Philip Keately and writer Paul St. Pierre, as well as the actors whose characters appeared in various episodes, all received direct and timely reactions from the ranchers and First Nations' peoples of the Cariboo, whose lives the series explored.

The series was a deliberate antithesis to the dominant North American television genre of the 1960s: the television western. It was set in the Chilcotin region of modern British Columbia. Guns were used for hunting only and were seldom seen. Horses and overused tractors shared the fields. The stories were told by a gently humorous narrator who ran the general store. Reflecting Canada's different culture and history, there were no stagecoach robberies, range wars, or wagon trains fending off hostile Indians with the help of the cavalry. When the Royal Canadian Mounted Police were introduced in one episode, they were parodied. There were no prim school marms or whores with hearts of gold. The women were occasionally in the foreground but only as full partners to the men—and they never needed rescue.

The series introduced actor Chief Dan George as Ol' Antoine and was distinguished in the 1960s by the fact that all actors representing Indian characters were members of the First Nations. *Cariboo Country* was shot in black and white in documentary style without programmatic music or rapid edits. It used laconic but superbly allusive dialogue, marked by silences and honed by St. Pierre's ear for dialect.

Notable episodes included the historical flashback called "The Strong Ones," about the reaction of a young man to the fact that his Indian mother and her children—who are involved in an "up-country" relationship with a successful rancher—are suddenly displaced by a "suitable" bride from the East. Another episode, "One Small Ranch," documents the struggles of Smith, a recurring character, and his wife to survive harsh weather, low prices, and government interference on their marginal ranch. It also explains with ironic humor why they refuse to sell it to wealthy hunters from "outside." In "Sarah's Copper," a young couple eventually refuse to sell a precious artifact—a "copper," which signifies for Northwest Coast aboriginal peoples wealth, prestige, and an honorable history—to a white collector for his apartment wall. Their choice is made more difficult because it means they will have to do without a new truck. "All Indian," like Keatley's *Beachcombers,* tried to be authentic and responsive to concerns about cultural appropriation long before the term was widely used. This episode refuted the myth that "all Indians are the same" by showing a cross-cultural conflict between a husband from the Cariboo and his coast Salish wife who is "kidnapped" by her people to become a spirit dancer. The episode included a trailer pointing out that none of the dances shown were authentic. Other episodes looked at an old rancher who competes in the rodeo until it kills him, and at the conflict between a métis and his wife who bears him an imperfect child and then leaves him. Like most of the episodes of *Cariboo Country,* few of these had linear plots or neatly wrapped endings.

Three specials were developed from the series. The award-winning *The Education of Phyllistine* (pulled together from two half-hour episodes) not only explains the roots of the heedless racism that drives an Indian child out of a small rural school but also explores the relationship between the child and Ol' Antoine, her grandfather. The second, *How to Break a Quarterhorse,* was commissioned for the prestigious anthology *Festival* during the 1967 centennial. It is a story of justice Cariboo style—the recent history of exploitation and racism that motivates a murder is taken into account when a fugitive surrenders after ten years on the run, and he is acquitted by a Cariboo jury. The story's other plotline focuses on how Smith, Ol' Antoine's old friend, gets involved in the outcome of the case. After a less-successful third drama special, *Sister Balonika,* Keately moved on to *Beachcombers,* while St. Pierre continued to write short stories about the Cariboo.

St. Pierre and Keately enjoyed the freedom of being away from Toronto, production headquarters of English Canada, and were thus able to make filmed drama when it was not usually done. *Cariboo Country* was broadcast on CBC-owned stations only and then was presented as part of *The Serial* (despite the fact that each episode was self-sufficient). It remains one of the very best works of television created in English Canada on the CBC or the private networks.

MARY JANE MILLER

See also **Canadian Programming in English**

Cast (irregular)

Arch MacGregor	Ted Stidder
Ken Larsen	Wally Marsh
Smith	David Hughes
Norah Smith	Lillian Carlson
Morton Dillonbeigh	Buck Kendt
Mrs. Dillonbeigh	Rae Brown
Ol' Antoine	Chief Dan George
Walter Charlie	Merv Campone
Sarah	Jean Sandy
Johnny	Paul Stanley
Frenchie	Joseph Golland

Producers

Philip Keatley, Frank Goodship

Programming History

CBC

1959	two episodes
July 1960–September 1960	13 half-hour episodes
1964–66	mixture of various episodes, repeats and new, aired intermittently
1967	one 1-hour special
1969	one 90-minute special

Further Reading

Miller, Mary Jane, "*Cariboo Country:* The CBC Response to the American Television Western," *American Journal of Canadian Studies* (Fall 1984)

Carney, Art (1918–2003)

U.S. Actor

Art Carney's many noteworthy achievements as an actor will always be overshadowed by one role: Ed Norton. Carney made his reputation as the loyal but dopey neighbor, Ed Norton, opposite Jackie Gleason's Ralph Kramden in the classic sketches and series *The Honeymooners.* So complete was Carney's transformation into the loose-limbed, bumbling sewer worker that he won five Emmy Awards for his work with Gleason, including three consecutive awards as Best Supporting Actor from 1953 to 1955.

Carney got his start in show business doing imitations and comedy bits with Horace Heidt's orchestra. Stints in radio and bit parts in films led to Carney's first regular role on television on *The Morey Amsterdam Show.* When Jackie Gleason took over as host of the DuMont network's *Cavalcade of Stars,* Carney became a principal supporting player. He moved with the show to CBS in 1952, where it was rechristened *The Jackie Gleason Show* and "The Honeymooners" became a regular sketch.

Ed Norton may have been second banana to Ralph Kramden, but Carney's performance never took a backseat to Gleason's. Indeed, the pair created a symbiosis of comic styles so unique that when Carney left the show in 1957 "The Honeymooners" went on hiatus until his return almost ten years later. In contrast to Gleason's broad, blustery Kramden, Carney's Norton was the personification of nonchalance. His casual delivery could make any statement sound vacuous. Even his typical greeting, "Hey-hey, Ralphie boy," announced Norton's childlike amicability as well as his lack of intelligence. Carney's face drooped into a slack-jawed expression that was perpetually blank. Coupled with his feebleminded manner was a body like a rubber band. It could be as slouched as the hat that was always perched on his head at one moment, then snapping into improbable contortions the next. Carney seemed to make up for Ed's lack of intelligence by investing the character with a host of broad physical tics that could turn a game of pool, a few moments on a pinball machine, or a mambo step, into a comic ballet. Much like the great silent comedians, Carney created a wholly original character who was recognizable at a glance. In Ed Norton we find the pathos of Chaplin, the earnestness of Lloyd, and the physical grace of Keaton.

Even though the *Gleason Show* and the role of Ed Norton cemented Carney's success as a comedian, he was never content to be known as merely a comic actor. When the program moved to CBS, Carney's agent negotiated for the actor to have three out of every 13 weeks off to perform in noncompetitive shows. Carney built up a solid background as a dramatic performer on episodes of *Studio One, Suspense, Kraft Television Theatre,* and *Playhouse 90,* and in special events such as a telecast of Thornton Wilder's *Our Town.* By the latter part of the decade, critics had come to take the excellence of Carney's dramatic performances for granted. When he appeared in the lead in Rod Serling's teleplay "The Velvet Alley" on *Playhouse 90,* the *Vari-*

Art Carney, c. late 1950s–early 1960s.
Courtesy of the Everett Collection

ety review of January 28, 1959, commented, "Carney achieved considerable stature as a dramatic actor with his remarkable performance."

In 1966 Carney returned to *The Jackie Gleason Show,* and the role of Norton. That same year, he captured one of the coveted slots as a guest villain ("The Archer") in ABC's wildly popular *Batman* series. He had achieved success on Broadway, creating the role of Felix Unger in the original run of Neil Simon's *The Odd Couple.* And he was maturing as an actor. Lacking any formal training in the profession, Carney drew from his own life to build performances. Overcoming battles with alcoholism and depression seemed to add depth and wisdom to his characterizations. His ability to convey a sense of loneliness and world-weary resignation tended to belie his relative youth. This was evident in his film work, including his Academy Award–winning portrayal as an old man traveling across the country with his cat in *Harry and Tonto* (1974), and as the aging hardboiled detective in *The Late Show* (1977). He also had impressive performances in television movies, such as his low-key portrayal of Robert Stroud, "the Birdman of Alcatraz," in *Alcatraz: The Whole Shocking Story* (1980). Despite a flourishing career for theatrical features, Carney continually returned to the medium that made him a star. He took the lead in the short-lived series *Lanigan's Rabbi* (1977), did guest appearances on shows such as *Alice* and *Fame,* and was featured in specials and telefilms. He won a sixth Emmy in a heartfelt performance as the loyal caretaker of an elderly boxing champion (played by Jimmy Cagney in his last role) in *Terrible Joe Moran* (1984).

Constant reruns of *The Honeymooners* and the packaging of the so-called lost "Honeymooners" sketches from *The Jackie Gleason Show* have guaranteed Art Carney's place in the pantheon of television comedians. But to be given his full due, Carney must be recognized as one of the most accomplished and multifaceted actors to emerge during television's "golden age."

ERIC SCHAEFER

See also **Gleason, Jackie; *Honeymooners, The***

Art Carney (Arthur William Matthew Carney). Born in Mount Vernon, New York, November 4, 1918. Attended A.B. Davis High School, Mount Vernon, New York. Married: 1) Jean Myers (twice), 1940 (divorced, 1965) and 1977 (divorced); children: Ellen, Brian, Paul; 2) Barbara Isaac. Served in U.S. Army, 1944–45. Began entertainment career as member of the Horace Heidt Orchestra, 1936–39; vaudeville and club performer, 1939–40; radio performer, 1942–44, 1945–49; began television career on *The Morey Amsterdam Show,* 1948; featured performer in various versions of *The Jackie Gleason Show,* 1952–70; various guest performances in television series from 1950s. Recipient: six Emmy Awards; two Sylvania Awards; Academy Award, 1974; Best Actor, National Society of Film Critics, 1977. Died in Chester, Connecticut, November 9, 2003.

Television

1948–50	*The Morey Amsterdam Show*
1952–59, 1966–70	*The Jackie Gleason Show*
1955–56	*The Honeymooners*
1966–68	*Batman*
1977	*Lanigan's Rabbi*
1986–89	*The Cavanaughs*

Made-for-Television Movies

1972	*The Snoop Sisters*
1975	*Katherine*
1975	*Death Scream*
1976	*Lanigan's Rabbi*
1979	*Letters from Frank*
1980	*Alcatraz: The Whole Shocking Story*
1980	*Fighting Back*
1981	*Bitter Harvest*
1984	*Terrible Joe Moran*
1984	*The Night They Saved Christmas*
1984	*The Emperor's New Clothes*
1984	*A Doctor's Story*
1985	*The Undergrads*
1985	*Izzy and Moe*
1985	*The Blue Yonder*
1986	*Miracle of the Heart: A Boys Town Story*
1990	*Where Pigeons Go to Die*

Films

Pot of Gold, 1941; *The Yellow Rolls-Royce,* 1965; *A Guide for the Married Man,* 1967; *Harry and Tonto,* 1974; *W.W. and the Dixie Dancekings,* 1975; *Won Ton Ton, the Dog Who Saved Hollywood,* 1976; *Scott Joplin,* 1977; *The Late Show,* 1977; *Movie Movie,* 1978; *House Calls,* 1978; *Sunburn,* 1979; *Ravagers,* 1979; *Going in Style,* 1979; *Steel,* 1980; *Roadie,* 1980; *Defiance,* 1980; *Take This Job and Shove It,* 1981; *St. Helens,* 1981; *Better Late Than Never,* 1982; *The Naked Face,* 1984; *The Muppets Take Manhattan,* 1984; *Firestarter,* 1984; *Night Friend,* 1987; *Last Action Hero,* 1993.

Stage

Harvey, 1956; *The Rope Dancers,* 1957; *Take Her, She's Mine,* 1961; *The Odd Couple,* 1965; *Lovers,* 1968; *The Prisoner of Second Avenue,* 1972; *The*

Odd Couple, 1974; *The Prisoner of Second Avenue, Long Island, New York,* 1974.

Further Reading

Bishop, Jim, *The Golden Ham: A Candid Biography of Jackie Gleason,* New York: Simon and Schuster, 1956
Crescenti, Peter, *The Official Honeymooners Treasury: To the Moon and Back with Ralph, Norton, Alice, and Trixie,* New York: Perigee, 1990
Hall, Jane, "Reunited for a Made-for-TV Movie, Jackie Gleason and Art Carney Savor a Wacky Second Honeymoon," *People Weekly* (September 23, 1985)
Henry, William A., *The Great One: The Life and Legend of Jackie Gleason,* New York: Doubleday, 1992
Marc, David, *Comic Visions: Television Comedy and American Culture,* Boston: Unwin Hyman, 1989; 2nd edition, Malden, Massachusetts: Blackwell, 1997
McCrohan, Donna, *The Honeymooners' Companion: The Kramdens and the Nortons Revisited,* New York: Workman, 1978
McCrohan, Donna, and Peter Crescenti, *The Honeymooners Lost Episodes,* New York: Workman, 1986
Meadows, Audrey, *Love Alice: My Life as a Honeymooner,* New York: Crown, 1994
Mitz, Rick, *The Great TV Sitcom Book,* New York: Marek, 1980
Waldron, Vince, *Classic Sitcoms: A Celebration of the Best of Prime-Time Comedy,* New York: Macmillan, 1987
Zolotow, Maurice, "The All-Out Art of Art Carney," *Reader's Digest* (October 1989)

Carol Burnett Show, The

U.S. Comedy/Variety Show

When *The Carol Burnett Show* aired in September 1967 on CBS, no one expected it to run 11 years. The show gave Carol Burnett, along with regulars Harvey Korman, Vicki Lawrence, Lyle Waggoner (who left in 1974), and Tim Conway (whose occasional guest appearances became permanent in 1975), an opportunity to fuse the best of live vaudeville-style performance with the creative benefits of time and tape. Burnett's ensemble quickly bonded into a tight unit of professionals who looked and acted as if performing on *The Carol Burnett Show* was the best fun an entertainer could have. In reality, the meticulously structured, musical-comedy program became one of the last, and one of the finest, prime-time variety shows to link the modern television age with Tin Pan Alley and the golden ages of motion pictures and television.

The show brought Carol Burnett's working-class persona into a unique relationship with her audience. There was a glamorous, celebrity-brushed side to her work: Burnett could wear exclusive Bob Mackie gowns, banter with popular celebrities, and illustrate her brilliant talent for physical and intellectual comedy in cleverly written and produced skits. Her musical abilities ranged from Shubert's Alley to more refined venues, and her voice could amuse and inspire. She vamped with Hollywood royalty: Lucille Ball, Liza Minnelli, Sammy Davis Jr. Even California governor Ronald Reagan joked and performed. On the other hand, Burnett's charwoman character; her dysfunctional and beleaguered "family" member, Eunice; her zestful Tarzan call; and her weekly question-and-answer sessions with the studio audience gave her an accessibility and down-to-earth warmth that firmly reinstated her within the world of her viewers. The dichotomy between the two Carols (one homespun, the other neon-minted) gave *The Carol Burnett Show* a flavor and personality that showcased the idiosyncrasies of its eponymous star. Only later did Burnett reveal the source of that working-class quality—the talented comedian had lifted herself from appalling poverty, a dysfunctional family, and emotional abuse to become a beloved star. One of Burnett's insightful actions, as she constructed her characters and her persona, was to draw on the contradictions that informed her artistic evolution.

Throughout the show's run, Burnett maintained, and increased, her creative input and control. She worked closely with a team of writers, among them Ken Welch and his wife, Mitzi, who had a strong sense of Burnett's attributes and strengths. (Ken Welch had written the famous "I Made a Fool of Myself over John Foster Dulles" routine that had catapulted comic chanteuse Burnett to fame in 1956.) The show combined musical comedy with humorous sketches, using the ensemble of players as well as weekly guest stars, such as Jim Naybors, Cher, and Julie Andrews.

Burnett's three-tiered abilities—singer, actress, comedian—allowed the writers to create and sustain

The Carol Burnett Show, Harvey Korman, Vicki Lawrence, Lyle Waggoner, Carol Burnett, 1967–79.
Courtesy of the Everett Collection

characters throughout the 11-year run. The charwoman, whose pantomimed mishaps often brought her into the shadow of greatness, became the show's trademark; a caricature of the dusty maid adorned credits and teasers for the program. Eunice, who was always under the abusive power of her mama, blended the kind of sharply sketched comedy and tragedy that marks the finest comedic characters. Eunice, Mama, and the rest of the working-class family members insulted, demeaned, and belittled one another in acrimonious skits that revealed the dark heart of a family in turmoil. Critics complained that Eunice became more disturbing, rather than amusing, as the show progressed. Eventually, the family skits were spun off into a situation comedy, without Burnett, titled *Mama's Family,* in which Vicki Lawrence reprised her role as the bilious Mama.

The *Carol Burnett Show* centered on Burnett, but its enduring qualities also arose from its talented ensemble of players, whose interactions contributed to the overwhelming sense of "live" performance exuded by the show. Vicki Lawrence was fresh out of high school when her resemblance to Burnett won her a role; her transformation from sprightly youth to dour Mama astonished and delighted audience and cast. The infamous comic rivalry between perennially bemused Harvey Korman and the irrepressible Tim Conway remains one of the show's most distinctive features, as Conway's scripted and ad-libbed high jinks forced Korman to battle uncontrollable laughter during skits. Bits would halt as Korman struggled to stay in character; Conway would continue to pile on more egregious additions, trying to break up his costar. While the other cast members joined in unexpected breakups, the anarchic camaraderie of Korman and Conway became legendary.

These refreshing ad-libs often appeared during movie parodies, another of the show's trademarks. Burnett had been deeply influenced by classical Hollywood films during her childhood, and she and her writers drew from a copious knowledge of motion pictures to design film-related skits. Nothing was sacred: genres, films, actors, and characters from familiar and obscure pictures provided fodder for the ensemble. A takeoff of *Gone with the Wind* ("Went with the Wind") found Burnett dressed in Bob Mackie window drapes, complete with curtain rods doubling as shoulder pads, rolling down the stairs as she deconstructed one of the film's most famous moments, Scarlett's miscarriage during a fight with Rhett. "From Here to Maternity," "Sunnyset Boulevard," "Lovely Story": Burnett and her ensemble paid tribute to a bygone golden age with arch and loving comic elegies.

The show ended in 1978, still attaining decent ratings at a time when variety shows no longer attracted large audiences. Burnett wished to go on to other projects and wanted to close *The Carol Burnett Show* while it could still entertain its viewers. The show periodically appears in syndication as *Carol and Company;* in 1992 *Carol Burnett: A Reunion* brought highlights of the run back to CBS prime time, where the special did well in the ratings. Ultimately, *The Carol Burnett Show* represents a sophisticated fusion of music, comedy, drama, celebrity, parody, and slapstick that both resurrected and archived the traditions of America's vaudeville-variety past.

KATHRYN C. D'ALESSANDRO

See also **Burnett, Carol**

Regular Performers
Carol Burnett
Harvey Korman (1967–77)
Lyle Waggoner (1967–74)
Vicki Lawrence
Tim Conway (1975–79)
Dick Van Dyke (1977)
Kenneth Mars (1979)
Craig Richard Nelson (1979)

Music
The Harry Zimmerman Orchestra (1967–71)
The Peter Matz Orchestra (1971–78)

Dancers
The Ernest Flatt Dancers

Programming History
CBS

September 1967–May 1971	Monday 10:00–11:00
September 1971–November 1972	Wednesday 8:00–9:00
December 1972–December 1977	Saturday 10:00–11:00
December 1977–March 1978	Sunday 10:00–11:00
June 1978–August 1978	Wednesday 8:00–9:00

ABC

August 1979–September 1979	Saturday 8:00–9:00

Further Reading

Beifuss, John, "So Glad We Had This Time Together," *The Commercial Appeal* (December 1, 2000)
King, Susan, "Q&A: Carol Burnett Videos Put Shows Back Together," *Los Angeles Times* (October 10, 2000)
Marc, David, "Carol Burnett: The Last of the Big-Time Comedy-Variety Stars," *Quarterly Review of Film Studies* (July 1992)
O'Connor, John J., "Funny Women of Television: A Museum of Television and Radio Tribute," *New York Times* (October 24, 1991)

Carsey, Marcy (1944–)

U.S. Producer

Marcy Carsey, one of the most successful situation comedy producers of the 1980s and 1990s, is co-owner of the Carsey-Werner Company, an independent television production company responsible for two of the most highly rated and longest running sitcoms on TV, *The Cosby Show* and *Roseanne.* Carsey has a number of notable accomplishments in the television industry: she developed the concept of building a sitcom around a single stand-up comedian; she established one of the first successful production companies to operate independently of the networks; and she is frequently named one of the most powerful women in show business.

Carsey began her career in television in the 1960s as a tour guide at NBC, later becoming a story editor for the Tomorrow Entertainment company. In 1974 she joined ABC as a program executive concentrating on comedy programming, rising to senior vice president of prime-time series in 1978. While at ABC, she developed some of the most successful shows of that era, including *Mork and Mindy, Soap,* and *Happy Days.* In 1980, she left ABC and in 1982 started Carsey Productions, an independent production company. She was joined in this venture a year later by Tom Werner, who had worked with her at ABC. They remain equal partners in the Carsey-Werner Company.

The programs produced by Carsey-Werner have been notable for their innovation in pushing the boundaries of traditional sitcom fare. *The Cosby Show,* the first sitcom about an African-American family to sustain wide, diverse, and enduring popularity, consistently led in the ratings for several years. It was Carsey-Werner's first hit show, employing the formula that helped to establish them as a television production powerhouse: building a family-based situation comedy around a popular, established stand-up comedian. *Cosby* aired in prime time for eight seasons and is currently in worldwide syndication. With virtually no track record when they sold *Cosby* to NBC, the company's success was firmly established, as well as its reputation as a source of programming.

In *Roseanne,* Carsey-Werner continued the concept of a show starring a well-known comedian, in this case Roseanne (then Roseanne Barr). *Roseanne* was a centerpiece of the ABC programming schedule from its debut in 1988 until it ceased production in 1997. In contrast to *Cosby,* which was about an upper-middle-class family, *Roseanne* featured a working-class woman with husband and children, a perspective not usually found in prime-time sitcoms. The character Roseanne was closely based on the persona evident in Barr's stand-up performances, which she derived from

Marcy Carsey, 1978.
Courtesy of the Everett Collection/CSU Archives

her personal experiences. Not only was the main character relatively authentic, the program received critical acclaim for the topics it addressed and the quality of the writing. It gained a reputation for scathing dialogue and controversial plotlines, while sustaining high ratings.

In addition to *Cosby* and *Roseanne,* Carsey and Werner have a number of other popular situation comedies to their credit, including *Grace Under Fire, A Different World,* and *Cybill.* Beginning with *The Cosby Show,* Carsey-Werner programs have emphasized nonmainstream, nontraditional, and ethnic family groupings. This can be seen in the flops as much as the hits—shows like *Chicken Soup,* starring Jewish comedian Jackie Mason, and *Frannie's Turn,* based on the life of a single working-class mother.

Carsey and Werner led the wave of independent production companies in the 1980s that resisted affiliation with a major network or distributor. Carsey-Werner shows have appeared on all three major broadcast networks. They retain (or have repurchased) control of syndication rights for reruns of their hit shows and have produced original programming for syndication—for example, a revival of the Groucho Marx quiz show *You Bet Your Life* hosted by Bill Cosby, which aired briefly in the early 1990s. In 1995 Carsey-Werner ventured into the feature film industry by founding Carsey-Werner Moving Pictures. Carsey has been quoted as saying that the secret of the success of Carsey-Werner's shows has to do with their preference for thinking up "people and ideas together" and for "atypical casting."

Carsey has been touted as one of the few women in a high-level executive position in television and one of the most successful American women in show business. She has been on the board of directors of the Academy of Television Arts and Sciences and is currently a member of the University of Southern California School of Cinema-Television's Executive Advisory Council.

KATHRYN CIRKSENA

See also ***Cosby Show, The; Different World, A; Roseanne***

Marcy Carsey (Marcia Lee Peterson). Born in South Weymouth, Maine, 1944. Attended the University of New Hampshire, Durham, New Hampshire, B.A. in English literature 1966. Married: John Carsey, 1969; children: Rebecca and John. Program supervisor, William Esty advertising agency, 1960s; story editor, Tomorrow Entertainment, Los Angeles, 1971–74; program executive, later senior vice president for prime-time series, ABC Television, 1974–80; founder, Carsey Productions, Los Angeles, 1982; co-owner, Carsey-Werner Productions, Los Angeles, from 1982; producer of numerous prime-time television series, including *The Cosby Show, A Different World,* and *Roseanne,* from 1982. Won an Emmy Award in 1985 for *The Cosby Show.* Nominated again in 1986 and 1987. Nominated again in 1998 for *3rd Rock from the Sun.* Won a Crystal Award in 1990 and a Lucy Award in 2000. Inducted into the PGA Hall of Fame for *The Cosby Show* in 2000.

Television (producer/executive producer)

1983	*Oh, Madeline*
1984–92	*The Cosby Show*
1987–93	*A Different World*
1988–97	*Roseanne*
1989–90	*Chicken Soup*
1990	*Grand*
1991	*Davis Rules*
1992–93	*You Bet Your Life (starring Bill Cosby)*
1992	*Frannie's Turn*
1993–98	*Grace Under Fire*
1995–98	*Cybill*
1996	*Cosby*
1996	*Townies*
1996–2001	*3rd Rock from the Sun*
1998	*Damon*
1998–	*That 70s Show*

2000	*God, the Devil and Bob*
2000	*Normal, Ohio*
2001–	*Grounded for Life*
2001	*You Don't Know Jack*
2001	*The Downer Channel*
2002	*That 80s Show*
2002	*The Cosby Show: A Look Back*
2003–	*The Tracey Morgan Show*
2003–	*Whoopi*

Further Reading

"Carsey-Werner: The Little Programming Engine That Did," *Broadcasting* (July 18, 1988)
Gerard, Jeremy, "What Have They Done for Us Lately?" *New York Times Magazine* (November 25, 1990)
Grover, Ronald, "Can This TV Team Go Five for Five?" *Business Week* (June 19, 1989)
Walley, Wayne, "Carsey-Werner: Cosby's Co-Pilots Stay Small and Lean," *Advertising Age* (June 16, 1986)

Carson, Johnny (1925–)

U.S. Comedian, Talk Show Host

Johnny Carson is best known as America's late-night king of comedy. For 30 years he hosted NBC television's *The Tonight Show;* his topical monologues, irreverent characters, comical double takes, and frivolous sketches entertained more people than any other performer in history. His late-night arena provided plugs for untold books, films, and products; created a springboard to stardom for an infinite number of new performers; and more than occasionally offered a secure refuge for aging legends.

Carson began performing professionally at the age of 14 as a magician-comic, "The Great Carsoni," for the local Rotary Club in his hometown of Norfolk, Nebraska. After a two-year stint as a Navy ensign during World War II and four years as a radio-drama major at the University of Nebraska, he plunged headfirst into the world of broadcasting as a radio announcer/disc jockey. When WOW in Omaha began television operations in 1949, Carson was there to host his first video program, *The Squirrel's Nest,* a daily early-afternoon show. The young performer told jokes, conducted humorous interviews, and staged various skits with wacky comic characters and premises. *Squirrel's Nest* gave Carson the opportunity to develop a good portion of his public persona and adjust his performance style to the intimate visual medium.

Relocating to Hollywood in the early 1950s, Carson's television career took a step forward with his weekly low-budget series, *Carson's Cellar,* on CBS's KNXT. Performing monologues and satirical sketches reminiscent of his later work, Carson attracted the attention of such stars as Fred Allen, Groucho Marx, and Red Skelton—all of whom dropped by to appear on the local show at no charge. Based on his work with *Carson's Cellar,* a more sophisticated *Johnny Carson Show* was created for regional broadcasts in the western United States. This program proved unsuccessful, and Carson subsequently began work for *The Red Skelton Show* as a writer.

Casting about for new on-air opportunities, Carson's first prime-time network television exposure happened in May 1954, as host of the short-lived quiz show *Earn Your Vacation.* Fortunately, working for Skelton provided more of a career boost. When Skelton was injured during a show rehearsal, the young Carson was thrust instantly into the limelight as substitute host. On the strength of this appearance, CBS created a new prime-time *Johnny Carson Show,* a traditional potpourri of comedy, music, dance, skits, and monologues. Working through seven writers and eight directors in 39 weeks, the troubled show left the air because of poor ratings.

As quizmaster of the ABC-TV daytime show *Who Do You Trust?* in 1957, Carson's career again took an upward turn. This highly rated daytime entry allowed Carson to display his engaging personality and quick wit through five years of continual give-and-take with a wide variety of guests. During this time, he also worked at extending his reputation and base of experience by appearing on a number of television musical variety shows and game shows, on Broadway, and as a guest actor in live television plays. Most importantly, Carson's successes brought him offers to substitute for Jack Paar as guest host on *The Tonight Show* and ultimately to replace Paar when the temperamental emcee retired.

Johnny Carson.
Photo courtesy of Carson Productions

On October 1, 1962, Carson broadcast his first *Tonight Show* as permanent host. Less excitable and emotional than his predecessor, Carson's relaxed pace, more casual interviewing style, impeccable timing, and ability to play straight man for other guests proved instantly popular with his viewing audience. Comparing differences between Paar and Carson, *Time* magazine reported on May 28, 1965, that "Paar's emotionalism had made the show the biggest sleep stopper since caffeine. By contrast, Carson came on like pure Sanka. But soon his low-key, affable humor began to prove addictive. Paar generated new interest, but Carson is watched."

Within four months of assuming the *Tonight Show* reins, Carson surpassed Paar's old record night-time ratings by nearly a half million viewers, adding approximately 20 stations to the NBC network—this despite heavy CBS competition from former *Tonight Show* host Steve Allen. Incredibly, over a 15-year period, with continual competitive threats from CBS and ABC, *The Tonight Show* doubled its audience. Observed Kenneth Tynan in his *New Yorker* portrait of Carson on February 20, 1978, this was "a feat that, in its blend of staying power and mounting popularity, is without precedent in the history of television."

Despite occasional contract squabbles, criticism over his numerous days off, marital conflicts, and assorted family problems, Carson continued to outdistance his competition for an additional 15 years. Without losing his timing, his unpredictability, or his perfectionist work ethic, for 30 years he kept his finger on the pulse of mainstream America's moods, attitudes, and concerns. Combining his verbal dexterity with a well-stocked supply of facial expressions and gestures, he became the acknowledged master at lampooning the pretentious, salvaging the boring, or sharpening a nervous guest's performance for maximum effect.

Through the years, Carson hosted a number of network television specials, including the Academy Awards and Emmy Awards, and performed stand-up comedy at the top hotels in Las Vegas. But it was *The Tonight Show* that guaranteed his place in American history. For 30 years, he entered U.S. homes to provide commentary on the day's news, to help determine the next day's conversational agenda, and, of course, to entertain. Over time, his mild-mannered, Midwestern brand of humor became more politically biting and sexually frank but never demeaning or offensive. His well-known characters, like Carnac, Aunt Blabby, and Art Fern, so familiar to multiple generations of American families, remained brash, silly, and, somehow, consistently funny.

On May 22, 1992, at the age of 66, Johnny Carson left *The Tonight Show*—a remarkable 30-year run in more than a half century of comedy performance that raised him to the level of national court jester and national treasure. Expected to maintain a comparable level of visibility in retirement, Carson has surprised his public by turning down nearly all requests for television appearances and interviews. Exceptions to this include cameos on Bob Hope's 90th birthday special in 1993 and on the *Late Show with David Letterman* in 1994. Substituting tennis, boating, and travel for the national limelight, Carson has led a somewhat reclusive life but generated major publicity on the occasion of his successful quadruple-bypass heart surgery on March 19, 1999. He has also been noted for his generous contributions, totaling millions of dollars, for charitable causes in the United States and Africa.

JOEL STERNBERG

See also **Talk Show; *Tonight Show, The***

Johnny (John William) Carson. Born in Corning, Iowa, October 23, 1925. Attended the University of Nebraska, Lincoln, B.A., 1949. Ensign, U.S. Navy, World War II. Married: 1) Jody Wolcott, 1948 (divorced, 1963), children: Chris, Ricky, Cory; 2) Joanne Copeland, 1963 (divorced); 3) Joanna Holland, 1972 (divorced, 1983); 4) Alexis Maas, 1987. Began career as radio announcer, KFAB, Lincoln, Nebraska, 1948; announcer, WOW and WOW-TV, Omaha, Nebraska; announcer, KNXT-TV, Los Angeles, California, 1950; began television with *Carson's Cellar,* a comedy-variety-talk show, KNXT-TV, 1951; writer, *The Red Skelton Show,* on-air replacement for the injured Skelton, 1954; host-star of quiz show, *The Johnny Carson Show,* 1955–56; succeeded Jack Paar as host of *The Tonight Show,* October 1, 1962; last telecast May 22, 1992. Recipient: four Emmy Awards; Friar's Club Entertainer of the Year Awards, 1965, 1969; Harvard Hasty Pudding Club Man of the Year, 1977.

Television

1951–52	*Carson's Cellar*
1954	*Earn Your Vacation*
1955–56	*The Johnny Carson Show*
1957–62	*Who Do You Trust?*
1961–62	*To Tell the Truth*
1962–92	*The Tonight Show Starring Johnny Carson*

Made-for-Television Movie

1993	*The Positively True Adventures of the Alleged Texas Cheerleader-Murdering Mom*

Film

Looking for Love, 1965

Publications

Happiness Is... a Dry Martini, 1965
Unhappiness Is... a Blind Date, 1967

Further Reading

"Carson to Library: Heeere's Money!" *Library Journal* (March 15, 2001)
Corkery, Paul, *Carson: The Unauthorized Biography,* Ketchum, Idaho: Randt, 1987
Cox, Stephen, *Here's Johnny!: Thirty Years of America's Favorite Late-Night Entertainment,* New York: Harmony, 1992
de Cordova, Fred, *Johnny Came Lately: An Autobiography,* New York: Simon and Schuster, 1988
"The Last Monologue: Nostalgia and a Few Political Digs," transcript, *New York Times* (May 23, 1992)
Leamer, Laurence, *King of the Night: The Life of Johnny Carson,* New York: Morrow, 1989
McMahon, Ed, with Carroll Carroll, *Here's Ed: The Autobiography of Ed McMahon,* New York: Berkley Medallion, 1976
Metz, Robert, *The Tonight Show,* Chicago: Playboy Press, 1980
Rosenfield, Paul, *The Club Rules: Power, Money, Sex, and Fear: How It Works in Hollywood,* New York: Warner, 1992
Smith, Ronald L., *Johnny Carson: An Unauthorized Biography,* New York: St. Martin's Press, 1987
Van Hise, James, *40 Years at Night: The Story of the Tonight Show,* Las Vegas, Nevada: Pioneer, 1992

Carter, Thomas

U.S. Actor, Director, Producer

Thomas Carter's award-winning career in television has included acting, directing, and producing. Carter also has directed major motion pictures such as *Metro* and *Save the Last Dance.* However, when Carter arrived in Hollywood in the mid-1970s, focused on an acting career, he claimed he could not find roles for African Americans like himself: "I had to learn to 'street it up' a bit to get work" (Gunther, p. C22).

Carter grew up in a small Texas town with no apparent hints of a regional accent, a result he credits to the voices he heard on TV. Ironically, after graduating from Southwest Texas State University, his career in television began by playing northern teenagers in two series, *Szysznyk* and *The White Shadow.* He also made guest appearances on such series as *M*A*S*H, Good Times, Lou Grant,* and *Hill Street Blues.* Interestingly, Carter ended his acting career in a role requiring a rich Jamaican accent, playing Orderly John in the film *Whose Life Is It Anyway?*

Carter gave up acting to become one of television's most sought-after dramatic directors. Following his role of James Hayward on *The White Shadow,* he had directed episodes of the series: "*White Shadow* was what did it. Just being on that set. My film school was the set" (Hughes, p. 1). But after a string of successful pilots for award-winning television dramas such as *St. Elsewhere, Miami Vice, I'll Fly Away,* and *Equal Justice,* he became known as Thomas Carter, "television pilot king." He also directed the pilots for *Call to Glory* and *Midnight Caller* and episodes for such television series as *Alfred Hitchcock Presents, Bret Maverick, Remington Steele, Amazing Stories,* and *Fame.* Despite these successful TV ventures, Carter still proclaimed, "I look at television and I don't see myself" (Gunther, p. C22), referring to a dearth of middle-class, mainstream, African-American characters on television. His production company created and produced episodes of excellent television series such as *Equal Justice* (1990–91). Though short-lived, this series included African-American characters such as Michael James, superbly played by Joe Morton.

By the mid-1990s, Carter had reached a high point and created *Under One Roof,* the first hour-long series to focus on the daily lives of an extended African-American family. The pilot received strong support at the African American Filmmakers Foundation in 1994. Picked up by CBS a year later, the series debuted in March as a mid-season replacement. *Under One Roof* received considerable attention, and as creator and executive producer Carter acknowledged the historical significance of the series: "No African American family with this kind of breadth and complexity has even been shown on a weekly drama. Never has there been one with the amount of talent and experience that has gone into this show" (Braxton, p. 7). Although Carter wanted stories that applied to people, not races, he also wanted an African-American family that debunked the misconception that blacks live lives that are vastly different from those of white people. He chose, however, not to dwell on the show's historical importance, concentrating instead on making an honest, revealing, and compelling drama.

Under One Roof starred James Earl Jones, Joe Morton, and Vanessa Bell Calloway, who, like Morton, had also appeared in *Equal Justice.* Like *Equal Justice, Under One Roof* was long on quality but short on viewers. Although CBS did not renew the series after its six-episode run, Carter credited the network for putting the show on the schedule.

Carter's awards include a Directors Guild of America Award for Outstanding Directorial Achievement in Dramatic Shows for *Hill Street Blues* (1981). He has received two Emmys, one for Outstanding Directing in a Drama Series for *Equal Justice* (1990), the other for Outstanding Made for Television Movie for *Don King: Only in America* (1998), which also received a Peabody Award. He has been nominated for the Emmy Award six times.

Carter is an advocate for increased African-American participation in Hollywood. He believes the resistance to telling stories about African-American experiences results from decision makers at studios and networks whose perceptions are dominated by the limitations of their own experiences with white society. Yet he remains optimistic, in part because of his own success as a pioneer: "When more Blacks in the industry reach my position—where they can breed familiarity with the real power brokers—then we'll get more significant shots." In Carter's opinion, this business does not have a closed door: "You just have to make your own opportunities. It may be harder for us to break in, but we can do it" (Brown, p. 100).

DWIGHT BROOKS

See also **Racism, Ethnicity and Television**

Television Series (director; miscellaneous episodes)

UC: Undercover
Bronx County
Michael Hayes
Divas
Under One Roof
Equal Justice
Midnight Caller
A Year in the Life
Under the Influence
Heart of the City
Alfred Hitchcock Presents
Amazing Stories
Miami Vice
Call to Glory
St. Elsewhere
Remington Steele
Fame
Bret Maverick
Hill Street Blues
The White Shadow
Trauma Center

Acting Appearances

1972	*Snatches*
1976	*Good Times* (Jerry)
1977	*Lou Grant* (Chris)
1977	*M*A*S*H* (patient)
1977	*Szysnyk* (Ray Gun)
1978	*Lou Grant* (Chris)
1978–80	*The White Shadow* (James Hayward)
1982	*Hill Street Blues* (Donald Lilly)

Further Reading

Braxton, Greg, "Drama of a Different Color," *Los Angeles Times* (March 12, 1995)
Brown, Carolyn M., "Fighting for Airtime," *African American Enterprise* (December 1994)
Gunther, Mark, "The Color Barrier: Why Can't Black-Oriented Dramas Find a Place on TV?" *Chicago Tribune* (March 5, 1995)
Hughes, Mike, "James Earl Jones, Others All 'Under One Roof,' " Gannett News Service (March 12, 1995)
Scott, Matthew S., and Tariq K. Muhammad, "Top 50 African American Powerbrokers in Entertainment," *African American Enterprise* (December 1994)

Cartier, Rudolph (1904–1994)

British Producer, Director

When Rudolph Cartier died in June 1994, his obituaries unanimously credited him as the "inventor of television drama" and "a television pioneer." He was a television drama director at the British Broadcasting Corporation (BBC) from 1952 to the late 1960s (although the BBC preferred the title "producer" for their directors until the 1960s), and he was one of the first innovative television stylists working in British television during this period. The range of his 120 television productions (all for the BBC) stretched from the science fiction serial (*The Quatermass Experiment,* 1953; *Quatermass II,* 1955; *Quatermass and the Pit,* 1958), drama documentary (*Lee Oswald—Assassin,* 1966), and adaptations of classics (*Wuthering Heights,* 1953; *Anna Karenina,* 1961) to crime serials (*Maigret,* 1961, and *Z Cars,* 1963) and opera.

He was born Rudolph Katscher in Vienna in 1904 and studied to be an architect before attending classes given by Max Reinhardt, which had an important impact on him. In 1929 he submitted a script to a film company in Berlin, which accepted it, and he was enrolled as a staff writer (paired with Egon Eis) scripting low-budget crime movies. He later moved on to writing for UFA and directed his first movie, *Unsichtbare Gegner,* in 1931. Cartier immigrated to Britain in 1935, but it was not until 1952 that he began work as a BBC television drama director. From this point until the mid-1960s, he directed more than 120 separate productions, most of them live studio plays, although he also had a penchant for televised opera adaptations.

Cartier did not expand the spectrum of BBC TV drama single-handedly, but he did offer some innovations both stylistically and thematically. BBC TV drama production has been perceived as consisting largely of adaptations of West End successes—theatrical, static stage performances respectfully and passively relayed by efficient BBC personnel—before Cartier's arrival on the scene. This is a false perception, although it captures the sense of impasse felt by a drama department that during the late 1940s was starved of funds, studio space, and equipment. The transformation of BBC drama in the early 1950s was the result of various factors, not simply Cartier's fortuitous arrival. By 1951 the expansion of television was under way: threats of a commercial competitor and increased funding for the TV department led to the acquisition of new studios, which were fitted with fresh equipment (new camera mountings, cranes, and so on). The largely ad hoc manner of production and training was formalized as training manuals and production courses were established.

The appointment of Michael Barry (a former drama director and an innovator in his own way, he had directed the first documentary-drama for the BBC) as head of drama established a continuity of drama policy that was to last a decade until Barry was replaced by Sydney Newman. Unlike his predecessors, Barry was convinced that TV drama had to rely less on dialogue and more on the "power of the image"; he contended that television had to be visibly televisual, not a discrete, passive relay medium. It was into this new, fertile environment that Cartier was employed, and he quickly took full advantage: "I said [to Barry] that the BBC needed new scripts, a new approach, a whole new spirit, rather than endlessly televising classics like Dickens or familiar London stage plays." Barry was initially receptive to these suggestions (drama directors were given a relative amount of freedom in the selection of their material).

One way of changing traditional approaches to drama direction was to change the material; instead of using current or recent West End successes, Cartier drew upon the science fiction genre and European modernist theater as well as the pulp-detective genres he had worked on in Germany. Initially, Cartier directed more unconventional, European modernist drama: Berthold Brecht, Jean-Paul Sartre, Jean Anouihl; later, he developed a partnership with the newly appointed BBC staff writer Nigel Kneale and directed works specifically written by Kneale for the medium, including the three *Quatermass* serials. Kneale later adapted George Orwell's *Nineteen Eighty-Four* for television and Cartier directed.

The impact of that play (transmitted live and repeated live a few days later, as was the norm) cannot be overstated. Produced in 1954, as cold war ideologies were being constructed and reinforced, the play's landscapes of totalitarian control resonated strongly with the public—some viewed the program as celebratory, as an anti-Soviet piece (an editorial in *The Times* praised the play for clarifying for the British public the "Communist practice of making words stand on their heads"); others were disgusted by the graphic depiction of torture (one letter to the BBC reads, "Dear Sir, *Nineteen Eighty-Four* was unspeakably putrid and depraved"). Questions were asked in Parliament about the tendency for BBC drama to "pander to sexual and sadistic tastes," and Cartier himself received death threats from those who considered the play antifascist (the BBC provided bodyguards for him).

Hidden behind the furor is an important point. If the 1953 BBC live broadcast of the coronation proved that television had a mass audience that could be united by a spectacle of national rebirth, Cartier's *Nineteen Eighty-Four* proved television's ability to influence, and frighten, a mass audience (one *Daily Express* headline read, "Wife Dies as She Watches"). It was the beginning of television's role as an agency of pernicious influence.

The power of that production rests with Cartier's explicit desire to influence and manipulate the television audience. *Nineteen Eighty-Four* is an exemplary instance of his technique: the mixture of powerful close-ups and expanded studio space. Writing in 1958, Cartier cited the close-up as a key tool of the TV director: "When the viewer was watching these 'horrific' TV productions of mine, he was completely in my power."

Another important element was his use of filmed inserts. The restrictive space of the Lime Grove studios meant that filmed inserts were usually location scenes introduced into the live studio action. In this way, scenery, camera, and costume changes could be made in the studio. But Cartier took this approach further; instead of filmed inserts for entire scenes, he often used telecine inserts (transfer of film to video) between shots, hence expanding the apparent studio space.

For example, a minor, almost unnoticeable case in *Nineteen Eighty-Four:* Winston Smith (Peter Cushing) is walking down a corridor past another employee working at a console. This movement consists of three shots: In the first, live in the studio, Winston walks past. In the second, a filmed insert, Winston walks past another console (in fact, the same one, filmed earlier with another actor). In the third—with Cushing having the chance to reposition—Winston walks past the same console again: the corridor appears to be long, but takes only a few steps to complete! This is a minor example of how confidently Cartier combined both live and telecine material seamlessly.

One criticism of this technique made by television purists at the time was that the expansion of space gave the plays a cinematic, rather than a strictly televisual, feel. One critic described Cartier's plays as "the trick of making a picture on a TV screen seem as wide and deep as Cinemascope."

Furthermore, Cartier's desire to expand the scale of television often brought him into conflict with Barry. In 1954 Barry sent Cartier a warning that his productions were becoming ambitious and, more important, expensive. He cited Cartier's recent version of *Rebecca:*

> I am unable to defend at a time when departmental costs and scene loads are in an acute state the load imposed by *Rebecca* on Design and Supply and the expenditure upon extras and costumes.... The leading performances were stagey and very often the actors were lost in the setting. Occasionally there were fine shots such as when Max was playing the piano with his wife beside him, and the composition of figures, piano top and vase made a good frame, but the vast area of the hall and the stairway never justified the great expenditure of effort required in building and one is left with a very clear impression of reaching a point where the department must be accused of not knowing what it is doing. (Michael Barry to Rudolph Cartier, memo, October 12, 1954, BBC Written Archives Centre, File number T5/424)

In effect, Barry was judging Cartier by the model of the small-scale "intimate style" espoused by many critics and television producers of the time—for them, television plays should be small with few characters, and nice close shots ("Max playing the piano with his wife beside him"). Cartier's television style was radically different: large spaces, long shots, *and* close-ups. Cartier responded to Barry: "the set should be large enough so that the small Mrs. de Winter should feel 'lost' enough and not 'cosy.' " Packed into this observation is the contrast between the early BBC drama style of directors such as Fred O'Donovan, George More O'Ferrall, Jan Bussell, and Royston Morley (longer-running shots, close-ups, the study of one or two characters), on the one hand, and Cartier and Kneale's conception of a wider canvas of shooting styles, a more integrated mixture of studio and film, larger sets, and multicharacter productions, on the other.

Cartier's difference from other directors did not simply lie in a greater use of film. His was a refusal to confine television within one essentialist style that required constant reference to its material base (intimate because the screen was small, the audience was at home, urgent because it was live, etc.). His use of film was not primarily dependent on the limitations of what could be achieved during live studio production; he used film as a material that could expand the space of the production.

Cartier never saw himself as a film director constrained by an imperfect medium; he preferred television production (although he returned once to cinema in 1958 to direct a striking melodrama, *The Passionate Summer*). Writing in 1958, when his stature was confirmed, he noted, "If the TV director knows his medium well and handles it skillfully, he can wield almost unlimited power over his mass audience; a power no other form of entertainment can give him—not even cinema."

JASON J. JACOBS

See also ***Quatermass; Z Cars***

Rudolph Cartier. Born Rudolph Katscher in Vienna, Austria, April 17, 1904. Attended the Vienna Academy of Music and Dramatic Art (Max Reinhardt's masterclass). Married: Margaret Pepper, 1949; two daughters. Film director and writer, Berlin; immigrated to the United Kingdom, 1935; joined BBC, 1952, and remained for 25 years as producer and director. Recipient: Guild of Television Producers and Directors Award, 1957. Died in London, June 7, 1994.

Television Series

1953 *The Quatermass Experiment*
1955 *Quatermass II*
1958–59 *Quatermass and the Pit*
1961 *Maigret*
1962–78 *Z Cars*
1974 *Fall of Eagles*

Television Plays (selected)

1951 *Man with the Twisted Lip*
1952 *Arrow to the Heart*
1952 *Dybbuk*
1952 *Portrait of Peter Perowne*
1953 *It Is Midnight, Doctor Schweitzer*
1953 *L'Aiglon*
1953 *Wuthering Heights*
1954 *Such Men Are Dangerous*
1954 *That Lady*
1954 *Rebecca*
1954 *Captain Banner*
1954 *Nineteen Eighty-Four*
1955 *Moment of Truth*
1955 *The Creature*
1955 *Vale of Shadows*
1955 *The Devil's General*
1955 *Thunder Rock*
1956 *The White Falcon*
1956 *The Mayerling Affair*
1956 *The Public Prosecutor*
1956 *The Fugitive*
1956 *The Cold Light*
1956 *The Saint of Bleecker Street*

1956	*Dark Victory*
1956	*Clive of India*
1956	*The Queen and the Rebels*
1957	*Salome*
1957	*Ordeal by Fire*
1957	*Counsellor-at-Law*
1958	*Captain of Koepenick*
1958	*The Winslow Boy*
1958	*A Tale of Two Cities*
1958	*A Midsummer Night's Dream*
1959	*Philadelphia Story*
1959	*Mother Courage and Her Children*
1959	*Otello*
1960	*The White Guard*
1960	*Glorious Morning*
1960	*Tobias and the Angel*
1961	*Rashomon*
1961	*Adventure Story*
1961	*Anna Karenina*
1961	*The Golden Fleece*
1961	*Liars*
1961	*Cross of Iron*
1962	*The Aspern Papers*
1962	*Doctor Korczuk and the Children*
1962	*Sword of Vengeance*
1962	*Carmen*
1963	*Anna Christie*
1963	*Night Express*
1963	*Stalingrad*
1963	*Peter the Lett*
1964	*Lady of the Camellias*
1964	*The Midnight Men*
1964	*The July Plot*
1965	*Wings of the Dove*
1965	*Ironhand*
1965	*The Joel Brand Story*
1966	*Gordon of Khartoum*
1966	*Lee Oswald—Assassin* (also writer)
1967	*Firebrand*
1967	*The Burning Bush*
1968	*The Fanatics*
1968	*Triumph of Death*
1968	*The Naked Sun*
1968	*The Rebel*
1969	*Conversation at Night*
1969	*An Ideal Husband*
1969	*Shattered Eye*
1970	*Rembrandt*
1970	*The Bear*
1970	*The Year of the Crow*
1971	*The Proposal*
1972	*Lady Windermere's Fan*
1973	*The Deep Blue Sea*
1976	*Loyalties*
1977	*Gaslight*

Film

Unsichtbare Gegner, 1931; *Corridor of Mirrors* (producer and writer), 1948; *Passionate Summer* (director), 1958.

Further Reading

Cartier, Rudolph, "A Foot in Both Camps," *Films and Filming* (September 1958)

Myles, L., and J. Petley, "Rudolph Cartier," *Sight and Sound* (Spring 1990)

Cartoon Network

Cartoon Network, part of the AOL Time Warner Turner Broadcasting System's family of cable channels, is a 24-hour basic cable network specializing in animated programming. Since launching on October 1, 1992, Cartoon Network has remained one of advertisement-supported basic cable's highest-rated offerings. The network's programming comprises original series, acquisitions, and programs from the Warner Brothers and Hanna-Barbera libraries. Its corporate headquarters are based in Atlanta, Georgia, but in 2000, the network opened Cartoon Network Studios, a 45,000-square-foot production space in Burbank, California.

Spirited by its first president, Betty Cohen, and a core of creative talent, as well as the financial backing of the Turner Broadcasting System, Cartoon Network has grown exponentially in its short history. In the early years, before establishing its own original programming, Cartoon Network was able to challenge Nickelodeon, its greatest competition for the young-audience demographic, with little more than repackaged classic Warner Brothers and Hanna-Barbera cartoons. Within two and a half years of its launch, the network had already begun to turn a profit and was attracting double the viewing time of any other new basic cable network. In November 1994, after the adoption of the FCC's "going forward" rules, virtually all basic cable channels increased their number of subscribers, but in 1995, Cartoon Network saw one of the largest increases in subscriptions. In 1994, Cartoon Network had 12.4 million viewers; in 2002, ten years after its launch, the network reached 80 million viewers nationally.

The network has had success internationally, as well, and in its first years the network often shared its international feeds with other Turner networks. In 1993 the network began broadcasting in Europe and Latin America. Already by 1994, Cartoon Network was broadcasting to 22 million homes in 29 countries in Europe alone. By 2001 Cartoon Network was running 24 hours and distributing internationally in 14 languages in 145 countries. International expansion has been easier for Cartoon Network than for many other American broadcast networks because its main programming products—animated shows—can be dubbed simply and inexpensively into a variety of languages.

Cartoon Network's core audience is children, ages two through 11. Like Nickelodeon, Cartoon Network quickly became known by children and their parents as a safe, 24-hour kid-friendly place on the dial. Some of its programs cater more to "tweens" (preteen children, approximately 9 through 12), an increasingly popular demographic for advertisers. And since its inception, a third of the network's viewers have been adults (18–34). While some of these are parents, a number of adults turn to Cartoon Network as loyal cult followers of classic favorites or of the network's more recent, innovative programming.

In 1991 Ted Turner purchased the Hanna-Barbera library, increasing a collection of animated programming that already included the MGM library, the Tom and Jerry cartoons, and pre-1950 Warner Brothers' Bugs Bunny and Daffy Duck cartoons. In its first few years, Cartoon Network filled its schedule with programs from Turner's vintage cartoon library. The network invested the profits from library programming into original production, and in April 1994, Cartoon Network's first original program aired, *Space Ghost Coast to Coast.* Still in production, *Space Ghost Coast to Coast* is not a series built around original cartoon characters and their adventures but a "talk show" hosted by a 1960s Hanna-Barbera cartoon superhero and modeled on major television networks' late-night interview programs.

Cartoon Network's original programming has continued to aim for the fearless, zany, and visually com-

Courtesy of Cartoon Network

pelling, but programs have ultimately been chosen for their success and their marketability. In 1995 Cartoon Network began *World Premiere Toons,* a program of original cartoon shorts created as pilots for original series. Using its own audience as a focus group, the network hosted a contest in which viewers voted for their favorite cartoons. The top four shorts picked by viewers—*Dexter's Laboratory, Johnny Bravo, The Powerpuff Girls,* and *Cow and Chicken*—were the first half-hour series launched by the network. *Dexter's Laboratory,* the network's first original series, has remained among the network's highest-rated programs since its debut in 1996. The series has been nominated for four Emmy Awards and has inspired a profitable line of licensed merchandise. The network has continued to use the Friday 7:30–11:00 P.M. time period as a key day-part for the launch and promotion of original programming.

The network's greatest success has come with its original series *The Powerpuff Girls,* created and coproduced by Craig McCracken. The program stars three doe-eyed, six-year-old sisters with super powers who frequently excuse themselves from kindergarten in order to save their city, Townsville, from an array of nefarious villains. Since its premiere in November 1998, *The Powerpuff Girls* has been one of the network's highest-rated programs among all its target demographics. The series has also become famous as a merchandising powerhouse: sales of *Powerpuff* merchandise exceeded $350 million in 2000 alone. A film based on the series, *The Powerpuff Girls: The Movie,* is the first full-length feature based on a Cartoon Network original series; it was produced at the Cartoon Network Studios.

In 1995 Turner Broadcasting System, Cartoon Network's parent company, merged with Time Warner, which was itself purchased in 2000 by AOL. These mergers required an adjustment for Cartoon Network and for the entire TBS family of networks. Management changes included a structure in which network executives no longer reported directly to Ted Turner, and other changes affected programming and marketing possibilities. Still, the first merger gave Cartoon Network access to new Warner Brothers animation, and both transitions provided new avenues for joint advertisement deals and programming diversity, including cross-platform entertainment.

The network's profitability can be attributed as much to its marketing strategies as its programming. By strongly branding itself through the use of extensive on- and off-air promotions, the treatment of its animated characters as celebrities, and the use of programming franchises, Cartoon Network has continued to increase its audience share. Through the use of savvy on-air promotions and franchised tie-ins, Cartoon Network has focused on making its audience dedicated, active fans. One campaign, "Dexter's Duplication Summer," garnered 35 million calls when the network asked audiences to vote by phone about whether to shift the program to a five-nights-a-week strip. The network has also put great effort into marketing campaigns with a number of its advertisers, tying its characters to packaged goods, fast food, clothing, and toys. Indeed, most Cartoon Network characters have their own line of licensed merchandise and many are used in promotions for the network or for tie-ins with commercial partners. Other marketing strategies for the network have focused on the treatment of animated characters as celebrities and the marketing of each program as an integrated entertainment experience. In recent years, the network has merged its advertising sales and promotions departments to provide a synergistic relationship for sponsors who may also wish to become promotional partners. In 1998 the same year its on-air promotional budget exceed $53 million, the network was named *Advertising Age*'s Cable TV Marketer of the Year.

In 2000 the network introduced "Cartoon Campaign 2000," a mock presidential campaign promoted as a way to teach kids about the electoral process but that also served as a method for the network to gauge the popularity of its programs and characters. Another strategy, the "Total Immersion Cartoon" events, use games and prizes to attract viewers onto the network's website. Cartoon Network has also been successful in using franchises, or particular packages of programming, to lure in viewers for a block of time, typically two to four hours. By combining a variety of programs from different studios, decades, and countries under a central theme and title, the network brands the programs as its own. "Toonami," Cartoon Network's weekday afternoon action-adventure lineup, for example, features a rotating series of Japanese animé. "Cartoon Theatre" is a twice-weekly presentation for contemporary animated films. And "Cartoon Cartoon Fridays," the network's Friday-night programming block, is designed to showcase back-to-back episodes of the network's original animated series.

The most recent franchise, "Adult Swim," is a new block of programming aimed at Cartoon Network's adult audience. This block, which premiered in September 2001 and airs on Saturday and Sunday nights, takes advantage of the one-third of its audience falling into the adult demographic. Saturday evening features a variety of action-adventure programming and Japanese animé series. Sunday nights are dedicated to comedy, including several original programs and popular acquisitions. This block is marketed as distinct from the rest of the network's programming, and often the types of advertisers represented reflect this more adult audience. With the help of "Adult Swim," Cartoon Network has recently jumped up two ranks, to number eight among all advertising-supported basic cable networks delivering adult audiences, ages 18 to 34.

Some of Cartoon Network's most recent original series have also earned both critical praise and ratings success, in part as the result of a $500 million investment in 2001 to develop and expand its original programming over a five-year period. Two of its most popular new programs are *Samurai Jack* and *Justice League.* Conceived by Cartoon Network veteran Genndy Tartakovsky (creator of *Dexter's Laboratory* and coproducer of *The Powerpuff Girls*), *Samurai Jack* debuted in August 2001 and follows the adventures of an ancient warrior stuck in a time portal. Witty and rife with action, like many Cartoon Network programs, this series is distinctive for its cinematic storytelling and highly stylized visual design. *Justice League,* which premiered in November 2001, follows the premise and storyline of the DC Comics series of the same title. Beautifully stylized, the program brings together classic superheroes, including Batman, Superman, and Wonder Woman, to fight crime and quash evildoers.

Cartoon Network has more recently integrated some of its programming and promotions with its sibling station, Kids' WB, sharing programs and allowing certain franchises to migrate between the two networks. The network also continues to expand into the digital realm on its official website, and in April 2000 launched Boomerang, a companion digital network showing only classic cartoons from its expansive library of Hollywood-produced animation. This new network, which has attracted 4.5 million subscribers since its launch, is designed to target the baby-boomer generation eager to watch favorite cartoons from childhood. Cartoon Network also spent $50 million redesigning its website in 2000 and expanded its presence within the America Online portal. For each of its series the website features unique areas that include short animations and games. Visitors to the site can also enter the "Department of Cartoons" and view storyboards, model sheets, and an animation primer explaining how cartoons are created. The *Powerpuff Girls* section is the most popular area of the site, averaging more than 6 million page views a month in early 2002.

In July 2000, Betty Cohen, who first began at Turner Broadcasting System in 1988 as senior vice president/general manager of TNT, left her position as president of Cartoon Network Worldwide. Bradley Sigel, previously the president of general entertainment networks for TBS Inc., is currently president of Cartoon Network Worldwide.

MIRANDA J. BANKS

See also **Cartoons; Children and Television; Time Warner; Turner Broadcasting Systems; Turner, Ted**

Further Reading

Carvell, Tim, and Joe McGowan, "Showdown in Toontown," *Fortune,* 134, no. 8 (October 28, 1996)

Ebenkamp, Becky, "Power to the Puff People," *Brandweek,* 42, no. 24 (June 11, 2001)

Littleton, Cynthia, "An Animated Conversation with Betty Cohen," *Broadcasting & Cable* (June 2, 1997)

Pursell, Chris, "Originals Widen Cartoon Net Base," *Variety* (October 18–24, 1999)

Ross, Chuck, "Cartoon Network: Cable TV Marketer of the Year," *Advertising Age* (November 30, 1998)

Stanley, T.L., "Marketers of the NextGeneration," *Brandweek,* 40, no. 45 (November 8, 1999)

Cartoons

Cartoons have long existed on the periphery of broadcast television, consigned to the shadowy regions of weekday afternoons, Saturday mornings, and, most recently, cable channels. Broadcast networks' prime-time programming has contained surprisingly few cartoon series. After *The Flintstones* (1960–66) went off the air, 23 years passed before *The Simpsons* (1989–) proved that animation could be successful with a general audience. Due to the initial lack of made-for-television cartoons, many of the "television" cartoon characters with which we are the most familiar (Bugs Bunny, Mickey Mouse, Daffy Duck, Popeye) were not actually designed for television, but rather were initially exhibited in cinema theaters. On any given day, one may view a short history of theatrical film animation on television, as cartoons from the 1930s and 1940s are juxtaposed with more recent offerings.

Cartoons initially evolved in the second decade of the 20th century, but their development was slowed by their prohibitive cost. After all, 24 entire pictures had to be drawn for every second of film. Animation became more economically feasible in 1914 when Earl Hurd patented the animation cel. The cel is a sheet of transparent celluloid that is placed on top of a background drawing. By using cels, the animator need only redraw the portions of the image that move, thus saving considerable time and expense. The acceptance of the cel was slowed by legal wrangling, however, and comparatively few silent cartoons were made.

At the same time that sound and color film technologies were popularized, studios also found ways to streamline the animation process by using storyboards (small drawings of frames that represented different shots in the cartoon) to plan the cartoon and departmentalizing the steps of the process. Thus, something resembling an assembly line was created for animation, making it much more cost effective. Producer Walt Disney was a leader in using these technologies and devising an efficient mode of cartoon production. *Steamboat Willie* (1928) was the first significant cartoon with synchronized sound, whereas *Flowers and Trees* (1932) was the first to use the three-color Technicolor process (which became the cinema's principal color process in the late 1930s). Disney was so protective of these new technologies that he negotiated an exclusive deal with Technicolor; for three years, no other animators could use it.

The final key to the success of the cartoon was an effective distribution system. During the silent era, cartoons had been created by small studios with limited access to cinema theaters. In the 1930s, major studios such as Paramount, Warner, Universal, and MGM each signed distribution deals with the cartoon studios, or they created their own cartoon departments (the output of which they then distributed themselves). Since the studios also owned the preeminent theaters, and since the standard way of exhibiting films at the time was two feature-length films separated by a newsreel and a cartoon, the animation studios and departments had a

Batman: The Animated Series, 1992–95.
Courtesy of the Everett Collection

steady, constant demand for their product. The late 1930s to 1950s were a "golden era" for the cartoon, and it is from this era that most theatrical cartoons on television are drawn.

Cartoons started their emigration to television in the late 1940s, when one of the smaller studios (Van Beuren) began marketing their catalog to early children's programs such as *Movies for Small Fry.* Other, larger studios were slower to take advantage of the electronic medium. In 1948 the major studios were forced by the U.S. Supreme Court to divest themselves of their theaters, which greatly weakened their ability to distribute their product. In this weakened state, the studios also had to compete with television for viewers. Disney, however, was among the first of the major cartoon studios to develop a liaison with television networks. When they premiered in the mid-1950s, Disney's long-running programs *Disneyland* (later known as, among other things, *The Wonderful World of Disney*) and *The Mickey Mouse Club* included cartoons among live-action shorts and other materials. The other studios soon followed suit, and, by 1960, most theatrical films and cartoons were also available to be shown on television.

Concurrent with these critical and, for the film studios, disastrous changes in the entertainment industry were significant transformations in the aesthetics of animation. Up until the 1950s, cartoonists, especially those with Disney, had labored under a naturalistic aesthetic, striving to make their drawings look as much like real-world objects as was possible in this medium. The apotheosis of this was Disney's *Snow White,* which traced the movements of dancer Marge Champion and transformed her into Snow White. But post–World War II art movements such as abstract expressionism rejected this naturalistic approach, and these avant-garde principles eventually filtered down to the popular cartoon. In particular, United Productions of America (UPA), a studio that contained renegade animators who had left Disney during the 1941 strike, nurtured an aesthetic that emphasized abstract line, shape, and pattern over naturalistic figures. UPA's initial success came in 1949 with the *Mr. Magoo* series, but its later, Academy Award–winning *Gerald McBoing Boing* (1951) is what truly established this new style.

The UPA style was characterized by flattened perspective, abstract backgrounds, strong primary colors, and "limited" animation. Instead of using perspective to create the illusion of depth in a drawing, UPA's cartoon objects looked flat, like the blobs of color that they were. Instead of filling in backgrounds with lifelike detail, as in, say, a forest scene in *Bambi,* UPA presented backgrounds that were broad fields of color, with small squiggles to suggest clouds and trees. Instead of varying the shades and hues of colors to imply the colors of the natural world, UPA's cartoons contained bold, bright, saturated colors.

Most important for the development of television cartoons, UPA used animation that was limited in three ways. First, the amount of movement within the frame was substantially reduced. Rather than have a cartoon woman move her entire head in a shot, a UPA cartoon might have her just blink her eyes. Second, in limited animation, figure movements are often repeated. A character waving good-bye, for instance, might contain only two distinct movements, which are then repeated without change. Full animation, in contrast, includes many unique movements. Third, limited animation uses fewer individual frames to represent a movement. If, for example, Yosemite Sam were to hop off his mule in a movement that takes one second, full animation might use 24 discrete frames to represent that movement. Limited animation, in contrast, might

Huckleberry Hound Show, Huckleberry Hound, 1958–62.
Courtesy of the Everett Collection

cut that number in half. The result is a slightly jerkier movement.

UPA's changes in animation appear to have been aesthetically inspired, but they also made good business sense. Flattened perspective, abstract backgrounds, strong primary colors, and limited animation result in cartoons that are quicker and cheaper to produce. When animators began creating programs specifically for television, they quickly adopted these economical practices.

The first successful designed-for-television cartoon was not created for a TV network, but rather was released directly into syndication. *Crusader Rabbit,* created by Jay Ward (of *Rocky and Bullwinkle* fame) and Alexander Anderson, was first distributed in 1949. Network television cartooning came along eight years later. The networks' first cartoon series was *The Ruff and Reddy Show,* which was developed by the most successful producers of television cartoons, Bill Hanna and Joe Barbera. *The Ruff and Reddy Show* was also the first made-for-TV cartoon show to be broadcast nationally on Saturday mornings; its popularity helped establish the feasibility of Saturday-morning network programming. Hanna-Barbera was also responsible for bringing cartoons to the prime-time network schedule, creating, in 1960, *The Flintstones,* prime time's first successful cartoon series.

With *Crusader Rabbit, The Ruff and Reddy Show,* and *The Flintstones,* the characteristics of the made-for-TV cartoon were established. UPA-style aesthetics (especially limited animation) were blended with narrative structures that developed in 1950s television. In particular, *The Flintstones* closely resembled live-action situation comedies and was often compared to Jackie Gleason's *The Honeymooners.* One final characteristic of the made-for-TV cartoon that distinguishes it from the theatrical cartoon is the former's emphasis on dialogue. Often dialogue in *The Flintstones* restates what is happening visually. Fred will cry out, "Pebbles is headed to the zoo," over an image of Pebbles's baby carriage rolling past a sign that reads, "Zoo, this way." Thus, television reveals its roots in radio. There is a reliance on sound that is missing from, say, *Roadrunner* or many other theatrical cartoons. Made-for-TV cartoons are often less visually oriented than theatrical cartoons from the "golden era."

Since the early 1960s, when cartoons became an established television feature, they have been the source of two major controversies: commercialization/merchandising and violence. These two issues have taken on special significance with the cartoon since so many of its viewers are impressionable children.

Commercialization and merchandising have been a part of cartooning since comic strips first began appearing in newspapers. The level of merchandising increased in the 1980s, however, as several cartoon programs were built around already-existing commercial products: *Strawberry Shortcake, The Smurfs,* and *He-Man.* Unlike the merchandising of, for instance, Mickey Mouse, these cartoon characters began as products, and thus their cartoons were little more than extended commercials for the products themselves. It became more and more difficult for child viewers to discern where the cartoon ended and the commercial began. The degree of cartoon merchandising did not lessen in the 1990s (as the popularity of the *Mighty Morphin Power Rangers* attested), but broadcasters did add short intros to the programs to try to better distinguish cartoon from commercial.

The complicated issue of violence on television and its potential impact on behavior has yet to be resolved, but in response to critics of cartoon violence, broadcasters have censored violent scenes from many theatrical films shown on television. Oddly enough, scenes that were considered appropriate for a general audience in a theater in the 1940s are now thought to be too brutal for today's Nintendo-educated children.

TV cartoons in the 1990s were dominated by the phenomenal success of Matt Groening's *The Simpsons,* which thrived after its series premiere in 1989 (having first appeared in 1988, in short form, on *The Tracey Ullman Show*). Its ratings triumph was largely responsible for establishing a new television network (FOX) and launching one of the biggest merchandising campaigns of the decade. In 1990 Bart Simpson was on t-shirts across the United States declaring, "Don't have a cow, man!" And yet, despite the trappings of success, *The Simpsons* was often a sly parody of popular culture, in general, and television cartoons, in particular—as was to be expected from Groening, who established himself as the artist of the satiric *Life in Hell* comic strip. The recurrent feature of "The Itchy and Scratchy Show," a cartoon within *The Simpsons,* allowed the program to critique violence in cartoons at the same time it reveled in the gore. In one episode, *The Simpsons* retold the entire history of cartooning as if Itchy and Scratchy had been early Disney creations.

The Simpsons proved that the market for cartoons extended beyond children. In 1993 MTV and Mike Judge capitalized on this new, young-adult market, with the debut of *Beavis and Butt-head* (1993–97). The program's title characters were two teenaged heavy-metal fans, who mostly sit around making rude comments about music videos. *Beavis and Butt-head* brought "adult" humor to television cartoons and established that cable networks could succeed with animated material that was too sexually explicit, scatological, and drug-oriented for broadcast networks. When Judge discontinued the program and developed *King of the Hill* (1997–) for *The Simpsons*' network (FOX), Trey Parker and Matt Stone picked up where *Beavis and Butt-head* left off. Their creation, *South Park* (1997–), on cable's Comedy Central, has touched on subjects as sensitive as child abuse and as offensive as a character made of feces.

Beavis and Butt-head and *South Park* exemplify the adult-oriented animation on cable networks, but by far the most common animation genre on television today is that which is developed for children and presented on such cable networks as Disney, Nickelodeon, and the Cartoon Network. For example, *Rugrats* (1991–94, 1997–), which chronicles a group of mischievous babies, has been such a success for Nickelodeon that it has spawned several movies. *SpongeBob SquarePants,* which first aired in 1999 as Nickelodeon's original Saturday-morning cartoon, is notable as a cartoon that both children and adults embrace. By April 2002, the series had surpassed *Rugrats* as Nickelodeon's most popular program. With a substantial number of adults among its more than 50 million viewers, *SpongeBob* has showcased an irreverent style for grownups while still appealing to enormous numbers of children.

The 1990s also saw the debut of the first animated program that was entirely created on computer. When *ReBoot* appeared in 1994, computer-generated imagery (CGI) was mostly limited to experimental shorts and commercials. Indeed, *ReBoot* was released before the first entirely CGI feature film (*Toy Story* [1995]). The cost of creating entire programs on computer remains relatively high, but digital technology can also save animators time and money. Much of the repetitive work of traditional animators has been usurped by computers, leading to faster, cheaper productions. It seems clear that computer-assisted and computer-generated cartoons will become more common in the future.

JEREMY G. BUTLER

See also ***Beavis and Butt-head; Flintstones, The; Simpsons, The; South Park***

Further Reading

Brasch, Walter M., *Cartoon Monikers: An Insight into the Animation Industry,* Bowling Green, Ohio: Bowling Green University Popular Press, 1983

Butler, Jeremy G., *Television: Critical Methods and Applications,* Belmont, California: Wadsworth, 1994

Cawley, John, and Jim Korkis, *Cartoon Superstars,* Las Vegas, Nevada: Pioneer, 1990

Crafton, Donald, *Before Mickey: The Animated Film, 1889–1928,* Cambridge, Massachusetts: MIT Press, 1982

Erickson, Hal, *Television Cartoon Shows: An Illustrated Encyclopedia, 1949–1993,* Jefferson City, North Carolina: McFarland, 1995

Grossman, Gary H., *Saturday Morning TV,* New York: Dell, 1981

Herdeg, Walter, *Film and TV Graphics: An International Survey of Film and Television Graphics,* Zurich: W. Herdeg, Graphis Press, 1967

Lenberg, Jeff, *The Encyclopedia of Animated Cartoons,* New York: Facts on File, 1991

Maltin, Leonard, with Jerry Beck, *Of Mice and Magic: A History of American Animated Cartoons,* New York: New American Library, 1980

Seiter, Ellen, *Sold Separately: Children and Parents in Consumer Culture,* New Brunswick, New Jersey: Rutgers University Press, 1993

Smoodin, Eric, *Animating Culture: Hollywood Cartoons from the Sound Era,* New Brunswick, New Jersey: Rutgers University Press, 1993

U.S. Congress, Senate Committee on Commerce, Science, and Transportation: Subcommittee on Communications, Education, Competitiveness, and Children's Television, *Hearings Before the Committee,* April 12, 1989, Washington, D.C.: Congressional Sales Office, 1989

Woolery, George W., *Children's Television, The First Thirty-Five Years: 1946–1981,* Metuchen, New Jersey: Scarecrow Press, 1985

Case, Steve (1958–)

U.S. Media Executive

Steve Case, a former marketing and brand manager at Procter and Gamble and Pizza Hut, helped to build a small online services company into one of the world's largest single online service provider, America Online (AOL). At the peak of the market for high-technology stocks at the end of the 1990s, Case was able to parlay the high value of AOL stock into a friendly takeover of the then-largest media conglomerate, Time Warner, which was consummated in early 2001. Case expected AOL Time Warner to use its assets in online services, film, broadcasting, cable, publishing, and music to lead a trend toward technological convergence. In a speech to investors in 2001, Case claimed that AOL Time Warner would be well positioned to "build bridges to link technologies, to blur the lines between industries, . . . to drive a fundamental transformation of the media and communications industries."

Case, a taciturn, reserved executive who prefers to operate behind the scenes, was nicknamed "The Wall" at AOL for his affectless, calm demeanor. However, despite his introversion, Case's skills in identifying consumer interests and in developing the social and communicative aspects of online services helped to fuel the explosive growth of online services in the 1990s. In his early online experiences, Case had been excited but frustrated by technological difficulties and complexities. He then realized that "if you made [online services] easy to use, useful and fun, and affordable, someday it would become a mass market." Case found his first opportunity in the computing industry when his older brother Dan invested in a small company named Control Video Corporation, which then recruited Steve in 1983 to help build its video game business. In 1985 Steve Case, along with partners Jim Kimsey and Marc Seriff, took over, renamed the company Quantum Computer Services, and started an online service named Q-Link for Commodore computer users. Seeking to expand, Quantum made deals with Apple Computer and Tandy, but when Apple opted out, Case reconfigured the company, renaming it America Online in 1989.

Named president of AOL in 1990, Case oversaw a marketing campaign that undercut the basic principles then prevalent in the software industry: instead of selling its software, AOL gave it away in order to sell its subscription service instead. Seeking to widen its market rapidly, AOL used direct mail, magazine inserts, and retail promotions to provide free AOL software to as many potential customers as possible. The free software provided an incentive to stay online by subscribing. AOL's strategies for subscriber retention included convenience, user friendliness, and services such as e-mail, games, chat rooms, and messaging. AOL then also provided professionally produced content, organized in "channels" for ease of access, aiming for a hybrid form of magazine information and television entertainment that would appeal to new users. While other online services kept tight control over their subscribers' communications by banning certain forms of speech, AOL encouraged an open, freewheeling, user-controlled communications environment. As Case formulated it, AOL had to develop the "three C's" of "communication, community, and clarity" in order to personalize online experiences and build subscriber loyalty. Case said, "We wanted people to think they were members and not customers." And by spending hours online interacting with subscribers himself, Case helped build a corporate image of AOL as accessible, friendly, and human. To many subscribers, investors, and employees, Steve Case was AOL personified.

By the time AOL sold stock in its first public offering in 1992, it had overtaken its competitors Prodigy and CompuServe. When the World Wide Web developed in the early 1990s, AOL was redesigned to allow Internet access from inside AOL. In 1996, after AOL switched from hourly pricing to a flat-rate subscription plan, AOL reversed its long-standing arrangements with outside professional content providers and began to charge them for access to AOL screen space (that is, AOL subscribers' attention). AOL had discovered that most of its subscribers logged on not to read repurposed magazine articles but to communicate with other subscribers through e-mail, instant messaging, and chat room—services that subscribers could find only online, not in magazines or on television.

As AOL resisted friendly and unfriendly takeover attempts in the late 1990s, it used its highly valued stock to acquire businesses including Netscape,

MovieFone, ICQ, Winamp, and CompuServe, and also expanded into Europe, Japan, and Latin America. Having proved that online services could appeal to a mass market by being user friendly, Case began to look for partners in building his vision of a converged media environment. Time Warner was an attractive candidate. Its subsidiaries Warner Bros. Television, Warner Bros. Animation, HBO Productions, Lorimar, and Telepicture Productions are major television producers, distributors, and syndicators of programs such as *Friends, ER, The West Wing, The Drew Carey Show,* and *Gilmore Girls.* In addition to its broadcast network, The WB, Time Warner controlled many top cable networks, including Home Box Office, Cinemax, and the Turner Networks (Cable News Network, Turner Network Television, Turner Broadcasting System, Cartoon Network, and Turner Classic Movies). Time Warner assets also included the film studios Warner Bros. (*Harry Potter*) and New Line (*The Lord of the Rings*); Time Warner trade book publishing (Little, Brown); Warner Music Group (Madonna, Britney Spears); and Time magazines (*Time, People, Sports Illustrated*). Time Warner had tried to break into the new-media world through online and interactive media and, as these attempts were perceived as failures, was receptive to Case's overtures.

Case initiated merger talks with Time Warner in part because its cable operating systems, then the second largest in the United States, offered broadband access via cable modems, as well as addressable cable set-top boxes, and it was working on video-on-demand, interactive programming, home shopping, and streaming video and audio. In explaining his motivation for the merger, Case said, "Having assets in the Internet space, having assets in the television space, allows you to make a difference if, for instance, one of your goals is to re-invent television." Having marketed online computing as a medium as easy to use as television, Case hoped to "re-invent" television as a medium as interactive as online computing.

However prescient Case's vision of interactive media may prove to be, the first years after the merger of AOL and Time Warner were difficult. As AOL Time Warner's stock price fell, in part because of the overall reevaluation of technology and communications companies, most of the major architects of the merger were forced out of the company. Case himself resigned as chairman of the board in 2003, his leadership contested by competing factions of the conglomerate. Although AOL Time Warner planned to build on the base of the millions of subscribers to its magazines, online services, and cable television to cross-promote broadband and interactive television services, as of this writing it has begun to divest some of its holdings, including AOL from its name. However, Case's idea of building a "synergistic" conglomerate that builds its online, cable, and broadband distribution services by offering user-friendly technologies and popular content brands may still yet be realized. As Case has insisted, "convergence is the wave of the future.... [I]t isn't science fiction, it's already happening."

CYNTHIA B. MEYERS

See also **Levin, Gerald; Media Conglomerates; Time Warner**

Stephen McConnell Case. Born in Honolulu, Hawaii, August 21, 1958. Married: 1) Joanne Barker (1985–96); three children; 2) Jean Villanueva (1996). B.A., political science, Williams College, 1980. Procter and Gamble, brand manager (1980–81 or 82); Pizza Hut, manager of new development (1981 or 1982–83); Control Video Corporation, marketing (1983–85); Quantum Computer Services, marketing director (1985–89); America Online, president (1990–93), CEO (1993–2001); AOL Time Warner, chairman of the board (2001–03).

Further Reading

Case, Stephen M., speech, UBS Warburg Annual Media Week Conference, New York City, December 4, 2001, www.aoltimewarner.com

Harmon, Amy, "AOL Chief Relaxes a Dress Code but Not His Vision of the Internet," *New York Times* (January 11, 2000)

Klein, Alec, *Stealing Time: Steve Case, Gerry Levin, and the Collapse of AOL Time Warner,* New York: Simon and Schuster, 2003

Loomis, Carol, "AOL Time Warner's New Math," *Fortune* (February 4, 2002)

Swisher, Kara, *AOL.com: How Steve Case Beat Bill Gates, Nailed the Netheads, and Made Millions in the War for the Web,* New York: Random House, 1999

Casualty

British Hospital Drama

Since it was launched in autumn 1986 as a 15-part series, the hospital drama *Casualty* has grown into one of the British Broadcasting Corporation's (BBC's) most successful programs. Eventually running to 24 episodes a year (plus a repeat season), and with ratings second only to those for soap operas *EastEnders* and *Neighbours, Casualty* was to become a linchpin of the schedule and crucial to the corporation's confidence in the run up to the renewal of its charter in 1996.

The series began as the brainchild of Jeremy Brock, a young BBC script editor, and Paul Unwin, a director at the Bristol Old Vic Theatre. A visit to a Bristol accident and emergency ward and conversation with one of the charge nurses prompted the idea of a series that would deal with the working lives of casualty staff but that would also have a campaigning edge at a time when the National Health Service in Britain was under increasing financial and political pressure. The proposal was taken up by the head of BBC drama, Jonathan Powell, who was convinced that a medical series was essential to a healthy schedule. The Bristol hospital became Holby General and the nurse, Peter Salt, one of the program's medical advisers and a model for the longest-serving central character, charge nurse (later nursing manager) Charlie Fairhead.

The foregrounding of a male nurse was one of several ways in which *Casualty* set out to contest the traditional values of hospital drama. The gender stereotyping associated with sluice-room romances of popular medical fiction was inverted (if not always subverted) in storylines such as Charlie's passionate involvement with a female house officer and the protracted consequences of nursing officer Duffin's pregnancy by a feckless doctor. The series has also attempted to address racial underrepresentation by placing black characters at the center of the drama and has carried storylines on racial prejudice and abuse.

What *Casualty* sought to achieve in its first series was a gritty realism, bordering on documentary authenticity, capable of dealing with the day-to-day stresses of frontline emergency care, and the further difficulties of working in a system coming apart at the seams. Brock claimed to have been influenced by the high-octane style of MTM Entertainment Inc. shows, especially *Hill Street Blues,* with their overlapping narratives and dialogue, rapid cutting, and wry humor, though the series never went for the sort of élan found in its U.S. counterparts. It began on a modest budget and was shot exclusively on video, with lightweight cameras to give it pace and fluidity: the technique of following dialogue down corridors and picking up on several overlapping conversations within the same take was to become a hallmark of the emerging production style.

The central storyline for the first two series was the campaign to keep the night shift open at Holby in the teeth of funding cuts. The shift also provided the setting and time frame for each episode and, improbably, a justification for focusing on the same eight members of staff. By the end of the first series, although another was in production, there was talk of *Casualty* being axed. There had been criticism of the show's stress-laden relentlessness and press coverage of protests from the medical professions about the disreputable image of staff conduct, though there was considerable support for the series' representation of health-service conditions. The program also came under attack from the ruling Conservative Party for its stand against such key Thatcherite policies as funding cuts and the contracting out of services and, along with news coverage of the bombing of Tripoli and the drama *The Monocled Mutineer,* was held up as an example of alleged left-wing bias at the BBC.

However, as audience figures for the second series began to climb to 8 million, the BBC started to invest more in it. New characters were brought in, and a sharper style began to emerge, particularly in the cross-weaving of storylines and the more honed gallows humor. By 1991 *Casualty* had an audience of 12 to 13 million and the formula was securely established: a basic structure created by the ten main characters' continuing stories, a major accident interwoven with six to eight further parallel storylines, and up to 80 short scenes per episode; a real-time feel based on the single-shift setting; sharp-cutting, mobile single-camera work; no background music; realistic lighting; an army of trauma-specific extras and models; and a range of 30 to 40 guest actors per series.

The casting of familiar, high-caliber performers in cameo roles was, for some time, one of the series' main attractions, along with its growing reputation for graphic authenticity in the depiction of injuries and their treatment. The series also shed its regional identity: although still shot in and around Bristol, this was no longer its ostensible setting and the characters came to reflect a more general population mix. A proposal by Powell, by now controller of BBC 1, to go to a twice-weekly, early-evening slot was rejected, but by this time, many would argue, the show had already softened into a standardized predictability. By 1993 audiences were peaking at 15.47 million and the program was tent-poling the Saturday evening schedule. A ruling in that year by the Broadcasting Standards Council concerning the pre-watershed unsuitability of a storyline about rent boys and male rape and further controversy over an episode showing teenagers rioting and burning down the ward forced the new BBC 1 controller, Alan Yentob, into a promise of greater "responsibility" in the handling of topical material. A year later, audiences stood at 17 million. By 2001, however, they had dropped to around 8 million. In January 1999, a spin-off series, *Holby Central,* was launched, set in the hospital's general wards and with some characters already established in *Casualty.*

Against the claim that *Casualty* had lost its earlier political abrasiveness, the producers would argue that public opinion had caught up with the program, that the once-controversial claims had become fact, and that the issues were more subtly woven into the fabric of the stories. By 1995, however, the series seemed to reach a final transformation into soap opera. It was the human-interest vignettes imported with each casualty case that now dominated, along with the lives and loves of the regular medical staff. Although the narratives have never fully lost their concern with the fabric of contemporary life, or with the social cohesion beyond the hospital doors, they have sometimes become more overtly theatrical. One later storyline followed two romantically involved characters to the Australian bush, while another dealt with a young, gay Asian male nurse whose HIV-positive status was leaked in the press and whose eventual departure was marked with a spirited gay wedding.

Casualty is a classic example of the intergeneric development of formula-based television fiction. All the attractions of hospital drama are there: life, death, and human vulnerability; institutional hierarchy; and personal and professional tensions. The show also chimes in with the ascendancy in the 1990s of a new genre of emergency service narrative on British television, from Carlton's drama *London's Burning* to such reconstruction programs as the BBC's *999.* Beneath the surface, however, the fictional structure rests on foundations tried and tested in the "cop-shop" police drama, and it is no coincidence that the background of founding producer Geraint Morris lay with series such as *Softly Softly* and *Juliet Bravo.* The accident and emergency ward, in particular the waiting area that provides the focal point of the production set, operates here as a classic frontline—a site of friction between the hospital community and life on the street, and a liminal space into which hundreds of individual cases are drawn, to be returned, in varying states of social and psychological repair, to the world beyond.

JEREMY RIDGMAN

Cast

Charlie Fairhead	Derek Thompson
Lisa (Duffy) Duffin	Catherine Shipton
Megan Roach	Brenda Fricker
Clive King	George Harris
Ewart Plimmer	Bernard Gallagher
Elizabeth Straker	Maureen O'Brien
Karen Goodlife	Suzanna Hamilton
Cyril James	Eddie Nestor
Dr. Andrew Bower	William Gaminara/Philip Bretherton
Martin (Ash) Ashford	Patrick Robinson
Adele Beckford	Doña Croll
Helen Chatsworth	Samantha Edmonds
Mike Barratt	Clive Mantle
Maxine Price	Emma Bird
Kenneth Hodges	Christopher Guard
Sandra Nicholl	Maureen Beattie
Dr. Robert Khalefa	Jason Riddington
Julian Chapman	Nigel le Vaillant
Dr. Beth Ramanee	Mamta Kaash
Dr. Lucy Perry	Tam Hoskyns
Dr. David Rowe	Paul Lacoux
Dr. Mary Tomlinson	Helena Little
Dr. Barbara "Baz" Samuels (Hayes)	Julia Watson
Alex Spencer	Belinda Davidson
Karen O'Malley	Kate Hardie
Andrew Ponting	Robert Pugh
Sandra Mute	Lisa Bowerman
Shirley Franklin	Ella Wilder
Keith Cotterill	Geoffrey Leesley
Frankie Drummer	Steven O'Donnell
Susie Mercier	Debbie Roza
Mie Nishi-Kawa	Naoko Mori
Josh Griffiths	Ian Bleasdale
Jane Scott	Caroline Webster
Liz Harker	Sue Devaney
Norma Sullivan	Anne Kristen
Kuba Trzcinski	Christopher Rozycki

Jimmy Powell
Kelly Liddle
Trish Baynes
Rachel Longworth
Kate Wilson
Jude Kocarnik
Daniel Perryman
Laura Milburn
Matt Hawley
Valerie Sinclair
Kate Miller
Simon Eastman
Mark Calder
Adam Cooke
Adam Osman
Alison McGrellis
Amy Howard
Anna Paul
Barney Wolfe
Brian Crawford
Chloe Hill
Colette Kierney
Dan Robinson
Dave Masters
Eddie Gordon
Elliot Matthews
Eve Montgomery
Finlay Newton
Gloria Hammond
Georgina (George) Woodman
Helen Green
Holly Miles
Jack Hathaway
Will Mellor
Julie Stevens
Kiran Joghill
Lucy Cooper
Robson Green
Adie Allen
Maria Freedman
Jane Gurnett
Sorcha Cusack
Lisa Coleman
Craig Kelly
Lizzy McInnerny
Jason Merrells
Susan Franklyn
Joanna Foster
Robert Dawe
Oliver Parker
Stephen Brand
Pal Aron
Julie Graham
Rebecca Wheatley
Zitta Sattar
Ronnie McCann
Brendan O'Hea
Jan Anderson
Adjoa Andoh
Grant Masters
Martin Ball
Joan Oliver
Peter Guiness
Barbara Marten
Kwame Kwei Armah
Ganiat Kasumu

Rebecca Lacey
Maggie McCarthy
Sandra Huggett
Peter Birch
Jack Vincent
Vivienne McKane
Shaheen Khan
Jo Unwin
Mark Grace
Mary Skillett
Max Gallagher
Mel Dyson
Patrick Spiller
Penny Hutchens
Richard McCraig
Sadie Tomkins
Sam Colloby
Sean Maddox
Spencer
Derek (Sunny) Sunderland
Tina Seabrook
Tom Harley
Tom Harvey
Tony Walker
Trevor Wilson
Paterson Joseph
Tara Moran
Robert Gwilym
Michelle Butterfly
Ian Kelsey
Donna Alexander
Gray O'Brien
Carole Leader
Jonathan Kerrigan
Gerald Kyd
Ben Keaton

Vincenzo Pellegrino
Claire Goose
David Ryall
Kieron Forsyth
Eamon Boland
Michael N. Harbour

Producer
Geraint Morris

Programming History
BBC
1986–

Further Reading

Kerr, Paul, "Drama out of a Crisis," *The Listener* (September 4, 1986)
Kingsley, Hilary, *Casualty: The Inside Story,* London: BBC Books, 1993
Lustig, Vera, "Emergency Ward Tenable?" *The Listener* (September 20, 1990)
Saynor, James, "Doctor, It's Something up My Nose," *Guardian* (February 22, 1993)
Smith, David James, "Close to the Bone," *7 Days* (September 3, 1989)

Cathy Come Home

British Docudrama

Cathy Come Home was screened by BBC 1 on December 16, 1966, within the regular *Wednesday Play* slot. The program is a "drama-documentary" concerning homelessness and its effect upon families. Written by Jeremy Sandford, produced by Tony Garnett, and directed by Ken Loach, *Cathy* has become a British TV "classic," regularly referred to by critics and researchers as well as by program makers themselves. Part of the status accorded to *Cathy* is undoubtedly due to its particular qualities of scripting, direction, and acting, but part follows from the way in which the film has been seen to focus and exemplify questions about the mixing of dramatic with documentary material and, more generally, about the public power of television in highlighting social problems. After the screening, the issue of homelessness, and the various measures adopted by local authorities to deal with that problem, became more prominent in public and political discussion, and the housing action charity "Shelter" was formed. The more long-term consequences, in terms of changes to the kinds of conditions depicted in the film, remain much more doubtful, of course.

Cathy is organized as a narrative about a young woman who marries, has children, and then—following an accident to her husband that results in his loss of job and the subsequent impoverishment of their family—suffers various states of homelessness in poor or temporary accommodation until her children are taken into care by the social services. The program adopts an episodic structure, depicting the stages in the decline of Cathy and her family across a number of years. Both as a play and as a kind of documentary, *Cathy Come Home* is held together by the commentary of Cathy herself, a commentary that is given in a self-reflective past tense and that not only introduces and ends the program but is heard regularly throughout it, providing a bridge between episodes and a source of additional explanation to that obtained by watching the dramatic action.

One "documentary" element in *Cathy* is seen in the program's visual style. In addition, the play resembles a documentary in that a large amount of research on the problem of homelessness went into the writing of the script and because the script devotes considerable time to depicting aspects of this problem as it advances the storyline concerning Cathy and her family.

Stylistically, a number of scenes in the program are shot in the documentary mode of action-led camera, with events appearing to develop spontaneously and to be "caught" by the filming. The resultant effect is one of high immediacy values, providing the viewer with a strong sense of being a "witness." Where the script broadens its scope to situate Cathy's story in the context of homelessness as a more general problem, camera work and sound recording produce a scopic field and address to the viewer that resemble conventional reportage. For instance, in a scene in a crowed tenement block, we hear the anonymous voices of occupants on the soundtrack while various shots are combined to produce a montage of "place," of "environment." Similarly, toward the end of the film, when Cathy and her children enter the lowest class of hostel accommodation, the camera not only situates them in the crowded dormitory they have entered but offers "snapshot" case histories of some of the other women living there. Some of this information comes through voice-over, some in speech to camera, as if addressed to Cathy herself. The documentarist element is more directly present in the use of commentary and brief "viewpoint" voice-over at several points in the film. These moments offer statistics on the housing situation and allow various perspectives on it to be heard in a manner that directly follows conventional documentary practice.

Thus, *Cathy* plays with the codes of reportage and merges them with those of realist drama. The developing story, however, often shown through an exploration of private, intimate space, requires that the film be organized principally as narrative fiction, moving outward to establish a documentary framing of context at a number of points and then closing back in on "story." Since the story is a particularization of the general problem, however, movement between "story" and "report" often involves no sharp disjunctions, substantive or stylistic.

The initial critical response to the program was generally positive, but public discussion tended to circulate around two issues—the possibility that the audience would be deceived into according a greater "truth" to *Cathy* than was warranted by its fictional status, and the way the account was a "biased" one, depicting officials as uncaring and often hostile in a way that would have been unacceptable in a conventional documentary.

It is hard to imagine a viewer so unskilled in the conventions of television as to believe that *Cathy* was "reality" footage, so extensively is it conceived of in terms of narrative fiction. However, doubt clearly existed in some viewers' minds as to whether it was a story based directly on a real incident or whether (as was actually the case) Cathy's tale was a construction developed from a range of research materials. Several commentators queried the legitimacy of combining the dramatic license to articulate a viewpoint through character and action, on the one hand, with the documentary requirement to be "impartial," on the other—a perspective that often revealed a certain amount of naiveté on the commentators' part about the veracity of "straight documentary."

Against these complaints, other critics defended the program makers' right to use dramatic emotional devices in order to engage the viewer with public issues, pointing to the way in which the program's view of officialdom was essentially the view held by Cathy herself—in their eyes, this was a perfectly proper use of character viewpoint from which audience members could measure their own empathetic distance.

In British television history, then, *Cathy Come Home* remains an important marker in the long-running debate about television and truth. This should not be allowed to overshadow its own qualities as a work of social imagination, however, and as an exploration in "hybridized" forms that sometimes brilliantly prefigures much later shifts in the modes of address of factual television.

JOHN CORNER

See also **Docudrama; Garnett, Tony; Loach, Ken; Sanford, Jeremy; *Wednesday Play***

Cast

Cathy	Carol White
Ray	Ray Brooks

Producer
Tony Garnett

Programming History
BBC
December 16, 1966

Further Reading

Brandt, George, editor, *British Television Drama,* London: Cambridge University Press, 1981
Sanford, Jeremy, *Cathy Come Home,* London: Boyars, 1976

Cavalcade of America

U.S. Anthology Drama

Cavalcade of America pioneered the use of anthology drama for company voice advertising. A knockoff of sponsor E.I. DuPont de Nemours and Company's long-running radio program, television's *Cavalcade* celebrated acts of individual initiative and achievement consistent with its sponsor's "Better things for better living" motto. The historical-documentary format especially fit the politically conservative DuPont Company, whose own history in the United States dated to 1802. The *Cavalcade* frequently touched on science and invention, often focusing its free-enterprise subtext on the early American republic. "Poor Richard," its first telecast on October 1, 1952, dramatized the wit and inventiveness of Benjamin Franklin. Developed from a back catalog of radio plays judged to have "picture qualities," the drama sent the "old and obstinate" Franklin to delay American surrender talks with the British, thereby allowing General George Washington to escape capture to fight another day. The denouement found Franklin "on his knees praying for Liberty and Peace and the ability to deserve them." Other first season telecasts reprised stories of *Cavalcade* favorites Samuel Morse, in "What Hath God Wrought"; electric motor inventor Thomas Davenport as "The Indomitable Blacksmith"; Samuel Slater in "Slater's Dream"; and Eli Whitney as "The Man Who Took a Chance."

For many viewers the *Cavalcade of America* was history on the air. DuPont Company publicist Lyman Dewey confidently asserted that the typical viewer "abstracts [sic] the meaning for himself" without explicit statement from the company, identifying DuPont with the "rugged scene of America's struggle." Program specialists exercised the format's malleable historical and dramatic properties under maximum editorial control. A complete reliance on telefilms ensured the prescribed interpretation of scripts, expanded the scope of production limited by the television studio, and lent programs a finished look that specialists felt reflected the company's stature. The use of telefilms allowed for additional economies in the rebroadcast and syndication of programs. Shorn of the "Story of Chemistry" commercials that concluded each program, telefilms were then placed in circulation on the club-and-school circuit. Merchandising directed to the general viewing public leavened the series' educational purpose with entertainment values. Promotional material accompanying the *Cavalcade*'s second telecast, titled "All's Well with Lydia," for example, described "the Revolutionary War story of Lydia Darragh, American patriot and Philadelphia widow, who by her cleverness gained information instrumental in an American victory." Spot announcement texts supplied to local stations read, "Was she minx or patriot?" A second exclaimed, "Lydia Darragh's receptive ear, ready smile and pink cheek are more dangerous to British hopes than a thousand muskets!"

In a bid to freshen up the series' historical venue with the trend toward "actuals" then in favor on *General Electric Theater* and *Armstrong Circle Theatre,* during the 1954–55 television season, *Cavalcade* introduced contemporary story subjects: "Saturday Story," with the football team the Cleveland Browns' Otto Graham, who played himself; "Man on the Beat," a police drama; "The Gift of Dr. Minot," the story of the 1934 Nobel laureate in medicine and his treatment of anemia; and "Sunrise on a Dirty Face," a juvenile-delinquent drama. The favorable reception of stories of "modern American life" led to a change of title for the 1955–56 television season. Retaining an option on the historical past, the new *DuPont Cavalcade Theater* debuted with "A Time for Courage," the story of "Nancy Merki and the swimming coach who led her to victory over polio and to Olympic stardom." In subsequent weeks *Cavalcade* featured a mix of contemporary and historical stories, including "Toward Tomorrow," a biography of Dr. Ralph Bunche; "Disaster Patrol," an adventure story about the Civil Air Patrol; "The Swamp Fox," featuring Hans Conried in the role of General Francis Marion; and "Postmark: Danger," a police drama drawn from the files of U.S. postal investigators.

DuPont's new interest in contemporary relevance, however, was occasionally misread by Batten, Barton, Durstine and Osborn, its Madison Avenue advertising agency and program producer. Rejecting a *Cavalcade Theater* script titled "I Lost My Job," a DuPont Company official testily explained to agency producers that

> on *Cavalcade* or in any other DuPont advertising, we do not want to picture business in a bad light, or in any way that can be interpreted as negative by even a single viewer. It just seems axiomatic that we'd be silly to spend advertising money to tear down the very concept we're trying to sell.

By the 1956–57 television season, that sale had moved to new settings and locations far from the *Cavalcade*'s capsule demonstrations of free enterprise at work. Spurred by editorial confidence in the value of entertainment, the newly renamed *DuPont Theatre* all but abandoned the historical past, at least as an educational prerequisite for an evening's entertainment. The following season the *DuPont Show of the Month* confirmed the trend with a schedule of 90-minute spectaculars, some in color, debuting September 29, 1957, with "Crescendo," a musical variety program costarring Ethel Merman and Rex Harrison.

WILLIAM L. BIRD, JR.

See also **Advertising, Company Voice; Anthology Drama; *Armstrong Circle Theatre; General Electric Theater***

Producers

Maurice Geraghty, Armand Schaefer, Gilbert A. Ralston, Arthur Ripley, Jack Denove, Jack Chertok

Programming History

NBC

October 1952–June 1953	Wednesday 8:30–9:00

ABC

September 1953–June 1955	Tuesday 7:30–8:00
September 1955–June 1957	Tuesday 9:30–10:00

Further Reading

Grams, Martin, *The History of the Cavalcade of America,* OTR, 1999

Hawes, William, *The American Television Drama: The Experimental Years,* University: University of Alabama Press, 1986

Sturcken, Frank, *Live Television: The Golden Age of 1946–1958 in New York,* Jefferson, North Carolina: McFarland, 1990

CBC. *See* **Canadian Broadcasting Corporation Newsworld**

CBS. *See* **Columbia Broadcasting System**

Censorship

Conceptions of censorship derive from Roman practice in which two officials were appointed by the government to conduct the census, award public contracts, and supervise the manners and morals of the people. Today, the scope of censorship has been expanded to include most media and involves suppressing any or all parts deemed objectionable on moral, political, military, or other grounds. While most Americans are fiercely protective of First Amendment rights and resent government control, they are more tolerant of self-imposed censorship. This is one reason many media industries, in the face of mounting criticism, would rather devise "rating systems" of their own that classify the content of their product or warn viewers of objectionable material than subject themselves to external censorship.

With regard to television in the United States, censorship usually refers to the exclusion of certain topics, social groups, or language from the content of broadcast programming. While censorship has often been constructed against the explicit backdrop of morality, it has been implicitly based on assumptions about the identity and composition of the audience for U.S. broadcast television at particular points in time. The economic drive to maximize network profits has helped to inspire the different conceptions of the audience that broadcasters have held. At times, the television audience has been constructed as an undifferentiated mass. During other periods, the audience has been divided into demographically desirable categories. As the definition of the audience has changed over time, so has the boundary between appropriate and inappropriate content. At times, different sets of moral values have often come into conflict with each other and with the economic forces of American broadcasting. The moral limits on content stem from what might be viewed as specific social groups' social and cultural taboos, particularly concerning religious and sexual topics.

During the 1950s and 1960s, the networks and advertisers measured the viewing audience as an undifferentiated mass. Despite the lumping together of all viewers, broadcasters structured programming content around the "normal," dominant values of white, middle-class Americans. Therefore, content centered around the concerns of the nuclear family. Topics such as racism or sexuality, which seemingly had little direct impact on this domestic setting, were excluded from content. Indeed, ethnic minorities were excluded, for the most part, from the television screen because they did not fit into the networks' assumptions about the viewing audience. Sexuality was a topic allocated to the private, personal sphere, rather than the public arena of network broadcasting. For example, during the mid-1960s, the sexual relationship between Rob and Laura Petrie in *The Dick Van Dyke Show* could only be implied. When the couple's bedroom was shown, twin beds diffused any explicit connotation that they had a physical relationship. Direct references to nonnormative heterosexuality were excluded from programming altogether. In addition, coarse language that described bodily functions and sexual activity or profaned sacred words was excluded from broadcast discourse.

However, conceptions about the viewing audience and the limits of censorship changed drastically during the early 1970s. To a large degree, this shift in censorship came about because techniques for measuring the viewing audience became much more refined at that time. Ratings researchers began to break down the viewing audience for individual programs according to specific demographic characteristics, including age, ethnicity, education, and economic background. In this context, the baby-boomer generation (younger, better educated, with more disposable income) became the desired target audience for television programming and advertising. Even though baby boomers grew up on television programming of the 1950s and 1960s, their tastes and values were often in marked contrast to that of their middle-class parents. Subjects previously excluded from television began to appear with regularity.

All in the Family was the predominant battering ram that broke down the restrictions placed on television content during the preceding 20 years. Frank discussions of sexuality, even outside of traditional heterosexual monogamy, became the focal point of many of the comedy's narratives. The series also introduced issues of ethnicity and bigotry as staples of its content. Constraints on the use of profanity began to crumble as well. Scriptwriters began to pepper dialogue with "damns" and "hells," language not permitted during the more conservative 1950s and 1960s.

While the redefinition of the desirable audience in

the early 1970s did expand the parameters of appropriate content for television programming, the new candor prompted reactions from several fronts and demonstrated large divisions within social and cultural communities. As early as 1973, the Supreme Court emphasized that community standards vary from place to place: "It is neither realistic nor constitutionally sound to read the First Amendment as requiring that people of Maine or Mississippi accept public depiction of conduct found tolerable in Las Vegas or New York City." Clearly, such a ruling leaves it to states or communities to define what is acceptable and what is not, a task that cannot be carried out to everyone's satisfaction. When applying community standards, the courts must decide what the "average person, in the community" finds acceptable or not, and some communities are clearly more conservative than others. These standards are particularly difficult to apply to television programming that is produced, for economic reasons, to cross all such regional and social boundaries.

In part as a result of these divisions, however, special-interest or advocacy groups began to confront the networks about representations and content that had not been present before 1971. For some social groups that had had very little, if any, visibility during the first 20 years of U.S. broadcast television, the expanding parameters of programming content were a mixed blessing. The inclusion of Hispanics, African Americans, and gays and lesbians in programming was preferable to their near invisibility during the previous two decades, but advocacy groups often took issue with the framing and stereotyping of the new images. From a contrasting perspective, conservative groups began to oppose the incorporation of topics within content that did not align easily with traditional American values or beliefs. In particular, the American Family Association decried the increasing presentation of nontraditional sexual behavior as acceptable in broadcast programming. Other groups rallied against the increased use of violence in broadcast content. As a result, attempts to define the boundaries of appropriate content have become an ongoing struggle, as the networks negotiate their own interests against those of advertisers and various social groups. Whereas censorship in the 1950s and 1960s was based on the presumed standards and tastes of the white, middle-class nuclear family, censorship in the 1970s became a process of balancing the often conflicting values of marginal social groups.

The proliferation of cable since the 1980s has only exacerbated the conflicts over programming and censorship. Because of a different mode of distribution and exhibition (often referred to as "narrowcasting") cable television has been able to offer more explicit sexual and violent programming than broadcast television. To compete for the viewing audience that increasingly turns to cable television channels, the broadcast networks have loosened restrictions on programming content, enabling them to include partial nudity, somewhat more graphic violence, and the use of coarse language. This strategy seems to have been partially successful in attracting viewers, as evidenced by the popularity of adult dramas such as *NYPD Blue*. However, this programming approach has opened the networks to further attacks from conservative advocacy groups, which have increased the pressure for government regulation (i.e., censorship) of objectionable program content.

As these issues and problems indicate, most Americans, because of cherished First Amendment rights, are extremely sensitive to any form of censorship. Relative to other countries, however, the United States enjoys remarkable freedom from official monitoring of program content. Negative reactions are often expressed toward imported or foreign programs when they do not reflect indigenous norms and values. "Cutting of scenes" is practiced far more in developing countries than in Western countries. Americans may find it interesting to note that even European countries consider exposure to nudity and sex to be less objectionable than abusive language or violence.

Sydney Head, Christopher Sterling, and Lemuel Schofield point out that the control of media and media content is also related to the type of government in power in a particular country. They identify four types of governmental philosophy related to the issue of censorship: authoritarian, paternalistic, pluralistic, and permissive. Of the four types, the first two are more inclined to exercise censorship because they assume they know what is best for citizens. Anything that challenges this exclusive view must be banned or excluded. Since most broadcasting in such countries is state funded, control is relatively easy for the government to impose. Exclusionary methods include governmental control of broadcast stations' licenses, jamming external broadcasts, promoting indigenous programming, imposing restrictions on imported programs, excluding newspaper articles, cutting scenes from films, and shutting down printing presses.

Pluralistic and permissive governments allow for varying degrees of private ownership of broadcasting stations. Such governments assume that citizens will choose what they consider best in a free market where competing media companies offer their products. Such an ideal can be effective, of course, only if the competitors are roughly equal and operate in the interests of the public. To maintain this "balance of ideas" in the United States, the Federal Communications Commission (FCC) established rules that regulate the formation of media monopolies and require stations to demonstrate they operate in the interests of their audiences' good. Despite such intentions, recent deregulation has disturbed the balance, allowing powerful media conglomerates to dominate the marketplace and reduce the number of voices heard.

Pluralistic and permissive governments also assume that competing companies will regulate themselves. Perhaps the best-known attempt at self-regulation is conducted by the Motion Picture Association of America (MPAA), which rates motion pictures for particular audiences. For example, the contents of "G" rated movies are considered suitable for all audiences and "PG" requires parental guidance, whereas "R," "X," and "NC17" are considered appropriate for adults only.

In the past, one of the arguments against censorship has been freedom of choice. Parents who object to offensive television programs can always switch the channel or choose another show. Unfortunately, parental supervision is lacking in many households. In the 1990s, this problem, coupled with political and interest group outrage against media producers, led many to debate the possibility of a self-imposed television rating system similar to that of the MPAA. To counter conservative criticism and government censorship, producers and the networks agreed to begin a ratings system that could be electronically monitored and blocked in the home. In 1996 the Telecommunications Act required new television sets sold in the United States to include the "V-chip," technology that allows home viewers to program their television sets to block reception of specific shows or of shows with particular ratings. In 1997 the U.S. television rating system—employing six grades that indicate the age-appropriateness of particular programs—was implemented, with the TV-Y (appropriate for very young children), TV-Y7 (suitable for children over 7 years), G (for general audiences), TV-PG (parental guidance suggested), TV-14 (not intended for children under 14 years), or TV-M (mature audiences only) symbol appearing on the upper-left-hand corner of the TV screen at the beginning of each program. In addition, to indicate whether the episode contains certain types of content, up to four additional symbols may be placed below the TV rating: V (violence), L (potentially offensive language), D (mature dialogue), and/or S (sexual situations). Ideally, with this technology and the ratings, parents could effectively censor programming they found unsuitable for their children, while still allowing the networks to air adult-oriented programming. However, the V-chip and the rating system have not been entirely successful, with some people complaining that the information provided is confusing and insufficient. Furthermore, not all the networks fully implemented the rating policy: NBC, in particular, uses the age-related ratings but does not indicate specific types of content.

In the 1970s, an early attempt at a similar sort of regulation came when the FCC encouraged the television industry to introduce a "family viewing concept," according to which television networks would agree to delay the showing of adult programs until children were, presumably, no longer among the audience. The National Association of Broadcasters (NAB) willingly complied with this pressure, but in 1979 a court ruled that the NAB's action was a violation of the First Amendment.

In the late 1990s, as networks relaxed corporate restrictions on content in their competition with cable and satellite programming, the early-evening hours once again took on special importance. In mid-1996, more than 75 members of the U.S. Congress placed an open letter to the entertainment industry in *Daily Variety.* The letter called on the creative community and the programmers to provide an hour of programming each evening that was free from sexual innuendo, violence, or otherwise troublesome material. Clearly, the question of censorship in television continues to vex programmers, producers, government officials, and viewers. No immediate solution to the problems involved is apparent. Indeed, the debate and struggle over censorship of programming will more than likely continue in the 21st century, as social groups with diverse values vie for increased influence over program content.

The terrorist attacks of September 11, 2001, on New York and Washington, D.C., and the subsequent war in Iraq (Operation Iraqi Freedom) have brought issues of censorship into sharper focus. The events of September 11 precipitated an atmosphere of national vulnerability and defensiveness. At this time, the American public seemed willing to tolerate an invasive police presence and a high level of surveillance, in exchange for security. Censorship in a variety of forms has also been accepted, within and without the country, provided it is justified by national security. To increase national security, the George W. Bush administration found it necessary to create a Department of Homeland Security, with sweeping authority and jurisdiction.

Under great pressure to reveal what the government knew about the activities of terrorists prior to September 11 and the soundness of intelligence reports used to justify the Iraq war, President Bush asked a Congressional Committee on Intelligence to published a detailed report. In the public sections, 28 pages that implicated members of the Saudi royal family were censored. This action is allegedly to protect sensitive relationships that might affect the war effort.

Under the U.S.A. Patriot Act of 2001 and the Homeland Security Act, notice was given to librarians that the activities of library patrons, including their World Wide Web browsing, might be subjected to government surveillance without the knowledge or consent of those patrons. In response to this notice, many librarians voiced their strong opposition to provisions of those acts, claiming that they violated their professional ethics, undermined the privacy of individuals, and would have a chilling effect on research and the free flow of information.

Reporting during Operation Iraqi Freedom was handled in a methodical and open manner. Reporters "embedded" in the army were allowed to file reports directly from the battlefront, providing frontline accounts. At times these field reports placed reporters in great jeopardy and several died in the war. The Basra Sheraton Hotel, which was being used by al-Jazeera journalists as a base, was bombed. Apparently no one was hurt, but al-Jazeera complained to the Pentagon. The news organization claimed that it had provided the Pentagon with all the relevant details about its reporters, as stipulated by international practice and conventions, governing the reporting of wars. An inquiry into this incident revealed that American forces may have believed sniper fire was coming from the building.

RICHARD WORRINGHAM AND ROBERT ERLER

See also ***All in the Family;*** **Narrowcasting;** ***NYPD Blue;*** **September 11, 2001; War on Television**

Further Reading

Brown, Les, *Television: The Business Behind the Box,* New York: Harcourt Brace Jovanovich, 1971

Cowan, Geoffrey, *See No Evil: The Backstage Battle over Sex and Violence on Television,* New York: Simon and Schuster, 1979

Head, Sydney, Christopher Sterling, and Lemuel Schofield, *Broadcasting in America: A Survey of Electronic Media,* Boston: Houghton Mifflin, 1972; 7th edition, Princeton, New Jersey: Houghton Mifflin, 1994

Marin, Rick, "Blocking the Box," *Newsweek* (March 11, 1996)

Montgomery, Kathryn C., *Target: Prime-Time Advocacy Groups and the Struggle over Entertainment Television,* New York and Oxford: Oxford University Press, 1989

Channel 4

British Programming Service

The fourth British channel arrived on the scene in 1982 after extensive debate between proponents of public service television on the one hand and of commercial broadcasting on the other. The timing was crucial, for the commercially funded ITV network was starting to outstrip combined BBC 1 and BBC 2 in terms of audience numbers. Channel 4 (C4) was a compromise between the two principles: it was to be financed by advertising revenue from the existing private companies, but governed independently from them, with a brief to provide minority and complementary programming to the three existing channels. It would make none of its own programming, but rather "publish" work produced by outside production companies, and indeed, a host of small independent producers sprung up in its wake, peddling their ideas to a group of "commissioning editors." It would be innovative in program styles and working practices and would find new audiences.

Piloted in its first years by Jeremy Isaacs, a veteran of documentary and current affairs television production who had given a noteworthy speech about his vision at an Edinburgh Television Festival, C4 saw its role as being "different, but not too different." It would stake its claim to being "alternative" by pioneering material new to British television (access, community, youth and minority programs), by catering to as-yet-untelevised sports and hobby enthusiasts (cycling, basketball, chess), and by giving new life to threatened genres like documentary, arts features, and independent film. Risk taking would include the first hour-long TV news and the first overtly "committed" current affairs magazines *(The Friday Alternative).* Dubbed "Channel Bore" by early critics put off by earnest late-night intellectual discussions, and afflicted with occasional censorship battles over certain programs that appeared overly partisan (toward the left), the channel saw its audience share gradually creep upward—though it never attained the 10 percent share it sought in a national television landscape as yet untouched by cable and satellite. Associated with yuppie and liberal values, it boasted a 90 percent satisfaction rate among its selective audience.

Channel 4 did not neglect popular genres, creating its own early-evening serial (*Brookside,* Liverpool-set, remains its most popular program) and launching *Max Headroom* and other avant-garde—or at least less classical than existing—series. It showed quality series imported from the United States like *Hill Street Blues* and *Cheers* and launched some of Britain's alternative comedians *(Comic Strip Presents...)*.

But its main success has been its feature film production; Channel 4 revitalized a moribund British film industry. It invested in a third of the feature films made in Britain in 1984, financing a number of low-budget films such as Stephen Frears's *My Beautiful Launderette* (shot on 16 millimeter in 1985) and coproducing medium-budget ones such as *The Draughtsman's Contract* (Peter Greenaway) and *Dance with a Stranger* (Mike Newell). "Film on Four," under David Rose, wooed writers like David Hare and directors like Mike Leigh from the BBC and attracted new ones like Neil Jordan and Derek Jarman. In contrast to the BBC, C4 policy has been to address contemporary issues and use experimental storytelling. It has backed a number of projects aimed at the European art film market: Wim Wender's *Paris, Texas;* Agnes Varda's *Vagabond;* Andre Tarkovsky's *The Sacrifice;* and Neil Jordan's *The Crying Game.* "Film Four International" showcases independent filmmakers from around the world.

In 1988 chief executive Isaacs stepped down and was replaced by Michael Grade, formerly controller of BBC 1 and scion of a family distinguished in commercial entertainment. Despite fears that he would be forced by commercial pressures to take the channel down a vulgarian path, Grade proved a populist in the best sense of the word, importing more U.S. shows (e.g., *Oprah Winfrey, Roseanne, ER*), although the gamble on American content did not always pay off (*Tales of the City*). The 1990 Broadcasting Act refined its remit to be "distinctive," that is, to include proportions that are European and are supplied by independent producers. More important, the act spun C4 off from the ITV companies by giving it the right to market its own advertising. Funding, like distribution, became a problem: Channel 4 has been so successful at marketing itself that subsidy is flowing the other way, as a share of its profits instead reverts back to the ITV companies' coffers—£38 million in 1994.

Channel 4 underwent significant organizational change under Grade. Under the 1990 Broadcasting Act, Channel 4 became a public cooperation. The service expanded under Grade's leadership. He stepped down in 1997.

Grade's successor, Michael Jackson, imbued the channel with a postmodern, pop cultural sensibility. During his tenure, several successful shows had their debuts, including *Da Ali G Show, Queer as Folk, So Graham Norton,* and the British version of *Big Brother.* Under Jackson, turnover was raised 30 percent in four years. Two new channels, Film Four and E4, were launched.

Since 2002, Mark Thompson has served as the current chief executive of Channel 4.

SUSAN EMMANUEL

See also **Grade, Michael; Isaacs, Jeremy; Jackson, Michael**

Further Reading

Isaacs, Jeremy, *Storm over Four: A Personal Account,* London: Weidenfeld and Nicholson, 1989

Pym, John, *Film on Four, 1981–1991,* London: British Film Institute, 1992

Stoneman, Rod, "Sins of Commission," *Screen* (Summer 1992)

Wyver, John, "The English Channel," *American Film* (July–August 1986)

Channel One News

U.S. Proprietary Programming Service

Channel One News is a 12-minute television news program targeted to teenagers and distributed via satellite to more than 12,000 middle and high schools across the United States each school day morning. This represents an audience of more than 8 million students, with thousands of other schools currently on a waiting list to receive the program. *Channel One News* became, almost from its inception, a highly controversial educational program offering, primarily because two minutes of each program are devoted to advertising. Its

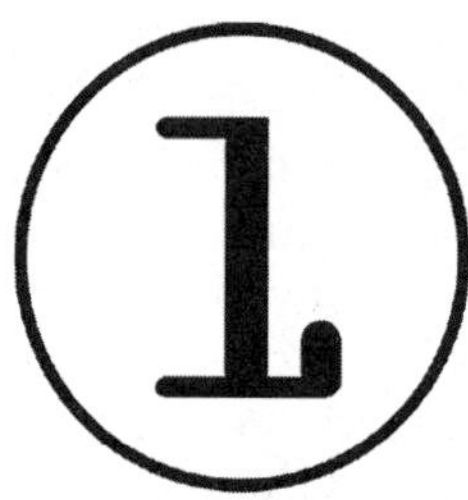

Channel One News™

critics came from both sides of the political spectrum and included such diverse and outspoken critics as Ralph Nader and Phyllis Schlafley.

Channel One News began its pilot phase in January 1989, originally as a production of Whittle Communications, Inc., in Knoxville, Tennessee, and was heavily promoted by the company's founder, Christopher Whittle. In 1995 Whittle Communications closed and sold *Channel One* to K-III Communications Corporation, a large diversified communications company focused on education, information, and magazine publishing. K-III Communications is now PRIMEDIA, Inc., a $1.6 billion corporation currently trading on the New York Stock Exchange as PRM. On its corporate website, PRIMEDIA proclaims it is the "#1 special interest magazine publisher in the U.S., with 250 titles such as *Automobile, Motor Trend, New York, Fly Fisherman, American Baby, Telephony and American Demographics;* the #1 producer and distributor of specialty video with 18 satellite and digital video product lines, including Channel One Network."

In order for a school to receive *Channel One News,* it must sign a three-year agreement to carry the program in its entirety each school day and make the telecast available to at least 90 percent of the student body. In return, each school receives a satellite dish (TVRO), two videocassette recorders, one 19-inch television set per classroom, and all of the necessary cabling. No money is exchanged. In a recent enhancement, the school will also have access to more than 100 hours of curriculum-specific, satellite-delivered programming.

Channel One News content is geared to teenagers and delivered by anchors and reporters typically in their early to mid-20s. Program content includes the latest news as well as weeklong series for more depth on such topics as jobs, drug abuse, science and technology, and international politics. According to *Channel One News,* its news programming has "five educational goals":

1. to enhance cultural literacy,
2. to promote critical thinking,
3. to provide a common language and shared experience,
4. to provide relevance and motivation, and
5. to strengthen character and build a sense of responsibility.

Channel One News has received many awards, including the Advertising Council's Silver Bell Award for "outstanding public service" and a George Foster Peabody Award for the series *A Decade of AIDS.*

In addition to the daily news program, schools are also provided approximately 250 hours per school year of noncommercial educational programming (through an agreement with Pacific Mountain Network) designed to serve as a supplemental teaching tool to support existing curricula.

Many in the educational community and elsewhere have decried *Channel One News* on the basis that it commercializes the classroom environment, and some have expressed concern that there may be an implicit endorsement of the products shown. *Channel One News* characterizes its role as a positive partnership between the educational and business communities. It cites, for example, a three-year study of *Channel One News* by a team, commissioned by Whittle, from the University of Michigan. Among the study's findings were apparent increases in awareness and knowledge of current events by the audience and the judgment by a majority of teachers surveyed that they would recommend the program to other teachers. Other studies have found that *Channel One News*' stated commitment to community service is evidenced by a high percentage (about 15 percent) of the commercial time being given to public service announcements. And in a 1993 report published in *Educational Leadership,* 90 percent of teachers thought *Channel One News* included the "most important events of the previous day." Other teachers, critics, and evaluators, however, still find the idea of students viewing advertising in the classroom anathema. The debate continues.

THOMAS A. BIRK

Further Reading

Greenberg, B.S., and J.E. Brand, "Television News and Advertising in Schools: The *Channel One* Controversy," *Journal of Communication* (1993)

Tiene, D., "Channel One: Good or Bad News for Our Schools?" *Educational Leadership* (May 1993)

Tiene, D., "Exploring the Effectiveness of the *Channel One* School Telecasts," *Educational Technology* (May 1993)

Wulfemeyer, K.T., and B. Mueller, "*Channel One* and Commercials in Classrooms: Advertising Content Aimed at Students," *Journalism Quarterly* (1992)

Charles, Glen and Les

U.S. Writers and Producers

When Glen and Les Charles watched television comedies in the early 1970s, they saw more than just clever entertainment and escape—they saw an opportunity to leave their unsatisfying jobs and become part of show business. While many people might share this dream, the Charles brothers had the talent, dedication, and luck to move from their sofa to behind the scenes of some of the most successful comedies in television history.

The Charleses were raised Mormon near Las Vegas, Nevada, exposed to the glitz of their hometown while absorbing their family's emphasis on education. They both received a liberal arts education at University of Redlands in Los Angeles. Les Charles followed in his mother's footsteps by teaching public school, while Glen Charles attended law school and eventually worked as an advertising copywriter. Neither brother was content in his job, and both dreamed of something more. On a Saturday night in 1974, they were watching their favorite night of television and they became inspired—instead of just watching CBS's Saturday lineup of *All in the Family, M*A*S*H, The Bob Newhart Show,* and *The Mary Tyler Moore Show,* they would write episodes for these television comedies.

They started by writing an episode of their favorite, *The Mary Tyler Moore Show,* and sending it to MTM Productions. After receiving no response, they persisted, writing a sample episode of every television comedy they enjoyed and sending it to the producers on spec. Confident in their talents, they both quit their jobs to dedicate more time to their writing; Les Charles and his wife were living out of their van when the Charles brothers received notification of their first sold script. They lived off the money and excitement generated from seeing their episode of *M*A*S*H* on the air, but no jobs followed immediately. Finally, after two years and dozens of unsolicited scripts, they received the phone call they had been waiting for—the producers at MTM had read their first script at last and offered them jobs as staff writers on the spin-off *Phyllis.*

Often referred to as "MTM Television University," MTM Productions was a training ground for young writers in the 1970s, offering a supportive atmosphere that emphasized talent and quality over commercial success and popularity. The Charles brothers quickly climbed up the ranks in MTM, moving from story editors to producers at *Phyllis* and eventually getting the opportunity to produce one of the programs that had first inspired them, *The Bob Newhart Show.* While at *Phyllis,* the brothers met a colleague with whom they would form a long fruitful working partnership—James Burrows. The Charles brothers and Burrows "graduated" from MTM together when four MTM veterans created *Taxi* and hired this team to oversee the daily production of the show. Glen and Les Charles left MTM to become writer-producers for *Taxi,* while Burrows directed the series.

Taxi brought both success and acclaim to the Charles brothers, as the program won Emmy Awards for their writing in addition to TV's top honor in their category—Outstanding Comedy Series. But Glen and Les Charles and Jim Burrows all wanted to work on a series that was uniquely their own, not the concept of other writers and producers. Therefore, after three highly successful years at *Taxi,* the trio left the show to form Charles-Burrows-Charles Productions and create their own signature brand of television comedy. Luckily for them, Grant Tinker had just taken over NBC and was looking for "quality" programming to fill out the last-place network's schedule. Without even a concept or script in hand, Tinker gave Charles-Burrows-Charles a deal to produce a new comedy for NBC.

All three partners were fans of the British comedy *Fawlty Towers* and thought that setting the series in a hotel would be a good choice. Like the British series, theirs would feature odd guests passing through and associating with the series regulars. But after sketching out their ideas, they realized that most scenes took place in the hotel bar and they could streamline the show by eliminating the hotel altogether. Unlike the seedy atmosphere commonly associated with bars, they envisioned a classy neighborhood tavern based on a Boston pub. To avoid any implication that they were glorifying drinking, they made the owner of the bar a recovering alcoholic. After casting a group of unknowns, many of whom had been guest stars on *Taxi, Cheers* was born.

While *Cheers* certainly bore many of the marks of MTM shows and *Taxi,* there were aspects distinct to Charles-Burrows-Charles. Unlike most MTM shows, there were no well-known actors on the show, which relied solely on the comedic talent of the cast and writing to draw in audiences. While *Taxi* had moved away from the middle-class and optimistic settings of MTM programs and toward a grittier and more pessimistic view of the world, *Cheers* found a middle ground—while no characters were truly happy with their jobs or circumstances, there was a contentedness in the bar where "everybody knows your name" that was never present in *Taxi.* The major adjustment the Charles brothers brought to *Cheers* was the presence of a long-term narrative arc concerning the tempestuous romance between Sam Malone and Diane Chambers; Glen and Les Charles wrote this aspect of the series in direct reaction to the static relationship between Mary Richards and Lou Grant, which never changed through the course of *The Mary Tyler Moore Show.*

Luckily for the Charles brothers, Tinker was willing to give *Cheers* a chance to develop this long-term arc. The program's first-season ratings were horrible (77th place), but both Tinker and his programming head Brandon Tartikoff were fans of *Cheers* and subsequently gave the show another chance. Emmy Awards followed, word of mouth grew, and the show gained in the ratings, but it was not until *The Cosby Show* found its place in the leadoff slot of NBC's Thursday night lineup that *Cheers* turned into a blockbuster show. The Charles brothers moved away from writing individual episodes and served as general overseers of the program from their executive producer chairs. They attempted to develop a stable of programs by introducing the *Cheers* spin-off *The Tortellis* and *All Is Forgiven,* but both shows bombed; after this failure, Glen and Les Charles decided that they were not the "comedy factory" type of producers. They needed direct, day-to-day control of their programs. They stuck with *Cheers* as executive producers throughout its 11-year run and returned to the writing table to script the series' final episode. Since *Cheers,* the Charles brothers have been inactive in television; their film work has been modest, featuring one produced screenplay, 1999's "dramedy" *Pushing Tin.* But even if they never write another script for television, their rise from comedy fans to creators of one of the most successful and acclaimed television series ever should be enough for a valued place in television history.

JASON MITTELL

See also ***Bob Newhart Show, The; Cheers; M*A*S*H; Taxi***

Glen Charles. Born in Henderson, Nevada. Attended University of Redlands, California, B.A. in English; San Francisco State University. Advertising copywriter; began television career as writer, with brother Les Charles; writer-producer, *The Bob Newhart Show;* formed Charles-Burrows-Charles production company with television director James Burrows, 1977; creator-producer, *Taxi, Cheers.*

Les Charles. Born in Henderson, Nevada. Attended University of Redlands, California, B.A. in English. High school English teacher; began television career as writer, with brother Glen Charles; writer-producer, *The Bob Newhart Show;* formed Charles-Burrows-Charles production company with television director James Burrows, 1977; creator-producer, *Taxi, Cheers.*

Television (Glen and Les Charles)

1972–78	*The Bob Newhart Show* (writer-producers)
1972–83	*M*A*S*H* (writers)
1975–77	*Phyllis* (writers)
1978–83	*Taxi* (writers, coproducers)
1982–93	*Cheers* (writers, coproducers)
1986	*All Is Forgiven* (coproducers)
1987	*The Tortellis* (coproducers)

Film (writers)

Pushing Tin, 1999

Further Reading

Sorensen, Jeff, *The Taxi Book,* New York: St. Martin's Press, 1987

Waldron, Vince, *Classic Sitcoms: A Celebration of the Best of Prime-Time Comedy,* New York: Macmillan, 1987

Charlie's Angels

U.S. Detective Drama

Charlie's Angels, the critically panned female detective series that heralded the age of "jiggle TV," aired on ABC from 1976 to 1981. The show, which featured three shapely, often scantily clad women solving crimes undercover for a boss they knew only as a godlike voice from a phone speaker, was an immediate sensation, landing the number five spot in the Nielsen ratings during the 1976–77 TV season. (This premiere-season record would remain unbroken until 1994–95, when NBC's new medical drama *E/R* finished number two for the year.) In its second year, following the departure of its most popular star, *Charlie's Angels* tied for number four with the critically acclaimed *60 Minutes* and *All in the Family.* However, by its third season, *Charlie's Angels* slipped out of the top ten, and by the 1980–81 season, the show's novelty had worn as thin as the Angels' slinky outfits; in that year *Charlie's Angels* placed 59 out of 65 shows and was canceled after 115 episodes.

Deemed "sexploitation" by its detractors, *Charlie's Angels* was the brainchild of producer Aaron Spelling, who in the early 1970s had found success in the TV detective genre with *The Mod Squad* and *The Rookies,* hip series shooting for young-adult audiences. With *Charlie's Angels,* Spelling spun a new formula that would attract desirable demographics among young men and women: he combined detective drama with the glamorous fantasy that would become his staple in the 1980s with *Dynasty* and the 1990s with *Beverly Hills, 90210* and *Melrose Place.* Not only were his Angels beautiful and sexy, they were smart and powerful heroines who used provocative attraction (and feminine, often feigned, vulnerability) to lure and capture unsuspecting male criminals. Although *Charlie's Angels* was among TV's first dramas to instill female characters with typically male "powers" via a dominant subject position, the show's critics, including infuriated feminists, countered that *Charlie's Angels* was little more than a patriarchal production that sexually objectified its characters.

The premise of *Charlie's Angels* placed the show's feminine heroes in a male-dominated workplace and a woman-as-victim society. The Angels—once "three little girls who went to the police academy"—worked under the auspices of a patriarchal, narrative voice they called "Charlie" (the never-seen John Forsythe), who ran from remote locations the Charles Townsend Detective Agency in Los Angeles. Bosley, Charlie's asexual (and thus unthreatening) representative (played by David Doyle), helped direct the Angels to meet Charlie's desired ends. Working undercover in women's prison camps, as showgirls, as prostitutes, and in other sexually suggestive locales and professions, the Angels inevitably found themselves in jeopardy each week, victimized either by evil men or unattractive (which in Spelling's lexicon meant "bad") women who underestimated the Angels' smarts and their strengths as beautiful, seemingly frail decoys.

The three original Angels included two decoys—brunette Kelly Garret (played by Jaclyn Smith, the only Angel to remain through the series' entire run) and blonde Jill Munroe (played by Farrah Fawcett, whose fluffy, feathered hairstyle became a nationwide 1970s fad and whose sexy posters became best-sellers). By contrast, the third, less glamorous Angel, Sabrina Duncan (played by Kate Jackson, who also starred in Spelling's *The Rookies*), became known as "the smart one." Sabrina's impish qualities—independence, athleticism, adventurism, and asexuality—often kept her working behind the scenes with Bosley, helping to rescue other Angels, and consequently often kept her out of the bikinis, braless t-shirts, and tight dresses with plunging necklines that her coworkers opted to wear. Sabrina, Jill, and Kelly (a martial arts expert) all participated in the show's choreographed violence, which included karate chops, kicks to the groin, and other sanitized brutality (guns seldom were fired).

Fawcett (then Farrah Fawcett-Majors during her brief marriage to *Six Million Dollar Man* star Lee Majors) broke her contract and left the series after one season to become a movie star. She was replaced by blonde actress Cheryl Ladd, who played Jill's younger sister, Kris, also a decoy character. (As part of her exit agreement, Fawcett was forced to make guest appearances through the show's fourth season.) After two seasons and struggles to insert more meaningful characterizations into the show, Jackson also retired her

Charlie's Angels, Farrah Fawcett, Kate Jackson, Jaclyn Smith, 1976–81.
©Columbia Pictures/Courtesy of the Everett Collection

wings. She was replaced in 1979 by blonde actress Shelley Hack, who in 1980 was replaced by brunette actress Tanya Roberts for the show's final season. Throughout these cast changes, the formula remained consistent, save the loss of the impish Sabrina.

All six Angels, especially Fawcett, Smith, Jackson, and Ladd, became media icons whose faces—and heavenly bodies—were plastered on magazine covers, posters, lunch boxes, and loads of other toys and related merchandise. *Charlie's Angels* was undoubtedly a fantasy whose trappings appealed to males and females, young and old. Whether the show ultimately helped or hurt female portrayals in TV drama remains debatable. But as pure camp, the show, highlighted by episodes with titles like "Angels in Chains," remains a cult classic. As the omniscient Charlie would say, "Good work, Angels."

CHRIS MANN

See also **Detective Programs; Forsythe, John; Gender and Television**

Cast

Sabrina Duncan (1976–79)	Kate Jackson
Jill Munroe (1976–77)	Farrah Fawcett-Majors
Kelly Garrett	Jaclyn Smith
Kris Munroe (1977–81)	Cheryl Ladd
Tiffany Welles (1979–80)	Shelley Hack
Julie Rogers (1980–81)	Tanya Roberts
John Bosley	David Doyle
Charlie Townsend (voice only)	John Forsythe

Producers

Leonard Goldberg, Aaron Spelling, Rich Husky, David Levinson, Barney Rosenzweig, Ronald Austin, James David Buchanan, Edward J. Lasko, Robert Janes, Elaine Rich

Programming History

108 episodes
ABC

September 1976–August 1977	Wednesday 10:00–11:00
August 1977–October 1980	Wednesday 9:00–10:00
November 1980–January 1981	Sunday 8:00–9:00
January 1981–February 1981	Saturday 8:00–9:00
June 1981–August 1981	Wednesday 8:00–9:00

Further Reading

D'Acci, Julie, *Defining Women: Television and the Case of Cagney and Lacey,* Chapel Hill: University of North Carolina Press, 1994

Fiske, John, *Television Culture,* New York: Routledge, 1987

Meehan, Diana, *Ladies of the Evening: Women Characters of Prime-Time Television,* Metuchen, New Jersey: Scarecrow, 1983

Chase, David (1945–)

U.S. Writer, Producer, Director

David Chase (born David DeCesare) once aspired to be a rock musician, but after studying at the School of Visual Arts in New York and acquiring a master's degree from Stanford University, he sought work in feature films. Despite some success in that arena, most of his work has been in television where, after 25 years as a writer, producer, director, and creator of some of the medium's most highly acclaimed series, he achieved "overnight" success as creator, writer, producer, and sometimes director of HBO's *The Sopranos.*

Chase's first writing credit was the adaptation of his story *The Still Life* as the low-budget horror film *Grave of the Vampire* (1972). Turning his attentions to television, his story *The Hunter* was adapted as the television film *Scream of the Wolf* (ABC, January 16, 1974). He worked as a story consultant/story editor for ABC's *Kolchak: The Night Stalker* (1974–75) and as a story consultant for *Switch* (CBS, 1975–78). As supervising producer for *The Rockford Files* (NBC, 1974–80) starring James Garner, Chase also wrote several episodes and in 1978 shared the Emmy for Outstanding Drama Series with fellow *Rockford* producers Stephen J. Cannell, Meta Rosenberg, and Charles Floyd Johnson. The series was also awarded a 1980 Golden Globe for Best Television Drama Series. That same year, Chase's teleplay for *Off the Minnesota Strip* (ABC, May 5, 1980) garnered him his first Emmy Award for writing as well as an award from the Writers Guild of America. Chase made his directorial debut on the 1985 revival of *Alfred Hitchcock Presents* (NBC, 1985–86), directing two episodes he wrote himself ("A Very Happy Ending," February 16, 1986, and "Enough Rope for Two," March 9, 1986). The new version of the classic anthology series lasted only one season but aired two additional seasons on the USA network.

In the fall of 1988, Chase created, executive produced, wrote, and directed the critically acclaimed drama *Almost Grown* (CBS), but lackluster ratings caused the show's cancellation after only nine episodes. The series, about a couple on the brink of divorce, incorporated Chase's love of music, using popular songs to trigger flashbacks relating various points in the couple's 30-year relationship. Subsequent television projects continued to enhance his reputation as a producer of quality dramas. With John Falsey and Joshua Brand he produced NBC's *I'll Fly Away* (1991–93), the story of a southern African-American woman in the midst of the 1950s civil rights movement. The series received numerous critical awards, and in 1993 Chase won the prestigious Golden Laurel from the Producers Guild of America as producer of the year. That same year he succeeded Falsey and Brand as executive producer of the popular *Northern Exposure* (CBS, 1990–95). In 1996 Chase wrote, produced, and directed the second TV film based on *The Rockford Files* (with James Garner reprising the title role), *The Rockford Files: Crime and Punishment* (CBS, September 18, 1996).

But it is his work as the creator, executive producer, writer, and sometimes director of HBO's *The Sopranos,* the story of a New Jersey mobster's relationship with his "families," that has brought Chase's name to the forefront of Hollywood. Like much of Chase's previous work, *The Sopranos* focuses on character rather than situation or action. The series is heavily influenced by his own fascination with 1930s gangster films and his New Jersey childhood. The characters are based on an amalgam of people he has known and he admits the family dynamics sometimes mirror his own. Although it depicts an organized crime family, the characters deal with human issues common to all families.

The Sopranos premiered on HBO on January 10, 1999. In its first season, the series began with a small cult following that eventually pulled in nearly 10 million viewers each week. The series has garnered Chase numerous nominations and awards, including one from the Directors Guild of America for directing the series' pilot episode, a Golden Globe Award for Best Television Drama Series, and Peabody Awards for quality television (2000 and 2001). In its first season, *The Sopranos* literally dominated the Emmy category Writing for a Drama Series (four out of five nominations, including one for Chase). In 2001 *The Sopranos* received 22 Emmy nominations, the third-highest number for any series in a single year, and a record-breaking number for a cable series.

Concerned that the quality of the show might deteriorate over time, Chase created a self-imposed limit of four seasons for the series. However, the show's enormous popularity, coupled with Chase's intrigue with new storylines, prompted him to agree to a fifth season. Chase has plans to return to feature films and is currently slated to write and direct feature films for HBO and Sony Pictures Entertainment.

SUSAN R. GIBBERMAN

See also **Sopranos, The**

David Chase. Born David DeCesare in Mount Vernon, New York, August 22, 1945. Educated at New York's School of Visual Arts and Stanford University. Recipient: Edgar Allan Poe Award nomination for Best Television Episode ("The Oracle Wore a Cashmere Suit," *The Rockford Files*), 1977; Emmy Award for Outstanding Drama Series (*The Rockford Files*), 1978; Emmy Award for Outstanding Writing in a Limited Series or Special (*Off the Minnesota Strip*), 1980; Producers Guild of America Award for Television Producer of the Year, 1993; Emmy Award for Outstanding Writing in a Drama Series ("College," *The Sopranos*), 1999; Directors Guild of America Award for Outstanding Directorial Achievement in a Dramatic Series (*The Sopranos*), 2000; Silver FIPA from the Biarritz International Festival of Audiovisual Programming (*The Sopranos*), 2000; Golden Laurel from the Producers Guild of America as Television Producer of the Year, 2000.

Television Series

1974–75 *Kolchak: The Night Stalker* (writer)
1975–78 *Switch* (writer)
1976–80 *The Rockford Files* (writer, producer)
1985 *Alfred Hitchcock Presents* (writer, director)
1988 *Almost Grown* (co-creator, producer, director)
1991–93 *I'll Fly Away* (producer, writer, director)
1993–95 *Northern Exposure* (producer, writer)
1999– *The Sopranos* (creator, producer, writer, director)

Television Films

1974 *Scream of the Wolf* (story)
1980 *Off the Minnesota Strip* (writer)
1982 *Moonlight* (writer)
1996 *The Rockford Files: Crime and Punishment* (writer, producer, director)

Films

Grave of the Vampire, 1972; *Kounterfeit,* 1996.

Further Reading

Carter, Bill, "He Engineered a Mob Hit, and Now It's Time to Pay Up," *New York Times* (January 11, 2000)
Carter, Bill, "The Roots of 'Sopranos' Grew from Cagney Film," *New York Times* (February 28, 2001)
Carter, Bill, "Stringing Together Taut Episodes, Not Codas, on 'The Sopranos,'" *New York Times* (July 16, 2001)
"David Chase," in *Current Biography,* New York: Bowker, 2001
Kelly, Audrey, "Made Man: Hit After Hit, David Chase Ushers *The Sopranos* into the Big Time," *The Fade In* (2000)
Rosenberg, Janice, "*The Sopranos;* David Chase," *Advertising Age* (June 26, 2000)

Chayefsky, Paddy (1923–1981)

U.S. Writer

Sydney "Paddy" Chayefsky was one of the most renown dramatists to emerge from the "golden age" of American television. His intimate, realistic scripts helped shape the naturalistic style of television drama in the 1950s. After leaving television, Chayefsky succeeded as a playwright and novelist. He won greatest acclaim as a Hollywood screenwriter, receiving Academy Awards for three scripts, including *Marty* (1955), based on his own television drama, and *Network* (1976), his scathing satire of the television industry.

Chayefsky began his television career writing episodes for *Danger* and *Manhunt* in the early 1950s. His scripts caught the attention of Fred Coe, the dynamic producer of NBC's live anthology dramas the *Philco Television Playhouse* and the *Goodyear Television Playhouse,* which were alternating series. Chayefsky's first script for Coe, "Holiday Song," won immediate critical acclaim when it aired in 1952. Subsequently, Chayefsky bucked the trend of the anthology writers by insisting that he would write only

Paddy Chayefsky.
Photo courtesy of Wisconsin Center for Film and Theater Research

original dramas, not adaptations. The result was a banner year in 1953. Coe produced six Chayefsky scripts, including "Printer's Measure" and "The Reluctant Citizen." Chayefsky became one of television's best-known writers, along with such dramatists as Tad Mosel, Reginald Rose, and Rod Serling.

Chayefsky's stories are notable for their dialogue, their depiction of second-generation Americans, and their infusions of sentiment and humor. They frequently draw on the author's upbringing in the Bronx, New York. The protagonists are generally middle-class tradesmen struggling with personal problems: loneliness, pressures to conform, blindness to their own emotions. The technical limitations of live broadcast suited these dramas. The stories take place in cramped interior settings and are advanced by dialogue, not action. Chayefsky said that he focused on "the people I understand; the $75 to $125 a week kind"; this subject matter struck a sympathetic chord with the mainly urban, middle-class audiences of the time.

"Marty," a typical Chayefsky teleplay and one of the most acclaimed of all the live anthology dramas, aired in 1953. Rod Steiger played the lonely butcher who believes that whatever women want in a man, "I ain't got it." When Marty finally meets a woman, his friends cruelly label her "a dog." Marty finally decides that he is a dog himself and has to seize his chance for love. The play ends happily, with Marty arranging a date. Critics have compared "Marty" and other Chayefsky teleplays to the realistic dramas of Arthur Miller and Clifford Odets. In Chayefsky's plays, however, positive endings and celebrations of love tend to emerge from the naturalistic framework. The Chayefsky plays also steered clear of social issues, like most of the anthology dramas.

After *Marty* enjoyed phenomenal success as a Hollywood film, Chayefsky left television in 1956. His exit narrowly preceded the demise of the live dramas, as sponsors began to prefer prerecorded shows. Even while the live dramas were declining, however, Chayefsky's teleplays found new life, as Simon and Schuster published a volume of them, and three of them, in addition to *Marty,* became Hollywood films: *The Bachelor Party* (1957) and *Middle of the Night* (1959), adapted by Chayefsky, and *The Catered Affair* (1957), adapted by Gore Vidal.

In the 1960s, Chayefsky abandoned the intimate, personal dramas on which he had built his reputation. His subsequent work was often dark and satiric, like the Academy Award–winning film *The Hospital* (1971). *Network,* Chayefsky's send-up of television, marked the apex of his satiric mode. He depicted an institution that had sold its soul for ratings and become "a goddamned amusement park," in the words of news anchor Howard Beale, the movie's main character. Before Chayefsky's death in 1981, he wrote one more screenplay, *Altered States* (1980), based on his own novel. He refused a script credit, however, due to disagreements with the film's director, Ken Russell.

Chayefsky wrote only one television script after 1956, an adaptation of his 1961 play *Gideon.* His reputation as a television dramatist rests on the 11 scripts he completed for the *Philco* and *Goodyear Playhouse* series. His influence on the live anthologies was considerable, but he is just as notable for the career he forged after television.

J.B. BIRD

See also **Anthology Drama; Coe, Fred; "Golden Age" of Television; Robinson, Hubbell; Writing for Television**

Paddy Chayefsky (Sidney Chayefsky). Born in Bronx, New York, January 29, 1923. City College of New York, B.S.S., 1943; studied languages, Fordham University, New York. Married Susan Sackler, 1949; one son. Served in U.S. Army, 1943–45. Dramatist from 1944; printer's apprentice, Regal Press (uncle's print shop), New York City, six months in 1945; wrote short stories, radio scripts full-time, late 1940s; gag writer for Robert Q. Lewis, late 1940s; with Garson Kanin, wrote documentary *The True Glory,* his first film, uncredited, 1945; first screenplay credit, for *As Young as You Feel,* 1951; adapted plays for *Theatre Guild of the Air,* 1952–53; first television script, "Holiday Song," 1952; teleplay "Marty," 1953; screenplay, *Marty,* 1955 (Academy Award for Best Screenplay and Best Picture); president, Sudan Productions, 1956; president, Carnegie Productions, from 1957; president S.P.D. Productions, from 1959; president, Sidney Productions, from 1967; president, Simcha Productions, from 1971; last screenplay, *Altered States,* credited under nom de plume Aaron Sydney, 1980. Member: New Dramatists' Committee, 1952–53; Writers Guild of America; Screen Writers Guild; American Guild of Variety Artists; American Guild of Authors and Composers; Screen Actors Guild; Council, Dramatists Guild, from 1962. Recipient: Purple Heart, 1945; private fellowship from Garson Kanin, 1948; Sylvania Television Award, 1953; Screen Writers Guild Awards, 1954 and 1971; Academy Awards, 1955, 1971, and 1976; Palme d'Or, Cannes Film Festival, 1955; *Look Magazine* Award, 1956; New York Film Critics Awards, 1956, 1971, and 1976; Venice Film Festival Awards, 1958; Edinburgh Film Festival Award, 1958; Critics' Prize, Brussels Film Festival, 1958; British Academy Award, 1976. Died in New York City, August 1, 1981.

Television Series

1948–55	*Philco Television Playhouse*
1950–55	*Danger*
1951–52	*Manhunt*
1951–60	*Goodyear Television Playhouse*

Television Plays (as episodes of anthology series; selected)

1952	"Holiday Song"
1953	"The Reluctant Citizen"
1953	"Printer's Measure"
1953	"Marty"
1953	"The Big Deal"
1953	"The Bachelor Party"
1953	"The Sixth Year"
1953	"Catch My Boy on Sunday"
1954	"The Mother"
1954	"Middle of the Night"
1955	"The Catered Affair"
1956	"The Great American Hoax"

Films

The True Glory (uncredited, with Garson Kanin), 1945; *As Young as You Feel,* with Lamar Trotti, 1951; *Marty,* 1955; *The Catered Affair,* 1956; *The Bachelor Party,* 1957; *The Goddess,* 1958; *Middle of the Night,* 1959; *The Americanization of Emily,* 1964; *Paint Your Wagon* (with Alan Jay Lerner), 1969; *The Hospital,* 1971; *Network,* 1976; *Altered States,* 1980.

Radio Plays (adapter)

"The Meanest Man in the World," "Tommy," "Over 21," for *Theater Guild of the Air* series, 1951–52.

Stage

No T.O. for Love, 1944; *Fifth from Garibaldi,* ca. 1944; *Middle of the Night,* 1956; *The Tenth Man,* 1959; *Gideon,* 1961; *The Passion of Josef D* (also director), 1964; *The Latent Heterosexual,* 1967.

Publications

" 'Art Films': They're Dedicated Insanity," *Films and Filming* (May 1958)
Altered States (novel), 1978

Further Reading

Brady, John, *The Craft of the Screenwriter,* New York: Simon and Schuster, 1981
"Chayefsky, Paddy," *Contemporary Authors,* New Revision Series 18, Detroit, Michigan: Gale Research, 1983
Clum, John M., *Paddy Chayefsky,* Boston: Twayne, 1976
Considine, Shaun, *Mad as Hell: The Life and Work of Paddy Chayefsky,* New York: Random House, 1994
Frank, Sam, "Paddy Chayefsky," *Dictionary of Literary Biography,* 44, Detroit: Gale Research, 1986
Marc, David, and Robert J. Thompson, *Prime Time, Prime Movers: From I Love Lucy to L.A. Law—America's Greatest TV Shows and the People Who Created Them,* Boston: Little Brown, 1992
Sturcken, Frank, *Live Television: The Golden Age of 1946–1958 in New York,* Jefferson, North Carolina: McFarland, 1990

Cheers

U.S. Situation Comedy

Cheers, NBC's longest-running comedy series, aired Thursdays from 1982 to 1993. The show narrowly escaped cancellation during its first season and took several years to develop a strong following. By 1985, however, *Cheers* was one of television's most popular shows. It garnered top-ten ratings for seven of its 11 seasons and often earned the number-one ranking in the weekly Nielsens. The final episode, aired May 20, 1993, received the second-best Nielsen ratings of all time for an episodic program. Numerous awards complemented *Cheers*' commercial success, and the show boosted the careers of all its stars.

This popular situation comedy is often cited for successfully blending elements of romance and soap opera into the sitcom format. Fans of the show enjoyed its witty dialogue and comic situations but also followed the twists and turns in the lives of the main characters. Would Sam and Diane get together? Would Rebecca marry Robin? These sorts of plot questions strung together episodes and whole seasons, which often ended with summer cliff-hangers—at the time, a rare device for television comedy.

The show was set at Cheers, the Boston bar "where everybody knows your name." Bar owner Sam Malone (Ted Danson), a former pitcher for the baseball team the Boston Red Sox and an irascible womanizer, served up beers and traded one-liners with regular customers Cliff (John Ratzenberger) and Norm (George Wendt). Carla (Rhea Perlman), a feisty waitress with a weakness for hockey players, kept the men in check with her acerbic comments. Bartender "Coach" (Nicholas Colasanto) was the slow-witted and ironically funny straight man of the ensemble cast. When Colasanto passed away in 1985, Woody Harrelson joined the cast as Woody, a young bartender who took slow-wittedness to new heights.

Sam's on-again, off-again romance with cocktail waitress Diane (Shelly Long) exemplified the show's serial-comedy mix. In the first season, Diane despised Sam and constantly rejected his come-ons. In the second season, she started a torrid affair with him. They broke it off in the third season, and Diane took up with a neurotic psychiatrist, Frasier Crane (Kelsey Grammer). Diane almost went back to Sam after the fourth season but then rejected his marriage proposal. The ongoing romantic tension allowed Sam and Diane to develop as characters. Flashbacks and references to past episodes gave the show a sense of continuous history, like an evening soap. Over the years, other characters developed their own plotlines. Rebecca (Kirstie Alley), who replaced Diane when actress Shelly Long left the show in 1987, pursued a futile romance with Robin Colcord (Roger Rees), a corporate raider who briefly owned the bar. Woody dated Kelly (Jackie Swanson), a wealthy socialite who matched him in naiveté. Frasier married Lilith (Bebe Neuwirth), an ice-cold psychiatrist who matched him in neurosis. Only Cliff and Norm remained essentially static, holding down the bar with their mutual put-downs.

The creators of *Cheers,* Glen Charles, James Burrows, and Les Charles, previously worked on various MTM Productions sitcoms, such as *The Mary Tyler Moore Show, Phyllis,* and *The Bob Newhart Show.* Like *Taxi,* another of their creations, *Cheers* inherited the MTM emphasis on character development. Upscale audiences appreciated this emphasis—and advertisers appreciated the upscale audiences. *Cheers* was not politically correct: the main character was a womanizer; Rebecca pretended to be a career woman but really just wanted a rich husband; and the collegial atmosphere centered around drinking. Though several of the characters were working class, the show completely avoided social issues. Indeed, *Cheers* never preached to its audience on any subjects whatsoever. Even the poignant moments of personal drama that quieted the set from time to time were quickly counterbalanced by sardonic one-liners before any serious message could take hold.

In 1993 Paramount announced that *Cheers* would go off the air. The show was still highly rated, but production costs had soared to record numbers—$65 million for the 1991–92 season. Star Ted Danson, who reportedly participated in making the decision to cancel the program, was earning $450,000 per episode. The network orchestrated a rousing finale, which garnered a 45.5 rating and a 64 audience share. On the evening of the finale, many local newscasts aired segments from bars, where fans saluted *Cheers* from an appropriate

Cheers, Nicholas Colasanto, Ted Danson, Rhea Perlman, Shelley Long, 1982–93.
Courtesy of the Everett Collection

setting. In 1994, Kelsey Grammer launched a spin-off, the long-running and highly rated *Frasier* (in which many *Cheers* characters have made appearances). George Wendt and Rhea Perlman have also starred in sitcoms, though to less success than Grammer. Woody Harrelson has landed numerous leading roles in Hollywood, following in the footsteps of his *Cheers* costars Alley and Danson. Both of them returned to television after *Cheers,* with Alley starring in the NBC sitcom *Veronica's Closet* and Danson playing the lead in two CBS sitcoms, the short-lived *Ink* and the more successful comedy *Becker.*

Over the years *Cheers* received 26 Emmy Awards and a record 111 Emmy nominations. Since the mid-1990s, it has been a major hit in syndication. As an inheritor of the MTM character-comedy tradition, *Cheers* pushed the "serialization" of sitcoms to new levels and was one of the most successful shows from the 1980s.

J.B. Bird

See also **Burrows, James; Charles, Glen and Les; *Frasier***

Cast

Sam Malone	Ted Danson
Diane Chambers (1982–87)	Shelley Long
Carla Tortelli LeBec	Rhea Perlman
Ernie "Coach" Pantusso (1982–85)	Nicholas Colasanto
Norm Peterson	George Wendt
Cliff Clavin	John Ratzenberger
Dr. Frasier Crane (1984–93)	Kelsey Grammer
Woody Boyd (1985–93)	Woody Harrelson
Rebecca Howe (1987–93)	Kirstie Alley
Dr. Lilith Sternin (1986–93)	Bebe Neuwirth
Evan Drake (1987–88)	Tom Skerritt
Eddie LeBec (1987–89)	Jay Thomas
Robin Colcord (1989–91)	Roger Rees
Kelly Gaines (1989–93)	Jackie Swanson
Paul (1991–93)	Paul Willson
Phil (1991–93)	Philip Perlman

Producers

Glen Charles, Les Charles, James Burrows

Programming History
274 episodes
NBC

September 1982–December 1982	Thursday 9:00–9:30
January 1983–December 1983	Thursday 9:30–10:00
December 1983–August 1993	Thursday 9:00–9:30
February 1993–May 1993	Thursday 8:00–8:30

Further Reading

Brooks, Tim, *The Complete Directory to Prime-Time Network TV Shows,* New York: Ballantine, 1992
Carter, Bill, "Why *Cheers* Proved So Intoxicating," *New York Times* (May 9, 1993)
Feuer, Jane, "Genre Study and Television," in *Channels of Discourse, Reassembled,* edited by Robert C. Allen, Chapel Hill: University of North Carolina Press, 1992
Hamamoto, Darrell Y., *Nervous Laughter: Television Situation Comedy and Liberal Democratic Ideology,* New York: Praeger, 1989
Long, Rob, "Three Cheers," *National Review* (June 7, 1993)
Marc, David, *Comic Visions: Television Comedy and American Culture,* Boston: Unwin Hyman, 1989; 2nd edition, Malden, Massachusetts: Blackwell, 1997
Marc, David, and Robert J. Thompson, *Prime Time, Prime Movers: From I Love Lucy to L.A. Law—America's Greatest TV Shows and the People Who Created Them,* Boston: Little Brown, 1992
Papazian, Ed, *Medium Rare: The Evolution, Workings, and Impact of Commercial Television,* New York: Media Dynamics, 1991
Sackett, Susan, *Prime-Time Hits: Television's Most Popular Network Programs,* New York: Billboard, 1993

Cheyenne

U.S. Western

Cheyenne was the first successful television series to be produced by the motion picture studio Warner Brothers. Originally one of the three rotating series in the studio's showcase series, *Warner Brothers Presents, Cheyenne* emerged as the program's breakout hit and helped to fuel ABC's ratings ascent during the mid-1950s. ABC had fewer national affiliates than CBS and NBC, but in markets with affiliates of all three networks, *Cheyenne* immediately entered the top ten; by 1957 it had become the number-one program in those markets. Although clearly successful, *Cheyenne* never stood alone as a weekly series, but alternated biweekly with other Warner Brothers series: *Casablanca* and *King's Row* in *Warner Brothers Presents* (1955–56), *Conflict* (1956–57), and two spin-off series, *Sugarfoot* (1957–61) and *Bronco* (1958–62). *Cheyenne*'s eight-year run produced only 107 episodes, an average of 13 per season.

Early network television was staked out by refugees from Hollywood's B-western backlots, who salvaged their careers by appealing to a vast audience of children. Cowboy stars Gene Autrey, Roy Rogers, and William "Hopalong Cassidy" Boyd made their fortunes in television with inexpensive little westerns made from noisy gunfights and stock-footage Indian raids. As television westerns were made to appeal to younger viewers, the movie industry shifted in the opposite direction, toward "adult" westerns in which the genre's familiar landscape became the setting for psychological drama or mythic allegory, as in *High Noon* (1952) and *The Searchers* (1956). With the 1955 premieres of *Cheyenne, Gunsmoke* (1955–75), and *The Life and Legend of Wyatt Earp* (1955–61), the networks attempted to import the adult western into prime time by infusing the genre with more resonant characters and psychological conflicts.

Cheyenne starred Clint Walker as Cheyenne Bodie, a former frontier scout who drifts through the old West, traveling without any particular motivation from one adventure to another. Along the way he takes a number of jobs, working on ranches or wagon trains, taking part in cattle drives, or protecting precious cargo. Sometimes he works for the federal government; at other times he finds himself deputized by local lawmen. Essentially, the producers of *Cheyenne* changed the character's circumstances at will in order to insert him into any imaginable conflict. Indeed, several *Cheyenne* episodes were remakes of such earlier Warner Brothers movies as *To Have and Have Not* (1944) and *Treasure of the Sierra Madre* (1948), with the character of Cheyenne Bodie simply inserted into the original plot.

With Walker as a lone redeemer wandering from community to community, *Cheyenne* had a thin,

Cheyenne, Clint Walker, 1955–63.
Courtesy of the Everett Collection

though extremely adaptable, premise for generating episodic stories. With its virtually unrelated individual episodes, this type of series bears many similarities to the anthology format. In *Cheyenne,* each episode featured a new conflict involving new characters, with only the recurring character of Cheyenne Bodie to connect one episode with another. Each time Cheyenne enters a new community, he either witnesses or provokes a new story in which he can participate to varying degree—though he is always the force of moral order able to resolve any conflict. This structure is particularly suited to the western's violent resolutions, since only one continuing character must remain alive when the dust settles.

The series was held together not so much by its premise as by its charismatic star, Walker, who rose from obscurity to become one of the icons of the TV western. With his powerful physique and towering height, Walker commanded the small screen through sheer presence; his performance gained gravity simply from the way his body dominated the screen. Walker's personal strength extended beyond the screen to his dealings with Warner Brothers, which exercised tight control over its contract performers. In battling the studio, Walker made *Cheyenne* one of the more tempestuous productions in the history of television.

For the 1957–58 season, ABC offered to purchase a full season of 39 episodes of *Cheyenne,* but Warner Brothers declined. Since each hour-long episode took six working days for principle photography alone, the studio could not supply a new episode each week. Because Walker appeared in virtually every scene, it was also impossible to shoot more than one episode at a time. Consequently, Warner Brothers developed a second series, *Sugarfoot,* to alternate with *Cheyenne.*

In a gesture that would characterize creativity at Warner Brothers, the studio designed *Sugarfoot* as only a slight variation on the *Cheyenne* formula. In *Sugarfoot,* Will Hutchins played Tom Brewster, a kindhearted young drifter who travels the West while studying to become a lawyer. Toting a stack of law books and an aversion to violence, he shares Cheyenne Bodie's penchant for meddling in the affairs of others. But whereas Cheyenne usually dispatches conflicts with firepower, Tom Brewster replaces gunplay with a gift for rhetoric—though he knows how to handle a weapon when persuasion fails. The series was more lighthearted than *Cheyenne,* but it otherwise held close to the formula of the heroic loner.

In May 1958, Clint Walker demanded to renegotiate his contract before returning for another season. Walker had signed his first contract at Warner Brothers in 1955 as a virtual unknown and had received an initial salary of $175 per week, which had risen gradually to $1,250 per week. After the second season of *Cheyenne,* Warner Brothers capitalized on Walker's rising popularity by casting him in a feature film, *Fort Dobbs* (1958), and by releasing a musical album on which he sang. However, Walker was still merely a contract performer who worked on the studio's terms. Walker timed his ultimatum carefully, assuming that he had acquired some leverage because *Cheyenne* finished the 1957–58 season as ABC's second-highest-rated series. He requested more freedom from his iron-clad contract, particularly the autonomy to decide which projects to pursue outside the series. "Television is a vicious, tiring business," he informed the press, "and all I'm asking is my fair share."

When Warner Brothers refused to negotiate, Walker left the studio and did not return for the entire 1958–59 season. After meeting with ABC and advertisers, Warner Brothers decided to continue the *Cheyenne* series without its star. In his place, the studio simply substituted a new charismatic drifter, a former Confederate captain named Bronco Layne (Ty Hardin). Warner Brothers received some puzzled fan mail, but the studio sustained an entire season without Walker—and finished among the top 20 programs—by interspersing Bronco Layne episodes with reruns of Walker episodes from previous seasons. If there was a difference between episodes of *Bronco* and *Cheyenne,* it was solely in the stars; otherwise, *Bronco* was a nearly identical clone.

Warner Brothers finally renegotiated Walker's contract after his boycott, and *Cheyenne* resumed with its star for the 1959–60 season. *Bronco* survived as a stand-alone series and alternated with *Sugarfoot* for the season. During the following season, the three shows alternated in *The Cheyenne Show;* occasionally, the characters would cross over into episodes of the other series.

By the end, the actors were numbed by the repetition of the scripts and by the dreary, taxing routine of production on series in which one episode was virtually indistinguishable from another. Even after returning from his holdout, Walker disliked working on *Cheyenne* and complained to the press that he felt "like a caged animal" pacing back and forth in a zoo. "A TV series is a dead-end street," he lamented. "You work the same set, with the same actors, and with the same limited budgets. Pretty soon you don't know which picture you're in and you don't care." Will Hutchins admitted hoping that *Sugarfoot* would be canceled. Its episodes, he complained, "are pretty much the same after you've seen a handful. They're moneymakers for the studio, the stations, and the actors, but there's a kind of empty feeling when you're through."

CHRISTOPHER ANDERSON

See also **Western**

Cast

Cheyenne Bodie	Clint Walker
Toothy Thompson	Jack Elam

Producers

William T. Orr, Roy Huggins, Arthur Silver, Harry Foster

Programming History

107 episodes

ABC

September 1955–September 1959	Tuesday 7:30–8:30
September 1959–December 1962	Monday 7:30–8:30
April 1963–September 1963	Friday 7:30–8:30

Further Reading

Anderson, Christopher, *Hollywood TV: The Studio System in the Fifties,* Austin: University of Texas Press, 1994

Jackson, Ronald, *Classic TV Westerns: A Pictorial History,* Seacaucus, New Jersey: Carol, 1994

MacDonald, J. Fred, *Who Shot the Sheriff?: The Rise and Fall of the Television Western,* New York: Praeger, 1987

West, Richard, *Television Westerns: Major and Minor Series, 1946–1978,* Jefferson, North Carolina: McFarland, 1987

Woolley, Lynn, Robert W. Malsbary, and Robert G. Strange, Jr., *Warner Bros. Television: Every Show of the Fifties and Sixties, Episode by Episode,* Jefferson, North Carolina: McFarland, 1985

Yoggy, Gary A., *Riding the Video Range: The Rise and Fall of the Western on Television,* Jefferson, North Carolina: McFarland, 1995

Chicago School of Television

During the late 1940s and early 1950s, broadcast television emanating from Chicago was noted for its original ideas, inventive production techniques, and significant contributions to the development of the new visual medium. Paying close attention to the problems of adjusting personal styles of writing, direction, and performance to television, and to the more theoretical questions of how television actually worked, Chicago broadcasters developed a style or technique that came to be known as the Chicago School of Television.

While all Chicago stations contributed to the school, most success with the distinctive approach to programming is attributed to the NBC-owned and -operated station WNBQ. Under the leadership of station manager Jules Herbuveaux and program manager Ted Mills, the NBC outlet went furthest in developing formats and ideas that would capitalize on television's idiosyncrasies.

Simply stated, the Chicago School worked at creating inventive programs different from both New York's theatrical offerings and Hollywood's screenplay-based productions. Utilizing an almost totally scriptless-improvisational approach reliant on interpretive camera work and creative use of scenery, costumes, props, and lighting, Chicago School practitioners produced successful programs in limited spaces with local talent and small budgets. Herbuveaux provided the freedom for his staff to create, and Mills theorized and experimented with a variety of ideas including Chinese opera, commedia dell'arte, and Pirandellian forms of reality in his search for new and effective television forms.

By late 1949, Chicago's low-cost television packages were making a ratings impact with such offerings as NBC's *Kukla, Fran, and Ollie,* ABC's *Super Circus,* and the piano talents of DuMont's Al Morgan. By the spring of 1950, the major body of Chicago School work focused on such NBC-WNBQ variety offerings as *Garroway at Large,* the *Wayne King Show, Hawkins Falls,* and *Saturday Square.* Children's shows consisted of an extraordinary number of award-winning entries including *Zoo Parade, Quiz Kids, Mr. Wizard, Ding Dong School, Pistol Pete and Jennifer,* and the highly rated, low-budgeted cowboy film series, *Cactus Jim.* For comedy and drama there was Studs Terkel's *Studs' Place, Portrait of America, Crisis,* and *Reported Missing.* Actuality programming featured *Walt's Workshop, The Pet Shop,* and *R.F.D. America.* Local news offered the unique *Five Star Final* with weatherman Clint Youle, news anchor Clifton Utley, Dorsey Connors with consumer tips, sportscaster Tom Duggan, and, reflecting Herbuveaux's sense of showmanship, Herbie Mintz with musical nostalgia.

As critically acclaimed as it proved to be, elements of the Chicago School's decline were seen as early as 1950. Chicago programs were shortened and/or removed from network schedules. Key personnel left Chicago to pursue more lucrative careers in New York and Los Angeles, and in 1953, with the opening of the coast-to-coast network cable, there was less and less need for Chicago productions. In 1953, 13 network programs originated from Chicago. By 1955, no Chicago-produced programs appeared on the DuMont network. CBS and NBC had no Chicago-network originations except occasional newscasts and a network radio farm program. The Chicago School of Television was becoming just a fond memory.

JOEL STERNBERG

See also **Allison, Fran; *Garroway at Large;* "Golden Age" of Television; *Kukla, Fran, and Ollie;* Tillstrom, Burr**

Further Reading

Fay, Bill, "Top TV Town," *Collier's* (March 17, 1951)
Nielsen, Ted, "Television: Chicago Style," *Journal of Broadcasting* (fall 1965)
Olson, John, "The Reward of Being Local, Live, Lively," *Broadcasting* (May 24, 1954)
Shayon, Robert Lewis, *Open to Criticism,* Boston: Beacon Press, 1971
Sternberg, Joel, "Television Town," *Chicago History* (Summer 1975)
"Telefile: Creative Programming Highlights WNBQ (TV) Success," *Broadcasting* (January 9, 1950)
Terkel, Studs, "Chi's TV Imagination vs. Radio City Panjandrums," *Variety* (May 27, 1953)
"TV Chicago Style," *Television Magazine* (March 1951)
Van Horne, Harriet, "The Chicago Touch," *Theatre Arts* (July 1951)

Children and Television

Children devote much of their free time to watching television—seemingly enamored of the screen—and continuous contact is thought to influence the way they understand and interpret both television and the world in which they live. Although children have everyday contact with other media and many other forms of expression and communication, visual media alone are seen as speaking a "universal language," accessible regardless of age. In the United States questions about program content and its use by children, about television's influence on children's attitudes, knowledge, and behavior, and about the appropriate public policy toward children's television have been central to the discussion of this medium throughout its half century as the electronic hearth.

Children's Programming

In the 1950s, children's programs and the benefits that television could presumably bring to the family were highly touted selling points for television sets. By 1951 the networks' schedules included up to 27 hours of children's programs. Like much of television programming, offerings for children continued radio's tradition of action-adventure themes and a pattern of late-afternoon and evening broadcasts. An early reliance on movies as a program staple was lessened in favor of half-hour live-action shows such as *The Lone Ranger, Sky King,* or *Lassie,* and host/puppet shows such as *The Howdy Doody Show* and *Kukla, Fran, and Ollie.* By the mid-1950s, programs had found their place on Saturday morning, and by decade's end the 30-minute, once-a-week format was established.

During the 1960s, almost all other forms gave way to animation. Reduced costs resulting from limited-action animation techniques and the clear appeal of cartoons to children transformed scheduling, and the institutionalization of Saturday-morning cartoons became complete—an unexpected lucrative time slot for the networks. Popular shows included *The Flintstones, The Jetsons, Bullwinkle,* and *Space Ghost.*

The 1970s have been described as a video mosaic in which 60- or 90-minute shows incorporated a number of segments under umbrella labels such as *The New Super Friends Hour* or *Scooby Laff-a-Lympics.* These extended shows were designed to increase audience flow across the entire morning.

Children's programming in the 1980s was influenced by the "television revolution," as the growth of cable and VCR penetration began to erode the network audience, and international co-ventures began to change the production process. Cartoons remained the standard children's fare, but live-action shows began to increase in number. Cable networks such as Nickelodeon and Disney, devoted primarily to children, as well as cable networks with extensive children's programming like Discovery, Learning Channel, USA, TBS, the Family Channel, and Lifetime, have experimented extensively in programming for children. They have produced live-action programs, including game shows, puppet shows, magazine-format news and variety programs, and live-action drama/adventure shows frequently incorporating anthropomorphic creatures into the storyline.

The 1990s have been influenced by the Children's Television Act with many educational shows joining the available programming. Since 1990, for example, eight of the nine Peabody Awards for children's programs were for informational or educational programs.

While it is the case that most of the television viewed by children is of programs not specifically considered "children's shows," the production of children's programming is big business, often defined by the ways in which such children's shows are distinctive. Children's shows are those that garner a majority of a child audience, traditionally the Saturday-morning programs. These shows are almost always profitable. Because the child audience changes rapidly, and because children do not seem to mind watching reruns, the programs are shown as many as four times a year, a factor that reduces production costs without reduction in program availability or profitability. Moreover, a strong syndication market for off-network children's shows adds to the profits.

For many of these reasons the major networks have traditionally exerted strong control over production in the five or six production houses they routinely use. Each network has a vice president for children's programming who uses other advisers and often relies on extensive marketing research, as do the Sesame Workshop and the Nickelodeon cable network.

Both those who purchase and those who produce children's programs operate with assumptions about the child audience that, although changing, remain important. They assume, for example, that there are gender differences in preferences, but an important corollary is the assumption that while girls will watch "boys' shows," boys will not watch "girls' shows." They assume that older children control the set, an assumption related to the axiom that younger children will watch "up" (in age appeal) but that older children will not watch "down." Producers and purchasers assume that children have a short attention span, that repetition is a key to education and entertainment, and that children prefer recognizable characters and stories.

The body of television content emerging from these economic and industrial practices, and based on these and similar assumptions, has been a central component of "childhood" since the 1950s. Because they are seen as a special "class" or "group" of both citizens and viewers, great concern for the role of television in the lives of children has accompanied the development of the medium. As a result of this concern, issues surrounding children and television have often been framed as "social problems," issues of central concern to numerous groups. Large-scale academic research enterprises have been mounted to monitor, analyze, and explain relationships between television and children. Congress, regulatory agencies, advocacy groups, and the television networks have struggled continuously over research findings, public responsibility, and popular response. And significant policy decisions continue to be made based both on that research and on the political and economic power that is brought to bear on these issues.

The Effects of Television Violence

Throughout all these policy debates, citizens' actions, and network responses, the issue of violence in television programming has been central to concerns regarding children and television. As an aspect of television content, violence has traditionally been measured

Ding Dong School.

quantitatively by researchers who count incidents of real or threatened physical injury. Gerbner and his colleagues have conducted such analyses yearly since 1967. Their violence index shows a fairly stable level of prime-time violence over the past 25 years. The question then becomes what is the effect of this type of programming on children.

In the 1960s, researchers used experimental methods to investigate the impact of media violence. Albert Bandura's social learning theory (also called observational learning or modeling theory) argued that children could easily learn and model behaviors observed on film or television. Sometimes known as the "Bobo doll" studies, these experiments demonstrated that children who viewed filmed violent actions were as likely to imitate those actions as were children who saw live modeling of those actions. Many extensions of this basic finding established that modeling was influenced by other attributes of the children such as their prior level of aggressiveness. Context and message, specifically the punishment or reinforcement of the filmed aggressor and the presence of an adult in the viewing or imitation context, emerged as other significant factors in the modeling behavior. Later laboratory studies used more realistic measures of aggression and programming that more closely resembled prime-time television. Field experiments were also conducted, in which viewing in real-life situations (home, camps, schools) was manipulated.

In a series of experiments, two opposing theories, catharsis and stimulation, were investigated. Catharsis holds that viewing violence purges the individual of negative feelings and thus lessens the likelihood of aggressive behavior. Stimulation predicted the opposite. No support for the catharsis theory emerged from the research; stimulation was found to be more likely.

Taken together, the experimental studies demonstrated that the process of televisual influence on children is indeed complicated. Still, the results from laboratory experiments do demonstrate that shortly after exposure to violent programming, children are more likely to show an increase in their own levels of

(left) *Barney & Friends.*
Courtesy of the Everett Collection

aggression. But how would these laboratory findings translate into real life?

Correlational studies, surveys, tell little about cause and effect, but they do avoid the artificiality of laboratory studies. If viewing is associated with television violence, then individuals who watch a great deal of violent television should also score high on survey scales that measure aggressive behavior. The results from a large number of such surveys are remarkably consistent: there is a small but consistent association between viewing violent television and aggressive tendencies. Yet another form of survey research, panel studies, tackles the question of causality by looking at the same individuals over time. In the case of television violence, the question is this: does television viewing at Time 1 relate to aggression at Time 2; or, conversely, could the causal linkage be reversed, suggesting that aggressive behavior leads to a propensity to view violent television content? Only a few such studies exist, but, again, the findings are generally consistent. Although the effect is small, watching television violence encourages aggression.

What conclusions can be reached from this large, ongoing body of research? Television does contribute to aggressive behavior—however, television is only one of many causes of aggression. Many other factors unrelated to television influence violence, and the precise impact of televised violence will be modified by age, sex, family practices, and the way violence is presented. One statement is frequently repeated: television has large effects on a small number of individuals, and modest effects on a large number of people. The questions and approaches continue to be refined, and currently, groups funded by both the cable and network industries are studying levels of violence and its appearance in context, in order to provide better information on the type of violence being shown.

Television and Cognitive Development

While televisual violence is often the most visible and debated aspect of questions linking children and television, it is hardly the only topic that concerns researchers. Other inquiries focus on potential effects of the medium on patterns of thinking and understanding. Posed negatively, the question is this: does television mesmerize attention, promote passive or overstimulated children, while wrecking creativity and imagination? To explore such concerns, cognitive developmental approaches to television and children have typically examined attention, comprehension, and inference.

Children's attention to television has often been characterized as "active" versus "passive." Popular concern about the "zombie" viewer suggests that children enter some altered state of consciousness when viewing television. But this generalization has received little research support. However, one notion that seems to underlie many implicit theories of children's attraction to the screen is that children's viewing is governed by the novelty of the visual stimulus—rapid formal features such as movements, visual complexity, cuts, pans, zooms, which produce an orienting reflex.

A theory of active television viewing suggests that attention is linked to comprehension. Thus, when visual or auditory features of television content suggest to the young viewer that it is designed "for children," attention is turned to that content. When material is no longer comprehensible or becomes boring, or when distractions occur, attention is deflected. This theory of child attentional patterns has received substantial support and has indicated specific stages. Attention to television is fragmentary before the age of two; visual attention increases during the preschool years, with a major shift in amount and pattern of attention occurring between 24 and 30 months. Frequently beginning around the age of eight, visual attention to TV decreases (presumably as the decoding of television becomes routine) and the attention pattern begins to resemble that of an adult.

With regard to perception and evaluation of television content, children clearly operate on different dimensions than adults who produce programs. Understanding television programming requires a fairly complex set of tasks for children, including selective attention to the events portrayed, perceiving an orderly organization of events, and making inferences about information given implicitly. Comprehension research has examined both verbal and visual decoding and determined that comprehension is a function of both cognitive development and experience. Younger children have difficulty with a number of tasks involved in understanding television programs: separating central from peripheral content, comprehending the sequence of events, recalling events and segments, and understanding causation. As well, they find it difficult to complete such inferential tasks as understanding intersections of motivation, action, and consequence, or evaluating the "reality" of programs and characters. The comprehension of forms and conventions—sometimes termed "formal features"—is similarly grounded in developmental stages, with surprisingly early recognition of the time-and-space ellipses of cuts or the part-whole relationship of zooms. Such complex storytelling functions as point-of-view shots or flashbacks, however, are unclear to children through much of the first decade.

Television Within the Family

In most cases, this viewing and the development of skills and strategies occurs within a family context filled with other activities and other individuals. The average child watches television a little more than four hours a day. Childhood viewing peaks somewhere around 12 years of age and declines during adolescence to a little more than three hours per day. Children do most of their viewing during the weekday hours with only 10 percent of their viewing on Saturday and Sunday mornings. Viewing amount varies by gender and race, with studies showing that blue-collar families average more television viewing than white-collar families and that blacks view more than whites. Television provides the backdrop for growing up, and studies show that children often play, eat, do homework, and talk while "watching TV."

Viewing is not usually solitary. Children and adults view together and do many other things while watching. The family has a say in creating the context in which television will be consumed, a context involving who decides what to watch, sibling or parental conflict over viewing, and the rules for decision making. Although many families report few rules, there may be subtle as well as direct rules about television use. For example, children may not be allowed to watch until they have completed important tasks such as homework or chores, or there may be a requirement that television must be turned off at a certain time. When parents report rules, they report control of when younger children can watch; older children have rules about what they can watch.

Often this context is modified by processes of "mediation," a term used to refer to the role of social interaction in relation to television's use in the home and the potential impact of television within the family. Some mediation is direct and intentional—parents make specific comments about programs. Other mediation may be indirect or unintentional, as in general comments about alternative activities, discussions of social or personal issues generated by media content, and talk loosely tied to content. Parents and siblings may respond to questions with evaluative comments, interpretive comments, explanations of forms and codes, or discussions of morality or desirability of behavior.

One result related to the complexity of viewing practices has emerged very clearly from research conducted within a number of different contexts: interaction with parents during viewing increases comprehension and learning from television. In middle childhood, peer and sibling co-viewing involves talk about television action and evaluation of that action. Parental comments on the importance, truthfulness, and relevance of media are common at this age.

Learning from Television

In many ways general notions of how children learn from television and specific aspects of educational television were revolutionized by the premier of *Sesame Street* in 1969. Viewed by more than 6 million preschoolers every week in the United States and internationally, this production is also one of the most studied television programs. Research focused on *Sesame Street* has provided ample evidence to suggest that young children can learn skills from the show, and that these skills will contribute to their early educational success. Many other programs produced by the Sesame Workshop and by public broadcasting stations, independent producers, and state departments of education have been constructed to teach educational concepts ranging from reading to international understanding.

Related to these educational programs are pro-social programs that model socially valued responses for viewers. Pro-social behavior is usually defined as "good for persons and society" and may include lessons on the value of cooperation, self-control, helping, sharing, and understanding those who are different. *Mr. Rogers' Neighborhood,* for example, is a classic pro-social program.

Even with the knowledge gained from research focused on television's ability to teach specific skills, the medium is frequently castigated for interfering in the education of children. Achievement, intellectual ability, grades, and reading show complex relationships with television viewing. For example, the relationship between television viewing and academic performance is not clear-cut. Children who spend a great deal of time watching television do poorly in school, but children who spend a moderate amount of time with TV perform better than nonviewers. The small negative relationship between IQ and television viewing masks some important subgroup differences, such as age (high IQ is positively correlated with viewing until the teens) and gender (with the negative relationship holding stronger for boys than for girls). Reading and television viewing are positively correlated up to a threshold of about ten hours of viewing per week. Only when television viewing rises above a certain level does it seem to be related to less reading. Overall, the data suggest that television has a small adverse effect on learning.

In addition to the many ways in which television can influence the learning of specific educational concepts, or the ways in which basic television behavior affects other forms of learning, the medium can also teach indirect lessons. Socialization, especially sex-role socialization, has been a continuing concern, because television so frequently presents basic images of gender. In prime-time programming, men outnumber women two or three to one. Women are younger than men and tend to be cast in more stereotypical roles, and tend to be less active, more likely to be victimized, less aggressive, and more limited in employment than men. Children's programs are similarly sex stereotyped; women are generally underrepresented, stereotyped, and less central to the program. Cultivation analysis suggests that a relationship exists between viewing and stereotypical conceptions about gender roles. Nonetheless, some improvement has been made. Research on the impact of gender representation reveals that children do understand the images and want to be like same-sex television characters, and it seems clear that counterstereotypical images are helpful in combating stereotypes.

Some research examining race-role socialization shows similar patterns, suggesting that limited portrayals and stereotyped roles can contribute to skewed perceptions by race. Although African Americans have frequently been portrayed negatively, other minority groups such as Asians and Hispanics have simply been missing from the screen world—a process sometimes called symbolic annihilation.

Beyond the content of fictional representations, parents would agree that children learn from television advertising. Researchers initially assumed children had minimal comprehension of the selling intent of advertising, and children verbally described advertisement as an "informational service." Nonverbal measures, however, demonstrated that children understood that commercials persuaded them to buy products. Social scientists have studied a number of potential effects of advertising. These include the frequent requests for products, the modification of self-esteem, and the relations of advertising to obesity and to alcohol and cigarette consumption. This research has been dominated by a deficit model in which children are defined as unable to distinguish selling intent, or as easily misled by what they see.

History and Policy

Such vulnerability on the part of children explains, in part, the designation of "children and television" as a specific topic for political as well as intellectual concern. Politicians and the public worried about the effects of media on children long before television, of course. Novels, movies, music, radio, and comic books all came under scrutiny for their potential negative consequences on the behaviors and attitudes of the young. But in the 1950s, the spotlight turned to television.

The first congressional hearings, predictably, addressed violence on television; they were held in the House Interstate and Foreign Commerce Subcommittee in June 1952. Network representatives were called to testify about television and violence before the Senate Subcommittee on Juvenile Delinquency headed by Estes Kefauver in 1954 and 1955. In 1964 the same committee again held hearings and issued a report critical of television programming and concluding that television was a factor in shaping the attitudes and character of young people.

In the wake of the urban unrest and violence of the 1960s, a Presidential Commission on the Causes and Prevention of Violence was formed to examine the issues of violence in society. The report, basing its conclusions on a review of existing research, indicted television as part of the problem of violence. At the instigation of Senator John Pastore of Rhode Island, the U.S. Surgeon General commissioned a series of studies of televised violence and its effects on children. This work resulted in what is popularly termed the Surgeon General's Report of 1972, in which 23 research projects in five volumes focused on many issues surrounding television. The committee's main conclusion was that there was a causal link between viewing television violence and subsequent antisocial acts. Despite some initial confused reporting of the findings, the consensus that had emerged among the researchers was made clear in subsequent hearings. In 1982 a ten-year update of the Surgeon General's Report was released. It underscored the findings of the earlier report and also documented other areas in which television was having an impact, particularly on perceptions of reality, social relationships, health, and education.

During this long history of public regulatory debate on television, government commissions and citizen action groups were pursuing related agendas. Key to these interactions were the Federal Communications Commission (FCC), the Federal Trade Commission (FTC), and citizens' advocacy and action groups. Always involved in these disputes, whether directly or indirectly, were the major television networks; their industry associations, usually the National Association of Broadcasters (NAB); and advertisers. Action for Children's Television (ACT) was the citizens' group most directly engaged in legal procedures and policy actions.

Founded in 1968 by Peggy Charren, Action for Children's Television was formed to increase availability of quality programming for children. Unsuccessful at obtaining cooperation from the networks directly, ACT turned to political action. In 1970 the organization presented a petition to the FCC intended to change a number of FCC policies regarding children's programming. A resulting inquiry launched unprecedented response. Hearings were held, and in 1974 the *FCC Children's TV Report and Policy Statement* offered specific guidelines: a limit of nine and a half advertising minutes per hour in children's programs, the use of separation devices indicating divisions between commercials and programs, the elimination of host selling, and the directive that children's programs not be confined to one day (Saturday morning television had become synonymous with children's television). Later reviews suggested that the networks were not meeting these requirements or their obligations to serve children, but further regulatory action in the 1980s was blocked by the shift toward a deregulatory stance at the FCC and in the courts.

At the Federal Trade Commission, ACT was also at work, petitioning for the regulation of advertising directed at children. In 1977 the group presented a petition requesting that advertising of candy in children's programs be banned. The FTC responded with a notice that it would consider rule making to ban all ads to audiences too young to understand selling intent, to ban ads for sugared products, or to require that counter- and corrective advertising be aired in order to counteract advertising of sugared products. Hearings were held, but lobbying efforts by networks and advertisers were very strong. Congress passed a bill eliminating the power of the FTC to rule on "unfair" practices and restricting its focus to the regulation of "deceptive" practices. In 1981 the FTC issued a formal report dropping the inquiry. Throughout the 1970s and 1980s, ACT was engaged with the FCC and FTC in many other ways, representing petitions dealing with matters such as the banning of program-length commercials (programs designed primarily to provide product exposure and create consumer demand) or the evaluation of individual ads deemed deceptive.

Other citizen action groups have also been involved with issues surrounding television. The National Coalition on Television Violence (NCTV) has focused on television violence and efforts to educate the public and curb such content. The National Citizen Committee for Broadcasting monitored programs and identified companies that support television violence. The PTA threatened boycott of products and programs. The Coalition for Better Television (CBTV) was successful in pressuring some advertisers to boycott sponsors of programs with sexual themes.

But by the 1990s, the regulation of children's media was back on the legislative agenda. The 1990 Children's Television Act was the first congressional act that specifically regulated children's television. Most importantly, it imposed an obligation on broadcasters to serve the educational and informational needs of children. These are further defined as cognitive/intellectual or social/emotional needs. Although no minimum number of hours was established as a requirement, the obligation of some regularly scheduled programming specifically designed for children was established. Stations were also mandated to keep a log of that programming and to make the log available in a public inspection file. In a 1992 move widely viewed as an effort to stave off a federally imposed ratings system for violence, the three networks announced new standards, forswearing gratuitous violence; later they agreed to include on-screen advisories prior to the presentation of strong programs. In spite of these proposals all the issues emerged again in the Telecommunications Act of 1996.

A major legislative package that rewrote the 1934 Communications Act, the many provisions of the act will take years to sort out. But, in February 1996, the Telecommunications Act was signed into law. Of relevance to the children and television arena were provisions requiring the installation of an electronic monitoring device in television sets, a "V-chip" that would "read" violence ratings and allow families to block violent programming. Moreover, the networks were charged with creating a self-designed and regulated ratings system, similar to that used by the Motion Picture Association of America, which would designate specific content depicting degrees of violence, sexual behavior, suitable language, and other controversial content. The bill includes the threat of a governmentally imposed system if the networks do not comply, but concerns about constitutionality and practicality of such a ratings system suggest that the issue will be under debate for many years.

In all these research and policy areas much of what we know comes from the study of children enjoying television as it has existed for almost half a century. But that traditional knowledge, like the traditional definition of television itself, is being challenged by emerging telecommunications technologies. Cable, video games, and VCRs (and later DVDs) changed the face of television within the home. The Internet, a 500-channel world, increasing international programming ventures, and regulatory changes will change the way children interact with electronic media. The special place of children in human societies ensures, however, that the concerns that have surrounded their interaction with television will remain central, even if they are shifted to new and different media.

ALISON ALEXANDER

See also **Action for Children's Television; Cartoons; Family Viewing Time; *Howdy Doody Show; Kukla, Fran, and Ollie;* Sesame Workshop**

Further Reading

Bryant, Jennings, and J. Alison Bryant, editors, *Television and the American Family,* 2nd edition, Mahwah, New Jersey: Erlbaum, 2001

Buckingham, David, et al., *Children's Television in Britain: History, Discourse, and Policy,* London: British Film Institute, 1999

Gunter, Barrie, and Jill L. McAleer, *Children and Television: The One-Eyed Monster?* New York: Routledge, 1990

Inglis, Ruth, *The Window in the Corner: A Half-Century of Children's Television,* London: P. Owen, and Chester Springs, Pennsylvania: Dafour Editions, 2003

Liebert, Robert M., and Joyce Sprafkin, *The Early Window: Effects of Television on Children and Youth,* New York: Pergamon, 1973; 3rd edition, 1988

Oswell, David, *Television, Childhood, and the Home: A History of the Making of the Child Television Audience in Britain,* Oxford: Clarendon Press, and New York: Oxford University Press, 2002

Pecora, Norma Odom, *The Business of Children's Entertainment,* New York: Guildford, 1998

Price, Monroe, and Stefaan G. Verhulst, editors, *Parental Control of Television Broadcasting,* Mahwah, New Jersey: Erlbaum, 2002

Signorielli, Nancy, *A Sourcebook on Children and Television,* New York: Greenwood, 1991

Singer, Dorothy G., and Jerome Singer, editors, *Handbook of Children and the Media,* Thousand Oaks, California: Sage, 2001

Van Evra, Judith, *Television and Child Development,* Hillsdale, New Jersey: Erlbaum, 1990

Children's Television Workshop. *See* **Sesame Workshop**

China

Since television emerged in China, the medium has experienced various drastic changes and become one of the largest and most sophisticated, advanced, and influential television systems in the world.

Developments and Setbacks

China's first TV station, Beijing Television, began broadcasting on May 1, 1958. Within just two years, dozens of stations were set up in major cities like Shanghai and Guangzhou, although most stations had to rely on using planes, trains, or cars to send tapes and films from one to another.

The first setback for Chinese television came in the early 1960s, when the former Soviet Union withdrew economic aid from China. Many TV stations were closed, and the total number was reduced from 23 to five. The second setback derived from an internal factor, the Cultural Revolution of 1966 to 1976. Beijing Television's regular telecasting was forced to a halt in January 1967 by the leftists of the Chinese Communist Party led by Mao Zedong. All other local stations followed its lead. Television stations were criticized for their bourgeois direction and changed to a new, revolutionary direction as a weapon for class struggle and anti-imperialism, antirevisionism, and anticapitalism.

Beginning in the late 1970s with the end of the Cultural Revolution and the start of the country's reform, television became the most rapidly growing medium. On May 1, 1978, Beijing Television changed to China Central Television (CCTV); as China's only national network, CCTV had the largest audience in the world. From the 1980s through the 1990s, television developed swiftly. The total number of TV stations once exceeded 1,000, with one national network, dozens of provincial and major city networks, and hundreds of regional and local ones. The government reregulated the development of television when it became out of control and chaotic in the late 1990s. In 2000 China had a total of 651 TV stations that generated programming, 42,228 TV-transmitting-and-relaying stations, and 368,553 satellite-TV-receiving-and-relaying stations. By the early 21st century, China had 270 million TV sets, becoming the nation with the most TV sets in the world. Statistically, there is one television set for each Chinese family. The penetration rate of television in China has reached 92.5 percent, covering a population of 1 billion people.

Television broadcasting technology has also developed very quickly. A few major stations have started using high technology for production and broadcasting, such as virtual field production technology and high-definition technology. CCTV opened its webcast service in 1996 to the worldwide audience, providing text, audio, and photographic and video images. Digital broadcasting technology has been set as one of the priorities of China's "Tenth Five-Year Plan" for 2001 to 2005. Based on that plan, by 2005 all television programming will be transmitted via digital technology.

System and Structure

The only form of television in China, as well as all other media in the country, is state owned. Neither privately owned nor foreign-owned television is allowed. Without government permission, receiving foreign TV programming via satellite is prohibited by law. There are no license fees for owning a TV set and no charge for viewing broadcast television. Until the late 1970s, Chinese television was not allowed to carry advertising. Instead, the medium was completely financed by the government.

Media theories undergirding the organization and uses of Chinese television flow directly from Marxist-Leninist doctrine. Mao Zedong, the founder and late chairman of the Chinese Communist Party, further embellished Marx's idea of the importance of the superstructure and ideological state apparatus and Lenin's concept of the importance of propaganda and media control, stressing that media must be run by the Communist Party and become the party's loyal eyes, ears, and mouthpiece. The current leadership of the Communist Party requires that broadcasting must keep in line with the party and serve the party's main tasks voluntarily, firmly, and in a timely manner.

Under these guidelines, television is regarded as part of the party's overall political machine. Television is used, to the greatest extent, by the party and state to impose ideological hegemony on the society. It is the party and the central government that set the tone of propaganda for television. Although TV stations provide news, entertainment, and educational programs, Chinese television's first function is to popularize party and government policies and motivate the masses in the construction of Communist ideology.

A tight control and administrative system has been used to run television. The Communist Party is actually the owner, manager, and practitioner of television. All TV stations are under the dual jurisdiction of the Communist Party's Propaganda Department and the government's Radio and Television Bureau, while the party's Central Propaganda Department is under the supervision of the Political Bureau of the Party's Central Committee. The Propaganda Department sets propaganda policies, determines programming content and themes, and issues operational directives. Technological, regulatory, and administrative affairs are generally the concern of the Radio and Television Bureau. As media are crucial political organs of the Communist Party, virtually no independence of media is allowed or envisioned. Except for those years in the 1980s that were criticized later by the party as the period of "Western liberalization" and the period of "bourgeois spiritual pollution," neither open debate on ideology nor criticism of the party, government policies, or high-ranking officials has been permitted in communist China. The self-censorship policy has been long and extensively used. Routine material does not require approval from the party authorities, but important editorials, news stories, and sensitive topics all require official endorsement prior to their dissemination.

Programming and Production

Television programming in China consists of five categories: news programs, documentary and magazine programs, educational programs, entertainment programs, and service programs. In 2000 roughly 10 percent of Chinese programming (in terms of total broadcasting hours) was news; 10 percent, documentary and magazine shows; 2 percent, educational; 60 percent, entertainment; and 18 percent, service oriented or advertising.

Although entertainment programs now occupy the bulk of the total broadcasting hours, before the reform in the late 1970s there were not many real entertainment programs. Prior to that period, most entertainment programs were just old films of revolutionary stories, with occasional live broadcast of modern operas about model workers, peasants, and soldiers. Newscasts from that era were mostly what the Chinese Communist Party's official newspaper, *The People's Daily,* and the official news agency, the *Xinhua News Agency,* reported. Production capability was low; production quality was poor; equipment and facilities were simple; and broadcasting hours, transmitting scales, and channel selections were limited. Television broadcast usually lasted three hours daily.

Television has developed explosively since the reform beginning in 1978. Many taboos were eliminated, restrictions lifted, and new production skills adopted. Entertainment programs in the form of TV plays, soap operas, Chinese traditional operas, game shows, and domestic and foreign feature films have become routine. News programs have also changed substantially and expanded enormously. International news coverage and live telecasts of important news events are now often seen in news programs. Educational programs in particular have received special treatment from the government. In addition to the 2 percent of total broadcasting hours for educational programs, China now has two satellite TV channels (CETV-1, CETV-2) and one Beijing-based regional TV station (CETV-3) designated to broadcast educational programs only. Altogether, in 2000 the three educational TV stations broadcast 17,864 hours of programs, more than 50 hours per day. College courses offered by China Central Broadcasting and Television University make up 45 percent of this programming; education-related newscasts, 4 percent; general education and science education programs, 24 percent; social/public education programs, 11 percent; and service programs and advertising, 16 percent.

Production capability has been remarkably enhanced since the reform. CCTV expanded from two channels in 1978 to nine channels in 2000, with Channel 1 focusing on news; Channel 2, economy and finance; and Channel 3, culture, arts, and music. Channel 4 is dedicated to overseas Chinese and international audiences. Channel 5 shows sports; Channel 6, movies; Channel 7, social programs, including children's programs; and Channel 8, TV plays and series. Channel 9 is an English-language channel that broadcasts 24 hours a day, targeting an international audience. Channel 10 focuses on science. Another new channel that will focus on tourism is to be launched soon.

Most provincial and major city networks have also increased the number of their broadcasting channels and offered more programs. In 2000 alone, a total of 455 TV plays with 7,535 episodes were produced, plus 12 TV plays with 263 episodes jointly produced by Chinese and foreign TV organizations. In contrast, in the two decades from 1958 to 1977, only 74 TV plays were produced. In 2000, TV stations across China produced 164,834 hours of news programs, 18.9 percent of that year's total television productions.

Broadcasting hours have increased considerably as well. In an average week of the year 1980, 2,018 hours of programs were broadcast. The number went up to 7,698 in 1985; 22,298 in 1990; and 83,373 in 2000, reflecting a 3.5-fold increase in five years, an 11-fold expansion in ten years, and a 41-fold explosion in 20 years.

Internationalization and Commercialization

One of the most important tokens of the internationalization of Chinese television is the change in the importation of programming. Before the reform of the late 1970s, TV imports were quantitatively limited and ideologically and politically oriented. From the late 1950s to the late 1970s, only the national network was authorized to import TV programs, and it did so under the tight control and close surveillance of the party and government. During those years, programs were imported almost exclusively from socialist countries, and the content usually concentrated on the Soviet Revolution and the U.S.S.R.'s socialist economic progress. Few programs were imported from Western countries, and those were restricted only to those that exemplified the principle that "socialism is promising, capitalism is hopeless."

During the reform period, the ban on most imports was gradually lifted. Today, although they still face various kinds of restrictions, central, provincial, regional, and even local television stations are all looking to other countries, mostly Western nations, as sources of programs. Moreover, import channels, import purposes, import criteria, import formats, and import categories have all changed, expanded, or developed significantly. In the early 1970s, imported programming occupied less than 1 percent of the total programming nationwide. The figure jumped to 8 percent in the early 1980s, to 15 percent in the early 1990s, and to around 25 percent in 2000. The Ministry of Radio, Film, and Television now dictates that, unless special permission is obtained, no imported programs are allowed to be shown during prime time (between the hours of 1900 and 2130) and that imported programs cannot fill more than 15 percent of prime time.

A second token of the internationalization of Chinese television is the organizing of TV festivals. In 1986, Shanghai Television held China's first international TV festival, with Sichuan Television organizing another festival in 1990. Since then, one international TV festival has been held in China each year. Recognized as the largest TV festival ever held in Asia, the 8th Shanghai International TV Festival (held October 2000) consisted of a programming competition, a program fair, an exhibition of television equipment and facilities, and an academic seminar on television. A total of 1,487 television organizations and companies from 47 countries attended the festival; 413 programs participated in the competition; and 9,328 episodes of programs were purchased.

A third token of internationalization is the effort to expand exportation of China-produced TV programs to other countries. Major Chinese TV stations have produced programs for the global TV program market and have even become main programming suppliers of some television stations in other Asian countries. In addition to holding TV program fairs at TV festivals to promote program exportation, CCTV and a few major city networks have set up offices in the United States, Britain, France, Belgium, Russia, Egypt, Japan, Hong Kong, Macao, India, Thailand, and Australia to promote business. In addition, CCTV and a few other major Chinese TV stations have established joint-venture business with television stations in North America, South America, Europe, Asia, and Oceania to broadcast programs via satellite. CCTV's international and English-language channels are now broadcast via China's own satellite and are available in most countries around the world.

In one sense, the most significant change in Chinese television since the reform is probably the medium's commercialization, that is, the resurrection of advertising on television and its impact on programming. Advertising was halted for three decades following the Communist Party ascent to power in 1949, but since the end of the Cultural Revolution, economic reforms have revived the importance of market forces and the power of advertising. Both domestic and foreign advertising were resurrected in the late 1970s. Throughout the 1980s, television's revenue from advertising increased at an annual rate of 50 to 60 percent and in 1990 reached 561 million Chinese yuan (about $100 million at that time), compared with no revenue 12 years before. In the 1990s, television became the most commercialized and market-oriented medium in China and attracted a large portion of advertising investment from both domestic and foreign clients. For the hundreds of television stations across the country, advertising and other commercial activities now constitute the majority of programming revenue, ranging from 90 percent as the high end to 40 percent as the low. In 2000 the nationwide total TV advertising revenue was approximately 1.7 billion yuan (about $2 billion), accounting for 23.7 percent of China's total advertising revenue. Among the top ten advertising revenue makers, four are television stations, with CCTV at number one on the list. In the 1990s, several fully commercialized television services, such as the Shanghai-based Oriental Television and the Guangzhou-based Zujiang Delta Television, were established. Their operation is stripping away all state financial support. To a certain degree, fewer government subsidies may give TV stations more programming flexibility.

New Trends and New Directions

Since the early 1980s, under the Communist Party's liberalization policies, Chinese television has become a most popular medium, a very technologically advanced broadcast system, and a service capable of highly professional performance. Moreover, Chinese television has also become much more open than before, unprecedentedly commercialized, and remarkably pluralized, except in political content. Both media practitioners and segments of the public have striven to make television a political forum, and their efforts have met with progress and setbacks, successes as well as failures. By and large, Chinese television in the early 21st century is still a state-owned and party-controlled political and ideological instrument. However, television in China has to a certain extent evolved to fulfill other purposes as well, serving not only the party and the state but also society and the public.

Both cable television and satellite television in China have developed rapidly since the early 1980s. During the 1980s and 1990s, cable television became an important presence in all provinces and major cities, and especially at the county level, as thousands of cable services were established. As both cable and satellite TV services swiftly grew, party and government officials came to worry that the state could not effectively administer, or politically and ideologically control, the expanding television industry. At the end of the 1990s, the central government restructured both the cable TV service and the satellite TV service. Many cable stations that generated small amounts of programming were forced to close by the government, a few satellite stations operating without government approval were stopped, and all remaining cable and satellite stations were merged into the main television stations in each place, forming one large TV unit.

Since the beginning of the 21st century, Chinese television has undergone another profound shift, this time moving toward conglomeration, as China aims to become more competitive both in the domestic television market and in the global television arena. An ambitious multimedia, multidimensional, multilevel, and multifunction operation, the China Radio, Television, and Film Conglomerate was formed in 2001. It consists of China Central Television, China Central Radio, Beijing International Radio, China Film Corporation, and China Radio and Television Online, making it the largest and most powerful media entity in China's history. Following suit, a few economically advanced provinces and big cities, such as Shanghai, Guangdong, and Hunan, have also started the conglomeration process in the media sector, especially in the broadcast media sector.

JUNHAO HONG

Further Reading

Bishop, Robert L., *Qi Lai!: Mobilizing One Billion Chinese: The Chinese Communication System,* Ames: Iowa State University Press, 1989

Chan, J., "Media Internationalization in China: Process and Tensions," *Journal of Communication,* 44, no. 3 (1994)
Chang, Won Ho, *Mass Media in China: The History and the Future,* Ames: Iowa State University Press, 1989
Hong, Junhao, "Changes in China's Television News Programming in the 1980s: The Case of Shanghai Television (STV)," *Media Asia,* 18, no. 2 (1991)
Hong, Junhao, "China's TV Program Import 1958–1988: Towards the Internationalization of Television," *Gazette,* 52 (1993)
Hong, Junhao, "CNN over the Great Wall: Transnational Media in China," *Media Information Australia,* 71 (1994)
Hong, Junhao, "CNN Sets Its Sights on the Asian Market," *Media Development,* 4 (1994)
Hong, Junhao, "The Resurrection of Advertising in China: Developments, Problems, and Trends," *Asian Survey,* 24, no. 4 (1994)
Hong, Junhao, "The Evolution of China's Satellite Policy," *Telecommunications Policy,* 19, no. 2 (1995)
Hong, Junhao, "Changes in China's Media Function in the 1980s: A New Model in a New Era?" in *Democratizing Communication?: Comparative Perspectives on Information and Power,* edited by Mashoed Bailie and Dwayne Winseck, Cresskill, New Jersey: Hampton Press, 1997
Hong, Junhao, "China's Satellite Technology: Developments, Policies, and Applications," in *Telecommunications and Development in China,* edited by Paul S.N. Lee, Cresskill, New Jersey: Hampton Press, 1997
Hong, Junhao, *The Internationalization of Television in China: The Evolution of Ideology, Society, and Media since the Reform,* Westport, Connecticut: Praeger, 1998.
Hong, Junhao, "China's Dual Perception of Globalization and Its Reflection on Media Policies," in *The New Communications Landscape: Demystifying Media Globalization,* edited by Georgette Wang et al., London: Routledge, 2000
Hong, Junhao, and M. Cuthbert, "Media Reform in China Since 1978: Background Factors, Problems, and Future Trends," *Gazette,* 47 (1991)
Huang, Y., "Peaceful Evolution: The Case of Television Reform in Post-Mao China," *Media, Culture, and Society,* 16 (1994)
Lee, Chin-Chuan, editor, *Voices of China: The Interplay of Politics and Journalism,* New York: Guilford Press, 1990
Lee, P., "Mass Communication and National Development in China: Media Roles Reconsidered," *Journal of Communication,* 44, no. 3 (1994)
Li, X., "The Chinese Television System and Television News," *China Quarterly,* 126 (1991)
Lull, James, *China Turned On: Television, Reform, and Resistance,* London: Routledge, 1991
Sun, L., "A Forecasting Study on Chinese Television Development, 1986 to 2001," *Media Asia,* 17, no. 2 (1989)

China Beach

U.S. War Drama

Situated at the televisual intersection of the soap opera, medical show, and war drama, *China Beach* took the pursuit of serial ensemble drama to a self-conscious, provocative extreme. The program's premise was the exploration of personal and professional entanglements among American soldiers and civilians staffing a hospital and entertainment company during the Vietnam War. But the show's hybridization of filmic and televisual genres, rhetorically complex invocation of popular music, and pointed modernist-cum-postmodern reflexivity eventually shifted the emphasis from the story to the telling. Ultimately, the series approached a convergence of televisual narrative association with collectively shared cultural remembrance. *China Beach*'s ensemble, the show ultimately implied, necessarily included the viewer inhabiting post-Vietnam America.

The program depicted issues familiar from such dark war comedies as *M*A*S*H* and revisionist allegories like *Apocalypse Now.* Storylines explored the corruption or ineptitude of military authority; soldiers' inability to function in "normal" interactions; the medical staff's necessary posture of mordant irony; and the war's sudden curtailment of friendship or romance.

However, the narration profoundly shifted the usual priorities of such plots by focusing on the women at the base, an emphasis fundamentally intended to undermine vainglorious heroism and to portray war instead, through "women's eyes," as a vast and elaborate conceit. Contemporary critics divided between those applauding the program's feminine deflation of war and those who regarded the characters and their orientations toward war as wholly stereotypical invocations of femininity. John Leonard, writing for *Ms.,* anticipated both camps in an early review: on the one hand, he identified the show's "war-movie foxhole principle of diversity-as-paradigm, which is to say that if you're stuck with all these women, one must be a Madonna, another a whore, a third, Mother Courage, and a fourth, Major Barbara." On the other hand, he reveled in the power of such stereotypes to multiply dramatic possibilities.

China Beach, 1988–89 Season.
©20th Century Fox/Courtesy of the Everett Collection

Certainly *China Beach*'s two crucial protagonists amounted to carefully elaborated formulas. The camp's head nurse was the willful Colleen McMurphy, a woman proud of her composure and careful in her moral convictions, compassionate but capable of a scathingly condemning glance. K.C. was the calculating madam, alluring but hard, for whom the war brought nothing but higher profits, better contacts, and escalating entrepreneurial opportunities. These two roles constituted an important dialectic not primarily in character conflict but in the orientation viewers were asked to take at any given time. They were played by exceptional performers whose portrayals complicated the stereotypes by importing still other formulas. Rather than a distanced Madonna, Dana Delany's McMurphy proved to be a passionate woman who—as a feminized, Irish Catholic version of *M*A*S*H*'s Hawkeye Pierce—found not mere escape but potential redemption in relationships. Rather than a whore with a heart of gold, Marg Helgenberger's K.C. emerged as chillingly objective, independent, self-isolated, and unaccountable, as formidable and unapologetic as any soap opera diva. If McMurphy sought to discover a sheltering and resilient humanity in the ensemble's reciprocities, K.C.'s continual interest was the manipulation of the ensemble's pitifully predictable foibles from without. McMurphy, K.C., and their supporting characters merged the sentimental education of women's melodrama, the life-and-death ethical discourse of medical dramas, and the lurid bathos of the apocalyptic war story in an ambitious format. Here the simultaneous development of serial plotlines created (as on *St. Elsewhere* and *Hill Street Blues*) an ongoing, organically changing, symbolically charged fictional world.

Both melodramatic sentiment and the psychic dislocation of war were conveyed not only through juxtaposed storylines and generic recombination but also through the show's evocative use of Vietnam-era soul, blues, and rock. *China Beach* frequently used such nostalgic music to frame the show's events as remembrances, laden with a sense of moral revisitation. Even more ambitiously, the program consistently invoked the audiences' feelings of nostalgic distance from the period in which the songs originated. That separation served as an analog for the feelings of distance that the protagonists, immersed in a war, were likely to feel from the society producing those songs. The viewer, like the dislocated combatant, was asked to yearn for the consolations of everyday 1960s American civilization (an invitation that drew on already prevalent revivals of 1960s counterculture among "baby boomers" and late-1980s youth).

In its final season, the show's convergence between the viewing audience and the protagonists took a considerable leap. The program now followed the characters into their postwar lives, reconstructing key events at China Beach—and the end of the war itself—through flashbacks. In an especially melodramatic plot, the show's narrative is controlled by the investigative efforts of K.C.'s dispossessed baby, now a film student whose handheld video camera (an instrument of 1980s culture) becomes the show's eye as she interviews her mother's acquaintances in an attempt to find where K.C. has gone. In this season, the original ensemble has dispersed geographically, historically, and socially. Their separation exacerbates the multiplicity of vantages that gestated at China Beach during the war and places the characters, sometimes disconcertingly and tragically, in situations that seem approachably contemporary with the viewing audience. Screen time became equally divided between fictive "past" and "present," making the entire narration an uprooted historical rumination. The viewer became implicated not just in a *Rashomon*-like reconstruction of the war, but in an equally segmented and self-conscious sense of present American society, and its shared reflections.

Formal complication was not confined to music or narrative. *China Beach* used self-conscious, often expressionist lighting, sets, sound, and camera movement, which could vary dramatically from subplot to subplot. The military company's role as an entertainment unit was sometimes exploited to set characters in ironic plays-within-the-show or to frame the allegorical dimension of musical performances.

For some critics, *China Beach* comprised, at its moment in the history of television production and viewership, a remarkable case of intrinsically televisual fiction. Others, however, regarded the program's overwrought televisual rhetoric differently. Such critics did not see *China Beach* as an exploration of the ethical and aesthetic possibilities of one of American culture's key sites for the fictional production of touchstone sentiments; rather, they interpreted the program to be a conceited diminishment of history. Richard Zoglin of *Time* (a considerable forge of collective memory in its own right) accurately perceived the show's postmodern efforts to collapse wartime tragedy into contemporary viewers' casual nostalgia. But he seemed to think he was indicting the show by suggesting it reflected "the way dissent [against Vietnam] has become domesticated in America; what were radical antiwar views in the '60s are now mainstream TV attitudes." His assessment was accurate but not necessarily lamentable. *China Beach* demonstrated the historical war's continuing ability to provoke special sentiments among contemporary audiences.

Zoglin and others' questionable worries over television's historical license were based in the assumption that *China Beach*'s version of the war would remain exclusive, definitive, and unrecognized as fiction. But television, with its multiple representations in fiction, documentary, and news programs dealing with Vietnam, clearly continues to deny that assumption.

MICHAEL SAENZ

See also **Vietnam on Television; War on Television**

Cast

Nurse Colleen McMurphy	Dana Delany
Cherry White (1988–89)	Nan Woods
Laurette Barber (1988)	Chloe Webb
Karen Charlene (K.C.) Koloski	Marg Helgenberger
Pvt. Sam Beckett	Michael Boatman
Dr. Dick Richard	Robert Picardo
Natch Austen (1988–89)	Tim Ryan
Maj. Lila Garreau	Concetta Tomei
Boonie Lanier	Brian Wimmer
Wayloo Marie Holmes (1988–89)	Megan Gallagher
Pvt. Frankie Bunsen	Nancy Giles
Dodger	Jeff Kober
Jeff Hyers (1989)	Ned Vaughn
Sgt. Pepper (1989–91)	Troy Evans
Holly the Donut Dolly (1989–90)	Ricki Lake

Producers

John Sacrett Young, William Broyles Jr.

Programming History

ABC

April 1988	Tuesday 9:00–10:00
April 1988–June 1988	Wednesday 10:00–11:00
August 1988–September 1988	Wednesday 10:00–11:00
November 1988–March 1990	Wednesday 10:00–11:00
April 1990	Monday 9:00–10:00
July 1990–August 1990	Wednesday 10:00–11:00
August 1990–December 1990	Saturday 9:00–10:00
June 1991–July 1991	Tuesday 10:00–11:00
July 1991	Monday 9:00–11:00

Further Reading

Auster, Albert, " 'Reflections of the Way Life Used to Be': *Tour of Duty, China Beach,* and the Memory of the Sixties," *Television Quarterly* (fall 1990)

Ballard-Reisch, Deborah, "*China Beach* and *Tour of Duty:* American Television and Revisionist History of the Vietnam War," *Journal of Popular Culture* (winter 1991)

Hanson, Cynthia A., "The Women of *China Beach,*" *Journal of Popular Film and Television* (winter 1990)

Leonard, John, "Networking: A Not-So-Frank Assessment of Prime-Time Women," *Ms.* (October 1988)

Morrison, Mark, "*China Beach* Salutes the Women of Vietnam," *Rolling Stone* (May 19, 1988)

Rasmussen, Karen, "*China Beach* and American Mythology of War," *Women's Studies in Communication* (fall 1992)

Schine, Cathleen, "TV's Women in Groups: They Work Together, They Sweat Together, They 'Care' Together," *Vogue* (September 1988)

Vande Berg, Leah R., "*China Beach,* Prime-Time War in the Postfeminist Age: An Example of Patriarchy in a Different Voice," *Western Journal of Communication* (summer 1993)

Christian Broadcasting Network. *See* **ABC Family Channel**

Chung, Connie (1946–)

U.S. Broadcast Journalist

Connie Chung is one of a very small group of women who have achieved prominence in American network news. Along with Barbara Walters, Diane Sawyer, and Jane Pauley, Chung is one of the leading female journalists on television. Until 1995 she coanchored the *CBS Evening News* with Dan Rather, as well as *Eye to Eye with Connie Chung,* a prime-time news hour. Following considerable controversy over her interviewing

Connie Chung.
Photo courtesy of Connie Chung/Tony Esparza

style and reportorial skills, and during which it was reported that Rather had never been happy with the coanchor arrangement, Chung parted ways with CBS in 1995.

Chung began her journalism career in 1969 as a copyperson at WTTG-TV, Washington, D.C., a Metromedia affiliate, where she later became a newswriter and on-air reporter. She first joined CBS News in 1971, working as a Washington-based correspondent from 1971 to 1976, covering Watergate, Capitol Hill, and the 1972 presidential campaign. In 1976 she joined KNXT (now KCBS-TV), the CBS-owned television station in Los Angeles, working on both local and network broadcasts. In her seven years in Los Angeles, Chung coanchored three daily newscasts and was a substitute anchor for the *CBS Morning News* and CBS News' weekend and evening broadcasts. She also anchored CBS News' *Newsbreak* for the Pacific time zones.

Chung left CBS to join NBC News as a correspondent and anchor. Her assignments included anchoring the Saturday edition of the *NBC Nightly News, NBC News at Sunrise, NBC News Digest,* several prime-time news specials, and the newsmagazine *1986.* She was also contributing correspondent and substitute anchor on the *NBC Nightly News* broadcast. Chung served as political analysis correspondent and podium correspondent during the 1988 presidential campaign and political conventions.

When she joined Dan Rather as coanchor of the *CBS Evening News,* Chung became only the second woman to hold a network anchor job, following Barbara Walters's brief stint as coanchor with Harry Reasoner on ABC in the mid-1970s. The male-female anchor pairing, already a staple of local news, seemed designed also to capitalize on Chung's recognizability. In the Q-ratings (a set of measurements provided by a company called Marketing Evaluations, which gauge the popularity of people who appear on television), Chung has always scored extremely high. At the time she was named coanchor, she had one of the highest Q-ratings of any woman in network news. In 1990 she was chosen "favorite interviewer" in *U.S. News and World Report's* Best of America survey.

In unexpected ways, Chung has foregrounded issues of concern to working women. In 1990 she took the unusual step of announcing plans to postpone her magazine series *Face to Face with Connie Chung* in order to take time to conceive a child with her husband, syndicated daytime television talk-show host Maury Povich.

Chung has also been part of the trend toward using newscast anchors on prime-time programs. Her work on nighttime news shows has sometimes drawn criticism, as when the short-lived *Saturday Night with Connie Chung* was tagged as "infotainment" and charged with undermining the credibility of network news by using controversial techniques such as news reenactments. Chung was again involved in controversy in early 1995, when in an interview with Kathryn Gingrich, the mother of Speaker of the House Newt Gingrich, Chung urged her subject to whisper her son's comments about First Lady Hillary Clinton "just between us." The whisper was picked up by the microphone and used by Chung for broadcast, drawing attacks on Chung's journalistic integrity. This incident was followed by conflict over Chung's assignment to cover the Oklahoma City bombing incident and CBS's apparent plans to "demote" her to the position of weekend anchor and possibly to cancel her prime-time program *Eye to Eye with Connie Chung.* Accompanied by an almost palpable strain on the set of the *CBS Evening News,* as well as by the program's declining ratings, these events led to Chung's departure from CBS amidst charges of sexism and countercharges of a lack of journalistic seriousness.

In December 1997, Chung joined ABC as a correspondent in the news division. She moved from ABC to CNN in January 2002 and hosted her own prime-time program, *Connie Chung Tonight.* However, CNN abruptly dropped the show in March 2003 in favor of more extensive coverage of the war in Iraq. Although the network asked Chung to stay on in another capacity, Chung declined the offer and left CNN.

DIANE M. NEGRA

Connie Chung. Born Constance Yu-Hwa Chung in Washington, D.C., August 20, 1946. Educated at University of Maryland, B.A. in journalism, 1969. Married: Maurice (Maury) Richard Povich, 1984; child: Matthew Jay. Reporter, WTTG-TV, Washington, 1969–71; correspondent, CBS News, Washington, 1971–76; anchor, KNXT-TV (CBS), Los Angeles, 1976–83; anchor, NBC News, 1983–89, and NBC news specials, 1987–89; anchor, *Saturday Night with Connie Chung,* CBS, *CBS Evening News* (Sunday), 1989–92; coanchor, *CBS Evening News,* 1993–95. Honorary degrees: D.J., Norwich University, 1974; L.H.D., Brown University, 1987. Honorary member: Pepperdine University Broadcast Club, 1981. Recipient: Metro Area Mass Media Award, American Association of University Women (AAUW), 1971; Outstanding Excellence in News Reporting and Public Service Award, Chinese-American Citizens Alliance, 1973; award for best TV reporting, Los Angeles Press Club, 1977; award for outstanding TV broadcasting, Valley Press Club, 1977; Emmy Awards, 1978, 1980, and 1987; Peabody Award, 1980; Newscaster of the Year Award, Temple Emmanuel Brotherhood, 1981; Portraits of Excellence Award, B'nai B'rith, Pacific S.W. Region, 1980; First Amendment Award, Anti-Defamation League of B'nai B'rith, 1981. Fellow, Harvard University's Joan Shorenstein Center on the Press, Politics, and Public Policy, 1997.

Television Series

1983–89 *NBC Nightly News* (anchor and reporter)
1983–89 *News Digest* (anchor and reporter)
1983–89 *NBC News at Sunrise* (anchor and reporter)
1985–86 *American Almanac* (cohost)
1985–86 *1986* (cohost)
1989–95 *CBS Evening News* (reporter)
1989–90 *Saturday Night with Connie Chung* (host)
1990 *Face to Face with Connie Chung* (host)
1993–95 *CBS Evening News* (coanchor)
1993–95 *Eye to Eye with Connie Chung*
2002–03 *Connie Chung Tonight*

Television Specials

1980 *Terra: Our World*
1987 *NBC News Report on America: Life in the Fat Lane*
1987 *Scared Sexless*
1988 *NBC News Reports on America: Stressed to Kill*
1988 *Everybody's Doing It*

Further Reading

Anderson, Kurt, "Does Connie Chung Matter?" *Time* (May 31, 1993)
Carter, Bill, "Chung to Join Rather," *New York Times* (May 18, 1993)
Conant, Jennet, "Broadcast Networking: Despite What You've Heard, the Women of TV News Feel a Strong Sense of Solidarity," *Working Woman* (August 1990)
Frank, Reuven, "Connie Chung at the Circus," *New Leader* (May 8, 1995)
"A Future Affair," *MediaWeek* (June 10, 1996)
Hosley, David H., and Gayle K. Yamada, *Hard News: Women in Broadcast Journalism,* New York: Greenwood, 1987
Reibstein, Larry, "Irreconcilable Ratings," *Newsweek* (June 5, 1995)
Westin, Av, *Newswatch: How TV Decides the News,* New York: Simon and Schuster, 1982
Wolf, Steve, "Weighing Anchors," *Time* (May 15, 1995)

Citytv

Canadian Television Station

Citytv, Toronto's fast-paced and image-driven independent television station, first aired on September 28, 1972, as a UHF channel. It was assured of financial security when the Canadian media giant CHUM Ltd., which had purchased a 45 percent interest in Citytv from Montreal-based Multiple Access in 1979, acquired the remainder of shares in the struggling station in 1981. ChumCity's total enterprise includes the cable and satellite music-video channels MuchMusic and MusiquePlus (also franchised in Latin America as MuchaMusica), the national arts and culture channel Bravo!, and international syndication sales of Citytv's magazine programs (such as *The New Music, Fashion Television, Media Television,* and *The Originals*). Citytv is now a consistently top-ranked channel within what is perhaps North America's most competitive market (Toronto has 53 television stations).

Built on the programming keystones of news, music, and movies, Citytv found early notoriety by broadcasting *Baby Blue Movies,* a series of late-night, soft-core porn films. While the "Baby Blues" are now off the air, Citytv still broadcasts an average of five movies a day, many of which are world or Canadian premiers. Similarly innovative in music programming, Citytv first telecast *The New Music,* a forerunner to both MTV and MuchMusic, in 1979. However, Citytv's most notable distinction lies in a conceptual approach that consistently attempts to expand the mobility and function of the medium. As Canada's first all-videotape station, Citytv initiated the practices of electronic news gathering and single-person reportage. Such techniques are exercised in the local news program *CityPulse,* which foregoes anchor desks and news studios for an unconventional and tabloidlike momentum. The emphasis on process, locality, and informal interactivity is particularly evidenced in the ChumCity building, a refurbished 19th-century gothic structure in which there are no studios, sets, or control rooms. Instead, the entire complex is wired to "shoot itself" through a series of strategically placed electronic "hydrants." In this manner, cameras are enabled to roam anywhere—the roof, stairwells, or the street—and are often integrated into the shot. Viewers then watch camera operators at work setting up, watch themselves viewing programs in process through the building's large ground-floor windows, or see an interview through the eyes of an interviewee, via a second Hi-8 camera provided to the story subject. The concept of public access is expanded through *Speaker's Corner,* a video booth where, for a charity-addressed dollar, passersby may confess their sins, declare their love, or sound off on pet peeves; the best of these are used as shorts between shows or collated into the weekly *Speaker's Corner* program.

Unlike many other Canadian networks or independent stations, Citytv does not bid for dramatic programs produced in the United States, with the exception of importing the contemporary *Star Trek* series (*The Next Generation, Deep Space Nine,* and *Voyager*) and the occasional made-for-TV movie or miniseries. Citytv does buy syndicated daytime talk shows from the United States, which it airs during its weekday schedule. There are no game shows, children's programs, soaps, sitcoms, or sports on Citytv. Saturday- and Sunday-morning schedules are given over to community ethnic programming.

While often favoring style and self-promotion over substance and self-reflexivity, Citytv's accomplished characteristic lies in its process-oriented format. This is evident not only within the programs per se but in the breaks between programs: station IDs, interstitials, and promotional spots are tailored to intervene, as well as interweave, within the overall effect and tenor of the show. In this respect, Citytv successfully capitalizes on the capacities of televisual "flow."

BETH SEATON

See also **Canada; Canadian Production Companies; Canadian Programming in English; MuchMusic; Znaimer, Moses**

Further Reading

McDonald, Marci, "The Gospel According to Moses (Znaimer)," *Maclean's* (May 8, 1995)

Murray, Ken, "Canadian TV Moguls Rev Engines in Race for U.K.'s Channel 5," *Variety* (June 1, 1992)

Robins, J. Max, "This Moses May Lead TV to Its Promised Land," *Variety* (July 26, 1993)

The Civil Rights Movement and Television

American television coverage of the civil rights movement ultimately contributed to a redefinition of the country's political as well as its televisual landscape. From the 1955 Montgomery bus boycotts to the 1964 Democratic National Convention in Atlantic City, New Jersey, technological innovations in portable cameras and electronic news gathering (ENG) equipment increasingly enabled television to bring the nonviolent civil disobedience campaign of the civil rights movement and the violent reprisals of

Dr. Martin Luther King Jr. speaks about his Montgomery, Alabama bus boycott arrest, ca. mid-1950s.
Courtesy of the Everett Collection

southern law enforcement agents to a newly configured mass audience.

The landmark U.S. Supreme Court case *Brown v. Board of Education* (1954), along with the brutal murder of 15-year-old Emmet Till in Mississippi and the subsequent acquittal of the two white men accused of his murder, marked the beginning of the modern civil rights movement in the United States. The unprecedented media coverage of the Till case rendered it a cause célèbre that helped to swell the membership ranks of civil rights organizations nationwide. As civil rights workers organized mass boycotts and civil disobedience campaigns to end legal segregation and white supremacist terror in the South, white segregationists mounted a counteroffensive that was swift and too often violent. Medgar Evers and other civil rights activists were assassinated. Black churches, businesses, and residences with ties to the movement were bombed. Although this escalation of terror was intended to thwart the civil rights movement, it had the unanticipated effect of broadening local and global support for civil rights.

These events were unfolding at the same time that the percentage of U.S. homes equipped with television sets jumped from 56 to 92 percent. This was 1955, and television was securing its place at the center of American society. Network news shows were also beginning to expand from the conventional 15-minute format to 30 minutes, splitting the time between local and national issues. From the mid- to late 1950s, these social, political, technological, and cultural events began to converge. The ascendancy of television as the new arbiter of public opinion became increasingly apparent at this time to civil rights leaders and television news directors alike. Thus, television's coverage of the civil rights movement changed considerably, especially as the "antiestablishment politics" of the 1960s erupted. When television covered the consumer boycotts and the school desegregation battles in the early days of the civil rights movement, it was usually in a detached manner, with a particular focus on the most dramatic and sensational occurrences. Furthermore, the coverage of the movement in the late 1950s was intermittent, typically with a field reporter conducting a stand-up report from a volatile scene. Alternatively, an in-studio anchor man would narrate the unfolding events captured on film. Rarely, if ever, did black participants speak for themselves or address directly the United States' newly constituted mass television audience. Nevertheless, civil rights leaders understood how central television exposure was becoming to the success of the movement.

The desire to bring the struggle for civil rights into American living rooms was not limited to civil rights workers, however. The drama and sensationalism of peaceful civil rights protesters in violent confrontation with brutal agents of southern segregation were not lost on news producers. News programmers needed to fill their expanded news programs with live telecasts of newsworthy events, and the public clashes around the civil rights movement were too violent and too important to ignore.

For example, the most enduring images telecast from this period include shots of numerous boycotted buses driving down deserted Alabama streets in 1955; angry white mobs of segregationists squaring off against black students escorted by a phalanx of federal troops in front of Ole Miss, the University of Mississippi (1957); and Dr. Martin Luther King Jr., leading a mass of black protesters across a bridge in Selma, Alabama (1965). Most memorable, perhaps, of all these dramatic video images is the 1963 attack on young civil rights protesters by the Birmingham, Alabama, police and their dogs, and the fire department's decision to turn on fire hydrants to disperse the young black demonstrators, most of whom were children. Television cameras captured the water's force pushing young black protesters down flooding streets like rubbish during a street cleaning. In contrast to the typical televisual landscape of formulaic game shows, "vaudeo" (video variety programs), westerns, and situation comedies, this was unquestionably compelling and revolutionary television.

By the early to mid-1960s, television was covering the explosive civil rights movement regularly and forcefully. It was at this time that the young, articulate, and telegenic Reverend Martin Luther King Jr., emerged from the Southern Christian Leadership Conference as the movement's chief spokesman. Commenting on King's oratory skills, one reporter noted that his "message and eloquence were met with rapt attention and enthusiastic support." He was the perfect visual symbol for a new era of American race relations. During this period, television made it possible for civil rights workers to be seen and heard on an international scale. King's historic "I Have a Dream" speech was delivered on August 28, 1963, at the March on Washington rally. King's speech not only reached the 300,000 people from civil rights organizations, church groups, and labor unions who gathered at the nation's capital to demonstrate for unity, racial tolerance, and passage of the civil rights bill—with the aid of television, it reached Americans nationwide as well.

Later that same year, television covered the assassinations of civil rights leader Medgar Evers and President John F. Kennedy. These deaths devastated the civil rights community, and television coverage of both events ensured that the nation mourned these losses as well.

In 1964 Fanny Lou Hamer's televised speech at the Democratic National Convention in Atlantic City signaled a pivotal moment in the history of television's relationship to the civil rights campaign. Hamer's now famous "Is This America?" speech infuriated President Lyndon Johnson, emboldened the networks, rallied the civil rights troops, and riveted the nation. Even though Johnson directed the networks to kill the live feed carrying her speech on voting rights on behalf of the African-American Mississippi Freedom Democratic Party (MFDP), the networks recognized the speech's powerful appeal and aired Hamer's address in its entirety later that night. Thus, Hamer, a black woman and a sharecropper, became one of the first black civil rights activists to address the nation directly and on her own terms.

This phase of the movement also saw an influx of white, liberal college students and adults from across the United States into the Deep South, during the so-called Freedom Summer of 1964. Civil rights organizers encouraged the participation of white liberals in the movement because organizers understood that the presence of whites in the struggle would attract the television cameras and, by extension, the nation. No one was prepared for the tragic events that followed. As it turns out, television's incessant probing into the murders and subsequent monthlong search for the bodies of two white, northern civil rights workers, Michael Schwerner and Andrew Goodman, and black southerner James Chaney did have a chilling effect on the nation. Now, with the deaths of innocent white volunteers, television helped convince its suburban viewers across the United States that the civil rights movement did concern them as well, as it was difficult to turn on the television without news of the Schwerner, Chaney, and Goodman search. From late June to August 4, 1964, television regularly and consistently transmitted news of the tragedy to the entire nation. Television ultimately legitimated and lent new urgency to the decade-long struggle for basic human and civil rights that the civil rights movement had difficulty achieving prior to the involvement of television. The incessant gaze of the television cameras on the murders and disappearance of Schwerner, Chaney, and Goodman, following on the heels of the Evers and Kennedy assassinations, resulted in mobilizing national support for the civil rights movement. In fact, it was television's coverage of the movement's crises and catastrophes that became a prelude to the medium's subsequent involvement with and handling of the later social and political chaos surrounding the Black Power, antiwar, free speech, and second-wave feminist movements. As veteran civil rights reporters went on to cover the assassinations of Malcolm X, Martin Luther King Jr., and Robert Kennedy, as well as the ghetto uprisings of the late 1960s, a whole new visual and aural lexicon of "crisis television" developed, one that in many ways still defines how television news is communicated.

By 1968 it was clear that television's powerful and visceral images of the civil rights struggle had permeated many levels of American social and political reality. These images had helped garner support for such liberal legislation as the 1964 Voting Rights Act and President Johnson's "Great Society" and "War on Poverty" programs, all of which were legatees of the civil rights movement.

However, as volatile pictures of Detroit, Michigan; Washington, D.C.; the Watts neighborhood in Los Angeles; and other U.S. cities going up in smoke hit the television airwaves in the late 1960s, they provoked a strong reaction, marked by the presidential campaign slogans calling for law and order. Consequently, many of the very images that supported the movement simultaneously helped to fuel the national backlash against it. This anti–civil rights backlash contributed to the 1968 presidential election of conservative Republican Richard M. Nixon.

While television news programs strove to cover the historic events of the day, entertainment shows responded to the civil rights movement in their own fashion. With their concern over advertising revenues and corporate sponsorship, the networks' entertainment divisions decided on a turn to social relevance, although they did not tackle the controversy and social conflict of the civil rights movement directly. Instead, they took the cautious route of slowly integrating (in racial terms) fictional programming by casting black characters in roles other than the usual domestic and comedic stereotypes. Beloved characterizations of domesticated blacks in such popular television shows as *Beulah, Amos 'n' Andy, The Jack Benny Show,* and *The Danny Thomas Show,* for example, slowly gave way to integrated-cast programs depicting the network's accommodationist position on the "New Frontier" ideology of Kennedy liberalism, wherein black characters were integrated into American society as long as they supported American law and order. Among these shows were *East Side/West Side* (1963–64), *The Defenders* (1961–65), *Naked City* (1958–63), *The Nurses* (1962–65), *I Spy* (1965–68), *Peyton Place* (1964–69), *Star Trek* (1966–69), *Mission: Impossible* (1966–73), *Daktari* (1966–69), *NYPD* (1967–69), and *The Mod Squad* (1968–73), to name but a few. Rather than reflect the intense racial conflicts of bombed-out churches, blacks being beaten by southern cops, and massive demonstrations, these dramatic programs portrayed interracial cooperation and peaceful coexistence between black and white characters. For the first time on network television, many of the black characters in these shows were depicted as intelligent and heroic. Although some of these shows were criticized for their lone black characters who staunchly upheld the status quo, these shows, nevertheless, did mark a significant transformation of the televisual universe. By contrast, CBS's spate of all-white-cast television shows, mainly set in the rural South—*The Andy Griffith Show* (1960–68), *The Beverly Hillbillies* (1962–71), *Petticoat Junction* (1963–70), and *Green Acres* (1965–71)—fictionalized lovable and hapless southern "hillbillies" that directly countered the real-life southern racists whose brutal repressions appeared nightly in network news coverage of the civil rights struggle. For mass audiences accustomed to traditional white and black shows, the civil rights movement brought a little more color to the television spectrum.

ANNA EVERETT

See also **Racism, Ethnicity, and Television**

Further Reading

Brooks, Tim, and Earle Marsh, editors, *The Complete Directory to Prime Time Network TV Shows: 1946–Present,* New York: Ballantine, 1979; 5th edition, 1992

Gitlin, Todd, *Inside Prime Time,* New York: Pantheon, 1985; revised edition, 1994

Hampton, Henry, *Voices of Freedom: An Oral History of the Civil Rights Movement from the 1950s through the 1980s,* New York: Bantam, 1990

Hill, George, et al., *Black Women in Television,* New York and London: Garland, 1990

Hine, Darlene Clark, et al., editors. *Black Women in America,* Bloomington: Indiana University Press, 1993

Kellner, Douglas, *Television and the Crisis of Democracy,* Boulder, Colorado: Westview Press, 1990

MacDonald, J. Fred, *Blacks and White TV: Afro-Americans in Television Since 1948,* Chicago: Nelson-Hall, 1983; 2nd edition, 1992

MacDonald, J. Fred, *One Nation Under Television: The Rise and Decline of Network TV,* New York: Pantheon, 1990

McNeil, Alex, *Total Television: A Comprehensive Guide to Programming from 1948 to 1980,* Harmondsworth, England, and New York: Penguin Books, 1980; 4th edition as *Total Television: A Comprehensive Guide to Programming from 1948 to the Present,* New York: Penguin Books, 1996

Mills, Kay, *This Little Light of Mine: The Life of Fannie Lou Hamer,* New York: Penguin, 1993

Newcomb, Horace, editor, *Television: The Critical View,* New York: Oxford University Press, 1976; 4th edition, 1987

O'Connor, John E., editor, *American History/American Television: Interpreting the Video Past,* New York: Ungar, 1983

Renov, Michael, editor, *Theorizing Documentary,* New York and London: Routledge, 1993

Williams, Juan, *Eyes on the Prize: America's Civil Rights Years, 1954–1965,* New York: Viking Penguin, 1987

Civil War, The

U.S. Compilation Documentary

The Civil War premiered on the Public Broadcasting Service (PBS) over five consecutive evenings (September 23 to 27, 1990), amassing the largest audience for any series in public television history. More than 39 million Americans tuned into at least one episode of the telecast, and viewership averaged more than 14 million viewers each evening. Subsequent research indicated that nearly half the viewers would not have been watching television at all if it had not been for *The Civil War.*

The widespread positive reaction to *The Civil War* was generally lavish and unprecedented. Film and television critics from across the country were equally attentive and admiring. *Newsweek* called the program "a documentary masterpiece"; *Time,* "eloquen[t]...a pensive epic"; and *U.S. News and World Report,* "the best Civil War film ever made." David Thomson in *American Film* declared that *The Civil War* "is a film Walt Whitman might have dreamed." And political pundit George Will wrote: "Our *Iliad* has found its Homer... if better use has ever been made of television, I have not seen it."

Between 1990 and 1992, accolades for producer Ken Burns and the series took on institutional proportions. He won Producer of the Year from the Producers Guild of America; two Emmys (for Outstanding Information Series and Outstanding Writing Achievement); a Peabody; a DuPont-Columbia Award; a Golden Globe; a D.W. Griffith Award; two Grammys; a People's Choice Award for Best Television Mini-Series; and eight honorary doctorates from various U.S. colleges and universities, along with literally dozens of other recognitions.

The Civil War also became a phenomenon of popular culture. The series was mentioned on episodes of *Twin Peaks, thirtysomething,* and *Saturday Night Live* during the 1990–91 television season. Ken Burns appeared on *The Tonight Show,* and he was selected by the editors of *People* magazine as one of their "25 most intriguing people of 1990." The series, moreover, developed into a marketing sensation. The companion volume, published by Knopf, *The Civil War: An Illustrated History,* became a runaway best-seller; as did the nine-episode videotaped version from Time-Life and the Warner soundtrack, featuring the bittersweet anthem "Ashokan Farewell" by Jay Ungar.

Several interlocking factors evidently contributed to this extraordinary level of interest, including the documentary's accompanying promotional campaign, the momentum of scheduling Sunday through Thursday, the synergetic merchandising of its ancillary products, and, of course, the quality of production itself. Most significantly, though, the series examined the United States' great civil conflict from a distinct perspective. A new generation of historians had already begun addressing the war from the so-called bottom-up point of view, underscoring the role of African Americans, women, immigrants, workers, farmers, and common soldiers in the conflict. This fresh emphasis on social and cultural history had revitalized the Civil War as a subject, adding a more inclusive and human dimension to the traditional preoccupations with "great men," transcendent ideals, and battle strategies and statistics. The time was again propitious for creating a filmed version of the war between the states that included the accessibility of the newer approach. In Ken Burns's own words, "I don't think the story of the Civil War can be told too often. I think it surely ought to be retold for every generation."

Much of the success of Ken Burns's *The Civil War* must be attributed to the ways in which his account made the 19th-century conflict immediate and comprehensible to viewers in the 1990s. The great questions of race and continuing discrimination, of the changing roles of women and men in society, of big government versus local control, and of the individual struggle for meaning and conviction in modern life all form essential parts of Burns's version of the war. In this way, *The Civil War* serves as an artistic attempt to better understand these enduring public issues and form a new consensus around them, functioning also as a validation for the members of its principal audience (which was older, white, male, and upscale in the ratings) of the importance of their past in an era of unprecedented multicultural redefinition. In Ken Burns's own words, "I realized the power that the war still exerted over us."

To define and present that power on television, Burns employed 24 prominent historians as consultants on the project. He melded together approximately 300 expert commentaries and another 900 first-person quotations from Civil War–era letters, diaries, and memoirs. Excerpts from these source materials were read by a wide assortment of distinguished performers, such as Sam Waterston, Jason Robards, Julie Harris, and Morgan Freeman, among many others.

Often these remarkable voices were attached to specific historical characters—foot soldiers from both armies, wives or mothers left behind, slaves who escaped to fight on behalf of their own freedom. One of Burns's extraordinary techniques was to follow some of these individuals through long periods of time, using their own words to chronicle the devastating sense of battle weariness, the loneliness of divided families, and both the pain and joy of specific moments in personal histories.

The Civil War, Shelby Foote, Ken Burns, 1990.
Courtesy of the Everett Collection

Just as significantly, he attached pictures to these words. Using a vast collection of archival images, some rarely seen, the primary visual production technique was the slow movement of the camera over the surfaces of still photographs. Audiences were allowed to move in for close-ups of faces and eyes, to survey spaces captured in more panoramic photos, and to see some individuals at different stages of their war experiences. The visual component of *The Civil War* also compared historical photographs of places with contemporary filmed shots of the same locations. The "reality" of bluffs over Vicksburg, a Chancellorsville battlefield, or the Appomattox Courthouse was established by these multiple pictorial representations.

All these visual and aural techniques combined in a

special sort of opportunity for the audience. The series invited one into a meditation more than an analysis, an intimate personal consideration of massive conflict, social upheaval, and cultural devastation.

Ken Burns, a hands-on and versatile producer, was personally involved in researching, fund-raising for, co-writing, shooting, directing, editing, scoring, and even promoting *The Civil War.* The series, a production of Burns's Florentine Films in association with WETA-TV in Washington, D.C., also boasted contributions by many of the filmmaker's usual collaborators, including his brother and coproducer, Ric Burns, writer Geoffrey C. Ward, and narrator David McCullough. Writer, historian, and master raconteur Shelby Foote emerged as the on-screen star of *The Civil War,* peppering the series with entertaining anecdotes during 89 separate appearances.

The Civil War took an estimated five years to complete and cost nearly $3.5 million, garnered largely from support by General Motors, the National Endowment for the Humanities, and the Corporation for Public Broadcasting. By any standard that has gone before, *The Civil War* is a masterful historical documentary. Through reruns and home videos, more than 70 million Americans have now seen the program. International audiences have also numbered in the tens of millions.

Burns now laughs about the apprehension he felt on the evening *The Civil War* premiered on prime-time television and changed his life forever. He remembers thinking long and hard about the remarks of several reviewers who predicted that the series would be "eaten alive," going head-to-head with network programming. He recalls being "completely unprepared for what was going to happen" next, as the series averaged a 9.0 rating, an exceptional performance for public television. Ken Burns admits, "I was flabbergasted! I still sort of pinch myself about it. It's one of those rare instances in which something helped stitch the country together, however briefly, and the fact that I had a part in that is just tremendously satisfying."

GARY R. EDGERTON

See also **Burns, Ken; Documentary**

Producers
Ken Burns, Ric Burns

Coproducers
Stephen Ives, Julie Dunfey, Mike Hill, Lynn Novick

Programming History
PBS
September 23–27, 1990

Further Reading

Burns, Ken, "In Search of the Painful, Essential Images of War," *New York Times* (January 27, 1991)

Censer, J.T., "Videobites: Ken Burns' *The Civil War* in the Classroom," *American Quarterly* (1992)

"*The Civil War:* Ken Burns Charts a Nation's Birth," *American Film* (September 1990)

DuBois, E., "The Civil War," *American Historical Review* (1991)

Duncan, D., "A Cinematic Storyteller," *Boston Globe Magazine* (March 19, 1989)

Edgerton, Gary R., "Ken Burns's Rebirth of a Nation: Television, Narrative, and Popular History," *Film and History* (1992)

Edgerton, Gary R., "Ken Burns's America: Style, Authorship, and Cultural Memory," *Journal of Popular Film and Television* (1993)

Edgerton, Gary R., "Ken Burns's American Dream—Histories-for-TV from Walpole, New Hampshire," *Television Quarterly* (1994)

Edgerton, Gary R., "Ken Burns—A Conversation with Public Television's Resident Historian," *Journal of American Culture* (1995)

Henderson, B., "*The Civil War:* 'Did It Not Seem Real?' " *Film Quarterly* (1991)

Koeniger, A.C., "Ken Burns's *The Civil War:* Triumph or Travesty?" *Journal of Military History* (April 1991)

Milius, J., "Reliving the War Between Brothers," *New York Times* (September 16, 1990)

Powers, R., "Glory, Glory," *GQ* (September 1990)

Purcell, H., "America's Civil Wars," *History Today* (May 1991)

Summers, M.W., "The Civil War," *Journal of American History* (December 1990)

Thomson, D., "History Composed with Film," *Film Comment* (September–October 1990)

Toplin, Robert Brent, editor, *Ken Burns' The Civil War: Historians Respond,* New York: Oxford University Press, 1996

Weisberger, B., "The Great Arrogance of the Present Is to Forget the Intelligence of the Past," *American Heritage* (September–October 1990)

Civilisation: A Personal View

British Arts Program

Kenneth Clark's 13-part series *Civilisation: A Personal View,* produced by the British Broadcasting Corporation's Channel 2 (BBC 2) in 1969 and released in the United States in 1970 on public television, remains a milestone in the history of arts television, the Public Broadcasting System, and the explication of high culture to interested laypeople. The series offers an extended definition of the essential qualities of Western civilization through an examination of its chief monuments and important locations. While such a task may seem both arrogant and impossible, Clark's views are always stimulating and frequently entertaining. Civilization, he suggests, is energetic, confident, humane, and compassionate, based on a belief in permanence and in the necessity of self-doubt.

As Clark would readily acknowledge, civilization is not always all of these things at once, which gives his chronological tour considerable drama inasmuch as episodes speak to each other; Abbot Suger enters into dialogue in the viewer's mind with Michelangelo, Beethoven, and Einstein. A self-confessed hero worshiper, Clark arranged each episode around one or more important figures, illustrating his Carlylean view that civilization is the product of great men. Given his exploration of the visual possibilities of television (not always utilized in previous arts programming) and his particular intellectual biases, the program draws its evidence primarily from art history but takes a wider view than that description might suggest. In his memoir *The Other Half,* Clark comments that "I always... based my arguments on things seen—towns, bridges, cloisters, cathedrals, palaces," but adds that he considers the visual a "poin[t] of departure" rather than a final destination: "When I set about the programmes I had in mind Wagner's ambition to make opera into a *Gesamtkunstwerk*—text, spectacle, and sound all united."

Clark's qualifications for the series included his position as a leading art historian and, beginning in 1937, his career as a pioneer of British television arts programming. He had also served in the Ministry of Information during World War II, an experience that seems to have contributed to his philosophy of arts television. "The first stage was to learn that every word must be scripted; the second that what viewers want from a programme on art is not ideas, but information; and the third that things must be said clearly, energetically and economically," he wrote. Thus, his first successful television series, *Five Revolutionary Painters* (which aired on ITA and which he discusses briefly in *The Other Half*), allowed him to test his theory that the viewing public wanted to learn about individual artists while also serving as a kind of dress rehearsal for the more ambitious *Civilisation.* As Clark noted, "I might not have been able to do the filmed sequences of *Civilisation* with as much vivacity if I had not 'come up the hard way' of live transmission."

Following the social and political upheavals that marked 1968 in both Europe and the United States, *Civilisation* teaches that hard times do not inevitably crush the humane tradition so central to Clark's view of Western civilization. Indeed, when David Attenborough suggested the title for the series, Clark's typically self-deprecating response was "I had no clear idea what [civilization] meant, but I thought it was preferable to barbarism, and fancied that this was the moment to say so." That the program offers a *personal* (and in some ways idiosyncratic) look at nine centuries of European intellectual life is thus a crucial part of its appeal, inasmuch as it argues that following cultural matters—and caring about them—is within the reach of television viewers.

Clark appreciated the fact that television remains a performer's medium even when it deals with the abstract. This conception of the medium established the pattern for later pundit programs such as Alistair Cooke's *America* and Jacob Bronowski's *The Ascent of Man,* which were, like *Civilisation,* directed by Michael Gill. In all three programs, the cultural cicerone and his locations are the stimulus for the presentation of ideas. "I am convinced that a combination of words and music, colour and movement can extend human experience in a way words alone cannot do," Clark remarks in the foreword to the book version of *Civilisation.* His series aired only two years after BBC 2 switched to full-color broadcasting and was intended in part as a dramatic introduction to the possibilities of the new technology.

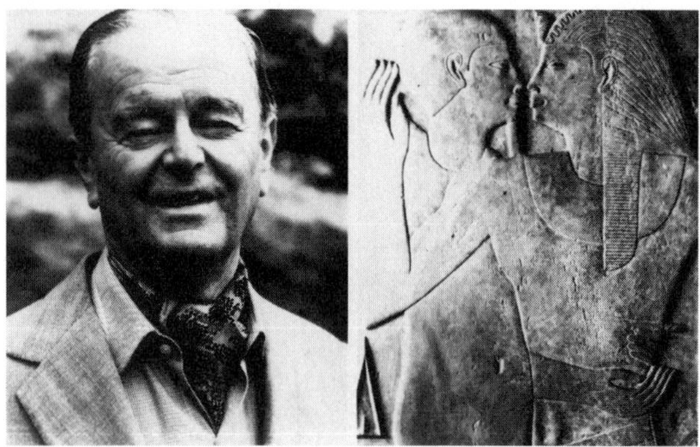

Civilisation: A Personal View.
Courtesy of the Everett Collection/CSU Archives

Civilisation came at an opportune time for U.S. public television, appearing in that venue after the BBC had tried in vain to place the series with the commercial networks. The program was underwritten by Xerox, which also provided $450,000 for an hour-long promotional program (produced by the BBC) to drum up business for the multipart broadcast. The nascent Public Broadcasting System received plaudits for carrying the program, and Clark undoubtedly found his largest audience in the United States. The series' reach in that country was demonstrated by the precedent-setting Harper and Row tie-in book, which became a best-seller despite its $15 price tag. Thus, in addition to promulgating its comforting message about the survival of a high culture besieged for a millennium by the forces of darkness, *Civilisation* had in the United States the serendipitous effect of demonstrating that high-culture television could in fact draw significant numbers of viewers.

ANNE MOREY

See also **Attenborough, Richard**

Host
Kenneth Clark

Producers
Michael Gill, Peter Montagnon

Programming History
BBC 2
13 episodes
February 23–May 18, 1969

Further Reading

Clark, Kenneth, *Civilisation: A Personal View,* New York: Harper and Row, 1969

Clark, Kenneth, *The Other Half: A Self-Portrait,* London: John Murray, 1977

A Guide to Civilisation: The Kenneth Clark Films on the Cultural Life of Western Man, New York: Time-Life, 1970

Secrest, M., *Kenneth Clark: A Biography,* London: Weidenfeld and Nicolson, 1984

Walker, John A., "Clark's *Civilisation* in Retrospect," *Art Monthly* (December–January 1988–89)

Walker, John A., *Arts TV: A History of Arts Television in Britain,* London: Libbey, 1993

Clark, Dick (1929–)

U.S. Producer, Media Personality

With a career spanning more than 50 years, Dick Clark is one of television's most successful entrepreneurs of program production. Often acknowledged more for his youthful appearance than for his business acumen, Clark nevertheless has built an impressive production record since the 1950s with teen dance shows, prime-time programming, television specials, daytime game shows, made-for-television movies, and feature films.

As a teenager, Clark began his career in broadcasting in 1945 in the mailroom of station WRUN in Utica, New York, working his way up to weatherman and then newsman. After graduating from Syracuse University in 1951, Clark moved from radio into television broadcasting at station WKTV in Utica. Here, Clark hosted *Cactus Dick and the Santa Fe Riders,* a country-music program that became the training ground for his later television hosting persona. In 1952, Clark moved to Philadelphia and radio station WFIL as a disc jockey for *Dick Clark's Caravan of Music.* At that time, WFIL was affiliated with a television station that carried *Bandstand,* an afternoon teen dance show. Clark often substituted for Bob Horn, the show's regular host. When Horn was jailed for drunken driving in 1956, Clark took over as permanent host, boosting *Bandstand* into Philadelphia's best-known afternoon show. From that point on, he became a fixture in the American television broadcasting arena.

In 1957 the American Broadcasting Corporation (ABC) picked up the program for its daytime schedule, changing the name to *American Bandstand.* As a cornerstone of the afternoon lineup through 1963, the program was a boon for ABC, an inexpensively produced success for the network's target audience of youthful demographics. From 1963 through 1987, *American Bandstand* ran on a weekly basis to become one of the longest-running shows in broadcast television.

In addition to Clark's hosting and producing duties for *American Bandstand,* he began to diversify in the 1950s by moving into the music publishing and recording industries. However, by the end of 1959, the federal government began to scrutinize Clark for a possible conflict between his broadcasting interests and his publishing and recording interests. At that time, payola, the practice of music industry companies paying radio personalities to play new records, was widespread in radio broadcasting. Clark, with the cultural scope of his network television program, became the prime target of the congressional investigation into this illegal activity. Pressured by ABC to make a choice between broadcast and music industry interests, Clark opted for the former, divesting himself of his publishing and recording companies. Even though Clark was cleared of any illegal behavior, he had to testify before the congressional committee on payola practices in 1960.

Given the present state of cross-corporate links among the recording, broadcasting, cable, and film industries, Clark's persecution would be highly unlikely now. Indeed, even at the time of the payola scandals, the networks and film studios, such as ABC and Disney, were already inextricably connected with program production, broadcasting, and profits. In retrospect, Clark's problems stemmed as much from his embrace of a somewhat raucous, interracial youth culture and his involvement in the conflict between ASCAP, representing the old guard of the music publishing business, and BMI, representing the new breed of rock-and-roll songwriters.

A somewhat tarnished reputation did not hinder Clark's further success in the area of broadcast programming and film production with Dick Clark Productions (DCP). DCP produced *Where the Action Is,* another daily teenage music show, during the late

Dick Clark.
Photo courtesy of Dick Clark Productions, Inc.

1960s, as well as feature exploitation films such as *Psych-Out, The Savage Seven,* and *Killers Three.* At this time, Clark also moved into the game show arena with *Missing Links* and *The Object Is,* culminating in the late 1970s with *The $25,000 Pyramid.*

In addition, DCP produced *Elvis, Murder in Texas* and *The Woman Who Willed a Miracle,* made-for-television movies that garnered impressive audience ratings. The latter won an Emmy Award. On a more lowbrow level, DCP also introduced *TV's Bloopers and Practical Jokes,* another inexpensive but extremely popular recurring television special. Clark also produces award shows, the *American Awards* and *The Golden Globe Awards.*

Often criticized for the lack of quality in DCP programs, Clark points to the networks and the audiences as the index of that quality. He gives them what they want, declaring in an interview in *Newsweek* magazine in 1986, "If I were given the assignment of doing a classical-music hour for PBS, it would be exquisite and beautifully done."

Clark shows little sign of slowing down in either his role as on-air personality or program producer. Indeed, Dick Clark Productions has now moved into the realm of special events planning, often building corporate conferences around the theme of *American Bandstand.* At the dawn of the 21st century, DCP continues to produce *Your Big Break* and *Beyond Belief: Fact or Fiction,* both syndicated programs, as well as the broadcast favorite *TV's Bloopers and Practical Jokes.* In 2001 Clark took on the patriarchal role on the all-male panel for *The Other Half: The World of Women Through the Eyes of Men,* an NBC morning talk show. In 2002, he became executive producer for the new drama *American Dreams,* which is set in the 1960s and revolves around Meg, a 15-year-old girl who dances on *American Bandstand.*

Despite the boyish good looks and charm that are the identifying characteristics of this American icon, it is Clark's economically efficient business savvy and his uncanny ability to measure the American public's cultural mood that have been his most important assets in television broadcasting.

RODNEY A. BUXTON

See also **American Bandstand; Music on Television**

Dick Clark (Richard Wagstaff Clark). Born in Mt. Vernon, New York, November 30, 1929. Graduated from Syracuse University, 1951. Married: 1) Barbara Mallery, 1952 (divorced, 1961); child: Richard Jr.; 2) Loretta Martin, 1962 (divorced, 1971); children: Duane and Cindy; 3) Karen Wigton, 1977. Announcer, station WRUN, Utica, New York, 1945–50; staff announcer, station WOLF, Syracuse, New York, 1950; announcer, WRUN, 1951; announcer, station WKTV, Utica, 1951; announcer, station WFIL, Philadelphia, 1952; host, *American Bandstand,* 1956–89; formed Dick Clark Productions, 1956, producing more than 7,500 hours of television programming, including more than 30 series and 250 specials, and more than 20 movies for theatrical release and television. Founder: Dick Clark Media Archives. Inductee: Hollywood Walk of Fame, 1976; Broadcasting Magazine Hall of Fame, 1992; Rock 'n' Roll Hall of Fame, 1993; Academy of Television Arts and Sciences Hall of Fame, 1993. Recipient: Emmy Awards, 1979, 1983, 1985, 1986, and Daytime Emmy, Lifetime Achievement Award, 1994; MTV Award, 1987; Grammy National Trustees Award, 1990; named International Person of Year, NAPTE, 1990; Distinguished Service Award, National Association of Broadcasting, 1991; American D.J. Association, Lifetime Achievement Award, 1995; Person of the Year, Philadelphia Advertising Club.

Television Series (selected)

1951	*Cactus Dick and the Santa Fe Riders* (host)
1956–89	*American Bandstand* (host, executive producer)
1958–60	*The Dick Clark Saturday Night Beechnut Show* (host)
1959	*Dick Clark's World of Talent* (host)
1959	*The Record Years* (host, executive producer)
1964	*Missing Links* (host)
1964	*The Object Is* (host)
1973–74	*Dick Clark Presents the Rock and Roll Years* (host, executive producer)
1973–75	*In Concert* (executive producer)
1973–89	*$10,000 Pyramid* (host) *$20,000 Pyramid* (host) *$25,000 Pyramid* (host) *$50,000 Pyramid* (host) *$100,000 Pyramid* (host)
1981	*The Krypton Factor* (host)
1984–86, 1988	*TV's Bloopers and Practical Jokes* (executive producer)
1985–88	*Puttin' on the Hits* (executive producer)
1988	*Live! Dick Clark Presents* (host, executive producer)
1990–91	*The Challengers* (host, executive producer)
1995	*Tempest* (executive producer)
2001–	*The Other Half: The World of Women Through the Eyes of Men*
2002–	*American Dreams* (executive producer)

Made-for-Television Movies (executive producer)

1979	*Elvis*
1979	*Man in the Santa Claus Suit*
1979	*Birth of the Beatles*
1981	*Murder in Texas*
1983	*The Demon Murder Case*
1983	*The Woman Who Willed a Miracle*
1985	*Copacabana*
1988	*Promised a Miracle*
1988	*The Town Bully*
1988	*Liberace*
1989	*A Cry for Help: The Tracy Thurman Story*
1991	*Death Dreams*
1993	*Elvis and the Colonel: The Untold Story*
1994	*Secret Sins of the Father*

Television Specials (selected; executive producer)

1965–67	*Where the Action Is*
1966	*Swinging Country*
1968–69	*Happening*
1970	*Get It Together*
1970	*Shebang*

1972–	*Dick Clark's New Year's Rockin' Eve*
1977	*Dick Clark's Good Ol' Days*
1978	*Dick Clark's Live Wednesday*
1980	*The Sensational, Shocking Wonderful Wacky 70's*
1981	*Whatever Became Of...?*
1981	*I've Had It Up to Here*
1982	*Inside America*
1983	*Hollywood's Private Home Movies*
1983	*The 1/2-Hour Comedy Hour*
1984	*Hollywood Stars Screen Test*
1984	*You Are the Jury*
1985	*Reaching for the Stars*
1985	*Rock 'n' Roll Summer Action*
1985	*Live Aid—An All-Star Concert for African Relief*
1985	*American Bandstand's 33 1/3 Celebration*
1985	*Dick Clark's Nighttime*
1986	*America Picks the #1 Songs*
1986	*Alabama... My Home's in Alabama*
1987	*Keep on Cruisin'*
1987	*Superstars and Their Moms*
1987	*In Person from the Palace*
1987	*Getting in Touch*
1988	*Sea World's All-Star Lone Star Celebration*
1989	*Freedom Festival '89*
1991, 1993	*Super Bloopers and New Practical Jokes*
1992	*1992 USA Music Challenge*
1992	*American Bandstand's 40th Anniversary*
1992	*The World's Biggest Lies*
1992	*A Busch Gardens/Sea World Summer Safari*
1992	*Golden Greats*
1992	*Olympic Flag Jam*
1993	*The Return of TV Censored Bloopers*
1993	*The Academy of Country Music's Greatest Hits*
1993	*The Olsen Twins Mother's Day Special*
1993	*American Bandstand: One More Time*
1993	*Caught in the Act*
1993, 1994	*Sea World/Busch Garden Summer Celebration*
1993–95	*The Jim Thorpe Pro Sports Awards*
1994	*Taco Bell's Battle of the Bands*
1994	*How I Spent My Summer Vacation*
1994	*Chrysler American Great 18 Golf Championships*
1994	*American Music Awards 20th Anniversary Special*
1994	*Golden Globes 50th Anniversary Celebration*
1994	*Hot Country Jam '94*
1994	*American Bandstand's Teen Idols*
1994	*American Bandstand's #1 Hits*
1994	*Universal Studios Summer Blast*
1994, 1995	*Will You Marry Me?*
1995	*We're Having a Baby*
1995	*The Making of the Adventures of Mary Kate and Ashley*
1995	*Christmas at Home with the Stars*
1995	*When Stars Were Kids*
1995	*Rudy Coby: The Coolest Magician in the World*
1995	*Sea World/Busch Gardens Party for the Planet*
1995	*All Star Ultra TV Censored Bloopers*
1995	*TNN Country Series*

Films

Because They're Young (actor), 1960; *The Young Doctors* (actor), 1961; *Wild in the Streets,* 1968; *Killers Three,* 1968; *Psych-Out* (producer), 1968; *The Savage Seven* (producer), 1968; *The Dark* (producer), 1970; *Remo Williams: The Adventure Begins* (producer), 1985.

Radio

Dick Clark's Caravan of Music; Dick Clark's Music Machine; Dick Clark's National Music Survey; Dick Clark's Rock, Roll, and Remember; Dick Clark's U.S. Music Survey.

Publications

Your Happiest Hears, 1959

To Goof or Not to Goof, 1963

Rock, Roll, and Remember, with Richard Robinson, 1976

Dick Clark's Program for Success in Your Business and Personal Life, 1980

Looking Great, Staying Young, with Bill Libby, 1980

Dick Clark's The First 25 Years of Rock 'n' Roll, with Michael Usland, 1981

The History of American Bandstand, with Michael Shore, 1985

Dick Clark's Easygoing Guide to Good Grooming, 1985

Further Reading

"*Bandstand* Ready to Rock Again," *Broadcasting* (May 21, 1990)

"Dick Clark on Dick Clark: The Flip Side," *Broadcasting* (May 1, 1989)

Miller, Holly G., "Dick Clark's Role After Rock," *Saturday Evening Post* (July–August 1995)
Schipper, Henry, "Dick Clark," *Rolling Stone* (April 19, 1990)
U.S. Congress, House of Representatives, *Responsibilities of Broadcasting Licensees and Station Personnel: Hearings Before a Subcommittee of the Committee on Interstate and Foreign Commerce, House of Representatives, Eighty-Sixth Congress, Second Session on Payola and Other Deceptive Practices in the Broadcasting Field,* Washington, D.C.: U.S. Government Printing Office, 1960

Clarkson, Adrienne (1939–)

Canadian Television Personality

Adrienne Clarkson has been a major cultural force in Canada for more than 35 years. She began her career in broadcasting in 1965 as a book reviewer on CBC-TV. She then became interviewer and host of the long-running CBC daytime magazine show *Take Thirty.* After ten years there, she spent seven years as host of *The Fifth Estate,* another long-running magazine program, this one in prime time.

In 1982 Clarkson was appointed agent general for Ontario in France, a high-level government position in which she promoted the province and acted as a cultural liaison between the two countries. When she returned to Canada in 1987, she became president and publisher of McClelland and Stewart, one of Canada's most prestigious publishing firms, where she maintained her own imprint, Adrienne Clarkson Books. At the same time, she resumed her work in television as host and executive producer of her own CBC program—*Adrienne Clarkson's Summer Festival*—in 1988. Its successor, *Adrienne Clarkson Presents,* was a prime-time cultural affairs series on which Clarkson offered profiles of Canadian and international figures from the worlds of opera, ballet, folksinging, and the other arts.

Despite the variety of her work in journalism, news, the arts, and cultural policy, Clarkson has been perceived as an elitist. For many years, she was lampooned by Canadian comics such as those of the *Royal Canadian Air Farce* and *Double Exposure.* In one skit, a haughty, modulated voice introduces itself, "*I'm* Adrienne Clarkson... and *you're* not." Because her most recent programs were arts oriented and because she was involved in arts activities and posts of distinction, Clarkson was regarded as having limited commercial appeal. Indeed, like most arts programs, hers did not garner high ratings, but they were highly regarded by critics.

Clarkson won numerous television awards, including three Association of Canadian Television and Radio Artists (ACTRA) Awards for *Take Thirty* and *The Fifth Estate.* In 1993 she was the recipient of a Gemini Award (which succeeded the ACTRA Awards as the national television awards) for Best Host in a Light Information, Variety, or Performing Arts Program for *Adrienne Clarkson Presents.*

In 1992 Clarkson wrote, produced, and directed her first film, a full-length drama-documentary for television, called *Artemisia,* about the 17th-century Italian painter Artemisia Gentileschi, whose rape by an artist friend of her father's informed her work. Clarkson was passionately involved in this production, which premiered at the 1992 Toronto International Film Festival and was then aired on Clarkson's series. She then wrote and directed three other documentaries for television between 1994 and 1996.

From 1995 to 1999, Clarkson was chairwoman of the board of the Canadian Museum of Civilization in Hull, Quebec. In 1999 Clarkson was appointed Canada's Governor General (representative for the queen of the British Commonwealth), a post she continues to hold; since this appointment, she no longer hosts or produces television programs.

JANICE KAYE

See also ***Fifth Estate, The***

Adrienne Clarkson. Born in Hong Kong, February 10, 1939. Educated at Trinity College; University of Toronto, B.A., 1960, M.A., 1962; Sorbonne, Paris, France, 1963–64. Married: author John Ralston Saul. Lecturer, University of Toronto, 1964–65; host and interviewer, *Take Thirty,* 1965–75; host, *Adrienne at Large,* 1975; host, *The Fifth Estate,* 1975–82; appointed agent general, France, 1982–87; producer and host of her own TV programs, 1988–98; president and publisher, McClelland and Stewart, 1987–88; pub-

Adrienne Clarkson, 1989.
Courtesy of CBC/Fred Phipps

lisher, Adrienne Clarkson Books, McClelland and Stewart, 1988; chairwoman of the board of the Canadian Museum of Civilization, Hull, Quebec, 1995–99; appointed governor general, 1999. Honorary degrees: Dalhousie University, Lakehead University, Acadia University. Recipient: Gordon Sinclair Award, 1979; ACTRA Awards, 1974, 1975, 1976; Order of Canada, 1992; Gemini Award, 1993.

Television Series

1965–75 *Take Thirty*
1974–75 *Adrienne at Large*
1975–82 *The Fifth Estate*
1988–98 *Adrienne Clarkson's Summer Festival* (became *Adrienne Clarkson Presents*)

Television Specials

1992 *Artemisia*
1994 *Borduas and Me*
1995 *The Lust of His Eye: The Vision of James Wilson Morris*
1996 *Black and White to Color: The Making of the English Patient*

Publications

A Lover More Condoling, 1968
Hunger Trace, 1970
True to You in My Fashion, 1971

Class. *See* **Social Class and Television**

Clearance

U.S. Broadcasting Policy

The term "clearance" as applied in the context of U.S. broadcasting refers to the acceptance by a local station of a program provided by a broadcasting network or a supplier of syndicated programming. Ideally, an affiliate will carry a program when the network specifies. The number of clearances determines the potential audience size of a program. Networks hope to clear their programs with as many stations as possible. This will ensure greater advertising revenues. Clearance of a network program by an affiliate is thus crucial to the network's profitability. Likewise, affiliates that frequently reject network offerings risk their survivability if they are dropped by the network. Networks provide programming certain to compete successfully with programs provided by the other local stations. Moreover, the networks compensate affiliates for carrying their programs. The practice of program clearance best illustrates the symbiotic nature of the network-affiliate relationship, a relationship established in law as well as in economic practice.

The Federal Communications Commission (FCC) recognized the problems inherent in "chain broadcasting" as early as 1943, when the Supreme Court attempted to clarify the role of networks as program suppliers in the "Network Case" (*NBC, Inc. et al. v. United States et al.*). To further prevent anticompetitive practices, the FCC implemented rules such as clearance and the Prime Time Access Rule. These regulations grant programming autonomy to affiliate stations, while in practice the stations are dependent on other program suppliers.

Clearances vary according to the part of the day to which they apply. Prime time commands the highest number of clearances by affiliates. The stations can charge high rates for advertising time during top-rated network programs. Low-rated programs run a greater risk of being rejected by stations. Because more commercial spots are available in a film, for example, than in a low-rated network offering, it might be more lucrative for an affiliate to substitute the movie for the network program.

An affiliate station will also sometimes reject a prime-time network program because of controversial subject matter. To appease the tastes and attitudes of their local communities, affiliates may not air particular programs, despite their potential for high ratings. In 1993, for example, the program *NYPD Blue* was rejected by 57 ABC affiliates before it aired because of objectionable material. It is an affiliate's legal right to reject any program in an attempt to serve the public interest. The choice to reject a program may prove most profitable to independent stations that opt to carry the "taboo" programs.

Preemption occurs when an affiliate cancels a program it has agreed to carry, or when a network interrupts a "cleared" program to broadcast a special event or breaking news story. Because of lost advertising time, such preemptions can prove costly to both parties.

Affiliates give low clearances to network programs during morning, late-afternoon, early-evening, and late-night segments of the day. During these times, the predominant source of programming is syndicated material, often consisting of older network programs with proven audience appeal.

Clearance of a syndicated program involves acceptance through purchase. To be truly profitable, syndicators must "clear" (sell) a program in enough markets to represent at least 70 percent of all television households.

SHARON ZECHOWSKI

See also **Networks: United States**

Further Reading

Eastman, Susan Tyler, Sydney W. Head, and Lewis Klein, *Broadcast/Cable Programming: Strategies and Practices,* Belmont, California: Wadsworth, 1981; 5th edition, 1997

Head, Sydney W., *Broadcasting in America: A Survey of Television and Radio,* Boston: Houghton Mifflin, 1956; 7th edition, with Christopher H. Sterling and Lemeul B. Schofield, as *Broadcasting in America: A Survey of Electronic Media,* 1994

Kahn, Frank J., editor, *Documents of American Broadcasting,* New York: Appleton Century Crofts, 1968; 4th edition, Englewood Cliffs, New Jersey: Prentice Hall, 1984

Cleese, John (1939–)

British Actor

John Cleese belongs to a tradition of university humor that has supplied a recognizable strand of comedy to British television and radio from *Beyond the Fringe* in the late 1950s to *Blackadder* and beyond. The brilliance of his writing, the dominant nature of his performances (due largely to his extraordinary height), and the variety of his successes have made him undoubtedly the most influential figure of this group. He has always shown an unerring instinct for how far to go with any one project or idea, with the result that there is little in his large body of work that could be counted as failure, although he is also highly critical, in hindsight, of anything he regards as not having worked precisely as he might have wanted it to.

Following the success of Cambridge Circus, the Cambridge University Footlights Club revue to which he contributed and which toured Britain and the world between 1963 and 1965, Cleese made his first big impact on television by writing and performing sketches on David Frost's *The Frost Report,* airing on the British Broadcasting Corporation (BBC). (Cleese had already written material for *That Was the Week That Was,* the seminal BBC satire show that had launched Frost's career.) Fellow performers included Ronnie Barker and Ronnie Corbett, with whom Cleese created the classic "class" sketch, and the show won the Golden Rose of Montreux in 1966. Cleese's written contributions were created in collaboration with his writing partner Graham Chapman, then still a medical student at Cambridge. At the same time, Cleese was also writing and performing in the cult BBC radio series *I'm Sorry, I'll Read That Again,* together with such Cambridge Circus colleagues as Tim Brooke-Taylor and Bill Oddie. There were a total of eight series of this show between 1964 and 1973, probably the only thing Cleese ever overdid.

Cleese was now much in demand, and his next major project, produced by David Frost for Rediffusion, was *At Last the 1948 Show,* a sketch-comedy series written and performed in collaboration with Chapman, Brooke-Taylor, and Marty Feldman, two series of which were transmitted in 1967. Although not seen throughout the country, the show gained a cult following for the brilliance and unpredictability of its comedy and the innovative nature of its structure, in which the show was linked by a dumb blonde called the Lovely Aimi MacDonald. Cleese was now developing a full range of comic personae, including manic bullies, unreliable authority figures (especially lawyers and government ministers), and repressed Englishmen, all of which were later to gel in the character of Basil Fawlty. The quality of invention in *At Last the 1948 Show* was consistently high, and it gave the world of television comedy one of its most enduring pieces—the "Four Yorkshiremen" sketch. It was also the recognized precursor to the series that remains, in spite of all his own retrospective criticism, Cleese's most significant contribution to television comedy, *Monty Python's Flying Circus* (BBC).

Beginning in 1969, *Monty Python's Flying Circus* teamed Cleese and Chapman with three other university comedians, Michael Palin and Terry Jones, who wrote together and had also contributed to *The Frost Report,* and Eric Idle. The team was completed by American animator Terry Gilliam. Four series were made between 1969 and 1974, though Cleese did not appear in the fourth, contributing only as a writer. This was probably the main reason for the comparative failure of the final series, because Cleese was clearly the dominant figure in the *Python* team and appeared in the sketches that made the greatest impact, thus becoming the figure most associated with the series in the public mind.

John Cleese.
Courtesy of the Everett Collection

Two sketches in particular stand out in this regard: the "Dead Parrot" sketch, in which Cleese returns a defective pet bird to the shop where he bought it; and the "Ministry of Silly Walks" sketch, in which Cleese used his angular figure to startling effect. He was to be constantly exasperated in future years by people asking him to "do the silly walk." In *At Last the 1948 Show,* Cleese's appearances with Marty Feldman have a particular resonance. In *Monty Python's Flying Circus,* his work with Michael Palin was similarly memorable.

The overall impact and influence of *Monty Python's Flying Circus* is difficult to overestimate. The intricate flow of each show, the abandonment of the traditional "punch line" to a sketch, the knowing experimentation with the medium, and the general air of silliness combined with obscure intellectualism set a standard—one that comedians thereafter found hard to get away from.

Producers such as John Lloyd and writer-performers such as Ben Elton acknowledge the enormous influence of *Monty Python's Flying Circus* on their own work. The word "pythonesque" entered the language, being used to describe any kind of bizarre juxtaposition.

Although there were no more series of *Monty Python* on television after 1974, largely because Cleese had had enough, the team continued to come together occasionally to make feature films, of which *Monty Python's Life of Brian* is the best and most controversial, given its religious theme. Cleese's discussion of the film with religious leaders on the chat show *Friday Night... Saturday Morning* in 1979 remains a television moment to cherish. The untimely death of Graham Chapman from cancer in 1989 put an end to the team for good.

By then, Cleese, having altered the world of sketch comedy forever, had done the same for the sitcom. He was no stranger to sitcoms, having written episodes of *Doctor in Charge* together with Chapman. For *Fawlty Towers,* he teamed up with his American wife Connie Booth to create a comedy of character and incident that is almost faultless in its construction. The "situation" is a small hotel in the genteel English resort of Torquay, run by Basil Fawlty (Cleese), his wife Sybil (Prunella Scales), the maid Polly (Booth), and the incompetent Spanish waiter Manuel (Andrew Sachs). Each episode is so packed with comic situations and complex plot developments, often bordering on farce, that it is no surprise that there were, in all, only 12 episodes ever made, in two series of six each from 1975 and 1979. Basil Fawlty is the ultimate Cleese creation—a manic, snobbish, repressed English stereotype with a talent for disaster, whether it be trying to dispose of the dead body of a guest or coping with a party of German visitors. In 2000 a poll of the British television industry, organized by the British Film Institute, voted *Fawlty Towers* the best British TV program of all time.

Cleese's television work after *Fawlty Towers* was sporadic and included the role of Petruchio in Jonathan Miller's production of *The Taming of the Shrew* for the BBC Television Shakespeare series and a guest appearance on the U.S. sitcom *Cheers,* as well as the two funniest *Party Political Broadcasts* (for the Social Democratic Party) ever made. He concentrated more on esoteric projects such as the comic training films he made through his own company, Video Arts, and books on psychotherapy written in collaboration with Dr. Robin Skynner. He also pursued his work in feature films, enjoying great success with *A Fish Called Wanda,* in which he returned to one of his favorite subjects—the differences between English and American characters—already explored in one memorable episode of *Fawlty Towers.* The film also saw him play the role of a lawyer, the profession he had lampooned throughout his career and that he had originally studied to join. In 2001 Cleese returned to British TV screens as the presenter of the documentary series *The Human Face,* which he also wrote. In 2002 he became a costar in a new U.S. sitcom, *Wednesdays 9:30 (8:30 Central),* a satirical look at work life at a television network with Cleese playing the owner of the fictional network. ABC canceled the comedy after only two episodes. In 2003 and 2004, he had a recurring guest role on the U.S. sitcom *Will & Grace.*

STEVE BRYANT

See also **Fawlty Towers; Monty Python's Flying Circus**

John (Marwood) Cleese. Born in Weston-super-Mare, Somerset, England, October 27, 1939. Attended Clifton Sports Academy; Downing College, Cambridge. Married: 1) Connie Booth, 1968 (divorced, 1978); child: Cynthia; 2) Barbara Trentham, 1981 (divorced, 1990); child: Camilla; 3) Alyce Faye Eichelberger, 1992. Appeared in London's West End, and later on Broadway, as member of the Cambridge Footlights company, 1963; first appeared on television in *The Frost Report* and *At Last the 1948 Show,* 1966; leading comedy star in *Monty Python* television series and films, from 1969, and subsequently as television's Basil Fawlty, *Fawlty Towers;* founder and director, Video Arts Ltd., company making industrial training films, 1972–89. LLD, University of St. Andrews. Recipient: Golden Rose of Montreux, 1966; *TV Times* Award for Funniest Man on TV, 1978–79; Emmy Award, 1987; British Academy of Film and Television Arts for Best Actor, 1988; Screen Actors Guild Jack Oakie Award, Outstanding Achievement in Comedy, 1994.

Television Series

1966–67	*The Frost Report*
1966–67	*At Last the 1948 Show*
1969–74	*Monty Python's Flying Circus*
1975–79	*Fawlty Towers*
2001	*The Human Face*
2002	*Wednesday 9:30 (8:30 Central)*
2003–04	*Will & Grace* (recurring guest role)

Television Specials

1977	*The Strange Case of the End of Civilization as We Know It*
1980	*The Taming of the Shrew*
1998	*Lemurs*

Films

Interlude, 1968; *The Bliss of Mrs. Blossom,* 1968; *The Best House in London,* 1968; *The Rise and Rise of Michael Rimmer* (also co-writer), 1970; *The Magic Christian,* 1970; *The Statue,* 1970; *The Bonar Law Story,* 1971; *And Now for Something Completely Different* (also co-writer), 1971; *It's a 2' 6" Above the Ground World (The Love Ban),* 1972; *Abbott and Costello Meet Sir Michael Swann,* 1972; *The Young Anthony Barber,* 1973; *Confessions of a Programme Planner,* 1974; *Romance with a Double Bass,* 1974; *Monty Python and the Holy Grail* (also co-writer), 1975; *Pleasure at Her Majesty's,* 1976; *Monty Python Meets Beyond the Fringe,* 1978; *Monty Python's Life of Brian* (also co-writer), 1979; *Away from It All* (voice only), 1979; *The Secret Policeman's Ball,* 1979; *Time Bandits,* 1981; *The Great Muppet Caper,* 1981; *The Secret Policeman's Other Ball,* 1982; *Monty Python Live at the Hollywood Bowl,* 1982; *Monty Python's The Meaning of Life,* 1983; *Yellowbeard,* 1983; *Privates on Parade,* 1984; *The Secret Policeman's Private Parts,* 1984; *Club Paradise,* 1985; *Gonzo Presents Muppet Weird Stuff,* 1985; *Silverado,* 1985; *Clockwise,* 1986; *S.D. Pete,* 1986; *The Secret Policeman's Third Ball,* 1987; *A Fish Called Wanda* (also executive producer and writer), 1988; *The Big Picture,* 1988; *Erik the Viking,* 1989; *Bullseye!* 1990; *An American Tail: Fievel Goes West* (voice only), 1991; *Splitting Heirs,* 1992; *Mary Shelley's Frankenstein,* 1994; *Rudyard Kipling's The Jungle Book,* 1994; *The Swan Princess,* 1994; *The Fine Art of Separating People from Their Money,* 1996; *Ferocidade MáXima,* 1997; *The Wind in the Willows,* 1997; *George of the Jungle* (voice), 1997; *Fierce Creatures,* 1997; *The Out-of Towners,* 1999; *The World Is not Enough,* 1999; *Isn't She Great,* 2000; *Rat Race,* 2001; *Harry Potter and the Sorcerer's Stone,* 2001; *Harry Potter and the Chamber of Secrets,* 2002.

Stage

Cambridge Footlights Revue, 1963; *Half a Sixpence,* 1965.

Publications

The Strange Case of the End of Civilization as We Know It, with Jack Hobbs and Joe McGrath, 1970
Fawlty Towers, with Connie Booth, 1979
Families and How to Survive Them, with Robin Skynner, 1983
The Golden Skits of Wing Commander Muriel Volestrangler FRHS and Bar, 1984
The Complete Fawlty Towers, with Connie Booth, 1988
Life and How to Survive It, with Robin Skynner, 1993

Further Reading

"And Now for Something Completely Different...." *The Economist* (October 20, 1990)
Bryson, Bill, "Cleese up Close," *New York Times Magazine* (December 25, 1988)
"Cleese on Creativity," *Advertising Age* (December 4, 1989)
Gilliat, Penelope, "Height's Delight," *New Yorker* (May 2, 1988)
Johnson, Kim, *The First 20 Years of Monty Python,* New York: St. Martin's Press, 1989
Johnson, Kim, *Life (Before and) After Monty Python: The Solo Flights of the Flying Circus,* New York: St. Martin's Press, 1993
Margolis, Jonathan, *Cleese Encounters,* New York: St. Martin's Press, 1992
McCall, Douglas L., *Monty Python: A Chronological Listing of the Troupe's Creative Output, and Articles and Reviews About Them,* Jefferson, North Carolina: McFarland, 1991
Wilmut, Roger, *From Fringe to Flying Circus,* London: Methuen, 1980

Clinton Impeachment Trial

On December 19, 1998, the U.S. House of Representatives approved two articles of impeachment against Democratic President William Jefferson Clinton in connection with Clinton's obstruction of justice and perjury about his relationship with former White House intern Monica Lewinsky. On February 12, 1999, Clinton was acquitted of the two articles of impeachment by the U.S. Senate. While Clinton was not the first president to be impeached by the House and acquitted by the Senate (President Andrew Johnson suffered a similar fate in 1868), the Clinton impeachment was uniquely marked by the characteristics of a powerful late-20th-century force: the electronic mass media.

The imprint of the electronic media on the impeachment of Clinton began when rumors of an affair between Clinton and Lewinsky appeared in an Internet gossip column, the *Drudge Report,* on January 19, 1998. The column alleged that *Newsweek* magazine had postponed running a piece on the relationship, and the Drudge website is reported to have received up to 300,000 hits per day as a result of this column (up from the typical 60,000 at that time). Television network news programs first aired the story on January 21, 1998, and television coverage would play a pivotal role in informing Americans about the fate of Clinton's presidency for the next 14 months.

The investigation of Clinton, and the Clinton-Lewinsky affair, prompted considerable television attention. During the summer of 1998, the Clinton investigation was the top news story, receiving more coverage than all other prominent events at that time combined (e.g., the civil war in Kosovo, the Russian economic crisis, the Asian economic crisis, the monitoring of Iraqi weapons, the crash of Swissair Flight 111, the U.S. retaliation for East African bombings, the campaign finance investigation, and baseball's home run record).

Burgeoning 24-hour cable news channels also allocated resources to this story, and one new cable network, MSNBC, was dubbed "all Monica, all the time" for its extensive treatment of the investigation. To prevent losing viewers to cable news stations, the network news programs expanded their evening coverage to a full hour, the first time since the Gulf War in 1991.

Late-night television comedians and reporters told a considerable number of jokes about the scandal. President Clinton was reported to be the subject of 1,712 jokes in 1998, more than in any other year of his presidency (*Media Monitor,* January–February 1999). When jokes about all individuals involved in the investigation of the Clinton scandal were tallied (Clinton, Hillary Rodham Clinton, Monica Lewinsky, Linda Tripp, and Special Prosecutor Kenneth Starr), 2,461 jokes about the scandal were shared on television (*Media Monitor,* January–February 1999).

Research on the quality of the coverage reveals that few sources were employed in reports on the investigation. Lawrence Grossman found that many of the allegations by major television programs, newspapers, and magazines "were not factual reporting at all . . . but were instead journalists offering analysis, opinion, speculation, or judgment." Jeff Elliott reported the findings from another study that found that only about half of the news in the *New York Times* came from a named source and that anonymous sources were used 84 percent of the time by the *Washington Post.* After the impeachment, journalists admitted that they had a difficult time finding sources that would go on the record on this sensitive story.

Those who did go on the record largely critiqued the president. A *Media Monitor* study (September–October 1998) discovered that more than 1,000 sources criticized Clinton on the evening news shows in a period of less than two months in 1998. Moreover, reporters' comments on Clinton were seven times more negative than positive. A primary reason for the negative coverage, according to communications scholar Kathleen Hall Jamieson, is that the investigation team was building a case against Clinton and was selective in the evidence it shared with the media; exculpatory material was not offered by the investigation team, so it did not appear in news reports on the Clinton scandal.

An irony throughout the investigation of Clinton was that he was the most publicly shamed president of modern time and also one of the most popular. After the first month of coverage, Clinton's public approval ratings increased in the Gallup poll from 60 to 67 percent. Over the course of the next year, citizens learned about his personal transgressions, and became even more adamant that he was performing well in office. Political pundits often doubted the president's approval in public opinion polls, suggesting that Clinton's public opinion ratings would decrease as citizens learned more about the scandal. This was not the case. Approval for Clinton in March 1999 hovered around 65 percent, a paradox that has been explained by several factors. Political scholars believe that despite 14 months of damaging news coverage, the American public approved of Clinton's moderate policies, rewarded him for the relative peace and prosperity of the late 1990s, questioned the motive of his accusers, disliked his accusers more than they disliked him, understood the pattern of lying about intimate sexual relations, and viewed the exhaustive coverage as an invasion of his privacy.

Sharon E. Jarvis

See also **Political Processes and Television**

Timeline of Key Televised Events in the Clinton Investigation and Impeachment

January 21, 1998	Television news stations broadcast rumors posted to the Internet that Clinton had an affair with a White House intern.
January 26, 1998	Clinton delivers a public statement claiming, "I did not have sexual relations with that woman, Miss Lewinsky."
March 15, 1998	Kathleen Willey appears on CBS's *60 Minutes* television program accusing Clinton of harassment.
April 30, 1998	Clinton holds first televised

news conference since the Lewinsky scandal broke.

August 17, 1998 — Clinton tells the nation he had an inappropriate relationship with Lewinsky after testifying before a grand jury.

September 21, 1998 — Television networks air more than four hours of Clinton's videotaped grand jury testimony released by the House Judiciary Committee featuring detailed information about the affair between Clinton and Lewinsky; the networks preempt their daily schedule of soap operas and talk shows to air Clinton's testimony, and their audience increases 32 percent; CNN reaches a record audience of its own, scoring its highest daytime rating of the year.

December 19, 1998 — Television news programs broadcast that the U.S. House of Representatives approved two articles of impeachment, charging President Clinton with lying under oath to a federal grand jury and obstructing justice.

January 7, 1999 — The perjury and obstruction of justice trial begins in the U.S. Senate.

January 25, 1999 — Senators hear arguments about dismissing the charges against Clinton and then deliberate in secret.

February 12, 1999 — Clinton is acquitted of the two articles of impeachment: on the first charge of perjury, ten Republicans and all 45 Democrats voted not guilty; on the charge of obstruction of justice, the Senate was split 50–50.

Further Reading

Drudge, Matt, *The Drudge Report,* http://www.drudgereport.com

Elliott, Jeff, "Counting Lewinskys: These Are Not Proud Times to Be a Journalist," *Albion Monitor* (March 1, 1998)

Grossman, Lawrence K., "Spot News: Reporting the Press and the Dress," *Columbia Journalism Review* (November–December 1998)

Mazza, Edward, "Last Bytes," *Government Technology* (July 1999)

Media Monitor, 12, no. 5 (September–October 1998)

Media Monitor, 13, no. 1 (January–February 1999)

Rozell, Mark J., and Clyde Wilcox, *The Clinton Scandal and the Future of American Government,* Washington, D.C.: Georgetown University Press, 2000

Sonner, Molly W., and Clyde Wilcox, "Forgiving and Forgetting: Public Support for Bill Clinton During the Lewinsky Scandal," *PS: Political Science and Politics,* 32 (1999)

Toobin, Jeffrey, *A Vast Conspiracy: The Real Story of the Sex Scandal That Nearly Brought Down a President,* New York: Random House, 1999

Zaller, John, "Monica Lewinsky's Contribution to Political Science," *PS: Political Science and Politics,* 31 (1998)

Closed Captioning

Closed captioning involves the display of subtitles superimposed over a portion of the television picture. These subtitles or captions are created to represent the audio portion of the television signal. Although initially developed for the hearing impaired, closed captioning can also be used as a teaching device by viewers learning a second language and by children, and even adults, who are learning to read.

Closed captioning can even be used as a convenience device by viewers who mute their TV to take a phone call but activate closed captioning to continue the program dialogue. Some newer television receivers automatically display this captioning when the mute button is pushed.

Perhaps the most novel use of closed captioning occurs in restaurants and bars where television sets are on but the audio portion is muted. Many bars will have multiple sets tuned to one or more channels of interest to their clientele. These channels might include the cable sports network ESPN, the cable news outlets CNN and CNBC, or various local stations.

The captions are "closed" to the general viewing audience because television producers believe that a continuous display of alphanumeric data across a TV screen is distracting and bothersome to the majority of viewers who are capable of following the dialogue aurally. Any viewer can choose to "open" the closed captioning, either by activating a switch on newer television sets or by using a separate decoder with older television sets that do not include the necessary decoder circuitry.

The decoder circuitry is designed to "read" the closed captions embedded in the vertical blanking interval. The vertical blanking interval is that 21-line portion of the 525-line National Television Systems Committee (NTSC) television signal that does not contain picture information. Various lines are used to carry technical data, and one of these lines is specifically reserved for closed captioning. The Advanced Television Systems Committee (ATSC) digital television signal carries closed captions as part of that signal's data bit stream.

The concept for closed captioning was conceived in 1971 by engineers at the National Bureau of Standards. Further development involved WGBH-TV, the Boston public television station; Gallaudet University, the leading U.S. university for the hearing impaired; and the National Technical Institute in Rochester, New York. In 1976 the Federal Communications Commission (FCC) formally authorized the use of line 21, the last line of the vertical blanking interval, for this purpose.

Closed captioning received a major boost with the passage of the Television Decoder Circuitry Act of 1990. This law mandated the inclusion of closed-captioned circuitry in every television receiver with a screen of 13 inches or more that was manufactured, assembled, imported, or shipped in interstate commerce beginning July 1, 1993. Most receivers sold prior to that date did not include the circuitry, and viewers who wanted to access closed captions were required to purchase a separate decoder box for approximately $160.

The National Captioning Institute, an independent, nonprofit corporation, worked with engineers to develop an inexpensive electronic chip that could perform the same function as the cumbersome decoder boxes. This chip, if included in every TV receiver, would cost as little as $5, and this expense would presumably be absorbed into the total production cost of the sets. Citizen groups representing the hearing impaired lobbied Congress to enact legislation requiring the inclusion of a decoder chip in all receivers. Some opposition from manufacturers' groups was voiced during congressional hearings, but the overwhelming number of those testifying supported the legislation. The bill passed both the House and the Senate and was signed into law October 15, 1990.

Closed captioning is program dependent, and not all programs are captioned. Most network and syndicated programs are captioned, however, and the percentage continues to grow. Locally produced programs are less likely to be captioned since stations lack the technical and financial resources to provide this service. Most cities do have one or more local newscasts with captions. Initially, the cost of this service was underwritten by a local health care provider or a charitable foundation. More recently, a number of advertisers have been willing to underwrite the cost in exchange for an announcement or credit at the end of the program.

Captions appear in either "roll-up" or "pop-up" fashion. The captions roll up the screen if the program is being aired live. Live captioning is done by skilled professionals using court stenographic techniques who can transcribe speech as rapid as 250 words per minute. The lag time between the spoken word and the caption is one to five seconds. The captions are not always word-for-word transcripts, but they do closely approximate the verbal message.

Pop-up captions are used for prerecorded programs and for commercials. These captions can be prepared more leisurely and are timed to match the flow of dialogue on the TV screen. Also, an attempt is made to place the caption under the person speaking at the time. In a two-person dialogue, the caption would pop-up on either the left or right half of the screen depending on the position of the speaker. Various icons are used to symbolize sounds; for example, a musical note is placed next to the caption when a person is singing.

The most challenging captions involve live sports coverage since there is no way to anticipate what program participants will say. Newscasts are less difficult because the same TelePrompTer that cues on-air talent also cues the person preparing the captions.

Since the captions are encoded as part of the electronic signal, a closed-captioned program may be transmitted in any form: over-the-air broadcast, satellite, cable, video cassette, or video disc. Programs containing captions are noted with a (CC) following the program title in *TV Guide* and similar listings.

NORMAN FELSENTHAL

See also **Language and Television**

Further Reading

Fantel, Hans, "Watch Television and Get the Word," *New York Times* (July 11, 1993)

Television Closed Captioning: Hearing Before the Subcommittee on Telecommunications and Finance of the Committee on Energy and Commerce on H.R. 4267, U.S. House of Representatives, 101st Congress, Second Session, May 2, 1990

Closed-Circuit Television

Closed-circuit television (CCTV) is a television transmission system in which live or prerecorded signals are sent over a closed loop to a finite and predetermined group of receivers, either via coaxial cable or as scrambled radio waves that are unscrambled at the point of reception.

CCTV takes numerous forms and performs functions ranging from image enhancement for the partially sighted to the transmission of pay-per-view sports broadcasts. Although cable television is technically a form of CCTV, the term is generally used to designate TV systems with more specialized applications than broadcast or cable television. In the United States, these specialized systems are not subject to regulation by the Federal Communications Commission (FCC), although CCTV systems using scrambled radio waves are subject to common carrier tariffs and FCC conditions of service.

CCTV has many industrial and scientific applications, including electron microscopy, medical imaging, and robotics, but the term "closed-circuit TV" refers most often to security- and surveillance-camera systems. Other common forms of CCTV include live, on-site video displays for special events (e.g., conventions, arena sports, rock concerts); pay-per-view telecasts of sporting events such as championship boxing matches; and "in-house" television channels in hospitals, airports, racetracks, schools, malls, grocery stores, and municipal buildings.

The conception of many of these uses of CCTV technology dates back to the earliest years of television. In the 1930s and 1940s, writers such as *New York Times* columnist Orrin Dunlap predicted that closed-circuit TV systems would enhance industry, education, science, and commerce. Dunlap and other writers envisioned CCTV systems for supervising factory workers and for visually coordinating production in different areas of a factory, and they anticipated CCTV systems replacing pneumatic tubes in office communications. In the world of science, closed-circuit television was heralded as a way of viewing dangerous experiments as they took place; in the sphere of education, CCTV was seen as a way of bringing lessons simultaneously to different groups of students in a school or university.

Many of today's CCTV systems were first implemented in the years following World War II. For example, pay-per-view closed-circuit sports broadcasts can be traced back to a postwar Hollywood invention known as "theater television," a CCTV system used for viewing sports in movie theaters that became a lucrative source of ancillary revenue for boxing promoters in the 1950s, 1960s, and 1970s. With the growth of cable television and satellite delivery systems, CCTV telecasts have become an integral part of the business of sports today, not only in the boxing industry but also in horseracing, baseball, and golf.

Educational TV and video advertising in retail stores are other CCTV applications that originated in the post–World War II period. The controversial *Channel One News,* a commercial CCTV news program for schools founded in the 1980s, is only the latest of several CCTV experiments in education dating back to the 1950s. Today's "on-site" media industry, which places video advertising monitors in grocery stores, shopping malls, and other retail sites, dates back to a series of tests involving closed-circuit advertising in department stores that took place in the 1940s.

Although all of these applications of CCTV are fairly common, perhaps the most pervasive use of CCTV is for surveillance. Security cameras are now a

Mrs. Hal Roach Jr., Shari Roach, Howard Duff watch closed circuit broad cast of Notre Dame-Southern California football game at the Palm Springs Racquet Club, 1953.
Courtesy of the Everett Collection/CSU Archives

ubiquitous feature of many institutions and places, from the corrections facility to the convenience store, from the traffic stop to the Super Bowl. In prisons, CCTV systems reduce the costs of staffing and operating observation towers and make it possible to maintain a constant watch on all areas of the facility. CCTV is also used as a means of monitoring performance in the workplace; in 1992, according to an article in *Personnel Journal,* there were 10 million employees in the United States whose work was monitored via electronic security systems. Retail stores often install CCTV cameras as a safeguard against theft and robbery, a practice that municipal authorities have adopted as a way of curtailing crime in public housing and even on city streets. In the United Kingdom and United States, for example, police in several cities have installed closed-circuit cameras in busy public areas. Similar measures are taken to deter or detect terrorist attacks at major sporting events and other crowded gatherings.

These uses of CCTV technology are not neutral; indeed, they are often a matter of some controversy. These controversies center on the status of legal evidence acquired via closed-circuit TV and on the Orwellian implications of constant perceived surveillance. Police use of CCTV security cameras has led to charges of civil liberties violations. A 1978 survey on the topic of CCTV in the workplace found that 77 percent of employers interviewed supported the use of CCTV on the job. However, it also found that a majority of employees felt that CCTV in the workplace constituted an unwarranted intrusion and favored the passage of laws prohibiting such surveillance. The ascendancy of other sophisticated electronic employee surveillance technologies, such as keystroke monitoring of information workers, can sometimes render CCTV somewhat less important as a visual management technology.

In addition to these civil liberties issues, another controversy surrounding security cameras concerns their effectiveness in crime prevention. The purpose of CCTV surveillance is usually deterrence of, rather than intervention in, criminal acts. Many security cameras go unmonitored and are thus ineffective as a means of halting crimes in progress. This fact was forcefully demonstrated by a highly publicized juvenile murder case in England in 1992. After the discovery of the victim's body and the apprehension of the perpetrators, police discovered that the initial abduction had been recorded by a shopping center's security cameras.

Another controversy surrounding CCTV is its use in the courtroom. In 1985 the state of California passed a law allowing children to testify via CCTV in child molestation cases. In response to a similar ruling, the Illinois Supreme Court ruled that this method of testimony was unconstitutional, as it violated a defendant's right to confront his or her accuser.

Although this particular case reflects a concern that the camera can somehow "lie" and that it is not equivalent to face-to-face interaction, the latest trends in CCTV applications seem to rely precisely on the equation of closed-circuit television with actual presence. New technological developments that seem to base themselves on this premise include "teleconferencing," an audiovisual communications form designed to allow individuals in different places to interact via CCTV hookups, and "virtual reality," imaging systems that use CCTV "goggles" in conjunction with advanced computer graphics and input devices to create the illusion of a three-dimensional, interactive environment for the viewer.

ANNA MCCARTHY

See also ***Channel One News***

Further Reading

Borow, Wendy, "Medical Television: Prescription for Progress," *Journal of the American Medical Association* (October 6, 1993)

Clement, Andrew, "Office Automation and the Technical Control of Information Workers," in *The Political Economy of Information,* edited by Vincent Mosco and Janet Wasko, Madison: University of Wisconsin Press, 1988

Constant, Mike, *The Principles and Practice of Closed Circuit Television,* Borehamwood, England: Paramount, 1994

Dawson, Tim, "Framing the Villains," *New Statesman and Society* (January 28, 1994)

Dunlap, Orrin, *The Outlook for Television,* 1932; reprinted, New York: Arno Press, 1971

Dunlap, Orrin, *The Future of Television,* New York: Harper, 1947

Gannon, Mary, "Retail Applications of Television," *Television Magazine* (November 1945)

Genensky, S.M., *Advances in Closed Circuit TV Systems for the Partially-Sighted,* Santa Monica, California: Rand, 1972

Goldberg, Stephanie, "The Children's Hour," *American Bar Association Journal* (May 1994)

Gomery, Douglas, "Theater Television: The Missing Link of Technological Change in the U.S. Motion Picture Industry," *Velvet Light Trap* (1985)

Laabs, Jennifer J., "Measuring Work in the Electronic Age," *Personnel Journal* (June 1992)

Levine, Barry, "TV Cameras in Prison: Providing Extra Eyes for Officers," *Corrections Today* (July 1989)

Newburn, Tim, and Stephanie Hayman, *Policing, Surveillance, and Social Control: CCTV and Police Monitoring of Suspects,* Devon, England: Willan, 2002

Norris, Clive, and Gary Armstrong, *The Maximum Surveillance Society: The Rise of CCTV,* Oxford: Oxford University Press, and New York: Berg, 1999

Painter, Kate, and Nick Tilley, editors, *Surveillance of Public Space: CCTV, Street Lighting, and Crime Prevention,* Monsey, New York: Criminal Justice Press, 1999

"Safe Testimony," *Time* (June 3, 1985)
Sambul, Nathan J., *The Handbook of Private Television: A Complete Guide for Video Facilities and Networks Within Corporations, Nonprofit Institutions, and Government Agencies,* New York: McGraw-Hill, 1982
Stevenson, Richard W., "They're Capturing Suspects on Candid Camera," *New York Times* (March 11, 1995)
Zworykin, Vladimir, *Television in Science and Industry,* New York: Wiley, 1958

CNN. *See* **Cable News Network**

Cock, Gerald (1887–1973)

British Broadcasting Executive and Producer

Gerald Cock was appointed by the British Broadcasting Corporation (BBC) in 1935 to run its first television service (under the title "director of television"). At the time many BBC executives were skeptical about the value and potential of the new medium, and Cock's achievement during his short reign—the pre–World War II service began in November 1936 and was closed in September 1939—was to push for the expansion of the television service in the face of the BBC's reluctance to fund adequately what became known as the "Cinderella Service." Unlike many senior BBC executives, Cock regarded television as a natural successor to radio, rather than as a luxury or novelty.

Before joining the BBC during the 1920s, Cock spent a colorful youth in the Americas, gold mining and ranching in Alaska, Utah, and Mexico; he also worked as an extra in Hollywood. He started working for BBC radio during the 1920s and was appointed director of the Outside Broadcasts Department in 1925, where he encouraged the deployment of new technology and the development of new program forms, while often dealing with a competitive press.

The Selsdon Report of 1935 recommended that the BBC be given responsibility for the development of a regular high-definition television service; at the time television's potential as a medium of live immediacy meant that Cock's experience in the Outside Broadcasts Department—which aspired to be topical and contemporary—made him an obvious choice to head the new division.

The service began regular transmissions in 1936 from Alexandra Palace. Despite few staff and two small studios, Cock was able to build up an effective and successful repertoire of program achievements—including the live televising of the coronation of George VI, tennis from Wimbledon, and even a program where Cock himself answered viewers' phoned-in questions. In fact, every type of program that was to become popular after the war was already attempted during these prewar years, in part because of the freedom to experiment that Cock allowed his producers.

The programming policy of the prewar service was overseen by Cock. He instigated a policy of "variety and balance," which was coordinated through Cecil Madden, program organizer and chief liaison with the producers. This policy was congruent with Cock's realization that television's main attraction was that it allowed viewers to "see at a distance" contemporary events. For him, this aspect of the medium was relevant not only to the relay of current showbiz personalities and sporting events but also to early television drama. As he put it in a 1939 *Radio Times* article:

> Television is essentially a medium for topicalities.... An original play or specially devised television production might be a weekly feature. If a National Theatre were in being, close co-operation between it and the BBC might

> have solved an extremely difficult problem. Excerpts from plays during their normal runs, televised from the studio or direct from the stage, with perhaps a complete play at the end of its run would have attractive possibilities as part of a review of the nation's entertainment activities. But, in my view television is from its very nature more suitable for the dissemination of all kinds of information than for entertainment.

Cock's view of television was clearly inflected by his previous career as director of Outside Broadcasts for BBC radio, where the broadcasts were conceived as informative and enabling rather than as entertainment; hence, the broadcast of "scenes" from current plays, congruent with Cock's overall attitude, served as informative views on the nature of contemporary drama and performance, while also providing a "what's on" function. Cock regarded television's function to be as a relay service, its key benefits and attractions provided by the Outside Broadcast. For Cock, therefore, there was no need for large studios to house spectacular drama productions.

However, the "Theatre Parade" relay of "scenes" from the West End theater was far less popular than the studio production of complete plays. This meant that the demands on studio time and space were heavy, demands that were exacerbated as the ambitions of producers and the length of programs increased.

Cock's vision for a topical television service was also undermined by underfunding and a general distrust of television by sports promoters and theater managers; contrary to received history, outside broadcasts of West End plays and scenes from plays were the exception after 1937, and the prewar television service largely consisted of what would later be considered studio-based light entertainment.

Unfortunately—and despite Cock's determined enthusiasm—current-affairs television was not developed until the mid-1950s, and BBC Television News in vision was not introduced until 1954 (this was because senior executives assumed that seeing the news announcer in vision would distract the viewer from important information).

However, Cock himself was indirectly responsible for the gradual development of current-affairs television. When the television service was closed in 1939, Cock went on to work as North American representative for the BBC in New York and California. He later gave evidence to the Hankey Committee, which was appointed to consider the resurrection of the television service after the war, and he wrote a key 1945 document, "Report on the Conditions for a Post-War Television Service," which stressed that news and current affairs should be "a main feature of the new service." However, senior BBC management were to disregard Cock's suggestions for another ten years.

By the late 1940s, Cock was seriously ill. In 1948 a young radio producer, Grace Wyndham Goldie, had been offered a post in the television service; at the time she was working for the prestigious and highbrow Third Programme. Despite discouragement from two senior radio executives, it was Cock who encouraged her to work in television. Goldie was to become the single most important personality in the development of British current-affairs television, overseeing the development of programs such as *Panorama* and *Tonight*—precisely the kind of programs that Gerald Cock had envisaged as the sine qua non of television programming.

JASON J. JACOBS

See also **British Television**

Gerald Cock. Born in 1887. Educated at Tonbridge School; Seafield Park. Commissioned Royal Engineers, BEF, France, and Belgium, 1915–20; served as captain, 1917. Traveled in United States, British Columbia, Mexico, working various jobs, including gold mining and ranching, 1909–15; returned to United Kingdom, 1915; conducted business in London, 1920–24; first director of Outside Broadcasts, BBC, 1925; appointed first director of television, 1935; organized and directed first television service to be established in Europe, 1936–39; served as North American representative, BBC, 1940–41; Pacific Coast representative, BBC, 1942–45; retired, 1946. Member: Reform Club; Royal Victorian Order, 1935. Died November 10, 1973.

Publication (selected)

"Looking Forward, a Personal Forecast of the Future of Television," *Radio Times* (October 29, 1936)

Codco

Canadian Sketch-Comedy Satire

The name *Codco,* short for Cod Company, makes humorous reference to the origins of the TV show's cast and its production roots on the Canadian East Coast. Founded as a theatrical revue in the early 1970s in St. John's, Newfoundland, *Codco* drew on the island province's cultural history of self-deprecating "Newfie" humor, adopting the cod-fishing industry as local, fringe identity. From these theatrical and regional roots, the cast subsequently developed the half-hour, television comedy program of the same name, produced in the regional studio of the Canadian Broadcasting Corporation (CBC) in Halifax, Nova Scotia, and on location in St. John's.

Codco was produced and nationally broadcast on the CBC for six seasons. In 1991 the program underwent a marked change without losing its satirical edge. In that year, Andy Jones, an original *Codco* theater cofounder and TV show member, left the TV cast to pursue solo theatrical projects. In 1993, just months before Tommy Sexton's death from AIDS-related causes, and Greg Malone's own departure, *Codco* went off the air. The death of the boyish, talented Sexton was a subject of national news and reflection on the role of humor in the television and cultural life of Canada from a Newfie point of view. The remaining core members of TV's *Codco,* Mary Walsh and Cathy Jones, teamed up with two fresh faces, East Coast writer-actors Rick Mercer and Greg Thomey, and returned in the 1993–94 season in a revamped half-hour newsmagazine satire, *This Hour Has 22 Minutes.*

Codco's satire took aim at regional differences and national assumptions within Canada, attacking politics and politicians, sexism and gender roles, and the gay subtext of straight characters in television genres. The format for *Codco*'s satire was sketch comedy, with sets, costumes, and makeup mimicking the sources under attack. The *Codco* members' theatrical roots trained them to develop detailed caricatures, performed with nuances that dismantled the source subjects, the CBC, and television itself as a medium compromised by commercialization. Spun from the collective writing and acting skills of the members, and ably directed by the experienced John Blanchard and David Acomba, *Codco* sketches revealed the tightness of well-rehearsed scene studies, exceeding the loose burlesque of *Saturday Night Live*'s broad spoofs.

All four *Codco* cast members continued to cross-dress as they made the transition from regional theater company to national television show, and their ability to traverse sex roles played to *Codco*'s long interest in social transgression and critique. Cathy Jones and Walsh portrayed a variety of males, from macho through wimpy, along with their femme fatales, "loud feminists," and pesky middle-aged, bingo-bent matrons. The sketches featuring the homely, dateless "Friday Night Girls" satirized the isolation of lone women who lack the glamour of the women they view on television. Walsh's Dakey Dunn, "Male Correspondent," replete with gold chain, hairy chest, cigarette, and beer in hand, might explain the local dilemma facing the Friday Night Girls. In one monologue, Dakey admits to not completing high school and, in crude English, lays out a macho view of economic and cultural matters as if his type is a male standard within Newfie life. Malone's Queen Elizabeth and Sexton and Malone's gay barristers personified a Canadian colonial condition and gay-rights emergence that only satire could accommodate on broadcast television.

In November 2001, nine years after Sexton's death, the CBC aired a retrospective biography, *Tommy: A Family Portrait,* chronicling Sexton's comedic legacy and struggle as gay son, valued sibling, and alternative performer working in the lively arts and music scene of St. John's. Part of Sexton's wider legacy includes the CBC special *The National Doubt* (1992), a collaboration with Malone and musical-theater satirist John Gray. *The National Doubt* featured two medieval characters (played by Sexton and Malone) crossing Canada to take the country's national pulse amid the regional climate that had developed since the Expo '67 celebrations 25 years earlier in Montreal.

Ivan Fecan, once the CBC's "wunderkind" and former director of television programming, nurtured *Codco*'s place on the network, first in a late-night slot and later in prime time. Placed back-to-back with *Kids in the Hall* to constitute a prime-time hour of "adult" CBC programming (9 to 10 P.M.), the satiric heft of *Codco* and the *Kids* was enhanced by this yoking of the two shows. Both were driven by sharp comedic misbehavior—prominently, in the hour before the CBC's flagship newscast, *The National.*

JOAN NICKS

Performers
Tommy Sexton
Greg Malone
Cathy Jones
Mary Walsh
Andy Jones

Programming History
CBC
63 episodes
1987–93

Further Reading

Hluchy, Patricia, "Cold War of the Sexes," *Maclean's* (March 2, 1987)
Peters, Helen, "From Salt Cod to Cod Filets," *Canadian Theatre Review* (fall 1990)
Peters, Helen, editor, *The Plays of Codco,* New York: Peter Lang, 1992

Coe, Fred (1914–1979)

U.S. Producer

A prolific television, theater, and film producer and director, Fred Coe is closely identified with the "Golden Age" of live television. His television career started in 1945, when he became production manager for NBC in New York and worked with Worthington Miner on *Studio One.* In 1948 Coe began production of NBC's *Philco Television Playhouse,* a live dramatic-anthology series broadcast on Sunday evenings from 9:00 to 10:00. From 1951 to 1955, *Philco Television Playhouse* alternated with *Goodyear Television Playhouse* and became one of the top-rated programs of the early 1950s. Live programming of this type was used by NBC's programming chief Pat Weaver to differentiate television from motion pictures, to strengthen the network's ties with its affiliates, and to enlarge the audience for TV sets (manufactured by NBC's parent company, RCA).

Coe was noted for using unknown writers and directors who were able to create works tailored for the new medium: the writers included Paddy Chayefsky, Tad Mosel, Horton Foote, Gore Vidal, J.P. Miller, and Robert Alan Arthur; and the directors included Delbert Mann, Arthur Penn, and Vincent Donehue. Setting anthology drama on a course that established it as the most prestigious format on live television, Coe relied at first on TV adaptations of Broadway plays and musicals, then on literary classics, biographies, and old Hollywood movies, and finally on original television drama. The Philco series opened on October 3, 1948, with a one-hour version of George S. Kaufman and Edna Ferber's *Dinner at Eight.* In 1952 Coe produced the first play of the first playwright to achieve fame in television. The playwright was Paddy Chayefsky, and the play, *Holiday Song.* In 1953 Coe produced Chayefsky's *Marty,* with Rod Steiger in the title role. Directed by Delbert Mann, *Marty* became the most popular anthology drama of the period, winning many awards and even initiating a Hollywood production trend of films based on TV drama. The film *Marty,* produced by Harold Hecht and released through United Artists in 1955, won Academy Awards for Best Picture, Best Actor (Ernest Borgnine), Direction (Delbert Mann), and Original Screenplay (Paddy Chayefsky). Other notable Coe productions included Chayefsky's *The Bachelor Party,* Horton Foote's *The Trip to Bountiful,* and Tad Mosel's *Other People's Houses.* Productions such as these earned Coe and the *Philco Playhouse* the George Foster Peabody Award in 1954 and many other honors.

In 1954 Coe began producing *Producer's Showcase,* a 90-minute anthology series that aired every fourth Monday for three seasons. One aim of the series was to broadcast expensive color spectaculars to promote RCA's new color television system. The best example of this strategy was *Peter Pan,* a successful Broadway production of Sir James M. Barrie's fantasy that Coe brought to television almost intact. Starring Mary Martin, *Peter Pan* was broadcast on March 7, 1955, and was viewed by an estimated 65 to 75 million people, becoming the highest-rated show in TV's brief history. As a result of this memorable production and adaptations of such plays as Sherwood Anderson's *The*

Fred Coe.
Photo courtesy of Wisconsin Center for Film and Theater Research

Petrified Forest (1955), which starred Humphrey Bogart and Lauren Bacall in their TV dramatic debuts, and Thornton Wilder's *Our Town,* which starred Paul Newman and Eva Marie Saint, Coe was awarded an Emmy for Best Producer of a Live Series in 1955.

NBC's programming strategies radically changed after 1956 to rely on the routines of series programming produced by West Coast suppliers on film. In 1957 Coe departed the network for CBS, where he produced *Playhouse 90* for three seasons. Among the best productions of the series were *Days of Wine and Roses* (1958), *The Plot to Kill Stalin* (1958), and *For Whom the Bell Tolls* (1959). Thereafter, Coe worked sporadically in television, producing specials for all three networks in the late 1960s and 1970s and producing and directing several episodes of *The Adams Chronicles* for PBS in 1976.

Anticipating the decline of live anthology drama on television, Coe brought anthology drama to Broadway by producing theatrical versions of TV plays by TV writers, among them William Gibson's *Two for the Seesaw* (1958) and *The Miracle Worker* (1959), Tad Mosel's *All the Way Home* (1960), and Herb Gardner's *A Thousand Clowns* (1962). Coe even converted two TV plays into films—*The Miracle Worker* (1962) and *A Thousand Clowns* (1966). Coe's legacy is a tradition of programming demonstrating television's unique aspects as a medium of dramatic expression.

TINO BALIO

See also **Anthology Drama; Chayefsky, Paddy; "Golden Age" of Television; *Goodyear Playhouse;* Mann, Delbert; *Peter Pan; Philco Television Playhouse; Playhouse 90***

Fred Coe. Born in Alligator, Mississippi, December 23, 1914. Attended Peabody Demonstration School, Nashville, Tennessee; attended Peabody College for Teachers, Nashville; studied at Yale Drama School, New Haven, Connecticut, 1938–40. Married: 1) Alice Griggs, 1940 (divorced), children: John and Laurence Anne; 2) Joyce Beeler, 1952; children: Sue Anne and Samuel Hughes. Ran community theater in Nashville; presented radio dramas on station WSM; production manager, NBC, New York (producing more than 500 hour-long teleplays), 1945; producer, *Philco-Goodyear Playhouse,* NBC, 1948–53; executive producer, *Mr. Peepers* series, 1952–53; producer, *Producers' Showcase,* 1954–55; producer, *Playwrights '56,* 1956; producer and director, *Playhouse 90,* CBS, produced such Broadway shows as *Two for the Seesaw, A Trip to Bountiful,* and *The Miracle Worker;* coproducer and director, various Broadway shows. Recipient: Writers Guild of America Evelyn Burkey Award; Peabody Award, 1954; Emmy Award, 1955. Died in Los Angeles, California, April 29, 1979.

Television Series

1948–53	*Philco Television Playhouse* and *Goodyear Television Playhouse*
1952–53	*Mr. Peepers* (executive producer)
1954–55	*Producers' Showcase*
1956	*Playwrights '56*
1956–61	*Playhouse 90* (also director)

Made-for-Television Movie

1979	*Miracle Worker* (producer)

Teleplays (selected)

1949	*Philco Television Playhouse: What Makes Sammy Run?*
1949	*Philco Television Playhouse: The Last Tycoon*
1953	*Philco Television Playhouse: Marty*
1955	*Producers' Showcase: Peter Pan*

Films

The Left-Handed Gun (producer), 1958; *Miracle Worker* (producer), 1962; *This Property Is Condemned* (writer), 1966.

Stage

Two for the Seesaw; A Trip to Bountiful; The Miracle Worker; All the Way Home (coproducer); *A Thousand Clowns* (coproducer and director).

Further Reading

Averson, Richard, editor, *Electronic Drama: Television Plays of the Sixties,* Boston: Beacon, 1971

"The Broadcasting and Cable Hall of Fame (Biographies of 17 Inductees)," *Broadcasting and Cable* (November 7, 1994)

Hawes, William, *The American Television Drama: The Experimental Years,* University: University of Alabama Press, 1986

Kindem, Gorham, editor, *The Live Television Generation of Hollywood Film Directors: Interviews with Seven Directors,* Jefferson, North Carolina: McFarland, 1994

Krampner, Jon, *The Man in the Shadows: Fred Coe and the Golden Age of Television,* New Brunswick, New Jersey: Rutgers University Press, 1997

Sturcken, Frank, *Live Television: The Golden Age of 1946–1958 in New York,* Jefferson, North Carolina: McFarland, 1990

Wilk, Max, *The Golden Age of Television: Notes from the Survivors,* New York: Delacorte Press, 1976

Cole, George (1925–)

British Actor

George Cole, as his alter ego Arthur Daley in the long-running series *Minder,* is to countless British viewers the quintessence of the cockney spiv, a mischief-causing small businessman always with an eye to the main chance and often caught treading on the toes of the law. Endearingly convinced against all the evidence of his own cunning, and equally often driven to distraction by the comical collapse of his schemes, the irrepressible Daley, with his salesman's patter and naive pretensions as a big-time wheeler and dealer, became an icon for the 1980s, representing the materialist sub-yuppie culture that was fostered under the capitalist leadership of Margaret Thatcher. Every episode of the comedy series, which costarred Dennis Waterman as Daley's dim-witted but resolutely honest bodyguard-cum-assistant Terry McCann, featured the launch of another of Daley's shady schemes, or "nice little earners" as he called them, and culminated in the hapless secondhand car salesman and would-be executive being exposed for some fiddle or other and having to be rescued from arrest, physical assault, or worse by his long-suffering minder. Other troubles in Daley's life, from which he took refuge in his drinking club, the Winchester, came from " 'Er indoors," the formidable Mrs. Daley, who was never seen.

Minder, written by Leon Griffiths and filmed in some of the less picturesque parts of London, was not an instant success. The first two series failed to convince audiences, who welcomed Cole but were confused at the sight of tough-guy Dennis Waterman, fresh from the police series *The Sweeney,* taking a comic part. Thames Television persevered, however, and the public were gradually won over, the two stars becoming the highest-paid television actors in Britain. After six series, each billed as the last, Waterman finally withdrew to concentrate on other work, but Cole continued just a little longer, now with his nephew Ray (played by Gary Webster) as Terry's replacement.

The part of Arthur Daley was perfect for Cole, who had in fact been playing variations of the character for years on both the large and small screen (he made his film debut as early as 1941). He had been schooled in the finer points of comic acting as the protégé of the film comedian Alistair Sim and as a young man made a memorable impression as the cockney spiv Flash Harry, an embryonic Daley figure complete with funny walk, loud suits, catchy signature tune, and suitcase bulging with dodgy merchandise, in the *St. Trinian's* films of the 1950s. His television career took off in 1960, when he was seen as David Bliss in *A Life of Bliss,* which had started out as a radio series. Subsequently, he continued to be associated chiefly with similar cockney roles, as in *A Man of Our Times,* in which he played the manager of a small furniture store, although in reality he has played a much wider variety of parts—including an aspiring playwright in *Don't Forget to Write,* a dedicated com-

George Cole.
Courtesy of the Everett Collection

munist in *Comrade Dad,* the aristocratic and much put-upon Sir Giles Lynchwood in Tom Sharpe's hilarious *Blott on the Landscape,* Henry Root in *Root into Europe,* and the absentminded central character in *Dad,* among other assorted characters.

It is, however, as the ever-likable if sometimes unscrupulous Arthur Daley that George Cole, an officer of the British Empire, is best known. Such is his identification with the part that the actor reports that he frequently has trouble getting people to accept his checks, fearing that they will not be honored by the banks because of his on-screen reputation. The extensive use of cockney rhyming slang by Daley in the 70-odd episodes that were made of *Minder* is also said, incidentally, to have done much to keep this linguistic oddity from extinction.

DAVID PICKERING

See also ***Minder; Sweeney, The***

George Cole. Born in Tooting, London, England, April 22, 1925. Attended Surrey County Council Secondary School, Morden. Married: 1) Eileen Moore, 1954 (divorced, 1966); one son and one daughter; 2) Penelope Morrell, 1967; children: Tara and Toby. Served in Royal Air Force, 1943–47. Began career as stage actor in *The White Horse Inn* on tour, 1939; discovered by Alistair Sim in 1940 to play a cockney evacuee in the film *Cottage to Let,* 1941; subsequently specialized in chirpy cockney roles, notably Flash Harry in the *St. Trinian's* films; established reputation on television with the role of David Bliss in *A Life of Bliss,* 1960–61; best known to television audiences as Arthur Daley in the long-running series *Minder.* Order of the British Empire, 1992.

Television Series

1960–61	*A Life of Bliss*
1968	*A Man of Our Times*
1977–79	*Don't Forget to Write*
1979–85	*Minder*
1982–83	*The Bounder*
1984–85	*Heggerty Haggerty*
1984, 1986	*Comrade Dad*
1985	*Blott on the Landscape*
1988–94	*Minder*
1992	*Root into Europe*
1995–96	*My Good Friend*
1997–99	*Dad*

Made-for-Television Movie (selected)

1985	*Minder on the Orient Express*

Films

Cottage to Let, 1941; *Those Kids from Town,* 1942; *Fiddling Fuel,* 1943; *The Demi-Paradise,* 1943; *Henry V,* 1944; *Journey Together,* 1945; *My Brother's Keeper,* 1948; *Quartet,* 1948; *The Spider and the Fly,* 1949; *Morning Departure,* 1949; *Gone to Earth,* 1949; *Flesh and Blood,* 1951; *Laughter in Paradise,* 1951; *Scrooge,* 1951; *Lady Godiva Rides Again,* 1951; *The Happy Family,* 1952; *Folly to Be Wise,* 1952; *Who Goes There?,* 1952; *Top Secret,* 1952; *The Clue of the Missing Ape,* 1953; *Will Any Gentleman,* 1953; *Apes of the Rock,* 1953; *The Intruder,* 1953; *Our Girl Friday,* 1953; *Happy Ever After,* 1954; *The Belles of St. Trinian's,* 1954; *An Inspector Calls,* 1954; *Where There's a Will,* 1955; *A Prize of Gold,* 1955; *The Constant Husband,* 1955; *The Adventures of Quentin Durward,* 1955; *It's a Wonderful World,* 1956; *The Weapon,* 1956; *The Green Man,* 1956; *Blue Murder at St. Trinian's,* 1957; *Too Many Crooks,* 1958; *Don't Panic Chaps,* 1959; *The Bridal Path,* 1959; *The Pure Hell of St. Trinian's,* 1961; *The Anatomist,* 1961; *Cleopatra,* 1962; *Dr. Syn Alias the Scarecrow,* 1963; *One Way Pendulum,* 1964; *The Legend of Young Dick Turpin,* 1965; *The Great St. Trinian's Train Robbery,* 1966; *The Green Shoes,* 1968; *The Right Prospectus,* 1970; *The Vampire Lovers,* 1970; *Girl in the Dark,*

1971; *Fright,* 1971; *Take Me High,* 1973; *Gone in 60 Seconds,* 1974; *The Blue Bird,* 1976; *Double Nickels,* 1978; *Mary Reilly,* 1996.

Radio

A Life of Bliss (series); *Sexton's Tales,* 1996, 1997.

Stage (selected)

The White Horse Inn, 1939; *Cottage to Let,* 1940; *Goodnight Children,* 1942; *Mr. Bolfry,* 1943; *Dr. Angelus,* 1947; *The Anatomist,* 1948; *Mr. Gillie,* 1950; *A Phoenix too Frequent,* 1951; *Thor with Angels,* 1951; *Misery Me,* 1955; *Mr. Bolfry,* 1956; *Brass Butterfly,* 1958; *The Bargain,* 1961; *The Sponge Room,* 1962; *Squat Betty,* 1962; *Meet Me on the Fence,* 1963; *Hedda Gabler,* 1964; *A Public Mischief,* 1965; *Too True to Be Good,* 1965; *The Waiting Game,* 1966; *The Three Sisters,* 1967; *Doubtful Haunts,* 1968; *The Passionate Husband,* 1969; *The Philanthropist,* 1971; *Country Life,* 1973; *Déjà Revue,* 1974; *Motive,* 1976; *Banana Ridge,* 1976; *The Case of the Oily Levantine,* 1977; *Something Afoot,* 1978; *Brimstone and Treacle,* 1979; *Liberty Hall,* 1980; *The Pirates of Penzance,* 1982; *A Month of Sundays,* 1986; *A Piece of My Mind,* 1987; *Peter Pan,* 1987; *The Breadwinner,* 1989; *Natural Causes,* 1993; *Theft,* 1995; *Lock Up Your Daughters,* 1996; *Heritage,* 1997.

Further Reading

Berkmann, Marcus, "Still a Nice Little Earner," *Daily Mail* (October 9, 1993)

Bradbury, Malcolm, "Requiem for an Old Rogue," *Daily Mail* (October 9, 1993)

Buss, Robin, "Minder," *Times Educational Supplement* (November 8, 1991)

Truss, Lynne, "Television Workhorses Finally Put Out to Grass," *The Times* (March 10, 1994)

Colgate Comedy Hour, The

U.S. Variety Show

For approximately five and a half seasons, NBC's *Colgate Comedy Hour* presented big-budget musical variety television as head-to-head competition for *Ed Sullivan's Toast of the Town* on CBS. Featuring the top names in vaudeville, theater, radio, and film, this live Sunday-evening series was the first starring vehicle for many notable performers turning to television. Reflecting format variations by host, *The Colgate Comedy Hour* initially offered musical comedy, burlesque sketches, opera, and/or nightclub comedy revues.

In his autobiography *Take My Life,* comedian Eddie Cantor recalled proposing to NBC that he was prepared to host a television show but only once every four weeks in rotation with other comics. Colgate-Palmolive-Peet picked up the tab for three of the four weeks, and *The Colgate Comedy Hour* was born with Cantor, Dean Martin and Jerry Lewis, and Fred Allen as hosts. The fourth show of the month was sponsored originally by Frigidaire and appeared for a short time under the title *Michael Todd's Revue,* with Todd producing and comic Bobby Clark scheduled to alternate with Bob Hope as host.

Cantor premiered *The Colgate Comedy Hour* on September 10, 1950, to rave reviews. Working the thread of a storyline into the show for continuity, the veteran performer took his material out of the realm of vaudeville and turned it into more of a legitimate Broadway attraction. Martin and Lewis met with similar success. Dominating their hour, the energetic duo created a nightclub setting whose intimacy and ambience the trade press found continuously funny. Allen, on the other hand, found the large-scale theatrical nature of the format too demanding and out of character for his more relaxed style of humor. Attempting to transfer elements of his successful radio show to video, he met only with disappointment. This was especially true when the characters of his famous Allen's Alley were foolishly turned into puppets. A kindly *Time* magazine reviewer noted in the October 2, 1950, issue of the magazine that the show did sizzle "with much of Allen at his best," but, realistically, it also "fizzled occasionally with some of Allen at his worst." Allen showed improvement on subsequent telecasts but was retired from the series after his fourth broadcast. Bitter about his experience, he promised he would not return to television unless provided a low-key format comparable to Dave Garroway's Chicago-based *Garroway at Large.* Clark produced better ratings and reviews than Allen, but ultimately he and the *Michael Todd Revue* suffered a similar fate.

Premiering with Jackie Gleason in its second season, *The Colgate Comedy Hour* was the highest-budgeted single-sponsor extravaganza on television, with Colgate-Palmolive-Peet picking up a $3 million a year talent-production-time tab. Back for their second year were Cantor and Martin and Lewis with Gleason, Abbott and Costello, Spike Jones, Tony Martin, and Ezio Pinza slotted as starters. Ratings remained high for the original hosts, but the Sullivan show began producing high-budget specials that chipped away at the Colgate numbers when the new hosts appeared.

During the second season, *The Colgate Comedy Hour* also became the first commercial network series to originate on the West Coast when Cantor hosted his program from Hollywood's El Capitan Theatre on September 30, 1951. Two years later, on November 22, 1953, a Donald O'Connor *Comedy Hour* became the first sponsored network program to be telecast in color. In an FCC-approved test of RCA's new compatible color system, several hundred persons monitored the broadcast in specially equipped viewing booths at a site distant from the Colgate production theater.

Despite an annual budget estimated at more than $6 million, during the 1953–54 season *The Colgate Comedy Hour* began to experience problems. Many performers, hard pressed to generate new material continually, were considered stale and repetitious. Cantor and Martin and Lewis were still highly rated regulars, but Cantor was feeling stressed. The diminutive showman had suffered a heart attack after a *Comedy Hour* appearance in September 1952, and now nearly 60 years of age, he felt the work too demanding. This would be his last season. To attract and maintain an audience, new hosts, including the popular Jimmy Durante, were absorbed from NBC's faltering *All Star Revue.* Occasional "book" musicals, top-flight shows such as *Anything Goes* with Ethel Merman and Frank Sinatra, were produced. *The Comedy Hour* also began to tour, providing viewers with special broadcasts from glamorous locations—New York seen from the deck of the SS *United States,* among others.

During the 1954–55 season, the Sullivan show made significant inroads on *The Colgate Comedy Hour*'s ratings. Martin and Lewis made fewer appearances, and an emphasis was placed on performers working in big settings such as the Hollywood Bowl and Broadway's Latin Quarter. During the summer, Colgate collaborated with Paramount Pictures, the latter supplying guest stars and film clips from newly released motion pictures. The show moved away from comedy headliners; actor Charlton Heston hosted as did orchestra leader Guy Lombardo and musical star Gordon MacRae. To reflect these differences, the show's name was changed to the *Colgate Variety Hour,* but despite the changes, for the first time in its history, the series dropped out of the top 25 in Nielsen ratings while Sullivan moved into the top five.

The Colgate Comedy Hour.
Photo courtesy of Wisconsin Center for Film and Theater Research

A feuding Martin and Lewis kicked off the last season of the *Colgate Variety Hour* to good reviews, but subsequent shows proved it had become increasingly difficult to sustain acceptable ratings for a series of this budget magnitude. On December 11, 1955, Sullivan drew an overnight Trendex of 42.6. The *Variety Hour*'s salute to theatrical legend George Abbott came in a distant third with a dismal 7.2. Two weeks later, on December 25, 1955, the Colgate series quietly left the air following a Christmas music broadcast by Fred Waring and his Pennsylvanians. Replaced with the poorly conceived *NBC Comedy Hour,* featuring unlikely host Leo Durocher, one of the most lavish, entertaining, and at times extraordinary musical variety series in television history was just a memory. In May 1967, NBC presented a *Colgate Comedy Hour* revival, but it was a revival in name only—not in format or in star value.

JOEL STERNBERG

Principal Hosts
Eddie Cantor (1950–54)
Dean Martin and Jerry Lewis (1950–55)
Fred Allen (1950)
Donald O'Connor (1951–54)
Lou Abbott and Bud Costello (1951–54)
Bob Hope (1952–53)
Jimmy Durante (1953–54)
Gordon MacRae (1954–55)
Robert Paige (1955)

Producers
Charles Friedman, Sam Fuller

Programming History
NBC
September 1950–December 1955 Sunday 8:00–9:00

Further Reading

Brooks, Tim, and Earle Marsh, *The Complete Directory to Prime Time Network TV Shows 1946–Present,* New York: Ballantine Books, 1979; 5th edition, 1992
Cantor, Eddie, with Jane Kesner Ardmore, *Take My Life,* Garden City, New York: Doubleday, 1957
Castleman, Harry, and Walter J. Podrazik, *Watching TV: Four Decades of American Television,* New York: McGraw-Hill, 1982
"Color TV Review: Colgate Comedy Hour," *Variety* (November 25, 1953)
"How the New Shows Are Doing," *Television* (November 1950)
Rosen, George, "Cantor Sock in Debut on Colgate Airer; Vet Showman a TV Natural," *Variety* (September 13, 1950)
"Tele Topics," *Radio Daily* (September 19, 1950)
Terrace, Vincent, *The Complete Encyclopedia of Television Programs, 1947–1979,* Vol. 1, A–Z, New York: Barnes, 1979

Collins, Bill (1935–)

Australian Television Personality

Bill Collins has been described as "Mr. Movies of Australia." He has presented films on television and on video since 1963 and has come to seem like a trusted and enthusiastic guarantor of whatever film he happens to be presenting. As a high school English teacher, long interested in the cinema and its possible role in the classroom, he completed a master's degree in education (studying the role of film in education) and took a position as a lecturer in English at the Sydney Teachers College. He regularly introduced trainee teachers to the place of film in the high school English curriculum.

In 1963, he made his first appearance on television, producing and presenting a series of filmed segments on film appreciation. That same year he compiled a weekly column in the better of Australia's television guides, *TV Times,* titled "The Golden Years of Hollywood." The column consisted of a series of reviews of upcoming Hollywood films to be screened on Australia's three commercial networks as well as the public broadcaster, the ABC. Collins's reviews were invariably to the point and reliable in their production credits at a time when that kind of information was not so easily available as it is nowadays. To write his reviews, Collins was having to preview many of the films. It seemed quite logical, then, when TCN Channel 9 (owned by Consolidated Press, which copublished *TV Times* with the ABC) decided to have Collins host a Saturday-night movie, with the generic name of *The Golden Years of Hollywood.* Collins continued to host the Saturday-night movie on Channel 9 in Sydney until 1975, when he moved to the Seven Network. Channel 9 disputed that Collins had the legal right to call his Saturday-night movie program *The Golden Years of Hollywood,* and so the Seven program became *Bill Collins' Golden Years of Hollywood.* The change suited Collins because his career as a movie host was now taking off. His Saturday-night movie was now increasingly seen nationally, and as his earnings increased Collins quit his teaching job to concentrate full time on his television work. At Seven, Collins began to host a Sunday daytime film, *Bill Collins' Picture Time,* and also a more general program featuring film clips and promotion for new releases, *Bill Collins' Show Business.*

Collins moved yet again in 1980 in a move that made him even busier. Rupert Murdoch had recently acquired the third commercial network, which he renamed Network Ten. The latter had always lagged in the ratings, and Murdoch was determined to change this situation even if it meant spending a lot of money—to hire Collins away. Collins now became a national figure to the point that other movie hosts on regional stations ceased to have any importance and little recognition. By this time he seemed to be everywhere. Not only did he host a double feature on Saturday night under the old title of *The Golden Years of Hollywood,* a double feature on Sunday lunchtime and afternoon, the midday movie during the week on a capital-city-by-capital-city basis but also an afternoon book review and promotion program. Thanks both to the size of his program budgets as well as his commercial standing, Collins was able to do live interviews with major Hollywood actors, including his favorite, Clint Eastwood. He also published two books, lavishly illustrated, on his favorite films. In addition Collins hosted his own series of Hollywood feature films on video: *Bill Collins' Movie Collection.* Collins also made professional visits to fans across the country, these taking the form of breakfasts and lunches. To carry out these massive commitments, Collins now had a staff of researchers and his own press and publicity agents. In 1987, because of the introduction of new cross-ownership rules in Australian media, Murdoch sold off Network Ten. Collins continued there until 1994. The network suffered from financial problems, so there was a curtailment of his programs. However, in 1995, he in effect rejoined the Murdoch camp when he began presenting films on Australia's first cable network, Foxtel, owned and operated by Murdoch's News Corporation and Telstra Corporation. Collins now hosts films produced by Twentieth Century Fox on Foxtel Channel.

There is no gainsaying the achievement of Bill Collins. He appeared on Australian television at a time when Hollywood films, not only of the 1930s and 1940s but also of the 1950s, were becoming available for television programming. He has helped to make Hollywood films popular with generations who were born after the Hollywood studio era. As befits a former teacher, his introductions to particular films are invariably interesting, enthusiastic, and well researched. He will often display a still or a poster, brandish the book on which a film is based (he has an extensive collection of these, often extremely rare books), or play some of a film's theme music. All of these ploys are in the service of not only giving the audience particular features to look for in the upcoming film but also contextualizing the film in terms of such frames as the biography of one of the leading figures. Nor has Collins been afraid to expose his audience to some of the fruits of more critical research with references to such material as a critical study of John Ford or an article in the U.S. film studies journal *The Velvet Light Trap.* Altogether Bill Collins is one of the most durable and valuable figures in the history of Australian television.

ALBERT MORAN

Bill Collins.
Photo courtesy of Bill Collins

Bill Collins. Born in Sydney, Australia, 1935. Educated at Sydney University, B.A., M.A., Dip.Ed., and M.Ed. Taught in high school for four years; university lecturer; began reviewing movies in print (*TV Times*) and on television (ABC Television), 1963; moved from ABC to commercial station TCN Channel 9, 1967–75; movie host, ATN Channel 7 Sydney, 1975–79; presented movies nationally on the Network Ten, 1980–94; currently presenting movies on the Foxtel movie network. Awarded the Order of Australia Medal (OAM) for his services to film and television in 1987.

Color Television

The early stages of color television experimentation in the United States overlap with the technological development of monochromatic television. Color television was demonstrated by John Logie Baird as early as 1928, and a year later by Bell Telephone Laboratories. Experimental color broadcasting was initiated in 1940, when the Columbia Broadcasting System (CBS) publicly demonstrated a field-sequential color television broadcasting system. This system employed successive fields scanned one at a time in one of three colors: red, blue, or green. On the receiver end, a mechanical color wheel was used to reconstitute these three colors in sequence enabling reproduction of the colors in the original scene. In their 1941 report confirming the National Television Systems Committee (NTSC) monochromatic standards, the Federal Communications Commission (FCC) noted the potential benefits of the CBS color system but concurred with the NTSC assessment that color television required further testing before it could be standardized.

Further refinement of color television was temporarily suspended during World War II. After the war, work on the development of color TV resumed, and engineers were able to design a system that would operate within the 6-megahertz channel allocation that had been established for black-and-white service. In a hearing that began on September 26, 1949, and lasted for 62 days, CBS petitioned the FCC for commercialization of its 6-megahertz, 405-line, 144-fields-per-second field-sequential color system. Because of the higher scanning rate, such a system was not compatible with the existing monochromatic standard.

The economic costs of adopting an incompatible system were a major factor in the FCC deliberations. If adopted, it appeared that consumers would carry the cost of modifying the existing 2 million monochrome receivers to follow the higher field-sequential scanning rates and reproduce color signal transmissions in monochrome. The projected costs of this modification varied, with a low figure of about $25. In addition, it was also argued that when broadcasters elected to begin color service, they would lose that portion of the audience that had not yet modified their monochrome receivers.

At the hearings, work on several experimental electronic color systems designed to be compatible with the existing monochrome system was presented to the commission. Color Television, Incorporated (CTI) demonstrated its line-sequential color system, which assigned the color portion of the signal to the successive lines of the image. In the first field, the uppermost line was scanned in green, the next line in blue, the next in red, and so on until the first field was complete. The second field was scanned in a similar manner, and the combination of the two fields produced a complete picture in color. The system operated at 525 lines, and 60 fields a second, corresponding to the existing monochrome service. The Radio Corporation of America (RCA) demonstrated its dot-sequential color system in which color is assigned to successive picture elements, or dots, of the image. With this system, each line of any field is composed of dots in the colors of red, blue, and green. The scanning system for this color design (525/60) was also identical to the existing monochrome standard. Both the CTI and RCA color system were formally proposed to the commission as potential standards. In addition to these proposals, preliminary development of several other color systems were also presented. To many of the industry witnesses appearing before the commission, the demonstrations and discussions indicated that a satisfactory compatible system could be developed in a reasonable period of time, and they urged that a decision regarding color be postponed.

Examining the various proposed color systems, the FCC determined that the shortcomings of the compatible systems were fundamental and noted that if a viable alternative compatible system could not be developed and the field-sequential color system was eventually adopted, the costs of modifying an even greater number of monochrome receivers would be prohibitive, denying the public color service altogether. The commission therefore concluded that it was unwise to delay the decision and on October 10, 1950, decided that the adoption of the color field-sequential system proposed by CBS was in the public interest. RCA appealed this decision all the way to the Supreme Court, but the commission's actions were upheld. The CBS station in New York began regular color broadcasts on June 25, 1951. However, because of the military demands of the Korean War and the reallocation of resources toward the war effort, color receiver production could not be dramatically increased. On October 19, 1951, CBS discontinued color broadcasts due to the limited numbers of color receivers.

It was in this context that the NTSC, the entity that played a key role in setting monochrome standards in the United States, was reactivated to investigate the status of compatible color systems. On July 21, 1953, two years after its first meeting, the second NTSC approved a compatible all-electronic color television dot-sequential system (a modified version of RCA's system) and petitioned the FCC for adoption. On December 17, 1953, the FCC formally adopted a compatible color standard.

After the color standard was set in 1953, broadcasting stations were fairly quick to upgrade their transmission facilities to provide for color programming. Of the 158 stations operating in the top 40 cities, 106 had adopted color capabilities by 1957. Color programming offerings, however, remained fairly limited for quite some time. Although NBC increased its output of color programming to help its parent company, RCA, sell color receivers, the other major networks were not as supportive of this new innovation. As late as 1965, CBS provided only 800 hours of color programming for the entire year, and ABC only 600 hours. In addition to the limited programming, early sets were somewhat cumbersome to adjust for proper color reception, receiver prices remained fairly high, and manufacturers were reluctant to promote color receivers until the lucrative black-and-white market had been saturated. Consequently, consumers were fairly slow to adopt color technology. As of 1965, only 10 percent of U.S. homes had a color set. It was not until the late 1960s, more than a decade after the standard was set, that color TV sales rose significantly. Today, approximately 95 percent of all U.S. homes have color television.

DAVID F. DONNELLY

See also **Technology, Television**

Further Reading

Crane, Rhonda J., *The Politics of International Standards: France and the Color TV War,* Norwood, New Jersey: Ablex, 1979

Fink, D., editor, *Color Television Standards: Selected Papers and Records of the National Television System Committee,* New York: McGraw-Hill, 1955

Radio Corporation of America, *Petition of Radio Corporation of America and National Broadcasting Company, Inc. for Approval of Color Standards for the RCA Color Television System,* New York: Federal Communications Commission, 1953

Rzeszewski, T., editor, *Color Television,* New York: Institute of Electrical and Electronics Engineers Press, 1983

Sterling, Christopher H., and John M. Kittross, *Stay Tuned: A Concise History of American Broadcasting,* Belmont, California: Wadsworth, 1978; 3rd edition, Mahwah, New Jersey: Erlbaum, 2002

Colorization

Colorization is a computerized process that adds color to a black-and-white movie or TV program. The process was invented by Wilson Markle and was first used in 1970 to add color to monochrome footage of the moon from the Apollo mission. In 1983 Markle founded Colorization, Inc. The word "colorization" soon became a generic name for the adding of color to black-and-white footage.

The process of colorizing a movie begins with a monochrome film print, preferably a new print struck from the original negative. From the film print, a high-quality videotape copy is made. Technicians, aided by a computer, determine the gray level of every object in every shot and note any movement of objects within shots. A computer adds color to each object, while keeping gray levels the same as in the monochrome original. Which color to use for which object is determined through common sense (green for grass, blue for the ocean) or by investigation. For example, movie studio photographs or costume vaults may provide guidance as to what color a hat should be. In cases where no such guidance is available, colorists pick their own colors, presumably with some aesthetic sensibility.

Colorization is an expensive and time-consuming process. *Popular Mechanics* reported in 1987 that colorizing a movie cost more than $3,000 per minute of running time. The economic justification for such an expenditure lay in audience demand. *Variety* estimated in 1988 that while it cost $300,000 to colorize an old movie, the revenue generated by the release of the colorized version was $500,000. This revenue came mostly from television syndication, although videocassette release was also important in some cases. Another important consideration was the opportunity to claim new copyrights on old films, thus extending the film's potential life as a profit center for the owner.

Colorization became extremely controversial in the late 1980s, especially with regard to "classic" monochrome films such as *Citizen Kane* (which ultimately was not colorized), *Casablanca, The Maltese Falcon,* and *It's a Wonderful Life.* With some exceptions, the dispute pitted film directors and critics (who opposed colorization) against copyright owners (who favored it). Among its opponents, TV critic Eric Mink viewed colorization as a "bastardization" of film. The Writers Guild of America West called it "cultural vandalism."

The case against colorization is most often couched in moral terms. According to this reasoning, colorization violates the moral right of the film director to create a work of art that has a final, permanent form and that will not be subject to alteration years later by unauthorized parties. *Moral* rights of artists, recognized in other countries, have no standing in U.S. law, which gives preference to the *property* rights of copyright holders. In film and television, the copyright holder is almost always a large film studio or production company, which employs the director as an author-for-hire, so to speak. To an extent, the battle over colorization was an attempt by directors and other creative artists to prevent further erosion of their power to control their own work.

This position was often framed, somewhat spuriously, in more high-minded terms. For example, it was argued that colorization is an affront to film history. According to this line of thinking, the color version of a film drives the original monochrome version out of circulation, with the result that some viewers may not understand that *Casablanca* was shot in black and white. Similarly, as Stuart Klawans notes, the viewer might erroneously conclude that a color film such as *Gone with the Wind* was originally shot in monochrome and later colorized. If colorization can deceive to this extent, it must have a fairly convincing appearance, and, indeed, image quality and craftsmanship were probably the least-often-heard objections to colorizing.

As more movie "classics" became involved, the reaction against colorization took on the flavor of a moral panic. With colorization frequently the object of ridicule, the case in favor of the process became largely a defensive one: colorization does not harm the black-and-white original, and in fact it encourages restoration of the original film and the striking of new prints; colorization is no more meddlesome than other, generally accepted practices in the televising of movies, such as interruption for commercials, editing for TV, cropping, time compression, and panning and scanning (not to mention the reduction in image size and the possibility of watching a color movie on a monochrome TV set); finally, any viewer who is offended by the color image can turn off the chroma on the TV set and watch in black and white.

It is worth emphasizing that the product of colorization is a video recording, not a film print. When a movie is colorized, nothing bad happens to the original film print, and the colorized version can only be watched on TV. Ultimately, the greatest impact of colorization may be upon old, monochrome TV series, if and when colorization loses its stigma. Indeed, one of the original ideas behind colorization was the creation of quasi-new TV series. As Earl Glick put it in 1984, "You couldn't make *Wyatt Earp* today for $1 million an episode. But for $50,000 a segment, you can turn it into color and have a brand new series—with no residuals to pay." As logical as this may sound, only *McHale's Navy* and a few other series have been colorized.

The controversy surrounding colorization rapidly died down after the late 1980s. Demand for colorized movies declined drastically. Ted Turner, owner of hundreds of MGM, Warner Bros., and RKO titles and colorization's most outspoken advocate at the height of the controversy, quietly stopped releasing colorized movies. As of 2001, existing colorized versions of movies and TV programs are only rarely aired on TV, and not many titles are available in video stores. The main legacy of colorization is the National Film Registry, established by Congress in 1988 in response to the colorization controversy. The registry is a list of films, selected by experts and expanded annually, that, if colorized, will have to be labeled with a disclaimer. As Klawans points out, the hundreds of thousands of dollars spent on compiling the registry would be much better spent on actual film (not to mention television) preservation.

GARY BURNS

See also **Movies on Television**

Further Reading

Cooper, Roger, "Colorization and Moral Rights: Should the United States Adopt Unified Protection for Artists?" *Journalism Quarterly* (autumn 1991)

Daniels, Charles B., "Note on Colourization," *British Journal of Aesthetics* (January 1990)

Dawson, Greg, "Ted Turner: Let Others Tinker with the Message. He Transforms the Medium Itself," interview, *American Film* (January–February 1989)

Leibowitz, Flo, "Movie Colorization and the Expression of Mood," *Journal of Aesthetics and Art Criticism* (Fall 1991)

Library of Congress, Copyright Office, *Technological Alterations to Motion Pictures: Implications for Creators, Copyright Owners, and Consumers: A Report of the Register of Copyrights,* Washington, D.C.: U.S. Copyright Office, 1989

Sherman, Barry L., "Perceptions of Colorization," *Journalism Quarterly* (Winter 1988)
U.S. Congress, House of Representatives, *Moral Rights and the Motion Picture Industry: Hearing Before the Subcommittee on Courts, Intellectual Property, and the Administration of Justice,* Washington, D.C.: U.S. Government Printing Office, 1991
Wagner, Craig A., "Motion Picture Colorization, Authenticity, and the Elusive Moral Right," *New York University Law Review* (June 1989)

Coltrane, Robbie (1950–)

British Actor

Robbie Coltrane is one of Britain's most popular and versatile actors. During the 1980s, he became a household name following a succession of spirited comedic stage, cinema, and small-screen appearances. In the 1990s, Coltrane's celebrity developed internationally, with his acting repertoire maturing to include dramatic roles, as befitted his more mellow temperament and professional confidence.

In the mid-1970s, Coltrane became involved in repertory theater in Edinburgh, before a brief stint in New York, where he participated in several experimental films. Returning to England, Coltrane achieved his first major stage success in *The Slab Boys,* a bittersweet trilogy about Glaswegian youth written by ex–college mate John Byrne. Relocating to London in the early 1980s, Coltrane became associated with the city's burgeoning, politically charged stand-up comedy movement. There he headlined alongside the likes of Rik Mayall, Jennifer Saunders, Ade Edmondson, and Dawn French—to name only a few of the talents who would soon become, collectively and individually, the core of British broadcasting's "alternative" comedy. Coltrane's first television credits were earned in various programs, taking first sketch then narrative forms, centered around the satirical humor generated by this new-wave troupe. He costarred in *A Kick Up the Eighties* and *Laugh??? I Nearly Paid My Licence Fee;* he was a regular in *The Comic Strip Presents;* and he frequently appeared as minor characters in shows such as *Blackadder's Christmas Carol.*

Effortlessly humorous, yet sharply critical, Coltrane proved to be an immediate audience favorite. Full-bodied and unpretentious, the Scotsman was often bracketed with his fellow comedic social commentator Alexei Sayle. But whereas Sayle was manic and edgy, constantly exposing his personal identity, Coltrane's exuberant delivery was channeled into his role-playing and his amazing ability to parody the self-righteous through imitation. The Scot's capacity to produce more mainstream material is evident in his prodigious work record, his marketability as a celebrity endorser of commercial products, and his mass appeal across a variety of audiences and age groups.

Coltrane's enthusiasm for his performances is unassailable. His own personal passions and vices—chain-smoking, 1950s cars, an appreciation for the style (if not the substance) of Chandleresque masculinity—have become recurrent motifs that function as backdrops to his stage and screen personae. Since the mid-1980s, Coltrane has rapidly progressed from supporting roles in such successful feature films as *Mona Lisa* and *Defence of the Realm* to made-to-measure, screen-stealing leads in *Henry V* (an homage to Orson Welles amid a tribute to Sir Laurence Olivier), *Nuns on the Run,* and *The Pope Must Die!* Occasionally miscast as a genial funnyman, Coltrane has starred in his share of lightweight comedies. However, as a known box-office property, he is now able to choose his Hollywood offers more selectively—for example, electing to play the villain in the James Bond revivals *Goldeneye* (1995) and *The World Is Not Enough* (1999), and taking on the role of Hagrid the giant caretaker in the blockbuster *Harry Potter and the Philosopher's Stone* (2001; U.S. release as *Harry Potter and the Sorcerer's Stone*).

Coltrane's maturity as a thespian has been achieved less in cinema than on the stage and in his television performances, where his ability to convincingly portray complex characters and convey contradictory emotions has more fully developed. His own enigmatic personality (jocular and acutely perceptive, sensitive, forthright, both worldly and down-to-earth) combined with his penchant for panache (with its mixture of grand style and garish display) often surface in his TV roles. As Danny McGlone in the hit 1987 miniseries *Tutti Frutti,* Coltrane portrayed the endearing,

Robbie Coltrane.
Courtesy of the Everett Collection

egotistical front man of the Majestics, a group of aging rock 'n' rollers touring Scotland in search of newfound fame and fortune. The critical and popular acclaim accorded this black comedy was due in large measure to the affectionately self-mocking tone of John Byrnes's screenplays. He and Coltrane again collaborated several years later on the seriocomic historical adaptation *Boswell and Johnson's Tour of the Western Isles.* Coltrane's theatrical versatility, comedic range, and gallery of accents were evident in his interpretation of Dario Fo's antiestablishment satire *Mistero Buffo.* Juggling the anger, hostility, and humor of the numerous characterizations required in this one-man show, Coltrane performed the play at British venues in 1990, prior to its broadcast as a BBC miniseries.

That year marked a turning point for the Scotsman, who married and retreated to the more sedate pace of a converted Stirlingshire farmhouse. Proclaiming his hell-raising years to be over, Coltrane consciously sought dramatic roles. In a part written for him by social realist Jimmy McGovern, Coltrane played Dr. Eddie Fitzgerald, a forensic psychologist for the Manchester police force, in Granada TV's *Cracker.* "Fitz" applies his incredible mental agility to outwit suspects and solve a series of heinous crimes, all the while evidencing shortcomings of his own brought on by personal overindulgence and "deviant" behavior (drinking, smoking, debt, domestic ruin). Extremely well received in Britain and North America, *Cracker*'s nine stories represent Coltrane's most accomplished screen performance to date—one rewarded with numerous industry honors, including the British Academy of Film and Television Arts' Award for Best Television Actor in 1995.

MATTHEW MURRAY

See also ***Cracker***

Robbie Coltrane. Born Anthony McMillan in Rutherglen, Glasgow, Scotland, March 31, 1950. Attended Trinity College, Glenalmond, Perthshire; Glasgow School of Art. One son with partner Rhona Irene Gemmell. Began career as actor with the Traverse Theatre Company and Borderline Theatre Company, Edinburgh; worked briefly as stand-up comedian in the United States, late 1970s, then returned to England to appear in various alternative television comedy shows and dramas; subsequently established reputation as character actor in films; returned to the United States to develop film career, 1989. Recipient: Montreux Television Festival Silver Rose Award, 1987; *Evening Standard* Peter Sellers Award, 1991; British Academy of Film and Television Arts Award, 1993, 1994, 1995; Monte Carlo Silver Nymph Best Actor Award, 1994; BPG Best Actor Award, 1994; Royal Television Society Best Actor Award, 1994; FIPA (French Academy) Best Actor Award, 1994; Cable Ace Best Actor Award, 1994; Cannes Film Festival Best Actor Award, 1994.

Television Series

1981–84	*A Kick Up the Eighties*
1987	*Tutti Frutti*
1992	*Coltrane in a Cadillac*
1993	*Boswell and Johnson's Tour of the Western Isles*
1993–96	*Cracker*

Made-for-Television Movies

1991	*Alive and Kicking*
1997	*Ebb Tide*
2000	*Alice in Wonderland*

Television Specials (selected)

1981	*81 Take 2*
1982–92	*The Comic Strip Presents* ("Five Go Mad in Dorset," "Beat Generation," "War," "Summer School," "Five Go Mad on Mescaline," "The Strike," "Gino: Full Story and Pics," "GLC," "South Atlantic Raiders," "Demonella," "Jealousy")
1983	*The Crystal Cube*
1985	*Laugh??? I Nearly Paid My Licence Fee*
1986	*Hooray for Hollywood*
1988	*Blackadder's Christmas Carol*
1990	*Mistero Buffo*
1992	*Open to Question*

Films

Flash Gordon, 1980; *Subway Riders,* 1981; *Krull,* 1983; *Chinese Boxes,* 1984; *Ghost Dance,* 1984; *Loose Connections,* 1984; *Scrubbers,* 1984; *The Supergrass,* 1985; *Revolution,* 1985; *National Lampoon's European Vacation,* 1985; *Defence of the Realm,* 1985; *Mona Lisa,* 1986; *The Secret Policeman's Third Ball,* 1987; *Caravaggio,* 1986; *Absolute Beginners,* 1986; *Eat the Rich,* 1987; *The Fruit Machine,* 1988; *Wonderland,* 1988; *Slipstream,* 1989; *Danny, the Champion of the World,* 1989; *Lenny—Live and Unleashed,* 1989; *Let It Ride,* 1989; *Henry V,* 1989; *Bert Rigby, You're a Fool,* 1989; *Where the Heart Is,* 1990; *Nuns on the Run,* 1990; *Perfectly Normal,* 1990; *The Pope Must Die!* (U.S.: *The Pope Must Diet!*), 1991; *Triple Bogey on a Par 5 Hole,* 1992; *Oh, What a Night,* 1992; *The Adventures of Huckleberry Finn,* 1993; *Goldeneye,* 1995; *Buddy,* 1997; *Montana,* 1998; *Frogs for Snakes,* 1998; *Message in a Bottle,* 1999; *The World Is Not Enough,* 1999; *From Hell,* 2001; *On the Nose,* 2001; *Harry Potter and the Philosopher's Stone* (U.S. release as *Harry Potter and the Sorcerer's Stone*), 2001; *Harry Potter and the Chamber of Secrets,* 2002; *Harry Potter and the Prisoner of Azkaban,* 2004.

Stage (selected)

Slab Boys Trilogy; Yr Obedient Servant, 1987; *Mistero Buffo,* 1990.

Publication

Coltrane in a Cadillac, 1993

Further Reading

Cosgrove, Stuart, "History Is Bunk," *New Statesman and Society* (February 16, 1990)

Leith, William, "A Big Star, but Shrinking," *The Independent* (May 16, 1993)

Linklater, Andro, "On the Road with Johnson and Boswell and Co.," *Daily Telegraph* (September 11, 1993)

Wilmut, Roger, and Peter Rosengard, *Didn't You Kill My Mother-in-Law?: The Story of Alternative Comedy in Britain from The Comedy Store to Saturday Live,* London: Methuen, 1989

Columbia Broadcasting System

U.S. Network

The network Columbia Broadcasting System (CBS), traditionally referred to as the "Tiffany network" among major television broadcasting systems, has in recent years come more and more to resemble Wal-Mart. Ironically, this often prestige-laden television institution began almost as an afterthought. In 1927, when David Sarnoff did not see fit to include any of talent agent Arthur Judson's clients in his roster of stars for the new NBC radio networks, Judson defiantly founded his own network—United Independent Broadcasters. Soon merged with the Columbia Phonograph Company, the network went on the air on September 18, 1927, as the Columbia Phonograph Broadcasting Company. Within a year, heavy losses compelled the sale of the company to Jerome Louchheim and Ike and Leon Levy, the latter the fiancée of the sister of William Paley. Paley, who had become enamored of radio as a result of advertising the family's La Palina brand cigars over a local station, bought the fledgling network, then consisting of 22 affiliates and 16 employees, for $400,000 on January 18, 1929, and renamed it the Columbia Broadcasting System.

Courtesy of CBS Worldwide, Inc.

Relatively untested as a business executive, Paley immediately showed himself a superb entrepreneur. He ensured the success of the new network by offering affiliates free programming in exchange for an option on advertising time, and he was extremely aggressive in gaining advertising for the network. Paley's greatest gift, however, was in recognizing talent. He soon signed singers such as Bing Crosby, Kate Smith, and Morton Downey for the network. Unfortunately, as soon as some of them gained fame at CBS, they were lured away by the far richer and more popular NBC.

This pattern of losing talent to the competition was not to be repeated in the news realm. Starved for programming, Paley initially allowed his network to be used by the likes of the demagogic Father Charles Coughlin. By 1931, however, Paley had terminated Coughlin's broadcasts, and under the aegis of former *New York Times* editor Edward Klauber and ex–United Press reporter Paul White, he began building a solid news division.

CBS News did not come of age, however, until Klauber assigned the young Edward R. Murrow to London as director of European talks. On March 13, 1937, at the time of the Anschluss, Murrow teamed with former newspaper foreign correspondent William L. Shirer and a number of others to describe those events in what would become the forerunner of *The CBS World News Roundup.* Subsequently, during World War II, Murrow assembled a brilliant team of reporters, known collectively as "Murrow's Boys," including Eric Sevareid, Charles Collingwood, Howard K. Smith, Winston Burdett, Richard K. Hottelet, and Larry LeSueur.

In 1948 Paley turned the tables on NBC and signed some of its premier talent, including Jack Benny, Red Skelton, and George Burns and Gracie Allen. He also stole a march on his rival in what NBC considered its undisputed realm—technology—when his CBS Research Center, under the direction of the brilliant inventor Peter Goldmark, developed the long-playing (LP) phonograph recording technique and color television.

Even with this success, Paley was still loathe to enter television broadcasting. However, with prodding from Frank Stanton, whom he had appointed CBS president in 1946, and his growing awareness of how rapidly television was expanding, Paley began increasing CBS investment in television programming. Indeed, with the talent that CBS had taken from NBC and homegrown artists and programming such as *I Love Lucy, Ed Sullivan, Arthur Godfrey,* and *Gunsmoke,* CBS dominated in the audience ratings race for almost 20 years.

The postwar years were hardly an undisturbed triumphal march for CBS. During the McCarthy era, the network found itself dubbed the "Communist Broadcasting System" by conservatives. Nor did CBS distinguish itself by requiring loyalty oaths of its staff and hiring a former FBI man as head of a loyalty clearance office. These actions were, however, redeemed to a large extent by Murrow's March 9, 1954, *See It Now* broadcast investigating Senator Joseph R. McCarthy. Unfortunately, Murrow's penchant for controversy tarnished him in the eyes of many CBS executives, and shortly thereafter, in 1961, he resigned to head the U.S. Information Agency.

More and more the news division, which thought of itself as the crown jewel at CBS, found itself subordinate to the entertainment values of the company, a trend highlighted at the end of the 1950s by the quiz show scandals. Indeed, Paley, who had taken CBS public in 1937, now seemed to make profits his priority. Perhaps the clearest evidence of this development occurred when Fred Friendly, one of Murrow's closest associates and then CBS News division president, resigned after reruns of *I Love Lucy* were shown instead of the 1966 Senate hearings on the Vietnam War.

This tendency to emphasize entertainment over news was only exacerbated in the 1960s, when, despite almost universal critical disdain, *The Beverly Hillbillies, Green Acres,* and *Petticoat Junction* were CBS's biggest hits. However, in the early 1970s, CBS abruptly shifted away from these programs, as programming executives Robert Wood and Fred Silverman inaugurated a series of sitcoms such as *All in the Family, The Mary Tyler Moore Show,* and *M*A*S*H.* These changes had less to do with any contempt for the rural idiocy of the "barnyard comedies" than the network's need to appeal to a younger, urban audience with larger disposable incomes. However, the newer programs, with their socially conscious themes, garnered both audience and critical acclaim.

During these years, profits increased to such an extent that by 1974 the Columbia Broadcasting System had become CBS, Inc., and consisted not only of radio and TV networks but a publishing division (Holt, Reinhart, and Winston), a magazine division (*Woman's Day*), a recording division (Columbia Records), and even for a time the New York Yankees (1964–73). Nevertheless, CBS, Inc., was hardly serene. Indeed, it was quite agitated over the question of who would succeed Paley.

In violation of his own rule, Paley refused to retire. He did, however, force the 1973 retirement of his logical heir, Stanton. Paley then installed and quickly forced the resignation of Arthur Taylor, John Backe, and Thomas Wyman as presidents and chief executive officers of CBS. Anxiety about the succession at CBS began to threaten the network's independence. Declining ratings left the company vulnerable. The biggest threat came from a takeover bid by cable mogul Ted Turner. To defend itself against a takeover, CBS turned to the president of the Loew's chain of movie theaters, Laurence Tisch, who soon owned a 25 percent share in the company and became president and CEO in 1986.

Within a year, Tisch's cuts in personnel and budget, and his sale of assets such as the recording, magazines, and publishing divisions, had alienated many. Dan Rather, who had succeeded the avuncular Walter Cronkite as the anchor on *The CBS Evening News* in 1981, wrote a scathing *New York Times* commentary called "From Murrow to Mediocrity." By 1990, the year of Paley's death, *The CBS Evening News,* which had led in the ratings for 18 years under Cronkite, and for a long period under Rather, fell to number three in the rankings.

After what seemed a brief ratings resurrection resulting from the success of the 1992 Winter Olympics, and the 1993 coup of wresting late-night host David Letterman away from NBC, CBS was outbid for the television rights to National Football League (NFL) games by the fledgling FOX network and watched the defection of 12 choice affiliates to the same company. Despite repeated denials that the company was for sale, Tisch shopped it to prospective buyers such as former Paramount and FOX president Barry Diller. In November 1995, CBS was sold to the Westinghouse Corporation for $5.4 billion, effectively bringing to a close CBS's history as an independent company.

In 1996 Westinghouse, under the leadership of its CEO Michael Jordan, merged with Infinity Broadcasting Corporation. The CEO of Infinity, Mel Karmazin, became the largest shareholder in the merged company, which was renamed CBS Corporation in 1997. In 1998 CBS reacquired the rights to NFL football for eight years for $4 billion dollars. The price of CBS stock fell as a result of this deal, and Karmazin supplanted Jordan as the CEO of the company. Realizing that the company was too small to stand on its own in an era of media megamergers such as that of Disney and ABC-TV, Karmazin successfully concluded a deal with Viacom's CEO Sumner Redstone to sell CBS for $37.3 billion in 1999. Karmazin became the chief operating officer of Viacom. Because Viacom already owned a network, the fledgling United Paramount Network (UPN), the Federal Communications Commission (FCC) carefully scrutinized this deal before finally permitting the duopoly.

Viacom's purchase of CBS coincided with an increase in the network's ratings. Despite Wall Street's misgivings, the NFL deal turned out to be profitable. In addition, in the summer of 2000, CBS introduced a miniseries called *Survivor,* which quickly was dubbed "reality TV." The program involved a group of people selected by the producers, such as the mephistophelean Richard Hatch, who were placed on a remote Pacific island and then tested with various trials that pitted one group against another until only one person remained. This individual was then awarded $1 million. The final episode of the first series received Super Bowl–like ratings and launched a trend of reality TV shows on virtually every network. While later editions of *Survivor* have not matched the hype or the ratings of the first version, they have performed well against stiff competition, such as NBC's hit sitcom *Friends.* In addition to *Survivor,* CBS's programming chief, Leslie Moonves, can also take credit for scheduling sitcoms such as *Everybody Loves Raymond* and *Becker* and dramas such as *C.S.I.* and *Judging Amy* that helped raise CBS's ratings in the early 21st century. In another key move to keep CBS's entertainment division healthy, Moonves managed to sign David Letterman in 2002 to a multiyear contract, thereby thwarting a highly publicized attempt by ABC to lure away the host of *The Late Show.*

Unfortunately for its network, in the early 2000s, CBS News continued to languish in third place in the network news race. However, *The CBS Evening News* under the aegis of Rather regarded itself as a "hard news" show that did not indulge in the soft features such as health, entertainment, and lifestyle news that appeared so frequently on its rivals. This dedication to hard news was most prominently on display during the summer of 2001, when *The CBS Evening News* stood out in its determination not to indulge in the media frenzy that surrounded the possible involvement of California congressman Gary Condit in the disappearance of Chandra Levy, who interned in Condit's Washington office. Needless to say, it was efforts such as these that helped restore some of the sheen to the reputation of CBS that it had lost during the Tisch years.

Albert Auster

Further Reading

Benjamin, Burton, *Fair Play: CBS, General Westmoreland, and How a Television Documentary Went Wrong,* New York: Harper and Row, 1988

Gates, Gary Paul, *Air Time: The Inside Story of CBS News,* New York: Harper and Row, 1978

Goldmark, Peter C., *Maverick Inventor: My Turbulent Years at CBS,* New York: Saturday Review Press, 1973

Joyce, Ed, *Prime Time, Bad Times,* New York: Doubleday, 1988

McCabe, Peter, *Bad News at Black Rock: The Sell-out of CBS News,* New York: Arbor House, 1987

Murray, Michael D., *The Political Performers: CBS Broadcasts in the Public Interests,* Westport, Connecticut: Praeger, 1994

Paley, William S., *As It Happened: A Memoir,* Garden City, New York: Doubleday, 1979

Paper, Lewis J., *Empire: William S. Paley and the Making of CBS,* New York: St. Martin's Press, 1987

Slater, Robert, *This Is CBS: A Chronicle of 60 Years,* Englewood Cliffs, New Jersey: Prentice Hall, 1988

Smith, Sally Bedell, *In All His Glory: The Life of William S. Paley, the Legendary Tycoon and His Brilliant Circle,* New York: Simon and Schuster, 1990

Winans, Christopher, *The King of Cash: The Inside Story of Laurence A. Tisch and How He Bought CBS,* New York: Wiley, 1995

Columbo

U.S. Police Drama

Columbo was a popular detective series featuring Peter Falk as Lieutenant Columbo. The character (who never had a first name) and the series were a creation of the writing/producing team of Richard Levinson and William Link. *Columbo* ran as a television series from 1971 to 1978, but the character had appeared in a short story, a live-television broadcast, and a stage play before making his first network television appearance in the made-for-television movie *Prescription: Murder* (1968). Originally written for Bing Crosby, the Columbo role went to Falk when Crosby opted not to end his retirement.

The series' original run was not in weekly hour-long episodes, but as a 90-minute "spoke" in the *NBC Mystery Movie* "wheel" concept: each week, one of three different series was shown on a rotating basis. *Columbo* was interspersed with *McMillan and Wife* (starring Rock Hudson and Susan St. James) and *McCloud* (starring Dennis Weaver). This suited Falk and the producers just fine since the pace of production would be much slower than was usually the case with weekly series. The 90-minute program length also allowed each episode to be more intricate than the typical one-hour installment, and intricacy was stock in trade for the character.

Columbo was not a whodunit. Indeed, the most distinguishing aspect of the series is the plot structure itself. Although this structure is just as rigid and successful as that in *Perry Mason, Dragnet,* or *The Rockford Files,* each episode is actually an inversion of the classic detective formula. In the classic formula, the crime is committed by an unknown person, a detective comes onto the case, clues are gathered, the detective solves the crime with the aid of his or her assistants, and the ability of the detective is proven true. In each *Columbo* plot, the crime *and* the culprit are shown in great detail. The audience sees the murder planned, committed, and covered up by the murderer. Since the audience knows who did it and how, the enigma becomes "How will Columbo figure it out?" The methods of the murderer are presented with such care that there is little doubt that the horrible crime will go unpunished—little doubt until Columbo comes onto the scene.

With his rumpled overcoat, stubby cigar, tousled hair, and (apparently) confused attitude, Columbo rambles around in his old Peugeot, doggedly following the suspect of a homicide. The attitude and behavior, however, are all an act. Columbo is not confused but acutely aware, like a falcon circling its prey, waiting for a moment of weakness. Columbo bumbles about, often interfering with the activities of the uniformed police and gathering what seem to be the most unimportant clues. All the while, he constantly pesters the person he has pegged as his central suspect.

At first, even the murderer is amused at the lieutenant's style and usually seems inclined to assume that if this is the best the Los Angeles police can offer, the murder will never be found out. But whenever the suspect seems to be rid of the lieutenant, Columbo turns with a bemused remark, something like "Oh, there's just one more thing...." By the end of the episode, Columbo has taken an apparently mi-

Columbo, Peter Falk, 1971–93.
Courtesy of the Everett Collection

nor discrepancy in the murderer's story and wound it into the noose with which to hang the suspect. Conclusions often feature a weary, yet agreeable, criminal admitting to his or her guilt as Columbo, in the form of some imaginative turnabout, delivers the final blow. If the suspect is a magician, the lieutenant uses a magic "trick." If the crime was done by knowledge of movie special effects, Columbo uses similar special effects.

Columbo is the only regular character in the series. There is no grizzled police commissioner, no confidant with whom the case could be discussed. For Columbo, each guest villain becomes something of an ironic "Watson." Columbo and the murderer spend most of the story playing off each other. The lieutenant discusses the twists and turns of the case, the possible motives, the implications of clues with his primary suspect, always rich, powerful, and arrogant, always happy to match wits with the apparently witless policeman on the doorstep. In the end, the working-class hero overcomes the wealthy, privileged criminal.

Many writers, directors, and producers influential in the 1980s and 1990s worked on this series. Stephen J. Cannell (*The Rockford Files, The A-Team, Wiseguy*), Peter S. Fisher (*Murder, She Wrote*), and Steven Bochco (*L.A. Law, Hill Street Blues*) were writers. Dean Hargrove (*Matlock, Perry Mason*) and Roland Kibbee (*Barney Miller*) were producers. The premiere episode was directed by a very young Steven Spielberg. Each episode featured a well-known character actor or minor star as the murderer. Robert Culp and Jack Cassidy had the highest number of returns as guest villain (three each).

Columbo won seven Emmys over the first run of the series, including three for Falk and one for the series itself. *Columbo* spawned only one spin-off, NBC's short-lived *Mrs. Columbo* (name later changed to *Kate Columbo, Kate the Detective,* and *Kate Loves a Mystery*) with Kate Mulgrew in the title role. This series played against *Columbo* in several ways. Instead of Mrs. Columbo being absent each episode (as she was from the original series), the lieutenant was "unavailable." And here the plot followed the traditional detective format instead of the inverted one. It is not clear what caused this series to fail, but *Mrs. Columbo* was ill-fated and ill-advised. Both Link and Levinson disavowed it, and Falk disliked the concept.

Following the success of Raymond Burr's return as Perry Mason in a series of made-for-television movies, Falk returned to *Columbo* on February 6, 1989, for a new "mystery wheel" concept (this time on ABC and alternating with Burt Reynolds in *B.L. Stryker* and Lou Gossett, Jr., in *Gideon Oliver*). Just as he left Rock Hudson and Dennis Weaver behind during his original run, the rumpled detective was the only one of the new "wheel" to survive. Indeed, like the character, *Columbo* always seems to be coming back as if to say, "Oh, there's just one more thing. . . ."

J. Dennis Bounds

See also **Falk, Peter; Link, William**

Producers

Richard Levinson and William Link, Dean Hargrove, Roland Kibbee, Richard Alan Simmons

Programming History

43 episodes in original series
NBC

September 1971–September 1972	Wednesday 8:30–10:00
September 1972–July 1974	Sunday 8:30–10:00

August 1974–August 1975	Sunday 8:30–10:30
September 1975–September 1976	Sunday 9:00–11:00
October 1976–September 1977	Sunday 8:00–9:30
ABC	
February 1989–May 1989	Monday 9:00–11:00
August 1989–July 1990	Saturday 9:00–11:00
August 1990	Sunday 9:00–11:00
January 1992–May 1992	Thursday 8:00–10:00
November 1992–February 1993	Saturday 8:00–10:00

Further Reading

Dawidziak, Mark, *The Columbo Phile: A Casebook,* New York: Mysterious, 1989

Marc, David, and Robert J. Thompson, *Prime Time, Prime Movers: From I Love Lucy to L.A. Law—America's Greatest TV Shows and the People Who Created Them,* Boston: Little, Brown, 1992

Meyers, Richard, *TV Detectives,* San Diego, California: Barnes, 1988

Meyers, Richard, *Murder on the Air: Television's Great Mystery Series,* New York: Mysterious, 1989

Newcomb, Horace, and Robert S. Alley, *The Producer's Medium: Conversations with Creators of American TV,* New York: Oxford University Press, 1983

Comedy Central

U.S. Cable Network

The first generation of cable channels in the United States focused on niche-programming genres—news, sports, religion, and music—all of which proved successful. By the late 1980s, two media companies believed the same could be true for comedy. On November 15, 1989, Time Warner, through its HBO subsidiary, launched The Comedy Channel with a subscriber base of 4.2 million. On April 1, 1990, Viacom, through its MTV Networks, launched HA!: The TV Comedy Network with 4 million subscribers. Both part-time networks (each network aired only 12 hours of programming a day, while also repeating a large portion of their programming several times each day) faced the same problem: few cable system operators found two comedy channels necessary. The two networks merged in a 50-50 joint ownership agreement between Viacom and Time Warner on April 1, 1991, becoming CTV: The Comedy Network and later renamed Comedy Central, with 12.5 million subscribers.

Early programming on the channel generally consisted of off-net reruns, stand-up comedy routines, British imports, and old movies. The acquisition-heavy lineup included programs such as *Monty Python, Dream On, The Tracey Ullman Show, Fawlty Towers, It's Gary Shandling's Show, Bob and Mary,* and *Saturday Night Live.* Two of the most popular acquisitions in the early years of the network were *Absolutely Fabulous,* a farcical series featuring two boozing, pill-popping middle-aged British women and their social excesses, and *Kids in the Hall,* a sketch-comedy series from a Canadian comedy troupe originally produced for the Canadian Broadcasting Company, CBS, and HBO.

One of the most important early programs appearing on Comedy Central was *Mystery Science Theater 3000* (*MST3K* to its fans). Beginning on HBO's Comedy Channel in 1989 with an original two-hour license fee of $125,000, the low-budget show featured a smart-mouthed janitor and his two robot pals condemned to watch, and offer running commentary on, cheesy B-grade sci-fi movies. The show won a Peabody Award in 1994, and it was nominated for two Emmys and six CableACEs over its seven-year run on the network. As a quirky low-budget show, however, *MST3K* had limited potential for attracting a mass audience.

In order to distinguish itself as a channel worthy of carriage and viewers, the network needed original programming. A cheap programming solution resulted in the network becoming more "topical," developing programming based on news and political events. One of the first efforts was its controversial satirical treatment of President George Bush's 1992 State of the Union Address, presented as the speech was being delivered. Titled "*State of the Union—Undressed,*" a panel of "commentators" (comedians) offered their humorous opinions during the natural pauses and breaks for applause throughout the speech (similar in format to an *MST3K* episode). The broadcast was a success, for the network not only doubled its January ratings but also garnered high-profile press coverage from the First Amendment–related controversy.

By April, the network had decided to continue its satirical treatment of politics by covering both the Democratic and Republican presidential nominating conventions to be held that summer. Labeled "*Indecision '92*" (the first of similar broadcasts during the 1996 and 2000 presidential elections), the network aired two hours of coverage each night of the Democratic and Republican conventions, offering what it called a "raised eye brow approach" to the proceedings for interested but bored convention viewers (Du Brow).

Though television critics and viewers warmly received these efforts, special-event coverage was not enough to convince many cable operators to include the channel in their lineup. Executives at the network were still clamoring for a signature show that would give the network an identity and get people talking about the network. In 1993 the network achieved that success with *Politically Incorrect,* a political discussion show hosted by comedian Bill Maher. *Politically Incorrect* was an original twist on two existing talk show genres, the political pundit and entertainment-variety talk shows. Featuring Maher and four nonexperts on politics discussing current events, the show garnered favorable reviews from critics as a smart, original, and daring contribution to American public discourse. The show became the network's flagship program in its search for brand identity (while continuing its success with political satire) and eventually ran for four seasons on Comedy Central before moving to the ABC network in early 1997—one of the first instances of programming moving from cable to a broadcast network.

Knowing that *Politically Incorrect* would depart at the end of the 1996 season, CEO Doug Herzog and programming chief Eileen Katz, both newly arrived from tenures at MTV, sought not only to find a replacement for *Politically Incorrect* but also to direct the network's focus to a younger audience. The first significant step in that regard was *The Daily Show,* a caustic news and talk show hosted by former ESPN SportsCenter anchor Craig Kilborn. *The Daily Show* is, as one critic described it, the network's "half-hour send up of news programs in general and sanctimonious news programs in particular" (Strum). Comedian Jon Stewart replaced host Kilborn in 1999, and the show received a Peabody Award in 2001.

With *The Daily Show* as its programming anchor, the network began a series of innovative and popular original programming moves under the tenure of Herzog (1995–98). On July 28, 1997, the game show *Win Ben Stein's Money* premiered, featuring the dry-witted Ben Stein, a former Nixon speechwriter, as host and co-contestant in a trivia game show. Almost two

Courtesy of Comedy Central

months later, the animated series *South Park* appeared. Developed by former University of Colorado at Boulder students Trey Parker and Matt Stone, the show featured potty-mouthed elementary school children in some of television's most biting social satire. The program became a breakout hit for the network, with $300 million in merchandising revenue in 1998 and a feature movie, *South Park: Bigger, Longer, & Uncut,* in 1999. The program also became one of the highest-rated shows on cable, garnering an 8.2 households (HH) rating in 1998, while helping the network achieve an additional 5 million subscriber homes in just six months' time (Lerman).

By 1999 programming consisted of a 50-50 split between original and acquired shows. With males making up 60 percent of its viewing audience, and 63 percent of the audience between the ages of 18 and 49, the network launched *The Man Show* in 1999, hosted by Jimmy Kimmel (formerly with *Win Ben Stein's Money*) and Adam Corrolla (from MTV's *Loveline*). Featuring scantily clad women and beer-drinking hosts and audience members, the show is, as one critic described it, "an unapologetic look at things men think, like and do" (Turegano). In terms of acquisitions, the network also began buying rights in 2000 to edgy new film comedies with marginal box office success (such as *Being John Malkovich, The Man on the Moon, Cecil B. Demented, Rushmore,* and *High Fidelity*).

In 2001 the network sought to combine its own history as a smart and daring political animal with the success of *South Park* by offering *That's My Bush!,* a live-action sitcom by *South Park* creators Trey Parker and Matt Stone. The program was a parody that placed newly elected President George W. Bush and his family in a sitcom setting. Though poking fun at Bush as a dim-witted but affable president, the program was also a send-up of the sitcom genre in general, with "typical" sitcom characters, plotlines, music, and so on. At $1 million an episode, it was the most expensive program in the network's history; it garnered marginal ratings and ran for only eight episodes. The series was daring and controversial, however, for parodying a sitting president and his family in such a scathing manner.

Comedy Central has consistently sought a provocative, edgy, and over-the-top position in the television programming landscape. Network executives contend, however, that they offer more than simply the comedic. "Comedy Central is not a lifestyle channel," one executive stated. "Dare to watch our programs and you might think in a different way" (Endrst). Whether such high-minded posturing is merited is questionable. Nevertheless, Comedy Central has proven to be one of the best locations on television for significant sociopolitical commentary as well as downright base and trivial entertainment.

JEFFREY P. JONES

See also **Comedy, Domestic Settings; *South Park***

Further Reading

Du Brow, Rick, "TV Comedy Channel: Politics and Punch Lines," *Los Angeles Times* (July 4, 1992)

Endrst, James, "Comedy Central Sends 'That's My Bush!' to the Movies," *Hartford Courant* (August 3, 2001)

Goodman, Tim, "Grand Central Station," *San Francisco Chronicle* (April 10, 2001)

Granville, Kari, "Laugh War Produces The Comedy Network," *Los Angeles Times* (April 2, 1991)

Herbert, Steven, "Comedy Central Hopes to Get First Laugh on State of the Union," *Los Angeles Times* (January 28, 1992)

Lerman, Laurence, "Comedy Central Moves Uptown," *Daily Variety* (October 12, 1998)

Strum, Charles, "Taste Schmaste! This Is Just About Laughs," *New York Times* (June 13, 1999)

Turegano, Preston, "Comedy Central; A Farce to be Reckoned With," *San Diego Union-Tribune* (March 10, 2002)

Werts, Diane, " 'Mystery Science Theater' Is Having Its Plug Pulled," *Newsday* (December 14, 1995)

Williams, Scott, "Not the News: Comedy Central Plans Convention Coverage," *Associated Press* (April 27, 1992)

Comedy, Domestic Settings

As was the case with many program formats, television inherited the situation comedy from radio. And again following the patterns of radio, TV sitcoms soon explored generic variations within the form. The two most identifiable versions could be classified as workplace comedies (*The Phil Silvers Show*) and domestic or family comedies (*Leave It to Beaver*). This division follows the underlying appeal of the "situations" themselves, with domestic comedies focused on the drama of family comportment, while workplace comedies deal often with sexual exploration. The latter are driven by sexual chemistry rather than occupational specificity, and routinely focus on characters and relationships rather than workplace situations as such, especially after successful seasons that extend the narrative arc of the series (*Taxi, Cheers, Drop the Dead Donkey*).

From the outset, domestic comedies explored identity and individual roles within the family rather than in the contexts of sexual relationships. In some ways, the form complements the soap opera genre, which specialized in neighborly comportment and focused on the drama among families. Soap opera covered the street, neighborhood, pub, or mall, while in domestic comedies, the point of social congregation was the living room couch (Hartley, p. 172). Like soaps, however, family comedy taught identity formation and life skills (how to talk rather than fight). Interestingly, while domestic comedy remained primarily a prime-time genre, its efficiency in the matter of family role-play and wish fulfillment, and its characterization of the family as a place of leisure, refuge, and talk rather than productivity, danger, and work, also made it a major component of children's TV.

Domestic comedy was well suited for broadcast television production methods, using a studio with one or at most two sets (living room and kitchen) and few or no film inserts. Stable characters in a given situation meant that it could be produced in-house in industrial quantities. It was tolerant of commercial imperatives,

The Munsters, Beverly Owen, Fred Gwynne, Al Lewis, Butch Patrick, Yvonne De Carlo, 1964–66.
Courtesy of the Everett Collection

allowing for segment-length acts, interrupted by commercial breaks, fitting into the TV hour or, more commonly, half hour. It could produce spin-off shows, such as *Rhoda* from the *Mary Tyler Moore* show, *Frasier* from *Cheers,* or *Whatever Happened to the Likely Lads?* from *The Likely Lads.* It was flexible enough to remain recognizable as a genre despite the variety of "situations"—from prehistoric grunts with a Welsh accent in the *Gogs* (S4C in the United Kingdom; FOX Family in the United States; ABC in Australia) to the almost imperially classy *Cosby Show.*

Minority TV channels rarely attempted domestic comedy for general audiences, unless the situation in question was an affront to everything held dear in "normal" families, as in U.K. Channel 4's *The Young Ones* or Fox's *The Simpsons.* Indeed, one of the pleasures of watching "normal" sitcoms was to observe how bizarre some of the family setups were, no matter what their surface smiles suggested about family values. After the pioneering and patriarchal *Father Knows Best,* traditional nuclear families became rarer: solo father and sons in *My Three Sons;* father, uncle, friend, and daughters in *Full House;* father and sons melded with mother and daughters in *The Brady Bunch*—with never an on-screen sexual frisson among them, and no talk of divorce to account for family melding. "Blood families" were monsters (*The Munsters*), witches (*Sabrina the Teenage Witch, Bewitched*), or aliens (*My Favorite Martian, Mork and Mindy, Alf*). This tendency suggests that like modernity, progress, science, and reason themselves, the modern suburban family was shadowed by darker and mostly unspoken "others" from premodern and irrational traditions (Spigel).

The Donna Reed Show, Shelly Fabares, Carl Betz, Donna Reed, Paul Petersen (in back), 1958–66.
Courtesy of the Everett Collection

Within the sphere of everyday ordinariness, then, families were fractured at best. *Cybill* was divorced, *Ellen* was gay, and *Murphy Brown* was a single parent. *One Foot in the Grave* was about a grouchy old man. Where families were intact they were dysfunctional, as in *Married... with Children,* the British *2.4 Children* and *My Family,* and *The Simpsons,* which combined cultural savvy and underlying decency with the most dysfunctional family situations imaginable. Homer Simpson's philosophy of family aspiration ("aim low and miss") began as a comment on the role model fathers of classic sitcoms. Perversely, it made him a more plausible model for many real families than the fathers who "knew best."

The Simpsons joined a long line of animated sitcoms going back to *The Flintstones* and *The Jetsons,* showing how the format could migrate happily away from live action and yet still improve the genre. There were animatronic family comedies too, notably *Dinosaurs*—which correctly identified the god of contemporary family life in its "Fridge Day" episode (see Hartley, pp. 99–107).

Sitcoms' attention to the downside of family life,

Home Improvement, (top) Tim Allen, Jonathan Taylor Thomas, Patricia Richardson, Zachery Ty Bryan, (bot) Taran Noah Smith, TV, 1992 (1991–99).
Courtesy of the Everett Collection

and to some of the grittier issues lurking under suburban consumerism (even as audiences lived in it and endorsed it at elections), made them active in cultural politics. Classic in this respect was *Till Death Us Do Part,* making a national hero out of a working-class bigot whose sexist, racist, xenophobic chauvinism and insularity were mercilessly lampooned by writer Johnny Speight. Speight thought he was inoculating the English against some of their nastier cultural heritage. But they loved Alf Garnett in their millions. In an early example of "re-versioning," Garnett crossed the Atlantic to become Archie Bunker in Norman Lear's *All in the Family,* which also politicized both traditional family values and the sitcom format. *Ellen* sparked public debate about gay and lesbian issues in families just as *Murphy Brown* did about single parents. *Roseanne* put working-class life and nonidealized body shapes into the prime-time sitcom.

Domestic comedies waxed and waned, hitting a low period in the 1980s (before *Cosby*) only to reemerge a little darker and wilder in the 1990s. In the meantime the format gravitated to television for children and adolescents. Here there seemed to be a need to delete the mother from the family in order to propel the situation. The family was intact in *Clarissa Explains It All,* but the perspective was that of the teenage daughter, not the parents (see Hartley, pp. 181–85). In *Sister Sister* the main characters were (and were played by) African-American twins who were supposed to have been brought up separately by different parents not married to each other. The white version of this was *Two of a Kind,* played by the Olsen twins (who debuted as the baby in *Full House*), whose mother was absent. In the highly successful *Sabrina* (Melissa Joan Hart), the central character lived with two witch aunts. *Moesha* featured an all-black leading cast, with a teenage girl (Brandy Norwood) having to deal with her father's new partner and the absence of her natural mother.

Kate & Allie, Jane Curtin and Susan Saint James, 1984–89.
©Reeves Entertainment Group/Courtesy of the Everett Collection

Although ethnic diversity was apparent in some more recent programs and was introduced very early through Lucille Ball's marriage to Cuban-American Desi Arnaz, the sitcom family tended to be monocultural (white or black) and rarely mixed or foreign. Minority identities were slow to appear in domestic comedies, but eventually black and Hispanic (although not Asian, indigenous, or mixed-race) shows proliferated on U.S. TV, leading Herman Gray to comment on the sitcom as "a site of some of the most benign but persistent segregation in American public culture" (Gray, p. 123).

In some cases sitcoms hybridized, joining aspects of the domestic sphere (a focus on living together and the home) with those of the workplace (presence of those beyond the family, presence of sexuality, flirting). *Friends* and *Seinfeld* are classic examples of this development. These 20- and 30-something heterosexual home-building shows sometimes eventually placed their characters in romantic relationships (such as in *Mad About You*). Significantly, many workplace sitcoms reproduced the family formula, such as *Just Shoot Me!,* where boss and employee are also father and daughter. In other programming strategies, many domestic comedies required a novel situation to appeal to younger audiences. For example, in the British *Game On,* the "family" was composed of three young flat-sharers who talked constantly about sex (as did characters in workplace sitcoms) but who lived in an internally celibate household.

Some sitcoms seemed so full of raw new energy that they could be viewed as products of Research and Development for the genre itself, renewing its very form for a new generation of writers, performers, and audiences. *The Young Ones* achieved this status in the United Kingdom, *The Simpsons* and *South Park* in the United States. More recently, *The Royle Family* managed the same rare trick of being "about" TV as well as life, testing its genre and any vestigial faith we may have had in the family.

Meanwhile, the family was redeemed in an unexpected way. Domestic comedy was invaded by reality TV. As the drama of family comportment, reality took the form of *The Osbournes*—MTV's fly-on-the-wall docudrama of life with Black Sabbath lead singer Ozzy Osbourne and his family. Its "actors" played it deadpan, but the combination of the family's underlying sensible good-heartedness with Ozzy's spectacularly feral appearance was pure domestic comedy, giving a new twist to Bill Cosby's famous catchphrase of the 1980s: "I just hope they get out of the house before we die."

JOHN HARTLEY

See also ***All in the Family; Bewitched; Brady Bunch, The; Cheers;*** **Comedy, Workplace;** ***Cosby Show, The; Ellen; Father Knows Best; Flintstones; Frasier; Friends; I Love Lucy; Leave It to Beaver; The Likely Lads; Married... with Children; Mary Tyler Moore Show, The; Murphy Brown; My Three Sons; One Foot in the Grave; Phil Silvers Show, The;*** **Reality Programming;** ***Roseanne; Royle Family; Seinfeld; Simpsons, The; South Park; Taxi; Till Death Us Do Part***

Further Reading

Gray, Herman, "Black Representations in the Post Network, Post Civil Rights World of Global Media," in *Ethnic Minorities and the Media,* edited by S. Cottle, Buckingham and Philadelphia: Open University Press, 2000

Hartley, John, *Uses of Television,* London and New York: Routledge, 1999

Newcomb, Horace, *TV: The Most Popular Art,* New York: Doubleday, 1974

Olson, R. Scott, *Hollywood Planet: Global Media and the Competitive Advantage of Narrative Transparency,* Mahwah, New Jersey: Erlbaum, 1999

Spigel, Lynn, "From Theatre to Space Ship: Metaphors of Suburban Domesticity in Postwar America," in *Visions of Suburbia,* edited by Roger Silverstone, London and New York: Routledge, 1996

Comedy, Workplace

Workplace comedies provide a convenient vehicle for the writers and producers of the television program to access all the essential components of series drama. The workplace frame adapts to changes in the production context, gives the characters a continuing mandate for action, provides the dramatic tension of continuing relationships among persons of different backgrounds, and offers the opportunity to introduce additional or visiting characters. The significant structural weakness of the workplace comedy is that it is deprived of the interaction between youth and maturity often central to situation and domestic comedy in television. But even this arrangement can be addressed by creating a work situation devoted to child nurturing or by introducing the workers' family members, who can appear regularly or randomly at the will of producers.

In pragmatic industrial terms, the workplace series provides a flexible format that can adapt to changes in the real-world production context. With the workplace series, the departure of a cast member allows a new performer to assume the job responsibility and simultaneously introduce a new interpersonal dynamic to the ensemble—as with the departures of McLean Stevenson (Lt. Colonel Henry Blake) and Wayne Rogers (Capt. John [Trapper John] McKenzie) on *M*A*S*H.* The characters introduced by Harry Morgan (Col. Sherman Potter) and Mike Farrell (Capt. B.J. Hunnicut) did not simply replace the job functions of

WKRP In Cincinnati, Richard Sanders, Frank Bonner, Gordon Jump, Loni Anderson, Gary Sandy, Howard Hesseman, Tim Reid, Jan Smithers, 1978–82.
Courtesy of the Everett Collection

Alice, Polly Holiday, Linda Lavin, Beth Howland, 1976–85.
Courtesy of the Everett Collection

their predecessors; they created new personalities that varied the mix of relationships within the ensemble. The death of Nicholas Colasanto (Coach) was mourned on *Cheers* and his character was replaced by the much younger Woody Harrelson (Woody Boyd), who portrayed a naive Indiana farm boy who had been taking a mail-order bartending course from Coach. *Cheers* writers and producers dealt with the departure of Shelley Long (Diane Chambers) with the introduction of Kirstie Alley's Rebecca Howe and an increased emphasis on the Kelsey Grammer (Dr. Frasier Crane) and Bebe Neuwirth (Dr. Lilith Stern) characters.

As these strategies indicate, the humor in the workplace comedy may come from the personalities of the characters, the interaction of the characters, or the situations encountered by the characters. The successful series draw on all these elements, but the balance differs from program to program. Some shows emphasize character relationships, others are best at creating comedic situations, and still others offer characters who are individually funny in their own right (often the case when a series is developed specifically to showcase the talents of a stand-up comedian). *The Office,* a BBC comedy set in a paper-supply office in Slough, England, draws most of its overt laughs from the office manager, David Brent, played by the English comedian Ricky Gervais. Brent has a fondness for jumbled corporate-speak that borders on the nonsensical. However, the supporting cast members highlight the humor inherent in the pettiness and absurdity that mark daily office life. However, they also subtly emphasize the bonds that form there (such as in the poignant, stifled attraction between secretary Dawn and frustrated sales representative Tim).

Series like *Our Miss Brooks, Newhart, The Andy Griffith Show, Night Court, Frasier,* and *The Mary Tyler Moore Show* drew many of their laughs from the antics of a few eccentric characters. Some of the comic characters were objects of ridicule, some were simply out of step with their surroundings, and some were so superior to their surroundings that they were humorous. Richard Crenna's dim-witted Walter Denton was often a source of amusement on *Our Miss Brooks;* Don Knotts made the bumbling Barney Fife a laugh getter on *The Andy Griffith Show;* and *Newhart*'s Larry, Darryl, and Darryl needed only to appear on screen to

Car 54, Where Are You?, Fred Gwynne, Joe E. Ross, 1961–63.
Courtesy of the Everett Collection

Night Court, Marsha Warfield, Charles Robinson, Harry Anderson, Richard Moll, Markie Post, John Larroquette, 1984–92.
Courtesy of the Everett Collection

draw anticipatory giggles from many viewers. Even *Rhoda*'s unseen Carleton the Doorman acquired a unique comedic persona. On *The Mary Tyler Moore Show,* the pompous Ted Baxter, acerbic Sue Ann Nivens, and ditzy Georgette Franklin Baxter were all ridiculous characters who inspired varying degrees of sympathy.

Workplace comedies can also draw on references to the popular forms they parody. The incompetent spy of *Get Smart* and the bumbling policemen of *Car 54, Where Are You?* developed the comedy line by contradicting the premise of a strong, competent leading character. *The Wild, Wild West* and *The Rockford Files* parodied the western and detective forms so well that they are generally categorized with those genres, respectively, as opposed to comedy.

Persons in a work situation are granted a franchise to action by the nature of their work—the job requires them to deal with problems or participate in events related to their work. Professions such as law enforcement, medicine, and media provide ready-made opportunities to place the characters in varied situations and involve them with a wide range of characters.

WKRP in Cincinnati, Barney Miller, ER, and *Taxi* often found their strength in creating bizarre situations, then letting the established characters play out the story. Episodes such as the *WKRP* Thanksgiving story in which Herb Tarlek and Mr. Carlson dropped live turkeys from a helicopter as a promotional gimmick take logical premises and carry them to illogical extremes.

The workplace setting facilitates interaction among characters of varied origin. Despite their diverse backgrounds, the characters on a workplace comedy are united by a common goal and are required to maintain even difficult relationships. Diahann Carroll's *Julia* was the first series to place a professional black woman in a starring role, but many other series have drawn humor from contrasting characters of different race, gender, ethnicity, class, or regional origin. *Barney Miller*'s Ron Glass, as Harris—a literate, urbane African-American man—constantly reminded his coworkers of racial stereotyping and his own departure from those stereotypes; Jack Soo as Yemana similarly made ironic reference to his Asian background. On

Designing Women there were frequent references to the "hillbilly" background of Jean Smart's Charlene, and Meschach Taylor's Anthony often made mention of his race. In *M*A*S*H,* Corporal Walter (Radar) O'Reilly's rural background and Major Charles Emerson Winchester's upper-class Boston upbringing were frequent sources of humor.

In some instances, workplace comedies require that individuals who are not merely different but actually hostile to one another maintain a relationship, and the resultant tension provides humor. In *The Dick Van Dyke Show,* Richard Deacon's character—the pompous producer Mel Cooley—was the butt of endless jokes by the writing staff. Robert Guillaume's *Benson* was constantly engaged in combat with Inga Swenson, who portrayed the cook Gretchen, and a truce between Craig T. Nelson's Hayden Fox and the women's basketball coach, Judy, in *Coach,* would have removed a consistent source of humor from that series.

The ability to introduce guest or visiting characters is another advantage of the workplace comedy. The criminals and complainants who visited the police station in *Barney Miller* or the varied defendants who appeared in *Night Court* all contributed to the general atmosphere of those series. Similarly, the patients on *The Bob Newhart Show* and *ER* added interest and facilitated the development of new plotlines. In some cases, guest performers appeared only once; others became semiregulars who would appear unexpectedly to add further complications to their stories. Such is the case with *Scrubs,* in which Dr. Perry Cox's (John C. McGinley) ex-wife, Jordan Sullivan (Christa Miller Lawrence), is initially introduced primarily to cause a rift between Cox and his protégé, intern J.D. (Zach Braff). However, as the series progresses, she comes into her own as a character, eventually becoming pregnant and reuniting romantically with Cox (which simply causes another set of problems to be addressed).

In some workplace series, the families and friends of the working group also participate in the storylines. In the case of *The Mary Tyler Moore Show,* Mary's friend Rhoda and landlady Phyllis became such important characters that each was given a spin-off series of her own. *Murphy Brown*'s resident housepainter Eldin became a significant component of the series, and *The Andy Griffith Show* drew heavily on Andy's relationships with Aunt Bea and son Opie. Even *Get Smart* assumed a family aspect when Smart and Agent 99 were married and became the parents of twins. The relationship between Gabriel and Julie Kotter was frequently the focus of *Welcome Back, Kotter* episodes, and *The Dick Van Dyke Show* included numerous segments dealing with Rob and Laura Petrie's home life.

The workplace comedy, like the society it portrayed, has both evolved and gone through cyclical changes. The form of the series has definitely evolved. Contrasting one of the earliest workplace comedies, *Private Secretary,* with more recent series shows changes in casting, relationships, and narrative structure. *Private Secretary* centered around the activities of Susie McNamara, a private secretary in a New York City talent agency, a vehicle that provided for the introduction of numerous guest characters who appeared as clients. All the cast members were middle-class and upper-middle-class whites. Although the relationship between Susie and her boss was congenial, there was no doubt that Susie was by no means as intellectually or emotionally competent as the male authority figure for whom she worked. While the men carried out business, the women worried about relationships—especially that special relationship that would take them out of the office and into a blissful married life. Susie was central to every episode, and each episode came to closure, bringing with it no memory of previous episodes and leaving no character or situation changes to affect subsequent episodes.

By contrast, more recent series portray a broad range of racial and ethnic characters. The cast of *Whoopi* includes an African-American hotel owner, her brother, his white girlfriend, and an Iranian handyman. On *Scrubs,* the white J.D.'s best friend, Chris Turk (Donald Adeosun Faison), is African American, and Turk's fiancée, Carla Espinosa (Judy Reyes), is Latina.

Along with this broader range of characters comes a broader distribution of storyline emphases. *The Mary Tyler Moore Show* and subsequent MTM productions are often cited as a turning point in the evolution of series structure, with their refinement of the ensemble cast. Rather than focusing every episode on the actions of one clearly defined lead character, the ensemble allows any of several central characters to provide the story focus. In some series—for example, *Murphy Brown*—a central character will provide the stimulus for the actions of the featured character, but that character is still the focus of the storyline.

The narrative structure has made distinct changes with the move to more open stories, allowing growth and change. The series is allowed memory of previous events, and stories are no longer required to return the situation to its state at the opening of the play. Episodes no longer require complete closure, and some problems require multiple episodes to reach resolution or may even continue indefinitely.

Topics addressed by the workplace comedy have

experienced cyclical popularity, influenced by the dominant concerns of the society and by the economic influence of other popular forms. Comedy has often addressed social concerns, and the workplace comedy has assumed that joint opportunity and responsibility. From direct confrontation—as when Mary Richards learned her male predecessor had been more highly paid—to implicit endorsement of the abilities of underrepresented groups—as in Benson's steady rise to gubernatorial candidacy—the workplace comedies provide a forum for the expression of social issues and offer opportunities to consider new ideas and challenges to the existing order. At the same time, television comedies are a commercial form, directly influenced by the need to remain commercially viable. Examining the popular topics for the workplace comedy reinforces Steve Allen's charge that "imitation is the sincerest form of television." Series do tend to borrow ideas from the headlines, from other media, and from one another. These notions receive broad attention for a time; some are then integrated into the form, and others disappear. In this process, the television workplace series operates in the same manner as many other elements of modern culture, evolving slowly in the process of contested change.

KAY WALSH

See also ***Amen; Andy Griffith Show, The; Bob Newhart Show, The/Newhart; Dad's Army; Desmonds'; Fawlty Towers; Frank's Place; Get Smart; It's Garry Shandling's Show/Larry Sanders Show, The; M*A*S*H; Mary Tyler Moore Show, The; Murphy Brown; Taxi; Yes Minister***

Further Reading

Attallah, Paul, "Situation Comedy and 'The Beverly Hillbillies': The Unworthy Discourse," Montreal, Canada: McGill University Graduate Communication Program Working Papers, 1983

Butsch, Richard, "Class and Gender in Four Decades of Television Situation Comedy: plus ça change . . . ." *Critical Studies in Mass Communication* (December 1992)

Feuer, Jane, Paul Kehr, and Tise Vahamagi, *MTM: Quality Television,* London: British Film Institute, 1985

Freeman, Lewis, "Social Mobility in Television Comedies," *Critical Studies in Mass Communication* (December 1992)

Hamamoto, Darrell Y., *Nervous Laughter: Television Situation Comedy and Liberal Democratic Ideology,* New York: Praeger, 1989

Javna, John, *The Best of TV Sitcoms: Burns and Allen to the Cosby Show, The Munsters to Mary Tyler Moore,* New York: Harmony Books, 1988

Jones, Gerard, *Honey, I'm Home!: Sitcoms, Selling the American Dream,* New York: Grove Weidenfeld, 1992

Leibman, Nina, *Living Room Lectures: The Fifties Family in Film and Television,* Austin: University of Texas Press, 1995

Lipsitz, George, "The Meaning of Memory: Family, Class, and Ethnicity in Early Network Television," *Camera Obscura* (January 1988)

Marc, David, *Demographic Vistas: Television in American Culture,* Philadelphia: University of Pennsylvania Press, 1984

Marc, David, *Comic Visions: Television Comedy and American Culture,* Boston: Unwin-Hyman, 1989

Mellencamp, Patricia, "Situation Comedy, Feminism, and Freud, Discourse of Gracie and Lucy," in *Studies in Entertainment: Critical Approaches to Mass Culture,* edited by Tanya Modleski, Bloomington: Indiana University Press, 1986

Mitz, Rick, *The Great TV Sitcom Book,* New York: Marek, 1980

Neale, Stephen, and Frank Krutnik, *Popular Film and Television Comedy,* London and New York: Routledge, 1990

Rowe, Kathleen, *The Unruly Woman: Gender and the Genres of Laughter,* Austin: University of Texas Press, 1995

Spigel, Lynn, *Make Room for TV: Television and the Family Ideal in Postwar America,* Chicago: University of Chicago Press, 1992

Taylor, Ella, *Prime-Time Families: Television Culture in Postwar America,* Berkeley: University of California Press, 1989

Commercials. *See* **Advertising**

Communications Act of 1934

U.S. Communications Policy Legislation

The Communications Act of 1934 remains the cornerstone of U.S. television policy nearly seven decades after its initial passage. Though often updated through amendments, and itself based on the pioneering Radio Act of 1927, the 1934 legislation that created the Federal Communications Commission (FCC) has endured remarkably well through an era of dramatic technical and social change.

Congress first specifically regulated broadcasting with the 1927 Radio Act, which created a Federal Radio Commission designed to regulate in "the public interest, convenience, or necessity." But federal regulation of communications was shared by the Department of Commerce and the Interstate Commerce Commission. By 1934 pressure to consolidate all telecommunications regulation for both wired and wireless services prompted new legislation with a broader purpose.

President Franklin Roosevelt's message requesting new legislation was published in January 1934; the Senate held hearings on several days in March; the House of Representatives held a single day of hearings in April; a conference report melding the two differing bills together appeared in early June; and the act was passed on June 19. The act generated little controversy at the time it was considered. Few proposed substantial alteration of the commercially based broadcast system encoded in the 1927 law. Some critics expressed concern about educational radio's survival—and although Congress mandated the new FCC to consider setting aside some frequencies for such stations, this occurred only in 1941 with approval of FM service.

In its original form, the act's text runs some 45 pages in the standard government-printed version and is divided into several dozen numbered sections of a paragraph or more, which are arranged in six parts called titles. The first title provides general provisions on the FCC; the second is devoted to common-carrier regulation; the third deals with broadcasting (and is of primary concern here), the fourth with administrative and procedural matters, the fifth with penal provisions and forfeitures (fines), and the sixth with miscellaneous matters (in 1984, a seventh title concerning cable television was added).

The act has been updated through amendment many times—chiefly with creation of public television in 1967 (provisions on the operation and funding of the Corporation for Public Broadcasting expanded title III) and the cable act of 1984 (which, as noted previously, created a new title devoted to cable regulation, sections of which were expanded in cable legislation of 1992).

Attempts to update substantially or replace totally the act have arisen in Congress several times, most notably during a series of "rewrite" bills from 1977 to 1982, and again in the mid-1990s. The Telecommunications Act of 1996 became the most extensive set of amendments to the 1934 law. Although focused largely on common-carrier concerns, the new amendments also extend broadcast station licenses to eight years and greatly ease ownership restrictions. Such efforts to change the law are driven partly by frustration with legislation based on analog radio and telephone technology still in force in a digital era of convergence. They are driven as well by increasing rivalries among competing industries—broadcast, cable, telephone, and others. They are also driven by political ideology that argues government should no longer attempt to do all things for all people, and by economic constraints that force government to operate more efficiently. Despite—or perhaps because of—its many amendments, the 1934 act has survived decades of technical, economic, and policy changes to remain at the heart of U.S. telecommunications.

CHRISTOPHER H. STERLING

See also **Allocation; Education Television; "Freeze" of 1948; License; Ownership; Public Interest, Convenience, and Necessity; U.S. Policy: Telecommunications Act of 1996**

Further Reading

Berry, Tyler, *Communications by Wire and Radio: A Treatise on the Law,* Chicago: Callaghan, 1937

"Communications Act of 1934: 50th Anniversary Supplement," *Federal Communications Law Journal* (January 1985)

Federal Communications Commission, *Annual Report,* Washington, D.C.: Government Printing Office, 1934–

McChesney, Robert W., *Telecommunications, Mass Media, and Democracy: The Battle for Control of U.S. Broadcasting, 1928–1935,* New York: Oxford University Press, 1993

McMahon, Robert S., *Regulation of Broadcasting: Half a Century of Government Regulation of Broadcasting and the Need for Further Legislative Action,* 85th Cong., 2nd sess., Subcommittee Print, Washington, D.C., 1958

Paglin, Max D., *A Legislative History of the Communications Act of 1934,* New York: Oxford University Press, 1989

Rosen, Philip T., *The Modern Stentors: Radio Broadcasters and the Federal Government, 1920–1934,* Westport, Connecticut: Greenwood, 1980

Communications Satellite Corporation

The Communications Satellite Corporation (COMSAT) was created in 1962 with the passage of the Communications Satellite Act. The act authorized the formation of a private corporation to administer satellite communications for the United States. COMSAT was given responsibility for many activities, including the development of a global satellite communications system, the acquisition and maintenance of ground stations around the world, and the development of new satellite technologies. COMSAT is governed by a board of directors elected by the company's shareholders and the president of the United States. Half of the company's shares are owned by major communications companies such as AT&T, ITT, and Western Union, and the rest are held by members of the public. COMSAT has offices worldwide, and its headquarters are located in Washington, D.C.

COMSAT emerged amid a public controversy staged in a series of congressional hearings in 1961 and 1962. During these hearings, public advocates and private businesses struggled for control over satellite communications in the United States. Senators Wayne Morse and Estes Kefauver and Representative Emanuel Celler formed an alliance against the privatization of COMSAT and rallied support from the American Communication Association—a union of telecommunications workers—as well as Assistant Attorney General Lee Loevinger and communications scholars Dallas Smythe and Herbert Schiller. Concerned that the privatization of COMSAT would strengthen the private sector's control over public airwaves, they called for further public participation in the hearings and government ownership of satellite communications. Senator Robert Kerr, on the other hand, formed an alliance led by major communications companies such as RCA and AT&T and proposed a bill that called for the privatization of satellite communications. Kerr insisted that space communication offered new business opportunities that would benefit the private sector, the nation, and the world. Pressure from both sides ultimately culminated in the creation of a "government corporation" designed to operate as a private business and yet act in the public interest. Throughout its history, COMSAT has faced the difficult challenge of negotiating the often contradictory interests of private enterprise and the public good. The organization has historically favored the business end of its mandate.

COMSAT was established as a "carrier's carrier." This meant that COMSAT could not sell satellite circuits directly to broadcasters, news agencies, or other customers for overseas communication. Rather, the company could only sell circuits wholesale to other communications carriers and allow them to resell them. COMSAT must pursue customers to buy satellite time in order to recover the high cost of developing new satellite systems. Its customers range from national governments to common carriers. COMSAT maintains liaisons with private businesses and national governments around the world, but at the same time, it must fill its mandate to conduct business negotiations in the interest of the American public.

In 1964 COMSAT representatives participated in international negotiations that led to the creation of Intelsat—the International Telecommunications Satellite Organization. Intelsat still exists today and is a global satellite network that provides developing nations access to communications satellites for domestic com-

Photo courtesy of COMSAT Corporation

munications. The United States owns more than 50 percent of Intelsat, and COMSAT has managed the organization since 1964.

In 1965 COMSAT launched Early Bird—the first commercial communications satellite. Early Bird relayed common-carrier network traffic, telephone, television, telegraph, and digital data, as well as voice bandwidth analog data such as facsimile and wire photo transmittals. The satellite was deployed to evaluate the viability of synchronous satellites for commercial communications and to supplement the capacity of transatlantic cables. In 1980 COMSAT formed a subsidiary company called the Satellite Television Company (STC) to design and launch the United States' first direct broadcast satellite. Despite the STC's efforts, its domestic satellite system was thwarted when the Federal Communications Commission (FCC) denied its application because of the STC's failure to demonstrate how satellite programming would differ from that offered by cable or network television.

COMSAT operates as the U.S. signatory to Intelsat and Inmarsat (International Maritime Satellite Organization). The company still sells satellite circuits to private companies and governments around the world for national and international communication. COMSAT laboratories located in Clarksburg, Maryland, have been responsible for a variety of technical developments in satellite and wireless communications, including coding and transmission, networking and multiple access, space-qualified electronics and power sources, antennas, and many others.

LISA PARKS

See also **Satellite**

Further Reading

Hudson, Heather E., *Communications Satellites: Their Development and Impact,* New York: Free Press, and London: Collier Macmillan, 1990

Kinsley, Michael E., *Outer Space and Inner Sanctums: Government, Business, and Satellite Communication,* New York: Wiley, 1976

Maddox, Brenda, *Beyond Babel: New Directions in Communications,* London: Deutsch, 1972

Schiller, Herbert I., *Mass Communications and American Empire,* Boulder, Colorado: Westview, 1992

Tedeschi, Anthony Michael, *Live via Satellite: The Story of COMSAT and the Technology That Changed World Communication,* Washington, D.C.: Acropolis Books, 1989

Computers in Television

The advent of computers has had a tremendous effect on the television and the video industry. Smaller, faster personal computers and computer chips have reduced camera sizes, revolutionized editing, and brought the process of video production to the desktop.

Cameras have benefited from the increased computer power and decreased chip size. Computer chips, called charged coupled devices (CCDs), have replaced tubes as image-processing devices in video cameras. Because CCDs are small and provide good resolution, high-quality cameras have become smaller, more portable, and better able to provide good pictures in low-light situations. Other types of computer chips are also used to control some studio cameras. These cameras have an internal memory that automatically retains the correct camera settings, ensuring accurate synchronization between camera and the camera control unit and allowing easy registration and alignment. Other cameras even have remote control capabilities that allow the camera operator to preload shots during rehearsal and then recall them at the appropriate moment with the touch of a button.

Computers have also enhanced other production equipment. Still-stores and frame stores, devices that capture one frame of video and store it in memory for future use, rely on computers. Still-stores and frame stores are often used to generate the graphics that accompany news anchors as they introduce news stories. Digital video effects, such as rotating images, morphing (when one image turns into another), and image stretching, previously sent out to specialty shops, can now be done on the premises, for less money, with a computer.

Computer-generated imaging is also on the rise and is used widely in a variety of applications such as computer graphics, titles, paint systems, and three-dimensional animation. Technology enables computer-generated images often to look "real" or to be so well integrated in postproduction that they appear to be a part of the camera-generated images. This area is likely to continue to increase in sophistication.

An example of computers used in television production.
Photo courtesy of Avid Technology, Inc.

Computerization has also allowed more automation. At NBC network studios, satellite feeds to affiliates and master control of programming are largely in the hands of a computer. Some local television stations also use computers to keep track of their air traffic and master control.

Perhaps the biggest change in the television production process has come in postproduction. The change began when computers were found to be useful in controlling videotape recorders using timecode. By adding a character generator and a switcher and using a computer-generated edit decision list, a new online editing process was born. Timecode and the computer provided an accuracy not achieved before.

Nonlinear editing has progressed beyond computer-controlled videotape recorders. Nonlinear editing is performed with a personal computer outfitted with hardware and software that enable it to digitize the video and audio and store them on computer disk. Nonlinear editing is often referred to as "random access editing" because it provides the editor with random access to the source material stored on a computer disk. Therefore, it is not necessary to wait for the source tape to fast-forward or rewind to a desired scene. One of the biggest advantages of nonlinear editing is that if the timing of an edit is unacceptable, it can be changed easily. Unlike linear editing, segments can be tightened or extended without revising subsequent edit points. Segments can also be effortlessly added, deleted, and moved around within the program. At present, nonlinear editing is most often used for offline editing because a high-quality digital-to-analog converter is needed to convert the finished product to a broadcast-quality product. Generally, an edit decision list is generated and online editing is done in a computer-controlled editing suite. However, companies such as Avid are developing high-quality online nonlinear editing systems.

In general, the introduction of computers to the television and video industry has demystified the industry and made it possible for individuals to produce video at a relatively affordable price. "Desktop video" has become a viable production process especially for independent and corporate producers. Small, portable, high-quality cameras and desktop editing systems can cost as little as $10,000 total. Macintosh-based systems such as Adobe Premiere and Avid Media Suite Pro provide special effects, transitions, filters, and a means for digitizing video. Similar systems exist for other platforms. Of particular note is the Video Toaster, which is on Commodore's Amiga platform and was specifically designed to interface with video systems. This system is capable of performing many functions of traditional video production and does not have the problems with conversion to analog that other systems have. However, because the Commodore is not a popular platform, the market for the Toaster is not very large and its future is unclear. What is clear is that the future of desktop video is bright. Television and video are no longer confined to the broadcast industry. Video on the computer, in educational settings, games, and other applications, will become even more commonplace. As interactive television and the information superhighway continue to develop, television, television equipment, and television production will continue to change.

PATTI CONSTANTAKIS-VALDES

See also **Technology, Television**

Further Reading

Borrell, Jerry, "The Future of Television and Computers; In 1991 Computers and Video Are Combining to Create New Media," *Macworld* (February 1991)

Churbuck, David C., "Desktop Television," *Forbes* (December 7, 1992)

Noll, M.A., *Television Technology: Fundamentals and Future Prospects,* Norwood, Massachusetts: Artech House, 1988

Ohanian, T. A., *Digital Non-Linear Editing,* Stoneham, Massachussetts: Focal Press, 1992

Smith, C.C., *Mastering Television Technology: A Cure for the Common Video,* Richardson, Texas: Newman-Smith, 1990

Verna, T., *Global Television: How to Create Effective Television for the Future,* Stoneham, Massachusetts: Focal Press, 1993

Wells, M., *Desktop Video,* White Plains, New York: Knowledge Industry Publications, 1990

Wurtzel, A., and J. Rosenbaum., *Television Production,* 5th edition, New York: McGraw-Hill, 1995

Conglomerates. *See* **Media Conglomerates**

Congress. *See* **United States Congress and Television**

Convergence

Convergence describes the combination of previously separate communication media, including telecommunications, television, and personal computing. This confluence of formats and capabilities creates technological and industrial convergences. As digitalization makes content delivery increasingly independent of traditional television, radio, or other media delivery formats, the media industry is also consolidating. Companies such as NewsCorp and Time Warner have interests in a variety of communication media—from television to the Internet and traditional newspapers—and technological convergence allows these historically disparate media services to come together, transmitted via fiber-optic cable or satellite. The trend of convergence is especially significant for television, as illustrated by the appearance of interactive television services such as video-on-demand, WebTV, and digital video recorders (DVRs), using technology like TiVo.

Although media convergence is often associated with digitalization, traditional media formats were already beginning to blend prior to the widespread diffusion of digital media platforms. The videocassette recorder (VCR) brought theatrical films to the television screen, eroding traditional media boundaries while allowing interactivity in the form of rewinding, pausing, and fast-forwarding. This sense of control and interactivity continues to be a primary characteristic of convergent media. With the diffusion of digital technologies, traditionally discrete media have continued to merge while allowing increased control for the user.

Nicholas Negroponte (among other media scholars) suggests that digitalization has reduced print, film, and video to a universal format of binary data, so that the only real difference among media is the choice of display technology. As these previously disparate media are digitized, image and text are translated into lines of ones and zeros, becoming a flexible stream of information to be transmitted through wireless satellite and microwave technologies, fiber-optic cables, or the copper wires of traditional telephone lines. The information can then be displayed on a television screen, a personal computer (PC), or a cellular phone. The primary limitations on this process are the storage capacity of the receiving device and the bandwidth of the transmission channel. With the ongoing diffusion of broadband technologies such as fiber-optic cable and wireless satellite transmission, it is increasingly easy for the media consumer to interact with a variety of formats over a single network. Digital cable service, for example, offers video-on-demand (VOD) as well as a plethora of video and audio channels, and the home consumer can also hook up a network-ready game console, such as Microsoft Xbox or Sony PlayStation, to use their television as a gaming display, while playing with distant users on the network. These digital networks allow both upstream and downstream data transmission and allow the user more control over the media product, whether through digital video recording, VOD, or access to information services. DVRs allow the television viewer to manipulate television content, skipping commercial breaks even while a program is still being broadcast, and later burn the edited program to a digital video disc (DVD) for future viewing. Home media servers integrate DVR technology with PCs, so that users can transmit movies, television, audio, and still-image programs to displays throughout the house from a single computer.

Efforts to market convergent technology to the home consumer include WebTV, DVR products such as TiVo and ReplayTV, and PC media servers. WebTV, founded in 1995 and purchased by Microsoft in 1997, was marketed as a device that would bring Internet connectivity to the television, bypassing the PC. To bring interactive television content to consumers, Microsoft formed an agreement with the CBS network to integrate interactive capabilities into dramas, sports programming, and reality shows, such as *CSI* and *Survivor.* Still, as PC prices fell in the late 1990s, there was little customer interest in using the television as an Internet interface. WebTV, now called MSN TV, has been considered a commercial failure. Microsoft's next attempt at converging television and Internet technologies was UltimateTV, a product that offered both DVR capabilities and Internet access via a satellite receiver. By 2000, however, other DVR products such as TiVo and ReplayTV were already on the market.

ReplayTV and TiVo decks were first available to consumers in spring 1999. With 10 gigabytes of hard drive space, these products could record 14 hours of video, providing the ability to pause and rewind a television program as it was broadcast. Both devices cost about $700, but TiVo became more commercially successful, possibly because of its enhanced capacity to learn the user's viewing preferences and record appropriate programs automatically. The user would connect the TiVo unit through the phone line or a broadband connection, allowing the unit to download and update program information. By choosing a particular program, the user could ensure that all new episodes of the selected program or similar programs would be automatically recorded.

In 2003 TiVo storage capacity had increased to 80 hours on the basic DVR model and TiVo had formed an agreement with DirecTV, the largest satellite television service in the United States. This connection to DirecTV helped TiVo revenues grow by almost 75 percent in the third quarter of 2003, and it is credited with adding 150,000 new subscriptions for TiVo in that quarter, out of a total of 209,000. In late 2003, TiVo was estimated to get about half of its subscribers from DirecTV customers, so that TiVo was expected to reach 1 million customers total by the end of 2003. This agreement with DirecTV has benefited TiVo substantially, but may lapse if NewsCorp follows through on its proposal to purchase DirecTV from its corporate parent, Hughes Electronics, in 2003. NewsCorp, which owns a rival DVR service, NDS, could either drop TiVo in favor of its own DVR technology or use this leverage to purchase TiVo at a reduced cost.

TiVo has also been unable to form an agreement with a major cable provider. Thus far, multiple system operators (MSOs) have been reluctant to commit to offering premium DVR services, although some MSOs, such as Time Warner Cable, do offer generic DVR capability with devices manufactured by companies such as Panasonic, Samsung, Toshiba, and Hitachi. These "generic" DVRs, like their brand name counterparts, are equipped with hard drives so that users can record television programs onto the drive, edit programs, and even write the finished program to a DVD for long-term storage. In addition, users can watch a program while it is still recording but are unable to access the program listings features provided by TiVo. Some of these hardware companies are also producing set-top boxes for TiVo and DirecTV use, allowing up to 120 hours of media storage, as well as DVD-recording capabilities. Meanwhile, other forms of interactive television are chiefly of the "two-screen" variety. Viewer surveys demonstrated that television program websites received a high number of hits during the actual broadcast, and in response, shows such as the CBS network's *CSI Miami* have included a variety of interactive activities targeted at audience members as they are watching the program. The interactivity is two-screen, because the user accesses both the television screen and the screen of the PC.

Media servers are another type of home entertainment technology taking advantage of convergence. Examples of these devices include products from Hewlett-Packard, Sony, and Prismiq. These servers tap into the home Ethernet network or can function through WiFi wireless networks. The user attaches such devices to a PC and makes it into a media server, sending videos and music to the home television and stereo. In addition, some products also allow the user to go online to check e-mail, weather, theater times, and other information services. Because some media servers only work with videos and music already purchased by the user, there is no subscription fee, as there is for TiVo or other similar DVRs receiving signals over cable or satellite. These media server devices incorporate digital-rights-management software and will not allow media from unrecognized sources to be displayed even if those sources are not illegal copies. This digital-rights-management code also will not break the encryption commonly used on DVDs, so such films cannot be shown on some of these devices. However, many media servers do make use of DVR technology, so the user is able to record, edit, and store television programs. In addition, many digital media servers and DVRs will now allow content to be delivered to any TV in the house, offering networked media services between multiple set-top boxes. In 2003 the cost for basic models of media servers was between $200 and $300. While some media server products are sold separately, to be hooked up to an already-purchased PC, Hewlett-Packard, Gateway, and other companies are also marketing PCs with built-in media server components, offering similar capabilities. The market for convergent television technology is expected to grow significantly in the next several years. In 2003 only about 1.5 percent of television viewers used personal video-recording technology, but market research firms such as the Yankee Group and Forrester Research predict that within four years, nearly a fourth of television households will have DVRs, many through cable and satellite providers.

The diffusion of convergent media products in the home creates new problems and opportunities for traditional media models. Two pressing issues surrounding DVR technology are the increasing ability for viewers to skip commercials and the problem of audience measurement, as fewer viewers watch shows in real time. According to surveys by Forrester Research, 60 to 70 percent of DVR users skip ads during playback. TiVo released information on viewing habits of 700,000 users in fall 2003, showing that prime-time advertisements, the most costly to purchase, are also the most likely to be skipped. According to the company research, over three-fourths of viewers who record shows to watch at a later time edit these commercials. The TiVo report also showed that about 60 percent of the DVR's use is for timeshifting, or recording shows for viewers to watch at a later time. Among programs typically viewed live, such as news and sports, only 17 percent of viewers use their TiVo devices to skip commercials.

Advertisers and television sales executives have responded to this perceived threat with a variety of strategies. Product placement is one option, as advertised products are integrated directly into the content of the programs, but this is not considered an adequate replacement for traditional commercials. Another possible strategy is for advertisers to sponsor entire shows, and in 2003, TiVo formed an agreement with Coca-Cola to sponsor an entire series of short programs on this model. Other broadcaster-oriented solutions include technology that prevents the user from fast-forwarding through the commercial or only allows the user to compress the advertisement, and not eliminate it entirely. However, DVR and VOD technologies also offer new opportunities for target marketing, so that in the future commercials may be selected and programmed by zip code or other similarly narrow parameters.

Technological convergence, primarily through the diffusion of digital networks and content, has produced a variety of new consumer products and may introduce new models for media sales, as subscription-based consumer relationships and target marketing become increasingly common. The phenomenon of convergence goes beyond technology, however, also characterizing industrial strategies. As media formats become less distinct and broadband networks become more common, many traditional media companies have merged with or purchased Internet firms, hedging their bets against the future of digitalization and convergent media. Relaxed regulatory structures have also enabled a spate of mergers, leading to the clustering of TV stations and cable systems, as well as increased cross-ownership of various media formats, such as television, print, and Internet sites. There are a variety of reasons for these mergers. The popularity and perceived importance of the Internet has led to fears of little future growth in mature, established media industries. Also, media firms are increasingly concerned with maintaining and building their appeal to advertisers. Mergers that bring together a variety of media enable conglomerates to offer a wide breadth of media properties as advertising platforms. One example of this desired breadth is ABC Unlimited, the cross-platform unit of the ABC network and its parent Disney properties, which includes a television network, cable networks like ESPN, radio, magazines, and cruise ships. With this broad variety of platforms, ABC Unlimited can offer advertisers diverse opportunities to purchase airtime and space. Media company mergers are justified by emerging models of programming economics, which dictate that breadth is desirable, hopefully leading to synergistic relationships between diverse media properties. Merger trends include efforts to buy out program suppliers and content and pursuit of paid-on-demand revenue models to supplement traditional advertising income, since this income may be threatened by the diffusion of DVR and VOD technology. These growing conglomerates (the results of multiple mergers) may also be a significant competitive threat to single-revenue-source media, such as the local broadcast affiliates of the conglomerates. Advertising income is increasingly siphoned off to cable systems, which are often part of the cable networks, owned, in turn, by the local affiliates' parent networks.

Some early attempts at embracing convergence earned poor financial returns. In the late 1990s, Michael Armstrong of AT&T focused on the strategy of buying up cable systems, assuming they would be an important broadband link to the home consumer. Investing $110 billion in these systems, AT&T overextended itself and was forced to begin selling off other parts of the massive corporation. AT&T's drive to enter the broadband market may have helped motivate another gigantic merger, that of Time Warner and America Online. The AOL–Time Warner merger of 2000—combining the impressive media library of Time Warner with the online acumen and reach of AOL—was based on hopes of convergence and the imminent combination of the computer and television. However, this allegedly strategic merger led to a loss of billions of dollars for the two companies within two years. There are a variety of explanations for the failure of these efforts at industrial convergence. Although huge media conglomerates may be able to spread risk more effectively, they may not be able to adapt as quickly to changing economic or technological conditions. In hindsight, these mergers have been viewed as unsuccessful, as the resulting firms have been unable to surmount the challenge of getting various parts of the newly formed conglomerate to act in harmony between multiple media platforms.

In 2002 there was little merger and acquisition activity, but this trend increased in 2003 and is expected to continue in 2004. Proposed acquisitions include NewsCorp's intended investment in DirecTV, the General Electric/NBC purchase of entertainment conglomerate Vivendi-Universal, and Spanish-language media company Univision's intended purchase of the Hispanic Broadcasting Company. NewsCorp's proposed investment in DirecTV has drawn some attention from the Federal Communications Commission (FCC), which has questioned whether NewsCorp's planned purchase of a controlling stake in DirecTV would allow the company undue influence over its cable competitors and affiliates. The National Association of Broadcasters, filing with the FCC, suggest that NewsCorp's FOX network would be dangerous to local broadcasters, in that FOX would be capable of shifting programming from local affiliates to DirecTV. Previously, the FCC blocked a proposed 2002 merger between consumer satellite services EchoStar and DirecTV because it would have virtually eliminated competition in the direct satellite industry. This decision is credited with creating the subscriber war between the two companies in 2003, where each service was using DVR as a means to attract customers.

The NBC/GE and Vivendi-Universal transaction is valued at about $14 billion, with Vivendi getting 20 percent of the new conglomerate and GE receiving control of the remaining 80 percent. Vivendi may be at a disadvantage in this agreement for a variety of reasons. It will not be allowed to begin selling its stake until 2006, when the total value of the company may have decreased. Meanwhile, GE's NBC will get control of the USA and Sci-Fi Channel cable television brands, and it will get Universal's film and television production business. The acquisition puts NBC in a better position to create, distribute, and cross-promote media content, taking advantage of synergy and advertising opportunities across a breadth of diverse media properties, as do other conglomerates such as Viacom and Time Warner.

With the merger of Univision and the Hispanic Broadcasting Corporation, Spanish-language media giant Univision moves into the radio medium, owning 53 Spanish-language television stations and 63 radio stations. Already, Univision's holdings are reflective of contemporary industrial convergence; they include a top Spanish-language website, a cable channel, and a record label. A minority of the FCC has been concerned that the merger could create anticompetitive conditions. Univision is dwarfed by media goliaths such as Time Warner and Viacom, but it is a powerful force in the Spanish-language media industries.

The current atmosphere of deregulation and media convergence leads many industry analysts to predict a variety of other mergers between conglomerates vying for strategic positions on the shifting terrain of the media landscape. This industrial convergence is facilitated by shifts in federal communications policy and a general trend toward deregulation. Whereas traditional policy has dictated a variety of market-entry rules, many restrictions surrounding cross-ownership and levels of concentration within national and regional markets have recently been loosened.

One of the primary arguments for deregulation in the 1980s and 1990s appealed to technological innovation and convergence. Theorists such as Ithiel de Sola Pool have argued that the convergence of traditional media models of broadcasting, print, and telecommunications necessitated deregulatory policy. As technological convergence changed the media landscape, traditional restrictions were no longer relevant, and were even harmful, to ongoing innovation and competition. The 1996 Telecommunications Act removed many of the historical limits on cross-ownership and market penetration, allowing a flurry of mergers between media companies. While these new policies were meant to promote competition between traditionally separate media formats, such as cable and telephony, the deregulation produced greater consolidation among media firms, with giants such as Time Warner and NewsCorp purchasing a variety of subsidiaries.

In June 2003, the FCC attempted to loosen market restrictions further, allowing newspaper and broadcasting cross-ownership within regional markets, allowing control of two or even three television stations in a single market, and permitting television station groups to reach up to 45 percent of the national audience. Although public interest groups and members of Congress protested that this shift would increase the potential for news monopolization in most U.S. media markets, proponents of the deregulation argued that online news content offers enough diversity to balance any increased concentration in news ownership. The FCC decision was blocked by a federal appeals court, and it remained a subject of controversy in Congress in late 2003.

KAREN GUSTAFSON

See also **AOL–Time Warner Merger; News Corporation, Ltd.; Univision; Vivendi Universal**

Further Reading

Brinkley, Joel, *Defining Vision: The Battle for the Future of Television,* New York and London: Harcourt Brace, 1997

Curran, Steve, *Convergence Design: Creating the User Experience for Interactive Television, Wireless, and Broadband,* Gloucester, Massachusetts: Rockport, 2002

Kovsky, Steve, *High-Tech Toys for Your TV: Secrets of TiVo, Xbox, ReplayTV, UltimateTV, and More,* Indianapolis: QUE, 2002

Negroponte, Nicholas, *Being Digital,* New York: Knofp, 1995

Pangani, Margherita, *Multimedia and Interactive Digital TV: Managing the Opportunities Created by Digital Convergence,* Hershey, Pennsylvania, and London: IRM Press, 2003

Swann, Phillip, *TV dot Com: The Future of Interactive Television,* New York: TV Books, 2000

Yoffie, David, B., editor, *Competing in the Age of Digital Convergence, Boston: Harvard Business School Press,* 1997

Cooke, Alistair (1908–2004)

U.S. Journalist, Television Personality

During some eras of history, significant individuals may serve as important cultural and social links of communication between countries. In the years following World War II and for many decades after, Alistair Cooke filled such a role. He served as British correspondent for the British Broadcasting Corporation (BBC) in the United States and as host of both British and American shows that revealed some of the finer aspects of American life.

As British correspondent for the BBC, Cooke lived in the United States and reported on American affairs, both political and cultural for half a century. In so doing, he became a kind of 20th-century Alexis de Tocqueville, noting those qualities of American life that only a foreigner could describe with such unique insight. In the early 19th century, Tocqueville marveled over a land of wonders where everything was in constant motion, and in his own time Cooke observed American life with a similar precision, but using tools common to that era—radio and television.

Cooke first achieved notice in Great Britain, for his weekly radio series on the BBC, *Letter from America.* The program continued for many decades, providing British audiences with perspectives unavailable from other sources and perhaps some appreciation for the American ethic. His real influence, however, came with his efforts to bring a refinement to American television. The program was *Omnibus,* and Cooke served as host and narrator. The program turned out to be the longest-running cultural series on U.S. commercial television. First seen on CBS in 1952, the show was scheduled for late afternoon and early evening on Sundays. In the era before Sunday afternoon/evening football and other sports, *Omnibus* served as a respite from the commercial chatter of the weekdays. It offered time to reflect at a leisurely pace on the cultural, historical, and artistic heritage of American society, aspects of American life rarely noticed by television.

Omnibus later moved to ABC, which scheduled the program from 9:00 to 10:00 P.M. on Sunday. Still later, NBC picked up the series and programmed it earlier, on Sunday afternoons. Cooke remained the host as *Omnibus* thus became one of the few programs to make the rounds to all three commercial U.S. networks. Although the program never achieved high ratings, it proved that a portion of the American television audience could appreciate program elements different from most television fare, elements traditionally thought of as part of high culture. *Omnibus* ended in 1961, having established an image of thoughtfulness

Alistair Cooke.
Photo courtesy of WGBH-TV/Boston

and wisdom for Cooke and earning him enormous respect.

Cooke returned to television as narrator and sometimes writer for the NBC program *America.* The program, a series of 13 one-hour documentaries, told the fascinating story of the growth of a country from its inception during colonial times into the then-current scene of the 1970s. Cooke regarded the series as a "personal history of America," and he told it in a way that was both entertaining as well as educational. He made it a point to examine events, individuals, locations, and controversies from both close and distant perspectives. He insisted on being on the scene, walking the paths where history was made. We see his face, we look at his hands handling objects; it was, indeed, a personal history. It carried his trademarks, his reminiscences, his feelings about his memories, and his knowledge.

Cooke also insisted on producing for "the box," for television's small screen. In order for television viewers to see the objects, there were many close-ups. In order for them to understand concepts, there were careful, unhurried examinations of ideas. Cooke brought together the words, sights, and sounds in a way that was to be recognized by the industry: he won an Emmy Award in 1973 for Individuals Contributing to Documentary Programs. Later, *America* would run on public television, one of the few programs originally produced for U.S. commercial television to do so.

During the years that *America* was broadcast, Cooke also appeared on television as host for a number of British productions shown on U.S. public television under the umbrella title *Masterpiece Theatre.* The program premiered in the United States in 1971. *Masterpiece Theatre* offered to American viewers adaptations of British and American novels (Jane Austen's *Emma* and Henry James's *The Golden Bowl,* for example) as well as original productions such as *Elizabeth R* and *The Six Wives of Henry VIII.* It is often remembered for its popular continuing serials such as *Upstairs, Downstairs,* which ran from 1974 until 1977.

Cooke acted as the host who introduced the program, making a few off-the-cuff observations about the style of the production or the ideas about British culture found therein. He referred to his role on *Masterpiece Theatre* as "headwaiter." "I'm there to explain for interested customers what's on the menu, and how the dishes were composed. But I'm not the chef." Nevertheless, in 1974 he won another Emmy Award for his role on the program as Special Classification of Outstanding Program and Individual Achievement. Cooke remained in this role for 22 years, until 1992, when he retired at 83. He continued to write and produce his weekly BBC *Letter from America* until shortly before his death in March 2004.

Val E. Limburg

Alfred Alistair Cooke. Born in Manchester, Lancashire, England, November 20, 1908; became U.S. citizen, 1941. Attended Blackpool Grammar School; Jesus College, Cambridge, B.A. in English, 1930; Commonwealth Fund Fellow, Yale University, 1932–33; Harvard University, 1933–34. Married: 1) Ruth Emerson, 1934; one son; 2) Jane White Hawkes, 1946; one daughter. BBC film critic, 1934–37; BBC commentator on U.S. affairs, from 1938; NBC London correspondent, 1936–37; special correspondent on U.S. affairs, *London Times,* 1938–42; U.S. feature writer, *Daily Herald,* 1941–43; U.N. correspondent, 1945–48, and chief U.S. correspondent, 1948–72, *Manchester Guardian;* best known for *Letter from America,* the world's longest-running solo radio feature program, first broadcast in 1946. Knight Commander of the Order of the British Empire, 1973. Honor Fellow: Jesus College, Cambridge, 1986. LLD: University of Edinburgh, 1969; University of Manchester, 1973. Litt.D: St. Andrew's University, 1976; Cambridge University, 1988; Yale University, 1993. Recipient: Peabody Awards, 1952, 1983; Writers Guild of Great Britain Award for Best Documentary, 1972; Society of Film and Television Arts Dimbleby Award, 1973; Royal Society of Arts Benjamin Franklin Medal,

1973; four Emmy Awards; Yale University Howland Medal, 1977. Died in New York City, March 30, 2004.

Television Series

1938–43	*The March of Time* (narrator)
1948	*Sorrowful Jones* (narrator)
1952–61	*Omnibus* (host)
1957	*Three Faces of Eve* (narrator)
1961–67	U.N.'s International Zone program (host and producer)
1971–92	*Masterpiece Theatre* (host)
1972–73	*America: A Personal History of the U.S.* (writer and narrator)
1973	*Hitler* (narrator)

Radio

Letter from America, 1946–2004.

Publications (selected)

Garbo and the Night Watchmen (editor), 1937
Douglas Fairbanks: The Making of a Screen Character, 1940
A Generation on Trial: USA v. Alger Hiss, 1950
Christmas Eve, 1952
A Commencement Address, 1954
Around the World in Fifty Years, 1966
Talk About America, 1968
Alistair Cooke's America, 1973
The American in Europe: From Emerson to S.J. Perelman, 1975
Six Men, 1977
Above London, with Robert Cameron, 1980
Masterpieces, 1981
The Patient Has the Floor, 1986
America Observed, 1988
Fun and Games with Alistair Cooke, 1994
Memories of the Great and the Good, 1999

Further Reading

Barnouw, Erik, *Tube of Plenty: The Evolution of American Television,* New York: Oxford University Press, 1975; 2nd revised edition, 1990
Brozan, Nadine, "Chronicle," *New York Times* (July 22, 1992)
Fireman, Judy, editor, *TV Book,* New York: Workman, 1977

Cooking Shows

Cooking programs have been integral, if often peripheral, to American television since its earliest postwar expansion. These shows usually assumed a pedantic mode of address, featuring an expert chef who offered instructive tips and recipes. *I Love to Eat,* part of NBC's inaugural 1946 season, introduced James Beard, TV's first celebrity chef. In 1947 the network offered *In the Kelvinator Kitchen,* and in 1948 CBS aired the similar *To the Queen's Taste,* which brought viewers into the kitchen of the Cordon Bleu restaurant in New York. More often, though, cooking programs have been scarce on prime-time network schedules, relegated instead to daytime syndicated slots and public and cable networks. Julia Child's *The French Chef* premiered on Boston's WGBH in 1963, and her subsequent programs have been public television staples for decades. A prominent symbol of PBS's "safely splendid" middlebrow programming, Child has become a cherished icon not only of contemporary American cooking but also of the cultural possibilities of educational television, earning her TV kitchen set a place in the Smithsonian Institution.

Child helped pave the way for the popular syndicated program *The Galloping Gourmet,* which ran from 1968 to 1971. The program's host was chef and nutritionist Graham Kerr, who has since created several other food-related programs for public television and cable. Similarly, Jeff Smith's *The Frugal Gourmet* began at a small public television station and eventually reached national prominence. Dozens of local, regional, and national programs have followed suit, often focusing on particular ethnic or regional cuisines and/or on the challenges of preparing home-cooked food quickly and inexpensively.

The number and range of food-related programs in the United States exploded with the creation of the Food Network cable channel in 1993. Initially, the channel targeted principally middle-class working mothers and "foodies"—serious cooks and restaurant fans. For its first two seasons, the network developed a small but dedicated audience through a mix of original programming and reruns of older favorites (including *The Galloping Gourmet* and Julia Child's various PBS shows). By 1996, the network began to air a number of series that challenged the pedantic conventions of traditional cooking shows, which nearly always featured a chef guiding viewers through a particular recipe or meal on a set equipped as a kitchen. *Two Fat Ladies* followed the exploits of a pair of happily indulgent motorcycle-riding middle-aged English women, while *Ready-Set-Cook* offered a game-show-like cooking competition hybrid, and Alton Brown's *Good Eats* enthusiastically explained the science behind particular techniques. Among the network's most remarkable departures from PBS-derived educational conventions is *Iron Chef,* a dubbed Japanese-cooking-competition program. Created in 1993 by Tokyo's Fuji-TV, *Iron Chef* pits chefs from around the world against one of the program's eponymous experts. In a 60-minute duel set in the torch-lit Kitchen Stadium, they each prepare a multicourse meal around a mystery theme ingredient. Borrowing equally from the stylistic conventions of video games, professional wrestling, Japanese game shows, and traditional cooking programs, the show abandons cooking shows' generic formula of instructive daytime lessons for women, instead embracing hypermasculine competition, intertextuality, and camp.

Cooking shows more typically navigate a path between discourses of expertise and certified technique and those of familial comfort. In a way that often mirrors other talk programs' use of experts, this tension takes an explicit gendered form of address, as the shows' hosts move between an often overtly masculine world of chefs and cooking schools and the implicitly feminized space of the domestic kitchen. This split was manifest in the very earliest programs on the air. NBC's 1949 TV adaptation of the radio program *The Mystery Chef,* for example, encouraged women to take a break from their daytime soaps to develop sophisticated but manageable meals, entreating them to "always be an artist at the stove, not just someone who cooks." The presumptive audience for many of these shows was middle-class women who didn't work outside the home, a mode of address succinctly lampooned by "The Happy Homemaker"—the fictional program produced on *The Mary Tyler Moore Show,* in which Betty White reminded her viewers that "a woman who does a good job in the kitchen is sure to reap her rewards in other parts of the house."

Extending this gendered convention is Martha Stewart, who built a synergistic media empire in the 1990s around cooking and home improvement. Her syndicated program *Martha Stewart Living* offers expert instruction on cooking, home decor, gardening, and crafts, all while constructing a soft-focus vision of upper-middle-class leisure and domestic femininity. As is the case with many other celebrity chefs and TV hosts, Stewart's television program is cross-promoted with a line of magazines, websites, cookbooks, and consumer products—a marketing arrangement with the Kmart discount chain offers moderately priced linens and housewares. From Julia Child forward, though, the neat gendered logic that equates cooking on television with normative femininity has never been uncomplicated. Child herself disrupted the largely masculine culture of professional chefs, as have more recent women television chefs like Sara Moulton, who trained at the Culinary Institute of America.

In its attempts to broaden its audience, the Food Network has both exploited and slightly shifted the gendered discourses surrounding food preparation. British cookbook author and self-described "domestic goddess" Nigella Lawson's *Nigella Bites* infuses cooking with sex appeal, and *Emeril Live* features chef Emeril Lagasse cooking for a rapt live audience. Though he is a professionally trained restaurateur, Lagasse eschews precise recipes in favor of carefree enthusiasm. Seemingly far from the effete world of professional chefs, Lagasse adopts a working-class machismo, treating cooking as a fun hobby. Similarly, *The Naked Chef* follows young British chef Jamie Oliver around London as he shops for produce, relaxes with friends, and listens to the latest club music. Both shows embrace working-class masculinity as a way to deflect anxieties about the potentially feminizing act of cooking. This strategy has apparently worked; half of the audience for the network's top-rated *Emeril Live* is men, and a significant portion of the network's overall audience reportedly is not interested in cooking at all.

MICHAEL KACKMAN

Further Reading

Adema, Pauline, "Vicarious Consumption: Food, Television, and the Ambiguity of Modernity," *Journal of American and Comparative Cultures,* 23, no. 3 (Fall 2000)

Hollows, Joanne, "Oliver's Twist," *International Journal of Cultural Studies,* 6, no. 2 (June 2003)

Williams, Mark, "Considering Monty Margett's *Cook's Corner:* Oral History and Television History," in *Television, History, and American Culture: Feminist Critical Essays,* edited by Mary Beth Haralovich and Lauren Rabinovitz, Durham, North Carolina, and London: Duke, 1999

Cooney, Joan Ganz (1929–)

U.S. Producer, Media Executive

Joan Ganz Cooney was the chief driving force behind the creation of Children's Television Workshop (CTW, now Sesame Workshop) and the most successful children's television show in the history of either commercial or educational television, *Sesame Street.* Before *Sesame Street,* successful children's programs were entertainment oriented and appeared on commercial television; educational programs were thought to be boring and pedantic, and they appeared on public television, which garnered a small, more affluent audience. Cooney recognized that television could do more than entertain; it could provide supplementary education at a fraction of the cost of classroom instruction. She demonstrated that quality educational programming could attract and hold a mass audience and established an organization that continues to produce innovative programming for all ages. And, through *Sesame Street,* a larger, more diverse audience discovered public television, bringing it to the forefront of the national consciousness.

Cooney had an early interest in education, earning a B.A. degree in education from the University of Arizona in 1951, but she gravitated toward the mass media in part as a result of the influence of the Christophers, a religious group that emphasizes utilizing communication technologies for humanitarian goals. Although she began her career as a reporter for the *Arizona Republic* in 1952, she moved into television in 1954, joining the NBC publicity department in New York. By 1955, she was handling publicity for the prestigious *U.S. Steel Hour.* However, public television offered greater opportunity to do in-depth analyses of major issues, and she moved to the noncommercial WNDT-TV (now WNET-TV) in New York in 1962, where she produced a number of documentaries, including *A Chance at the Beginning,* a Harlem precursor of Project Head Start, and the Emmy Award–winning *Poverty, Anti-Poverty, and the Poor.*

At a 1966 dinner party at her apartment, Lloyd N. Morrisett, vice president of the Carnegie Corporation, wondered aloud whether television could be a more effective educator. Realizing that she could continue to produce documentaries without having a lasting effect on the disadvantaged, Cooney undertook a study called "The Potential Uses of Television in Preschool Education." This vision was the genesis of a proposal she submitted to Carnegie in February 1968, a proposal that resulted in the establishment of CTW and the creation of *Sesame Street.* Morrisett was particularly active in developing the proposal and raising the initial funds, and he remains a guiding force of CTW, as chair of the board of directors. But it was Cooney who articulated the creative vision and established the organization that brought it to reality.

Cooney proposed taking advantage of commercial production techniques, such as the fast pacing and repetition of advertisements and the multiple formats of *Rowan and Martin's Laugh-In,* to give life to the curriculum. Although she hoped the program would educate all preschool children, she stated that if the needs of disadvantaged children were not met, the program would be a failure.

Cooney also recognized that educational programs often fail because they are planned by educators and implemented by production personnel. Shortly after the creation of CTW in March 1968, therefore, she established a series of seminars in collaboration with Gerald S. Lesser (a Harvard educational psychologist who became chairman of the board of advisers). Production personnel (under David D. Connell, executive producer) worked with educators, child development experts, and research personnel (under Edward L. Palmer, director of research) to plan the show. Cooney, as executive director of CTW, established the guidelines, stressing the importance of exploiting the unique features of television to present a well-defined curriculum designed to supplement rather than replace classroom activity. She indicated that there was to be no star but rather a multiracial cast including both sexes and that the primary goal was to produce an excellent program, not more academic research. The working environment she established was one that fostered mutual confidence and participation among its diverse members.

Once her vision was articulated, Cooney developed an organization that guaranteed the production team the freedom to focus on the creative task. Although required by funding agencies to establish an affiliation with National Educational Television (NET), CTW remained semiautonomous and self-contained, utilizing some administrative functions of NET, but retaining all rights to the program. Cooney traveled the country,

Joan Ganz Cooney.
Courtesy of Sesame Workshop

ensuring morning airtime for the new show. CTW also used unprecedented means of informing the potential audience, enlisting commercial networks in promotional efforts. Those efforts were coupled with more personal means of reaching disadvantaged families—using sound trucks and door-to-door representatives, for example.

Sesame Street first aired in November 1969, on nearly 190 public and commercial stations, and by all measures has been a continuing success. In large-scale studies, the Educational Testing Service of Princeton concluded that *Sesame Street* generally reached its educational goals. The show also rapidly gained a mass audience, which it currently maintains. And there have been numerous critical measures of success, including a Peabody Award and three Emmys after the first year and 58 Emmys to date.

After the first successful season, CTW dissolved its relationship with NET, and Cooney became its president. The impetus was there to develop other projects, so Cooney guided the fund-raising and creative vision for a second show, airing in 1971, called *The Electric Company.* This program provided basic reading instruction for 8-to-12-year-old children. Although by 1973 Cooney described her work as mostly administrative, her vision of using the unique features of television coupled with methodical planning and research to produce programming to address identified needs was evident in other innovative CTW productions, including *Feelin' Good* (1974), *The Best of Families* (1977), *3-2-1 Contact* (1980), and *Square One TV* (1987).

Since the role of foundations is usually to provide start-up money, and since government support of public television has declined, Cooney has extended the influence of CTW productions and ensured the organization's survival by guiding the licensing of an array of commercial products and developing foreign distribution and production agreements. Product and international revenues have often provided as much as two-thirds of the budget, helping to sustain CTW and provide money for new projects. Cooney has also led CTW down the narrow road between commercial and public television, developing tax-paying subsidiaries that operate in commercial broadcasting, such as Distinguished Productions, which produced *Encyclopedia* in 1988 in collaboration with HBO.

In 1990 Cooney stepped down as president to become chair of the CTW executive committee, thus allowing her more time for creative development. Still actively involved in the creation of *Sesame Street,* she also focuses on strategic planning, with more recent projects involving interactive software and a multimedia project titled *Ghostwriter,* which debuted in 1992.

Cooney has enriched children's television with her vision, altered public perception and introduced record-setting audiences to public television, and raised the level of expectation for children entering school.

SUZANNE WILLIAMS-RAUTIOLLA

See also **Children and Television; *Sesame Street;* Sesame Workshop**

Joan Ganz Cooney. Born in Phoenix, Arizona, November 30, 1929. University of Arizona, B.A. in education, 1951. Married: 1) Timothy J. Cooney, 1964 (divorced, 1975); 2) Peter G. Peterson, 1980. Reporter, *Arizona Republic,* Phoenix, 1952–54; publicist, NBC, 1954–55; publicist, *U.S. Steel Hour,* 1955–62; producer, Channel 13, New York City, 1962–67; TV consultant, Carnegie Corporation, New York City, 1967–68; executive director, Children's Television Workshop (producers of *Sesame Street, Electric Company, 3-2-1 Contact, Square One TV,* and *Ghostwriter*), New York City, 1968–70, president and trustee, 1970–88, chair and chief executive officer, 1988–90, chair, executive committee, since 1990; director, Johnson and Johnson, Metropolitan Life Insurance Company. Trustee: Channel 13/Educational Broadcasting Corporation; Museum of Television and Radio; Columbia Presbyterian Hospital. Member: President's Commission on Marijuana and Drug Abuse, 1971–73; National News Council, 1973–81; Council on Foreign Relations, since 1974; Advance Committee for Trade Negotiations, 1978–80; Governor's Commission on International Year of the Child, 1979; President's Commission for Agenda for the 1980s, 1980–81; Carnegie Foundation National Panel on High Schools, 1980–82; National Organization for Women (NOW), National Academy of Television Arts and Sciences, National Institute of Social Sciences, International Radio and TV Society, American Women in Radio and TV. Honorary degrees: Boston College, 1970; Hofstra University, Oberlin College, Ohio Wesleyan University, 1971; Princeton University, 1973; Russell Sage College, 1974; University of Arizona and Harvard University, 1975; Allegheny College, 1976; Georgetown University, 1978; University of Notre Dame, 1982; Smith College, 1986; Brown University, 1987; Columbia University and New York University, 1991. Recipient: Christopher Award, 1970; National Institute for Social Sciences Gold Medal, 1971; Frederick Douglass Award, New York Urban League, 1972; Silver Satellite Award, American Women in Radio and TV; Woman of the Decade Award, 1979; National Endowment for the Arts, Friends of Education Award; Kiwanis Decency Award; National Association of Educational Broadcasters Distinguished Service Award; Stephen S. Wise Award, 1981; Harris Foundation Award, 1982; Emmy Award for Lifetime Achievement, 1989; named to Hall of Fame Academy of Television Arts and Sciences, 1989; Presidential Medal of Freedom, 1995. Inducted into the National Women's Hall of Fame, 1998.

Television (publicist)

1955–62 *U.S. Steel Hour*

Television Documentaries (producer)

1962–67 *Court of Reason*
A Chance at the Beginning
Poverty, Anti-Poverty, and the Poor
1968–90 *Children's Television Workshop* (executive)

Further Reading

"The First Lady of *Sesame Street:* Joan Ganz Cooney," *Broadcasting* (June 7, 1971)
Gilbert, Lynn, and Gaylen Moore, *Particular Passions: Talks with Women Who Have Shaped Our Times,* New York: Potter, 1981
Gratz, Roberta Brandes, "*Sesame:* An Open-End Play Street," *New York Post* (November 8, 1969)
Heuton, Cheryl, "TV Learns How to Teach. . . ." *Channels: The Business of Communication* (October 22, 1990)
Kramer, Michael, "A Presidential Message from Big Bird," *U.S. News and World Report* (June 13 , 1988)
Lesser, Gerald, *Children and Television: Lessons from Sesame Street,* New York: Random House, 1974
Moreau, Dan, "Joan Ganz Cooney Created Sesame Street 20 Years Ago. Now It's an Institution," *Changing Times* (July 1989)
O'Dell, Cary, *Women Pioneers in Television,* Jefferson, North Carolina: McFarland, 1996
Polsky, Richard M., *Getting to Sesame Street: Origins of the Children's Television Workshop,* New York: Praeger, 1974
Sheldon, Alan, "Tuning In with Joan Cooney," *Public Telecommunications Review* (November–December 1978)
Sklar, Robert, "Growing Up with Joan Ganz Cooney," *American Film* (November 1977)
"TV's Switched-On School," *Newsweek* (June 1, 1970)
Tyler, Ralph, "Cooney Cast Light on a Vision," *Variety* (December 13 , 1989)

Coproduction, International

"Coproduction" is a generic term that covers a variety of production arrangements between two or more companies undertaking a television (or film or other video) project. "International coproduction" refers to the situation of two or more organizations from different countries undertaking such projects. It encompasses everything from a straightforward cofinancing arrangement, in which one partner provides partial funding while another company undertakes the actual production, to more complex arrangements that involve joint creative control over projects. In all cases, the allocation of distribution rights and other aftermarket rights is a standard element of the negotiation. Complex coproduction agreements generally involve more permutations in such matters. While coproductions in film have a history dating from the 1920s, in television they were rarely popular until the 1980s. They now appear to be more and more common, as the cost of production rises and as international markets for television change through deregulation and the rise of a digital, multichannel environment in which the same media operators straddle several countries.

Simple coproductions (those that provide financing in return for distribution rights) offer significant advantages to the production partners and have been undertaken for many years. Having multiple partners means more money for a project, and in an era of escalating production costs, the financial needs of television production can be tremendous, particularly for certain genres. Most coproduction arrangements address the level and source of resource contributions, what each partner receives (such as distribution rights in certain territories), the controls and approvals each partner can wield (such as choice of actors and locations), and how the venture's credits will appear on the final product.

Coproductions have been especially popular with television networks that require long-format programs or films but do not have a sufficiently large budget to produce programs of their own. In the United States, for example, coproductions first became common between the public broadcasting stations in major markets (Boston, Maryland, New York City) and the British Broadcasting Corporation (BBC). Coproductions offered U.S. public television stations the opportunity to produce high-quality products at a fraction of the costs of creating such programs independently. In return, the arrangements offered the BBC, with its huge expenditures on production facilities, a means of stretching its budget with no threat to its other distribution rights or its own primary market, the United Kingdom. The first such coproduction, a 1971 U.S. public broadcaster/BBC venture called *The First Churchill,* was a BBC period saga that won an Emmy. Since then, such ventures have become common fare for PBS stations.

In the 1990s coproductions also became popular production vehicles for numerous U.S.-based cable services such as A&E (Arts and Entertainment), Bravo, TLC (The Learning Channel), and Discovery. Since many of those networks have sister operations based in numerous countries, their use of international coproductions is increasingly common. Similarly, as so many American commercial broadcasters have merged with other companies and become integrated into global enterprises, international production arrangements have become more common. U.S. commercial television producers have typically partnered with other English-language broadcasting systems, but since the late 1990s, U.S. TV producers also have turned to partners from non-English-language countries, notably Germany and Japan, to stretch finances and reach broader markets.

Coproduction treaties serve to regularize the government benefits that accrue to undertaking international coproductions. Such treaties establish terms that, when met, enable productions to qualify for various forms of government support. While the specifics of such treaties vary, they generally ensure that creative, technical, and financial contributions will be balanced, over time, among the participating countries; the treaties may scrutinize crew composition, investment, actors, sites, and perhaps even the language of the production. For countries such as Canada and France, as well as other European Union (EU) members, coproduction treaties ensure that the resulting product qualifies as "domestic," a category crucial in meeting legally established quotas determining allowable amounts of imported television content. The treaties also ensure that coproduced material is eligible for government financing or investor tax credits in terms of the national policies. Organizations such as Eurimages, a Council of Europe production fund, have been created specifically to foster increased coproductions among European countries, thereby encouraging the vitality of filmmaking throughout the continent.

The increase in cable, satellite, and commercial television channels that occurred around the world in the 1980s and 1990s prompted an intensified search for affordable programming and made coproductions even more attractive for maximizing production and distribution. The international aspects of television programming now receive greater scrutiny from the outset of program planning; no longer are domestic markets the sole or even necessarily the primary consideration in the planning process. Making television programs that can cater to multiple audiences across national boundaries increasingly requires care and an awareness of audiences as well as broadcasting conventions around the globe. France's Canal Plus is a leader in this effort, crafting production arrangements with numerous European pay-TV operations as well as Hollywood ventures.

Another notable consequence involves the range of content accommodations that coproductions entail when the products must satisfy different national audiences. A great deal of scholarly interest and some attention by policymakers have been directed at the perceived threat to "national" television that international coproductions may represent. In its most extreme version, this threat invokes a scenario of homogeneous, global programs driving out national television production that caters to and captures what is meaningful to local audiences. In a sense, some concern over coproduction joins the worry focused on

"Americanization" or "cultural imperialism" of international television programming. Selection of the primary language in which to record dialogue and the choice to dub or subtitle also figure into this issue. The response of the European Union to such problems to date has included a loosely worded 1989 Broadcasting Directive urging members to ensure that at least 50 percent of their television programming originated from within the EU. The EU also established several programs (such as the MEDIA program) to support and invigorate the production and exhibition infrastructure within member countries. In 2001, for example, the European Commission and the European Investment Bank assembled a $445.2 million financial support package to nurture the European film industry for a few years, and one initiative that received funding was the digitization of film archives belonging to Canal Plus. The program specifically did not request that the financers retain copyright to the funded projects, a possible sticking point in encouraging production.

As financing vehicles, coproductions have emerged as particularly significant means for smaller-market countries to ensure that some local production remains possible. Insofar as the television schedules in many countries rely heavily on films (indeed, in certain countries, such as France, broadcasters are major investors in film), the financial clout available through coproduction is almost mandatory for film production destined for television airing. The ability to produce high-budget feature films is moving out of the reach of single companies, but with partners from several countries or companies the opportunities still exist.

One consequence of the demand for more video product has been intensified competition for coproduction partners, a factor that has driven up the cost of coproductions and threatened arrangements for financially strapped public broadcasting in the United States. Moreover, the process of coproducing is itself not without problems. On the one hand, coproductions offer a mechanism for films and higher-budget television to garner the capital they require, as well as ways to penetrate other markets, but coproductions may also create production headaches emerging from the very difficult process of being accountable to multiple funders and multiple audiences. Coproductions also must deal with issues related to multiple styles and cultures among the cast and crew. Many efforts have floundered when partners could not agree on script, production technique, cast, or postproduction issues. One of the earliest and most notorious failed coproduction efforts was *Riviera,* a $35 million project involving several European broadcasters. This soap opera, set on the Côte d'Azur, ultimately pleased none of its backers (nor their audiences), and it has gone down in history as a costly lesson in the frailties of joint production efforts. On the other hand, when coproductions use known actors and actresses and have a firm hand guiding their creative effort, tremendous success can be achieved. The 1999 production of *The Count of Monte Cristo*—a $20 million miniseries sponsored by France's TF1, Germany's KirchGroup, and Italy's Mediaset, and starring well-known French actor Gerard Depardieu and Italian actress Ornella Muti—was a huge success in its European markets and an ideal example of the pan-European production and distribution network arrangements that are becoming popular in the early 21st century.

Coproductions will continue to figure into the growth of international media corporations looking for ways to maximize their investments in productions; partnering with local media companies in various countries has become a way to guarantee broad distribution, as well as a method of obviating certain national restrictions on "imported" television product, and that trend shows no evidence of slowing. However, coproduction does seem to be yielding some production lessons, with the consequence that partners and contracts are more carefully initiated now than was perhaps the case in earlier years. The "Europuddings" and failed efforts that garnered trade press headlines in the late 1980s have given way to growing understanding that coproduction makes most sense only under certain conditions, and only for certain types of projects.

Coproduction's partner vehicle, format licensing, has also became more popular since the 1980s, and it is now pursued actively by many networks with active production schedules. Format licensing represents a useful scheme for adapting tested, lower-budget formula programming (especially quiz shows, such as *Jeopardy* or *Who Wants to Be a Millionaire,* and soap operas) for new markets in a way that allows such programs to be tailored to local tastes and styles. For example, Skyquest Television of Miami, Florida, produced the *telenovela A Todo Corazón* for broadcast in Venezuela and later sold the format to television networks in Argentina and Spain, which hired their own actors but used Skyquest's directors and sets. Format licensing eliminates many of the production problems coproduction may present and effectively domesticates a successful content and a format originated and tested elsewhere.

SHARON STROVER

See also **Geography and Television**

Further Reading

Becker, Jurgen, *European Coproduction in Film and Television: Second Munich Symposium on Film and Media Law, Munich Symposium on Film and Media Law,* Baden-Baden, Germany: Verlagsgellschaft, 1989

Hill, J., "Contemporary British Cinema: Industry, Policy, Identity," *Cineaste,* 26, no. 4 (Fall 2001)

Hill, J., Martin McLoone, and Paul Hainsworth, editors, *Border Crossing: Film in Ireland, Britain, and Europe,* Belfast: Belfast Institute of Irish Studies, 1994

Hoskins, Colin, Stuart McFadyen, and Adam Finn, *Global Television and Film: An Introduction to the Economics of the Business,* Oxford and New York: Oxford University Press, 1997

Jackel, A., "Cultural Cooperation in Europe: The Case of British and French Cinematographic Co-productions with Central and Eastern Europe," *Media, Culture, and Society,* 19, no. 1 (January 1997)

Johnston, C., *International Television Co-production: From Access to Success,* Stoneham, Massachusetts: Butterworth-Heinemann, 1992

McFadyen, Stuart, et al., "Cultural Industries from an Economic/Business Research Perspective," *Canadian Journal of Communication,* 25, no. 1 (winter 2000)

Negrine, R., and S. Papathanassopoulos, *The Internationalisation of Television,* London: Pinter, 1990

Renaud, J., and B. Litman, "Changing Dynamics of the Overseas Marketplace for TV Programming," *Telecommunications Policy* (September 1985)

Schlesinger, P., "Wishful Thinking: Cultural Politics, Media, and Collective Identities in Europe," *European Journal of Communications* (1993)

Strover, Sharon, "Recent Trends in Coproductions: Demise of the National," in *Democracy and Communications in the New Europe: Change and Continuity in East and West,* edited by F. Corcoran and P. Preston, Cresskill, New Jersey: Hampton Press, 1995

COPS

U.S. Reality Series

COPS has become one of the most successful and long-running television reality series of all time. Premiering on the FOX network on March 11, 1989, *COPS* changed the face of crime programming and helped fuel a global thirst for reality-based shows. From its video vérité form to its continual top spot in the ratings, *COPS* has become an icon in the reality television genre.

During the late 1980s and early 1990s, *COPS* was instrumental in shaping a new form of reality television programming, reality crime television. In the basic format for the show, video crews follow police officers on their daily beat, capturing events in each tour of duty. Shoulder-held cameras capture high-speed chases, drug busts, domestic disputes, and traffic stops. There are no reporters or narrators to provide context for or information about the images being seen. The only explanations given are the occasional observations made by the police officers featured in each episode. Thus, *COPS* allows viewers to witness the gritty and dangerous life of police work from the comfort of their couch. The daily events and experiences are heavily edited, however, into what the series presents as "real-life drama and adventure of crime fighting cops."

COPS is unlike its predecessors, *Unsolved Mysteries* and *America's Most Wanted,* which utilize an interactive element in which viewers call in with information, and thus participate in apprehending criminals. Rather, *COPS* employs a passive format. Viewers do not watch *COPS* to help solve a crime, but merely to gaze at police procedures and practices and at criminal behavior and its potential consequences.

The voyeuristic format of *COPS* has been strongly criticized from its inception. Much of the criticism surrounding *COPS* stems from the show's content, blurring the line between information and entertainment. In an attempt to make the program entertaining for viewers, hours of video, which show police officers merely sitting in their squad car or filling out paperwork, are edited out or not recorded at all. In addition, because *COPS* is a highly successful program, often achieving number-one ratings in its time period for key adult demographics, ontological incongruities and their potential effects on society are of great concern for critics. *COPS* has the power to shape how society views crime, criminal behavior, and police officers. Studies conducted on reality crime programs, like *COPS,* have shown that violent crimes, such as murder, rape, and assault, are overemphasized. This mis-

COPS, 1989–present, Los Angeles police officer with a suspect.
Courtesy of the Everett Collection

representation of reality, researchers warn, could be harmful to society by reinforcing false notions of crime and criminal behavior. Additional criticism is directed at the characterizations constructed for both law enforcement professionals and criminals, characterizations that often fall along lines of social class. These depictions tend to reinforce certain stereotypes, with the frequently inebriated criminals exhibiting violent behavior and strongly expressed antisocial attitudes.

Not only does *COPS* have the ability to affect society's views of the criminal justice system, it has also affected the criminal justice system itself. The possible effect of having cameras present at real-life crime scenes has been a heated topic and has even been subject to judicial debate. At issue are the property rights of the videographic evidence taken at the scene of a crime as well as the protection of privacy rights for the alleged criminals who unknowingly become the stars of reality crime shows. As a consequence of court battles, such programs now face stricter guidelines and scrutiny over how they obtain their graphic docu-cop footage.

Despite its critics, *COPS* continues to enjoy tremendous success. The first-run syndicated series has featured more than 104 different U.S. cities. In addition, *COPS* has ventured outside the United States. Episodes have featured police in London, Hong Kong, Central and South America, Leningrad, and even Moscow, where *COPS* became the first American television show allowed to follow the police in the former Soviet Union. The format has also been marketed on a global scale, increasing its popularity and significance in the reality television genre. *COPS* also achieved critical recognition in 1993 when the show was named the Best Reality Show by the American Television Awards. The series has also regularly received Emmy nominations throughout its 14 seasons on the air.

The popularity of the *COPS* series has stretched into other media ventures. First, the demand for more *COPS* footage spawned the *COPS* home video market. Several videos, including *COPS: Too Hot for TV, COPS: Caught in the Act, COPS: In Hot Pursuit,* and *Best of COPS,* feature highlights from the show or exclusive footage that was edited out for television. In addition to video sales, the *COPS* series has produced several spin-offs including *CODE 3* (FOX) and *Cop Files* (UPN).

LISA JONIAK

See also **Reality Television**

Creators
Malcomb Barbour and John Langley

Executive Producer
John Langley

Producer
Murray Jordan

Production Company
Barbour/Langley Productions

Distribution
Twentieth Television

Musical Theme
"Bad Boys" performed by Inner Circle, music and lyrics by Ian Lewis

Programming History
500-plus episodes
FOX Broadcast Network
March 1989– Saturday 8:00–8:30
Saturday 8:30–9:00

Further Reading

Andersen, R., "'Reality' TV and Criminal Justice," *The Humanist,* 54, no. 5 (1994)

Carmody, Dianne Cyr, "Mixed Messages: Images of Domestic Violence on 'Reality' Television," in *Entertaining Crime: Television Reality Programs,* edited by Mark Fishman and Gray Cavender, New York: De Gruyter, 1998

Cavender, Gray, and Mark Fishman, "Television Reality Crime Programs: Context and History," in *Entertaining Crime: Television Reality Programs,* edited by Mark Fishman and Gray Cavender, New York: De Gruyter, 1998

Denniston, L., "The Risk of Getting Too Close to the Cops," *American Journalism Review,* 15, no. 5 (1993)

Doyle, Aaron, " 'Cops': Television Policing as Policing Reality," in *Entertaining Crime: Television Reality Programs,* edited by Mark Fishman and Gray Cavender, New York: De Gruyter, 1998

Fishman, Mark, "Ratings and Reality: The Persistence of the Reality Crime Genre," in *Entertaining Crime: Television Reality Programs,* edited by Mark Fishman and Gray Cavender, New York: De Gruyter, 1998

Fishman, Mark, and Gray Cavender, editors, *Entertaining Crime: Television Reality Programs,* New York: De Gruyter, 1998

Goodwin, Andrew, "Riding with Ambulances: Television and Its Uses," *Sight and Sound,* 3, no. 1 (1993)

Joniak, Lisa, "Understanding Reality Television: A Triangulated Analysis," Ph.D. diss., University of Florida, 2001

Katz, Jon, "Covering the Cops: A TV Show Moves in Where Journalists Fear to Tread," *Columbia Journalism Review* (January–February 1993)

Kilborn, Richard, " 'How Real Can You Get?': Recent Developments in 'Reality' Television," *European Journal of Communication,* 9 (1994)

Oliver, Mary Beth, and G. Blake Armstrong, "Predictors of Viewing and Enjoyment of Reality-Based and Fictional Crime Shows," *Journalism and Mass Communication Quarterly,* 72, no. 3 (1995)

O'Neill, Edward R., "The Seen of the Crime: Violence, Anxiety, and the Domestic in Police Reality Programming," *Cineaction,* 38 (1995)

Copyright Law and Television

Copyright law is the economic linchpin of the television broadcasting business. In nearly every country of the world, the domestic law permits the owner of the copyright in a literary or artistic work to prevent that work from being copied, broadcast, or communicated to the public. The copyright owner can then license other parties to use the work on either an exclusive or a nonexclusive basis. As broadcasting becomes ever more international in scope and reach, the international framework of copyright law has become as important as the national laws themselves.

The International Framework

The basic principles governing copyright protection at the international level have been laid down in the Berne Convention for the Protection of Literary and Artistic Works, which was last revised in 1979. The convention implements the minimum requirements for the national laws of all signatory states. At the time of this writing, at least 150 countries are members of the Berne Convention, which is administered by the World Intellectual Property Organization (WIPO). A second international convention, the Universal Copyright Convention (UCC), was drawn up to establish a system of international copyright protection under the auspices of the United Nations Educational, Scientific, and Cultural Organization (UNESCO) in 1952. The Berne Convention offers far more copyright protection than the UCC. In essence, the UCC merely says copyright owners in any member country have whatever rights local citizens have in other countries. The Berne Convention, on the other hand, sets minimum standards for copyright protection, requiring each member country to provide at least that much protection.

There is another international convention, the Rome Convention for the Protection of Performers, Producers of Phonograms, and Broadcasting Organizations, which dates from 1961 and extends protection to performers, record producers, and broadcasters. This convention, ratified by 76 countries so far, extended copyright protection to neighboring rights: performing artists enjoy rights over their performances, producers of phonograms over their recordings, and radio and television organizations over their programs. A key reason for negotiating the Rome Convention was to afford international protection to holders of neighboring rights, including broadcasters. By protecting the rights of performers, as well as those of phonogram producers and broadcasters, however, the Rome Convention gave performers rights that many countries, such as the United States, considered excessive. Such countries have therefore declined to ratify the Rome Convention.

Finally, a chapter protecting Trade-Related Aspects of Intellectual Property Rights (TRIPS) is included in the WTO Agreement, which was accepted in 1994 and is administered by the World Trade Organization. The TRIPS Agreement was developed to ensure the provision of proper standards and principles concerning intellectual property rights, and at the same time to foresee means for the enforcement of such rights. The TRIPS Agreement includes some, but not all, of the provisions of the Rome Convention. It only protects performers against the unauthorized recording and broadcasting of live performances (i.e., bootleg recordings and broadcasts). However, the main reason for establishing a parallel system of protecting intellectual property rights within the TRIPS Agreement was to strengthen enforcement procedures for protecting intellectual property rights. Each country must ensure that its laws provide enforcement procedures that are backed by rapid and effective action. Judicial authorities must be given powers to serve an injunction requiring an alleged infringer to desist and to require the destruction of infringing goods or the tools and materials with which the infringing activities were carried out. They must also require the infringer to pay damages and costs to the right holder. Furthermore, under the most-favored-nation clause of the TRIPS Agreement, each country must afford equal, immediate, and unconditional protection to nationals from all other signatories. Finally, any dispute as to the implementation of the provisions of the TRIPS Agreement must be settled under its dispute settlement procedures. This is a new departure, as there are no enforceable dispute procedures in other conventions.

Copyright and Broadcasts

In general, the owner of a literary or artistic work—copyrighted work—has the exclusive right to reproduce the copyrighted work, to create derivative work based on it, and to distribute copies of or perform or display the work to the public. As most broadcasts include literary or artistic works, the broadcaster must normally acquire these exclusive rights to license the work to be produced or broadcast in advance. In the television, music, and motion picture industries, complex business arrangements have been developed to compensate the copyright owners of literary and artistic works that go into television productions.

When recorded music is used, the broadcaster is required to acquire a separate neighboring right in the sound recording of the performance; and in many countries performers also have a separate right in their performance. Therefore, broadcasters wishing to use the music as part of their programming usually enter into an agreement with copyright holders of the music, and they mostly pay them a license fee for the music used in programming. The fee paid is based on the market size of the medium and the amount of music used. If a cinematographic recording is used during a broadcast, the broadcaster must also acquire its broadcasting right. By acquiring the broadcasting rights in all the constituent literary or artistic works that are included in a broadcast, the broadcaster can thus protect the broadcast itself from being copied, broadcast, or communicated to the public.

The broadcaster has five key issues to negotiate when acquiring a license to broadcast a literary or artistic work: (a) the territories for which the right should be acquired; (b) the period of time for which the right should be acquired; (c) whether the right should be licensed on an exclusive or nonexclusive basis; (d) whether to acquire any ancillary rights, such as cable rights; and (e) whether payment to the original right holders should be made immediately or stage by stage with each successive broadcast. Thus, once the broadcaster has acquired the constituent rights in the broadcast, these can form the basis of protection for the broadcast itself.

In some broadcasts, however, there may be no constituent literary or artistic work. The broadcaster cannot rely therefore on the licenses to the constituent works to protect the broadcast itself. Two typical examples would be a live broadcast of a sports event or a discussion program. In common law countries, the broadcaster is normally granted a copyright in the broadcast itself. But in Roman law countries, a broadcaster is only given a neighboring right. Therefore, the international protection afforded by the Berne Convention does not extend to these broadcasts. Under the Berne Convention, states are required to provide copyright protection for a term of the life of the author plus 50 years. However, the convention permits parties to provide for a longer term of protection. Recently, the duration of copyright protection has been extended in both the European Union and the United States. In 1993 the European Union issued a directive on harmonizing the term of copyright protection. The goal was to ensure that there was a single duration for copyright protection across all EU countries. The directive chose the term of Germany, which had the longest copyright term of any EU country, lasting 70 years after the death of the author.

In order to facilitate international trade in television programs, a number of European states used the umbrella of the Council of Europe to establish the European Agreement Concerning Program Exchanges by Means of Television Films in 1958 and the European Agreement to Protect Television Broadcasts in 1960. But in the following year, broadcasters were also afforded more limited, although more widespread, protection by the Rome Convention for the Protection of Performers, Phonogram Producers, and Broadcasting Organizations. Even so, broadcasters that are established in states that are not signatories to the Rome Convention may have to rely for protection on bilateral agreements between the country where they are established and that where protection is claimed. Elsewhere, the broadcaster's only protection could depend on the terms of the contract between the broadcaster and the foreign user.

To bring U.S. law into conformity with that of many European countries, the United States also extended the term in the Sonny Bono Copyright Term Extension Act of 1998. The basic term now is the author's life plus 70 years, or 95 years for works created for hire, which means most corporate copyrights are valid for 95 years.

The Collective Administration of Rights

For many broadcasters, the time and effort in negotiating copyright clearance for all the literary, musical, and artistic works used in their broadcasts is potentially extremely expensive and time-consuming. Conversely, many copyright owners have neither the means nor the ability to monitor the use of their work by broadcasters. In practice, therefore, many rights are collectively administered by collecting societies. These collecting societies are effectively cooperatives between different categories of rights holders.

Originally, this form of administration was mainly confined to musical works. But when sound recording and radio broadcasting arrived, composers and music publishers soon realized that the performing rights of their works in gramophone recordings and radio broadcasts would far outstrip sales of sheet music. They therefore transferred the right to authorize the use of their works to a collecting society. The collecting society can, in turn, authorize recording companies and broadcasters to use a wide range of music in one general contract. Depending on the agreement, the fee the broadcaster has to pay may either be standard or vary according to some agreed criterion, such as the broadcaster's net advertising revenue. The collecting society then passes its revenues back to its members, after deducting its administration costs. On the other hand, broadcasting licenses for cinematographic or musical works are still normally acquired by individual negotiation and the payment of a specific fee.

In the United States, broadcasters and cable operators pay a license fee to the three major music performing rights organizations: the American Society of Composers, Authors, and Publishers (ASCAP), Broadcast Music Incorporated (BMI), and SESAC (formerly Society of European Stage Authors and Composers).

Founded as an international organization in 1926, the International Confederation of Societies of Authors and Composers (CISAC) has provided an international framework of cooperation and financial exchange between national collecting societies. In many countries, similar collecting organizations, or sometimes the same ones, have also been established to license the recording rights for musical works. A parallel international bureau of societies administering those rights, BIEM, has also been set up, which negotiates model agreements with broadcasters and others that serve as the basis for licensing recordings throughout many parts of the world. Today collecting societies administer collectively the author's rights and neighboring rights for broadcasting, the public reception of broadcasts, and cable transmission (including retransmission of broadcasts). In Europe, the simultaneous cable transmission of broadcasts, both domestic and foreign, has led to the formation of "supercollectives," which are able to grant licenses on behalf of several different collective licensing organizations.

Cable Relays of Broadcasts

Once a television program has been broadcast, it is technically possible to capture it and relay it to new audiences by cable. In the early days of the technology, cable was often used to improve signal reception, particularly in the so-called shadow zones, or to distribute the signal through large buildings. The Berne Convention permits states to determine the conditions under which authors of literary and artistic works may exercise their rights to communicate their works to the public by wire, provided that those conditions are prejudicial neither to the moral rights of the author nor to the right to receive equitable remuneration. Many states therefore impose compulsory licenses on the cable rights of literary and artistic works that were incorporated in broadcasts.

The Rome Convention affords even less protection. It denies a performer the right to prevent a performance from being communicated to the public by cable when the performance is already part of a broadcast; and it only allows a broadcaster a separate cable right in its television broadcasts if they are relayed to places where the public must pay an entrance fee. In many countries, therefore, cable operators can relay both domestic and foreign broadcasting services to their subscribers without a sublicense from the original broadcaster.

The U.S. Supreme Court originally held that it was not an infringement of copyright to relay broadcasts to paying subscribers. But the 1976 Copyright Act drew a distinction between "secondary transmissions," which simultaneously retransmit network programs or programs within the local service area of a broadcaster, and the retransmission of far-away nonnetwork programs. The former are deemed to have no adverse economic effect on the copyright owners, whereas the latter are determined to have such an effect, since they distribute the broadcast to a new audience that the original right owner did not anticipate when the works were first licensed. Each distant signal is therefore given a "distant signal equivalent," with different values for independent station networks and educational stations.

In the United States, the compulsory license originally provided for semiannual royalty payments by cable operators to the Copyright Royalty Tribunal (CRT). In 1993 Congress passed legislation to abolish the CRT. As a result, royalty rates are now determined by binding arbitration. The royalties are set by an entity within the U.S. Copyright Office, the Copyright Arbitration Royalty Panel. Every six months, cable operators must provided the Copyright Office with information about retransmitted broadcast signals and the system's gross subscriber receipts from secondary retransmission of local and distant broadcast signals.

In Europe the situation is variable. The United Kingdom permits licensed cable operators to retransmit the broadcasts of British broadcasting organizations. But in Germany, copyright owners are fully protected against their works being retransmitted by cable. In addition, both broadcasters and cable operators have a 25-year neighboring right against rebroadcasting and retransmission. In Austria, complete and unaltered transmissions of the public broadcaster ORF can be retransmitted throughout the country. On the other hand, cable retransmissions of foreign broadcasts are subject to copyright under a statutory license that sets out the remuneration criteria.

A cable operator can now pick up a broadcast signal from a foreign satellite and relay it to its domestic subscribers. In its Council Directive on the coordination of certain rules concerning copyright and rights related to copyright applicable to satellite broadcasting and cable retransmission (93/83), the European Union harmonized the rules for the internal market between its 15 member states. When a program from another member state is retransmitted by cable, the applicable copyrights and related rights must be observed. Any retransmission must be licensed by individual or collective contractual arrangements between cable operators and the relevant right holders. But this provision does not automatically apply to cable retransmissions of broadcasts from countries outside the European Union. Furthermore, although there are several European states that are members of the Council of Europe but not of the European Union, the parallel convention of the Council of Europe (the European Convention Relating to Questions of Copyright Law and Neighboring Rights in the Framework of Transfrontier Broadcasting by Satellite) does not cover the simultaneous, complete, and unchanged retransmission of satellite broadcasts by terrestrial means.

Satellite Broadcasting

Satellite technologies recently have made transfrontier broadcasting possible. In some situations, the signals are broadcast direct to home; elsewhere they are relayed by cable. Some channels, financed by advertising and sponsorship, broadcast open signals. Others, which are financed by subscription, broadcast encrypted signals. But in practice, every satellite service also has to negotiate the appropriate copyright clearances, both for the literary and artistic works in the program and for the broadcast itself.

The Rome Convention of 1961, which for the first time dealt with related or neighboring rights, made no reference to satellite broadcasting. Instead, the 1974 Brussels Convention Relating to the Distribution of Program-Carrying Signals Transmitted by Satellite dealt with the protection of satellite signals by which programs are transmitted between broadcasting organizations or between such organizations and cable distributors. As of this writing, while only 24 countries signed on to the Brussels Convention, the relevant jurisdiction for a transfrontier broadcast is a key issue that the international community has still to resolve.

In 1999 the United States passed legislation enacting the Satellite Home Viewer Improvement Act, which amended the copyright and communications law with respect to satellite delivery to subscribers of over-the-air television broadcast stations. The act provides satellite carriers with a royalty-free copyright license to clear the copyrights to local television broadcast programming in all television markets across the United States. As a result, some satellite carriers have already begun to offer packages of local network stations in certain markets.

Home Taping

While broadcasters and program producers have been battling over copyright protection, another intense battle has been waged over the advent of new technologies such as home video recording and the exchange of copyrighted material on the Internet. Ordinary television audiences can now tape television programs off air, to be stored and replayed at a later time. Many educational institutions also tape broadcasts off air for educational use. There is still no firm agreement at the international level as to whether these activities are a breach of copyright. There are two distinct, but related, issues. First, does the act of making a video or audio recording infringe copyright? And second, does the replaying of the recording infringe copyright?

The Berne Convention allows countries to permit the reproduction of literary and artistic works "in certain special cases, provided that such reproduction does not conflict with a normal exploitation of the work and does not unreasonably prejudice the legitimate interests of the author" (Article 9); and there is a parallel provision for broadcasts in the Rome Convention (Article 15). Therefore, it is not necessarily an infringement of copyright to make an off-air video recording, provided that the manner in which the recording is used does not conflict with the normal exploitation of the work and does not unreasonably prejudice the legitimate interests of the author.

In general, common law countries, such as the United States, permit video recording for domestic use. In the United States, for example, the home videotaping of broadcast television programs was deemed to be fair use by the Supreme Court. In *Sony Corp. v. Universal Studios Inc.* (1984), the Court held that noncommercial in-home use of videotaped programs was not copyright infringement. This case has been referred to as the Betamax case, so named because of Sony's tape format at the time. The decision in the Betamax case opened the door to legal home videotaping of broadcast programs and spurred the purchase of home videotape recorders in the 1980s.

Since the United States is in the midst of moving toward digital television (DTV), there is a far-reaching legal debate about copyright protection in the digital age. As of the time of writing, the "broadcast flag" system is now the subject of a major rule-making proceeding at the Federal Communications Commission. The broadcast flag proposal is a combination of technical standards and federal regulations designed to prevent unauthorized redistribution of digital television broadcasts. It is a set of regulations requiring that DTV receivers and devices that receive content from them—such as TV sets, computers, DVD recorders, and other digital video recorders—be built to protect DTV content marked by digitally encrypted code called the "flag." Overall, a consensus is emerging among industry groups that the digital hardware will include provisions to prevent home videotaping once the DTV transition is complete.

Although most countries in continental Europe consider video recording to be a breach of the author's right, they simultaneously recognize that they cannot prevent the onward march of technology. Many therefore impose a levy, either on the sale of video recorders or on the sale of blank recording tape, or both, to "compensate" right owners for their "lost" revenues. As emerged first in Germany and spread to other states, currently, 12 EU member states have put in place a levy system. Conversely, many right owners consider these levies to be a compulsory license that has been imposed on their right to license the video recordings of television broadcasts of their works. In some countries, however, these levies are also used to subsidize the domestic film production industry. The principles on which such levies have been established and the levels at which they have been set have often been ambiguous.

The regulations governing the educational use of video recordings are even more confused. The Berne Convention allows states to permit the use of literary or artistic works by way of illustration in broadcasts or visual recordings for teaching, provided such use is compatible with fair practice. In the United States, the fair use doctrine, outlined in Section 107 of the U.S. Copyright Act, states that under certain conditions, copyrighted works may be used for teaching, research, scholarship, criticism, or similar purpose without specific permission of the copyright holder. The federal fair use guidelines for off-air recording cover the recording of off-air programs simultaneously with broadcast transmission (including simultaneous cable transmission), which serve as primary criteria when courts assess fair use in cases involving off-air videotaping for educational purposes. Although they do not have the force of law, the guidelines have been considered a safe harbor for educational use. If a particular instance of off-air videotaping is not covered by a specific negotiated agreement with the copyright holder, the fair use guidelines for off-air recording may apply. These guidelines apply to off-air recording by nonprofit educational institutions only.

The policy differences between individual states carry significant implications for domestic educational policies, but some degree of international harmonization may emerge. The EU Commission has prepared a draft directive to introduce a system of blank tape levies in all member states, although at the time of this writing, this proposal has not commanded the consent of a qualified majority in the Council of Ministers. Furthermore, a producer state could choose to use the stronger mechanism for resolving international disputes set down in the TRIPS Agreement in order to challenge a lax interpretation by a user state of the ambiguous provisions in the Berne Convention regulating off-air recording.

VINCENT PORTER AND SEUNG-HWAN MUN

Further Reading

Becker, Jurgen, and Manfred Rehbinder, editors, *European Coproduction in Film and Television: Second Munich Symposium on Film and Media Law,* Baden-Baden: Nomos Verlagsgesellschaft, 1989

Besen, Stanley M., *Copyright Liability for Cable Television: Is Compulsory Licensing the Solution?* Santa Monica, California: Rand Corporation, 1977

Dittrich, Robert, et al., *Intellectual Property Rights and Cable Distribution of Television Programmes: Report Prepared by a Working Party,* Strasbourg: Council of Europe, 1983

Goldstein, Paul, *International Copyright: Principles, Law, and Practice,* Oxford: Oxford University Press, 2001

Mosteshar, Said, and Stephen de B. Bate, *Satellite and Cable Television: International Protection: A Specially Commissioned Report,* London: Longman Professional Intelligence Reports, 1986

Patrick, Dennis R., "Cable Systems Held Ready for Full Copyright Liability; Consumer Seen Benefiting (Inside the FCC)," *Television-Radio Age* (December 29, 1986)

Pichler, Marie Helen, *Copyright Problems of Satellite and Cable Television in Europe,* London and Boston, Massachusetts: Graham and Trotman/Nijhoff, 1987

Porter, Vincent, "The Re-regulation of Television: Pluralism, Constitutionality, and the Free Market in the U.S., West Germany, France, and the United Kingdom," *Media, Culture, and Society* (January 1989)

Porter, Vincent, *Beyond the Berne Convention: Copyright, Broadcasting, and the Single European Market,* London: Libbey, 1991

Porter, Vincent, *Copyright and Information: Limits to the Protection of Literary and Pseudo-literary Works in the Member States of the European Communities: A Report Prepared for the Commission of the European Communities* (DG IV), Luxembourg: Office for Official Publications of the European Communities, and Lanham, Maryland: UNIPUB (distributor), 1992

U.S. Senate Committee on the Judiciary, *Satellite Compulsory License Extension Act of 1994: Report (To accompany S. 1485, as amended),* Washington, D.C.: U.S. Government Printing Office, 1994

Veraldi, Lorna, "Newscasts as Property: Will Retransmission Consent Stimulate Production of More Local Television News?" *Federal Communications Law Journal* (June 1994)

Willard, Stephen Hopkins, "A New Method of Calculating Copyright Liability for Cable Rebroadcasting of Distant Television Signals," *Yale Law Journal* (May 1985)

Corbett, Harry H. (1925–1982)

British Actor

British actor Harry H. Corbett is best remembered for the single role that dominated his career: Harold Steptoe in the BBC's popular and successful sitcom *Steptoe and Son.* Corbett added the "H" to his stage name to distinguish himself from the children's entertainer Harry Corbett (creator of *Sooty*). He did not display any particular leaning toward comedy in his early career, which consisted both of supporting and lead roles in film and television. His bulky frame made him a natural to play tough-guy roles. Corbett appeared regularly in ABC's groundbreaking anthology drama series, *Armchair Theatre,* contributing at least two performances to each season between 1957 and 1961. Notable productions included the death row drama *The Last Mile* (1957), directed by Philip Saville, and Eugene O'Neill's *The Emperor Jones* (1958).

When creating *Steptoe and Son* in 1962, writers Ray Galton and Alan Simpson wanted to cast straight actors, rather than comedians, in the lead roles of Harold and Albert Steptoe. Wilfrid Brambell was cast as Albert, and Corbett given the role of his son Harold. Corbett was later to claim credit for altering Galton and Simpson's original conception by lowering the ages of these characters, making Harold a man approaching his 40s (his own age).

Albert and Harold Steptoe run the business referred to by the show's title. Albert is a widower and Harold does most of the work. But Harold has dreams of advancement; he wants to be sophisticated, to get out of the business he is in, marry, and, most of all, get away from his father. However, these remain dreams, and he knows that his life will not change, and the struggle with his father will go on. The pilot episode, "The Offer," ends with Harold pitifully failing to drag his belongings away to a new life on the back of a cart, a heavily symbolic scene that set the tone for the series as a whole. Over the next four seasons of *Steptoe and Son,* Harold had all his dreams shattered by Albert, whether it was his cultural pursuits (classical music, antiques, and foreign films) or his romantic involvements.

Harry H. Corbett brought great dramatic pathos to the part of Harold, creating a character who struck a nerve in the audience. He had ambitions and pretensions beyond his abilities and social position and was often left bitterly disappointed, but he remained a decent and honest man. Corbett enriched Galton and Simpson's scripts and gave them a character to develop further as the series progressed. His own comic timing also developed with his character, particularly his delivery of the predictable catchphrase "You dirty old man!" when his father displayed his more earthy characteristics.

Between series, and when Galton and Simpson brought *Steptoe and Son* to an end in 1965, both Corbett and Brambell were sought for movie roles because

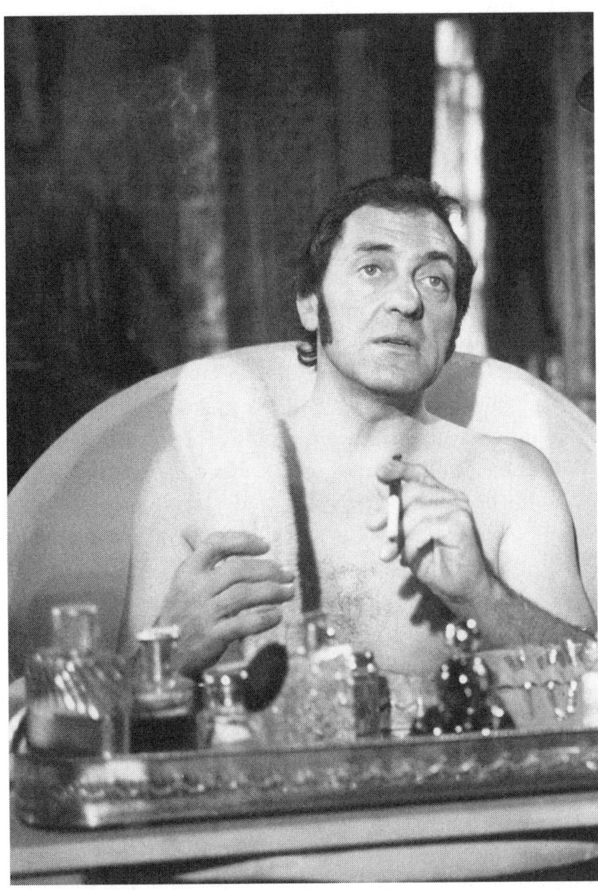

Harry H. Corbett.
Courtesy of the Everett Collection

of their popularity, although Corbett's starring roles in *Ladies Who Do, The Bargee,* and *Rattle of a Simple Man* are barely remembered today. Corbett also became a regular on the chat show scene, particularly as a frequent guest on the *Eamonn Andrews Show.* The audience expected him to be funny and he knew it, but his failure only pointed up the fact that Harold Steptoe was his career.

Fortunately, the BBC brought *Steptoe and Son* back for another four seasons, in color, between 1970 and 1974, and there were two *Steptoe and Son* movies as well. The new episodes simply took up where the series had left off and achieved the same level of popularity and quality as before.

STEVE BRYANT

See also **Steptoe and Son**

Harry H. Corbett. Born in Rangoon, Burma, February 28, 1925. Attended schools in Manchester. Married: 1) Sheila Steafel (divorced); 2) Maureen Blott; two children. Served in Royal Marines during World War II. Trained as radiographer before embarking on career as an actor; joined the Chorlton Repertory Company, later recruited by Joan Littlewood's Theatre Workshop in Stratford East, London; acted extensively in the theater and in films before achieving fame as Harold Steptoe in long-running *Steptoe and Son* comedy series, 1962–65 and 1970–75. Officer, Order of the British Empire, 1976. Died in Hastings, Kent, United Kingdom, March 21, 1982.

Television Series

1962–65, 1970–75	*Steptoe and Son*
1967	*Mr. Aitch*
1969	*The Best Things in Life*
1979–83	*Potter*
1980	*Grundy*

Films

The Passing Stranger, 1954; *Floods of Fear,* 1958; *Nowhere to Go,* 1958; *In the Wake of a Stranger,* 1959; *Shake Hands with the Devil,* 1959; *The Shakedown,* 1960; *Cover Girl Killer,* 1960; *The Big Day,* 1960; *The Unstoppable Man,* 1960; *Marriage of Convenience,* 1960; *Wings of Death,* 1961; *Time to Remember,* 1962; *Some People,* 1962; *Sparrows Can't Sing,* 1963; *Sammy Going South,* 1963; *Ladies Who Do,* 1963; *What a Crazy World,* 1963; *The Bargee,* 1964; *Rattle of a Simple Man,* 1964; *Joey Boy,* 1965; *Carry on Screaming,* 1966; *The Vanishing Busker,* 1966; *The Sandwich Man,* 1966; *Crooks and Coronets,* 1969; *Magnificent Seven Deadly Sins,* 1971; *Steptoe and Son,* 1972; *Steptoe and Son Ride Again,* 1973; *Percy's Progress,* 1974; *Hardcore,* 1976; *The Chiffy Kids,* 1976; *Adventures of a Private Eye,* 1977; *Jabberwocky,* 1977; *What's Up Superdoc,* 1979; *Silver Dream Racer,* 1980; *The Moles,* 1982.

Radio

Steptoe and Son.

Stage (selection)

Hamlet; The Power and the Glory; The Way of the World.

Further Reading

Burke, Michael, "You Dirty Old Man!" *The People* (January 9, 1994)

"How We Met: Ray Galton and Alan Simpson," *The Independent* (June 11, 1995)

Corday, Barbara (1944–)

U.S. Television Producer

Barbara Corday is one of several dozen women who first entered the television business in the early 1970s. She began her entertainment career with a small theatrical agency in New York and later worked there as a publicist. In 1967 she moved to Los Angeles and joined Mann Scharf Associates.

In 1972 she met Barbara Avedon, who had been a television writer for several years, at a political activist group. They began discussing writing and Corday sensed that her experience gave her a certain discipline and ability to tell a story succinctly and "in a kind of a linear fashion." She and Avedon became writing partners and came up with a project that "got us in the door" and that became their calling card. This led to their being hired as a writing team to do several projects, and as freelance writers they wrote numerous episodes for television series and a few pilots from 1972 to 1979.

It was during that period that the two women developed the idea for their best-known television creation, *Cagney and Lacey.* They began the project in 1974 as a theatrical film intended as a comedy feature. Written in a year when "buddy" movies had become popular, their project was a crazy comedy featuring two women, originally planned as a spoof of the police genre. Unable to get the movie made as a feature, they tried to sell it as a television series—and all three networks rejected it. Nobody wanted a television series about two women cops. But when they tried to sell it as a television movie, CBS said "maybe," and the two women rewrote the script completely, adjusting for budget and language and story. As Corday noted, "Here we had written this insane, irreverent feature with all kinds of chases and things exploding and clearly we couldn't do that for television. We retained a lot of what we thought was the feminist point of view."

However, there was a vast difference between what they created in 1974 and what it became by 1982. As Corday commented in an interview, "By the time the show went on as a television series, it was no longer necessary to say a lot of the things we had started out saying; and I think the show became far more intelligent and sensitive and interesting. The characters deepened and broadened and became much more real." Produced by Barney Rosenzweig, *Cagney and Lacey* first appeared as a TV movie in 1981 and then was scheduled as a CBS series beginning in 1982.

In 1979 Avedon returned to freelancing on her own. Corday had by then determined that she was not able to sit down at the typewriter and create without the incentive of a particular show or episode. She liked going into the studio every day and working on projects that kept her really busy. A neighbor, an executive at ABC, offered her a position at the network. Corday surmised that the company wanted someone experienced in production and writing who could deal with writers and producers making shows for ABC. She took the job as vice president of comedy series development at ABC, where she remained for three years.

In 1982 she was offered a position with Columbia Pictures, where she started her own production company, Can't Sing, Can't Dance Productions. Having demonstrated that she could bring projects to completion, she was appointed president of Columbia Pictures Television in 1984, and in March 1987 took on the additional duties of overseeing another Coca-Cola television subsidiary, Embassy Communications. She became president and chief operating officer of Columbia/Embassy Television, overseeing production and development at both units. In October of that same year, she resigned as president.

In July 1988, Corday was named vice president of prime-time programs at CBS. The appointment, announced by network entertainment president Kim LeMasters, placed her in the number-two position behind LeMasters in overseeing the prime-time schedule and gave her broader programming responsibilities than any other woman had ever had at one of the three major television networks. By December 1989, LeMasters resigned after CBS failed to climb out of the third-place position in the ratings, and Corday left shortly thereafter.

In the spring of 1992, Lorimar Television hired Corday to be co–executive producer of the CBS evening serial *Knots Landing.* In the fall of 1993, she was appointed president of New World Television, where she was to create programming for first-run syndication. Following a managerial shakeup, Corday resigned after ten months. In 1996 she was named chair of the film and television production division at the University of Southern California School of Cinema-Television. She stepped down from the position in 2003, but continues to teach at the university.

Corday is a founding member of the Hollywood Women's Political Committee and a member of the Board of Governors of the Academy of Television Arts and Sciences. An outspoken advocate of equality in the workplace, she is one of the most articulate television executives. Her perceptive assessment of the role of women in the television industry coupled with her executive skills has earned her wide respect among her peers.

ROBERT S. ALLEY

See also ***Cagney and Lacey***

Corday, Barbara. Born in New York City, October 15, 1944. Married: 1) Barney Rosenzweig, 1979 (divorced, 1990); 2) Roger Lowenstein, 1992. Began career as publicist in New York and Los Angeles; switched to TV writing; vice president for comedy series development, ABC-TV, 1979–82; co-creator (with Barbara Avedon), *Cagney and Lacey* TV series; president, Columbia Pictures TV, 1984–87; executive vice president, prime-time programming, CBS Entertainment, 1988–90; producer, *Knots Landing* TV series, 1992; president, New World Television, 1993–94; formerly chair of film and television production division, School of Cinema-Television, University of Southern California. Member: Caucus of Writers, Producers and Directors; founding member, Hollywood Women's Political Committee.

Television Series

1979 *American Dream* (writer for pilot)
1981 *Cagney and Lacey* (co-creator)
1992 *Knots Landing* (producer)

Made-for-Television Movie

1980 *Cagney and Lacey*

Further Reading

Battaglio, Stephen, "Woman of the Year," *Adweek's Marketing Week* (June 5, 1989)

D'Acci, Julie, *Defining Women: Television and the Case of Cagney and Lacey,* Chapel Hill: University of North Carolina Press, 1994

McHenry, Susan, "Cagney and Lacey," review, *Ms.* (April 1984)

Tobenkin, David, "Seismic Shift at New World," *Broadcasting and Cable* (August 8, 1994)

Weller, Sheila, "The Prime Time of Barbara Corday," *Ms.* (October 1988)

Coronation Street

British Soap Opera

Coronation Street, the longest-running and most successful British soap opera, was first transmitted on ITV on Friday, December 9, 1960. Made by Granada Television, a Manchester-based commercial company, the *Street,* as it is affectionately known, has been at the top of the British ratings for more than 30 years.

The program is perhaps best known for its realistic depiction of everyday working-class life in a northern community. Set in a fictional area of Weatherfield in a working-class region of northwest England, it grew out of the so-called kitchen sink drama style popularized in the late 1950s. The series, originally called *Florizel Street* by its creator, Tony Warren, began as a limited 13 episodes, but its cast of strong characters, its northern roots, and its sense of community immediately created a loyal following. These factors, combined with skillfully written and often amusing scripts, have ensured its continued success.

From its opening titles with scenes of terraced houses, there is a strong sense of regional and local identity, which is echoed in the language of its characters. Set in a domestic existence of various homes, pubs, and shops, which are all set out to be part of everyday life, *Coronation Street* is imbued with a definite feeling of community. Through its account of supposedly everyday life, the program shows a high degree of social realism. A close parallel is made between the fictional world of Weatherfield and the everyday world inhabited by its audience, whose loyalty is encouraged by the sense of close community, the predictability of plot, and the regular transmission times.

The storylines of *Coronation Street* tend to concen-

Coronation Street.
Courtesy of the Everett Collection

trate on relationships within and between families rather than on topical or social issues, as is the case with the newer soaps such as *Brookside* and *East-Enders.* Critics might argue that the celebration of a mutually supportive community has more than a touch of nostalgia, whilst its fans would argue that the program reflects shifts in social attitudes in Britain.

Early episodes were recorded live without editing, requiring a high standard of performance. This theatrical style of production has influenced the character of the program, resulting in a reliance on good writing and ensemble performance. For many years *Coronation Street* was produced on a studio set and shot on multicamera with few exterior film inserts. The advent of the social realism soaps and introduction of lightweight video cameras have resulted in a dramatic increase in the number of exterior scenes. The *Street* itself has been expanded to incorporate such filming with a specially constructed exterior set, although interior filming is still multicamera.

The *Street,* in common with other soaps, has always been noted for its independent and assertive women characters, such as Ena Sharples, Elsie Tanner, Annie Walker, and more recently Bet Lynch and Rita Fairclough. Even a more downtrodden character such as Hilda Ogden produced a huge amount of affection from the program's audience. The men in the cast often seem weak by comparison. The viewer of *Coronation Street* is often encouraged to make a moral judgment on the behavior of a particular character, and it is generally the stronger women characters who set the tone. Tony Warren summed up the program as "a fascinating freemasonry, a volume of unwritten rules.... *Coronation Street* sets out to explore these values and in doing so, to entertain."

Only two characters have remained on the program

since its launch—Ken Barlow, played by William Roache, and Emily Bishop, née Nugent, played by Eileen Derbyshire. However, the program has been the ground for many actors who have gone on to greater fame, such as Davy Jones (later of the Monkees), Joanna Lumley, and Ben Kingsley. The *Street* has also nurtured many novice writers such as Jack Rosenthal and Jimmy McGovern, while the award-winning, feature-film director Michael Apted has also been part of the production team.

The deaths and departures in recent years of several well-established characters combined with the introduction of *EastEnders, Brookside,* and the Australian soaps have resulted in a shift toward the lives of its younger characters.

The success of *Coronation Street* has resulted in a series of merchandising and promotional ventures by Granada, many of them focused around the soap's local pub and center of gossip, the Rover's Return. By providing a secure economic base through high ratings, *Coronation Street* has enabled Granada to build a wide range of programs. Because of the long-standing cultural ties and familiarity with the world it evokes, *Coronation Street* has also built up a sizable audience in Australia, Canada, and New Zealand.

In 1989 the *Street* went from two to three episodes a week, and in autumn 1996 this was increased to four. Granada was confident that a more pressurized production line would not affect *Coronation Street*'s reputation for quality writing. Instead, it planned to develop secondary characters more strongly. *Coronation Street* celebrated its 40th anniversary in 2000 and continues to top the ratings with an average audience of 16 million. Its longevity and success are testament to the firm place it holds in the hearts of the British public.

JUDITH JONES

See also **Soap Opera**

Producers

Stuart Latham, Derek Granger, Tim Aspinall, Harry Kershaw, Peter Eckersley, Jack Rosenthal, Michael Cox, Richard Doubleday, John Finch, June Howson, Leslie Duxbury, Brian Armstrong, Eric Prytherch, Susi Hush, Bill Podmore, Pauline Shaw, Mervyn Watson, John G. Temple, Carolyn Reynolds, H.V. Kershaw, Richard Everitt, David Liddiment

Programming History

Granada Television
1960–

Further Reading

Dyer, Richard, et al., *Coronation Street,* London: British Film Institute, 1981

Geraghty, Christine, *Women and Soap Opera: A Study of Prime-Time Soaps,* Oxford: Blackwell, 1991

Kilborn, Richard, *Television Soaps,* London: Batsford, 1992

Nown, Graham, editor, *Coronation Street: 25 Years (1960–1985),* London: Ward Lock, in association with Granada Television, 1985

Cosby, Bill (1937–)

U.S. Comedian, Actor

Bill Cosby is a successful comedian, product representative, television producer, storyteller, author, and film and television actor. His work in the media has been recognized by his peers and critics, and acclaimed by audiences.

Cosby began his career as a stand-up comedian and in that arena developed his trademark of using "raceless" humor to capture audience appeal. His "humor for everyone" cast him less as a jokester than as a storyteller, commenting on the experiences of life from a personal point of view. Immensely popular on the nightclub circuit, Cosby translated his act to phonograph recordings and won five Grammys and seven gold records for his comedy albums.

His first starring role on television, however, came not in comedy but in the 1960s action-adventure series *I Spy* (1965–68). Producer Sheldon Leonard fought network hesitance to cast him as costar for Robert Culp, making Cosby one of the first African-American players to appear in a continuing dramatic role on U.S. television. More than the faithful sidekick to the star, Cosby's role developed into an equal partner, winning him three Emmy Awards. His portrayal in this series introduced viewers to an inoffensive African-

American feature character who seldom addressed his blackness or another character's whiteness.

When Cosby began to produce his own comedy series, however, this disassociation with black culture ended. The programs he produced were noted not only for their wit but for introducing a side of African-American life never portrayed on the small screen. Cosby's comedies share several common characteristics. Each has been a trendsetter, has included characters surrounded by family and friends, and has specialized in plots with universal themes and multidimensional characters.

As Chet Kincaid in *The Bill Cosby Show* (1969–71), Cosby defied the typical image of the militant black man depicted on 1960s television by expressing his blackness in more subtle, nonverbal ways. Starting with the opening music by Quincy Jones, the program created a black ambience unique to the African-American experience. The character Kincaid wore dashikis, listened to black music, and had pictures of Martin Luther King and H. Rap Brown and prints by black artist Charles White hanging on the walls of his home. He worked with less-privileged children and ordered "soul" food in black restaurants. Kincaid was pictured as a colleague, friend, teacher, and member of a close, supportive family unit. Audiences experienced his failures and successes in coping with life's everyday occurrences.

Fat Albert and the Cosby Kids (1972–77) was the first animated show to include value-laden messages instead of the slapstick humor used in most cartoons to that time. Plots featured Fat Albert and the Kids playing, going to school, and sharing experiences. After the success of *Fat Albert* on CBS, ABC and NBC also added children's shows to the Saturday-morning schedule that presented specific value-oriented material.

Cosby's most notable success in series television, *The Cosby Show* (1984–92), departed from familiar sitcom formulas filled with disrespectful children and generational conflict; it presented instead a two-parent black family in which both partners worked as professionals. In the Huxtable household, viewers were exposed to the existence and culture of historically black colleges and universities. Prints by black artist Varnette Honeywood decorated the walls. The music of African-American jazz artists was woven into the background or featured for discussion. Events in black history and signs calling for an end to apartheid became elements of plots. Just as Chet Kincaid and the Cosby Kids portray their frailties and personality traits, the Huxtables followed this Cosby pattern by depicting imperfect but likable people in realistic situations.

Even when he turned to the police genre with *The Cosby Mysteries* (1994–95), Cosby continued his exploration and presentation of his fundamental concerns. His use of nonverbal symbols (e.g., pictures, magazines, a fraternity paddle) attached his character, Guy Hanks, a retired criminologist (who recently won the lottery), to African-American culture.

To ensure that universal themes were depicted in his series, Cosby hired professionals to serve as consultants to review scripts. *A Different World* (1987–93) was the spin-off series from *The Cosby Show* that portrayed life on the fictional Hillman College campus. It floundered during its first year on the air, and Cosby hired director and choreographer Debbie Allen to lend her expertise to focus and give direction to writers and actors. The ratings improved significantly, and *A Different World* became a top 20 program for the 1991 season.

Cosby premiered in September 1996 to solid ratings. CBS Television executive Leslie Moonves credited the series with helping to spark a turnaround at the network. Cosby portrayed Hilton Lucas, a curmudgeon and cranky-but-lovable airline employee, forced to readjust when he was laid off, after 30 years, when the company decided to downsize. Lucas spent his days sitting home complaining to his wife Ruthie, who patiently listened to his gripes. Frequent visitors to the Lucas household included grown daughter and law school graduate Erica, Ruthie's friend Pauline, and next-door neighbor Griffin.

The series, based on a British sitcom, *One Foot in the Grave,* initially met with harsh reviews. Some critics felt the Lucas character was too far removed from America's favorite father depicted on *The Cosby Show.* Others believed the storylines were lethargic and the characters poorly developed. After the original writer and executive producer, Richard Day, was fired, the series changed and began to look more like a traditional Cosby sitcom. The Lucas character softened and stopped complaining; upbeat and brighter storylines aired; children appeared in the cast; and a more congenial relationship developed between Lucas and Griffin. The series, though not a ratings winner comparable to *The Cosby Show,* still survived four seasons before going off the air in 2000.

In the 1990s, Cosby also starred in new versions of two old television favorites: *You Bet Your Life,* originally hosted by Groucho Marx, and Art Linkletter's *Kids Say the Darndest Things.* Neither was a hit.

Commercials began to interest Cosby in the mid-1970s, and he has become one of the most respected and believable product spokespersons on television. He has represented Coca-Cola, Jello, Ford Motor Company, Texas Instruments, and Del Monte Foods. Marketing Evaluations, Inc.'s TVQ index, the U.S. television industry's annual nationwide survey of a performer's popularity with viewers, and Video Storyboard Tests, a firm that ranks the most persuasive entertainers in television commercials, rated Cosby the

Bill Cosby.
Courtesy of the Everett Collection

number-one entertainer for five consecutive years during the 1980s.

In 1974 Cosby teamed with Sidney Poitier in the film *Uptown Saturday Night.* This duo was so popular with audiences that two sequels followed, *Let's Do It Again* (1975) and *A Piece of the Action* (1977). Cosby has also starred in a number of other movies, but his Everyman character, so successful on the small screen, has not translated into box office revenues in theatrical releases.

As a creative artist, Cosby's forte is the half-hour comedy. In this form his application and exploration of universal themes and multidimensional characters create situations common to audiences of all ages and races. He counters the accepted practice of portraying African Americans as sterile reproductions of whites, as trapped in criminality, or as persons immersed in abject poverty performing odd jobs for survival. Instead, he creates black characters who are accepted or rejected because they depict real people, rather than "types." These characters emanate from his own experience, not through reading the pages of 18th-century literature or viewing old tapes of *Amos 'n' Andy. The Bill Cosby Show* presented a more realistic image of the black male than had been seen previously. *Fat Albert* significantly altered Saturday-morning network offerings. And with *The Cosby Show,* a standard was set to which all television portrayals of the black family and African-American culture will be compared. Cosby's personal style is stamped on all his products, and his creative technique and signature are reflected in each book he writes or series he produces. As the 21st century begins, Cosby remains one of the few African-American television stars with the clout to determine his destiny on and off the small screen.

BISHETTA D. MERRIT

See also ***Cosby Show, The; Different World, A; I Spy***

Bill Cosby. Born in Germantown, Pennsylvania, July 12, 1937. Served in U.S. Navy, 1956–60. Attended Temple University; University of Massachusetts, M.A., 1972, Ed.D., 1977. Married: Camille Hanks, 1965; children: Erika Ranee, Erinn Chalene, Ennis William, Ensa Camille, and Evin Harrah. Worked as stand-up comedian through college; appeared on *The Tonight Show,* 1965; starred in TV's *I Spy,* 1965–68; guest appearances on shows, including *The Electric Company,* 1971–76; host and voices, *Fat Albert and the Cosby Kids,* 1972–79; star and producer, various television programs, since 1984. Recipient: four Emmy Awards; eight Grammy Awards for comedy recordings.

Television Series

1964–65	*That Was the Week That Was*
1965–68	*I Spy*
1969–71	*The Bill Cosby Show*
1971–76	*The Electric Company*
1972–73	*The New Bill Cosby Show*
1972–77	*Fat Albert and the Cosby Kids*
1976	*Cos*
1981	*The New Fat Albert Show*
1984–92	*The Cosby Show*
1987–93	*A Different World* (executive producer)
1992–93	*You Bet Your Life*
1992–93	*Here and Now* (executive producer)
1994–95	*The Cosby Mysteries*
1996–2000	*Cosby*
1998	*Kids Say the Darndest Things* (host)

Made-for-Television Movies

1971	*To All My Friends on Shore*
1978	*Top Secret*
1994	*I Spy Returns*

Television Specials

1968	*The Bill Cosby Special*
1969	*The Second Bill Cosby Special*
1970	*The Third Bill Cosby Special*
1971	*The Bill Cosby Special, Or?*
1972	*Dick Van Dyke Meets Bill Cosby*
1975	*Cos: The Bill Cosby Comedy Special*
1977	*The Fat Albert Christmas Special*
1977	*The Fat Albert Halloween Special*
1984	*Johnny Carson Presents The Tonight Show Comedians*
1986	*Funny*

Films

Hickey and Boggs, 1972; *Man and Boy,* 1972; *Uptown Saturday Night,* 1974; *Let's Do It Again,* 1975; *Mother, Jugs, and Speed,* 1976; *A Piece of the Action,* 1977; *California Suite,* 1978; *The Devil and Max Devlin,* 1981; *Bill Cosby, Himself,* 1982; *Leonard: Part VI,* 1987; *Ghost Dad,* 1990; *The Meteor Man,* 1993; *Jack,* 1996; *Men of Honor* (executive producer), 2000.

Recordings

Bill Cosby Is a Very Funny Fellow... Right!; I Started Out as a Child; Why Is There Air?; Wonderfulness; Revenge; To Russell My Brother with Whom I Slept; Bill Cosby Is Not Himself These Days; Rat Own Rat Own Rat Own; My Father Confused Me; What Must I Do? What Must I Do?; Disco Bill; Bill's Best Friend; Cosby and the Kids; It's True It's True; Bill Cosby—Himself; 200 MPH; Silverthroat; Hooray for the Salvation Army Band; 8:15 12:15; For Adults Only; Bill Cosby Talks to Kids About Drugs; Inside the Mind of Bill Cosby.

Publications

The Wit and Wisdom of Fat Albert, 1973
Bill Cosby's Personal Guide to Tennis Power, 1975
Fatherhood, 1986
Time Flies, 1988
Love and Marriage, 1989
Little Bill Books (series for children), 1997–
Kids Say the Darndest Things, 1998
Congratulations! Now What?: A Book for Graduates, 1999
Cosbyology: Essays and Observations from the Doctor of Comedy, 2001
It's All Relative: A Field Guide to the Modern Family, 2001

Further Reading

Adams, Barbara Johnston, *The Picture Life of Bill Cosby,* New York: Watts, 1986
Adler, Bill, *The Cosby Wit: His Life and Humor,* New York: Carroll and Graf, 1986
Behrens, Steve, "Billion Dollar Bill," *Channels of Communication* (January–February 1986)
Britt-Gibson, Donna, "Cover Story: The Cos, Family Man for the 80s," *USA Today* (December 23, 1986)
Cohen, Joel H., *Cool Cos: The Story of Bill Cosby,* New York: Scholastic, 1969
Darrach, Brad, "Cosby!" *Life* (June 1985)
Fuller, Linda K., *The Cosby Show: Audiences, Impact, and Implications,* Westport, Connecticut: Greenwood, 1992
Goodgame, Dan, " 'I Do Believe in Control'; Cosby Is a Man Who Gets Laughs and Results—By Doing Things His Way," *Time* (September 28, 1987)
Griffin, Cynthia, and George Hill, "Bill Cosby: In Our Living Rooms for 20 Years," *Ebony Images: Black Americans and Television,* Los Angeles: Daystar, 1986
Jhally, Sut, and Justin Lewis, *Enlightened Racism: The Cosby Show, Audiences, and the Myth of the American Dream,* Boulder, Colorado: Westview, 1992
Klein, Todd, "Bill Cosby: Prime Time's Favorite Father," *Saturday Evening Post* (April 1986)
Lane, Randall, "Bill Cosby, Capitalist," *Forbes* (September 28, 1992)
McClellan, Steve, "Wussler, Cosby Eye NBC Bid," *Broadcasting and Cable* (July 19, 1993)
Merritt, Bishetta D., "Bill Cosby: TV Auteur?" *Journal of Popular Culture* (Spring 1991)
Smith, Ronald L., *Cosby,* New York: St. Martin's Press, 1986
"Someone at the Top Has to Say: 'Enough of This,' " interview, *Newsweek* (December 6, 1993)

Cosby Show, The

U.S. Situation Comedy

The Cosby Show, one of the biggest surprise hits in American television history, dominated Thursday evenings from 1984 to 1992. Focusing on the everyday adventures of an upper-middle-class black family, the series revived a television genre (situation comedy), saved a beleaguered network (NBC), and sparked controversy about race and class in the United States.

The Cosby Show premiered September 20, 1984, and shot to the top of the ratings almost immediately. The series finished third in the ratings its first season (1984–85) and first for the next four seasons. *The Cosby Show* fell from the very top of the ratings only after its sixth season (1989–90), when it finished second behind another family-oriented situation comedy, *Roseanne.*

The Cosby Show was almost not to be. NBC recruited Marcy Carsey and Tom Werner to develop the sitcom after a Bill Cosby monologue about child rearing on NBC's *Tonight* show impressed the network's entertainment chief, Brandon Tartikoff. However, despite Cosby's widespread popularity—he had registered one of the highest audience appeal ratings in history as a commercial pitchman—programmers initially viewed his star potential with suspicion. His television career history was mixed. After costarring in the hit series *I Spy* (1965–68), Cosby appeared in a string of ratings failures: *The Bill Cosby Show* (1969), *The New Bill Cosby Show* (1972), and *Cos* (1976). While NBC fretted over questions concerning Cosby's viability as a television star and situation comedy's status as a dying genre, Carsey and Werner presented the idea to ABC. That network was not interested. At the last minute, just in time for inclusion in the fall schedule, NBC gave a firm commitment to Carsey and Werner to produce a pilot and five episodes for the sitcom. The extraordinary success of the show quickly propelled also-ran NBC into first place in the prime-time ratings.

Set and taped before a studio audience in Brooklyn, New York, *The Cosby Show* revolved around the day-to-day situations faced by Cliff (Bill Cosby) and Clair Huxtable (Phylicia Ayers-Allen, later Phylicia Rashad) and their five children. This family was unlike other black families previously seen on television in that it was solidly upper-middle-class: the Huxtables lived in a fashionable Flatbush brownstone; the father was a respected gynecologist; and the mother a successful attorney. Theo (Malcolm Jamal-Warner), the only son, was something of an underachiever who enjoyed a special relationship with his father. The oldest daughter, Sondra (Sabrina LeBeauf), was a college student at prestigious Princeton University. The next-oldest daughter, Denise (Lisa Bonet), tested her parents' patience with rather eccentric, new-age preoccupations. Denise left the series after the third season to attend the fictitious, historically black Hillman College; her experiences there became the basis of a spin-off, *A Different World* (1987–93). The two younger daughters, Rudy (Keisha Knight Pulliam) and Vanessa (Tempestt Bledsoe), were cute preteens who served admirably as foils to Cosby's hilarious child-rearing routines. Secure in a cocoon of loving parents and affluence, the Huxtable kids steered clear of trouble as they grew up over the series' eight-year run. Indeed, *TV Guide* compared the Huxtables' lifestyle with that of other black families in the United States and described the family as the most "atypical black family in television history."

For many observers, *The Cosby Show* was unique in other ways as well. For example, unlike many situation comedies, the program avoided one-liners, buffoonery, and other standard tactics designed to win laughs. Instead, series writers remained true to Cosby's vision of finding humor in realistic family situations, in the minutiae of human behavior. Thus, episodes generally shunned typical sitcom formulas, featuring instead a rather loose story structure and unpredictable pacing. Moreover, the soundtrack was sweetened with jazz, and the Huxtable home prominently featured contemporary African-American art. Several observers described the result as "classy."

In many respects, *The Cosby Show* and its "classy" aura were designed to address a long history of negative portrayals of blacks on television. Indeed, Alvin Poussaint, a prominent black psychiatrist, was hired by producers as a consultant to help "recode blackness" in the minds of audience members. In contrast to the families in other popular situation comedies about blacks—for example, those in *Sanford and Son* (1972–77), *Good Times* (1974–79), and *The Jeffersons* (1975–85)—the Huxtables were given a particular mix of qualities that its creators thought would challenge common stereotypes of African Americans. These qualities included a strong father figure; a strong nuclear family; parents who were professionals; affluence and fiscal responsibility; a strong emphasis on education; a multigenerational family; multiracial friends; and low-key racial pride.

This project, of course, was not without its critics. Some observers described the show as a 1980s version of *Father Knows Best,* with the Huxtables as a white family in blackface. Moreover, as the show's debut coincided with President Reagan's landslide reelection, and as many of the Huxtables' "qualities" seemed to echo key Republican themes, critics labeled the show's politics as "reformist conservatism." The Huxtables' affluence, they argued, worked to obscure persistent inequalities in the United States—especially those faced by blacks and other minority groups—and to validate the myth of the American Dream. One audience study suggested that the show "strikes a deal" with white viewers, absolving them of responsibility for racial inequality in the United States in exchange for inviting the Huxtables into their living room. Meanwhile, the same study found that black viewers tended to embrace the show for its positive portrayals of blackness but ex-

The Cosby Show, Sabrina LeBeauf, Keshia Knight Pulliam, Lisa Bonet, Malcolm-Jamal Warner, Phylicia Rashad, Bill Cosby, Tempestt Bledsoe, 1984–92.
Courtesy of the Everett Collection

pressed misgivings about the Huxtables' failure to regularly interact with less-affluent blacks.

On an April evening in 1992—when the United States was being saturated with images of fires and racial and economic turmoil from Los Angeles—many viewers opted to tune in to the farewell episode of *The Cosby Show.* In Los Angeles, at least, this viewing choice was almost not an option. KNBC-TV's news coverage of the civil unrest seemed certain to preempt the show, much as news coverage would preempt other network affiliates' regular prime-time programming that evening. But as Los Angeles mayor Tom Bradley worked to restore order to a war-torn city, he offered, perhaps, the greatest testament to the social significance of the series: he successfully lobbied KNBC-TV to broadcast the final episode as originally scheduled.

DARNELL M. HUNT

See also **Cosby, Bill; Comedy, Domestic Settings; Racism, Ethnicity, and Television**

Cast

Dr. Heathcliff (Cliff) Huxtable	Bill Cosby
Clair Huxtable	Phylicia Rashad
Sondra Huxtable Tibideaux	Sabrina Le Beauf
Denise Huxtable Kendall	Lisa Bonet
Theodore Huxtable	Malcolm-Jamal Warner
Vanessa Huxtable	Tempestt Bledsoe
Rudy Huxtable	Keisha Knight Pulliam
Anna Huxtable	Clarice Taylor
Russel Huxtable	Earl Hyman
Peter Chiara (1985–89)	Peter Costa
Elvin Tibideaux (1986–92)	Geoffrey Owens
Kenny ("Bud") (1986–92)	Deon Richmond
Cockroach (1986–87)	Carl Anthony Payne II
Denny (1987–91)	Troy Winbush
Lt. Martin Kendall (1989–92)	Joseph C. Phillips
Olivia Kendall (1989–92)	Raven-Symone
Pam Tucker (1990–92)	Erika Alexander
Dabnis Brickey (1991–92)	William Thomas, Jr.

Producers

Marcy Carsey, Tom Werner, Caryn Sneider, Bill Cosby

Programming History

200 episodes
NBC

September 1984–June 1992	Thursday 8:00–8:30
July 1992–September 1992	Thursday 8:30–9:00

Further Reading

Beller, Miles, "The Cosby Show," *Hollywood Reporter* (September 29, 1986)

Bogle, Donald, *Blacks in American Films and Television: An Encyclopedia,* New York: Fireside, 1988

Brown, Judy, "Leave It to Bill: The Huxtables, the Cleavers of the '80s," *L.A. Weekly* (December 27–January 2, 1985)

Cantor, Muriel, "The American Family on Television: From Molly Goldberg to Bill Cosby," *Journal of Comparative Family Studies* (Summer 1991)

Carson, Tom, "Cosby Knows Best," *Village Voice* (October 23, 1984)

Carter, Richard G., "TV's Black Comfort Zone for Whites," *Television Quarterly* (Fall 1988)

Downing, John D.H., "*The Cosby Show* and American Racial Discourse," in *Discourse and Discrimination,* edited by Geneva Smitherman-Donaldson and Teun A. van Dijk, Detroit, Michigan: Wayne State University Press, 1988

Frazer, June M., and Timothy C. Frazer, "*Father Knows Best* and *The Cosby Show:* Nostalgia and the Sitcom Tradition," *Journal of Popular Culture* (Winter 1993)

Fuller, Linda K., *The Cosby Show: Audiences, Impact, and Implications,* Westport, Connecticut: Greenwood, 1992

Gray, Herman, "Television, Black Americans, and the American Dream," *Critical Studies in Mass Communication* (December 1989)

Gray, Herman, "Response to Justin Lewis and Sut Jhally," *American Quarterly* (March 1994)

Gray, Herman, *Watching Race: Television and the Struggle for "Blackness,"* Minneapolis: University of Minnesota Press, 1995

Inniss, Leslie B., "*The Cosby Show:* The View from the Black Middle Class," *Journal of Black Studies* (July 1995)

Jhally, Sut, and Justin Lewis, *Enlightened Racism: The Cosby Show, Audiences, and the Myth of the American Dream,* Boulder, Colorado: Westview Press, 1992

Johnson, Robert B., "TV's Top Mom and Dad," *Ebony* (February 1986)

Kalu, Anthonia C., "Bill Cosby, Blues, and the Reconstruction of African-American Literary Theory," *The Literary Griot: International Journal of Black Oral and Literary Studies* (Spring–Fall 1992)

McNeil, Alex, *Total Television: A Comprehensive Guide to Programming from 1948 to 1980,* Harmondsworth, England, and New York: Penguin Books, 1980; 4th edition as *Total Television: A Comprehensive Guide to Programming from 1948 to the Present,* New York: Penguin Books, 1996

Merritt, Bishetta D., "Bill Cosby: TV Auteur," *Journal of Popular Culture* (Spring 1991)

Nelson, Carlos, "White Racism and *The Cosby Show:* A Critique," *Black Scholar* (Spring 1995)

Palmer, Gareth, "*The Cosby Show*—An Ideologically Based Analysis," *Critical Survey* (1994)

Payne, Monica A., "The 'Ideal' Black Family? A Caribbean View of *The Cosby Show,*" *Journal of Black Studies* (December 1994)

Real, Michael R., *Super Media: A Cultural Studies Approach,* London: Sage, 1989

Cost-per-Thousand and Cost-per-Point

Media Efficiency Measurement Ratios

Cost-per-thousand (CPM) and cost-per-point (CPP) are two methods of evaluating media efficiency. CPM is a ratio based on how much it costs to reach 1,000 people. CPP is a ratio based on how much it costs to buy one rating point, or 1 percent of the population in an area being evaluated.

Cost-per-thousand is calculated by using the following formula:

Cost of advertising schedule purchased
CPM = 1,000 gross impressions

Cost-per-point is calculated by using the following formula:

Cost of advertising schedule purchased
CPP = gross rating points (GRPs or "grips")

Some explanations: The area being evaluated might be a country, such as the United States, or a television market, such as New York. The major networks cover virtually all of the United States, and their audiences are measured by ACNielsen, the company that provides television networks, television stations, and advertisers with audience measurement, or rating, information.

Television markets typically cover an area inside a circle with a radius of about 75 miles from television stations' transmitter sites plus those homes reached by cable television systems that carry local TV station signals. Such an area is referred to as a "designated marketing area" (DMA) by ACNielsen. DMAs can encompass several counties and many cities and are usually designated by the largest city in the area. For example, the New York market includes Newark, New Jersey; Long Island and White Plains, New York; and Stamford, Connecticut.

The average television network program achieves about an 11.0 rating, which means it reaches 11 percent of the 94 million homes in the United States with television sets, or approximately 10.3 million homes. If an advertiser were to buy 10 commercials each with a rating of 11.0 on a network (ABC, for example), then it would make 10 times 10.3 million, or 103 million gross impressions. If ABC charged an average of $150,000 per 30-second commercial (the typical television commercial length), the total cost of a 10-commercial schedule would be $1.5 million. The CPM of the schedule would be:

$1.5 million
CPM = 103,000 (103 million gross impressions ÷ 1,000)
CPM = $14.56 ($1.5 million divided by 103,000; the cost of making 1,000 impressions)

Advertisers and their advertising agencies and media-buying services evaluate television networks based on CPM because it is a good comparative measure of media efficiency across several media. Thus, the efficiency of reaching 1,000 viewers with the above theoretical schedule on ABC could be compared, for example, with how much it cost to reach 1,000 readers with an ad in *Cosmopolitan.*

There are two primary buying methods, or markets, in which advertising time is purchased on network television. These are referred to as the "upfront" market and the "scatter" market. The upfront buying market is usually active in the spring of each year. Advertisers place orders for commercials that will appear in television programs run during the television season beginning in the fall of each year. By buying in advance and committing for a full network season (which runs until roughly the second week in April) advertisers are given lower prices than they would pay in the later, scatter, market. The scatter market is active at a period much closer to the actual time when the advertising is to appear. Advertisers may purchase time in September, for example, in order for their ads to run during a fourth-quarter schedule, from October through December.

The networks give advertisers CPM guarantees for buying in the upfront market. If a network does not deliver the guaranteed ratings, it will run free commercials, called "make-goods," to compensate for the rating shortfall.

In the past, CPMs for television networks have been based on the number of households watching. However, the use of newer technologies such as VCRs and cable television networks has increasingly fragmented the television audience. Recognizing this change, advertisers have tended to evaluate and compare network schedules based on persons reached rather than on households. Even more specifically, they have based their analysis and spending on numbers of persons within demographic groups. The two most desirable demographics for advertisers are women 18 to 49 years old and all adults 25 to 54.

Advertisers evaluate local television stations based on cost-per-point because the method provides a good comparative measure of media efficiency within a broadcast medium. Rating points are also used by advertising agency media departments as a planning tool to make very rough estimates of how many times an average viewer might be reached by a particular advertisement placed within the television schedule. For example, a media plan might call for 300 rating points to be purchased in a television market with the hope that 100 percent of the viewers in the market might see a commercial three times (a frequency of three). Thus, using rating points and CPP serves both an evaluative function and a planning function.

CHARLES WARNER

See also **Market; Ratings; Share**

Further Reading

Warner, C., and J. Buchman, *Broadcast and Cable Selling,* Belmont, California: Wadsworth, 1993

Webster, James G., and Lawrence W. Lichty, *Ratings Analysis: Theory and Practice,* Hillsdale, New Jersey: Erlbaum, 1991

Country Music Television

U.S. Cable Network

Country Music Television (CMT), a 24-hour, advertiser-supported music video channel that airs videos exclusively on basic cable systems, has emerged in recent years as one of the fastest growing cable channels in the United States. In a symbiotic relationship with record companies and radio stations, CMT has become the most influential aspect in the introduction and popularity of new artists in the country music entertainment field. CMT is also credited with creating the "young country" format that many radio stations have adopted, and with shaping other new trends in the country music genre.

The channel went on the air in March 1983 with about 20 videos and a very small audience. Many observers in the country music industry did not take the channel seriously because they were too concerned about the image already created by Music Television (MTV), an image decidedly at odds with that created by the country music establishment in Nashville. After several years of struggle, CMT was acquired in 1991 by Gaylord Communications and Group W Satellite Communications. In 1999 it was purchased by Viacom, Inc., in a group deal for MTV Networks.

In 1992 CMT was launched in Europe. It went on the air in the Asia-Pacific region in 1994 and in Latin America in 1995. According to the ACNielsen ratings service, CMT now reaches almost 57 million domestic subscribers. CMT also offers an extensive Internet website designed for a younger audience featuring artist appearances, play lists, reviews, and television schedules.

The popularity of country music was not truly realized until the use of Soundscan, a computerized tabulation technique. This system, which reads a barcode and counts the actual number of record, cassette, and compact disc sales, is used at discount stores such as Wal-Mart and Kmart, where a significant number of purchases of country music are made. ACNielsen reports that CMT is the number-one choice for cable programming among women aged 18 to 49.

Based in Nashville, CMT has become a major influence in the success of country music artists and their records. The network features live specials including the Farm Aid benefit concert and sponsors the popular Fan Fair in Nashville annually. CMT develops original programming and houses a library of 4,000-plus music videos. Its promotional fleet includes several 53-foot promotional trucks that regularly promote special events and enhance more than 1,200 local events across the United States.

The Gavin Reports, a music industry publication, noted that much of the popularity of country music artists is attributed to CMT and the impact it has had on the marketing of country music. Another indication of this effect is evidenced through the tracking of CMT's "pick hits," videos selected each week to receive additional play. In 1993, 68 percent of the recordings supported by pick hit videos reached the top ten charts of *Radio and Records,* a major music industry trade publication.

MARGARET MILLER BUTCHER

See also **MTV; Music on Television**

Further Reading

Malone, Bill C., *Country Music U.S.A.,* 2nd rev. edition, Austin, Texas: University of Texas Press, 2002

Wolfe, Charles K., and James Edward Akenson, editors, *The Women of Country Music: A Reader,* Lexington, Kentucky: University Press of Kentucky, 2003

Country Practice, A

Australian Drama Series

A Country Practice, one of Australia's longest-running and most successful drama series, aired on Australian Television Network (Channel 7) in Sydney and networked stations across Australia from 1981 to 1994. Produced by Sydney-based company JNP, the series consistently drew high ratings in Australia and also screened on the ITV network in Britain, on West German cable television, and on the European satellite system Sky TV, as well as in the United States, Italy, Sweden, New Zealand, Ireland, Zimbabwe, Zambia, Malta, and Hong Kong. In the mid-1980s, executive producer James Davern estimated an audience worldwide of between 5 and 6 million people.

In their comprehensive, book-length treatment of the series, John Tulloch and Albert Moran identify *A Country Practice* as "quality soap." While produced on a modest budget, it was noted for the high priority given to creative script development and its sometimes provocative treatment of topical social issues. It was particularly important in the context of Australian television for staking a position somewhere between the high-cultural production values of the government-funded Australian Broadcasting Corporation and the often narrow commercialism of Australian drama screened on the privately owned networks.

Set in Wandin Valley, a fictional location in rural New South Wales, the series focused on a small medical practice, a site that provides a window into the life of the wider community. Key founding characters were Dr. Terence Elliott (Shane Porteous); his junior partner, Dr. Simon Bowen (Grant Dodwell); the doctors' receptionist, Shirley Dean (Lorraie Desmond); and her daughter Vicky (Penny Cook), a local vet. The mainstay of narrative development was romance, the most notable instance being the evolving relationship of Simon and Vicky, which culminated, at the high point of the series' ratings, in their wedding in 1983. Against this background and the general peace of the rural community, disruptive and confrontational episodes often dealt with illnesses or deaths encountered in the medical practice but also took up issues such as youth unemployment, the problems of aging, or the position of aboriginal people in Australian society.

Much of the interest of the series was generated by the ongoing tension between romanticism and realism. On the one hand, it was a conscious policy, as producer James Davern put it, "to reinforce the positive values of human relationships." The series rarely featured violence, frankly presenting itself as an es-

A Country Practice.
Photo courtesy of JNP Films Pty. Ltd.

cape from the harsher realities of news and current affairs, and implicitly distancing itself both from the dominant strain in imported U.S.-produced drama and from other long-running Australian series such as *Prisoner* and *Homicide.* The rural setting provided ample opportunity for midrange shots of outdoor scenes as well as the inclusion of animals. It also established the series within the tradition that has been most successful in giving Australian audiovisual products international exposure, a tradition that includes feature films such as *Picnic at Hanging Rock, The Man from Snowy River,* and *Crocodile Dundee.* More recently, the international appeal of Australian settings as a site of innocence and harmonious community has been spectacularly demonstrated by the success of *Neighbours* and *Home and Away* in the United Kingdom.

On the other hand, the series became widely recognized for its topicality on medical and social issues and responded closely to the immediate concerns of its largely urban audience. Material for episodes was often directly inspired by news or current-affairs stories or by suggestions from viewers and organizations such as the Australian Medical Association. Particularly in the medical area, *A Country Practice* was overtly pedagogical, providing basic information on problems such as heart failure, leukemia, epilepsy, alcoholism, and leprosy. Working from the relative safety of this base of technical expertise, it also took positions on more controversial issues—for example, suggesting in one notable episode that unemployment cannot be blamed on a lack of motivation of the unemployed themselves. The series employed naturalistic dialogue, sets, and action, and it strove to avoid what is often identified in Australia as "Hollywood" sentimentality.

A Country Practice ceased production in 1993, largely as a result of staff losses. In the history of Australian television, it remains a landmark for its success in overseas markets and for setting a standard in quality, low-budget production.

MARK GIBSON

Cast

Ben Green	Nick Bufalo
Alex Fraser/Elliott	Di Smith
Jo Loveday/Langley	Josephine Mitchell
Cathy Hayden/Freeman	Kate Raison
Matt Tyler	John Tarrant
Lucy Gardiner/Tyler	Georgie Parker
Dr. Chris Kouros	Michael Muntz
Jessica Kouros	Georgina Fisher
Julian "Luke" Ross	Matt Day
Dr. Terence Elliott	Shane Porteous
Sister Shirley Dean/Gilroy	Lorraie Desmond
Sgt. Frank Gilroy	Brian Wenzel
Vet Vicky Dean/Bowen	Penny Cook
Dr. Simon Bowen	Grant Dodwell
Melissa "Molly" Jones	Anne Tenney
Brendan Jones	Shane Withington
Vernon "Cookie" Locke	Syd Heylen
Bob Hatfield	Gordon Piper
Miss Esme Watson	Joyce Jacobs
Nurse Judy Loveday	Wendy Strethlow
Matron Sloan	Joan Sydney

Producers

James Davern, Lynn Bayonas, Marie Trevor, Bruce Best, Forrest Redlich, Bill Searle, Denny Lawrence, Robyn Sinclair, Peter Dodds, Mark Callam

Programming History

1,058 episodes
Seven Network

November 1981–January 1982	Monday and Thursday 7:30–8:30
February 1982–March 1987	Tuesday and Wednesday 7:30–8:30
March 1987–April 1993	Monday and Tuesday 7:30–8:30

29 episodes
Ten Network

April 1994–May 1994	Wednesday 7:30–8:30
June 1994–July 1994	Saturday 7:30–8:30
July 1994–November 1994	Saturday 5:30–6:30

Further Reading

Day, Christopher, editor, *A Country Practice: 10th Birthday Souvenir,* Sydney: Express, 1991

McKee, Alan, "*A Country Practice:* Making Issues Social," in his *Australian Television: A Genealogy of Great Moments,* Melbourne: Oxford University Press, 2001

Tulloch, John, and Albert Moran, *A Country Practice: Quality Soap,* Sydney: Currency Press, 1986

Couric, Katie (1957–)

U.S. Anchor

Katie Couric became a national celebrity on April 5, 1991, the day she began her tenure as the female coanchor on NBC's *Today.* Her arrival in that position was also tinged with notoriety, as she replaced Deborah Norville, then on maternity leave with some expectation of returning to the post. Barbara Walters, Jane Pauley, and Norville had previously filled the same position, with Walters and Pauley each spending 13 years welcoming viewers to the peacock network's morning news and talk show. Couric is expected to outlast her predecessors. In December 2001, she agreed to stay with *Today* until 2006 and will earn more than $13 million per year. When the contract was signed, Couric became the highest-paid woman in television news.

Historically, *Today* has garnered more viewers than its chief competitor, ABC's *Good Morning America. Today*'s ratings plunged when Pauley left, however, and for 34 weeks, while Norville served as *Today* coanchor with Bryant Gumbel, ABC attracted a larger audience at 7 A.M. than NBC. Soon after Couric began her hosting duties, Gumbel left for vacation. That week, *Today* overtook *Good Morning America* as the nation's most-watched morning show. Since then, Couric has helmed *Today* through a cohost change (when Gumbel departed the show), guest anchored the *Nightly News,* and provided coverage for NBC's sports, newsmagazines, and parades.

Katherine Anne Couric was born January 7, 1957, in Arlington, Virginia, to Elinor and John Couric, a journalist. She majored in American studies at the University of Virginia, graduating with honors. Twenty-two-year-old Couric impressed veteran television journalist Sam Donaldson, who appointed her as a desk assistant at ABC network news. A year later, she joined Cable News Network (CNN) in a behind-the-scenes capacity. CNN transferred Couric between venues and eventually gave her on-air exposure. She worked at WTVJ in Miami from 1984 to 1986 as a general assignment reporter.

Couric changed employers again in 1987, moving to Washington, D.C.'s NBC affiliate, WRC-TV. While there, Couric won both a local Emmy and an Associated Press award for a feature about a dating service for the handicapped. In 1989 NBC promoted her to the post of deputy Pentagon correspondent. She joined *Today* as its first national news correspondent in 1990 and in January 1991, became interim host of *Today.* Three months later she accepted the permanent anchor position.

Viewers found Couric to be a compelling personality. The *Washington Journalism Review* named her Best in the Business in 1993, and *Glamour* magazine recognized her as a Woman of the Year. In 2001 the Harris Poll asked a national sample of men and women, "Who is your favorite TV personality?" Couric ranked ninth. In feature articles, she is frequently categorized in terms of her energy and attitude. *Salon Magazine* called her "a chipper everywoman," the *Boston Globe* said Couric was "both impish and assertive," and a satirist described her as "the queen of perky."

NBC capitalized on Couric's popularity by extending her exposure within prime-time news programming. Her assignments included stints as coanchor for *Dateline NBC,* the network's coverage of the XIX Winter Olympic Games from Salt Lake City, and the defunct shows *Now, with Tom Brokaw and Katie Couric* and cable channel MSNBC's interview program *Internight.* Couric has been nominated for 12 national Emmys and has won the award five times for hosting Macy's Thanksgiving Day parades.

Couric has interviewed many of the nation's leading newsmakers. More notable interviewees included Supreme Court justice Sandra Day O'Connor; Colin Powell in 1993 just after his stint with the Joint Chiefs of Staff and again as secretary of defense on September 12, 2001; Reverend Billy Graham; Bill Gates; and Amazon.com's Jeff Bezos. Couric conducted Hillary Clinton's initial TV interview as First Lady and John Kennedy Jr.'s final interview prior to his death in July 2000. Often, however, her subjects are common people faced with extraordinary challenges.

Couric has guest-starred as herself on the television programs *Murphy Brown* and *Will & Grace;* she played a prison guard in the 2002 movie *Austin Powers in Goldmember.* Couric also has publishing credits. She coauthored the children's book *The Brand New Kid,* about how school children interact with classmates from other ethnic groups. Couric penned an introduction for *Life Magazine*'s photograph collection

Katie Couric.
Courtesy of Allison Gollust/NBC

Life with Mother, and she also wrote the foreword for *Childhood Revealed: Art Expressing Pain, Discovery, and Hope,* a collection of drawings from adolescents with emotional, mental, or physical problems.

Couric's personal life has been a success story laden with profound family tragedies. In 1988 she met Washington, D.C., attorney John Paul "Jay" Monahan III, and they married in 1989. The couple had two children, Elinor born in 1990 and Caroline born in 1996. Monahan was diagnosed with colorectal cancer in 1997 and died nine months later in January 1998. Couric's eldest sister, Virginia state senator Emily Couric, died of pancreatic cancer in October 2001.

When Couric's husband began his health struggle, she became a champion for colon cancer awareness, testing, and research. With the Entertainment Industry Foundation and philanthropist Lilly Tartikoff, Couric founded the National Colorectal Cancer Research Alliance (NCCRA). In 2001 she won a George Foster Peabody Award for televising her own colonoscopy examination. In 2002 Couric spoke with cancer survivor and activist Molly McMaster on *Today.* The show premiered public service announcements about the disease prepared at Couric's request by top New York, Boston, and Austin advertising agencies and to be used throughout the United States.

Besides her advocacy on *Today,* Couric has used her connections to influence government policy. In 1998 Hillary Rodham Clinton hosted a White House event focusing on colorectal cancer awareness and screenings. Prior to her death, Couric's sister Emily sponsored a new Virginia law that requires insurance companies to pay for colon cancer screenings. In 2000 Couric testified before Congress about how the disease has affected her life.

It is likely that Katie Couric will be remembered in years to come as an energetic and intelligent woman, someone who used her strength to ask newsmakers tough questions and her compassion to champion children's literacy, intercultural understanding, and cancer education.

JOAN STULLER-GIGLIONE

See also **Morning Television Programs**

Further Reading

Peyser, Marc, "Tops of the Morning: Katie Couric and Matt Lauer Talk About Life on and off 'Today,' " *Newsweek* (January 14, 2002)

Courtroom Television

In the United States, the question of whether to permit television coverage of court proceedings has evolved from a tension created by conflicting rights in the First and Sixth Amendments to the Constitution. Among its several guarantees, the First Amendment dictates that the Congress shall make no law abridging freedom of speech or of the press. The Sixth Amendment grants citizens accused of committing a crime the right to a speedy and public trial by an impartial jury of their peers drawn from the state and district where the crime has taken place. Additionally, the accused is to be informed of the basis for the accusation, is allowed to be confronted by any witnesses testifying against her or him, has the right to secure witnesses on her or his behalf, and can have the assistance of legal representation to counsel her or his case.

At first examination, these rights may not appear to clash. However, the sensational press coverage practiced by the tabloids during the late 19th century, combined with the development of the flash camera in the early 20th, led to the inevitable legal test of these competing rights. Most legal historians refer to the Lindbergh kidnapping trial in 1935 as initiating the hostility to cameras in the courts. Bruno Hauptmann was accused of kidnapping and killing the 18-month-old son of aviation hero Charles Lindbergh. While only a small number of cameras were actually permitted inside the courtroom and photographers generally followed the court order prohibiting taking pictures while court was in session, a few years after the trial's conclusion the American Bar Association (ABA) passed Canon 35 of the association's Canons of Professional and Judicial Ethics, recommending cameras be banned from trials. Although Canon 35 did not have the weight of law, such ABA recommendations are often consulted by state legislatures, state bar associations, and judges writing case opinions. Radio was similarly barred by the ABA in 1941, and television cameras were added to the list in 1963.

As television became a part of life in the United States in the 1950s and early 1960s, most states continued to prohibit any form of camera coverage in their courts. By 1962 only a couple of states permitted television coverage of courtroom trials. In Texas that year, the pretrial hearing of accused scam artist Billie Sol Estes played to live television and radio coverage. Broadcast equipment jammed the courtroom to the degree that, by the time Estes's actual trial began, the judge restricted television cameras to a booth in the back of the courtroom. Live coverage was allowed only periodically, and most trial coverage was done during news reports. Despite these precautions, Estes appealed his conviction by claiming his Sixth Amendment rights had been denied him because of the broadcast coverage. In 1965 the U.S. Supreme Court ruled five to four in Estes's favor. On retrial, Estes was again convicted.

In *Estes v. Texas,* the court majority ruled the Sixth Amendment guarantee to a fair trial was paramount in relation to the press's right to cover the proceeding. Four of the five majority justices wrote that they believed the Sixth Amendment was violated simply by the presence of the television cameras. The majority stated cameras caused a distraction, had a negative impact on testimony, presented mental and physical distress for defendants, placed additional burdens on judges, and allowed judges to utilize televised trials for political purposes.

Many of these concerns were evident to the justices the following year when the Supreme Court addressed the negative influence of media coverage in *Sheppard v. Maxwell* (1966). This was the celebrated case where Dr. Sam Sheppard was accused of murdering his wife in their suburban Cleveland, Ohio, home. Sheppard maintained his innocence throughout, claiming he had wrestled in the bedroom with a shadowy intruder, who knocked the doctor unconscious. According to Sheppard, when he awoke his wife was already dead, bludgeoned to death on the bed. The case, and the ensuing nationwide publicity it received, later provided the basis for the popular television series *The Fugitive.*

Sheppard was arrested and tried in the press even before the coroner's inquest, which was held in a high school gymnasium in front of live broadcast microphones to accommodate media coverage and public interest. The Supreme Court ruled that during both the inquest and trial proceedings, the coroner and judge failed to ensure Sheppard's Sixth Amendment rights by their inability to control the media, jurors, and court officers, as well as by allowing the release of information to the press during the actual trial. The judge, who was up for reelection, was also rebuked for failing to shield jurors from pretrial publicity. While live television coverage of the trial itself was prohibited, the labyrinth of cable and extra lighting needed to cover the trial snaked throughout the courthouse and contributed to the case's carnival atmosphere.

While the Sheppard courtroom was not affected by television coverage to the degree seen in the Estes case, the Supreme Court, in an opinion written by Justice Tom Clark, was explicit when it came to setting forth guidelines judges should follow to ensure a fair trial. These instructions provided the foundation for states and their courts to follow in the future to guarantee proper use of television cameras in courtrooms. As specified by Justice Clark, judges sitting on highly publicized cases in the future were instructed to adopt strict rules governing courtroom use by the media by considering the following: (1) The number of reporters in the courtroom itself should be limited at the first sign that their presence would disrupt the trial. (2) The court should insulate prospective witnesses from the news media. (3) The court should make some effort to control the release of leads, information, and gossip to the press by proscribing extrajudicial statements by police, counsel for both sides, witnesses, and officers of the court. (4) The judge could continue the case or transfer it to another county whenever "there is reasonable likelihood that prejudicial news prior to trial will prevent a fair trial." (5) The judge should discuss with counsel the feasibility of sequestering the jury. In the end, the U.S. Supreme Court ruled that Sheppard deserved a retrial. He was eventually found not guilty.

In the years following *Sheppard,* television technol-

The Menendez trial.
Photo courtesy of CourtTV

ogy improved dramatically as cameras became more portable and required less light to obtain broadcast-quality pictures. While these improvements were being implemented and refined, in 1980 the U.S. Supreme Court ruled in *Richmond Newspapers v. Virginia* that members of the public and the media have a constitutionally guaranteed right to attend criminal trials. This opinion reflected an ongoing trend in the states to open their courts by experimenting with television coverage. By December 1980, 22 states allowed cameras into their court systems to some degree, with 12 more studying such implementation.

In 1976 Florida had led the way by attempting to allow camera coverage of civil and criminal trials. The initial guidelines necessitated agreement from all trial participants, however, and this requirement stifled television coverage in most instances. In July 1977, the Florida State Supreme Court began a one-year study that placed responsibility for opening a trial to television coverage solely on the presiding judge. The state guidelines specified the type of equipment to be used. Additionally, no more than one television camera and camera operator were permitted, and broadcasters could only use a courtroom's existing audio recording system for sound pickup. Broadcast equipment was to remain stationary; no extra lighting beyond existing light in the courtroom was allowed; and film, videotape, and lenses could not be changed while court was in session. The lone camera was to serve as a pool camera if more than one television station desired footage.

After the year-long program was completed, a study discovered that the presence of a television camera was generally not a problem. This conclusion and the state's guidelines were challenged by two Miami Beach police officers who had been found guilty of conspiring to burglarize an area restaurant. Because the case involved two local law enforcement officers who were caught by luck when a local amateur radio operator accidentally overheard them planning the heist, the case drew above-average media attention. The officers' attorney requested Florida's new courtroom rules (Canon 3A[7]) be declared unconstitutional, but the state Supreme Court declined to decide on grounds the rules were not directly relevant to the criminal charges against the officers. Eventually, the trial was held and the defendants found guilty. An appeal was filed claiming the officers had been denied a fair trial because of the trial's television coverage. They were denied appeal throughout the Florida system, but the case was scheduled for hearing by the U.S. Supreme Court. In *Chandler v. Florida* (1981), Chief Justice Warren Burger wrote, "the Constitution does not prohibit a state from experimenting with the program authorized by revised Canon 3A(7)." The Florida procedures provided restrictions on television coverage that worked with technological advances to ensure defendants a fair trial, and since the U.S. Supreme Court found no constitutional issues threatened by Florida's guidelines, the request for a new trial was found lacking.

Shortly following the *Chandler* decision, the majority of states decided to allow camera coverage of some levels of their court systems. By 2001 all 50 states had decided to permit some form of camera coverage of their courts while proceeding to define those contexts in which a camera's presence violates a defendant's rights, especially since this issue was not clarified by the U.S. Supreme Court in *Estes* or *Chandler.*

Broadcast journalists gained entry to most state courts as a result of the latter decision, but they still faced closed doors to the federal court system. On March 12, 1996, the Judicial Conference of the United States voted 14 to 12 to allow cameras to cover federal appeals court cases. The decision allowed each of the 13 federal appellate circuits to determine whether to admit coverage. At the same time the conference voted not to open federal district courtrooms to television. The change of heart by the conference allowed for television coverage of civil cases but left broadcast journalists uncertain whether they could gain access to federal criminal cases.

One change at the U.S. Supreme Court level occurred during the Court's hearings regarding the contentious Florida vote counts in the 2000 presidential election. While not opening the courtroom itself to live video coverage, the justices chose to make available to the media audio transcriptions of oral arguments almost immediately following their conclusion in *Bush v. Gore* (2000).

The U.S. Supreme Court's decision in *Chandler* came at a time when cable television entered a phenomenal growth phase. As the 1980s progressed, cable television networks were created to serve an increasing variety of programming niches. By the decade's conclusion, many cable systems looked like the electronic equivalent of a well-stocked magazine rack, providing special interest material on almost any subject imaginable. Such special interest programming was evident in the July 1991 launch of the Courtroom Television Network (Court TV). The brainchild of Steven Brill, legal journalist and editor of *The American Lawyer,* the channel initially programmed its day to emphasize two or three courtroom trials from around the country. During evening prime time, Court TV's schedule provided a summary of the day's court cases and various original materials. During the weekend, trial highlights from the preceding week were paired with special programming oriented specifically for lawyers. Criticized by some for the "play-by-play" commentary by the channel's legal experts during trial coverage, the service developed a reputation for aggressive trial reporting while fulfilling its mission of demystifying the national court system for the public.

The channel's ratings were often moribund, however, especially when there were no trials available for coverage that caught the public's imagination. In addition, ownership of the channel began changing hands when NBC acquired Cablevision's percentage of Court TV in 1995. In February 1997, Time Warner bought out Steven Brill's stake, with Brill leaving the network he had founded. Time Warner and Liberty Media then purchased NBC's interest in May 1998, becoming equal partners. The key to the channel's revival took place during the fall of 1998, when ex-lawyer Henry Schleiff was brought in as chairman and chief executive officer after stints with Viacom and Studios USA. Schleiff's vision for the service paired daytime's live coverage of trials with off-network crime-and-justice dramas during the evening. At the same time, funding was made available for producing what became the highly acclaimed documentary miniseries *Brooklyn North Homicide Squad.* The new owners' commitment to original programming has been supplemented with purchases of synergistic fare such as reruns of the dramatic crime series *Homicide: Life on the Street* and *NYPD Blue,* while also establishing Internet sites that have proven to be among the best sampled in the cable television universe. These programming changes led to Court TV being named cable's fastest-growing network in 2001 and being established as *the* cable channel for law buffs.

Cable network presence in well-publicized trials was established in the 1980s by Ted Turner's Cable News Network. CNN provided coverage ranging from the Klaus von Bulow attempted murder case and the William Kennedy Smith rape trial to the network's lengthy presentation of the O.J. Simpson murder case. The legal issues discussion show *Burden of Proof,* created during the Simpson trial, became a part of CNN's schedule of specialty news-related fare.

The rise of Court TV, CNN's live coverage of trials, and the use of courtroom footage by local and network television news organizations have brought up issues beyond the constitutional ones posed by the First and Sixth Amendments. Many judges and attorneys still question the effect a television camera's presence has on witnesses, jury members, and counsel during a trial and how these often-subtle nuances contribute to a trial's outcome. Others are concerned that television coverage of cases may be incomplete and contribute to rioting or public misperception and trivialization of crucial issues affecting a case, rather than positively informing viewers about the court system. At the same time, court journalists point out their cameras often act as the public's representative at a trial, while helping the news media provide oversight of the nation's judicial system.

ROBERT CRAIG

See also **Cable Networks**

Further Reading

Bart, Peter, "Trial by Tube," *Variety* (March 27, 1995)

"Court TV at 10," special supplement to *Broadcasting & Cable, Multichannel News, and Cablevision* (July 2001)

Cox, Gail Diane, "TV Changed Politics and Football: What Will It Do to Our System of Justice?" *National Law Journal,* 29 (January 1996)

Craig, R. Stephen, "Cameras in Courtrooms in Florida," *Journalism Quarterly* (winter 1979)

Denniston, Lyle, "Are Federal Cases Headed for Television?" *American Journalism Review* (June 1994)

Diuguid, Carol, "Court Touts Integrity over Sensationalism," *Variety* (December 11, 1995)

Drucker, Susan, "The Televised Mediated Trial: Formal and Substantive Characteristics," *Communication Quarterly* (fall 1989)

Drucker, Susan, "Cameras in the Court Revisited," *New York State Bar Journal* (July–August 1992)

Hernandez, Debra, "Courtroom Cameras Debated," *Editor and Publisher* (February 17, 1996)

"High Court Says No to TV, Radio," *Broadcasting* (November 6, 1989)

Landau, Jack, "The Challenge of the Communications Media," *American Bar Association Journal,* 62 (1976)

Middleton, Kent R., and Bill F. Chamberlin, *The Law of Public Communication,* White Plains, New York: Longman, 1988; 5th edition, with Robert Trager, New York: Longman, 2000
Minow, Newton, and Fred Cate, "Who Is an Impartial Juror in an Age of Mass Media?" *American University Law Review,* 40 (1991)
Pryor, Bert, et al., "The Florida Experiment: An Analysis of On-the-Scene Responses to Cameras in the Courtroom," *Southern Speech Communication Journal* (fall 1979)
Thaler, Paul, *The Watchful Eye: American Justice in the Age of the Television Trial,* Westport, Connecticut: Praeger, 1994

Cousteau, Jacques (1910–1997)

French Scientist and Television Producer

Jacques Cousteau was television's most celebrated maker and presenter of documentaries about the underwater world. Setting the standard for such programs for decades to come, he had a profound influence upon succeeding generations of television documentary makers around the world.

Cousteau was the virtual creator of the underwater documentary, having helped to develop the world's first aqualung diving apparatus in 1943 while a lieutenant in the French Navy and having pioneered the process of underwater television. The aqualung afforded divers a freedom underwater that they had not hitherto enjoyed, and the arrival of equipment to film underwater scenes opened the door to documentary makers for the first time (he also had a hand in the development of the bathyscaphe, which allowed divers to descend to great depths).

Founder of the French Navy's Undersea Research Group in 1946, Cousteau became commander of the research ship *Calypso* (a converted minesweeper) in 1950, and most of his epoch-making films were subsequently made with this vessel as his base of operations (he made a total of some 30 voyages in all). Cousteau's early films were made for the cinema, and he earned Oscars for *The Silent World, The Golden Fish,* and *World Without Sun,* as well as other top awards such as the Palme d'Or at the Cannes Film Festival. Later documentaries were made for television, and such series as *Under the Sea, The World About Us,* and *The Cousteau Odyssey* consistently attracted large audiences when shown in the United Kingdom. *The World of Jacques Cousteau,* first broadcast in 1966, proved internationally successful, running for some eight years (later retitled *The Undersea World of Jacques-Yves Cousteau*) and drawing fascinated audiences of millions all around the globe. When this series ended in 1976, Cousteau concentrated on one-off specials on selected subjects (titles including *Oasis in Space, The Cousteau/Amazon,* and *Cousteau Mississippi*).

The appeal of Cousteau's films was not limited to the subject matter, for Cousteau's narrative, delivered in his distinctive nasal, unremittingly French accent, was part of the character of his work. His narration was occasionally humorous and tended to personalize the species under discussion, with fish being described as "cheeky" or "courageous." The inclusion of members of his family, his wife, Simone, and his two sons (one of whom later died), in his films also added a humanizing touch. Such an approach did much to rouse awareness of the richness of life beneath the waves and underlined the responsibility humankind has toward other species.

The winner of numerous accolades and awards over the years, Cousteau was also respected as an outspoken commentator on a range of environmental issues, particularly noted for his uncompromising stand on such matters as nuclear waste and oil pollution. He also wrote numerous books based on his research and was until 1988 director of the Oceanic Museum of Monaco (a similar institution opened in Paris in 1989 failed to prosper and closed its doors two years later).

DAVID PICKERING

Jacques-Yves Cousteau. Born in Saint-Andre-de-Cubzac, Gironde, France, June 11, 1910. Educated at Stanislas Academy in Paris, Bachelier, 1930; Ecole Navale in Brest, France, 1933. Married: Simone Melchior, 1937 (died, 1990); children: Diane, Elizabeth, Pierre-Yves Daniel, Phillipe (died, 1979). Served in the French Navy, entering as a second lieutenant, 1933; assigned to the naval base at Toulon; served as a gunnery officer, 1939–40; active in the French under-

Jacques-Ives Cousteau, naturalist and undersea explorer, undated.
Courtesy of the Everett Collection/CSU Archives

ground resistance; founded and became head of the French Navy's Undersea Research Group, 1946; resigned from French Navy, 1956. Coinvented the first aqualung, 1943; set a world's free-diving record, 1947; founded and became president, Campagnes Oceanographiques Francaises, 1950, and the Centre d'Etudes Marines Acancees, 1952; as scientific leader, conducted field expeditions aboard his oceanographic research vessel named *Calypso,* 1950–96, and *Calypso II,* from 1996; director, Oceanographic Institute and Museum, Monaco, 1957–88; promoted the Conshelf Saturation Dive Program, 1962; general secretary, International Commission for the Scientific Exploration of the Mediterranean (ICSEM), 1966; author of numerous books, from 1953; author and producer of numerous documentary films and television series; environmental advocate; inventor of turbosail system, 1985. Member: National Academy of Sciences; Académie Française. Recipient: Academy Awards, 1957, 1959, 1965; Cannes Film Festival, Gold Palm Award, 1959; Potts Medal of the Franklin Institute, 1970; Presidential Medal of Freedom, 1985; inducted into the Television Hall of Fame, 1987; National Geographic Society's Centennial Award, 1988; numerous Emmys and Oscars; the Legion of Honor. Died in Paris, June 25, 1997.

Television Series

1966–68	*The World of Jacques Cousteau*
1968–76	*The Undersea World of Jacques Cousteau*
1977	*Oasis in Space*
1977–81	*The Cousteau Odyssey*
1982–84	*The Cousteau/Amazon*
1985–91	*Cousteau's Rediscovery of the World I*
1992–94	*Rediscovery of the World II*

Television Specials (selected)

The Tragedy of the Red Salmon
The Desert Whales; Lagoon of Lost Ships
Dragons of Galapagos; Secrets of the Sunken Caves
The Unsinkable Sea Otter
A Sound of Sea Dolphins
South to Fire and Ice
The Flight of Penguins
Beneath the Frozen World
Blizzard of Hope Bay
Life at the End of the World
Jacques Cousteau's Calypso's Legend
Lilliput Conquers America
Outrage at Valdez
Lilliput in Antarctica

Films (selected)

The Silent World, 1956; *The Golden Fish,* 1959; *World Without Sun,* 1965.

Publications (selected)

The Silent World, with Frederic Dumas, 1952
The Living Sea, with James Dugan, 1963
World Without Sun, edited by James Dugan, 1965
The Shark: Splendid Savage of the Sea, with Phillipe Cousteau, 1970
Diving for Sunken Treasure, with Philippe Diole, 1971
The Ocean World of Jacques Cousteau (21 vols.), 1973
Jacques Cousteau's Calypso, with Alexis Sivirine, 1983
Jacques Cousteau's Amazon Journey, with Mose Richards, 1984

Jacques Cousteau: Whales, with Yves Paccalet, 1988
Cousteau's Great White Shark, with Mose Richards, 1992
Cousteau's Australian Journey, with Mose Richards, 1993

Further Reading

Dunaway, Philip, and George De Kay, editors, *Turning Point,* New York: Random House, 1958
Jonas, Gerald, "Jacques Cousteau: Oceans' Impresario Dies," *New York Times* (June 26, 1997)
Madsen, Axel, *Cousteau: An Unauthorized Biography,* New York: Beaufort, 1986
Wagner, Frederick, *Famous Underwater Adventurers,* New York: Dodd, 1962

Cracker

U.K. Detective Drama

Cracker arrived on British screens in September 1993, a new addition to a schedule already crowded with crime drama. At a time when the genre was dominated by the comfortable whodunit formula of *Inspector Morse* and the soap-opera-like *The Bill,* the series, alongside the contemporary (and similarly impressive) *Between the Lines,* marked a more hard-edged and less flattering approach to the police than had typically been seen in British television drama. Despite an initially lukewarm critical response, the series was a surprise hit, and two further series (24 episodes in all) were made for Granada before the show was retired in 1996.

The series benefited from the inspired casting of Robbie Coltrane, a Scottish actor known chiefly for comic roles (and his recent turn as Hagrid in the *Harry Potter* films), who brought a vicious wit and an imposing physical presence to the part of Fitz, the overweight, arrogant, hard-drinking, chain-smoking, compulsive gambler who was the series' unlikely hero. Detectives with troubled personal lives have been a staple of crime fiction, but it is hard to imagine any so abundantly dysfunctional. Fitz's personal inadequacies, however, were balanced by a razor-sharp mind and an uncanny ability to pinpoint character and to locate the weak spots of his opponents, qualities that placed him in the lineage of Sherlock Holmes.

Fitz was a triumph of characterization for Coltrane and for series creator Jimmy McGovern. But the key to *Cracker*'s success was the fact that its rotund hero was not a policeman at all, but a criminal psychologist. This gave McGovern a distance from the police that enabled a more critical approach. Writers like Conan Doyle, Chandler, and Hammett had previously used an independent detective as a device to make a dig at police incompetence, but the savagery of McGovern's critique was unusual.

The first two stories of the first series, dealing respectively with an apparent case of amnesia and a latter-day Bonnie and Clyde, introduced Fitz's chaotic home life, including a tempestuous relationship with his wife, Judith (admirably played by the underrated Barbara Flynn), and the prolonged psychological cross-examinations that were to be the program's stock-in-trade. Such scenes were a showcase for Fitz's combative interrogation style and his incisive intelligence, but they also illustrated an attention to criminal motivation and psychology that was unusual in a genre that typically prefers its villains two-dimensional.

It was the third and final story of the first season, "One Day a Lemming Will Fly," in which the latent anger in McGovern's writing was given full expression. The story begins with the sexual murder of a sensitive young boy, the suspicion falling on a socially awkward teacher at his school. In an atmosphere of mounting tension, and with a mob outside the police station baying for blood, Fitz secures a confession, only to find that the suspect is actually innocent and the true killer is still at large. The police, however, are satisfied that the case is closed, despite Fitz's protests.

The story was a ferocious piece of social criticism, railing against the police, media, and public hysteria surrounding pedophilia and demonstrating how the search for justice is sacrificed in the cynical pursuit of a "result" to satisfy a political leadership obsessed with statistics and a public thirsty for revenge. Perhaps most extraordinary, the writer calls into question his hero's own previously faultless professional judgment.

Equally powerful was "To Be a Somebody," in which a disturbed young man (memorably played by Robert Carlyle) attempts to avenge the 1986 Hillsborough disaster (in which 96 soccer fans, many of them children, were crushed to death as a result of serious errors in police crowd control, compounded by the insensitivity of some tabloid newspapers). A particularly memorable scene had Christopher Eccleston's Detective Chief Inspector Bilborough, stabbed and slowly bleeding to death, delivering his testimony by radio while his horrified colleagues listen helplessly. McGovern would return to this subject in his 1996 documentary-style drama *Hillsborough.*

McGovern also brought to *Cracker* a fascination with Catholicism, which he would continue to explore in his later work, notably in his screenplay for the feature film *Priest* (directed by Antonia Bird, 1994) and in the BBC series *The Lakes* (1997). McGovern situated *Cracker* in Manchester (a city with a strong Catholic tradition, in part due to its historical ties with Ireland) and themes of guilt, confession, and redemption echo through the series. The villain in one story pretends to be a priest, while another has a priest covering up his brother's crime. Other characters, including the boorish and emotionally unstable Irish policeman Beck (Lorcan Cranitch), struggle with issues of faith and morality. Moreover, Fitz is himself a Catholic-turned-atheist, but when he interrogates suspects he explicitly offers redemption through confession.

Similarly intriguing was the awkward relationship between Fitz and the ambitious but undervalued detective Penhaligon (Geraldine Somerville). Coltrane and Somerville created a tangible sexual chemistry, despite their apparent mismatch in size and temperament. Their relationship, growing from an initial mutual hostility and thriving on a shared intellectual combativeness, was a refreshing departure from conventional representations of sexual attraction.

The brilliance of the early stories proved difficult to sustain, but nevertheless the series continued to offer surprises. Particularly impressive was the unraveling of Beck following Bilborough's death, culminating in his rape of Penhaligon. Other issues tackled in later stories included a murderous Christian sect and a mixed-race rapist driven by insecurity about his ethnicity.

Following McGovern's departure, writers included Paul Abbott, initially one of the show's producers and subsequently creator of the excellent blue-collar drama series *Clocking Off.* Directors included Michael Winterbottom, who has since become one of Britain's most consistently innovative film directors with credits including *Welcome to Sarajevo* (1997) and *Wonderland* (1999), and Simon Cellan Jones, who also moved into feature films with *Some Voices* (2000).

Cracker, Robbie Coltrane, Clive Russell, 1993–95.
Courtesy of the Everett Collection

A one-off special set in Hong Kong failed to recapture the success of the early episodes, and Fitz was retired from British screens in 1996. The following year, an attempt was made to recreate the series, retitled *Fitz,* for an American audience, but, although well written and performed, the show failed to find a large audience.

MARK DUGUID

See also **Coltrane, Robbie; Detective Programs; *Hillsborough;* McGovern, Jimmy**

Cast

Fitz	Robbie Coltrane
Judith Fitzgerald	Barbara Flynn
DCI Bilborough (1993–94)	Christopher Eccleston
DS Beck (1993–95)	Lorcan Cranitch
DS Penhaligan	Geraldine Somerville
DCI Wise (1994–96)	Ricky Tomlinson

Producers
Sally Head, Neal Gub, Paul Abbott, Hilary Bevan Jones

Writers
Jimmy McGovern, Ted Whitehead, Paul Abbott

Production History
24 episodes
ITV (Granada)
1993–96 Mondays 9:00–10:00 (except October 22, 1995: Sunday 9:00–10:00)

Further Reading

Crace, John, *Cracker: The Truth Behind the Fiction,* London: Boxtree in association with Granada Television, 1994
Day Lewis, Sean, *Talk of Drama: Views of the Television Dramatist Now and Then,* Luton, England: John Libbey Media/University of Luton Press, 1998
Page, Adrian, *Cracking Morse Code: Semiotics and Television Drama,* Luton, England: University of Luton Press, 2000

Craft, Christine (1943–)

U.S. Broadcast Journalist

Christine Craft is a broadcast journalist who will be remembered not for what she said on the air but rather for what she said, and what was said about her, in a federal district courtroom. It was there that she challenged the different standards by which male and female on-air broadcast news anchors were being judged in the U.S. media industries.

Craft's broadcast career began in 1974, when, at the age of 29, she took a job as a weather reporter with KSBW-TV in Salinas, California. During her tenure at Channel 8 in Salinas, as well as her next position at KPIX-TV, the CBS affiliate in San Francisco, Craft filled every on-air position in the newsroom, from weather to sports to news reporting.

In 1977 Craft was hired by CBS Television to do features on women athletes for a *CBS Sports Spectacular* segment titled "Women in Sports." According to Craft, this was her first experience with being "made over," and she hated it. Among the physical characteristics that were altered was her hair, bleached so that she appeared on camera as a platinum blonde. After a year at CBS, Craft returned to California, where she again worked in several news positions including coanchor for the ABC affiliate in Santa Barbara, KEYT-TV.

Her life inexorably changed when she received a phone call from the Metromedia, Inc., ABC affiliate in Kansas City, Missouri, KMBC-TV Channel 9. According to Craft, a consulting firm had made a tape of her without her permission or knowledge and marketed it around the country. Executives at KMBC saw the tape and called her to Kansas City for an interview and audition. Given her experience at CBS, Craft stated that she told the station management that she "showed signs of her age and experience" and was not willing to be made over. She interviewed and auditioned in the KMBC studios and was hired as coanchor with a two-year contract. Eight months later, in July 1981, Craft was informed that she had been demoted to reporter because focus group research had indicated that she was "too old, too unattractive, and wouldn't defer to men." Craft decided to challenge the action of management, and when asked for a comment on why she was no longer anchor, she told a Kansas City newspaper what had occurred.

Craft left the station in Kansas City and returned to television news in Santa Barbara, where for two years she prepared a breach-of-contract lawsuit against Metromedia. In August 1983, a ten-day trial was held at Federal District Court in Kansas City, at the conclusion of which the jury unanimously returned a verdict in favor of Craft, awarding her $500,000 in damages. U.S. District Court judge Joseph E. Stevens Jr., then threw out the verdict and called for a second trial in Joplin, Missouri. After a six-day trial in 1984 in Joplin, the jury again returned a verdict in favor of Craft. Metromedia appealed, and the 8th Circuit Court threw out the second verdict. When the U.S. Supreme Court would not hear the case, Craft's years of litigation ended.

In 1986 Craft wrote *Too Old, Too Ugly, Not Deferential to Men* about her experiences. She practices law and continues to appear as a broadcast journalist on both radio and television, most recently in the San Francisco Bay area.

THOMAS A. BIRK

See also **Anchor**

Christine Craft. Born in 1943. Graduated from the University of the Pacific McGeorge School of Law, 1995. Competitive surfer and teacher; weather reporter, KSBW-TV, Salinas, California, 1974; reporter, KPIX-TV, San Francisco; worked at KEYT-TV, Santa Barbara, California; coanchor, KMBC-TV, Kansas City, Missouri, 1981; returned briefly to KEYT-TV, 1983; lecturer, 1983–84; currently works as radio talk show host and attorney in San Francisco Bay area.

Publications

Christine Craft: An Anchorwoman's Story, 1986
Too Old, Too Ugly, Not Deferential to Men, 1986

Further Reading

Smith, S.B., "Television Executives Upset by Kansas City Finding," *New York Times* (August 9, 1983)
Thornton, M., "Newscaster Wins $500,000," *Washington Post* (August 9, 1983)
"Woman in TV Sex Bias Suit Is Awarded $500,000 by Jury," *New York Times* (August 9, 1983)

Craig, Wendy (1934–)

British Actor

In the 1970s and 1980s, Wendy Craig emerged as one of the most familiar faces of British domestic situation comedy, starring in a string of series in which she typically played a self-searching housewife and mother struggling to cope with the various demands made by her family, her home, and life in general.

Craig began a career on the stage as a very young child and later entered films before establishing herself as a television performer. *Not in Front of the Children* was the first of the sitcoms in which she was cast in the role of harassed mother, a role she was later to make peculiarly her own. Resilient and yet sensitive (or, according to critics of the program and its successors, simpering and middle class), her character, Jennifer Corner, held the family together through crises both trivial and serious. The character appealed to thousands of real women whose days were similarly filled. Newly widowed Sally Harrison in *And Mother Makes Three* (later retitled *And Mother Makes Five* after Sally remarried) and Ria Parkinson in Carla Lane's *Butterflies* were essentially extensions of the same character; only the members of the families and the details of the kitchen decor changed.

Butterflies, with Carla Lane's fluent scripts, was perhaps the most assured of the sitcoms in which Craig was invited to explore the state of mind of a flustered contemporary housewife facing a midlife crisis. Supported by the lugubrious but always watchable Geoffrey Palmer as her husband and the up-and-coming Nicholas Lyndhurst as one of her two sons (the other was played by Andrew Hall), Craig played the part at a high pitch—sometimes arguably overhysterically—as she debated ways to break out of the confinements of the life imposed upon her by her family (chiefly through seemingly endless contemplation of an affair with the smooth and wealthy businessman Leonard Dunn, played by Bruce Montague). The comedy was often obvious (Ria's failure to cook anything without destroying it risked becoming tiresome), the pathos was sometimes painful, and the central character's self-absorption and inability to help herself was irritating to many more liberated viewers, but the skillful characterizations and the pace at which events were played, together with the quality of the support, kept the series fresh and intriguing and ensured a large and faithful audience.

Nanny, about the experiences of a children's nanny in the 1930s, represented something of a variation upon the matriarchal roles with which Craig had become associated. The story of nanny Barbara Gray, caring for the children of the rich and well connected, was in fact Craig's own idea, submitted and accepted under a pen name after she got the idea while flicking through advertisements for children's nurses in *The*

Wendy Craig, *Nanny,* 1981–83.
Courtesy of the Everett Collection

Lady magazine. The program eschewed comedy for a straighter dramatic approach. Comparisons between Craig's enlightened nanny Gray adding a helping hand to obviously dysfunctional upper-crust families and cinema's Mary Poppins were inevitable but did not detract from the success of the series, and an increase in the numbers of girls planning careers as nannies was duly reported as a result.

Since the late 1980s, perhaps reflecting changes in society in general, Craig's matriarch has largely disappeared from the screen. *Laura and Disorder,* which Craig and her real-life son had a hand in writing, depicted her as an accident-prone divorcée newly returned from the United States, but this program proved weak and was only short-lived. Even more misjudged was the attempt to make a British version of the highly acclaimed U.S. comedy series *The Golden Girls,* under the title *Brighton Belles,* with Craig cast as Annie, the equivalent of Rose in the original. The scripts failed entirely to match the wit and vivacity of the U.S. original, and the project was quickly abandoned. Craig has remained busy as a stage actress and in 2001 was cast as Aunt Juley in a major remake of the classic television serial *The Forsyte Saga.*

DAVID PICKERING

Wendy Craig. Born in Sacriston, County Durham, England, June 20, 1934. Attended Central School of Speech and Drama, London; Ipswich Repertory Theatre. Married: Jack Bentley; children: Alaster and Ross. Won first acting award at the age of three; popular star of domestic situation comedy series. Recipient: British Academy of Film and Television Arts Award, 1968; Variety Club TV Personality of the Year Awards, 1969 and 1973; *TV Times* Readers' Funniest Woman on TV, 1972–74; BBC Woman of the Year, 1984.

Television Series

1964	*Room at the Bottom*
1967–70	*Not in Front of the Children*
1971–74	*And Mother Makes Three*
1974–76	*And Mother Makes Five*
1978–82	*Butterflies*
1981–83	*Triangle*
1981–83	*Nanny*
1989	*Laura and Disorder* (also co-writer)
1993	*Brighton Belles*

Films

Room at the Top, 1959; *The Mind Benders,* 1963; *The Servant,* 1963; *The Nanny,* 1965; *Just Like a Woman,* 1966; *I'll Never Forget Whatshisname,* 1967; *Joseph Andrews,* 1977; *Kindergarten Cop,* 1990; *Blown Away,* 1994; *A Family Thing,* 1996; *Girl, Interrupted,* 1999.

Stage (selected)

The Secret Place, 1957; *Heart to Heart,* 1962; *Late Summer Affair,* 1962; *Room at the Top; Easy Virtue,* 1999; *The Rivals,* 2000.

Crawford, Hector (1913–1991)

Australian Producer and Media Executive

Hector Crawford was a Melbourne-based producer of radio and television programs. The most nationalist of Australian producers, his company was a family company not only in the sense of being dominated by the Crawford family but also in the sense of being vertically organized so that every production was controlled from the top of the company. The company was also family oriented in terms of the values esteemed in many of its programs: respect for authority, espousal of domestic values, celebration of Australian history and society. However, these were old-fashioned values and practices, and they were found especially wanting in the 1980s when Crawford was to lose control, some years before his death, of the company he founded.

Hector Crawford was born in 1913 in Melbourne, where he acquired a musical training. While working as a clerk in the late 1930s, he began the *Music for the People* outdoor concerts, which were broadcast by the *Herald and Weekly Times*' own radio station 3DB. In 1940 he became music and recording director of Broadcast Exchange, an Australian recording and radio production company, and in 1942 he rose to the position of managing director. His sister, Dorothy Crawford, trained at the Melbourne Conservatorium and was a professional singer. She worked for the Australian Broadcasting Commission (ABC) in radio and drama productions before joining Broadcast Exchange in 1944 as drama producer. With the encouragement of 3DB, the two set up their own radio program production company, Hector Crawford Productions, in 1945.

Thanks to its special relationship with 3DB and sister stations in the Major Network, Crawford's was very successful in radio. In addition, the market for local radio programs, which had developed considerably in wartime, continued to expand, and by 1950 the company was one of the largest in radio. The company's radio output specialized in music and drama series and features. Some of its important programs were *Melba, Melba Sings, The Blue Danube, John Turner's Family, D24,* and *No Holiday for Halliday.*

When HSV Channel 7 (owned by the *Herald and Weekly Times* newspaper group) went to air on television in late 1956, Crawford Productions was producing a quiz/game show, *Wedding Day,* for the station within a week. However, between 1956 and 1960, HSV Channel 7 bought little except for some quiz shows and a modest sitcom series, *Take That.* In 1961 the company's fortunes improved, with HSV committing itself to the courtroom drama series *Consider Your Verdict.* Its modest success helped pave the way for Crawford's next major development. In 1964 the company sold the police series *Homicide* to HSV and the Seven Network. *Homicide* spawned two other Crawford police series, *Division 4* and *Matlock Police.* These, together with other company series such as *Ryan, Showcase,* and *The Box,* made Crawford Productions a veritable "Hollywood on the Yarra." The company employed hundreds and had construction departments, sound stages, and its own studios. Crawford's hiccuped briefly in 1975, with the cancellation of the three police series, but in late 1976, *The Sullivans* began on the Nine Network. It was the quintessential Crawford series, notable for its good production values and solid entertaining drama that treated traditional institutions—most especially the Australian family in wartime—with great respect. The company was less successful with serials such as *Carson's Law, Skyways, Holiday Island,* and *Good Vibrations.* However, Crawford's was much more successful with two other serials, *Cop Shop* and *The Flying Doctors.* In 1983 Crawford's made its first miniseries, the enormously successful *All the Rivers Run.* Other miniseries included *The Flying Doctors; Alice to Nowhere; My Brother Tom; Whose Baby?; All the Rivers Run II; This Man, This Woman;* and *Jackaroo.* In addition, Crawford's made several films for theatrical release. It also made two children's series, *The Henderson Kids* and *The Zoo Family.*

In 1974 Dorothy Crawford retired from the company because of ill health. Her son, Ian, then shared executive producer credits with Hector Crawford on all Crawford programs.

The larger companies in television drama packaging in Australia have weathered periods of financial difficulty not only because of the cash flow from past successes but also because of other sources of financial stability. In the case of Crawford's, it was sustained by the special relationship it enjoyed with HSV Channel 7 and the Seven Network, which bought a large number of programs from the company. The *Herald and*

Hector Crawford.
Photo courtesy of Crawford Productions Pty. Ltd.

Weekly Times was also ready to help Crawford's with loans in times of need.

In 1972, for example, Hector Crawford privately sold the company to the *Herald and Weekly Times*, only to buy it back a year later. Again, in 1985 Crawford sold 40 percent of shares to the group, as well as a further 10 percent to Gordon and Gotch. This was the situation in early 1987, when Rupert Murdoch's News Ltd. bought out the *Herald and Weekly Times* group and, already owning Gordon and Gotch, found itself owning half of Crawford Productions. With the special relationship with HSV Channel 7 at an end, in poor health after a throat operation, and deciding to capitalize on Crawford's extensive library, Hector Crawford sold the company to Ariadne, a property and tourist company in 1987. Hector Crawford continued as honorary chair and died early in 1991.

ALBERT MORAN

See also **Australian Production Companies; *Homicide***

Hector Crawford. Born in Melbourne, Australia, August 14, 1913. Studied at the Melbourne Conservatorium of Music. Married: Glenda Raymond, 1950; two children. Began career as a choral conductor at the Conservatorium; musical and recording director of radio broadcasting house, Broadcast Exchange of Australia, 1940, managing director, 1942; formed Hector Crawford Productions with older sister, Dorothy, 1945; began producing musical radio programs such as *Music for the People, Opera for the People, The Melba Story, The Amazing Oscar Hammerstein, The Blue Danube;* produced dramatic radio shows *Sincerely Rita Marsden, My Imprisoned Heart, A Woman in Love, Inspector West,* and *Lone Star Lannigan;* entered Melbourne television with game show productions, 1956; produced first one-hour drama series, *Consider Your Verdict,* 1961, followed by the immensely successful police series *Homicide,* 1964; production expanded, at one time having five one-hour drama series playing on all three of the Australian commercial television networks, 1974; sold controlling interests in Crawford Productions, 1985; retired in 1989. Member: Australian Film Commission, 1974; Australian Film and Television School, 1972–76. Died in Melbourne, March 11, 1991.

Television Series (selected)

1961–64	*Consider Your Verdict*
1964–75	*Homicide*
1966–68	*Hunter*
1974–77	*The Box*
1976–82	*The Sullivans*

Television Miniseries (selected)

1983	*All the Rivers Run*

Radio

Music for the People; Opera for the People; The Melba Story; The Amazing Oscar Hammerstein; The Blue Danube; Sincerely Rita Marsden; My Imprisoned Heart; A Woman in Love; Inspector West; Lone Star Lannigan; Consider Your Verdict.

Criticism, Television (Journalistic)

From the early 1900s, U.S. newspapers carried brief descriptions of distant reception of wireless radio signals and items about experimental stations innovating programs. After station KDKA in Pittsburgh inaugurated regular radio broadcast service in 1920, followed by hundreds of new stations, newspaper columns noted distinctive offerings in their schedules. In 1922 the *New York Times* started radio columns by Orrin E. Dunlap Jr. From 1925, Ben Gross pioneered a regular column about broadcasting in the *New York Daily News,* which he continued for 45 years. Newspapers across the country added columns about schedules, programs, and celebrities during radio's golden age in the 1930s and 1940s. During those decades experiments in "radio with pictures" received occasional notice; attention to the new medium of television expanded in the late 1940s as TV stations went on the air in major cities, audiences grew, and advertisers and stars forsook radio for TV networks.

Chronicling those early developments were Jack Gould of the *New York Times* and John Crosby of the *New York Herald Tribune,* in addition to reviewer-critics of lesser impact in other metropolitan areas. From 1946 to 1972, Gould meticulously and even-handedly reported technical, structural (networks, stations), legal (Congress and Federal Communications Commission), economic (advertising), financial, and social aspects of TV as well as programming trends. Crosby began reviewing program content and developments in 1946 with stylistic vigor, offering a personalized judgment that could be caustic. As the medium matured in the 1960s and 1970s, Lawrence Laurent of the *Washington Post* joined the small group of influential media critics writing for major metro newspapers. He explored trends and causal relations and reported interrelations of federal regulatory agencies and broadcast corporations while also appraising major program successes and failures. On the West Coast, where TV entertainment was crafted, the *Los Angeles Times*' Hal Humphrey and Cecil Smith covered the creative community's role in television, emphasizing descriptive reviews of individual programs and series. Other metro dailies and their early, influential program reviewer-critics included the *San Francisco Chronicle*'s Terrance O'Flaherty, *Chicago Sun-Times*' Paul Malloy, and *Chicago Tribune*'s Larry Wolters.

Meanwhile most newspapers carried popular columns about daily program offerings, reported behind-the-scenes information, and relayed tidbits about TV stars. Some referred to this kind of column as "racing along in shorts," a series of brief items each separated by three dots. Complementing local columns were syndicated wire services, featuring a mix of substantive pieces and celebrity interviews. Among long-time syndicated columnists, in addition to *New York Times* and *Washington Post* columnists distributed nationally, were the Associated Press's Cynthia Lowrey and Jay Sharbut.

Weekly and monthly magazines also published analyses of broader patterns and implications of television's structure, programming, and social impact. They featured critics such as *Saturday Review*'s Gilbert Seldes and Robert Lewis Shayon, *Time*'s "Cyclops" (John McPhee, among others), John Lardner and Jay Cocks in *Newsweek,* Marya Mannes in *The Reporter,* and Harlan Ellison's ideosyncratic but trenchant dissections in *Rolling Stone.* Merrill Panitt, Sally Bedell Smith, Neil Hickey, and Frank Swertlow offered serious analysis in weekly *TV Guide;* often multipart investigative reports, those extended pieces appeared alongside pop features and interviews, plus think-pieces by specialists and media practitioners all wrapped around massive TV and cable local listings of regional editions across the country. Reporter-turned-critic Les Brown wrote authoritatively for trade paper *Variety,* then the *New York Times,* then as editor of *Channels of Communication* magazine. Weekly *Variety* published critical reviews of all new entertainment and documentary or news programs, both one-time-only shows and initial episodes of series; the news-magazine's staff faithfully analyzed themes, topics, dramatic presentation, acting, sets, and scenery, including complete listings of production personnel and casts. Reflecting shifting perspectives on the significance of modern mass media, Ken Auletta (*Wall Street Journal, New Yorker*) monitored in exhaustive detail the media megamergers of the 1980s and 1990s.

In the 1950s, TV columnists tended to be reviewers after the fact, offering comments about programs only after they aired, because almost all were "live." (Comedian Jackie Gleason quipped that TV critics merely reported accidents to eye witnesses.) They could also appraise continuing series, based on previous episodes. As more programs began to be filmed, following *I Love Lucy*'s innovation, and videotape was introduced in the late 1950s for entertainment and news-related programs alike, critics were able to preview shows. Their critical analyses in advance of broadcast helped viewers select what to watch. Producers and network executives could monitor print reviewers' evaluations of their product. Those developments increased print critics' influence, though their authority never approached New York drama critics' impact on Broadway's theatrical shows. Typically, many of a season's critically acclaimed new programs tend to be driven off the schedule by mass audience preferences for other less challenging or subtle programming. Praised, award-winning new series often find themselves canceled for lack of popular ratings. Some might apply to television movie-critic Pauline Kael's aphorism about films; she cynically described the image industry as "the art of casting sham pearls before real swine."

Television critics often use a program or series as the concrete basis for examining broader trends in the industry. Analyzing a new situation comedy or action-adventure drama or documentary-like news magazine is more than an exercise in scrutinizing a 30- or 60-minute program; it serves as a paradigm representing larger patterns in media and society. The critical review traces forces that shape not only programming but media structures, processes, and public perceptions. Often reviewers not only lament failures but question factors influencing success and quality. They challenge audiences to support superior programming by selective viewing just as they challenge producers to create sensitive, authentic depictions of deeper human values. Yet Gilbert Seldes cautioned as early as 1956 that the critic must propose changes that are feasible in the cost-intensive mass media system; this would be "more intellectually honest and also save a lot of time" while avoiding pointless hostility and futility.

Over the decades studies of audiences and program patterns, and surveys of media executives, have generally discounted print media criticism as a major factor in program decision making, particularly regarding any specific program content or scheduling. But critics are not wholly disregarded. Those published in media centers and Washington, D.C., serve as reminders to media managers of criteria beyond ratings and revenues. Critics in trade and metropolitan press are read by government agency personnel as well, to track reaction to pending policy moves. The insightful comments of critics have come in many forms: courteous and cerebral (veteran John O'Connor and Walter Goodman, longtime columnists at the *New York Times*), stylistically sophisticated and witty (Tom Shales, still the lead critic at the *Washington Post*), sometimes abrasive (Ron Powers, formerly of the *Chicago Sun-Times*), even cynical (Howard Rosenberg, who recently left the *Los Angeles Times*). Each of these may have illuminated lapses in artistic integrity or "good taste" and prod TV's creators and distributors to reflect on larger aesthetic and social implications of their lucrative, but ephemeral, occupations. Those published goadings enlighten readers, serve as a burr under the saddle of broadcasters and creators, and provide an informal barometer to federal lawmakers and regulators.

At the same time television criticism published in print media serves the publisher's primary purpose of gaining readership among a wide and diverse circulation. That goal puts a premium on relevance, clarity, brevity, cleverness, and attractive style. The TV column is meant to attract readers primarily by entertaining them, while also informing them about how the system works. And at times columns can inspire readers to reflect on their use of television and how they might selectively respond to the medium's showcases of excellence, plateaus of mediocrity, and pits of meretricious exploitation and excess. Balanced criticism avoids blatant appeals and gratuitous savaging of media people and projects. The critic serves as a guide, offering standards or criteria for judgment along with factual data, so readers can make up their own minds. A test of successful television criticism is whether readers enjoy reading the articles as they grow to trust the critic's judgment because they respect his or her perspective. The critic-reviewer's role grows in usefulness as video channels proliferate; viewers inundated by dozens of cable and over-air channels can ensure optimum use of leisure viewing time by following critics' tips about what is worth tuning in and what to avoid.

Reflecting the quality of published television criticism in recent years, distinguished Pulitzer Prizes have been awarded to Ron Powers (1973), William Henry III (1980, *Boston Globe*), Howard Rosenberg (1985), and Tom Shales (1988). Early on, influential *Times* critic Jack Gould set the standard when in 1957 he won a special George Foster Peabody Award for his "fairness, objectivity and authority." Prerequisites for proper critical perspective outlined by Lawrence Laurent three decades ago remain apt today: sensitivity and reasoned judgment, a renaissance knowledge, coupled with exposure to a broad range of art, culture, technology, business, law, economics, ethics, and social studies all fused with an incisive writing style causing commentary to leap off the page into the reader's consciousness, possibly influencing their TV behavior as viewers or as professional practitioners.

In the late 1970s, the Television Critics Association (TCA) was formed in the United States to represent professional critics in relations with the television industry. In part the association was formed to offset criticism that critics could be swayed by favors—travel, meetings, interviews—provided by the television industry. The TCA now coordinates annual visits by members to Los Angeles and other industry sites. There they have access to network programmers and other executives, to producers, and to stars of television programs, all seeking publicity and commentary from the critics. Press tours are scheduled for two and a half weeks in July, when networks and studios present new programs for review prior to placement on the regular television schedules. A second tour is arranged in January to review "midseason" alterations in the schedule. In addition to attending presentations in major hotel settings, the TCA tours now include visits to sets and discussions with businesses ancillary to the primary television providers. The association has also established the TCA Awards and recognizes television programs and personalities in a variety of categories.

James A. Brown

Further Reading

Adkins, Gale, "Radio-Television Criticism in the Newspapers: Reflections on a Deficiency," *Journal of Broadcasting* (Summer 1983)

Gould, Jack, *Watching Television Come of Age: The New York Times Reviews,* edited with an introduction by Lewis Gould, Austin: University of Texas Press, 2002

Laurent, Lawrence, "Wanted: The Complete Television Critic," in *The Eighth Art,* New York: Holt, Rinehart, and Winston, 1962

Orlik, Peter B., *Critiquing Radio and Television Content,* Boston: Allyn and Bacon, 1988

Rossman, Jules, "The TV Critic Column: Is It Influential?" *Journal of Broadcasting* (fall 1975)

Seldes, Gilbert, *The Public Arts,* New York: Simon and Schuster, 1956

Shales, Tom, *On the Air!* New York: Summit Books, 1982

Shayon, Robert Lewis, *Open to Criticism,* Boston: Beacon Press, 1971

Smith, Ralph Lewis, *A Study of the Professional Criticism of Broadcasting in the United States,* New York: Arno Press, 1973

Watson, Mary Ann, "Television Criticism in the Popular Press," *Critical Studies in Mass Communication* (March 1985)

Cronkite, Walter (1916–)

U.S. Broadcast Journalist

Walter Cronkite is the former *CBS Evening News* anchorman whose commentary defined issues and events in the United States for almost two decades. Cronkite, whom a major poll once named the "most trusted figure" in American public life, often saw every nuance in his nightly newscasts scrutinized by politicians, intellectuals, and fellow journalists, looking for clues to the thinking of mainstream America. In contrast, Cronkite viewed himself as a working journalist, epitomized by his title of "managing editor" of the *CBS Evening News.* His credo, adopted from his days as a wire service reporter, was to get the story, "fast, accurate, and unbiased"; his trademark exit line was, "And that's the way it is."

After working at a public relations firm, for newspapers, and in small radio stations throughout the Midwest, in 1939 Cronkite joined United Press (UP) to cover World War II. There, as part of what some reporters fondly called the "Writing 69th," he went ashore on D-Day, parachuted with the 101st Airborne, flew bombing missions over Germany, covered the Nuremberg trials, and opened the UP's first postwar Moscow bureau.

Though he had earlier rejected an offer from Edward R. Murrow, Cronkite joined CBS in 1950. First at CBS's Washington, D.C., affiliate and then over the national network, Cronkite paid his dues to the entertainment side of television, serving as host of the early CBS historical recreation series, *You Are There.* He even briefly cohosted the *CBS Morning Show* with the puppet Charlemagne. In a more serious vein, he narrated the CBS documentary series *The Twentieth Century.* Earlier, Cronkite had impressed many observers when he anchored CBS's coverage of the 1952 presidential nominating conventions.

In April 1962, Cronkite took over from Douglas Edwards the anchorman's position on the *CBS Evening News.* Less than a year later, the program was expanded from 15 to 30 minutes. Cronkite's first 30-minute newscast included an exclusive interview with President John F. Kennedy. Barely two months later, Cronkite was first on the air reporting Kennedy's assassination, and in one of the rare instances when his journalist objectivity deserted him, Cronkite shed tears.

Cronkite's rise at CBS was briefly interrupted in 1964, when the network, disturbed by the ratings beating *CBS Evening News* was taking from NBC's Huntley and Brinkley, decided to replace him as anchor at the 1964 presidential nominating conventions with the team of Robert Trout and Roger Mudd. Publicly accepting the change, but privately disturbed, Cronkite contemplated leaving CBS. However, more than 11,000 letters protesting the change undoubtedly helped convince both Cronkite and CBS executives that he should stay on. In 1966, Cronkite briefly overtook the *Huntley-Brinkley Report* in the ratings, and in 1967 his newscast took the lead. From that time until his retirement, the *CBS Evening News* was the ratings leader.

Initially, Cronkite was something of a "hawk" on the Vietnam War, although his program did broadcast controversial segments, such as Morley Safer's famous "Zippo lighter" report. However, returning from Vietnam after the Tet offensive, Cronkite addressed his massive audience with a different perspective. "It seems now more certain than ever," he said, "that the bloody experience of Vietnam is a stalemate." He then urged the government to open negotiations with the North Vietnamese. Many observers, including presidential aide Bill Moyers speculated that Cronkite's views were a major factor contributing to President Lyndon B. Johnson's decision to offer to negotiate with the enemy and not to run for president in 1968.

A year later Cronkite was one of the foremost boosters of the United States' technological prowess, anchoring coverage of the flight of Apollo XI. Again his vaunted objectivity momentarily left him as he shouted, "Go, Baby, Go," when the mission rocketed into space. For some time Cronkite had seen the space story as one of the most important events of the future, and his coverage of the space shots was as long on information as it was on his famed endurance. In what critics referred to as "Walter to Walter coverage," Cronkite was on the air for 27 of the 30 hours that Apollo XI took to complete its mission.

By the same token, Cronkite never stinted on coverage of the Watergate scandal and subsequent hearings. In 1972, following on the heels of the *Washington Post*'s Watergate revelations, the *CBS Evening News* presented a 22-minute, two-part overview of Watergate that is generally credited with keeping the issue alive and making it intelligible to most Americans.

Cronkite could also influence foreign diplomacy, as evidenced in a 1977 interview with Egyptian president Anwar Sadat, in which he asked Sadat if he would go to Jerusalem to confer with the Israelis. A day after Sadat agreed to such a visit, an invitation came from Israeli prime minister Menachem Begin. It was a step that would eventually pave the way for the Camp David accords and an Israeli-Egyptian peace treaty.

Many have criticized Cronkite for his refusal to take more risks in TV news coverage. Others have argued that his credibility and prestige had greater impact because of his judicious display of those qualities. Cronkite was also criticized for his preference for short "breaking stories," many of them originating from CBS News' Washington bureau, rather than longer "enterprisers," which might deal with long-range and non-Washington stories. In addition, many have contended that Cronkite's demand for center stage—an average of six minutes out of the 22 minutes on an evening newscast focused on him—took time away from in-depth coverage of the news. Some have referred to this time in the spotlight as "the magic."

In 1981, in accord with CBS policy, Cronkite retired. Since then, however, he has hardly been inactive. His annual hosting of PBS's broadcast of the Vienna Philharmonic has become a New Year's Eve tradition. He has also hosted PBS documentaries on health, old age, and poor children. In 1993 he signed a contract with the Discovery Channel and the Learning Channel to do 36 documentaries in three years. He followed that deal with the publication in 1996 of his autobiography, *A Reporter's Life.* This endeavor was succeeded by an eight-part series on the Discovery Channel titled *Cronkite Remembers,* which was dubbed "Walter's Greatest Hits." In 1998 Cronkite returned, albeit briefly, to the anchor's chair to coanchor CNN's coverage of the return to Earth from space of the then 70-year-old former astronaut turned U.S. senator, John Glenn.

Cronkite's legacy of separating reporting from advocacy has become the norm in television news. His name has become virtually synonymous with the position of news anchor worldwide—Swedish anchors are known as *Kronkiters,* while in Holland they are *Cronkiters.*

ALBERT AUSTER

See also **Anchor; Kennedy, John F.: Assassination and Funeral; News, Network; Space Program and Television**

Walter Cronkite. Born in St. Joseph's, Missouri, November 4, 1916. Attended University of Texas, 1933–35. Married: Mary Elizabeth Maxwell, 1940; three children. News writer and editor, Scripps-Howard, also United Press, Houston, Texas; Kansas City, Missouri; Dallas, Austin, and El Paso, Texas; and New York City; United Press war correspondent, 1942–45, foreign correspondent, reopening bureaus in Amsterdam, Brussels; chief correspondent, Nuremberg war crimes trials, bureau manager, Moscow, 1946–48, manager and contributor, 1948–49, CBS News correspondent, 1950–81, special correspondent, since 1981; managing editor, *CBS Evening News with Walter Cronkite,* 1962–81. Honorary degrees: American International College; Harvard University; LL.D., Rollins College, Bucknell University, Syracuse University; L.H.D., Ohio State University. Member: Academy of Television Arts and Sciences (president, national academy, New York chapter, 1959, Governor's Award, 1979); Association Radio News Analysts. Recipient: several Emmy Awards; Peabody Awards, 1962 and 1981; William A. White Award for journalistic merit, 1969; George Polk Journalism Award, 1971; Gold Medal, International Radio and Television Society, 1974; Alfred I. DuPont-Columbia University Award in Broadcast Journalism, 1978 and 1981; Presidential Medal of Freedom, 1981.

Television Series

1953–57 *You Are There*
1957–67 *The Twentieth Century*
1961–62 *Eyewitness to History*
1961–79 *CBS Reports*
1962–81 *The CBS Evening News with Walter Cronkite* (managing editor)
1967–70 *21st Century*
1980–82 *Universe* (host)
1991 *Dinosaur!*

Television Specials (selected)

1975 *Vietnam: A War That Is Finished*
1975 *In Celebration of US*
1975 *The President in China*
1977 *Our Happiest Birthday*
1984 *Solzhenitsyn: 1984 Revisited*
1994 *The Holocaust: In Memory of Millions* (host)
2000 *Fail Safe* (host)
2000 *Good Grief, Charlie Brown: A Tribute to Charles Schultz* (host)
2001 *Korean War Stories* (host)

Publications

The Challenges of Change, 1971
Eye on the World, 1971
A Reporter's Life, 1996

Further Reading

Attanasio, Paul, "Anchors Away: Good Evening Dan, Tom, and Peter. Now Buzz Off," *New Republic* (April 23, 1984)
"Covering Religion," interview, *Christian Century* (December 14, 1994)
Cronkite, Kathy, *On the Edge of the Spotlight: Celebrities' Children Speak Out About Their Lives,* New York: Morrow, 1981
Rottenberg, Dan, "And That's the Way It Is," *American Journalism Review* (May 1994)
Snow, Richard F., "He Was There," interview, *American Heritage* (December 1994)
Unger, Arthur, " 'Uncle Walter' and the 'Information Crisis,' " interview, *Television Quarterly* (winter 1990)

C-SPAN

U.S. Cable Network

Founded in 1979 by Brian Lamb with the support of the cable industry, C-SPAN (Cable Satellite Public Affairs Network) is now available on three 24-hour cable channels and on WCSP, as well as satellite radio. C-SPAN 1, with a primary mission to cover the House of Representatives when in session, can be seen in more than 86 million homes and is available in all of the top 100 television markets. Brought online in 1986 to cover Senate proceedings, C-SPAN 2 reaches 98 percent of the top 100 markets and is accessible in 72 million households. Launched in 2001, C-SPAN 3 is a national digital network carrying events live on weekdays and long-form programming in the evening and on weekends. It has a potential audience of 7 million and can be seen in 54 percent of the top 100 markets.

Unique in the world of American television, C-SPAN is the only unfiltered national public affairs network available to the public. In a news world too often devoted to sound bites and instant analysis, it stands virtually alone as an example of long-form, noncommercial television. What began in a small office in Crystal City, Virginia, with four employees and no ability to pick up the signal it sent into 3.5 million homes has now become a fixture on cable television and in American politics.

C-SPAN owes its origin to the confluence of three forces, each with different missions and needs. As the cable industry developed in the 1970s it sought programming, visibility, and respect. The quality and content of cable programming had caused concern among certain civic groups and the legislators they supported. The House of Representatives, disappointed by network television's emphasis on presidential politics, searched for a way to become more visible. Televising sessions from the floor offered a possible solution, so

C-SPAN®

Courtesy of C-SPAN

long as those doing the televising did not turn hours of debate into sound bites.

Motivated by what he saw as the broadcast networks' stranglehold on the news, Brian Lamb (then the Washington bureau chief for *Cablevision* magazine) managed to soothe congressional concerns about how they would be covered while giving the cable industry the respect it needed on the hill. Lamb was no stranger to the world of Washington politics or to its coverage in the media. As a naval officer he had served as a White House social aide and as a Pentagon press spokesman. During the Nixon administration, he became assistant to the director of the Office of Telecommunications Policy. As a result, he knew leaders in the cable industry well.

Industry support freed C-SPAN from the responsibility of delivering eyeballs to advertisers. In time, it extended its reach, without having to sell itself to sponsors. In 2001 C-SPAN reached more cable and satellite homes than MTV. An estimated 28.5 million people tune in to C-SPAN weekly. While just over half of all American voters went to the polls in the 2000 presidential campaign, 90 percent of C-SPAN viewers did.

Known for its gavel-to-gavel coverage, C-SPAN actually devotes more time to public policy forums, special events, and signature programming. Only 13 percent of the network's time is spent covering House sessions. *The Washington Journal,* C-SPAN's regularly scheduled version of a call-in program, illustrates the network's mission and its presentational style. Its objective is to give viewers the opportunity to both learn from and question politicians, policymakers, and those who cover them in the news. Hosts are schooled to stay out of the way of the conversation. Constant efforts are made to balance points of view both in guest selection and in access to those on the air. Still there are always callers from both the right and the left who are sure they detect bias in programming. Long-term, long-form coverage of presidential campaigns too has become a C-SPAN hallmark. Its signature program, *The Road to the White House,* first took to the campaign trail during the 1988 election. Coverage broadened during each of the following contests. *Booknotes,* another signature program, first aired in 1989. The hour-long in-depth interviews with authors of serious nonfiction books is unique in American television. The interest generated by it within and without C-SPAN led to the development of a network within a network, *Book TV,* carried weekends on C-SPAN 2. As the network has continued to grow so too has interest in developing series exploring the American past. From its first effort, coverage of the reenactment of the Lincoln-Douglas debates, to its ten-month series *American Writers: A Journey Through History,* C-SPAN has used the format to broaden its appeal to the viewing audience. One thing is certain: C-SPAN does more than carry signals from the House and Senate floors.

In spring 2004, C-SPAN turned 25. Over the years it had gathered more than a handful of awards from the cable industry for programming and service. Its series *American Presidents: Life Portraits* won a prestigious Peabody Award. In 2002 its chairman became the 13th recipient of the National Press Club's Fourth Estate Award, given annually to an individual who has achieved distinction for a lifetime of contributions to American journalism, joining Walter Cronkite and Theodore White on the list of winners. A year later, Brian Lamb was one of eight individuals to receive a National Humanities Medal from President Bush. Still, a not-for-profit network supported by a nickel-a-month fee from subscribers is always subject to the unintended effects of legislation and FCC regulation designed for the major players in a commercial industry. Media consolidation and technological developments can shift the playing field and, in doing so, threaten C-SPAN as viewers now see it. Almost from the beginning citizen's groups have formed to protect the network. Its work has changed the landscape of American politics and given citizens wider access to the ways in which government works. Its impact on the world of journalism is undoubted. C-SPAN is a unique network in the world of commercial television.

JOHN SULLIVAN

See also **Cable Networks; Lamb, Brian**

Further Reading

CBS News Sunday Morning (October 13, 2002) Academic Universe, Lexis-Nexis, http://web.lexis-nexis.com, accessed November 1, 2003

"C-SPAN 25th Anniversary Milestones," http://www.c-span.org/25th_anniversary/milestones.asp

Devlin, Ann, "An Interview with Brian Lamb" (May 18, 1999) http://www.annononline.com/interviews/990518/

Frantzich, Stephen, and John Sullivan, *The C-SPAN Revolution,* Norman and London: University of Oklahoma Press, 1996

Lamb, Brian, "Debunking the Myths," speech at the National Press Club, January 6, 1997, www.c-span.org/about brian/2.asp

Lamb, Brian, and the C-SPAN staff, *C-SPAN: America's Town Hall,* Washington D.C.: Acropolis Books, 1988

Lardner, James, "The Anti-Network," *New Yorker* (March 14, 1994)

CTV. *See* **Canadian Television Network**

Cuba

The history of television in Cuba is generally missing from the contemporary bibliography surrounding telecommunications and media studies. Few are aware of the groundbreaking role Cuba has played in Ibero-America and its major role in world broadcasting.

The Beginning of Commercial TV in Cuba

Development of the telecommunications sector in Cuba is best understood within historical, political, and economic contexts, such as relations between Cuba and the United States, laws regulating specific sectors of communications in Cuba, and the geographic proximity of Cuba to the United States. These factors contributed to the situation in which, during the first decade of Cuban television broadcasting, countless elements of the industry were imported. Among them were capital financing and technologies such as television transmitters and receivers, professional organizational patterns, marketing practices, and commercial communication and market research strategies applied to electronic communications media. In terms of content, TV programs and news from U.S. networks were imported, as were assorted models of programs created in the United States, which were then converted into Spanish-language versions.

Cuba became, in some ways, a unique laboratory for the United States. Experiments involving technologies, TV program genres, and the practices surrounding production, communication, and trade were carried out in Cuba—a small market but one that represented Spanish-speaking culture. These strategies were later generalized to the Caribbean and Latin American region by different means. Among these were the application of transnational structures of TV stations, the use of international publicity agencies, and the presence of Cuban artists and technicians in the creation and development of TV stations in different countries throughout Ibero-America.

These developments were first seen during one week in December 1946, when station CM-21P transmitted an experimental broadcast of a live TV show between two distant points of La Habana (Havana) city. This broadcast displayed the possibilities of the new audiovisual electronic technique. By 1950, Cuba had become the third country in Latin America with regular TV broadcasts. This was an initiative of private enterprises that, like those in the United States, were financially based on the marketing and commercial practices of TV, a system of sponsors and advertisers. Most of the earliest television managers came from radio and, to a lesser extent, from the film industry, other productive sectors of the economy, and even some posts in the national government.

The first TV channel, Union Radio TV (Channel 4), was arranged and directed by Gaspar Pumarejo Such, then general director of the radio network of the same name. Union Radio TV was supported by RCA representatives in Cuba and other participants in the commercially based national communications sectors. The station began television test-broadcasting with interviews and shows October 14, 1950. Its official opening took place with the broadcasting of a ceremony via remote control from the Presidential Palace (now the Museum of the Revolution) on October 24, 1950. Later, this TV station would be affiliated with DuMont, a U.S. television network.

On December 18, 1950, the second Cuban TV channel, CMQ-TV (Channel 6), began experimental broadcasting. It was directed by Goar Mestre Espinosa, also chief executive of CMQ S.A., which at the same time owned the CMQ radio network. It was officially inaugurated on March 11, 1951, and later became affiliated with the U.S. television network NBC.

Other channels—CMBF-TV (Channel 7); CMBA-TV, Telemundo (Channel 2); and TV Caribe (Channel 11)—were established in 1953. Telemundo later joined the CBS network (U.S.). In 1955 TV Habanera (Channel 10) appeared and also soon became an associate of NBC. Gaspar Pumarejo was again a pioneer when his Channel 12, Telecolor S.A., began in 1957 to broadcast daily for more than 16 hours. This commercial, color television station continued the daily broadcast in La Habana for almost two years.

This concentration of channels broadcasting from the capital city of Cuba unleashed a frenzy of competition for the television market. Competition centered on TV networks in La Habana, and later in the provincial capitals, but it also involved the remaining media-announcers, publicity firms, and U.S. producers of TV transmitters and receivers, most of them represented in Cuba at that time.

This multiple participation within the exceptional 1950s economic-cultural environment in La Habana led to a heavy financial investment and a rapid increase in commercial channels. The channels supported their positions in the competitive mix with an emphasis on designing TV programs, experimenting with technological systems and communications equipment, and/or developing commercial communication practices and market research. These experiments contributed to Cuba's role as a leader in developing diverse TV technologies in Ibero-America and throughout the world.

Notable developments and innovations in the history of television in Cuba include the following:

1950: Two Cuban commercial TV channels begin broadcasting from La Habana in the same quarterly time frame.

1952: A video network covering the main provincial capitals, CMQ-TV, Channel 6, is established.

1952: Regular use of the kinescope at CMQ-TV, Channel 6.

1954: CMQ-TV, Channel 6, transmits a live TV program (Major League Baseball's World Series) between two countries using an airplane as a relay.

1954: The teleprompter is used regularly as an assisting device for dramatic and news programs in Gaspar Pumarejo's organization, then on Channel 2.

1957: Direct transmission of regular, live TV signal between the United States and Cuba (sometimes vice-versa) occurs, using the Over the Horizon System on CMQ-TV, Channel 6.

1957: Local color, commercial TV channel, Telecolor S.A., Channel 12, broadcasts 16 hours daily.

1958: Videotape is used experimentally.

The overall design of Cuban television programs favored not only entertainment, variety shows, and commercials but also other cultural forms. Despite its heavy commercial focus, television looked for settings for actors and communications and economic agents, providing opportunities in the specific environment of the new medium. Many scriptwriters, adapters, producers, directors, actors, and technicians came to television from varying backgrounds, including the radio, theater, and film industries. These opportunities developed because La Habana was one of the leading cultural industry locations; this centrality offered unique conditions for assimilating the most deeply rooted cultural patterns of Cuba, for speeding up the creation of an audience for program design and commercial messages, and for increasing the number of consumers of TV receivers. The migration to the new medium became prominent early in the Cuban television industry, which though it broadcast typical commercial programs, poured into Cuban television the different cultural expressions and genres deeply rooted in the audience. Among these are *bufo* and zarzuela (types of operetta); universal, classic, and contemporary theater; ballet; opera; humor; music; and sports. In fact, some television genres and programs that later evolved into worldwide paradigms were created and broadcast first in Cuba.

Examples of these developments include the following:

1950: A complete baseball game, with full remote control, is broadcast from a stadium, as TV programs from two early channels developed from that very year to the most diverse sports programming.

1950: Images of a surgical operation performed in a La Habana hospital are broadcast to different parts of the capital city.

1952: A Spanish-language *telenovela* (soap opera) is broadcast every afternoon, Monday through Saturday, on CMQ-TV, Channel 6.

1953: The Miss Universe pageant is sponsored by and broadcast on Union Radio TV, Channel 4.

1953: A telethon is first broadcast as a fund-raising device by Union Radio TV, Channel 4.

Public Service Television

In 1960 the Cuban government took over the administration of communications media, shifting their focus to public service. Since May 24, 1962, the activities of electronic media have been coordinated by the Radio and TV Coordination Office, the predecessor of the Cuban Broadcasting Institute (Instituto Cubano de la Radiodifusión, ICR), which was officially renamed the Cuban Institute of Radio and Television (Instituto Cubano de Radio y Television, ICRT) in 1976. Today this organization constitutes the strongest public radio and television system in the Ibero-American region. The first decade of public service television in Cuba also established decisive links among historical, political, economic, and technological factors.

Amid a radical social transformation of television, La Habana became a network stronghold. Some networks had repeaters at main province capitals, but their entire coverage only reached 50 percent of the Cuban territory through use of a transmitting-receiving technology imported mainly from the United States and a microwave network mostly controlled by radio and television consortiums. With the beginning of the U.S. economic blockade in 1962, however, and the breaking of commercial, political, and financial ties, the bulk of available, U.S.-derived technology grew obsolete.

The main challenge of Cuban public service television has always been to serve increasing demands concerning coverage, technological diversification, and programming content—for the state as well as every other aspect of Cuban society—without taking into account ideal technological and financial resources to fulfill these aims. In the 1960s, electricity reached the most remote areas of the country, and the number of television sets owned by people increased. Meanwhile, the basis of a national-coverage broadcast system (including Isle of Youth, formerly the Isle of Pines), and rural and/or mountain range zones, had to be implemented with the least financial investment, the highest efficiency, and technological and communicative effectiveness.

The reorganization, rationalization, and centralization process of Cuban television at a national level of technological and enterprise infrastructure led to the redistribution of television transmitters, which were transferred to the Ministry of Communications in 1967. It also led to the merging of existing TV channels and networks and the creation of new operational structures.

TV Station and Producing Houses

By this time, the Cuban television system was made up of two national networks, Channels 6 and 2. A third system, Telerebelde, was created later, having a regional character. Telerebelde broadcast from the eastern province of Santiago de Cuba, sending its own programs to the five surrounding eastern provinces. Some time later, Canal 2 was renamed Telerebelde and Santiago de Cuba's channel became a territorial center of the system.

An important step in the expansion of the national system of Cuban television was the progressive creation of the Regional Network of 15 territorial television stations, which today covers all 14 provinces and the Isle of Youth, a special municipality. These territorial channels, or *telecentros,* produce and make their own programming according to the informational needs and unique traditions of their respective audiences. These programs are broadcast during a set schedule, in the assigned area, and when they sign off, their frequency is transferred to national networks. A selection of the aforementioned regional programming also feeds national networks.

The international Cuban TV satellite channel Cubavision Internacional began operation in 1986. Its assorted cultural and informative programming concerning Cuba was initially oriented toward Cuban students and workers living temporarily in Africa. Today, its 24-hour coverage has been widened to North America, Latin America, and Africa, and its content has been diversified with other dramatic and regular genres from Cuban television.

TV Serrana, a UNESCO and ICRT joint project, began in 1993 at the San Pablo del Yao, Buey Arriba, Sierra Maestra mountain range (Granma province) in the eastern part of the country. TV Serrana is both a producer and community territorial cultural center, opening its production and video exhibits (documentary and news reports) on diverse themes concerning the community and its environment to community inhabitants who also work as creators of these audiovisual productions. Its productions are also screened in international events and festivals, as well as in national TV programming.

In November 2001, the third Cuban national network, Canal Educativo, began broadcasting from La Habana. In its first stage its signal covered La Habana's two provinces; by 2002 the entire national territory was covered. This network produces and disseminates direct and indirect educational content, from TV classes for every educational level to didactic programs such as *Mi TV* (for child audiences) and *Universidad para Todos* (general population). It also airs foreign and domestic documentaries and reports on arts, history, nature, and languages. The opening of a second network also specializing in educational themes is expected in the first quarter of 2004.

Mayra Cue Sierra

Curtin, Jane (1947–)

U.S. Actor

Comic actor Jane Curtin made her mark in television with three successful series each begun in and representative of a different decade. Her first two series coincided with and participated in the revival and redefinition of two familiar televisual forms: live comedy-variety and situation comedy. The former resurgence was initiated by Curtin's show NBC's *Saturday Night Live* (*SNL*) in 1975. The later revival encompassed many new sitcoms in 1984, among them *Kate and Allie,* in which Curtin played divorced homemaker-mom Allie Lowell. Then, in 1996, capitalizing on the audience's support of science fiction in film and television, situation comedy's proven endurance, and Curtin's proven record, *Third Rock from the Sun* debuted, casting Curtin as colleague, then love interest, to the (undercover) commander of a troupe of alien visitors to Earth.

One of the original "Not-Ready-for-Prime-Time Players" on *SNL,* Curtin had the distinction of being the only cast member producer Lorne Michaels hired cold. Though she had, like other cast members, worked in improvisational theater ("The Proposition"), Michaels had not met her or worked with her before, as he had with the rest of the cast. Less facile with physical comedy than Chevy Chase, less disposed to creating the broad characters of Gilda Radner, with a less elastic face than John Belushi, Curtin's perfect posture, cool, sophisticated demeanor, and classic strong-boned beauty made her a fitting choice for many "straight" parts. While Curtin would do a fair share of absurd characters (e.g., the nasal Mrs. Loopner, the mother in the Big Butts family; Prymaat Conehead, the mother in a family from another planet), more often than other women in the cast from 1975 to 1980 she played the "serious" roles (e.g., weekend anchor, Shana Alexander–type political combatant to Dan Akroyd's James Kilpatrick). Where Gilda Radner would outrageously parody journalist Barbara Walters (as Baba WaWa), Jane Curtin would do a deadpan imitation of liberal commentator Shana Alexander, maintaining her élan even as Akroyd's conservative Kilpatrick character began his rebuttal with the infamous line, "Jane, you ignorant slut." Yet, despite her cool, square-jawed stoicism, Curtin could instantly abandon herself to riotous slapstick, using the break in her persona to comic effect. This yin-yang style became something of a trademark in scenes from all three series.

In an interview with James Brady years later Curtin was asked how she would rate her experience on *SNL.* She said on a scale of one to ten, it was a ten. Curtin was nominated for two Emmy Awards for her work on *SNL* before she left the show in 1980. She did not return to a television series until 1984.

Kate and Allie, premiering in March 1984, was a part of a resurgence in the sitcom genre. The family consisted of two divorced mothers, Kate McArdle and Allie Lowell, who decide to rent an apartment and raise their three children together. Once again Curtin played the more conventional character: abandoned traditional wife and mother Allie.

During the program's six-year run, Allie grew from a shy homebody through a returning college student to an entrepreneur running her own catering business through her domestic culinary and organizational skills. Thus, Curtin was again playing a many-sided woman who seemed easily stereotyped at first glance but exhibited hidden resources. She won two Emmy Awards for her portrayals for the 1983–84 and the 1984–85 seasons. She stayed with the show until it ended in 1990.

Curtin worked on stage and appeared in a number of movies, both for the big screen and for television, during and after *Kate and Allie,* and she tried another series that was not successful (*Working It Out,* 1990). It wasn't until January 1996 that she again "hit" with a program that drew on both sitcom formula and the growing popularity of science fiction TV programs, *Third Rock from the Sun.*

The premise of *Third Rock* was reminiscent of the Coneheads, as a group of aliens land on Earth and live as a human family. The leader, played by John Lithgow, posed as a professor colleague of anthropologist Mary Allbright (Curtin). The interplay between the characters drew on Curtin's past style. Her Dr. Allbright, a conventional professional academic with a sober exterior, often broke character to partake in the absurd behaviors of the aliens (e.g., breaking into show tunes in a

Jane Curtin.
Courtesy of the Everett Collection

diner, getting aroused by a slap in the face). *Third Rock from the Sun* ran from January 1996 to May 2001.

Curtin has done a number of straight dramatic roles on stage and in made-for-television movies. Those arenas were bridged in 2003 when she took part in the Westport County Playhouse production of Thornton Wilder's *Our Town,* which aired on Showtime and PBS. The play, starring Paul Newman, featured Curtin in a supporting role. Praised for her understated performance and comic timing, Curtin seemed to have found yet another milieu in which to mix and rebalance her comic and dramatic talents.

Meanwhile, *Saturday Night Live, Kate and Allie,* and *Third Rock from the Sun* play in perpetual syndication, making the programs, and Jane Curtin, an enduring part of television.

IVY GLENNON

See also ***Kate & Allie; Saturday Night Live***

Jane (Therese) Curtin. Born in Cambridge, Massachusetts, September 6, 1947. Attended Elizabeth Seton Junior College, A.A., 1967; attended Northwestern University, 1967–68. Married Patrick F. Lynch, 1975; one child: Tess. Began comedy career as company member of "The Proposition" comedy group, 1968–72; contributing writer and actor in off-Broadway production *Pretzels,* 1974–75; original cast member of Saturday Night Live, NBC-TV, 1975–80; roles in several stage productions and TV programs. Recipient: Emmy Awards 1983–84 and 1984–85.

Television Series

1975–80	*Saturday Night Live*
1978	*What Really Happened to the Class of '65*
1984–89	*Kate & Allie*
1990	*Working It Out*
1996–2001	*3rd Rock from the Sun*

Made-for-Television Movies

1982	*Divorce Wars: A Love Story*
1987	*Suspicion*
1988	*Maybe Baby*
1990	*Common Ground*
1995	*Tad*
2000	*Catch a Falling Star*
2003	*Our Town*

Theatrical Releases

Mr. Mike's Mondo Video, 1979; *Bob & Ray, Jane, Laraine, & Gilda,* 1979; *How to Beat the High Cost of Living,* 1980; *O.C. & Stiggs,* 1985; *Coneheads,* 1993; *Antz,* 1998.

Stage

"The Proposition" (comedy group), 1968–72; *Pretzels,* 1974–75; *Candida,* 1981; *The Last of the Red Hot Lovers; Our Town,* 2002.

Czech Republic, Slovakia

From its inception in 1953, television in Czechoslovakia was a tool of communist propaganda. In the late 1960s, state-owned Czechoslovak Television played an important role in the gradual liberalization of the totalitarian state, which culminated in the short-lived period of media freedom during the "Prague Spring" of 1968. After the Warsaw Pact invasion of Czechoslovakia in August 1968, which stopped the liberalizing reforms, Czechoslovak Television was again turned into a mouthpiece of communist, progovernment propaganda for two more decades. After the fall of communism in 1989, attempts were made in Czechoslovakia to produce a dual, public service/commercial television broadcasting system, according to West European (primarily British) examples. The majority of these attempts have not been successful. Because of legal and regulatory problems, Czech and Slovak television broadcasting has continued to experience difficulties.

The first experiments with television broadcasting were made in Czechoslovakia by Jaroslav Šafránek in the period before World War II, on an amateur basis. After the war, television broadcasting was shown to the Czechoslovak public at the 1948 International Radio Exhibition. Public television broadcasting began in Prague on May 1, 1953, within the framework of state-owned Czechoslovak Radio. In subsequent years, television broadcasting was extended throughout Czechoslovakia, and the country had nationwide television broadcasting from 1958 onward. Nevertheless, the impact of television was considerably smaller than that of radio, since only about half of the households owned a TV set still in the 1960s. In 1957–58 state-run Czechoslovak Television was instituted as an entity separate from Czechoslovak Radio. State-owned Czechoslovak Television enjoyed a broadcasting monopoly, confirmed by Czechoslovak Law No. 18/1964.

In the early years of its existence, Czechoslovak Television did not broadcast its own television news; at 7:00 P.M., the main evening radio news was transmitted while the television picture showed a test card. From October 1, 1956, the occasional current-affairs program *Televizní aktuality a zajímavosti* (*Topical Newsitems*) was broadcast daily. On January 1, 1958, nightly *Televizní noviny* (*Television News*) went on the air at 7:00 P.M. The programming schedule was set thus: after the main evening news at 7:00 P.M., a documentary was usually shown at 7:30, and a feature film followed at 8:00. Czechoslovak Television advertised itself as "Your Small Cinema at Home."

From the mid-1960s, the communist regime in Czechoslovakia found itself on the defensive. Reformers within the system, mostly writers, artists, and intellectuals, initiated a sustained push for freedom, using contemporary literature and culture as an instrument of democratization. From the mid-1960s, Czechoslovak Television, at least in certain areas of its broadcasting, freed itself of strict ideological censorship, especially in entertainment, where it broadcast its own popular drama (*Jaroslav Dietl*), and, partially, also in the area of current affairs. Thus, for instance, on April 22, 1966, Czechoslovak Television aired a special program, *Spor* (*Argument*), in which an "indictment," drafted by members of the younger generation criticizing the older generation and their Stalinist activism of the early 1950s, was debated. Although the program could not openly discuss the crimes committed by the ruling Communist Party in the 1950s, the broadcasting of *Spor* was interpreted by the Czechoslovak public as a signal that democratic debate was now possible. The program produced a large response from viewers. However, a follow-up debate, titled *Porota* (*The Jury*), made a few months later, which openly criticized Communist Party policy, was banned by the government and could not be broadcast until the period of the Prague Spring, in March 1968.

The campaign for democratic reform culminated in the Prague Spring, a period that lasted from March until August 1968, when Czechoslovakia enjoyed an almost absolute freedom of expression and engaged in an intensive debate about the totalitarian excesses of its immediate past and the alternatives for its political future. This was a remarkable period in the history of the Czech media: newspapers, radio, and television provided professional and highly sophisticated coverage of the issues under debate. A number of leading broadcasters emerged as figures of national importance. Czechoslovak Television, under its then-director Jiří Pelikán, a reformist communist, played a significant role in this period.

Equally remarkable was the work of the Czechoslovak media during the first week of Soviet occupation following the Warsaw Pact military invasion of August 21, 1968, which put an end to the Prague Spring. From the early hours of the invasion, the media went underground, defying the invading forces and provided a round-the-clock, independent news service, calling for sensible, peaceful resistance and preventing chaos and bloodshed. While Czechoslovak television attempted to broadcast in certain regions during the invasion, sometimes directly from television transmitters, the occupying armies mostly managed to silence those broadcasts. It was the voice of "Free Czechoslovak Radio" that the invading armies failed to silence and that became the focus of national resistance.

There was a postinvasion "interregnum" after August 1968 because the occupying authorities did not manage to bring Czechoslovakia fully to heel until the spring of 1970. In spite of a certain amount of censorship (it was not possible to mention the invasion or to criticize the Soviet Union), Czechoslovak Television remained a strong voice of freedom throughout the autumn of 1968, in both its political and entertainment programming, and it again played a major role during the crisis of January 1969, when Jan Palach, a Prague university student, immolated himself in protest against the Warsaw Pact invasion and when about a million people attended his funeral.

The Soviet Union threw the country into a harsh, neo-Stalinist mode within a couple of years after the invasion and instigated a direct assault on the Czechoslovak intelligentsia. The media were purged of all the reformists and turned into a machine that produced emotional, ideological propaganda, the intensity of which remained practically unchanged until the fall of communism in 1989. Political purges took place in Czechoslovakia from 1969 through 1971, and some three quarters of a million supporters of democratic reform were sacked from their jobs.

Most professional journalists had to leave Czechoslovak Television and were replaced by ideological zealots who were at first so unprofessional that for a period of time after the purges, the new presenters of the evening news were incapable of broadcasting live and the news bulletin had to be prerecorded earlier in the day. In the mid-1970s, the Communist Party ordered Czechoslovak Television to move its evening news from 7:00 to 7:30 P.M. in order to increase its viewing figures (which peaked at about 8:00 P.M. when the feature film of the night started). This strategy also allowed them to compete with the evening news on Austrian Television, which was broadcast at 7:30 and which people in the border areas in Czechoslovakia watched in large numbers, as an antidote to communist propaganda.

In the 1970s, there were ties between Czechoslovak Television's News and Current Affairs Department and the Czechoslovak secret police (STB). Czechoslovak Television occasionally broadcast programs, based on secret police material, that scandalized the banned democratic reformers and human rights activists. Czechoslovak Television also transmitted popular, consumerist entertainment in the 1970s and 1980s.

The Second Program of Czechoslovak Television began broadcasting on May 10, 1970; from May 9, 1973, the Second Program broadcast in color. The First Program started broadcasting in color on May 9, 1975. From 1983 onward, Czechoslovakia showed the first program of Russian television for the occupying Soviet troops. In the late 1980s, when reform began in the Soviet Union, Russian television broadcast many programs that questioned the authoritarian communist establishment. The occupation regime in Czechoslovakia would have never allowed such programs on its own indigenous TV channels (many Czechs understand Russian since the two Slavic languages are related). Thus, paradoxically, Russian television broadcasts became a voice of freedom in Czechoslovakia in the late 1980s.

After the fall of communism, state-owned Czechoslovak Television was turned into a public service system. From 1992 there was a federal, Czechoslovak channel and separate Czech and Slovak television stations. In May 1990, the Soviet TV channel in Czechoslovakia was temporarily turned into an "open channel," OK3, which broadcast a selection of international satellite programming until the end of 1992. After the division of Czechoslovakia in 1993 into Czech Republic and Slovakia, Czech Television retained two nationwide terrestrial channels: the mainstream program ČT 1 and the cultural program ČT 2. In Slovakia, Slovak Television also retained two nationwide terrestrial channels: STV 1 and STV 2.

Attempts have been made since the fall of communism to turn the former Czechoslovak Television into a public service station, but they have not been on the whole successful. During the semiauthoritarian government of Vladimír Mečiar and his Movement for Democratic Slovakia, Slovak public service television sided with the government, producing propaganda for them.

From 1993 to 1998, Czech Television's chief executive, Ivo Mathé, continued to place emphasis on entertainment. News and current affairs remained relatively undeveloped. In the first half of the 1990s, Czech Television reporters and interviewers also often sided with the government. In the wake of Mathé's departure, several attempts have been made since 1998 to professionalize Czech TV, in particular its news and current-affairs department, and to open up its finances to public scrutiny. Between 1998 and 2001, Czech Television had four different chief executives.

A fourth attempt at reform failed spectacularly in

December 2000 and January 2001, when the Council for Czech Television, a regulatory body, appointed a former BBC journalist, Jiří Hodač, as Czech Television's chief executive. This appointment resulted in a rebellion by Czech TV employees, led by the news and current-affairs department, whose members turned an internal labor dispute into a public political struggle.

In December 2000, upon learning of Hodač's appointment, the TV rebels began to transmit emotional broadcasts, hijacking the output of the station for their own ends. Defending their working practices, they aligned themselves with an opposition political party (the Freedom Union) and used popular discontent with the government to urge some 80,000 people to demonstrate in the streets of Prague against an alleged government attempt to stifle the independence of Czech TV. The new chief executive was deposed within a matter of days. The Council for Radio and Television Broadcasting characterized the Czech TV rebellion as "probably the most serious crisis since the fall of communism in 1989" and imposed the highest possible fine (2 million Czech crowns) on Czech TV for the behavior of its employees during the TV rebellion.

A number of well-known Prague cultural figures supported the Czech TV rebellion, fearing with some justification that the opening of the finances of Czech Television might compromise the often informal, subcontractors' infrastructure on which many filmmakers and other cultural workers were financially dependent. They feared that the role of Czech Television as the only major surviving source of cultural subsidy supporting the work of Prague artists and intellectuals might be threatened.

In 1993 the regulatory authority, the Council for Radio and Television Broadcasting, awarded a free television license for a commercial, culturally oriented nationwide terrestrial television station to CET 21. This company was a consortium of six Czech and Slovak individuals, headed by Vladimír Železný, and Ronald Lauder's American company Central European Development Corporation, which later became Central European Media Enterprises (CME). The new commercial television station, Nova TV, operated by Česká nezávislá televizní společnost (ČNTS, Czech Independent Television Company), began broadcasting on February 4, 1994. From its inception, it dropped the cultural remit and went aggresively for downmarket, tabloid broadcasting, including pornography. The station was financially very successful. According to estimates, in the first years of its existence it was watched by some 70 percent of the Czech audiences. In the third year of its broadcasting, Nova TV recorded an operational profit of $45 million (U.S.) on the basis of a turnover of $109 million (U.S.). In 1995 a dividend of $12 million (U.S.) was paid out by the TV company. Vladimír Železný, chief executive of Nova Television, used his TV station for the support of his own political and business interests, in particular in his weekly program *Volejte řediteli* (*Call the Director*), broadcast on Saturdays at lunchtime. He often lambasted his political and business opponents, providing no opportunity for them to respond.

The American company CME bought out the participation interest in ČNTS from the original Czech and Slovak founders of the station, achieving 99 percent ownership. At the same time, CME made it possible for Vladimír Železný to acquire a 60 percent majority in CET 21, the license holder, hoping that he would always represent CME's interests. But from 1998, Železný began secretly to act against the interests of CME, and in April 1999, he was fired from the post of chief executive of ČNTS. Železný then found indigenous financial backers in the Czech Republic, and in August 1999, he took the American-backed Nova TV (ČNTS) off the air, replacing it with his own Nova TV Mark 2 with funds that are still characterized by mysterious origins. CME sued Železný and the Czech Republic at the international chamber of commerce in Amsterdam and the Czech side lost. Železný is to repay CME $28 million, and the Czech Republic is to pay CME $500 million in damages. Information about the ultimate owners of Nova TV is not available: their identities are covered by a number of front organizations. In June 2002, CET 21, the company controlling Nova Television, attempted to sack Vladimír Železný from the post of chief executive of Nova TV for alleged financial irregularities.

Another commercial TV broadcaster in the Czech Republic, TV Prima (on air in its present form from January 1997), apparently has close ties with the CET 21 television empire and takes over some of its programming. TV Prima developed from a regional broadcaster and was temporarily owned by the Czech Investment and Postal Bank (IPB). This bank had succumbed to corruption and had to be renationalized by the Czech government. The true identity of the owners of the station is not known, but in spring 2001, problems arose between the bank, which now controls IPB, and Domeana, the firm that represents the current owners of TV Prima.

In Slovakia, the U.S. company Central European Media Enterprises launched Markíza TV (Marchioness TV) as a nationwide television station on August 31, 1996, using the model of Czech Nova TV. Markíza TV immediately made significant inroads in the viewing figures of public service Slovak Television. CME owns an 80 percent noncontrolling economic interest and a 49 percent voting interest in Slovenská Televizná Spoločnosť (STS, Slovak Television Company), which operates Markíza TV. The Slovak director of Markíza TV, Pavol Rusko, openly uses the TV station for his own political and business ends, having founded his own political party, Ano ("Yes"), which is supported by Markíza TV. A number of Rusko's collaborators held posts also in the public service Slovak Television in 2002, which assumed a hostile attitude toward the current right-of-center Slovak government coalition. On March 2, 2002, the Czech company CET 21, then still headed by Vladimír Železný, launched Joj TV in Slovakia. Joj TV has been mostly transmitting Nova TV repeats, and its viewing figures were only some 7 percent throughout the spring of 2002.

JAN ČULÍK

Further Reading

Čulík, Jan, articles on the Czech media in *Central Europe Review,* http://www.ce-review.org/authorarchives/culik_archive/culik_main.html

Čulík, Jan, and Tomáš Pecina, *V hlavních zprávách: Televize,* Prague: ISV, 2001

Council of Europe, *Radio and Television Systems in Central and Eastern Europe,* Council of Europe, 1998

Czech Council for Radio and Television Broadcasting, various reports, http://www.rrtv.cz/en/

Kaid, Lynda Lee, *Television and Politics in Evolving European Democracies,* Nova Science, 1999

Kroupa, Vladimír, and Milan Šmíd, "The Limitations of a Free Market: Czech Republic," in *The Development of the Audiovisual Landscape in Central Europe Since 1989,* Luton, England: ULP/John Libbey Media, 1998

Quarterly and annual reports, submitted to the U.S. Securities and Exchange Commission, http://www.sec.gov

Šmíd, Milan, *Média, internet, Nova a já,* Prague: ISV, 2000